Boone&Kurtz

Contemporary Marketing

2011

DAVID L. KURTZ

*Distinguished Professor of Marketing and
R.A. and Vivian Young Chair of Business Administration*

University of Arkansas

SOUTH-WESTERN
CENGAGE Learning™

Australia • Brazil • Japan • Korea • Mexico • Singapore • Spain • United Kingdom • United States

Contemporary Marketing, 2011 Edition
David L. Kurtz

VP of Editorial, Business: Jack W. Calhoun

Editor-in-Chief: Melissa Acuña

Acquisitions Editor: Mike Roche

Vice President of Marketing: Bill Hendee

Developmental Editor: Erin Guendelsberger

Sr. Marketing Comm. Manager: Sarah Greber

Marketing Coordinator: Shanna Shelton

Content Project Manager: Scott Dillon

Managing Media Editor: Pamela Wallace

Media Editor: John Rich

Manufacturing Coordinator: Miranda Klapper

Production House: Bill Smith Group

Sr. Art Director: Stacy Jenkins Shirley

Photo Permissions Manager: Deanna Ettinger

Text Permissions Manager: Mardell Glinski-Schultz

Cover/Internal Designer: KeDesign, Mason, OH

Cover Image: © PhotoDisc/Alamy

For product information and technology assistance, contact us at
Cengage Learning Customer & Sales Support, 1-800-354-9706
For permission to use material from this text or product, submit all requests online at **www.cengage.com/permissions**
Further permissions questions can be emailed to
permissionrequest@cengage.com

Exam*View*® is a registered trademark of eInstruction Corp. Windows is a registered trademark of the Microsoft Corporation used herein under license. Macintosh and Power Macintosh are registered trademarks of Apple Computer, Inc. used herein under license.

© 2008 Cengage Learning. All Rights Reserved.

Cengage Learning WebTutor™ is a trademark of Cengage Learning.

Library of Congress Control Number: 2009940478

Student Edition ISBN 13: 978-0-538-74689-2

Student Edition ISBN 10: 0-538-74689-0

South-Western Cengage Learning
5191 Natorp Boulevard
Mason, OH 45040
USA

Cengage Learning products are represented in Canada by Nelson Education, Ltd.

For your course and learning solutions, visit **www.cengage.com**
Purchase any of our products at your local college store or at our preferred online store **www.ichapters.com**

Printed in Canada
2 3 4 5 13 12 11 10

This edition of *Contemporary Marketing* is dedicated to Mike Roche, longtime editor and longtime friend.

ABOUT THE AUTHOR

DAVE KURTZ

During **Dave Kurtz's** high school days, no one in Salisbury, Maryland, would have mistaken him for a scholar. In fact, he was a mediocre student, so bad that his father steered him toward higher education by finding him a succession of backbreaking summer jobs. Thankfully, most of them have been erased from his memory, but a few linger, including picking peaches, loading watermelons on trucks headed for market, and working as a pipefitter's helper. Unfortunately, these jobs had zero impact on his academic standing. Worse yet for Dave's ego, he was no better than average as a high school athlete in football and track.

But four years at Davis & Elkins College in Elkins, West Virginia, turned him around. Excellent instructors helped get Dave on a sound academic footing. His grade point average soared—enough to get him accepted by the graduate business school at the University of Arkansas, where he met Gene Boone. Gene and Dave became longtime co-authors; together they produced more than 50 books. In addition to writing, Dave and Gene were involved in several entrepreneurial ventures.

Today, Dave is back teaching at the University of Arkansas, after tours of duty in Ypsilanti, Michigan; Seattle, Washington; and Melbourne, Australia. He is the proud grandfather of five "perfect" kids and a sportsman with a golf handicap too high to mention. Dave, his wife, Diane, and four demanding canine companions (Daisy, Lucy, Molly, and Sally) live in Rogers, Arkansas. Dave holds a distinguished professorship at the Sam M. Walton College of Business in nearby Fayetteville, home of the Arkansas Razorbacks.

BRIEF CONTENTS

CONTENTS

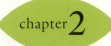

chapter **2** **Strategic Planning in Contemporary Marketing   32**

chapter **3** **The Marketing Environment, Ethics, and Social Responsibility   58** chapter **4**   **E-Business: Managing the Customer Experience   94**

PART 2   UNDERSTANDING BUYERS AND MARKETS   131

chapter 5   Consumer Behavior   132

chapter 6   Business-to-Business (B2B) Marketing   164

chapter 7   **Global Marketing 200**

PART 3   TARGET MARKET SELECTION   237

chapter **8**   **Marketing Research and Sales Forecasting   238**

chapter 9 Market Segmentation, Targeting, and Positioning 272

chapter 10 Relationship Marketing and Customer Relationship Management (CRM) 308

PART 4 PRODUCT DECISIONS 341

chapter 11 Product and Service Strategies 342

chapter **12** **Developing and Managing Brand and Product Categories 376**

PART 5   DISTRIBUTION DECISIONS   413

chapter 13   Marketing Channels and Supply Chain Management   414

OPENING VIGNETTE
Burlington Northern Santa
Fe Rides Green Rails   414

ETIQUETTE TIPS FOR
MARKETING PROFESSIONALS
Anatomy of a Successful
Sales Call   420

MARKETING FAILURE
Recycling Programs
Trashed by Recession   430

SOLVING AN ETHICAL
CONTROVERSY
The Battle over "Blue
Gold"   438

chapter 14   Retailers, Wholesalers, and Direct Marketers   450

PART 6   PROMOTIONAL DECISIONS   487

chapter 15   Integrated Marketing Communications   488

chapter **16**   **Advertising and Public Relations**   **528** chapter 17 **Personal Selling and Sales Promotion 564**

OPENING VIGNETTE
Vivek Gupta: IBM India's Go-to Guy 564

ETIQUETTE TIPS FOR MARKETING PROFESSIONALS
Dressing Like a Sales Pro 573

SOLVING AN ETHICAL CONTROVERSY
Limiting Sweepstakes Fraud 591

MARKETING SUCCESS
Coast to Coast, It's the Eco Trade Show 592

PART 7   PRICING DECISIONS   605

chapter 18   Pricing Concepts   606

chapter 19 Pricing Strategies 640

PREFACE

Continuing a Legacy of Excellence— Boone & Kurtz … In a Class by Itself!

Products often begin their lives as something extraordinary, and as they grow they continue to evolve. The most successful products in the marketplace are those that know their strengths and have branded and marketed those strengths to form a passionate emotional connection with loyal users and relationships with new users every step of the way. Just like the very best brands in the business world, Boone & Kurtz, *Contemporary Marketing,* continues to evolve, both as a product and as a brand. This 2011 edition of *Contemporary Marketing* continues to develop and grow with new cases and examples, as well as a new emphasis on Green Marketing. As with every good brand, though, the patterns of innovation and excellence established at the beginning remain steadfast. The goals and standards of Boone & Kurtz, *Contemporary Marketing,* remain intact and focused on excellence, as always. I present to you a text and supplement package that will not only show you why we've been the standard-bearer for so long but also prove to YOU and your STUDENTS why Boone & Kurtz remains … IN A CLASS BY ITSELF!

PUTTING INSTRUCTORS IN A CLASS BY THEMSELVES

This new edition's supplement package is designed to propel the instructor into the classroom with all the materials needed to engage students and help them understand text concepts. All the major teaching materials have been combined into one resource—the Instructor's Manual. While this might not sound revolutionary, good brands know that the heart of the product is in its core strengths. In the same way, our Instructor's Manual combines all of the most important teaching materials in one place. The lecture outline walks step-by-step through chapter content. And for your convenience, we've included references to the tables, figures, and PowerPoint slides throughout the lecture notes. Greensburg, Inc., our brand-new continuing case, is highlighted in all-new part videos, while chapter videos showcase a stellar list of companies from a variety of industries, including Flight 001, Ogden Publications, and Numi Organic Tea.

We've heard your appreciation for our PowerPoint presentations and have once again tailored these to meet the needs of all instructors, offering two versions: our expanded collection and the basic collection. In addition, our CERTIFIED TEST BANK, which has been verified, gives instructors that extra edge needed to drive home key concepts, ignite critical thinking, and boost confidence and assurance when creating and issuing tests.

The evolution of a brand or product can be a powerful and compelling undertaking involving every aspect of the marketing process. Understanding this evolution can be a student's best help in understanding how marketing is conducted every day. Every chapter begins with EVOLUTION OF A BRAND, which discusses the evolution of the company or product that is the focus of the opening vignette. We've focused our efforts on showing how stellar brands evolve and what this evolution means in the grander scheme of marketing and product management.

HELPING STUDENTS STAND IN A CLASS BY THEMSELVES

A new, intriguing series of continuing videos—Greensburg, Inc.—detail the rebuilding of Greensburg, Kansas, following a devastating tornado that destroyed much of the town. Students will find the look into this town's "green" reconstruction efforts interesting and insightful. As always, every chapter is loaded with up-to-the-minute marketing issues and examples to liven up classroom discussion and debate. Processes, strategies, and procedures are brought to life through videos highlighting real companies and employees, an inventive business model, and collaborative learning exercises. Voice of Experience interviews are placed at the end of each part so that students can see how real-life marketing careers are conducted. And to further enhance the student learning process, a number of text-specific quizzes, games, and videos are available within the WebTutor platform.

How Boone & Kurtz's *Contemporary Marketing* Evolved into the Leading Brand in the Market

For more than three decades, *Contemporary Marketing* has provided the latest in content and pedagogy. Our *current* editions have long been the model for our competitors' next editions. Consider Boone & Kurtz's proven record of providing instructors and students with pedagogical firsts:

▷ *Contemporary Marketing* was the first introductory marketing text written specifically for the student—rather than the instructor—featuring a conversational style that students readily understand and enjoy.

▷ *Contemporary Marketing* has always been based on marketing research, written the way instructors actually teach the course.

▷ *Contemporary Marketing* has always employed extensive pedagogy—such as opening vignettes and boxed features—to breathe life into the exciting concepts and issues facing today's marketers.

▷ *Contemporary Marketing* was the first business text to offer end-of-chapter video cases as well as end-of-part continuing video cases filmed by professional producers who include text concepts in each video.

▷ *Contemporary Marketing* was the first to use multimedia technology to integrate all ancillary components—videos, overhead transparencies, and PowerPoint CD-ROMs for both instructors and students—enabling instructors to customize lively lecture presentations.

▷ *Contemporary Marketing* received the William Holmes McGuffey Award for Excellence and Longevity, a testament to its many contributions to the field of marketing.

Going Green

In addition to a continuing commitment to focus on brand evolution, this new edition of *Contemporary Marketing* takes a hard look at an important new topic in the marketing world—green marketing. Throughout the book, opening vignettes, boxed features, cases, and text references are dedicated to the discussion of how the trend to "go green" has affected the world of marketing. A green leaf icon is included throughout to signify "green" topics. Plus, the book itself has gone "green" and is printed on recycled paper.

Environmental issues are prevalent in every industry, including publishing! Here is a sample look at the "green" scene, written in the style of an opening vignette:

Are You Consuming This Book in Paper or Plastic?

You may be reading this book either in paper form, or in an e-book. One of the things that both consumers and businesses must address in today's environment

is how their products, processes, and consumption affect the environment. This edition of *Contemporary Marketing* has been printed on recycled paper and is also available in e-book form. Which of the versions—print or e-book—is the most ecologically sound?

You would think that reading an e-book would be more ecologically friendly than a traditional printed book, but when one compares the environmental costs for each medium, a traditional printed book or an e-book, interesting issues emerge. Overall, e-books win out for their reduced carbon footprint, but they still generate some potentially hazardous waste when the readers or PCs are thrown out. Greg Kozak was on the cutting edge four years ago when, for his master's degree thesis at the University of Michigan, he conducted a lifecycle assessment (LCA), comparing e-readers with paper college textbooks. An LCA is sometimes called a cradle-to-

grave analysis because it adds up all of the environmental impacts of a product or service from its manufacture to its disposal, including the use of energy, water, and natural resources. It's a great way to compare two products.

First, Kozak outlined all of the potential impacts of the e-book reader and the paper book for each phase of its lifecycle, starting with its manufacture from raw materials and continuing through its distribution to consumers, use, and disposal. For each stage, Kozak calculated the materials used, total energy consumed, air and water emissions, and total solid wastes on the basis of published values or through his own experiments if no published data existed.

In Kozak's analysis, e-textbooks won out overall for environmental friendliness. He found that over its lifecycle, a paper textbook created more greenhouse gas emissions, ozone-depleting substances, and chemicals than an e-book reader. Conventional

books also required more raw materials and water consumption than e-books. For e-book readers, most of the energy consumed is from the electricity used while reading. "Although [it was] the most significant contributor to the e-reader's LCA results, electricity generation for e-reader use had less of an environmental impact than did paper production for the conventional book system," Kozak writes. The paper book's biggest green advantage is that no electricity is needed to read it.

Sources: css.snre.umich.edu/ css_doc/CSS03-04.pdf, Greg Kozak, LCA Analysis of Paper and e-Textbooks; Erica Engelhaupt, "Would you like that book in paper or plastic?" *Environmental Science and Technology* (May 7, 2008); "Paper versus Paperless: Which Makes Reading Greener?," LA Times online edition, June 2, 2008, http://latimesblogs.latimes. com/emeraldcity/2008/06/ paper-vs-paperl.html.

Pedagogy

The reason Boone & Kurtz came together to write the first edition of *Contemporary Marketing* was revolutionary. They wanted to write a book about marketing that wasn't an encyclopedia: a text students would find interesting, a text filled with interesting examples and pedagogy. As with every edition of *Contemporary Marketing*, the 2011 edition is packed with new pedagogical features to keep students interested and bring the text topics to life:

▷ **Assessment, Assessment, Assessment:** In every marketing department in the country, assessment and assurance of learning among students has become increasingly important. As a result, we've provided you with assessment checks after every main head in every chapter. In addition, the end-of-part video cases have been specifically designed to allow instructors to embed a signature assignment that not only can be used to assess the marketing competency and understanding of concepts by students, but also has an associated rubric for assessing student communication ability, understanding of ethics, or application of technology that can then be used for a school's assurance of learning compliance.

▷ **Assurance of Learning Review:** Assurance of learning is further enhanced by end-of-chapter self-quizzes: In addition to ensuring that students are learning throughout the chapter, we've taken assessment one step further by incorporating self-quizzes called Assurance of Learning Review at the end of each chapter. These questions are designed to quickly assess whether students understand the basic concepts covered in the chapter.

▷ **Evolution of a Brand:** Products, brands, and people that evolve are the ones that succeed. The evolution of *Contemporary Marketing* is what has put BOONE & KURTZ ... IN A CLASS BY ITSELF. Every chapter begins with a new Evolution of a Brand feature. This feature discusses the evolution of the company or product that is the focus of the opening vignette and what this evolution means in the larger picture of marketing strategy and product management.

▷ **Business Etiquette:** Schools realize it has become increasingly important to understand proper business etiquette when entering the business world, so more and more schools are adding business etiquette to their curriculums. Every chapter of *Contemporary Marketing* contains an Etiquette Tips for Marketing Professionals box, addressing all aspects of proper behavior, including communications etiquette, business dinners, and even the most effective way to create customer relationships.

▷ **Voice of Experience:** Students often have an amazing ability to grasp chapter concepts and intellectually understand marketing and what a marketing career entails. However, they often do not understand how careers are created and maintained and fail to understand in a real-life sense what a career in marketing may involve on a day-to-day basis. Every part in the text ends with an interview of an actual marketing professional and includes information about his or her education, career path, and day-to-day responsibilities. These professionals come from all aspects of marketing, from entrepreneurs to vice presidents at some of students' favorite companies. The traits all of them have in common are their hard work, dedication, professionalism, and success. This feature gives students a true understanding of how to launch a real marketing career for themselves through the Voices of Experience.

Continuing to Build the Boone & Kurtz Brand

Because the business world moves at an unprecedented pace today, the Principles of Marketing course must race to keep up. Trends, strategies, and practices are constantly changing, though a few things remain the same—the need for excellence and the necessity to evolve and innovate.

You've come to trust *Contemporary Marketing* to cover every aspect of marketing with a critical but fair eye. Let's face it: there are best practices and those we'd never want to repeat.

However, both provide learning opportunities and we've always chosen to take a critical look at the way business is being done in the world and help students understand what they need to know in order to have a long and illustrious career in marketing. Keeping this in mind, here are just a few of the important trends and practices we've focused on for this edition:

▷ "Your Career in Marketing," which appeared as a prologue in the previous edition, has been moved to the end of the text as Appendix A. As in the previous edition, the section is chock full of practical advice for the student who is looking at career options in the field of marketing.

▷ Chapter 1 includes the American Marketing Association (AMA) definition of marketing and covers the most cutting-edge marketing technologies in use today. As always, boxed features have been updated in Chapter 1, which now covers everything from Colgate-Palmolive to IBM, and throughout the text.

▷ In-text examples in Chapter 2 are all new or updated from the previous edition. The appendix, "Developing an Effective Marketing Plan," which was previously placed just after Chapter 2, has been moved to the end of the text as Appendix B.

▷ Chapter 3 has a strong focus on green marketing practices, including coverage of the Peanut Corporation of America, Chipotle Mexican Grill, and electronic recyclers. There is also a new section on the global economic crisis.

▷ Chapter 4 has been thoroughly updated, including a new section titled "The Digital World," as well as up-to-date information on visual Web searches, behavioral targeting, social networking, use of video and multimedia promotion tools, and copyright disputes.

▷ Chapter 5 contains new examples to illustrate Maslow's hierarchy as well as fully updated statistics and examples.

▷ Several "green" items have been added to Chapter 7, including a focus on McDonald's going "Glocal." Examples, statistics, and details have been carefully updated to give the most current view of global marketing.

▷ Chapter 8 now includes information on new types of customer observation, including social networking sites and Internet phone observation.

▷ Coverage of customer churn has been added to Chapter 10 as well as fully updated boxed features, including one featuring Google.

▷ Chapter 12 received a major overhaul, with new and updated in-text examples and boxed features. Also, all key term definitions were carefully checked against the American Marketing Association definitions.

▷ Chapter 14 received a thorough revision, including the addition of examples from retailing giants Wal-Mart and Macy's.

▷ Discussion of athletic endorsement deals has been bolstered in Chapter 15, including information on Olympic gold medalist Michael Phelps's probable endorsement worth in the marketplace.

▷ Chapter 17 includes the most up-to-date statistics on base salary, bonuses, and compensation for sales account managers. And, of course, all examples and boxed features are new or updated.

▷ An in-depth example of yield management has been added to Chapter 18.

▷ An additional short case has been added to the end of each chapter to give variety and options for the student and instructor. Now, instead of one end-of-chapter case, there are two to explore.

Greensburg, Inc. Continuing Video Case

You've come to expect only the best from us in choosing our continuing video case concepts, and we do not disappoint with our new focus on a fresh, environmentally minded topic. Greensburg, Inc. is a series of videos that describes the rebuilding of Greensburg, Kansas, into a model green community following a tornado that destroyed much of the town. The rebuilding process has taken organization, coordination, determination, and a large amount of marketing. Students will hear from the town leaders instrumental in the rebuilding process as well as everyday people involved in the tragedy and reconstruction efforts. Students and instructors will see how the town is rebuilding from the ground up, brick by brick, focusing at each step on creating a sustainable community that can serve as an example to other communities—small and large—across the nation.

Written case segments at the end of each part of the text contain critical-thinking questions designed to provoke discussion and interaction in the classroom setting. Answers to the questions are in the Instructor's Manual, as well as a complete video synopsis, a list of text concepts covered in the videos, and even more critical-thinking exercises.

End-of-Chapter Video Cases

In addition to a stellar, continuing video case, we've produced a whole new batch of video cases for each and every chapter, designed to exceed your every expectation. Students need to know the basics about life in the real world of marketing and how businesses succeed and grow—but they don't need a bunch of talking heads putting them to sleep. So although we admit that you will indeed see a few talking heads, they're just there because they really do know what they're talking about, and they have something important for students to hear. But do trust us . . . the videos we've created for this new edition of *Contemporary Marketing* contain so much more!

A complete set of written cases accompanies these chapter videos and are located in the end-of-book video case appendix, beginning on page VC-1. The written segments contain discussion questions. As with the Greensburg, Inc. cases, answers to the questions are in the Instructor's Manual, as well as a complete video synopsis, a list of text concepts covered in the videos, and even more critical-thinking exercises. The video cases are as follows:

Chapter 1: Marketing: Satisfying Customers at Flight 001

Chapter 2: Strategic Planning and the Marketing Process at Recycline

Chapter 3: The Marketing Environment, Ethics, and Social Responsibility at Scholfield Honda

Chapter 4: E-business at Evo

Chapter 5: Consumer Behavior at Scholfield Honda

Chapter 6: Business-to-Business Marketing at Flight 001

Chapter 7: Global Marketing at Evo

Chapter 8: Marketing Research and Sales Forecasting at Ogden Publications

Chapter 9: Targeting and Positioning at Numi Tea

Chapter 10: Relationship Marketing and CRM at Numi Tea

Chapter 11: Product and Service Strategy at Recycline

Chapter 12: Devoloping and Managing Brand and Product Categories at Maine Media Workshops

Chapter 13: Marketing Channels and Supply Chain Management at Recycline

Chapter 14: Retailing at Flight 001

Chapter 15: Integrated Marketing Communications at Ogden Publications

Chapter 16: Advertising and Public Relations at Ogden Publications

Chapter 17: Personal Selling and Sales Promotion at Scholfield Honda

Chapter 18: Pricing Concepts at Evogear.com

Chapter 19: Pricing Strategy at Standard Renewable Energy

The *Contemporary Marketing* Resource Package

Since the first edition of this book was published, Boone & Kurtz has exceeded the expectations of instructors, and it quickly became the benchmark for other texts. With its precedent-setting learning materials, *Contemporary Marketing* has continued to improve on its signature package features—equipping students and instructors with the most comprehensive collection of learning tools, teaching materials, and innovative resources available. As expected, the 2011 edition continues to serve as the industry benchmark by delivering the most extensive, technologically advanced, user-friendly package on the market.

For the Instructor

INSTRUCTOR'S MANUAL WITH MEDIA GUIDE AND COLLABORATIVE LEARNING EXERCISES

The 2011 edition of *Contemporary Marketing* has a completely updated Instructor's Manual. This valuable tool integrates the various supplements and the text. A detailed lecture outline provides guidance about how to teach the chapter concepts. Collaborative learning exercises are included for each chapter, giving students a completely different way to apply chapter concepts to their own lives. References to the PowerPoint slides are included in the lecture outline. You'll also find answers to all of the end-of-chapter materials and various critical-thinking exercises. Full descriptions of all technology offerings can be found in the Media Guide along with complete video synopses, outlines, and extra questions. For this edition, the Instructor's Manual is available on the Instructor's Resource CD-ROM or can be downloaded from the product support Web site.

CHAPTER VIDEO CASES ON DVD (ISBN: 0-324-78769-3)

Brand-new end-of-chapter video cases for every chapter of the text focus on successful real companies' processes, strategies, and procedures. Real employees explain real marketing situations with which they have been faced, bringing key concepts from the chapter to life.

GREENSBURG, INC. CONTINUING CASE VIDEO ON DVD (ISBN: 0-324-78769-3)

This brand-new continuing video case details the "green" reconstruction of Greensburg, Kansas, after a devastating tornado destroyed much of the town. These videos examine the rebuilding efforts of companies and individuals as well as the formation of new organizations to deal with the disaster. Each piece of the reconstruction has taken organization, coordination, determination, and marketing. The written and video cases are divided into seven sections and are created to be used at the end of each part of the text.

CERTIFIED TEST BANK

Containing more than 4,000 questions, this Test Bank has been thoroughly verified to ensure accuracy—with each question and answer read and reviewed. The Test Bank includes true/false, multiple choice, essay, and matching questions. Each question in the Test Bank is labeled with text objective, text page reference, level of difficulty, and type. Each question is also tagged to AACSB, Marketing Discipline, and Dierdorff/Rubin guidelines. For this edition, the Test Bank is available on the Instructor's Resource CD-ROM or can be downloaded from the product support Web site.

EXAMVIEW® TESTING SOFTWARE

Available on the Instructor's Resource CD-ROM, ExamView contains all of the questions in the Test Bank with all question tags described above. This program is easy-to-use test creation software and is compatible with Microsoft® Windows®. Instructors can add or edit questions, instructions, and answers, and select questions (randomly or numerically) by previewing them on the screen. Instructors can also create and administer quizzes online, whether over the Internet, a local-area network (LAN), or a wide-area network (WAN).

BASIC AND EXPANDED POWERPOINT PRESENTATIONS

After reviewing competitive offerings, we are convinced that our PowerPoint presentations are the best you'll find. We offer two separate collections. The Basic PowerPoint collection contains 10 to 20 slides per chapter. This collection is a basic outline of the chapter, with Web links that bring chapter concepts to life; it also includes figures and tables from the text. The Expanded PowerPoint collection includes 20 to 40 slides per chapter and provides a more complete overview of the chapter. The Expanded collection includes figures and tables from the chapter as well as Web links. For this edition, the Basic and Expanded PowerPoint Presentations are available on the Instructor's Resource CD-ROM or can be downloaded from the product support Web site.

INSTRUCTOR'S RESOURCE CD (ISBN: 0-538-47234-0)

The Instructor's Resource CD-ROM includes electronic versions of all of the instructor supplements: Instructor's Manual with Media Guide and Collaborative Learning Exercises, Test Bank, ExamView testing files and software, and Basic and Expanded PowerPoint Presentations.

WEBTUTOR™ (FOR WEBCT® AND BLACKBOARD®)

Online learning is growing at a rapid pace. Whether you are looking to offer courses at a distance or in a Web-enhanced classroom, South-Western, a part of Cengage Learning, offers you a solution with WebTutor. WebTutor provides instructors with text-specific content that interacts with the two leading systems of higher education course management: WebCT and Blackboard.

WebTutor is a turnkey solution for instructors who want to begin using technology like Blackboard or WebCT but do not have Web-ready content available or do not want to be burdened with developing their own content. WebTutor uses the Internet to turn everyone in your class into a front-row student. WebTutor offers interactive study guide features including quizzes, concept reviews, animated figures, discussion forums, video clips, and more. Instructor tools are also provided to facilitate communication between students and faculty.

BUSINESS & COMPANY RESOURCE CENTER (BCRC)

Available as an optional resource, BCRC puts a complete business library at your students' fingertips. BCRC is a premier online business research tool that allows students to seamlessly search thousands of periodicals, journals, references, financial information sources, market share reports, company histories, and much more. View a guided tour of the Business & Company Resource Center at gale.com/BusinessRC.

CONTEMPORARY MARKETING, 2011 EDITION WEB SITE

Our text Web site (cengage.com/marketing/boone) is filled with a whole set of useful tools. Instructors will find all the key instructor resources in electronic format: Test Bank, PowerPoint collections, and Instructor's Manual with Media Guide and Collaborative Learning Exercises. Students will find quizzes, key words, and other valuable materials.

RESOURCE INTEGRATION GUIDE (RIG)

The RIG is written to provide the instructor with a clear and concise guide to all of the ancillaries that accompany the text as well as how best to use these items in teaching a Principles of Marketing course. Not only are all of the book's ancillaries organized clearly for you, but we also provide planning suggestions, lecture ideas, and help in creating assignments. This guide will help instructors prepare for teaching the course, execute teaching plans, and evaluate student performance. The RIG can be found on the text Web site (cengage.com/marketing/boone) in the Instructor's Resource section.

CUSTOM SOLUTIONS FOR *CONTEMPORARY MARKETING,* 2011 EDITION

Cengage Learning Custom Solutions develops personalized solutions to meet your business education needs. Match your learning materials to your syllabus and create the perfect learning solution. Consider the following when looking at your customization options for *Contemporary Marketing,* 2011 edition:

▷ Remove chapters you do not cover or rearrange their order, creating a streamlined and efficient text students will appreciate.

▷ Add your own material to cover new topics or information, saving you time and providing students with a fully integrated course resource.

Cengage Learning Custom Solutions offers the fastest and easiest way to create unique customized learning materials delivered the way you want. Our custom solutions also include: accessing on-demand cases from leading business case providers such as **Harvard Business School Publishing, Ivey, Darden,** and **NACRA;** building a tailored text online with www.textchoice2.com; and publishing your original materials. For more information about custom publishing options, visit cengage.com/custom/ or contact your local Cengage Learning representative.

For the Student

WEBTUTOR™ (FOR BOTH WEBCT® AND BLACKBOARD®)

This online learning system gives students a host of interactive study guide features including quizzes, concept reviews, animated figures, discussion forums, video clips, and more.

CONTEMPORARY MARKETING, WEB SITE

Our text Web site (cengage.com/marketing/boone) includes valuable resources such as key terms with definitions, flashcards, and quizzes for each chapter.

CHAPTER AUDIO REVIEWS

These audio reviews, found in the WebTutor product, contain short summaries of the chapter objectives and major concepts in each chapter and are a good review of reading assignments. Listen to them before you read the chapter as a preview of what's to come—or after you read the chapter as reinforcement of what you've read. Listen to them on the way to class as a refresher before the lecture—or after you've left class as a review of what the instructor just discussed. However you choose to listen to them, these concise summaries are helpful in reinforcing all the major concepts for each chapter.

Acknowledgments

Over the years, *Contemporary Marketing* has benefited from the suggestions of hundreds of marketing instructors. I am most appreciative of their efforts and thoughts. These people provide valuable feedback for the current revision:

Nathan Himelstein
Essex County College

Jack J. Rose
Johnson & Wales University

Buffie Schmidt, MBA, EdS
Augusta State University

Sue Taylor
Southwestern Illinois College

Pam Uhlenkamp
Iowa Central Community College

Earlier reviewers and contributors include the following: Keith Absher, Kerri L. Acheson, Zafar U. Ahmed, Alicia T. Aldridge, M. Wayne Alexander, Bruce Allen, Linda Anglin, Allen Appell, Paul Arsenault, Dub Ashton, Amardeep Assar, Tom F. Badgett, Joe K. Ballenger, Wayne Bascom, Richard D. Becherer, Tom Becker, Richard F. Beltramini, Michael Bernacchi, Robert Bielski, Carol C. Bienstock, Roger D. Blackwell, David Blanchette, Jocelyn C. Bojack, Barbara Brown, Reginald E. Brown, Michele D. Bunn, Marvin Burnett, Scott Burton, James Camerius, Les Carlson, John Carmichael, Jacob Chacko, Robert Collins, Elizabeth Cooper-Martin, Deborah L. Cowles, Howard B. Cox, James Coyle, John E. Crawford, Elizabeth Creyer, Geoff Crosslin, Michael R. Czinkota, Kathy Daruty, Grant Davis, Gilberto de los Santos, William Demkey, Carol W. DeMoranville, Fran DePaul, Gordon Di Paolo, John G. Doering, Jeffrey T. Doutt, Michael Drafke, Sid Dudley, John W. Earnest, Joanne Eckstein, Philip E. Egdorf, Michael Elliot, Amy Enders, Bob Farris, Lori Feldman, Sandra M. Ferriter, Dale Fodness, Gary T. Ford, Michael Fowler, John Frankel, Edward Friese, Sam Fullerton, Ralph M. Gaedeke, G. P. Gallo, Nimish Gandhi, Sheryl A. Gatto, Robert Georgen, Don Gibson, David W. Glascoff, Robert Googins, James Gould, Donald Granbois, John Grant, Arlene Green, Paul E. Green, William Green, Blaine Greenfield, Matthew Gross, Robert F. Gwinner, Raymond M. Haas, John H. Hallaq, Cary Hawthorn, E. Paul Hayes, Hoyt Hayes, Joel Haynes, Betty Jean Hebel, Debbora Heflin-Bullock, John (Jack) J. Heinsius, Sanford B. Helman, Robert D. Hisrich, Mabre Holder, Ray S. House, Andrew W. Honeycutt, George Housewright, Dr. H. Houston, Donald Howard, John Howe, Michael D. Hutt, Gregory P. Iwaniuk, Don L. James, James Jeck, Tom Jensen, Candida Johnson, David Johnson, Eugene M. Johnson, James C. Johnson, Harold H. Kassarjian, Bernard Katz, Stephen K. Keiser, Michelle Keller, J. Steven Kelly, Marcella Kelly, James H. Kennedy, Charles Keuthan, Maryon King, Stephen C. King, Randall S. Kingsbury, Donald L. Knight, Linda S. Koffel, Philip Kotler, Kathleen Krentler, Terrence Kroeten, Russell Laczniak, Martha Laham, L. Keith Larimore, Edwin Laube, Ken Lawrence, Francis J. Leary, Jr., Mary Lou Lockerby, Laddie Logan, James Lollar, Paul Londrigan, David L. Loudon, Kent Lundin, Dorothy Maass, Patricia Macro, James C. Makens, Lou Mansfield, Frank Markley, Tom Marshall, Warren Martin, Dennis C. Mathern, James McCormick, Carl McDaniel, Lee McGinnis, Michael McGinnis, James McHugh, Faye McIntyre, H. Lee Meadow, Norma Mendoza, Mohan Menon, William E. (Gene) Merkle, John D. Milewicz, Robert D. Miller, Laura M. Milner, Banwari Mittal, Anthony Miyazaki, Harry J. Moak, J. Dale Molander, John F. Monoky, James R. Moore, Jerry W. Moorman, Linda Morable, Thomas M. Moran, Diane Moretz, Eugene Moynihan, Margaret Myers, Susan Logan Nelson, Colin F. Neuhaus, Robert T. Newcomb, Jacqueline Z. Nicholson, Thomas S. O'Connor, Robert O'Keefe, Nita Paden, Sukgoo Pak, George Palz, Eric Panitz, Dennis D. Pappas, Constantine Petrides, Barbara Piasta, Dennis D. Pitta, Barbara Pletcher, Carolyn E. Predmore, Arthur E. Prell, George Prough, Warren Purdy, Bill Quain, Salim Qureshi, Rosemary Ramsey, Thomas Read, Thomas C. Reading, Joel Reedy, Gary Edward Reiman, Dominic Rella, Ken Ridgedell, Glen Riecken, Arnold M. Rieger, C. Richard Roberts, Patrick J. Robinson, William C. Rodgers, Fernando Rodriguez, William H. Ronald, Bert Rosenbloom, Barbara Rosenthal, Carol Rowery, Lillian Roy, Ronald S. Rubin, Don Ryktarsyk, Arthur Saltzman, Rafael Santos, Elise T. Sautter, Duane Schecter, Dennis W. Schneider, Jonathan E. Schroeder, Larry J. Schuetz, Bruce Seaton, Howard Seigelman, Jack Seitz, Steven L. Shapiro, Farouk Shaaban, F. Kelly Shuptrine, Ricardo Singson, Norman Smothers, John Sondey, Carol S. Soroos, James Spiers, Miriam B. Stamps, William Staples, David Starr, Bob Stassen, David Steenstra, Bruce Stern, Robert Stevens, Kermit Swanson, G. Knude Swenson, Cathy Owens Swift, Clint B. Tankersley, Ruth Taylor, Donald L. Temple, Vern Terpstra, Ann Marie Thompson, Howard A. Thompson, Lars Thording, John E. Timmerman, Frank Titlow, Rex Toh, Dennis H. Tootelian, Fred Trawick, Richard Lee Utecht, Rajiv Vaidyanathan, Toni Valdez, Peter Vanderhagen, Dinoo T. Vanier, Sal Veas, Charles Vitaska, Cortez Walker, Roger Waller, Gayle D. Wasson, Mary M. Weber, Donald Weinrauch, Fred Weinthal, Susan B. Wessels, Vicki L. West, Elizabeth White, John J. Whithey, Debbora Whitson, David Wiley, William Wilkinson, James

Williams, Robert J. Williams, Nicholas C. Williamson, Cecilia Wittmayer, Mary Wolfindarger, Joyce Wood, Van R. Wood, Julian Yudelson, and Robert J. Zimmer.

In Conclusion

I would like to thank Karen Hill and Susan Nodine of Elm Street Publishing Services. Their ability to meet tight deadlines is truly appreciated.

Let me conclude by mentioning that the new edition would never have become a reality without the superior efforts of the South-Western Cengage Learning production and marketing teams. My editors—Michael Roche, Erin Guendelsberger, Scott Dillon, and John Rich—provided another *Contemporary Marketing* winner.

Dave Kurtz

Designing Customer-Oriented Marketing Strategies

© Getty Images

CHAPTER 1

Marketing: The Art and Science of Satisfying Customers

© Kurt Brady/Alamy

Colgate-Palmolive Faces the Future with a Smile

When the economy is sluggish, consumers choose their products carefully, weighing each purchase. To anticipate the needs and wants of consumers, companies have to work hard, create items

that interest consumers, and send out information to attract them. Colgate-Palmolive offers consumers value when they are ready to buy.

Global consumer-goods company Colgate-Palmolive has been making and selling products for more than two centuries. Despite the recent economic downturn, the company has managed not only to survive but to thrive. Sales of its products jumped

11 percent worldwide during a recent year. Why the positive news? One reason is that the firm manufactures basics that consumers need every day—from hand soap and toothpaste to laundry detergent and pet

food. These products also must be replaced regularly. Another reason for Colgate-Palmolive's continued success is the widespread recognition of its brands, which include Colgate Total Advanced Toothpaste, Softsoap, Speed Stick and Mennen deodorants, Irish Spring bath soap, Palmolive dishwashing liquid, and Hill's Science Diet pet food. These major brands provide familiarity, high quality—and ultimately value. Finally, Colgate-Palmolive has been developing new products in oral care and liquid soaps. Regardless of the economy, consumers are interested in oral health—especially whiter teeth and fresher breath—and sales of dental-care products are shining, thanks to some innovative products.

Recently, Colgate launched the Wisp, a disposable miniature toothbrush with a "breath-freshening bead" embedded in the bristles. The bead dissolves as the user brushes, avoiding the need to add toothpaste. Consumers who tested the product before its launch said they didn't even have

to rinse after brushing. This simple innovation allows people to brush at the office, in school, before meeting clients—anywhere they need to freshen up. In addition, the firm has expanded its more traditional line of Total toothpastes to include Colgate Total Advanced Whitening and Colgate Advanced Fresh, along with the Colgate 360 degree Deep Clean manual toothbrush and its battery-operated counterpart, the Sonic. For those with sensitive teeth, the company offers a new version of Colgate Sensitive Enamel Protect.

Sales of toothpaste won't carry the entire company, however. One industry observer warns, "What Colgate has been lacking is a home run," meaning a truly revolutionary product. Although the Wisp won't clear the bases, it's a start. Colgate CEO Ian Cook remains optimistic, pointing out some recent company changes. "There are many things that are different . . . and one is a greater focus on innovation," he says. The company has allocated resources to its three new U.S.-based long-term innova-

tion centers. Cook also announced a 14-percent increase in advertising spending worldwide to inform consumers about new products.

The company is also focusing on its impact on the environment. Colgate-Palmolive has worked for nearly a decade to reduce its use of energy and raw materials in producing, packaging, distributing, and promoting its products. Through various projects, it realigned power distribution for greater efficiency, recovered waste heat to power other processes, and installed new units to reduce carbon dioxide emissions at its manufacturing plants. It has cut the amount of plastic used in packaging and reduced the overall weight of small items such as toothpaste tubes—which lowers the fuel needed for transportation.

Meanwhile, Colgate-Palmolive continues to look for the grand slam. "We believe we will sustain the growth of the company by a relentless focus on big hits," says Cook. In Colgate's new playbook, no strikeouts are allowed.[1]

OBJECTIVES

1 Define *marketing,* explain how it creates utility, and describe its role in the global marketplace.

2 Contrast marketing activities during the four eras in the history of marketing.

3 Explain the importance of avoiding marketing myopia.

4 Describe the characteristics of not-for-profit marketing.

5 Identify and briefly explain each of the five types of nontraditional marketing.

6 Explain the shift from transaction-based marketing to relationship marketing.

7 Identify the universal functions of marketing.

8 Demonstrate the relationship between ethical business practices, social responsibility, and marketplace success.

evolution of a brand

Colgate has been in business since 1806. The first Colgate advertisement appeared in a New York newspaper in 1817. Palmolive soap was introduced to the marketplace in 1898, and the two firms merged in 1928. Over the years, Colgate-Palmolive brands have become synonymous with everyday homemaking. The firm continues to innovate in product development, package design, and manufacturing and distribution processes to meet the needs of consumers and create an environmentally sustainable business. As far back as 1908, the firm devised a marketing strategy that involved updating its product packaging. "We couldn't improve the product [toothpaste]," said one of founder William Colgate's sons, "so we improved the tube."

- Take a quick inventory of your apartment or dorm room. How many Colgate-Palmolive products do you use regularly? Were you aware of their identity before reading this story?

- How might Colgate create marketing messages that let consumers know about the firm's environmentally friendly practices in addition to new products and packaging?

chapter overview

- "I'll only drink caffeine-free Diet Coke."

- "I buy all my clothes at American Eagle."

- "The next car I drive will be a Toyota Prius."

- "I go to all the Detroit Lions games at Ford Field."

briefly speaking

"A sign at Dell headquarters reads 'Think Customer.' A full 90 percent of employees deal directly with customers. What are the universal attributes of the Dell brand? Customer advocacy."

—Mike George
U.S. CONSUMER VICE PRESIDENT, DELL

These words are music to a marketer's ears. They may echo the click of an online purchase, the ping of a cash register, the cheers of fans at a stadium. Customer loyalty is the watchword of 21st-century marketing. Individual consumers and business purchasers have so many goods and services from which to choose—and so many different ways to purchase them—that marketers must continually seek out new and better ways to attract and keep customers. Sometimes they miss the boat, allowing other companies to make the most of opportunities. Apple's successful introduction of the iPhone took business away from Palm and T-Mobile, which have hurried to catch up with the compact Centro and the user-friendly Shadow. T-Mobile even hired away Apple's vice president of product development, who says, "Entrants like the Apple iPhone have actually upped the ante for carriers and manufacturers to improve the consumer experience."[2]

The technology revolution continues to change the rules of marketing in the 21st century and will continue to do so in years beyond. The combined power of telecommunications and computer technology creates inexpensive global networks that transfer voice messages, text, graphics, and data within seconds. These sophisticated technologies create new types of products and demand new approaches to marketing existing products. Newspapers are learning this lesson the hard way, as circulation continues to decline around the country, victim in large part to the rising popularity of blogs and auction and job-posting sites. Newspapers have increased their online presence but still find it difficult to adapt to the new competitors and new revenue models.[3]

Communications technology also contributes as to the globalization of today's marketplace where businesses manufacture, buy, and sell across national borders. You can bid at eBay on a potential bargain or eat a Big Mac or drink Coca-Cola almost anywhere in the world, and your DVD or MP3 player was probably manufactured in China or South Korea. Both Mercedes-Benz and Hyundai SUVs are assembled in Alabama, while some Volkswagens are imported from Mexico. Finished products and components routinely cross international borders, but successful global marketing also requires knowledge to tailor products to regional tastes. A chain restaurant in the South might offer grits as an option to hash browns on its breakfast menu.

Rapidly changing business landscapes create new challenges for companies, whether they are giant multinational firms or small boutiques, profit oriented or not-for-profit. Organizations must react quickly to shifts in consumer tastes, competitive offerings, and other market dynamics. Fortunately, information technologies give organizations fast new ways to interact and develop long-term relationships with their customers and suppliers. Such links have become a core element of marketing today.

Every company must serve customer needs—create customer satisfaction—to succeed. We call customer satisfaction an art because it requires imagination and creativity and a science because it requires technical knowledge, skill, and experience. Marketing strategies are the tools that marketers use to identify and analyze customers' needs, then show that their company's goods and services can meet those needs. Tomorrow's market leaders will be companies that can make the most of these strategies to create satisfied customers.

This new edition of *Contemporary Marketing* focuses on the strategies that allow companies to succeed in today's interactive marketplace. This chapter sets the stage for the entire text, examining the importance of creating satisfaction through customer relationships. Initial sections describe the historical development of marketing and its contributions to society. Later sections introduce the universal functions of marketing and the relationship between ethical business practices and marketplace success. Throughout the chapter—and the entire book—we discuss customer loyalty and the lifetime value of a customer.

What Is Marketing?

The production and marketing of goods and services—whether it's a new crop of organically grown vegetables or digital cable service—are the essence of economic life in any society. All organizations perform these two basic functions to satisfy their commitments to society, their customers, and their owners. They create a benefit that economists call **utility**—the want-satisfying power of a good or service. Table 1.1 describes the four basic kinds of utility: form, time, place, and ownership.

Form utility is created when the company converts raw materials and component inputs into finished goods and services. By combining glass, plastic, metals, circuit boards, and other components, Nikon makes a digital camera and Panasonic produces a plasma television. With fabric and leather, Prada manufactures its high-fashion line of handbags. With a ship and the ocean, a captain and staff, food and entertainment, Carnival Cruise Lines creates a cruise. Although the marketing function focuses on influencing consumer and audience preferences, the organization's production function creates form utility.

❙ Define *marketing*, explain how it creates utility, and describe its role in the global marketplace.

utility Want-satisfying power of a good or service.

table 1.1 Four Types of Utility

Type	Description	Examples	Organizational Function Responsible
Form	Conversion of raw materials and components into finished goods and services	Dinner at Outback Steakhouse; HP Pavilion; T-shirt from Urban Outfitters	Production*
Time	Availability of goods and services when consumers want them	Dental appointment; digital photographs; LensCrafters eyeglass guarantee; FedEx Overnight	Marketing
Place	Availability of goods and services at convenient locations	Mechanic available at an auto repair facility; on-site day care; banks in grocery stores	Marketing
Ownership (possession)	Ability to transfer title to goods or services from marketer to buyer	Retail sales (in exchange for currency, credit, or debit card payment)	Marketing

*Marketing provides inputs related to consumer preferences, but creating form utility is the responsibility of the production function.

Redbox Automated Retail takes advantage of time and place utility, positioning their movie-rental kiosks in high-traffic supermarkets, drugstores, and food stores around the country.

© George Frey/Stringer/Getty Images

Marketing creates time, place, and ownership utilities. *Time and place utility* occur when consumers find goods and services available when and where they want to purchase them. Vending machines and convenience stores focus on providing place utility for people buying newspapers, snacks, and soft drinks. Redbox Automated Retail has nearly 7,000 movie-rental kiosks in supermarkets, drugstores, and food stores around the country. Walgreens is expanding its deal with Redbox to increase the number of its stores offering movie-rental kiosks from 250 to about 2,000 following a successful test in several cities.[4]

The transfer of title to goods or services at the time of purchase creates *ownership utility.* Signing up for the Carnival Cruise Lines cruise or buying a digital TV creates ownership utility.

All organizations must create utility to survive. Designing and marketing want-satisfying goods, services, and ideas are the foundation for the creation of utility. But where does the process start? In the toy industry, manufacturers try to come up with items that children will want to play with—creating utility. But that's not as simple as it sounds. At the Toy Fair held each February in New York, retailers pore through the booths of manufacturers and suppliers, looking for the next Webkinz toys or Lego building blocks—trends that turn into classics and generate millions in revenues over the years. Marketers also look for ways to revive flagging brands. Mattel hopes to capitalize on children's interest in computer play sites with its Barbie Girls site. While there, children can create their own characters, design a room, and go shopping at the virtual mall to try on clothes. Up next is a Barbie-themed MP3 music device to provide another link.[5]

But how does an organization create a customer? Most take a three-step approach: identifying needs in the marketplace, finding out which needs the organization can profitably serve, and developing goods and services to convert potential buyers into customers. Marketing specialists are responsible for most of the activities necessary to create the customers the organization wants. These activities include the following:

▷ identifying customer needs;

▷ designing products that meet those needs;

▷ communicating information about those goods and services to prospective buyers;

▷ making the items available at times and places that meet customers' needs;

▷ pricing merchandise and services to reflect costs, competition, and customers' ability to buy; and

▷ providing the necessary service and follow-up to ensure customer satisfaction after the purchase.[6]

A DEFINITION OF MARKETING

The word *marketing* encompasses such a broad scope of activities and ideas that settling on one definition often is difficult. Ask three people to define marketing, and three different definitions are likely to follow. We are exposed to so much advertising and personal selling that most people link marketing only to those activities. But marketing begins long before a product hits the shelf. It involves analyzing customer needs, obtaining the information necessary to design and produce goods or services that match buyer expectations, satisfying customer preferences, and creating and maintaining relationships with customers and suppliers. Marketing activities apply to profit-oriented businesses such as Apple and Zappos.com as well as not-for-profit organizations such as Save the Children and the Red Cross. Even government agencies such as the U.S. Postal Service engage in marketing activities. Today's definition takes all these factors into account. **Marketing** is an organizational function and a set of processes for creating, communicating, and delivering value to customers and for managing customer relationships in ways that benefit the organization and its stakeholders.[7]

The expanded concept of marketing activities permeates all functions in businesses and not-for-profit organizations. It assumes that organizations conduct their marketing efforts ethically and that these efforts serve the best interests of both society and the organization. The concept also identifies the marketing variables—product, price, promotion, and distribution—that combine to provide customer satisfaction. In addition, it assumes that the organization begins by identifying and analyzing who its potential customers are and what they need. At all points, the concept emphasizes creating and maintaining long-term relationships with customers and suppliers.

marketing Organizational function and a set of processes for creating, communicating, and delivering value to customers and for managing customer relationships in ways that benefit the organization and its stakeholders.

TODAY'S GLOBAL MARKETPLACE

Several factors have forced marketers—and entire nations—to extend their economic views to events outside their own national borders. First, international agreements are negotiated to expand trade among nations. Second, the growth of electronic business and related computer technologies allows previously isolated countries to enter the marketplace for buyers and sellers around the globe. Third, the interdependence of the world's economies is a reality because no nation produces all of the raw materials and finished goods its citizens need or consumes all of its output without exporting some to other countries. Evidence of this interdependence is illustrated by the introduction of the euro as a common currency to facilitate trade among the nations of the European Union and the creation of trade agreements such as the North American Free Trade Agreement (NAFTA) and the World Trade Organization (WTO).

Rising oil prices affect the price that U.S. consumers pay for just about everything—not just gasoline at the pump. Dow Chemical raised the prices of its products up to 20 percent to adjust to its rising cost for energy. The largest U.S. chemical company, Dow supplies companies in industries from agriculture to health care, all of whom will be affected by the price hike. Airlines, too, are trying to respond to a near-doubling of the cost of jet fuel. Many have started charging customers for redeeming their reward miles, and American Airlines and United Airlines are charging passengers $15 for the first checked bag.[8]

To remain competitive, companies must continually search for the most efficient manufacturing sites and most lucrative markets for their products. U.S. marketers now find tremendous opportunities serving customers not only in traditional industrialized nations but also in Latin America and emerging economies in central Europe, the Middle East, Asia, and Africa where rising standards of living create increased customer demand for the latest products. Expanding operations beyond the U.S. market gives domestic companies access to 6.5 billion international customers. China is now the second-largest market in the world—only the United States is larger.

briefly
speaking

"Too often we measure everything and understand nothing. The three most important things you need to measure in a business are customer satisfaction, employee satisfaction, and cash flow. If you're growing customer satisfaction, your global market share is sure to grow, too. Employee satisfaction gets you productivity, quality, pride, and creativity. And cash flow is the pulse—the key vital sign of a company."

—Jack Welch
(b. 1935)
FORMER CEO OF GENERAL ELECTRIC

Rising oil prices affect the price U.S. consumers pay for just about everything. To offset the rising cost of jet fuel, most airlines have started charging passengers for checking baggage.

© Caro/Alamy

And Chinese customers will soon purchase 9.5 million cars, trucks, and other vehicles a year, so automakers worldwide are extending their operations to China.[9] In addition, companies based in these emerging economies are beginning to compete in the global market. Over a recent two-year period, Chinese exports to the United States increased by more than 32 percent. In contrast, overall imports into the United States rose less than 17 percent during the same period.[10] Interestingly, however, signs are mounting that China's increasing prosperity may be reducing its attractiveness as a low-cost labor source. Rising costs already are driving some U.S. manufacturers out of the country, according to the American Chamber of Commerce. "The competitive labor market poses difficulties for export-oriented manufacturers, especially in low-margin sectors such as toys, garments, and shoes," says the organization's chairman. "They are looking to India, Vietnam, and other places."[11]

Service firms also play a major role in today's global marketplace. Telecommunications firms like South Africa's MTN, Luxembourg's Millicom International, and Egypt's Orascom Telecom Holding have carved out new global markets for their products by following the lead of Finnish firm Nokia, among the first high-tech firms to create durable and affordable cell phones specifically designed for emerging markets. The opportunities for such telecom innovators will continue to grow as long as electricity-reliant personal computers remain out of reach for millions in the developing world. "Like a lot of people who made their first call on a mobile [phone], they will have their first experience with the Internet on a mobile," says one industry analyst.[12]

The United States is also an attractive market for foreign competitors because of its size and the high standard of living American consumers enjoy. Companies such as Nissan, Sony, and Sun Life of Canada operate production, distribution, service, and retail facilities in the United States. Foreign ownership of U.S. companies has increased also. Pillsbury and MCA are two well-known firms with foreign parents.

Although many global marketing strategies are almost identical to those used in domestic markets, more and more companies are tailoring their marketing efforts to the needs and preferences of consumers in foreign markets. It is often difficult to standardize a brand name on a global basis. The Japanese, for example, like the names of flowers or girls for their automobiles—names like Bluebird, Bluebonnet, Violet, and Gloria. Americans, on the other hand, prefer rugged outdoorsy names like Chevy Tahoe, Jeep Cherokee, and Dodge Challenger.

assessment check

1. Define *marketing* and explain how it creates utility.

2. What three factors have forced marketers to embrace a global marketplace?

---

2 **Contrast marketing activities during the four eras in the history of marketing.**

exchange process
Activity in which two or more parties give something of value to each other to satisfy perceived needs.

Four Eras in the History of Marketing

The essence of marketing is the **exchange process,** in which two or more parties give something of value to each other to satisfy perceived needs. Often people exchange money for tangible goods such as groceries, clothes, a car, or a house. In other situations, they exchange money for intangible services such as a haircut or a college education. Many exchanges involve a combination of goods and services, such as dinner in a restaurant—where dinner represents the good and the wait staff represents the service. People also make exchanges when they donate money or time to a charitable cause such as Habitat for Humanity.

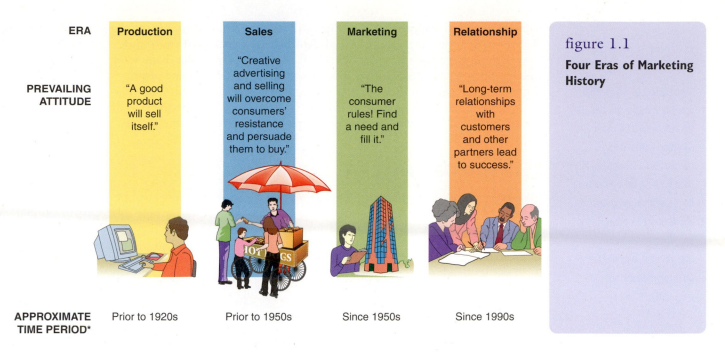

ERA	Production	Sales	Marketing	Relationship
PREVAILING ATTITUDE	"A good product will sell itself."	"Creative advertising and selling will overcome consumers' resistance and persuade them to buy."	"The consumer rules! Find a need and fill it."	"Long-term relationships with customers and other partners lead to success."
APPROXIMATE TIME PERIOD*	Prior to 1920s	Prior to 1950s	Since 1950s	Since 1990s

figure 1.1

Four Eras of Marketing History

Although marketing has always been a part of business, its importance has varied greatly. Figure 1.1 identifies four eras in the history of marketing: (1) the production era, (2) the sales era, (3) the marketing era, and (4) the relationship era.

THE PRODUCTION ERA

Before 1925, most firms—even those operating in highly developed economies in western Europe and North America—focused narrowly on production. Manufacturers stressed production of quality products and then looked for people to purchase them. The prevailing attitude of this era held that a high-quality product would sell itself. This **production orientation** dominated business philosophy for decades; business success often was defined solely in terms of production successes.

The production era reached its peak during the early part of the 20th century. Henry Ford's mass-production line exemplifies this orientation. Ford's slogan, "They [customers] can have any color they want, as long as it's black," reflected the prevalent attitude toward marketing. Production shortages and intense consumer demand ruled the day. It is easy to understand how production activities took precedence.

However, building a new product is no guarantee of success, and marketing history is cluttered with the bones of miserable product failures despite major innovations—more than 80 percent of new products fail. Inventing an outstanding new product is not enough because it must also fill a perceived marketplace need. Otherwise, even the best-engineered, highest-quality product will fail. Even Henry Ford's horseless carriage took a while to catch on. People were afraid of motor vehicles: they spat out exhaust, stirred up dust on dirt roads, got stuck in mud, and tied up horse traffic. Besides, at the speed of seven miles per hour, they caused all kinds of accidents and disruption. It took savvy marketing by some early salespeople—and eventually a widespread perceived need—to change people's minds about the product. Today, most of us could not imagine life without a car and have refined that need to preferences for certain types of vehicles, including SUVs, convertibles, trucks, and hybrids.

THE SALES ERA

As production techniques in the United States and Europe became more sophisticated, output grew from the 1920s into the early 1950s. As a result, manufacturers began to increase their emphasis on effective sales forces to find customers for their output. In this era, firms attempted to match their output to the potential number of customers who would want it. Companies with a

consumer orientation
Business philosophy incorporating the marketing concept that emphasizes first determining unmet consumer needs and then designing a system for satisfying them.

marketing concept
Companywide consumer orientation with the objective of achieving long-run success.

sales orientation assume that customers will resist purchasing nonessential goods and services and that the task of personal selling and advertising is to persuade them to buy.

Although marketing departments began to emerge from the shadows of production and engineering during the sales era, they tended to remain in subordinate positions. Many chief marketing executives held the title of sales manager. But selling is only one component of marketing. As marketing scholar Theodore Levitt once pointed out, "Marketing is as different from selling as chemistry is from alchemy, astronomy from astrology, chess from checkers."

THE MARKETING ERA

Personal incomes and consumer demand for goods and services dropped rapidly during the Great Depression of the 1930s, thrusting marketing into a more important role. Organizational survival dictated that managers pay close attention to the markets for their goods and services. This trend ended with the outbreak of World War II, when rationing and shortages of consumer goods became commonplace. The war years, however, created only a pause in an emerging trend in business: a shift in the focus from products and sales to satisfying customer needs.

Emergence of the Marketing Concept

The marketing concept, a crucial change in management philosophy, can be linked to the shift from a **seller's market**—one in which there were more buyers for fewer goods and services—to a **buyer's market**—one in which there were more goods and services than people willing to buy them. When World War II ended, factories stopped manufacturing tanks and ships and started turning out consumer products again, an activity that had, for all practical purposes, stopped in early 1942.

The advent of a strong buyer's market created the need for **consumer orientation** by businesses. Companies had to market goods and services, not just produce and sell them. This realization has been identified as the emergence of the marketing concept. Marketing would no longer be regarded as a supplemental activity performed after completing the production process. Instead, the marketer played a leading role in product planning. *Marketing* and *selling* would no longer be synonymous terms.

Today's fully developed **marketing concept** is a *company-wide consumer orientation* with the objective of achieving long-run success. All facets—and all levels, from top to bottom—of the organization must contribute first to assessing and then to satisfying customer wants and needs. From marketing manager to accountant to product designer, every employee plays a role in reaching potential customers. Even during tough economic times, when companies tend to emphasize cutting costs and boosting revenues, the marketing concept focuses on the objective of achieving long-run success instead of short-term profits. Because the firm's survival and growth are built into the marketing concept, companywide consumer orientation should lead to greater long-run profits.

Google exemplifies the marketing concept in every aspect of its business. Even as it has grown in a few short years from a Silicon Valley start-up to a global Internet search and advertising company with more than 16,000 employees and $14 billion in annual revenue, it has retained the spirit of quirky innovation and relentless drive for quality that have set it apart from other successful technology firms. When prospective employees are asked how they would change the world using Google's resources, it's not a trick question—the company really wants to know. Google treats information as a natural resource to be widely distributed. It believes in doing "one thing really, really well" and that "great just isn't good enough." But above all, and the first of its ten principles, is the directive, "Focus on the user and all else will follow."[13]

A strong market orientation—the extent to which a company adopts the marketing concept—generally improves market success and overall performance. It also has a positive effect on new-product development and the introduction of innovative products. Companies that implement market-driven strategies are better able to understand their customers' experiences, buying habits, and needs. Like Google, these companies can, therefore, design products with advantages and levels of quality compatible with customer requirements.

THE RELATIONSHIP ERA

The fourth era in the history of marketing emerged during the final decade of the 20th century and continues to grow in importance. Organizations now build on the marketing era's customer orientation by focusing on establishing and maintaining relationships with both customers and suppliers. **Relationship marketing** involves developing long-term, value-added relationships over time with customers and suppliers. Strategic alliances and partnerships among manufacturers, retailers, and suppliers often benefit everyone. It took a decade and more than $13 billion from four countries to launch the world's largest passenger plane, the Airbus A380. To develop the new aircraft, Airbus merged its partner companies into one large firm. Then it worked with more than 60 airports during the design phase to make sure that they could accommodate the huge aircraft. By the time Singapore Airlines conducted the first test flight, 13 other airlines had already placed orders for the Airbus A380, and it was highly successful in the United States when it recently debuted on a special celebratory flight around Manhattan.[14] The concept of relationship marketing, which is the current state of customer-driven marketing, is discussed in detail later in this chapter and in Chapter 10. On a personal level, see the "Etiquette Tips for Marketing Professionals" feature for suggestions on creating your own personal network, a key to success in marketing and in business generally.

THE FIRST AIRLINE TO FLY THE A380 BRINGS YOU TRAVEL IN A NEW LIGHT
DEPARTING DAILY FROM LONDON TO SINGAPORE STARTING 18 MARCH 2008

singaporeair.com

© Leon Neal/AFP/Getty Images

It took a decade and more than $13 billion from four countries to launch the world's largest passenger plane, the Airbus A380. Relationship marketing involves developing long-term, value-added relationships that make large projects like this possible.

relationship marketing Development and maintenance of long-term, cost-effective relationships with individual customers, suppliers, employees, and other partners for mutual benefit.

CONVERTING NEEDS TO WANTS

Every consumer must acquire goods and services on a continuing basis to fill certain needs. Everyone must satisfy the fundamental needs for food, clothing, shelter, and transportation by purchasing items or, in some instances, temporarily using rented property and hired or leased transportation. By focusing on the benefits resulting from these goods and services, effective marketing converts needs to wants. A need for a pair of pants may be converted to a desire for jeans—and further, a desire for jeans from Abercrombie & Fitch or Lucky Brand Jeans. The need for food may be converted to a desire for dinner at Pizzeria Uno or groceries from Trader Joe's. But if the need for transportation isn't converted to a desire for a Ford Focus or Mini Cooper, extra vehicles may sit unsold on a dealer's lot.

Consumers need to communicate. But converting that need to the desire for certain types of communication requires skill. It also requires listening to what consumers want. Consumers' demand for more cell phone and wireless services seems nearly unlimited—providing tremendous opportunities for companies. New products appear continually to feed that demand, such as increasingly popular broadband wireless services now offered by all cell phone carriers in a market currently dominated by Verizon Wireless and Sprint Nextel. Though many consumers who use Internet-friendly phones and other devices tend to be business travelers, the wireless broadband industry is intent on improving its appeal to the mass market, perhaps with flexible service plans and lower fees. Some believe the technology can offer more than just Internet access. Says Ericsson's president and CEO, "It is important, if you really want to have a society that works, to use communications to reduce travel and make this planet work for the long perspective."[15]

assessment check

1. What is the major distinction between the production era and the sales era?

2. What is the marketing concept?

3. Describe the relationship era of marketing.

Etiquette Tips for Marketing Professionals

How to Network

You may think only extroverts and social butterflies can build the personal networks that lead to business and career success. Not so! Networking is a skill anyone can learn. Here are some tips to get you started.

- Think of building your personal connections as making an investment in your future. It requires time and effort to become fruitful.

- Work on your network a little at a time. Start by attending one or two promising events a month or joining one or two professional groups such as the local Chamber of Commerce and stick with them.

- If you join a group or network that doesn't look immediately promising but you really enjoy it, keep going.

- Talk to new people everywhere, including social events like weddings and everyday places like checkout lines in stores.

- Don't hesitate to invite people to join you for coffee or a quick meal after work. Some of the most interesting contacts might just be shy or hesitant to speak.

- Carry information about yourself or your company to give out, such as an up-to-date brochure or business card.

- Remember, it's not all about you. Talk about relevant activities you've done, but be ready to ask questions that help others talk about themselves and their company or organization.

- Look for a few people who know a lot of other people, rather than many people in specific positions or types of businesses.

- Keep a record of people you want to stay in touch with, and don't wait for an occasion to get together. Follow-up and reciprocating are the keys to being remembered.

- Evaluate your results periodically. Which networking strategies are working best for you, and which can you improve?

Sources: Rob May, "How to Network: For Introverts," *Business Pundit,* www.businesspundit.com, accessed April 16, 2009; "How to Network Effectively," *eHow,* www.ehow.com, accessed April 16, 2009; C. J. Hayden, "Network Your Way to a New Job or Career, *About.com,* humanresources.about.com, accessed April 16, 2009.

---

③ **Explain the importance of avoiding marketing myopia.**

marketing myopia Management's failure to recognize the scope of its business.

Avoiding Marketing Myopia

The emergence of the marketing concept has not been devoid of setbacks. One troublesome problem led marketing scholar Theodore Levitt to coin the term **marketing myopia.** According to Levitt, marketing myopia is management's failure to recognize the scope of its business. Product-oriented rather than customer-oriented management endangers future growth. Levitt cites many service industries, such as dry cleaning and electric utilities, as examples of marketing myopia. But many firms have found innovative ways to reach new markets and develop long-term relationships.

Most people wouldn't think of waste vegetable oil as an attractive product, for instance. But for a Wisconsin-based company called INOV8 International, waste oil is an exciting opportunity to help the environment and serve customers at the same time. INOV8 has found a way to provide the hotel and restaurant industry with drinkable hot water by using the waste oil as fuel in specially designed boiler systems that boast clean emissions and fail-proof operation. "I was consistently looking for cost reductions," says the company's project manager, "and here it is—the technology, the fuel, and the need for hot water—talk about win–win. Once business owners realize that our … systems typically pay for themselves in less than one year, and that the systems will then save them literally thousands of dollars each year, they will know that [our system] is the logical choice for fueling their business."[16] Table 1.2 illustrates how firms in a number of industries have overcome myopic thinking by developing broader marketing-oriented business ideas that focus on consumer need satisfaction.

assessment check

1. What is marketing myopia?

2. Give an example of how a firm can avoid marketing myopia.

table 1.2 **Avoiding Marketing Myopia**

Company	Myopic Description	Company Motto—Avoiding Myopia
BMW	Automobile	The Ultimate Driving Machine
Disneyland	Amusement park	The Happiest Place on Earth
American Express	Credit card company	Don't Leave Home Without It
Rolaids	Antacid	How Do You Spell Relief?
Michelin	Tire manufacturer	A Better Way Forward
Avis	Car rental company	We Try Harder

Extending the Traditional Boundaries of Marketing

Today's organizations—both profit oriented and not-for-profit—recognize universal needs for marketing and its importance to their success. During a television commercial break, viewers might be exposed to an advertisement for a Kia Spectra, an appeal to help feed children in foreign countries, a message by a political candidate, and a commercial for McDonald's—all in the space of about two minutes. Two of these ads are paid for by firms attempting to achieve profitability and other objectives. The appeal for funds to feed children and the political ad are examples of communications by not-for-profit organizations and individuals.

MARKETING IN NOT-FOR-PROFIT ORGANIZATIONS

More than a quarter of all U.S. adults volunteer in one or more of the 1.5 million not-for-profit organizations across the country.[17] In total, these organizations generate hundreds of billions of dollars of revenues each year through contributions and from fund-raising activities. That makes not-for-profit organizations big business.

Not-for-profit organizations operate in both public and private sectors. Federal, state, and local firms pursue service objectives not keyed to profitability targets. The Federal Trade Commission oversees business activities; a state's department of motor vehicles issues car registrations and driver's licenses; a local school board is responsible for maintaining educational standards for its district. The private sector has an even greater array of not-for-profit organizations, including hospitals, libraries, the American Kennel Club, and the American Heart Association. Regardless of their size or location, all of these organizations need funds to operate. Adopting the marketing concept can make a great difference in their ability to meet their service objectives.

Conner Prairie in Fishers, Indiana, is an open-air re-creation of rural life in 1830s Indiana that features historic areas to explore, including a Lenape Indian camp, the Conner Homestead, a modern museum, and 800 acres of undeveloped land along with indoor play and learning areas for young children. Costumed staff host events that range from a festive wedding to the experience of slaves seeking freedom through the Underground Railroad. Thousands of families and school groups visit each year.[18]

Some not-for-profits form partnerships with business firms that promote the organization's cause or message. Target Stores funds a facility called Target House, which provides long-term housing for families with children treated at St. Jude Children's Research Hospital. The house has apartments and common areas where families can gather and children can play. Celebrities have also contributed to the house. Golf pro Tiger Woods sponsored a library, singer Amy Grant furnished a music room, and Olympic gold-medalist Scott Hamilton donated a fitness center and art room. Sponsors like Yahoo! and Brooks Brothers also support the house.[19]

Generally, the alliances formed between not-for-profit organizations and commercial firms and their executives benefit both. The reality of operating with multimillion-dollar budgets requires not-for-profit organizations to maintain a focused business approach. Consider some current examples:

▷ Feeding America (formerly known as America's Second Harvest) receives assistance from food manufacturers and grocery stores in distributing more than 2 billion pounds of food and grocery products to needy Americans. Participating businesses include Cott Beverages, the Dannon Company, Heinz North America, the Kellogg Company, Sam's Club, and Tropicana Products.[20]

▷ Corporate Angel Network works with the National Business Aviation Association to provide free transportation for cancer patients traveling to and from their treatments using empty seats on corporate jets.

▷ Lowry Mays, former chairman, CEO, and founder of Clear Channel Communications Inc., and his wife Peggy gave $20 million to the M.D. Anderson Cancer Center at the University of Texas in support of the Red and Charline McCombs Institute for the Early Detection and Treatment of Cancer.[21]

The diversity of not-for-profit organizations suggests the presence of numerous organizational objectives other than profitability. In addition to their organizational goals, not-for-profit organizations differ from profit-seeking firms in several other ways.

4 **Describe the characteristics of not-for-profit marketing.**

CHARACTERISTICS OF NOT-FOR-PROFIT MARKETING

The most obvious distinction between not-for-profit organizations and for-profit—commercial—firms is the financial **bottom line,** business jargon that refers to the overall profitability of an organization. For-profit organizations measure profitability in terms of sales and revenues, and their goal is to generate revenues above and beyond their costs to make money for all stakeholders involved, including employees, shareholders, and the organization itself. Not-for-profit organizations hope to generate as much revenue as possible to support their causes, whether it is feeding children, preserving wilderness areas, or helping single mothers find work. Historically, not-for-profits have had less exact goals and marketing objectives than for-profit firms, but in recent years, many of these groups have recognized that to succeed, they must develop more cost-effective ways to provide services and they must compete with other organizations for donors' dollars. Marketing can help them accomplish these tasks. Some groups are finding, for instance, that online social network sites, such as Facebook and MySpace, can bring them increased attention through general communities. But they are also using specialized networks devoted to social causes like YourCause.com to generate funds.[22]

Other distinctions exist between for-profit and not-for-profit organizations as well, each of which influences marketing activities. Like profit-seeking firms, not-for-profit organizations may market tangible goods or intangible services. The Lance Armstrong Foundation offers cotton T-shirts and the familiar yellow wristbands—tangible items—as well as cancer patient support and referrals—intangible services.[23] But profit-seeking businesses tend to focus their marketing on just one public—their customers. Not-for-profit organizations, however, often must market to multiple publics, which complicates decision making about the correct markets to target. Many deal with at least two major publics—their clients and their sponsors—and often many other publics as well. A college or university targets prospective students as recipients of its marketing program, but it also markets to current students, parents of students, major donors, alumni, faculty, staff, local businesses, and local government agencies.

A service user of a not-for-profit organization may have less control over the organization's destiny than customers of a profit-seeking firm. Not-for-profit organizations also often possess some degree of monopoly power in a given geographic

assessment check

1. What is the most obvious distinction between a not-for-profit organization and a commercial organization?

2. Why do for-profit and not-for-profit organizations sometimes form alliances?

area. An individual contributor might object to United Way's inclusion of a particular local agency, but that agency will receive a portion of any donor contribution.

Nontraditional Marketing

As marketing evolved into an organization-wide activity, its application has broadened far beyond its traditional boundaries of for-profit organizations that create and distribute tangible goods and intangible services. In many cases, broader appeals focus on causes, events, individuals, organizations, and places. Table 1.3 lists and describes five major categories of nontraditional marketing: person marketing, place marketing, cause marketing, event marketing, and organization marketing. These categories can overlap—promotion for an organization may also encompass a cause or a promotional campaign may focus on both an event and a place.

PERSON MARKETING

Person marketing involves efforts designed to cultivate the attention, interest, and preferences of a target market toward a celebrity or authority figure. Celebrities can be real people or fictional characters. Political candidates engage in person marketing as they promote their candidacy for office. Authors such as Suze Orman of *The Road to Wealth* use person marketing to promote their books. Oprah Winfrey uses person marketing to promote her *O* magazine, where she appears on every cover.

An extension of person marketing is *celebrity endorsements,* in which well-known athletes, entertainers, and experts or authority figures promote products for companies or social causes for not-for-profit organizations. Singer Clint Black does commercials for Wal-Mart, which distributes his CDs. Actor William Shatner was seen in ads for Priceline.com, while his former *Star Trek* co-star Leonard Nimoy promoted the pain reliever Aleve. Athletes are the big winners in the celebrity endorsement arena—NBA Cleveland Cavaliers star LeBron James has multimillion-dollar endorsement deals with Nike, Upper Deck, and The Coca-Cola Company. New York Giants quarterback Eli Manning already had millions of dollars worth of deals with Citizen Watch, Reebok, and Nabisco's Oreo brand before his Super Bowl upset win, which will likely increase his endorsement earnings. Tennis star Maria Sharapova promotes Canon's PowerShot camera. But few athletes approach the $100 million earned by Tiger Woods for endorsing Tag Heuer watches, American Express cards, and other goods and services.[24]

person marketing
Marketing efforts designed to cultivate the attention, interest, and preferences of a target market toward a person (perhaps a political candidate or celebrity).

briefly speaking

"How bad a day can it be if you're looking at the right side of the grass?"

—Michael Bloomberg (b. 1942)
MAYOR OF NEW YORK CITY

table 1.3 Categories of Nontraditional Marketing

Type	Brief Description	Examples
Person marketing	Marketing efforts designed to cultivate the attention and preference of a target market toward a person	Athlete Eli Manning, New York Giants quarterback Celebrity Toby Keith, country singer Political candidate James DeMint, U.S. Senator from South Carolina
Place marketing	Marketing efforts designed to attract visitors to a particular area; improve consumer images of a city, state, or nation; and/or attract new business	Las Vegas: "What happens here stays here." Oklahoma: "Native America."
Cause marketing	Identification and marketing of a social issue, cause, or idea to selected target markets	"Click it or ticket." "Refill, not landfill."
Event marketing	Marketing of sporting, cultural, and charitable activities to selected target markets	Vancouver Olympics Susan G. Komen Race for the Cure
Organization marketing	Marketing efforts of mutual-benefit organizations, service organizations, and government organizations that seek to influence others to accept their goals, receive their services, or contribute to them in some way	American Red Cross: "Together, we can save a life." March of Dimes: "Saving babies, together" "United Way brings out the best in all of us."

An extension of person marketing is celebrity endorsements, such as New York Giants quarterback Eli Manning appearing in an advertisement for Citizen Watch.

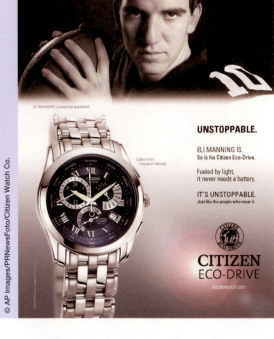

© AP Images/PRNewsFoto/Citizen Watch Co.

UNSTOPPABLE.

ELI MANNING IS.
So is his Citizen Eco-Drive.

Fueled by light,
it never needs a battery.

IT'S UNSTOPPABLE.
Just like the people who wear it.

CITIZEN
ECO-DRIVE
citizenwatch.com

place marketing
Marketing efforts to attract people and organizations to a particular geographic area.

PLACE MARKETING

Another category of nontraditional marketing is **place marketing,** which attempts to attract customers to particular areas. Cities, states, regions, and countries publicize their tourist attractions to lure vacation travelers. They also promote themselves as good locations for businesses. Place marketing has become more important in the world economy—not only for tourism but also to recruit business and workers. MGM Mirage is building a new casino and resort hotel in Atlantic City that, at nearly $5 billion, will be one of the most expensive such projects in history. MGM and other casino operators such as Harrah's and Pinnacle Entertainment are betting hundreds of millions of dollars on the future of Atlantic City as a younger, hipper entertainment destination than Las Vegas that will prove attractive to free-spending tourists lured by fine food, lavish stage shows, and, of course, gambling.[25]

Place marketing can be a showcase for ingenuity. Although commercial space travel remains a somewhat distant possibility, the New Mexico Spaceport Authority has already designed what it says will be the world's first public launch and landing site for space vehicles. Spaceport America, with a budget of $225 million in state tax dollars, will house seven spacecraft and includes a passenger terminal. It's planned to open by 2010 and will be home to Virgin Galactic, whose president calls the sci-fi-looking building "a vision of the future, not the past."[26]

New York City wants to increase the number of international tourists who visit by the year 2015. Its marketing campaign begins at JKF International Airport with welcome signs, personal greetings, maps, and other information. "Just Ask the Locals" is a larger-scale campaign that offers advice from well-known residents of the city such as actors Robert DeNiro and Julianne Moore and former Giants football player Tiki Barber. Teams of "ambassadors" from the city's tourism office hand pedestrians tip sheets with advice about navigating the city's crowded streets. The campaign will unfold at other city ports and even includes activities in Shanghai, Tokyo, Madrid, Moscow, and Seoul.[27]

In another area of the country, you wouldn't necessarily think of West Virginia as a hub for skiers. But the town of Davis is home to Timberline Four Seasons Ski Resort, which boasts up to 160 inches of snow per year on its Herz Mountain. Although often overlooked by skiers who routinely travel north and west, locals are convinced that their mountain, which recently upgraded the snowmaking capacity of its 37 slopes and trails, is about to be discovered. In addition to skiing, the area promotes mountain bike races and hiking in the summer.[28]

Place marketing, such as this ad for Barbados, attempts to attract customers to particular areas.

© Image courtesy of The Advertising Archives

Waking to the music of tropical birds greeting the sunrise
An afternoon stroll on the golden beaches
Dinner at one of the best restaurants in the world

It doesn't get better than Barbados

BARBADOS
www.visitbarbados.co.uk

CAUSE MARKETING

A third category of nontraditional marketing, **cause marketing,** refers to the identification and marketing of a social issue, cause, or idea to selected target markets. Cause marketing covers a wide range of issues, including literacy, physical fitness, awareness of childhood obesity, environmental protection, elimination of birth defects, child-abuse prevention, and preventing drunk driving.

As mentioned earlier, an increasingly common marketing practice is for profit-seeking firms to link their products to social causes. Saving Paws Animal Rescue, for example, relies for help on numerous veterinary practices in its area in Wisconsin. The vets are acknowledged on its Web site as are PetSmart stores for housing pets in need of adoption.[29]

Surveys show strong support for cause-related marketing by both consumers and company employees. In a recent survey, 92 percent of consumers had a more positive image of companies that support important social causes, and four of five respondents said that they would change brands to support a cause if the price and quality of the two brands remained equal. Cause marketing can help build relationships with customers.

EVENT MARKETING

Event marketing refers to the marketing of sporting, cultural, and charitable activities to selected target markets. It also includes the sponsorship of such events by firms seeking to increase public awareness and bolster their images by linking themselves and their products to the events. Sports sponsorships have gained effectiveness in increasing brand recognition, enhancing image, boosting purchase volume, and increasing popularity with sports fans in demographic segments corresponding to sponsor business goals.

Some people might say that the premier sporting event is baseball's World Series. Others claim it's the Olympics. Still others might argue that it's the Super Bowl, which some consumers claim they watch only to see the debut of commercials. Those commercials are expensive, costing as much as $2.7 million for 30 seconds of airtime, or $90,000 a second.[30] But they reach an estimated 90 million viewers. Companies now also feed their commercials to Web sites and make them available for downloading to personal computers and video iPods. Experienced marketers caution that firms planning such a big expenditure should make it part of a larger marketing plan, not just a single shot at fame.

For those who prefer the international pageantry of the Olympics, marketers have plenty of plans. The promotion of upcoming Olympics—both summer and winter—begins years in advance. Before the end of each Olympics, hosts of the next games unveil their logo, and the marketing takes off from there. Corporate sponsors such as Adidas and Nike try to target the next Olympic gold medal winners, draping them in clothing and gear with company logos. The Olympics in Beijing, China, were particularly important because of the huge consumer market there. Nike sponsored three-quarters of the Chinese athletes, including hurdler Liu Xiang, and both Nike and Adidas, which reportedly paid $80 million to be an official sponsor of the games, hoped to earn $1 billion a year in China following the competition. Both firms are opening apparel stores in China at record rates but believe the investment will pay off in sales and long-term relationships with Chinese consumers.[31]

cause marketing
Identification and marketing of a social issue, cause, or idea to selected target markets.

event marketing
Marketing of sporting, cultural, and charitable activities to selected target markets.

vancouver 2010

© Newscom

Event marketing for the Olympics begins years in advance. Here is the logo for the 2010 winter olympics in Vancouver.

ORGANIZATION MARKETING

organization marketing Marketing by mutual-benefit organizations, service organizations, and government organizations intended to persuade others to accept their goals, receive their services, or contribute to them in some way.

Organization marketing attempts to persuade people to accept the goals of, receive the services of, or contribute in some way to an organization. Organization marketing includes mutual-benefit organizations such as Service Employees International Union and the Republican and Democratic political parties; service and cultural organizations such as DePaul University, Baylor College of Medicine, St. Louis's Barnes-Jewish Hospital, and Little Rock's Clinton Presidential Library; and government organizations such as the U.S. Coast Guard, the Newark Police Department, the Sacramento Fire Department, and the U.S. Postal Service. Colleges and universities use organizational marketing to help raise funds. The University of Texas now leads all colleges and universities in the sale of licensed merchandise— the school receives around $3.5 million a year from these sales.[32]

assessment check

1. Identify the five major categories of nontraditional marketing.

2. Give an example of a way in which two or more of these categories might overlap.

6   **Explain the shift from transaction-based marketing to relationship marketing.**

From Transaction-Based Marketing to Relationship Marketing

As marketing progresses through the 21st century, a significant change is taking place in the way companies interact with customers. The traditional view of marketing as a simple exchange process, or **transaction-based marketing,** is being replaced by a different, longer-term approach that emphasizes building relationships with one customer at a time. Traditional marketing strategies focused on attracting customers and closing deals. Today's marketers realize that, although it's important to attract new customers, it's even more important to establish and maintain a relationship with them so they become loyal repeat customers. These efforts must expand to include suppliers and employees as well. Over the long term, this relationship may be translated to the **lifetime value of a customer**—the revenues and intangible benefits that a customer brings to an organization over an average lifetime, minus the investment the firm has made to attract and keep the customer.

Marketers realize that consumers are becoming more and more sophisticated. They quickly recognize marketing messages and may turn away from them if the messages don't contain information that consumers want and need. So marketers need to develop new techniques to establish and build trusting relationships between companies and their customers. As defined earlier in this chapter, relationship marketing refers to the development, growth, and maintenance of long-term, cost-effective exchange relationships with individual customers, suppliers, employees, and other partners for mutual benefit. It broadens the scope of external marketing relationships to include suppliers, customers, and referral sources. In relationship marketing, the term *customer* takes on a new meaning. Employees serve customers within an organization as well as outside it; individual employees and their departments are customers of and suppliers to one another. They must apply the same high standards of customer satisfaction to intradepartmental relationships as they do to external customer relationships. Relationship marketing recognizes the critical importance of internal marketing to the success of external marketing plans. Programs that improve customer service inside a company also raise productivity and staff morale, resulting in better customer relationships outside the firm.

Relationship marketing gives a company new opportunities to gain a competitive edge by moving customers up a loyalty ladder—from new customers to regular purchasers, then to loyal supporters of the firm and its goods and services, and finally to advocates who not only buy its products but recommend them to others, as shown in Figure 1.2.

Relationship building begins early in marketing. It starts with determining what customers need and want, then developing high-quality products to meet those needs. It continues with excellent customer service during and after purchase. It also includes programs that encourage

briefly speaking

"The best way to get what you want is to help other people get what they want."

—Zig Ziglar (b. 1926)
AMERICAN MOTIVATIONAL SPEAKER

repeat purchases and foster customer loyalty. Marketers may try to rebuild damaged relationships or rejuvenate unprofitable customers with these practices as well. Sometimes modifying a product or tailoring customer service to meet the needs of these customers can go a long way toward rebuilding a relationship.

USING INTERACTIVE MARKETING TO BUILD RELATIONSHIPS

Today's technology allows people to transmit memos, reports, and drawings quickly and inexpensively over phone lines, cables, or wireless devices. People can subscribe to personalized news services that deliver article summaries on specified topics directly to their computers or cell phones. They can communicate via e-mail, voice mail, text messages, fax, videoconferencing, and computer networks; pay bills using online banking services; and use online resources to get information about everything from theater events to a local Toyota dealer's special sale. As an increasing number of Internet users in the United States use wireless devices such as smart phones or notebook computers to access the Web and check their e-mail, the stage is set for **mobile marketing**—marketing messages transmitted via wireless technology.

figure 1.2

Converting New Customers to Advocates

Interactive media technologies combine computers and telecommunications resources to create software that users can control. Putting power into the hands of customers allows better communication, which can build relationships. **Interactive marketing** refers to buyer–seller communications in which the customer controls the amount and type of information received from a marketer. This technique provides immediate access to key product information when the consumer wants it. Interactive marketing allows marketers and consumers to customize their communication. Customers may come to companies for information, creating opportunities for one-to-one marketing. They also can tell the company what they like or dislike about a product, and they can just as easily click the exit button and move on to another area. As interactive promotions grow in number and popularity, the challenge is to attract and hold consumer attention.

High-end bicycle manufacturer Cannondale hosts a company blog that it sees as a lively alternative to its customer-service department. "One of the key benefits that we've seen through the blog is the ability to acknowledge and respond to technical product-related questions directly and less formally, and post the answers in an open forum for others to see and comment on," says the head of the company's Web operations. "It puts a face on our customer support function, and I believe it has had a direct impact on increasing sales."[33]

Through ads on YouTube, Google, CNN.com, and online communities, Dunkin' Donuts invited customers to upload their own videos about "How do you keep America running?" on its YouTube channel. Fifty winners received a year's supply of Dunkin' Donuts coffee, and the top 10 videos had a chance to appear on the company's Web site and other Internet locations. In other interactive efforts, Dunkin' Donuts customers were asked to send stories about and share personal experiences with the chain's coffee drinks. Some of the best were even made into commercials.[34]

Interactive marketing can also allow larger exchanges in which consumers can communicate with one another using e-mail or social networking sites. These electronic conversations establish innovative relationships between users and the business, providing customized information based on users' interests and levels of understanding.

The increasing number of Internet users in the United States using wireless devices has set the stage for mobile marketing—marketing messages transmitted via wireless technology.

By converting indifferent customers into loyal ones, companies generate repeat sales. The cost of maintaining existing customers is far below the cost of finding new ones, and these loyal customers are profitable. Some of the best repeat customers are those who are also willing to spread the word—create a buzz—about a product. **Buzz marketing** can be very effective in attracting new customers by bridging the gap between a company and its products. Companies as diverse as Microsoft and KFC have tapped customers to create a buzz about their products. Firms that make the most efficient use of buzz marketing warn that it is not a "one-way" approach to building customer relationships.

Acknowledging the growing importance of public opinion, NASCAR uses a new Web-based research tool called Buzz Manager to cull information from sports blogs, podcasts, YouTube videos, and other online sources to find out what fans are saying about a particular racecar driver or corporate sponsor. The results are boiled down to an at-a-glance Buzz Rating from 1 to 10. "It's online word of mouth," says the tool's developer, who designed it to apply to all sports and whose other clients include ESPN and the NBA. "The value of listening to it is amazing."[35]

Effective relationship marketing often relies heavily on information technologies such as computer databases that record customers' tastes, price preferences, and lifestyles. This technology helps companies become one-to-one marketers that gather customer-specific information and provide individually customized goods and services. The firms target their marketing programs to appropriate groups rather than relying on mass-marketing campaigns. Companies that study customer preferences and react accordingly gain distinct competitive advantages.

DEVELOPING PARTNERSHIPS AND STRATEGIC ALLIANCES

Relationship marketing does not apply just to individual consumers and employees. It also affects a wide range of other markets, including business-to-business relationships with the firm's suppliers and distributors as well as other types of corporate partnerships. In the past, companies often have viewed their suppliers as adversaries against whom they must fiercely negotiate prices, playing one off against the other. But this attitude has changed radically as both marketers and their suppliers discover the benefits of collaborative relationships.

strategic alliance
Partnerships in which two or more companies combine resources and capital to create competitive advantages in a new market.

The formation of **strategic alliances**—partnerships that create competitive advantages—is also on the rise. Alliances take many forms, including product development partnerships that involve shared costs for research and development and marketing, and vertical alliances in which one company provides a product or component to another firm, which then distributes or sells it under its own brand. Major League Baseball is a revenue-sharing partner with online ticket agency StubHub, owned by eBay, which connects sports fans who have event tickets to buy and sell. "The taboo of the secondary ticket market has been all but eliminated," according to one professor of sports business at the University of Southern California, who believes sports franchises are asking themselves, "Why not capture some of the revenue that for years has been left on the table to scalpers?"[36]

Not-for-profit organizations often use strategic alliances to raise awareness and funds for their causes. *National Geographic* teamed up with Oriental Weavers to create a line of rugs inspired by world cultures. The National Geographic Society's proceeds from this collection go to its World Cultures Fund, which supports the study and preservation of world cultures.

assessment check

1. How does relationship marketing give companies a competitive edge?

2. Why is interactive marketing an important tool for marketers?

3. What is a strategic alliance?

7 **Identify the universal functions of marketing.**

Costs and Functions of Marketing

Firms must spend money to create time, place, and ownership utilities. Numerous attempts have been made to measure marketing costs in relation to overall product costs, and most estimates have ranged between 40 and 60 percent of total costs. On average, half of the costs involved in a product, such as a Subway sandwich, a Toyota Prius, or a trip to Costa Rica, can be traced directly to marketing. These costs are not associated with wheat, metal, or other raw materials nor are they associated with baking, welding, or any of the other production functions necessary for creating form utility. What functions does marketing perform, and why are they important in creating customer satisfaction?

As Figure 1.3 reveals, marketing is responsible for the performance of eight universal functions: buying, selling, transporting, storing, standardizing and grading, financing, risk taking, and securing marketing information. Some functions are performed by manufacturers, others by retailers, and still others by marketing intermediaries called **wholesalers.**

Buying and selling, the first two functions shown in Figure 1.3, represent **exchange functions.** Buying is important to marketing on several levels. Marketers must determine how and why consumers buy certain goods and services. To be successful, they must try to understand consumer behavior. In addition, retailers and other intermediaries must seek out products that will appeal to their customers. Because they generate time, place, and ownership utilities through these purchases, marketers must anticipate consumer preferences for purchases to be made several months later. Selling is the second half of the exchange process. It involves advertising, personal selling, and sales promotion in an attempt to match the firm's goods and services to consumer needs.

Transporting and storing are **physical distribution functions.** Transporting involves physically moving goods from the seller to the purchaser. Storing involves warehousing goods until they are needed for sale. Manufacturers, wholesalers, and retailers typically perform these functions.

The final four marketing functions—standardizing and grading, financing, risk taking, and securing marketing information—often are called **facilitating functions** because they help the marketer perform the exchange and physical distribution functions. Quality and quantity control standards and grades, frequently set by federal or state governments, reduce the need for purchasers to inspect each item. For example, if you request a certain size tire for your automobile, you expect to get it.

Financing is another marketing function because buyers often need access to funds to finance inventories prior to sales. Manufacturers often provide financing for their wholesale and retail customers. Some types of wholesalers perform similar functions for their markets. Finally, retailers frequently allow their customers to buy on credit with either store charge cards or major credit cards.

The seventh function, risk taking, is part of most ventures. Manufacturers create goods and services based on research and their belief that consumers need them. Wholesalers and retailers acquire inventory based on similar expectations of future consumer demand. Entrepreneurial risk takers accommodate these uncertainties about future consumer behavior when they market goods and services.

figure 1.3

Eight Universal Marketing Functions

1. **Buying**
Ensuring that product offerings are available in sufficient quantities to meet customer demands

2. **Selling**
Using advertising, personal selling, and sales promotion to match products to customer needs

3. **Transporting**
Moving products from their point of production to locations convenient for purchasers

4. **Storing**
Warehousing products until needed for sale

5. **Standardizing and Grading**
Ensuring that product offerings meet quality and quantity controls of size, weight, and other variables

6. **Financing**
Providing credit for channel members (wholesalers and retailers) and consumers

7. **Risk Taking**
Dealing with uncertainty about future customer purchases

8. **Securing Marketing Information**
Collecting information about consumers, competitors, and channel members for use in making marketing decisions

The final marketing function involves securing marketing information. Marketers gather information about potential customers: who they are, what they buy, where they buy, and how they buy. By collecting and analyzing marketing information, marketers can understand why consumers purchase some goods while passing others by. This information also helps determine what consumers want and need—and how to offer goods and services to satisfy them. So marketing is the direct connection between a firm and its customers, the link that helps build and maintain lasting relationships.

assessment check

1. Which two marketing functions represent exchange functions?

2. Which two functions represent physical distribution functions?

3. Which four functions are facilitating functions?

8 Demonstrate the relationship between ethical business practices, social responsibility, and marketplace success.

Ethics and Social Responsibility: Doing Well by Doing Good

Ethics are moral standards of behavior expected by a society. Most companies do their best to abide by an ethical code of conduct, but sometimes organizations and their leaders fall short. Several years ago, the Texas-based energy giant Enron collapsed, taking with it the retirement savings of its employees and investors. In another scandal, executives from Tyco were convicted of using millions of company dollars for their personal benefit. And chemical manufacturer Monsanto was convicted not only of polluting water sources and soil in a rural Alabama area for decades but of ignoring evidence its own scientists had gathered indicating the extent and severity of the pollution.

Despite these and other alleged breaches of ethical standards, most businesspeople follow ethical practices. More than half of all major corporations now offer ethics training to employees, and most corporate mission statements include pledges to protect the environment, contribute to communities, and improve workers' lives. This book encourages you to follow the highest ethical standards throughout your business and marketing career. Because ethics and social responsibility are so important to marketers, each chapter in this book contains a critical-thinking feature titled "Solving an Ethical Controversy." This chapter's feature explores the unanswered questions about new energy-saving compact fluorescent light bulbs.

Social responsibility involves marketing philosophies, policies, procedures, and actions whose primary objective is to enhance society. Wal-Mart, for instance, has made great strides in reducing its use of energy in its stores; see the "Marketing Success" feature for details. Social

MARKETING SUCCESS

Wal-Mart's Big Environmental Push: Green SuperCenters

Background. Wal-Mart, the world's largest retailer, withstood criticism from environmental groups to pursue unique energy-saving innovations, including auditing the energy use of its suppliers in seven product areas like DVDs, toothpaste, milk, soft drinks, and beer. It also cut energy use throughout its stores and opened high-efficiency supercenters. The logical next step? To create climate-specific stores that reduce energy use even more.

The Challenge. "Difficult, yes. Impossible, no." That's how Wal-Mart's vice-president of prototype design and construction standards viewed the challenge of designing a new type of store that would take the hot climate of Western states into account.

The Strategy. Engineers, architects, and quality-control experts devised a prototype that recently rolled out in the desert environment of Las Vegas. The new store uses natural

Solving an ethical controversy

Does "Green" Light Have a Dark Side?

The U.S. Department of Energy believes if every household replaced just five incandescent bulbs with new compact fluorescents, the effect on greenhouse emissions would equal taking 10 million cars off the road. Compact fluorescents use 75 percent less energy, emit 90 percent less heat, and last up to 10 times longer than conventional bulbs. Manufacturer General Electric, energy supplier Con Edison, and retailers Home Depot and Wal-Mart are joining the push to get the public to make the switch. By 2012, the new bulbs may be virtually mandatory, since by law all bulbs must soon meet strict efficiency standards.

But each compact bulb contains a tiny amount of mercury, a highly toxic element whose presence is critical to the bulb's functioning but poses a potential risk. That makes disposing of the bulbs problematic and breaking them at home hazardous to your health.

Are compact fluorescent bulbs really environmentally friendly?

PRO

1. Compact fluorescent bulbs significantly reduce the amount of pollutants in the environment because we burn less coal to use them.

2. The improvement in efficiency means we save energy now and use less energy to produce and distribute replacement bulbs.

CON

1. Compact fluorescents can end up in landfills with other trash, and their mercury can leak into the ground, contaminating water supplies.

2. The bulbs emit a harsher quality of light than consumers are used to, and few lighting fixtures are designed to accommodate them, slowing public adoption.

Summary

Wal-Mart reports compact fluorescents still make up fewer than 20 percent of bulb sales, but some cities are addressing the disposal problem by collecting used bulbs with other hazardous waste like paint and batteries, and home furnishings marketer Ikea accepts bulbs for safe disposal. Meanwhile, manufacturers promise a wider variety of bulbs and fixtures is on the way.

Sources: "How Compact Fluorescents Compare with Incandescents," U.S. Department of Energy: Energy Efficiency and Renewable Energy, eere.energy.gov, accessed April 16, 2009; Julie Scelfo, "Any Other Bright Ideas?" *The New York Times*, January 10, 2008, www.nytimes.com; Alex Matthiessen, "The Dark Side of Green Light," *The New York Times*, July 29, 2007, wwwnytimes.com.

cooling systems on the roof to chill water that circulates through pipes in the floor of the 210,000-square-foot interior and keeps the temperature of the shopping area a comfortable 67 degrees. The same cooled water helps chill the grocery and freezer cases. The store needs only ten air-handling units to circulate fresh outdoor air inside, compared with 40 for a conventional store. That means less noise, fewer materials, and lower maintenance costs. Meanwhile, waste heat from the refrigeration system supplies hot water to the kitchen and rest rooms, and skylights provide most of the daytime lighting.

The Outcome. The prototype store is 45 percent more energy efficient than stores built just a few years ago and far surpasses the company's goals. It represents the first in "a new series of prototypes designed for specific climates," and many observers, including once-skeptical environmentalists, believe it will help the company to make a real difference in pushing green initiatives. Says the research director at Greenpeace, "Wal-Mart has the power to coax suppliers into changing. They're taking on a daunting task, which is pretty cool."

Sources: Company Web site, "Sustainability Fact Sheets," http://walmartstores.com, accessed April 16, 2009; Andrew Jensen, "Wal-Mart Prototype Team Embraces Efficiency Challenges," *Northwest Arkansas Business Journal*, May 5, 2008, p. 17; "Wal-Mart's Latest Green Store Slashes Energy Use," *GreenBiz.com*, March 19, 2008, www.greenbiz.com; "Wal-Mart's 'Greenest' Store Devours 45% Less Energy," *NetworkWorld*, March 18, 2008, www.networkedworld.com.

responsibility often takes the form of philanthropy, which involves making gifts of money or time to humanitarian causes. Many firms, both large and small, include social responsibility programs as part of their overall mission. These programs often produce such benefits as improved customer relationships, increased employee loyalty, marketplace success, and improved financial performance. Timberland, a manufacturer of boots, outdoor clothing, and accessories, is well known for its high ethical standards and socially responsible programs. The company donates large sums of money to charities each year, and its employees are given paid time off to volunteer for their favorite organizations, from the animal shelter to the local preschool. The company also welcomes ideas for socially responsible programs from its employees.[37] As part of an ongoing project to benefit St. Helena's Residence, a foster-care home for girls in New York City, Ernst & Young has provided employee mentors for students at New York's Stevenson High School for many years.[38]

Recent recipients of the prestigious annual awards given by the Committee Encouraging Corporate Philanthropy (CECP) include the PNC Financial Services Group, which won for its 10-year, $100 million investment in the Grow Up Great program, designed to improve school readiness in young children from birth to five years. Considered the most comprehensive such corporate endeavor in the country, Grow Up Great is designed to engage children, families, and communities in fostering a child's cognitive, social, and emotional skills. The program partners with Sesame Workshop and Family Communications, Inc.[39]

Strategic Implications of Marketing in the 21st Century

Unprecedented opportunities have emerged out of electronic commerce and computer technologies in business today. These advances and innovations have allowed organizations to reach new markets, reduce selling and marketing costs, and enhance their relationships with customers and suppliers. Thanks to the Internet, business has grown into a global market.

Both profit-seeking and not-for-profit organizations must broaden the scope of their activities to prevent myopic results in their enterprises. If they fail to do so, they lose out on promising opportunities.

Marketers must constantly look for ways to create loyal customers and build long-term relationships with those customers, often on a one-to-one basis. They must be able to anticipate customer needs and satisfy them with innovative goods and services. They must do this faster and better than the competition. And they must conduct their business according to the highest ethical standards.

Review of Chapter Objectives

1 Define *marketing,* explain how it creates utility, and describe its role in the global marketplace.

Marketing is an organizational function and a set of processes for creating, communicating, and delivering value to customers and for managing customer relationships in ways that benefit the organization and its stakeholders. Utility is the want-satisfying power of a good or service. Four basic kinds of utility exist: form, time, place, and ownership. Marketing creates time, place, and ownership utilities. Three factors have forced marketers to embrace a global marketplace: expanded international trade agreements, new technologies that have brought previously isolated nations to the marketplace, and greater interdependence of the world's economies.

2 Contrast marketing activities during the four eras in the history of marketing.

During the production era, businesspeople believed that quality products would sell themselves. The sales era emphasized convincing people to buy. The marketing concept emerged during the marketing era, in which there was a company-wide focus on consumer orientation with the objective of achieving long-term success. The relationship era focuses on establishing and maintaining relationships between customers and suppliers. Relationship marketing involves long-term, value-added relationships.

3 Explain the importance of avoiding marketing myopia.

Marketing myopia is management's failure to recognize a company's scope of business. It focuses marketers too narrowly on products and thus misses potential opportunities to satisfy customers. To avoid it, companies must broadly define their goals so that they focus on fulfilling consumer needs.

4 Describe the characteristics of not-for-profit marketing.

Not-for-profit organizations operate in both public and private sectors. The biggest distinction between not-for-profits and commercial firms is the bottom line—whether the firm is judged by its profitability levels. Not-for-profit organizations may market to multiple publics. A customer or service user of a not-for-profit organization may have less control over the organization's destiny than customers of a profit-seeking firm. In addition, resource contributors to not-for-profits may try to influence the organization's activities. Not-for-profits and for-profits may form alliances that effectively promote each other's causes and services.

5 Identify and briefly explain each of the five types of nontraditional marketing.

Person marketing focuses on efforts to cultivate the attention, interest, and preferences of a target market toward a celebrity or noted figure. Place marketing attempts to attract visitors and businesses to a particular destination. Cause marketing identifies and markets a social issue, cause, or idea. Event marketing promotes sporting, cultural, charitable, or political activities. Organization marketing attempts to influence others to accept an organization's goals or services and contribute to it in some way.

6 Explain the shift from transaction-based marketing to relationship marketing.

Relationship marketing represents a dramatic change in the way companies interact with customers. The focus on relationships gives a firm new opportunities to gain a competitive edge by moving customers up a loyalty ladder from new customers to regular purchasers and then to loyal supporters and advocates. Over the long term, this relationship may be translated to the lifetime value of a customer. Interactive technologies allow marketers direct communication with customers, permit more meaningful exchanges, and put the customer in control. Organizations may form partnerships—called *strategic alliances*—to create a competitive advantage. These alliances may involve product development, raising awareness, and other activities.

7 Identify the universal functions of marketing.

Marketing is responsible for eight universal functions, divided into three categories: (1) exchange functions (buying and selling); (2) physical distribution (transporting and storing); and (3) facilitating functions (standardization and grading, financing, risk taking, and securing market information).

8   **Demonstrate the relationship between ethical business practices, social responsibility, and marketplace success.**

Ethics are moral standards of behavior expected by a society. Companies that promote ethical behavior and social responsibility usually produce increased employee loyalty and a better public image. This image often pays off in customer growth, since many buyers want to associate themselves with—and be customers of— such firms. Social responsibility involves marketing philosophies, policies, procedures, and actions whose primary objective is the enhancement of society. These actions also generally promote a firm's public image.

assessment check: **answers**

1.1   Define *marketing* and explain how it creates utility.

Marketing is an organizational function and a set of processes for creating, communicating, and delivering value to customers and for managing customer relationships in ways that benefit the organization and its stakeholders. It creates time, place, and ownership utilities.

1.2   What three factors have forced marketers to embrace a global marketplace?

International agreements are negotiated to expand trade among nations. The growth of technology is bringing previously isolated countries into the marketplace. The interdependence of the world's economies is now a reality.

2.1   What is the major distinction between the production era and the sales era?

During the production era, businesspeople believed that quality products would sell themselves. But during the sales era, emphasis was placed on selling—persuading people to buy.

2.2   What is the marketing concept?

The marketing concept is a companywide consumer orientation with the objective of achieving long-term success.

2.3   Describe the relationship era of marketing.

The relationship era focuses on building long-term, value-added relationships over time with customers and suppliers.

3.1   What is marketing myopia?

Marketing myopia is management's failure to recognize the scope of a company's business.

3.2   Give an example of how a firm can avoid marketing myopia.

A firm can find innovative ways to reach new markets with existing goods and services.

4.1   What is the most obvious distinction between a not-for-profit organization and a commercial organization?

The biggest distinction between for-profit and not-for-profit organizations is the bottom line—whether an organization is judged by its profitability.

4.2 Why do for-profit and not-for-profit organizations sometimes form alliances?

For-profits and not-for-profits may form alliances to promote each other's causes and services. For-profits may do so as part of their social responsibility efforts.

5.1 Identify the five major categories of nontraditional marketing.

The five categories of nontraditional marketing are person, place, cause, event, and organization marketing.

5.2 Give an example of a way in which two or more of these categories might overlap.

Overlap can occur in many ways. An organization might use a person to promote its cause or event. Two organizations might use one marketing effort to promote an event and a place; for example, NBC Sports and the National Thoroughbred Racing Association combining to promote the Kentucky Derby at Churchill Downs.

6.1 How does relationship marketing give companies a competitive edge?

Relationship marketing can move customers up a loyalty ladder, generating repeat sales and long-term relationships.

6.2 Why is interactive marketing an important tool for marketers?

Interactive marketing technologies create direct communication with customers, allow larger exchanges, and put the customer in control.

6.3 What is a strategic alliance?

A strategic alliance is a partnership formed between two organizations to create a competitive advantage.

7.1 Which two marketing functions represent exchange functions?

Buying and selling are exchange functions.

7.2 Which two functions represent physical distribution functions?

Transporting and storing are physical distribution functions.

7.3 Which four functions are facilitating functions?

The facilitating functions are standardization and grading, financing, risk taking, and securing market information.

8.1 Define *ethics*.

Ethics are moral standards of behavior expected by a society.

8.2 What is *social responsibility*?

Social responsibility involves marketing philosophies, policies, procedures, and actions whose primary objective is the enhancement of society.

Marketing Terms You Need to Know

utility 5
marketing 7
exchange process 8
consumer orientation 10
marketing concept 10

relationship marketing 11
marketing myopia 12
person marketing 15
place marketing 16
cause marketing 17

event marketing 17
organization marketing 18
strategic alliance 20

Other Important Marketing Terms

production orientation 9
sales orientation 10
seller's market 10
buyer's market 10
bottom line 14
transaction-based marketing 18

lifetime value of a customer 18
mobile marketing 19
interactive marketing 19
buzz marketing 20
wholesalers 21
exchange functions 21

physical distribution functions 21
facilitating functions 21
ethics 22
social responsibility 22

Assurance of Learning Review

1. Identify the four types of utility and give an example of each.

2. What condition in the marketplace gave rise to the need for a consumer orientation by businesses after World War II?

3. Define *relationship marketing* and describe how it fits into the marketing concept.

4. Why do not-for-profit organizations need to engage in marketing efforts?

5. Give an example of how Big Apple Bagels could use one or more of the nontraditional marketing techniques to promote the opening of a new franchise.

6. What might be some of the benefits of mobile marketing for firms that use it to reach out to consumers?

7. Describe the significance of the shift from transaction-based marketing to relationship marketing. When does relationship building begin?

8. Identify the two exchange functions of marketing and explain why they are important to the overall marketing program.

9. How does the physical distribution function create utility?

10. How do ethics and social responsibility help a firm achieve marketplace success?

Projects and Teamwork Exercises

1. Consider each of the following firms and describe how the firm's goods and/or services can create different types of utility. If necessary, go online to the company's Web site to learn more about it. You can do this alone or in a team.
   a. Olive Garden, Red Robin, Chili's, or another restaurant chain
   b. Flickr or other online digital photo service
   c. Busch Gardens
   d. eBay
   e. SuperValu supermarkets

2. With a classmate, choose a U.S.-based company whose products you think will do well in certain overseas markets. Suggestions include Pizza Hut, Cuts Fitness (for Men) or Curves (for Women), StubHub, ColdPlay, or American Eagle Outfitters. The company can be anything from a music group to a clothing retailer—anything that interests you. Then write a plan for how you would target and communicate with overseas markets.

3. Choose a company that interests you from the following list or select one of your own. Research the company online, through business magazines, or through other sources to identify the scope of its business. Write a brief description of the company's current scope of business. Then describe strategies for avoiding marketing myopia, expanding the company's scope of business over the next ten years.
   a. UPS (delivery service)
   b. Walt Disney World
   c. Sony
   d. E*Trade
   e. Apple Inc.

4. With a classmate, choose one of the following not-for-profit organizations. Then come up with a for-profit firm with which you think your organization could form a strategic alliance. Create a presentation—an ad, a poster, or the like—illustrating and promoting the partnership.
    a. U.S. Postal Service
    b. Make-a-Wish Foundation
    c. Habitat for Humanity
    d. American Cancer Society
    e. American Kennel Club

5. With a classmate, choose one of the following for-profit organizations. Then create a presentation using person, place, cause, event, or organization marketing to promote its products.
    a. MasterCard
    b. L'Oréal Paris
    c. Trek bicycles
    d. T-Mobile
    e. Subway

Critical-Thinking Exercises

1. How does an organization create a customer?

2. How can marketers use interactive marketing to convert needs to wants and ultimately build long-term relationships with customers?

3. Why is utility such an important feature of marketing?

4. What benefits—monetary and nonmonetary—do social responsibility programs bring to a business?

5. Why is determining the lifetime value of a customer an important analysis for a company to make?

6. Why is it important for a firm to establish high ethical standards for its business practices? What role do you think marketers play in implementing these high standards?

Ethics Exercise

You are having lunch with a friend who works for a marketing agency that competes with yours. Suddenly he remembers an errand he has to run before returning to work, and he rushes off with a hasty good-bye after giving you some money to cover his lunch. As you gather your things to leave a few minutes later, you realize your friend left a folder on the table with a client's name on the cover. Your company is very interested in doing some work for this client in the future.

1. Would you take a quick look at the contents of the folder before you return it to your friend? Why or why not?

2. Would you show the folder to anyone in your office? Why or why not?

3. When you return the folder to your friend, would you mention the contents and offer your own commentary on them? Why or why not?

Internet Exercises

1. **Careers in marketing.** Visit the U.S. Bureau of Labor Statistics Web site (www.bls.gov) and click on "Occupational Outlook Handbook." Next, click on "Management" and then "Advertising, Marketing, Promotion, Public Relations, and Sales Managers." Review the material and answer the following questions:
   a. What is the outlook for growth in various marketing-related occupations over the next few years?
   b. Which industry employs the largest number of sales managers?

2. **Marketing definitions.** Go to the Web site of the American Marketing Association (www.marketingpower.com). Click on "Resource Library" and then "Dictionary." Define the following marketing terms: above the fold, back haul, gatekeeper, package, and safety stock.

3. **Strategic alliances.** Computer networking firm Cisco Systems has developed many strategic alliances with other firms. Visit the Web site listed and review two of Cisco's current strategic alliances. Prepare a brief report on the overall purposes of benefits of these arrangements. (cisco.com/web/partners/pr67/part_strat_alliance_category.html)

Note: **Internet Web addresses change frequently. If you don't find the exact site listed, you may need to access the organization's home page and search from there or use a search engine such as Google.**

Case 1.1   Reinventing IBM

IBM's successful management of globalization and technological change amounts to a reinvention of the company known as "Big Blue." A firm whose original name was International Business Machines and that relied nearly exclusively on computer manufacturing is now turning to software and services to provide it with a competitive edge in today's marketplace. To increase its margins, IBM first reduced its costs, in part by hiring lower-cost labor in India to run its data centers and to help its customers maintain their IBM software products. Big Blue also addressed flattening profits in its service businesses by automating as many tasks as possible. Its senior vice president for global business services says, "The goal is to replace a lot of labor but to do it with software, not … with lower-cost labor."

The firm is also looking for profits in the higher-margin software sphere. "Software had to play a bigger role," says CEO Samuel Palmisano. "Then we could offset the transition in services." To achieve its goals, IBM bought more than 50 smaller software and service companies that specialized in security, data management, and e-commerce. "Software is now the largest provider of IBM profit, and our most stable source of growth," says the company's chief financial officer.

Higher-end services are proving profitable for IBM in new fields like energy management and conservation, fraud detection, traffic management using variable-pricing models, personalized medicine based on genetics, and Internet-based supercomputing known as *cloud computing,* which many believe is the next step in information technology. Blue Cloud, as IBM's supercomputing initiative is known, relies on open-source programming but will ultimately help sell more IBM software, hardware, and services that assist corporate clients become more efficient, reduce power usage, and save costs.

IBM is also tackling social media, testing in-house versions of networking and blogging tools like Facebook and Twitter. It currently uses them to connect and strengthen links among its 400,000 far-flung employees and work teams, but it also hopes they will attract bright new hires. And farther down the line, IBM hopes products like its new Atlas Connections, which digests e-mail and chat content to help users build networks of contacts, will become industry-leading innovations that also become profitable. The company maintains that Atlas is already "the fastest-growing software product in IBM history."

And Big Blue still hopes to challenge Microsoft in the office software arena. It's joined forces with Google and Sun Microsystems to offer free alternatives to Microsoft's popular Word, Excel, and PowerPoint programs.

Questions for Critical Thinking

1. How do IBM's plans for its goods and services meet the definition of marketing? How do you think they help create utility?

2. IBM has inked partnerships with Google and Sun Microsystems. What other partnerships do you think might be useful to its future plans? Why?

Sources: Company Web site, "IBM Social Computing Guidelines," http://www .ibm.com, accessed April 16, 2009; Stephen Baker, "Big Blue Embraces Social Media," *BusinessWeek,* May 22, 2008, www.businessweek.com; Steve Lohr, "IBM to Push 'Cloud Computing,' Using Data from Afar," *The New York Times,* November 15, 2007, www.nytimes.com; Steve Lohr, "IBM to Offer Office Software Free in Challenge to Microsoft's Line," *The New York Times,* September 18, 2007, www. nytimes.com; Steve Lohr, "IBM Showing that Giants Can Be Nimble," *The New York Times,* July 18, 2007, www.nytimes.com.

Video Case 1.2   Marketing: Satisfying Customers at Flight 001

The written video case on Flight 001 appears on page VC-2. The Flight 001 video is designed to expand and highlight the concepts in this chapter and the concepts and questions covered in the written video case.

CHAP**2**TER

Strategic Planning in Contemporary Marketing

© Scott Olson/Getty Images

Target's Strategy: Low Prices, High Design, Green Practices

Target's crisp, red and white logo seems to be everywhere—on television, on the side of a bus, online, even at unlikely places like New York's Museum of Modern Art. When consumers see it, they

identify the red circle within a circle immediately. According to one recent survey, 97 percent of U.S. consumers recognize the logo—an achievement that is an inspiration to other firms. The target logo, along with

the retail chain's mascot Bullseye the bull terrier, are part of Target's strategic plan to be the store where consumers "expect more, [but] pay less." To that end, Target strives to offer shoppers more quality,

more innovative design, and more selection than its competitors—but at a lower price. Partnerships with name designers like Isaac Mizrahi and Loeffler Randall help give the Target image prestige, while prices remain significantly lower than those of many department stores. Even when economic times grow challenging, Target sticks to its strategy. "A strategy is a strategy," insists CEO Gregg Steinhafel. "Sometimes we focus a little bit more on the 'pay less,' sometimes on the 'expect more,' but the guardrails are here." Tactics for surviving when consumer confidence is down include revising the messages in store circulars to emphasize price—particularly in advertisements for food and other essentials—and cutting back on worker hours when store traffic is light anyway. But every five years, Target unveils a new prototype for its stores, and Steinhafel shows no signs of veering from this strategy.

Part of Target's strategic planning includes an emphasis on environmentally sound practices, including reusing existing buildings and refurbishing them to be energy efficient for its new store prototypes. Target's objectives include reducing waste, using energy more wisely, and operating a more sustainable business model.

Every action counts, a message that reaches consumers. In one recent year, Target reused 385 million garment hangers and recycled 2.1 million pounds of plastic and 153,000 pounds of metal from *broken* hangers. The firm also recycled 4.3 million pounds of plastic shrink-wrapping and recycled or refurbished 47,000 broken shopping carts. Partnering with its customers, Target collected 10,400 pounds of their rechargeable batteries for recycling.

In an effort to conserve energy, Target uses compact fluorescent lighting and has installed motion-sensor lighting in its stockrooms to provide light only when someone is in the room. Eighteen Target stores in California receive 20 percent of their electricity from rooftop solar-panel systems, and other sources of renewable energy are used whenever possible at different locations around the country. Finally, Target is committed to offering consumers goods made from recycled-content materials such as greeting cards, office paper, doormats, and gardening products. All of these activities are tied to Target's promise to consumers that they can expect more from their shopping experience—without paying more.[1]

OBJECTIVES

1 Distinguish between strategic planning and tactical planning.

2 Explain how marketing plans differ at various levels in an organization.

3 Identify the steps in the marketing planning process.

4 Describe successful planning tools and techniques, including Porter's Five Forces model, first and second mover strategies, SWOT analysis, and the strategic window.

5 Identify the basic elements of a marketing strategy.

6 Describe the environmental characteristics that influence strategic decisions.

7 Describe the methods for marketing planning, including business portfolio analysis and the BCG matrix.

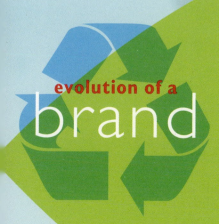

evolution of a brand

Target opened its doors in 1962, the same year as Wal-Mart and Kmart. While Kmart went bankrupt and reorganized and Wal-Mart became the biggest retailer in the world, Target sits somewhere in between, with 1,500 stores in 47 states. "[Wal-Mart] is a hell of a competition," concedes former CEO Robert Ulrich, "but ours is dependent on innovation, on design, and on quality."

• The Target brand—including the logo and Bullseye the mascot—has become one of the most recognizable in the world. Going forward, in what ways do you think Target can use these symbols to attract and build relationships with consumers?

• Target embraces green practices on both a broad scale and a small one. For instance, collecting batteries from consumers is a small step toward connecting with customers and creating a more sustainable business. How do you think Target can tie these practices in with the future growth and development of its brand?

chapter overview

• More and more consumers are purchasing smaller, more fuel-efficient vehicles, including hybrid models. The market for large SUVs is dwindling. Are fuel-efficient vehicles the wave of the future? Should we commit to building more of them and feature them prominently in our marketing?

• We have fewer customers eating at our restaurant on weekends. Should we revamp our menu? Lower our prices? Use special promotions? Update the dining room décor?

• Recent marketing research shows that we are not reaching our customer target—consumers in their early to mid-20s. Should we consider another advertising agency?

Marketers face strategic questions every day—planning strategy is a critical part of their job. The marketplace changes continually in response to changes in consumer tastes and expectations, technological developments, competitors' actions, economic trends, and political and legal events, as well as product innovations and pressures from suppliers and distributors.

Although the causes of these changes often lie outside a marketer's control, effective planning can anticipate many of the changes.

As the price of gas and jet fuel soared recently, travelers opted to stay close to home instead of booking vacations to exotic, faraway places. This represented an opportunity for places like Ocean City, Maryland, and Branson, Missouri. Any destination that promoted itself to potential vacationers within a short drive could find itself adding up the profits.

This chapter provides an important foundation for analyzing all aspects of marketing by demonstrating the importance of gathering reliable information to create an effective plan. These activities provide a structure for a firm to use its unique strengths. Marketing planning identifies the markets a company can best serve as well as the most appropriate mix of approaches to satisfy the customers in those markets. While this chapter focuses on planning, we will examine in greater detail the task of marketing research and decision making in Chapter 8.

briefly speaking

"Those who look only to the past or present are certain to miss the future."

—**John F. Kennedy (1917–1963)**
35TH PRESIDENT OF THE UNITED STATES

Marketing Planning: The Basis for Strategy and Tactics

planning Process of anticipating future events and conditions and of determining the best way to achieve organizational objectives.

Everyone plans. We plan which courses we want to take, which movie we want to see, and which outfit to wear to a party. We plan where we want to live and what career we want to pursue. Marketers plan as well. **Planning** is the process of anticipating future events and conditions and of determining the best way to achieve organizational objectives. Of course, before marketing planning can even begin, an organization must define its objectives. Planning is a continuous process that includes identifying objectives and then determining the actions through which a firm can attain those objectives. The planning process creates a blueprint for marketers, executives, production staff, and everyone else in the organization to follow for achieving organizational objectives. It also defines checkpoints so that people within the organization can compare actual performance with expectations to indicate whether current activities are moving the boost organization toward its objectives.

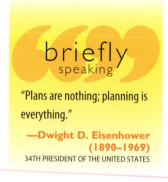

Planning is important for small and large companies. Small and large joined forces when the founder of Dagoba Organic Chocolate agreed to an acquisition by Hershey.

Planning is important for both large and small companies. In an effort to keep flying despite rising jet fuel costs and a reduction in passengers, Delta Air Lines and Northwest Airlines agreed to merge. If details are finalized, the merger would create the world's largest airline. Prior to the agreement, both airlines had filed and emerged from bankruptcy protection. Plans for the combined airline included offering flights to 400 destinations in 67 countries and providing competitive fares. In addition, executives noted that no major hubs would be closed.[2]

At the other end of the size spectrum, Frederick Schilling founded a small company called Dagoba Organic Chocolate in the hope that his product would eventually reach health-conscious consumers around the country through health-food stores and premium markets. When Dagoba became a hit, the big companies called on Schilling with a plan to buy out his operation. Surprising some of his friends and fans, Schilling agreed to an acquisition by Hershey. "There's only so much impact a small company can have on environmental restoration and social justice for farmers," reasoned Schilling. "Now I can use Hershey's distribution framework to reach more customers and bring Dagoba to full fruition."[3]

Marketing planning—implementing planning activities devoted to achieving marketing objectives—establishes the basis for any marketing strategy. Product lines, pricing decisions, selection of appropriate distribution channels, and decisions relating to promotional campaigns all depend on plans formulated within the marketing organization. In today's boundaryless organizations, many planning activities take place over the Internet with *virtual conferences*—teleconferences with computer interfaces. These conferences represent a new way to build relationships among people who are in different geographic locations. The "Etiquette Tips for Marketing Professionals" feature describes how to make these meetings work.

An important trend in marketing planning centers on relationship marketing, a firm's effort to develop long-term, cost-effective links with individual customers and suppliers for mutual benefit. Good relationships with customers can arm a firm with vital strategic weapons, and that's as true in business-to-business industries as anywhere else.

Many companies now include relationship-building goals and strategies in their plans. Relationship marketers frequently maintain databases to track customer preferences. These marketers may also manipulate product spreadsheets to answer what-if questions related to prices and marketing performance. At Procter & Gamble, the inspiration for new or better products often comes from customers themselves. The company operates in more than 150 countries with 138,000 employees, many of whom serve as the eyes and ears of the firm. Many P&G executives and marketers actually spend time in the homes of consumers, observing how they cook and eat meals, when they play, and where they shop. Other employees are trained simply to have conversations with friends and family about their lifestyles and the products or services they use. All of this interaction helps build relationships, and the information helps develop products.[4]

briefly
speaking

"Plans are nothing; planning is everything."

—**Dwight D. Eisenhower**
(1890–1969)
34TH PRESIDENT OF THE UNITED STATES

marketing planning
Implementing planning activities devoted to achieving marketing objectives.

Etiquette Tips for Marketing Professionals

Planning Virtual Meetings

many companies now encourage virtual meetings to save time and travel costs. These meeting also offer the opportunity to gather people together who might not otherwise be available or able to attend. But some pitfalls exist in adapting to this virtual world of business relationships. Holding a conference over the phone or Internet can work if you follow some simple guidelines for success:

- Be sure everyone is available to sign on at the appointed time and remind participants of the time and duration of the meeting ahead of time.

- Begin the meeting with a quick introduction or reintroduction of all participants and identify the goals.

- Request that anyone who needs to leave the conversation because of prior commitments announce when she or he is doing so.

- If your meeting doesn't involve video, state your name, such as, "This is Emma," at the beginning of each time you speak.

- Speak clearly and slowly.

- Do not engage in other tasks during the conference. For example, don't read a memo or check your e-mail during the meeting. Keep your full attention on the conference at hand.

- At the conclusion of the conference, designate someone to prepare minutes highlighting discussion points of the meeting and any conclusions, and e-mail them to all participants.

Sources: Kate Harper, "Virtual Meetings That Work," *Kate Harper Coaching,* www.kateharper.com, accessed April 16, 2009; "Effective Meetings by Phone," *Article Trader,* www.articletrader.com, accessed June 3, 2008; Karen Sobel Lojeski and Richard R. Reilly, "How Virtual Teams Can Succeed," *BusinessWeek,* May 16, 2008, www.businessweek.com.

❘ **Distinguish between strategic planning and tactical planning.**

strategic planning
Process of determining an organization's primary objectives and adopting courses of action that will achieve these objectives.

STRATEGIC PLANNING VERSUS TACTICAL PLANNING

Planning often is classified on the basis of its scope or breadth. Some extremely broad plans focus on long-range organizational objectives that will significantly affect the firm for five or more years. Other more targeted plans cover the objectives of individual business units over shorter periods.

Strategic planning can be defined as the process of determining an organization's primary objectives and adopting courses of action that will achieve these objectives. This process includes, of course, allocation of necessary resources. The word

assessment check

1. Define *planning*.

2. Give an example of strategic planning and tactical planning.

When Wendy's and Arby's united under Triarc Companies, one of their first tactical moves was to expand their breakfast and snack menus to compete directly with McDonald's and Burger King.

© AP Images/Rogelio V. Solis

strategy dates back to a Greek term meaning "the general's art." Strategic planning has a critical impact on a firm's destiny because it provides long-term direction for its decision makers.

Strategic planning is complemented by **tactical planning,** which guides the implementation of activities specified in the strategic plan. Unlike strategic plans, tactical plans typically address shorter-term actions that focus on current and near-future activities that a firm must complete to implement its larger strategies. When Wendy's and Arby's united under Triarc Companies—the franchisor of Arby's restaurant system—one of their first tactical moves was to expand their breakfast and snack menus to compete directly with McDonald's and Burger King. The combination of the two chains involved more than 10,000 restaurants nationwide, making it the third-largest fast-food company in the United States.[5]

tactical planning
Planning that guides the implementation of activities specified in the strategic plan.

PLANNING AT DIFFERENT ORGANIZATIONAL LEVELS

Planning is a major responsibility for every manager, so managers at all organizational levels devote portions of their workdays to planning. Top management—the board of directors, chief executive officers (CEOs), chief operating officers (COOs), and functional vice presidents, such as chief marketing officers—spend greater proportions of their time planning than do middle-level and supervisory-level managers. Also, top managers usually focus their planning on long-range strategic issues. In contrast, middle-level managers—such as advertising executives, regional sales managers, and marketing research directors—tend to focus on operational planning, which includes creating and implementing tactical plans for their own units. Supervisors often develop specific programs to meet goals in their areas of responsibility. Table 2.1 summarizes the types of planning undertaken at various organizational levels.

When it is most effective, the planning process includes input from a wide range of sources: employees, suppliers, and customers. Some marketing experts advocate developing a network of "influencers"—people who have influence over other people's opinions through authority, visibility, or expertise—to provide input and spread the word about company plans and products. However, assertions that social media outlets such as blogs and MySpace have the greatest influence on consumer decisions are proving false. According to one recent study, nearly 80 percent of participants said they were more likely to consider products recommended by "real-world" friends and family as opposed to virtual friends or bloggers. "This shows that popularity doesn't always equate to credibility," warns researcher Robert Hilton. "Marketers might have to reconsider who the real influencers are out there."[6]

2 **Explain how marketing plans differ at various levels in an organization.**

assessment check

1. How do marketing plans vary at different levels of the organization?
2. Why is it important to get input from others when planning?

table 2.1   Planning at Different Managerial Levels

Management Level	Types of Planning Emphasized at This Level	Examples
Top Management		
Board of directors	Strategic planning	Organization-wide objectives; fundamental strategies; long-term plans; total budget
Chief executive officer (CEO)		
Chief operating officer (COO)		
Chief financial officer (CFO)		
Middle Management		
General sales manager	Tactical planning	Quarterly and semiannual plans; business unit budgets; divisional policies and procedures
Team leader		
Director of marketing research		
Supervisory Management		
Regional sales manager	Operational planning	Daily and weekly plans; unit budgets; departmental rules and procedures
Supervisor—telemarketing office		

briefly speaking

"Marketing and innovation produce results: All the rest are costs."

—**Peter F. Drucker
(1909–2005)**
U.S. MANAGEMENT THEORIST

3 Identify the steps in the marketing planning process.

Steps in the Marketing Planning Process

The marketing planning process begins at the corporate level with the definition of a firm's mission. It then determines its objectives, assesses its resources, and evaluates environmental risks and opportunities. Guided by this information, marketers within each business unit then formulate a marketing strategy, implement the strategy through operating plans, and gather feedback to monitor and adapt strategies when necessary. Figure 2.1 shows the basic steps in the process.

DEFINING THE ORGANIZATION'S MISSION AND OBJECTIVES

mission Essential purpose that differentiates one company from others.

The planning process begins with defining the firm's **mission,** the essential purpose that differentiates the company from others. The mission statement specifies the organization's overall goals and operational scope and provides general guidelines for future management actions. Adjustments in this statement reflect changing business environments and management philosophies.

Although business writer Peter Drucker cautioned that an effective mission statement should be brief enough "to fit on a T-shirt," organizations typically define themselves with slightly longer statements. A statement may be lengthy and formal or brief and informal. Here are several examples:

briefly speaking

"If you are not No. 1 or No. 2 ... fix it, sell it, or close it."

—John F. Welch, Jr. (b. 1935)
RETIRED CHAIRMAN AND CEO, GENERAL ELECTRIC

▷ Boeing: "People working together as one global company for aerospace leadership."

▷ Avon: "The company for women."

▷ Whole Foods: "Whole foods, whole people, whole planet."

▷ Costco: "To continually provide our members with quality goods and services at the lowest possible prices."

▷ Southwest Airlines: "Dedication to the highest quality of Customer Service delivered with a sense of warmth, friendliness, individual pride, and Company Spirit."

▷ MD Anderson Cancer Center: "Making cancer history."

▷ Google: "To organize the world's information and make it universally accessible and useful."

An organization lays out its basic **objectives,** or goals, in its complete mission statement. These objectives guide development of supporting marketing objectives and plans. Soundly conceived objectives should state specific intentions such as the following:

▷ Generate a 12 percent profit over the next 18 months.

▷ Attain a 15 percent share of the market by 2012.

▷ Add 75 new outlets within the next two years.

▷ Develop 15 new products within the next 36 months.

▷ Improve or re-engineer six products within the next 12 months.

figure 2.1

The Marketing Planning Process

▷ Expand operations to the Pacific Rim by 2015.

▷ Cut manufacturing costs by 15 percent.

▷ Create energy savings of 10 percent.

ASSESSING ORGANIZATIONAL RESOURCES AND EVALUATING ENVIRONMENTAL RISKS AND OPPORTUNITIES

The third step of the marketing planning process is to assess an organization's strengths, weaknesses, and available opportunities. Organizational resources include the capabilities of the firm's production, marketing, finance, technology, and employees. An organization's planners pinpoint its strengths and weaknesses. Strengths help them set objectives, develop plans for meeting those objectives, and take advantage of marketing opportunities.

Chapter 3 will discuss environmental factors that affect marketing opportunities. Environmental effects can emerge both from within the organization and from the external environment. For example, the technological advances provided by the Internet have transformed how people communicate and do business around the world. In fact, the Internet itself has created entirely new categories of business.

FORMULATING, IMPLEMENTING, AND MONITORING A MARKETING STRATEGY

Once a firm's marketers figure out their company's best opportunities, they can develop a marketing plan designed to meet the overall objectives. A good marketing plan revolves around an efficient, flexible, and adaptable marketing strategy.

A **marketing strategy** is an overall, companywide program for selecting a particular target market and then satisfying consumers in that market through a careful blending of the elements of the marketing mix—product, distribution, promotion, and price—each of which is a subset of the overall marketing strategy.

In the two final steps of the planning process, marketers put the marketing strategy into action; then they monitor performance to ensure that objectives are achieved. Sometimes strategies need to be modified if the product's or company's actual performance is not in line with expected results. Until recently, U.S. consumers were forced to choose a cell phone service provider before selecting the phone, which came from a list of models approved by the provider. Often this restriction resulted in frustration because consumers could not always get the features they wanted and needed. But Verizon has broken rank by announcing that it will let its customers choose any cell phone, device, or software compatible with its network. If other providers follow Verizon's lead, consumers may soon enjoy a more open cell phone market.[7] Occasionally, a strategy meets with controversy or criticism, as in the case of companies that decided to send marketing messages to people's smart phones without their permission. This situation is described in the "Solving an Ethical Controversy" feature.

Successful Strategies: Tools and Techniques

We can identify a number of successful marketing planning tools and techniques. This section discusses four of them: Porter's Five Forces model, first and second mover strategies, SWOT analysis, and the strategic window. All planning strategies have the goal of creating a **sustainable**

> **briefly**
> speaking
>
> "One minor invention every ten days, a major invention every six months."
>
> **—Thomas A. Edison (1847–1931)**
> INVENTOR OF THE PHONOGRAPH, INCANDESCENT LIGHT BULB, AND MORE

assessment check

1. Distinguish between an organization's mission and its objectives.

2. What is the importance of the final step in the marketing planning process?

4 **Describe successful planning tools and techniques, including Porter's Five Forces model, first and second mover strategies, SWOT analysis, and the strategic window.**

Solving an **ethical** controversy

Ads on Smart Phones: Personalized Information or Privacy Invasion?

Just when you thought you were safe from unwanted marketing messages, your cell phone beeps. It's not a message from a friend; it's an ad telling you about a product or an event. Do you want this information, or is it an invasion of your privacy? One consumer describes receiving a text message from AT&T while he was in a business meeting. The message was an ad promoting TV show "American Idol," which AT&T sponsors. The consumer was not happy. AT&T defended the move by saying, "We want people to watch the show and participate." But this marketing strategy is not necessarily popular with everyone.

Should there be tighter restrictions on advertising messages sent to individuals' phones?

PRO

1. Just like the National Do Not Call Registry for land line phones, the government should form a registry for consumers to join if they do not want to receive unsolicited marketing messages by cell phone. "Mobile spam invades both a consumer's cell phone and the monthly bill," points out Senator Olympia Snow, cosponsor of a bill to limit these messages.

2. Location-based advertisements delve deeply into consumers' lives, tracking their movements to target ads where they are. "It's potentially a portable, personal spy," says Jeff Chester of the Center for Digital Democracy. "Users are going to be inclined to say, sure, what's harmful about a click, not realizing that they've consented to give up their [personal] information."

CON

1. As technology changes, marketers must be able to keep up with consumers' communications. Smart phones now make up more than one-third of all cell phones, which makes them a natural medium for marketers to reach customers.

2. Mobile advertising connects with consumers in a way that other types of advertising do not, tailoring messages for individual preferences, which many busy consumers appreciate.

Summary

Sending ads over smart phones stirs up heated debate. While it has huge potential for success, this strategy could backfire if marketers are not careful. The consumer who received the "American Idol" text message during a meeting was annoyed with AT&T—and could have decided to change carriers. In addition, industry observers worry that mobile messages could contain viruses and malicious spyware. But marketers insist that smart phone advertising isn't just the wave of the future—it's already here and gives companies a competitive edge.

Sources: Stephanie Condon, "Senators Introduce Bill to Curb Mobile Spam," *CNET News*, April 3, 2009, http://news.cnet.com; Antony Bruno, "Billboard Mobile Entertainment Live: Smartphones Driving Ad Revenue," *Billboard*, April 1, 2009, http://www.billboard.biz; Tom Hespos, "The Trick to Marketing on Smartphones," *iMedia Connection*, March 26, 2009, http://imediaconnection.com; Stephanie Clifford, "Advertisers Get a Trove of Clues in Smartphones," *The New York Times*, March 11, 2009, http://www.nytimes.com; Matt Richtel, "A Text Arrives. Oh, It's Just an 'Idol' Ad.," *The New York Times*, January 13, 2009, http://www.nytimes.com; Judy Mottl, "Mobile Ads Find a Welcome on Smartphones," *Internet News.com*, January 12, 2009, http://www.internetnews.com.

Porter's Five Forces Model developed by strategy expert Michael Porter that identifies five competitive forces that influence planning strategies: the threat of new entrants, the bargaining power of buyers, the bargaining power of suppliers, the threat of substitute products, and rivalry among competitors.

competitive advantage for a firm in which other companies simply cannot provide the same value to their customers that the firm does—no matter how hard they try.

PORTER'S FIVE FORCES MODEL

A number of years ago, renowned business strategist and academic Michael E. Porter identified five competitive forces that influence planning strategies in a model called **Porter's Five Forces.** Porter later updated his model to include the impact of the Internet on the strategies that businesses use. As illustrated in Figure 2.2, the five forces are potential new entrants, bargaining power of buyers, bargaining power of suppliers, threat of substitute products, and rivalry among competitors.

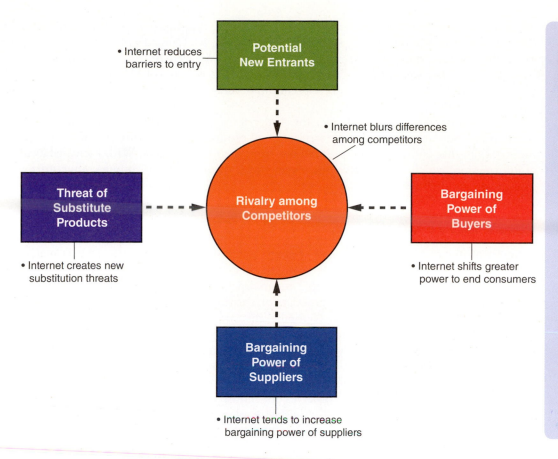

figure 2.2

Porter's Five Forces Model

Source: Adapted with permission of The Free Press, a division of Simon & Schuster Adult Publishing Group. From *Competitive Strategy: Techniques for Analyzing Industries and Competitors* by Michael E. Porter. Copyright © 1980, 1998 by The Free Press. All rights reserved.

Potential new entrants sometimes are blocked by the cost or difficulty of entering a market. It is a lot more costly and complicated to begin building aircraft than it is to start up an Internet résumé service. The Internet has reduced the barriers to market entry in many industries.

If customers have considerable bargaining power, they can greatly influence a firm's strategy. The Internet can increase a customer's buying power by providing information that might not otherwise be easily accessible such as alternate suppliers and price comparisons. Nearly two-thirds of consumers shop for information online before making an actual online or in-store purchase, according to one survey. Ninety percent of those surveyed report that they have a "better overall shopping experience" when they research goods and services online before visiting a store to make a purchase.[8]

The number of suppliers available to a manufacturer or retailer affects their bargaining power. If a seafood restaurant in the Midwest has only one supplier of Maine lobsters, that supplier has significant bargaining power. But seafood restaurants along the coast of Maine have many lobster suppliers, which gives their suppliers less bargaining power.

If customers have the opportunity to replace a company's products with goods or services from a competing firm or industry, the company's marketers may have to find a new market, change prices, or compete in other ways to maintain an advantage. McDonald's made what some considered a bold move

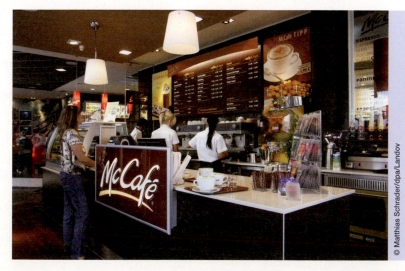

When McDonald's started offering high-end coffee drinks, they entered into direct competition with Starbucks. The threat of a substitute product can create a need for a company's marketers to find new ways to compete.

when the firm announced that it would be offering lattes, cappuccinos, espressos, and other high-end coffee drinks—in direct competition with Starbucks. McDonald's plans to install coffee bars in 14,000 of its locations. While some remain skeptical, "We were hearing loud and clear from our customers that they were ready for this," asserts Lisa Frick, director of McDonald's combined beverage business. If McDonald's can serve premium beverages at a competitive price, it may become a major player in the coffee game.[9]

The four previous forces influence the rivalry among competitors. In addition, issues such as cost and differentiation or lack of differentiation of products—along with the Internet—influence the strategies that companies use to stand out from their competitors. With increased availability of information, which tends to level the playing field, rivalry heats up among competitors who try to differentiate themselves from the crowd.

FIRST MOVER AND SECOND MOVER STRATEGIES

first mover strategy
Theory advocating that the company first to offer a product in a marketplace will be the long-term market winner.

Some firms like to adopt a **first mover strategy,** attempting to capture the greatest market share and develop long-term relationships by being the first to enter the market with a good or service, as McDonald's did when it increased its hours of operation to 24/7. Being first may also refer to entering new markets with existing products or creating significant innovations that effectively turn an old product into a new one. Naturally, this strategy has its risks—companies that follow can learn from mistakes by first movers. Apple has held firmly to the lead it established with its iTunes online music store, recently passing the 1 billion mark in downloads purchased. That success grew directly from Apple's leading the way in the market for digital music players, in which the iPod still dominates, having sold more than 100 million players. "I don't think anybody knows what it takes to knock [Apple] off," observes one industry watcher. "They are in a leadership position that is not threatened by anyone." Another Apple product, the iPhone, was also a first-mover success, with 1.4 million sold within the first 90 days.[10]

second mover strategy Theory that advocates observing closely the innovations of first movers and then improving on them to gain advantage in the marketplace.

On the other hand, Apple failed terribly with another first mover introduction, its Newton handheld computer, while other firms overtook the lead in the market. Businesses often thrive on a **second mover strategy,** observing closely the innovations of first movers and then improving on them to gain advantage in the marketplace. Target has benefited greatly from being next in line to industry leader Wal-Mart, for instance. Although Wal-Mart was the first to offer a $4 prescription program, later followed by $10 for a 90-day supply, Target has enjoyed the benefits of following Wal-Mart's lead, matching Wal-Mart's strategy.[11]

SWOT ANALYSIS

SWOT analysis
Review that helps planners compare internal organizational strengths and weaknesses with external opportunities and threats.

An important strategic planning tool, **SWOT analysis,** helps planners compare internal organizational strengths and weaknesses with external opportunities and threats. (SWOT is an acronym for *strengths, weaknesses, opportunities,* and *threats.*) This form of analysis provides managers with a critical view of the organization's internal and external environments and helps them evaluate the firm's fulfillment of its basic mission.

A company's strengths reflect its **core competencies**—what it does well. Core competencies are capabilities that customers value and competitors find difficult to duplicate. As Figure 2.3 shows, matching an internal strength with an external opportunity produces a situation

Apple's first mover strategy, introducing iTunes online music store as well as the iPod into the market, has proven successful. They still lead the way in the digital music market.

© Justin Sullivan/Getty Images

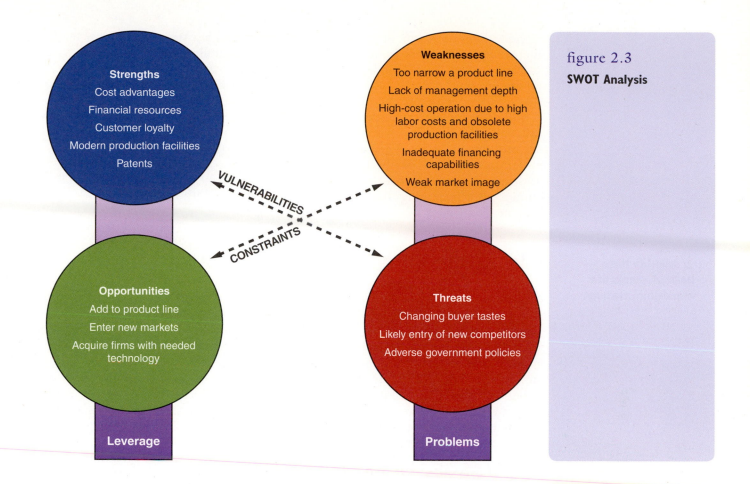

figure 2.3
SWOT Analysis

Strengths
Cost advantages
Financial resources
Customer loyalty
Modern production facilities
Patents

Weaknesses
Too narrow a product line
Lack of management depth
High-cost operation due to high labor costs and obsolete production facilities
Inadequate financing capabilities
Weak market image

VULNERABILITIES

CONSTRAINTS

Opportunities
Add to product line
Enter new markets
Acquire firms with needed technology

Threats
Changing buyer tastes
Likely entry of new competitors
Adverse government policies

Leverage

Problems

known as *leverage.* Marketers face a problem when environmental threats attack their organization's weaknesses. Planners anticipate constraints when internal weaknesses or limitations prevent their organization from taking advantage of opportunities. These internal weaknesses can create vulnerabilities for a company—environmental threats to its organizational strength.

HP is recognized the world over for its excellence in hardware—one of its greatest strengths. But to make the most of the opportunities represented by the $1.1 trillion information technology market, the firm knows that it must address its weaknesses. Specifically HP has been burdened by its own bureaucracy. "We know we are not perfect," admits CEO Mark Hurd, adding that he is working hard to "eradicate bureaucracy from HP. Our challenge is to make sure our complexity becomes an asset to customers and not a problem." The company plans to invest more time and money developing its software business despite threats that come in the form of competitors like IBM. "We are not interested in protecting the old," says Hurd. "We are interested in diving into the new."[12]

Even if a company focuses on its core competencies, sometimes it needs to broaden its offerings to maintain a competitive edge. One way to accomplish this is through a merger or an acquisition, as was the case between Wrigley and Mars, described in the "Marketing Success" feature.

THE STRATEGIC WINDOW

The success of products is also influenced by conditions in the market. Professor Derek Abell has suggested the term **strategic window** to define the limited periods during which the key requirements of a market and the particular competencies of a firm best fit together.[13] The view through a strategic window shows planners a way to relate potential opportunities to company capabilities. Such a view requires a thorough analysis of (1) current and projected external environmental conditions; (2) current and projected internal company capabilities; and (3) how, whether, and when the firm can feasibly reconcile environmental conditions and company capabilities by implementing one or more marketing strategies.

briefly speaking

"Innovation is the central issue in economic prosperity."

—**Michael Porter (b. 1947)**
AMERICAN MANAGEMENT THEORIST
AND WRITER

strategic window
Limited periods when key requirements of a market and a firm's particular competencies best fit together.

During one recent year, automakers drove through a strategic window by dramatically increasing their investment in the Indian market and doubling their production of vehicles there. General Motors, Fiat, Honda, Nissan, and Hyundai all announced Indian investments totaling about $1.5 billion, with production to reach nearly 3 million vehicles in one year. These figures fall way behind China, which has surpassed 10 million, but they represent a commitment to producing and selling cars for Indian consumers with increasing disposable income.[14]

assessment check

1. Briefly explain each of Porter's Five Forces.

2. What are the benefits and drawbacks of a first mover strategy?

3. What are the four components of the SWOT analysis? What is a strategic window?

5 **Identify the basic elements of a marketing strategy.**

Elements of a Marketing Strategy

Success for a product in the marketplace—whether it is a tangible good, a service, a cause, a person, a place, or an organization—depends on an effective marketing strategy. It's one thing to develop a great product, but if customers don't get the message about it, the product will die. An effective marketing strategy reaches the right buyers at the right time, persuades them to try the product, and develops a strong relationship with them over time. The basic elements of a marketing strategy consist of (1) the target market and (2) the marketing mix variables of product, distribution, promotion, and price that combine to satisfy the needs of the target market. The outer circle in Figure 2.4 lists environmental characteristics that provide the framework within which marketing strategies are planned.

THE TARGET MARKET

A customer-driven organization begins its overall strategy with a detailed description of its **target market:** the group of people toward whom the firm aims its marketing efforts and ultimately its merchandise. Kohl's department stores serve a target market of consumers purchasing for themselves and their families. Other companies, such as Boeing, market most of their products to business buyers such as American Airlines and government purchasers. Still other firms provide goods and services to retail and wholesale buyers. In every instance, however, marketers pinpoint their target markets as accurately as possible. Although the concept of dividing markets into specific segments is discussed in more detail in Chapter 9, it's important to understand the idea of targeting a market from the outset.

Although it may be hard to imagine the classic Oreo cookie as anything other than two discs of chocolate with a white cream filling, Kraft has reformulated the favorite to market it in China. The Chinese version is four layers of long, thin biscuits coated in chocolate, which is more appealing to consumers there. The move reflects Kraft CEO Irene Rosenberg's strategy of placing

MARKETING SUCCESS   Wrigley and Mars Concoct a Sweet Connection

Background. For some observers, the acquisition of chewing gum icon Wrigley by candymaker Mars represented the end of an era. For others, it appeared to be a sweet deal. Either way, when CEO William Wrigley Jr. agreed to a buyout by the Mars family, the merger created a stir in the confection business.

The Challenge. William Wrigley knew that, for his company to grow through the next century, it had to expand on what it already did well. "If you're limited to chewing gum, there's a limit to your importance with retailers," says an industry observer with Credit Suisse. "Wrigley has always

more authority in the hands of local business units around the world, trusting that people who live and work there know better what consumers want than the top Kraft executives located at the firm's Illinois headquarters. In addition to the Oreo reformulation, Kraft is introducing more dark chocolate products in Germany to appeal to the palates of German consumers, and it is planning to launch a premium instant coffee in Russia, where consumers prefer that beverage.[15]

Diversity plays an ever-increasing role in targeting markets. According to the U.S. Census Bureau, the rapidly growing Hispanic population in the United States surpassed African Americans as the largest minority group. The census reports more than 48 million Hispanics in America, or nearly 16 percent of the U.S. population.[16] With this phenomenal growth, marketers would be wise to pay attention to these and other markets—including women, seniors, and children of baby boomers—as they develop goods and services to offer consumers. CVS Caremark has set its aim squarely on women consumers, who make up 80 percent of the pharmacy chain's customers. Company marketers know that women are the ultimate multitaskers, so CVS is taking steps to make life easier for them. "Women are really stressed out across the country," notes the head of the pharmacy chain's mid-Atlantic region. So to assist these time-pressed consumers, CVS recently redesigned more than 1,200 of its 6,200 stores to appeal to women, providing shorter wait times for prescriptions, wider and better-lit shopping aisles, and more beauty products.[17]

figure 2.4

Element of a Marketing Strategy and Its Environmental Framework

MARKETING MIX VARIABLES

After marketers select a target market, they direct their company's activities toward profitably satisfying that segment. Although they must manipulate thousands of variables to reach this goal, marketing decision making can be divided into four strategies: product, distribution, promotion, and pricing strategies. The total package forms the **marketing mix**—the blend of four strategic elements to fit the needs and preferences of a specific target market. While the fourfold classification is useful to study and analyze, remember that the marketing mix can—and should—be an ever-changing combination of variables to achieve success.

Figure 2.4 illustrates the focus of the marketing mix variables on the central choice of the target market. In addition, decisions about product, distribution, promotion, and price are affected by the environmental factors in the outer circle of the figure. The environmental variables may play a major role in the success of a marketing program, and marketers must consider their probable effects.

marketing mix
Blending of the four strategy elements—product, distribution, promotion, and pricing—to fit the needs and preferences of a specific target market.

wanted to expand into the broader confectionary arena, and maybe they realize this is the best way to do that and keep their jobs."

The Strategy. Immediately, executives at both companies acknowledged the strengths of each other and saw that those strengths would carry the new firm forward. "The strong cultural heritage of two legendary American companies with a shared commitment to innovation, quality, and best-in-class global brands provides a great basis for this combination," said Paul S. Michaels, global president of Mars. "We are looking forward to continuing on our path of growth by jointly developing those values even further."

The Outcome. The combined company represents almost 15 percent of the confectionary market worldwide, second only to Cadbury Schweppes. The makers of Wrigley chewing gum, Milky Way candy bars, and M&Ms are now a sweet combination.

Sources: Company Web site, http://www.mars.com, accessed April 16, 2009; Pallavi Gogol, "A Bittersweet Deal for Wrigley," *BusinessWeek,* May 12, 2008, p. 34; Mike Hughlett, "Mars to Buy Wrigley Co.," *Chicago Tribune,* April 29, 2008, www.chicagotribune.com; Andrew Ross Sorkin, "Mars Acquires Wrigley's for $23 Billion," *The New York Times,* April 28, 2008, www.nytimes.com.

Product Strategy

In marketing, the word *product* means more than a good, service, or idea. Product is a broad concept that also encompasses the satisfaction of all consumer needs in relation to a good, service, or idea. So **product strategy** involves more than just deciding what goods or services the firm should offer to a group of consumers. It also includes decisions about customer service, package design, brand names, trademarks, patents, warranties, the lifecycle of a product, positioning the product in the marketplace, and new-product development. As U.S. consumers became wary of the unpredictable swings in the cost of fuel, Ford Motor Company announced its "One Ford" plan. Under the plan, the company is looking at all of the company's global divisions and using whatever expertise it has locally in other markets. Ford has developed a lineup of small, stylish cars that are popular in Europe, so the company wants to build on that advantage to offer a wider variety of smaller vehicles in the United States.[18]

Distribution Strategy

Marketers develop **distribution strategies** to ensure that consumers find their products in the proper quantities at the right times and places. Distribution decisions involve modes of transportation, warehousing, inventory control, order processing, and selection of marketing channels. Marketing channels are made up of institutions such as retailers and wholesalers—intermediaries that may be involved in a product's movement from producer to final consumer.

Technology is opening new channels of distribution in many industries. Computer software, a product made of digital data files, is ideally suited to electronic distribution. But all kinds of other products are now bought and sold over the Internet as well. By affecting everything from warehousing to order processing, technology has made possible the success of Amazon.com and eBay. Although these firms operate differently, both rely on technology for various distribution tasks. Netflix is another firm that relies on technology for its distribution. Recently the company began offering unlimited streaming video to its 7 million rental subscribers. "Unlimited has always been a very powerful selling point with our subscribers and a large part of what set us apart in the marketplace," explains the firm's chief marketing officer. "In talking with members about our streaming feature during the past year, it became clear that, as with DVDs, the idea of streaming unlimited movies and TV episodes on a PC resonated quite strongly. And we're now in a good position to offer that."[19]

Promotion Strategy

Promotion is the communications link between sellers and buyers. Organizations use varied ways to send messages about their goods, services, and ideas. They may communicate messages directly through salespeople or indirectly through advertisements and promotions. Recently Starbucks gave away 50 million free digital songs to customers who visited Starbucks locations around the United States. The marketing effort was designed to promote a new wireless iTunes music service that would be available in a select number of markets. During the giveaway, Starbucks *baristas* handed out 1.5 million "Song of the Day" cards each day, which could be redeemed at Apple's iTunes Store online.[20]

In developing a promotional strategy, marketers blend

Netflix relies on technology for its distribution.

© AP Images/Paul Sakuma

the various elements of promotion to communicate most effectively with their target market. Many companies use an approach called **integrated marketing communications (IMC)** to coordinate all promotional activities so that the consumer receives a unified and consistent message. Consumers might receive newsletters, e-mail updates, discount coupons, catalogs, invitations to company-sponsored events, and any number of other types of marketing communications about a product. Toyota dealers mail maintenance and service reminders to their customers. New England–based Shaw's Supermarkets places discount coupons in local newspapers. A political candidate may send volunteer workers through a neighborhood to invite voters to a special reception.

Promotion can occur indirectly, through advertisements like this one for Caribou Coffee.

© AP Images/PRNewsFoto/Caribou Coffee

Pricing Strategy

Pricing strategy deals with the methods of setting profitable and justifiable prices. It is closely regulated and subject to considerable public scrutiny. One of the many factors that influence a marketer's pricing strategy is competition. The computer industry has become all too familiar with price cuts by both current competitors and new market entrants. After years of steady growth, the market has become saturated with low-cost computers, driving down profit margins even farther. A good pricing strategy should create value for customers, building and strengthening their relationship with a firm and its products. But sometimes conditions in the external marketing environment cause difficulties in pricing strategies. The soaring cost of fuel has forced airlines to increase fares, cut the number of flights, and charge extra for checked baggage. As a result, travelers are scrambling for nearly nonexistent bargains or choosing to remain closer to home. Despite measures designed to keep planes in the air, industry analysts predict more airline bankruptcies in the coming months and years.[21] One company that appears to have dodged this bullet is Southwest, which locked in a purchase price for its fuel before the spike. While it was a gamble at the time, competitors and analysts are now praising the firm for its foresight. "Southwest is sitting there looking really good," observes one analyst.[22]

assessment check

1. What are the two components of every marketing strategy?
2. Identify the four strategic elements of the marketing mix.

THE MARKETING ENVIRONMENT

6 Describe the environmental characteristics that influence strategic decisions.

Marketers do not make decisions about target markets and marketing mix variables in a vacuum. They must take into account the dynamic nature of the five dimensions of the marketing environment shown back in Figure 2.4: competitive, political-legal, economic, technological, and social-cultural factors.

Concerns about the natural environment have led to new regulations concerning air and water pollution. Automobile engineers, for instance, have turned public concerns and legal issues into opportunities by developing hybrid cars. These new models are fueled by dual energy: a gasoline engine and an electric motor. Toyota was the first to enter the market with its Prius model. Note that the marketing environment is fertile ground for innovators and entrepreneurs.

Marketers must take into account public concerns about the environment, including energy conservation.

Tomorrow **begins today.**

We're defined by what we pass on to the next generation. That's why ConocoPhillips is working with Rebuilding Together to help homes and communities across our country become energy efficient. In the process, we're teaching our children about the importance of giving back and making better use of energy supplies. So we can pass on what matters . . . to the ones who matter most.

ConocoPhillips
Energy for tomorrow
www.conocophillips.com

Rebuilding Together.

Businesses are increasingly looking to foreign shores for new growth markets. Recently the Mexican conglomerate Grupo Salinas entered into an agreement with China's FAW Group Corp., one of that country's largest automakers, to build its cars in Mexico. "Most of the world's investments used to go to China," observed Mexican President Felipe Calderon, "and today China has come to invest in our country because it recognizes an enormous opportunity in Mexico, thanks to its domestic market." In addition, Mexico's position near the United States and other Central and South American countries makes it a prime location for China's entry into these markets.[23]

Technology has changed the marketing environment as well, partly with the advent of the Internet. Throughout this text, you will encounter examples of the ways the Internet and other technological developments continuously alter how firms do business. And as technology forces these changes, other aspects of the environment must respond.

Technology now produces a new formulation of diesel fuel that burns cleaner and is more efficient than earlier versions of diesel, as well as gasoline. The U.S. Environmental Protection Agency has endorsed this low-sulfur fuel, which now meets its standards for being as green as some hybrid vehicles. This change has attracted the attention of consumers searching for better, cleaner fuel; however, the price of diesel remains higher than that of gasoline, representing a challenge for marketers.[24]

Competition is never far from the marketer's mind. Among the companies finding themselves increasingly vulnerable to competition from the Internet, for instance, are media giants such as *The New York Times,* Walt Disney, major TV networks, and magazine and book publishers. Digital and online business entrepreneurs are looking for versatile ways to offer competing content and services to users everywhere, faster and more cheaply than ever before. Google, Yahoo!, and Comcast are posting record earnings. Microsoft is shifting more and more resources to the Internet, as evidenced by its investment in Facebook.[25]

Some experts have coined the phrase **rule of three,** meaning that in any industry, the three strongest, most efficient companies dominate between 70 and 90 percent of the market. Here are a few examples—all of which are household names:

▷ *Cereal manufacturers:* General Mills, Kellogg's, Post

▷ *Running shoes:* Nike, Fila USA, Reebok

▷ *Supermarkets:* Wal-Mart, Kroger, Supervalu

▷ *Pharmaceuticals:* Merck, Pfizer, Bristol-Myers Squibb

While it may seem like an uphill battle for the remaining companies in any given industry, they can find a strategy for gaining competitive ground.

The social-cultural environment includes a variety of factors, including prevailing cultural norms. As the novelty of bidding for auction items on eBay has worn off for consumers who don't necessarily have the time or desire to wait several days or a week for auction results, eBay has begun to reshape itself. Fixed-price purchase items are becoming the new norm. The "Buy It Now" option on most auctions now accounts for 42 percent of all items sold on eBay and is the fastest-growing feature on the site. CEO John Donahue predicts that this is the wave of the future for his company.[26]

The marketing environment provides a framework for all marketing activity. Marketers consider environmental dimensions when they develop strategies for segmenting and targeting markets and when they study consumer and organizational buying behavior.

assessment check

1. What are the five dimensions of the marketing environment?
2. How does technology influence the marketing environment?

Methods for Marketing Planning

As growing numbers of companies have discovered the benefits of effective marketing planning, they have developed planning methods to assist in this important function. This section discusses two useful methods: the strategic business unit concept and the market share/market growth matrix.

7 Describe the methods for marketing planning, including business portfolio analysis and the BCG matrix.

BUSINESS PORTFOLIO ANALYSIS

Although a small company may offer only a few items to its customers, a larger organization frequently offers and markets many products to widely diverse markets. Bank of America offers a wide range of financial products to businesses and consumers; Kraft Foods stocks supermarket shelves with everything from macaroni and cheese to mayonnaise. Top managers at these larger firms need a method for spotting product lines that deserve more investment as well as lines that aren't living up to expectations. So they conduct a **portfolio analysis,** in which they evaluate their company's products and divisions to determine the strongest and weakest. Much as securities analysts review their portfolios of stocks and bonds, deciding which to retain and which to discard, marketing planners must assess their products, the regions in which they operate, and other marketing mix variables. This is where the concept of an SBU comes in.

Strategic business units (SBUs) are key business units within diversified firms. Each SBU has its own managers, resources, objectives, and competitors. A division, product line, or single product may define the boundaries of an SBU. Each SBU pursues its own distinct mission and often develops its own plans independently of other units in the organization.

strategic business unit (SBU) Key business units within diversified firms.

Strategic business units, also called **categories,** focus the attention of company managers so that they can respond effectively to changing consumer demand within limited markets. Companies may have to redefine their SBUs as market conditions dictate. While the parents of today's college students will remember General Electric as the company that produced most or all of their household appliances, students themselves will probably associate the GE name with other businesses altogether. That's because GE has decided to shed its appliance division as it establishes itself in other business arenas. For instance, GE now operates a significant health-care division, and owns NBC. "Most young people know GE as a media company," observes Andrew Zolli, founder of his own innovation consulting firm.[27]

Companies redefine their strategic business units as market conditions dictate. GE, previously known for producing household appliances, has established itself in other business arenas. Here is a GE turbine for a Boeing 777.

© Frederick Florin/AFP/Getty Images

THE BCG MATRIX

To evaluate each of their organization's strategic business units, marketers need some type of portfolio

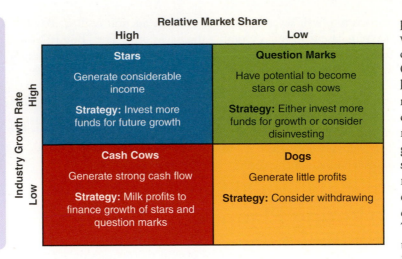

figure 2.5

BCG Market Share/ Market Growth Matrix

performance framework. A widely used framework was developed by the Boston Consulting Group. This **market share/market growth matrix** places SBUs in a four-quadrant chart that plots market share against market growth potential. **Market share** is the percentage of a market that a firm currently controls (or company sales divided by total market sales). The position of an SBU along the horizontal axis indicates its market share relative to those of competitors in the industry. Its position along the vertical axis indicates the annual growth rate of the market. After plotting all of a firm's business units, planners divide them according to the matrix's four quadrants. Figure 2.5 illustrates this matrix by labeling the four quadrants: stars, cash cows, question marks, and dogs. Firms in each quadrant require a unique marketing strategy.

Stars represent units with high market shares in high-growth markets. These products or businesses are high-growth market leaders. Although they generate considerable income, they need inflows of even more cash to finance further growth. Apple's popular iPod is the number one selling portable digital music player in the world, but Apple has already introduced upgrades and new models to remain competitive. The iPod touch is one recent offering. Consumers can also choose from the iPod Shuffle and iPod Nano, among others.[28]

Cash cows command high market shares in low-growth markets. Marketers for such an SBU want to maintain this status for as long as possible. The business produces strong cash flows, but instead of investing heavily in the unit's own promotions and production capacity, the firm can use this cash to finance the growth of other SBUs with higher growth potentials. For instance, Microsoft uses the profits from sales of its Windows operating system to finance research and development for new Internet-based technologies.[29]

Question marks achieve low market shares in high-growth markets. Marketers must decide whether to continue supporting these products or businesses because question marks typically require considerably more cash than they generate. If a question mark cannot become a star, the firm should pull out of the market and target other markets with greater potential. When some of its business units, most notably Ask.com and Ticketmaster, did not perform as expected, media giant InterActive Corp., headed by Barry Diller, sought to break IAC into five separate companies to compete more effectively with smaller firms. However, IAC's largest shareholder, Liberty Media, argued against the breakup. In the end, Diller took his argument to court and won.[30]

Dogs manage only low market shares in low-growth markets. SBUs in this category promise poor future prospects, and marketers should withdraw from these businesses or product lines as quickly as possible. In some cases, these products can be sold to other firms, where they are a better fit. IBM sold its PC business to Chinese firm Lenovo so that it could concentrate on its business services.

assessment check

1. What are SBUs?

2. Identify the four quadrants in the BCG matrix.

Strategic   Implications of   **Marketing**   **21st Century**   in the

never before has planning been as important to marketers as the 21st century speeds ahead with technological advances. Marketers need to plan carefully, accurately, and quickly if their companies are to gain a competitive advantage in today's global marketplace. They need to define their organization's mission and understand the different methods for formulating a successful marketing strategy. They must consider a changing, diverse population and the boundaryless business environment created by the Internet. They must be able to evaluate when it's best to be first to get into a market and when it's best to wait. They need to recognize when they've got a star and when they've got a dog—when to hang on and when to let go. As daunting as this seems, planning can reduce the risk and worry of bringing new goods and services to the marketplace.

Review of Chapter Objectives

1   Distinguish between strategic planning and tactical planning.

Strategic planning is the process of identifying an organization's primary objectives and adopting courses of action toward these objectives. In other words, strategic planning focuses on the big picture of which industries are central to a firm's business. Tactical planning guides the implementation of the activities specified in the strategic plan. Once a strategy is set, operational managers devise methods (tactics) to achieve the larger goals.

2   Explain how marketing plans differ at various levels in an organization.

Top management spends more time engaged in strategic planning than middle- and supervisory-level managers, who tend to focus on narrower, tactical plans for their units. Supervisory managers are more likely to develop specific plans designed to meet the goals assigned to them, for example, streamlining production processes so that they operate more efficiently.

3   Identify the steps in the marketing planning process.

The basic steps in the marketing planning process are defining the organization's mission and objectives; assessing organizational resources and evaluating environmental risks and opportunities; and formulating, implementing, and monitoring the marketing strategy.

4   Describe successful planning tools and techniques, including Porter's Five Forces model, first and second mover strategies, SWOT analysis, and the strategic window.

Porter's Five Forces are identified as the five competitive factors that influence planning strategies: potential new entrants, bargaining power of buyers, bargaining power of suppliers, threat of substitute products, and rivalry among competitors. With a first mover strategy, a firm attempts to capture the greatest market share by being first to enter the market; with a second mover strategy, a firm observes the innovations of first movers and then attempts to improve on them to gain advantage. SWOT analysis (strengths, weaknesses, opportunities, and threats) helps planners compare internal organizational strengths and weaknesses with external opportunities and threats. The strategic window identifies the limited periods during which the key requirements of a market and the competencies of a firm best fit together.

5   Identify the basic elements of a marketing strategy.

Development of a marketing strategy is a two-step process: (1) selecting a target market and (2) designing an effective marketing mix to satisfy the chosen target. The target market is the group of people toward whom a company decides to direct its marketing efforts. The marketing mix blends four strategy elements to fit the needs and preferences of a specific target market: product strategy, distribution strategy, promotion strategy, and pricing strategy.

6   Describe the environmental characteristics that influence strategic decisions.

The five dimensions of the marketing environment are competitive, political-legal, economic, technological, and social-cultural. Marketers must be aware of growing cultural diversity in the global marketplace.

7   Describe the methods for marketing planning, including business portfolio analysis and the BCG matrix.

The business portfolio analysis evaluates a company's products and divisions, including strategic business units (SBUs). The SBU focuses the attention of company managers so that they can respond effectively to changing consumer demand within certain markets. The BCG matrix places SBUs in a four-quadrant chart that plots market share against market growth potential. The four quadrants are stars, cash cows, dogs, and question marks.

assessment check: answers

1.1   Define *planning*.

Planning is the process of anticipating future events and conditions and of determining the best way to achieve organizational objectives.

1.2   Give an example of strategic planning and tactical planning.

To survive in a challenging environment that includes soaring fuel costs, several airlines have decided to merge as part of their strategic planning. Tactical plans include cutting the number of flights and charging passengers extra for checked baggage.

2.1   How do marketing plans vary at different levels of the organization?

Top managers usually focus their planning activities on long-range strategic issues. In contrast, middle-level managers focus on operational planning, which includes creating and implementing tactical plans for their own units. Supervisors develop specific programs to meet the goals in their areas of responsibility.

2.2   Why is it important to get input from others when planning?

Input from a variety of sources—other employees, suppliers, or customers—helps ensure that many ideas are considered. Involving those people in planning can also turn them into advocates for the plan.

3.1   Distinguish between an organization's mission and its objectives.

The firm's mission is the essential purpose that differentiates the company from others. Its objectives guide development of supporting marketing objectives and plans. Avon's mission is to be "the company for women." One of its objectives might be to convert all its packaging to recycled materials.

3.2   What is the importance of the final step in the marketing planning process?

In the final step of the marketing planning process, managers monitor performance to ensure that objectives are achieved.

4.1   Briefly explain each of Porter's Five Forces.

Porter's Five Forces are the threats of potential new entrants, which increases competition in a market; bargaining power of buyers, which can depress prices; bargaining power of suppliers, which can increase cost or reduce selection; threat of substitute products, which can lure customers to other products; and rivalry among competitors, which can bring about price wars or divert companies from their main goals.

4.2   What are the benefits and drawbacks of a first mover strategy?

The benefits of a first mover strategy include capturing the greatest market share and developing long-term relationships with customers. Disadvantages include the possibility that companies that follow can learn from mistakes by first movers. Apple has been a first mover with its iPod products.

4.3   What are the four components of the SWOT analysis? What is a strategic window?

SWOT analysis helps planners compare internal organizational strengths and weaknesses with external opportunities and threats. SWOT is an acronym for *strengths, weaknesses, opportunities,* and *threats.* A strategic window defines the limited periods when key requirements of a market and a firm's particular competencies best fit together.

5.1   What are the two components of every marketing strategy?

The basic elements of a marketing strategy are (1) the target market and (2) the marketing mix variables.

5.2   Identify the four strategic elements of the marketing mix.

The marketing mix consists of product, distribution, promotion, and price strategies.

6.1   What are the five dimensions of the marketing environment?

The five dimensions of the marketing environment are competitive, political-legal, economic, technological, and social-cultural factors.

6.2   How does technology influence the marketing environment?

The Internet and other technological developments continuously alter how firms do business. And as technology forces these changes, other aspects of the environment must respond.

7.1   What are SBUs?

Strategic business units (SBUs) are key business units within diversified firms. Each SBU has its own managers, resources, objectives, and competitors.

7.2   Identify the four quadrants in the BCG matrix.

The BCG matrix labels SBUs stars, cash cows, question marks, and dogs. Stars are the products with high market shares in high-growth markets; cash cows command high market shares in low-growth markets; question marks achieve low market shares in high-growth markets; and dogs manage only low market shares in low-growth markets.

Marketing Terms You Need to Know

planning 34
marketing planning 35
strategic planning 36
tactical planning 37

mission 38
Porter's Five Forces 40
first mover strategy 42
second mover strategy 42

SWOT analysis 42
strategic window 43
marketing mix 45
strategic business units (SBUs) 49

Other Important Marketing Terms

objectives 38
marketing strategy 39
sustainable competitive advantage 39
core competencies 42
target market 44

product strategy 46
distribution strategy 46
promotion 46
integrated marketing communications (IMC) 47
pricing strategy 47

rule of three 48
portfolio analysis 49
category 49
market share/market growth matrix 50
market share 50

Assurance of Learning Review

1. State whether each of the following illustrates strategic or tactical planning:
   a. China decides to enter the U.S. auto market.
   b. A local take-out restaurant decides to add more tables for eat-in dining.

2. Imagine you had a chance to interview the CEO and COO of Apple. What types of questions might you ask about their planning? Now imagine these two executives introduce you to a middle-level manager. In what kind of planning would you expect this manager to be involved?

3. What is the difference between a firm's mission and its objectives?

4. Define *marketing strategy*. Give an example of a marketing strategy practiced by a company whose products you know well.

5. Over which of Porter's Five Forces do consumers have the greatest influence?

6. What are the advantages of the first-mover strategy? The second-mover strategy? What are the drawbacks of each?

7. When using the strategic window, what three factors must marketers analyze?

8. Why is identifying a target market so important to a company?

9. Give an example of each of the four strategies in the marketing mix.

10. What is the *rule of three?* How might marketers at a small firm actually use that rule to gain competitive ground in their industry?

11. What is a *portfolio analysis?* What purpose does it serve for marketers?

12. Describe the characteristics of each of the four quadrants in the BCG matrix.

Projects and Teamwork Exercises

1. Choose one of the following companies, or select another one whose goods and services are familiar to you. On your own or with a classmate, formulate a mission statement for that company. Then create a list of objectives that reflect your company's mission.
   a. Sephora
   b. Marriott Hotels & Resorts
   c. Whole Foods Markets
   d. Southwest Airlines

2. Choose one of the companies listed or another firm that interests you. On your own or with a classmate, go online to research how technology affects its marketing strategy—how the firm uses technology and how technology might affect its marketing environment. Try to predict how technology will affect the firm's marketing strategy over the next five years.
   a. Vespa scooters
   b. QVC or HSN (shopping channels)
   c. Polaroid
   d. Friendly Planet (travel company)

3. Create a SWOT analysis for yourself, listing your own personal strengths, weaknesses, opportunities, and threats. How would you use this evaluation to move ahead in your future professional career?

4. Use your library or an Internet search engine to collect information on one of the following companies (or select one of your own). Identify the firm's target market(s). Note that a large company might have more than one target market. Write a brief proposal for a marketing strategy to reach that market.
   a. Chase Freedom Visa
   b. Sam's Club
   c. Barnes & Noble
   d. Hollister

5. With a classmate, choose a company whose products you have purchased in the past. Create two ads for one of the company's products (or product lines). One ad should focus on the product itself—its features, packaging, or brand name. The second ad should focus on pricing. Present your ads to the class for discussion. Which ad is more effective for the product and why?

Critical-Thinking Exercises

1. Suppose you are a marketer for a U.S. toy manufacturer. Two top executives have proposed getting into an entirely different field—pet supplies. What are the potential benefits and drawbacks if your firm strays from its core competencies? How would you advise your company to proceed?

2. Netflix has made thousands of streaming videos available to its unlimited subscribers. How does this strategy demonstrate a strategic window for the company?

3. Describe a consumer product that you think is particularly vulnerable to substitution. If you were a marketer for that product, what steps would you take to defend your product's position?

4. Research a company such as L.L. Bean or General Mills that has a number of different successful SBUs. What factors do you think make these units—and this company—successful from a marketing standpoint?

5. Suppose you were a marketer for a small, regional airline. Taking into consideration both the rule of three and rapidly rising fuel costs, what type of marketing strategy would you select, and why?

Ethics Exercise

Suppose you are hired as a marketer for a firm that sells bottled water. The firm's mission is "to provide the water that everyone drinks." One of its stated objectives is to reduce the amount of plastic used in its bottles. This is also part of the firm's tactical planning. But the information given to you by the design and engineering department clearly shows that they have not yet found a cost-effective way to achieve this. Still, you are pressured to advertise the bottles as eco-friendly.

1. Would you show the design information to your manager, then proceed as instructed?

2. Would you alert any outside sources about the situation? Why or why not?

Internet Exercises

1. **BCG matrix.** Visit the Web site of Procter & Gamble (www.pg.com). Select five product lines and classify each in the BCG matrix. Justify your classifications.

2. **Strategic versus tactical planning.** Review the chapter material on the differences between strategic and tactical planning. Visit the Web site of a large retailer such as Home Depot, Target, or Costco. Review the company's expansion plans, both domestic and international. Were decisions regarding expansion a result of strategic planning, tactical planning, or a combination of the two? Be prepared to defend your conclusions.

3. **Divestitures.** Occasionally companies sell individual products, or even entire product lines, to other companies. Two recent examples are Pfizer selling its consumer health products division to Johnson & Johnson, and Cadbury Schweppes divesting its soft-drinks business. Using Google or another Internet search engine, find another recent product sale. Using business portfolio analysis or the BCG matrix, prepare a brief report discussing why the seller sold the product and why the buyer purchased it.

Note: Internet Web addresses change frequently. If you don't find the exact site listed, you may need to access the organization's home page and search from there or use a search engine such as Google.

Case 2.1 Chrysler Retools for a Rebound

The U.S. auto industry has faced many roadblocks over the years, none more challenging than today's high fuel costs and

consumer reluctance to spend. Automakers are trying short-term tactics to attract buyers even as they refocus their long-term marketing strategies. Chrysler has faced several changes in ownership and leadership over the past decade. The company has changed hands three different times in the past 10 years, starting with the 1998 deal between Chrysler and Germany's Daimler. Daimler then sold its stake in 2007 to private equity firm Cerberus Capital Management, who was unable to turn around the company in time. Robert Nardelli, former Chrysler CEO during the Cerberus ownership, said, "During my 38 years in business, I've never faced a tougher challenge. Even with our early and aggressive restructuring efforts, we could not offset the negative impact of the financial crisis and the severe economic recession." In the middle of this crunch, Chrysler's new marketing chief operates with cool capability. Deborah Wahl Meyer says that the chance to refurbish Chrysler's status is what lured her away from her position at Toyota, already on a roll with new models of hybrids and other fuel-efficient vehicles. "The chance to really work and develop and expand [Chrysler's] brands and take them to the next level is the opportunity of a lifetime," she explains. "You don't have many of those chances in your career."

Part of Meyer's strategic planning includes experimenting with new marketing media. Although Chrysler already uses targeted Internet advertisements, the firm is researching ways to target advertising by Zip code. Meyer believes that one of the major keys to future success for the firm is to take marketing local so that dealers can zero in on specific customers. In addition, she wants to continue to court Hispanic consumers and younger customers—those who are just learning to drive. She wants to get a very clear sense of who Chrysler's customers are—and who they will be in the future. "As a marketer, the challenge is phenomenal," says Meyer enthusiastically. "Chrysler's been through a lot of different phases and has had incredible success, and with the way the company's structured now, it's an opportunity to put into play all the things that we know we can do to make it strong."

Meanwhile, Chrysler has also been engaged in a marketing tactic that has won praise from consumers and competitors alike. Its incentive program, "Let's Refuel America," allows buyers of most Chrysler, Dodge, and Jeep models to sign up for a gas card that locks in the price of gasoline to $2.99 per gallon for a period of three years or 36,000 miles. Launched at a time when the national average price of gas had reached $4.00 per gallon, many hailed the program as the perfect patch on a painful wound. "It's a brilliant bit of marketing—gas is on every potential car buyer's mind these days," complimented an editorial in the trade magazine *Kicking Tires*. Despite the fact that Chrysler stands to pay out less cash for the program than it has for other incentives in the past, this one has consumers considering trading in their old wheels for something new.

In the coming months and years, Chrysler executives and marketers will continue to examine closely the firm's strengths and weaknesses. Although Chrysler is still the industry leader in minivans, sales of the vehicles are slower than hoped, despite the addition of new features. The company is likely to manufacture fewer of these vehicles for the consumer market, at least over the short term, but there has been an initiative to sales in the non-consumer market. Chrysler announced that the company intends to apply to the U.S. Department of Energy's (DoE) Transportation Electrification stimulus program for a federal grant, which would enable Chrysler to establish a nationwide demonstration fleet of zero-emission electric minivans that could be used by the U.S. Postal Service for mail delivery. Meyer says her company is up to the task of facing the tough choices. "Chrysler has always been the scrappy brand," she observes with pride. "As a marketer, you'd rather be at the edge than way back there." She believes that with

good planning—even on a tight budget—she can get the right message about Chrysler products to the right consumers. "The consumer has so many messages coming at them, they're looking for a different voice to respond to," she asserts. "It's not such much a matter of absolute dollars; it's more the way we get at it."

Questions for Critical Thinking

1. Describe the difference between Chrysler's strategic plans and its tactics. Should both have the same objective? Why or why not?

2. Chrysler's motto is, "If You Dream It, We Can Build It." In what ways can the firm use strategic planning to reflect this mission?

Sources: Company Web site, www.chryslergroupllc.com and www.chrysler.com, accessed August 4, 2009; Adam Shapiro, Jeff Flock, Ken Sweet, and Joanna Ossinger, "Chrysler-Fiat Deal Signed, Company Exits Chap. 11" *Fox Business*, June 10, 2009; "Chrysler Celebrates Earth Day by Revealing All-new Electric Concepts to U.S. Postal Service" *The Auto Channel*, April 23, 2009; Melanie Lindner, "Should You Offer Incentives in a Recession?" *Forbes*, May 21, 2008, www.forbes.com; "Chrysler Extends $2.99 Gas Offer," *U.S. News & World Report*, May 20, 2008, usnews.rankingsandreviews.com; Christine Tierney, "Chrysler Offer: $2.99 Gas for 3 Years," *The Detroit News*, May 6, 2008, www.detnews.com; Dee-Ann Durbin, "Launch of Chrysler's New Minivans May Have Gotten Off to a Slower Start than Company Expected," *The San Diego Union-Tribune*, December 14, 2007, www.signonsandiego.com; Dee-Ann Durbin, "New Chrysler Marketing Head Enthusiastic," *The Boston Globe*, October 7, 2007, www.boston.com.

Video Case 2.2 Strategic Planning and the Marketing Process at Recycline

The written video case on Recycline appears on page VC-3. The Recycline video is designed to expand and highlight the concepts in this chapter and the concepts and questions covered in the written video case.

The Marketing
Environment,
Ethics, and Social
Responsibility

© AP Images/Ric Feld

Peanut Corporation of America's Safety Standards Fail Customers

"Effective immediately, all corporate operations will cease." These chilling words spelled the end of the family-run Peanut Corporation of America (PCA) but not the end of its troubling story. The

Virginia-based peanut-processing company first made headlines when a nationwide outbreak of salmonella sickened several hundred people in more than 40 states and killed as many as nine. Federal investiga-tors traced the contamination to peanuts processed in PCA's Blakeley, Georgia, plant. Those products were sold as ingredients for a number of food items, including peanut butter shipped to schools. A second plant in Texas was also closed after it tested positive for possible contamination. Hundreds of other products containing processed pea-nuts—from snack bars to TV dinners—were recalled.

PCA faces Chapter 7 bankruptcy to pay off its debts, estimated between $1 and $10 million. More than a dozen civil lawsuits are pending against the firm, and a criminal investigation is under way. The main charge against PCA is likely to be that its executives knew its products were tainted but ordered them to be shipped to its food-company customers anyway. Stewart Parnell, the company's president, would not comment on e-mails that appeared to implicate him.

The company's problems with food safety are long-standing. Its facilities should have been kept completely dry, for instance, because moisture promotes salmonella growth. Yet the roof "leaked when it rained," said the plant's assistant manager. "Different crews would come to work on it, but it would still leak." Workers reported seeing puddles on the floor under open gaps in the roof. Other chronic problems included poor storage procedures that allowed raw peanuts to come

into contact with processed ones, flaking rust, roasters that were not hot enough to destroy germs, grease buildup on equipment, and the presence of rodents, roaches, and mold.

"It was pretty filthy around there," said one former worker. "I never ate the peanut butter," admitted a former PCA cook, "and I wouldn't allow my kids to eat it." Other workers claimed the company put new date stamps on out-of-date containers of peanut paste and mended holes made by rats in packaging, all to continue sending products out.

Food safety audits failed to turn up any problems, but the audit company, American Institute of Baking International, was hired by PCA. The audit firm "realized that if they didn't give PCA a glowing review, they were not going to get hired again," said Henry Waxman, chairman of the House Energy and Commerce Committee. Even PCA's own inspections yielded worrisome results, but they were ignored.

Nestlé USA, a PCA customer, conducted its own on-site audits and rejected PCA products after finding rat droppings and insects at both the Georgia and Texas plants. Kellogg, which has about 1,000 different suppliers, relied on third-party audits of PCA and usually purchased between $5 and $10 million worth of peanut ingredients from the firm each year. Recalls of many of its Keebler and Famous Amos products have since cost Kellogg about $70 million. "It's extremely difficult," said Kellogg's CEO, "when you have an unethical and dishonest supplier, to manage this."

The Georgia State Agriculture Department found repeated safety violations at the Blakeley plant, but PCA documents suggest its managers would either ship contaminated products anyway or send samples out for repeated testing until they received a good result and then ship them, without correcting the factory conditions that promoted salmonella.[1]

Evidence suggests PCA officials not only knew plant conditions were unsanitary but actively tried to conceal problems. They arranged to be notified of pending inspections ahead of time, manipulated product testing, and shipped products they knew posed a public health risk. "So we appear to have a total systemic breakdown," said the chairman of the Senate investigations panel, "with severe consequences for hundreds of victims."

- PCA reportedly stopped using one testing lab that found more contaminants in its products than other labs did. But neither the company nor the lab was legally bound to report the bad test results to the government. What problems did this loophole cause? Should it be closed?

- Kellogg says it will follow Nestlé's example and pay for its own audits of peanut-processing companies on which it relies, but it cannot audit all its 1,000 food suppliers. Since state and federal food safety inspectors also conduct such audits, how much responsibility should companies like Kellogg bear for the safety of their products? What can they do to ensure that third-party audits of their suppliers are reliable?

evolution of a
brand

evolution of a brand
continued

- PCA issued a public statement saying, "We are sorry our process fell short of not only our goals, but more importantly, your expectations." Do you think the company handled the public health consequences of its lax standards well? What could it have done better in the aftermath of the salmonella outbreak?

chapter overview

❚ **Identify the five components of the marketing environment.**

Change is a fact of life for all people, including marketers. Adapting to change in an environment as complex and unpredictable as the world's energy usage is perhaps the supreme challenge. In response to the rising cost of fuel, many airlines—including American, Delta, and United—are taking their less fuel-efficient aircraft out of service and eliminating flights.[2]

Although some change may be the result of sudden crises, more often it is the result of a gradual trend in lifestyle, income, population, and other factors. Consumers are increasingly interested in buying "green" products—goods that minimize their impact on the environment. Technology can trigger a sudden change in the marketplace: in one fell swoop, it appeared that Internet music downloads had replaced traditional CDs. And within mere months of offering its iPhone, Apple introduced the iPod touch MP3 player, which borrowed touch-screen technology from the iPhone.

Marketers must anticipate and plan for change. They must set goals to meet the concerns of customers, employees, shareholders, and the general public. Industry competition, legal constraints, the impact of technology on product designs, and social concerns are some of the many important factors that shape the business environment. All potentially have an impact on a firm's goods and services. Although external forces frequently are outside the marketer's control, decision makers must still consider those influences together with the variables of the marketing mix in developing, and occasionally modifying, marketing plans and strategies that take these environmental factors into consideration.

This chapter begins by describing five forces in marketing's external environment: competitive, political-legal, economic, technological, and

> **briefly**
> speaking
>
> "If you look at a typical week I have, it's a combination of trying to lead a company in change in an industry in change."
>
> —**Susan Whiting** (b. 1957)
> CEO OF NIELSEN MEDIA RESEARCH

social-cultural. Figure 3.1 identifies them as the foundation for making decisions that involve the four marketing mix elements and the target market. These forces provide the frame of reference within which all marketing decisions are made. The second focus of this chapter is marketing ethics and social responsibility. That section describes the nature of marketers' responsibilities both to business and to society at large.

figure 3.1

Elements of the Marketing Mix within an Environmental Framework

Environmental Scanning and Environmental Management

Marketers constantly monitor crucial trends and developments in the business environment. **Environmental scanning** is the process of collecting information about the external marketing environment to identify and interpret potential trends. The goal of this process is to analyze the information and decide whether these trends represent significant opportunities or pose major threats to the company. The firm can then determine the best response to a particular environmental change.

Nearly 80 percent of the toys sold in the United States are made in China. After learning that some of their Chinese-made products were unsafe for children, several American toy retailers—including Mattel, the nation's largest—issued a series of massive product recalls. Some product failures involved the presence of tiny magnets in the toys. If swallowed, the magnets could prove harmful or even fatal. In another recall, more than 4 million craft kits were pulled off store shelves because they contained a dangerous chemical. Millions more recalled toys contained lead paint, a toxic substance linked to brain damage and other serious health problems. The use of lead paint in toys has long been prohibited by the U.S. Consumer Product Safety Commission (CPSC). Mattel moved quickly to investigate the problems and notified the CPSC of its findings. The company vowed to immediately tighten its quality-control procedures and more closely monitor its production facilities.[3]

Environmental scanning is a vital component of effective **environmental management.** Environmental management involves marketers' efforts to achieve organizational objectives by predicting and influencing the competitive, political-legal, economic, technological, and social-cultural environments. In the political-legal environment, managers who seek modifications of regulations, laws, or tariff restrictions may lobby legislators or contribute to the campaigns of sympathetic politicians. At the height of the U.S. mortgage crisis, Congress considered passing laws that would allow the bankruptcy courts to revise the terms of troubled mortgages and offer borrowers some financial relief. The Mortgage Bankers Association, the mortgage industry's largest trade group, spent $3.7 million lobbying legislators and federal agencies in an attempt to avoid increasing regulation.[4]

environmental scanning Process of collecting information about the external marketing environment to identify and interpret potential trends.

environmental management Attainment of organizational objectives by predicting and influencing the competitive, political-legal, economic, technological, and social-cultural environments.

Strategic alliances allow firms to combine resources and capital to create competitive advantages in the market.

Joining forces
AkzoNobel and ICI

Together, we're stronger. The integration of ICI into AkzoNobel has created a major industrial company. We now have the combined creative force of more than 60,000 individuals. The new AkzoNobel is the world's largest coatings manufacturer, the number one in decorative paints, and a leading supplier of specialty chemicals. We not only think with passion, but we also have the expertise to deliver on our ideas. By pushing our imagination beyond the normal limits, we're continuing to color, protect and transform virtually every aspect of daily life. For everyone across the globe. We're AkzoNobel. We're committed to delivering Tomorrow's Answers Today.

Glidden sikkens Dulux International

To see our complete brand portfolio please visit AkzoNobel.com

AkzoNobel
Tomorrow's Answers Today

© Courtesy of Akzo Nobel

For many domestic and international firms, competing with established industry leaders frequently involves **strategic alliances**—partnerships with other firms in which the partners combine resources and capital to create competitive advantages in a new market. Strategic alliances are especially common in international marketing, in which partnerships with local firms provide regional expertise for a company expanding its operations abroad. Members of such alliances share risks and profits. Alliances are considered essential in a country such as China where laws require foreign firms doing business there to work with local companies.

Through successful research and development efforts, firms may influence changes in their own technological environments. A research breakthrough may lead to reduced production costs or a technologically superior new product. While changes in the marketing environment may be beyond the control of individual marketers, managers continually seek to predict their impact on marketing decisions and to modify operations to meet changing market needs. Even modest environmental shifts can alter the results of those decisions.

assessment check

1. Define *environmental scanning*.
2. How does environmental scanning contribute to environmental management?

The Competitive Environment

competitive environment
Interactive process that occurs in the marketplace among marketers of directly competitive products, marketers of products that can be substituted for one another, and marketers competing for the consumer's purchasing power.

As organizations vie to satisfy customers, the interactive exchange creates the **competitive environment.** Marketing decisions by individual firms influence consumer responses in the marketplace. They also affect the marketing strategies of competitors. As a consequence, marketers must continually monitor their competitors' marketing activities: their products, distribution channels, prices, and promotional efforts.

Few organizations have **monopoly** positions as the sole supplier of a good or service in the marketplace. Utilities, such as natural gas, electricity, water, and cable TV service have traditionally accepted considerable regulation from local authorities who controlled such marketing-related factors as rates, service levels, and geographic coverage. In exchange, the utilities gained exclusive rights to serve a particular group of consumers. But the **deregulation movement** of the past three decades has ended total monopoly protection for most utilities. Many shoppers can choose from alternative cable TV and Internet providers, cell phone and traditional telephone carriers, and even gas and electric utilities. Some firms, such as pharmaceutical giants Merck and Pfizer, have *temporary* monopolies provided by patents on new drugs. When the FDA approves a new drug for lowering cholesterol or improving sleep, its manufacturer typically is granted exclusive rights to produce and market the product during the life of the patent. This gives the manufacturer a chance to recoup the millions spent on developing and launching the drug. Once the patent expires, all bets are off, and competitors can flood the market with generic versions of the drug.

For years, real estate firms enjoyed a kind of monopoly when they limited other firms' access to their property listings, called the Multiple Listing Service. Most recently, the firms prevented

Web-based real estate companies, a growing industry segment, from viewing the multiple listings. The U.S. Justice Department sued the National Association of Realtors, the industry's trade group, claiming that the practice constituted a monopoly and falls under the government's **antitrust** remedies. The association reached a settlement with the government, agreeing to change the rules to permit online access to the listings. Under the settlement, home buyers may pay lower commissions to brokers.[5]

Rather than seeking sole dominance of a market, corporations increasingly prefer to share the pie with just a few rivals. Referred to by economists as an **oligopoly,** this structure of a limited number of sellers in an industry in which high start-up costs form barriers to keep out new competitors deters newcomers from breaking into markets while ensuring that corporations remain innovative. Commercial airplane manufacturers operate within an oligopolostic industry, currently dominated by Europe-based Airbus Industrie and U.S.-based Boeing. After earlier failures at building and marketing commercial airplanes, the Chinese government once again is attempting to enter this exclusive club. With the increasing numbers of Chinese air travelers, the government founded Commercial Aircraft Company of China to build jets domestically, in the hope that China can "buy local" and reduce its dependence on aircraft made in the West.[6]

TYPES OF COMPETITION

Marketers face three types of competition. The most *direct* form occurs among marketers of similar products, as when an ExxonMobil station opens across the street from a Shell retail outlet. The cell phone market provides consumers with such alternative suppliers as Verizon, AT&T, and T-Mobile.

Costco, which sells everything from home generators to birthday cakes, also takes direct aim at luxury retailers. The largest U.S. warehouse club operator, Costco offers diamond jewelry, cashmere sweaters, Fendi handbags, and more. And in a new venture with Synergy Brands, the retailer will sell Synergy's line of designer luxury items, including handbags, wallets, briefcases, and other goods.[7]

A second type of competition is *indirect,* involving products that are easily substituted. In the fast-food industry, pizza competes with chicken, hamburgers, and tacos. In entertainment, a movie could be substituted for a concert or a night at the bowling alley. Six Flags and Universal Studios amusement parks—traditional hot spots for family vacations—now compete with outdoor adventure trips. Many adults in the United States will decide not to make this year's vacation a tranquil week at the beach or a trip to Disney World. Instead, they'll choose to do something more adventurous— thrill-filled experiences such as skydiving, whitewater rafting, or climbing Mount Rainier. So marketers have to find ways to attract consumers to their specific brand as well as to their type of product.

A change such as a price increase or an improvement in a product's attributes can also affect demand for substitute products. As the prices for one type of energy soar, consumers look for cheaper, and more environmentally friendly, alternatives. Siemens Energy chose Boulder, Colorado, as the site of its first U.S. research and development facility for wind turbines. The company, which has other wind turbine R&D centers in Europe, said the Boulder facility will work to design more efficient wind turbine components and conduct research in atmospheric science.[8]

Advances in technology can give rise to other substitute products. Wireless fidelity, or Wi-Fi, makes the Internet available via radio waves and can be accessed at any number of public "hot spots" in a variety of locations, including airports, coffee shops, hotels, and libraries. The number of registered hot spots continues to grow worldwide, with nearly 240,000 in existence.[9] While some hosts charge a fee, Wi-Fi increasingly is offered at no charge.

Some industry observers claim WiMax will replace Wi-Fi as the wireless standard because it represents improved technology. For example, because Wi-Fi operates on unlicensed radio frequencies, users often experience interference. WiMax, on the other hand, uses a licensed radio channel that enables a clearer, stronger, more secure signal. This stronger WiMax signal also provides significantly greater range: up to 30 miles compared with Wi-Fi's typical 75 to 100 feet. Sprint currently is testing its WiMax network in Baltimore, Chicago, and Washington, D.C. With its enhanced capability, WiMax offers a wealth of potential applications.[10]

The final type of competition occurs among all organizations that compete for consumers' purchases. Traditional economic analysis views competition as a battle among companies in the same industry (direct competition) or among substitutable goods and services (indirect competition). But marketers know that *all* firms compete for a limited number of dollars that consumers can or will spend. In this broader sense, competition means that purchase of a Honda Accord might compete with a Holland America cruise.

2 Explain the types of competition marketers face and the steps necessary for developing a competitive strategy.

Because the competitive environment often determines the success or failure of a product, marketers must continually assess competitors' marketing strategies. New products, updated features or technology, increased service, and lower prices are variations that marketers look for. When changes occur in the competition, marketers must decide how to respond. Chipotle Mexican Grill competes in the fast-food industry by offering choice, fresh ingredients, as the "Marketing Success" feature describes.

DEVELOPING A COMPETITIVE STRATEGY

Marketers at every successful firm must develop an effective strategy for dealing with the competitive environment. One company may compete in a broad range of markets in many areas of the world. Another may specialize in particular market segments, such as those determined by customers' geographic location, age, or income characteristics. Determining a **competitive strategy** involves answering the following three questions:

1. Should we compete?

2. If so, in what markets should we compete?

3. How should we compete?

The answer to the first question depends on the firm's resources, objectives, and expected profit potential. A firm may decide not to pursue or continue operating a potentially successful venture that does not mesh with its resources, objectives, or profit expectations. Semiconductor manufacturer Texas Instruments shed its defense electronics business unit, which made missile sensors and radar and night-vision systems, to an aircraft company where this unit was a better fit. After pressure from investors to separate its candy and beverage businesses, Cadbury Schweppes spun off its highly popular beverage brands, which include Dr Pepper, 7UP, and Snapple.[11]

Answering the second question requires marketers to acknowledge their firm's limited resources—sales personnel, advertising budgets, product development capability, and the like. They must allocate these resources to the areas of greatest opportunity. Some companies gain access to new markets or new technologies through acquisitions or mergers. When Verizon Wireless acquired competitor Alltel Corporation, it added more than 13 million customers to its business. The $28 billion acquisition gave Verizon a total of more than 80 million customers, allowing Verizon to overtake AT&T as the number one wireless service in the United States.[12]

Answering the third question on the list requires marketers to make product, distribution, promotion, and pricing decisions that give the firm a competitive advantage in the marketplace. Firms can compete on a variety of bases, including product quality, price, and customer service. Stonyfield Farms, the world's largest maker of organic yogurt, competes on an environmental basis by using organic ingredients. And although it's higher-priced, the Stonyfield Farms brand has risen to number three in the United States—behind Yoplait and Dannon—because customers support the company's commitment to organic foods.[13]

Marketing Success   Chipotle Mexican Grill Turns Up the Heat

Background. When did eating a burrito become cool? Since it underwent a makeover at Chipotle Mexican Grill. Chipotle opened its first restaurant in 1993. Today it has well over 700 outlets across the United States and continues to grow. What's the secret of Chipotle's success?

The Challenge. Chipotle was entering the crowded "fast casual" restaurant category. It didn't want to be perceived as just another Mexican restaurant, so the chain's marketers needed to find ways to differentiate Chipotle and appeal to customers.

TIME-BASED COMPETITION

With increased international competition and rapid changes in technology, a steadily growing number of firms use time as a strategic competitive weapon. **Time-based competition** is the strategy of developing and distributing goods and services more quickly than competitors. Although a video option on cell phones came late to the U.S. market, the new feature was a big hit, attracting new customers to cell phone providers. The flexibility and responsiveness of time-based competitors enable them to improve product quality, reduce costs, and expand product offerings to satisfy new market segments and enhance customer satisfaction.

In rapidly changing markets, particularly those that involve technology, time-based competition is critical to a firm's success. The Transportation Security Administration, partnering with Continental and Delta airlines, has begun using technology to move passengers through airports more quickly and to reduce the incidence of phony boarding passes. The solution? Paperless boarding passes. Traditionally, airlines issued paper boarding passes, but the electronic pass, with its encrypted barcode, is transmitted directly to a passenger's cell phone or PDA. At check-in, the passenger simply presents the phone or PDA to a TSA officer, who uses a hand-held scanner to validate the barcode.[14]

Great organic taste at a fair price. We milk cows, not people.

Yeo Valley organic
A breath of fresh air from the country.

© Image courtesy of The Advertising Archives

Firms compete on a variety of bases, including product quality, price, and customer service. This ad focuses on price and quality.

assessment check

1. Distinguish between direct and indirect competition and give an example of each.
2. What is time-based competition?

The Political-Legal Environment

Before you play the game, learn the rules! You may find it hard to win a new game without first understanding the rules. Yet some businesspeople exhibit a lack of knowledge about marketing's **political-legal environment**—the laws and their interpretations that require firms to operate under competitive conditions and to protect consumer rights. Ignorance of laws, ordinances, and regulations or noncompliance with them can result in fines, negative publicity, and expensive civil damage suits.

The existing U.S. legal framework was constructed piecemeal, often in response to issues that were important when individual laws were enacted. Businesspeople must be diligent to understand the legal system's relationship to their marketing decisions. Numerous laws and regulations affect those decisions, many of them vaguely stated and inconsistently enforced by a multitude of different authorities.

political-legal environment
Component of the marketing environment consisting of laws and their interpretations that require firms to operate under competitive conditions and to protect consumer rights.

The Strategy. Chipotle operates under the message "Food with Integrity." It uses fresh ingredients, most of them organic, and spends more on them than the industry norm. In addition, Chipotle serves only meat and animal products fed with natural products such as grass on the free range; it serves more naturally raised meat than any other restaurant in the world. Chipotle also keeps the menu simple, offering only burritos, tacos, and salads. Chipotle hires strategically. Instead of building a workforce of part-timers and temporary employees, like most competitors, Chipotle looks for full-time, permanent workers who understand the cuisine.

The Outcome. Chipotle's annual sales volume per store averages $1.7 billion—significantly higher than the average in this category. About 80 percent of its workforce is Hispanic, and it has one of the lowest employee turnover rates in the industry.

Sources: Courtney Dentch, "Chipotle Earnings Climb on Higher Prices, New Restaurants," *Bloomberg*, April 22, 2009, www.bloomberg.com; Anna Kuchment, "A Chain That Pigs Would Die For," *Newsweek*, May 12, 2008, pp. 45–46; "Chipotle Is First Restaurant to Serve 100 Percent Naturally Raised Chicken," *The New York Times*, May 5, 2008, www.reuters.com; Alex Markels, "Chipotle's Secret Salsa," *U.S. News & World Report*, January 9, 2008, www.usnews.com.

Federal, state, and local regulations affect marketing practices, as do the actions of independent regulatory agencies. These requirements and prohibitions touch on all aspects of marketing decision making: designing, labeling, packaging, distributing, advertising, and promoting goods and services. To cope with the vast, complex, and changing political-legal environment, many large firms maintain in-house legal departments; small firms often seek professional advice from outside attorneys. All marketers, however, should be aware of the major regulations that affect their activities.

3 **Describe how marketing activities are regulated and how marketers can influence the political-legal environment.**

GOVERNMENT REGULATION

The history of U.S. government regulation can be divided into four phases. The first phase was the *antimonopoly period* of the late 19th and early 20th centuries. During this era, major laws such as the Sherman Antitrust Act, Clayton Act, and Federal Trade Commission Act were passed to maintain a competitive environment by reducing the trend toward increasing concentration of industry power in the hands of a small number of competitors. Laws enacted more than 100 years ago still affect business in the 21st century.

The Microsoft case is a good example of antitrust legislation at work. The U.S. Department of Justice was successful in proving Microsoft guilty of predatory practices designed to crush competition. By bundling its own Internet Explorer browser with its Windows operating system—which runs 90 percent of the world's personal computers—Microsoft grabbed the majority of the market from rival Netscape. It also bullied firms as large as America Online to drop Netscape Navigator in favor of its browser. Microsoft's supporters countered that consumers have clearly benefited from the integrated features in Windows and that its bundling decisions were simply efforts to offer customer satisfaction through added value.

The second phase, aimed at *protecting competitors,* emerged during the Great Depression era of the 1930s, when independent merchants felt the need for legal protection against competition from larger chain stores. Among the federal legislation enacted was the Robinson-Patman Act. The third regulatory phase focused on *consumer protection.* The objective of consumer protection underlies most laws, with good examples including the Sherman Act, FTC Act, and Federal Food and Drug Act. Additional laws have been enacted over the past 40 years. The fourth phase, *industry deregulation,* began in the late 1970s and continues to the present. During this phase, government has sought to increase competition in such industries as telecommunications, utilities, transportation, and financial services by discontinuing many regulations and permitting firms to expand their service offerings to new markets.

The newest regulatory frontier is *cyberspace.* Federal and state regulators are investigating ways to police the Internet and online services. The FTC, along with private organizations and other government agencies, has created a site, **www.onguardonline.gov,** where consumers can take quizzes designed to educate them about ID theft, spam (junk e-mail), phishing (luring consumers to provide personal information), and online shopping scams. But cybercrime is spreading quickly. Attacks by malicious software that contain codes capable of stealing account logons, passwords, and other confidential data are on the rise. The Identity Theft Enforcement and Restitution Act enables victims of identity theft to seek restitution and makes it easier for the government to prosecute phishing and those who threaten to steal or divulge information from a computer.[15]

Privacy and child protection issues are another important—but difficult—enforcement challenge. With the passage of the Children's Online Privacy Protection Act, Congress took the first step in regulating what children are exposed to on the Internet. The primary focus is a set of rules regarding how and when marketers need to get parental permission before obtaining marketing research information from children over the Web. Finally, the government's Do Not Call Registry, a list to which consumers can add their phone numbers, including cell phones, to avoid telemarketing calls, provides protection for consumers who do not want to be contacted by telemarketers. The law exempts callers representing not-for-profit organizations, companies with which the consumer has an existing relationship, and political candidates. Telemarketing firms must check the list quarterly, with fines of as much as $11,000 per occurrence. Since establishing the list, the government has aggressively pursued offenders, resulting in settlements often totaling millions of dollars: DirecTV paid $5.3 million and Craftmatic Industries, $4.4 million.[16]

Table 3.1 lists and briefly describes the major federal laws affecting marketing. Legislation covering specific marketing practices, such as product development, packaging, labeling, product warranties, and franchise agreements, is discussed in later chapters.

table 3.1 Major Federal Laws Affecting Marketing

Date	Law	Description
A. LAWS MAINTAINING A COMPETITIVE ENVIRONMENT		
1890	Sherman Antitrust Act	Prohibits restraint of trade and monopolization; identifies a competitive marketing system as a national policy goal.
1914	Clayton Act	Strengthens the Sherman Act by restricting such practices as price discrimination, exclusive dealing, tying contracts, and interlocking boards of directors where the effect "may be to substantially lessen competition or tend to create a monopoly;" amended by the Celler-Kefauver Antimerger Act to prohibit major asset purchases that would decrease competition in an industry.
1914	Federal Trade Commission Act (FTC)	Prohibits unfair methods of competition; establishes the Federal Trade Commission, an administrative agency that investigates business practices and enforces the FTC Act.
1938	Wheeler-Lea Act	Amends the FTC Act to outlaw additional unfair practices; gives the FTC jurisdiction over false and misleading advertising.
1998	Digital Millennium Copyright Act	Protects intellectual property rights by prohibiting copying or downloading of digital files.
B. LAWS REGULATING COMPETITION		
1936	Robinson-Patman Act	Prohibits price discrimination in sales to wholesalers, retailers, or other producers; prohibits selling at unreasonably low prices to eliminate competition.
1993	North American Free Trade Agreement (NAFTA)	International trade agreement between Canada, Mexico, and the United States and designed to facilitate trade by removing tariffs and other trade barriers among the three nations.
C. LAWS PROTECTING CONSUMERS		
1906	Federal Food and Drug Act	Prohibits adulteration and misbranding of food and drugs involved in interstate commerce; strengthened by the Food, Drug, and Cosmetic Act (1938) and the Kefauver-Harris Drug Amendment (1962).
1970	National Environmental Policy Act	Establishes the Environmental Protection Agency to deal with various types of pollution and organizations that create pollution.
1971	Public Health Cigarette Smoking Act	Prohibits tobacco advertising on radio and television.
1972	Consumer Product Safety Act	Created the Consumer Product Safety Commission, which has authority to specify safety standards for most products.
1998	Children's Online Privacy Protection Act	Empowers FTC to set rules regarding how and when marketers must obtain parental permission before asking children marketing research questions.
1998	Identity Theft and Assumption Deterrence Act	Makes it a federal crime to unlawfully use or transfer another person's identification with the intent to violate the law.
1999	Anticybersquatting Consumer Protection Act	Bans the bad-faith purchase of domain names that are identical or confusingly similar to existing registered trademarks.

table 3.1 *continued*

Date	Law	Description
2001	Electronic Signature Act	Gives electronic signatures the same legal weight as handwritten signatures.
2005	Real ID Act	Sets minimum standards for state driver's licenses and ID cards. To be phased in from 2010 through 2013.
2006	Consumer Telephone Records Act	Prohibits the sale of cell phone records.
D. LAWS DEREGULATING SPECIFIC INDUSTRIES		
1978	Airline Deregulation Act	Grants considerable freedom to commercial airlines in setting fares and choosing new routes.
1980	Motor Carrier Act and Staggers Rail Act	Significantly deregulates trucking and railroad industries by permitting them to negotiate rates and services.
1996	Telecommunications Act	Significantly deregulates the telecommunications industry by removing barriers to competition in local and long-distance phone and cable and television markets.
2003	Amendments to the Telemarketing Sales Rule	Created the national Do Not Call Registry prohibiting telemarketing calls to registered telephone numbers. Restricted the number and duration of telemarketing calls generating dead air space with use of automatic dialers; cracked down on unauthorized billing; and required telemarketers to transmit their caller ID information.
2007	Do-Not-Call Improvement Act	Extends Telemarketing Sales Rule; allows registered numbers to remain on Do Not Call list permanently.
2007	Fee Extension Act	Extends Telemarketing Sales Rule; sets annual fees for telemarketers to access the Do Not Call Registry.

Marketers must also monitor state and local laws that affect their industries. Many states, for instance, allow hard liquor to be sold only in liquor stores while others prohibit the sale of alcoholic beverages on Sunday. California's stringent regulations for automobile emissions require special pollution control equipment on cars sold in the state.

GOVERNMENT REGULATORY AGENCIES

Federal, state, and local governments have established regulatory agencies to enforce laws. At the federal level, the Federal Trade Commission (FTC) wields the broadest powers of any agency to influence marketing activities. The FTC enforces laws regulating unfair business practices and stops false and deceptive advertising. It regulates communication by wire, radio, and television. Other federal regulatory agencies include the Consumer Product Safety Commission, the Federal Power Commission, the Environmental Protection Agency (EPA), and the Food and Drug Administration (FDA). The FDA, stung by criticisms over lax oversight of new-drug side effects, recently rejected a new cholesterol drug offered by pharmaceutical giant Merck. According to Merck, the new medication, which it had planned to name Cordaptive, raises "good" levels of cholesterol and prevents heart attack and stroke. Rejections by U.S. government regulators can come even after companies, like Merck, spend years developing a new product.[17]

The FTC uses several procedures to enforce laws. It may issue a consent order through which a business accused of violations can agree to voluntary compliance without admitting guilt. If a business refuses to comply with an FTC request, the agency can issue a cease-and-desist order, which gives a final demand to stop an illegal practice. Firms often challenge cease-and-desist orders in court. The FTC can require advertisers to provide additional information about products in their advertisements, and it can force firms using deceptive advertising to correct earlier claims with new promotional messages. In some cases, the FTC can require a firm to give refunds to consumers misled by deceptive advertising.

The FTC and U.S. Department of Justice can stop mergers if they believe the proposed acquisition will reduce competition by making it harder for new companies to enter the field. In recent years, these agencies have taken a harder line on proposed mergers, especially in the computer, telecommunications, financial services, and healthcare sectors.

Removing regulations also changes the competitive picture considerably. Following deregulation of the telecommunications and utilities industries, suppliers no longer have exclusive rights to operate within a territory. Natural gas utilities traditionally competed with electric companies to supply homeowners and businesses with energy needs. Because of deregulation, they now also compete with other gas companies. The restructuring of the electricity industry by state took hold immediately in the Northeast, ranging from Maine to Virginia and reaching through the Midwest in Ohio, Michigan, and Illinois. Indiana and Vermont abstained. Texas, Arizona, and Oregon also jumped on the bandwagon. But several states delayed deregulation activities, and California actually suspended them altogether. Restructuring caused major headaches for some utilities, leading to shortages and an inability to coordinate service with needs, nonmaintenance of power lines, and lack of funds for operating or decommissioning nuclear power plants. Thus, while deregulation may be designed to promote competition and provide better service and prices for consumers, it doesn't always work as planned.

The latest round of deregulation began with the passage of the Telecommunications Act of 1996 and its 2003 amendment, the Do Not Call law mentioned earlier. The Telecommunications Act removed barriers between local and long-distance phone companies and cable companies. It allowed the so-called Baby Bells—the regional Bell operating companies—to offer long-distance service; at the same time, long-distance companies offered local service. Satellite television providers such as Dish Network and DirecTV and cable companies such as Comcast can offer phone service, while phone companies can get into the cable business. The change promises huge rewards for competitive winners. Consumers can shop around for the best deals and packages as more companies compete for their business by packaging services at reduced prices.

OTHER REGULATORY FORCES

Public and private consumer interest groups and self-regulatory organizations are also part of the legal environment. Consumer interest organizations have mushroomed since the late 1970s, and today hundreds of groups operate at national, state, and local levels. These organizations seek to protect consumers in as many areas as possible. Citing the need for a standardized credit scoring system, the three major credit-reporting agencies—Equifax, Experian, and TransUnion—collaborated to create VantageScore. But consumer groups and other industry observers have criticized the system for being inconsistent and of questionable value to consumers.[18] The Coalition for Fire-Safe Cigarettes is working state-by-state to pressure tobacco companies to produce cigarettes that will not smolder and start fires if left unattended. Bills mandating fire-safe cigarettes have been passed in Canada and in 35 U.S. states.[19]

Other groups attempt to advance the rights of minorities, senior citizens, and other causes. The power of these groups has also grown. AARP (formerly known as the American Association of Retired Persons), wields political and economic power, particularly as more and more people reach retirement age. Animal rights groups are also a powerful influence on business. The American Humane Association grants the disclaimer "No Animals Were Harmed" to moviemakers who use animals in their films. It is the only organization authorized by movie studios to monitor the use and care of animals on the set. The AHA also advocates technology in the film industry, encouraging the use of computer-generated imagery and animatronics to minimize the use and possible injury of animals on the set.[20]

Self-regulatory groups represent industries' attempts to set guidelines for responsible business conduct. The Council of Better Business Bureaus is a national organization devoted to consumer service and business self-regulation. The council's National Advertising Division promotes truth and accuracy in advertising. It reviews and advocates voluntary resolution of advertising-related complaints between consumers and businesses. If NAD fails to resolve a complaint, an appeal can

As more people reach retirement age, AARP gains additional political and economic power.

© Dennis MacDonald/PhotoEdit

be made to the National Advertising Review Board, composed of advertisers, ad agency representatives, and public members. In addition, many individual trade associations set business guidelines and codes of conduct and encourage members' voluntary compliance.

The Direct Marketing Association supports consumer rights through its Commitment to Consumer Choice. Under this principle, all 275,000 DMA member organizations are required to inform consumers of their right to modify or discontinue receiving solicitations.[21]

As mentioned earlier, regulating the online world poses a challenge. Favoring self-regulation as the best starting point, the FTC sponsored a privacy initiative for consumers, advertisers, online companies, and others as a way to develop voluntary industry privacy guidelines. The Interactive Services Association is also working on its own privacy standards.

CONTROLLING THE POLITICAL-LEGAL ENVIRONMENT

Most marketers comply with laws and regulations. Doing so not only serves their customers but also avoids legal problems that could ultimately damage a firm's image and hurt profits. But smart marketers get ahead of the curve by providing products that will meet customers' future needs while also addressing government goals. Showing remarkable forward thinking, Toyota was one of the first automakers to commit to building hybrid cars. Its efforts were supported by a government tax break for purchasers of the first hybrids.

Consumer groups and political action committees within industries may try to influence the outcome of proposed legislation or

assessment check

1. Identify the four phases of U.S. government regulation of business. What is the newest frontier?

2. Which federal agency wields the broadest regulatory powers for influencing marketing activities?

change existing laws by engaging in political lobbying or boycotts. Lobbying groups frequently enlist the support of customers, employees, and suppliers to assist their efforts.

The Economic Environment

The overall health of the economy influences how much consumers spend and what they buy. This relationship also works the other way. Consumer buying plays an important role in the economy's health; in fact, consumer spending accounts for nearly 70 percent of the nation's total **gross domestic product (GDP),** the sum of all goods and services produced by a nation in a year.[22] Because marketing activities are directed toward satisfying consumer wants and needs, marketers must first understand how economic conditions influence the purchasing decisions consumers make.

Marketing's **economic environment** consists of factors that influence consumer buying power and marketing strategies. They include the stage of the business cycle, the global economic crisis, inflation and deflation, unemployment, income, and resource availability.

STAGES IN THE BUSINESS CYCLE

Historically, the economy has tended to follow a cyclical pattern consisting of four stages: prosperity, recession, depression, and recovery. Consumer buying differs in each stage of the **business cycle,** and marketers must adjust their strategies accordingly. In times of prosperity, consumer spending maintains a brisk pace, and buyers are willing to spend more for premium versions of well-known brands. Growth in services such as banking and restaurants usually indicates a strong economy. When economists predict such conditions as low inflation and low unemployment, marketers respond by offering new products, increasing their promotional efforts, and expanding distribution. They might even raise prices to widen profit margins. But high prices for some items, such as energy, can affect businesses and consumers alike. Skyrocketing gasoline prices and the growing wellness trend are good news for bicycle shops because more people become interested in riding a bike, either to save money or to get healthier. Says Rebecca Anderson, advocacy director for bicycle manufacturer Trek, "People are looking at the bicycle as more than just a toy."[23]

During economic slowdowns, consumers focus on more basic, functional products that carry lower price tags. They limit travel, restaurant meals, and entertainment. They skip expensive vacations and cook their own meals. During a recession, marketers consider lowering prices and increasing promotions that include special offers to stimulate demand. They may also launch special value-priced products likely to appeal to cost-conscious buyers.

Consumer spending sinks to its lowest level during a depression. The last true depression in the United States occurred during the 1930s. Although a severe depression could occur again, most experts see it as a slim possibility. Through its monetary and fiscal policies, the federal government attempts to control extreme fluctuations in the business cycle that lead to depression.

In the recovery stage, the economy emerges from recession and consumer purchasing power increases. But while consumers have money to spend, caution often restrains their willingness to buy. A family might buy a new car if no-interest financing is available. A couple might decide to book a trip through a discount travel firm such as Expedia.com or Travelocity. Companies like these can make the most of an opportunity and develop loyal customers by offering superior service at lower prices. Recovery still remains a difficult stage for businesses just climbing out of a recession because they must earn profits while trying to gauge uncertain consumer demand. Many cope by holding down costs. Some trim payrolls and close branch offices. Others cut back on business travel budgets, substituting teleconferencing and videoconferencing.

Business cycles, like other aspects of the economy, are complex phenomena that, despite the efforts of government, businesspeople, and others to control them, sometimes have a life of their own. Unforeseen natural disasters, such as the recent spate of tornadoes and flooding across the United States; major tragedies such as the attacks of September 11, 2001; and the effects of war or peace all have an impact on business and the economy as a whole. The most effective marketers know how to recognize ways to serve their customers during the best of times—and the worst of times.

4 **Outline the economic factors that affect marketing decisions and consumer buying power.**

economic environment
Factors that influence consumer buying power and marketing strategies, including stage of the business cycle, inflation and deflation, unemployment, income, and resource availability.

briefly *speaking*

"The future, according to some scientists, will be exactly like the past, only far more expensive."

—**John Sladek (1937–2000)**
AMERICAN AUTHOR

THE GLOBAL ECONOMIC CRISIS

Sometimes business cycles take a severe turn and affect consumers and businesses across the globe. That is the case with the recent recession, which is the worst economic downturn since the Great Depression of the 1930s. Typically, nations' GDP rates grow—some modestly at 2 to 4 percentage points a year and some, such as rapidly expanding India and China, at or near double digits. With the crisis, economists predicted that the world economy might shrink for the first time in 60 years.

The downturn could be seen most vividly in financial institutions. Banks large and small recorded huge losses, and some failed, which nearly brought the banking system to its knees. Because financial firms are at the center of global economic activity, governments and international agencies such as the International Monetary Fund intervened to stabilize the system. The U.S. government passed a $700 billion dollar bailout program and later an economic stimulus package. The nation's bank, the Federal Reserve, lowered interest rates to spur growth. Stock markets around the world swung wildly as investors tried to make sense of the situation.

With the tightening of credit, consumers found it difficult to pay or obtain loans for houses, cars, and other big-ticket items. And they faced increasing uncertainty about their jobs—would they remain employed, and if so, would their hours or salaries be cut? As mentioned previously, the uncertainty that mushrooms in a recession forces consumers to rethink their buying habits, and some believe that the downturn may have a long-term effect on purchasing behavior. Such curtailing of buying globally lowers trade between nations and slows growth.

One bright spot involved the price of oil. Once trading near $150 per barrel, the price plummeted to about a third. The drop made the cost of gasoline, home heating oil, and other oil-based energy more affordable. As a result, consumers could allocate more of their budgets to other necessities.

Marketers responded to consumers' concerns by emphasizing value in their products. Some slashed prices or offered sales to help customers stretch their budget dollars. Others, such as auto companies Ford and Hyundai, assured new-car buyers that they would assist them with payments for a period of time if they lost their jobs or would take the cars back to avoid damaging consumers' credit. Retailers that emphasized affordable products such as Wal-Mart and McDonald's saw their sales increase. With the severity of the recession, all marketers needed to reevaluate their strategies and concentrate on their most promising products. But it remains to be seen whether or how much consumers, now used to price reductions and special offers, will change their habits once their regain their economic footing in a recovery.

INFLATION AND DEFLATION

A major constraint on consumer spending, which can occur during any stage of the business cycle, is **inflation**—rising prices caused by some combination of excess demand and increases in the costs of raw materials, component parts, human resources, or other factors of production. Inflation devalues money by reducing the products it can buy through persistent price increases. These rising prices increase marketers' costs, such as expenditures for wages and raw materials, and the resulting higher prices may therefore negatively affect sales. U.S. inflation hit a heart-stopping high in 1979 of 13.3 percent. Recently, annual inflation hovered around 4.2 percent.[24]

If inflation is so bad, is its opposite, *deflation,* better? At first, it might seem so. Falling prices mean that products are more affordable. But deflation can be a long and damaging downward spiral, causing a freefall in business profits, lower returns on most investments, and widespread job layoffs. The last time the United States experienced significant deflation was in the Great Depression of the 1930s.

Unemployment

Unemployment is defined as the proportion of people in the economy who are actively seeking work but do not have jobs. Unemployment rises during recessions and declines in the recovery and prosperity stages of the business cycle. Like inflation, unemployment affects the way consumers behave. Unless unemployment insurance, personal savings, and union benefits effectively offset lost earnings, unemployed people have relatively little money to spend; they buy food, pay the rent or mortgage, and try to keep up with utility bills. Currently, unemployment stands at about 8.5 percent nationally. Not surprisingly, job cuts have a direct effect on consumer spending.

Income

Income is another important determinant of marketing's economic environment because it influences consumer buying power. By studying income statistics and trends, marketers can estimate market potential and plan to target specific market segments. A rise in income represents potential for increasing overall sales. Many marketers are particularly interested in **discretionary income,** the amount of money people have to spend after buying necessities such as food, clothing, and housing. Those whose industry involves the necessities seek to turn those needs into preferences for their goods and services. With slowdowns in the U.S. economy, American consumers experienced a drop in their net worth because their homes and stock investments lost value. At the same time, Americans are spending more for food and other necessities, which means they have less money available for other items.[25]

Changes in average earnings powerfully affect discretionary income. Historically, periods of major innovation have been accompanied by dramatic increases in living standards and rising incomes. Automobiles, televisions, telephones, and computers are just a few of the innovations that have changed consumers' lives—and standards of living. The Bureau of Economic Analysis, a division of the U.S. Department of Commerce, tracks personal income and discretionary income in the United States, then determines how much of that income is spent on personal consumption.[26] Marketers can use these figures to plan their approaches to everything from product development to the promotion of their goods and services.

Not only does income affect how much money individuals donate to not-for-profit organizations, but it can also affect the amount of time they're willing to spend on charitable efforts. The "Etiquette Tips for Marketing Professionals" feature discusses how the most successful organizations structure their workplace volunteer programs.

RESOURCE AVAILABILITY

Resources are not unlimited. Shortages, temporary or permanent, can result from several conditions, including lack of raw materials, component parts, energy, or labor. U.S. business executives and government officials continue to be concerned about the nation's dependence on imported oil and the effect shortages have on the economy. Increased demand for oil throughout Asia has worsened the situation. The price of a gallon of oil doubled in a recent year, forcing people the world over to take a closer look at their consumption levels.[27]

One reaction to a shortage is **demarketing,** the process of reducing consumer demand for a product to a level that the firm can reasonably supply. Oil companies publicize tips for consumers on how to cut gasoline consumption, and utility companies encourage homeowners to install more insulation to reduce heating costs. Many cities promote mass transit and carpooling for consumers, and the federal government has created tax deductions for employers that subsidize their employees' transportation costs.[28] A shortage presents marketers with a unique set of challenges. They may have to allocate limited supplies, a sharply different activity from marketing's traditional objective of expanding sales volume. Shortages may require marketers to decide whether to spread limited supplies over all customers or limit purchases by some customers so that the firm can completely satisfy others.

Marketers have also devised ways to deal with increased demand for fixed amounts of resources. In its annual *Green Book,* the American Council for an Energy Efficient Economy (ACEEE) gives cars a "green score," rating vehicles on their manufacturers' use of scarce resources and attention to the environment in the production process. The recent winner? The ACEEE rated the Civic GX, powered by emission-friendly compressed natural gas, at the top.[29]

> **demarketing** Process of reducing consumer demand for a good or service to a level that the firm can supply.

THE INTERNATIONAL ECONOMIC ENVIRONMENT

In today's global economy, marketers must also monitor the economic environment of other nations. Just as in the United States, a recession in Europe or Japan changes consumer and business buying habits. Changes in foreign currency rates compared with the U.S. dollar also affect marketing decisions. Labor costs and other factors affect firms' decisions to shift manufacturing operations overseas, decisions that may result in cutbacks in U.S. jobs and boosts to other nations' workforces. Although U.S. workers worry about the number of jobs sent overseas, some

Etiquette Tips for Marketing Professionals

To Give . . . or Not to Give?

a s a marketing professional, you may expect to work long hours at the office or travel for your company. But you may be surprised if you're asked to donate money or "free time" to build a house, tutor a child, or pack food boxes for the hungry. Employers increasingly look to enhance their public image by involving their workforce in charitable efforts. Larger organizations often support comprehensive employee volunteer programs, typically managed in the marketing, human resource, or community affairs departments. Studies show some employers believe such programs help them attract high-potential young job candidates, create opportunities for skill development, and increase employee loyalty.

What if you don't *want* to give a percentage of your hard-earned pay to a charity or install drywall on your day off? Before you say no, better check with coworkers about the company's position. In some organizations, you could be labeled as not being a team player. Getting involved may give you an opportunity to meet people from other departments in your organization.

What if you are responsible for managing an employee volunteer program? These tips may help.

- *Brand it.* Giving the volunteer program a name lets employees feel they "belong" to something.

- *Personalize it.* Vividly show why the program needs employees' help. Include testimonials from coworkers about how it made them feel to paint that house or help that fourth grader master the multiplication table. In short, show employees what's in it for them.

- *Communicate results meaningfully.* Did employees' total volunteer hours increase by 10 percent? Show what that means in human terms: one more apartment was remodeled or six more kids had tutors.

- *Acknowledge people's efforts.* Everyone hopes their work made a difference. Find ways, big and small, to recognize volunteers: an e-mailed thank-you, copying the manager; a story in the company newsletter; a barbeque celebrating volunteers.

Sources: "Why Have an Employee Volunteer Program?" VolunteerMatch Web site, www.volunteermatch.org, accessed April 28, 2009; "How the Best Employee Volunteer Programs Structure Themselves," Points of Light Foundation Benchmarks of Excellence Series, Volume 1, Washington D.C., www.pointsoflight.org, accessed April 28, 2009; Penelope Trunk, "What Gen Y Really Wants," *Time*, July 5, 2007, www.time.com.

---

manufacturing remains strong in the United States. While workers in Asia assemble computers, production of computer chips often remains in the United States.

As China exports more and more goods to the world and to the United States in particular, some people voice concern over the widening trade gap. Only recently have broad economic reforms allowed China to play in the global marketplace. Some wonder if China's entry into world markets might help the West economically. However, with its gross domestic product still only a fraction of the U.S. GDP, economists say China cannot rescue the world economy—yet. But they point to China's rapidly expanding economy, fueled in part by a growing middle class with vast, untapped marketing potential.[30]

Politics in other countries affects the international economic environment as well. Elections in countries like Russia could result in a shift away from free-market policies. Turmoil in Venezuela affects the oil industry.

But some valuable lessons have been learned. Whereas developing nations often relied on private funds from industries and organizations to jump-start their economies a decade ago, they now look to establish and build strong export industries. Global demand for certain commodities can help developing nations strengthen their economy and even achieve unaccustomed bargaining power. Protesting their nation's soybean tax, Argentine farmers recently blocked grain shipments and threatened even further disruption.[31]

assessment check

1. Identify and describe briefly the four stages of the business cycle.

2. Explain how inflation and income affect consumer buying decisions.

The Technological Environment

5 Discuss the impact of the technological environment on a firm's marketing activities.

technological environment Application to marketing of knowledge based on discoveries in science, inventions, and innovations.

The **technological environment** represents the application to marketing of knowledge based on discoveries in science, inventions, and innovations. Technology leads to new goods and services for consumers; it also improves existing products, offers better customer service, and often reduces prices through new, cost-efficient production and distribution methods. Technology can quickly make products obsolete—e-mail, for example, quickly eroded both letter writing and the market for fax machines—but it can just as quickly open new marketing opportunities sometimes in entirely new industries.

Pets have been wearing RFID—radio-frequency identification—transmitters for years, in case they got lost. Now RFID tags are used in many industries to locate everything from library books to laundry detergent. An RFID tag contains a computer chip with an antenna. A reader scans the tag and transmits the data from the tag to a computer. This innovation means that retailers, manufacturers, and others can locate and track inventory without opening packages. Dow AgroSciences, a division of Dow Chemical, recently won an award for its use of RFID technology in an electronic system that detects and eliminates termites. When the system detects termite activity, it activates the RFID tag to send a signal to the exterminator. And to enhance security and student safety, researchers at the University of Washington are piloting the use of RFID tags on campus. But the use of RFID to track the movement of humans is controversial because of the privacy implications.[32]

Technology can address social concerns. In response to pressure from the World Trade Organization and the U.S. government, automakers used technology to develop more fuel-efficient vehicles and reduce dangerous emissions. Increased use of ethanol made from corn was another solution, as discussed in the "Solving an Ethical Controversy" feature. But researchers have stepped up efforts to develop biofuels like cellulosic ethanol to replace gasoline. Unlike the corn ethanol currently sold in some gas stations, cellulosic ethanol comes from cellulose—grass clippings, wood chips, yard waste—anything organic, even old tires. Pennsylvania-based Coskata announced it will produce cellulosic ethanol for sale at $1 a gallon. The biofuel emits about 85 percent less greenhouse gases than gasoline.[33] Dependence on corn ethanol will remain for some time, however.

Industry, government, colleges and universities, and other not-for-profit institutions all play roles in the development of new technology. Research and development efforts by private organizations represent a major source of innovation. To help remedy cutbacks in federal funding for scientific research due to tight budgets, the Howard Hughes Medical Institute recently granted $600 million in funding for long-term biomedical research at 31 of the nation's universities and research institutions.[34]

Another major source of technology is the federal government, including the military. Air bags originated from Air Force ejection seats, digital computers were first designed to calculate artillery trajectories, and the microwave oven is a derivative of military radar systems. Even the Internet was first developed by the U.S. Department of Defense as a secure military communications system. Although the United States has long been the world leader in research, competition from rivals in Europe, Japan, and other Asian countries is intense.

briefly speaking

"If you really care about the environment, you want to develop green technologies that are so inexpensive that it is profitable to be environmentally sensitive."

—Newt Gingrich (b. 1943)
PROFESSOR, AUTHOR, AND FORMER SPEAKER OF THE U.S. HOUSE OF REPRESENTATIVES

APPLYING TECHNOLOGY

Marketers monitor the technological environment for a number of reasons. Creative applications of new technologies not only give a firm a definite competitive edge but can also benefit society. Marketers who monitor new technology and successfully apply it may also enhance customer service.

VoIP—*voice over Internet protocol*—is an alternative to traditional telecommunications services provided by companies such as Qwest. The telephone is not connected to a traditional phone jack but instead is connected to a personal computer with any type of broadband Internet connection. Special software transmits phone conversations over the Internet, rather than through telephone lines. A VoIP user dials the phone as usual. Recipients can receive calls made using VoIP through regular telephone connections, land or wireless. Moreover, you

Solving an **ethical** controversy

Diverting Corn from Food to Fuel

Once upon a time, corn was food for humans and livestock. Then, scientists put corn under the microscope, so to speak, and discovered it could be made into a fuel that replaces gasoline.

In some circles, ethanol has been hailed as a remedy to America's overreliance on foreign oil, but as the price of oil has soared, so too have food prices worldwide. Critics point to the production of ethanol as the cause of this inflation. The ethanol industry says it's the high price of oil, not the use of corn to make fuel, that's to blame.

Should corn for ethanol be shelved in favor of corn as a feed crop?

PRO

1. Corn ethanol yields only 25 percent more energy than it takes to grow, harvest, and process. When you use farmland to grow corn for ethanol, you have less acreage for corn as a feed crop. The shortage of feed corn is already reflected in higher grain prices worldwide.

2. There are other, better biofuels. Cellulosic ethanol can be made from anything containing cellulose including plants, yard waste, and other garbage. Switchgrass, an inedible plant, can grow even on land not well suited for farming and yields 540 percent more energy than was required to grow and process it.

CON

1. Data shows that corn prices have had little effect on food costs over the past 20 years and should not be blamed for food inflation today. For every dollar Americans spend on food, only 19 cents goes to a farmer. The rest goes to labor, fuel, transportation, and packaging.

2. Advances in seed technology are improving crop yields and will help corn keep pace with demands. Meanwhile, it could be years before other biofuels are as readily available as corn ethanol.

Summary

Biofuels may ease U.S. dependence on oil, but some bring their own environmental implications. In the short term, it's clear that we must find a way to balance our need for food and fuel without sacrificing our environment.

Sources: Ethanol Facts Web site, www.ethanolfacts.com, accessed April 28, 2009; Joshua Boak, "Ethanol versus Food Debate Growing," *Chicago Tribune*, May 1, 2008, www.chicagotribune.com; Bryan Walsh, "Solving the Biofuels versus Food Problem," *Time*, January 7, 2008, www.time.com; Christine Stebbins, "Corn Ethanol Not Culprit for Food Inflation," *Reuters*, December 10, 2007, www.reuters.com.

A growing number of consumers and businesses have embraced voice over Internet protocol (VoIP) because of cost savings and extra features offered.

© Alex Segre/Alamy

can call another person who has VoIP using a regular landline or cell phone. A growing number of consumers and businesses have embraced VoIP, mainly because of the cost savings and the extra features it offers. One of the largest VoIP providers, with nearly 3 million business and residential customers, is New Jersey–based Vonage. The company offers business and residential customers calling plans priced well below those offered by traditional telecommunications companies and include services such as call waiting and three-way calling at no extra charge.[35]

As convenient as the Internet, cell phones, and Wi-Fi are for businesspeople and consumers, the networks that facilitate these connections aren't yet compatible with each other. So engineers are working on a new standard that would enable these networks to connect with each other, paving the way for melded services such as video exchanges between a cell phone and a computer. Called the Internet Protocol Multimedia Subsystem (IMS), the new standard is attempting to create a common interface so that data can be carried across networks between different devices.[36] The implications for various communications providers are enormous—not only will they find new ways to cooperate, but they will also find new ways to compete. Subsequent chapters discuss in more detail how companies apply technologies—such as databases, blogs, and interactive promotional techniques—to create a competitive advantage.

assessment check

1. What are some of the consumer benefits of technology?
2. Why must marketers monitor the technological environment?

The Social-Cultural Environment

As a nation, the United States is becoming older, more affluent, and more culturally diverse. The birthrate is falling, and subculture populations are rising. People express concerns about the natural environment, buying ecologically friendly products that reduce pollution. They value their time with family and friends, cooking meals at home and exchanging vacation photos over the Internet. Marketers need to track these trends to be in tune with consumers' needs and desires. These aspects of consumer lifestyles help shape marketing's **social-cultural environment**—the relationship between marketing, society, and culture.

To remain competitive, marketers must be sensitive to society's demographic shifts and changing values. These variables affect consumers' reactions to different products and marketing practices. The baby boom generation—the 78 million Americans born between 1946 and 1965—represents a $2.1 trillion market. As boomers approach and enter retirement, marketers are scrambling to identify their needs and wants. With a longer life expectancy and the hope of more time and money to spend, baby boomers view retirement much differently than earlier generations did. Marketers already know that boomers feel young at heart and enjoy their leisure time, but they aren't playing canasta and shuffleboard—they're taking up fly fishing, yoga, and kayaking. Some even launch a second career, starting their own small business. And boomers have a whole new take on the concept of grandparenting. More than past generations, boomer grandparents get actively involved in their grandchildren's daily lives and are more inclined to spend money on them. An estimated 20 percent of all travel involves grandchildren with grandparents, with or without their parents along. As they age, boomers will need healthcare goods and services and, should they live longer, they may need everything from physical therapy for a repaired knee to a motorized scooter to get around.[37]

Another social-cultural consideration is the increasing importance of cultural diversity. The United States is a mixed society composed of various submarkets, each with its unique values, cultural characteristics, consumer preferences, and purchasing

6 **Explain how the social-cultural environment influences marketing.**

social-cultural environment Component of the marketing environment consisting of the relationship between the marketer, society, and culture.

We stop millions of visitors in their tracks every year.

SEE AMERICA'S NATIONAL PARKS

HELP PRESERVE AMERICA.
Buy a National Parks Pass.

Buy a National Parks Pass at www.SeeAmerica.org where you will also find detailed travel information, deals and tips for all of the 388 National Parks in America including national monuments, historic sites, trails, battlefields and more. Experience the best America has to offer starting at SeeAmerica.org.

SEE AMERICA.ORG

Marketers track trends, such as a growing concern for the natural environment, to stay in tune with consumers' needs and desires.

behaviors. In an effort to attract the millions of Hispanic viewers in the United States, satellite and cable TV companies now offer more Spanish-language programming. Spanish-language networks Univision and Telemundo, which once dominated the Hispanic TV market, now face competition from Comcast, Cablevision, Time Warner Cable, Dish Network, and DirecTV. Traditional media companies are creating networks that target online financial advertising and investment news to Latin American audiences. More than 340 Hispanic media outlets operate on the Web, with nearly 100 of the sites online only.[38]

Marketers also need to learn about cultural and societal differences among countries abroad, particularly as business becomes more and more global. Marketing strategies that work in the United States often fail when used in other countries, and vice versa. In many cases, marketers must redesign packages and modify products and advertising messages to suit the tastes and preferences of different cultures. Chapter 7 explores the social-cultural aspects of global marketing.

CONSUMERISM

consumerism Social force within the environment that aids and protects the consumer by exerting legal, moral, and economic pressures on business and government.

Changing societal values have led to **consumerism,** defined as a social force within the environment that aids and protects the consumer by exerting legal, moral, and economic pressures on business and government. Today everyone—marketers, industry, government, and the public—is acutely aware of the impact of consumerism on the nation's economy and general well-being.

Marketers see a rise in consumer activism. The $4 billion plastic bag industry, with its traditional bags used in most retail establishments, has come under fire. Americans use an estimated 110 billion bags a year, accounting for 0.5 percent of the solid waste in landfills. Some supermarkets, like Whole Foods, have stopped using plastic bags; and many chains offer in-store bag recycling and reasonably priced, reusable cloth alternatives.[39]

But firms cannot always adjust to meet the demands of consumer groups. The choice between pleasing all consumers and remaining profitable—thus surviving—defines one of the most difficult dilemmas facing business. Given these constraints, what do consumers have the right to expect from the companies from which they buy goods and services? The most frequently quoted answer to this question comes from a speech made by President John F. Kennedy more than four decades ago. Although this list does not amount to a definitive statement, it offers good rules of thumb that

consumer rights List of legitimate consumer expectations suggested by President John F. Kennedy.

explain basic **consumer rights:**

1. *The right to choose freely.* Consumers should be able to choose from among a range of goods and services.

2. *The right to be informed.* Consumers should be provided with enough education and product information to enable them to be responsible buyers.

3. *The right to be heard.* Consumers should be able to express their legitimate displeasure to appropriate parties—that is, sellers, consumer assistance groups, and city or state consumer affairs offices.

Due to environmental concerns, some stores and consumers have stopped using plastic bags and instead utilize reusable cloth alternatives.

© David McNew/Getty Images

THIS BAG IS MADE FROM RECYCLED PLASTIC BOTTLES AND COTTON

4. *The right to be safe.* Consumers should be assured that the goods and services they purchase are not injurious with normal use. Goods and services should be designed so that the average consumer can use them safely.

These rights have formed the conceptual framework of much of the legislation enacted during the first four decades of the consumer rights movement. However, the question of how best to guarantee them remains unanswered. Sometimes local, state, or federal authorities step in. New York City requires fast-food and casual-dining restaurants to post calorie counts of the various items displayed on their menu. According to local officials, the regulation is designed to address the issue of obesity—a serious health problem not only in New York City but nationwide as well.[40]

Consumers' right to safety encompasses a vast range of products, from automobiles to children's toys. Sometimes it seems as though safety recalls are reported in the media too regularly. You might even receive a letter in the mail from a manufacturer informing you of a recall for a part on your refrigerator or car. To streamline the exchange of information among federal agencies and to make it more convenient for consumers to learn about product recalls, the U.S. government has established the Web site **www.Recalls.gov.** This Web site consolidates recall information generated by the six federal agencies empowered to issue recalls, including the Consumer Product Safety Commission, the Food and Drug Administration, and others. The user-friendly site organizes information into broad categories: Boats, Consumer Products, Cosmetics, Environmental Products, Food, Medicine, and Motor Vehicles.[41]

Consumerism, along with the rest of the social-cultural environment for marketing decisions at home and abroad, is expanding in scope and importance. Today no marketer can initiate a strategic decision without considering the society's norms, values, culture, and demographics. Understanding how these variables affect decisions is so important that some firms have created a new position—typically, manager of public policy research—to study the changing societal environment's future impact on their organizations.

Ethical Issues in Marketing

The five environments described so far in this chapter do not completely capture the role that marketing plays in society and the resulting effects and responsibilities of marketing activities. Because marketing is closely connected with various public issues, it invites constant scrutiny. Moreover, since marketing acts as an interface between an organization and the society in which it operates, marketers often carry much of the responsibility for dealing with social issues that affect their firms.

Marketing operates outside the firm. It responds to that outside environment, and in turn is acted on by environmental influences. Relationships with employees, suppliers, the government, consumers, and society as a whole frame the social issues that marketers must address. The way that marketers deal with these social issues has a significant effect on their firm's eventual success. The diverse social issues that marketers face can be divided into two major categories: marketing ethics and social responsibility. While these two categories certainly overlap, this simple classification system provides a method for studying these issues.

Environmental influences have directed increased attention toward **marketing ethics,** defined as marketers' standards of conduct and moral values. Ethics concern matters of right and wrong: the responsibility of individuals and firms to do what is morally right. As Figure 3.2 shows, each element of the marketing mix raises its own set of ethical questions. Before any improvements to a firm's marketing program can be made, each element must be evaluated.

Creating an ethics program may be complicated and time consuming, but worthwhile. Some firms take their cue from the U.S. Federal Sentencing Guidelines for Organizations, which provides a framework for evaluating misconduct in business activities such as fraud or price fixing. After discovering that similar cases had been resolved differently by courts, the U.S. Sentencing Commission enacted guidelines in 1991 that rely on what legislators call the "stick-and-carrot" approach to corporate ethics: the financial penalties that the courts can impose for wrongdoing are the stick, while the existence of an effective ethics program can reduce the fines the courts can set, which serves as the carrot. Sentencing guidelines act as an incentive for corporations to implement effective ethics compliance programs—if they are hauled into court, the existence of such a program can help reduce penalties.

7 **Describe the ethical issues in marketing.**

marketing ethics
Marketers' standards of conduct and moral values.

briefly
speaking

"Thou shalt not use profanity. Thou shalt not covet thy neighbor's putter. Thou shalt not steal thy neighbor's ball. Thou shalt not bear false witness in the final tally."

—**Ground rules for a Grand Rapids, Michigan, ministers' golf tournament**

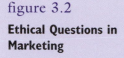

figure 3.2

Ethical Questions in Marketing

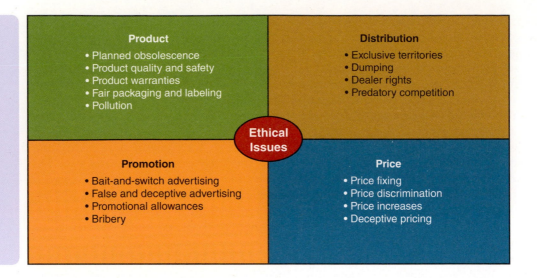

Product
- Planned obsolescence
- Product quality and safety
- Product warranties
- Fair packaging and labeling
- Pollution

Distribution
- Exclusive territories
- Dumping
- Dealer rights
- Predatory competition

Ethical Issues

Promotion
- Bait-and-switch advertising
- False and deceptive advertising
- Promotional allowances
- Bribery

Price
- Price fixing
- Price discrimination
- Price increases
- Deceptive pricing

In some industries, organizations are required by law to maintain corporate-level positions responsible for ethics and legal compliance. Typically, ethics officers are charged with creating and maintaining an ethical culture within the organization. They ensure that ethical protocols are established and enforced, and they serve as the chief source of information to all stakeholders inside and outside the organization regarding ethics.[42] Figure 3.3 presents a step-by-step framework for building an effective program.

Because ethical behavior is so important to business conduct, some firms and universities have taken an unusual step. They invite convicted corporate criminals to speak to employees and students about their mistakes and the consequences of their actions.[43]

Ensuring ethical practices means promising customers and business partners not to sacrifice quality and fairness for profit. In exchange, organizations hope for increased customer loyalty toward their brands. Yet issues involving marketing ethics are not always clear-cut. The issue of cigarette advertising, for example, has divided the ranks of advertising executives. Is it right for advertisers to promote a product that, while legal, has known health hazards?

For years, charges of unethical conduct have plagued the tobacco industry. In the largest civil settlement in U.S. history, tobacco manufacturers agreed to pay $206 billion to 46 states. Four other states—Florida, Minnesota, Mississippi, and Texas—had separate settlements totaling another $40 billion. The settlement freed tobacco companies from state claims for the cost of treating sick smokers. For their part, cigarette makers could no longer advertise on billboards or use cartoon characters in ads, nor could they sell nontobacco merchandise containing tobacco brands or logos. However, several years later, the penalties were softened, particularly those that involved funding smoking-cessation programs—fines dropped from $130 billion to $10 billion. The state courts continue to hear tobacco cases and award damages to smokers and their survivors.[44]

People develop standards of ethical behavior based on their own systems

figure 3.3

Ten Steps for Corporations to Improve Standards of Business Ethics

Source: Adapted from O.C. Ferrell, John Fraedrich, and Linda Ferrell, *Business Ethics: Ethical Decision Making and Cases,* Seventh Edition, pp. 212–224. Copyright © 2008 by Houghton Mifflin Company. Reprinted with permission

1. Appoint a senior-level ethics compliance officer.

2. Set up an ethics code capable of detecting and preventing misconduct.

3. Distribute a written code of ethics to employees, subsidiaries, and associated companies and require all business partners to abide by it.

4. Conduct regular ethics training programs to communicate standards and procedures.

5. Establish systems to monitor misconduct and report grievances.

6. Establish consistent punishment guidelines to enforce standards and codes.

7. Encourage an open-door policy, allowing employees to report cases of misconduct without fear of retaliation.

8. Prohibit employees with a track record of misconduct from holding positions with substantial discretionary authority.

9. Promote ethically aware and responsible managers.

10. Continually monitor effectiveness of all ethics-related programs.

of values, which help them deal with ethical questions in their personal lives. However, the workplace may generate serious conflicts when individuals discover that their ethical beliefs are not necessarily in line with those of their employer. For example, employees may think that shopping online during a lunch break using a work computer is fine, but the company may decide otherwise. The questionnaire in Figure 3.4 highlights other everyday ethical dilemmas. (See page 92 for the answers.)

Due to ethical issues, cigarette makers for the most part can no longer advertise on billboards or use cartoon characters in ads. The pictured billboard ad is largely a thing of the past.

© A. Ramey/Photo Edit

How can these conflicts be resolved? In addition to individual and organizational ethics, individuals may be influenced by a third basis of ethical authority—a professional code of ethics that transcends both organizational and individual value systems. A professional peer association can exercise collective oversight to limit a marketer's individual behavior. Any code of ethics must anticipate the variety of problems marketers are likely to encounter. Promotional matters tend to receive the greatest attention, but ethical considerations also influence marketing research, product strategy, distribution strategy, and pricing.

ETHICS IN MARKETING RESEARCH

Invasion of personal privacy has become a critical issue in marketing research. The proliferation of databases, the selling of address lists, and the ease with which consumer information can be gathered through Internet technology have increased public concern. The issue of privacy will be

---

Office Technology

1. Is it wrong to use company e-mail for personal reasons?
   ❑ Yes   ❑ No

2. Is it wrong to use office equipment to help your children or spouse do schoolwork?
   ❑ Yes   ❑ No

3. Is it wrong to play computer games on office equipment during the workday?
   ❑ Yes   ❑ No

4. Is it wrong to use office equipment to do Internet shopping?
   ❑ Yes   ❑ No

5. Is it unethical to blame an error you made on a technological glitch?
   ❑ Yes   ❑ No

6. Is it unethical to visit pornographic Web sites using office equipment?
   ❑ Yes   ❑ No

Gifts and Entertainment

7. What's the value at which a gift from a supplier or client becomes troubling?
   ❑ $25   ❑ $50   ❑ $100

8. Is a $50 gift to a boss unacceptable?
   ❑ Yes   ❑ No

9. Is a $50 gift from the boss unacceptable?
   ❑ Yes   ❑ No

10. Of gifts from suppliers: Is it OK to take a $200 pair of football tickets?
    ❑ Yes   ❑ No

11. Is it OK to take a $120 pair of theater tickets?
    ❑ Yes   ❑ No

12. Is it OK to take a $100 holiday food basket?
    ❑ Yes   ❑ No

13. Is it OK to take a $25 gift certificate?
    ❑ Yes   ❑ No

14. Can you accept a $75 prize won at a raffle at a supplier's conference?
    ❑ Yes   ❑ No

Truth and Lies

15. Due to on-the-job pressure, have you ever abused or lied about sick days?
    ❑ Yes   ❑ No

16. Due to on-the-job pressure, have you ever taken credit for someone else's work or idea?
    ❑ Yes   ❑ No

---

figure 3.4

Test Your Workplace Ethics

*Ethics questionnaire answers are on page 92.

Source: Ethics Officer Association, Belmont, Massachusetts; Leadership Group, Wilmette, Illinois; survey sampled a cross-section of workers at large companies and nationwide; used with permission from Ethics Officer Association

explored in greater detail in Chapter 4. One marketing research tool particularly problematic is the promise of cash or gifts in return for marketing information that can then be sold to direct marketers. Consumers commonly disclose their personal information in return for an e-mail newsletter or a favorite magazine.

Privacy issues have mushroomed with the growth of the Internet, with huge consequences to both consumers and marketers. A hacker break-in into the computer network of TJX, the parent of discount retail chains TJ Maxx and Marshalls, resulted in the theft of credit and debit card data for millions of accounts. Authorities believe the data was later used to make fraudulent purchases both in the United States and overseas.[45] A messenger service recently lost a computer disc it was transporting for its client, HSBC Group, a global financial services firm. Although the disc contained date of birth and insurance data for 370,000 of HSBC's customers, it listed no addresses or bank account information. For this reason, HSBC believes the potential for its customers' exposure is limited.[46] Incidents like these point to the importance of using encryption programs to safeguard data.

Several agencies, including the FTC, offer assistance to Internet consumers. Consumers can go to **ftc.gov/privacy** for information. The Direct Marketing Association also provides services, such as the Mail, Telephone, and E-Mail Preference Services, to help consumers get their names removed from marketers' targeted lists. Registration for the U.S. government's Do Not Call Registry is available at (888) 382–1222 and **www.donotcall.gov.** Unlistme.com and Junkbusters are free Web services that also help consumers remove their names from direct mail and telemarketing lists.

ETHICS IN PRODUCT STRATEGY

Product quality, planned obsolescence, brand similarity, and packaging all raise ethical issues. Feeling the competition, some marketers have tried packaging practices that might be considered misleading, deceptive, or unethical. Larger packages take up more shelf space, and consumers notice them. An odd-sized package makes price comparisons difficult. Bottles with concave bottoms give the impression that they contain more liquid than they actually do. Are these packaging practices justified in the name of competition, or are they deceptive? Growing regulatory mandates appear to be narrowing the range of discretion in this area.

How do you evaluate the quality of a product like a beverage? By flavor or by ingredients? Citing several studies, some consumer advocates say that the ingredients in soft drinks—mainly the high sugar content—are linked to obesity in consumers, particularly children. Not surprisingly, the beverage industry disagrees, arguing that lack of exercise and a poor diet in general are greater contributors to weight gain than regular consumption of drinks.

ETHICS IN DISTRIBUTION

Two ethical issues influence a firm's decisions regarding distribution strategy:

1. What is the appropriate degree of control over the distribution channel?

2. Should a company distribute its products in marginally profitable outlets that have no alternative source of supply?

The question of channel control typically arises in relationships between manufacturers and franchise dealers. For example, should an automobile dealership, a gas station, or a fast-food outlet be forced to purchase parts, materials, and supplementary services from the parent organization?

The second question concerns marketers' responsibility to serve unsatisfied market segments even if the profit potential is slight. Should marketers serve retail stores in low-income areas, serve users of limited amounts of the firm's product, or serve a declining rural market? These problems are difficult to resolve because often they involve individuals rather than broad segments of the general public. An important first step is to ensure that the firm consistently enforces its channel policies.

ETHICS IN PROMOTION

Promotion raises many ethical questions because it is the most direct link between a firm and its customers. Personal selling has always been a target of criticism—and jokes about untrustworthiness. Used-car dealers, horse traders, and purveyors of quack remedies have been the targets of such barbs. But promotion covers many areas, ranging from advertising to direct marketing, and it is vital for marketers to monitor their ethics in all marketing communications. Truth in advertising—representing accurately a product's benefits and drawbacks, warranties, price, and availability—is the bedrock of ethics in promotion.

Marketing to children has been under close scrutiny for many years because children have not yet developed the skills to receive marketing messages critically. They simply believe everything they see and hear. With childhood obesity now a serious concern in America, Kellogg Company has changed how it advertises its breakfast cereals to children worldwide, focusing solely on products that meet nutrition guidelines.[47] Other organizations like General Mills, Kraft Foods, McDonald's, and Quaker Oats have modified how they advertise their products to children and have pledged to emphasize healthy choices. Yet snack foods, candy, soft drinks, and other junk foods continue to be offered for sale in many schools throughout the country. And in Seminole County, Florida, McDonald's partnered with the school district to print report cards and offer Happy Meals and other food prizes to reward students with good grades. In some communities, including Denver and Miami, organizations can pay to advertise on school buses. Critics argue that such practices continue to target children inappropriately. The International Council of Beverages Associations recently established guidelines on marketing beverages to children. Its two largest members, The Coca-Cola Company and PepsiCo, agreed to comply.[48]

Promoting certain products to college students can raise ethical questions as well. College students are a prime market for firms that sell everything from electronics to beer. And although laws prohibit the sale of alcohol to anyone under 21, companies often advertise beer through popular items like hats, shirts, bar signs, and other collectibles. Critics have long claimed this practice supports underage drinking.

Another ethical issue involves paying universities for the use of their logo, team name, or mascot in advertising products and services to its students. The government recently reached a settlement with a loan consolidation company that marketed student loans in this way on campus, including the Go Hoyas Loan to students at Georgetown University and the Tiger Loan to Auburn students. According to the suit, the use of such logos or names leads students to mistakenly assume their school endorses the loans.[49]

ETHICS IN PRICING

Pricing is probably the most regulated aspect of a firm's marketing strategy. As a result, most unethical price behavior is also illegal. Some aspects of pricing, however, are still open to ethics abuses. For example, should some customers pay more for merchandise if distribution costs

Many organizations have modified how they advertise their products to children and have pledged to emphasize healthy snacks. This ad highlights the health benefits of Capri-Sun.

© Image courtesy of The Advertising Archives

are higher in their areas? Do marketers have an obligation to warn vendors and customers of impending price, discount, or return policy changes?

Some credit card companies target consumers with poor credit ratings and offer them what industry observers call "subprime" or "fee-harvesting" credit cards. Under such an arrangement, the company lures consumers to sign up for the card, promising to improve their credit rating. The cardholder is then charged exorbitant annual fees, leaving them in worse financial shape than before.[50]

While consumers are almost always informed of credit card terms in their agreements, the print often is tiny and the language may be hard to understand. For instance, a credit card issuer might advertise the benefits of its premium card, but the fine print explains that the firm is allowed to substitute a different plan—with a higher interest rate—if the applicant doesn't qualify for the premium card. In addition, certain laws allow companies to levy charges that consumers might not be aware of. For example, under a provision called *universal default,* a company may legally raise its interest rate on a card if the customer is late paying other bills, even if that credit card is paid on time. The *double-cycle billing* provision allows a company to apply finance charges to a two-month, rather than a one-month, billing period. Under this practice, a cardholder could end up paying interest on a balance that was already paid off.

Consumer groups are urging Congress to pass legislation to curb abuses in the credit card industry. Hoping to avoid government intervention, credit card issuer Citi stopped using the universal default provision and Chase ended double-cycle billing.[51]

All these concerns must be dealt with in developing a professional ethic for pricing products. The ethical issues involved in pricing for today's highly competitive and increasingly computerized markets are discussed in greater detail in Chapters 18 and 19.

⑧ Identify the four levels of the social responsibility pyramid.

social responsibility
Marketing philosophies, policies, procedures, and actions that have the enhancement of society's welfare as a primary objective.

assessment check

1. Define *marketing ethics.*

2. Identify the five areas in which ethics can be a problem.

Social Responsibility in Marketing

In addition to measuring sales, revenues, and profits, a firm must consider ways in which it has contributed to the overall well-being of society. This ad shows Timberland's awareness of environmental issues.

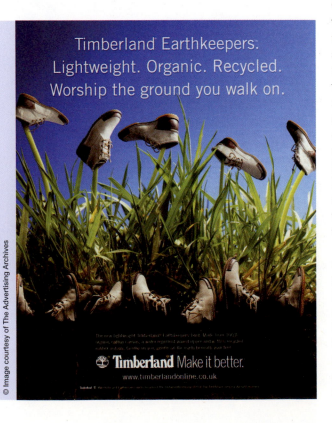

Timberland Earthkeepers: Lightweight. Organic. Recycled. Worship the ground you walk on.

Timberland Make it better.
www.timberlandonline.co.uk

© Image courtesy of The Advertising Archives

Companies can do business in such a way that everyone benefits—customers, the companies themselves, and society as a whole. While ethical business practices are vital to a firm's long-term survival and growth, **social responsibility** raises the bar even higher. In marketing, social responsibility involves accepting an obligation to give equal weight to profits, consumer satisfaction, and social well-being in evaluating a firm's performance. In addition to measuring sales, revenues, and profits, a firm must also consider ways in which it contributes to the overall well-being of its customers and society.

Social responsibility allows a wide range of opportunities for companies to shine. If reluctant at first, government legislation can mandate socially responsible actions. Government may require firms to take socially responsible actions in matters of environmental policy, deceptive product claims, and other areas. Also, consumers, through their power to repeat or withhold purchases, may force

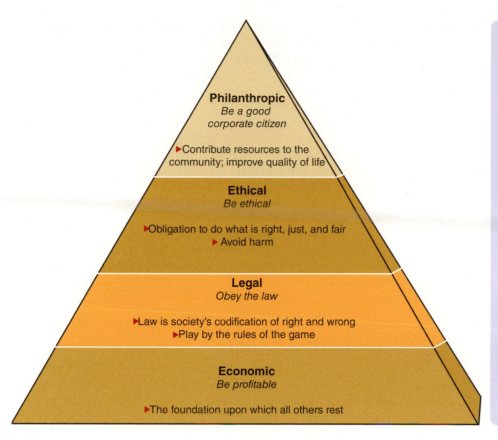

figure 3.5

The Four Step Pyramid of Social Responsibility

Source: The Four Step Pyramid of Corporate Social Responsibility from *Business Horizons,* Vol. 34, 1991, page 92, Freeman & Liedtka, "Corp. Social Responsibility." Reprinted from *Business Horizons* © 1991 with permission from Elsevier.

marketers to provide honest and relevant information and fair prices. The four dimensions of social responsibility—economic, legal, ethical, and philanthropic—are shown in Figure 3.5. The first two dimensions have long been recognized, but ethical obligations and the need for marketers to be good corporate citizens have increased in importance in recent years.

The locus for socially responsible decisions in organizations has always been an important issue. But who should accept specific accountability for the social effects of marketing decisions? Responses include the district sales manager, the marketing vice president, the firm's CEO, and even the board of directors. Probably the most valid assessment holds that all marketers, regardless of their stations in the organization, remain accountable for the social aspects of their decisions.

MARKETING'S RESPONSIBILITIES

The concept of business's social responsibility traditionally has concerned managers' relationships with customers, employees, and stockholders. In general, managers traditionally have felt responsible for providing quality products at reasonable prices for customers, adequate wages and decent working environments for employees, and acceptable profits for stockholders. Only occasionally did the concept extend to relations with the government and rarely with the general public.

Today, corporate responsibility has expanded to cover the entire framework of society. A decision to temporarily delay the installation of a pollution-control device may satisfy the traditional sense of responsibility. Customers would continue to receive an uninterrupted supply of the plant's products, employees would not face layoffs, and stockholders would still receive reasonable returns on their investments. Contemporary business ethics, however, would not accept this choice as socially responsible.

Contemporary marketing decisions must consider their global effect. Some clothing manufacturers and retailers have come under fire for buying from foreign suppliers who force employees to work in dangerous conditions or pay less than a living wage. The Chinese government is investigating the possibility that hundreds, perhaps thousands, of children from impoverished areas have been kidnapped or sold into slavery and sent to booming industrial cities. In some factories, children reportedly were forced to work as much as 300 hours a month for little pay.[52]

Marketers must also consider the long-term effects of their decisions and the well-being of future generations. Manufacturing processes that damage the environment or that use up natural energy resources are easy targets for criticism.

Marketers can use several methods to help their companies behave in socially responsible ways. Chapter 1 discussed cause marketing as one channel through which firms can promote social causes and at the same time benefit by linking their people and products to worthy undertakings. Socially responsible marketing involves campaigns that encourage people to adopt socially beneficial behaviors such as safe driving, eating more nutritious food, or improving the working conditions of people half a world away. And organizations that sponsor socially responsible programs not only help society but also develop goodwill for an organization, which could help the bottom line in the long run.

One way entire communities can benefit is through socially responsible investing. Many local banks and credit unions are committed to investing in their own communities. When consumers purchase certificates of deposit or open money market accounts or savings accounts, the bank or credit union can use the money to finance loans for affordable housing or for small businesses. The U.S. Treasury Department has certified over 800 community development financial institutions that serve neighborhoods that might otherwise be overlooked and educating low-income borrowers.[53]

MARKETING AND ECOLOGY

Ecology—the relationship between organisms and their natural environments—has become a driving force in influencing how businesses operate. Many industry and government leaders rank the protection of the environment as the biggest challenge facing today's corporations. Environmental issues such as water pollution, waste disposal, acid rain, depletion of the ozone layer, and global warming affect everyone. They influence all areas of marketing decision making, including product planning and public relations, spanning such topics as planned obsolescence, pollution control, recycling waste materials, and resource conservation.

In creating new-product offerings that respond to consumer demands for convenience by offering extremely short-lived products such as disposable diapers, ballpoint pens, razors, and cameras, marketers occasionally find themselves accused of intentionally offering products with limited durability—in other words, of practicing **planned obsolescence.** In addition to convenience-oriented items, other products become obsolete when rapid changes in technology create superior alternatives. In the computer industry, changes take place so quickly that lawmakers in several states have proposed legislation to force manufacturers to take back "e-waste"—used PCs and other technology products that contain toxic chemicals. For example, HP now supplies its printers with two cartridges—one for color and one for black. The replacement packs for each cartridge come with a self-addressed, postage-paid pouch to mail empty cartridges back to the company for reuse.

Public concern about pollution of such natural resources as water and air affects some industries, such as pharmaceuticals or heavy-goods manufacturing, more than others. Still, the marketing system annually generates billions of tons of packaging materials such as glass, metal, paper, and plastics that add to the world's growing piles of trash and waste. Recycling such materials, as HP does, is another important aspect of ecology. Recycling can benefit society by saving natural resources and energy as well as by alleviating a major factor in environmental pollution—waste disposal.

Unwanted and outdated electronic waste is the latest trash to overrun landfills as technology

Best Buy and Intel sponsored an event collecting computers, cell phones, and other technology-related gadgets. Consumers are increasingly interested in recycling unwanted electronics.

© Richard B. Levine/Newscom

advances motivate Americans to ditch their old electronics for newer models. Increasingly, consumers wonder how to dispose of their old computers, monitors, printers, TVs, phones, cameras, and other gadgets, especially since many of the older models contain lead and other hazardous materials requiring special handling. Best Buy, the nation's largest electronics retailer, is piloting a recycling program in 117 of its U.S. stores. Under the program, customers can drop off unwanted electronics equipment for recycling at no charge—even if it wasn't sold at Best Buy.[54] The case at the end of this chapter discusses electronic waste in greater detail.

Many companies respond to consumers' growing concern about ecological issues through **green marketing**—production, promotion, and reclamation of environmentally sensitive products. In the green marketing revolution of the early 1990s, marketers were quick to tie their companies and products to ecological themes. Consumers have responded by purchasing more and more of these goods, providing profits and opportunities for growth to the companies that make and sell them. Auto manufacturers such as Toyota and Honda already are making second-generation hybrid autos. Honda's FCX electric car uses no gasoline or diesel fuel and is powered by hydrogen gas.[55] Starwood Hotels recently introduced its Element brand, a chain of "green" hotels designed to create minimal impact on the environment. The hotels are built with technology that saves water and promotes energy efficiency. Guests with hybrid cars receive preferred parking; in the guest rooms, laundry bags are reusable and recycling is made easy through special receptacles.[56]

One area of green marketing that is booming is the organic food industry. Recent studies say 39 percent of the U.S. population uses organic products, and organics represent nearly 3 percent of total food sales in the United States.[57] But marketers and consumers alike have struggled to understand exactly what *organic* means. Marketers must use the term accurately in labeling, and consumers want to know what they are buying. According to the U.S. Department of Agriculture, "Organic food is produced by farmers who emphasize the use of renewable resources and the conservation of soil and water to enhance environmental quality for future generations." The USDA also specifies that certified organic meat, poultry, eggs, and dairy products must be produced by animals raised without antibiotics or growth hormones. A product that has a "USDA organic" seal certifies that it is at least 95 percent organic. Because it takes an average of three years for a farmer to receive USDA certification—an expensive process—prices for organic products are usually higher.[58]

briefly speaking

"Air pollution is turning Mother Nature prematurely gray."

—**Irv Kupcinet (1912–2003)**
AMERICAN NEWSPAPER COLUMNIST

green marketing
Production, promotion, and reclamation of environmentally sensitive products.

assessment check

1. Identify the four levels of the social responsibility pyramid.
2. What are the benefits of green marketing?

Strategic Implications of Marketing in the 21st Century

marketing decisions that businesses make are influenced by changes in the competitive, political-legal, economic, technological, and social-cultural environments. Marketing ethics and social responsibility will continue to play important roles in business transactions in your hometown and around the globe.

As the Internet and the rapid changes in technology that it represents are fully absorbed into the competitive environment, competition is even more intense than before. Much of the competition results from innovations in technology and scientific discoveries. Business in the 21st century is propelled by information technologies

but sustained by creative thinking and the willingness of marketers to meet challenges. Marketers face new regulations as the political and legal environment responds to changes in the United States and abroad. As the population ages and the social-cultural environment evolves, marketers will seek to meet the demands for new goods and services for consumers, such as increased health care. As always, they will try to anticipate and make the most of every opportunity afforded by the business cycle.

Ethics and social responsibility must underlie everything that marketers do in the 21st century—those who find ways to "do well by doing good" will succeed.

Review of Chapter Objectives

1   Identify the five components of the marketing environment.

The five components of the marketing environment are (1) the *competitive environment*—the interactive process that occurs in the marketplace as competing organizations seek to satisfy markets; (2) the *political-legal environment*—the laws and interpretations of laws that require firms to operate under competitive conditions and to protect consumer rights; (3) the *economic environment*—environmental factors resulting from business fluctuations and resulting variations in inflation rates and employment levels; (4) the *technological environment*—application to marketing of knowledge based on discoveries in science, inventions, and innovations; and (5) the *social-cultural environment*—the component of the marketing environment consisting of the relationship between the marketer and society and its culture.

2   Explain the types of competition marketers face and the steps necessary for developing a competitive strategy.

Three types of competition exist: (1) direct competition among marketers of similar products; (2) competition among goods or services that can be substituted for one another; and (3) competition among all organizations that vie for the consumer's purchasing power. To develop a competitive strategy, marketers must answer the following questions: (1) Should we compete? The answer depends on the firm's available resources and objectives as well as its expected profit potential. (2) If so, in what markets should we compete? This question requires marketers to make product, pricing, distribution, and promotional decisions that give their firm a competitive advantage. (3) How should we compete? This question requires marketers to make the technical decisions involved in setting a comprehensive marketing strategy.

3   Describe how marketing activities are regulated and how marketers can influence the political-legal environment.

Marketing activities are influenced by federal, state, and local laws that require firms to operate under competitive conditions and to protect consumer rights. Government regulatory agencies such as the Federal Trade Commission enforce these laws and identify and correct unfair marketing practices. Public and private consumer interest groups and industry self-regulatory groups also affect marketing activities. Marketers may seek to influence public opinion and legislative actions through advertising, political action committees, and political lobbying.

4   Outline the economic factors that affect marketing decisions and consumer buying power.

The primary economic factors are (1) the stage in the business cycle, (2) inflation and deflation, (3) unemployment, (4) income, and (5) resource availability. All are vitally important to marketers because of their effects on consumers' willingness to buy and consumers' perceptions regarding changes in the marketing mix variables.

5   Discuss the impact of the technological environment on a firm's marketing activities.

The technological environment consists of application to marketing of knowledge based on discoveries in science, inventions, and innovations. This knowledge can provide marketing opportunities: it results in new products and improves existing ones and it is a frequent source of price reductions through new production methods or materials. Technological applications also pose a threat because they can make existing products obsolete overnight. The technological environment demands that marketers continually adapt to change because its scope of influence reaches into consumers' lifestyles, competitors' products, and industrial users' demands.

6   Explain how the social-cultural environment influences marketing.

The social-cultural environment is the relationship between marketing, society, and culture. To remain competitive, marketers must be sensitive to society's demographic shifts and changing values, which affect consumers' reactions to different products and marketing practices. Marketers must consider the increasing importance of cultural diversity, both in the United States and abroad. Changing societal values have led to consumerism, the social force within the environment designed to aid and protect the consumer by exerting legal, moral, and economic pressures on business. Consumer rights include the following: (1) the right to choose freely, (2) the right to be informed, (3) the right to be heard, and (4) the right to be safe.

7 Describe the ethical issues in marketing.

Marketing ethics encompass the marketer's standards of conduct and moral values. Each element of the marketing mix raises its own set of ethical questions. Ethics in product strategy may involve quality and safety, packaging and labeling, and pollution. Ethics in distribution may involve territorial decisions. In promotion, ethical issues include honesty in advertising and promotion to children. Pricing may raise questions about price fixing and discrimination, increases deemed excessive, and deceptive pricing.

8 Identify the four levels of the social responsibility pyramid.

The four levels of social responsibility are (1) *economic*—to be profitable, the foundation upon which the other three levels of the pyramid rest; (2) *legal*—to obey the law, society's codification of right and wrong; (3) *ethical*—to do what is right, just, and fair and to avoid wrongdoing; and (4) *philanthropic*—to be a good corporate citizen, contributing to the community and improving quality of life.

assessment check: answers

1.1 Define *environmental scanning.*

Environmental scanning is the process of collecting information about the external marketing environment to identify and interpret potential trends.

1.2 How does environmental scanning contribute to environmental management?

Environmental scanning contributes to environmental management by providing current information about the five different environments so marketers can predict and influence changes.

2.1 Distinguish between direct and indirect competition and give an example of each.

Direct competition occurs among marketers of similar products, such as auto manufacturers or gas stations. Indirect competition involves products that are easily substituted. Pizza could compete with fried chicken or tacos. Six Flags could compete with a trip to a baseball game.

2.2 What is time-based competition?

Time-based competition is the strategy of developing and distributing goods and services more quickly than competitors.

3.1 Identify the four phases of U.S. government regulation of business. What is the newest frontier?

The four phases of government regulation of business are the antimonopoly period, protection of competitors, consumer protection, and industry regulation. The newest frontier is cyberspace.

3.2 Which federal agency wields the broadest regulatory powers for influencing marketing activities?

The Federal Trade Commission has the broadest regulatory authority.

4.1 Identify and describe briefly the four stages of the business cycle.

The four stages of the business cycle are prosperity, recession, depression, and recovery.

4.2 Explain how inflation and income affect consumer buying decisions.

Inflation devalues money and therefore may restrict some purchasing, particularly goods and services not considered necessary. Income also influences consumer buying power—the more discretionary income a household has, the more goods and services can be purchased.

5.1   What are some of the consumer benefits of technology?

Technology can lead to new or improved goods and services, offer better customer service, and reduce prices. It can also address social concerns.

5.2   Why must marketers monitor the technological environment?

Marketers need to monitor the technological environment to stay current with—and possibly ahead of—competitors. If they don't, they may wind up with obsolete offerings.

6.1   Define *consumerism*.

Consumerism is a social force within the environment that aids and protects the buyer by exerting legal, moral, and economic pressures on business.

6.2   Identify the four consumer rights.

The four consumer rights are the right to choose freely, the right to be informed, the right to be heard, and the right to be safe.

7.1   Define *marketing ethics*.

Marketing ethics refers to the marketer's standards of conduct and moral values.

7.2   Identify the five areas in which ethics can be a problem.

The five areas of ethical concern for marketers are marketing research, product strategy, distribution, promotion, and pricing.

8.1   Identify the four levels of the social responsibility pyramid.

The four levels of social responsibility are economic, legal, ethical, and philanthropic.

8.2   What are the benefits of green marketing?

Green marketing, which responds to consumers' growing concerns about ecological issues, offers consumers high-quality products without health risks or damage to the environment. Marketers who engage in green marketing may find themselves in a booming industry such as organic foods.

Marketing Terms You Need to Know

environmental scanning 61	*demarketing 73*	*marketing ethics 79*
environmental management 61	*technological environment 75*	*social responsibility 84*
competitive environment 62	*social-cultural environment 77*	*green marketing 87*
political-legal environment 65	*consumerism 78*	
economic environment 71	*consumer rights 78*	

Other Important Marketing Terms

strategic alliance 62	*competitive strategy 64*	*unemployment 72*
monopoly 62	*time-based competition 65*	*discretionary income 73*
deregulation movement 62	*gross domestic product (GDP) 71*	*VoIP 75*
antitrust 63	*business cycle 71*	*ecology 86*
oligopoly 63	*inflation 72*	*planned obsolescence 86*

Assurance of Learning Review

1. Why is environmental scanning an important activity for marketers?

2. What are the three different types of competition? Give an example of each.

3. What are the three questions marketers must ask before deciding on a competitive strategy?

4. What is the function of the Federal Trade Commission? The Food and Drug Administration?

5. Describe an industry or firm that you think might be able to weather an economic downturn and explain why.

6. Why do marketers monitor the technological environment?

7. How might marketers make the most of shifts in the social-cultural environment?

8. Describe the importance of consumer rights in today's marketing activities.

9. Why is it worthwhile for a firm to create an ethics program?

10. How can social responsibility benefit a firm as well as the society in which it operates?

Projects and Teamwork Exercises

1. With a classmate, choose two firms that compete directly with each other. Select two of the following or choose your own. Then develop a competitive strategy for your firm while your partner develops a strategy for his or hers. Present the two strategies to the class. How are they similar? How are they different?
   a. Home Depot and Lowe's
   b. Apple and Dell
   c. Busch Gardens and Six Flags
   d. Visa and MasterCard
   e. Honda and Ford
   f. Sara Lee and Kraft Foods

2. Track your own consumer purchasing decisions as they relate to your income. Compare your decisions during the college year and the summer. Do you have a summer job that increases your income? How does that affect your decisions?

3. The U.S. Postal service essentially enjoys a monopoly on the delivery of most mail. With a classmate, develop a strategy for a business that would compete with the USPS in areas that firms—such as UPS and FedEx—do not already address.

4. Choose one of the following products. Working in pairs or small groups, present arguments for and against having the United States impose certain regulations on the advertising of your product. (Note that some products already do have regulations—you can argue for or against them.)
   a. alcoholic beverages
   b. tobacco
   c. casinos
   d. prescription medications

5. With a classmate, research one of the recent large cases involving unethical and illegal activities by executives for companies such as Enron, Tyco, and Bear Stearns. Describe the charges made against these executives and the outcome. Do you think they were fairly charged and punished? Why or why not?

Critical-Thinking Exercises

1. Suppose you and a friend want to start a company that markets frozen fish dinners. What are some of the questions about the competitive environment you would like to have answered before you begin production? How will you determine whom your customers are likely to be? How will you reach them?

2. Emissions standards for motorcycles took effect in 2006 under rules adopted by the Environmental Protection Agency. There were no previous emissions controls for motorcycles at all, but even under the new laws, "dirt" bikes for off-road use will be exempt. The new standards add about $75 to the average cost of a motorcycle according to the EPA, but $250 according to the Motorcycle Industry Council. Why do you think motorcycle makers did not adopt voluntary emissions standards? Should they have done so? Why or why not?

3. The social-cultural environment can have a strong influence on the decisions marketers must make. In recent years, animal rights groups have targeted the manufacture and sale of *foie gras,* a European food delicacy made from goose and duck liver. Activists cite the cruel treatment of these birds, while chefs and restaurant owners claim otherwise. Animal rights groups are pressuring restaurants to stop serving *foie gras.* Others argue that consumers should be allowed a choice. What aspects of the social-cultural environment are affecting the marketing of *foie gras?* Which of the other components of the marketing environment may come into play, and how?

4. Nearly 400 million rebates—worth about $6 billion—are offered to U.S. consumers by marketers every year. But do consumers like them? Often rebates require more effort than

a consumer is willing to make to receive the cash back. Critics of the promotional effort say that marketers know this and are banking on consumers' not redeeming them, resulting in extra income for retailers and manufacturers. Do you think rebate programs are ethical? Why or why not?

5. The safe disposal of nuclear waste has been the topic of continuing public debate and an ongoing issue for marketers who work for nuclear power companies. This material is currently stored at 126 sites around the nation. To build a nuclear waste site, the U.S. Department of Energy must apply for and obtain a license. Supporters of such sites argue that they are important to building America's nuclear power capacity, while critics question their safety and usefulness. As a marketer, how would you approach this issue?

Ethics Exercise

Some retail firms protect their inventory against theft by locking their premises after hours even though maintenance and other workers are inside the stores working all night. Employees have charged that they are forbidden to leave the premises during these hours and that during an emergency, such as illness or injury, precious time is lost waiting for a manager to arrive who is authorized to unlock the doors. Although workers could open an emergency exit, in some cases they claim that they will be fired for doing so. Employers assert that managers with keys are on the premises (or minutes away) and that locking employees in ensures their own safety as well as cutting down on costly "shrinkage."

1. Under what circumstances, if any, do you think locking employees in at night is appropriate?

2. If you feel this practice is appropriate, what safeguards do you think should be put into effect? What responsibilities do employers and employees have in such circumstances?

Internet Exercises

1. **Competitive strategies.** Nike and New Balance are two of the largest manufacturers of athletic footwear in the world. Visit both firms' Web sites (www.nike.com, www.newbalance.com) and prepare a report comparing and contrasting the ways in which both have built their respective brands. How has each answered the five questions listed in the chapter concerning the development of a competitive strategy?

2. **Corporate social responsibility.** Visit the Starbucks Web site (www.starbucks.com) and click on the "corporate social responsibility" link. What are the key elements of the company's social responsibility efforts? How have they changed over the past couple of years?

3. **Economic environment.** High gas prices have forced auto manufacturers to make changes in the way they market their products. Pick at least three different companies, go to their Web sites, and prepare a report summarizing how each has responded to high gas prices. Which, in your opinion, has done the best job?

Note: **Internet Web addresses change frequently. If you don't find the exact site listed, you may need to access the organization's home page and search from there or use a search engine such as Google.**

Ethics Questionnaire Answers

Questionnaire is on page 81.

1. 34% said personal e-mail on company computers is wrong.
2. 37% said using office equipment for schoolwork is wrong.
3. 49% said playing computer games at work is wrong.
4. 54% said Internet shopping at work is wrong.
5. 61% said it's unethical to blame your error on technology.
6. 87% said it's unethical to visit pornographic sites at work.
7. 33% said $25 is the amount at which a gift from a supplier or client becomes troubling, while 33% said $50, and 33% said $100.
8. 35% said a $50 gift to the boss is unacceptable.
9. 12% said a $50 gift from the boss is unacceptable.
10. 70% said it's unacceptable to take the $200 football tickets.
11. 70% said it's unacceptable to take the $120 theater tickets.
12. 35% said it's unacceptable to take the $100 food basket.
13. 45% said it's unacceptable to take the $25 gift certificate.
14. 40% said it's unacceptable to take the $75 raffle prize.
15. 11% reported they lied about sick days.
16. 4% reported they have taken credit for the work or ideas of others.

Case 3.1 Electronic Recyclers International Puts a Dent in E-Waste

It's like a junkyard for abandoned electronics. But for John S. Shegerian, CEO of Electronic Recyclers International (ERI),

the heaps of TVs, computers, monitors, keyboards, speakers, and cell phones collecting in his Fresno, California, recycling center represent a chance to do well by doing good.

Shegerian bought the struggling firm—then known as Computer Recyclers of America—in 2002, changed its name to Electronic Recyclers International, and transformed it into the state's leading recycling operation dedicated to the responsible dismantling of consumer electronics. Through his business, Shegerian has found a way to help people *and* the environment.

According to the Environmental Protection Agency, Americans create nearly 1.9 million tons of electronic waste, or e-waste, per year, chiefly because of technology advances and Americans' insatiable appetite for the latest gadgetry. Electronic waste contaminates groundwater, pollutes the air, and endangers people. Traditional TV tubes and computer monitors are especially hazardous because they contain lead, cadmium, chromium, and other cancer-causing metals. In California alone, where e-waste is banned from landfills, over 200 million pounds of e-waste goes to recycling plants annually. With the 2009 conversion to digital broadcasting in America, an estimated 80 million analog TVs are being junked nationwide.

Despite laws in California and ten other states prohibiting e-waste in landfills, the EPA says landfills currently hold nearly 90 percent of the waste. Of the 10 percent that gets recycled, about 165,000 tons a year is shipped to developing nations like Africa, China, India, and Southeast Asia. There, impoverished workers, including children, pick through the wreckage in search of stray bits of copper or gold that can be sold. They work without tools or protective gear, exposing themselves to toxins.

ERI doesn't export any of the 8 million pounds of electronic waste it processes monthly. Its equipment produces minimal impact on the environment, ensuring that toxins are trapped and disposed of properly. Besides receiving government payments for processing waste, ERI sells what it salvages. Although such commodities as plastic, steel, and aluminum bring in less than a dollar a pound, computer microchips with precious metals sell for $75 a pound. Grossing $30 million during the last fiscal year, growth projections for ERI are extremely positive and plans for five more U.S. sites are underway.

And as ERI works to salvage e-waste, it also looks to rescue people. Nearly a third of ERI's 200 employees are part of its "second chances" program, an initiative that gives jobs to ex-convicts and recovered addicts. Turnover for this group stands at 17 percent— half that of the rest of Shegerian's workforce.

Questions for Critical Thinking

1. How do each of the five components of the marketing environment come into play for ERI?

2. The ERI case illustrates how a business can generate profit while operating in a way that benefits society. What kinds of alliances could a company like ERI form to widen its impact in the consumer electronics industry?

Sources: Electronic Recyclers International, Inc. Web site, www.electronicrecyclers .com, accessed April 28, 2009; Steve Miller, "Recycling Becomes Electric for CE Brands," *BrandWeek*, May 11, 2008, www.brandweek.com; Erika Brown, "Rehab, Reuse, Recycle," *Forbes*, April 21, 2008, pp. 70–72; Michael Kanellos, "Companies to Watch in Green Tech: Recycling," *CNET News*, April 21, 2008, news.cnet.com; Kent Garber, "Technology's Morning After," *U.S. News & World Report*, December 31, 2007–January 7, 2008, p. 24.

Video Case 3.2 The Marketing Environment, Ethics, and Social Responsibility at Scholfield Honda

The written video case on Scholfield Honda appears on page VC-4. The Scholfield Honda video is designed to expand and highlight the concepts in this chapter and the concepts and questions covered in the written video case.

CHAP**4**TER

E-Business: Managing the Customer Experience

Amazon.com Hopes to Re-Kindle E-Book Reading

Would you want to own a copy of a current bestseller that won't tear, wrinkle, or fall apart—for only $9.99? If so, you might be a customer for the Kindle 2, Amazon.com's newest portable book reader.

The Kindle 2 follows on the heels of Amazon's enormously successful Kindle reader, which sold out its initial inventory within hours of its launch on the retailer's popular Web site. Like its predecessor, the Kindle 2 is smaller and weighs less than an average paperback. It fits in one hand, runs cool and quiet, holds more titles than ever—over 1,500 books—and can download any of a quarter million books and magazines wirelessly within seconds. The new version has a 25 percent longer battery life so that users can read longer between recharges, and its screen can display 16 different shades of gray, producing clearer images that look more like real ink on paper.

With a new Broadsheet microchip, the Kindle 2's screen is also more responsive and allows for faster page turns. "It's the same brightness," said the CEO of the company that contributed some of the new screen technology, "but it's night and day for user activity . . . zooming in, [looking] up words, whatever, you really appreciate the speed. It's a major change." Its keyboard has also been redesigned.

The Kindle 2 can even read aloud. It has two small speakers on the back. It is priced at $359, the same as the original.

Amazon continues to back the Kindle brand with plenty of services. In fact, says company founder and CEO Jeff Bezos, "This isn't a device, it's a service." Popular features of the Kindle Web site include customized recommendations, one-click purchasing, and access to customer reviews. You can also link to online resources like Wikipedia and the New Oxford American Dictionary to check facts and learn vocabulary as you read. Book files are searchable, and you can highlight passages with the Kindle's built-in pen. The wireless connection comes free, along with an e-mail box, and Amazon makes a back-up copy of every purchased title so that customers can delete books to make room for new ones without losing books they've paid for. Subscriptions to magazines, blogs, and ad-free newspapers are available for a monthly fee. Amazon will even offer Kindle 2 users exclusive access to a new novel by best-selling author Stephen King, in which a Kindle is rumored to play a role.

According to Bezos, in its first six months the original Kindle accounted for 6 percent of total sales of books available in both print and electronic form. By the time the Kindle 2 was released, its predecessor had sold an estimated 500,000 units, 30 percent more than its closest competitor, the Reader from Sony. "This is the best solution we've seen so far," a personal computing research manager said of the original device. Bezos confirmed, "Our top design objective was for Kindle to disappear in your hands—to get out of the way—so you can enjoy your reading . . . . Whether you're lying in bed or riding a train, you can think of a book and have it in less than 60 seconds."

Has the Kindle brand proven itself to be the iPod of books? Many think so. "It's all about getting people the content they want in an easy and fast way," says one industry observer. "That's the single most important factor in driving adoption." Given all the improvements the Kindle 2 offers, it looks like Amazon.com's biggest problem might once again be keeping the reader in stock.[1]

OBJECTIVES

1 Describe the growth of Internet use worldwide.

2 Define *e-business* and *e-marketing,* and list the opportunities e-marketing presents.

3 Distinguish between a corporate Web site and a marketing Web site.

4 List the major forms of B2B e-marketing.

5 Explain business-to-consumer (B2C) e-marketing.

6 Identify online buyers and sellers.

7 Describe some of the challenges associated with online marketing and e-business.

8 Discuss how marketers use the communication function of the Web as part of their online marketing strategies.

9 Outline the steps involved in developing successful e-business Web sites and identify methods for assessing Web site effectiveness.

evolution of a brand

Amazon.com's Jeff Bezos, an avid reader married to a novelist, calls the traditional book "an incredible device" but also "the last bastion of analog." One factor he believes is critical for the Kindle brand's success is for it "to be as good as the book in a lot of respects. But we also have to look for things that ordinary books can't do."

- What are some Kindle 2 features and services that don't come with the purchase of ordinary books? How big a role do you think they'll play in the Kindle brand's success? What new options, such as content written specifically for Kindle users, might also be important in marketing the device? Which ones matter to you?

- Would you expect Amazon to market the Kindle 2 more heavily on its Web site or in print and television advertising? Why?

chapter overview

During the past decade, marketing has become the cutting-edge tool for success on the Internet. Profit-seeking organizations are not the only benefactors of the Internet; organizations of all kinds are emphasizing marketing's role in achieving set goals. Colleges and universities, charities, museums, symphony orchestras, and hospitals now employ the marketing concept discussed in Chapter 1: providing customers the goods and services they want to buy when they want to buy them. Contemporary marketing continues to perform its function of bringing buyers and sellers together; it just does it faster and more efficiently than ever before. With just a few ticks of the clock and a few clicks of a mouse, the Internet revolutionizes every aspect of life. New terms have emerged such as *shopping blog, RSS, VoIP,* and *XML*; and old words have new meanings never imagined a few years ago: *Web, Net, surfer* and *server, banner* and *browser, online* and *offline.*

Electronic business or **e-business** refers to conducting business via the Internet and has turned virtual reality into reality. With a computer and Internet access, a virtual marketplace is open 24/7 to provide almost anything anywhere to anyone, including clothes, food, entertainment, medicine, and information. You can pay your cell phone bill, make travel reservations, do research for a term paper, post a résumé at an employment bulletin board, or buy a used car—perhaps at a lower price than you could in person.

Internet marketers can reach individual consumers or target organizations worldwide through a vast array of computer and communications technologies. In just a few short years, hundreds of thousands of companies large and small have been connected to electronic marketing channels. The size and scope of e-business is difficult to understate. For instance, according to the U.S. Census Bureau, online retail sales in the United States totaled $107 billion in a recent year during which online retail sales grew by 22 percent, or more than four times the overall growth rate in retail sales.[2]

E-business involves much more than just buying and selling goods and services. Some surveys suggest that the Web is the number one medium for new-product information, eclipsing catalogs, print ads, and trade shows. The Internet allows retailers and vendors to exchange vital information, improving the overall functioning of supply and distribution, lowering costs, and increasing profits. Moreover, an increasing number of Americans now get some of their news and information from *blogs* (online journals) rather than from traditional media such as television and newspapers. Consequently, a growing number of businesses use blogs to put human faces on their organizations and communicate directly with customers.

This chapter examines the current status and potential of e-business and online marketing.

e-business Conducting online transactions with customers by collecting and analyzing business information, carrying out the exchanges, and maintaining online relationships with customers.

briefly speaking

"The Internet has been the most fundamental change during my lifetime and for hundreds of years. Someone the other day said, 'It's the biggest thing since [the printing of the Gutenberg Bible],' and then someone else said, 'No, it's the biggest thing since the invention of writing.'"

—**Rupert Murdoch**
(b. 1931)
U.S. PUBLISHER AND BUSINESSMAN

We begin by describing the growth of Internet use throughout the world. Next, we explore the scope of e-business and outline how marketers use the Internet to succeed, and then distinguish different types of Web business models. This discussion is followed by a review of the major types of B2B marketing online. We then explore the types of goods and services most often traded in B2C marketing on the Internet, along with a profile of online buyers and sellers. We then describe some of the challenges associated with marketing on the Web, followed by a discussion of how marketers use the communication function of the Internet. We conclude the chapter by examining how to build an effective Web presence.

The Digital World

In the past decade, the number of Internet users in the United States and worldwide has grown dramatically. Today, an estimated 218 million U.S. citizens—almost three-quarters of the U.S. population—access the Internet at home, school, work, or public access sites. Worldwide, the number of Internet users has reached almost 1.5 billion.[3] The map in Figure 4.1 shows the number of Internet users and Internet penetration for each of the world's continents and regions. Internet penetration is the percentage of a region's population who use the Internet.

Asia leads the world in the sheer number of users and the speed of growth in Internet use. Among individual countries with the highest number of Internet users, the United States ranks first, but the next three countries are all in Asia—China, Japan, and India.[4] India's Internet audience grew by more than 25 percent in a recent year, while China's grew 14 percent.[5] Japan has the fastest Internet service in the world, with broadband connections running from 8 to 30 times faster than in the United States. This network speed allows broadcast-quality, full-screen television viewing over the Internet and costs far less than U.S. broadband service.[6]

What do people do online? Let's look at the two countries with the most Internet users—the United States and China. In the United States, Net usage is mostly about communication, information, and purchases. Nearly three-quarters of U.S. users say they use e-mail; between 26 and 40 percent get news, shop for personal consumption items, pay bills, and use an instant messaging service.[7] Almost half of U.S. adults have logged on from a handheld or wireless device including

❙ Describe the growth of Internet use worldwide.

figure 4.1

Number of Internet Users and Internet Penetration Rate (by region)

Source: Data from Internet World Stats, "Internet Usage Statistics," www. internetworldstats.com, accessed April 28, 2009.

laptops, and many say they'd rather give up television than the Internet.[8] In China, users log on for different reasons. Nearly 80 percent of Chinese Web users log on primarily to visit social networking sites; this compares to just under half in the United States. Chinese users also far outnumber U.S. adults in playing online games and frequenting virtual worlds.[9] Among the reasons for the absence of online shopping in China is that the government controls the online payment system, unwieldy enough to keep most people shopping in person. Further, because the government has long restricted access to information and the media, including the Internet, Chinese users—almost three-quarters of whom are under 30—find the Internet most conducive to entertainment and social interaction.[10]

So where is e-business going and how can marketers capitalize on the digital links with consumers? In spite of the past success and future potential of the Internet, issues and concerns relating to e-business remain. Some highly touted e-business applications have proven less than successful, cost savings and profits have occasionally been elusive, and many privacy and security issues still linger. Nevertheless, the benefits and potential of e-business outweigh the concerns and problems.

assessment check

1. How would you describe the growth of Internet use worldwide?

2. What do most U.S. consumers do online?

E-Business and E-Marketing

2 Define *e-business* and *e-marketing,* and list the opportunities e-marketing presents.

Today, *e-business* describes the wide range of business activities taking place via Internet applications such as e-mail and virtual shopping carts. E-business can be divided into the following five broad categories: (1) *e-tailing* or virtual storefronts on Web sites; (2) business-to-business transactions; (3) electronic data interchanges (EDI), the business-to-business exchange of data; (4) e-mail, instant messaging, blogs, podcasts, and other Web-enabled communication tools and their use as media for reaching prospective and existing customers; and (5) the gathering and use of demographic, product, and other information through Web contacts.

The component of e-business of particular interest to marketers is *electronic marketing* or **e-marketing,** the strategic process of creating, distributing, promoting, and pricing goods and services to a target market over the Internet or through such digital tools as smart phones. E-marketing is the means by which e-business is achieved. It encompasses such activities as the following:

e-marketing Strategic process of creating, distributing, promoting, and pricing goods and services to a target market over the Internet or through digital tools.

Using Expedia.com to book a flight to Atlanta for a job fair is an example of e-marketing.

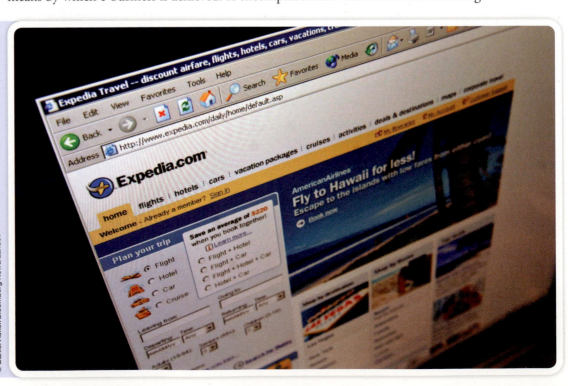

© Daniel Acker/Bloomberg News/Landov

▷ viewing your favorite band's latest videos on YouTube;

▷ booking a flight to Atlanta on Expedia.com to attend a job fair;

▷ researching MP3 accessories on Shopzilla and then placing an order; and

▷ accessing research site ProQuest through your college's network, allowing you to work on a paper, and then checking apartment rentals online.

The application of these electronic tools to contemporary marketing has the potential to greatly reduce costs and increase customer satisfaction by increasing the speed and efficiency of marketing interactions. Just as e-business is a major function of the Internet, e-marketing is an integral component of e-business.

A closely related but somewhat narrower term than e-marketing is *online marketing*. While electronic marketing can encompass digital technologies ranging from DVDs to interactive store kiosks that do not involve computers, online marketing refers to marketing activities that connect buyers and sellers electronically through interactive computer systems.

OPPORTUNITIES OF E-MARKETING

E-marketing offers countless opportunities to reach consumers. This radical departure from traditional brick-and-mortar operations provides the following benefits to contemporary marketers (summarized in Table 4.1).

▷ *Global reach.* The Net eliminates the geographic protections and limitations of local business and gives smaller firms a wider audience. Independent filmmakers often have a difficult time forging relationships with traditional distributors who buy the rights to films and promote them as they see fit. As a result, independent films sometimes have a limited audience. But the Internet is allowing filmmakers to organize their own screenings, send messages to interested online communities, and sell DVDs directly through their Web sites.[11]

▷ *Personalization.* Seven Cycles, a maker of customized bicycle frames, uses its Web site to introduce cyclists to its extensive Custom Kit data-gathering process, explain the required specifications and measurements, offer a timeline for order fulfillment, and provide forms for customers to print out and send to their preferred retailer.[12]

▷ *Interactive marketing.* Using a concept called **interactive marketing,** the Web site for the hit TV show "American Idol" lets users interact with the show and with each other, offering opportunities for blogging, messaging, and downloading show footage and videos sponsored by advertisers.[13]

interactive marketing
Buyer–seller communications in which the customer controls the amount and type of information received from a marketer through such channels as the Internet and virtual reality kiosks.

table 4.1 E-Marketing Capabilities

Capability	Description	Example
Global reach	The ability to reach anyone connected to the Internet anywhere in the world.	Independent filmmakers use the Internet to generate audiences and DVD sales for their films.
Personalization	Creating products to meet customer specifications.	Eddie Bauer has a Web site feature that allows buyers to mix and match items to complete outfits to suit their individual tastes.
Interactive marketing	Buyer–seller communications through such channels as the Internet and interactive kiosks.	Dell maintains an IdeaStorm site where users trade ideas, information, and product feedback.
Right-time marketing	The ability to provide a product at the exact time needed.	The Southwest Airlines Web site lets customers make advance reservations, check-in online, check flight status, and sign up for the carrier's rewards program.
Integrated marketing	Coordination of all promotional activities to produce a unified, customer-focused promotional message.	Michelin uses the slogan "A better way forward" in both online and offline promotions.

The Web site for the TV show "American Idol" uses interactive marketing, letting users interact with the show and with each other. Other Web sites also use the show's popularity to fuel e-marketing.

© Newscom

▷ *Right-time marketing.* Online retailers, such as BN.com and REI.com, can provide products when and where customers want them.

▷ *Integrated marketing.* The Internet enables the coordination of all promotional activities and communication to create a unified, customer-oriented promotional message.

In addition to the benefits listed here, an effective online presence can improve the performance of traditional marketing operations. Recent surveys of consumers found that, whether they purchase online or in person, well over half of shoppers do online product research before buying. Nearly three-quarters use the Internet as a first step in holiday shopping, and about nine in ten say they find online research improves their in-store shopping experience.[14] The Internet is thus a powerful force in shaping consumer behavior, even if it is seldom the only avenue most consumers pursue in their search for product information. Nearly half of all respondents to a recent Pew Internet survey say they use the Internet to research real estate purchases, in addition to looking at newspaper ads and talking to agents. More than half sample music online before purchase, but more than 80 percent have first found out about a song from radio, television, or a movie. About 40 percent of music buyers go on to visit artists' Web sites, however, and about the same number say online information helps them save on their purchases and influences them to buy more music than they otherwise would.[15]

assessment check

1. Define *e-marketing*.

2. Explain the difference between e-business and e-marketing.

3. What are the major benefits of e-marketing?

3 **Distinguish between a corporate Web site and a marketing Web site.**

corporate Web site
Site designed to increase a firm's visibility, promote its offerings, and provide information to interested parties.

WEB BUSINESS MODELS

Virtually all businesses today have Web sites. They may offer general information, electronic shopping, and promotions such as games, contests, and online coupons. Type in the firm's Internet address, and the Web site's home page appears on your computer screen.

Two types of company Web sites exist. Many firms have established **corporate Web sites** to increase their visibility, promote their offerings, and provide information to interested parties. Rather than selling goods and services directly, these sites attempt to build customer goodwill and assist channel members in their marketing efforts. For example, Burger King's Web site offers menus and nutrition information, a store locator, and videos and other types of promotions.[16] In addition to using the Web to communicate product information and build relationships with customers, many companies also use their corporate Web sites for a variety of other purposes, including disseminating financial information to investors; giving prospective employees the opportunity to apply online for jobs; and providing a communication channel for customers and other interested parties via e-mail, blogs, and online forums.

The Dunkin' Donuts Web site offers information traditionally found on a corporate Web site but also includes an online store for gift cards, merchandise, or purchase of its coffee to perk at home.

© Balkis Press/ABACAPRESS.com/Newscom

Although **marketing Web sites** often include information about company history, products, locations, employment opportunities, and financial information, their goal is to increase purchases by visitors. For instance, the Dunkin' Donuts Web site contains all of the information traditionally found on a corporate Web site, but it also includes an online store selling everything from coffee beans to tea, mugs, coffee machines, and apparel.

Many marketing Web sites try to engage consumers in interactions that will move them closer to a demonstration, trial visit, purchase, or other marketing outcome. Some marketing Web sites, such as Canon.com, are quite complex. Visitors can compare the company's different models of digital cameras and other products, selecting three at a time for detailed feature comparisons as well as find product registration and support, sign up for news and promotions, and locate a Canon dealer.[17] But not all products lend themselves to sales on the Internet. Complex products or those requiring demonstration or trials may be better sold in person. And some companies have relationships with partners, such as dealers and franchisees, that sell their products, which we discuss later in the chapter.

marketing Web site Site whose main purpose is to increase purchases by visitors.

assessment check

1. Explain the difference between a corporate Web site and a marketing Web site.

2. Why would companies *not* sell products on their Web sites?

B2B E-Marketing

FedEx's Web site is not designed to be flashy. Although it contains some graphics and minimal video clips, its main purpose is not entertainment. Instead, it provides lots of practical information to help the firm's customers. The site enables customers to check rates, compare services, schedule package pickups and deliveries, track shipments, and order shipping supplies. This information is vital to FedEx's customers, most of whom are businesses. Customers access the site thousands of times a day.

Business-to-business (B2B) e-marketing is the use of the Internet for business transactions between organizations. Although most people are familiar with such online firms as Amazon.com and eBay, consumer transactions are dwarfed by their B2B counterparts. According to the U.S. Census Bureau, 93 percent of e-business activity consists of B2B transactions.[18]

4 **List the major forms of B2B e-marketing.**

business-to-business (B2B) e-marketing Use of the Internet for business transactions between organizations.

In addition to generating sales revenue, B2B e-marketing also provides detailed product descriptions whenever needed. Payments and other information are exchanged on the Web, and B2B e-marketing can slash order-processing expenses. Business-to-business transactions, which typically involve more steps than consumer purchases, can be much more efficient on the Internet. Orders placed over the Internet usually contain fewer errors than handwritten ones, and when mistakes occur, the technology can quickly locate them. So the Internet is an attractive option for business buying and selling. In some industries, relying on the Internet to make purchases can reduce costs by almost 25 percent.

B2B e-marketing activity has become more varied in recent years. In addition to using the Web to conduct individual sales transactions and provide product information, companies use such tools as EDI, Web services, extranets, private exchanges, electronic exchanges, and e-procurement.

PROPRIETARY B2B TRANSACTIONS

One of the oldest applications of technology to business transactions is *electronic data interchange (EDI)*, computer-to-computer exchanges of price quotations, purchase orders, invoices, and other sales information between buyers and sellers. EDI requires compatible hardware and software systems to exchange data over a network. Use of EDI cuts paper flow, speeds the order cycle, and reduces errors. In addition, by receiving daily inventory status reports from vendors, companies can set production schedules to match demand.

Early EDI systems were limited due to the requirement that all parties had to use the same computer operating system. That changed with the introduction of *Web services*—Internet-based systems that allow parties to communicate electronically with one another regardless of the computer operating system they use. Web services rely on open source XML (Extensible Markup Language, a formatting language) standards. EDI and Web services are discussed further in Chapter 10.

The Internet also offers an efficient way for businesses to collaborate with vendors, partners, and customers through *extranets*, secure networks used for e-marketing and accessible through the firm's Web site by external customers, suppliers, or other authorized users. Extranets go beyond ordering and fulfillment processes by giving selected outsiders access to internal information. Like other forms of e-marketing, extranets provide additional benefits such as enhanced relationships with business partners. Harley-Davidson created an extranet called H-D.Net to help dealers complete warranty claims and order parts on the company's Web site.[19]

Security and access authorization remain critical issues, and most companies create virtual private networks that protect information traveling over public communications media. These networks control who uses a company's resources and what users can access. Also, they cost considerably less than leasing dedicated lines.

The next generation of extranets is the *private exchange*, a secure Web site at which a company and its suppliers share all types of data related to e-marketing, from product design through order delivery. A private exchange is more collaborative than a typical extranet, so this type of arrangement is sometimes called *c-business*. The participants can use it to collaborate on product ideas, production scheduling, distribution, order tracking, and any other functions a business wants to include. For example, Wal-Mart Stores has a private exchange it calls *retail link*. The system permits Wal-Mart employees to access detailed sales and inventory information. Suppliers such as Procter & Gamble and Nestlé, in turn, can look up Wal-Mart sales data and forecasts to manage their own inventory and logistics, helping them better meet the needs of the world's largest retailer and its millions of customers worldwide.

E-PROCUREMENT ON OPEN EXCHANGES

In the early stages of B2B transactions, marketers believed all types of products would be traded online. Entrepreneurs created **electronic exchanges** to bring buyers and sellers together in one electronic marketplace and cater to a specific industry's needs. Many believed electronic exchanges would become one of the most popular uses of the Internet. It didn't quite work out that way. Approximately 15,000 electronic exchanges were launched within a few years. Today, however, less than 20 percent remain. The others either merged or simply disappeared.

Why was the performance of many electronic exchanges so disappointing? Experts believe that many suppliers weren't happy with the pressure to come in with the lowest bid each time a satisfied long-term buyer decided to make a new purchase. Moreover, many buyers decided they preferred to cultivate long-term relationships with their suppliers, even if those suppliers charged slightly higher prices occasionally. Purchasing agents simply didn't see enough benefits from electronic exchanges to abandon suppliers they knew.

Evolving from electronic exchanges is **e-procurement,** Web-based systems that enable all types of organizations to improve the efficiency of their bidding and purchasing processes. Tea from India, for instance, is going digital as the Indian Tea Board moves its regular auction online to lower transaction costs and achieve fair prices. Now the board can accept bids from buyers anywhere in the world, instead of having to be physically present in the Guwahati trading hall. Says one industry consultant who assisted with the move to computerized trading, "That means buyer participation will be more, competition will be more. Greater competition ensures that the true price is discovered."[20] Eastman Kodak Co. used electronic bidding to select 150 contractors for a $200 million environmentally friendly upgrade of its Rochester, New York, facility. Demolition, construction, restoration, asbestos abatement, and other "green" improvements were covered by 1,600 different contracts over four years.[21]

E-procurement also benefits the public sector. The state government of Michigan maintains a Web site called Bid Contract. The site lists government contracts, bids, auctions, requests for proposals (RFPs), and other opportunities for firms to do business with the state and its cities, counties, and government-run entities such as police and fire departments.[22]

assessment check

1. What is B2B e-marketing? How large is it relative to consumer e-marketing?

2. Define *EDI* and *Web services.*

3. Briefly explain how e-procurement works.

B2C E-Marketing

5 Explain business-to-consumer (B2C) e-marketing.

business-to-consumer (B2C) e-marketing Selling directly to consumers over the Internet.

One area of e-business that consistently grabs news headlines is Internet shopping. Known as **business-to-consumer (B2C) e-marketing,** it involves selling directly to consumers over the Internet. Driven by convenience and improved security for transmitting credit card numbers and other financial information, online retail sales—sometimes called *e-tailing*—have grown rapidly in recent years. According to the U.S. Census Bureau, online retail sales now amount to more than 3 percent of all retail sales; five years ago, online retail sales made up around 0.05 percent of retail sales.[23] Currently, an estimated 66 percent of the U.S. population that is online has shopped there.[24] Some observers see e-tailing as a bright spot in retailing and project growth of up to 17 percent in the near future.[25]

Most people think of the Web as a giant cybermall of retail stores selling millions of goods online. However, service providers are also important participants in e-marketing, including providers of financial services. Brick-and-mortar banks such as PNC Financial and brokerage firms such as Charles Schwab have greatly expanded their online services. In addition, many new online service providers are rapidly attracting customers who want to do more of their own banking and investment trading at whatever time and day suits them.

ELECTRONIC STOREFRONTS

electronic storefronts Company Web site that sells products to customers.

Virtually all major retailers have staked their claims in cyberspace by setting up **electronic storefronts,** Web sites where they offer items for sale to consumers. Clothing retailer American Eagle sees e-retailing as a "significant growth opportunity" for all its brands and has been enjoying double-digit increases in electronic sales from year to year. The company's attractive Web site offers a store locator and wish list feature, gift card purchasing, a feedback link, and the opportunity to sign up for sales and other promotions. Clothing is organized by category—tops, bottoms, accessories, footwear, and so on—and the site has separate sections for sales and clearance items as well as for new arrivals and Web exclusives.[26]

Generally, online retailers—such as LLBean.com and BestBuy.com—provide an online catalog where visitors click on items they want to buy. These items are placed in a file called an **electronic shopping cart** or *shopping bag*. When the shopper indicates that he or she wants to complete the transaction, the items in the electronic shopping cart are listed on the screen, along with the total amount due, so the customer can review the whole order and make changes before paying.

One factor having a significant influence on the growth of online shopping is the increased availability of wireless access via laptops, cell phones, and smart phones. More than two-thirds of U.S. adults use cell phones and PDAs for purposes other than voice communication, including Internet use, and access is now faster and more reliable than before.[27] According to research on cell phone trends by Nielsen Mobile, 6.5 million mobile phone users have sent text messages to retailers and service providers to make online purchases.[28] Amazon.com is among many retailers who now let cell phone users browse, price-check, and purchase via text messages.[29]

BENEFITS OF B2C E-MARKETING

Many consumers prefer shopping online to the time needed to drive to a store and select purchases. Why do consumers shop online? Three main reasons are most often cited in consumer surveys: competitive pricing, access and convenience, and personalized service.

Competitive Pricing

Many of the best deals on products, such as airfares and hotels, can be found on the Internet. Expedia.com offers packages with combinations of flight, hotel, and car rental, plus special sales and last-minute flight specials at attractive prices organized by city and date of travel.[30] Bookseller Barnes and Noble's Web site offers member discounts up to 40 percent on hardcover best-sellers and other title-by-title price cuts.[31] One development that threatens online sales is the push to collect sales tax on online purchases, as the "Marketing Failure" features explains.

The Web is an ideal method for savvy shoppers to compare prices from dozens—even hundreds—of sellers. Online shoppers can compare features and prices at their leisure. Say, for instance, you're in the market for a new computer monitor. **Bots** aid consumers in comparison shopping. Bots—short for *robots*—are search programs that check hundreds of sites, gather and assemble information, and bring it back to the sender. For instance, at PriceGrabber.com, you can specify the type and size of monitor you're looking for, and the Web site displays a list of the highest-ranked monitors, along with the e-tailer offering the best price on each item and estimated shipping expenses. The Web site even ranks the e-marketers by customer experience and tells you whether a particular model is in stock. Amazon.com's text messaging system now lets shoppers compare prices as well.[32]

MARKETING FAILURE   Taxing Online Purchases

Background. The U.S. Supreme Court says only sellers with a physical presence in a given state—an office, store, or warehouse—can be forced to collect sales tax on behalf of that state. Tax law has not caught up with the economic and legal complexities of the rapid growth of Internet retailing, however. Many online retailers have little or no physical presence in any state, so most collect no state sales tax.

The Challenge. Under current laws that leave consumers to self-report sales tax owed on online purchases, as much as $4 billion in Internet-generated sales tax revenue goes uncollected by state governments each year, says the Direct Marketing Association. With Internet sales expected to pass the $200 billion mark, officials in many states facing huge budget deficits want to change this situation. But as one researcher points out, "Though sales taxes could potentially have a profound impact on what people buy and from where they buy it, there have been few marketing studies on how sales tax and the Internet relate."

Access and Convenience

A second important factor in prompting online purchases is shopper convenience. Cybershoppers can order goods and services from around the world at any hour of the day or night. Most e-marketers allow customers to register their credit card and shipping information for quick use in making future purchases. Customers are required to select a user name and password for security. Later, when they place another order, registered customers are asked to type in their password. E-marketers typically send an e-mail message confirming an order and the amount charged to the buyer's credit card. Another e-mail is sent once the product is shipped, along with a tracking number, which the customer can use to follow the order through the delivery process. A new service provided by *Elle* magazine's British Web site is the ability to use online photos to conduct visual matches for desired shopping items. In other words, using a digital picture of what you want, say, a pair of shoes, you can locate similar items for sale online. In the United States, Like.com will soon allow users to upload their own photos to find matches. "It's the first time you can search by submitting a photo," says the CEO of Like.com's parent company.[33]

Personalized Service

While online shopping transactions often operate with little or no human interaction, successful B2C e-marketing companies know how important personalization is to the quality of the shopping experience. Customer satisfaction is greatly affected by the marketer's ability to offer service tailored to many customers. But each person expects a certain level of customer service. Consequently, most leading online retailers offer customized features on their Web sites.

The early years of e-business saw Web marketers casting their nets broadly in an effort to land as many buyers as possible. Today, the emphasis has turned toward creating loyal customers likely to make repeat purchases. How does personalized marketing work online? Say you buy a book at Amazon.com and register with the site. The site welcomes you back for your next purchase by name. Using special software that analyzes your previous purchases, it also suggests several other books you might like. You even have the option of receiving periodic e-mails from Amazon.com informing you of new products. Many other leading e-marketers have adopted similar types of personalized marketing.

Some Web sites offer customized products to match individual consumer requirements. For instance, Nike offers online shoppers the opportunity to customize a running shoe, personalizing such features as the outsole, the amount of cushioning, and the width. The personalized shoe costs about $10 more than buying a product off store shelves. Some sites provide product use demonstrations and other product videos, and some, like Nordstrom's, offer 3-D product images and allow shopping by cost and by feature.

assessment check

1. What is B2C e-marketing?

2. Explain the difference between a shopping Web site and an informational Web site.

3. Discuss the benefits of B2C e-marketing.

The Outcome. The state of New York believes it can recover about $50 million in unreported sales tax with a new law requiring Internet retailers to collect sales tax from New York customers. While similar laws have been pending in Congress for some time, Amazon.com and Overstock.com immediately sued New York over the law; the case awaits resolution.

Lessons Learned. E-retailers value the advantage they gain over brick-and-mortar competitors by not collecting sales tax, which effectively lowers their prices. As Amazon and Overstock's reactions show, they won't willingly give this advantage up. Some already avoid creating physical presence in states with high sales tax rates, which may cost those states some jobs. While research is scarce, one recent study does suggest the imposition of a sales tax could depress online purchasing by as much as 16 percent. Related factors in consumers' decisions to shop online include the distance to a brick-and-mortar store, the ease of comparing prices on the Internet, whether the desired item is on sale, and even at what point in the transaction the consumer becomes aware that sales tax is being collected. "It's a legal morass," said one observer about taxing Internet commerce. "In a best-case scenario, it's going to take a while to sort everything out."

Sources: "A (Sales) Taxing Proposition," based on research by Eric T. Anderson, Nathan M. Fong, Duncan I. Simester, and Catherine E. Tucker, *Kellogg Insight*, February 2009, http://insight.kellogg.northwestern.edu; "Buying on Web to Avoid Sales Taxes Could End Soon," *Yahoo! Tech*, January 12, 2009, http://tech.yahoo.com; Candice Novak, "The Future of Internet Taxation," *U.S. News & World Report*, November 26, 2008, http://www.usnews.com; Anne Broache, "Tax-free Internet Shopping Days Could Be Numbered," *CNET News*, April 15, 2008, http://news.cnet.com.

Some sites provide product use demonstrations, such as My Virtual Model, which utilizes 3-D product images.

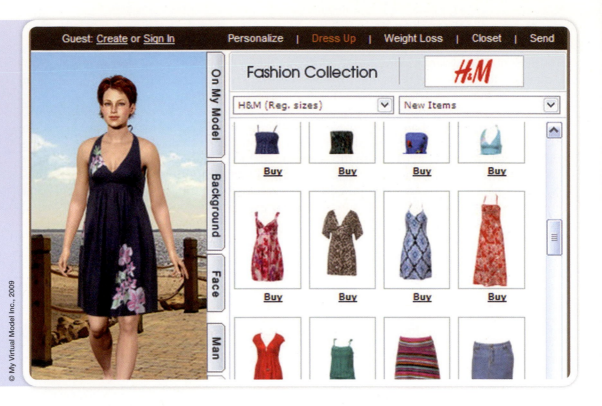

© My Virtual Model Inc., 2009

6 Identify online buyers and sellers.

ONLINE BUYERS AND SELLERS

A recent survey paints a picture of the characteristics of online users and buyers. Some of the key findings of the report are summarized in Figure 4.2. The typical Internet user is now likely to be between 35 and 64 years of age and will spend an average of 66 hours a month viewing more than 2,300 Web pages, including home and office Internet use. Moreover, today a broader range of Internet users now purchase products online compared with a few years ago. In 2000, men made up the majority of online shoppers. Today, women outshop men online.[34]

Realizing that customers would have little or no opportunity to rely on many of the sense modes—smelling the freshness of direct-from-the-oven bread, touching the soft fabric of a new cashmere sweater, or squeezing fruit to assess its ripeness—early online sellers focused on offering products consumers were familiar with and tended to buy frequently, such as books and music. Other popular early online offerings included computer hardware and software and airline tickets.

Figure 4.3 shows the top five products sold online during a recent year. Travel tops the list, with computer hardware and software tied with autos and auto parts for second place. Apparel and footwear is next, with home furnishings in fifth place. Other fast-growing categories include pet supplies, event and movie tickets, cosmetics and fragrance products, and gift cards—which all increased more than 20 percent in a recent year.[35]

Thanks to retailers' efforts, consumers' online shopping experiences have been steadily improving in quality and convenience. To keep up with rising expectations, some observers predict that

figure 4.2

Characteristics of U.S. Internet Users

Source: Data from Nielsen Online, as cited in "Nielsen Online Reports Topline U.S. Data," *Market Wire,* June 2008, accessed at FindArticles, www .findarticles.com, April 28, 2009.

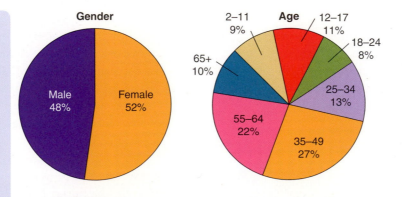

Average time online in a month (home and work) ≈ 66 hours
Average number of Web pages viewed per person in a month (home and work): 2,335

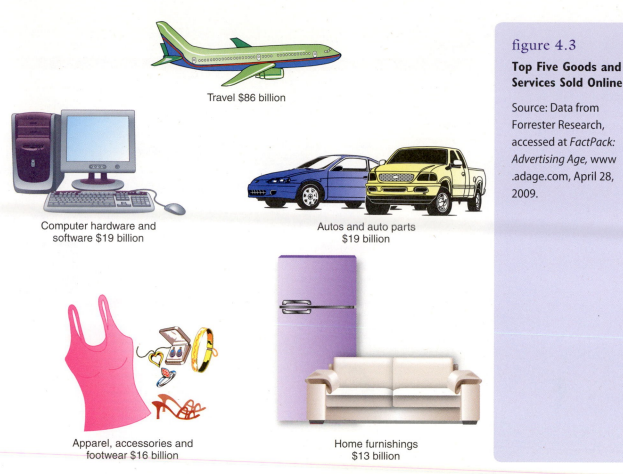

Travel $86 billion

Computer hardware and
software $19 billion

Autos and auto parts
$19 billion

Apparel, accessories and
footwear $16 billion

Home furnishings
$13 billion

figure 4.3

**Top Five Goods and
Services Sold Online**

Source: Data from
Forrester Research,
accessed at *FactPack:
Advertising Age,* www
.adage.com, April 28,
2009.

e-businesses will have to continually update their offerings at an increasing rate, speed the checkout process by eliminating the need to click from page to page, add video segments to their online product catalogs, and implement advanced, intuitive, and easy-to-use search and navigation technologies. Finally, e-tailers might look to the socializing capabilities of networking sites like Facebook and MySpace and start capitalizing on customer loyalty to initiate conversations with and between their customers.[36]

assessment check

1. Who shops online? Are the characteristics of online shoppers changing?

2. What are some of the capabilities e-marketers might add to their Web sites in the future?

Challenges in E-Business and E-Marketing

7 Describe some of the challenges associated with online marketing and e-business.

For all their advantages, e-business and e-marketing face some problems and challenges. Some of the most significant include developing safe online payment systems, protecting consumer privacy, preventing fraud and scams, improving site design and customer service, and reducing potential channel conflicts and copyright disputes.

SAFETY OF ONLINE PAYMENT

In response to consumer concerns about the safety of sending credit card numbers over the Internet, companies have developed secure payment systems. Internet browsers, such as Microsoft Internet Explorer, contain sophisticated encryption systems to protect sensitive information. **Encryption** is the process of encoding data for security purposes. When such a system is active, users see a special icon that indicates they are at a protected Web site.

VeriSign is one of the leading providers of Secure Sockets Layer (SSL) technology, which provides security for personal information provided online.

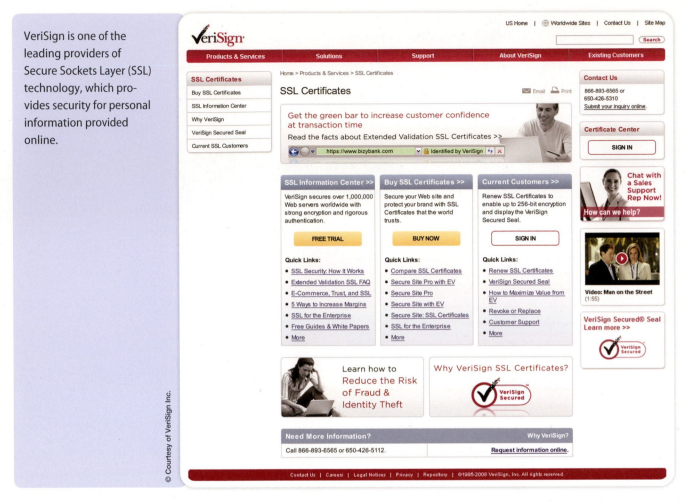

To further increase consumer security, most companies involved in e-business—including all major credit card companies—use **Secure Sockets Layer (SSL)** technology to encrypt information and provide authentication. SSL consists of a public key and a private key. The public key is used to encrypt information and the private key is used to decipher it. When a browser points to a domain with an SSL certificate, the technology authenticates the server and the visitor and establishes an encryption method and a unique session key. Both parties can then begin a secure session that guarantees message privacy and integrity. VeriSign is one of the leading providers of SSL technology used by more than 90 percent of *Fortune* 500 companies and the nation's ten largest banks.[37]

Many online shoppers are switching to online payment services such as Bill Me Later, Google Checkout, eBillme, and PayPal. Such services tend to speed checkout and make shopping more secure. They ensure that fewer merchants actually see the shopper's personal information and thus make it less vulnerable to hackers. These services benefit e-marketers, too, since they incur minimal marketing costs that then allow them to charge merchants lower transaction fees than credit card companies. About a third of 100 major e-marketers have recently added one or more new payment methods, and quite a few now offer at least three.[38]

PRIVACY ISSUES

Consumers worry that information about them will become available to others without their permission. Marketing research indicates privacy as one of the top concerns of many Internet users, although some recent studies suggest a generational split in privacy concerns: teens and young adults—more used to posting personal information—are less concerned. "I am constantly broadcasting who I am," says one 22-year-old from Texas. "It's the age of information; I'm used to giving and receiving tons."[39] As the earlier discussion of Internet payments explained, concern about the privacy of credit card numbers has led to the use of secure payment systems. To add to those security systems, e-marketing sites involving personal information require passwords as a form of authentication, that is, to determine if the person using the site actually is the one authorized to access the account. More recently, **electronic signatures** have become a way to enter into legal contract policies online. With an e-signature, an individual obtains a form of electronic identification and installs it in his or her Web browser. Signing the contract involves looking up and verifying the buyer's identity with this software.

Thanks to *cookies* and *spyware*—software used to automatically collect data from Internet browsers—online companies can track their customers' shopping and viewing habits. Amazon.com, for instance, has long employed sophisticated data collection systems to track customer preferences, and Google and other search engines gather users' search terms as a way to better target the ads that provide their revenue. The way companies use this technology has the potential both to make visits to the Web site more convenient and to invade computer users' privacy.

Now privacy advocates have proposed a Do Not Track list that would allow consumers to request online sellers *not* track their online habits, much as the Do Not Call list protects consumers who sign up from unwanted telemarketing approaches.[40] Congress is also considering legislation, known as the Counter Spy Act, to protect consumers from spyware that steals contact information without their knowledge.[41] Some Internet retailers prefer self-regulation. Google, for instance, avoids *behavioral targeting*, which collects search items over time—instead of per search—to develop a significantly detailed user profile. "That is not something that we have participated in, for a variety of reasons," the company's president of product management for advertising says. "We always want to be very careful about what information would or would not be used."[42]

Most consumers want assurances that any information they provide won't be sold to others without their permission. In response to these concerns, online merchants take steps to protect consumer information. For example, many Internet companies have signed on with Internet privacy organizations such as TRUSTe. By displaying the TRUSTe logo on their Web sites, they indicate their promise to disclose how they collect personal data and what they do with the information. Prominently displaying a privacy policy is an effective way to build customers' trust.

Such privacy features may become a necessary feature of Web sites if consumer concerns continue to grow. They also may become legally necessary. Already in the United States, the *Children's Online Privacy Protection Act* (*COPPA*) requires that Web sites targeting children younger than age 13 obtain "verifiable parental consent" before collecting any data that could be used to identify or contact individual users, including names and e-mail addresses.

Organizations, too, are concerned about the privacy of their data, and with good reason. A recent study by Verizon Business found nine of ten security breaches of corporate data were preventable if appropriate security had been in place. Three-quarters of the data breaches Verizon studied were made from outside the organization, and an equally high number were discovered by third parties rather than by the organizations themselves. The Identity Theft Resource Center (ITRC) found that, in more than half of identity fraud cases, the stolen data were used to open lines of credit and order cable and other utilities services.[43]

The government, too, frets about data security. Federal information technology employees are more worried than ever and cite bots and spyware, effects of security breaches, poorly trained users, and loss of employee and citizen data privacy due to security breaches among their nightmares, along with social networking and file sharing. Only half say they feel more secure than they did three years ago. Funding, training, and more embedded security protocols in existing network architecture were the top solutions they believed would increase data security.[44]

To prevent intrusions, companies install combinations of hardware and software called *firewalls* to keep unauthorized Net users from tapping into private corporate data. A **firewall** is an electronic barrier between a company's internal network and the Internet that limits access into and out of the network. However, an impenetrable firewall is difficult to find. A determined and skilled hacker often can gain access, so it is important for firms to test their Web sites and networks for vulnerabilities and back up critical data in case an intruder breaches security measures.

FRAUD AND SCAMS

Fraud is another impediment to the growth of e-business and e-marketing. The FBI, the National White Collar Crime Center, and the Bureau of Justice Assistance have formed a partnership called the Internet Crime Complaint Center (IC3) to receive and refer criminal complaints about cyberfraud and other Internet crime. In a recent year, it reported a record number of complaints—more than 206,000—and referred more than 90,000 of them, with $240 million in reported losses, to law enforcement officials. Auction fraud was the most frequent complaint, but other fraudulent activity included nondelivery of purchased items and credit and debit card fraud.[45]

phishing High-tech scam that uses authentic-looking e-mail or pop-up messages to get unsuspecting victims to reveal personal information.

One growing type of Internet fraud is called **phishing.** It is a high-tech scam that uses e-mail or pop-up messages that claim to be from familiar businesses or organizations such as banks, Internet service providers, or even government agencies. The message usually asks the reader to "update" or "validate" account information, often stating that some dire consequence will occur if the reader doesn't respond. The purpose of phishing is to get unsuspecting victims to disclose personal information such as credit card numbers, bank account numbers, Social Security numbers, or computer passwords. One recent e-mail example was a message, designed to look like an IRS letter, that included a link described as "the fastest and easiest way" to receive the 2008 Economic Stimulus Refund but that was actually an attempt to steal consumer information.[46] Phishing is also commonly used to distribute viruses and malicious spyware programs to computer users. In **vishing,** the voice equivalent of phishing, an e-mail or VoIP phone call requests the user to make a phone call to a voice response system that asks for the caller's credit card number.[47]

Payment fraud is another growing problem for many e-marketers. Orders are placed online and paid for using a credit card, and the retailer ships the merchandise. Then the cardholder asks the credit card issuer for a chargeback to the e-tailer, claiming he or she never made the purchase or never received the merchandise. Some claims are legitimate, but many involve fraud. Because an online purchase doesn't require a customer's signature or credit card imprint, the merchant—not the card issuer—bears the liability in most fraud cases.

SITE DESIGN AND CUSTOMER SERVICE

For firms to attract—and keep—customers, e-marketers must meet buyers' expectations. For instance, customers want to find products easily and have questions answered quickly. However, Web sites are not always well designed and easy to use. Competition and customer expectations will also drive more sites to include three-dimensional product photos and video demonstrations, because industry experts estimate better site design can quadruple the number of shoppers who actually buy what they put in their shopping carts. Product reviews, shopping information, pop-up discount offers, and instant messaging for customer questions are other features that can help online retailers to close sales.[48]

Another challenge to successful e-business is merchandise delivery and returns. Retailers sometimes have trouble making deliveries to on-the-go consumers. And consumers don't want to wait for packages to be delivered. Also, if customers aren't satisfied with products, then they have to arrange for pickup or send packages back themselves.

Retailers are addressing these issues. Most have systems on their Web sites that allow customers to track orders from placement to delivery. E-marketers have also worked hard on a process known as *reverse logistics*. Detailed directions on how to return merchandise, including preprinted shipping labels, are included in orders. A few, such as Nordstrom's and Zappos.com, even pay the shipping cost for returns.

Many of the so-called "pure play" dot-com retailers—those without traditional stores or catalogs—didn't survive for very long. They had no history of selling and satisfying customers. Because of expertise in all parts of retailing, companies that combine their store and catalog operations with e-business, such as Eddie Bauer and REI, generally have been more successful than those with little or no retail experience. That's probably part of the reason why seven of the top ten online retailers—like Target, Wal-Mart, and Best Buy—are companies that have traditional bricks-and-mortar stores. The three pure-play firms are eBay, Amazon, and Overstock.com, ranking first, second, and ninth respectively. Online shoppers also exhibit a strong streak of loyalty; six in ten make most of their purchases from sites they are already familiar with.[49]

The same lesson also applies to other service industries. To be successful at e-business, firms must establish and maintain competitive standards for customer service. When it began offering customers the opportunity to check flight schedules and purchase tickets online, Southwest Airlines worked hard to make sure its Web site had the same high service standards the airline is known for. Southwest.com has proved very popular and profitable for the airline.

Target, a traditional brick-and-mortar store, is also one of the top ten online retailers.

CHANNEL CONFLICTS AND COPYRIGHT DISPUTES

Companies spend time and money nurturing relationships with their partners. But when a manufacturer uses the Internet to sell directly to customers, it can compete with its usual partners. Retailers often have their own Web sites, so they don't want their suppliers competing with them for sales. As e-business broadens its reach, producers must decide whether these relationships are more important than the potential of selling directly on the Web. Conflicts between producers, wholesalers, and retailers are called **channel conflicts.**

Mattel, well known for producing toys such as Barbie, Cabbage Patch dolls, and Matchbox cars, sells most of its products in toy stores and toy departments of other retailers such as Target and Wal-Mart. The company wants an Internet presence, but it would cut the retailers out of this important source of revenue if it sold toys online to consumers. Mattel cannot afford to lose the goodwill and purchasing power of major retailers such as Toys "R" Us, so the company sells only specialty products online, including pricey American Girl dolls.

Solving an ethical controversy

Viacom vs. YouTube: Whose Property Is It?

In a $1 billion dispute, media giant Viacom is suing YouTube, the Internet's most popular video hosting site, for "massive" copyright infringement. Viacom claims that when YouTube, owned by Google, allows users to post clips from copyrighted works like films and television shows, it violates the law. YouTube can, and does, pull copyrighted material once it or the content owner identifies it as such, but it cannot prevent users from posting the content in the first place. Some observers think Viacom's suit also threatens the business models of such popular hosting sites as Flickr, eBay, and MySpace, which depend on user participation.

Should Web companies be held liable for copyright infringement by their users?

PRO

1. Companies that allow unauthorized posting of copyrighted material essentially are stealing from the content creators who are entitled to royalties for the use of protected material.

2. Content creators like Viacom are increasingly looking for ways to generate ad revenue from their content on their own Web sites, and illegal posting dilutes that content's value.

CON

1. The vast majority of clips on YouTube are just that—clips, not entire films or episodes. Thus, they are protected under the "fair use" doctrine.

2. Sites that remove illegal material once notified are protected by the Digital Millennium Copyright Act (DMCA), which makes their existence as Web communities possible.

Summary

While courts in the past have said that Web companies are not liable for user violations, some recent cases have been decided in favor of rights owners instead. If the courts begin to interpret the law to mean that Web companies are responsible for user behavior, many will have to reconsider their business models and their dependence on user participation.

Sources: Catherine Holahan, "Viacom vs. YouTube: Beyond Privacy," *BusinessWeek*, July 3, 2008, www.businessweek.com, accessed April 28, 2009; Clive Thompson, "YouTube versus Boob Tube," *New York* magazine, April 2, 2007, www.nymag.com; John Letzing, "Google Unveils Copyright Protection Tools," *Market Watch*, October 15, 2007, www.marketwatch.com.

Another conflict arises in the area of copyright, usually when a site hosts content to which someone else holds the rights. Over the last several years, Google has scanned more than a million books from libraries at Oxford and Harvard Universities and the New York Public Library to make them searchable online. But the Authors Guild has filed a copyright infringement suit to stop the project; a decision is still pending on what one observer calls "the vastest stand-alone case out there ... one [that] could shape copyright law for a generation."[50] Meanwhile, the world's largest music company, Universal Music, has accused Veoh Networks—a Web site for video and file sharing with financial backing from Time Warner and former Disney executive Michael Eisner—of large-scale copyright infringement, saying Veoh engages in "high-tech theft in the name of sharing."[51] The "Solving an Ethical Controversy" feature discusses a copyright infringement dispute between Viacom and YouTube, owned by Google.

assessment check

1. What are the major challenges to growth in e-business and e-marketing?

2. Describe phishing and vishing.

3. Explain how e-marketing can create channel conflicts and copyright disputes.

Marketing and Web Communication

8 Discuss how marketers use the communication function of the Web as part of their online marketing strategies.

There are four main functions of the Internet: e-business, entertainment, information, and communication. Even though e-business is growing rapidly, communication still remains the most popular Web function. The volume of e-mail today exceeds regular mail (sometimes called *snail mail*) by something like ten to one. Contemporary marketers also use the communication function of the Internet to advance their organizational objectives.

Companies have long used e-mail to communicate with customers, suppliers, and other partners. Most companies have links on their Web sites that allow visitors to send e-mail directly to the most appropriate person or division within the company. For instance, if you have a question concerning an online order from Williams-Sonoma, you can click on a link on the retailer's Web site and send an e-mail to a customer service representative. Many online retailers have gone even further by offering their customers live help. Using a form of instant messaging, live help provides a real-time communication channel between customers and customer service representatives.

Firms also use e-mail to inform customers about events such as new products and special promotions. While using e-mail in this manner can be quite cost effective, companies have to be careful. A growing number of customers consider such e-mails to be **spam,** the popular name for junk e-mail. A recent study found as much as 95 percent of all e-mail is spam, up from 70 percent three years before and only 5 percent six years ago. More than half the respondents in one poll considered e-mail the "worst" form of junk advertising, nearly twice as many as chose postal junk mail.[52] It is no wonder many Internet users employ *spam filters* that automatically eliminate junk e-mail from their in-boxes.

spam Popular name for junk e-mail.

ONLINE COMMUNITIES AND SOCIAL NETWORKS

In addition to e-mail, many firms use Internet forums, newsgroups, electronic bulletin boards, and social networks that appeal to people with common interests. All of these sites take advantage of the communication power of the Internet. Members congregate online and exchange views and information on topics of interest. These communities may be organized for commercial or noncommercial purposes.

Online communities can take several forms, but all offer specific advantages to users and organizations alike. Online forums, for instance, are Internet discussion groups. Users log in and participate by sending comments and questions or receiving information from other forum members. Forums may operate as electronic bulletin boards, as libraries for storing information, or even as a type of classified ad directory. Firms often use forums to ask questions and exchange information with customers. Digg started as a community for technophiles, but its audience has since grown into millions of increasingly diverse users. Some users who preferred the original focus are not as happy. Says Jay Adelson, one of Digg's founders, "Now that nontech stories have exceeded the tech stories [on the site], the challenge is on us to provide what our community needs." The answer, he believes, is a set of social networking tools to let users create their own communities.[53]

Newsgroups are noncommercial Internet versions of forums. Here, people post and read messages on specific topics. Tens of thousands of newsgroups are on the Internet, and the number continues to rise. **Electronic bulletin boards** are specialized online services that center on a specific topic or area of interest. For instance, mountain bikers might check online bulletin boards to find out about the latest equipment, new places to ride, or current weather conditions in popular biking locations. While newsgroups resemble two-way conversations, electronic bulletin boards are more like announcements.

Social networking sites have grown dramatically. MySpace's users recently numbered nearly 61 million, with Facebook running second at 26 million, and Classmates Online and LinkedIn following.[54] Community Connect is an umbrella site for niche social networking sites, many of which, like AsianAvenue.com and Blackplanet.com, are geared to specific ethnic and racial groups.[55] Marketers are still assessing the value of advertising on such sites, which remains difficult to measure.[56]

Online communities are not limited to consumers. They also facilitate business-to-business marketing. Using the Internet to build communities helps companies find other organizations, including suppliers, distributors, and competitors, that may be interested in forming an alliance. Marketers wanting to expand internationally frequently seek advice from other members of their online community.

briefly speaking

"The new information technology, Internet and e-mail, have practically eliminated the physical costs of communications."

—Peter Drucker (1909–2005)
MANAGEMENT AUTHOR AND EDUCATOR

Social networking sites, such as Facebook, have grown dramatically. Marketers are still assessing the value of advertising on such sites.

© Jonathan Ernst/Reuters/Landov

BLOGS AND PODCASTS

blog Short for *Web log*—an online journal for an individual or organization.

Another popular online communication method is the **blog.** Short for *Web log*, a blog is a Web page that serves as a publicly accessible journal for an individual or organization. Typically updated daily or even more frequently, these hybrid diary-guide sites are read regularly by almost 30 percent of American Internet users. Using *RSS (Really Simple Syndication)* software, readers continually are kept up-to-date on new material posted on their favorite blogs whenever they are online. Unlike e-mail and instant messaging, blogs let readers post comments and ask questions aimed at the author, called a *blogger*. Some blogs also incorporate **wikis.** A wiki is a Web page anyone can edit so a reader can, in addition to asking questions or posting comments, actually make changes to the Web page. **Podcasts** are another emerging technology. Anyone from bloggers to traditional media sources can prepare an audio or video recording and then post it to a Web site from which it can be downloaded to any digital device that can play the file.

Given the growing interest in blogs and podcasts, it hasn't taken long for marketers to incorporate them into their e-business strategies. Of particular interest to marketers are blogs that focus on new technology products, because they can prove effective at quickly forming public opinion. To try to reduce the damage from rumors and misinformation, some companies have decided to treat bloggers as members of the press and acknowledge their ability to spread news and influence. Sprint developed such close relationships of trust with some bloggers that it was able to have them sign nondisclosure agreements covering the release of Sprint's new Instinct phone. "These guys are specialists," says the U.S. public relations head of Samsung, which manufactures the phone. "They don't just know what a phone looks like. They really deep-dive into the industry—the mechanics of a particular device, the technology. These are very sharp people we're dealing with."[57] Moreover, many believe that corporate blogs, if done properly, can also help build brand trust.

Many companies allow, and even encourage, employees to start their own blogs, believing that employee blogs can serve useful functions. Wal-Mart operates a company blog called Check Out, where employees of Wal-Mart and Sam's Club discuss and invite reader comments about games, gadgets, phones, and other tech products. The employee entries are subject to company blogging rules, but they feature product announcements, photos, and chatty comments as well as announcements of sales and special prices on items featured in the stores.[58]

Some companies, however, have strict policies about the content of employee blogs, and some employees have even been disciplined over what their employers thought was improper blogging. However, most

Etiquette Tips for Marketing Professionals

Blogging on Your Best Behavior

The Internet is a very public place. That means writing a blog is like renting a billboard—anyone in the world can read what you write at any time, including family, friends, clients, colleagues, competitors, and current and future employers. Here are some guidelines for blogging that should help keep your online words from coming back to bite you.

- First, if you can't say something nice, don't say anything. Although you can delete posts you later regret, others can copy and redistribute them first, ensuring they will live forever.

- Avoid posting minute-by-minute details of your daily life. The blogosphere is clogged with such personal revelations, and they seldom find a wide or loyal readership.

- Choose a specific area or subject you know something about or feel passionately about and create a topical blog for a specific audience.

- Avoid posting copyrighted material, give credit for any text or image you legitimately copy or link to, and use your own image hosting site to avoid hogging others' bandwidth.

- Be honest but be respectful. Remember that everyone has an opinion, and you can have a healthy and informative debate without necessarily changing the other person's mind.

- Don't respond emotionally, or at all, to inappropriate or irresponsible posts by others; you will only fan the fire and you may be tempted to say something you'll wish you hadn't.

- If you choose to blog under a screen name, remember that it's always possible your real identity will become known. Don't use your Internet persona as a shield to hide behind.

- Never implicate or attack your employer, even if you think you've disguised the details. The odds are against your getting away with it.

Sources: "Blogging Etiquette," Deloitte, www.deloitte.com, accessed April 28, 2009; "The Social Etiquette of Blogging," September 14, 2007, www.customercrossroads.com; Zona Marie Tan, "Blogging Etiquette," *Suite 101*, May 28, 2007, blogs.suite101.com.

companies today still have no official policies regarding employee blogs. The "Etiquette Tips for Marketing Professionals" feature provides some hints on writing your own blog and keeping it trouble-free.

PROMOTIONS ON THE WEB

Rather than rely completely on their Web sites to attract buyers, companies frequently expand their reach in the marketplace by placing ads on sites their prospective customers are likely to visit. **Banner ads,** the most common form of Internet advertising, are typically small, strip messages placed in high-visibility areas of frequently visited Web sites. **Pop-up ads** are separate windows that pop up with an advertising message. The effectiveness of pop-up ads, however, is questionable. First, scam artists use pop-ups. Second, many Internet users simply hate pop-up ads—even those from legitimate companies. Consequently, most ISPs now offer software that blocks pop-up ads. Google and Microsoft also offer free pop-up ad-blocking software.

Preroll video ads, marketing messages that play before an online video, are becoming more popular. Although users have shown some resistance, NBC and YouTube are among those increasing their use of these 15- to 30-second videos.[59] **Widgets** are tiny interactive applications Internet users can copy and add to their MySpace or Facebook pages or their personal Web sites to play music, video, or slide shows. Marketers are adopting the use of widgets at a rapid rate, and Google has developed a development standard, called OpenSocial, that allows the programs to run on many different sites. "I'd say widgets are extremely useful, both as marketing tools and as a business tool in general," says one marketing consultant. "It would behoove anyone in business to learn how to use them."[60]

Another type of online advertising is so-called **search marketing.** Most firms make sure they are listed with the major search engines such as Google. But that is not enough to ensure visibility with consumers. A single search for an item—say, plastic fasteners—may yield thousands of sites, many of which may not even be relevant. To overcome this problem, companies pay search engines fees to have their Web sites or ads pop up after a user enters certain words into the search engine, or to make sure their firm's listing appears toward the top of the search results. Google and other search engines now include "Sponsored Links" on the right side of the search results page. A user who clicks on one of the sites listed under Sponsored Links is taken to that site, and

search marketing Paying search engines, such as Google, a fee to make sure the company's listing appears toward the top of the search results.

the company pays the search engine a small fee. Many experts consider search marketing the most cost-effective form of Web-based advertising. As a result, it is growing rapidly. Google, Yahoo, and AOL are spending billions to acquire popular sites they hope can help them expand their reach and refine their ad targeting. Google purchased YouTube for nearly $2 billion; Google agreed to spend $3.1 billion to buy online ad firm DoubleClick; and AOL bought Tacoda Inc. and its ad-targeting technology. "Everyone still wants to be your home page," says one marketing research executive.[61]

Another way companies use the Web to promote their products is through online coupons. For instance, customers can visit a company's Web site—for example, Procter & Gamble (www.pg.com)—to learn about a new product and then print a discount coupon redeemable at participating retailers.

assessment check

1. What are online communities and social networks? Explain how online communities can help companies market their products and improve customer service.

2. What are blogs, wikis, and podcasts?

3. Explain the difference between a banner ad, a pop-up ad, preroll video ad, widget, and search marketing.

9 Outline the steps involved in developing successful e-business Web sites and identify methods for assessing Web site effectiveness.

Building an Effective Web Presence

An e-business Web site can serve many purposes. It can broaden customer bases, provide immediate access to current catalogs, accept and process orders, and offer personalized customer service. As technology becomes increasingly easy to use, anyone with Internet access can open an account and place a simple Web site on the Internet. How people or organizations use their sites to achieve their goals determines whether their sites will succeed. Figure 4.4 lists some key questions to consider in developing a Web site.

SUCCESSFUL SITE DEVELOPMENT

Most Web experts agree: "It is easier to build a bad Web site than a good one." When judging Web sites, success means different things to different businesses. One firm might be satisfied by maintaining a popular site that conveys company information or reinforces name recognition—just as a billboard or magazine ad does—without requiring any immediate sales activity. Web sites like those of the *Los Angeles Times* and *USA Today* draw many visitors who want the latest news, and Yahoo!, Google, and ESPN.com are successful because they attract heavy traffic. As well as enhancing their brands, popular Web sites such as these add to their success by selling advertising space to other businesses.

Internet merchants need to attract customers who conduct business on the spot. Entrepreneurs are wise to clearly define their business goals, perhaps by creating a community of enthusiasts to

figure 4.4

Questions to Consider in Developing a Web Site

- What is the purpose of the Web site?
- How can we attract repeat visitors?
- What external links should be established to draw visitors to the site?
- What internal links to databases and other corporate resources are needed?
- What should the domain name be?
- What should the site contain?
- How should it work?
- Who should put the site on the Net—company or Web host?
- How much money should be spent to set up and maintain the site?
- How current does information on the site need to be?

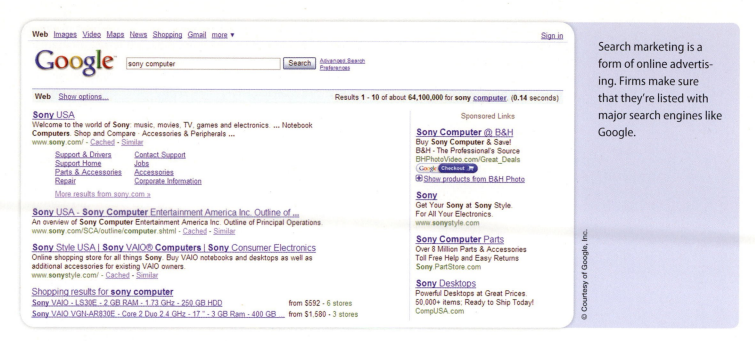

Search marketing is a form of online advertising. Firms make sure that they're listed with major search engines like Google.

build up sales in advance and to pay due attention to tried-and-true marketing tools that can complement Internet efforts, including television advertising. Listening to consumers is as important as talking to them via a company Web site or blog.[62]

ESTABLISHING GOALS

What is the company's goal for its Web site? Answering this question is the first and most important step in the Web site development process. For broadband telephone service provider Vonage, the primary objective is to sign up new customers. So the Web site designers put a link called "Sign Up Now" prominently in the upper portion of the home page.

Objectives for the Web site also determine the scope of the project. If the company's goal is to sell merchandise online, the site must incorporate a way for customers to place orders and ask questions about products, as well as links to the company's databases to track inventory and deliveries. The plan should include not only the appearance of the Web site but also the company's behind-the-scenes resources for making the Web site deliver on its promises.

Other key decisions include whether to create and maintain a site in-house or to contract with outside designers. Some companies prefer to retain control over content and design by producing their own sites. However, because acquiring the expertise to develop Web sites can be very time-consuming, hiring specialists may be more cost effective.

Naming the Web site is another important early step in the planning process. A domain name should reflect the company and its products and be easy to remember. However, with millions of domain names already registered, the search for a unique, memorable, and easily spelled name can be difficult.

IMPLEMENTATION AND INTEREST

Implementing the goals of the site is the next stage, and content is one of the most important factors in determining whether visitors return to a site. People obviously are more inclined to visit a site that provides material that interests them. Many e-business Web sites try to distinguish themselves by offering additional features. For example, Williams-Sonoma's Web site lures traffic to the site with weekly menu planners; printer-ready recipes; and features that convert menus between metric and U.S. measurement systems, adjust measurements for different numbers of servings, and create shopping lists for menus. Many sites offer links to other sites that may interest visitors.

Standards for good content vary for every site, but available resources should be relevant to viewers, easy to access and understand, updated regularly, and written or displayed in a compelling, entertaining way. When the World Wide Web was a novelty, a page with a picture and a couple of paragraphs of text seemed entertaining. But such "brochureware" falls far short of meeting today's standards for

interactivity, including the ability to accept customer data and orders, keep up-to-the-minute inventory records, and respond quickly to customer questions and complaints. Also, today's Internet users are less patient about figuring out how to make a site do what it promises. They won't wait ten minutes for a video clip to download or click through five different pages to complete a purchase. Revamping a site can help maintain interest and keep users on the site longer. MySpace recently completed a major redesign that improved the site's home page, profile editor, TV player, and navigation and search tools.[63]

After making content decisions and designing the site, the next step is connecting to the Internet by placing the required computer files on a server. Companies can have their own dedicated Web servers or contract to place their Web sites on servers at ISPs or other host companies. Most small businesses lack the necessary expertise to set up and run their own servers; they are better off outsourcing to meet their hosting and maintenance needs. They also need to draw business to their site. This usually requires a listing with the major search engines, such as Google, Ask.com, and Yahoo!.

PRICING AND MAINTENANCE

As with any technological investment, Web site costs are an important consideration. The highly variable cost of a Web site includes not only development expenses but also the cost of placing the site on a Web server, maintaining and updating it, and promoting it. A reasonably tech-savvy employee with off-the-shelf software can create a simple piece of brochureware for a few hundred dollars. A Web site that can handle e-business will cost at least $10,000. Creating it requires understanding how to link the Web site to the company's other information systems.

Although developing a commercial Web site with interactive features can cost tens of thousands of dollars, putting it online can cost as little as $30 a month for a spot on the server of a Web host such as Yahoo! And Web hosts deliver a huge audience.[64]

It's also important for a Web site to stay current. Visitors don't return to a site if they know that the information never changes or that claims about inventory or product selection are not current. Consequently, updating design and content is another major expense. Virgin Holidays experienced a 25 percent increase in online sales after working with a software design firm to redesign its site.[65] In addition, site maintenance should include running occasional searches to test that links to the company's Web site are still active.

Assessing Site Effectiveness

How does a company gauge the return from investing in a Web site? Measuring the effectiveness of a Web site is tricky, and the appropriate process often depends on the purpose of the Web site. Figure 4.5 lists some measures of effectiveness. Profitability is relatively easy to measure in companies that generate revenues directly from online product orders, advertising, or subscription sales. Southwest Airlines generates more than 74 percent of its bookings online at Southwest.com. However, what's not clear is how many of those tickets Southwest would have sold through other channels if Southwest.com did not exist. Also, evidence exists that so-called **Web-to-store shoppers**—a group that favors the Internet primarily as a research tool and time-saving device for retail purchases made in stores—are a significant consumer niche.

For many companies, revenue is not a major Web site objective. Most company Web sites are classified as corporate Web sites, not shopping sites, meaning that firms use their sites to showcase their products and to offer information about their organizations. For such companies, online success is measured by increased brand awareness and brand loyalty, which presumably translates into greater profitability through offline transactions.

Some standards guide efforts to collect and analyze traditional consumer purchase data, such as how many

figure 4.5

Measures of Web Site Effectiveness

Research studies · Profitability · Web site traffic counts · Click-through rates · Conversion rates · Web Site Effectiveness Measures

Illinois residents purchased new Toyotas the previous year, watched "American Idol" on Fox, or tried the new Starbucks Gazebo Blend coffee. Still, the Internet presents several challenges for marketers. Although information sources are getting better, it is difficult to be sure how many people use the Internet, how often, and what they actually do online. Some Web pages display counters that measure the number of visits. However, the counters can't tell whether someone has spent time on the page or skipped over it on the way to another site, or whether that person is a first-time or repeat viewer.

Advertisers typically measure the success of their ads in terms of **click-through rates,** meaning the percentage of people presented with a banner ad who click on it, thereby linking to a Web site or a pop-up page of information related to the ad. Recently, the average click-through rate has been declining to about 0.5 percent of those viewing an ad. This rate is much lower than the 1.0 to 1.5 percent response rate for direct-mail advertisements. Low click-through rates have made Web advertising less attractive than when it was new and people were clicking on just about anything online. Selling advertising has therefore become a less reliable source of e-business revenue.

click-through rate Percentage of people presented with a banner ad who click on it.

As e-business gains popularity, new models for measuring its effectiveness are being developed. A basic measurement is the **conversion rate,** the percentage of visitors to a Web site who make purchases. A conversion rate of 3 to 5 percent is average by today's standards. A company can use its advertising cost, site traffic, and conversion rate data to find out the cost to win each customer. E-business companies are trying to boost their conversion rates by ensuring their sites download quickly, are easy to use, and deliver on their promises. Many are turning to one of several firms that help companies improve the performance of their Web sites. Nielsen/Net Ratings developed a new way to rate Web sites that measures **engagement,** or how much time users spend on sites, rather than counting how many pages of a site they view. The change vaulted AOL to first place among U.S. Web sites, thanks to the 25 billion minutes users logged there, and dropped Google from third to fifth place, with about 7 billion minutes measured.[66] Microsoft, too, is testing an "engagement mapping" project. "Customers are exposed to one hundred times the online media today" than in the past, says one of the company's ad marketers. That means it's more important for marketers to know more about a customer than just the last ad clicked before purchase. "[With] an engagement model," says the media director for one agency that participated in the Microsoft project, "we'll now be able to see how a user was first encountered. We won't just pay the network where the last ad was clicked; we should be paying the previous network as well."[67]

conversion rate Percentage of visitors to a Web site who make a purchase.

assessment check

1. What are the basic questions a company should ask itself when planning a Web site?

2. How does the type of Web site affect measures of effectiveness?

3. Explain the difference between click-through rate, conversion rate, and engagement.

Strategic Implications of Marketing in the 21st Century

the future is bright for marketers who continue to take advantage of the tremendous potential of e-business and e-marketing. Online channels, such as podcasts, that seem cutting edge today will be eclipsed within the next decade by newer technologies, some of which haven't even been invented yet. First and foremost, e-business empowers consumers. For instance, already a significant percentage of car buyers show up at a dealership armed with information on dealer costs and option packages—information they obtained online. And the percentage of informed buyers is only going to increase. This trend isn't about being market led or customer focused; it is about consumer control. Some argue that the Internet represents the ultimate triumph of consumerism.

Since the end of World War II, there has been a fundamental shift in the retailing paradigm from Main Street to malls to superstores. Each time the framework shifted, a new group of leaders emerged. The old leaders often missed the early warning signs because they were easy to ignore. When the first Wal-Mart and Home Depot stores appeared, how many really understood what impact these large retailers would have on the marketing environment? Similarly, marketers must understand the potential impact of the Web. Initially, some experts predicted the death of traditional retailing. This hasn't happened and probably will never happen. Rather, a marketing evolution for organizations has occurred, one that embraces Internet technologies as essential parts of their marketing strategies. E-business is fueled by information; marketers who effectively use the wealth of data available will survive—and thrive—in cyberspace.

Review of Chapter Objectives

1   Describe the growth of Internet use worldwide.

Worldwide, the number of Internet users has reached almost 1.5 billion. Among individual countries with the highest number of Internet users, the United States is first with 218 million users, and the next three countries are in Asia: China, Japan, and India. India's Internet audience grew by more than 25 percent in a recent year, while China's grew 14 percent.

2   Define *e-business* and *e-marketing,* and list the opportunities e-marketing presents.

E-business involves targeting customers by collecting and analyzing business information, conducting customer transactions, and maintaining online relationships with customers by means of computer networks such as the Internet. E-marketing is the strategic process of creating, distributing, promoting, and pricing goods and services to a target market over the Internet or through digital tools. The capabilities and benefits of e-business and e-marketing include the elimination of geographical boundaries, personalized marketing, interactive marketing, right-time marketing, and integrated marketing.

3   Distinguish between a corporate Web site and a marketing Web site.

Virtually all businesses have Web sites. Generally, these sites can be classified as either corporate Web sites or marketing Web sites. Corporate Web sites are designed to increase the firms' visibility, promote their offerings, and provide information to interested parties. Marketing Web sites are also designed to communicate information and build customer relationships, but the main purpose of marketing Web sites is to increase purchases by site visitors.

4   List the major forms of B2B e-marketing.

B2B e-marketing is the process of selling goods and services through online transactions. B2B e-marketing includes product information; ordering, invoicing, and payment processes; and customer service. In a B2B context, e-business uses Internet technology to conduct transactions between two organizations via electronic data interchange, Web services, extranets, private exchanges, electronic exchanges, and e-procurement.

5   Explain business-to-consumer (B2C) e-marketing.

Business-to-consumer (B2C) e-marketing is maturing. B2C uses the Internet to connect companies directly with consumers. E-tailing and electronic storefronts are the major forms of B2C online sales channels. B2C Web sites are either shopping sites or informational sites. Products can be purchased on shopping sites, while informational sites provide product information along with links to sellers. Benefits of B2C e-marketing include competitive prices, increased access and convenience, and personalized service.

6   Identify online buyers and sellers.

Today's typical Internet user is from 35 to 64 years of age and spends about 66 hours online in a month both at home and at work. Women now outnumber men online. The top products sold online are travel; computer hardware and software; autos and auto parts; apparel, accessories, and footwear; and home furnishings. Other fast-growing online product sales involve pet supplies, cosmetics and fragrances, gift cards, and movie and event tickets.

7   Describe some of the challenges associated with online marketing and e-business.

One of the challenges to e-business is developing safe online payment methods. Most firms involved in e-business use Secure Sockets Layer technology to encrypt information and provide authentication. The growth of e-business has also been hampered by consumer security and privacy concerns and fraud. In addition, poor Web site design and service, unreliability of delivery and returns, and lack of retail expertise has limited e-business success. The Internet can also generate conflict among manufacturers, wholesalers, and retailers and present another avenue for copyright disputes.

Discuss how marketers use the communication function of the Web as part of their online marketing strategies.

Communication remains the most popular function of the Internet. Companies have long used e-mail to communicate with customers, suppliers, and other partners. Online communities are groups of people who share common interests. Companies use online communities, such as forums and electronic bulletin boards, and social networking sites to communicate with and obtain feedback from customers and other partners. Blogs are online journals that have gained popularity in recent years. Wikis are Web pages anyone can edit, and podcasts are audio and video files that can be downloaded from the Web to any digital device. Web-based promotions include advertising on other Web sites using banner ads and pop-up ads, preroll video ads, widgets, and search marketing. Banner ads are strip messages placed in high-visibility areas of frequently visited Web sites. A pop-up ad is a separate window that pops up with an advertising message. Preroll video ads appear before a selected video, and widgets are interactive applications users can add to their pages to play music, video, and slide shows. Search marketing is an arrangement by which a firm pays a search engine such as Google a fee to make sure the firm's listing appears toward the top of the search results.

Outline the steps involved in developing successful e-business Web sites, and identify methods for assessing Web site effectiveness.

Businesses establish Web sites to expand their customer bases, increase buyer awareness of their products, improve consumer communications, and provide better service. Before designing a Web site, a company's decision makers must first determine what they want to achieve with the site. Other important decisions include who should create, host, and manage the site; how to promote it; and how much funding to allocate. Successful Web sites contain informative, up-to-date, and visually appealing content. Sites should also download quickly and be easy to use. Finally, management must develop ways of assessing how well a site accomplishes its objectives. Common methods of measuring the effectiveness of Web sites include profitability, click-through rates, conversion rates, and engagement.

assessment check: answers

1.1 How would you describe the growth of Internet use worldwide?

Worldwide, the number of Internet users has reached almost 1.5 billion. Among individual countries with the highest number of Internet users, the United States is first with almost three-quarters of the population online, but the next three countries are in Asia: China, Japan, and India. Growth in Asia has been rapid.

1.2 What do most U.S. consumers do online?

Nearly three-quarters of U.S. users check their e-mail; between 26 and 40 percent get news, shop for personal consumption items, pay bills, and use an instant messaging service.

2.1 Define *e-marketing.*

E-marketing is the strategic process of creating, distributing, promoting, and pricing goods and services to a target market over the Internet.

2.2 Explain the difference between e-business and e-marketing.

E-business involves a wide range of activities that take place via the Internet. It is divided into five broad categories: (1) e-tailing; (2) business-to-business transactions; (3) electronic data interchanges; (4) e-mail, instant messaging, blogs, podcasts, and other Web-enabled communication; and (5) gathering and use of information through Web contacts. E-marketing transfers the traditional marketing functions of creating, distributing, promoting, and pricing goods and services to the Internet or through digital tools.

2.3   What are the major benefits of e-marketing?

The major benefits of e-business include the elimination of geographical boundaries, personalized marketing, interactive marketing, right-time marketing, and integrated marketing.

3.1   Explain the difference between a corporate Web site and a marketing Web site.

A corporate Web site is designed to increase a firm's visibility, promote its offerings, and provide information for interested parties. A marketing Web site generally includes the same information found on a corporate Web site but is also designed to increase sales by site visitors.

3.2   Why would companies *not* sell products on their Web sites?

Their products might not lend themselves to online sales, or the firms may have relationships with partners, such as dealers or franchisees, that sell their products instead.

4.1   What is B2B e-marketing? How large is it relative to consumer e-marketing?

B2B e-marketing is the use of the Internet for business transactions between organizations. By some estimates, 93 percent of all e-marketing activity consists of B2B transactions.

4.2   Define *EDI* and *Web services.*

An EDI is a computer-to-computer exchange of invoices, purchase orders, price quotations, and other sales information between buyers and sellers. All parties must use the same computer operating system. Web services consist of Internet-based systems that allow parties to communicate and exchange data regardless of the computer operating system they used.

4.3   Briefly explain how e-procurement works.

E-procurement systems are Web-based systems that enable all types of organizations to improve the efficiency of their bidding and purchasing processes.

5.1   What is B2C e-marketing?

B2C e-marketing uses the Internet to connect companies directly with consumers through either shopping sites or informational sites.

5.2   Explain the difference between a shopping Web site and an informational Web site.

Consumers can purchase products on shopping sites, while informational sites provide product information along with links to sellers. However, consumers cannot actually purchase products on informational sites.

5.3   Discuss the benefits of B2C e-marketing.

Benefits of B2C e-marketing include competitive prices, increased access and convenience, and personalized service.

6.1   Who shops online? Are the characteristics of online shoppers changing?

The typical Internet user now is likely to be between 35 and 64 years of age and spend an average of 66 hours a month viewing more than 2,300 Web pages, including home and office Internet use. While men used to shop more frequently online than women did, today women shoppers outnumber men.

6.2   What are some of the capabilities e-marketers might add to their Web sites in the future?

E-marketers need to update their offerings at their Web sites at an increasing rate, speed the checkout process, add video segments to their online product catalogs, implement advanced and easy-to-use search and navigation technologies, and initiate network-type conversations with and between their customers.

7.1   What are the major challenges to growth in e-business and e-marketing?

The major challenges include developing safe online payment, privacy concerns, and fraud and scams. In addition, poor site design and customer service, unreliability of delivery and returns, and lack of retail expertise have limited e-business success.

7.2   Describe phishing and vishing.

Phishing is a scam that uses e-mail or pop-up messages that claim to be from familiar banks, Internet service providers, or other organizations asking for personal information. The purpose of phishing is to get unsuspecting victims to disclose personal information such as credit card numbers. Vishing is the voice equivalent of phishing, and consists of a voice message or e-mail telling the user to make a phone call designed to elicit credit card information.

7.3   Explain how e-marketing can create channel conflicts and copyright disputes.

The Internet can generate conflict among manufacturers, wholesalers, and retailers—so-called *channel conflicts*. For instance, a channel conflict could be created when a manufacturer sells its products online and competes with its retail partners. Copyright disputes usually arise when a site hosts content to which someone else holds the rights.

8.1   What are online communities and social networks? Explain how online communities can help companies market their products and improve customer service.

Online communities and social networks can take several forms and include Internet discussion groups and electronic bulletin boards, as well as networking sites like MySpace and Facebook. Users log in and participate by sending comments and questions or receiving information from other forum members. Companies use online communities to ask questions and exchange information with customers.

8.2   What are blogs, wikis, and podcasts?

A blog, short for *Web log,* is a Web page that serves as a publicly accessible journal for an individual or organization. A wiki is a Web page anyone can edit. A podcast is an audio or video file that can be downloaded from a Web site to a digital device. Companies are starting to use blogs, wikis, and podcasts as tools to build and maintain customer relationships.

8.3   Explain the difference between a banner ad, pop-up ad, preroll video ad, widget, and search marketing.

Banner ads are strip messages placed in high-visibility areas of frequently visited Web sites. A pop-up ad is a separate window that pops up with an advertising message. Preroll video ads are brief marketing messages that appear before expected video content. Widgets are tiny interactive applications Internet users can copy and add to their own pages to play music, video, or slide shows. Search marketing is an arrangement by which a firm pays a search engine—such as Google—a fee to make sure the firm's listing appears toward the top of the search results.

9.1   What are the basic questions a company should ask itself when planning a Web site?

The first question deals with the purpose of the Web site. The second deals with whether the firm should develop the site itself or outsource it to a specialized firm. The third question is determining the name of the site.

9.2   How does the type of Web site affect measures of effectiveness?

For a shopping site, profitability is an important measure of effectiveness, though profitability can be difficult to measure given the presence of Web-to-store shoppers. For company Web sites, online success is measured by increased brand awareness and loyalty, which presumably translate into greater profitability through offline transactions.

9.3   Explain the difference between click-through rate, conversion rate, and engagement.

The click-through rate is the percentage of viewers who, when presented with a banner ad, click on it. The conversion rate is the percentage of visitors to a Web site who actually make purchases. Engagement measures how long a user spends on a site instead of how many pages he or she views.

Marketing Terms You Need to Know

e-business 96

e-marketing 98

interactive marketing 99

corporate Web site 100

marketing Web site 101

business-to-business (B2B) e-marketing 101

business-to-consumer (B2C) e-marketing 103

electronic storefronts 103

phishing 110

spam 113

blog 114

search marketing 115

click-through rate 119

conversion rate 119

Other Important Marketing Terms

electronic exchange 102

e-procurement 103

electronic shopping cart 104

bot 104

encryption 107

Secure Sockets Layer (SSL) 108

electronic signatures 109

firewall 109

vishing 110

channel conflict 111

electronic bulletin board 113

wiki 114

podcast 114

banner ad 115

pop-up ad 115

preroll video ad 115

widget 115

Web-to-store shoppers 118

engagement 119

Assurance of Learning Review

1. List the five e-business categories.

2. Explain how a Web presence can improve the performance of traditional brick-and-mortar operations.

3. Describe the type and purpose of information found on a corporate Web site.

4. Which is larger, B2B or B2C e-marketing?

5. How is wireless access changing e-marketing?

6. List the reasons consumers give for why they shop online.

7. Describe how firms can alleviate some of the privacy concerns of online shoppers.

8. What is purchase fraud?

9. How can companies benefit from blogs and avoid their downsides?

10. Describe the issues that go into developing a successful Web site. How does the purpose of the Web site affect its implementation and cost?

Projects and Teamwork Exercises

1. In small teams, research the benefits of purchasing the following products online:
   a. notebook computers
   b. hotel rooms in Orlando
   c. women's businesswear
   d. auto insurance

2. Assume your team is assigned to develop the Web site for a large online clothing retailer that also has traditional retail stores. Research the characteristics of Web users and online shoppers. What features would you want to incorporate into your Web site?

3. How can marketers use the concept of community to add value to their products? Give a real-world example of each of the types of communities discussed in the chapter.

4. Working with a small group, assume your group designs e-business Web sites. Identify a local company that operates with little or no online presence. Outline a proposal that explains the benefits to the firm of either going online or significantly expanding its online presence. Sketch out what the firm's Web site should look like and the functions it should perform.

5. Working with a partner, identify and visit ten different e-business Web sites. These can be either B2C or B2B sites. Which of these sites, in your opinion, have the highest and lowest conversion rates? Explain your choices and suggest some ways in which the conversion rates of all ten sites could be improved.

6. Identify a local company with an extensive online presence. Arrange to interview the person in charge of the company's Web site. Ask him or her the following questions:
   a. How was the Web site developed?
   b. Did the company develop the site in-house or did it outsource the task?
   c. How often does the company make changes to the site?
   d. In the opinion of the company, what are the advantages and disadvantages of going online?

Critical-Thinking Exercises

1. Who are typical online buyers and sellers? What are some of the strategic implications of these facts to online marketers?

2. Some marketers argue that search marketing is a more effective means of using the Web to advertise than traditional pop-up or banner ads. Research the concept of search marketing. What are some of the benefits of using search marketing?

3. Assume you work for a U.S. company that markets its products throughout the world. Its current online presence outside the United States is limited. Outline some steps the company should take to expand its online presence internationally.

4. Visa offers a service called Verified by Visa. The purpose is to reduce Internet-related fraud (MasterCard and American Express have similar services). Research "Verified by Visa" and prepare a report summarizing the program and how it protects both buyers and sellers.

5. One factor that appears to impede growth in online sales is consumers' fear of receiving unsolicited e-mail after a purchase is made. Given that fear, should companies continue to use e-mail to communicate with customers? If so, how?

Ethics Exercise

One of the lingering impediments to e-business revolves around privacy concerns. Virtually all Web sites collect user data. Internet service providers, for example, can track where users go on the Web and store that information. Search engines keep detailed data on Internet searches by users. Those arguing that additional privacy laws and regulations are needed claim that users never know exactly what information is collected, nor when it is collected. Moreover, there is no means for determining whether Web sites follow their own privacy policies.

On the other hand, some say current laws and regulations are adequate because they make it illegal for firms to misrepresent their privacy policies or fail to disclose the type of information collected. Furthermore, there is no evidence that Internet companies are quietly passing on specific customer information to outside parties. Aside from the strictly legal issues, Web privacy raises a number of ethical issues as well.

Assume your company collects and stores personal information about its online customers. The company's privacy policy allows the company to give limited amounts of that information to "selected" third parties.

1. Is this policy, in your opinion, appropriate and adequate? What ethical issues does your company's policy raise?

2. How would you change the privacy policy to reflect your ethical concerns?

3. From strictly an economic perspective, is the company's existing policy adequate and appropriate?

Internet Exercises

1. **Trends in Web usage.** Two sources of statistics on Web usage and related trends are ClickZ Network (www.clickz.com) and Internet World Stats (www.internetworldstats.com). Visit both sites and answer the following questions:

   a. Which countries have experienced the fastest growth in Internet usage over the past three years, in terms of number of users and penetration rates? What explains these trends? Do you expect them to continue? Why or why not?

   b. How much country-by-country variation is there in online activities? For instance, are residents of some countries more likely to shop online?

2. **Impediments to the growth in online shopping.** The Pew Internet and American Life Project (www.pewinternet.org) conducts regular surveys about online shopping habits. Go to the Pew Internet Web site and review the most recent survey.

   What do consumers commonly cite as their concerns about online shopping? Do these concerns impede the growth in online shopping? Prepare a report on how online retailers should address these concerns.

3. **B2B.** IBM and Arriba are two firms that offer extensive consulting services and software for firms engaged in e-business. Assume you're an entrepreneur and you'd like to expand your presence on the Web. Go to the IBM and Arriba Web sites (www.ibm.com and www.arriba.com). Read about the products offered and review some of the case studies. Prepare a report on what you learn.

Note: Internet Web addresses change frequently. If you don't find the exact site listed, you may need to access the organization's home page and search from there or use a search engine such as Google.

Case 4.1 Are Customers Wandering from Online Travel Sites?

For the first time in several years, the online travel industry has recorded a drop in the number of shoppers. Although online travel bookings are still expected to follow the trend for all e-marketing sectors and grow annual revenue by at least 10 percent, the percentage of Internet users who booked trips online declined from 68 to 62 percent in one recent year. A nearly corresponding increase in the number who reported booking offline suggests people are traveling in the same numbers but not booking online as frequently.

Other studies show that travelers who do book online are often booking directly through hotel Web sites, particularly for economy chains like Choice Hotels and Best Western, rather than using online travel agencies like Expedia, Travelocity, Priceline, and Orbitz as frequently. These agencies appear to be losing ground on two fronts.

"This is a wake-up call for the industry," says one online travel expert. "Customers are tired of spending two or three hours trying to find the airline or hotel or vacation package that meets their needs." The expert warned that online travel agencies might need to change the way they serve their customers by upgrading to newer technology with more features. For instance, current online travel searches use travel dates and destinations as search terms, bringing up a list of options that don't take into account travelers' other preferences such as budget, interests, and goals of the trip. The problem, the analyst says, is that while online retailers have improved their customers' shopping experience in recent years, the travel industry has been standing still.

Travelocity's vice president of business development agrees it is very important for online travelers to establish their preferences. Thus, the company recently debuted a new personalized search service called Road Trip Wizard. After inputting their interests and preferences, travelers get an itinerary with maps, directions, hotels, and local attractions. They can go on to book rooms and attraction tickets through Travelocity's Web site. "It's not just about the destination," says the CEO of LeisureLogix, which created the system, "but the things you do along the way."

To personalize its service more by suggesting appropriate hotels, Expedia uses information about the customer's travel plans to infer whether the trip is for business or pleasure; staying only one midweek night in a city suggests a business traveler, for instance. The company's president for North America explains, "I won't say there aren't upsides to understanding more about the person traveling. But we believe knowing about the occasion behind the trip, in many cases, is more important." Orbitz has also added new sections to its Web site that cater to family travelers as well as "road warriors," featuring destination recommendations and nearby hotels.

Questions for Critical Thinking

1. To improve their services and regain market share, do you think online travel agencies should increase the amount of personalization they offer customers? Why or why not? What other solutions could they try?

2. What would an online agency need to know about you to help you plan a vacation? How much and what kind of information would you be willing to provide, and why?

Sources: "Internet Travel Searches Drop," *m-Travel.com*, January 9, 2009, www.m-travel.com; "OTAs Continue to Lose Out to Supplier Sites for Hotel Bookings," *Hotel Marketing*, June 5, 2008, www.hotelmarketing.com; "Online Hotel Bookings Shift from Travel Agencies to Supplier Sites," *Marketing Vox*, June 5, 2008, www.marketingvox.com; Bob Tedeschi, "Travel Sales Still Growing, but Numbers of Customers Are Declining," *The New York Times*, October 29, 2007, www.nytimes.com.

Video Case 4.2   E-business at Evo

The written video case on Evo appears on page VC-5. The Evo video is designed to expand and highlight the concepts in this chapter and the concepts and questions covered in the written video case.

Talking about Marketing Careers with...
Michael L. Hutzel, Jr.

Knowledge is power, especially in today's competitive business environment. Organizations and their marketers continually look for ways to understand their customers and the products they purchase—or would like to purchase. The day-to-day contact firms have with those customers can provide key insights. Ohio-based RDI Marketing Services, Inc., helps contemporary marketers with their customer contact and research needs by providing inbound and outbound telemarketing services. Its staff offer customized, personal service for such major business initiatives as marketing research for new-product development, understanding customer perceptions of current practices or special promotions, sales, and industry-wide product recalls.

RDI is a strategic partner to its clients, tailoring its services to fit the project. Its employees consult with an organization's staff and offer expertise in developing marketing plans, drafting questionnaires and scripts, and using technology effectively to reach different markets. Here to discuss RDI's current activities and future plans is Michael L. Hutzel, Jr., the company's director of strategic initiatives. He agreed to a brief Q&A session to give us some background on building and maintaining a successful operation.

Q: Providing service and expertise to help Fortune 500 companies in their marketing efforts is a high-profile position. What is your educational background, and what experiences helped you work your way up the career ladder?

Ironically, most of my education in the marketing field is hands-on. I do have, however, a bachelor's degree in English as well as a master's in English education, both from The Ohio State University. This educational background has been extremely helpful in the writing of client scripts and proposals and in the bidding process. It has also been helpful with client meetings. My five years of experience in the classroom prepared me very well for the types of individual and group interactions that I now experience on a daily basis.

As for marketing experiences, nothing has proven more valuable to me. I remained tied to the marketing industry, one way or another, throughout my college career, mostly with part-time work. Initially, it was the type of job that allowed flexibility around constantly changing college courses, and it turned into a career. Learning to be flexible, understanding client needs, and embracing the changes of technology are key to developing a career in this field. And, of course, there is no substitute for hard work. Projects in this industry, much like the creation of a Web site, tend to be very "front-end" loaded. A lot of thankless hours go into the beginning of a project or new client relationship, but normally it is worth the haul.

Q: You are the Director of Strategic Initiatives at RDI. Tell us a bit about what your job involves. What is a typical day like for you?

First, there is no such thing as "typical." Honestly, though, that is part of the appeal. We have dozens of clients with very distinct needs that are ever changing. The reality of what we do is to service those clients in the best ways possible, which often means change, sometimes as frequently as by the hour.

My job entails two major aspects: operations and client relations. I serve as a client liaison to see that new projects get up and running as efficiently and effectively as possible. This means that I am involved in client meetings, normally to discuss upcoming needs and to evaluate the best plan of attack that is cost-effective for all involved. I have to stay intricately involved with operations so that I see the project though from inception to implementation. Because of this function, I need to have a thorough understanding of how the call center works—the human and technological resources—and be able to appropriately identify what is the best plan of action. After a project is under way, I facilitate necessary changes and maintain an ongoing relationship with the client.

Q: Your firm depends on solid relationships with such major clients as General Electric, Integrity Pharmaceuticals, and Sara Lee Corp. How do you develop and help strengthen those relationships?

Client relationships are the nucleus around which we all function. Quite simply, without them we would not be in existence. The initial development of these relationships comes from a wide variety of places. We are fortunate to have solid history, which allows us to work a great deal from client referrals. However, we never rest on our laurels and have an executive team, of which I am part, that focuses on exploring opportunities with clients in industries with which we are familiar, since we have a good understanding of what some of their needs might be. We also are constantly looking into other industries as well, to see if there is another niche we can explore. The premise from which we work is simple: to seek out and foster relationships in any industry in which the relationship can be mutually beneficial.

As for strengthening current relationships, this too has a high priority. Regular and positive contact seems to be the most effective for us. Each client is given several points of contact, typically executives, who can be available to address ongoing needs and concerns.

MICHAEL L. HUTZEL JR.
Director of Strategic Initiatives
RDI Marketing Services, Inc.

Photo: Courtesy of Michael L. Hutzel, Jr.

Q: We hear a lot about the importance of quality in providing services these days. How does RDI set quality standards, train employees, monitor their performance, and motivate them to perform their best for your clients?

RDI has worked very diligently to develop some of the highest standards in the business. Quality control is taken very seriously. So much so, that an entire department is dedicated just to that. Most of the quality control begins in the human resources department and is followed through with our Quality Assurance department. We have folks working literally around the clock to assure that the standards of our clients are met.

We are also very proud that we adopt a "promote from within" policy. This serves as incredible motivation for those who are beginning a career here. I have seen folks in my tenure here begin as hourly CSRs (client service representatives), spending their entire day on the phone in a cubicle, rise to team leads, supervisors, and even full-blown managers. It does wonders for maintaining team rapport and motivates those who want to grow within the company.

Q: We noticed that your firm provides multilingual call center services for clients at its center in Nogales, Arizona. How important is that service to your firm? Is this a growing part of your business?

To be competitive, offering such services is absolutely crucial. Our clients appeal to a wide range of consumers, and we have to adjust to fit their needs. The world is no longer a place of "us and them." Almost every major successful industry embraces diversity and utilizes the skills multiple cultures possess. The consumer base is the quintessential melting pot, and consumers are becoming increasingly informed. It used to be that offering such services was considered cutting edge; now I would argue it is essential as a fundamental service. Ultimately, it is the consumer who drives the market, and their needs must be met, by both our firm and our clients.

Q: We read nearly every week about the importance of outsourcing to today's marketers. As a company providing such services, how does your firm help clients formulate their strategic marketing plans?

We become as involved as our clients need us to be. Unfortunately, this too has no "typical" parameters. We do attempt to initiate our service in a standard approach, but normally it is very quickly tailored to what the client's ongoing needs may be. Often, we start with successful strategies that are time tested, particularly if a new client is in an industry with which we are familiar. If both the client and the industry are new to us, we try to draw from past success with clients who are most like the new client, or spend a great deal of effort to research the particular industry our new client is in. Understanding a client's industry, and more specifically their customer base, can go a long way in helping to determine a client's potential needs.

Q: Critical to developing and keeping customers' trust is operating in an ethical manner. In your field, confidentiality is an issue that must surface often. How important are confidentiality and security to RDI? How do you ensure the safety of client information?

Technology being what it is, this is probably a question better suited for our I.T. department. I can tell you, though, that we go to extreme measures in this age of constant security risks to protect our clients' data. We have security clearance in our buildings, electronic badges with varying levels of clearance, and similar clearance levels for logging in and out of computers, the server, and any of our storage databases. We expend a great deal of financial and human resources to ensure this.

Q: Marketers have been quick to adopt new technologies to help them achieve their goals. What new technologies, such as the Internet and telecommunications, do you use in your daily work? How have they helped your firm compete in the marketplace?

Depending on the project and its needs, different sources of technology are used. Telephony, point-to-point communication, I3 for remote access, INT5 dedicated servers, virtual private networks (VPNs), Internet, interactive voice response (IVR) are all just a few of the systems we use. The bottom line is that technology is one of the pillars in what we do on a daily basis. The trick to staying competitive is not always having the latest, greatest equipment. I would argue it is more about understanding what the available technologies have to offer, exploiting those technologies to their utmost capacities, and making sure that any new technologies will communicate efficiently with the current ones already in place.

Q: Students are always interested to hear advice on how to get started in their marketing careers. They read about the importance of gaining experience through volunteer activities and internships. What practical insights can you give to our readers to give them a head start?

I would say that getting as much exposure to as many firms as possible would be a good start. Do homework on each firm before volunteering or interning so there is a good base from which to make a decision. I would also say that it would be smart to get some idea of what interests them the most. Is it marketing or operations, sales or client development? There are several distinct courses that a professional can run in this industry, and although they may intertwine, they require very different skill sets. Look, listen, and be willing to learn from those who are successful; they have gems of wisdom to share, said or unsaid. Most important, never forget that at the end of the day, all successful firms are fueled by the consumer. Consumers are what make us possible.

Interview used with permission of RDI Marketing Services.

GREENSBURG, INC.

Marketing Is Not a Dirty Word

© Steven J. Eliopoulos

May 4, 2007 started out more or less like any other spring day for the 1,500 residents of Greensburg, Kansas. There was talk of storms later in the day, but few paid much attention—the folks in this rural community had seen their share of storms and knew what to do. Around 9:20 p.m., the storm sirens went off and the residents gathered in their bathrooms and basements to ride out the storm. Minutes later, the town was gone.

"My town is gone," announced Town Administrator Steve Hewitt in the first press conference on the next morning. "I believe 95 percent of the homes are gone. Downtown buildings are gone, my home is gone, and we've got to find a way to make this work and get this town back on its feet." With 700 homes to rebuild, the town was essentially a clean slate. Hewitt rallied the town and in the coming days and weeks, vowed to rebuild to the highest standard of energy efficiency and sustainability in accordance with the U.S. Green Building Council's *Leadership in Energy and Environmental Design* (LEED) rating system.

Thirty five miles away, Daniel Wallach's wife Catherine Hart wept as he read the first words of his new business plan: "What if we turned this tragedy into something beautiful?" Wallach and Hart had long been interested in sustainable, green living. Their home was not impacted by the storm, but their hearts were. Daniel and Catherine used their experience developing nonprofits to launch Greensburg GreenTown, an organization designed to support resident and business green building efforts through education and fundraising as well as provide public and media relations for the town.

In the aftermath of the storm, the town received generous donations and media attention, but all too often today's tragedy quickly becomes tomorrow's old news. GreenTown must work every day to keep this unique town on the map and the much needed contributions flowing. "I don't think marketing is a dirty word," says Hart. "I think marketing is relationship building. That's what we strive to do."

One year later, as most of Greensburg is still operating out of temporary FEMA trailers, Greensburg GreenTown serves as the front line for those who want to help in the rebuilding efforts. Companies have given tremendous donations of products and services for GreenTown to distribute on their behalf. They hand out everything from high-end, low-flow toilets to reusable grocery bags.

A large part of GreenTown's mission is to provide a green think-tank or "grink-tank" as Wallach calls it, for residents and businesses, the media and individuals interested in greening up their own lives. They host free seminars in green buildings and organic farmers organize a farmer's market, provide on-line resources and a place for residents still without electricity or computers to get on line and do their own research. They are working closely with manufacturers, builders, and architects to create a series of green model homes throughout the town where residents and tourists can check out different techniques, products, technologies—and even spend the night. Wallach believes these partnerships work

both ways. If successful, the model homes and eventually the town itself will become a living design magazine for all things green.

They've still got a long way to go in this very conservative town. Historically, the idea of green conjures up visions of politically radical, hippie tree-hugger types in Birkenstocks. While you may catch a glimpse of the ubiquitous footwear around the GreenTown office, Greensburg GreenTown strives to de-politicize green by making it easy and convenient for people to achieve. "If all you can do is build your deck out of recycled lumber, wonderful!" says Wallach. "We're gonna sing your praises as much as we will anybody else."

The long-term plans for Greensburg include a state of the art business incubator to help displaced businesses get back on their feet and bring new business to the town, a green industrial park, new highways, a green museum, green school system, wireless access throughout the city, and a community of green homes and businesses. While the city of Greensburg will take on the bulk of the financial responsibility for these projects, they will need GreenTown's help to continue to keep the cause on the radar of donors large and small to fund the gaps.

Questions

1. What is LEED, and how does adhering to LEED standards help create a story to market the town to the world?

2. What are the major challenges Greensburg GreenTown faces in gaining support for the green rebuilding efforts? What social and political views might they have to change?

3. Who is Greensburg GreenTown's "customer"?

4. Do you think Greensburg GreenTown's website (www. greensburggreentown.org) is an effective marketing tool?

5. Place yourself in the role of assisting Daniel Wallach and write a report (3 to 5 pages) that comments and provides recommendations on a specific product (i.e., low-flush toilet, solar or wind technology for power generation) and how to maximize the use of this technology.

Understanding Buyers and Markets

CHAP5TER Consumer Behavior

© JOHN LEE/CHICAGO TRIBUNE/Newscom

Paco Underhill: Master of Consumer Behavior

Consumers are mysterious. Why do we walk into one store and not another? What makes us buy some products and walk past others? Do we take longer to make purchase decisions when we

have less money to spend? Do we respond more positively to certain words, images, and signs than others? Paco Underhill and his associates at Envirosell set out to answer questions such as these every day for retail-

ers across the globe.

Underhill really is a hero to market-ers. He and his employees dig up all kinds of information about the way consumers behave that is helpful. In an economy

where every sale—and every customer—counts, the insights provided by Envirosell's research are pure gold. Underhill and his team gather information about the habits of consumers for major retailers such as

Wal-Mart, Best Buy, and Gap, as well as smaller companies. They videotape the actions of shoppers, learning which aisles they spend the most time in and which they tend to skip, what types of products they pick up, whether they spend time reading labels, how they respond to signs, and which items they actually purchase. In all, the Envirosell team collects nearly 50,000 hours of video in a year. Then they analyze it to help their clients make sense of it all.

One trend that Underhill has noticed is that consumers generally make more purchase decisions when they are actually in a store than beforehand—even if they come armed with a shopping list. As a result, stores can take advantage of an opportunity to market products with signs and displays that are attractive and convey the right marketing messages. "It's all about in-store marketing," says Underhill. "It's making things occur to the shopper." Another trend is that shoppers are currently spending

about 20 percent more time in stores than they did during more prosperous times. They are taking time to read labels, compare prices, and think about what they are buying. In addition, in grocery stores they are more frequently taking items out of their carts as they reach the checkout line. "They are trading out or experiencing buyer's remorse," notes Underhill. If retailers observe and understand these trends, they can tailor their marketing to influence shoppers to make purchases. For example, if a retailer realizes that more than 60 percent of a shopper's time in the store may actually be spent waiting in line for a cashier, the retailer might put more effort into making attractive products available within reach from the line.

One of Underhill's favorite sleuthing expeditions involves evaluating the signage used by various stores. He believes that a good sign has a great deal to do with a consumer's choice to buy an item. "Merchants have to take

some control over the consumer's eye," he explains. He suggests posting a sign that is creative and attractive but easy to read. It shouldn't take a shopper longer than 15 seconds to take in what the sign has to say. Signs that are handwritten on glass or a white board—like you'd see in a deli—convey the message that the product is new or somehow special. Signs that provide a smattering of information—such as the importance of buying something organic or green—make shoppers feel good about their purchases. Sometimes retailers forget the basics, such as placing a sign where most shoppers are likely to see it or making sure the lighting is good.

Underhill and his team strive to provide information to retailers that will help them—and their customers—make the most of the shopping experience. Consumers buy things—and don't—for reasons. Underhill is convinced that understanding these reasons is the key to any retailer's success.[1]

OBJECTIVES

1 Define *consumer behavior* and describe the role it plays in marketing decisions.

2 Describe the interpersonal determinants of consumer behavior: cultural, social, and family influences.

3 Explain each of the personal determinants of consumer behavior: needs and motives, perceptions, attitudes, learning, and self-concept theory.

4 Distinguish between high-involvement and low-involvement purchase decisions.

5 Outline the steps in the consumer decision process.

6 Differentiate among routinized response behavior, limited problem solving, and extended problem solving by consumers.

evolution of a brand

Paco Underhill founded Envirosell about 20 years ago. The firm offers marketing research services to help clients understand consumer behavior and increase retail sales. As the economy changes, Envirosell must monitor trends in consumer behavior. "The era of conspicuous consumption is over," observes Underhill. He recommends that retailers adapt. "Chains are going to have to get smaller."

In addition to working with individual clients, Underhill spreads the word about consumer behavior and the Envirosell brand through his popular books, *Why We Buy* and *Call of the Mall*. He predicts that the retail world "will change more in the next five years than it has in the past 100."

- Do you agree with Underhill that the retail world is changing drastically? Why or why not? If so, what changes do you foresee?

- What steps do you think Envirosell can take to remain relevant as a brand over the next decade?

chapter overview

Why do you head for Papa John's Pizza whenever you have a craving for extra cheese and pepperoni? Why does your roommate stock Jones soda in the fridge? Why does your best friend drive five miles out of the way for Caribou Coffee—when the local coffee shop is much closer? The answers to these questions aren't obvious, and they directly affect every aspect of marketing strategy, including the development of a product, the level at which it is priced, and the way it is promoted. Developing a marketing strategy requires an understanding of the process by which individual consumers buy goods and services for their own use and organizational buyers purchase business products for their organizations.

A variety of influences affect both individuals buying items for themselves and personnel purchasing products for their firms. This chapter focuses on individual purchasing behavior, which applies to all of us as consumers. **Consumer behavior** is the process through which the ultimate buyer makes purchase decisions from toothbrushes to autos to vacations. Chapter 6 will shift the focus to business buying decisions.

The study of consumer behavior builds on an understanding of human behavior in general. In their

briefly
speaking

"When you go to buy, use your eyes, not your ears."

—*Czech proverb*

efforts to understand why and how consumers make buying decisions, marketers borrow extensively from the sciences of psychology and sociology. The work of psychologist Kurt Lewin, for example, provides a useful classification scheme for influences on buying behavior. Lewin's proposition is

$$B = f(P, E)$$

This statement means that behavior (*B*) is a function (*f*) of the interactions of personal influences (*P*) and pressures exerted by outside environmental forces (*E*).

The statement usually is rewritten to apply to consumer behavior as follows:

$$B = f(I, P)$$

Consumer behavior (*B*) is a function (*f*) of the interactions of interpersonal influences (*I*)—such as culture, friends, classmates, coworkers, and relatives—and personal factors (*P*) such as attitudes, learning, and perception. In other words, inputs from others and an individual's psychological makeup affect his or her purchasing behavior. Before looking at how consumers make purchase decisions, we first consider how both interpersonal and personal factors affect consumers.

Define *consumer behavior* and describe the role it plays in marketing decisions.

consumer behavior
Process through which buyers make purchase decisions.

assessment check

1. Why is the study of consumer behavior important to marketers?
2. Describe Kurt Lewin's proposition.

Interpersonal Determinants of Consumer Behavior

2 Describe the interpersonal determinants of consumer behavior: cultural, social, and family influences.

You don't live in a bubble—and you don't make purchase decisions there. You might not be aware of it, but every buying decision you make is influenced by a variety of external and internal factors. Consumers often decide to buy goods and services based on what they believe others expect of them. They may want to project positive images to peers or satisfy the expectations of family members. They may buy a certain book because someone they respect recommended it. Or they may make reservations at a particular restaurant based on a good review in the newspaper. They may even buy a home in a neighborhood they think will impress their family and friends. Marketers recognize three broad categories of interpersonal influences on consumer behavior: cultural, social, and family influences.

CULTURAL INFLUENCES

Culture can be defined as the values, beliefs, preferences, and tastes handed down from one generation to the next. Culture is the broadest environmental determinant of consumer behavior. Marketers need to understand its role in consumer decision making, both in the United States and abroad. They must also monitor trends in cultural values as well as recognize changes in these values. As attention to the environment becomes more prevalent in U.S. and other cultures, marketers are responding to this change by offering products that either contain environmentally friendly components or are made with energy-saving processes. One example is Frito-Lay's line of SunChips multigrain snack chips, discussed in the "Marketing Success" feature.

Marketing strategies and business practices that work in one country may be offensive or ineffective in another. Strategies may even have to be varied from one area of a country to another. Nowhere is that more true than the United States, where the population continues to diversify at a rapid rate. When you insert your bank card into an ATM, the first option on the screen often is what language you prefer for the transaction. Depending on where you live, you may choose between Spanish and English or French and English. The Las Vegas Convention and Visitors Authority has been advertising in Spanish, placing commercials completely in Spanish on English-language programs on A&E, Bravo, Fox Sports Net, and Logo. Why do marketers believe this is an effective strategy? "The strength of the brand is really so incredible that you don't have to understand what they are saying to get it," explains a spokesperson for the ad agency that created the commercials.[2]

culture Values, beliefs, preferences, and tastes handed down from one generation to the next.

Core Values in U.S. Culture

Some cultural values change over time, but basic core values do not. The work ethic and the desire to accumulate wealth are two core values in American society. Even though the typical family structure and family members' roles have shifted over the years, American culture still emphasizes the importance of family and home life. This value is strengthened during times of upheaval such as natural disasters—tornadoes, floods, and extreme droughts. Other core values include the importance of education, individualism, freedom, youth, health, physical activity, humanitarianism, and efficiency. You can probably recognize yourself in some of these core values. Each of these values influences consumer behavior, including your own.

Values that change over time also have their effects. As technology rapidly changes the way people exchange information, consumers adopt values that include communicating with anyone, anytime, anywhere in the world. The generation that includes older teens and young twenties is the most skilled at using new communication technologies. They keep in touch with friends, classmates, and coworkers via laptop, iPhone, BlackBerry, and other devices. Though it comes less naturally, their parents are learning, too. More parents are using text messaging to reach their kids and each other. Messages like "Running L8" and "CU soon" zip from parents' to kids' phones regularly. "Parents like the immediacy of it and that it is not intrusive," observes Ralph de la Vega, chief executive of AT&T Mobility. "It's become an important way of communicating with their kids." Parents agree, noting that they are determined to learn the new technology so they don't fall behind the times the way *their* parents did.[3]

briefly speaking

"Culture is simply how one lives and is connected to history by habit."

—LeRoi Jones,
aka Amiri Baraka
(b. 1934)
AMERICAN POET AND PLAYWRIGHT

Frito-Lay reengineered its SunChips manufacturing process to rely more heavily on solar power, a move that was good for the environment and, ultimately, good for the company. Consumers have responded well to this new, greener practice.

We're living up to our name.

SunChips® snacks are now made with the help of solar energy in California.

As of April 22nd, one of our plants is using solar energy to help make SunChips® snacks. Not just because it's in our name, but because it's part of our vision for a healthy planet. It's a small step, but a step in the right direction.

live brightly

www.sunchips.com

Actual solar collectors at our SunChips® plant in Modesto, California

© Advertisement provided courtesy of Frito-Lay, Inc.

International Perspective on Cultural Influences

Cultural differences are particularly important for international marketers. Marketing strategies that prove successful in one country often cannot extend to other international markets because of cultural variations. Europe is a good example, with many different languages and a wide range of lifestyles and product preferences. Even though the continent is becoming a single economic unit as a result of the expansion of the European Union and the widespread use of the euro as currency, cultural divisions continue to define multiple markets.

McDonald's is known worldwide—its global business operations are now far greater than those in the United States and continue to grow faster. One reason for McDonald's success overseas is that the firm allows local managers to run their own advertising campaigns tailored to the preferences of their customers—including language—although the traditional logo remains intact. Also, McDonald's has worked hard for years to develop products that cater to the tastes of its local customers. One of its most successful products, the Big Tasty burger, isn't even available in the United States. It was developed in Germany and now is a top seller on menus in Brazil, Italy, and Portugal. In countries where people don't eat beef, as in India, McDonald's serves up items like the Maharaja Mac, made from chicken. In England, consumers can order porridge for breakfast.[4]

MARKETING SUCCESS

SunChips Live Up to Their Name

Background. SunChips multigrain snack chips have been on the market for a while. But the snack's maker, Frito-Lay, wanted to improve its operations in such a way that the environment, consumers, and the company itself would benefit.

The Challenge. Frito-Lay needed to find a new way to manufacture its SunChips, and researchers came up with an idea that would allow the product to live up to its name—literally.

"The companies and brands that are successful don't treat green as a promotional strategy," explains Gannon Jones, vice president for marketing at Frito-Lay. "They embrace it throughout their business strategy." That's exactly what his company did.

The Strategy. Frito-Lay decided to reengineer its manufacturing processes to rely more heavily on solar power. At the company's California plant, ten acres of solar collectors

McDonald's worldwide business operations are larger and growing faster than those in the United States. One reason for their international success is that the company has worked to develop products that cater to the tastes of local customers.

© AP Images/Anat Givon

Subcultures

Cultures are not homogeneous groups with universal values, even though core values tend to dominate. Each culture includes numerous **subcultures**—groups with their own distinct modes of behavior. Understanding the differences among subcultures can help marketers develop more effective marketing strategies.

The United States, like many nations, is composed of significant subcultures that differ by ethnicity, nationality, age, rural versus urban location, religion, and geographic distribution. The southwestern lifestyle emphasizes casual dress, outdoor entertaining, and active recreation. Mormons refrain from buying or using tobacco and liquor. Orthodox Jews purchase and consume only kosher foods. Understanding these and other differences among subcultures contributes to successful marketing of goods and services.

America's population mix is changing. By the year 2050, the U.S. population will total about 420 million, up from more than 305 million today. Eighty-two percent of that increase will come from immigrants and their U.S.-born children and grandchildren. The Hispanic population will

were installed, providing nearly 75 percent of the energy required to make the chips. The firm is also using less water and power, purchasing more fuel-efficient ovens, and expanding its use of solar power to more locations.

The Outcome. As Frito-Lay made these changes, the company incorporated them into its marketing efforts, letting consumers know what it has achieved and what it plans for the future. Television commercials, print advertisements, billboards, and information on SunChips packages have been part of the campaign. Consumers are

responding well to the green marketing messages because they are backed by action. "What we're talking about is what we're doing or what we've done," says Jones.

Sources: "Snacks Made with the Help of the Sun," company Web site, http://www.fritolay.com, accessed April 21, 2009; Christina Salerno, "Frito-Lay Solar System Puts the Sun in SunChips," *Modesto Bee,* May 29, 2008, www.modbee.com; "SunChips Gathers Energy from Its Namesake," *GreenBiz,* April 7, 2008, www.greenbiz.com; Stuart Elliott, "Trumpeting a Move to Put the Sun in SunChips," *The New York Times,* March 27, 2008, www.nytimes.com.

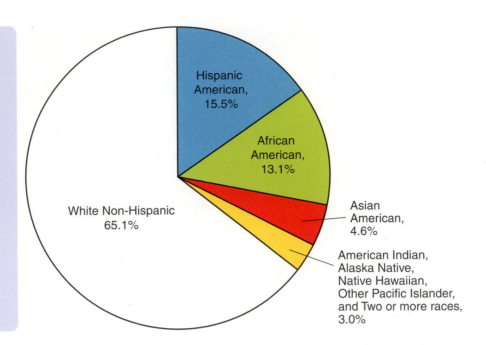

figure 5.1

Ethnic and Racial Minorities as a Percentage of the Total U.S. Population

Note: Percentages do not total to 100 percent due to overlap of some racial and ethnic categories.

Source: Data from the U.S. Census Bureau, "Projected Population of the United States, by Race and Hispanic Origin: 2000 to 2050," www.census.gov, accessed April 21, 2009.

triple, continuing to be the nation's largest minority group, representing more than one quarter of the total U.S. population. The number of African Americans is expected to reach 61 million, accounting for 14.6 percent of the population; Asians will represent 8 percent of the population; women will continue to outnumber men; and the number of senior citizens will double.[5] On a nearer horizon, as of 2010, the Hispanic population reached nearly 48 million, the African American population hit a little over 40 million, and the number of Asian Americans increased to more than 14 million.[6]

Marketers need to be sensitive to these changes and to the differences in shopping patterns and buying habits among ethnic segments of the population. Businesses can no longer succeed by selling one-size-fits-all products; they must consider consumer needs, interests, and concerns when developing their marketing strategies. Marketing concepts may not always cross cultural boundaries without changes. For example, new immigrants may not be familiar with cents-off coupons and contests. Marketers may need to provide specific instructions when targeting such promotions to these groups.

According to the U.S. Census Bureau, the three largest and fastest-growing U.S. ethnic subcultures are Hispanics, African Americans, and Asians. Figure 5.1 shows the proportion of the U.S. population made up of minority groups. Although no ethnic or racial subculture is entirely homogeneous, researchers have found that each of these three ethnic segments has identifiable consumer behavior profiles.

As important as differences in national origin may be the differences in **acculturation,** or the degree to which newcomers have adapted to U.S. culture. Acculturation plays a vital role in consumer behavior. For instance, marketers should not assume that all Hispanics understand Spanish. Whereas new immigrants are considered largely unacculturated and are likely to speak Spanish only, by the third generation after immigration, most Hispanic Americans are highly acculturated and speak only English. In addition, all Asians do not come from the same country, speak the same language, or eat the same foods, and black American immigrants may come from Central or South America as well as Africa.

Hispanic American Consumers

Marketers face several challenges in appealing to Hispanic consumers. The nearly 48 million Hispanics in the United States are not a homogeneous group. They come from a wide range of countries, each with its own culture. Two-thirds come from Mexico, one in seven is Central and South American, one in 12 is Puerto Rican, and nearly 4 percent are Cuban.[7] The common trait they share is a connection to Latin America, through either immigration or ancestry.

As the Hispanic population shifts to include second- and third-generation immigrants, changes in attitudes and values may occur as well. Even the word *Hispanic* is not universal; Puerto Ricans and Dominicans in New York and Cubans in southern Florida refer to themselves as Hispanic, but many Mexican and Central Americans in the southwestern United States prefer to be called Latinos. Not surprisingly, the cultural differences among these distinct segments often affect consumer preferences. In addition, although the Hispanic population was once concentrated in certain areas of the

United States, now these consumers are located everywhere, from South Carolina to Nebraska to Tennessee. So cultural aspects of these regions make their way into Hispanic consumer preferences as well. Salsa has now surpassed ketchup as the number-one selling U.S. condiment, and the traditional holiday Cinco de Mayo now is celebrated in many communities, including those that do not have a large Hispanic population.[8]

Despite differences among the various Hispanic segments, the Hispanic market in general is large and fast growing, with the greatest surge in population coming from children born to Hispanics who already live in the United States. "The Hispanic population has taken on a momentum of its own," observes Kenneth Johnson of the University of New Hampshire's Carsey Institute.[9]

Some other important trends for marketers to consider include the following:

As the U.S. Hispanic population has grown and dispersed, Hispanic consumer preferences have gained prevalence. Salsa, for example, has surpassed ketchup as the number-one selling U.S. condiment.

© iStockphoto.com/Rob Belknap

▷ Hispanics control more disposable income than any other minority group, a figure expected to hit $1.3 *trillion* by 2012.

▷ During recent years, large consumer goods companies such as Procter & Gamble have invested huge sums in advertising to Hispanic consumers, in both English and Spanish.

▷ Hispanic families tend to be somewhat larger than those of other population groups. They also tend to be younger, so deaths don't balance out births.[10]

African American Consumers

The continuously growing African American market offers a tremendous opportunity for marketers who understand its buying patterns. The African American population stands at more than 40 million people, but is expected to grow to more than 61 million by 2050.[11] The buying power of these consumers is projected to hit $1.1 trillion by 2012, roughly equal to that of Hispanics.[12]

A couple of unique trends that marketers should consider include the following:

▷ In general, African American consumers make more shopping trips per year than other consumers. They shop at beauty supply stores at triple the rate of other consumer groups and frequent automotive supply and electronics stores.[13]

▷ African American college students consume a lot of media, purchase technology products, and are active consumers. Female students tend to watch more television than males, and about 43 percent read at least one nationally distributed newspaper a week. Eighty-five percent of African American students go online daily, with Facebook.com and BlackPlanet.com the most popular Web sites. They also shop online, search for jobs, and complete homework assignments there.[14]

Despite these trends, as with any other subculture, marketers must avoid approaching all African American consumers in the same way; demographic factors such as income, age, language, and educational level must be considered. Most African Americans are descended from families who have lived in the United States for many generations, but some are recent immigrants. And they are members of every economic group.

Marketing to Asian Americans can be challenging because the population is spread among culturally diverse groups, many retaining their own languages. This billboard, written in Korean, is geared toward a specific segment of the population.

© Bill Aron/Photo Edit

Asian American Consumers

Marketing to Asian Americans presents many of the same challenges as reaching Hispanics. Like Hispanics, the country's more than 14 million Asian Americans are spread among culturally diverse groups, many retaining their own languages.[15] The Asian American subculture consists of more than two dozen ethnic groups, including Chinese, Filipinos, Indians, Japanese, Koreans, and Vietnamese. Each group brings its own language, religion, and value system to purchasing decisions. Forty-eight percent of Asian Americans hold a college degree or higher, and 60 percent own their own homes. Asian American consumers are expected to wield $670 billion in buying power by 2012.[16]

Sorabol Korean BBQ & Asian Noodles is the first Korean fast-food chain in the United States. Its mission is to make Korean food mainstream for all U.S. consumers, not just Asian Americans. While other restaurants are trying hard to add Asian items to their menus, Sorabol has actually "Americanized" its menu to appeal to a broader range of consumers. So consumers can try Korean BBQ dishes like *bulgogi* and *kalhi,* traditional Korean spicy soups and tofu stew, along with milder offerings. "People are realizing that there is more to Asian cuisine than Chinese and Japanese," says Sorabel CEO Richard Hong.[17]

Marketers in various industries are trying much harder than they did in the past to learn what Asian American consumers really want and need. One research firm for the grocery industry conducted a survey that included visiting people's homes to see what products they used and how they used them. Companies that make skin care products have recently developed more products targeted for Asian American consumers. One marketing report reveals that nine out of ten Asian women use skin care products—more than any other ethnic group. Mother-daughter team May and Michelle Wong developed a skin care line called Timeless Secret, which contains an ingredient found in Chinese recipes from 2,000 years ago.[18]

SOCIAL INFLUENCES

As a consumer, you belong to a number of social groups. Your earliest group experience came from membership in a family. As you began to grow, you might have joined a group of friends in elementary school or in the neighborhood. Later, you might have played on a soccer team, joined the drama club at school, or worked as part of a volunteer group in the community. By the time you became an adult, you had already been a member of many social groups—as you are now.

Group membership influences an individual consumer's purchase decisions and behavior in both overt and subtle ways. Every group establishes certain norms of behavior. **Norms** are the values, attitudes, and behaviors a group deems appropriate for its members. Group members are expected to comply with these norms. Members of such diverse groups as the Harley Owners Group (H.O.G.), Friends of the Earth, and the local country club tend to adopt their organization's norms of behavior. Norms can even affect nonmembers. Individuals who aspire to membership in a group may adopt its standards of behavior and values.

Differences in group status and roles can also affect buying behavior. **Status** is the relative position of any individual member in a group; **roles** define behavior that members of a group expect of individuals who hold specific positions within that group. Some groups (such as the American Medical Association) define formal roles, and others (such as a book club among friends) impose informal expectations. Both types of groups supply each member with both status and roles; in doing so, they influence that person's activities—including his or her purchase behavior.

People often make purchases designed to reflect their status within a particular group, particularly when the purchase is considered expensive by society. In the past few years, affluent consumers spent money on home redecorating and remodeling, as well as new cars. They also achieved status through the purchase of an experience, such as a mountaineering expedition, a Caribbean cruise, or a kayaking trip. As the economy fluctuates, affluent shoppers actually achieve status by shopping in warehouse club stores, perhaps showing off their bargain-hunting savvy. But they are willing to spend more on fresh or organic produce, often found at upscale grocery markets.[19]

In a countertrend, as gasoline prices rose to record levels, some drivers challenged themselves and others to consume as little fuel as possible. These so-called *hypermilers* took pride in squeezing every last mile out of a gallon of gasoline and presented their tips on TV talk shows and the Internet.

The Asch Phenomenon

Groups influence people's purchase decisions more than they realize. Most people adhere in varying degrees to the general expectations of any group they consider important, often without conscious awareness. The surprising impact of groups and group norms on individual behavior has been called the **Asch phenomenon,** named after social psychologist S. E. Asch, who first documented characteristics of individual behavior. Through his research, Asch found that individuals conformed to majority rule, even if it went against their beliefs. The Asch phenomenon can be a big factor in many purchase decisions, from major choices such as buying a car to deciding whether to buy a pair of shoes on sale.

Reference Groups

Discussion of the Asch phenomenon raises the subject of **reference groups**—groups whose value structures and standards influence a person's behavior. Consumers usually try to coordinate their purchase behavior with their perceptions of the values of their reference groups. The extent of reference group influence varies widely among individuals. Strong influence by a group on a member's purchase requires two conditions:

reference groups People or institutions whose opinions are valued and to whom a person looks for guidance in his or her own behavior, values, and conduct, such as spouse, family, friends, or celebrities.

1. The purchased product must be one that others can see and identify.

2. The purchased item must be conspicuous; it must stand out as something unusual, a brand or product that not everyone owns.

Reference group influence would significantly affect the decision to buy a luxury home in an upscale neighborhood but probably wouldn't have an impact on the decision to buy a loaf of bread, unless that loaf of bread was purchased at a gourmet bakery. Reference group influence can create what some marketers call "elastic consumers"—consumers who make decisions to save or splurge in the same economy. During a slow economy, a consumer might purchase generic brands at the supermarket but, because of reference group influence, spend those savings on designer jeans or a flat-screen TV. "It's a balancing act," observes Barb Fabing, senior vice president of retail design and strategy at Leo Burnett in Chicago. "Consumers have become very savvy at that." Reference group influence can also render bargain hunting fashionable if the economy is under strain. Conversely, a booming economy can make building a vacation home or buying a boat the desirable thing to do.[20]

Children are especially vulnerable to the influence of reference groups. They often base their buying decisions on outside forces such as what they see on television, opinions of friends, and fashionable products among adults. Understanding this phenomenon, marketers sometimes take a step back so that older children, preteens, and teens can shop—even if they don't have their own money to spend. More retailers now welcome teens who browse but don't buy. These retailers know they are still developing loyal customers—the teens will return when they have their own or their parents' money. "Kids really do influence where parents shop," observes Wendy Liebmann, president of WSL Strategic Retail. "The teenager can work both ways. They bring their own money, and they bring their parents' money." In addition, retailers that offer a range of goods—including items for adults—lay the groundwork for teen consumers to continue shopping as adults. "If a retailer can make an impact on them at this stage, it's likely to pay off in later life," predicts Jie Zhang of the University of Maryland.[21]

opinion leaders
Trendsetters who purchase new products before others in a group and then influence others in their purchases.

Social Classes

W. Lloyd Warner's research identified six classes within the social structures of both small and large U.S. cities: the upper-upper, lower-upper, upper-middle, and lower-middle classes, followed by the working class and lower class. Class rankings are determined by occupation, income, education, family background, and residence location. Note that income is not always a primary factor; pipe fitters paid at union scale earn more than many college professors, but their purchase behavior may be quite different. Still, the ability to make certain purchases, such as a private jet or an ocean-view home, is an important factor in determining class.

Family characteristics, such as the occupations and incomes of one or both parents, have been the primary influences on social class. As women's careers and earning power have increased over the past few decades, marketers have begun to pay more attention to their position as influential buyers.

People in one social class may aspire to a higher class and therefore exhibit buying behavior common to that class rather than to their own. Middle-class consumers often buy items they associate with the upper classes. Marketers of certain luxury goods appeal to these consumers. Coach, Tiffany, and Bloomingdale's—all traditionally associated with high-end luxury goods—now offer their items in price ranges and locations accessible to middle-class consumers. Although the upper-income classes themselves account for a very small percentage of the population, many more consumers now treat themselves to prestigious products, such as antique carpets or luxury cars.

Marketers for exclusive credit cards try to attract new customers in a variety of ways. The simplest tactic is to create an unusual-looking card that consumers will recognize as a status symbol. British bank Coutts' World MasterCard Signia Card is purple. Shoppers who present one don't need to tell anyone they are wealthy. Those who are invited to join this exclusive credit card club are in posh company; celebrities like Victoria "Posh Spice" Beckham and Queen Elizabeth are said to be card holders. American Express offers its black Centurion card by invitation, as well. A survey by the Luxury Institute of consumers with a minimum net worth of $5 million ranked the black card number one for their needs. "Special access, unparalleled benefits, and enhanced customer service" were the reasons given for the card's popularity.[22]

Middle-class consumers often buy items they associate with the upper class, such as Coach products.

© PHOTOEDIT/Photo Edit

Opinion Leaders

In nearly every reference group, a few members act as **opinion leaders.** These trendsetters are likely to purchase new products before others in the group and then share their experiences and opinions via word of mouth. As others in the group decide whether to try the same products, they are influenced by the reports of opinion leaders. Generalized opinion leaders are rare; instead, individuals tend to act as opinion leaders for specific goods or services based on their knowledge of and interest in those products. Their interest motivates them to seek out information from mass media, manufacturers, and other sources and, in turn, transmit this information to associates through interpersonal communications. Opinion leaders are found within all segments of the population.

Information about goods and services sometimes flows from the Internet, radio, television, and other mass media to opinion leaders and then from opinion leaders to others. In other instances, information flows directly from media sources to all consumers. In still other instances, a multistep flow carries information from mass media to opinion leaders and then on to other opinion leaders before dissemination to the general public.

Some opinion leaders influence purchases by others merely through their own actions. Oprah Winfrey is one such leader. Through her on-air book club, she encouraged millions of viewers to read. And through many on-air wellness programs, she motivated viewers to eat healthful meals and monitor their weight. Winfrey participated in these activities herself, holding book group discussions and allowing cameras to follow her as she exercised. Recently, Winfrey announced an agreement with the Discovery Health Network in which she will take over the network, renaming it OWN—Oprah Winfrey Network. With a network under her name, Winfrey hopes to inspire viewers to greater action. "I said from the beginning that this was an opportunity to step out of the box and make the kinds of shows that make my heart sing," she notes. "It's about unleashing the power of human potential; that's what it's all about."[23]

Oprah Winfrey is an opinion leader. She influences decisions made by others through her on-air book club and wellness programs.

© Kimberly White/Reuters/Landov

FAMILY INFLUENCES

Most people are members of at least two families during their lifetimes—the ones they are born into and those they eventually form later in life. The family group is perhaps the most important determinant of consumer behavior because of the close, continuing interactions among family members. Like other groups, each family typically has norms of expected behavior and different roles and status relationships for its members.

According to the U.S. Census Bureau, the structure of families has changed greatly over the last century. Today, only about half of all households are headed by married couples. Many couples are separated or divorced, so single heads of households are more common. In addition, there has been an increase in households headed by same-sex couples. Women are having fewer children, giving birth later in life, and spacing their children farther apart. More women are choosing to live alone, with or without children. And more senior citizens are living alone or without younger generations present in their homes. Still, to target a market for their goods and services, marketers find it useful to describe the role of each spouse in a household in terms of the following four categories:

1. *Autonomic role* is seen when the partners independently make equal numbers of decisions. Personal-care items would fall into the category of purchase decisions each would make for himself or herself.

2. *Husband-dominant role* occurs when the husband usually makes certain purchase decisions. Buying a life insurance policy is a typical example.

3. *Wife-dominant role* has the wife making most of certain buying decisions. Children's clothing is a typical wife-dominant purchase.

4. *Syncratic role* refers to joint decisions. The purchase of a house follows a syncratic pattern.

The increasing occurrence of the two-income family means that women have a greater role in making family purchase decisions. Today, women have more say in large-ticket family purchases such as homes, vacations, automobiles, and computers. One study revealed that 85 percent of all car-buying decisions are influenced by women.[24] And studies show that women take the lead in choosing entertainment, such as movies and restaurants. Women now outspend men in electronics purchases, at $55 billion compared with $41 billion for men.[25] These statistics mean that marketers must take note of the factors women consider when buying goods and services and the way they make their purchases. General Motors not only taps the brains of female customers to learn what they want, GM has female engineers on staff designing and building cars. Liz Pilibosian, chief engineer for the 2008 Cadillac CTS observes, "When you make a car for a woman, you are going to satisfy everybody."[26]

briefly
speaking

"Happy is the child whose father died rich."

—**Anonymous**

Preteens and teens represent a huge market. This group's familiarity with technology and desire to communicate with each other leads to ads like this.

© Image courtesy of The Advertising Archives

Studies of family decision making have also shown that households with two wage earners are more likely than others to make joint purchasing decisions. Members of two-income households often do their shopping in the evening and on weekends because of the number of hours spent at the workplace. Shifting family roles have created new markets for a variety of products. Goods and services that save time, promote family togetherness, emphasize safety, or encourage health and fitness appeal to the family values and influences of today.

Children and Teenagers in Family Purchases

Children and teenagers represent a huge market—more than 50 million strong—and they influence what their parents buy, from cereal to automobiles. These consumers are exposed to many marketing messages, and they are far more sophisticated than their parents or grandparents were at the same age. They also have greater influence over the goods and services their families purchase—in addition to the spending power they bring to their own purchases. Preteens and teens will spend a whopping $200 billion each year by 2011, and marketers are taking notice.[27] Familiarity with technology and individualism are two important characteristics of this group. "Teens living [now] have never known a world without personal computers and the Internet," says marketer Don Montuori. "Teens are in the vanguard of the digital revolution in the media and marketing worlds, and they're helping to change the way media, marketing, and advertising executives approach the American consumers."[28]

Products such as Apple's iPod and iPod touch allow teens to load and play whatever music they want. In addition, cell phones with texting capability and Web sites like Facebook allow teens—and their younger siblings—to communicate with each other. "What we're talking about is a generation that has the ability to be in touch with each other immediately at earlier and earlier ages," notes Nancy Robinson, a consumer strategist. "If you asked someone ten years ago about the necessity of a cell phone for a five-year-old, they would have laughed and walked away; now you can buy that at Target."[29] Knowledge about these changes in products, and the way consumers use them, is vital to any company's success.

assessment check

1. List the interpersonal determinants of consumer behavior.

2. What is a subculture?

3. Describe the Asch phenomenon.

3 Explain each of the personal determinants of consumer behavior: needs and motives, perceptions, attitudes, learning, and self-concept theory.

Personal Determinants of Consumer Behavior

Consumer behavior is affected by a number of internal, personal factors in addition to interpersonal ones. Each individual brings unique needs, motives, perceptions, attitudes, learned responses, and self-concepts to buying decisions. This section looks at how these factors influence consumer behavior.

NEEDS AND MOTIVES

Individual purchase behavior is driven by the motivation to fill a perceived need. A **need** is an imbalance between the consumer's actual and desired states. A person who recognizes or feels a significant or urgent need then seeks to correct the imbalance. Marketers attempt to arouse this sense of urgency by making a need "felt" and then influencing consumers' motivation to satisfy their needs by purchasing specific products.

Motives are inner states that direct a person toward the goal of satisfying a need. The individual takes action to reduce the state of tension and return to a condition of equilibrium.

need Imbalance between a consumer's actual and desired states.

motive Inner state that directs a person toward the goal of satisfying a need.

Maslow's Hierarchy of Needs

Psychologist Abraham H. Maslow developed a theory that characterized needs and arranged them into a hierarchy. Maslow identified five levels of needs, beginning with physiological needs and progressing to the need for self-actualization. A person must at least partially satisfy lower-level needs, according to Maslow, before higher needs can affect behavior. In developed countries, where relatively large per-capita incomes allow most people to satisfy the basic needs on the hierarchy, higher-order needs may be more important to consumer behavior. Table 5.1 illustrates products and marketing themes designed to satisfy needs at each level.

Physiological Needs

Needs at the most basic level concern essential requirements for survival, such as food, water, shelter, and clothing. Pur promotes its water filtration system with the slogan, "Your water should be Pur." Its ads emphasize the need for clean water: "When you realize how often water touches your family's life, you discover just how important healthy, great-tasting water is."

Safety Needs

Second-level needs include security, protection from physical harm, and avoidance of the unexpected. To gratify these needs, consumers may buy disability insurance or security devices. Aetna,

table 5.1 **Marketing Strategies Based on Maslow's Hierarchy of Needs**

Physiological Needs	Products	Vitamins and medicines, food, bottled water, exercise equipment, cleansing products, sleep
	Marketing themes	Dove body wash—"Go fresh"; Neutrogena Wave—"Maybe the best thing to happen to your skin"; Goya—"If it's Goya, it's got to be good"; Tempur-Pedic—"Welcome to bed"
Safety Needs	Products	Auto air bags, burglar alarm systems, retirement investments, insurance, computer antivirus software, smoke and carbon monoxide detectors
	Marketing themes	Michelin tires—"A better way forward"; ADT—"Always there"; Mozilla Firefox—"The browser that has it all"
Belongingness	Products	Beauty aids, entertainment, clothing, cars, clubs, fashion
	Marketing themes	Keds—"An attitude you can wear"; Mark cosmetics—"Make your mark"; Macy's—"The magic of Macy's"
Esteem Needs	Products	Clothing, cars, jewelry, hobbies, beauty spa services
	Marketing themes	Lexus automobiles—"The relentless pursuit of perfection"; Mad River Glen—"Ski it if you can"; Dillard's—"The style of your life"
Self-Actualization	Products	Education, cultural events, sports, hobbies, luxury goods, technology, travel
	Marketing themes	Alaska travel bureau—"Beyond your dreams. Within your reach"; Tiffany—"After all"; Southwest Airlines—"You are now free to move about the country"

which provides a wide range of insurance products, uses the slogan "We want you to know." Its ads focus on the power of information in making educated insurance purchases.

Social/Belongingness Needs

Satisfaction of physiological and safety needs leads a person to attend to third-level needs—the desire to be accepted by people and groups important to that individual. To satisfy this need, people may join organizations and buy goods or services that make them feel part of a group. American Express advertises its Membership Rewards program, which features the ability to use its frequent-flyer points on almost any airline, as if it is an exclusive club.

Esteem Needs

People have a universal desire for a sense of accomplishment and achievement. They also wish to gain the respect of others and even exceed others' performance once lower-order needs are satisfied. Las Vegas's luxury hotel Bellagio advertises with the slogan, "Look behind you. That's the pecking order."

Self-Actualization Needs

At the top rung of Maslow's ladder of human needs is people's desire to realize their full potential and find fulfillment by expressing their unique talents and capabilities. Companies specializing in exotic adventure or educational trips aim to satisfy consumers' needs for self-actualization. Not-for-profit organizations that invite paying volunteers to assist in such projects as archaeological digs or building homes for the needy appeal to these needs as well. MasterCard's well-known "priceless" ads often feature the satisfaction of self-actualization needs.

perception Meaning that a person attributes to incoming stimuli gathered through the five senses.

Maslow noted that a satisfied need no longer has to be met. Once the physiological needs are met, the individual moves on to pursue satisfaction of higher-order needs. Consumers periodically are motivated by the need to relieve thirst and hunger, but their interests soon return to focus on satisfaction of safety, social, and other needs in the hierarchy. But people may not always progress through the hierarchy; they may fixate on a certain level. For example, consumers who live through an economic downturn may always be motivated to save money. Marketers can use this as an opportunity by offering money-saving goods and services.

Critics have pointed out a variety of flaws in Maslow's reasoning. For example, some needs can be related to more than one level, and not every individual progresses through the needs hierarchy in the same order; some bypass social and esteem needs and are motivated by self-actualization needs. But the hierarchy of needs can offer an effective guideline for marketers who want to study consumer behavior.

PERCEPTIONS

Perception is the meaning that a person attributes to incoming stimuli gathered through the five senses—sight, hearing, touch, taste, and smell. Certainly a buyer's

MasterCard's well-known "priceless" ads often feature the satisfaction of self-actualization needs.

Courtesy of MasterCard Worldwide

behavior is influenced by his or her perceptions of a good or service. Researchers now recognize that people's perceptions depend as much on what they *want* to perceive as on the actual stimuli. For this reason, Nordstrom and Target are perceived differently, as are Godiva chocolates and Hershey bars. A person's perception of an object or event results from the interaction of two types of factors:

1. *Stimulus factors*—characteristics of the physical object such as size, color, weight, and shape

2. *Individual factors*—unique characteristics of the individual, including not only sensory processes but also experiences with similar inputs and basic motivations and expectations

Perceptual Screens

The average American consumer constantly is bombarded by marketing messages. According to the Food Marketing Institute, a typical supermarket now carries 30,000 different packages, each serving as a miniature billboard vying to attract consumers' attention. More than 6,000 commercials are aired on network TV each week. However, marketers have learned that people spend less time at home watching television than they used to, so they have begun to plaster just about every surface imaginable outside the home with promotional messages. "We never know where the consumer is going to be at any point in time, so we have to find a way to be everywhere," explains marketing consultant Linda Kaplan Thaler. "Ubiquity is the new exclusivity." Consumers might find their supermarket eggs stamped with the name of a CBS television show or their Chinese food cartons bearing ads for Continental Airways. Anyone passing through the turnstile of a subway is reminded of the benefits of Geico auto insurance. Old-style billboards are now converted to digital screens that change messages frequently from remote computers.[30]

This marketing clutter has caused consumers to ignore many promotional messages. People respond selectively to messages that manage to break through their **perceptual screens**—the mental filtering processes through which all inputs must pass. In fact, some marketing efforts actually backfire. When San Francisco commuters realized that the "Got Milk?" billboards near their bus stops were emitting the scent of chocolate chip cookies, they complained about the intrusion to their senses. The city ordered the California Milk Processing Board to turn off the scent.[31]

All marketers struggle to determine which stimuli evoke positive responses from consumers. They must learn how to grab a consumer's attention long enough to watch a commercial, read an advertisement, listen to a sales pitch, or react to a point-of-purchase display. Marketers want their messages to stand out in the crowd.

One way to break through clutter is to run large ads. Doubling the size of an ad in printed media increases its attention value by about 50 percent. Other methods for enhancing contrast include arranging a large amount of white space around a printed area or placing white type on a dark background. Vivid illustrations and photos can also help to break through clutter in print ads. Using color creatively can help break through clutter. Color is so suggestive that its use on product packaging and logos often is the result of a long and careful selection process. Red grabs the attention, and orange has been shown to stimulate appetite. Blue is associated with water— you'll find blue on cleaning products. Green connotes low-fat or healthful food products.

The psychological concept of closure also helps marketers create messages that stand out. *Closure* is the human tendency to perceive a complete picture from an incomplete stimulus. Advertisements that allow consumers to do this often succeed in breaking through perceptual screens. In an ad campaign for its cars and trucks that includes the tagline, "AN AMERICAN REVOLUTION," Chevrolet marketers replaced the *E* in *REVOLUTION* with three red bars so that it appears to be an American flag. The word is still legible, as readers mentally change the bars into the letter. The effect is subtle, but it helps reinforce the "made in America" concept.

Word-of-mouth marketing can be another effective way to break through consumers' perceptual screens. Marketers have taken this old-fashioned form of marketing to new levels with technology via Internet social networking sites like MySpace, Facebook, and others. Facebook is a prime example. Now that the site is open to the general public, marketing messages can shoot from user to user so rapidly that they can actually increase tenfold within minutes.[32]

A new tool that marketers are exploring is the use of virtual reality. Some companies have created presentations based on virtual reality that display marketing messages and information in a three-dimensional format. Eventually, experts predict, consumers will be able to tour resort areas via virtual reality before booking their trips or walk through the interiors of homes they are considering buying via virtual reality. Virtual reality technology may allow marketers to penetrate consumer perceptual filters in a way not currently possible with other forms of media.

With selective perception at work screening competing messages, it is easy to see the importance of marketers' efforts in developing brand loyalty. Satisfied customers are less likely to seek information about competing products. Even when competitive advertising is forced on them, they are less apt than others to look beyond their perceptual filters at those appeals. Loyal customers simply tune out information that does not agree with their existing beliefs and expectations.

Subliminal Perception

More than 50 years ago, a New Jersey movie theater tried to boost concession sales by flashing the words "Eat Popcorn" and "Drink Coca-Cola" between frames of actress Kim Novak's image in the movie *Picnic.* The messages flashed on the screen every five seconds for a duration of one three-hundredth of a second each time. Researchers reported that these messages, though too short to be recognizable at the conscious level, resulted in a 58 percent increase in popcorn sales and an 18 percent increase in Coke sales. After the findings were published, advertising agencies and consumer protection groups became intensely interested in **subliminal perception**—the subconscious receipt of incoming information.

Subliminal advertising is aimed at the subconscious level of awareness to circumvent the audience's perceptual screens. The goal of the original research was to induce consumer purchases while keeping consumers unaware of the source of the motivation to buy. All later attempts to duplicate the test findings were unsuccessful. Although subliminal advertising is considered manipulative, it is exceedingly unlikely to induce purchasing except by people already inclined to buy. There are three reasons for this:

1. Strong stimulus factors are required just to get a prospective customer's attention.

2. Only a very short message can be transmitted.

3. Individuals vary greatly in their thresholds of consciousness. Messages transmitted at the threshold of consciousness for one person will not be perceived at all by some people and will be all too apparent to others. The subliminally exposed message "Drink Coca-Cola" may go unseen by some viewers, while others may read it as "Drink Pepsi-Cola," "Drink Cocoa," or even "Drive Slowly."

Despite the findings about subliminal advertising, however, neuroscientists know that thoughts and emotions, including those a person may not be consciously aware of, play a vital role in decision making, and marketers are looking to find ways to elicit emotions that motivate people toward a purchase. *Neuromarketing* has already taken some concrete forms. Retailers such as SuperValu and Walgreens have adopted hypersonic sound technology, which beams commercials to individual customers in stores, say, when they are standing in the checkout line or in the cereal aisle. And teams of neuromarketers have begun to study people's brains using magnetic resonance imaging (MRI) machines to read how their neurons respond to certain products and marketing messages. By observing how different neural circuits light up or go dark during marketing and purchasing experiences, researchers have discovered that they can fairly accurately predict whether a person will actually buy an item or leave it on the shelf.[33] The results of these findings could have a real impact on the way marketers create messages for consumers.

ATTITUDES

attitudes Person's enduring favorable or unfavorable evaluations, emotions, or action tendencies toward some object or idea.

Perception of incoming stimuli is greatly affected by attitudes. In fact, a consumer's decision to purchase an item is strongly based on his or her attitudes about the product, store, or salesperson. **Attitudes** are a person's enduring favorable or unfavorable evaluations, emotions, or action tendencies toward some object or idea. As they form over time through individual experiences and group contacts, attitudes become highly resistant to change. New fees, a change in service hours, or other policy changes can be difficult for customers to accept. Because favorable attitudes likely affect brand preferences, marketers are interested in determining consumer attitudes toward their offerings. Numerous attitude-scaling devices have been developed for this purpose.

Attitude Components

An attitude has cognitive, affective, and behavioral components. The *cognitive* component refers to the individual's information and knowledge about an object or concept. The *affective* component deals with feelings or emotional reactions. The *behavioral* component involves tendencies to act in a certain manner. For example, in deciding whether to shop at a floor covering store, a consumer might obtain information about what the store offers from advertising, personal visits, and input from family, friends, and associates—the cognitive component. The consumer might also receive affective input by listening to others about their shopping experiences at this store. Other affective information might lead the person to make a judgment about the type of people who seem to shop there and whether they represent a group with which he or she would like to be associated. Then, the consumer may ultimately decide to have the store install carpet in the living room—the behavioral component. All three components maintain a relatively stable and balanced relationship to one another. Together, they form an overall attitude about an object or idea.

Changing Consumer Attitudes

As a favorable consumer attitude provides a vital condition for marketing success, how can a firm lead prospective buyers to adopt such an attitude toward its products? Marketers have two choices: (1) attempt to produce consumer attitudes that will motivate purchase of a particular product or (2) evaluate existing consumer attitudes and then make the product features appeal to them. It's always easier to create and maintain a positive attitude toward a product than it is to change an unfavorable one to favorable, as discussed in the "Etiquette Tips for Marketing Professionals" feature.

If consumers view an existing good or service unfavorably, the seller may redesign it or offer new options. Or an attitude may not be unfavorable—just one that does not motivate the consumer toward a purchase. When FedEx acquired Kinko's several years ago, the intention was to keep the Kinko's name because of the nostalgic, corner copy-shop image it conveyed. But FedEx quickly discovered that people also associated the Kinko's name with limited offerings. Consumers just didn't realize how many services FedEx really offered under the Kinko's brand. So the firm changed the name to FedEx Office, promoting the digital printing services, direct mail, signage, and other goods and services that FedEx provides business customers, traveling businesspeople, and consumers. But the FedEx Kinko's logo remains intact, at least for awhile. That way, customers know that the traditional services still remain.[34]

Modifying the Components of Attitude

Attitudes frequently change in response to inconsistencies among the three components. The most common inconsistencies result when new information changes the cognitive or affective components of an attitude. Marketers can modify attitudes by providing evidence of product benefits and by correcting misconceptions. Marketers may also change attitudes by engaging buyers in new behavior. Free samples, for instance, can change attitudes by getting consumers to try a product.

Sometimes new technologies can encourage consumers to change their attitudes. Some people are reluctant to purchase clothing online because they are afraid it will not fit properly. To address these concerns, e-retailer Lands' End (part of Sears) introduced a "virtual model" feature on its Web site. People who visit the site answer a series of questions about height, body proportions, and hair color, and the software creates a three-dimensional figure reflecting their responses. Consumers can then adorn the electronic model with Lands' End garments to get an idea of how various outfits might look on them. Of course, for the electronic model to be correct, shoppers must enter information about their bodies accurately instead of simply relying on their perception of themselves.

Etiquette Tips for Marketing Professionals

How to Deal with Product Returns

as a consumer, you know how frustrating it can be to deal with a firm that has an inconvenient return policy. If you have a poor experience trying to return an item, you are likely to develop a negative attitude not only toward the product but also toward the company. As a marketer, you can use this knowledge to your company's benefit by handling returns in a prompt, courteous, professional manner. If you do this, you are likely to create loyal customers who have a positive attitude toward your firm. Here are a few tips for handling customers who want to make returns:

- *Head the problem off prior to the sale.* If you are in a position to do so, try to ensure that your customer is making an educated purchase. Explain product features, answer questions, and allow the customer to try the product, if possible. Most customers don't want to go through the inconvenience of returning an item; they want to make the right purchase in the first place.

- *Inform the customer of your firm's return policy.* If you work in a retail store, point out the return policy that is usually displayed by the cash register. If you work in another sales environment, take the time to inform your customer of the return policy, which should be clear and easy to understand.

- *Respond immediately.* If a customer calls or arrives on site with a complaint or wishes to return a purchased item, respond as quickly as you can. Prompt service increases the likelihood that the shopper will buy something else.

- *Be courteous and professional.* A customer may already be frustrated and angry because an item is defective or performed poorly. Stay calm and friendly. Keep in mind how you would feel if roles were reversed. If you can create a positive experience from a return, the chances are much greater that your customer will give your store or firm a second chance.

- *If your firm has a guarantee, honor it.* Don't backpedal. Your company has made a promise to stand behind its products, and that promised must be fulfilled. This is another opportunity to instill a positive attitude in customers.

Sources: David Yakubik, "Six Tips for Creating Customer Loyalty through Strong Service," *Volusion,* onlinebusiness.volusion.com, accessed April 21, 2009; "Tips for Handling Consumer Complaints," *Better Business Bureau,* tucson.bbb.org, accessed April 21, 2009; "Top 10 Reasons to Rethink Merchandise Returns Processes," *About.com Retailing,* retailindustry.about.com, accessed April 21, 2009; "Handle a Customer Return or Refund," *Microsoft Office Online,* office.online.com, accessed April 21, 2009.

LEARNING

learning Knowledge or skill acquired as a result of experience, which changes consumer behavior.

Marketing is concerned as seriously with the process by which consumer decisions change over time as with the current status of those decisions. **Learning,** in a marketing context, refers to immediate or expected changes in consumer behavior as a result of experience. The learning process includes the component of **drive,** which is any strong stimulus that impels action. Fear, pride, desire for money, thirst, pain avoidance, and rivalry are examples of drives. Learning also relies on a **cue,** that is, any object in the environment that determines the nature of the consumer's response to a drive. Examples of cues are a newspaper advertisement for a new Thai restaurant (a cue for a hungry person) and a Shell sign near an interstate highway (a cue for a motorist who needs gasoline).

A **response** is an individual's reaction to a set of cues and drives. Responses might include reactions such as purchasing Frontline flea and tick prevention for pets, dining at Quizno's, or deciding to enroll at a particular community college or university.

Reinforcement is the reduction in drive that results from a proper response. As a response becomes more rewarding, it creates a stronger bond between the drive and the purchase of the product, likely increasing future purchases by the consumer. Reinforcement is the rationale that underlies frequent-buyer programs that reward repeat purchasers for their loyalty. These programs may offer points for premiums, frequent-flyer miles, and the like. However, so many companies now offer these programs that marketers must find ways to differentiate them. And firms that don't offer the programs quickly learn that consumers will bypass their products and move on to those of competitors. Customization is the latest trend toward attracting reward

briefly speaking

"A man who carries a cat by the tail learns something he can learn in no other way."

—**Mark Twain**
(1835–1910)
AMERICAN AUTHOR

Programs that reward repeat purchasers for their loyalty are often based on the principle of reinforcement.

card users. The Chase Freedom card allows its members to switch back and forth from cash back to rewards on a monthly basis if they want, and the program automatically awards the most points or cash each month toward the types of purchases a customer makes most frequently, such as gasoline or groceries.[35]

Applying Learning Theory to Marketing Decisions

Learning theory has some important implications for marketing strategists, particularly those involved with consumer packaged goods. Marketers must find a way to develop a desired outcome such as repeat purchase behavior gradually over time. **Shaping** is the process of applying a series of rewards and reinforcements to permit more complex behavior to evolve.

Both promotional strategy and the product itself play a role in the shaping process. Marketers want to motivate consumers to become regular buyers of certain merchandise. Their first step in getting consumers to try the product might be to offer a free-sample package that includes a substantial discount coupon for the next purchase. This example uses a cue as a shaping procedure. If the item performs well, the purchase response is reinforced and followed by another inducement—the coupon. The reason a sample works so well is that it allows the consumer to try the product at no risk. Supermarket shoppers have the opportunity to sample products on a regular basis—crackers, cheese, appetizers, salad dressings, and the like. Generally a display is set up near the aisle where the item is sold, staffed by an individual who dispenses the sample along with a coupon for future purchase.

The second step is to entice the consumer to buy the item with little financial risk. The discount coupon enclosed with the free sample prompts this action. Suppose the package that the consumer purchases has still another, smaller discount coupon enclosed. Again, satisfactory product performance and the second coupon provide reinforcement.

The third step is to motivate the person to buy the item again at a moderate cost. A discount coupon accomplishes this objective, but this time the purchased package includes no additional coupon. The only reinforcement comes from satisfactory product performance.

The final test comes when the consumer decides whether to buy the item at its true price without a discount coupon. Satisfaction with product performance provides the only continuing reinforcement. Repeat purchase behavior literally is shaped by effective application of learning theory within a marketing strategy context.

SELF-CONCEPT THEORY

self-concept Person's multifaceted picture of himself or herself.

The consumer's **self-concept**—a person's multifaceted picture of himself or herself—plays an important role in consumer behavior. Say a young woman views herself as bright, ambitious, and headed for a successful marketing career. She'll want to buy attractive clothes and jewelry to reflect that image of herself. Say a middle-aged man views himself as young for his age; he may purchase a sports car and stylish clothes to reflect his self-concept.

The concept of self emerges from an interaction of many of the influences—both personal and interpersonal—that affect buying behavior. A person's needs, motives, perceptions, attitudes, and learning lie at the core of his or her conception of self. In addition, family, social, and cultural influences affect self-concept.

A person's self-concept has four components: real self, self-image, looking-glass self, and ideal self. The *real self* is an objective view of the total person. The *self-image*, the way an individual views himself or herself, may distort the objective view. The *looking-glass self*, the way an individual thinks others see him or her, may also differ substantially from self-image because people often choose to project different images to others than their perceptions of their real selves. The *ideal self* serves as a personal set of objectives, because it is the image to which the individual aspires. When making purchasing decisions, consumers likely will choose products that move them closer to their ideal self-images.

4 Distinguish between high-involvement and low-involvement purchase decisions.

assessment check

1. Identify the personal determinants of consumer behavior.

2. What are the human needs categorized by Abraham Maslow?

3. How do perception and learning differ?

Purchasing a candy bar is a good example of a low-involvement purchase decision.

© Image courtesy of The Advertising Archives

MAY CONTAIN TRACES OF "OOOOOOOOOH" AND "MMMMMMMMMM"

Aero Chocolate TRUFFLE New

HAVE YOU FELT THE TRUFFLE & BUBBLES MELT?

Nestlé

The Consumer Decision Process

Although they might not be aware of it, consumers complete a step-by-step process in making purchasing decisions. The time and effort devoted to a particular purchasing decision depend on how important it is.

Purchases with high levels of potential social or economic consequences are said to be **high-involvement purchase decisions.** Buying a car, purchasing a condominium, or deciding where to go to college are examples of high-involvement decisions. Routine purchases that pose little risk to the consumer are **low-involvement purchase decisions.** Purchasing a jug of milk from a convenience store is a good example.

Consumers generally invest more time and effort in buying decisions for high-involvement products than in those for low-involvement products. A home buyer will visit a number of listings, compare asking prices, apply

for a mortgage, have the selected house inspected, and even have friends or family members visit the home before signing the final papers. Few buyers invest that much effort in choosing a brand of orange juice at the supermarket. Believe it or not, though, they will still go through the steps of the consumer decision process—but on a more compressed scale.

Figure 5.2 shows the six steps in the consumer decision process. First, the consumer recognizes a problem or unmet need, searches for appropriate goods or services, and evaluates the alternatives before making a purchase decision. The next step is the actual purchase. After buying the item, the consumer evaluates whether he or she made the right choice. Much of marketing involves steering consumers through the decision process in the direction of a specific product.

Consumers apply the decision process in solving problems and taking advantage of opportunities. Such decisions permit them to correct differences between their actual and desired states. Feedback from each decision serves as additional experience in helping guide subsequent decisions.

assessment check

1. Differentiate between high-involvement decisions and low-involvement decisions.

2. Categorize each of the following as a high- or low-involvement product: toothpaste, laptop, apartment, cup of coffee, cell phone service.

PROBLEM OR OPPORTUNITY RECOGNITION

5 Outline the steps in the consumer decision process.

During the first stage in the decision process, the consumer becomes aware of a significant discrepancy between the existing situation and a desired situation. You have experienced this yourself. Perhaps you open the refrigerator door and find little food there. By identifying the problem—not enough food in the refrigerator—you can resolve it with a trip to the grocery store. Sometimes the problem is more specific. You might have a full refrigerator, but no mustard or mayonnaise for sandwiches. This problem requires a solution as well.

Suppose you are unhappy with a particular purchase, say, a brand of cereal. The cereal might be too sweet or too crunchy. Or maybe you just want a change from the same old cereal every morning. This is the recognition of another type of problem or opportunity—the desire for change.

What if you just got a raise at work? You might decide to splurge on dinner at a restaurant. Or you might want to try a gourmet, prepared take-home dinner from the supermarket. Both dinners are more expensive than the groceries you have always bought, but now they are within

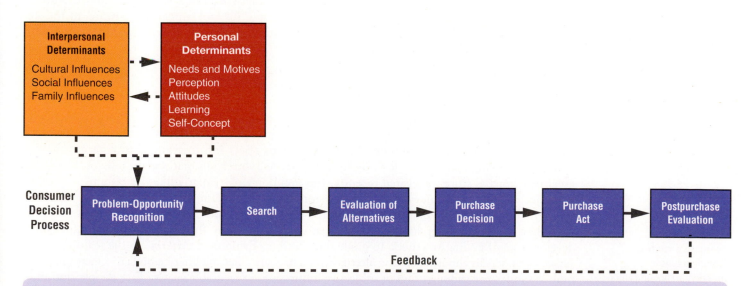

figure 5.2

Integrated Model of the Consumer Decision Process

Source: Roger Blackwell, Paul W. Miniard, and James F. Engel, *Consumer Behavior,* 10th ed. (Mason, OH: South-Western, 2006).

financial reach. The marketer's main task during this phase of the decision-making process is to help prospective buyers identify and recognize potential problems or needs. This task may take the form of advertising, promotions, or personal sales assistance. A supermarket employee might suggest appetizers or desserts to accompany the gourmet take-home dinner.

SEARCH

During the second step in the decision process, a consumer gathers information about the attainment of a desired state of affairs. This search identifies different ways to solve the problem. A high-involvement purchase might mean conducting an extensive search for information, whereas a low-involvement purchase might require much less research.

The search may cover internal or external sources of information. An internal search is simply a mental review: Is there past experience with the product? Was it good or bad? An external search involves gathering information from all kinds of outside sources—for instance, family, friends, coworkers or classmates, advertisements or salespeople, online reviews, and consumer magazines. Because conducting an external search requires time and effort, it usually is done for high-involvement purchases.

evoked set Number of alternatives a consumer actually considers in making a purchase decision.

The search identifies alternative brands or models for consideration and possible purchase. The number of alternatives a consumer actually considers in making a purchase decision is known in marketing as the **evoked set.** In some searches, consumers already know of the brands that merit further consideration; in others, their external searches develop such information. The number of brands included in the evoked set vary, depending on both the situation and the person. An immediate need, such as filling a nearly empty gas tank during a road trip, might limit the evoked set. But a driver with half a tank of gas, with more time to make a decision, might expand the evoked set to choose from a broader range of options.

Consumers now choose among more alternative products than ever before. This variety can confuse and complicate the analysis that narrows the range of choices. Instead of comparing one or two brands, a consumer often faces a dizzying array of brands and subbrands. Products that once included only regular and decaffeinated coffee now are available in many different forms— cappuccino, latté, skinny latté, flavored coffee, espresso, and iced coffee, just to name a few possibilities. Recognizing this, and wanting to help consumers find their way through the maze of choices, some firms have set up online shopping sites where consumers can compare products. The Biz Rate Web site has a free comparison shopping site that consumers can use to compare everything from air conditioners to GPS devices to barbecue grills and sunglasses. Visitors to the site can compare features, prices, and reviews of all the products listed, giving them information with which to make the best choices for their needs.[36]

EVALUATION OF ALTERNATIVES

The third step in the consumer decision process is to evaluate the evoked set of options. Actually, it is difficult to completely separate the second and third steps because some evaluation takes place as the search progresses; consumers accept, distort, or reject information as they receive it. For example, knowing that you are looking for a new jacket, your roommate might tell you about this great new apparel store she visited recently. But you don't particularly like her taste in clothes, so you reject the information, even though the store might have some nice things.

evaluative criteria Features a consumer considers in choosing among alternatives.

The outcome of the evaluation stage is the choice of a brand or product in the evoked set, or possibly a decision to keep looking for alternatives. To complete this analysis, the consumer must develop a set of evaluative criteria to guide the selection. **Evaluative criteria** are the features a consumer considers in choosing among alternatives. These criteria can either be objective facts (an automobile's miles-per-gallon rating) or subjective impressions (a favorable view of Free People clothing). Common criteria include price, brand name, and country of origin. Evaluative criteria can vary with the consumer's age, income level, social class, and culture; what's important to a senior citizen might not matter at all to a college student. If you were in the market for a flat-panel HDTV, your criteria might include price, brand name, and features. You might lean toward a Pioneer or Sony because you know the name but discover that the price of a set from Vizio is much less. If you look a bit

Solving an ethical controversy

Greenwashing: Truth or Myth?

s green marketing enters the mainstream, some critics of the practice are alerting the public that not every green message is based in fact. Calling the practice "greenwashing," critics charge that firms are rushing to jump on the green bandwagon, and many have been stretching the truth in their efforts to gain attention for their goods and services. As they shop, how do consumers know which products are green and which aren't?

Should marketers have stricter guidelines when creating green messages about their products?

PRO

1. Marketers need guidelines to avoid misleading consumers. A report by TerraChoice Environmental Marketing reveals that "greenwashing is pervasive" and that businesses selling everything from shampoo to computer printers are making environmental claims that "are either demonstrably false or that risk misleading intended audiences."

2. Consumers want to make informed, educated purchase decisions. "People are expecting a higher level of scrutiny than they used to need for these kinds of claims," notes Scot Case, vice president of TerraChoice.

CON

1. Consumers already know how and where to get the information they need about the products they buy. "The average consumer is well educated and will see beyond the smoke and mirrors," predicts Brian Mullis, president of Sustainable Travel International.

2. It would be nearly impossible to enforce such guidelines in a global business environment. "A global standard would be very difficult to do," argues Ayako Ezaki of the International Ecotourism Society. "There are social and political differences between countries and states."

Summary

Some standards for green marketing messages will likely emerge over the next few years. Officials in the ecotourism industry, for instance, have proposed that a single governing body be created to grant certification to travel and tour agencies, resorts, and hotels that engage in environmentally friendly practices. But regulation of any sort will probably differ among industries and is likely to cause dissent among those involved. Meanwhile, consumers can educate themselves by reading the fine print on packages and in advertisements.

Sources: "The Six Seven Sins of Greenwashing," TerraChoice, http://www .terrachoice.com, accessed April 21, 2009; Maura Judkis, "Deceptive Greenwashing Aims to Trick Ecotourists," *U.S. News & World Report,* May 23, 2008, www.usnews .com; Keith Johnson, "Greenwashing or Green Business?" *The Wall Street Journal,* January 30, 2008, blogs.wsj.com; "Most Green Marketing Claims Aren't True, Says New Report," *GreenBiz,* November 20, 2007, www.greenbiz.com; "The Six Sins of Greenwashing," *TerraChoice,* November 2007; Sarah Rich, "Are You Being Greenwashed?" *BusinessWeek,* March 27, 2007, www.businessweek.com.

---

further, you would discover that Westinghouse—a well-known brand name—offers a good TV at a lower price than those offered by Pioneer or Sony.[37]

Marketers attempt to influence the outcome of this stage in three ways. First, they try to educate consumers about attributes they view as important in evaluating a particular class of goods. They also identify which evaluative criteria are important to an individual and attempt to show why a specific brand fulfills those criteria. Finally, they try to induce a customer to expand the evoked set to include the marketed product. As marketing efforts designed to influence consumers to make decisions based on green—or ecofriendly—messages become more widespread, critics of this practice allege that not all green marketing is based in truth. Should guidelines be created for marketers of such messages? This situation is described in the "Solving an Ethical Controversy" feature.

PURCHASE DECISION AND PURCHASE ACT

The search and alternative evaluation stages of the decision process result in the purchase decision and the actual purchase. At this stage, the consumer has evaluated each alternative in the evoked set based on his or her personal set of evaluative criteria and narrowed the alternatives down to one.

The consumer then decides where—or from whom—to make the purchase. Sometimes this decision is part of the evaluation; perhaps one seller is offering a better price or better warranty than another. The purchase may be made online or in person at a retail store. The delivery options might also influence the decision of where to purchase an item. For example, a local electronics store might deliver your flat-panel TV for free, whereas an online retailer might charge $50 for delivery.

POSTPURCHASE EVALUATION

The purchase act produces one of two results. The buyer feels either satisfaction at the removal of the discrepancy between the existing and desired states or dissatisfaction with the purchase. Consumers are generally satisfied if purchases meet—or exceed—their expectations.

Sometimes, however, consumers experience postpurchase anxieties called **cognitive dissonance.** This anxiety results from an imbalance among a person's knowledge, beliefs, and attitudes. You might experience some dissonance once your flat-panel TV is delivered if you can't figure out how to use it, if you are worried about spending too much money, or if you discover that the one you chose doesn't have all the features you thought it had.

Dissonance is likely to increase (1) as the dollar value of a purchase increases, (2) when the rejected alternatives have desirable features that the chosen alternatives do not provide, and (3) when the purchase decision has a major effect on the buyer. In other words, dissonance is more likely with high-involvement purchases than with those that require low involvement. If you buy a diet soda and don't like the flavor, you can toss it and buy a different one. But if you have spent more than $1,000 on a flat-panel TV and you aren't satisfied with it, you will most likely experience dissonance. You might try to reduce the dissonance by focusing on good reviews about your choice or show a friend all the neat features on your TV—without pointing out anything you find dissatisfactory. Or you might read ads for your selected brand while ignoring advertisements for the one you didn't choose.

Marketers can help buyers reduce cognitive dissonance by providing information that supports the chosen item. Automobile dealers recognize the possibility of "buyer's remorse" and often follow up purchases with letters or telephone calls from dealership personnel offering personal attention to any customer problems. Advertisements that stress customer satisfaction also help reduce cognitive dissonance.

A final method of dealing with cognitive dissonance is to change products. The consumer may ultimately decide that one of the rejected alternatives would have been the best choice and vows to purchase that item in the future. Marketers may capitalize on this with advertising campaigns that focus on the benefits of their products or with tag lines that say something like, "If you're unhappy with them, try us." But making a different choice isn't always an option, particularly if the item requires a large investment in time and money. Homebuyers who decide they are not satisfied with their purchase once they move in usually can't change options quickly or easily, so they must find another way to reduce dissonance.

cognitive dissonance
Imbalance among knowledge, beliefs, and attitudes that occurs after an action or decision, such as a purchase.

assessment check

1. List the steps in the consumer decision process.

2. What is meant by the term *evoked set*?

3. What are evaluative criteria?

6 **Differentiate among routinized response behavior, limited problem solving, and extended problem solving by consumers.**

CLASSIFYING CONSUMER PROBLEM-SOLVING PROCESSES

As mentioned earlier, the consumer decision processes for different products require varying amounts of problem-solving efforts. Marketers recognize three categories of problem-solving behavior: routinized response, limited problem solving, and extended problem solving. The classification of a particular purchase within this framework clearly influences the consumer decision process.

Routinized Response Behavior

Consumers make many purchases routinely by choosing a preferred brand or one of a limited group of acceptable brands. This type of rapid consumer problem solving is referred to as **routinized response behavior.** A routine purchase of the same brand of dog food or the renewal of a magazine subscription are examples. The consumer has already set evaluative criteria and identified available options. External search is limited in such cases, which characterize extremely low-involvement products.

Limited Problem Solving

Consider the situation in which the consumer previously set evaluative criteria for a particular kind of purchase but then encounters a new, unknown brand. The introduction of a new shampoo is an example of a **limited problem-solving** situation. The consumer knows the evaluative criteria for the product but has not applied these criteria to assess the new brand. Such situations demand moderate amounts of time and effort for external searches. Limited problem solving is affected by the number of evaluative criteria and brands, the extent of external search, and the process for determining preferences. Consumers making purchase decisions in this product category will likely feel involvement in the middle of the range.

Extended Problem Solving

Extended problem solving results when brands are difficult to categorize or evaluate. The first step is to compare one item with similar ones. The consumer needs to understand the product features before evaluating alternatives. Most extended problem-solving efforts involve lengthy external searches. High-involvement purchase decisions—cars, homes, and colleges—usually require extended problem solving.

assessment check

1. What is routinized response behavior?
2. What does limited problem solving require?
3. Give an example of an extended problem-solving situation.

Strategic
Implications of
Marketing
21st Century
in the

marketers who plan to succeed with today's consumers need to understand how their potential market behaves. Cultural influences play a big role in marketers' relationships with consumers, particularly as firms conduct business on a global scale but also as they try to reach diverse populations in the United States. In addition, family characteristics are changing—more women are in the workforce, more senior citizens are living alone—which forecasts a change in the way families make purchasing decisions. One of the biggest shifts in family spending involves the amount of power that children and teens wield in

the marketplace. These young consumers are more and more involved, in some cases know more about certain products—such as electronics—than their parents do, and very often influence purchase decisions. This holds true even with high-involvement purchases such as autos and computers.

Marketers constantly work toward changing or modifying components of consumers' attitudes about their products to gain a favorable attitude and purchase decision. Finally, they refine their understanding of the consumer decision process and use their knowledge to design effective marketing strategies.

Review of Chapter Objectives

1   **Define *consumer behavior* and describe the role it plays in marketing decisions.**

Consumer behavior refers to the buyer behavior of individual consumers. Consumer behavior plays a huge role in marketing decisions, including what goods and services to offer, to whom, and where. If marketers can understand the factors that influence consumers, they can develop and offer the right products to those consumers.

2   **Describe the interpersonal determinants of consumer behavior: cultural, social, and family influences.**

Cultural influences, such as the general work ethic or the desire to accumulate wealth, come from society. Core values may vary from culture to culture. Group or social influences include social class, opinion leaders, and reference groups with which consumers may want to be affiliated. Family influences may come from spouses, parents, grandparents, or children.

3   **Explain each of the personal determinants of consumer behavior: needs and motives, perceptions, attitudes, learning, and self-concept theory.**

A need is an imbalance between a consumer's actual and desired states. A motive is the inner state that directs a person toward the goal of satisfying a need. Perception is the meaning that a person attributes to incoming stimuli gathered through the five senses. Attitudes are a person's enduring favorable or unfavorable evaluations, emotions, or action tendencies toward something. In self-concept theory, a person's view of himself or herself plays a role in purchasing behavior. In purchasing goods and services, people will likely choose products that move them closer to their ideal self-images.

4   **Distinguish between high-involvement and low-involvement purchase decisions.**

Purchases with high levels of potential social or economic consequences are called high-involvement purchase decisions. Examples include buying a new car or home. Routine purchases that pose little risk to the consumer are called low-involvement purchase decisions. Choosing a candy bar or a newspaper are examples.

5   **Outline the steps in the consumer decision process.**

The consumer decision process consists of six steps: problem or opportunity recognition, search, alternative evaluation, purchase decision, purchase act, and postpurchase evaluation. The time involved in each stage of the decision process is determined by the nature of the individual purchases.

6   **Differentiate among routinized response behavior, limited problem solving, and extended problem solving by consumers.**

Routinized response behavior refers to repeat purchases made of the same brand or limited group of items. Limited problem solving occurs when a consumer previously set criteria for a purchase but then encounters a new brand or model. Extended problem solving results when brands are difficult to categorize or evaluate. High-involvement purchase decisions usually require extended problem solving.

assessment check: answers

1.1   Why is the study of consumer behavior important to marketers?

If marketers can understand the behavior of consumers, they can offer the right products to consumers who want them.

1.2   Describe Kurt Lewin's proposition.

Kurt Lewin proposed that behavior *(B)* is the function *(f)* of the interactions of personal influences *(P)* and pressures exerted by outside environmental forces *(E)*. This research sheds light on how consumers make purchase decisions.

2.1   List the interpersonal determinants of consumer behavior.

The interpersonal determinants of consumer behavior are cultural, social, and family influences.

2.2   What is a subculture?

A subculture is a group within a culture that has its own distinct mode of behavior.

2.3   Describe the Asch phenomenon.

The Asch phenomenon is the impact of groups and group norms on individual behavior.

3.1   Identify the personal determinants of consumer behavior.

The personal determinants of consumer behavior are needs and motives, perceptions, attitudes, learning, and self-concept theory.

3.2   What are the human needs categorized by Abraham Maslow?

The human needs categorized by Abraham Maslow are physiological, safety, social/belongingness, esteem, and self-actualization.

3.3   How do perception and learning differ?

Perception is the meaning that a person attributes to incoming stimuli. Learning refers to immediate or expected changes in behavior as a result of experience.

4.1   Differentiate between high-involvement decisions and low-involvement decisions.

High-involvement decisions have high levels of potential social or economic consequences, such as selecting an Internet service provider. Low-involvement decisions pose little financial, social, or emotional risk to the buyer, such as a magazine or gallon of milk.

4.2   Categorize each of the following as a high- or low-involvement product: toothpaste, notebook computer, apartment, cup of coffee, cell phone service.

High-involvement products are the notebook, apartment, and cell phone service. Low-involvement products are the toothpaste and cup of coffee.

5.1   List the steps in the consumer decision process.

The steps in the consumer decision process are problem or opportunity recognition, search, alternative evaluation, purchase decision, purchase act, and postpurchase evaluation.

5.2   What is meant by the term *evoked set*?

The evoked set is the number of alternatives a consumer actually considers in making a purchase decision.

5.3   What are evaluative criteria?

Evaluative criteria are the features a consumer considers in choosing among alternatives.

6.1   What is routinized response behavior?

Routinized response behavior is the repeated purchase of the same brand or limited group of products.

6.2   What does limited problem solving require?

Limited problem solving requires a moderate amount of a consumer's time and effort.

6.3   Give an example of an extended problem-solving situation.

An extended problem-solving situation might involve the purchase of a car or a college education.

Marketing Terms You Need to Know

consumer behavior 134
culture 135
reference groups 141
opinion leaders 142
need 145

motive 145
perception 146
attitudes 148
learning 150
self-concept 152

evoked set 154
evaluative criteria 154
cognitive dissonance 156

Other Important Marketing Terms

subcultures 137
acculturation 138
norms 140
status 140
roles 140
Asch phenomenon 141

perceptual screen 147
subliminal perception 148
drive 150
cue 150
response 150
reinforcement 150

shaping 151
high-involvement purchase decision 152
low-involvement purchase decision 152
routinized response behavior 157
limited problem solving 157
extended problem solving 157

Assurance of Learning Review

1. What are core values? Describe what you think are three core values of American society.

2. Why is the concept of acculturation important to marketers who want to target such groups as Hispanic, Asian, or African American consumers?

3. Choose a group you identify with or are a member of. Identify the norms of that group. What is your status in the group? What is your role?

4. Describe three ways in which family members might influence a purchase.

5. How does Maslow's hierarchy of needs relate to marketing decisions?

6. What are the two factors that interact to create a person's perception of an object? How is this important for marketers?

7. What is subliminal perception? Is it an effective marketing tool? Why or why not?

8. How do marketers modify the components of attitude?

9. Identify the five steps of the consumer decision process.

10. Describe the two results produced by the purchase act. What steps might a purchaser take to resolve one of the results, if necessary?

11. Why is it important for marketers to recognize into which category of problem solving their goods and services fall?

Projects and Teamwork Exercises

1. Consider your participation in family purchases. How much influence do you have on your family's decisions? Has this influence changed over time? Why or why not? Compare your answers with those of classmates. Do they have more or less influence than you? If so, why?

2. On your own or with a classmate, choose a subculture. Then select a product from the following list, or choose one of your own. Describe the factors you would consider in creating marketing messages about your product for this subculture.
   a. flavored water
   b. hybrid vehicle
   c. day spa
   d. new magazine
   e. organic produce
   f. digital TV service

3. With a classmate, select a good or service that may have suffered from a poor image recently—it may have performed poorly or simply gone out of style. Think about how you would go about changing consumers' attitudes toward the product and present your plan to the class.

4. Ecotourism has become popular in the last few years, with companies offering adventurous travelers the opportunity to visit remote habitats, build wells and schools for needy communities, and have a hand in preserving endangered plant and animals species. For these types of vacations to be successful, however, a number of factors must be considered, including cultural influences, social influences, needs and motives, perceptions, and attitudes. Finally, regardless of consumers' incomes, a trip is likely to be a high-involvement purchase. On your own or with a classmate, create a travel brochure designed to attract consumers to the trip you are offering, keeping in mind these factors. Choose one of the following destinations, or create one of your own:
   a. viewing turtle nesting in the Bahamas
   b. visiting a rainforest in South America
   c. replanting trees destroyed by fire in the West
   d. hiking the glaciers in Alaska

5. Choose a partner and select a low-involvement, routinized consumer product such as toothpaste, a jar of spaghetti sauce, laundry detergent, or kitchen trash bags. Create an ad you think could stimulate consumers to change their preferred brand to yours.

Critical-Thinking Exercises

1. Identify the two conditions that must exist for a consumer to be influenced by a referent group. Have you been influenced by a referent group when making a purchase? Discuss the experience.

2. Choose one of the following combinations and explain why each is perceived differently by consumers:
   a. Seven jeans and Levi's
   b. Saks Fifth Avenue and Sears
   c. Hyundai Sonata and Jaguar XK
   d. Motel 6 and the Ritz-Carlton

3. Describe a good or service toward which you have changed your attitude. What influences caused you to make the change? If you haven't experienced a change, describe a good or service toward which you have a strong attitude—and how marketers might be able to change your attitude.

4. Outline three of the four components of your self-concept: self-image, looking-glass self, and ideal self. How close do you think these are to your real self?

5. Suppose you are working for a company getting ready to launch a new line of powdered flavorings that consumers can add to bottled water. How would you use shaping to entice people to try—and ultimately buy—your new product?

Ethics Exercise

Teenagers now wield enormous buying power in U.S. society. They influence purchases made by the entire family, both high-involvement and low-involvement decisions. While teens often are savvy about the goods and services they think they want, responsible marketers need to be careful about the messages they send to these consumers. Suppose you are hired by a firm to work on marketing a new social networking Web site for teens. Respond to the following questions to outline an ethical marketing campaign for your targeted market.

1. How would you break through the perceptual screens of your teen market?

2. How would you apply learning theory to the marketing messages you create?

3. Using Maslow's hierarchy of needs, create a slogan for your Web site.

Internet Exercises

1. **Maslow's hierarchy.** Choose a product listed in Table 5.1 in each of Maslow's Hierarchy of Needs. Identify a brand or producer, if one is given, and visit the company's Web site. Based on your review of each Web site, how are the products' marketing strategies designed to appeal to the specific need in Maslow's hierarchy?

2. **Marketing to Hispanic consumers.** HispanoClick.com is a marketing consulting and advertising firm that helps companies market products to Hispanic consumers. Visit the firm's Web site (www.hispanoclick.com). Click on the "solutions" link and prepare a report summarizing the services offered by HispanoClick.com. Who are the firm's primary clients?

3. **Consumer decision process.** Assume you are in the market for a new cell phone and cell phone provider. Follow the first three steps in the consumer decision process model discussed in the text—problem-opportunity recognition, search, and evaluation of alternatives. Use the Web to aid in your decision process. Do you think you can apply what you learned from this experience to the consumer decisions that you actually make, or will make in the near future? Why or why not?

Note: Internet Web addresses change frequently. If you don't find the exact site listed, you may need to access the organization's home page and search from there or use a search engine such as Google.

Case 5.1 Green Choices for Consumers

As consumers in the free enterprise system, we enjoy many choices among goods and services. As a marketer, you want to

find ways to differentiate the products you offer shoppers, making your products the most attractive for purchase. During the past few years, firms have rushed to promote their products and processes as green—using renewable energy sources, less packaging, and recycled materials. When consumers recognize a need for a certain product, these firms hope the search will lead to their goods and services.

One way to distinguish among the various items is to participate in a certification program. Green-e is one such program, established by the Center for Resource Solutions, an independent not-for-profit organization. Green-e offers product certification and verification of renewable energy sources and greenhouse gas mitigation to companies that apply for and complete the process. When they complete the certification, firms may display the Green-e logo in their offices, on their corporate communications, on their product packaging, and in other marketing communications. To qualify for the Green-e logo, companies must buy or generate a certain amount of Green-e certified renewable energy. In addition, all of the demand for electricity used to manufacture the firm's qualified goods must be met with Green-e certified renewable energy.

The Green-e logo benefits qualified firms by giving them credibility in their green marketing messages. The ultimate goal is to build trust and loyalty among customers. As consumers sift through the hundreds of products for sale, a quick, reliable way to identify those that have the desired qualities can make the difference in a purchase decision. Richvale, California–based Lundberg Family Farms, which makes rice-based foods, began its Green-e

certification with nine labeled products. Sales for these products jumped dramatically, so Lundberg sought certification for more of its goods. Timberland received the logo for covering 100 percent of the electricity needed for making its Mion line of footwear, including sandals, slides, and flip-flops. The maker of Silk Soymilk advertises its use of wind power on the side panel of its cartons, and Silk's Web site links interested consumers to the Green-e Web site.

Green-e certification allows companies to get their message across to consumers, educating them about their products and processes. As shoppers gather information about the many products they use, the Green-e label helps them evaluate the alternatives efficiently. Decisions in the supermarket, the drugstore, a restaurant, a convenience store, and many other retail outlets can be made in a matter of seconds. Many marketers now want those choices to be green.

Questions for Critical Thinking

1. Describe how the Green-e logo may affect the entire consumer decision process.

2. How might the Green-e logo change a consumer's attitude about a company or its products?

Sources: Green-e Web site, www.green-e.org, accessed April 21, 2009; "Green-e Product Labeling," U.S. EPA Web site, www.epa.gov, accessed April 21, 2009; "Get Certified!" *Buyer Be Fair*, www.buyerbefair.org, accessed April 21, 2009; Jeremy Faludi, "Toward an Eco-Label," *Package Design*, www.packagedesignmag.com, accessed April 21, 2009.

Video Case 5.2   Consumer Behavior at Scholfield Honda

The written video case on Scholfield Honda appears on page VC-6. The Scholfield Honda video is designed to expand and highlight the concepts in this chapter and the concepts and questions covered in the written video case.

CHAPTER 6

Business-to-Business (B2B) Marketing

Seafood Shortages Hurt Suppliers, Sellers, Shoppers

Seafood lovers, and those who make their living fishing, see rough waters ahead. Environmental and human factors have drastically reduced the size of the world's fish harvests,

resulting in supply shortages and price increases.

Demand has soared as the world's appetite for new dishes and healthful menu choices has grown. The increasing popularity of sushi and sashimi in growing economies like Russia and South Korea is depleting bluefin tuna supplies and driving prices up. In Japan, where all fish is highly prized, "it's like America running out of steak," says the vice-chairman of Japan's sushi chef's union.

Quality problems have also contributed to seafood shortages, especially with farm-raised fish. The Food and Drug

Administration announced restrictions on imports of catfish, shrimp, eel, basa, and dace from China due to concerns about the presence of carcinogens and antibiotic residues in those fish. That could affect up to 22 percent of U.S. seafood imports, which originate there, and reduce supply.

U.S. fish supplies are also suffering. A virus that acts like Ebola is killing off all kinds of freshwater fish in the Great Lakes. "It's killing fish from so many species and with amazingly high mortality levels," says Professor Paul Bowser of Cornell University. To contain the virus and protect the $4.5 billion Great Lakes commercial and sport fishing industry, local governments have closed three major fish hatcheries.

Commercial fishing enterprises—those who supply wholesale and retail outlets—are experiencing limits on their livelihoods. Enforced closure of the Great Barrier Reef to allow fish to spawn have reduced Australian suppliers' catches. "We've only been able to access the reef 14 days out of the last 51 days," said the chair of the Queensland Seafood Industry Association. "We're having trouble keeping crew … we're just not going to have an industry left at all if they keep this up."

Perhaps worst of all for the U.S. fishing industry, harvests of wild-caught king salmon (chinook) have been shut down for one year off the California and Oregon coasts. Officials hope the closure will be temporary, but they—and fish wholesalers—worry about the inexplicable crash in the salmon population that prompted the ban: only 10 percent of the expected number of fish returned to the Sacramento River to spawn. Nutrient-poor oceans and pollution, dams that hinder salmon migration, and agricultural irrigation that deplete local waterways are believed to contribute. "The salmon have gone off a cliff," says the owner of wholesaler Seafood Suppliers in San Francisco. "It's disastrous."[1]

OBJECTIVES

1 Explain each of the components of the business-to-business (B2B) market.

2 Describe the major approaches to segmenting business-to-business (B2B) markets.

3 Identify the major characteristics of the business market and its demand.

4 Discuss the decision to make, buy, or lease.

5 Describe the major influences on business buying behavior.

6 Outline the steps in the organizational buying process.

7 Classify organizational buying situations.

8 Explain the buying center concept.

9 Discuss the challenges of and strategies for marketing to government, institutional, and international buyers.

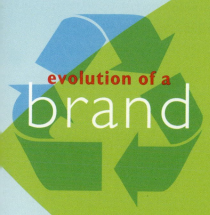
evolution of a **brand**

Seafood is growing in popularity across the globe. The trend toward more healthful diets is one factor driving up demand. U.S. consumers have traditionally relied on many sources, both foreign and local, to put fish on their tables. But quality and environmental concerns may threaten the supply.

- To ensure the public's safety, the U.S. government is beginning to inspect imported bluefin tuna more carefully now that the fish is catching up to yellowfin and albacore in popularity. To try to stabilize the bluefin population throughout the world, dozens of countries are reducing their Atlantic and Mediterranean tuna harvests. How will these events interact to affect bluefin demand? How much do you think consumer preferences can be changed to help protect declining fish populations? What can suppliers do to help improve fish farming in stabilizing the world's seafood populations?

- Salmon fishermen can't easily switch to other species because they require different equipment, types of boats, and even different licenses. Although

evolution of a brand
continued

most are resigned to waiting for stocks to replenish themselves, the restaurants, hotels, and supermarkets that make up their customers in this short supply chain will suffer as farm and wild salmon prices rise. Woodbury Fisheries, a wholesaler in New York State, absorbed a price increase in farm-raised salmon from Scotland. "We're taking most of the loss on our end so that we don't pass it on to the consumer," the owner said. "The last thing we want is to scare consumers away with prices." Given how short the fresh seafood supply chain is, what role do you think price will play during the shortage? Who will likely absorb any further price increases?

chapter overview

business-to-business (B2B) marketing
Organizational sales and purchases of goods and services to support production of other products, to facilitate daily company operations, or for resale.

We are all aware of the consumer marketplace. As consumers, we're involved in purchasing needed items almost every day of our lives. In addition, we can't help noticing the barrage of marketing messages aimed at us through a variety of media. But the business-to-business marketplace is, in fact, significantly larger. U.S. companies pay more than $300 billion each year just for office and maintenance supplies. Government agencies contribute to the business-to-business market even further; for example, the Department of Defense budget for one recent year was over $515 billion.[2] U.S. business-to-business commerce conducted over the Internet now totals nearly $3 trillion.[3] Whether through face-to-face transactions, via telephone, or over the Internet, business marketers each day deal with complex purchasing decisions involving multiple decision makers. They range from simple reorders of previously purchased items to complex buys for which

materials are sourced from all over the world. They often involve the steady building of relationships between companies and customers as well as the ability to respond to changing circumstances in existing markets. Customer satisfaction and customer loyalty are major factors in the development of these long-term relationships.

This chapter discusses buying behavior in the business or organizational market. **Business-to-business (B2B) marketing** deals with organizational sales and purchases of goods and services to support production of other products, to facilitate daily company operations, or for resale. But you ask, "How do I go about distinguishing between consumer purchases and B2B transactions?" Actually, it's pretty simple. Just ask yourself two questions:

1. Who is buying the good or service?

2. Why is the purchase being made?

Consumer buying involves purchases made by individuals. We purchase items for our own use and enjoyment—and not for resale. By contrast, B2B purchases are made by businesses, government, and marketing intermediaries to be resold, combined with other items to create a finished product for resale, or used up in the day-to-day operations of the organization. So answer the two questions—"Who is buying?" and "Why?"—and you have the answer.

Nature of the Business Market

Firms usually sell fewer standardized products to organizational buyers than to ultimate consumers. Although you might purchase a cell phone for your personal use, a company generally has to purchase an entire communications system from a supplier such as AT&T, whose OneNet Service offers digital voice and Internet technology in a single business network.[4] Purchases such as this require greater customization, more decision making, and usually more decision makers. So the buying and selling process becomes more complex, often involving teams of decision makers and taking an average of six to 36 months to complete. Because of the complexity of the purchases, customer service is extremely important to B2B buyers. Advertising plays a much smaller role in the business market than in the consumer market, although advertisements placed in business magazines or trade publications are common. Business marketers advertise primarily to announce new products, to enhance their company image and presence, and to attract potential customers who would then deal directly with a salesperson. Personal selling plays a much bigger role in business markets than in consumer markets, distribution channels are shorter, customer relationships tend to last longer, and purchase decisions can involve multiple decision makers. Table 6.1 compares the marketing practices commonly used in both B2B and consumer marketing.

Like final consumers, an organization purchases products to fill needs. However, its primary need—meeting the demands of its own customers—is similar from firm to firm. A manufacturer buys raw materials such as wood pulp, fabric, or grain to create the company's product. A wholesaler or retailer buys the manufactured products—paper, clothing, or cereal—to resell. Mattel buys everything from plastic to paints to produce its toys; Toys "R" Us buys finished toys to sell to the public. And passenger airlines buy and lease aircraft from manufacturers such as Boeing and Airbus. Wilson Sporting Goods supplies the National Football League with its official game ball, "The Duke." Institutional purchasers such as government agencies and nonprofit organizations also buy products to meet the needs of their constituents, whether it is global positioning system (GPS) mapping devices or meals ready to eat (MRE) for troops in the field.

table 6.1 **Comparing Business-to-Business Marketing and Consumer Marketing**

	Business-to-Business Marketing	**Consumer Marketing**
Product	Relatively technical in nature; exact form often variable; accompanying services very important	Standardized form; service important but less than for business products
Promotion	Emphasis on personal selling	Emphasis on advertising
Distribution	Relatively short, direct channels to market	Product passes through a number of intermediate links en route to consumer
Customer Relations	Relatively enduring and complex	Comparatively infrequent contact; relationship of relatively short duration
Decision-making Process	Diverse group of organization members makes decision	Individual or household unit makes decision
Price	Competitive bidding for unique items; list prices for standard items	List prices

Manufacturers like Mattell buy everything from plastic to paint to produce toys. Retailers like Toys "R" Us buy finished toys to sell to the public.

© Don Emmert/AFP/Getty Images

Companies also buy services from other businesses. A firm may purchase law and accounting services, an office-cleaning service, a call center service, or a recruiting service. Jan-Pro is a commercial cleaning service company in business since 1991. The chain has more than 75 master franchise offices throughout the United States and Canada and more than 7,000 individual franchise operations in the United States alone.[5]

Environmental, organizational, and interpersonal factors are among the many influences in B2B markets. Budget, cost, and profit considerations all play parts in business buying decisions. In addition, the business buying process typically involves complex interactions among many people. An organization's goals must also be considered in the B2B buying process. Later sections of the chapter will explore these topics in greater detail.

Some firms focus entirely on business markets. For instance, DuPont sells materials such as polymers, coatings, and color technologies to manufacturers that use them in a variety of products. Caterpillar makes construction and mining equipment, diesel and natural gas engines, and industrial gas turbines. SAP America provides collaborative business software that lets companies work with customers and business partners using databases and other applications from every major software vendor. Other firms sell to both consumer and business markets. Herman Miller makes award-winning office furniture as well as stylish furniture for the home, and Intel's digital and wireless computer technology is found in business computing systems and personal computers. Note also that marketing strategies developed in consumer marketing often are appropriate for the business sector, too. Final consumers often are the end users of products sold into the business market and, as explained later in the chapter, can influence the buying decision.

The B2B market is diverse. Transactions can range from orders as small as a box of paper clips or copy machine toner for a home-based business to transactions as large as thousands of parts for an automobile manufacturer or massive turbine generators for an electric power plant. As mentioned earlier, businesses are also big purchasers of services such as telecommunications, computer consulting, and transportation services. Four major categories define the business market: (1) the commercial market, (2) trade industries, (3) government organizations, and (4) institutions.

▌ Explain each of the components of the business-to-business (B2B) market.

commercial market
Individuals and firms that acquire products to support, directly or indirectly, production of other goods and services.

COMPONENTS OF THE BUSINESS MARKET

The **commercial market** is the largest segment of the business market. It includes all individuals and firms that acquire products to support, directly or indirectly, production of other goods and services. When Dell buys computer chips from Intel, when Sara Lee purchases wheat to mill into flour for an ingredient in its breads, and when a plant supervisor orders light bulbs and cleaning supplies for a factory in Tennessee, these transactions take place in the commercial market. Some products aid in the production of other items (the computer chips). Others are physically used up in the production of a good or service (the wheat). Still others contribute to the firm's day-to-day operations (the maintenance supplies). The commercial market includes manufacturers, farmers,

At Herman Miller,
we've managed to take our company philosophy and bottle it.

In 1995, we moved into the GreenHouse, our new, environmentally friendly manufacturing and office facility in Holland, Michigan. One day, we noticed large colonies of angry paper wasps had decided to make the exterior of our building their new home. But we weren't about to reach for the pesticides. Our solution? Bees. Six-hundred thousand of them, housed in 12 beehives on the GreenHouse grounds. Before long, the bees had persuaded the wasps to move elsewhere. And our new friends cross-pollinated the surrounding fields, giving us spectacular wildflowers. We also had another favorable result: Honey. And lots of it. So we began harvesting and bottling about 5,000 pounds of GreenHouse honey a year as gifts for our guests. And while the honey may only come in a 4-ounce bottle, we believe the story behind it speaks volumes. To us, the honey exemplifies our commitment to the environment, to those who live in it, and to those who will inherit it. Angry wasps included. If you'd like to learn more about what we're doing for a better world around you, visit hermanmiller.com/environment.

© Courtesy of Herman Miller, Inc.

Environmental factors influence the B2B market. Here, Herman Miller markets its environmentally friendly manufacturing and office facility.

and other members of resource-producing industries, construction contractors, and providers of such services as transportation, public utilities, financing, insurance, and real-estate brokerage.

The second segment of the organizational market, **trade industries,** includes retailers and wholesalers, known as **resellers,** who operate in this sector. Most resale products such as clothing, appliances, sports equipment, and automobile parts are finished goods that buyers sell to final consumers. Acco supplies paper clips, ring binders, vinyl envelopes, sheet protectors, and fasteners to Office Depot.[6] In other cases, the buyers may complete some processing or repackaging before

trade industries Retailers or wholesalers that purchase products for resale to others.

reseller Marketing intermediaries that operate in the trade sector.

reselling the products. A retail meat market may purchase a side of beef and then cut individual pieces for its customers. Lumber dealers and carpet retailers may purchase in bulk and then provide quantities and sizes to meet customers' specifications. In addition to resale products, trade industries buy computers, display shelves, and other products needed to operate their businesses. All of these goods—as well as maintenance items and specialized services such as scanner installation, newspaper inserts, and radio advertising—represent organizational purchases.

The government category of the business market includes domestic units of government—federal, state, and local—as well as foreign governments. This important market segment makes a wide variety of purchases, ranging from highways to social services. The primary motivation of government purchasing is to provide some form of public benefit such as national defense or pollution control. But government agencies have also become creative when it comes to selling; local police departments and state and federal agencies sell unclaimed shipments, confiscated goods, and unclaimed items found in safe-deposit boxes on eBay. Lucky bidders might be able to buy a custom yacht for their business, a sausage grinder for their restaurant, or an auto transmission for their delivery truck through an Internet auction.[7]

Institutions, both public and private, are the fourth component of the business market. This category includes a wide range of organizations such as hospitals, churches, skilled care and rehabilitation centers, colleges and universities, museums, and not-for-profit agencies. Some institutions—such as in public higher education—must rigidly follow standardized purchasing procedures, but others have less formal buying practices. Business-to-business marketers often benefit by setting up separate divisions to sell to institutional buyers.

B2B MARKETS: THE INTERNET CONNECTION

While consumers' use of Internet markets receives the bulk of public attention, about 93 percent of all Internet sales are B2B transactions.[8] Many business-to-business marketers have set up private portals that allow their customers to buy needed items. Service and customized pages are accessed through passwords provided by B2B marketers. Online auctions and virtual marketplaces offer other ways for buyers and vendors to connect with each other over the Internet.

During the early Internet boom, start-up companies rushed to connect buyers and sellers without considering basic marketing principles such as targeting their market and making sure to fulfill customers' needs. As a result, many of these companies failed. But the companies that survived—and new firms that have learned lessons from the mistakes of the old—have established a much stronger marketing presence. For instance, they recognize their business customers have a lot at stake and expect greater value and utility from the goods and services they purchase as well as streamlined marketing communications such as e-mail, blogs, and podcasts.[9]

The Internet also opens up foreign markets to sellers. One such firm, which began as a cotton exchange called The Seam, survived the Internet boom and bust and is now bringing together global buyers of commodities like cotton, peanuts, and grain.[10]

DIFFERENCES IN FOREIGN BUSINESS MARKETS

When The Seam first moved into other countries, its marketers had to consider the fact that foreign business markets may differ due to variations in government regulations and cultural practices. Some business products need modifications to succeed in foreign markets. In Australia, Japan, and Great Britain, for instance, motorists drive on the left side of the road. American-made automobiles must be modified to accommodate such differences.

Business marketers must be willing to adapt to local customs and business practices when operating abroad. They should also research cultural preferences. Factors as deceptively simple as the time of a meeting and methods of address for associates can make a difference. A company even needs to consider what ink colors to use for documents because colors can have different meanings in different countries.

assessment check

1. Define *B2B marketing*.
2. What is the commercial market?

Segmenting B2B Markets

2 **Describe the major approaches to segmenting business-to-business (B2B) markets.**

Business-to-business markets include wide varieties of customers, so marketers must identify the different market segments they serve. By applying market segmentation concepts to groups of business customers, a firm's marketers can develop a strategy that best suits a particular segment's needs. The overall process of segmenting business markets divides markets based on different criteria, usually organizational characteristics and product applications. Among the major ways to segment business markets are demographics (size), customer type, end-use application, and purchasing situation.

SEGMENTATION BY DEMOGRAPHIC CHARACTERISTICS

As in consumer markets, demographic characteristics define useful segmentation criteria for business markets. For example, firms can be grouped by size, based on sales revenues or number of employees. Marketers may develop one strategy to reach *Fortune 500* corporations with complex purchasing procedures and another strategy for small firms in which decisions are made by one or two people. According to one research study, many firms are actually increasing their outreach to small and mid-size businesses. Microsoft, for instance, targets small-business customers online but also recently went on the road with a tour to promote Office Live to entrepreneurs in Atlanta, Portland, Oregon, and Tempe. Bank of America offers online services for small businesses that include payroll, accounting, and health insurance. "Small business is a very significant opportunity for us," says the company's small-business marketing executive. "We have been increasingly focused on this segment."[11]

SEGMENTATION BY CUSTOMER TYPE

Another useful segmentation approach groups prospects according to type of customer. Marketers can apply this concept in several ways. They can group customers by broad categories—manufacturer, service provider, government agency, not-for-profit organization, wholesaler, or retailer—and by industry (see the "Marketing Success" feature on page 173 for an example). These groups may be further divided using other segmentation approaches discussed in this section.

Customer-based segmentation is a related approach often used in the business-to-business marketplace. Organizational buyers tend to have much more precise—and complex—requirements for goods and services than ultimate consumers do. As a result, business products often fit narrower market segments than consumer products, which leads some firms to design business goods and services to meet detailed buyer specifications. Pasadena-based Tetra Tech provides a variety of environmental services, including technology development, design, engineering, and pollution remediation for organizations around the world. Because the company's customers include government agencies as well as private firms—and because customers' needs are different—Tetra Tech has 275 offices worldwide that offer a range of programs to suit each type of customer. For instance, the firm provides consulting services for utilities, helps communities clean up polluted water sources, and even conducts programs to clear public and private sites of unexploded ordnance.[12]

customer-based segmentation Dividing a business-to-business market into homogeneous groups based on buyers' product specifications.

North American Industry Classification System (NAICS)

In the 1930s, the U.S. government set up a uniform system for subdividing the business marketplace into detailed segments. The Standard Industrial Classification (SIC) system standardized efforts to collect and report information on U.S. industrial activity.

SIC codes divided firms into broad industry categories: agriculture, forestry, and fishing; mining and construction; manufacturing; transportation, communication, electric, gas, and sanitary services; wholesale trade; retail trade; finance, insurance, and real-estate services; public administration; and nonclassifiable establishments. The system assigned each major category within these classifications its own two-digit number. Three-digit and four-digit numbers further subdivided each industry into smaller segments.

For roughly 70 years, B2B marketers used SIC codes as a tool for segmenting markets and identifying new customers. The system, however, became outdated with implementation of the

North American Industry Classification System (NAICS) Classification used by NAFTA countries to categorize the business marketplace into detailed market segments.

North American Free Trade Agreement. Each NAFTA member—the United States, Canada, and Mexico—had its own system for measuring business activity. NAFTA required a joint classification system that would allow marketers to compare business sectors among the member nations. In effect, marketers required a segmentation tool they could use across borders. The **North American Industry Classification System (NAICS)** replaced the SIC and provides more detail than previously available. The NAICS created new service sectors to better reflect the economy of the 21st century. They include information; health care and social assistance; and professional, scientific, and technical services.

Table 6.2 demonstrates the NAICS system for wholesale stationery and office supplies. The NAICS uses six digits, compared with the four digits used in the SIC. The first five digits are fixed among the members of NAFTA. The sixth digit can vary among U.S., Canadian, and Mexican data. In short, the sixth digit accounts for specific data needs of each nation.[13]

SEGMENTATION BY END-USE APPLICATION

end-use application segmentation Segmenting a business-to-business market based on how industrial purchasers will use the product.

A third basis for segmentation, **end-use application segmentation,** focuses on the precise way in which a business purchaser will use a product. For example, a printing equipment manufacturer may serve markets ranging from a local utility to a bicycle manufacturer to the U.S. Department of Defense. Each end use of the equipment may dictate unique specifications for performance, design, and price. Praxair, a supplier of industrial gases, for example, might segment its markets according to user. Steel and glass manufacturers might buy hydrogen and oxygen, while food and beverage manufacturers need carbon dioxide. Praxair also sells krypton, a rare gas, to companies that produce lasers, lighting, and thermal windows. Many small and medium-sized companies also segment markets according to end-use application. Instead of competing in markets dominated by large firms, they concentrate on specific end-use market segments. The 32 companies that manufacture wooden baseball bats for Major League Baseball focus on specific end users who are very different from the youth and high-school players using aluminum bats.

SEGMENTATION BY PURCHASE CATEGORIES

Firms have different structures for their purchasing functions, and B2B marketers must adapt their strategies according to those organizational buyer characteristics. Some companies designate centralized purchasing departments to serve the entire firm, and others allow each unit to handle its own buying. A supplier may deal with one purchasing agent or several decision makers at various levels. Each of these structures results in different buying behavior.

When the buying situation is important to marketers, they typically consider whether the customer has made previous purchases or this is the customer's first order, offering special rates or programs for valued clients. Verizon Wireless offers government customers cell phone discounts as either credits or reimbursements.[14]

Increasingly, businesses that have developed **customer relationship management (CRM)** systems—strategies and tools that reorient an entire organization to focus on satisfying customers—can segment customers in terms of the stage of the relationship between the business and the customer. A

briefly speaking

"No matter what your product is, you are ultimately in the education business. Your customers need to be constantly educated about the many advantages of doing business with you, trained to use your products more effectively, and taught how to make never-ending improvement in their lives."

—**Robert G. Allen**
AUTHOR OF *THE ONE-MINUTE MILLIONAIRE*

table 6.2   NAICS Classification for Stationery and Office Supplies Merchant Wholesalers

42	Merchant wholesalers
424	Merchant wholesalers; nondurable goods
4241	Paper and paper product merchant wholesalers
42412	Stationery and office supplies merchant wholesalers
424120	Stationery and office supplies merchant wholesalers in the U.S. industry

Source: NAICS, U.S. Census Bureau, www.census.gov, accessed April 21, 2009.

B2B company, for example, might develop different strategies for newly acquired customers than it would for existing customers to which it hopes to sell new products. Similarly, building loyalty among satisfied customers requires a different approach than developing programs to "save" at-risk customer relationships. CRM will be covered in more depth in Chapter 10.

assessment check

1. What are the four major ways marketers segment business markets?
2. What is the NAICS?

Characteristics of the B2B Market

3 Identify the major characteristics of the business market and its demand.

Businesses that serve both B2B and consumer markets must understand the needs of their customers. However, several characteristics distinguish the business market from the consumer market: (1) geographic market concentration, (2) the sizes and numbers of buyers, (3) the purchase

MARKETING SUCCESS   PolyCon's E-Krete Turns Roads Green

Background. The network of roads and highways that spreads across the United States has been falling into disrepair because of budget cuts and the swings in the cost of the oil required to manufacture asphalt. PolyCon Manufacturing says it can remedy this problem with a new product called E-Krete. Made of part concrete and part flexible polymer, E-Krete can be applied over an old coat of crumbling blacktop at a relatively low cost. E-Krete is also much more environmentally friendly than traditional oil-based materials.

The Challenge. PolyCon must reach government agencies, organizations, and other businesses in order to educate them about E-Krete. States, counties, and towns are currently paving about 275,000 miles of road each year, which translates to a promising market for E-Krete.

The Strategy. The federal government, state departments of transportation, and towns are all searching for a new answer to their paving problems. Publicly funded contracts are now requiring that manufacturers' bids include hefty warranties or maintenance contracts that protect against repair costs. In answer to this problem, PolyCon offers a 10-year warranty on its E-Krete product, which extends the life of a paving project more than 20 years. The warranty could save states a total of $300 million each year. No other paving manufacturer offers this type of protection.

In addition to the warranty, PolyCon markets the benefits of E-Krete in terms of strength, durability, and reduced impact on the environment. E-Krete is made from water-based, nonhazardous materials and does not create dangerous "heat islands"—areas that radiate absorbed heat from dark pavement—as traditional pavement does because it is lighter colored and more reflective. E-Krete coats old asphalt, making it nearly impervious to water and ultraviolet light. The firm's CEO says that his product can almost make the pavement last indefinitely.

The Outcome. PolyCon, which is a small firm, has been able to create partnerships with companies both in the United States and abroad to make E-Krete more available in the marketplace. Contractors have inked agreements with PolyCon to apply E-Krete to roads. Government agencies such as the Florida, New York, and Texas departments of transportation have approved E-Krete for use on their roadways. "[E-Krete] has great possibilities and potential," says one contractor. "It's going to revolutionize the paving of secondary roads."

Sources: Company Web site, http://www.polyconmfg.com, accessed April 10, 2009; Jeff Ayres, "Environmentally Green Road Surface Company Expanding," *The Clarion-Ledger*, March 4, 2009, http://www.clarionledger.com; Barbara Quinn, "Green Connections: A Different Kind of Repair," *Pollution Engineering*, March 1, 2009, http://www.pollutionengineering.com; "Roads: A Part-Concrete Solution," *BusinessWeek*, February 16, 2009, www.businessweek.com; "Pavements, Wastewater, Erosion Control," *CENews.com*, January 31, 2009, http://www.cenews.com; "E-Krete Turns Asphalt Green, Dramatically Extending its Life," *Hard Hat News*, January 30, 2009, http://hardhat.com.

decision process, and (4) buyer–seller relationships. The next sections consider how these traits influence business-to-business marketing.

GEOGRAPHIC MARKET CONCENTRATION

The U.S. business market is more geographically concentrated than the consumer market. Manufacturers converge in certain regions of the country, making these areas prime targets for business marketers. For example, the Midwestern states that make up the East North Central region—Ohio, Indiana, Michigan, Illinois, and Wisconsin—lead the nation in manufacturing concentration, followed by the Middle Atlantic and South Atlantic regions.[15]

Certain industries locate in particular areas to be close to customers. Firms may locate sales offices and distribution centers in these areas to provide more attentive service. It makes sense that the Washington, D.C. area is favored by companies that sell to the federal government.

In the automobile industry, suppliers of components and assemblies frequently build plants close to their customers. Ford recently established a first-of-its-kind campus for suppliers near its Chicago assembly plant. The campus allows suppliers to produce or assemble products close to the plant, reducing costs, controlling parts inventory, and increasing flexibility.[16] As Internet-based technology continues to improve, allowing companies to transact business even with distant suppliers, business markets may become less geographically concentrated. Much of government spending, for example, is now directed through the Internet.

SIZES AND NUMBERS OF BUYERS

In addition to geographic concentration, the business market features a limited number of buyers. Marketers can draw on a wealth of statistical information to estimate the sizes and characteristics of business markets. The federal government is the largest single source of such statistics. Every five years, it conducts both a Census of Manufacturers and a Census of Retailing and Wholesaling, which provide detailed information on business establishments, output, and employment. Many government units and trade organizations also operate Web sites that contain helpful information.

Many buyers in limited-buyer markets are large organizations. The international market for jet engines is dominated by three manufacturers: United Technology's Pratt & Whitney unit, General Electric, and Rolls-Royce. These firms sell engines to Boeing and the European consortium, Airbus Industrie. These aircraft manufacturers compete for business from passenger carriers such as American Airlines, British Airways, Emirates Air Lines, and Singapore Airlines, along with cargo carriers such as Federal Express and United Parcel Service.

Trade associations and business publications provide additional information on the business market. Private firms such as Dun & Bradstreet publish detailed reports on individual companies. These data serve as a useful starting point for analyzing a business market. Finding data in such a source requires an understanding of the NAICS, which identifies much of the available statistical information.

THE PURCHASE DECISION PROCESS

To market effectively to other organizations, businesses must understand the dynamics of the organizational purchase process. Suppliers who serve business-to-business markets must work with multiple buyers, especially when selling to larger customers. Decision makers at several levels may influence final orders, and the overall process is more formal and professional than the consumer purchasing process. Purchasers typically require a longer time frame because B2B involves more complex decisions. Suppliers must evaluate customer needs and develop proposals that meet technical requirements and specifications. Also, buyers need time to analyze competing proposals. Often decisions require more than one round of bidding and negotiation, especially for complicated purchases.

briefly speaking

"I would rather have a million friends than a million dollars."

—Edward V. Rickenbacker (1890–1973)
AMERICAN AVIATOR

BUYER–SELLER RELATIONSHIPS

An especially important characteristic of B2B marketing is the relationship between buyers and sellers. These relationships often are more complex than consumer relationships, and they require superior communication among the organizations' personnel. Satisfying one major customer may mean the difference of millions of dollars to a firm.

Relationship marketing involves developing long-term, value-added customer relationships. A primary goal of business-to-business relationships is to provide advantages that no other vendor can provide—lower price, quicker delivery, better quality and reliability, customized product features, more favorable financing terms, and so on. For the business marketer, providing these advantages means expanding the company's external relationships to include suppliers, distributors, and other organizational partners. CDW, for instance, relies on a variety of vendors to meet its own business, government, and education customers' technology needs with hardware, software, networking, and data storage. It has developed a CDW Supplier Diversity Program to increase and improve relationships with small business suppliers owned by minorities, women, and veterans and thus must manage its supplier as well as its customer relationships successfully.[17]

Close cooperation, whether through informal contacts or under terms specified in contractual partnerships and strategic alliances, enables companies to meet buyers' needs for quality products and customer service. This holds true both during and after the purchase process. Tetra Tech, mentioned earlier, has formal Client Service Quality and Shared Vision programs, designed to engage customers in continuous communication leading to customer satisfaction. For some tips on developing good relationships with potential customers at trade shows, see the "Etiquette Tips for Marketing Professionals" feature.

Relationships between for-profit and not-for-profit organizations are just as important as those between two commercial organizations. Wal-Mart is a longtime corporate sponsor of Children's Miracle Network, an international organization that helps improve children's health and welfare by raising funds for state-of-the-art care, cutting-edge research, and education. Wal-Mart has raised and donated an amount approaching $400 million to 170 children's hospitals in the network.[18]

EVALUATING INTERNATIONAL BUSINESS MARKETS

Business purchasing patterns differ from one country to the next. Researching these markets poses a particular problem for B2B marketers. Of course, as explained earlier, the NAICS has corrected this problem in the NAFTA countries.

In addition to assessing quantitative data such as the size of the potential market, companies must also carefully weigh its qualitative features. This process includes considering cultural values, work styles, and the best ways to enter overseas markets in general. Nokia is supporting its push into cell phone markets in emerging economies by establishing nine satellite studios in China, India, and Brazil. There its designers can customize products and approaches to each market. "Our process starts with a team of anthropologists and psychologists working in our design group," says the company's design director. "They spend time with specific types of people around the world to understand how they behave and communicate. This helps us to understand better and to spot early signals of new patterns of behavior that could be harnessed into mobile communication."[19]

In today's international marketplace, companies often practice **global sourcing,** purchasing goods and services from suppliers worldwide. This practice can result in substantial cost savings, although product quality must be carefully monitored. China, India, Mexico, Brazil, and Malaysia are the world's top destinations for global sourcing by companies like Best Buy, Carrefour, Philips, Sears, and Lowe's.[20]

Global sourcing requires companies to adopt a new mindset; some must even reorganize their operations. Among other considerations, businesses sourcing from multiple multinational locations should streamline the purchase process and minimize price differences due to labor costs, tariffs, taxes, and currency fluctuations.

global sourcing
Purchasing goods and services from suppliers worldwide.

assessment check

1. Why is geographic segmentation important in the B2B market?

2. In what ways is the buyer–seller relationship important in B2B marketing?

3. What is global sourcing?

Etiquette Tips for Marketing Professionals

How to Work a Trade Show

representing your company at a trade show is a challenging but rewarding experience. It takes some planning to put your best foot forward when meeting prospective clients. Here are some tips for avoiding common mistakes in the booth.

- Make sure there is always one person in the booth who's an expert in your company's offerings and can answer questions from the most casual to the most interested.

- Prepare a script for everyone in the booth to ensure they all greet visitors quickly and pleasantly, with a competent one-minute introduction to the company and the benefits your goods or services offer.

- Don't overstaff the booth or let employees block the entrance to your exhibit.

- Remain standing to greet visitors. If you need a seat, get a tall stool so that you can stay at eye level with attendees.

- Keep the booth neat, clean, and well stocked at all times.

- Always leave the booth to eat or use your cell phone.

- Don't use the trade show as an opportunity to catch up or gossip with your coworkers or the folks in the next booth. Nothing turns off potential visitors to your booth faster than the appearance that *they* are not the reason you're there.

- Remember that every impression you make during a show or convention is a first impression, and first impressions count. Spend most of your time listening to your visitors, not talking.

- Ask whether you can help answer any particular questions, and if you can, follow up by ensuring you've satisfied the potential customer and given them any appropriate literature or contact information.

- Always thank your visitors for stopping by.

Sources: "Trade Show Staffing Strategies," Trade-Show-Advisor.com, www.trade-show-advisor.com, accessed April 21, 2009; Ron Hard, "Trade Show Booth Etiquette Can Attract or Repel Attendees," *About.com Event Planning,* eventplanning.about.com, accessed June 13, 2008; "Boothmanship: The Etiquette to Man a Trade Show Booth," *Catalyst Exhibits,* www.catalystexhibit.com, accessed June 13, 2008; "Trade Show Etiquette," *BIG Images,* www.big-images.com, April 10, 2007.

Business Market Demand

The previous section's discussion of business market characteristics demonstrated considerable differences between marketing techniques for consumer and business products. Demand characteristics also differ in these markets. In business markets, the major categories of demand include derived demand, volatile demand, joint demand, inelastic demand, and inventory adjustments. Figure 6.1 summarizes these different categories of business market demand.

figure 6.1

Categories of Business Market Demand

[Pie chart: Business Market Demand Categories — Inventory Adjustments, Derived Demand, Joint Demand, Inelastic Demand, Volatile Demand]

DERIVED DEMAND

The term **derived demand** refers to the linkage between demand for a company's output and its purchases of resources such as machinery, components, supplies, and raw materials. The demand for computer microprocessor chips is *derived* from the demand for personal computers. If more businesses and individuals buy new computers, the demand for chips increases; if fewer computers are sold, the demand for chips decreases. Michigan-based Lear Corporation, for instance, supplies auto seats and other interior parts to companies like Ford and General Motors. In the wake of the car makers' recent plant closings and reduced production plans, demand for Lear products has declined, and Lear expects its own earnings to drop. It will close some facilities and may have to lay off some employees. "Like our customers, we are continuing to aggressively realign our capacity and implement structural cost reductions to improve our long-term competitiveness," says the company's CEO.[21]

Organizational buyers purchase two general categories of business products: capital items and expense items. Derived demand ultimately affects both. Capital items are long-lived business assets that must be depreciated over time. *Depreciation* is an accounting term that refers to charging a portion of a capital item's cost as a deduction against the company's annual revenue for purposes of determining its net income. Examples of capital items include major installations such as new manufacturing plants, office buildings, and computer systems.

Expense items, in contrast, are items consumed within short time periods. Accountants charge the cost of such products against income in the year of purchase. Examples of expense items include the supplies necessary to operate the business, ranging from copy paper to machine lubricants.

VOLATILE DEMAND

Derived demand creates volatility in business market demand. Assume the sales volume for a gasoline retailer is increasing at an annual rate of 5 percent. Now suppose the demand for this gasoline brand slows to a 3 percent annual increase. This slowdown might persuade the firm to keep its current gasoline pumps and replace them only when market conditions improve. In this way, even modest shifts in consumer demand for a gasoline brand would greatly affect the pump manufacturer.

JOINT DEMAND

Another important influence on business market demand is **joint demand,** which results when the demand for one business product is related to the demand for another business product used in combination with the first item. Both lumber and concrete are required to build most homes. If the lumber supply falls, the drop in housing construction will most likely affect the demand for concrete. Another example is the joint demand for electrical power and large turbine engines. If consumers decide to conserve power, demand for new power plants drops, as does the demand for components and replacement parts for turbines.

INELASTIC DEMAND

Inelastic demand means that demand throughout an industry will not change significantly due to a price change. If the price of lumber drops, a construction firm will not necessarily buy more lumber from its suppliers unless another factor—such as lowered mortgage interest rates—causes more consumers to purchase new homes.

INVENTORY ADJUSTMENTS

Adjustments in inventory and inventory policies can also affect business demand. Assume manufacturers in a particular industry consider a 60-day supply of raw materials the optimal inventory level. Now suppose economic conditions or other factors induce these firms to increase their inventories to a 90-day supply. The change will bombard the raw-materials supplier with new orders.

Furthermore, **just-in-time (JIT)** inventory policies seek to boost efficiency by cutting inventories to absolute minimum levels and by requiring vendors to deliver inputs as the production process needs them. JIT allows companies to better predict which supplies they will require and the timing for when they will need them, markedly reducing their costs for production and storage. Widespread implementation of JIT has had a substantial impact on organizations' purchasing behavior. Firms that practice JIT tend to order from relatively few suppliers. In some cases, JIT may lead to **sole sourcing** for some items, that is, buying a firm's entire stock of a product from just one supplier. Electronic data interchange (EDI) and quick-response inventory policies have produced similar results in the trade industries. The latest inventory trend, **JIT II,** leads suppliers to place representatives at the customer's facility to work as part of an integrated, on-site customer–supplier team. Suppliers plan and order in consultation with the customer. This streamlining of the inventory process improves control of the flow of goods.

Although inventory adjustments are critical in manufacturing processes, they are equally vital to wholesalers and retailers. Perhaps nowhere is inventory management more complex than at Wal-Mart, the largest retailer in the world, with sales approaching $400 billion per year. With no signs of slowing down, suppliers such as Procter & Gamble and Unilever—giants themselves—work closely with Wal-Mart to monitor and adjust inventory as necessary. Other suppliers such as Mega Toys, Parkway Imaging and Graphics, and Ruiz Foods generate a large portion of their total income from Wal-Mart, so inventory management is critical for those companies as well.[22]

assessment check

1. How does derived demand create volatile demand?

2. Give an example of joint demand.

3. How might JIT II strengthen marketing relationships?

4 Discuss the decision to make, buy, or lease.

The Make, Buy, or Lease Decision

Before a company can decide what to buy, it should decide whether to buy at all. Organizational buyers must figure out the best way to acquire needed products. In fact, a firm considering the acquisition of a finished good, component part, or service has three basic options:

1. Make the good or provide the service in-house.

2. Purchase it from another organization.

3. Lease it from another organization.

If the company has the capability to do so, manufacturing the product itself may be the best route. It may save a great deal of money if its own manufacturing division does not incur costs for overhead that an outside vendor would otherwise charge.

On the other hand, most firms cannot make all the business goods they need. Often it would be too costly to maintain the necessary equipment, staff, and supplies. As a result, purchasing from an outside vendor is the most common choice. Xerox manufactures more than 50 different types of color printers to meet nearly any business need—from affordable color laser printers to high-performance ink-jet printers. Its wide array of products, coupled with its track record of a century of supplying businesses, has made it a leader in the B2B printer market.[23] Companies can also look outside their own plants for goods and services formerly produced in-house, a practice called *outsourcing* that the next section will describe in more detail.

In some cases, however, a company may choose to lease inputs. This option spreads out costs compared with lump-sum costs for up-front purchases. The company pays for the use of equipment for a certain time period. A small business may lease a copier for a few years and make monthly payments. At the end of the lease term, the firm can buy the machine at a prearranged price or replace it with a different model under a new lease. This option can provide useful flexibility for a growing business, allowing it to easily upgrade as its needs change.

Companies can also lease sophisticated computer systems and heavy equipment. For example, some airlines prefer to lease airplanes rather than buy them outright because short-term leases allow them to adapt quickly to changes in passenger demand.

THE RISE OF OFFSHORING AND OUTSOURCING

Chances are, if you dial a call center for a firm such as Dell, GE, American Express, or Nestlé, your call may be answered by someone in India. In recent years, a political firestorm has been ignited by the movement of U.S. jobs to lower-cost overseas locations, a business practice referred to as **offshoring.** Microsoft recently increased the number of its employees abroad to about 40 percent of its total workforce.[24] This relocation of business processes to a lower-cost location can involve production offshoring or services offshoring. China has emerged as the preferred destination for production offshoring, while India has emerged as the dominant player in services offshoring.

Some U.S.-based firms want to remain closer to home but take advantage of the benefits of locating some of their operations overseas. Mexico and Canada are attractive locations for these **nearshoring** operations. In today's highly competitive marketplace, firms look outside the United States to improve efficiency and cut costs on just about everything including customer service, human resources, accounting, information technology, manufacturing, and distribution. **Outsourcing,** using outside vendors to produce goods and services formerly produced in-house, is a trend that continues to rise. Businesses outsource for several reasons: (1) they need to reduce costs to remain competitive; (2) they need to improve the quality and speed of software maintenance and development; and (3) outsourcing has begun to offer greater value than ever before.

Outsourcing allows firms to concentrate their resources on their core business. It also allows access to specialized talent or expertise that does not exist within the firm. The most frequently outsourced business functions include information technology (IT) and human resources, with other white-collar service jobs such as accounting, drug research, technical R&D, and film animation. Although most outsourcing is done by North American–based companies, the practice is rapidly becoming commonplace in Asia, Europe, and Central America.

China has been leading the way in offshore manufacturing, making two-thirds of the world's copiers, microwaves, DVD players, and shoes, and virtually all the world's toys. The size of its manufacturing workforce in Guangdong province is estimated to rival that of the entire United States. In recent years, however, China's very success and the resulting rise of an increasingly wealthy middle class have pushed up its labor and management costs and may have helped lure many companies to suppliers in Vietnam and India, where such costs are still low. For instance, management compensation in China increased over 9 percent in a recent year, while support staff wages climbed more than 10 percent, and blue-collar wages and the cost of raw materials both climbed more than 7 percent. The American Chamber of Commerce in Shanghai found that about one-fifth of companies it surveyed were considering leaving China, and some Chinese factories already face reduced profit margins and even bankruptcy and closure. The government sees potential good in this shift away from low-value, labor-intensive exports that pollute and waste energy; it wants industry to focus on higher-quality cars, biotech products, and software for the home market. "We are not abandoning the [exporters]," says the governor of Guangdong Province. "[But] selling domestically is good for the country, good for the collective, and good for the people."[25]

Outsourcing can be a smart strategy if a company chooses a vendor that can provide high-quality products and perhaps at a lower cost than could be achieved on the company's own. This priority allows the outsourcer to focus on its core competencies. Successful outsourcing requires companies to carefully oversee contracts and manage relationships. Some vendors now provide performance guarantees to assure their customers they will receive high-quality services that meet their needs.

PROBLEMS WITH OFFSHORING AND OUTSOURCING

Offshoring and outsourcing are not without their downsides. Many companies discover their cost savings are less than vendors sometimes promise. Also, companies that sign multiyear contracts may find their savings drop after a year or two. When proprietary technology is an issue, outsourcing raises security concerns. Similarly, companies protective of customer data and relationships may think twice about entrusting functions such as customer service to outside sources.

In some cases, outsourcing and offshoring can reduce a company's ability to respond quickly to the marketplace, or they can slow efforts in bringing new products to market. Suppliers that fail to deliver goods promptly or provide required services can adversely affect a company's reputation with its customers.

offshoring Movement of high-wage jobs from one country to lower-cost overseas locations.

nearshoring Moving jobs to vendors in countries close to the business's home country.

outsourcing Using outside vendors to provide goods and services formerly produced in-house.

Outsourcing and offshoring are controversial topics with unions, especially in the auto industry, as the percentage of component parts made in-house has steadily dropped. These practices can create conflicts between nonunion outside workers and in-house union employees, who fear job loss. Management initiatives to outsource jobs can lead to strikes and plant shutdowns. Even if they do not lead to disruption in the workplace, outsourcing and offshoring can have a negative impact on employee morale and loyalty.

assessment check

1. Identify two potential benefits of outsourcing.

2. Identify two potential problems with outsourcing.

5 Describe the major influences on business buying behavior.

The Business Buying Process

Suppose that MyMap, Inc., a hypothetical manufacturer of GPS devices for automakers, decides to upgrade its manufacturing facility with $5 million in new automated assembly equipment. Before approaching equipment suppliers, the company must analyze its needs, determine goals the project should accomplish, develop technical specifications for the equipment, and set a budget. Once it receives vendors' proposals, it must evaluate them and select the best one. But what does *best* mean in this context? The lowest price or the best warranty and service contract? Who in the company is responsible for such decisions?

The business buying process is more complex than the consumer decision process. Business buying takes place within a formal organization's budget, cost, and profit considerations. Furthermore, B2B and institutional buying decisions usually involve many people with complex interactions among individuals and organizational goals. To understand organizational buying behavior, business marketers require knowledge of influences on the purchase decision process, the stages in the organizational buying model, types of business buying situations, and techniques for purchase decision analysis.

INFLUENCES ON PURCHASE DECISIONS

B2B buying decisions react to various influences, some external to the firm and others related to internal structure and personnel. In addition to product-specific factors such as purchase price, installation, operating and maintenance costs, and vendor service, companies must consider broader environmental, organizational, and interpersonal influences.

Environmental Factors

Environmental conditions such as economic, political, regulatory, competitive, and technological considerations influence business buying decisions. MyMap may wish to defer purchases of the new equipment in times of slowing economic activity. During a recession, sales to auto companies might drop because households hesitate to spend money on a new car. The company would look at the derived demand for its products, possible changes in its sources of materials, employment trends, and similar factors before committing to such a large capital expenditure.

Environmental factors can also include natural disasters such as the recent floods that struck the U.S. Midwest and devastated the corn crop. Food producers, manufacturers of animal feed, ethanol plants, and livestock farmers who depend on corn as a raw material for their businesses face higher input prices and possibly reduced supplies. One commodities broker estimated that 2 million acres of corn might be lost. Corn farmers could recoup some of their own losses by planting soybeans, but their corn customers will face a possible shortage of more than 300 million bushels when supplies are already tight and demand is rising.[26]

Political, regulatory, and competitive factors also come into play in influencing purchase decisions. Passage of a privacy law that restricted GPS tracking would affect demand, as would competition from smart phones and other devices containing map features. Finally, technology plays a role in purchase decisions. When GPS systems were first introduced, many customers bought separate units to install in their cars. But as more new cars come factory equipped with the units, the market for stand-alone boxes naturally decreases.

Organizational Factors

Successful business-to-business marketers understand their customers' organizational structures, policies, and purchasing systems. A company with a centralized procurement function operates differently from one that delegates purchasing decisions to divisional or geographic units. Trying to sell to the local store when head office merchandisers make all the decisions would clearly waste salespeople's time. Buying behavior also differs among firms. For example, centralized buying tends to emphasize long-term relationships, whereas decentralized buying focuses more on short-term results. Personal selling skills and user preferences carry more weight in decentralized purchasing situations than in centralized buying.

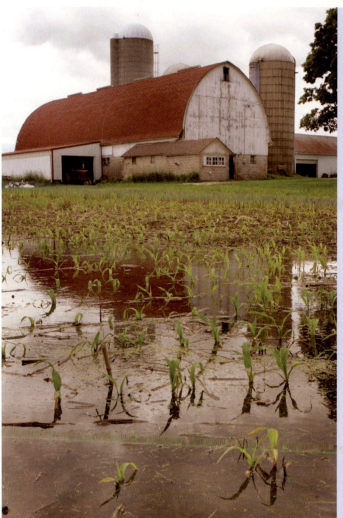

© Maryjo Walicki/MCT/Landov

Environmental factors can include natural disasters such as the recent floods that struck the U.S. Midwest and devastated the corn crop.

How many suppliers should a company patronize? Because purchasing operations spend more than half of each dollar their companies earn, consolidating vendor relationships can lead to large cost savings. However, a fine line separates maximizing buying power from relying too heavily on a few suppliers. Many companies engage in **multiple sourcing**—purchasing from several vendors. Spreading orders ensures against shortages if one vendor cannot deliver on schedule. However, dealing with many sellers can be counterproductive and take too much time. Each company must set its own criteria for this decision.

Interpersonal Influences

Many people may influence B2B purchases, and considerable time may be spent obtaining the input and approval of various organization members. Both group and individual forces are at work here. When committees handle buying, they must spend time to gain majority or unanimous approval. Also, each individual buyer brings to the decision process individual preferences, experiences, and biases.

Business marketers should know who in an organization will influence buying decisions for their products and should know each of their priorities. To choose a supplier for an industrial press, for example, a purchasing manager and representatives of the company's production, engineering, and quality-control departments may jointly decide on a supplier. Each of these principals may have a different point of view that the vendor's marketers must understand.

To effectively address the concerns of all people involved in the buying decision, sales personnel must be well versed in the technical features of their products. They must also interact well with employees of the various departments involved in the purchase decision. Sales representatives for

briefly speaking

"Tell me who's your friend and I'll tell you who you are."

—**Russian proverb**

medical products—traditionally called "detailers"—frequently visit hospitals and doctors' offices to discuss the advantages of their new products and leave samples with clinical staff. Representatives for IBM would most likely try to talk with staff who would potentially use its Linux application.

The Role of the Professional Buyer

Many large organizations attempt to make their purchases through systematic procedures employing professional buyers. In the trade industries, these buyers, often referred to as **merchandisers,** secure needed products at the best possible prices. Nordstrom has buyers for shoes and clothing that will ultimately be sold to consumers. Ford has buyers for components that will be incorporated into its cars and trucks. A firm's purchasing or merchandising unit devotes all of its time and effort in determining needs, locating and evaluating alternative suppliers, and making purchase decisions.

Purchase decisions for capital items vary significantly from those for expense items. Firms often buy expense items routinely with little delay. Capital items, however, involve major fund commitments and usually undergo considerable review.

One way a firm may attempt to streamline the buying process is through **systems integration,** or centralization of the procurement function. One company may designate a lead division to handle all purchasing. Another firm may choose to designate a major supplier as the systems integrator. This vendor then assumes responsibility for dealing with all of the suppliers for a project and for presenting the entire package to the buyer. In trade industries, this vendor is sometimes called a **category advisor** or **category captain.**

A business marketer may set up a sales organization to serve national accounts that deals solely with buyers at corporate headquarters. A separate field sales organization may serve buyers at regional production facilities.

Corporate buyers often use the Internet to identify sources of supplies. They view online catalogs and Web sites to compare vendors' offerings and obtain product information. Some use Internet exchanges to extend their supplier networks.

6 Outline the steps in the organizational buying process.

MODEL OF THE ORGANIZATIONAL BUYING PROCESS

An organizational buying situation takes place through a sequence of activities. Figure 6.2 illustrates an eight-stage model of an organizational buying process. Although not every buying situation requires all these steps, this figure provides a good overview of the whole process.

Stage 1: Anticipate or Recognize a Problem/Need/Opportunity and a General Solution

Both consumer and business purchase decisions begin when the recognition of problems, needs, or opportunities triggers the buying process. Perhaps a firm's computer system has become outdated or an account representative demonstrates a new service that could improve the company's performance. Companies may decide to hire an outside marketing specialist when their sales stagnate.

figure 6.2

Stages in the B2B Buying Process

Source: Based on Michael D. Hutt and Thomas W. Speh, *Business Marketing Management; B2B,* 10th ed. (Mason, OH: South-Western, 2010).

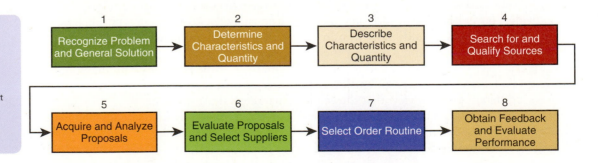

The problem may be as simple as needing to provide a good cup of coffee to a firm's employees. The founders of Keurig Incorporated, which supplies about 2.5 million individually brewed cups of coffee to U.S. homes and offices each day, started by asking themselves, "Why do we brew coffee a pot at a time when we drink it a cup at a time?"[27]

Now Serving: Our 2 Billionth K-Cup®

*I*n North America, the Keurig® system has generated over 2 billion cups of Keurig Brewed® gourmet coffee, tea and hot cocoa. That is a great milestone—but it is merely a measurement of what got us there:

- Leadership in single-cup brewing technology—for small, medium, and large offices

- A network of Keurig Authorized Distributors that are the best of the best

No wonder these brands have chosen to partner with us—offering over 190 K-Cup portion pack® varieties including hot cocoa.

KEURIG
www.keurig.com
©2008 Keurig, Incorporated

> The founders of Keurig recognized an opportunity when they asked themselves, "Why do we brew coffee a pot at a time when we drink it a cup at a time?"

Stage 2: Determine the Characteristics and Quantity of a Needed Good or Service

The coffee problem described in Stage 1 translated into a service opportunity for Keurig.® The small firm was able to offer a coffee system that would brew one perfect cup of coffee at a time, according to the preferences of each employee. After finding success in the offices of many accounting, law, and medical practices, the company developed a single-cup brewer for home use and has most recently introduced a model for hotel rooms at premier hotels such as Loews, Intercontinental, and LXR.[28]

Stage 3: Describe Characteristics and the Quantity of a Needed Good or Service

After determining the characteristics and quantity of needed products, B2B buyers must translate these ideas into detailed specifications. Customers told Keurig they wanted a foolproof, individual coffee maker. The Keurig system supplies a plastic K-Cup® portion pack, containing ground coffee that the individual simply places in the coffee maker—no measuring of water or coffee is required. Out comes the perfect cup of coffee. Firms could easily base the quantity requirements of the Keurig system on the number of coffee-drinking employees they have or the amount of space they occupy.

Stage 4: Search for and Qualify Potential Sources

Both consumers and businesses search for good suppliers of desired products. The choice of a supplier may be relatively straightforward—because there was no other machine like it, its early adopters had no trouble selecting the Keurig coffee system. Other searches may involve more complex decision making. A company that wants to buy a group life and health insurance policy, for example, must weigh the varying provisions and programs of many different vendors.

Stage 5: Acquire and Analyze Proposals

The next step is to acquire and analyze suppliers' proposals, often submitted in writing. If the buyer is a government or public agency, this stage of the purchase process may involve competitive bidding. During this process, each marketer must develop its bid, including a price, that will

satisfy the criteria determined by the customer's problem, need, or opportunity. While competitive bidding is less common in the business sector, a company may follow the practice to purchase nonstandard materials, complex products, or products made to its own specifications.

Stage 6: Evaluate Proposals and Select Suppliers

Next in the buying process, buyers must compare vendors' proposals and choose the one that seems best suited to their needs. Proposals for sophisticated equipment, such as a large computer networking system, can include considerable differences among product offerings, and the final choice may involve trade-offs.

Price is not the only criterion for the selection of a vendor. Relationship factors such as communication and trust may also be important to the buyer. Other issues include reliability, delivery record, time from order to delivery, quality, and order accuracy. In addition to speed and reliability, UPS offers specialized services such as consolidated shipments, real-time order tracking, and supply-chain management and reengineering to such valued customers as Harley-Davidson, Honeywell, and Cisco Systems. "UPS Supply Chain Solutions has helped us reduce our transportation costs, improve our delivery speed, keep our inventory lean, and improve service to our internal and external customers," said Harley-Davidson's director of transportation logistics.[29]

Stage 7: Select an Order Routine

Once a supplier has been chosen, buyer and vendor must work out the best way to process future purchases. Ordering routines can vary considerably. Most orders will, however, include product descriptions, quantities, prices, delivery terms, and payment terms. Today, companies have a variety of options for submitting orders: written documents, phone calls, faxes, or electronic data interchange (EDI).

Stage 8: Obtain Feedback and Evaluate Performance

At the final stage, buyers measure vendors' performances. Sometimes this judgment may involve a formal evaluation of each supplier's product quality, delivery performance, prices, technical knowledge, and overall responsiveness to customer needs. At other times, vendors may be measured according to whether they have lowered the customer's costs or reduced its employees' workloads. In general, bigger firms are more likely to use formal evaluation procedures, while smaller companies lean toward informal evaluations. Regardless of the method used, buyers should tell vendors how they will be evaluated.

Sometimes firms rely on independent organizations to gather quality feedback and summarize results. J. D. Power and Associates conducts research and provides information to a variety of firms so they can improve the quality of their goods and services.

assessment check

1. Why does the organizational buying process contain more steps than the consumer buying process?

2. List the steps in the organizational buying process.

---

7 Classify organizational buying situations.

CLASSIFYING BUSINESS BUYING SITUATIONS

As discussed earlier, business buying behavior responds to many purchasing influences such as environmental, organizational, and interpersonal factors. This buying behavior also involves the degree of effort the purchase decision demands and the levels within the organization where it is made. Like consumer behavior, marketers can classify B2B buying situations into three general categories, ranging from least to most complex: (1) straight rebuying, (2) modified rebuying, and (3) new-task buying. Business buying situations may also involve reciprocity. The following sections look at each type of purchase.

Straight Rebuying

The simplest buying situation is a **straight rebuy,** a recurring purchase decision in which a customer reorders a product that has satisfied needs in the past. The buyer already likes the product and terms of sale, so the purchase requires no new information. The buyer sees little reason to assess competing options and so follows a routine repurchase format. A straight rebuy is the business market equivalent of routinized response behavior in the consumer market. Purchases of low-cost items such as paper clips and pencils for an office are typical examples of straight rebuys. Reorders of coffee from Keurig would also be straight rebuys. Marketers who maintain good relationships with customers by providing high-quality products, superior service, and prompt delivery can go a long way toward ensuring straight rebuys.

Modified Rebuying

In a **modified rebuy,** a purchaser is willing to reevaluate available options. Buyers may see some advantage in looking at alternative offerings within their established purchasing guidelines. They might take this step if their current supplier has let a rebuy situation deteriorate because of poor service or delivery performance. Price, quality, and innovation differences can also provoke modified rebuys. Modified rebuys resemble limited problem solving in consumer markets.

B2B marketers want to induce current customers to make straight rebuys by responding to all of their needs. Competitors, on the other hand, try to lure those buyers away by raising issues that will persuade them to reconsider their decisions.

New-Task Buying

The most complex category of business buying is **new-task buying**—first-time or unique purchase situations that require considerable effort by the decision makers. Many companies decide, for instance, that they want to buy a customized data center rather than try to build their own. Companies like Procter & Gamble, Nokia, Ericsson, Unilever, and Pfizer have contracted with Hewlett-Packard (HP) to outsource their data center or information technology functions. These one-time purchases require customers and HP to work closely together to determine which functions to outsource, which to keep in house, if any, and which hardware and software configurations best meet their needs.[30] The consumer market equivalent of new-task buying is extended problem solving.

A new-task buy often requires a purchaser to carefully consider alternative offerings and vendors. A company entering a new field must seek suppliers of component parts that it has never before purchased. This new-task buying would require several stages, each yielding a decision of some sort. These decisions would include developing product requirements, searching out potential suppliers, and evaluating proposals. Information requirements and decision makers can complete the entire buying process, or they may change from stage to stage.

Reciprocity

Reciprocity—a practice of buying from suppliers who are also customers—is a controversial practice in a number of procurement situations. An office equipment manufacturer may favor a particular supplier of component parts if the supplier has recently made a major purchase of the manufacturer's products. Reciprocal arrangements traditionally have been common in industries featuring homogeneous products with similar prices such as the chemical, paint, petroleum, rubber, and steel industries.

Reciprocity suggests close links among participants in the organizational marketplace. It can add to the complexity of B2B buying behavior for new suppliers trying to compete with preferred vendors. Although buyers and sellers enter into reciprocal agreements in the United States, both the Department of Justice and the Federal Trade Commission view them as attempts to reduce competition. Outside the United States, however, governments may take more favorable views of reciprocity. In Japan, close ties between suppliers and customers are common.

ANALYSIS TOOLS

Two tools that help professional buyers improve purchase decisions are value analysis and vendor analysis. **Value analysis** examines each component of a purchase in an attempt to either delete the item or replace it with a more cost-effective substitute. Airplane designers have long recognized the need to make planes as light as possible. Value analysis supports using composite materials such as

Kevlar in airplane construction because it weighs less than the metals it replaces. The resulting fuel savings are significant for buyers in this marketplace.

Vendor analysis carries out an ongoing evaluation of a supplier's performance in categories such as price, EDI capability, back orders, delivery times, liability insurance, and attention to special requests. In some cases, vendor analysis is a formal process. Some buyers use a checklist to assess a vendor's performance. A checklist quickly highlights vendors and potential vendors that do not satisfy the purchaser's buying requirements.

assessment check

1. What are the four classifications of business buying situations?

2. Differentiate between value analysis and vendor analysis.

⑧ Explain the buying center concept.

buying center Participants in an organizational buying action.

The Buying Center Concept

The buying center concept provides a model for understanding B2B buying behavior. A company's **buying center** encompasses everyone involved in any aspect of its buying activity. A buying center may include the architect who designs a new research laboratory, the scientist who works in the facility, the purchasing manager who screens contractor proposals, the chief executive officer who makes the final decision, and the vice president of research who signs the formal contracts for the project. Buying center participants in any purchase seek to satisfy personal needs, such as participation or status, as well as organizational needs. A buying center is not part of a firm's formal organizational structure. It is an informal group whose composition and size vary among purchase situations and firms.

BUYING CENTER ROLES

Buying center participants play different roles in the purchasing decision process. **Users** are the people who will actually use the good or service. Their influence on the purchase decision may range from negligible to extremely important. Users sometimes initiate purchase actions by requesting products, and they may also help develop product specifications. Users often influence the purchase of office equipment.

Gatekeepers control the information that all buying center members will review. They may exert this control by distributing printed product data or advertisements or by deciding which salespeople may speak to which individuals in the buying center. A purchasing agent might allow some salespeople to see the engineers responsible for developing specifications but deny others the same privilege. The office manager for a medical group may decide whether to accept and pass along sales literature from a pharmaceutical detailer or sales representative.

At AFLAC, the supplemental insurance provider, decisions about whether to adopt new information technologies involve three levels of management—a high-level steering committee chaired by the company's U.S. president is the first; a review board headed by executives such as the chief administration officer, the chief information officer, and the chief accounting officer; and project boards run by different vice presidents. The company's U.S. president, Brian Abeyta, credits the layered system with saving the company time and money. "Because our governance process is gated," he says, "we've been able to ... make decisions to stop working on a project if we have found, as an organization, that it's not worth doing anymore."[31]

Influencers affect the buying decision by supplying information to guide evaluation of alternatives or by setting buying specifications. Influencers typically are technical staff such as engineers or quality-control specialists. Sometimes a buying organization hires outside consultants such as architects who influence its buying decisions.

The **decider** chooses a good or service, although another person may have the formal authority to do so. The identity of the decider is the most difficult role for salespeople to pinpoint. A firm's buyer may have the formal authority to buy, but the firm's chief executive officer may actually make the buying decision. Alternatively, a decider might be a design engineer who develops specifications that only one vendor can meet.

The **buyer** has the formal authority to select a supplier and to implement the procedures for securing the good or service. The buyer often surrenders this power to more influential members of the organization, though. The purchasing manager often fills the buyer's role and executes the details associated with a purchase order.

B2B marketers face the task of determining the specific role and the relative decision-making influence of each buying center participant. Salespeople can then tailor their presentations and information to the precise role an individual plays at each step of the purchase process. Business marketers have found their initial—and in many cases, most extensive—contacts with a firm's purchasing department often fail to reach the buying center participants who have the greatest influence, because these people may not work in that department at all.

Consider the selection of meeting and convention sites for trade or professional associations. The primary decision maker could be an association board or an executive committee, usually with input from the executive director or a meeting planner; the meeting planner or association executive might choose meeting locations, sometimes with input from members; finally, the association's annual-meeting committee or program committee might make the meeting location selection. Because officers change periodically, centers of control may change frequently. As a result, destination marketers and hotel operators must constantly assess how an association makes its decisions on conference locations.

INTERNATIONAL BUYING CENTERS

Two distinct characteristics differentiate international buying centers from domestic ones. First, marketers may have trouble identifying members of foreign buying centers because of cultural differences in decision-making methods. Second, a buying center in a foreign company often includes more participants than U.S. companies involve. International buying centers employ from one to 50 people, with 15 to 20 participants commonplace. Global B2B marketers must recognize and accommodate this greater diversity of decision makers.

International buying centers can change in response to political and economic trends. Many European firms once maintained separate facilities in each European nation to avoid tariffs and customs delays. When the European Union lowered trade barriers between member nations, however, many companies closed distant branches and consolidated their buying centers. The Netherlands has been one of the beneficiaries of this trend.

assessment check

1. Identify the five roles of people in a buying center decision.

2. What are some of the problems that U.S. marketers face in dealing with international buying centers?

Developing Effective Business-to-Business Marketing Strategies

9 Discuss the challenges of and strategies for marketing to government, institutional, and international buyers.

A business marketer must develop a marketing strategy based on a particular organization's buying behavior and on the buying situation. Clearly, many variables affect organizational purchasing decisions. This section examines three market segments whose decisions present unique challenges to B2B marketers: units of government, institutions, and international markets. Finally, it summarizes key differences between consumer and business marketing strategies.

CHALLENGES OF GOVERNMENT MARKETS

Government agencies—federal, state, and local—together make up the largest customer group in the United States. More than 85,000 government units buy a wide variety of products, including office supplies, furniture, concrete, vehicles, grease, military aircraft, fuel, and lumber, to name just a few.

To compete effectively, business marketers must understand the unique challenges of selling to government units. One challenge results because government purchases typically involve dozens of interested parties who specify, evaluate, or use the purchased goods and services. These parties may or may not work within the government agency that officially handles a purchase.

Government purchases are also influenced by social goals, such as "Buy American" provisions and minority subcontracting programs. Government entities such as the U.S. Postal Service strive to maintain diversity in their suppliers by making a special effort to purchase goods and services from small firms and companies owned by minorities and women. The Postal Service has developed a Supplier Diversity Corporate Plan to show its commitment to "providing opportunities to small, minority-owned, and women-owned businesses ... as an important business imperative."[32] The government also relies on its prime suppliers to subcontract to minority businesses.

Contractual guidelines create another important influence in selling to government markets. The government buys products under two basic types of contracts: fixed-price contracts, in which seller and buyer agree to a set price before finalizing the contract, and cost-reimbursement contracts, in which the government pays the vendor for allowable costs, including profits, incurred during performance of the contract. Each type of contract has advantages and disadvantages for B2B marketers. Although the fixed-price contract offers more profit potential than the alternative, it also carries greater risks from unforeseen expenses, price hikes, and changing political and economic conditions.

Government Purchasing Procedures

Many U.S. government purchases go through the General Services Administration (GSA), a central management agency involved in areas such as procurement, property management, and information resources management. The GSA buys goods and services for its own use and for use by other government agencies. In its role as, essentially, the federal government's business manager, it purchases billions of dollars' worth of products. The Defense Logistics Agency (DLA) serves the same function for the Department of Defense.

By law, most federal purchases must be awarded on the basis of bids, or written sales proposals, from vendors. As part of this process, government buyers develop specifications—detailed descriptions of needed items—for prospective bidders. U.S. government purchases must comply with the Federal Acquisition Regulation (FAR), an approximately 30,000-page set of standards originally designed to cut red tape in government purchasing. FAR standards have been further complicated by numerous exceptions issued by various government agencies. Because they provide services to various federal government agencies such as the Department of Energy, Environmental Protection Agency, and Department of Defense, large environmental engineering firms such as MACTEC, Tetra Tech, and Weston Solutions typically have procurement and contract specialists on staff. These specialists stay current with FAR standards and conduct internal quality-assurance and quality-control programs to make sure these standards are followed by their companies. Sometimes, despite safeguards, the process can become controversial. See the "Solving an Ethical Controversy" feature for one story.

State and local government purchasing procedures resemble federal procedures. Most states and many large cities have created buying offices similar to the GSA. Detailed specifications and open bidding are common at this level as well. Many state purchasing regulations give preference to in-state bidders.

Government spending patterns may differ from those in private industry. Because the federal government's fiscal year runs from October 1 through September 30, many agencies spend much of their procurement budgets in the fourth quarter, from July 1 to September 30. They hoard their funds to cover unexpected expenditures, and if they encounter no such problems, they find themselves with money to spend in late summer. Companies understand this system and keep their eyes on government bulletins so that they can bid on the listed agency purchases, which often involve large amounts of money.

Online with the Federal Government

Like their colleagues in the private sector, government procurement professionals are streamlining purchasing procedures with new technology. Rather than paging through piles of paper catalogs

Solving an ethical controversy

Is Government Purchasing a Level Playing Field?

In a government purchasing decision some are calling "the tanker soap opera," the Government Accountability Office (GAO) recently ruled that the U.S. aircraft manufacturer Boeing was right to protest the Air Force's award of a contract for an air refueling tanker. The purchase, worth about $108 billion over the next 25 years, had been awarded to a joint venture between Northrop Grumman and Airbus, a consortium of European companies—and Boeing's chief rival. But the GAO found the Air Force made several major errors in its buying process—including giving Northrop credit for designing a larger tanker than requested while underestimating the cost—and recommended that, in addition to bidding the job out again, the Air Force should "reimburse Boeing the costs of filing and pursuing the protest, including reasonable attorneys' fees."

Should the government be required to rebid the tanker contract?

PRO

1. Like other B2B purchasing decisions, the government's buying process should be above reproach. If that means rebidding a project, then it should be done.

2. The Air Force's failure to provide the two suppliers with the same information clearly biased the purchase decision.

CON

1. Boeing unfairly won the tanker contract several years ago when an Air Force procurement officer granted it special favors; she was later jailed. Northrop/Airbus should get it now.

2. Northrop/Airbus ultimately offers a better product in the larger plane and should be given the contract.

Summary

The Air Force had to respond to the GAO, whose opinion is influential but not binding. And after deliberations, the Pentagon announced that it would rebid the project. While Boeing executives praised the decision as a vindication, observers warned Northrop could still win the rebid. "The problem here was not with their plane—the GAO was explicit about that," said one defense analyst. "The problem here was with the way the Air Force went about evaluating the two planes being offered." Considering the controversial nature of the tanker bid, the Secretary of Defense announced that the Defense Department—not the Air Force—would handle the rebidding process.

Sources: Emma Vandore, "EADS Would Bid for $35 Billion Air Force Tanker Contract even if It Has to Share with Boeing," *Yahoo! Finance*, April 17, 2009, http://www.finance.yahoo.com; "Air Force Rebid May Favor Rival of Boeing," *The Seattle Times,* July 10, 2008, seattletimes.nwsource.com; Christopher Hinton, "Air Force Tanker Mishap Highlights Wider Problems," *Market Watch,* June 20, 2008, www.marketwatch.com; Dominic Gates, "Boeing Tanker 'Back in the Game' after GAO Backs Company's Protest," *The Seattle Times,* June 19, 2008, seattletimes.nwsource.com; James Wallace, "Boeing Back in Tanker Running," *Seattle Post-Intelligencer,* June 19, 2008, seattlepi.nwsource.com.

and submitting handwritten purchase orders, government buyers now prefer online catalogs that help them compare competing product offerings. In fact, vendors find doing business with the government almost impossible unless they embrace electronic commerce.

Vendors can sell products to the federal government through three electronic options. Web sites provide a convenient method of exchanging information for both parties. Government buyers locate and order products, paying with a federally issued credit card, and the vendors deliver the items within about a week. Another route is through government-sponsored electronic ordering systems, which help standardize the buying process. GSA Advantage allows federal employees to order products directly over the Internet at the preferred government price. The Electronic Posting System sends automatic notices of opportunities to sell to the government to more than 29,000 registered vendors. The Phoenix Opportunity System, set up by the Department of Commerce, provides a similar service for minority-owned companies. A pilot program at the Treasury is testing an electronic check-payment system to speed up the settling of vendor invoices.

Despite these advances, many government agencies remain less sophisticated than private-sector businesses. The Pentagon, for instance, is still coping with procurement procedures that

The Phoenix Opportunity System, set up by the Department of Commerce, provides a government-sponsored electronic ordering system for minority-owned companies.

© The Minority Business Development Agency (MBDA), www.mbda.gov

were developed over the last 50 years. However, it is introducing a streamlined approach to defense contracting that reduces the time necessary to develop specifications and select suppliers.

CHALLENGES OF INSTITUTIONAL MARKETS

Institutions constitute another important market. Institutional buyers include a wide variety of organizations such as schools, hospitals, libraries, foundations, clinics, churches, and not-for-profit agencies.

Institutional markets are characterized by widely diverse buying practices. Some institutional purchasers behave like government purchasers because laws and political considerations determine their buying procedures. Many of these institutions, such as schools and prisons, may even be managed by government units.

Buying practices can differ between institutions of the same type. In a small hospital, the chief dietitian may approve all food purchases, while in a larger medical facility, food purchases may go through a committee consisting of the dietitian and a business manager, purchasing agent, and cook. Other hospitals may belong to buying groups, perhaps health maintenance organizations or local hospital cooperatives. Still others may contract with outside firms to prepare and serve all meals.

Within a single institution, multiple buying influences may affect decisions. Many institutions, staffed by professionals such as physicians, nurses, researchers, and instructors, may also employ purchasing managers or even entire purchasing departments. Conflicts may arise among these decision makers. Professional employees may prefer to make their own purchase decisions and resent giving up control to the purchasing staff. This conflict can force a business marketer to cultivate both professionals and purchasers. A detailer for a pharmaceutical firm must convince physicians of the value to patients of a certain drug while simultaneously convincing the hospital's purchasing department that the firm offers competitive prices, good delivery schedules, and prompt service.

Group purchasing is an important factor in institutional markets because many organizations join cooperative associations to pool purchases for quantity discounts. Universities may join the Education and Institutional Purchasing Cooperative; hospitals may belong to regional associations; and chains of profit-oriented hospitals such as HCA Healthcare can also negotiate quantity discounts. Central headquarters staff usually handles purchasing for all members of such a chain.

Buying practices differ among institutions of the same type. In a small hospital, the chief dietitian may approve food purchases, while in a larger facility, food purchases may go through a committee.

© Rui Vieira/PA Photos/Landov

Diverse practices in institutional markets pose special challenges for B2B marketers. They must maintain flexibility in developing strategies for dealing with a range of customers, from large cooperative associations and chains to midsize purchasing departments and institutions to individuals. Buying centers can work with varying members, priorities, and levels of expertise. Discounts and effective distribution functions play important roles in obtaining—and keeping—institutions as customers.

CHALLENGES OF INTERNATIONAL MARKETS

To sell successfully in international markets, business marketers must consider buyers' attitudes and cultural patterns within areas where they operate. In Asian markets, a firm must maintain a local presence to sell products. Personal relationships are also important to business deals in Asia. Companies that want to expand globally often need to establish joint ventures with local partners. International marketers must also be poised to respond to shifts in cultural values.

Local industries, economic conditions, geographic characteristics, and legal restrictions must also be considered in international marketing. Many local industries in Spain specialize in food and wine; therefore, a maker of forklift trucks might market smaller vehicles to Spanish companies than to German firms, which require bigger, heavier trucks to serve the needs of that nation's large automobile industry.

Remanufacturing—efforts to restore worn-out products to like-new condition—can be an important marketing strategy in a nation that cannot afford to buy new products. Developing countries often purchase remanufactured factory machinery, which costs 35 to 60 percent less than new equipment.

Foreign governments represent another important business market. In many countries, government or state-owned companies dominate certain industries such as construction and other infrastructure sales. Additional examples include airport and highway construction, telephone system equipment, and computer networking equipment. Sales to a foreign government can involve an array of regulations. Many governments, like that of the United States, limit foreign participation in their defense programs. Joint ventures and countertrade are common, as are local content laws, which mandate domestic production of a certain percentage of a business product's components.

assessment check

1. What are some influences on government purchases?

2. Why is group purchasing important in institutional purchases?

3. What special factors influence international buying decisions?

Strategic
Implications of
Marketing
21st Century
in the

to develop marketing strategies for the B2B sector, marketers must first understand the buying practices that govern the segment they are targeting, whether it is the commercial market, trade industries, government, or institutions. Similarly, when selling to a specific organization, strategies must take into account the many factors that influence purchasing. B2B marketers must identify people who play the various roles in the buying decision and understand how these members interact with one another, other members of their own organizations, and outside vendors. Marketers must be careful to direct their marketing efforts to their organization, to broader environmental influences, and to individuals who operate within the constraints of the firm's buying center.

Review of Chapter Objectives

1 Explain each of the components of the business-to-business (B2B) market.

The B2B market is divided into four segments: the commercial market, trade industries, governments, and institutions. The commercial market consists of individuals and firms that acquire products to be used, directly or indirectly, to produce other goods and services. Trade industries are organizations such as retailers and wholesalers that purchase for resale to others. The primary purpose of government purchasing at federal, state, and local levels is to provide some form of public benefit. The fourth segment, institutions, includes a diverse array of organizations such as hospitals, schools, museums, and not-for-profit agencies.

2 Describe the major approaches to segmenting business-to-business (B2B) markets.

Business markets can be segmented by (1) demographics, (2) customer type, (3) end-use application, and (4) purchasing situation. The North American Industry Classification System (NAICS), instituted after the passage of NAFTA, helps further classify types of customers by the use of six digits.

3 Identify the major characteristics of the business market and its demand.

The major characteristics of the business market are geographic concentration, size and number of buyers, purchase decision procedures, and buyer–seller relationships. The major categories of demand are derived demand, volatile demand, joint demand, inelastic demand, and inventory adjustments.

4 Discuss the decision to make, buy, or lease.

Before a company can decide what to buy, it must decide whether to buy at all. A firm has three options: (1) make the good or service in-house; (2) purchase it from another organization; or (3) lease it from another organization. Companies may outsource goods or services formerly produced in-house to other companies either within their own home country or to firms in other countries. The shift of high-wage jobs from the home country to lower-wage locations is known as *offshoring*. If a company moves production to a country close to its own borders, it uses a *nearshoring* strategy. Each option has its benefits and drawbacks, including cost and quality control.

5 Describe the major influences on business buying behavior.

B2B buying behavior tends to be more complex than individual consumer behavior. More people and time are involved, and buyers often seek several alternative supply sources. The systematic nature of organizational buying is reflected in the use of purchasing managers to direct such efforts. Major organizational purchases may require elaborate and lengthy decision-making processes involving many people. Purchase decisions typically depend on combinations of such factors as price, service, certainty of supply, and product efficiency.

6 Outline the steps in the organizational buying process.

The organizational buying process consists of eight general stages: (1) anticipate or recognize a problem/need/opportunity and a general solution; (2) determine characteristics and quantity of needed good or service; (3) describe characteristics and quantity of needed good or service; (4) search for and qualify potential sources; (5) acquire and analyze proposals; (6) evaluate proposals and select supplier(s); (7) select an order routine; and (8) obtain feedback and evaluate performance.

7 Classify organizational buying situations.

Organizational buying situations differ. A straight rebuy is a recurring purchase decision in which a customer stays with an item that has performed satisfactorily. In a modified rebuy, a purchaser is willing to reevaluate available options. New-task buying refers to first-time or unique purchase situations that require considerable effort on the part of the decision makers. Reciprocity involves buying from suppliers who are also customers.

8 Explain the buying center concept.

The buying center includes everyone who is involved in some fashion in an organizational buying action. There are five buying center roles: users, gatekeepers, influencers, deciders, and buyers.

9 Discuss the challenges of and strategies for marketing to government, institutional, and international buyers.

A government purchase typically involves dozens of interested parties. Social goals and programs influence government purchases. Many U.S. government purchases involve complex contractual guidelines and often require detailed specifications and a bidding process. Institutional markets are challenging because of their diverse buying influences and practices. Group purchasing is an important factor because many institutions join cooperative associations to get quantity discounts. An institutional marketer must be flexible enough to develop strategies for dealing with a range of customers. Discounts and effective distribution play an important role. An effective international business marketer must be aware of foreign attitudes and cultural patterns. Other important factors include economic conditions, geographic characteristics, legal restrictions, and local industries.

assessment check: answers

1.1 Define B2B marketing.

Business-to-business, or B2B, marketing deals with organizational purchases of goods and services to support production of other products, to facilitate daily company operations, or for resale.

1.2 What is the commercial market?

The commercial market consists of individuals and firms that acquire products to be used, directly or indirectly, to produce other goods and services.

2.1 What are the four major ways marketers segment business markets?

Business markets can be segmented by (1) demographics, (2) customer type, (3) end-use application, and (4) purchasing situation.

2.2 What is the NAICS?

The North American Industry Classification System (NAICS) is a unified system for Mexico, Canada, and the United States to classify B2B market segments and ease trade.

3.1 Why is geographic segmentation important in the B2B market?

Certain industries locate in particular areas to be close to customers. Firms may choose to locate sales offices and distribution centers in these areas to provide more attentive service. For example, the Washington, D.C., area is favored by companies that sell to the federal government.

3.2   In what ways is the buyer–seller relationship important in B2B marketing?

Buyer–seller relationships often are more complex than consumer relationships, and they require superior communication among the organizations' personnel. Satisfying one major customer may mean the difference of millions of dollars to a firm.

3.3   What is global sourcing?

Global sourcing involves contracting to purchase goods and services from suppliers worldwide.

3.4   How does derived demand create volatile demand?

Business demand often is derived from consumer demand. Even modest shifts in consumer demand can produce disproportionate—and volatile—shifts in business demand.

3.5   Give an example of joint demand.

Both lumber and concrete are required to build most homes. If the lumber supply falls, the drop in housing construction will most likely affect the demand for concrete.

3.6   How might JIT II strengthen marketing relationships?

Under JIT II, suppliers place representatives at the customer's facility to work as part of an integrated, on-site customer–supplier team. Suppliers plan and take orders in consultation with the customer. This streamlining of the inventory process improves control of the flow of goods.

4.1   Identify two potential benefits of outsourcing.

Outsourcing allows firms to concentrate their resources on their core business. It also allows access to specialized talent or expertise that does not exist within the firm.

4.2   Identify two potential problems with outsourcing.

Many companies discover their cost savings are less than vendors sometimes promise. Also, companies that sign multiyear contracts may find their savings drop after a year or two.

5.1   Identify the three major factors that influence purchase decisions.

In addition to product-specific factors such as purchase price, installation, operating and maintenance costs, and vendor service, companies must consider broader environmental, organizational, and interpersonal influences.

5.2   What are the advantages and disadvantages of multiple sourcing?

Spreading orders ensures against shortages if one vendor cannot deliver on schedule. However, dealing with many sellers can be counterproductive and take too much time.

6.1   Why does the organizational buying process contain more steps than the consumer buying process?

The additional steps arise because business purchasing introduces new complexities that do not affect consumers.

6.2   List the steps in the organizational buying process.

The steps in organizational buying are (1) anticipate or recognize a problem/need/opportunity and a general solution; (2) determine characteristics and quantity of a needed good or service; (3) describe characteristics and quantity of needed good or service; (4) search for and qualify potential sources; (5) acquire and analyze proposals; (6) evaluate proposals and select supplier(s); (7) select an order routine; and (8) obtain feedback and evaluate performance.

7.1   What are the four classifications of business buying situations?

The four classifications of business buying are (1) straight rebuying, (2) modified rebuying, (3) new-task buying, and (4) reciprocity.

7.2   Differentiate between value analysis and vendor analysis.

Value analysis examines each component of a purchase in an attempt to either delete the item or replace it with a more cost-effective substitute. Vendor analysis carries out an ongoing evaluation of a supplier's performance in categories such as price, EDI capability, back orders, delivery times, liability insurance, and attention to special requests.

8.1   Identify the five roles of people in a buying center decision.

There are five buying center roles: users (those who use the product), gatekeepers (those who control the flow of information), influencers (those who provide technical information or specifications), deciders (those who actually choose the product), and buyers (those who have the formal authority to purchase).

8.2   What are some of the problems that U.S. marketers face in dealing with international buying centers?

International buying centers pose several problems. First, there may be cultural differences in decision-making methods. Second, a buying center in a foreign company typically includes more participants than is common in the United States. Third, international buying centers can change in response to political and economic conditions.

9.1   What are some influences on government purchases?

Social goals and programs often influence government purchases.

9.2   Why is group purchasing important in institutional purchases?

Group purchasing is an important factor because many institutions join cooperative associations to get quantity discounts.

9.3   What special factors influence international buying decisions?

An effective international business marketer must be aware of foreign attitudes and cultural patterns. Other important factors include economic conditions, geographic characteristics, legal restrictions, and local industries.

Marketing Terms You Need to Know

business-to-business (B2B) marketing 166
commercial market 168
trade industries 169
reseller 169
customer-based segmentation 171

North American Industry Classification System (NAICS) 172
end-use application segmentation 172
global sourcing 175
offshoring 179

nearshoring 179
outsourcing 179
buying center 186

Other Important Marketing Terms

customer relationship management (CRM) 172
derived demand 176
joint demand 177
inelastic demand 177
just-in-time (JIT)/just-in-time II (JIT II) 177
sole sourcing 177
multiple sourcing 181
merchandisers 182

systems integration 182
category advisor (category captain) 182
straight rebuy 184
modified rebuy 185
new-task buying 185
reciprocity 185
value analysis 185
vendor analysis 186

user 186
gatekeeper 186
influencer 186
decider 186
buyer 187
remanufacturing 191

Assurance of Learning Review

1. Which is the largest segment of the business market? What role does the Internet play in the B2B market? What role do resellers play in the B2B market?

2. How is customer-based segmentation beneficial to B2B marketers? Describe segmentation by purchasing situation.

3. How do the sizes and numbers of buyers affect B2B marketers? Why are buyer–seller relationships so important in B2B marketing?

4. Give an example of each type of demand.

5. For what reasons might a firm choose an option other than making a good or service in-house? Why is outsourcing on the rise? How is offshoring different from outsourcing?

6. What are some of the environmental factors that may influence buying decisions? Identify organizational factors that

may influence buying decisions. Describe the role of the professional buyer.

7. Why are there more steps in the organizational buying process than in the consumer buying process? Explain why feedback between buyers and sellers is important to the marketing relationship.

8. Give an example of a straight rebuy and a modified rebuy. Why is new-task buying more complex than the first two buying situations?

9. What buying center participant is a marketer likely to encounter first? In the buying center, who has the formal authority to make a purchase?

10. Describe some of the factors that characterize U.S. government purchases. Why are institutional markets particularly challenging?

Projects and Teamwork Exercises

1. In small teams, research the buying process through which your school purchases the following products:
   a. lab equipment for one of the science labs
   b. the school's telecommunications system
   c. food for the cafeteria
   d. classroom furniture
   Does the buying process differ for any of these products? If so, how?

2. As a team or individually, choose a commercial product—such as computer chips, flour for baking, paint, or equipment—and research and analyze its foreign market potential. Report your findings to the class.

3. In pairs or individually, select a firm in your area and request an interview with the person in charge of purchasing. In particular, ask this individual about the importance of buyer–seller relationships in his or her industry. Report your findings to the class.

4. In pairs, select a business product in one of two categories—capital or expense—and determine how derived demand will affect the sales of the product. Create a chart showing your findings.

5. As a team, research a firm such as Microsoft or Boeing to learn how it uses outsourcing or offshoring. Then report on what you think the benefits and drawbacks to the firm might be.

6. Imagine you and your teammates are buyers for a firm such as Olive Garden, Dick's Sporting Goods, Marriott, or another firm you like. Map out a logical buying process for a new-task purchase for your organization.

7. Form a team to conduct a hypothetical team selling effort for the packaging of products manufactured by a food company such as Kraft or General Mills. Have each team member cover a certain concern such as package design, delivery, and payment schedules. Present your marketing effort to the class.

8. Conduct research into the U.S. government's purchasing process. Select a federal agency or department such as the Environmental Protection Agency, National Aeronautics and Space Administration (NASA), or the Department of Health and Human Services. What types of purchases does it make? What is the range of contract amounts? Who are the typical suppliers? What type of process is involved in buying?

9. Find an advertisement with marketing messages targeted for an institutional market. Analyze the ad to determine how the marketer has segmented the market, who in the buying center might be the target of the ad, and what other marketing strategies may be apparent.

10. In teams, research the practice of remanufacturing business products such as factory machinery for foreign markets. What challenges do marketers of such products face?

Critical-Thinking Exercises

1. Imagine you are a wholesaler for dairy products such as yogurt and cheese, which are produced by a cooperative of small farmers. Describe what steps you would take to build relationships with both the producers—farmers—and retailers such as supermarkets.

2. Describe an industry that might be segmented by geographic concentration. Then identify some of the types of firms that might be involved in that industry. Keep in mind that these companies might be involved in other industries as well.

3. Imagine you are in charge of making the decision to lease or buy a fleet of automobiles for the limousine service for which you work. What factors would influence your decision and why?

4. Do you think online selling to the federal government benefits marketers? What might be some of the drawbacks to this type of selling?

Ethics Exercise

Suppose you work for a well-known local restaurant, and a friend of yours is an account representative for a supplier of restaurant equipment. You know the restaurant owner is considering upgrading some of the kitchen equipment. Although you have no purchasing authority, your friend has asked you to arrange a meeting with the restaurant owner. You have heard unflattering rumors about this supplier's customer service.

1. Would you arrange the meeting between your friend and your boss?

2. Would you mention the customer-service rumors either to your friend or your boss?

3. Would you try to influence the purchase decision in either direction?

Internet Exercises

1. **Marketing of ships.** Aker Yards (www.akeryards.com) is one of the world's largest ship builders. Visit the firm's Web site. Who are some of its largest customers? Click on the "vision and values" link at the site. List the firm's vision and values and discuss how they form the core of Aker Yard's marketing strategy.

2. **Small business assistance.** American Express offers a wide range of tools to assist small business. Go the American Express Small Business Web site (www.americanexpress.com/open) and prepare a report summarizing the types of services American Express offers to small businesses.

3. **Selling to government.** Federal, state, and local governments purchase billions of dollars worth of products each year. Most governments have established procurement systems and requirements for vendors. Visit the procurement site for the State of Florida (dms.myflorida.com/purchasing). Click on the "Doing Business with the State of Florida" link to learn more about what it takes to sell products to Florida.

Note: Internet Web addresses change frequently. If you don't find the exact site listed, you may need to access the organization's home page and search from there or use a search engine such as Google.

Case 6.1　Peerless Pump Puts Customers First

Pumps are the world's second most commonly used machines. They supply almost a quarter of global demand for electric

motor energy. Peerless Pump Co. of Indianapolis has been providing high-end industrial customers with reliable pumps and fire-protection systems for more than 85 years. By focusing on safety, quality, schedule, and cost—in that order—the firm has enjoyed steady growth and even increased its revenue expectations for the future. "Given the enthusiasm and management commitment, they are very attainable goals," says Vice President of Marketing and Business Planning Fred Bock.

A recent companywide marketing initiative called "One Peerless" focused the attention of the company's 430 employees, who work in five different U.S. locations, on improving flexibility, communication, value, and the speed of fulfilling business processes. "It is really easy to focus on needs, but we have taken a proactive approach to focusing on what our customers—both internal and external—truly want," Bock says. "One Peerless is a well-rounded operations, sales, and marketing plan that involves everyone associated with our company, from suppliers to employees to distributors to end users."

The company, with $120 million in annual sales, was spun from a private equity firm in 2007 to the Grundfos Group, a Danish pump company (the third largest in the world) that has been expanding rapidly in Eastern Europe, Asia, and North America and that sees "significant growth potential" in the U.S. market. "The synergies between our organizations are significant and will allow Peerless to accelerate the rapid growth we have enjoyed over the last few years," says Peerless CEO Dean Douglas.

Peerless, originally founded in California to supply agricultural irrigation pumps to orange growers, now counts city wastewater facilities, sports stadiums, airports, and skyscrapers around the world among its clients. With fuel and energy costs increasing, such customers are eager to save money on operations wherever they can. Peerless helps its clients cut costs by applying a "life cycle cost" approach to evaluating solutions to problems, and examining the costs—in both time and money—of repairing rather than replacing parts and equipment.

Looking at the costs of installation, maintenance, miscellaneous items, and especially energy in terms of a 20-year life cycle allows Peerless to compare several different possible solutions for its customers to choose from. The company identifies the particular pump features and specifications in each option that can best improve pump reliability and conserve energy, even in pump systems that move large volumes of water 24 hours a day. Market growth for new equipment far exceeds repairs as a revenue source, however, in order to minimize downtime from breakdowns and help customers make the right repair/replace decision, Peerless advocates ongoing training of its engineers and its customers in preventive maintenance and management of spare parts inventories. This strategy calls for maintaining a continuously open line of communication between Peerless and its end-user customers.

Questions for Critical Thinking

1. Do you think Peerless focuses on safety, quality, schedule, and cost in the right order to meet its customers' and distributors'

needs? Why or why not? How do you think a B2B company can most accurately determine what its business customers need and want?

2. What benefits does Peerless gain from helping its customers evaluate system repair as a potential alternative to costly replacement of a pump system? What strategies and business tools do you think the company must have in place to fulfill this customer need? Why is it important for Peerless to address it, if it is not as profitable for the firm as selling a new system?

Sources: Personal communication with Fred Bock, Peerless Pump, February 2009 and June 2008; Dean Douglas, "Aftermarket Business in 2007 and 2008," *Pumps & Systems,* February 2008, www.pump-zone.com; Peter Noll, "Determining the Real Cost of Powering a Pump," *World Pumps,* January 2008, pp. 32–33; "Peerless Pump Acquired," *Inside Indiana Business,* December 4, 2007, www.insideindianabusiness .com; Tom Spalding, "Acquisition Is Good News to Peerless," *Indianapolis Star,* December 4, 2007, p. C1.

Video Case 6.2   Business-to-Business Marketing at Flight 001

The written case on Flight 001 appears on page VC-6. The Flight 001 video is designed to expand and highlight the concepts in this chapter and the concepts and questions covered in the written video case.

Global Marketing

CHAP**7**TER

© Ted Aljibe/AFP/Getty Images

i'm lovin' it™
www.mcdonalds.com.hk

脆雞 飯tastic™

同維港一樣咁Fantastic!

"Global" Focus Drives McDonald's

"I'm lovin' it!" Since the mid-1950s, McDonald's has been dishing up hamburgers to a hungry public. The original McDonald's restaurant, a busy hamburger stand in San Bernardino, California, was the

joint venture of entrepreneurial brothers Dick and Mac McDonald. When a milkshake–mixer salesman named Ray Kroc paid them a visit in 1954, he persuaded the brothers to let him help them expand their

business to eight restaurants. The following year, Kroc opened a McDonald's in Des Plaines, Illinois. On its first day, sales totaled $366.12. The rest, as they say, is history.

Today, McDonald's restaurants can be found in more than 100 countries worldwide. The company grew through franchising: 70 percent of the more than 30,000 McDonald's restaurants are privately owned and operated.

But McDonald's success has an appeal that transcends culture. What was once a purely American phenomenon is now growing at a faster rate overseas than at home. With nearly 40 percent of total revenues, Europe has for the past few years regularly topped the United States in sales; U.S. revenues represent about 36 percent of the total. Moreover, McDonald's U.S. business grew a modest 7 percent during a recent year, while business in Europe grew 32 percent and in the Asia-Pacific market, an astonishing 69 percent.

As it extended its global reach, however, McDonald's has had to weather many storms. The company faced a beef scare connected to mad cow disease, and environmentalists accused McDonald's of using soybeans grown in an illegally deforested area of the Amazon rain forest. As a successful U.S.–based company expanding into developing nations, McDonald's periodically ends up as the poster child for numerous anti-American and globalization protests. The company learns something from each experience—and continues to move forward. For example, it leads the fast-food industry in its efforts to conserve the environment: developing green technologies for its restaurants and product packaging, working with its supply chain to minimize environmental impacts, and sponsoring local anti-littering and community beautification programs.

Although McDonald's operates on a global scale, does that mean the Big Mac rules supreme from Amsterdam to Mumbai? Not exactly. The operating formula behind the company's global growth has become "freedom within a framework." Under this decentralized model, the business units are "glocal"—managed not by American expatriates, as in earlier years, but by local talent. Country managers also have latitude to develop their own ad campaigns, make their own product decisions, and cater to local tastes.

The French enjoy a McDonald's concoction known as a "Croque McDo," a sandwich made from ham and melted Swiss cheese on toasted bread. In India, where religious dietary laws forbid the consumption of beef, the Maharaja Mac is a popular sandwich made of two chicken patties and smoky-flavored mayonnaise. Where the culture consumes more rice than potatoes, McDonald's restaurants may leave french fries off the menu in favor of, say, the Rice Burger in Taiwan, which consists of shredded beef between two rice patties. And Sweden was the site of a recent rollout of the Big Tasty: a 5.5-ounce beef patty doused with barbeque sauce and sharing a bun with three slices of cheese, lettuce, and tomatoes. The

OBJECTIVES

1
Describe the importance of global marketing from the perspectives of the individual firm and the nation.

2
Identify the major components of the environment for global marketing.

3
Outline the basic functions of GATT, WTO, NAFTA, FTAA, CAFTA-DR, and the European Union.

4
Identify the alternative strategies for entering foreign markets.

5
Differentiate between a global marketing strategy and a multidomestic marketing strategy.

6
Describe the alternative marketing mix strategies used in global marketing.

7
Explain the attractiveness of the United States as a target market for foreign marketers.

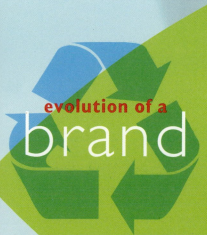

evolution of a brand

McDonald's Corporation provides a classic example of the challenges facing organizations that seek to grow their business by offering their products to customers worldwide. When the company first opened restaurants outside the United States, it operated on the belief that customers should have the same dining experience whether they were in Kalamazoo or Kuwait City. In those days, McDonald's relied almost exclusively on Americans living abroad to manage the overseas business. Over time, however, McDonald's has achieved success with local talent in the countries where it operates—and it has discovered it can maintain brand consistency even when catering to local taste preferences.

- Was it important for McDonald's to begin hiring local nationals to manage business units outside the United States? Why? In your opinion, could the company have achieved the same level of success with American managers in leadership positions?

evolution of a brand
continued

840-calorie sandwich was such a hit that it now sells all over Europe, Latin America, and Australia. But don't expect to find the Big Tasty on the menu at your local McDonald's: in a country where drive-throughs account for 70 percent of sales, consumer testers reported the enormous sandwich was too messy to eat in the car.[1]

- To elevate young people's skills, the British government has named McDonald's basic staff management training program equivalent to an advanced high-school diploma in that country. Some observers believe the training program could help equip McDonald's workers for entry to technical college or university. What do you see as the career advantages or disadvantages of such training?

chapter overview

importing Purchasing foreign goods and services.

exporting Marketing domestically produced goods and services in foreign countries.

Global trade now accounts for roughly 29 percent of the U.S. gross domestic product (GDP), compared with 10 percent 30 years ago.[2] Figure 7.1 shows the top ten nations with which the United States trades. Those ten countries account for nearly 63 percent of U.S. imports and 58 percent of U.S. exports.

Global trade can be divided into two categories: **exporting,** marketing domestically produced goods and services abroad, and **importing,** purchasing foreign goods and services. Global trade is vital to a nation and its marketers for several reasons. It expands markets, makes production and distribution economies possible, allows companies to explore growth opportunities in other nations, and makes them less dependent on economic conditions in their home nations. Many also find that global marketing and trade can help them meet customer demand, reduce costs, and provide valuable information on potential markets around the world.

figure 7.1

Top U.S. Trading Partners—Total Trade Including Exports and Imports

Source: Data from U.S. Census Bureau, "Top Trading Partners—Total Trade, Exports, Imports," Foreign Trade Division, census.gov/foreign-trade/statistics, accessed May 5, 2009

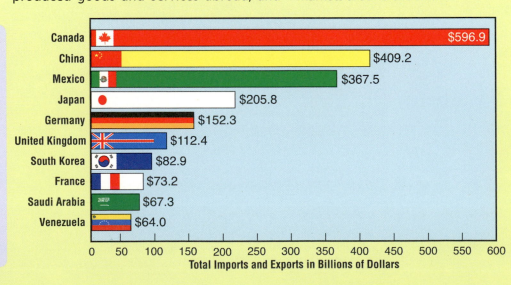

Country	Total Imports and Exports in Billions of Dollars
Canada	$596.9
China	$409.2
Mexico	$367.5
Japan	$205.8
Germany	$152.3
United Kingdom	$112.4
South Korea	$82.9
France	$73.2
Saudi Arabia	$67.3
Venezuela	$64.0

For North American marketers, trade with foreign markets is especially important because the U.S. and Canadian economies represent a mature market for many products. Outside North America, however, it is a different story. Economies in many parts of sub-Saharan Africa, Asia, Latin America, Eastern Europe, and the Middle East are growing rapidly. This opens up new markets for U.S. products as consumers in these areas have more money to spend and as the need for American goods and services by foreign companies expands.

Global trade also builds employment. The United Nations estimates that 65,000 transnational corporations are operating today, employing more than 54 million workers directly and through subsidiaries. Many of these companies and their subsidiaries represent **related party trade,** which includes trade by U.S. companies with their subsidiaries overseas as well as trade by U.S. subsidiaries of foreign-owned firms with their parent companies. According to the U.S. Department of Commerce, related party trade in a recent year accounted for over 40 percent of total goods traded.[3] Because importing and exporting of so many goods and services play such an important role in the U.S. economy, your future job might very well involve global marketing, either here in the United States or overseas.

Global marketers carefully evaluate the marketing concepts described in other chapters. However, transactions that cross national borders involve additional considerations. For example, different laws, varying levels of technological capability, economic conditions, cultural and business norms, and consumer preferences often require new strategies. Companies that want to market their products worldwide must reconsider each of the marketing variables—product, distribution, promotion, and price—in terms of the global marketplace. To succeed in global marketing, today's marketers answer questions such as these:

- How do our products fit into a foreign market?

- How can we turn potential threats into opportunities?

- Which strategic alternatives will work in global markets?

Many of the answers to these questions can be found by studying techniques used by successful global marketers. This chapter first considers the importance and characteristics of foreign markets. It then examines the international marketing environment, the trend toward multinational economic integration, and the steps that most firms take to enter the global marketplace. Next, the importance of developing a global marketing mix is discussed. The chapter closes with a look at the United States as a target market for foreign marketers.

The Importance of Global Marketing

As the list of the world's ten largest corporations shown in Table 7.1 reveals, half of these companies are headquartered in the United States. For most U.S. companies—both large and small—global marketing is rapidly becoming a necessity. The demand for foreign products in the fast-growing economies of the Pacific Rim and other Asian nations offers one example of the benefits of thinking globally. In a recent year, U.S. exports to China alone rose nearly 20 percent.[4] This increase was due partly to a weak American dollar but also because Asian consumers believe American

❘ Describe the importance of global marketing from the perspectives of the individual firm and the nation.

table 7.1   World's Ten Largest Marketers (Ranked by Annual Sales)

Rank	Company	Country	Industry	Sales (in billions of dollars)
1	Royal Dutch Shell	Netherlands	Oil and gas	$458
2	ExxonMobil	United States	Oil and gas	426
3	Wal-Mart Stores	United States	Retailing	406
4	BP	United Kingdom	Oil and gas	361
5	Toyota Motor	Japan	Consumer durable goods	263
6	Chevron	United States	Oil and gas	255
7	ConocoPhillips	United States	Oil and gas	225
8	Total	France	Oil and gas	223
9	ING Group	Netherlands	Insurance	214
10	General Electric	United States	Conglomerate	183

Source: Data from "The Global 2000: Ranked by Annual Sales," *Forbes*, April 8, 2009, www.forbes.com.

goods are higher quality than those made in their own countries. International marketers recognize how the slogan "Made in the USA" yields tremendous selling power.

Over the last decade, U.S. goods and services exports have increased about 72 percent.[5] In a recent year, the United States produced nearly $14 trillion in goods and services, with manufacturing exports rising by $80 billion and farm exports by $20 billion. Some economists say this increase, which sent nearly one in nine dollars' worth of produced goods and services overseas, helped delay the U.S. economy's recession.[6] Among the leading U.S. firms in revenues generated from exports are Boeing, Intel, Motorola, and Caterpillar.

Wal-Mart currently ranks as the world's largest private employer—with about 2.2 million employees—and the largest retailer; its annual sales are 50 percent greater than those of Target, Sears, Costco, and Kmart combined. The retail giant is currently devoting billions of dollars in expansion efforts abroad in Canada, China, Central America, India, Japan, South America, and the United Kingdom.[7]

The rapid globalization of business and the boundless nature of the Internet have made it possible for every marketer to become an international marketer. And while it isn't easy to be a successful marketer on the Web and larger firms have the advantage of more resources and wider distribution systems, smaller companies can build Web sites for as little as a few hundred dollars and can bring products to market quickly. Bidz.com, an online jewelry auctioneer, has seen its profits grow nearly sevenfold since it was founded a few years ago. Small companies like Bidz.com can succeed by being nimble and capitalizing on downturns in the economy. The company looked beyond its usual merchandising source—buying inventory closeouts from jewelry makers—to shopping at bankruptcy auctions, where it picked up new merchandise at pennies on the dollar.[8]

Just as some firms depend on foreign and Internet sales, others rely on purchasing raw materials abroad as input for their domestic manufacturing operations. A North Carolina furniture manufacturer may depend on purchases of South and Central American teak, while 21st-century furniture retailers take advantage of increased Chinese-made styling and quality and their traditionally low prices. Among the top U.S. imports are crude oil, computers and computer accessories, foods and livestock feed, and pharmaceuticals.[9]

SERVICE AND RETAIL EXPORTS

The United States has seen great shifts in the sources of its annual production over the years. In the 1800s, more than 90 percent of Americans worked in farming; today, less than 1.5 percent do.

Wal-Mart currently ranks as the world's largest employer, with about 2.2 million associates. They are devoting billions of dollars to expansion efforts abroad.

Likewise, manufactured goods no longer account for the lion's share of U.S. production output; today, only about 16 percent of the workforce works in manufacturing. Despite these shifts in the work population, the United States continues to produce record volumes of agricultural and manufactured goods.

The service industry has seen steady growth, with 82 percent of Americans now working in services. Nearly four of every five dollars in the nation's gross domestic product (GDP) comes from services such as banking, entertainment, business and technical services, retailing, and communications.[10] Although manufacturing exports are healthier than they were a decade ago, these figures represent a profound change from a largely manufacturing to a largely service economy. Still, manufacturers as diverse as General Motors and Procter & Gamble strive to serve growing markets such as China. GM offers a wide range of car models to Chinese consumers, while P&G offers some of its most popular brands such as Tide and Crest.

In addition to agricultural products and manufactured goods, the United States is the world's largest exporter of services and retailing. Of the approximately $497 billion in annual U.S. service exports, much of it comes from travel and tourism—money spent by foreign nationals visiting the United States.[11] But China is expected to become the number one tourist destination in the world before 2020, as well as the fourth-largest source of tourists; in a recent year, nearly 35 million Chinese traveled outside their country. Hong Kong, the United States, and the United Kingdom together account for 70 percent of the overseas investment in China's tourism industry.[12]

The most profitable U.S. service exports are business and technical services such as engineering, financial, computing, legal services, insurance, and entertainment. The financial services industry, already a major presence outside North America, is expanding globally via the Internet. Nearly half the world's active Web population visit a finance Web site at least once a month, with online stock trading and banking leading the way. And more than one of every four Europeans with Internet access currently banks online. A glance at the increasing number of foreign companies listed on the New York Stock Exchange illustrates the importance of global financial services. A number of global service exporters are household names in the United States: American Express, AT&T, Citigroup, Disney, and Allstate Insurance. Many earn a substantial percentage of their revenues from international sales. Others are smaller firms, such as the many software firms that

"Globalization and free trade do spur economic growth, and they lead to lower prices on many goods."

—Robert Reich (b. 1946)
FORMER U.S. SECRETARY OF LABOR

have found overseas markets receptive to their products. Still others are nonprofit organizations such as the U.S. Postal Service, which is attempting to increase overall revenues by operating a worldwide delivery service. The USPS competes with for-profit firms such as UPS and Federal Express.

The entertainment industry is another major service exporter. Movies, TV shows, and music groups often travel to the ends of the earth to entertain their audiences. Almost a century of exposure to U.S.-made films, television programs, and, more recently, music video clips has made international viewers more familiar with American culture and geography than that of any other nation on earth. Fox TV Studios is collaborating with production companies overseas on a TV drama series, reality shows, and game shows. Fox programs produced in Colombia and Chile are filmed in English and Spanish. The company is also in talks with producers in Poland and Bulgaria.[13]

U.S. retailers, ranging from Foot Locker and The Gap to Office Depot and Costco, have opened stores around the world. Wal-Mart, which operates in Japan and the United Kingdom, is considering opening stores in Russia. Earlier, the company pulled out of Germany and South Korea when its stores there were unprofitable.[14]

BENEFITS OF GOING GLOBAL

Besides generating additional revenue, firms expand operations outside their home country to gain other benefits, including new insights into consumer behavior, alternative distribution strategies, and advance notice of new products. By setting up foreign offices and production facilities, marketers may encounter new products, new approaches to distribution, or clever new promotions that they may apply successfully in their domestic market or in other international markets.

Global marketers typically are well positioned to compete effectively with foreign competitors. A major key to achieving success in foreign markets is the ability to adapt products to local preferences and culture. As discussed earlier, McDonald's succeeded outside the United States by paying attention to local tastes and modifying its menu. Similarly, Yum! Brands, parent of KFC and Pizza Hut, has been highly successful in China by catering to Chinese tastes. Its KFC brand became the first fast-food chain in China when it opened a restaurant there in 1987. KFC augmented its familiar chicken-based menu with such Chinese staples as fish, porridge, fried dough, beef rice, bean curd, and egg tarts. Today, Yum! is China's largest restaurant chain, with more than 2,500 KFC and Pizza Hut locations and over $2 billion in annual sales.[15]

A product as seemingly universal as pizza must be localized as well. Papa John's has over 3,200 pizza shops worldwide, including 450 in 28 countries outside the United States. Expansion plans are under way to serve the booming middle classes in China and Russia and to support a growing population in the Middle East. But buying behaviors differ around the globe. While Americans tend to prefer carryout or home delivery, customers in China and Russia like to eat their pizza in a restaurant, so Papa John's built attractive seating areas and added soups and salads to the menu. Portion sizes differ, too. Pizzas in the Middle East are one inch smaller than in the United States, and while China has the same pizza sizes as America, more Chinese tend to order the small pizza. In addition, as local tastes differ, so do pizza toppings. In Korea, potato wedges are common; in China, it's shrimp. And if you want green peas on your pizza, try a Papa John's in the Middle East.[16]

Because companies must perform the marketing functions of buying, selling, transporting, storing, standardizing and grading, financing, risk taking, and obtaining market information in both domestic and global markets, some may question the wisdom of treating global marketing as a distinct subject. But as this chapter will explain, there are similarities and differences that influence strategies for both domestic and global marketing.

assessment check

1. Define *importing* and *exporting*.

2. What is the largest category of exports from the United States?

3. What must global marketers do effectively to reach foreign markets?

Papa John's has over 3,200 pizza shops worldwide. As local tastes differ, so do pizza toppings.

The International Marketing Environment

As in domestic markets, the environmental factors discussed in Chapter 3 have a powerful influence on the development of a firm's global marketing strategy. Marketers must pay close attention to changing demand patterns as well as competitive, economic, social-cultural, political-legal, and technological influences when they venture abroad. The need for energy has hit the global market, so search for new, clean energy sources is a worldwide phenomenon, as the "Marketing Success" feature describes.

INTERNATIONAL ECONOMIC ENVIRONMENT

A nation's size, per-capita income, and stage of economic development determine its prospects as a host for international business expansion. Nations with low per-capita incomes may be poor markets for expensive industrial machinery but good ones for agricultural hand tools. These nations cannot afford the technical equipment that powers an industrialized society. Wealthier countries may offer prime markets for many U.S. industries, particularly those producing consumer goods and services and advanced industrial products.

But some less industrialized countries are growing fast. India and China, for example, may rival the United States in world economic importance in a generation or two. Although the U.S. per-capita GDP of $45,800 ranks way above China's $5,300 and India's $2,700, these nations have far larger populations and thus more potential human capital to develop in the future.[17] Their ability to import technology and foreign capital, as well as to train scientists and engineers and invest in research and development, ensures that their growth will be rapid and their income gaps with the United States will close quickly. In a recent year, India's GDP rose 9.2 percent and China's rose 11.4 percent, but the United States' GDP grew only 2.2 percent.[18]

Infrastructure—the underlying foundation for modern life and efficient marketing that includes transportation, communications, banking, utilities, and public services—is another important economic factor to consider when planning to enter a foreign market. An inadequate infrastructure may constrain marketers' plans to manufacture, promote, and distribute goods and services in

2 **Identify the major components of the environment for global marketing.**

In countries including Thailand, rivers are used to transport crops. The boats can become retail outlets in so-called floating markets.

© Hiroyuki Matsumoto/Photographer's Choice/Getty Images

a particular country. People living in countries blessed by navigable waters often rely on them as inexpensive, relatively efficient alternatives to highways, rail lines, and air transportation. Thai farmers use their nation's myriad rivers to transport their crops. Their boats even become retail outlets in so-called *floating markets*, like the one located outside the capital city of Bangkok. Often the population in rural areas begins to shift to where the infrastructure is more developed. This change is happening in both China and India. Current projections say that in 20 years China's cities will have an additional 350 million people—more than the total population of the United States today. And 20 years from now, it's estimated that more than two-fifths of India's population will live in its cities, as compared with just over one-quarter of India's urban population today.[19] Marketers expect

MARKETING SUCCESS　Scotland Rides the Wave

Background. With skyrocketing oil prices, the search for alternative energy has stepped up worldwide. In Germany and the United States, companies look to convert wind energy with turbines. Since the 1930s, Iceland has used geothermal power to heat its capital city of Reykjavik. Brazil, the United States, and other countries are experimenting with ethanol from sugar cane, corn, and other organic materials. Meanwhile, Scotland is looking to its seacoasts for answers.

The Challenge. From water comes wave power. The powerful waves of the North Sea and Atlantic Ocean hold

the promise of this predictable, renewable energy—cleaner, more efficient, and more cost-effective than any other energy source to date. Experts say the United Kingdom has sufficient wave capacity to generate up to a quarter of its annual energy demand. According to the World Energy Council, wave energy has a market potential of more than $1 trillion, roughly equivalent to the existing markets for nuclear and hydroelectric power.

The Strategy. Pledging that one-third of its electricity will come from renewable resources by 2011, the Scottish

developing economies to have substandard utility and communications networks. China encountered numerous problems in establishing a 21st-century communications industry infrastructure. The Chinese government's answer was to bypass the need for landline telephone connections by leapfrogging technologies and moving directly to cell phones.

Changes in exchange rates can also complicate international marketing. An **exchange rate** is the price of one nation's currency in terms of another country's currency. Fluctuations in exchange rates can make a nation's currency more or less valuable compared with those of other nations. In today's global economy, imbalances in trade, dependence on fossil fuels, and other conditions affect the currencies of many countries, not just one or two. The rising cost of energy and raw materials, stricter business standards, and a faltering U.S. dollar contributed to price increases for most goods produced in China.[20]

At the beginning of the 21st century, most members of the European Union (EU) switched to the euro as the replacement to their traditional francs and liras. The long-range idea behind the new currency is that switching to a single currency will strengthen Europe's competitiveness in the global marketplace. Russian and many eastern European currencies are considered *soft currencies* that cannot be readily converted into such hard currencies as the dollar, euro, or Japanese yen.

INTERNATIONAL SOCIAL-CULTURAL ENVIRONMENT

Before entering a foreign country, marketers should study all aspects of that nation's culture, including language, education, religious attitudes, and social values. The French love to debate and are comfortable with frequent eye contact. In China, humility is a prized virtue, colors have special significance, and it is insulting to be late. Swedes value consensus and do not use humor in negotiations. Navigating these rules that are commonly understood among the citizens of a foreign country takes time, patience, and a willingness to learn about other cultures. The "Etiquette Tips for Marketing Professionals" feature presents just a few tips on doing business globally.

Language plays an important role in global marketing. Table 7.2 lists the world's ten most frequently spoken languages. Marketers must make sure not only to use the appropriate language or languages for a country but also to ensure the message is correctly translated and conveys the intended meaning.

Firms that rely on call centers located in India and staffed by Indian nationals have discovered an occasional language gap. But these employees do speak English, which is the second most spoken language in the world. Despite some glitches, the call centers, along with other outsourced

exchange rate Price of one nation's currency in terms of another country's currency.

briefly speaking

"There have been many definitions of hell, but for the English the best definition is that it is a place where the Germans are the police, the Swedish are the comedians, the Italians are the defence force, Frenchmen dig the roads, the Belgians are the pop singers, the Spanish run the railways, the Turks cook the food, the Irish are the waiters, the Greeks run the government, and the common language is Dutch."

—**David Frost (b. 1939)**
ENGLISH AUTHOR AND TV SHOW HOST

government built the European Marine Energy Centre. The world's only test facility for tidal and wave energy, the center is a floating laboratory in the Orkney Islands off the coast of Scotland. The waters that separate the Orkneys from the Scottish mainland are known as "the Saudi Arabia of tidal power" for their rich energy supply. Scientists at the research center are working to harness the power of the waves and ready it for commercial consumption. In 1998, General Electric helped fund Pelamis Wave Power, a Scottish energy company headquartered there.

The Outcome. Since its founding, Pelamis has won global awards for wave-technology innovation. Recently it installed three turbines off the coast of Portugal. The power generated from these turbines will light an estimated 15,000 homes. Additional projects are under way, including the installation of the "world's largest

wave energy farm" in the Orkney Islands, which ultimately could help supply 20 percent of the United Kingdom's electricity needs. While wave technology is still in the early stages, the Scottish government is funding it aggressively. To further expedite global development of wave power, the government recently introduced its Saltire Prize, a $20 million award for scientists who harness marine energy.

Sources: Company Web site, www.pelamiswave.com, accessed May 5, 2009; "£10m Marine Energy Prize Unveiled," *BBC News,* April 2, 2008, news.bbc.co.uk; Matthew Boyle, "Scottish Power," *Fortune,* March 17, 2008, p. 28; "Europe Is Leading the Way in Marine Energy," *Reuters,* January 17, 2008, www.reuters.com; Paul Davidson, "Marine Energy Can Be Forecast," *USA Today,* April 20, 2007, www.usatoday.com; Lester Haines, "Scotland to Float 'World's Biggest' Wave Farm," *The Register,* February 20, 2007, www.theregister.co.uk; Scottish government Web site, "Scotland Seeks World Lead in Marine Power," February 20, 2007, www.scotland.gov.uk.

Etiquette Tips for Marketing Professionals

Global Business Etiquette

One of the first lessons marketing professionals learn about global markets is that no single set of rules applies to all the world's cultures. Customs, traditions, and cultural cues vary widely. For instance, while meetings typically start late in Latin America, Japan does not have a word for "late." Doing your homework about countries and cultures with which you'll come in contact is the best way to ensure that you demonstrate respect for the ways in which they differ from your own.

Here are a few social and cultural differences you may come across.

- U.S. executives often prize quick decisions that reduce the need for meetings; in Sweden detailed debates and multiple meetings are welcomed.
- Women are greeted before men in Denmark; in Russia women are normally not greeted at all during introductions.
- The French may introduce themselves with last name first and consider it rude to call a colleague by his or her first name. Danes and North Americans often use first names only.
- Alcohol is not generally ordered during business lunches in Canada. In New Zealand, business is discussed only before or after the meal, not during.
- Business gifts are usually exchanged in Japan, Indonesia, the Philippines, and the Middle East, but not in Africa and Australia.
- While consensus in decision-making is the norm in both Japan and Latin America, the Japanese begin with the younger members of any group. In Latin America the group defers to the eldest members.
- Many Asian cultures value business cards as representative of the person giving them. To show respect, accept business cards with both hands in Japan, China, Singapore, and Hong Kong; place them carefully with other important documents; and never write on them.
- In India business cards are exchanged with the right hand. Because English is widely spoken among businesspeople, they need not be translated into Hindi, although translation into the local language is recommended in most other countries.

Sources: Lydia Ramsey, "Minding Your Global Manners in Business," *Home Office Weekly*, http://www.homeofficeweekly.com, accessed April 16, 2009; Neil Payne, "Going Global? Your Passport to Business Card Etiquette," Clark & Reid, http://www.clarkreid.com/newsletter, accessed April 16, 2009; "Global Guide to Business Etiquette," *Monocle* magazine, http://www.monocle.com, accessed April 16, 2009; "Global Business Etiquette," *Expat Focus*, http://www.expatfocus.com, accessed April 16, 2009; "Global Workers Seek Etiquette Training," *Inc.*, April 16, 2008, http://www.inc.com.

table 7.2   **The World's Most Frequently Spoken Languages**

Rank	Language	Number of Speakers
1	Mandarin (Chinese)	1 billion
2	English	514 million
3	Hindustani	496 million
4	Spanish	425 million
5	Russian	275 million
6	Arabic	256 million
7	Bengali	215 million
8	Portuguese	194 million
9	Malay-Indonesian	176 million
10	French	129 million

Source: Data from "Most Widely Spoken Languages in the World," www.infoplease.com, accessed May 5, 2009.

operations, are booming—creating jobs and a new middle class in India. The country's economy has benefited hugely from the influx of foreign direct investment that came after the country loosened restrictions on foreign ownership. India now boasts the fastest-growing market for wireless services; mobile-phone sales tripled in a two-year period recently. Computer equipment maker Cisco Systems expects to triple its employee population in India to 10,000 by 2010.[21]

INTERNATIONAL TECHNOLOGICAL ENVIRONMENT

More than any innovation since the telephone, Internet technology has made it possible for both large and small firms to connect to the entire world. The Internet transcends political, economic, and cultural barriers, reaching every corner of the globe. It has made it possible for traditional brick-and-mortar retailers to add new business channels. It also helps developing nations compete with industrialized nations. However, a huge gap still exists between the regions with the greatest Internet usage and those with the least. Asia, Europe, and North America together account for more than 82 percent of the world's total Internet usage. Latin America and the Caribbean follow with nearly 10 percent, while Africa accounts for nearly 4 percent, the Middle East 3 percent, and Oceania/Australia just below 2 percent. Despite those numbers, usage in the Middle East jumped nearly 1,200 percent in just one year, and Africa's usage grew more than 1,000 percent.[22]

Technology presents challenges for global marketers that extend beyond the Internet and other telecommunications innovations. A major issue involving food marketers is genetic reengineering. Although U.S. grocery shelves are filled with foods grown with genetically modified organisms (GMOs), most Americans are unaware they are eating GMO foods because no labeling disclosures are required. However, in Europe, several organizations have moved to ban these foods. Local and regional authorities have declared themselves "GMO-free," but the European Court of Justice has yet to issue a ruling that would ban GMOs throughout the European Union. With soaring food prices and global grain shortages, governments the world over are rethinking their position on foods made from crops that are engineered to resist pests and drought.[23] This complex issue affects almost every marketer in the global food industry.

INTERNATIONAL POLITICAL-LEGAL ENVIRONMENT

Global marketers must continually stay abreast of laws and trade regulations in each country in which they compete. Political conditions often influence international marketing as well. Political unrest in places such as the Middle East, Africa, eastern Europe, Spain, and South America sometimes results in acts of violence such as destruction of a firm's property or even deaths from bombings or other terrorist acts. As a result, many Western firms have set up internal **political risk assessment (PRA)** units or turned to outside consulting services to evaluate the political risks of the marketplaces in which they operate.

Internet technology has made it possible for large and small firms to be connected to the entire world. Infosys Technologies Limited is India's second biggest software exporter.

© Namas Bhojani/Bloomberg News/Landov

The political environment also involves labor conditions in different countries. For decades, Chinese laborers have suffered workplace abuses including forced labor, withholding of pay, and other unfair practices. But that may be changing with the recent passage of a labor law that gives workers more rights.[24]

The legal environment for U.S. firms operating abroad results from three forces: (1) international law, (2) U.S. law, and (3) legal requirements of host nations. International law emerges from treaties, conventions, and agreements among nations. The United States has many **friendship, commerce, and navigation (FCN) treaties** with other governments. These agreements set terms for various aspects of commercial relations with other countries such as the right to conduct business in the treaty partner's domestic market. Other international business agreements concern worldwide standards for various products, patents, trademarks, reciprocal tax treaties, export control, international air travel, and international communications.

Since the 1990s, Europe has pushed for mandatory **ISO (International Organization for Standardization) certification**—internationally recognized standards that ensure a company's goods, services, and operations meet established quality levels. The organization has two sets of standards: the ISO 9000 series of standards sets requirements for quality in goods and services and the ISO 14000 series sets standards for operations that minimize harm to the environment. Today, many U.S. companies follow these certification standards as well. Currently, organizations in 157 countries participate in both series.[25] The International Monetary Fund, another major player in the international legal environment, lends foreign exchange to nations that require it to conduct international trade. These agreements facilitate the entire process of world marketing.

The second dimension of the international legal environment, U.S. law, includes various trade regulations, tax laws, and import and export requirements affecting international marketing. One important law, the Export Trading Company Act of 1982, exempts companies from antitrust regulations so they can form export groups that offer a variety of products to foreign buyers. The law seeks to make it easier for foreign buyers to connect with U.S. exporters. The controversial Helms-Burton Act of 1996 strengthened international trade sanctions against the Cuban government. More than a decade later, argument still raged over whether the law should remain on the books or be repealed. Another important law is the Foreign Corrupt Practices Act, which makes it illegal to bribe a foreign official in an attempt to solicit new or repeat sales abroad. This act has had a major impact on international marketing and mandates that adequate accounting controls be installed to monitor internal compliance. Violations can result in a $1 million fine for the firm and a $10,000 fine and five-year imprisonment for the individuals involved. This law has been controversial, mainly because it fails to clearly define what constitutes bribery. The 1988 Trade Act amended the law to include more specific statements of prohibited practices.

Finally, legal requirements of host nations affect foreign marketers. Despite China's many advances in recent years—and even as it attempts to build a modern economy—the Chinese government continues to censor the Internet. More than 233 million Chinese currently use the Internet—more than the number of Americans on the Web—and an active cadre of Chinese "hacktivists" works to outwit the government's firewall and help fellow citizens gain unfettered access.[26]

TRADE BARRIERS

tariff Tax levied against imported goods.

Assorted trade barriers also affect global marketing. These barriers fall into two major categories: **tariffs**—taxes levied on imported products—and administrative, or nontariff, barriers. Some tariffs impose set taxes per pound, gallon, or unit; others are calculated according to the value of the imported item. Administrative barriers are more subtle than tariffs and take a variety of forms such as customs barriers, quotas on imports, unnecessarily restrictive standards for imports, and export subsidies. Because the GATT and WTO agreements (discussed later in the chapter) eliminated tariffs on many products, countries frequently use nontariff barriers to boost exports and control the flows of imported products.

The United States and other nations continually negotiate tariffs and other trade agreements. One such recent agreement, the U.S.–Central American Free Trade Agreement and Dominican Republic (CAFTA-DR), streamlines and reduces the costs of exporting goods among the countries covered by the agreement—Costa Rica, El Salvador, Guatemala, Honduras, Nicaragua, and the

Dominican Republic. While the United States already considered these nations trading partners, the agreement paves the way for smoother exchanges over time. Better infrastructures as well as increasing incomes make these promising markets for global firms.[27]

Tariffs

Tariffs can be classified as either revenue or protective tariffs. **Revenue tariffs** are designed to raise funds for the importing government. For years, most U.S. government revenue came from this source. **Protective tariffs,** usually higher than revenue tariffs, are designed to raise the retail price of an imported product to match or exceed that of a similar domestic product. Some countries use tariffs in a selective manner to discourage certain consumption practices and thereby reduce access to their local markets. For example, the United States has tariffs on luxury items such as Rolex watches and Russian caviar. In 1988, the United States passed the Omnibus Trade and Competitiveness Act to remedy what it perceived as unfair international trade conditions. Under the so-called *Super 301 provisions* of the law, the United States can now single out countries that unfairly impede trade with U.S. domestic businesses. If these countries do not open their markets within 18 months, the law requires retaliation in the form of U.S. tariffs or quotas on the offenders' imports into this country.

Tariffs can also be used to gain bargaining clout with other countries, but they risk adversely affecting the fortunes of domestic companies. One industry that causes ongoing debate between countries is agriculture. Currently, the World Trade Organization is mediating a long-standing trade dispute between the United States and countries of the European Union over genetically modified crops.[28]

Other Trade Barriers

In addition to direct taxes on imported products, governments may erect a number of other barriers, ranging from special permits and detailed inspection requirements to quotas on foreign-made items in an effort to stem the flow of imported goods—or halt them altogether. European shoppers pay about twice as much for bananas as North Americans pay. The reason for these high prices? Through a series of import license controls, Europe limits the importation of bananas, and demand exceeds supply. Even worse, the European countries set up a quota system designed to support banana growing in former colonies in Africa, Asia, and the Caribbean, restricting imports from Latin American countries. The WTO ruled that European import tariffs on bananas unfairly discriminate against Latin American banana growers. The WTO ruling paves the way for countries like Ecuador to seek sanctions against the EU.[29]

Other forms of trade restrictions include import quotas and embargoes. **Import quotas** limit the number of units of products in certain categories that can cross a country's border for resale. The quota is supposed to protect domestic industry and employment and preserve foreign exchange, but it doesn't always work that way. Since the late 1950s, the United States has had quotas affecting the apparel industry, whether they involve certain textiles or the manufacturing of the clothes themselves. However, foreign companies often find loopholes in the quota systems and wind up not only with huge profits but also plenty of jobs for their own workers. For many years, China and the United States have engaged in a running battle

import quotas Trade restrictions limiting the number of units of certain goods that can enter a country for resale.

European shoppers pay about twice as much for bananas as North American shoppers because, through a series of import license controls, Europe limits the importation of bananas, and demand exceeds supply.

© Saul Loeb/AFP/Getty Images

over quotas on textiles and apparel, with global trade experts claiming the import quotas on textiles have not helped the U.S. economy.[30]

The ultimate quota is the **embargo**—a complete ban on the import of a product. In 1960, the United States instituted an embargo against Cuba in protest of Fidel Castro's dictatorship and the expropriation of property and disregard for human rights. Not only do the sanctions prohibit Cuban exports—cigars and sugar are the island's best-known products—to enter the country, but they also apply to companies that profit from property that Cuba's communist government expropriated from Americans following the Cuban Revolution. Several years ago, the discovery of mad cow disease and the potential for contaminated beef resulted in a number of embargoes. South Korea, an important market for American beef, banned the product. But the two countries eventually reached an agreement to modify the ban to accept beef products from cattle under 30 months old, the age at which animals are believed to be at greater risk for mad cow disease.[31]

Other trade barriers include **subsidies.** China has long subsidized the cost of gasoline so that its drivers paid less, but recently the government lifted its subsidy. The price of gasoline, diesel, and aviation fuel in China quickly rose.[32] Some nations also limit foreign ownership in the business sectors. And still another way to block international trade is to create so many regulatory barriers that it is almost impossible to reach target markets. China has a maze of regulations controlling trade, and while the government continues to lift the barriers, experienced businesspeople agree that it's important to have personal connections, or *guanxi,* to help navigate the bureaucratic challenges.[33]

Foreign trade can also be regulated by exchange control through a central bank or government agency. **Exchange control** means that firms that gain foreign exchange by exporting must sell foreign currencies to the central bank or other foreign agency, and importers must buy foreign currencies from the same organization. The exchange control authority can then allocate, expand, or restrict foreign exchange according to existing national policy.

DUMPING

The practice of selling a product in a foreign market at a price lower than it commands in the producer's domestic market is called **dumping.** Critics of free trade often argue that foreign governments give substantial support to their own exporting companies. Government support may permit these firms to extend their export markets by offering lower prices abroad. In retaliation for this interference with free trade, the United States adds import tariffs to products that foreign firms dump on U.S. markets to bring their prices in line with those of domestically produced products. However, businesses often complain that charges of dumping must undergo a lengthy investigative and bureaucratic procedure before the government assesses import duties. U.S. firms claiming that dumping threatens to hurt their business can file a complaint with the U.S. International Trade Commission (ITC), which—on average—rejects about half the claims it receives.

The European Union is investigating a dumping claim from the European Biodiesel Board. According to the board, the United States flooded the European market with a biodiesel fuel eligible for subsidies from both Europe and the United States, making the U.S.-made fuel significantly less costly than the biofuel made in Europe.[34]

assessment check

1. What are the three criteria that determine a nation's prospects as a host for international business expansion?

2. What is an FCN treaty?

3. What are the two major categories of trade barriers?

3 Outline the basic functions of GATT, WTO, NAFTA, FTAA, CAFTA-DR, and the European Union.

Multinational Economic Integration

A noticeable trend toward multinational economic integration has developed over the nearly seven decades since the end of World War II. Multinational economic integration can be set up in several ways. The simplest approach is to establish a **free-trade area** in which participating nations agree to the free trade of goods among themselves, abolishing tariffs and trade restrictions. A **customs union** establishes a free-trade area plus a uniform tariff for trade with nonmember nations, and a **common market** extends a customs union by seeking to reconcile all government regulations affecting trade. Despite the many factors in its favor, not everyone is enthusiastic about free trade. For more than a decade, Americans have lost jobs when employers outsourced their work to countries like Mexico, where wages are lower. Now, workers in Mexico face the same outsourcing threat as their employers begin outsourcing work to China, where wages are even lower. Although productivity and innovation are said to grow more quickly with free trade, workers often find themselves working longer and for reduced pay as operations move overseas. But many firms view the change as a collaboration and a way to offer superior service.[35] The "Solving an Ethical Controversy" feature debates another issue related to trade: whether fair-trade practices actually help the people they are intended to help in the long run.

GATT AND THE WORLD TRADE ORGANIZATION

The **General Agreement on Tariffs and Trade (GATT),** a trade accord that has sponsored several rounds of major tariff negotiations, substantially reducing worldwide tariff levels, has existed for six decades. In 1994, a seven-year series of GATT conferences, the Uruguay Round, culminated in one of the biggest victories for free trade in decades. The Uruguay Round reduced average tariffs by one-third, or more than $700 billion. Among its major victories:

> reduced farm subsidies, which opened vast new markets for U.S. exports;

> increased protection for patents, copyrights, and trademarks;

> included services under international trading rules, creating opportunities for U.S. financial, legal, and accounting firms; and

> phased out import quotas on textiles and clothing from developing nations, a move that cost textile workers thousands of jobs when their employers moved many of these domestic jobs to lower-wage countries, but benefited U.S. retailers and consumers.

A key outcome of the GATT talks was establishment of the **World Trade Organization (WTO),** a 152-member organization that succeeds GATT. The WTO oversees GATT agreements, serves as a forum for trade negotiations, and mediates trade disputes. It also monitors national trade policies and works to reduce trade barriers throughout the world. Unlike GATT, WTO decisions are binding. Countries that seek to become members of the WTO must participate in rigorous rounds of negotiations. Vietnam, one of the newer members of the WTO, was granted membership only after more than 10 years of negotiations.[36]

To date, the WTO has made slow progress toward its major policy initiatives: liberalizing world financial services, telecommunications, and maritime markets. Trade officials have not agreed on the direction for the WTO. Big differences between developed and developing nations create a major roadblock to its progress, and its activities thus far have focused more on dispute resolution through its Dispute Settlement Body than on reducing trade barriers. But the WTO also provides important technical assistance and training for the governments of developing countries—recently, several developed countries, among them Australia, Japan, Liechtenstein, and the United States, have helped fund the training.[37]

THE NAFTA ACCORD

More than a decade after the passage of the **North American Free Trade Agreement (NAFTA),** an agreement between the United States, Canada, and Mexico that removes trade restrictions among the three nations, negotiations among the nations continue. The three countries insist that they will not create a trade bloc similar to the European Union, that is, they will not focus on political integration but instead on economic cooperation. NAFTA is particularly important to U.S. marketers because Canada and Mexico are two of its largest trading partners.

General Agreement on Tariffs and Trade (GATT) International trade accord that has helped reduce world tariffs.

World Trade Organization (WTO) Organization that replaces GATT, overseeing GATT agreements, making binding decisions in mediating disputes, and reducing trade barriers.

North American Free Trade Agreement (NAFTA) Accord removing trade barriers between Canada, Mexico, and the United States.

Solving an ethical controversy

How Fair Is Fair Trade?

Wal-Mart works with local farmers in Guatemala, offering their produce in its stores nearby. So Wal-Mart shoppers in Guatemala have the benefit of fresh, local produce—and Wal-Mart makes good on its pledge to support the local economy. Wal-Mart's wholesale outlet, Sam's Club, offers fair-trade coffee. *Fair trade* offers small growers a chance to create a sustainable business by guaranteeing them a minimum price over their production costs. Sam's is also looking into carrying other fair-trade products like tea, sugar, vanilla, and fruit.

But some critics charge that fair-trade policies don't work because they reward the use of antiquated, uncompetitive farming techniques. They claim that free trade offers a better weapon against poverty because it encourages nations to industrialize and develop more efficient farming practices.

Is fair trade an effective business practice in the long run?

PRO

1. When managed properly, fair-trade policies help farmers build a sustainable business because they offer opportunities that would not otherwise be available to them.

2. Under a prudent fair-trade arrangement, farmers learn about environmentally sound growing practices and socially responsible working conditions. They are also required to invest in their business.

CON

1. The benefits of fair trade go to only a small number of farmers in a geographic area, with the rest of the growers suffering as a result.

2. Fair trade has the effect of keeping poor, underdeveloped countries poor and underdeveloped. What's more, fair trade redistributes the wealth by taxing or regulating others who have been more successful.

Summary

Some critics say fair-trade certification is merely a marketing gimmick that not only doesn't improve life for farmers but actually keeps them poor. Yet many coffee sellers—among them Starbucks and Intelligentsia—point to the success farmers have achieved through environmentally sustainable farming methods that increase their farms' profitability.

Sources: "Ethical Sourcing," Starbucks company Web site, http://www.starbucks.com, accessed May 5, 2009; Kimberly Morrison, "Wal-Mart Aims to Buy Local Farmers' Produce," *Morning News*, June 6, 2008, pp. 1D–2D; Janet Daley, "Forget Fair Trade: Only Free Trade Can Help Poor," *Telegraph*, February 25, 2008, telegraph.co.uk; Richard Gray, "Fair Trade Fails to Tackle Poverty, Report Says," *Telegraph*, February 24, 2008, telegraph.co.uk; Janet Rausa Fuller, "'Fair Trade' Gives Coffee Growers a Fighting Chance," *Chicago Sun-Times*, April 19, 2007, www.chicagosuntimes.com.

briefly speaking

"NAFTA recognizes the reality of today's economy— globalization and technology."

—John F. Kerry (b. 1943)
U.S. SENATOR, MASSACHUSETTS

But NAFTA is a complex issue, and from time to time groups in one or more of the three countries chafe under the agreement. In Mexico, farm workers have charged that NAFTA puts their industry at a disadvantage. In Canada, some observers claim NAFTA has compromised their country's oil reserves. And in the United States, critics argue that U.S. workers lose jobs to cheap labor south of the border. Yet since NAFTA's passage, these three countries daily conduct nearly $2.3 billion in trade with each other and have experienced GDP growth as a result.[38]

THE FREE TRADE AREA OF THE AMERICAS AND CAFTA-DR

NAFTA was the first step toward creating a **Free Trade Area of the Americas (FTAA),** stretching the length of the entire Western Hemisphere, from Alaska's Bering Strait to Cape Horn at South America's southern tip, encompassing 34 countries, a population of 800 million, and a combined gross domestic product of more than $11 trillion. The FTAA would be the largest free-trade zone on earth and would offer low or nonexistent tariffs, streamlined customs, and no quotas, subsidies, or other barriers to trade. In addition to the United States, Canada, and Mexico, countries expected to become members of the proposed FTAA include Argentina, Brazil, Chile, Colombia, Ecuador, Guatemala, Jamaica, Peru, Trinidad and Tobago, Uruguay, and Venezuela. The United States is a staunch supporter of the FTAA, which still has many hurdles to overcome as countries wrangle for conditions most favorable to them.

As FTAA negotiations continue, the United States entered into an agreement with the Dominican Republic and Central American nations known as the **Central American Free Trade Agreement-DR (CAFTA-DR).** Some of its provisions took effect immediately, while others will phase in over the next two decades. Supporters of the agreement say it will help American workers, farmers, and small businesses thrive and grow; critics worry that more American agricultural and manufacturing jobs will be lost. However, both sides agree that CAFTA's economic impact is likely to be relatively small compared with NAFTA.[39]

THE EUROPEAN UNION

The best-known example of a multinational economic community is the **European Union (EU).** As Figure 7.2 shows, 27 countries make up the EU: Austria, Belgium, Bulgaria, Cyprus, the Czech Republic, Denmark, Estonia, Finland, France, Germany, Greece, Hungary, Ireland, Italy, Latvia, Lithuania, Luxembourg, Malta, the Netherlands, Poland, Portugal, Romania, the Slovak Republic, Slovenia, Spain, Sweden, and the United Kingdom. Three countries—Croatia, Macedonia, and Turkey—have applicant status. With a total population of more than 491 million people, the EU forms a huge common market.[40]

The goal of the EU, whose council is based in Belgium, is eventually to remove all barriers to free trade among its members, making it as simple and painless to ship products between England and Spain as it is between New Jersey and Pennsylvania. Also involved is the standardization of currencies and regulations that businesses must meet. Introduced in 1999, the EU's euro is the common currency in 15 member countries, with nine other EU countries planning to phase it in over time. Only Denmark, Sweden, and the United Kingdom have declined to use the euro.

In addition to simplifying transactions among members, the EU looks to strengthen its position in the world as a political and economic power. Its Treaty of Lisbon is designed to further streamline operations and will enable the EU to enter into international agreements as a political entity. All EU member countries must ratify the treaty before it can go into effect.[41]

In some ways, the EU is making definite progress toward its economic goals. It is drafting standardized eco-labels to certify that products are manufactured according to certain environmental standards, as well as creating guidelines governing marketers' uses of customer information. Marketers can also protect

European Union (EU)
Customs union that is moving in the direction of an economic union by adopting a common currency, removing trade restrictions, and permitting free flow of goods and workers throughout the member nations.

figure 7.2

The 27 Members of the European Union

some trademarks throughout the entire EU with a single application and registration process through the Community Trademark (CTM), which simplifies doing business and eliminates having to register with each member country. Yet marketers still face challenges when selling their products in the EU. Customs taxes differ, and no uniform postal system exists. Using one toll-free phone number for several countries will not work, either, because each country has its own telephone system for codes and numbers.

Mexico negotiated a trade agreement with the EU that makes it easier for European companies to set up operations in Mexico. The agreement gives EU companies the same privileges enjoyed by the United States and Canada and brings new investors to Mexico.

Going Global

Globalization affects almost every industry and individual throughout the world, at least in some way. Traditional marketers who take their firms global may do so because they already have strong domestic market shares or their target market is too saturated to offer any substantial growth. Sometimes, by evaluating key indicators of the marketing environment, marketers can move toward globalization at an optimal time. The German footwear firm Adidas made a big jump into the global market after its successful "Impossible Is Nothing" ad campaign, announcing it would purchase rival Reebok in an effort to overtake number one competitor Nike. Using the benefits of the EU while also making a play for the Asian market, Adidas marketers believe they have a good chance at winning the global game. Making deals with athletes such as British soccer legend David Beckham and Chinese-born basketball star Yao Ming, as well as licensing agreements for major U.S. sports leagues, has helped Adidas strengthen its brand in major markets around the world. Recently, the firm scored one of its biggest goals yet: sponsorship of the Beijing Olympics. Adidas has 4,000 retail outlets in China alone.[42]

German footwear firm Adidas made a jump into the global market after its successful "Impossible Is Nothing" ad campaign, announcing it would purchase rival Reebok.

© Image courtesy of The Advertising Archives

Most large firms—and many smaller businesses—already participate in global commerce, and virtually every domestic marketer, large or small, recognizes the need to investigate whether to market its products overseas. It is not an easy step to take, requiring careful evaluation and preparation of a strategy. Common reasons that marketers cite for going global include globalization of customers, new customers in emerging markets, globalization of competitors, reduced trade barriers, advances in technology, and enhanced customer responsiveness.

4 **Identify the alternative strategies for entering foreign markets.**

Strategies for Entering Foreign Markets

Successful global marketing starts at the top. Without the enthusiasm and support of senior managers, an initiative is likely to fail. Once marketers have researched and identified markets for expansion and won the support of leadership, they may choose from

figure 7.3

Levels of Involvement in Global Marketing

three basic strategies for entering foreign markets: importing and exporting; contractual agreements such as franchising, licensing, and subcontracting; and international direct investment. As Figure 7.3 shows, the level of risk and the firm's degree of control over international marketing increase with greater involvement. Firms often use more than one of these entry strategies.

IMPORTING AND EXPORTING

An importer is a firm that brings in goods produced abroad to sell domestically or to be used as components in its products. In making import decisions, the marketer must assess local demand for the product, taking into consideration factors such as the following:

▷ ability of the supplier to maintain agreed-to quality levels;

▷ flexibility in filling orders that might vary considerably from one order to the next;

▷ response time in filling orders; and

▷ total costs—including import fees, packaging, and transportation—in comparison with costs of domestic suppliers.

Exporting, another basic form of global marketing, involves a continuous effort in marketing a firm's merchandise to customers in other countries. Many firms export their products as the first step in reaching foreign markets. Furniture manufacturer IKEA has built an entire exporting strategy around its modular furniture. Because IKEA's furniture is lightweight, packs flat, and comes in components that customers can assemble, the firm can ship its goods almost anywhere in the world at a low cost, unlike manufacturers of traditional furniture.[43]

First-time exporters can reach foreign customers through one or more of three alternatives: export-trading companies, export-management companies, or offset agreements. An export-trading company (ETC) buys products from domestic producers and resells them abroad. While manufacturers lose control over marketing and distribution to an ETC, it helps them export through a relatively simple and inexpensive channel, in the process providing feedback about the overseas market potential of their products.

The second option, an export-management company (EMC), provides the first-time exporter with expertise in locating foreign buyers, handling necessary paperwork, and ensuring that its goods meet local labeling and testing laws. However, the manufacturer retains more control over the export process when it deals with an EMC than if it were to sell the goods outright to an export-trading company. Smaller firms can get assistance with administrative needs such as financing and preparation of proposals and contracts from large EMC contractors.

The final option, entering a foreign market under an offset agreement, teams a small firm with a major international company. The smaller firm essentially serves as a subcontractor on a large foreign project. This entry strategy provides new exporters with international experience, supported by the assistance of the primary contractor, in such areas as international transaction documentation and financing.

CONTRACTUAL AGREEMENTS

As a firm gains sophistication in global marketing, it may enter contractual agreements that provide several flexible alternatives to exporting. Both large and small firms can benefit from these methods. Franchising and foreign licensing, for example, are good ways to take services abroad. Subcontracting agreements may involve either production facilities or services.

Franchising

franchise Contractual arrangement in which a wholesaler or retailer agrees to meet the operating requirements of a manufacturer or other franchiser.

A **franchise** is a contractual arrangement in which a wholesaler or retailer (the franchisee) agrees to meet the operating requirements of a manufacturer or other franchiser. The franchisee receives the right to sell the products and use the franchiser's name as well as a variety of marketing, management, and other services. Fast-food companies such as McDonald's have been active franchisers around the world.

One advantage of franchising is risk reduction by offering a proven concept. Standardized operations typically reduce costs, increase operating efficiencies, and provide greater international recognizability. However, the success of an international franchise depends on its willingness to balance standard practices with local customer preferences. McDonald's, Pizza Hut, and Domino's are expanding into India with special menus that feature lamb, chicken, and vegetarian items, in deference to Hindu and Muslim customers who do not eat beef and pork.

Foreign Licensing

foreign licensing Agreement that grants foreign marketers the right to distribute a firm's merchandise or to use its trademark, patent, or process in a specified geographic area.

A second method of going global through the use of contractual agreements is **foreign licensing.** Such an agreement grants foreign marketers the right to distribute a firm's merchandise or to use its trademark, patent, or process in a specified geographic area. These arrangements usually set certain time limits, after which agreements are revised or renewed.

Licensing offers several advantages over exporting, including access to local partners' marketing information and distribution channels and protection from various legal barriers. Because licensing does not require capital outlays, many firms, both small and large, regard it as an attractive entry strategy. Like franchising, licensing allows a firm to quickly enter a foreign market with a known product. The arrangement also may provide entry into a market that government

The World Poker Tour has grown tremendously, partly due to foreign licensing agreements.

© Shelly Castellano ICON SMI/Newscom

restrictions close to imports or international direct investment. The World Poker Tour has grown tremendously, partly due to foreign licensing agreements. Following the model of golf's PGA Tour, founder of the poker tournament TV show Steve Lipscomb created a way for individual poker enthusiasts to sign up and play in tournaments around the world. By licensing the show in different countries such as France and Italy, Lipscomb maintains a company standard that can be translated—literally—to different markets. The televised tournaments on the World Poker Tour have become extremely popular, having already awarded players around the globe more than $300 million in prize money.[44]

Subcontracting

A third strategy for going global through contractual agreements is **subcontracting,** in which the production of goods or services is assigned to local companies. Using local subcontractors can prevent mistakes involving local culture and regulations. Manufacturers might subcontract with a local company to produce their goods or use a foreign distributor to handle their products abroad or provide customer service. Manufacturing within the country can provide protection from import duties and may be a lower-cost alternative that makes it possible for the product to compete with local offerings. But it can also have a downside when local suppliers don't make the grade. When Nike pulled shoe orders from two local Indonesian manufacturers, citing quality concerns, the Indonesian government stepped in to press Nike to keep its business in Indonesia.[45]

INTERNATIONAL DIRECT INVESTMENT

Another strategy for entering global markets is international direct investment in foreign firms, production, and marketing facilities. Because the United States is the world's largest economy, its foreign direct investment inflows and outflows—the total of American firm investments abroad and foreign firm investments in the United States—are one-third greater than Germany's and twice as much as Japan's, its two largest competitors. U.S. direct investment abroad is nearly $2.4 trillion, with its greatest presence in the United Kingdom, Canada, and the Netherlands. On the other hand, foreign direct investment in the United States in a recent year totaled almost $277 billion and originated through investors in Europe, the United Kingdom, Canada, and Asia.[46]

Although high levels of involvement and high risk potential are characteristics of investments in foreign countries, firms choosing this method often have a competitive advantage. Direct investment can take several forms. A company can acquire an existing firm in a country where it wants to do business, or it can set up an independent division outside its own borders with responsibility for production and marketing in a country or geographic region. Chinese firms have been seeking to purchase U.S. businesses, mostly in industries involving natural resources such as oil, natural gas, metals, and coal. However, they have been making inroads in consumer products and technology companies as well.[47] And a true American icon, St. Louis–based Anheuser-Busch agreed to be bought by Belgian brewer InBev for $52 billion. Anheuser-Busch was the largest U.S. brewer, with more than 48 percent of the market. With the merger, InBev—the maker of Stella Artois and Becks—became the world's largest brewer, helping it compete with SABMiller. The company plans to use St. Louis as its North American headquarters.[48]

Companies may also engage in international marketing by forming joint ventures in which they share the risks, costs, and management of the foreign operation with one or more partners. These partnerships join the investing companies with nationals of the host countries. While some companies choose to open their own facilities overseas, others share with their partners. Because India puts limits on foreign direct investment, Wal-Mart formed a partnership with Indian conglomerate Bharti Enterprises to open wholesale cash-and-carry stores in India. The stores do business under the name Bharti Wal-Mart.[49]

Although joint ventures offer many advantages, foreign investors have encountered problems in several areas throughout the world, especially in developing economies. Lower trade barriers, new technologies, lower transport costs, and

assessment check

1. What are the three basic strategies for entering foreign markets?

2. What is a franchise?

3. What is international direct investment?

vastly improved access to information mean that many more partnerships will be involved in international trade.

From Multinational Corporation to Global Marketer

A **multinational corporation** is a firm with significant operations and marketing activities outside its home country. Examples of multinationals include General Electric, Siemens, and Mitsubishi in heavy electrical equipment, and Timex, Seiko, and Citizen in watches. Since they first became a force in international business in the 1960s, multinationals have evolved in some important ways. First, these companies are no longer exclusively U.S. based. Today, it is as likely for a multinational to be based in Japan, Germany, or Great Britain as in the United States. Second, multinationals no longer think of their foreign operations as mere outsourcing appendages that carry out the design, production, and engineering ideas conceived at home. Instead, they encourage constant exchanges of ideas, capital, and technologies among all the multinational operations.

Multinationals often employ huge foreign workforces relative to their American staffs. More than half of all Ford and IBM personnel are located outside the United States. These workforces are no longer seen merely as sources of cheap labor; on the contrary, many multinationals center technically complex activities in locations throughout the world. Texas Instruments does much of its research, development, design, and manufacturing in East Asia. It is increasingly common for U.S. multinationals to bring product innovations from their foreign facilities back to the States.

Multinationals have become global corporations that reflect the interdependence of world economies, the growth of international competition, and the globalization of world markets. However, many people worry that this globalization means that U.S. dominance in many markets will decline and disappear. Sixty percent of households in Hong Kong get their television services through ultrahigh-speed broadband connections that turn their TVs into computers, a concept still catching on slowly in the United States. European and Asian consumers now use smart cards with embedded memory chips instead of traditional credit cards or cash for retail purchases. And many American travelers discover that their cell phone service works better when they're overseas: when Internet service provider EarthLink went looking for a partner to launch a cell phone service in the United States, it approached not a U.S. firm but SK Telecom of South Korea because that country outperforms the United States in cell phone technology. EarthLink and SK Telecom subsequently created a joint venture known as Hello. After Hello recently received an infusion of an additional $70 million from SK, the South Korean firm gained controlling rights in the company.[50]

assessment check

1. What is a multinational corporation?

2. What are two ways in which multinationals have changed since the 1960s?

5 **Differentiate between a global marketing strategy and a multidomestic marketing strategy.**

Developing an International Marketing Strategy

In developing a marketing mix, international marketers may choose between two alternative approaches: a global marketing strategy or a multidomestic marketing strategy. A **global marketing strategy** defines a standard marketing mix and implements it with minimal modifications in all foreign markets. This approach brings the advantage of economies of scale to production and

Procter & Gamble marketers follow a global marketing strategy for Pringles potato chips, its leading export brand.

© Jeff Greenberg/Alamy

marketing activities. Procter & Gamble marketers follow a global marketing strategy for Pringles potato chips, its leading export brand. P&G sells one product with a consistent formulation in every country and meets 80 percent of worldwide demand with only six flavors of Pringles and one package design. This standardized approach saves money because it allows large-scale production runs and reinforces the brand's image.

A global marketing perspective can effectively market some goods and services to segments in many nations that share cultures and languages. This approach works especially well for products with strong, universal appeal such as McDonald's, luxury items such as Rolex watches, and high-tech brands such as Microsoft. Global advertising outlets such as international editions of popular consumer and business magazines and international transmissions of TV channels such as CNN, MTV, and the CNBC financial network help marketers deliver a single message to millions of global viewers. International satellite television channels such as Star TV reach more than 300 million viewers in more than 50 Asian countries through a host of sports, news, movie, music, and entertainment channels programmed in nine languages.[51]

A global marketing strategy can also be highly effective for luxury products that target upscale consumers everywhere. Marketers of diamonds and luxury watches, for instance, typically use advertising with little or no copy—just a picture of a beautiful diamond or watch with the name discreetly displayed on the page.

But a global strategy doesn't always work. After a quick spike in sales of its computers in China, Dell saw just as rapid a decline. The firm discovered that competitors such as Hewlett-Packard and the Chinese firm Lenovo were more successful at selling their computers through retail stores. Dell's well-known practice of building computers to order and shipping them directly to consumers was not succeeding in China. After modifying its marketing strategy to include selling Dell computers in retail outlets, the company experienced a surge in market share.[52]

A major benefit of a global marketing strategy is its low cost to implement. Most firms, however, find it necessary to practice market segmentation outside their home markets and tailor their marketing mixes to fit the unique needs of customers in specific countries. This **multidomestic marketing strategy** assumes that differences between market characteristics and competitive situations in certain nations require firms to customize their marketing decisions to effectively reach individual marketplaces. Many marketing experts believe that most products demand multidomestic marketing strategies to give them realistic global marketing appeal. Cultural, geographic, language, and other differences simply make it difficult to send the same message to many countries. Specific situations may allow marketers to standardize some parts of the marketing process but customize others.

assessment check

1. What is the difference between a global marketing strategy and a multidomestic marketing strategy?

6   **Describe the alternative marketing mix strategies used in global marketing.**

INTERNATIONAL PRODUCT AND PROMOTIONAL STRATEGIES

Global marketers can choose from among five strategies for selecting the most appropriate product and promotion strategy for a specific foreign market: straight extension, promotion adaptation, product adaptation, dual adaptation, and product invention. As Figure 7.4 indicates, the strategies center on whether to extend a domestic product and promotional strategy into international markets or adapt one or both to meet the target market's unique requirements.

A firm may follow a one-product, one-message straight extension strategy as part of a global marketing strategy. This strategy permits economies of scale in production and marketing. Also, successful implementation creates universal recognition of a product for consumers from country to country. FedEx's global advertising campaign, "Behind the Scenes," has run in China, Hong Kong, Japan, Korea, Singapore, Taiwan, and several other strategic markets. The campaign highlights the role FedEx plays in helping businesses tackle opportunities, whether local or global.[53]

Other strategies call for product adaptation, promotion adaptation, or both. In Taiwan, 7-Eleven takes the convenience-store concept to a new level. At a Taiwanese 7-Eleven, not only can shoppers buy a Slurpee but they can also send documents, book travel plans, pay bills, buy Wi-Fi cards, settle parking tickets, and more. The Taiwanese government is even considering instituting a needle-exchange program for drug addicts at—you guessed it—their local 7-Eleven. Introduced in Taiwan in 1980, 7-Eleven stores now number nearly 4,800 on the island.[54]

figure 7.4

Alternative International Product and Promotional Strategies

Product Strategy

Promotion Strategy		Same Product	Product Adaptation	New Product
Same Promotion		**Straight Extension** General Mills Cheerios Coca-Cola Mars Snickers candy bar	**Product Adaptation** Campbell's soup Exxon gasoline	**Product Invention** Nonelectric sewing machines Manually operated washing machines
Different Promotion		**Promotion Adaptation** Bicycles/motorcycles Outboard motors	**Dual Adaptation** Coffee Some clothing	

Finally, a firm may select product invention to take advantage of unique foreign market opportunities. To match user needs in developing nations, an appliance manufacturer might introduce a hand-powered washing machine even though such products became obsolete in industrialized countries years ago. Although Chapter 12 discusses the idea of branding in greater detail, it is important to note here the value of a company's recognizable name, image, product, or even slogan around the world.

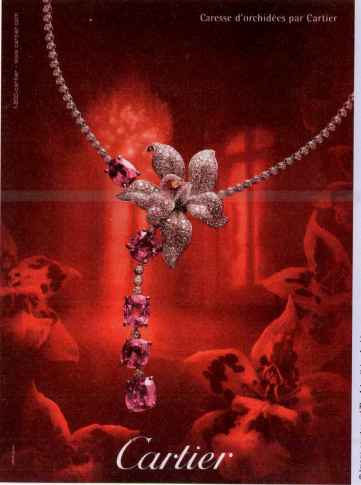

Caresse d'orchidées par Cartier

Cartier

A global marketing strategy can be highly effective for luxury products like Cartier that target upscale consumers everywhere.

© Image courtesy of The Advertising Archives

INTERNATIONAL DISTRIBUTION STRATEGY

Distribution is a vital aspect of overseas marketing. Marketers must set up proper channels and anticipate extensive physical distribution problems. Foreign markets may offer poor transportation systems and warehousing facilities—or none at all. Global marketers must adapt promptly and efficiently to these situations to profit from overseas sales.

A distribution decision involves two steps. First, the firm must decide on a method of entering the foreign market. Second, it must determine how to distribute the product within the foreign market through that entry channel. Daimler AG had been marketing its subcompact car, the Smart Fortwo, through its Mercedes-Benz division for at least a decade in Europe. Seeing Americans' growing interest in fuel-efficient cars, Daimler decided to enter the U.S. market, establishing Smart USA with headquarters in a Detroit suburb. Daimler ships the cars to ports in California, Florida, and Maryland, from which they are delivered to nearly 70 dealerships across the country.[55]

PRICING STRATEGY

Pricing can critically affect the success of an overall marketing strategy for foreign markets. Considerable competitive, economic, political, and legal constraints often limit pricing decisions. Global marketers can succeed if they thoroughly understand these requirements.

Companies must adapt their pricing strategies to local markets and change them when conditions change. In India, Unilever's partner Hindustan Lever offers "penny packets" of shampoo to lower-income consumers who typically cannot afford to buy an entire bottle of shampoo. Although local firms follow the same practice, Hindustan Lever wants to develop loyalty among these consumers so that when they move up the income scale, they will be more apt to buy the firm's higher-priced products as well.

An important development in pricing strategy for international marketing has been the emergence of commodity marketing organizations that seek to control prices through collective action. The Organization of the Petroleum Exporting Countries (OPEC) is a good example of this kind of collective export organization. Pricing agreements such as fair trade pricing in the coffee industry have drawn criticism from those who believe that the agreements do not benefit everyone.

COUNTERTRADE

countertrade Form of exporting whereby goods and services are bartered rather than sold for cash.

In a growing number of nations, the only way a marketer can gain access to foreign markets is through **countertrade**—a form of exporting in which a firm barters products rather than selling them for cash. Less developed nations sometimes impose countertrade requirements when they lack sufficient foreign currency to attain goods and services they want or need from exporting countries. These nations allow sellers to exchange their products only for domestic products as a way to control their balance-of-trade problems.

Countertrade became popular two decades ago, when companies wanted to conduct business in eastern European countries and the former Soviet Union. Those governments did not allow exchanges of hard currency, so this form of barter facilitated trade. PepsiCo made one of the largest countertrades ever when it exchanged $3 billion worth of Pepsi-Cola for Russian Stolichnaya vodka, a cargo ship, and tankers from the former Soviet Union.

assessment check

1. What are the five strategies for selecting the most appropriate product and promotion strategy for a specific foreign market?

2. What is countertrade?

---

7 Explain the attractiveness of the United States as a target market for foreign marketers.

The United States as a Target for International Marketers

Foreign marketers regard America as an inviting target. It offers a large population of more than 306 million people. In addition, U.S. consumers have a high level of discretionary income, with a GDP per capita estimated at nearly $46,000 and a median gross family income of $61,500.[56] Risks to foreign marketers are also low due to the United States' political stability, generally favorable attitude toward foreign investment, and growing economy.

South Korean consumer electronics giant LG Electronics counts the United States as its second most profitable market; Asia ranks first. Since establishing a North American headquarters in the United States, sales there topped $10 billion annually. The firm markets cell phones; TVs; computers, MP3 players and other digital media; and home appliances.[57] As mentioned earlier in the chapter, Cuba would benefit from trade with the United States, but the U.S. embargo prohibits any trade with that country.

Among the best-known industries in which foreign manufacturers have established U.S. production facilities is automobiles. Most of the world's leading auto companies built assembly facilities in the United States: Honda, Hyundai, Mercedes-Benz, and Toyota in Alabama; Kia in Georgia; BMW in South Carolina; Toyota in Kentucky and Mississippi; and Nissan and Honda in Tennessee, Mississippi, and Ohio.[58]

As we discussed earlier, foreign investment continues to grow in the United States. Increasingly, foreign multinationals will invest in U.S. assets as they seek to produce goods locally and control distribution channels.

assessment check

1. What characteristics of the United States make it an inviting target for foreign marketers?

2. Why would U.S. automobile manufacturing be a target for foreign companies?

Strategic Implications of Marketing in the 21st Century

t he first decade of the new century has marked a new era of truly global marketing, in which the world's marketplaces are accessible to nearly every firm. Marketers in both small, localized firms and giant businesses need to reevaluate the strengths and weaknesses of their current marketing practices and realign their plans to meet the new demands of this era.

Marketers are the pioneers in bringing new technologies to developing nations. Their successes and failures will determine the direction global marketing will take and the speed with which it will be embraced. Actions of international marketers will influence every component of the marketing environment: competitive, economic, social-cultural, political-legal, and technological.

The greatest competitive advantages will belong to marketers who capitalize on the similarities of their target markets and adapt to the differences. In some instances, the actions of marketers today help determine the rules and regulations of tomorrow.

Marketers need flexible and broad views of an increasingly complex customer. Goods and services will likely become more customized as they are introduced in foreign markets—yet some recognizable brands seem to remain universally popular just as they are. New and better products in developing markets will create and maintain relationships for the future.

Review of Chapter Objectives

1 Describe the importance of global marketing from the perspectives of the individual firm and the nation.

Global marketing expands a company's market, allows firms to grow, and makes them less dependent on their own country's economy for success. For the nation, global trade provides a source of needed raw materials and other products not available domestically in sufficient amounts, opens up new markets to serve with domestic output, and converts countries and their citizens into partners in the search for high-quality products at the lowest possible prices. Companies find that global marketing and international trade can help them meet customer demand, reduce certain costs, provide information on markets around the world, and increase employment.

2 Identify the major components of the environment for global marketing.

The major components of the international environment are economic, social-cultural, technological, political-legal, and competitive. A country's infrastructure also plays an important role in determining how effective marketers will be in manufacturing, promoting, and distributing their goods and services.

3 Outline the basic functions of GATT, WTO, NAFTA, FTAA, CAFTA-DR, and the European Union.

The General Agreement on Tariffs and Trade is an accord that has substantially reduced tariffs. The World Trade Organization oversees GATT agreements, mediates disputes, and tries to reduce trade barriers throughout the world. The North American Free Trade Agreement removes trade restrictions among Canada, Mexico, and the United States. The proposed Free Trade Area of the Americas seeks to create a free-trade area covering the entire Western hemisphere. As another step in that direction, the United States has made an agreement with the Dominican Republic and Central American nations known as the Central American Free Trade Agreement-DR (CAFTA-DR). The European Union is a customs union whose goal is to remove all barriers to free trade among its members.

4 Identify the alternative strategies for entering foreign markets.

Several strategies are available to marketers, including exporting, importing, franchising, foreign licensing, subcontracting, and direct investment. This progression moves from the least to the most involvement by a firm.

5   Differentiate between a global marketing strategy and a multidomestic marketing strategy.

A global marketing strategy defines a standard marketing mix and implements it with minimal modifications in all foreign markets.

A multidomestic marketing strategy requires firms to customize their marketing decisions to reach individual marketplaces.

6   Describe the alternative marketing mix strategies used in global marketing.

Product and promotional strategies include the following: straight extension, promotion adaptation, product adaptation, dual

adaptation, and product invention. Marketers may also choose among distribution, pricing, and countertrade strategies.

7   Explain the attractiveness of the United States as a target market for foreign marketers.

The United States has a large population, high levels of discretionary income, political stability, a favorable attitude toward foreign investment, and a steadily growing economy.

assessment check: **answers**

1.1   Define *importing* and *exporting*.

Importing involves purchasing foreign goods and services. Exporting refers to marketing domestically produced goods and services abroad.

1.2   What is the largest category of exports from the United States?

The largest category of exports from the United States is services.

1.3   What must global marketers do effectively to reach foreign markets?

Global marketers must adapt their goods and services to local preferences.

2.1   What are the three criteria that determine a nation's prospects as a host for international business expansion?

A nation's size, per-capita income, and stage of economic development determine its prospects as a host for international business expansion.

2.2   What is an FCN treaty?

FCN stands for friendship, commerce, and navigation. These treaties set terms for various aspects of commercial relations with other countries.

2.3   What are the two major categories of trade barriers?

The two categories of trade barriers are tariffs and nontariffs.

3.1   What is the World Trade Organization?

The World Trade Organization (WTO) oversees GATT agreements and mediates disputes. It also continues efforts to reduce trade barriers around the world.

3.2   What countries are parties to the NAFTA accord?

The United States, Canada, and Mexico are members of NAFTA.

3.3 What is the goal of the European Union (EU)?

The European Union seeks to remove all barriers to free trade among its members and strengthen its position in the world as an economic and political power.

4.1 What are the three basic strategies for entering foreign markets?

The three basic strategies are importing and exporting, contractual agreements, and international direct investment.

4.2 What is a franchise?

A franchise is a contractual agreement in which a wholesaler or retailer (the franchisee) agrees to meet the operating requirements of a manufacturer or other franchiser.

4.3 What is international direct investment?

International direct investment is direct investment in foreign firms, production, and marketing facilities.

5.1 What is a multinational corporation?

A multinational corporation is a firm with significant operations and marketing activities outside the home country.

5.2 What are two ways in which multinationals have changed since the 1960s?

Two ways these firms have changed are that they are no longer exclusively U.S. based, and they no longer think of their foreign operations as mere outsourcing appendages.

5.3 What is the difference between a global marketing strategy and a multidomestic marketing strategy?

A global marketing strategy defines a marketing mix and implements it with minimal modifications in all foreign markets. A multidomestic marketing strategy requires that firms customize their marketing decisions to reach individual marketplaces.

6.1 What are the five strategies for selecting the most appropriate product and promotion strategy for a specific foreign market?

The five strategies are straight extension, promotion adaptation, product adaptation, dual adaptation, and product invention.

6.2 What is countertrade?

Countertrade is a form of exporting in which a firm barters products rather then selling them for cash.

7.1 What characteristics of the United States make it an inviting target for foreign marketers?

The characteristics making the United States an attractive target for foreign marketers are a large population to sell products to and high levels of discretionary income that make purchases possible. In addition, it has low risks to foreign marketers due to a stable political environment, favorable attitude toward foreign investment, and a growing economy.

7.2 Why would U.S. automobile manufacturing be a target for foreign companies?

Since the United States has a large population and high income levels, foreign car manufacturers would find the country an attractive and lucrative market. The size and weight of cars make them bulky to transport long distances, so firms might find local manufacturing a profitable alternative to exporting.

Marketing Terms You Need to Know

exporting 202
importing 202
exchange rate 209
tariff 212
import quota 213

General Agreement on Tariffs and Trade (GATT) 215
World Trade Organization (WTO) 215
North American Free Trade Agreement (NAFTA) 215

European Union (EU) 217
franchise 220
foreign licensing 220
countertrade 226

Other Important Marketing Terms

related party trade 203
infrastructure 207
political risk assessment (PRA) 211
friendship, commerce, and navigation (FCN) treaties 212
ISO (International Organization for Standardization) certification 212
revenue tariff 213

protective tariff 213
embargo 214
subsidy 214
exchange control 214
dumping 214
free-trade area 214
customs union 215
common market 215

Free Trade Area of the Americas (FTAA) 216
Central American Free Trade Agreement-DR (CAFTA-DR) 217
subcontracting 220
multinational corporation 222
global marketing strategy 222
multidomestic marketing strategy 223

Assurance of Learning Review

1. What are the benefits to firms that decide to engage in global marketing?
2. Why is a nation's infrastructure an important factor for global marketers to consider?
3. What are the two different classifications of tariff? What is each designed to do?
4. How does an import quota restrict trade?
5. What are two major victories achieved by the Uruguay Round of GATT conferences?
6. Why has the progress of the WTO been slow?
7. What are the three alternatives for first-time exporters to reach foreign customers?
8. Define and describe the different types of contractual agreements that provide flexible alternatives to exporting.
9. In what conditions is a global marketing strategy generally most successful?
10. What type of nation benefits most from countertrade? Why?

Projects and Teamwork Exercises

1. Imagine you and a classmate are marketers for one of the following companies: Apple Inc., Burger King, General Mills, or Mattel Toys. Choose one of the following markets into which your company could expand: Mexico, India, or China. Research the country's infrastructure, social-cultural environment, technological environment, and any possible trade barriers your firm might encounter. Then present your findings to the class, with a conclusion on whether or not you think the expansion would be beneficial.

2. Assume you work for Domino's Pizza, which already has 3,500 outlets in more than 60 overseas markets. With a classmate, identify a country that Domino's has not yet reached and write a brief plan for entering that country's market. Then create a print ad for that market (you can write the ad copy in English). It may be helpful to visit Domino's Web site for some ideas.

3. London is hosting the 2012 Summer Olympics. By yourself or with a classmate, identify a company that might benefit from promoting its goods or services at the London Olympics. In a presentation, describe which strategy you would use: straight extension, product or promotion adaptation, dual adaptation, or product invention. Consider the fact that England is a member of the European Union.

4. Suppose you work for a firm that is getting ready to introduce its brand of MP3 player to the Chinese marketplace. With a classmate, decide which strategies your firm could use most effectively for entering this market. Present your ideas either in writing or to the class.

5. Chinese automaker Geely (pronounced *jeely*) recently announced plans to enter the U.S. market. With a classmate, research Geely to find out more about its cars, then create an ad for the firm, targeting U.S. consumers.

Critical-Thinking Exercises

1. Few elements in the global marketing environment are more difficult to overcome than the unexpected, such as natural disasters or outbreaks of disease such as the avian flu. Travel may be curtailed or halted by law, by a breakdown in infrastructure, or simply by fear on the part of consumers. Suppose you work for a firm that has resorts on several continents. As a marketer, what kinds of contingency plans might you recommend for your firm in the event of an unexpected disaster?

2. Zippo lighters have been around for more than 75 years. But as the number of smokers in the United States continues to decline, Zippo has spent the last half-century scouting the world for new markets. Today, Zippo is a status symbol among Chinese consumers, who prefer U.S. products. To reduce the sale of made-in-China knockoffs, Zippo's ads show Chinese consumers how to identify a real Zippo. In addition, Zippo

has worked with U.S. government officials to find a safe way to package its lighters for air travel. Both of these examples demonstrate a firm adapting to requirements of a new marketplace. Do you think a global marketing strategy or a multidomestic strategy would work best if Zippo decided to enter other markets? Explain the reasons for your choice.

3. Do you agree with the goals and ideas of the proposed FTAA? Why or why not?

4. Do you agree with countertrade as a legitimate form of conducting business? Why or why not? Describe a countertrade agreement that Microsoft might make in another country.

5. Foreign investment continues to grow in the United States. Do you think this is a positive trend for U.S. businesses and consumers? Why or why not?

Ethics Exercise

Cheap—and illegal—copies of pirated popular movies, video games, and music often are available for sale in Asia within days of their worldwide release. The entertainment industry has so far had little success in stopping the flow of these copies into consumers'

hands. Do you think multinational economic communities should be more effective at combating piracy? Why or why not? What actions could they take?

Internet Exercises

1. **International product strategies.** Visit the Web site of a U.S. company with an extensive presence internationally. Examples include The Coca-Cola Company and Johnson & Johnson. Note two or three differences in product strategies you found between the company's products sold domestically and those sold internationally. Next, visit the Web site of Swiss firm Nestlé or Dutch firm Unilever and repeat the exercise. Based on your findings, did you find any differences between the U.S. and non-U.S. companies?

2. **Treaty of Lisbon.** Search Google news (news.google.com) and review several recent articles on the Treaty of Lisbon. Prepare a brief report on the treaty and its current status. What impact will the treaty have on marketers doing business in the European Union?

3. **World Trade Organization.** Visit the Web site of the World Trade Organization (www.wto.org). Make a list of the current policy initiatives and their current status. Then, review two recent trade disputes. What type (or types) of products are involved? Which nations are involved? How does the WTO resolve such disputes?

Note: Internet Web addresses change frequently. If you don't find the exact site listed, you may need to access the organization's home page and search from there or use a search engine such as Google.

Case 7.1 Fresh & Easy: Not So Easy

Fresh & Easy Neighborhood Market represents the latest "British invasion" of America. It's backed by UK-based

Tesco, the world's third-largest retailer. Tesco's vision is that Fresh & Easy will change the way Americans shop for groceries. The retailer expects Fresh & Easy stores eventually to outnumber Safeway in the United States and take on the likes of Whole Foods and Wal-Mart.

Tesco's strategy is to open small stores—about the size of your average Trader Joe's—with lots of natural foods like Whole Foods but low prices like Costco. The "Fresh & Easy" name says it all. Tesco wants to offer fresh, high-quality food in a convenient setting.

Here's an example of what the brand means by "easy"— shoppers are encouraged to sample the wares before they buy. They can bring almost any grocery item to the store's "Kitchen Table" area, where a staff member will open it, cook it, and serve a sample.

To keep costs low, Fresh & Easy uses only a self-checkout system; the stores employ no cashiers. The stores also have no loyalty cards; all shoppers receive the same savings. And Fresh & Easy does little or no advertising, preferring instead to mail area residents a $5-off coupon when it enters a market.

The Fresh & Easy stores were designed with the environment in mind. They use 30 percent less energy than other supermarkets their size, and they emphasize recycling. Store-brand products are packaged minimally so that shoppers can see what they're buying, and all fresh food—even produce—carries expiration dates.

So far, the offbeat look and feel of these stores has thrown American shoppers for a loop. They are confused about what Fresh & Easy actually is. As a result, U.S. sales are said to be performing well below expectations. Tesco announced it would take a three-month break and review its tactics from opening its first 50-plus stores before continuing to launch additional outlets.

That Fresh & Easy hasn't hit a home run in its first at bat is probably frustrating to the retail giant, who industry experts say spent an unprecedented amount of time and money studying American consumers up close before it entered the U.S. market.

Questions for Critical Thinking

1. In their first days of operation, some Fresh & Easy stores sold out of certain items, leaving the shelves empty. In the United States, where abundance is an important cultural trait, the image of empty shelves created a poor first impression. What can Fresh & Easy do to correct this impression?

2. Some observers criticized Fresh & Easy for not tailoring its stores to their specific neighborhoods. For example, in one store in a heavily Hispanic area, none of the signs were in Spanish. What advice would you give Tesco management about tailoring their stores to specific markets?

3. To be successful, global marketers must consider whether their product or concept fits in a foreign market. In your opinion, does the Fresh & Easy concept fit the U.S. market?

Sources: Fresh & Easy company Web site, http://www.freshandeasy.com, accessed May 5, 2009; Bruce Horovitz, "British Invasion Hits Grocery Stores," *USA Today,* April 7, 2008, pp. B1–B2; Kelly Johnson, "Tesco Delays Openings to 'Smooth Out Any Wrinkles,'" *Sacramento Business Journal,* March 31, 2008, sanfrancisco.bizjournals.com; Nancy Luna, "Tesco's Fresh & Easy Off to Rocky Start, Industry Watchers Say," *Orange County Register,* February 28. 2008, goliath.exnet.com; Matthew Boyle, "Tesco Needs a Fresh Start in the U.S.," *Fortune,* December 4, 2007, money.cnn.com.

Video Case 7.2   Global Marketing at Evo

The written video case on Evo appears on page VC-7. The Evo video is designed to expand and highlight the concepts in this chapter and the concepts and questions covered in the written video case.

Talking about Marketing Careers with...
Anne Saunders

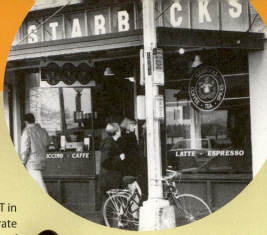

ANNE SAUNDERS
Senior Vice President, Global Brand
Strategy & Communications
Starbucks Coffee Company

Millions of people around the world just can't start their day off right without a steaming cup of Starbucks coffee. Whether they opt for the full Starbucks experience at a retail store, grind and brew their own cups at home, or serve themselves at a hotel breakfast buffet or their college's foodservice, consumers can satisfy their craving for rich, flavorful coffees or other beverages nearly anytime they choose. And that's the way Starbucks planned it. The firm has outlets in all 50 U.S. states and the District of Columbia and operates in 37 countries worldwide. It has more than 12,000 locations globally to serve customers—from Australia to Japan to Chile and on through the United Arab Emirates, to name just a few.

The company's attention to quality in its roasting and blending process is legendary. So no matter where you prefer to relax with your latte or espresso, you'll find the same premium drink you have come to expect from Starbucks. The firm is even working with other business partners to bring its products to new communities and venues, such as vending machines. Anne Saunders, senior vice president of Global Brand Strategy & Communications, took some time recently to discuss her firm's expansion plans and her own marketing career with us.

Q: Anne, most students would jump at the chance to be part of such a respected company as Starbucks. How did your education and career stepping stones prepare you for your current position with the company?
Prior to joining Starbucks, I was the chief executive officer and president of E-Society, a business-to-business e-commerce company. I also spent nine years at AT&T in a variety of positions, including corporate officer. I joined AT&T via its acquisition of McCaw Communications where I led the marketing function.

My undergraduate work was at Northwestern University, where I majored in economics, and I later earned a master's degree in management from Fordham University.

I consider myself a management generalist, with a strong interest in marketing and branding activities. In terms of "stepping stones," I advise people to develop their strength as leaders and to get experience in the basics of management—planning, setting direction, and delivering measurable results. While functional experience is extremely helpful, in a fast-growing company like Starbucks, we find that attributes like the ability to deal with ambiguity and to create a productive work environment are the most valuable leadership skills.

Q: What is involved in managing global brand strategy day to day? Do you have a team helping you with major activities? If so, would you describe their roles briefly?
Starbucks's brand has been developed through a unique approach. Rather than relying on traditional advertising, we have essentially considered our stores as our billboards and also leveraged public relations activities to build connections with the communities we serve.

Our brand strategy team includes our creative department, communications (which works as much with our partners [employees] and other stakeholders as it does with the media), and other teams who work in concert with our marketing department. Each function is led by a vice president, who helps to set the vision and strategy for the team and ensures a cohesive approach between departments.

Q: Coffee is enjoyed in many societies around the world. But does Starbucks need to tailor its selection of beverages or other products for different countries? Can you give us an example?
We pride ourselves on delivering a consistent experience throughout our entire organization. If you order a nonfat latte in Sheboygan, Wisconsin, it should taste the same as the one that you ordered last week in London. But we definitely adjust our food and beverage offerings to local tastes. For instance, one of our most popular Frappuccino blended beverages in our Asia market has cubes of coffee jelly in it. Our Strawberries & Cream Frappuccino blended beverage was developed in our United Kingdom market and was later released in North America.

Q: Starbucks opened its first coffeehouse in Japan a decade ago. What drives the company in its global expansion? What are its goals in reaching more people?
Starbucks has always been a growth company, and we see enormous untapped potential both in North America and certainly around the world. There are more than 12,000 Starbucks stores as of this writing, and we believe that we will ultimately have at least 40,000 locations worldwide, with at

least half of those outside the United States. And beyond our store projections, we want to be available everywhere that our customers want to experience Starbucks—in foodservice locations, at home, and more.

Q: There is often a lot of skepticism in the world about the motivations and actions of large companies. In many instances, companies that market or communicate their corporate social responsibility activities risk being accused of "greenwashing." How does Starbucks approach this subject?

Effectively communicating a company's social responsibility efforts can be one of the greatest challenges in marketing. At Starbucks, we try to "bake in" corporate social responsibility messaging throughout all of our internal and external communications. We also do our best to ensure that those messages are clearly linked to our overall commitment to be a positive member of the communities we serve—and to the coffee farmers who supply our beans. Perhaps our most crucial tool is our annual corporate social responsibility report. By providing audited, verifiable updates on the key issues that Starbucks and our stakeholders value, we demonstrate our commitment to economic transparency and to upholding our own guiding principles.

Q: How do you get the message out about Starbucks in countries outside the U.S.? What sort of promotions do you plan? Do local partners provide assistance with your marketing? And do you need to adjust the messages or means of communication from country to country or region to region?

As in North America, we do very little traditional advertising in our international markets. We use local public relations agencies and leverage our teams in Europe, the Middle East and Africa, the Asia-Pacific region, and Latin America to create locally relevant promotions. We also have a number of business partners who use their experience to find just the right mix of local taste with Starbucks brand.

Q: We've seen Starbucks coffee in many places other than retail coffeehouses these days. What type of business relationships have you developed with other companies? How do you select a partner who would be a good fit? Is anything new on the horizon?

Over the years, Starbucks has formed a number of very successful strategic partnerships. By teaming with Pepsi, for instance, we were able to offer bottled Frappuccino® in the grocery aisle and to create Starbucks DoubleShot®. We have a variety of business relationships, from joint ventures to partnerships to licensing, which allow us to both expand the reach of the *Starbucks Experience* and ensure that our brand is communicated consistently. When we explore potential partnerships, we use our Mission Statement and Guiding Principles as the benchmark. It's important that our organizations have similar values and approaches to business in general. Then we match up our capabilities to see whether there is a complementary fit that benefits us both.

Q: What would you advise students to help them get a solid start in a marketing career? Do internships or other experiences play a role?

Internships, job shadowing, and other types of exploratory experiences are a great way to get started in any profession. I definitely recommend that students start actively working in the field during their school years. There are usually many short-term opportunities on campus or with nonprofit organizations. There is nothing like getting that experience in the basics—writing press releases, managing events, contributing content to newsletters or websites—to get a jumpstart on your career. I also encourage students to keep moving and trying new roles either within a large, growing organization such as Starbucks or by exploring various types of companies and organizations. Getting a wide range of experiences and "sampling" provides a strong base from which to go in any direction your career may take.

Interview courtesy of Starbucks Coffee Company

GREENSBURG, INC.

Rebuilding: They Didn't Ask for This

© Steven J. Eliopoulos

On May 4, 2007, the Green Acres Bed & Breakfast at 122 W. Iowa in Greensburg, Kansas was destroyed by an F5 tornado. To innkeepers Janice and John Haney, this wasn't just the loss of a business, but also of their home. The brick, split-level house was built in 1926 by a high school shop teacher. It was tidy, charming, and filled with period detail and Janice's hand-made quilts. "We had never had any intentions of ever building a new house, we were just very happy with the house we had," Janice said. As inviting as the home was, Janice admits that it was drafty and in need of some energy-efficient upgrades. "This was an opportunity for us to want to do something bigger and better and a once-in-a-lifetime opportunity to make it as green as possible," she said. The Haneys did not decide to rebuild right in town, instead choosing to build a larger, more energy-efficient home on some family land about eight miles out of town. For the most part, Janice left the construction to contractors and kept the decorating for herself.

Farrell Allison lived right off Route 54 in a beautiful 100-year-old Victorian with stained glass and elaborate woodwork artfully restored by Allison and his wife. It was a lifelong labor of love, but when the tornado seriously damaged the home and plans were announced to reroute a new highway right through the Allisons' backyard, it was time to move on. Never one to shy from a challenge, Allison hit the books and set out to build the greenest house in Greensburg. His new home is truly state-of-the-art, even for the new Greensburg. Unlike the Haneys, Allison, a soil consultant, is acting as his own contractor, sourcing his own materials, hiring crews and subcontractors and, of course, managing the budget.

"Contractors are a different breed," says Allison. "I had one, the heating and air guy say, 'You know you are really particular!' and I said, 'I'm payin' the bills, I'm the one who's gonna be living in this house, you're not, and this is the way we're gonna build it.'"

Allison has become such an expert in green building that contractors and even government agencies such as the USDA's Rural Development arm have come to him for advice on building green.

Mike Boyles, owner of Calmarc Construction, had been building homes in the Wichita, Kansas, area for years, but when the tornado destroyed 700 houses in Greensburg, he knew exactly what he had to do.

He went home.

"We couldn't be here by ourselves," says Boyles, speaking about B&B Lumber, their regular lumber vendor in Wichita. Even before the tornado, Greensburg residents had a tough time getting contractors, repair services, and supplies. After the tornado, it was impossible to source materials locally, especially the environmentally friendly products Greensburg residents are demanding.

Calmarc's ability to serve these customers relies on the existing relationships with vendors like B&B. Randy Mude, a sales representative with B&B, doesn't mind going the extra mile. "Every stick you move and every piece of plywood you sell is a benefit to your company," says Mude, adding that if the tragedy hadn't happened, he'd probably be doing the same volume of work with Calmarc in Wichita. "If we give Mike and the homeowners out here some extra attention and time, we have to [do it] to make things right." Randy even takes their Greensburg clients to his own home to get ideas and see what some of the products will look like. In turn, Randy gets the opportunity to learn about and try new green materials, which he hopes someday to sell to larger developers.

While the town provides residents with a list of reliable contractors, most are not from the area and don't understand the needs of the people the way Boyles does. "They didn't ask for this, and we have to understand that," he says. Those who choose to build back green are constantly researching and bringing questions and ideas to Mike and Randy. Boyles often incorporates pieces from the old homes into the new homes he builds, and spends a lot of extra time working with his Greensburg clients, adding, "if this was a different place and I didn't know the people, it wouldn't be worth it."

When it comes to buyers and sellers, regardless of whether you're talking business-to-consumer or business-to-business, the same principles apply; caveat emptor, buyer beware! The Haneys, like most homeowners, put their trust and dollars in an outside contractor and luckily for them, their new home came out beautifully. Sadly, not all Greensburg residents have been this lucky. A few homeowners have fallen victim to shady contractors who have overcharged or left them with half-finished homes.

Farrell Allison's do-it-yourself plan saves him money by not paying the markup an outside contractor would charge, and he gets ultimate control over the project. On the other hand, he lacks the leverage and buying power companies like Calmarc have with B&B.

Mike Boyles lives in the best (or worst) of both worlds. He's got all the power and none of it, depending on whether he's dealing with a client or dealing with a supplier.

Questions

1. How are the Haneys, Farrell Allison, and Mike Boyles similar in terms of their consumer behavior? How are they different?

2. Would you consider Mr. Allison a regular consumer or a B2B buyer?

3. Why is it important that Calmarc maintain a good buyer–seller relationship with B&B? What does Calmarc get out of it and what's in it for B&B?

4. Write a report on the advantages and disadvantages of working with customers who want to act as their own contractors.

PART 3

Target Market Selection

© Getty Images

CHAP8TER

Marketing Research
and Sales
Forecasting

© Terri Miller/E-Visual Communications, Inc.

Procter & Gamble's Research for a Better Environment

Big companies have a big impact on customers' lives—and the world in general. Consumer products giant Procter & Gamble (P&G) takes its position in the market seriously. Not only does

P&G work to make its customers' lives easier, but it also wants to lessen its impact on the environment. So the company created the position of vice president–global sustainability. Len Sauers, who currently holds that

office, defines sustainability "very broadly and very simply: ensuring a better quality of life for everyone, and for generations to come." To achieve that goal, the firm spends considerable time and money developing

sustainable innovations, lightening the company's environmental footprint, and standing firm against "greenwashing," pretending a run-of-the-mill product is really green. Another mandate, expressed by a researcher who has worked with the firm, is helping to make environmentally friendly products easy to use. "Finding the 'right thing to do' won't help much if most people won't do it," he says.

A long tradition of marketing research lies behind P&G's ability to pair green initiatives with brands and products that meet consumers' needs. It developed its highly profitable Swiffer floor cleaner by observing average people in their homes and watching "in excruciating detail" how they cleaned their floors. Discovering that most people used lots of hot water to clean the floor and then clean the mop, and that water was ineffective at removing the real problem—dust—led to Swiffer's electrostatic disposable cloths, which the company believes saves water and energy and reduces

the amount of chemicals released into the environment.

Taking its observation methods to Mexico, P&G adopted a "consumer closeness" program that allowed employees to live with lower-income Mexican customers for several days, sharing meals, shopping, and other everyday activities. The "Living It" program helped the company understand why its Downy fabric softener wasn't a bigger hit with homemakers, who take such pride in caring for their family's clothes that they devote more time to laundry than to the rest of their household chores combined. Nearly all use softener, even when washing by hand. "By spending time with women, we learned that the softening process is really demanding," said the Downy brand manager. The reason? Millions of families have

running water only a few hours a day and still bring buckets to neighborhood wells. Most have washing machines that are only semiautomatic, meaning the user must add and extract the water by hand. At the same time, Mexican women put their laundry through a labor- and water-intensive six-step process, including four rinse cycles that consumed a great deal of water. The turning point came with P&G's realization that water was extremely valuable to its Mexican customers. "And we only got that by experiencing how they live their life," says the brand manager.

The result was Downy Single Rinse, which reduces the laundry process to three steps—with one rinse cycle—which saves huge amounts of time, labor, and water. The product has been a hit since its introduction.[1]

OBJECTIVES

1 Describe the development of the marketing research function and its major activities.

2 Explain the steps in the marketing research process.

3 Distinguish between primary and secondary data and identify the sources of each type.

4 Explain the different sampling techniques used by marketing researchers.

5 Identify the methods by which marketing researchers collect primary data.

6 Explain the challenges of conducting marketing research in global markets.

7 Outline the most important uses of computer technology in marketing research.

8 Identify the major types of forecasting methods.

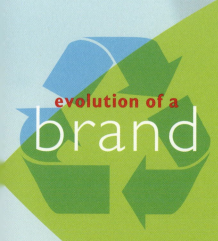

evolution of a
brand

P&G was the first company to have a marketing research department, and it has long been known for conducting thousands of hours of customer interviews, focus groups, and product testing each year. Sometimes the company conducts this research in specially created environments—a simulated drugstore, grocery store, living room, baby play center, and so on. Several years ago, P&G also became the first company to issue a corporate sustainability report.

- What do you think is the link between sustainable products and marketing research?

- P&G created another intensive marketing research effort called "Working It," in which its employees gain insight into how shopkeepers operate their stores and how shoppers make buying choices by actually working the counter in small Mexican stores. What sorts of lessons or ideas about "green" products do you think participants in "Working It" might learn?

chapter overview

marketing research
Process of collecting and using information for marketing decision making.

Collecting and managing information about what customers need and want is a challenging task for any marketer. **Marketing research** is the process of collecting and using information for marketing decision making. Data comes from a variety of sources. Some results come from well-planned studies designed to elicit specific information. Other valuable information comes from sales force reports, accounting records, and published reports. Still other data emerges from controlled experiments and computer simulations. Thanks to new database technologies, some data companies collect is compiled for them by research specialists, and some is collected and compiled by in-house marketing researchers. Marketing research, by presenting pertinent information in a useful format, aids

decision makers in analyzing data and in suggesting possible actions.

This chapter discusses the marketing research function. Marketers use research to understand their customers, target customer segments, and develop long-term customer relationships—all keys to profitability. Information collected through marketing research underlies much of the material on market segmentation discussed in the following chapter. Clearly, the marketing research function is the primary source of information needed to make effective marketing decisions. The use of technology to mine data and gather business and competitive intelligence is also discussed, as is technology's vast impact on marketing research decision making and planning. This chapter also explains how marketing research techniques are used to make accurate sales forecasts, a critical component of marketing planning.

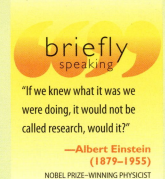

briefly speaking

"If we knew what it was we were doing, it would not be called research, would it?"

—Albert Einstein (1879–1955)
NOBEL PRIZE–WINNING PHYSICIST

The Marketing Research Function

Before looking at how marketing research is conducted, we must first examine its historical development, the people and organizations it involves, and the activities it entails. Because an underlying purpose of research is to find out more about consumers, research is clearly central to effective customer satisfaction and customer relationship programs. Media technologies such as the Internet and virtual reality are opening up new channels through which researchers can tap into consumer information.

⬛ Describe the development of the marketing research function and its major activities.

DEVELOPMENT OF THE MARKETING RESEARCH FUNCTION

It has been 130 years since advertising pioneer N. W. Ayer conducted the first organized marketing research project in 1879. A second important milestone in the development of marketing research occurred 32 years later, when Charles C. Parlin organized the nation's first commercial research department at Curtis Publishing, publisher of *The Saturday Evening Post*.

Parlin got his start as a marketing researcher by counting soup cans in Philadelphia's garbage. Here is what happened. Parlin, an ad salesman, was trying to persuade the Campbell Soup

Company to advertise in *The Saturday Evening Post.* Campbell Soup resisted, believing that the *Post* reached primarily working-class readers, who they thought preferred to make their own soup. Campbell Soup marketers were targeting higher-income people who could afford to pay for the convenience of soup in a can. To prove Campbell wrong, Parlin began counting soup cans in the garbage collected from different neighborhoods. His research revealed that working-class families bought more canned soup than wealthy households, who had servants to cook for them. Campbell Soup soon became a regular *Post* client. It is interesting to note that garbage remains a good source of information for marketing researchers even today. Prior to the current cutbacks in food service, some airlines studied the leftovers from onboard meals to determine what to serve passengers.

Early on, Campbell Soup marketers targeted higher-income people who could afford to pay for the convenience of soup in a can, until market research revealed that working-class families bought more canned soup than wealthy households.

Most early research gathered little more than written testimonials from purchasers of firms' products. Research methods became more sophisticated during the 1930s as the development of statistical techniques led to refinements in sampling procedures and greater accuracy in research findings.

In recent years, advances in computer technology have significantly changed the complexion of marketing research. Besides accelerating the pace and broadening the base of data collection, computers have aided marketers in making informed decisions about problems and opportunities. Simulations, for example, allow marketers to evaluate alternatives by posing "what-if" questions. Marketing researchers at many consumer goods firms simulate product introductions through computer programs to determine whether to risk real-world product launches or even to subject products to test marketing.

WHO CONDUCTS MARKETING RESEARCH?

The size and organizational form of the marketing research function usually are tied to the structure of the company. Some firms organize research units to support different product lines, brands, or geographic areas. Others organize their research functions according to the types of research they need to perform such as sales analysis, new-product development, advertising evaluation, or sales forecasting.

Many firms outsource their research needs and depend on independent marketing research firms. These independent organizations might specialize in handling just part of a larger study such as conducting consumer interviews. Firms can also contract out entire research studies.

Marketers usually decide whether to conduct a study internally or through an outside organization based on cost. Another major consideration is the reliability and accuracy of the information collected by an outside organization. Because collecting marketing data is what these outside organizations do full time, the information they gather often is more thorough and accurate than that collected by less experienced in-house staff. Often an outside marketing research firm can provide technical assistance and expertise not available within the company's marketing department. Interaction with outside suppliers also helps ensure that a researcher does not conduct a study only to validate a favorite viewpoint or preferred option.

Marketing research companies range in size from sole proprietorships to national and international firms such as ACNielsen, Information Resources, and Arbitron. They can be classified as syndicated services, full-service suppliers, or limited-service suppliers depending on the types of services they offer to clients. Some full-service organizations are also willing to take on limited-service activities.

Marketers usually decide whether to conduct a study internally or externally based on cost as well as reliability and accuracy of the information collected by an outside organization. This ad touts quality and dependability.

© Courtesy of Thoroughbred Opinion Research

Pedigree Does Matter

Our senior partners and project managers are collaborative. The interviewers are highly trained. Your team communicates with you throughout the project. That's market research with a pedigree.

Thoroughbred Opinion Research, your winner in field research.

To learn more call

Vic Walsh
502.338.6375 or
Karen Flannery
312.573.9960

THOROUGHBRED
OPINION RESEARCH
Consultative. Trusted. Dependable.
www.torinc.net

Syndicated Services

An organization that regularly provides a standardized set of data to all customers is called a **syndicated service.** Mediamark Research, for example, operates a syndicated product research service based on personal interviews with adults regarding their exposure to advertising media. Clients include advertisers, advertising agencies, magazines, newspapers, broadcasters, and cable TV networks.

Another syndicated service provider is J. D. Power and Associates, a global marketing information firm headquartered in California that specializes in surveying customer satisfaction, product quality, and buyer behavior. Among its customers are companies in the telecommunications, travel and hotel, marine, utilities, healthcare, building, consumer electronics, automotive, and financial services industries.[2]

Full-Service Research Suppliers

An organization that contracts with clients to conduct complete marketing research projects is called a **full-service research supplier.** Brain Research Group, a Mexican marketing research firm, provides quantitative and qualitative research and various field studies, including face-to-face and telephone interviews, online interviews, multinational studies, B2B interviews, and even "mystery shopper" research to collect information about retail outlets. The company also studies public opinion and buyer behavior and evaluates Web pages and work environments. Its editing department reviews questionnaires before they are used, under strict supervision, by Brain Research's staff in interviews, focus groups, and other types of observation techniques, including video.[3] A full-service supplier becomes the client's marketing research arm, performing all of the steps in the marketing research process (discussed later in this chapter).

Limited-Service Research Suppliers

A marketing research firm that specializes in a limited number of activities, such as conducting field interviews or performing data processing, is called a **limited-service research supplier.** Nielsen Media Research specializes in tracking what people watch on TV, and who watches what, in more than 40 countries.[4] The firm also prepares studies to help clients develop advertising strategies and to track awareness and interest. Syndicated services can also be considered a type of limited-service research supplier.

CUSTOMER SATISFACTION MEASUREMENT PROGRAMS

In their marketing research, firms often focus on tracking the satisfaction levels of current customers. Austin, Texas–based Bazaarvoice charges a monthly fee to clients and does everything from designing and managing a firm's customer feedback area on its Web site to moderating online discussion groups and analyzing comments.[5] Some marketers have also gained valuable insights by tracking the dissatisfaction that led customers to abandon certain products for those of competitors. Some customer defections are only partial; customers may remain somewhat satisfied with a business but not completely satisfied. Such attitudes could lead them to take their business elsewhere. Studying the underlying causes of customer defections, even partial defections, can be useful for identifying problem

Some organizations conduct their own measurement programs through online or phone polls and surveys.

areas that need attention. Since 1991, the annual Airline Quality Rating survey has scored specific carriers and the airline industry in general on such measures as on-time performance, baggage handling, diverted and cancelled flights, overbooking, and number of customer complaints. The national study, sponsored by the Aviation Institute at the University of Nebraska at Omaha and Wichita State University, recently reported "the worst year ever for the U.S. airlines" in terms of overall performance quality.[6]

Some organizations conduct their own measurement programs through online polls and surveys. California Pizza Kitchen's servers point out to customers a special code number printed on their check. Entering the code number on the company Web site brings up a customer satisfaction survey that offers respondents free food or discounts on their next meal.[7]

assessment check

1. Identify the different classifications of marketing research suppliers and explain how they differ from one another.

2. What research methods can be used to measure customer satisfaction?

The Marketing Research Process

2 Explain the steps in the marketing research process.

As discussed earlier, business executives rely on marketing research to provide the information they need to make effective decisions regarding their firm's current and future activities. The chances of making good decisions improve when the right information is provided at the right time during decision making. To achieve this goal, marketing researchers often follow the six-step process shown in Figure 8.1. In the initial stages, researchers define the problem, conduct exploratory research, and formulate a hypothesis to be tested. Next, they create a design for the research study and collect needed data. Finally, researchers interpret and present the research information. The following sections take a closer look at each step of the marketing research process.

DEFINE THE PROBLEM

A popular anecdote advises that well-defined problems are half solved. A well-defined problem permits the researcher to focus on securing the exact information needed for the solution. Clearly defining the question that research needs to answer increases the speed and accuracy of the research process.

Researchers must carefully avoid confusing symptoms of a problem with the problem itself. A symptom merely alerts marketers that a problem exists. For example, suppose that a maker of frozen pizzas sees its market share drop from 8 to 5 percent in six months. The loss

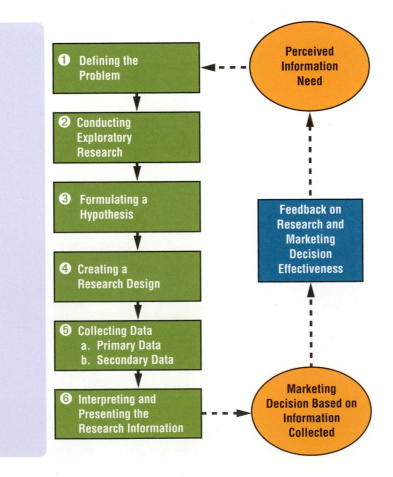

figure 8.1

The Marketing Research Process

of market share is a symptom of a problem the company must solve. To define the problem, the firm must look for the underlying causes of its market share loss.

A logical starting point in identifying the problem might be to evaluate the firm's target market and marketing mix elements. Suppose, for example, a firm has recently changed its promotional strategies. Research might then seek to answer the question "What must we do to improve the effectiveness of our marketing mix?" The firm's marketers might also look at possible environmental changes. Perhaps a new competitor entered the firm's market. Decision makers will need information to help answer the question "What must we do to distinguish our company from the new competitor?"

The Kmart chain, owned by Sears Holding Corp., has lost sales and market share to Wal-Mart, which typically beats it on price, and to Target, whose stores often are better designed and more conveniently located. An earlier attempt to convert old Kmart locations into Sears stores failed to help either brand because their customer bases do not overlap. Now Sears is exploring its problem by trying to pinpoint what products customers like and how they should be displayed. Company marketers are conducting experiments with two Kmart test stores in Rockford, Illinois, that it has quietly remodeled and restocked. A smaller city but one the chain believes reflects the core of its target customer segment, Rockford is "the testing ground for what will resonate with our customers around the Kmart brand," says Sears Holdings vice president for store initiatives. "Not what we think about the customer, but what we really get firsthand. If something isn't working, we will try and make it better."[8] Through the test stores, marketers can identify its problems and find out what its target market really prefers.

CONDUCT EXPLORATORY RESEARCH

Once a firm has defined the question it wants to answer, researchers can begin exploratory research. **Exploratory research** seeks to discover the cause of a specific problem by discussing the problem with informed sources both within and outside the firm and by examining data from other information sources. Marketers at Romano's Macaroni Grill, part of Dallas-based Brinker International, might talk with their customers, suppliers, and retailers. Executives at Brinker might also ask for input from the sales force or look for overall market clues. In addition, exploratory research can include evaluation of company records, such as sales and profit analyses, and available competitive data. Marketing researchers often refer to internal data collection as situation analysis. The term *informal investigation* often is used for exploratory interviews with informed people outside the researchers' firms.

exploratory research
Process of discussing a marketing problem with informed sources both within and outside the firm and examining information from secondary sources.

Using Internal Data

Marketers can find valuable data in their firm's own internal records. Typical sources of internal data are sales records, financial statements, and marketing cost analyses. Marketers analyze sales performance records to gain an overall view of company efficiency and to find clues to potential problems. Easily prepared from company invoices or a computer database system, this **sales analysis** can provide important details to management. The study typically compares actual and expected sales based on a detailed sales forecast by territory, product, customer, and salesperson. Once the sales quota—the level of expected sales to which actual results are compared—has been established, it is a simple process to compare actual results with expected performance. St. Louis–based Emerson Electric, a growing industrial conglomerate that makes everything from telecommunications wires to appliance parts, asks its managers to categorize sales of new products according to whether they represent minor improvements, major improvements, products new to the business, or products new to the world. Using these measures for strategic planning "just gives us better data about where our resources are going," says the CEO of Emerson Climate Technologies. The goal is to free up those resources for a concentrated push on creating products that are truly ground breaking.[9]

Other possible breakdowns for sales analysis separate transactions by customer type, product, sales method (Internet, mail, telephone, or personal contact), type of order (cash or credit), and order size. Sales analysis is one of the least expensive and most important sources of marketing information available to a firm.

Accounting data, as summarized in the firm's financial statements, can be another good tool for identifying financial issues that influence marketing. Using ratio analysis, researchers can compare performance in current and previous years against industry benchmarks. These exercises may hint at possible problems, but only more detailed analysis would reveal specific causes of indicated variations.

A third source of internal information is *marketing cost analysis*—evaluation of expenses for tasks such as selling, warehousing, advertising, and delivery to determine the profitability of particular customers, territories, or product lines. Firms often examine the allocation of costs to products, customers, and territories. Marketing decision makers then evaluate the profitability of particular customers and territories on the basis of the sales produced and the costs incurred in generating those sales. Sometimes internal data can produce remarkably detailed customer profiles.

Like sales analysis and financial research, marketing cost analysis is most useful when it provides information linked to other forms of marketing research. A later section of this chapter will address how computer technologies can accomplish these linkages and move information among a firm's units.

FORMULATE A HYPOTHESIS

After defining the problem and conducting an exploratory investigation, the marketer needs to formulate a **hypothesis**—a tentative explanation for some specific event. A hypothesis is a statement about the relationship among variables that carries clear implications for testing this relationship. It sets the stage for more in-depth research by further clarifying what researchers need to test. For example, Olive Garden restaurants might want to see whether good customer service is related to its increased sales, so its marketers would conduct a survey of customers to test this hypothesis.

Not all studies test specific hypotheses, however, a carefully designed study can benefit from the rigor introduced by developing a hypothesis before beginning data collection and analysis.

CREATE A RESEARCH DESIGN

To test hypotheses and find solutions to marketing problems, a marketer creates a **research design,** a master plan or model for conducting marketing research. In planning a research project, marketers must be sure the study will measure what they intend to measure. A second important research design consideration is the selection of respondents. Marketing researchers use sampling techniques (discussed later in the chapter) to determine which consumers to include in their studies.

Test kitchens and willing palates are indispensable in the prepared-food business. At Kraft's test kitchen, brand managers are among those who sample frozen pizza products headed for supermarket aisles and weigh in on their flavor subtleties. With adult consumers craving the gourmet toppings and thin crusts available in restaurants and pizza chains, exotic ingredients like eggplant, caramelized onions, cilantro, artichoke, Gouda, and kalamata olives are tested against standby cheeses and pepperoni slices. While not always precise or scientific, comments like "Bring up the salt. Take the olives down," may shape what consumers find in their freezer aisle.[10]

3 **Distinguish between primary and secondary data and identify the sources of each type.**

COLLECT DATA

Marketing researchers gather two kinds of data: secondary data and primary data. **Secondary data** is information from previously published or compiled sources. Census data is an example. **Primary data** refers to information collected for the first time specifically for a marketing research study. An example of primary data is statistics collected from a survey that asks current customers about their preferences for product improvements. Global research firm Synovate collects primary data in the Americas, Asia, Europe, and the Middle East for its clients. The com-

secondary data Previously published information.

primary data Information collected for a specific investigation.

pany operates in 115 cities in 51 countries around the world, conducts thousands of projects and focus groups and millions of interviews, and employs nearly 6,000 people with "one thing in common: boundless curiosity."[11]

Secondary data offers two important advantages: (1) it is almost always less expensive to gather than primary data and (2) researchers usually spend less time to locate and use secondary data. A research study that requires primary data may take three to four months to complete, while a researcher often can gather secondary data in a matter of days.

Secondary data has limitations that primary data does not. First, published information can quickly become obsolete. A marketer analyzing the population of various areas may discover that even the most recent census figures already are out of date because of rapid growth and changing demographics. Second, published data collected for an unrelated purpose may not be completely relevant to the marketer's specific needs. For example, census data do not reveal the brand preferences of consumers.

Although research to gather primary data can cost more and take longer, the results can provide richer, more detailed information than secondary data offers. The choice between secondary and primary data is tied to cost, applicability, and effectiveness. Many marketing research projects combine secondary and primary data to fully answer marketing questions. This chapter examines specific methods for collecting both secondary and primary data in later sections.

The Wheel.
The Lightbulb.
The Microchip.
Sliced bread.

Where would the world be without curiosity?

Global research firm Synovate collects primary data around the world, conducting thousands of projects and focus groups and millions of interviews.

INTERPRET AND PRESENT RESEARCH DATA

The final step in the marketing research process is to interpret the findings and present them to decision makers in a format that allows managers to make effective judgments. Possible differences in interpretations of research results may occur between marketing researchers and their audiences due to differing backgrounds, levels of knowledge, and experience. Both oral and written reports should be presented in a manner designed to minimize such misinterpretations.

Marketing researchers and research users must cooperate at every stage in the research process. Too many studies go unused because management fears that the results are of little use, once they hear lengthy discussions of research limitations or unfamiliar terminology. Marketing researchers must remember to direct their reports toward management and not to other researchers. They should spell out their conclusions in clear and concise terms that can be put into action. Reports should confine technical details of the research methods to an appendix, if they

assessment check

1. What are the six steps in the marketing research process?

2. What is the goal of exploratory research?

are included at all. By presenting research results to all key executives at a single sitting, researchers can ensure that everyone will understand the findings. Decision makers can then quickly reach consensus on what the results mean and what actions need to be taken.

Marketing Research Methods

Clearly, data collection is an integral part of the marketing research process. One of the most time-consuming parts of collecting data is determining what method the marketer should use to obtain the data. This section discusses the most commonly used methods by which marketing researchers find both secondary and primary data.

SECONDARY DATA COLLECTION

Secondary data comes from many sources. The overwhelming quantity of secondary data available at little or no cost challenges researchers to select only data relevant to the problem or issue studied.

Secondary data consists of two types: internal and external data. Internal data, as discussed earlier, includes sales records, product performance reviews, sales force activity reports, and marketing cost reports. External data comes from a variety of sources, including government records, syndicated research services, and industry publications. Computerized databases provide access to vast amounts of data from both inside and outside an organization. The following sections on government data, private data, and online sources focus on databases and other external data sources available to marketing researchers.

Government Data

The federal government is the nation's most important source of marketing data. Census data provides the most frequently used government statistics. A census of population is conducted every ten years and is made available at no charge in local libraries, on computer disks, and via the Internet. Because of problems implementing a computerized system, the U.S. Census Bureau recently abandoned plans to go high-tech with handheld computers for data collection. Instead, it will count the country's more than 306 million residents by training 600,000 workers to collect data with pen and paper from those who don't respond to its mailed survey.[12] The Census Bureau also conducts a periodic census of housing, population, business, manufacturers, agriculture, minerals, and governments.

The U.S. Census of Population contains a wealth of valuable information for marketers. It breaks down the population by very small geographic areas, making it possible to determine population traits by city block or census tract in large cities. It divides the populations of nonmetropolitan areas into census tracts, which are important for marketing analysis because they highlight populations of about 1,500 to 8,000 people with similar traits. This data helps marketers, such as local retailers and shopping center developers, gather vital information about customers in an immediate neighborhood without spending time or money to conduct comprehensive surveys. The Census Bureau uses a variety of statistical techniques to group households into homogeneous clusters of people with similar lifestyles and spending habits and who listen to similar kinds of broadcast media.[13]

Marketing researchers have found even more valuable resources in the government's computerized mapping database originally called the TIGER system, for Topographically Integrated Geographic Encoding and Referencing system. This system overlays topographic features such as railroads, highways, and rivers with census data such as household income figures. Recently updated with an Oracle relational database, the new TIGER/Line Shapefiles are downloadable and cover all 50 states, the District of Columbia, and Puerto Rico.[14]

Marketers often get other information from the federal government, such as the following:

▷ *Monthly Catalog of United States Government Publications* and *Statistical Abstract of the United States,* published annually and available online as the *Catalog of U.S. Government Publications (CGP);*

▷ *Survey of Current Business,* updated monthly by the Bureau of Economic Analysis; and

▷ *County and City Data Book,* typically published every three years and available online, providing data on all states, counties, and cities of more than 25,000 residents.

State and city governments serve as additional important sources of information on employment, production, and sales activities. In addition, university bureaus of business and economic research frequently collect and disseminate valuable information.

Private Data

Many private organizations provide information for marketing decision makers. A trade association may be an excellent source of data on activities in a particular industry. Thomson Gale's *Encyclopedia of Associations,* available in many libraries, can help marketers track down trade associations that may have pertinent data. Also, the advertising industry continuously collects data on audiences reached by various media.

Business and trade magazines also publish a wide range of valuable data. Ulrich's *Guide to International Periodicals,* another common library reference, can point researchers in the direction of trade publications that conduct and publish industry-specific research. General business magazines can also be good sources. *Sales & Marketing Management,* for instance, publishes an annual *Survey of Media Markets* that combines statistics for population, effective buying income (EBI), and retail sales into buying power indexes that indicate each geographic market's ability to buy.

Because few libraries carry specialized trade journals, the best way to gather data from them is either directly from the publishers or through online periodical databases such as ProQuest Direct's ABI/Inform, available at many libraries. Increasingly, trade publications maintain Web home pages that allow archival searches. Larger libraries often can provide directories and other publications that can help researchers find secondary data. For instance, Guideline's *FindEx: The Directory of Market Research Reports, Studies, and Surveys* lists a tremendous variety of completed research studies available for purchase.

Several national firms offer information to businesses by subscription. RoperASW is a global database service; its Roper Reports Worldwide provides continuing data on consumer attitudes, life stages, lifestyle, and buying behavior for more than 30 developed and developing countries.

Electronic systems that scan UPC bar codes speed purchase transactions and provide data used for inventory control, ordering, and delivery. Scanning technology is widely used by grocers and other retailers, and marketing research companies such as ACNielsen and Information Resources store this data in commercially available databases. These scanner-based information services track consumer purchases of a wide variety of UPC-coded products. Retailers can use this information to target customers with the right merchandise at the right time.

Scanning technology is widely used by grocers and other retailers. Marketing research companies, such as ACNielsen and Information Resources, store these data in databases.

© Mark Douet/Stone/Getty Images

Newer techniques that rely on radio-frequency identification (RFID) technology are in growing use. Wal-Mart has run successful tests showing that RFID reduced out-of-stocks and cut down dramatically on manual orders and excess inventory, with the potential to save almost $300 million a year, and a study by the University of Kansas showed that stores could replace out-of-stock items three times faster if they carried RFID labels instead of standard bar codes.[15] Use of RFID to track an individual's purchase and use of products is, however, controversial because of privacy concerns. Currently, the technology is used for aggregate data.

ACNielsen SalesNet uses the Internet to deliver scanner data quickly to clients. Data is processed as soon as it is received from supermarkets and is then forwarded to marketing researchers so they can perform more in-depth analysis. At the same time, Nielsen representatives summarize the data in both graphic and spreadsheet form and post it on the Internet for immediate access by clients.

Online Sources of Secondary Data

The tools of cyberspace sometimes simplify the hunt for secondary data. Hundreds of databases and other sources of information are available online. A well-designed, Internet-based marketing research project can cost less yet yield faster results than offline research.

The Internet has spurred the growth of research aggregators—companies that acquire, catalog, reformat, segment, and then resell premium research reports that have already been published. Aggregators put valuable data within reach of marketers who lack the time or the budget to commission custom research. Because Web technology makes their databases easy to search, aggregators such as Datamonitor and eMarketer can compile detailed, specialized reports quickly and cost-effectively.[16]

Social networking sites also yield valuable marketing information. YouTube now offers a service called YouTube Insight that gives its video-uploading account holders an array of statistics, graphs, and maps about the audiences they attract, far more specific than just the number of views it used to collect. "It's been hard [until now] to measure the success of online advertising campaigns," says the executive vice president of an interactive ad agency. But with innovations like Insight, and a similar weekly report from Facebook, "people are trying to dig down into the numbers." Web companies that advertise on other sites can now also track visitors' activities on more home pages than just their own and collect far more information about potential markets than just their size. Such information helps companies target online ads to the people who might be interested in them. The CEO of Web ad agency Carat Americas said, "That's the whole idea here: put dog food ads in front of people who have dogs."[17]

Researchers must, however, carefully evaluate the validity of information they find on the Internet. People without in-depth knowledge of the subject matter may post information in a newsgroup. Similarly, Web pages might contain information gathered using questionable research methods. The phrase *caveat emptor* ("let the buyer beware") should guide evaluation of secondary data on the Internet.

Companies must also be careful about how they interpret what they learn. When online language-training company GlobalEnglish surveyed customers about its products, user satisfaction was high, but a frequent complaint arose that the programs required too much repetitive vocabulary drill. After studying the comments in depth, the company decided the right response was to do nothing, because repetition is essential to learning a new language successfully.[18]

SAMPLING TECHNIQUES

sampling Process of selecting survey respondents or research participants.

4 **Explain the different sampling techniques used by marketing researchers.**

Before undertaking a study to gather primary data, researchers must first identify which participants to include in the study. **Sampling** is the process of selecting survey respondents or research participants. Sampling is important because, if a study fails to involve consumers who accurately reflect the target market, the research is likely to yield misleading conclusions.

The total group of people the researcher wants to study is called the **population** or **universe.** For a political campaign study, the population would be all eligible voters. For research about a new lipstick line, it might be all women in a certain age bracket. The sample is a representative group chosen from this population. Researchers rarely gather information from a study's total population, resulting in a census. Unless the total population is small, the costs of a census are simply too high. Sometimes limitations can reduce the size of the sample. Online surveys, for instance, often draw large but self-selected, rather than random, groups of respondents who don't usually represent the total population. And when research firms offer incentives to respond to surveys and questionnaires, these rewards often help skew the results even further.[19]

Samples can be classified as either probability samples or nonprobability samples. A **probability sample** is one that gives every member of the population a chance of being selected. Types of probability samples include simple random samples, stratified samples, and cluster samples.

In a **simple random sample,** every member of the relevant universe has an equal opportunity of selection. The draft lottery of the Vietnam era is an example. The days of the year were drawn and set into an array. The placement of a person's birthday in this list determined his likelihood of being called for service. In a **stratified sample,** randomly selected subsamples of different groups are represented in the total sample. Stratified samples provide efficient, representative groups that are relatively homogeneous for a certain characteristic for such studies as opinion polls in which groups of individuals share various divergent viewpoints. In a **cluster sample,** researchers select a sample of subgroups (or clusters) from which they draw respondents. Each cluster reflects the diversity of the whole population being sampled. This cost-efficient type of probability sample is widely used when the entire population cannot be listed or enumerated.

In contrast, a **nonprobability sample** relies on personal judgment somewhere in the selection process. In other words, researchers decide which particular groups to study. Types of nonprobability samples are convenience samples and quota samples. A **convenience sample** is a nonprobability sample selected from among readily available respondents; this sample often is called an *accidental sample* because those included just happen to be in the place where the study is being conducted. Mall intercept surveys and TV call-in opinion polls are good examples. Marketing researchers sometimes use convenience samples in exploratory research but not in definitive studies. A **quota sample** is a nonprobability sample divided to maintain the proportion of certain characteristics among different segments or groups seen in the population as a whole. In other words, each field worker is assigned a quota that specifies the number and characteristics of the people to contact. It differs from a stratified sample in which researchers select subsamples by some random process; in a quota sample, they handpick participants.

probability sample
Sample that gives every member of the population a chance of being selected.

nonprobability sample
Sample that involves personal judgment somewhere in the selection process.

assessment check

1. What is sampling?
2. Explain the different types of probability samples.
3. Identify the types of nonprobability samples.

PRIMARY RESEARCH METHODS

Marketers use a variety of methods for conducting primary research, as Figure 8.2 shows. The principal methods for collecting primary data are observation, surveys, and controlled experiments. The choice among these methods depends on the issues under study and the decisions that marketers need to make. In some cases, researchers may decide to combine techniques during the research process.

5 Identify the methods by which marketing researchers collect primary data.

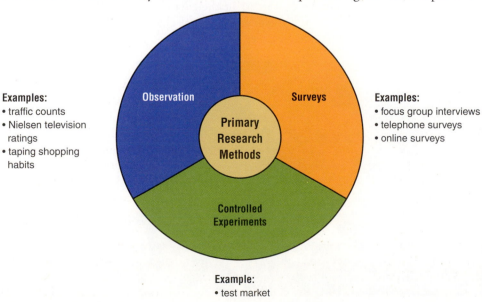

Examples:
- traffic counts
- Nielsen television ratings
- taping shopping habits

Observation

Surveys

Primary Research Methods

Controlled Experiments

Examples:
- focus group interviews
- telephone surveys
- online surveys

Example:
- test market

figure 8.2

Types of Primary Research

Observation Method

In observational studies, researchers view the overt actions of subjects being studied. Marketers trying to understand how consumers behave in certain situations find observation a useful technique. Observation tactics may be as simple as counting the number of cars passing by a potential site for a fast-food restaurant or checking the license plates at a shopping center near a state line to determine where shoppers live.

Technological advances provide increasingly sophisticated ways for observing consumer behavior. The television industry relies on data from people meters, electronic remote-control devices that record the TV viewing habits of individual household members to measure the popularity of TV shows. Traditional people meters require each viewer to press a button each time he or she turns on the TV, changes channels, or leaves the room.

Nielsen Customized Research recently studied supermarket shoppers' habits in stores by observing how much attention they paid to selecting discounted products. The observations revealed that some marketers may be spending too much money unnecessarily redesigning products in ways that merely make them harder to identify, such as canned coffee and mayonnaise, and giving up profit by discounting in categories like energy drinks and soft drinks where price is less of a factor than brand name.[20]

Pudding Media in San Jose is introducing a new Internet phone service, similar to Skype, that charges no tolls but instead uses voice recognition software to monitor conversations and display relevant ads on the subscriber's computer screen even before he or she has hung up the call. "We saw that when people are speaking on the phone, typically they were doing something else," says Pudding Media's CEO. "So we said, 'Let's use that,' and actually present them with things that are relevant to the conversation while it's happening." Some advertising executives are cautious, however. "We're getting more intrusive with each passing technology," one warns.[21]

Videotaping consumers in action is also gaining acceptance as a research technique. Cookware manufacturers may videotape consumers cooking in their own kitchens to evaluate how they use their pots and pans. A toothbrush manufacturer asked marketing research firm E-Lab to videotape consumers brushing their teeth and using mouthwash in its quest to develop products that would leave behind the sensation of cleanliness and freshness.

In an effort to understand what makes younger consumers tick, a trend-forecasting firm called Teenage Research Unlimited has auditioned and hired a panel of more than 300 "diverse, trend-setting, savvy teens" to participate in focus groups and research queries for its Trendwatch Panel. The company has also interviewed more than 1 million young people in 15 countries around the world for its annual TRU Study report.[22]

Interpretative Research

interpretative research
Observational research method developed by social anthropologists in which customers are observed in their natural setting and their behavior is interpreted based on an understanding of social and cultural characteristics; also known as ethnography, or "going native."

Another type of primary research is **interpretative research,** a method in which a researcher observes a customer or group of customers in their natural setting and interprets their behavior based on an understanding of the social and cultural characteristics of that setting. We discuss interpretative research in more detail later.

To discover information on attitudes, motives, and opinions, as well as demographic information, researchers can use either interviews or questionnaires.

© AP Images/Alden Pellett

SURVEY METHODS

Observation alone cannot supply all of the desired information. Researchers must ask questions to get information on attitudes, motives, and opinions. It is also difficult to get exact demographic information, such as income levels, from observation. To discover this information, researchers can use either interviews or questionnaires. Philadelphia-based Dorland Healthcare Information provides market research for the healthcare and managed-care market and relies heavily on mail, phone, and fax surveys as well as interviews with knowledgeable sources.[23]

Telephone Interviews

Telephone interviews are a quick and inexpensive method for obtaining a small quantity of relatively impersonal information. Simple, clearly worded questions are easy for interviewers to pose over the phone and are effective at drawing appropriate responses. Telephone surveys have relatively high response rates, especially with repeated calls; calling a number once yields a response rate of 50 to 60 percent, but calling the same number five times raises the response rate to 85 percent. To maximize responses and save costs, some researchers use computerized dialing and digitally synthesized voices that interview respondents.

However, phone surveys have several drawbacks. Most important, many people refuse to take part in them. Their reasons include lack of time, the nuisance factor, negative associations of phone surveys with telemarketing, and poorly designed surveys or questions that are difficult to understand. The National Do Not Call Registry, which regulates telemarketing, excludes calls made for research purposes.[24]

Many respondents hesitate to give personal characteristics about themselves over the telephone. Also, results may be biased by the omission of typical households in which adults are working during the day. Other households, particularly market segments such as single women and physicians, are likely to have unlisted numbers. While computerized random dialing can give access to unlisted numbers, it is restricted in several states.

The popularity of Caller ID systems to screen unwanted calls is another obstacle for telephone researchers. State laws on Caller ID vary. Some require vendors to offer a blocking service to callers who wish to evade the system. Marketers face other problems in obtaining responses from a representative sample of respondents using phone surveys: consumer perception of intrusion into their privacy and the number of consumers in the national Do Not Call Registry.

Other obstacles restrict the usefulness of telephone surveys abroad. In areas where telephone ownership is rare, survey results will be highly biased. Telephone interviewing is also difficult in countries that lack directories or charge landline telephone customers on a per-minute basis, or where call volumes congest limited phone line capacity.

Personal Interviews

The best means for obtaining detailed information about consumers usually is the personal interview because the interviewer can establish rapport with respondents and explain confusing or vague questions. In addition to contacting respondents at their homes or workplaces, marketing research firms can conduct interviews in rented space in shopping centers where they gain wide access to potential buyers of the merchandise they are studying. These locations sometimes feature private interviewing space, videotape equipment, and food preparation facilities for taste tests. As mentioned earlier, interviews conducted in shopping centers typically are called **mall intercepts.** Downtown retail districts and airports provide other valuable locations for marketing researchers.

Focus Groups

Marketers also gather research information through the popular technique of focus group interviews. A **focus group** brings together eight to 12 individuals in one location to discuss a subject of interest. Unlike other interview techniques that elicit information through a question-and-answer format, focus groups usually encourage a general discussion of a predetermined topic. Focus groups can provide quick and relatively inexpensive insight into consumer attitudes and motivations.

In a focus group, the leader, or moderator, typically begins by explaining the purpose of the meeting and suggesting an opening topic. The moderator's main purpose, however, is to stimulate interaction among group members to encourage their discussion of numerous points. The moderator may occasionally interject questions as catalysts to direct the group's discussion. The moderator's job is difficult, requiring preparation and group facilitation skills.

Focus group sessions often last one or two hours. Researchers usually record the discussion on tape, and observers frequently watch through a one-way mirror. Some research firms also allow clients to view focus groups in action through videoconferencing systems.

focus group Simultaneous personal interview of a small group of individuals that relies on group discussion about a certain topic.

Focus groups are a particularly valuable tool for exploratory research, developing new-product ideas, and preliminary testing of alternative marketing strategies. They can also aid in the development of well-structured questionnaires for larger scale research.

Focus groups have a few drawbacks. For instance, one argumentative participant can intimidate everyone else in the group, just as one person who won't open up in the discussion can hold others back. In addition, some group members may say what they think researchers want to hear, offer ideas and opinions for which they have no supporting evidence or experience, or assume everyone feels the same way they do.[25]

Researchers are finding ways to re-create the focus group environment over the Internet. With experienced moderators who have the technical skills to function fluently online, it is possible to gain valuable qualitative information at a fraction of the cost of running a traditional focus group session. Online focus groups can be both cost and time efficient, with immediate results in the form of chat transcripts. The convenience of online conversations tends to improve attendance as well, particularly among those who are otherwise difficult to include, such as professionals and people who travel frequently, and the problem of peer pressure virtually is eliminated. Some drawbacks include the lack of ability to see body language and nonverbal cues, the difficulty of testing any products in which taste or smell is relevant, and the potential for samples to be nonrepresentative because they are limited to those who have Internet access and a certain comfort level with technology.

Mail Surveys

Although personal interviews can provide very detailed information, cost considerations usually prevent an organization from using personal interviews in a large-scale study. A mail survey can be a cost-effective alternative. Mail surveys can provide anonymity that may encourage respondents to give candid answers. They can also help marketers track consumer attitudes through ongoing research and sometimes provide demographic data that may be helpful in market segmentation.

Mail questionnaires do, however, have several limitations. First, response rates typically are much lower than for personal interviews. Second, because researchers must wait for respondents to complete and return questionnaires, mail surveys usually take a considerably longer time to conduct. A third limitation is that questionnaires cannot answer unanticipated questions that occur to respondents as they complete the forms. In addition, complex questions may not be suitable for a mail questionnaire. Finally, unless they gather additional information from nonrespondents through other means, researchers must worry about possible bias in the results stemming from differences between respondents and nonrespondents.

Researchers try to minimize these limitations by carefully developing and pretesting questionnaires. Researchers can boost response rates by keeping questionnaires short and by offering incentives—typically, discount coupons or a dollar bill.

Fax Surveys

The low response rates and long follow-up times associated with mail surveys have spurred interest in the alternative of faxing survey documents. In some cases, faxes may supplement mail surveys; in others, they may be the primary method for contacting respondents. Because millions of households do not have fax machines, securing a representative sample of respondents is a difficult undertaking in fax surveys of final consumers. As a result, most of these surveys focus on business-related research studies.

The federal junk fax law prohibits the sending by fax of "any material advertising the commercial availability or quality of any property, goods, or services which is transmitted to any person without that person's prior express invitation or permission, in writing or otherwise." The first page of any fax solicitation must now include information for the recipient about how to opt out of similar messages in the future.[26]

Online Surveys and Other Internet-Based Methods

The growing population of Internet users has spurred researchers to conduct online surveys. Using the Web, they are able to speed the survey process, increase sample sizes, ignore geographic boundaries, and dramatically reduce costs. While a standard research project can take up to eight weeks to complete, a thorough online project may take two weeks or less. Less

The growing population of Internet users has spurred researchers to conduct online surveys. Using the Web, they are able to expedite the survey process, increase sample size, and reduce costs. This ad focuses on fast feedback.

intrusive than telephone surveys, online research allows participants to respond at their leisure. The novelty and ease of answering online may even encourage higher response rates. For some tips on creating online surveys, see the "Etiquette Tips for Marketing Professionals" feature.

Businesses are increasingly including questionnaires on their Web pages to solicit information about consumer demographics, attitudes, and comments and suggestions for improving goods and services or improving marketing messages. Marketers also experiment with electronic bulletin boards as an information-gathering device. On a password-protected Web site, moderators pose questions to selected respondents—usually just 15 to 25—over a predetermined period of time. Respondents have a chance to try out new products and submit feedback at their leisure. Online polling is also increasingly popular. The Nielsen Company reports that the global appeal of social networking sites, which attract almost 87 million unique users a month, shows no sign of slowing down with MySpace, Facebook, and Classmates Online leading the way in the creation of a virtual global village and consumer forum. Nielsen has its own social network, Hey! Nielsen, which tracks consumer buzz on movies, TV shows, music, video games, and other forms of entertainment by user profile and activity.[27]

The growth of the Internet is creating a need for new research techniques to measure and capture information about Web site visitors. At present, no industry-wide standards define techniques for measuring Web use. Some sites ask users to register before accessing the pages; others merely keep track of the number of "hits," or number of times a visitor accesses a page. Marketers have tried to place a value on a site's "stickiness"—longer-lasting site visits—as a means of measuring effectiveness. Others use "cookies," which, as Chapter 4 explained, are electronic identifiers deposited on viewers' computers, to track click-through behavior—the paths users take as they move through the site. However, because some consumers change their Internet service providers frequently and special software is available to detect and remove them, cookies have lost some of their effectiveness. Because some marketers fear Web traffic is not reported accurately, the Interactive Advertising Bureau recently asked the two big Internet traffic measuring firms, ComScore and Nielsen/Net Ratings, to submit to third-party audits to verify their figures on the Internet's most heavily trafficked sites.[28]

Observing consumers online, where users spend more time than with any other medium including TV, offers marketers the opportunity to monitor the buying decision process, understand what turns a browser into a buyer, see how shoppers compare product features, and grasp the relative impacts on purchase decisions of marketing and price. Details like these help advertisers grow increasingly accurate about where they place their messages. A ComScore analysis conducted for *The New York Times* found that Yahoo!, Google, Microsoft, AOL, and MySpace together record data such as ZIP code and search queries from at least 336 billion user searches and video and page views a month. Traditional media companies such as The Walt Disney Company and magazine publisher Condé Nast lag well behind these Internet giants.[29] Some companies combine

Etiquette Tips for Marketing Professionals

How to Conduct Online Surveys

Online surveys are significantly less expensive than paper questionnaires and telephone interviews. They offer respondents anonymity, which helps most people speak more freely, and the chance to answer questions at their own pace. They do require a bit of planning, however, to make sure that you get the results you want and don't waste respondents' time. Here are some tips for creating successful online surveys.

- Find out what you want to know. List items you want customers to tell you, and prioritize them. Then create and rank a list of your own questions about your business, its goals, or its products. Write a third list of recent customer complaints or suggestions. Compare the lists. Issues appearing on two or more lists are those you'll want to ask about.

- Decide how to organize the results. This will help you determine whether to ask about category breakdowns like age, sex, income bracket, geographic location, and educational attainment.

- Determine how much effort you want to spend analyzing write-in comments, as opposed to easy-to-tabulate multiple-choice and yes/no responses.

- Recognize that people won't spend a long time answering questions. Keep the survey and its instructions short and to the point.

- Word questions carefully. Avoid complex constructions like double negatives, keep questions neutral (don't lead respondents to the answer), and weed out acronyms and abbreviations.

- Have at least two people proofread the questionnaire carefully.

- Test the survey on people in different departments of your firm. You may get valuable insights from their different points of view.

- Tabulate the test surveys to make sure there won't be any technical glitches in the live survey.

- Edit once more to make sure each question will provide you with information that's really useful to your business.

- Consider e-mail reminders, or even an incentive like a gift-certificate drawing, to boost your response rate.

Sources: "How to Conduct an Online Survey and Engage Customers in a Dialogue," *SurveyPro*, www.surveyspro.com, accessed May 5, 2009; "How to Conduct an Online Customer Survey," EHow, www.ehow.com, accessed May 5, 2009; "Guidelines for Conducting an Online Survey," *Survey-Hosting.com*, www.survey-hosting.com, accessed June 16, 2008.

their online marketing research efforts with attempts to manage what others say about them. The "Solving an Ethical Controversy" feature discusses the pros and cons of this strategy.

Experimental Method

The third—and least-used—method for collecting primary data is the **controlled experiment.** A marketing research experiment is a scientific investigation in which a researcher controls or manipulates a test group (or groups) and compares the results with those of a control group that did not receive the experimental controls or manipulations.

The most common use of this method by marketers is **test marketing,** or introducing a new product in a specific area and then observing its degree of success. Up to this point, a product development team may have gathered feedback from focus groups. Other information may have come from shoppers' evaluations of competing products. Test marketing is the first stage at which the product performs in a real-life environment.

To preview a new Internet series called "Quarterlife," scheduled to run on MySpace, the producers arranged screenings of the first six episodes for several live audiences in New York, including viewings at Columbia and New York University. The eight-minute episodes were well received by the 20-something audience members who make up the primary intended audience for the show. "It's HBOish," said a 19-year-old from Brandeis University who saw the show at a downtown film festival. "It really captures your attention."[30]

Some firms omit test marketing and move directly from product development to full-scale production. These companies cite three problems with test marketing:

1. Test marketing is expensive. A firm can spend more than $1 million depending on the size of the test market city and the cost of buying media to advertise the product.

Solving an ethical controversy

Online Reputation Management: Legitimate Marketing or Cover-Up?

When an Internet post revealed that a pen could pick a pricey bike lock, word spread online like wildfire, and maker Kryptonite Lock hastened to make amends. That post was true, but other news spreads online whether it is true or not. A burgeoning industry, *search engine optimization,* uses search results to track and repair or contain such damage to corporate names. No one knows how big the market for online reputation management is; its vendors can boost traffic to legitimate sites, recruit bloggers to write positively about clients on third-party sites, create new sites to suppress harmful ones on search engine results, and ask host sites to remove damaging material.

Some critics call such efforts unfair, and they can backfire. But companies tracking unfavorable information about them by monitoring online discussions say they also learn what current and potential customers think about them and their products.

Is online reputation management a legitimate marketing tool?

PRO

1. Companies use reputation management techniques to better understand customer preferences and complaints and to respond to problems.

2. Most vendors of reputation management services say they won't lie or pretend to be legitimate customers when they post notices or blog for clients.

CON

1. Most companies wish negative comments would disappear. Instead of fixing a problem, says one analyst, "they just want to make sure that other people can't find it."

2. Opportunity for abuse exists. Paid bloggers, even if they are told to be truthful, can't be objective about their client.

Summary

microsoft uses vendors to test-monitor social networking sites, weighing whether that helps it understand customers' experiences. But most observers agree a firm must take responsibility for protecting its own reputation. "It's not something that you can simply provide a credit card number to a company and they can take care of it," says one. A first line of defense: Google your company's name on a regular basis.

Sources: John Tozzi, "Do Reputation Management Services Work?" *BusinessWeek*, April 30, 2008, www.businessweek.com, accessed May 5, 2009; Thomas Hoffman, "7 Cheap Ways to Manage Your Online Reputation," *ComputerWorld*, February 12, 2008, www.computerworld.com; Thomas Hoffman, "Online Reputation Management Is Hot, But Is It Ethical?" *ComputerWorld*, February 12, 2008, www.computerworld.com.

2. Competitors quickly learn about the new product. By studying the test market, competitors can develop alternative strategies.

3. Some products are not well suited to test marketing. Few firms test market long-lived, durable goods such as cars because of the major financial investments required for their development, the need to establish networks of dealers to distribute the products, and requirements for parts and servicing.

Companies that decide to skip the test-marketing process can choose several other options. A firm may simulate a test-marketing campaign through computer-modeling software. By plugging in data on similar products, it can develop a sales projection for a new product. Another firm may offer an item in just one region of the United States or in another country, adjusting promotions and advertising based on local results before going to other geographic regions. Another option may be to limit a product's introduction to only one retail chain to carefully control and evaluate promotions and results.

assessment check

1. Distinguish between primary and secondary data.

2. What are the major methods of collecting secondary data?

3. What are the major methods of collecting primary data?

6 Explain the challenges of conducting marketing research in global markets.

Conducting International Marketing Research

As corporations expand globally, they need to gather correspondingly more knowledge about consumers in other countries. Although marketing researchers follow the same basic steps for international studies as for domestic ones, they often face some very different challenges.

U.S. organizations can tap many secondary resources as they research global markets. One major information source is the U.S. government, particularly the Department of Commerce, which regularly publishes two useful reports—*Export America* magazine (monthly) and *Overseas Business Reports* (annual)—that discuss marketing activities in more than 100 countries. The Department of State offers commercial guides to almost every country in the world, compiled by the local embassies. Other government sources include state trade offices and small-business development centers.

When conducting international research, companies must be prepared to deal with both language issues—communicating their message in the most effective way—and cultural issues, or capturing local citizens' interests while avoiding missteps that could unintentionally offend them. Companies also need to take a good look at a country's business environment, including political and economic conditions, trade regulations affecting research studies and data collection, and the potential for short- and long-term growth. Many marketers recommend tapping local researchers to investigate foreign markets.

Businesses may need to adjust their data collection methods for primary research in other countries because some methods do not easily transfer across national frontiers. Face-to-face interviewing, for instance, remains the most common method for conducting primary research outside the United States.

While mail surveys are a common data collection method in developed countries, they are useless in many other nations because of low literacy rates, unreliable mail service, and a lack of address lists. Telephone interviews may also not be suitable in other countries, especially those where many people do not have phones. Focus groups can be difficult to arrange because of cultural and social factors. In Latin American countries, for example, highly educated consumers make up a sought-after and opinionated minority, but they have little time to devote to lengthy focus group discussions. Middle- to lower-income Latin Americans may not be accustomed to articulating their opinions about products and grow reticent in the presence of others, whereas in some countries where violence and kidnapping are common, affluent consumers are reluctant to attend any meetings with strangers. To help with such difficulties, a growing number of international research firms offer experience in conducting global studies.

assessment check

1. What are some U.S. organizations that can serve as sources of international secondary marketing data?

2. What is the most common method of primary data collection outside the United States?

A growing number of international research firms offer experience in conducting global studies.

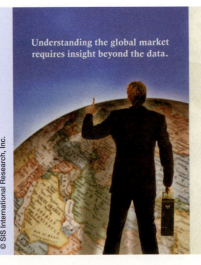

Interpretative Research

We mentioned earlier that interpretative research is a method that observes a customer or group of customers in their natural settings and then interprets their behavior based on an understanding of social and cultural characteristics of that setting.

Interpretative research has attracted considerable interest in recent years. Developed by social anthropologists as a method for explaining behavior that operates below the level of conscious thought, interpretative research can provide insights into consumer behavior and the ways in which consumers interact with brands.

The researcher first spends an extensive amount of time studying the culture, and for that reason, the studies often are called *ethnographic* studies. The word *ethnographic* means that a researcher takes a cultural perspective of the population being studied. For that reason, interpretative research often is used to interpret consumer behavior within a foreign culture where language, ideals, values, and expectations are subject to different cultural influences. But ethnographic research is also used domestically by looking at the consumer behavior of different groups of people. To help engineers and technology specialists understand how people interact and communicate in social settings, Motorola employs social scientists who conduct field research in communications, including a project called Social TV that explores how people bond over TV shows. The company's principal staff anthropologist says the studies are the first step in helping his company develop innovative products.[31]

Interpretative research focuses on understanding the meaning of a product or the consumption experience in a consumer's life. Its methods capture consumers interacting with products in their environment—in other words, capturing what they actually do, not what they say they do. Typically, subjects are filmed in specific situations, such as socializing with friends in a bar for research into beverage consumption, or for extended periods of time for paid participants. Paid participants may be followed by a videographer who records their day-to-day movements and interactions, or they may film themselves. Some companies even pay consumers to wear mini video cameras attached to visors and linked to a sound recorder. These systems record consumer behavior while participants are shopping or doing chores.

Cost is an issue in interpretative research. This type of study takes time and money, and sometimes the results can verge on the abstract. In its first series of Social TV observations, for instance, Motorola's team discovered "universally that people watch TV with their feet up and no socks. We couldn't use that data." But the program has survived budget-cutting at the firm.[32] Because of its expense, interpretative research is used only when a company needs detailed information about how consumers use its products.

assessment check

1. How is interpretative research typically conducted?
2. When should ethnographic research be employed?

Computer Technology in Marketing Research

7 Outline the most important uses of computer technology in marketing research.

The ability to quickly gather and analyze business intelligence can create a substantial strategic advantage. Computer databases provide a wealth of data for marketing research, whether they are outside the company or designed specifically to gather important facts about its customers. The "Marketing Failure" feature discusses what happened when a computerized system failed at the Census Bureau. Chapter 10 explores how companies use internal databases and customer relationship management technology. This section addresses important uses of computer technology related to marketing research: marketing information systems (MISs), marketing decision support systems (MDSSs), data mining, business intelligence, and competitive intelligence.

MARKETING INFORMATION SYSTEMS (MISs)

In the past, many marketing managers complained that their information problems resulted from too much rather than too little information. Reams of data were difficult to use and not always relevant. At times, information was almost impossible to find. Modern technological advances have made constraints like these obsolete.

A **marketing information system (MIS)** is a planned, computer-based system designed to provide decision makers with a continuous flow of information relevant to their areas of responsibility. A component of the organization's overall management information system, a marketing information system deals specifically with marketing data and issues.

A well-constructed MIS serves as a company's nerve center, continually monitoring the market environment—both inside and outside the organization—and providing instantaneous information. Marketers can store data for later use, classify and analyze that data, and retrieve it easily when needed.

MARKETING DECISION SUPPORT SYSTEMS (MDSSs)

marketing decision support system (MDSS) Marketing information system component that links a decision maker with relevant databases and analysis tools.

A **marketing decision support system (MDSS)** consists of software that helps users quickly obtain and apply information in a way that supports marketing decisions. Taking MIS one step further, it allows managers to explore and connect such varying information as the state of the market, consumer behavior, sales forecasts, competitors' actions, and environmental changes. MDSSs consist of four main characteristics: they are interactive, investigative, flexible, and accessible. An MDSS can create simulations or models to illustrate the likely results of changes in marketing strategies or market conditions.

While an MIS provides raw data, an MDSS develops this data into information useful for decision making. For example, an MIS might provide a list of product sales from the previous day. A manager could use an MDSS to transform this raw data into graphs illustrating sales trends or reports estimating the impact of specific decisions, such as raising prices or expanding into new regions.

DATA MINING

Data mining is the process of searching through computerized data files to detect patterns. It focuses on identifying relationships not obvious to marketers—in a sense, answering questions that marketing researchers may not even have thought to ask. The data is stored in a huge database called a *data warehouse.* Software for the marketing decision support system often is associated with the data warehouse and is used to mine data. Once marketers identify patterns and connections, they use this intelligence to check the effectiveness of different strategy options.

Data mining is an efficient way to sort through huge amounts of data and to make sense of that data. It helps marketers create customer profiles, pinpoint reasons for customer loyalty or the lack thereof, analyze potential returns on changes in pricing or promotion, and forecast sales. Data mining offers considerable advantages in retailing, the hotel industry, banking, utilities, and many other areas and holds the promise of providing answers to many specific strategic questions.

San Diego research firm Strategic Vision conducted a data-mining study of sales and ownership data to identify preferences and perceptions among minority new-car buyers in the United States. Results of the data mining turned up links among different ethnic groups and car features. According to the study of 200,000 survey respondents—of whom 10,000 identified themselves as African American, Hispanic, or Asian American—African Americans look

MarKeting FaiLure   Technology System Failure Jeopardizes 2010 Census

Background. The 2010 Census must, by constitutional mandate, count every citizen living within U.S. borders. At stake in an accurate count are representation in the U.S. House of Representatives, the borders of state election districts, and distribution of $300 billion annually in state and federal funding. Census data also serve as a resource for marketing research.

The Challenge. Data gatherers face citizens' privacy concerns, uncertainty among immigrants, and a highly mobile and

diverse population speaking dozens of languages. Among the Census Bureau's tools are a multibillion-dollar budget, an army of 3 million temporary workers, and new handheld computers that were meant to streamline the March 2010 head count.

In 2006, Harris Corp. of Florida was awarded a $600 million contract to develop a computerized data-gathering system, including GPS mapping technology for address verification. But the Census Bureau changed more than 400 technical specifications for the

for characteristics like "powerful" and "classy" in new vehicles and for "things that set them apart from others"; Hispanics look for "aggressive and powerful, but confident and protective" features; and Asians choose "pleasant yet powerful ... with modern design and technology."[33] Discovering such patterns can help auto manufacturers tailor specific models for ethnic groups as well as target their marketing efforts more effectively.

BUSINESS INTELLIGENCE

Business intelligence is the process of gathering information and analyzing it to improve business strategy, tactics, and daily operations. Using advanced software tools, marketers gather information from within and outside the organization. Business intelligence can thus tell the firm how its own sales operation is doing or what its top competitors are up to.

The key is not only gathering the information but also getting it into a form that employees can make sense of and use for decision making and strategizing. Software can help users collect, aggregate, and create reports with outside information available on the Web from such databases as, say, Dun & Bradstreet. Hewlett-Packard used a business intelligence application from SmartOrg to identify market opportunities for its image-display technology. HP executives needed to determine which of its marketing plans would be most beneficial to the bottom line, and it used the business intelligence software to quickly sort through data. "You have all these great plans and you can only do a couple," said an HP executive. Thanks to its ability to answer key questions, business intelligence software is expected to grow at about twice the rate of the rest of the business software industry.[34]

COMPETITIVE INTELLIGENCE

Competitive intelligence is a form of business intelligence that focuses on finding information about competitors using published sources, interviews, observations by salespeople and suppliers in the industry, government agencies, public filings such as patent applications, and other secondary sources, including the Internet. Its aim is to uncover the specific advantages a competitor has, such as new-product launches, new features in existing goods or services, or new marketing or promotional strategies. Even a competitor's advertising can provide clues. Marketers use competitive intelligence to make better decisions that strengthen their own competitive strategy in turn.

assessment check

1. Distinguish between an MIS and an MDSS.

2. What is data mining?

3. Describe the process of collecting business and competitive intelligence.

---

system two years later, and just two years before the count. Problems developed during program testing—the computers proved too complex for some census workers and had difficulty transmitting large amounts of data. With the census date fast approaching, the bureau's expert panel advised using the handhelds only for the initial address canvassing but traditional paper methods for the required door-to-door follow-up for those who do not complete the mailed census questionnaire.

The Outcome. Because the process won't be entirely computerized, despite 10 years of planning, the Census Bureau's budget for the 2010 count is expected to grow by as much as $2 billion, even as accuracy may suffer. Any data errors are likely to persist for years.

Lessons Learned. "This is a management problem. It's an organizational problem," said a former U.S. Commerce Secretary. The census director pledged to conduct "a complete and accurate census," while acknowledging that "communication problems" with Harris Corp. delayed resolution of the computer problems. A Harris representative maintained that the computers were as easy to use as a cell phone and had a lower than 1 percent failure rate.

Sources: "Census Bureau Has $1B Plan for 2010," *Business First of Buffalo*, April 13, 2009, http://www.bizjournals.com; "Census Crunch Time," *New York Times* editorial, January 8, 2009, http://www.nytimes.com; "Statement of U.S. Secretary of Commerce Carlos M. Gutierrez before the United States Senate Committee on Homeland Security and Governmental Affairs," April 15, 2008, http://www.commerce.gov; "2010 Census: Little Time Remains to Address Operational Challenges", U.S. Government Accountability Office, March 5, 2009, www.gao.gov.

8   **Identify the major types of forecasting methods.**

sales forecast Estimate of a firm's revenue for a specified future period.

Sales Forecasting

A basic building block of any marketing plan is a **sales forecast,** an estimate of a firm's revenue for a specified future period. Sales forecasts play major roles in new-product decisions, production scheduling, financial planning, inventory planning and procurement, distribution, and human resources planning. An inaccurate forecast may lead to incorrect decisions in each of these areas.

Marketing research techniques are used to deliver effective sales forecasts. A sales forecast is also an important tool for marketing control because it sets standards against which to measure actual performance. Without such standards, no comparisons can be made.

Planners rely on short-run, intermediate, and long-run sales forecasts. A short-run forecast usually covers a period of up to one year, an intermediate forecast covers one to five years, and a long-run forecast extends beyond five years. Although sales forecasters use an array of techniques to predict the future—ranging from computer simulations to studying trends identified by futurists—their methods fall into two broad categories: qualitative and quantitative forecasting.

Qualitative forecasting techniques rely on subjective data that reports opinions rather than exact historical data. **Quantitative forecasting** methods, by contrast, use statistical computations such as trend extensions based on past data, computer simulations, and econometric models. As Table 8.1 shows, each method has benefits and limitations. Consequently, most organizations use a combination of both techniques.

QUALITATIVE FORECASTING TECHNIQUES

Planners apply qualitative forecasting methods when they want judgmental or subjective indicators. Qualitative forecasting techniques include the jury of executive opinion, Delphi technique, sales force composite, and survey of buyer intentions.

Jury of Executive Opinion

The technique called the **jury of executive opinion** combines and averages the outlooks of top executives from such areas as marketing, finance, production, and purchasing. Top managers bring the following capabilities to the process: experience and knowledge about situations that influence sales, open-minded attitudes toward the future, and awareness of the bases for their judgments.

table 8.1   **Benefits and Limitations of Various Forecasting Techniques**

Techniques	Benefits	Limitations
Qualitative Methods		
Jury of executive opinion	Opinions come from executives in many different departments; quick; inexpensive	Managers may lack background knowledge and experience to make meaningful predictions
Delphi technique	Group of experts can accurately predict long-term events such as technological breakthroughs	Time-consuming; expensive
Sales force composite	Salespeople have expert customer, product, and competitor knowledge; quick; inexpensive	Inaccurate forecasts may result from low estimates of salespeople concerned about their influence on quotas
Survey of buyer intentions	Useful in predicting short-term and intermediate sales for firms that serve selected customers	Intentions to buy may not result in actual purchases; time-consuming; expensive
Quantitative Methods		
Market test	Provides realistic information on actual purchases rather than on intent to buy	Alerts competition to new-product plans; time-consuming; expensive
Trend analysis	Quick; inexpensive; effective with stable customer demand and environment	Assumes the future will continue the past; ignores environmental changes
Exponential smoothing	Same benefits as trend analysis, but emphasizes more recent data	Same limitations as trend analysis, but not as severe due to emphasis on recent data

This quick and inexpensive method generates good forecasts for sales and new-product development. It works best for short-run forecasting.

Delphi Technique

Like the jury of executive opinion, the **Delphi technique** solicits opinions from several people, but it also gathers input from experts outside the firm, such as academic researchers, rather than relying completely on company executives. It is most appropriately used to predict long-run issues, such as technological breakthroughs, that could affect future sales and the market potential for new products.

The Delphi technique works as follows: A firm selects a panel of experts and sends each a questionnaire relating to a future event. After combining and averaging the answers, the firm develops another questionnaire based on these results and sends it back to the same people. The process continues until it identifies a consensus. Although firms have successfully used Delphi to predict future technological breakthroughs, the method is both expensive and time-consuming.

Sales Force Composite

The **sales force composite** technique develops forecasts based on the belief that organization members closest to the marketplace—those with specialized product, customer, and competitive knowledge—offer the best insights concerning short-term future sales. It typically works from the bottom up. Management consolidates salespeople's estimates first at the district level, then at the regional level, and finally nationwide to obtain an aggregate forecast of sales that reflects all three levels.

The sales force composite approach has some weaknesses, however. Because salespeople recognize the role of their sales forecasts in determining sales quotas for their territories, they are likely to make conservative estimates. Moreover, their narrow perspectives from within their limited geographic territories may prevent them from considering the impact on sales of trends developing in other territories, forthcoming technological innovations, or the major changes in marketing strategies. Consequently, the sales force composite gives the best forecasts in combination with other techniques.

Survey of Buyer Intentions

A **survey of buyer intentions** gathers input through mail-in questionnaires, online feedback, telephone polls, and personal interviews to determine the purchasing intentions of a representative group of present and potential customers. This method suits firms that serve limited numbers of customers but often proves impractical for those with millions of customers. Also, buyer surveys gather useful information only when customers willingly reveal their buying intentions. Moreover, customer intentions do not necessarily translate into actual purchases. These surveys may help a firm predict short-run or intermediate sales, but they employ time-consuming and expensive methods.

QUANTITATIVE FORECASTING TECHNIQUES

Quantitative techniques attempt to eliminate the subjectiveness of the qualitative methods. They include such methods as market tests, trend analysis, and exponential smoothing.

Test Markets

One quantitative technique, the test market, frequently helps planners assess consumer responses to new-product offerings. The procedure typically begins by establishing one or more test markets to gauge consumer responses to a new product under actual marketplace conditions. Market tests also permit experimenters to evaluate the effects of different prices, alternative promotional strategies, and other marketing mix variations by comparing results among different test markets.

The primary advantage of test markets is the realism they provide for the marketer. On the other hand, these expensive and time-consuming experiments may also communicate marketing plans to competitors before a firm introduces a product to the total market.

briefly speaking

"There are many methods for predicting the future. For example, you can read horoscopes, tea leaves, tarot cards, or crystal balls. Collectively, these methods are known as 'nutty methods.' Or you can put well-researched facts into sophisticated computer models, more commonly referred to as 'a complete waste of time.'"

—Scott Adams (b. 1957)
U.S. CARTOONIST, IN *THE DILBERT FUTURE*

Trend Analysis

Trend analysis develops forecasts for future sales by analyzing the historical relationship between sales and time. It implicitly assumes the collective causes of past sales will continue to exert similar influences in the future. When historical data is available, planners can quickly and inexpensively complete trend analysis. Software programs can calculate the average annual increment of change for the available sales data. This average increment of change is then projected into the future to come up with the sales forecast. So if the sales of a firm have been growing $15.3 million on average per year, this amount of sales could be added to last year's sales total to arrive at next year's forecast.

Of course, trend analysis cannot be used if historical data is not available, as in new-product forecasting. Also, trend analysis makes the dangerous assumption that future events will continue in the same manner as the past. Any variations in the determinants of future sales will cause deviations from the forecast. In other words, this method gives reliable forecasts during periods of steady growth and stable demand. If conditions change, predictions based on trend analysis may become worthless. For this reason, forecasters have applied more sophisticated techniques and complex, new forecasting models to anticipate the effects of various possible changes in the future.

Exponential Smoothing

A more sophisticated method of trend analysis, the **exponential smoothing** technique, weighs each year's sales data, giving greater weight to results from the most recent years. Otherwise, the statistical approach used in trend analysis is applied here. For example, last year's sales might receive a 1.5 weight, while sales data from two years ago could get a 1.4 weighting. Exponential smoothing is considered the most commonly used quantitative forecasting technique.

assessment check

1. Describe the jury of executive opinion.
2. What is the Delphi technique?
3. How does the exponential smoothing technique forecast sales?

Strategic Implications of Marketing in the 21st Century

marketing research can help an organization develop effective marketing strategies. Most new products eventually fail to attract enough buyers to remain viable. Why? A major reason is the seller's failure to understand market needs.

Consider, for example, the hundreds of dot-com companies that went under. A characteristic shared by all of those failing businesses is that virtually none of them was founded on sound marketing research. Very few used marketing research techniques to evaluate product potential, and even fewer studied consumer responses after the ventures were initiated. While research might not have prevented every dot-com meltdown, it may have helped a few of those businesses survive.

Marketing research ideally matches new products to potential customers. Marketers also conduct research to analyze sales of their own and competitors' products, to gauge the performance of existing products, to guide the development of promotional campaigns and product enhancements, and to develop and refine products. All of these activities enable marketers to fine-tune their marketing strategies and reach customers more effectively and efficiently.

Marketing researchers have at their disposal a broad range of techniques with which to collect both quantitative and qualitative data on customers, their lifestyles, behaviors, attitudes, and perceptions. Vast amounts of data can be rapidly collected, accessed, interpreted, and applied to improve all aspects of business operations. Because of customer relationship management technology, that information is no longer generalized to profile groups of customers—it can be analyzed to help marketers understand every customer.

Review of Chapter Objectives

1 Describe the development of the marketing research function and its major activities.

Marketing research, or the collection and use of information in marketing decision making, reached a milestone when Charles C. Parlin, an ad salesman, counted empty soup cans in Philadelphia's trash in an effort to persuade the Campbell Soup Company to advertise in *The Saturday Evening Post*. Today, the most common marketing research activities are (1) determining market potential, market share, and market characteristics and (2) conducting sales analyses and competitive product studies. Most large consumer goods companies now have internal marketing research departments. However, outside suppliers still remain vital to the research function. Some perform the complete research task, while others specialize in a limited area or provide specific data services.

2 Explain the steps in the marketing research process.

The marketing research process can be divided into six specific steps: (1) defining the problem, (2) conducting exploratory research, (3) formulating hypotheses, (4) creating a research design, (5) collecting data, and (6) interpreting and presenting the research information. A clearly defined problem focuses on the researcher's search for relevant decision-oriented information. Exploratory research refers to information gained outside the firm. Hypotheses, tentative explanations of specific events, allow researchers to set out specific research designs—that is, the series of decisions that, taken together, comprise master plans or models for conducting the investigations. The data collection phase of the marketing research process can involve either or both primary (original) and secondary (previously published) data. After the data is collected, researchers must interpret and present it in a way that is meaningful to management.

3 Distinguish between primary and secondary data and identify the sources of each type.

Primary data can be collected by the firm's own researchers or by independent marketing research companies. Three principal methods of primary data collection are observation, survey, and experiment. Secondary data can be classified as either internal or external. Sources of internal data include sales records, product evaluation, sales force reports, and records of marketing costs. Sources of external data include the government and private sources such as business magazines. Both external and internal data can also be obtained from computer databases.

4 Explain the different sampling techniques used by marketing researchers.

Samples can be categorized as either probability samples or nonprobability samples. A probability sample is one in which every member of the population has a known chance of being selected. Probability samples include simple random samples, in which every item in the relevant universe has an equal opportunity to be selected; stratified samples, in which randomly selected subsamples of different groups are represented in the total sample; and cluster samples, in which geographic areas are selected from which respondents are drawn. A nonprobability sample is arbitrary and does not allow application of standard statistical tests. Nonprobability sampling techniques include convenience samples, in which readily available respondents are picked, and quota samples, divided so that different segments or groups are represented in the total sample.

5 Identify the methods by which marketing researchers collect primary data.

Observation data is gathered by observing consumers via devices such as people meters or videotape. Survey data can be collected through telephone interviews, mail or fax surveys, personal interviews, focus groups, or a variety of online methods. Telephone interviews provide more than half of all primary marketing research data. They give the researcher a fast and inexpensive way to get small amounts of information but generally not detailed or personal information. Personal interviews are costly but allow researchers to get detailed information from respondents. Mail surveys are a means of conducting national studies at a reasonable cost; their main disadvantage is potentially inadequate response rates. Focus groups elicit detailed, qualitative information that provides insight not only into behavior but also into consumer attitudes and perceptions. Online surveys can yield fast responses but face obstacles such as the adequacy of the probability sample. The experimental method creates verifiable statistical data through the use of test and control groups to reveal actual benefits from perceived benefits.

6   Explain the challenges of conducting marketing research in global markets.

Many resources are available to help U.S. organizations research global markets. Government resources include the Department of Commerce, state trade offices, small-business development centers, and foreign embassies. Private companies, such as marketing research firms and companies that distribute research from other sources, are another resource. Electronic networks offer online international trade forums, in which marketers can establish global contacts.

7   Outline the most important uses of computer technology in marketing research.

Important uses of computer technology in marketing research include (1) a marketing information system (MIS)—a planned, computer-based system designed to provide managers with a continuous flow of information relevant to their specific decision-making needs and areas of responsibility; (2) a marketing decision support system (MDSS)—a marketing information system component that links a decision maker with relevant databases and analysis tools; (3) data mining—the process of searching through consumer information files or data warehouses to detect patterns that guide marketing decision making; (4) business intelligence—the process of gathering information and analyzing it to improve business strategy, tactics, and daily operations; and (5) competitive intelligence—the form of business intelligence that focuses on finding information about competitors using published sources, interviews, observations by salespeople and suppliers in the industry, government agencies, public filings such as patent applications, and other secondary methods including the Internet.

8   Identify the major types of forecasting methods.

There are two categories of forecasting methods. Qualitative methods are more subjective because they are based on opinions rather than exact historical data. They include the jury of executive opinion, the Delphi technique, the sales force composite, and the survey of buyer intentions. Quantitative methods include more factual and numerical measures such as test markets, trend analysis, and exponential smoothing.

assessment check: **answers**

1.1   Identify the different classifications of marketing research suppliers and explain how they differ from one another.

Marketing research suppliers can be classified as syndicated services, which regularly send standardized data sets to all customers; full-service suppliers, which contract to conduct complete marketing research projects; or limited-service suppliers, which specialize in selected activities.

1.2   What research methods can be used to measure customer satisfaction?

Some companies look at feedback from existing customers, for instance, hiring marketing research firms to collect and analyze customer feedback at their Web sites. Other firms collect feedback about customer defections—why a customer no longer uses a product. Other organizations conduct research through online polls and surveys.

2.1   What are the six steps in the marketing research process?

The marketing research process can be divided into six specific steps: (1) defining the problem, (2) conducting exploratory research, (3) formulating hypotheses, (4) creating a research design, (5) collecting data, and (6) interpreting and presenting the research information.

2.2   What is the goal of exploratory research?

Exploratory research seeks to discover the cause of a specific problem by discussing the problem with informed sources within and outside the firm and examining data from other information sources.

3.1   Distinguish between primary and secondary data.

Primary data is original; secondary data has been previously published.

3.2 What are the major methods of collecting secondary data?

Sources of internal data include sales records, product evaluation, sales force reports, and records of marketing costs.

3.3 What are the major methods of collecting primary data?

Three principal methods of primary data collection are observation, survey, and experiment.

4.1 What is sampling?

Sampling is the process of selecting representative survey respondents or research participants from the total universe of possible participants.

4.2 Explain the different types of probability samples.

Types of probability samples include simple random samples, stratified samples, and cluster samples.

4.3 Identify the types of nonprobability samples.

Nonprobability samples are convenience samples and quota samples.

5.1 How is interpretative research typically conducted?

Interpretative research observes a customer or group of customers in their natural setting and interprets their behavior based on social and cultural characteristics of that setting.

5.2 When should ethnographic research be employed?

Ethnographic research is used to look at the consumer behavior of different groups of people.

6.1 What are some U.S. organizations that can serve as sources of international secondary marketing data?

The Departments of Commerce and State offer reports and guides to many countries. Other sources include state trade offices, small-business development centers, and U.S. embassies in various nations.

6.2 What is the most common method of primary data collection outside the United States?

Face-to-face interviewing remains the most common method for conducting primary research outside the United States.

7.1 Distinguish between an MIS and an MDSS.

A marketing information system (MIS) is a planned, computer-based system designed to provide managers with a continuous flow of information relevant to their specific decision-making needs and areas of responsibility. A marketing decision support system (MDSS) is a marketing information system component that links a decision maker with relevant databases and analysis tools to help ask "what-if" questions.

7.2 What is data mining?

Data mining is the process of searching through huge consumer information files or data warehouses to detect patterns that can help marketers ask the right questions and guide marketing decision making.

7.3 Describe the process of collecting business and competitive intelligence.

Business intelligence is the process of gathering information and analyzing it to improve business strategy, tactics, and daily operations. Competitive intelligence focuses on finding information about competitors using published sources, interviews, observations by salespeople and suppliers in the industry, government agencies, public filings such as patent applications, and other secondary methods including the Internet.

8.1　Describe the jury of executive opinion.

The jury of executive opinion combines and averages the outlooks of top executives from areas such as marketing, finance, production, and purchasing.

8.2　What is the Delphi technique?

The Delphi technique solicits opinions from several people but also includes input from experts outside the firm such as academic researchers.

8.3　How does the exponential smoothing technique forecast sales?

Exponential smoothing weighs each year's sales data, giving greater weight to results from the most recent years.

Marketing Terms You Need to Know

marketing research 240	sampling 250	focus group 253
exploratory research 245	probability sample 251	marketing decision support system (MDSS) 260
secondary data 246	nonprobability sample 251	sales forecast 262
primary data 246	interpretative research 252	

Other Important Marketing Terms

syndicated service 243	cluster sample 251	quantitative forecasting 262
full-service research supplier 243	convenience sample 251	jury of executive opinion 262
limited-service research supplier 243	quota sample 251	Delphi technique 263
sales analysis 245	mall intercept 253	sales force composite 263
hypothesis 246	controlled experiment 256	survey of buyer intentions 263
research design 246	test marketing 256	trend analysis 264
population (universe) 250	marketing information system (MIS) 259	exponential smoothing 264
simple random sample 251	data mining 260	
stratified sample 251	qualitative forecasting 262	

Assurance of Learning Review

1. Outline the development and current status of the marketing research function.

2. What are the differences between full-service and limited-service research suppliers?

3. List and explain the steps in the marketing research process. Trace a hypothetical study through the stages in this process.

4. Distinguish between primary and secondary data. When should researchers collect each type of data?

5. What is sampling? Explain the differences between probability and nonprobability samples and identify the various types of each.

6. Distinguish among surveys, experiments, and observational methods of primary data collection. Cite examples of each method.

7. Define and give an example of each of the methods of gathering survey data. Under what circumstances should researchers choose a specific approach?

8. Describe the experimental method of collecting primary data and indicate when researchers should use it.

9. Describe business intelligence.

10. Contrast qualitative and quantitative sales forecasting methods.

Projects and Teamwork Exercises

1. ACNielsen offers data collected by optical scanners from the United Kingdom, France, Germany, Belgium, the Netherlands, Austria, Italy, and Finland. This scanner data tracks sales of UPC-coded products in those nations. In small teams, imagine you are Nielsen clients in the United States. One team might be a retail chain, another an Internet company, and still another a toy manufacturer. Discuss the types of marketing questions this data might help you answer. Share your list with other teams.

2. Today, one in three new homes sold in America is likely to be a manufactured home. New manufactured homes are built using higher-quality materials than those of the past. As a result, the market for manufactured homes has grown to include more affluent buyers. Alabama-based Southern Energy Homes tries to appeal to upscale buyers by custom-building its homes according to customer specifications. What type of data and information should Southern Energy gather through its ongoing marketing intelligence to predict demand for its products? Would primary or secondary methods work best? Name some specific secondary sources of data that Southern Energy might study to find useful business intelligence.

3. Discuss some of the challenges Pizza Hut might face in conducting marketing research in potential new international markets. What types of research would you recommend the company use in choosing new countries for expansion?

4. Which sales forecasting technique(s) are most appropriate for each of the following products? Prepare your arguments in pairs or teams:
   a. Post Shredded Wheat breakfast cereal
   b. Coach handbags
   c. UPS Store copy shops
   d. *Time* magazine

5. Assume you are responsible for launching a new family of skin-care products for teens, with separate product lines for males and females. You would like to collect primary data from a sampling of each market before you prepare your marketing campaign. Let one team make the case for using a focus group and another team devise a plan supporting the use of an online chat room. Present the class with the benefits of each method and the ways in which each team plans to overcome its method's possible shortcomings. Now take this project one step further by having a classroom discussion on whether a decision support system could enhance the data collected from each method. How could an MDSS make the data more useful?

6. Interpretative research offers marketing researchers many possibilities, including the opportunity to improve product features such as packaging for food or over-the-counter medication that is difficult for seniors or the disabled to open. List some other ways in which you think this observation method can help make existing product offerings more appealing or more useful to specific users. What kind of products would you choose, and how would you test them?

7. Use the Internet to research the details of the National Do Not Call Registry and prepare a report outlining what it does and does not allow marketers to do. Research the effects of the registry to date. Do you think the public understands the purpose of the registry? Why or why not, and if not, what do you think marketers can do to clarify it?

8. McDonald's conducts extensive marketing research for all its new products, including new menu items for its overseas stores. Because of cultural and other differences and preferences, the company cannot always extrapolate its results from one country to another. For instance, Croque McDo fried ham-and-cheese sandwiches are unlikely to be as popular in the United States as they are in France, which invented the *croque monsieur* sandwich on which the McDonald's product is based. Can you think of any other kinds of firms that share this limitation on global applications of their research? In contrast, what sorts of questions *could* multinational firms answer on a global basis? Why?

Critical-Thinking Exercises

1. Some companies are broadening their markets by updating classic products to appeal to younger people's tastes and preferences. What primary and secondary market information would you want to have if you were planning to reinvigorate an established brand in each of the following categories? Where and how would you obtain the information?
   a. household cleaner
   b. moist packaged cat food
   c. spray starch
   d. electrical appliances

2. Marketers sometimes collect primary information by using so-called *mystery shoppers* who visit stores anonymously (as if they were customers) and note such critical factors as store appearance and ambiance, items in stock, and quality of service including waiting time and courtesy of employees. (The CEO of Staples has gone on mystery shopper trips and sometimes asked his mother to make similar trips.) Prepare a list of data you would want to obtain from a mystery shopper surveying a chain of gas stations in your area. Devise a format for gathering the information that combines your need to

compile the data electronically and the researcher's need to remain undetected while visiting the stores.

3. Select a sales forecasting method (or combination of methods) for each of the following information needs and explain your pick(s).
    a. prediction of next year's sales based on last year's figures
    b. prediction of next year's sales based on weighted data from the last five years
    c. expected sales categorized by district and by region

d. estimated product usage for the next year by typical consumers
e. probable consumer response to a new product

4. The Internet provides ready access to secondary market information but is also a portal to an almost limitless store of primary information via social networking sites, message boards, chat rooms, e-mail questionnaires, newsgroups, and Web site registration forms. What are some specific drawbacks of each of these methods for obtaining primary information from customers?

Ethics Exercise

Consumer groups sometimes object to marketers' methods of collecting primary data from customers. They object to such means as product registration forms; certain types of games, contests, or product offers; and "cookies" and demographic questionnaires on company Web sites. Marketers believe that such tools offer them an easy way to collect market data. Most strictly control the use of such data and never link identifying information with consumers' financial or demographic profiles. However, the possibility of abuse or error always exists.

Research the code of ethics of the American Marketing Association (AMA). Note especially the guidelines for use of the Internet in marketing research.

1. Check the Web sites of a few large consumer products companies. How effectively do you think these sites are at informing visitors about the use of "cookies" on the sites? Do you think marketers could or should improve their protection of visitors' privacy? If so, how?

2. Do you think the AMA's code of ethics would be violated if marketers compiled a mailing list from information provided on warranty and product registration cards and then used the list to send customers new-product information? Why or why not? Does your opinion change if the company also sends list members special discount offers and private sale notices?

Internet Exercises

1. **Marketing research tools.** SAS and SPSS offer statistical analysis products widely used by marketing professionals. Visit each company's Web site (www.sas.com and www.spss.com) and learn more about their products, including actual customer experiences. Prepare a brief report on what you learned.

2. **Qualitative marketing research.** e-Focus Groups is a San Francisco–based firm offering assistance to companies in conducting focus groups and other forms of qualitative marketing research. Visit the firm's Web site (www.e-focusgroups.com) and summarize the services offered. Who are the clients? What are some of the advantages of conducting focus groups and other forms of qualitative marketing research online?

3. **Census data.** An enormous amount of statistical data is available from the U.S. Census Bureau. One of the best summaries of Census data is the *Statistical Abstract of the United States,* published annually. Access the Web site of the *Statistical Abstract* (www.census.gov/compendia/statab/). Follow the links listed and answer the following questions:

a. Under the population section, how is the age distribution of Americans expected to change over the next ten years?
b. Under the population section, Hispanics make up what percentage of the U.S. population? What is expected to happen to that percentage over the next ten years?
c. Under the income section, which state has the highest median income? Which state has the fastest rising median income? What is the relationship between median income and the age of the householder (head of house)?
d. Under the construction and housing section, how many U.S. households are homeowners? Has this percentage changed in the last 30 years? Which state has the highest percentage of homeowners?

Note: Internet Web addresses change frequently. If you don't find the exact site listed, you may need to access the organization's home page and search from there or use a search engine such as Google.

Case 8.1 The NPD Group Scans the Globe for Marketing Data

Almost every day, it seems, we hear something on the news about the eating habits of U.S. adults and children. For instance, you

may hear a piece saying kids under six years of age snack mostly on fruit, and dieting may be on the wane. But how do we know this? Where does such information come from?

The NPD Group is one source. A leading global marketing researcher, the NPD Group was founded in 1967 and now provides research information and expertise in more industries, national and global, than any other research firm. Using tools such as customer panels, retail sales tracking, and customized research projects, the company works with clients in the automotive, beauty, technology, entertainment, fashion, office supplies, software, sports, toys, and wireless industries. It is also expert in the food service and food and beverage industries. The NPD Group helps more than 1,600 clients identify new markets, develop new products and marketing strategies, analyze pricing strategies, find out what's selling and where across the retail network, and understand consumer buying decisions and satisfaction. The result for clients is a deeper, broader view of the market, and often an increased share of the market as well.

The NPD Group also has a network of ongoing relationships with over 600 retailers that send it a steady stream of point-of-sale data. These sources include department and specialty stores, mass merchants, catalog and direct-mail companies, e-stores, distributors, resellers, and national chains. Their data helps the NPD Group conduct its retail tracking service; major clients for that service include Wal-Mart and Sam's Club.

In compiling national data on kids' snacks and adult eating habits, the NPD Group relied on 14-day food and beverage diaries kept by 500 moms in 1985–1987 and 600 moms in 2005–2007. By writing down everything their children ate, the women supplied the NPD Group with evidence of a healthful trend. During the 1985–1987 period, cookies were the top snack for children under six, followed by fruit, milk, juice, and candy. In 2005–2007, not only was fruit first, followed by cookies, milk, crackers, and juice, but candy didn't even make the list. These data show "moms … are

starting to make subtle changes" in the way they feed their kids, says an NPD vice president, who also notes that rates of childhood obesity are now holding steady, not increasing.

The NPD Group's recent research on adult eating habits indicates almost three-quarters of U.S. adults are choosing reduced-fat, reduced-calorie, whole grain, or fortified foods at least once every two weeks, making better food choices a preferred strategy over dieting for health and weight control. The number of adults on a diet has actually declined by 10 percent since 1990, while the number eating healthier is increasing. The average consumer, NPD finds, is eating one of these items or a light, diet, reduced sodium or cholesterol, caffeine or sugar free, or organic item at least twice a day. "A generation ago," says the company's vice president, "it was about subtracting bad things from your diet, but today healthy eating is more a matter of addition *and* subtraction." An NPD survey also found that even those who described themselves as financially worse off than a year ago still considered healthy eating a top priority for their households.

Questions for Critical Thinking

1. Snacking behavior tends to turn into lifelong eating choices. What implications do you think the NPD Group's findings about childhood snacking patterns and the drop-off in dieting might suggest for food manufacturers? For farmers? For schools, employers, and government agencies?

2. Which of NPD Group's data-collecting methods do you think would yield the most accurate information about consumers' food purchases? Why?

Sources: Company Web site, www.npd.com, accessed May 5, 2009; "NPD Finds Fewer Americans Dieting but More Eating 'Better for You' Foods," company press release, June 16, 2008; Nanci Hellmich, "Cookies' Perch as No. 1 Snack for Kids Starts to Crumble," *USA Today*, June 11, 2008, p. 1A.

Video Case 8.2   Marketing Research and Sales Forecasting at Ogden Publications

The written video case on Ogden Publications appears on page VC-8. The Ogden Publications video is designed to expand and highlight the concepts in this chapter and the concepts and questions covered in the written video case.

CHAP**9**TER Market Segmentation, Targeting, and Positioning

© MARIO ANZUONI/Reuters/Landov

Outback Steakhouse Returns to its Roots

How often do you go out for dinner? Does it depend on when you get your paycheck or whether you have a job at all? How do you decide where to eat? Does your criteria include price, menu choices,

the distance you have to travel, or your friends' preferences? OSI Restaurant Partners, the third-largest operator of casual dining restaurants in the United States, recently examined these and other

questions to determine exactly who its customers were and what factors were important in their decision to eat at one restaurant instead of another.

After posting a loss of nearly $740 mil-

lion in one year, OSI knew it had to change its marketing strategy to survive and ultimately grow again. All of its dining chains, including Carrabba's Italian Grill, Bonefish Grill, Cheeseburger in Paradise, and Blue

Coral Seafood & Spirits, suffered flat or falling sales. But most concerning to OSI was its flagship chain, Outback Steakhouse, which saw sales drop more than 9 percent across its 970 locations during one quarter. But difficult circumstances can spur creative thinking in marketers.

Targeting its market—understanding who its customers are—has been an important part of OSI's regrouping effort for Outback Steakhouse. OSI marketers realized that consumers still like to eat dinner out when they can afford it and that people do enjoy Outback's food. So they began developing menu choices and pricing options to appeal to its value-driven customers. These changes actually represented a return to Outback's original premise—offering a variety of high-quality menu selections at prices lower than those of a typical steak house and serving them in an atmosphere that resembled the Australian Outback. The challenge was to make the modifications while cutting costs to offset losses.

First, Outback eliminated some food items that weren't as popular as others or were too expensive to prepare. Second, the restaurant reassured regular customers that their favorites would remain on the menu, including the Bloomin' Onion appetizer, baby back ribs, and the "special" steak. Third, it spent more than a year formulating new, tasty meals that would appeal to the palates and wallets of price-conscious diners. Ultimately, Outback launched a new menu featuring 15 meals priced under $15, including some priced as low as $9.95. The new offerings included savory pepper mill steak—slices of New York strip steak encrusted with black pepper and served with potato wedges—and Sweet Glazed Pork Tenderloin. A new seafood dish, Shrimp en Fuego, featured large, crispy shrimp served with mushrooms and tomatoes in a cream sauce. Those who couldn't decide on a single

dish could select the new Ribs and Alice Spring Chicken, a one-third rack of baby back ribs paired with a grilled chicken breast topped with bacon, honey-mustard sauce, sautéed mushrooms, and melted cheeses. Regulars would be pleased with the customary side of Aussie Fries. With its new meals, Outback Steakhouse hoped to refurbish its reputation as a chain of restaurants providing the highest quality at "Down Under Prices."

In addition to updating the menu, Outback freshened up the appearance of its restaurants. Remaining true to its Australian image, the restaurants' updated décor encouraged consumers to feel as if they were sampling a new dining spot. "A new look delivers an experience that we believe reaches beyond the existing interpretation of Australia and the Outback in our restaurants, and it is expressed in updated fabrics, textures, art, lighting, props, and murals," states a company document. "Our marketing

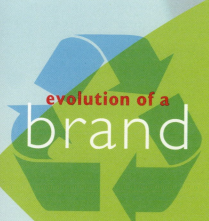

evolution of a brand

Outback Steakhouse is a casual dining chain that was founded on the premise that diners enjoy eating good food in an exotic environment. "Australia is a place of adventure and wonder. Make a discovery of your own at Outback Steakhouse with our new menu," invites the company's Web site. After some serious setbacks, Outback has returned to its roots—serving hearty food in a setting that echoes the Australian Outback. "We know consumers crave great tasting, high quality appetizers, entrées, and desserts," says Jeff Smith, president of Outback Steakhouse. "Our new menu features classic favorites and new culinary creations, at prices that are easy on the wallet."

- Outback is boosting its brand with a new menu that features generous portions of good food at affordable prices. How is this strategy helping to position Outback in consumers' minds?

evolution of a brand
continued

- With its new menu choices and its updated décor, what group or groups of consumers do you think Outback is attempting to attract? Do you predict it will be successful? Why or why not?

- Why is it important to modify a chain's image from time to time? How might Outback further develop its brand going forward?

strategy of getting people to visit frequently and also recommending our restaurants to others comple ments what we believe are the fundamental elements of success: convenient sites, service-oriented employees, and flawless execution in a well-managed restaurant."

A challenging business environment encourages the best marketing minds to think creatively about who their customers are and how their company should be positioned to serve them. Outback Steakhouse now invites diners to "Think Australian. Live Adventurous." And that means eating good food at a great price—an old trend made new again.[1]

chapter overview

market Group of people with sufficient purchasing power, authority, and willingness to buy.

Each of us is unique. We come from different backgrounds, live in different households, and have different interests and goals. You and your best friend may shop at different stores, listen to different music, play different sports, and take different courses in college. Suppose you like country music, but your best friend prefers rock. Marketers for all kinds of music-related products, ranging from digital songs to live concerts, want to capture your interest as well as that of your friends. Do you play an instrument or sing, or are you a fan who goes to clubs and downloads music? As OSI Restaurant Partners did recently after a fall-off in sales, marketers look at customers and potential customers to figure out what their characteristics are, whether they can identify certain subgroups, and how they can best offer products to meet their needs. Your interests and needs, your lifestyle and income, the town where you live, and your age all contribute to the likelihood that you will listen to and buy certain types of music—say, Jack Johnson or the score to *Wicked*. All of these factors make up a market. A **market** is composed of people with sufficient purchasing power, authority, and willingness to buy. Marketers must use their expertise to understand the market for a good or service, whether it's a room for a business traveler at a Marriott Hotel or a vacation timeshare at Disney World.

Many markets include consumers with different lifestyles, backgrounds, and income levels. Nearly everyone buys toothpaste, but that does not mean every consumer has the same lifestyle, background, or income. So it is unusual for a single marketing mix strategy to attract all sectors of a market. By identifying, evaluating, and selecting a target market to pursue, such as consumers who prefer toothpaste made with all-natural ingredients or those who want an extra-whitening formula—marketers develop more efficient and effective marketing strategies. On the other hand, some products, such as luxury sports cars and fly-fishing supplies, are intended for a more specific market. In either case, the **target market** for a product is the specific segment of consumers most likely to purchase a particular item.

Marketing now takes place on a global basis more than ever, incorporating many target markets. To identify those markets, marketers must determine useful ways for segmenting different populations and communicating with them successfully. This chapter discusses useful ways to accomplish this objective, explaining the steps of the market segmentation process and surveying strategies for reaching target markets. Finally, it looks at the role of positioning in developing a marketing strategy.

target market Group of people to whom a firm decides to direct its marketing efforts and ultimately its goods and services.

Types of Markets

Products usually are classified as either consumer products or business products. **Consumer products** are bought by ultimate consumers for personal use, for example, cell phones, sports tickets, or fashion magazines. **Business products** are goods and services purchased for use either directly or indirectly in the production of other goods and services for resale. Most goods and services purchased by individual consumers, such as DVDs and restaurant meals, are considered consumer products. Rubber and raw cotton are examples of items generally purchased by manufacturers and therefore classified as business products. B. F. Goodrich buys rubber to manufacture tires; textile manufacturers such as Burlington Industries convert raw cotton into cloth.

However, in many cases, a single product can serve different uses. Tires purchased for the family car constitute consumer products, but tires purchased by Ford Motor Company to be mounted on its Ford Focus are business products because they become part of another product destined for resale. Or, a product that was once a business product might be modified for consumer use, and vice versa. A line of professional cookware sold to restaurants—a business product—could be adapted by its manufacturer to become a line of cookware for home use—a consumer product. If you want to determine the classification of an item, just think about who is going to buy the product, who will use it, and how or why the product will be used. The bottle of mouthwash you buy at the supermarket is a consumer product, but if a large hotel chain purchases large quantities of the same mouthwash from a wholesaler, it becomes a business product.

1 Identify the essential components of a market.

consumer products Products bought by ultimate consumers for personal use.

business products Goods and services purchased for use either directly or indirectly in the production of other goods and services for resale.

assessment check

1. Define *target market*.
2. Distinguish between a consumer product and a business product.

The Role of Market Segmentation

There are 6.8 billion people in the world today; more than 306 million live in the United States.[2] In today's business world, too many variables exist in consumer needs, preferences, and purchasing power to attract all consumers with a single marketing mix. That's not to say that firms must actually change products to meet the needs of different market segments—although they often do—but they must attempt to identify the factors that affect purchase decisions and then group consumers according to the presence or absence of these factors. Finally, they adjust marketing strategies to meet the needs of each group.

Consider motor vehicles. Unlike a century ago, when Henry Ford pronounced that customers could order any color of car they liked—as long as it was black—today there is a make, model, and color for every taste and budget. But auto manufacturers need to adjust their messages for different markets. And savvy marketers look toward markets that show growth, such as the U.S. Hispanic population—now the largest ethnic group in the country—and aging baby boomers, whose needs for goods and services are changing.

2 Outline the role of market segmentation in developing a marketing strategy.

market segmentation
Division of the total market into smaller, relatively homogeneous groups.

3 **Describe the criteria necessary for effective segmentation.**

The division of the total market into smaller, relatively homogeneous groups is called **market segmentation.** Both profit-oriented and not-for-profit organizations practice market segmentation.

CRITERIA FOR EFFECTIVE SEGMENTATION

Segmentation doesn't automatically guarantee success in the marketing arena; instead, it is a tool for marketers to use. Its effectiveness depends on four basic requirements.

First, the market segment must present measurable purchasing power and size. With jobs, incomes, and decision-making power, female consumers represent a hefty amount of purchasing power, approaching $1 trillion, or 60 percent of the nation's wealth. Women control or influence the purchase of 80 percent of all consumer goods, including such items as stocks for investment, personal computers, and family vehicles.[3] With this information in mind, car manufacturers and dealers now market directly to women. In addition, Web sites like AskPatty.com offer advice to women on making car purchases—and certify dealerships that "provide women consumers with an automotive retail experience based on relationship building, trust, respect, and improved communications," according to the site's promise to female consumers.[4]

Second, marketers must find a way to effectively promote and serve the market segment. Because women now wield purchasing power in the technology market, marketers need to find different ways to appeal to them. Some companies have taken this advice to heart. T-Mobile and BlackBerry have created ads featuring working moms.

Third, marketers must then identify segments large enough to give them good profit potential. Because women significantly influence 90 percent of home purchases, homebuilders have turned their marketing efforts to them. Design Basics, the largest home-plan design company in the country, now focuses on designs aimed at women. Its guidelines include improving storage options, creating multipurpose rooms, and emphasizing the practicality of the back-door entry—with space for muddy boots and school backpacks, car keys, mail, and a plug to recharge cell

Because women control or influence the purchase of 80 percent of all consumer goods, many companies choose ads that feature women and appeal to women.

© Image courtesy of The Advertising Archives

phones. A spokesperson for the firm explains that designers now think more about how a family actually lives.[5]

Fourth, the firm must aim for segments that match its marketing capabilities. Targeting a large number of small markets can be an expensive, complex, and inefficient strategy, so smaller firms may decide to stick with a particular niche, or target market. But Harley-Davidson, once thought the domain of men, is now experiencing a surge in purchases by women, the fastest-growing segment of the motorcycle business. So the firm runs targeted ads in women's magazines and recently held its first Women's Day at the Sturgis Motorcycle Rally in Rapid City, South Dakota, featuring demonstrations, social gatherings, and events targeted for women.[6]

assessment check

1. Identify the four criteria for effective segmentation.

2. Give an example of a market segment that meets these criteria.

Segmenting Consumer Markets

Market segmentation attempts to isolate the traits that distinguish a certain group of consumers from the overall market. An understanding of the group's characteristics—such as age, gender, geographic location, income, and buying patterns—plays a vital role in developing a successful marketing strategy. In most cases, marketers seek to pinpoint a number of factors affecting buying behavior in the target segment. Marketers in the travel industry consider employment trends, changes in income levels and buying patterns, age, lifestyle, and other factors when promoting their goods and services. To boost flagging attendance at its theme parks, Disney World advertises to "empty nesters" and groups of friends instead of focusing entirely on families with young children. Marketers rarely identify totally homogeneous segments, in which all potential customers are alike; they almost always encounter some differences among members of a target group, but must be careful to ensure their segments accurately reflect consumers.

In the next sections, we discuss the four common bases for segmenting consumer markets: geographic segmentation, demographic segmentation, psychographic segmentation, and product-related segmentation. These segmentation approaches offer important guidance for marketing strategies, provided they identify significant differences in buying behavior.

Geographic Segmentation

Marketers have long practiced **geographic segmentation**—dividing an overall market into homogeneous groups based on their locations. Geographic location does not ensure all consumers in a location will make the same buying decisions, but this segmentation approach helps identify some general patterns.

The approximately 306 million people living in the United States are not scattered evenly across the country. For instance, many are concentrated in major metropolitan areas; New York is the largest U.S. city, with more than 8.2 million citizens, but the metropolitan area surrounding it includes nearly 19 million people. Los Angeles ranks second, with 3.8 million, and a surrounding area of nearly 13 million.[7] Figure 9.1 shows populations of the ten largest cities in the United States and the ten states with the largest populations. California tops the list at 38 million residents. Wyoming is the least-populated state, with 520,000. In addition to total population, marketers need to look at the *fastest-growing* states to plan their strategies for the future. Nevada and Arizona are the fastest-growing states, but Louisiana is rebounding from its population loss after Hurricane Katrina.[8]

A look at the worldwide population distribution illustrates why so many firms pursue customers around the globe. China has the most citizens, with 1.3 billion people, and India is second with 1.1 billion. The United States is third with about 306 million, and Indonesia is fourth with 237 million. Japan is a distant tenth with 127 million.[9] As in the United States, much of the world's population lives in urban environments. The two largest cities in the world are Shanghai,

4 **Explain the geographic approach to segmenting consumer markets.**

geographic segmentation Division of an overall market into homogeneous groups based on their locations.

figure 9.1

The Ten Largest Cities and Ten Most Populous States in the United States

Sources: "Interim Projections of the Total Population for the United States and States: July 1, 2010," U.S Census Bureau, http://www.census .gov, accessed May 12, 2009; "Population Estimates for the 25 Largest U.S. Cities Based on July 1, 2006, Population Estimates," U.S. Census Bureau, http://www.census.gov, accessed May 12, 2009.

China, with 15.5 million and Bombay, India, with 13.6 million. The two largest metropolitan areas are Tokyo, Japan, with more than 37 million and Mexico City, with nearly 23 million.[10]

Population size alone, however, may not be reason enough for a business to expand into a specific country. Businesses also need to look at a wide variety of economic variables. Some businesses may decide to combine their marketing efforts for countries that share similar population and product-use patterns instead of treating each country as an independent segment. This grouping is taking place with greater frequency throughout the European Union as the currency and trade laws of the member nations become more unified.

While population numbers indicate the overall size of a market, other geographic indicators such as job growth give useful guidance to marketers, depending on the type of products they sell. Automobile manufacturers might segment geographic regions by household income because it is an important factor in the purchase of a new car.

Geographic areas also vary in population migration patterns. Job transfer and retirement are two circumstances that cause people to move. Major natural disasters may affect population migration, as in the case of Hurricane Katrina, which devastated Louisiana and neighboring states. It's also important for marketers to observe who is moving where: people who leave the East Coast aren't necessarily jumping to the West, and vice versa. New Yorkers tend to gravitate to the South or even to Connecticut or New Jersey. Californians often move to other western states instead of coming farther east. The metropolitan area surrounding Atlanta gained nearly 900,000 new residents during one six-year period, while Dallas-Fort Worth gained 825,000.[11]

The move from urban to suburban areas after World War II created a need to redefine the urban marketplace. This trend radically changed cities' traditional patterns of retailing and led to decline in many downtown shopping areas. Subsequently, traditional city boundaries become almost meaningless for marketing purposes. However, marketers now observe a trend toward the revitalization of downtown urban areas as the cost of fuel and other factors contribute to the rising expenses associated with living in the suburbs.

In an effort to respond to these changes, the government now classifies urban data using the following categories:

▷ The category of **core based statistical area (CBSA)** became effective in 2000 and refers collectively to metropolitan and micropolitan statistical areas. Each CBSA must contain at least one urban area with a population of 10,000 or more. Each metropolitan statistical area must have at least one urbanized area of 50,000 or more inhabitants. Each micropolitan statistical area must have at least one urban cluster with a population of at least 10,000 but less than 50,000. There are 361 metropolitan and 575 micropolitan statistical areas in the United States. Of the 361 metropolitan statistical areas, 170 are classified as large, meaning they contain more than 250,000 people.[12]

briefly
speaking

"Consumers are statistics. Customers are people."

**—Stanley Marcus
(1905–2002)**
AMERICAN MERCHANT

▷ A **metropolitan statistical area (MSA)** is a free-standing urban area with a population in the urban center of at least 50,000 and a total metropolitan statistical area population of 100,000 or more. Buyers in metropolitan statistical areas exhibit social and economic homogeneity and usually border on nonurbanized counties. Examples include Rochester, New York; Albuquerque, New Mexico; and Kalamazoo–Battle Creek, Michigan. Figure 9.2 identifies the ten largest metropolitan areas in the United States.

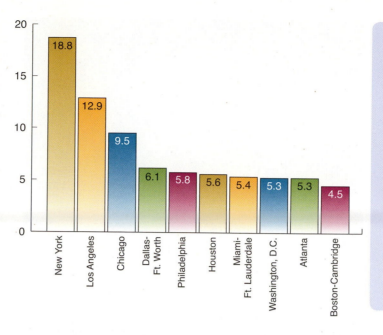

figure 9.2

The Ten Largest Metropolitan Areas in the United States

Source: "Large Metropolitan Statistical Areas—Population: 1990 to 2007," *Statistical Abstract of the United States, 2009,* U.S. Census Bureau, www.census.gov, accessed May 12, 2009.

▷ A **micropolitan statistical area** has at least one town of 10,000 to 49,999 people—it can have several such towns—and proportionally few of its residents commuting outside the area. Recently, the government counted 575 such areas in the continental United States. Examples of micropolitan statistical areas include Granbury, Texas; Marion, Ohio; Alamogordo, New Mexico; and Yazoo City, Mississippi.

▷ The category of **consolidated metropolitan statistical area (CMSA)** includes the country's 25 or so urban giants such as Detroit–Ann Arbor–Flint, Michigan; Los Angeles–Riverside–Orange County, California; and Philadelphia–Wilmington–Atlantic City. (Note in the third example, three states are involved: Pennsylvania, Delaware, and New Jersey.) A CMSA must include two or more primary metropolitan statistical areas, discussed next.

▷ A **primary metropolitan statistical area (PMSA)** is an urbanized county or set of counties with social and economic ties to nearby areas. PMSAs are identified within areas of 1-million-plus populations. Olympia, Washington, is part of the Seattle–Tacoma–Bremerton PMSA. Bridgeport, Connecticut, is part of the New York–northern New Jersey–Long Island PMSA, and Riverside–San Bernardino, California, is a PMSA within the Los Angeles–Riverside–Orange County PMSA.[13]

USING GEOGRAPHIC SEGMENTATION

Demand for some categories of goods and services can vary according to geographic region, and marketers must be aware of how these regions differ. Marketers of major brands are particularly interested in defining their **core regions,** the locations where they get 40 to 80 percent of their sales.

Residence location *within* a geographic area is an important segmentation variable. City dwellers often rely on public transportation and may get along fine without automobiles, whereas those who live in the suburbs or rural areas depend on their own cars and trucks. Also, those who live in the suburbs spend more on lawn and garden care products than city dwellers. Climate is another important segmentation factor; consumers in cold northern states eat more soup than people in warmer southern markets. But here's a surprise—they also eat more ice cream! One recent survey revealed that residents of Chicago drink more coffee, caffeinated cola, and energy drinks—and eat more chocolate—than other city dwellers. However, those who live in Seattle rank highest in consumption of coffee alone. Marketers can use this information to determine where their products are most likely to be successful.[14]

Geographic segmentation provides useful distinctions when regional preferences or needs exist. A consumer may not want to invest in a snowblower or flood insurance, but may *have* to because of the location of his or her home. But it's important for marketers not to stop at geographic location

Seattle ranks high in consumption of coffee. Marketers can use such information to determine where their products are most likely to be successful.

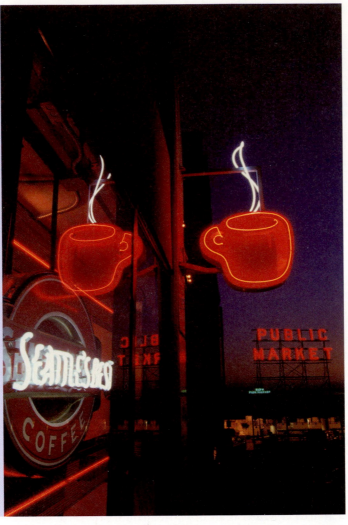

© Chuck Pefley/Alamy

as a segmentation method because distinctions among consumers also exist within a geographic location. Consider those who relocate from one region to another for work or family reasons. They may bring with them their preferences from other parts of the country. Using multiple segmentation variables is probably a much better strategy for targeting a specific market.

GEOGRAPHIC INFORMATION SYSTEMS (GISs)

Super Bowl Sunday is more than a sporting event—it is also the single biggest sales day of the year for a pizza company such as Domino's. On that day alone, Domino's delivers 1.2 million pizzas around the nation. The firm built its reputation as the number-one pizza delivery company in the world, which means its delivery system must be as streamlined and efficient as possible. To achieve its objectives, Domino's invested in new technology systems like its "pizza tracker," which allows football fans to order their favorite pizzas ahead of time online with PCs or mobile phones via Domino's and track the delivery status of their pies.[15] This new feature is part of the firm's geographic information system.

Once used mainly by the military, **geographic information systems (GISs)** are computer systems that assemble, store, manipulate, and display data by their location. GISs simplify the job of analyzing marketing information by relating data to their locations. The result is a geographic map overlaid with digital data about consumers in a particular area. A growing number of companies benefit from using a GIS to locate new outlets, assign sales territories, plan distribution centers—and map out the most efficient delivery routes. Google Earth is a recent application of GIS technology that allows computer users to view different parts of the country up close. Users simply type in an address and zoom into it, whether it's a house, a theme park, a school, or a store.

5 Discuss the demographic approach to segmenting consumer markets.

demographic segmentation Division of an overall market into homogeneous groups based on variables such as gender, age, income, occupation, education, sexual orientation, household size, and stage in the family life cycle; also called *socioeconomic segmentation*.

assessment check

1. Under what circumstances are marketers most likely to use geographic segmentation?

2. What are the five main categories for classifying urban data?

Demographic Segmentation

The most common method of market segmentation—**demographic segmentation**—defines consumer groups according to demographic variables such as gender, age, income, occupation, education, sexual orientation, household size, and stage in the family lifecycle. This approach is also called *socioeconomic segmentation*. Marketers review vast quantities of available data to complete

Communicating with Your Target Market

a s a marketer, you learn to create and communicate messages for the people you want to purchase your firm's goods and services. The messages you send can have a major impact on potential customers' decisions to buy your products or those offered by a competitor. Understanding the needs and preferences of your target market will help you communicate effectively with the right people. The following suggestions will help you succeed:

- Develop an understanding of your target market before attempting to market products to them. This way, you will gain credibility among your consumers.

- Tailor your message directly to the group of consumers you want to reach—whether they are senior citizens, women, or African Americans. Don't try to sell your products to everyone.

- Use language appropriate for the recipients of your message. Become familiar with the conventional sayings, wording, and tone suitable for your audience.

- Use images that illustrate to your market segment that you understand their culture, beliefs, and lifestyle. This will also communicate that you understand their needs and preferences.

- Create messages that provide clear solutions to specific problems or needs consumers may have.

- Always be respectful of the consumers you intend to serve. Address their needs and preferences seriously.

Sources: Laura Lake, "In Marketing You Must Know Your Target," *About.com Marketing*, marketing.about.com, accessed May 12, 2009; "Target Marketing: Reasons to Know Your Target Business Market," *More Business.com*, www.morebusiness.com, accessed May 12, 2009; Caroline Middlebrook, "Communicating with Your Target Market," *Promotion*, September 12, 2007, www.caroline-middlebrook.com.

a plan for demographic segmentation. One of the primary sources for demographic data in the United States is the Census Bureau. Marketers can obtain many of the Census Bureau's statistics online at www.census.gov.

The following discussion considers the most commonly used demographic variables. Keep in mind, however, that while demographic segmentation is helpful, it can also lead to stereotyping—a preconception about a group of people—which can alienate a potential market or cause marketers to miss a potential market altogether. The idea is to use segmentation as a starting point, not as an endpoint. Demographic segmentation can help marketers communicate effectively with their target markets, as described in the "Etiquette Tips for Marketing Professionals" feature.

SEGMENTING BY GENDER

Gender is an obvious variable that helps define the markets for certain products, but segmenting by gender can be tricky. In some cases, the segmenting is obvious—lipstick for women, facial shaving products for men. However, in recent years, the lines have increasingly blurred. Some men wear earrings and use skin-care products, once both the province of women. Some of today's women purchase power tools and pickup trucks, once considered traditionally male purchases. So marketers of cars and trucks, power tools, jewelry, and skin-care products have had to change the way they segment their markets. Nivea, well known for its skin-care products for women and babies, created an entire line of men's skin-care products called Nivea for Men. Some companies successfully market the same—or similar—products to both men and women. Visa markets its small-business credit card services to firms owned by both men and women.

As purchasing power in many households has shifted toward women, marketers learned that female consumers who regularly use the Internet make most of the decisions about retail items. Based on this information, Yahoo! recently launched Shine, a site specifically for women. The site offers content in a variety of areas ranging from entertainment to finance, and provides opportunities for advertisers to reach a targeted female audience. Skype, Perfect Escapes, and Herbal Essences are among the brands advertised on the site.[16]

SEGMENTING BY AGE

Age is another variable marketers use to segment their markets. As with gender, age seems an easy distinction to make—baby food for babies, retirement communities for seniors. But the distinctions become blurred as consumers' roles and needs change, and as age distribution shifts and changes in each group take place. St. Joseph's baby aspirin is no longer marketed just to parents for their infants; now it is also marketed to adults to help prevent heart disease.

The Cohort Effect

Marketers can learn from a sociological concept called the **cohort effect,** the tendency of members of a generation to be influenced and bound together by significant events occurring during their key formative years, roughly ages 17 to 22. These events help define the core values of the age group that eventually shape consumer preferences and behavior. For advanced seniors, the events would be the Great Depression, World War II, and Korea because many were in this age bracket at that time. Later groups were influenced by the *Cold War.* For older baby boomers, it would be the Vietnam War and the civil rights movement. Marketers have already labeled people who were in the 17-to-22 age bracket at the time of the September 11, 2001 terrorist attacks the **9/11 Generation.** This group's previous priorities and values changed in light of the attacks, and those changes become more evident as time passes.

The significance of the cohort effect for marketers lies in understanding the general characteristics of each group as it responds to its defining life events. The social and economic influences each group experiences help form their long-term beliefs and goals in life—and can have a lasting effect on their buying habits and the product choices they make. For marketers to be effective in reaching their targeted age segments, they need to understand some basic characteristics of each age group. We highlight a few of the distinguishing characteristics next and briefly discuss how some marketers are providing products to meet each age segment's wants and needs.

School-Age Children

School-age children—and those even younger—exert considerable influence over family purchases, as marketers are keenly aware, particularly in the area of food. Children as young as 2 make choices about what they want to eat, play with, and wear. Marketers spend more than $900 million a year on television commercials for products such as breakfast cereals, snack foods, and beverages of all kinds. These advertisements are designed to attract the attention of children under the age of 12—who in turn persuade their families to purchase them. With childhood obesity on the rise, nutritionists and pediatricians are concerned about the nutritional value of foods marketed to children. McDonald's, Campbell's Soup, and PepsiCo recently agreed to stop advertising directly to children under age 12 foods that do not meet specific nutritional standards.[17]

Tweens and Teens

Tweens—also called *preteens*—and teens are a rapidly growing market. Known as *Generation Y* or the *Millenials,* this group is 71 million strong and packs a wallop when it comes to spending; some researchers estimate as much as $200 billion. But they also influence billions of dollars' worth of purchases made by their families.[18] Although members of this group don't fall into a single category—they reflect the diversity of the U.S. population in general—the most popular purchases include candy and snacks, soft drinks, clothing, music, and electronics. If marketers could describe this group with one characteristic, it would likely be *interactive.* They grew up with the Internet, and they expect to be actively involved in their own entertainment. They might rather determine the outcome of a video game than watch to see who won a football game on TV. Even the TV shows they watch—like *American Idol*—provide opportunities for input. They are completely comfortable in a digital world, and many cannot imagine life without their cell phones and iPods. When they want to communicate with friends—or parents—they send text messages. They expect a vast array of choices when it comes to programming, media alternatives, and interactive experiences. The big challenge for marketers is keeping up with them—let alone staying a step ahead. Phone companies and car companies have increased their spending on advertising to older teens, while snacks, clothing, and video games claim the attention of the younger set.[19]

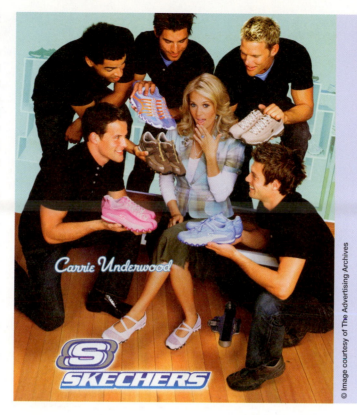

Tweens and teens are a rapidly growing market: 71 million strong and packing a wallop when it comes to spending on items including soft drinks, music, and clothing.

© Image courtesy of The Advertising Archives

Some companies have expanded their product lines to include specific offerings to tweens and teens. Pottery Barn devotes an entire catalog to this group, PB Teen. Teen consumers—both boys and girls—can decorate their bedrooms or dorm rooms with coordinating furniture, bedding, pillows, curtains, corkboards, and even retro-styled telephones from PB Teen. Free People is a clothing and accessories company aimed entirely at teen girls. Although the company is based in South Carolina, the fashions have an international flair, with styles reminiscent of those found in Mexico, Belize, Nepal, and India. Blogs are posted by Free People employees on the company's Web site, and teen shoppers are encouraged to communicate.[20]

Generation X

The group born between 1966 and 1981, now between ages 27 and 42, often are referred to as *Generation X.* This group of nearly 50 million faced some economic and career challenges as they began their adult lives and started families: housing costs were high and debt associated with college loans and credit cards was soaring. But their financial squeeze should ease as they enter their prime earning years. This group is very family oriented—not defining themselves by their careers as much as previous generations—well educated, and optimistic. Like their younger counterparts, Gen Xers are comfortable with the Internet; even if they make a purchase at a retail store, they are likely to have researched their choices online. But like their elders, they were raised on television—so the TV is still an important marketing tool.[21]

As this generation matures, they are growing more concerned about social issues and protecting the natural environment, both of which they view as affecting the well-being of their children. As a result, they are turning to goods and services that support certain causes. Singer-songwriter Jack Johnson, in his mid-thirties, recorded an album using solar energy. He requires his concert promoters to recycle and launched an online social networking site, All At Once, where fans can support environmental not-for-profit organizations. Johnson, a member of Generation X, appeals both to his own age group and older teens in Generation Y.[22]

Baby Boomers

Baby boomers—those born between 1946 and 1965—are a popular segment to target because of their numbers and income levels. Approximately 78 million people were born during this period.[23] The values of this age group were influenced both by the Vietnam War era and the career-driven era that followed. They also came of age with early television, with TV commercials serving as a backdrop to most of their lives. They tried new breakfast cereals, ate TV dinners, and recall when cigarettes were advertised on television.

Vespa Motor Scooters has baby boomers clearly in its sights. When the firm rolled its scooters back onto U.S. streets after a 15-year absence, marketers discovered that consumers aged 50 and older were snapping them up.

© Kim Karpeles/Alamy

Not surprisingly, baby boomers are a lucrative segment for many marketers. Baby boomers wield spending power estimated at $2.1 trillion, which is why businesses try to woo this group.[24] Different subgroups within this generation complicate segmentation and targeting strategies. Some boomers put off having children until their 40s, while others their age have already become grandparents. Boomers tend to value health and quality of life—a fact not lost on marketers for products such as organic foods, financial investments, travel, and fitness. But boomers are also quick to embrace new technology, even as they age. While some firms have hesitated to promote new products to this age group, others have learned these consumers are just as quick to embrace something new as they were when they were in their early twenties. "Boomers are leading the companies that are bringing new technologies to the world," says one marketing researcher. "They're using it at work, and at home, and their kids are using it, too. Their entire lives have been about change."[25]

Vespa Motor Scooters is another firm that has boomers clearly in its sight. When the firm rolled its scooters back onto U.S. streets after a 15-year absence, marketers discovered consumers age 50 and older were snapping them up. It seemed these consumers were nostalgic for the old candy-colored bikes of their childhood, and the new scooters made them feel good. Although baby boomers now have more money to spend on leisure goods, the rising cost of fuel also makes the Vespa a bargain for quick trips around the neighborhood or town. Parent company Piaggio understands the importance of marketing to this group as well as older consumers: "No age limit" is the Vespa motto.[26]

Seniors

As Americans continue to live longer, the median age of the U.S. population has dramatically increased. More than 36 million people are now over age 65. In the United States, heads of households of age 55-plus control about three-quarters of the country's total financial assets. Their discretionary incomes and rates of home ownership are higher than those of any other age group. They account for about 40 percent of new-car sales and most of the travel dollars spent. These numbers show why many marketers should target this group. Although many seniors live on modest, fixed incomes, those who are well off financially have both time and money to spend on leisure activities and luxury items. Knowing this, some unethical marketers try to take advantage of seniors, as discussed in the "Solving an Ethical Controversy" feature.

Other important characteristics of this group include the following:

▷ Families experienced economic hardship during this group's childhood.

▷ They built the suburbs.

▷ They value hard work.

▷ They like to associate with people who have similar views and backgrounds.

▷ They are concerned with personal safety.

▷ They spend money conservatively, but have reached a level of financial comfort where they like to indulge in some luxury.

▷ They are not likely the first to try new products.[27]

Solving an ethical controversy

Targeting Seniors with Unclear Messages

While seniors control 75 percent of the nation's financial assets, they also account for nearly 30 percent of reported fraud victims. As baby boomers age into seniors, financial regulators predict the number of financial scams targeted at this group to increase dramatically. Seniors are vulnerable to unethical—if not illegal—practices, particularly in the areas of insurance, mortgages, and investments. Having accumulated a certain amount of wealth, they want to safeguard both their assets and their health. Because of this, seniors become prime targets for financial scams. Consumer and elder advocacy groups, along with the Securities and Exchange Commission, are working to stop such practices.

Should marketers have special rules on marketing to seniors to protect against abuses?

PRO

1. Seniors are consumers. Marketers should be allowed to gather information on them and target them for purchases just like any other group of consumers in a free enterprise economic system.

2. All consumers can be targets of fraud. Seniors do not need special protection from the Securities and Exchange Commission or other agencies.

CON

1. Investing events are particularly problematic for seniors. "Free" lunch or dinner seminars, often held at upscale restaurants or hotels, are marketed as educational workshops when they are actually sales presentations. Seniors are pressured to open an account at the event and invest or deposit funds immediately, without being fully informed of the risks involved.

2. Some insurance firms prey on the fears of seniors, pushing them to purchase coverage they neither need nor can afford. "Abusive Medicare insurance sales practices are spreading rapidly through [California]," reports one state senator. Generally, the plans are so confusing that seniors do not understand the terms, and their care is not managed carefully.

Summary

Regulators, consumers, and advocacy groups agree there is no place for unethical behavior in the marketplace. However, they may not agree about what type—and how much—action to take. The insurance commissioner for the state of Georgia describes the arrest of two insurance agents. "[They] signed up unwilling consumers and even deceased individuals for private Medicare plans," he says. "This appears to be a national problem, based on my conversations with insurance officials around the country." In the meantime, seniors, like all consumers, need to be wary of claims that seem too good to be true or pitches that are a little too slick.

Sources: Lois Center-Shabazz, "The Pitfalls of Reverse Mortgages for Senior Citizens," *MsFinancialSavvy.com*, www.msfinancialsavvy.com, accessed May 12, 2009; March Gordon, "Firms Faulted over Misleading Seniors at Investing Events," *The Washington Post*, September 10, 2007, www.washingtonpost.com; Robert Pear, "Methods Used by Insurers Are Questioned," *The New York Times*, May 7, 2007, www.nytimes.com.

Understanding just a few of these characteristics helps marketers develop goods and services and create marketing messages that will reach this group. When it was founded over two decades ago, Overseas Adventure Travel offered trekking, mountaineering, safari, and kayaking trips geared toward younger travelers. Today, OAT is part of the Grand Circle Travel Company and focuses on outdoor travel experiences for active baby boomers and seniors. The trips are less rigorous than the original itineraries, but still provide access to places off the beaten path. The company knows its customers have both the time and income for such excursions and appreciate the adventure experience.[28]

SEGMENTING BY ETHNIC GROUP

According to the Census Bureau, America's racial and ethnic makeup is constantly changing. The three largest and fastest-growing racial/ethnic groups are Hispanics, African Americans, and Asian Americans. From a marketer's perspective, it is important to note that spending by these groups is rising at a faster pace than for U.S. households in general.

Hispanics and African Americans

Hispanics and African Americans are currently the largest racial/ethnic minority groups in the United States, with Hispanics surpassing African Americans at nearly 48 million, according to the most recent census data.[29] The Hispanic population is growing much faster than the African American population and will account for 24 percent of the total population by the year 2050.[30] The South is expected to experience a 30 percent increase Hispanic residents by 2025, and the West should anticipate growth of 50 percent.[31] Just as important for marketers, U.S. Hispanics' disposable income has increased by nearly one-third over a two-year period, double the rate of the rest of the population—although it is still significantly less than that of non-Hispanic whites.[32]

Many marketers have focused their efforts on the Hispanic population in the United States. Procter & Gamble, The Coca-Cola Company, and Wal-Mart are among the largest advertisers to target this group of consumers. Still, many companies find it a challenge to reach Hispanic consumers and turn them into customers. Consorte Media specializes in gathering and analyzing data about the Hispanic market for clients such as Best Buy and Monster.com. One thing founder and CEO Alicia Morga has learned is "it's not just about language. It's about culture." Morga focuses on the online habits of Hispanic consumers, more than 22 million of whom visit the Internet regularly. She helped Best Buy build a better recruitment site for Hispanic job candidates and used her research to assist BuenaMusica.com in developing a more effective ad campaign.[33]

As is the case with Hispanics—whose origins may be from a variety of countries—African Americans do not represent a single category. Instead, they represent a wide range of diversity ranging from country of origin to income, age, education, and geographic location. However, market segmentation experts note that African American identity as a whole remains strong throughout the United States. Studies show these consumers tend to plan for the future and are generally optimistic about it.[34] Affluent African Americans are having a significant impact on the consumer economy. Nearly half of African American households earn $75,000 or more, and they are likely to focus their luxury spending on designer clothing, beauty supplies, and cruise vacations.[35] Significant advertising campaigns targeted at African Americans include Gatorade's alliance with Michael Jordan, featuring the tag line "I Wanna Be Like Mike," and McDonald's theme "I'm Lovin' It," which has its roots in urban African American teen culture.[36]

Asian Americans

Although Asian Americans represent a smaller segment than either the African American or Hispanic populations, they are the second-fastest-growing segment of the U.S. population. The Census Bureau estimates this group will grow to 18 million by the year 2020, representing more than 5 percent of the U.S. population.[37] Asian Americans are an attractive target for marketers because they also have the fastest-growing income.

Asian Americans, the second fastest growing segment of the U.S. population, are an attractive target for marketers because they also have the fastest growing income. This ad features actress Lucy Liu, who is of Chinese descent.

The Asian American population is concentrated in fewer geographic areas than other ethnic markets. Half of Asians live in California, Texas, and New York. More than half of Asian Americans hold college degrees or higher, and

60 percent own their own homes.[38] They are very diverse, representing more than 15 different cultures, and speak languages that include Cantonese, Hawaiian, Hindi, Japanese, Korean, Mandarin, Tagalog, Urdu, and Vietnamese. However, according to one study, 86 percent of Asian Americans are literate in English, suggesting that marketing obstacles may be more cultural than language based.[39]

Many companies find advertising to Asian Americans in local markets better than launching a national campaign. Honda's first Asian American advertising campaign, "Calligraphy," was launched in Los Angeles.

Native Americans

Another important minority group is Native Americans, whose current population numbers about 4.3 million, or 1.5 percent of the total U.S. population, including both American Indians and Alaska natives. In addition to tribes located in the continental United States, such as Apache, Navaho, Pueblo, and Iroquois, the Census Bureau includes Alaska native tribes such as Aleut and Eskimo.[40] The Native American population is growing at double the rate of the U.S. population in general.

In addition to population growth, Native American businesses are growing. There are more than 200,000 non-farm Native American firms in the United States.[41] Native American businesses are increasing in the service, construction, and retail areas in particular. Reservation-based casinos and related gaming activities make up a multi-billion-dollar industry, but plenty of other businesses are thriving as well. The Native American Business Alliance Fund fosters relationships between Native American-owned firms and other corporations. Recently NABA hosted a golf outing and cultural event that featured sponsors such as Ford, General Motors, Kellogg, and AAA.[42] *Rez-Biz*, a magazine published by the Navaho nation, is aimed at Native American entrepreneurs and includes blogs from other entrepreneurs, business stories, advertisements, and contacts. The magazine encourages entrepreneurial ventures and economic development on reservations and other locations where Native Americans are concentrated.[43]

People of Mixed Race

U.S. residents completing census forms now have the option of identifying themselves as belonging to more than one racial category. According to the Census Bureau, more than 7 million U.S. residents classify themselves this way.[44] Marketers need to be aware of this change. On one hand, it benefits marketers by making racial statistics more accurate; on the other hand, marketers may find it difficult to compare the new statistics with data from earlier censuses. In some cases, people of mixed race prefer to emphasize one part of their heritage over another; in other cases, they prefer not to make a choice. When professional golfer Tiger Woods first appeared in the national media, he referred to himself as Cablinasian, acknowledging his Caucasian, African American, American Indian, and Asian heritages. Although the most recent census reveals that 41 percent of the U.S. mixed-race population was under the age of 18, these consumers are growing into adults—and having their own families.[45] Forward-thinking marketers should keep tabs on this group, identifying their needs and preferences.

SEGMENTING BY FAMILY LIFECYCLE STAGES

Still another form of demographic segmentation employs the stages of the **family lifecycle**—the process of family formation and dissolution. The underlying theme of this segmentation approach is that life stage, not age per se, is the primary determinant of many consumer purchases. As people move from one life stage to another, they become potential consumers for different types of goods and services.

An unmarried person setting up an apartment for the first time is likely a good prospect for inexpensive furniture and small home appliances. This consumer probably must budget carefully, ruling out expenditures on luxury items. Alternatively, a young single person still living at home will probably have more money to spend on products such as a car, entertainment, and clothing. As couples marry, their consumer profiles change. Couples without children are frequent buyers of personalized gifts, power tools, furniture, and homes. Eating out and travel may also be part of their lifestyles.

The birth or adoption of a first child changes any consumer's profile considerably; parents must buy cribs, changing tables, baby clothes, baby food, car seats, and similar products. Parents usually spend less on the children who follow because they have already bought many essential items for the first child. Today, the average woman gives birth to fewer children than she did a century ago and usually waits until she is older to have them. Although the average age for American women to have their first child is 25, many women wait much longer, often into their 30s and even 40s. This means that, if they work outside the home, older women are likely more established financially with more money to spend. However, if a woman chooses to stay home after the birth of a child, income can drop dramatically.

Families typically spend the most during the years their children are growing—on everything including housing, food, clothing, braces, and college. Thus, they often look to obtain value wherever they can. Marketers can create satisfied and loyal customers among this group by giving them the best value possible.

Once children are grown and on their own—or at least off to college—married couples enter the "empty nest" stage. Empty nesters may have the disposable incomes necessary to purchase premium products once college tuitions and mortgages are paid off. They may travel more, eat out more often, redecorate the house, or go back to school themselves. They may treat themselves to a new and more luxurious car or buy a vacation home. In later years, empty nesters may decide to sell their homes and become customers for retirement or assisted-living communities. They may require home-care services or more healthcare products as well. However, more older adults report they have not saved enough for retirement, which may include this type of care. People currently in this stage of life now say they would advise younger adults to address issues of a lifetime income, the cost of healthcare, and less reliance on Social Security benefits for income. To meet expenses, many retired adults are returning to work at least part time—consulting in their field of expertise or doing something entirely different like working in a retail store.[46]

One trend noted by researchers in the past decade is an increase in the number of grown children who have returned home to live with their parents. Called "boomerangs," some of these grown children bring along families of their own. Another trend is the growing number of grandparents who care for grandchildren on a regular basis—making them customers all over again for baby and child products such as toys, food, and safety devices. In China, empty nesters whose children have left the country for work or education are informally "adopting" local adult children to spend weekends and holidays with them, creating a sense of family that both sides feel they are missing.[47]

SEGMENTING BY HOUSEHOLD TYPE

The first U.S. census in 1790 found an average household size of 5.8 people. Today, that number is below 3, although demographers are reporting the possibility of a baby boomlet, the largest number of babies born in nearly half a century.[48] The U.S. Department of Commerce cites several reasons for the trend toward smaller households: lower fertility rates (including the decision to have fewer children or no children at all), young people's tendency to postpone marriage, the frequency of divorce, and the ability and desire of many people to live alone.

People live alone for a variety of reasons. In response, marketers have modified their products to meet the needs of single-person households.

© AP Images/PRNewsFoto/The J.M. Smucker Company

Today's U.S. households represent a wide range of diversity. They include households with a married couple and their children; households blended through divorce or loss of a spouse and remarriage; those headed by a single parent, same-sex parents, or grandparents; couples without children; groups of friends; and single-person households.

Couples without children may be young or old. If they are seniors, their children may have already grown and be living on their own. Some older couples choose to live together without marriage because they prefer to keep their finances separate and because they could lose valuable health or pension benefits if they married. Younger couples without children are considered attractive to marketers because they often have high levels of income to spend. These couples typically eat out often, take expensive vacations, and buy luxury cars.

Same-sex couples who share households—with or without children—are on the rise. More than 400,000 U.S. children are raised by same-sex couples. While the social debate over same-sex marriage and civil unions continues, marketers recognize these households as important customers. Wal-Mart has introduced a line of wedding cards and commitment rings designed for same-sex couples. Companies such as American Airlines, BMW, and Xerox have also created ad campaigns aimed at gay and lesbian households.[49]

People live alone for a variety of reasons—sometimes by choice and sometimes by necessity, such as divorce or widowhood. In response, marketers have modified their messages and their products to meet the needs of single-person households. Food industry manufacturers are downsizing products, offering more single-serving foods, ranging from soup to macaroni and cheese.

<aside>
briefly speaking

"We have become not a melting pot but a beautiful mosaic. Different people, different beliefs, different yearnings, different hopes, different dreams."

—**Jimmy Carter (b. 1924)**
39TH PRESIDENT OF THE UNITED STATES
</aside>

SEGMENTING BY INCOME AND EXPENDITURE PATTERNS

Part of the earlier definition of *market* described people with purchasing power. Not surprisingly, then, a common basis for segmenting the consumer market is income. Marketers often target geographic areas known for the high incomes of their residents. Or they might consider age or household type when determining potential buying power.

Engel's Laws

How do expenditure patterns vary with income? Over a century ago, Ernst Engel, a German statistician, published what became known as **Engel's laws**—three general statements based on his studies of the impact of household income changes on consumer spending behavior. According to Engel, as household income increases, the following will take place:

1. A smaller percentage of expenditures goes for food.

2. The percentage spent on housing, household operations, and clothing remains constant.

3. The percentage spent on other items (such as recreation and education) increases.

Are Engel's laws still valid? Recent studies say yes, with a few exceptions. Researchers note a steady decline in the percentage of total income spent on food, beverages, and tobacco as income increases. Although high-income families spend greater absolute amounts on food items, their purchases represent declining percentages of their total expenditures compared with low-income families. In addition, that percentage has declined over the last century.[50] But as food prices grow inflated, consumers change how they shop—they may spend the same to buy fewer items, spend more to buy the same items, or try to spend less and buy as many items as possible within the new budget. Marketers note that consumers are more selective, on the alert for bargains at the supermarket. Ground beef, milk, chicken, apples, tomatoes, lettuce, coffee, and orange juice have all increased dramatically in price according to the Bureau of Labor Statistics.[51] One other recent finding splits the food dollar according to meals cooked and eaten at home versus meals eaten out at restaurants. U.S. consumers now eat nearly 49 percent of their food away from home, a dramatic increase over the last few decades.[52]

The second law remains partly accurate. However, the percentage of fixed expenditures for housing and household operations has increased over the past 30 years. And the percentage spent on clothing rises with increased income because of choice. Also, expenditures may vary from region to region. In general, residents of the Northeast and West spend more on housing than people who live in the Midwest and South. The third law remains true, with the exception of medical and personal-care costs, which appear to decline as a percentage of increased income.

Engel's laws can help marketers target markets at all income levels. Regardless of the economic environment, consumers still buy luxury goods and services. One reason is some companies now offer their luxury products at different price levels. Mercedes-Benz has its lower-priced C-class models, while Tiffany sells a $100 sterling silver heart pendant with chain. Both of these firms continue to offer their higher-priced items but have broadened their market by serving other consumers.

DEMOGRAPHIC SEGMENTATION ABROAD

Marketers often face a difficult task in obtaining the data necessary for demographic segmentation abroad. Many countries do not have scheduled census programs. Germany skipped counting from 1970 to 1987, and France conducts a census about every seven years. By contrast, Japan and Canada conduct censuses every five years; however, the mid-decade assessments are not as complete as the end-of-decade counts.

Also, some foreign data include demographic divisions not found in the U.S. census. Canada collects information on religious affiliation, for instance. On the other hand, some of the standard segmentation data for U.S. markets are not available abroad. Many nations do not collect income data. Great Britain, Japan, Spain, France, and Italy are examples. Similarly, family lifecycle data are difficult to apply in global demographic segmentation efforts. Ireland acknowledges only three marital statuses—single, married, and widowed—while Latin-American nations and Sweden count their unmarried cohabitants.

One source of global demographic information is the International Programs Center (IPC) at the U.S. Census Bureau. The IPC provides a searchable online database of population statistics for many countries on the Census Bureau's Web page. Another source is the United Nations, which sponsors national statistical offices that collect demographic data on a variety of countries.

In addition, private marketing research firms can supplement government data. Firms like Boston Consulting Group have been gathering data on income of consumers around the world, focusing in particular on millionaire households. The top five countries with the most millionaire households are the United States, Japan, Britain, Germany, and China. But the United Arab Emirates and Switzerland have the highest *density* of millionaire households, nearly nine times the global average.[53]

⑥ Outline the psychographic approach to segmenting consumer markets.

Psychographic Segmentation

Marketers have traditionally referred to geographic and demographic characteristics as the primary bases for dividing consumers into homogeneous market segments. Still, they have long recognized the need for fuller, more lifelike portraits of consumers in developing their marketing programs. As a result, psychographic segmentation can be a useful tool for gaining sharper insight into consumer purchasing behavior.

WHAT IS PSYCHOGRAPHIC SEGMENTATION?

psychographic segmentation Division of a population into groups having similar attitudes, values, and lifestyles.

Psychographic segmentation divides a population into groups with similar psychological characteristics, values, and lifestyles. Lifestyle refers to a person's mode of living and describes how an individual operates on a daily basis. Consumers' lifestyles are composites of their individual psychological profiles, including their needs, motives, perceptions, and attitudes. A lifestyle also bears the mark of many other influences such as family, job, social activities, and culture.

The most common method for developing psychographic profiles of a population is to conduct a large-scale survey asking consumers to agree or disagree with a collection of several hundred AIO statements. These **AIO statements** describe various activities, interests, and opinions. The resulting data allow researchers to develop lifestyle profiles. Marketers can then develop a separate marketing strategy that closely fits the psychographic makeup for each lifestyle segment.

Marketing researchers have conducted psychographic studies on hundreds of goods and services, such as beer and air travel. Hospitals and other healthcare providers use such studies to assess consumer behavior and attitudes toward health care in general, to learn the needs of consumers in particular marketplaces, and to determine how consumers perceive individual institutions. Many businesses turn to psychographic research to learn what consumers in various demographic and geographic segments want and need.

VALS™

A quarter century ago, research and consulting firm SRI International developed a psychographic segmentation system, VALS. Today VALS is owned and managed by SRI Consulting Business Intelligence (SRIC-BI), an SRI spin-off. VALS originally stood for "values and lifestyles" because it categorized consumers by their social values—how they felt about issues such as legalization of marijuana or abortion rights, for example. A decade later, SRIC-BI revised the system to link it more closely with consumer buying behavior. The revised VALS system categorizes consumers by psychological characteristics that correlate with purchase behavior. It is based on two key concepts: resources and self-motivation. **VALS** divides consumers into eight psychographic categories: innovators, thinkers, achievers, experiencers, believers, strivers, makers, and survivors. Figure 9.3 details the profiles for these categories and their relationships.

The VALS framework in the figure displays differences in resources as vertical distances, and primary motivation is represented horizontally. The resource dimension measures income, education, self-confidence, health, eagerness to buy, and energy level. Primary motivations divide consumers into three groups: principle-motivated consumers who have a set of ideas and morals—principles—they live by; achievement-motivated consumers, influenced by symbols of success; and action-motivated consumers who seek physical activity, variety, and adventure. Marketers of new lines of eco-friendly fashions are likely to create appeals for principle-motivated consumers who want to wear their environmental commitment—literally—as described in the "Marketing Success" feature.

SRIC-BI has created several specialized segmentation systems based on this approach. GeoVALS™, for instance, estimates the percentage of each VALS type in each U.S. residential zip code. Marketers can identify zip codes with the highest concentrations of the segment they want to reach; they can use the information to choose locations for retail outlets; and they can tailor marketing messages for a local audience. For example, one GeoVALs study revealed that 26 percent of consumers who live in Goldfield, Nevada, are classified as believers—information marketers can use to customize goods and services.[54] Japan-VALS segments the Japanese marketplace with an emphasis on early adopters of new ideas and products. With a questionnaire of 49 items, marketers using Japan-VALS zero in on consumer needs, differentiate their brands, and develop more targeted tools and strategies.[55]

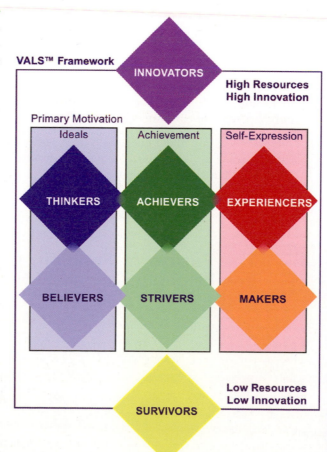

figure 9.3
The VALS Network

Source: SRI Consulting Business Intelligence (SRIC-BI); www. src-bi.com/VALS

Marketers of new types of eco-friendly fashion, such as items made from recycled materials, are likely to create appeal for environmentally motivated consumers.

Other tools available include LifeMatrix, developed by RoperASW and Mediamark Research. LifeMatrix crunches the numbers on hundreds of personal variables that include political views, religious affiliations, and social attitudes and comes up with ten psychographic categories reflecting today's lifestyles. Participants are asked to indicate how many hours each week they spend on certain activities, which helps shape the overall picture of their lives.[56]

PSYCHOGRAPHIC SEGMENTATION OF GLOBAL MARKETS

As Japan-VALS suggests, psychographic profiles can cross national boundaries. Marketing research firm RoperASW, now part of Germany-based GfK NOP, surveyed 7,000 people in 35 nations. From the data, Roper identified six psychographic consumer segments that exist in all 35 nations, although to varying degrees:

▷ *Strivers,* the largest segment, value professional and material goals more than the other groups. One-third of the Asian population and one-fourth of Russians are strivers. They are slightly more likely to be men than women.

▷ *Devouts* value duty and tradition. While this segment comprises 22 percent of all adults, they are most common in Africa, the Middle East, and developing Asia. They are least common in western Europe and developed Asian countries. Worldwide, they are more likely to be female.

▷ *Altruists* emphasize social issues and societal well-being. Comprising 18 percent of all adults, this group shows a median age of 44 and a slightly higher percentage of women.

▷ *Intimates* value family and personal relationships. They are divided almost equally between males and females. One American or European in four would be categorized as intimates, but only 7 percent of consumers in developing Asia fall into this category.

▷ *Fun seekers,* as you might guess from their name, focus on personal enjoyment and pleasurable experiences. They comprise 12 percent of the world's population, with a male–female ratio of 54 to 46. Many live in developed Asia.

MARKETING SUCCESS The Future of Fashion: Designers Market Eco-Friendly Threads

Background. Not long ago, the phrase "eco-friendly fashion" conjured up images of dresses made of feed sacks, shoes made of recycled tires, and shapeless skirts or tops in dull colors. Those images are now changing fast. As designers and retailers recognize that consumers want eco-friendly—and stylish—clothing, they are creating new duds that are anything but dull.

The Challenge. Designers and clothing manufacturers face several challenges as they attempt to design and make

clothing that conservation-minded consumers want to buy. High-quality sustainable fabrics are difficult to find. "Most designers with existing labels are finding there aren't comparable fabrics that can just replace what you're doing and what your customers are used to," observes one fashion marketer. Overcoming a frumpy image is another challenge: people need to see how comfortable and beautiful the clothing can be. They also need to accept that green synthetic fabrics can be an even better alternative to some natural fabrics.

▷ *Creatives*, the smallest segment, account for just 10 percent of the global population. This group seeks education, technology, and knowledge; their male–female ratio is roughly equal.

Roper researchers note that some principles and core beliefs—such as protecting the family—apply to more than one psychographic segment. In addition to Roper, GfK operates 115 companies in more than 100 countries, generating a wide range of marketing research. A recent venture involves a partnership between GfK Roper Public Affairs & Media Partners and the government advisor and author Simon Anholt to provide an expanded Nation Brands Index, which will compile and analyze the perceptions of 20,000 people around the world.[57]

USING PSYCHOGRAPHIC SEGMENTATION

No one suggests that psychographic segmentation is an exact science, but it does help marketers quantify aspects of consumers' personalities and lifestyles to create goods and services for a target market. Psychographic profile systems such as those of Roper and SRIC-BI can paint useful pictures of the overall psychological motivations of consumers. These profiles produce much richer descriptions of potential target markets than other techniques can achieve. The enhanced detail aids in matching a company's image and product offerings with the types of consumers who use its products.

Identifying which psychographic segments are most prevalent in certain markets helps marketers plan and promote more effectively. Often segments overlap. One study revealed that people who are early to adopt new technology devices generally have leadership qualities, are highly dynamic, and assertive. They rarely are considered modest; however, these consumers may represent either gender and just about any age or income.[58] When it comes to technology though, change is the norm—so early users must cope with the fact that the new gizmo they bought a few months ago may become obsolete quickly. Some experts warn that these consumers will likely add a touch of wariness to their purchasing outlook.[59]

Psychographic segmentation is a good supplement to segmentation by demographic or geographic variables. For example, marketers may have access to each consumer type's media preferences in network television, cable television, Internet use, radio format, magazines, and newspapers. Psychographic studies may then refine the picture of segment characteristics to give a more elaborate lifestyle profile of the consumers in the firm's target market. A psychographic study could help marketers of goods and services in Philadelphia, New Orleans, or Las Vegas predict what kinds of products consumers in those cities would be drawn to and eliminate those that are not attractive.

assessment check

1. What is demographic segmentation?
2. What are the major categories of demographic segmentation?
3. What is psychographic segmentation?
4. Name the eight psychographic categories of the U.S. VALS.

The Strategy. As designers and manufacturers hunt for the best materials, groups like Earth Pledge and FutureFashion are organizing fashion shows and events to showcase the new lines, that are produced not only by smaller firms but also by couture names like Calvin Klein, Givenchy, Ralph Lauren, and Versace. High-end retailer Barney's New York has helped sponsor such events. In addition, mainstream retailers like Banana Republic and Guess have come out with their own green lines.

The Outcome. Although eco-friendly fashions still occupy only a small portion of the total clothing market, as word spreads about new fabrics and the processes used to make them, more consumers are looking for these clothes. "The coolest stuff is tech-driven, and that's what people get excited about," notes organic fashion marketer Scott Hahn. He believes green is the future of fashion. "Mainstream is about to occur," he predicts.

Sources: Rebecca Eve Schweitzer, "Target Debuts Eco-Friendly Fashion Line," *Earth Wind & Power Blogazine*, April 20, 2009, http://blog.earthwindpower.net; Anna Kuchment, "Sense and Sensibility," *Newsweek*, April 14, 2008, p. 68; Suzy Menkes, "Moving beyond Fast Fashion to Sustainable Styles," *International Herald Tribune*, February 14, 2008, www.iht.com; Jasmin Malik Chua, "Future Fashion: Fashion Week's Green Kickoff," *Treehugger.com*, February 6, 2008, www.treehugger.com.

product-related segmentation Division of a population into homogeneous groups based on their relationships to a product.

Product-Related Segmentation

Product-related segmentation involves dividing a consumer population into homogeneous groups based on their relationships to the product. This segmentation approach can take several forms:

1. segmenting based on the benefits people seek when they buy a product;
2. segmenting based on usage rates for a product; or
3. segmenting according to consumers' brand loyalty toward a product.

SEGMENTING BY BENEFITS SOUGHT

This approach focuses on attributes people seek and benefits they expect to receive from a good or service. It groups consumers into segments based on what they want a product to do for them.

Consumers who quaff Starbucks premium coffees are not just looking for a dose of caffeine. They are willing to pay extra to savor a pleasant experience, one that makes them feel pampered and appreciated. Women who work out at Curves want to look their best and feel healthy. Pet owners who feed their cats and dogs Science Diet believe they are giving their animals a great-tasting, healthful pet food.

Even if a business offers only one product line, however, marketers must remember to consider product benefits. Two people may buy the same product for very different reasons. A box of Arm & Hammer baking soda could end up serving as a refrigerator freshener, a toothpaste substitute, an antacid, or a deodorizer for a cat's litter box.

Segmenting by benefits sought focuses on the attributes that people seek and the benefits they expect to receive from a good or service. This ad focuses on the healthy benefits of milk.

Pass by Steve.
Body by milk.

Off the court, milk provides the perfect assist. Its protein helps build muscle and studies suggest teens who choose milk over sugary drinks tend to be leaner. Staying active, eating right and drinking three glasses of lowfat or fat free milk a day helps you look great and stay in shape. Score three for milk.

got milk?

bodybymilk.com

© AP Images/PRNewsFoto/MilkPEP

SEGMENTING BY USAGE RATES

Marketers may also segment a total market by grouping people according to the amounts of a product they buy and use. Markets can be divided into heavy-, moderate-, and light-user segments. The **80/20 principle** holds that a big percentage of a product's revenues—maybe 80 percent—comes from a relatively small, loyal percentage of total customers, perhaps 20 percent. The 80/20 principle is sometimes referred to as *Praedo's law*. Although the percentages need not exactly equal these figures, the general principle holds true: relatively few heavy users of a product can account for the bulk of its consumption.

Depending on their goals, marketers may target heavy, moderate, or light users as well as nonusers. A company may attempt to lure heavy users of another product away from their regular brands to try a new brand. Nonusers and light users may be attractive prospects because other companies are ignoring them. Usage rates can also be linked to other segmentation methods such as demographic and psychographic segmentation.

SEGMENTING BY BRAND LOYALTY

A third product-related segmentation method groups consumers according to the strength of the brand loyalty they feel toward a product. A classic example of brand loyalty segmentation is the frequent-purchase program—it might be frequent flyer, frequent stay, or frequent purchase of books or gasoline. Other companies attempt to segment their market by developing brand loyalty over a period of time, through consumers' stages of life. New Balance recently launched a line of sneakers for infants and preschoolers, accompanied by an impressive array of celebrity endorsers: Elmo, Cookie Monster, and Oscar the Grouch. Reebok launched a collection of toddler and children's shoes featuring the Incredible Hulk and Iron Man. Marketers for these companies are intent on creating brand loyalty for their shoes at the earliest stages of life.[60]

Companies spar for loyalty on just about every front. Recently, when Starbucks announced it was closing nearly all of its stores for three hours to accommodate an employee training event, Dunkin' Donuts announced a special promotion coinciding with those hours, during which its coffee drinks sold for 99 cents.[61]

USING MULTIPLE SEGMENTATION BASES

Segmentation can help marketers increase their accuracy in reaching the right markets. Like other marketing tools, segmentation is probably best used in a flexible manner—for instance, combining geographic and demographic segmentation techniques or dovetailing product-related segmentation with segmentation by income and expenditure patterns. An important point to keep in mind is that segmentation is a tool to help marketers get to know their potential customers better and ultimately satisfy their needs with the appropriate goods and services.

assessment check

1. List the three approaches to product-related segmentation.
2. What is the 80/20 principle?

The Market Segmentation Process

8 Identify the steps in the market segmentation process.

To this point, the chapter has discussed various bases on which companies segment markets. But how do marketers decide which segmentation base—or bases—to use? Firms may use a management-driven method, in which segments are predefined by managers based on their observation of the behavioral and demographic characteristics of likely users. Or they may use a market-driven method, in which segments are defined by asking customers which attributes are important. Then, marketers follow a four-stage process.

DEVELOP A RELEVANT PROFILE FOR EACH SEGMENT

After identifying promising segments, marketers should understand the customers in each one. This in-depth analysis of customers helps managers accurately match buyers' needs with the firm's marketing offers. The process must identify characteristics that both explain the similarities among customers within each segment and account for differences among segments.

The task at this stage is to develop a profile of the typical customer in each segment. Such a profile might include information about lifestyle patterns, attitudes toward product attributes and brands, product-use habits, geographic locations, and demographic characteristics.

FORECAST MARKET POTENTIAL

In the second stage, market segmentation and market opportunity analysis combine to produce a forecast of market potential within each segment. Market potential sets the upper limit on the demand competing firms can expect from a segment. Multiplying by market share determines a single firm's maximum sales potential. This step should define a preliminary go or no-go decision from management because the total sales potential in each segment must justify resources devoted to further analysis. For example, in deciding whether to market a new product to teens, electronics firms need to determine the demand for it and the disposable income of that group.

FORECAST PROBABLE MARKET SHARE

Once market potential has been estimated, a firm must forecast its probable market share. Competitors' positions in targeted segments must be analyzed, and a specific marketing strategy must be designed to reach these segments. These two activities may be performed simultaneously. Moreover, by settling on a marketing strategy and tactics, a firm determines the expected level of resources it must commit, that is, the costs it will incur to tap the potential demand in each segment.

Apple's iPod took the marketplace by storm, followed by the iPhone, and analysts believe these two products helped boost sales of the iMac computer as well—Apple's overall share of the U.S. consumer computer market now stands at 21 percent. As iPod and iPhone users are ready to upgrade their computers, they are purchasing iMacs instead of new PCs.[62]

SELECT SPECIFIC MARKET SEGMENTS

The information, analysis, and forecasts accumulated throughout the entire market segmentation decision process allow management to assess the potential for achieving company goals and to justify committing resources in developing one or more segments. Demand forecasts, together with cost projections, determine the profits and the return on investment the company can expect from each segment. Marketing strategy and tactics must be designed to reinforce the firm's image, yet keep within its unique organizational capabilities.

At this point in the analysis, marketers weigh more than monetary costs and benefits; they also consider many difficult-to-measure but critical organizational and environmental factors. The firm may lack experienced personnel to launch a successful attack on an attractive market segment. Similarly, a firm with 60 percent of the market faces possible legal problems with the Federal Trade Commission if it increases its market concentration. This assessment of both financial and nonfinancial factors is a difficult but vital step in the decision process.

assessment check

1. Identify the four stages of market segmentation.

2. Why is forecasting important to market segmentation?

9 Discuss four basic strategies for reaching target markets.

Strategies for Reaching Target Markets

Marketers spend a lot of time and effort developing strategies that will best match their firm's product offerings to the needs of particular target markets. An appropriate match is vital to the firm's marketing success. Marketers have identified four basic strategies for achieving consumer satisfaction: undifferentiated marketing, differentiated marketing, concentrated marketing, and micromarketing.

UNDIFFERENTIATED MARKETING

undifferentiated marketing Strategy that focuses on producing a single product and marketing it to all customers; also called *mass marketing*.

A firm may produce only one product or product line and promote it to all customers with a single marketing mix; such a firm is said to practice **undifferentiated marketing,** sometimes called *mass marketing*. Undifferentiated marketing was much more common in the past than it is today.

While undifferentiated marketing is efficient from a production viewpoint, the strategy also brings inherent dangers. A firm that attempts to satisfy everyone in the market with one standard product may suffer if competitors offer specialized alternatives to smaller segments of the total market and better satisfy individual segments. In fact, firms that implement strategies of differentiated marketing, concentrated marketing, or micromarketing may capture enough small segments of the market to defeat another competitor's strategy of undifferentiated marketing. The golden arches of McDonald's have always stood for quick, inexpensive meals. Consumers could count on the same food and same dining experience at every McDonald's they visited. But McDonald's marketers are changing the firm's strategy somewhat in response to a trend that says consumers want a little luxury with their burger and fries and a more varied dining experience from restaurant to restaurant. At some stores—including those in India—diners can sit on soft couches instead of hard plastic chairs. In addition, menu changes include multigrain breads and fruit juices.[63]

DIFFERENTIATED MARKETING

Firms that promote numerous products with differing marketing mixes designed to satisfy smaller segments are said to practice **differentiated marketing.** By providing increased satisfaction for each of many target markets, a company can produce more sales by following a differentiated marketing strategy than undifferentiated marketing would generate. Oscar Mayer, a marketer of a variety of meat products, practices differentiated marketing. It increased its sales by introducing Lunchables, aimed at children. The original Lunchables were so successful that Oscar Mayer introduced more choices in the line, including snack versions. In general, however, differentiated marketing also raises costs. Production costs usually rise because additional products and variations require shorter production runs and increased setup times. Inventory costs rise because more products require added storage space and increased efforts for record keeping. Promotional costs also rise because each segment demands a unique promotional mix.

Despite higher marketing costs, however, an organization may be forced to practice differentiated marketing to remain competitive. The travel industry now recognizes the need to target smaller groups of travelers with specialized interests. History buffs can attend special events at Colonial Williamsburg or at George Washington's estate, Mount Vernon.[64] The Sierra Club and other environmental organizations—in addition to commercial travel operators—offer hikes, kayaking expeditions, and birdwatching trips for outdoor enthusiasts.[65] Luxury travel agency Tauck Tours now offers a series of trips called Tauck Bridges, designed with traveling families or grandparents and their grandchildren in mind.[66]

differentiated marketing
Strategy that focuses on producing several products and pricing, promoting, and distributing them with different marketing mixes designed to satisfy smaller segments.

CONCENTRATED MARKETING

Rather than trying to market its products separately to several segments, a firm may opt for a concentrated marketing strategy. With **concentrated marketing** (also known as **niche marketing),** a firm focuses its efforts on profitably satisfying a single market segment. This approach can appeal to a small firm lacking the financial resources of its competitors and to a company offering highly specialized goods and services. American Express, a large firm with many financial products, recently introduced two new credit cards designed for very specific markets: The Knot, for engaged couples, and The Nest, for newlyweds.

Peanut Butter & Co. appeals to the peanut butter lovers of the world with its proprietary brand of gourmet, natural peanut butter flavors including Smooth Operator, Crunch Time, and Dark Chocolate Dreams. Its Mighty Maple is intended for pancake lovers, and The Bee's Knees can replace a humdrum jar of honey. Fans can visit the flagship store in New York City, where they can sample favorites such as "ants on a log" or grilled peanut butter, banana, honey, and bacon sandwiches; or, they can shop for their favorite blends online.[67] But along with its benefits, concentrated marketing has its dangers. Because the strategy ties a firm's growth to a specific segment, sales can suffer if new competitors appeal successfully to the same target. If another firm targets peanut butter lovers in the same manner, Peanut Butter & Co. may face a struggle. In addition, errors in forecasting market potential or customer buying habits can lead to severe problems, particularly if the firm has spent substantially on product development and promotion. If more

concentrated marketing
Focusing marketing efforts on satisfying a single market segment; also called *niche marketing.*

briefly
speaking

"Put all your eggs in one basket, and watch the basket."

—**Mark Twain
(1835–1910)**
AMERICAN AUTHOR

Peanut Butter & Co. is an example of concentrated marketing. It appeals to peanut butter lovers with its proprietary brand of gourmet, natural peanut butter flavors.

people—children in particular—continue to develop peanut allergies, sales of Peanut Butter & Co.'s products may begin to decline. Anticipating this, the company could begin to diversify product offerings to include nonallergenic foods.

MICROMARKETING

The fourth targeting strategy, still more narrowly focused than concentrated marketing, is **micromarketing,**—targeting potential customers at a very basic level, such as by zip code, specific occupation, or lifestyle. Ultimately, micromarketing can target even individuals. The salesperson at your favorite clothing boutique may contact you when certain merchandise she thinks you might like arrives at the store. The Internet allows marketers to make micromarketing even more effective: by tracking specific demographic and personal information, marketers can send e-mail directly to individual consumers most likely to buy their products.

micromarketing
Targeting potential customers at very narrow, basic levels such as by zip code, specific occupation, or lifestyle—possibly even individuals themselves.

Best Buy, known for its broad appeal to what it refers to as "Middle America," altered its marketing strategy to zero in on specific customers at specific stores. Although the retailer's "Planagans"—store layouts—are determined at headquarters, local managers have the authority to move products around to appeal to the needs of their customers. One Texas store experienced an influx of Eastern European workers on shore leave from cargo ships and tankers; these customers were on the hunt for hot products such as iPods. So the manager moved the iPods and other small electronics to the front of the store, where the ship crews—on a tight schedule—could snap them up in a hurry. In anticipation of nearly 10,000 U.S. soldiers returning from military bases overseas, the Savannah, Georgia, store stocked up on such items as flat-panel TVs and video-game systems. A Best Buy store manager in North Carolina realized many local customers were senior

Best Buy store layouts are determined at headquarters, but local managers have the authority to move products around to appeal to the needs of their customers. In anticipation of U.S. soldiers returning from military bases overseas, a Georgia store stocked up on such items as flat-panel TVs.

citizens who might buy new electronics if they knew how to use these products. So the store held a special instructional event for these customers, who attended the seminar and spent $350,000 on electronics.[68]

But micromarketing, like niche marketing, can become too much of a good thing if companies spend too much time, effort, and marketing dollars to unearth a market too small and specialized to be profitable. In addition, micromarketing may cause a company to lose sight of other, larger markets. So it's important for marketers to assess the situation and pursue the most profitable markets.

assessment check

1. Explain the difference between undifferentiated and differentiated marketing strategies.

2. What are the benefits of concentrated marketing?

Selecting and Executing a Strategy

10 **Summarize the types of positioning strategies, and explain the reasons for positioning and repositioning products.**

Although most organizations adopt some form of differentiated marketing, no single choice suits all firms. Any of the alternatives may prove most effective in a particular situation. The basic determinants of a market-specific strategy are (1) company resources, (2) product homogeneity, (3) stage in the product life cycle, and (4) competitors' strategies.

A firm with limited resources may have to choose a concentrated marketing strategy. Small firms may be forced to select small target markets because of limitations in their sales force and advertising budgets. On the other hand, an undifferentiated marketing strategy suits a firm selling items perceived by consumers as relatively homogeneous. Marketers of grain, for example, sell standardized grades of generic products rather than individual brand names. Some petroleum companies implement undifferentiated marketing to distribute their gasoline to the mass market.

The firm's strategy may also change as its product progresses through the stages of the life-cycle. During the early stages, undifferentiated marketing might effectively support the company's effort to build initial demand for the item. In the later stages, however, competitive pressures may force modifications in products and in the development of marketing strategies aimed at segments of the total market.

The strategies of competitors also affect the choice of a segmentation approach. A firm may encounter obstacles to undifferentiated marketing if its competitors actively cultivate smaller segments. In such instances, competition usually forces each firm to adopt a differentiated marketing strategy.

Having chosen a strategy for reaching their firm's target market, marketers must then decide how best to position the product. The concept of **positioning** seeks to put a product in a certain position, or place, in the minds of prospective buyers. Marketers use a positioning strategy to distinguish their firm's offerings from those of competitors and to create promotions that communicate the desired position. Restaurants that position themselves as "fast-casual" continue to outperform most other categories of restaurants. Top menu choices in this segment include Mexican, bakery café, pizzas, Asian, chicken, and hamburgers. Analysts believe fast-casual restaurants provide consumers with the chance to sit down to a dinner priced lower than what is offered at an upscale restaurant yet of higher quality than a fast-food restaurant. Fast-casual provides good value in the minds of many consumers. Many fast-casual restaurants currently are trying to increase breakfast traffic, adding new menu items, and offering Wi-Fi and adult beverages to attract even more customers.[69]

positioning Placing a product at a certain point or location within a market in the minds of prospective buyers.

To achieve the goal of positioning, marketers follow a number of positioning strategies. Possible approaches include positioning a product according to the following categories:

1. *Attributes*—Kraft Foods, "Deliciously simple. Every day."

2. *Price/quality*—Omega watches, "We measure the 100th of a second that separates winning from taking part."

3. *Competitors*—Nantucket Nectars, "Real is better."

4. *Application*—Merry Maids, "Relax, it's done."

5. *Product user*—Crane's stationery "for the writer somewhere in each of us."

6. *Product class*—BMW, the "ultimate driving machine."

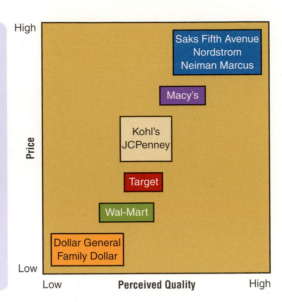

figure 9.4

Hypothetical Positioning Map for Selected Retailers

Whatever strategy they choose, marketers want to emphasize a product's unique advantages and to differentiate it from competitors' options. A **positioning map** provides a valuable tool in helping managers position products by graphically illustrating consumers' perceptions of competing products within an industry. Marketers can create a competitive positioning map from information solicited from consumers or from their accumulated knowledge about a market. A positioning map might present two different characteristics—price and perceived quality—and show how consumers view a product and its major competitors based on these traits. The hypothetical positioning map in Figure 9.4 compares selected retailers based on possible perceptions of the prices and quality of their offerings.

Sometimes changes in the competitive environment force marketers to **reposition** a product—changing the position it holds in the minds of prospective buyers relative to the positions of competing products. Repositioning may even be necessary for already successful products or firms in order to gain greater market share. Once positioned as the mid-priced car for the average driver, Saturn has taken a turn—repositioning itself to attract performance-minded drivers. Its Sky roadster and Astra are marketed as stylish, enhanced-performance vehicles for drivers who want their "daily dose of fun."[70]

Strategic *Implications of* **Marketing** **21st Century** *in the*

To remain competitive, today's marketers must accurately identify potential customers. They can use a variety of methods to accomplish this, including segmenting markets by gender and by geographic location. The trick is to figure out the best combination of methods for segmentation to identify the most lucrative, long-lasting potential markets. Marketers must also remain flexible, responding to markets as they change—for instance, following a generation as it ages or reaching out to new generations by revamping or repositioning products.

The greatest competitive advantage will belong to firms that pinpoint and serve markets without segmenting them to the point at which they are too small or specialized to garner profits. Marketers who reach and communicate with the right customers have a greater chance of attracting and keeping those customers than marketers who search for the wrong buyers in the wrong place.

Review of Chapter Objectives

1 Identify the essential components of a market.

A market consists of people and organizations with the necessary purchasing power, willingness, and authority to buy. Consumer products are purchased by the ultimate consumer for personal use.

Business products are purchased for use directly or indirectly in the production of other goods and services. Certain products may fall into both categories.

2 Outline the role of market segmentation in developing a marketing strategy.

Market segmentation is the process of dividing a total market into several homogeneous groups. It is used in identifying a target market for a good or service. Segmentation is the key to deciding a marketing strategy.

3 Describe the criteria necessary for effective segmentation.

Effective segmentation depends on these four basic requirements: (1) the segment must have measurable purchasing power and size, (2) marketers can find a way to promote to and serve the market, (3) marketers must identify segments large enough for profit potential, and (4) the firm can target a number of segments that match its marketing capabilities.

4 Explain the geographic approach to the segmentation of consumer markets.

Geographic segmentation divides the overall market into homogeneous groups according to population locations.

5 Discuss the demographic and psychographic approaches to segmenting consumer markets.

Demographic segmentation classifies the market into groups based on characteristics such as age, gender, and income level. Psychographic segmentation uses behavioral profiles developed from analyses of consumers' activities, opinions, interests, and lifestyles to identify market segments.

6 Describe product-related segmentation.

Product-related segmentation can take three basic forms: segmenting based on the benefits people seek when buying a product; segmenting based on usage rates for a product; and segmenting according to consumers' brand loyalty toward a product.

7 Identify the steps in the market segmentation process.

Market segmentation is the division of markets into relatively homogeneous groups. Segmentation follows a four-step sequence: (1) developing user profiles, (2) forecasting the overall market potential, (3) estimating market share, and (4) selecting specific market segments.

8 Discuss four basic strategies for reaching target markets.

Four strategies are (1) undifferentiated marketing—uses a single marketing mix; (2) differentiated marketing—produces numerous products, each with its own mix; (3) concentrated marketing— directs all the firm's marketing resources toward a small segment; and (4) micromarketing—targets potential customers at basic levels, such as zip code or occupation.

9 Summarize the types of positioning strategies, and explain the reasons for positioning and repositioning products.

Positioning strategies include positioning a good or service according to attributes, price/quality, competitors, application, product user, and product class. Positioning helps distinguish a firm's products from those of competitors and provides a basis for marketing communications. Repositioning a product—changing the position it holds in consumers' minds—may be necessary to gain greater market share.

assessment check: answers

1.1   Define *target market*.

A target market is the specific segment of consumers most likely to purchase a particular product.

1.2   Distinguish between a consumer product and a business product.

A consumer product is purchased by the ultimate buyer for personal use. A business product is purchased for use directly or indirectly in the production of other goods and services.

2.1   Define *market segmentation*.

Market segmentation is the process of dividing a total market into several homogeneous groups.

2.2   Describe the role of market segmentation.

The role of market segmentation is to identify the factors that affect purchase decisions and then group consumers according to the presence or absence of these factors.

3.1   Identify the four criteria for effective segmentation.

The four criteria for effective segmentation are (1) the market segment must present measurable purchasing power and size, (2) marketers must find a way to promote effectively and serve the market segment, (3) marketers must identify segments sufficiently large to give them good profit potential, and (4) the firm must aim for segments that match its marketing capabilities.

3.2   Give an example of a market segment that meets these criteria.

Examples might include women, teenagers, Hispanics, empty nesters, and NASCAR enthusiasts.

4.1   Under what circumstances are marketers most likely to use geographic segmentation?

Marketers usually use geographic segmentation when regional preferences exist and when demand for categories of goods and services varies according to geographic region.

4.2   What are the five main categories for classifying urban data?

The five categories are core based statistical area (CBSA), metropolitan statistical area (MSA), micropolitan statistical area, consolidated metropolitan statistical area (CMSA), and primary metropolitan statistical area (PMSA).

5.1   What is demographic segmentation?

Demographic segmentation defines consumer groups according to demographic variables such as gender, age, income, occupation, household, and family lifecycle.

5.2   What are the major categories of demographic segmentation?

The major categories of demographic segmentation are gender, age, ethnic group, family life cycle, household type, income, and expenditure patterns.

5.3   What is psychographic segmentation?

Psychographic segmentation divides a population into groups with similar psychological characteristics, values, and lifestyles.

5.4   Name the eight psychographic categories of VALS.

The eight categories are: innovators, thinkers, achievers, experiencers, believers, strivers, makers, and survivors.

6.1   List the three approaches to product-related segmentation.

The three approaches are segmenting by benefits sought, segmenting by usage rates, and segmenting by brand loyalty.

6.2   What is the 80/20 principle?

The 80/20 principle states that a big percentage (80 percent) of a product's revenues comes from a relatively small number (20 percent) of loyal customers.

7.1   Identify the four stages of market segmentation.

The four stages are developing user profiles, forecasting the overall market potential, estimating market share, and selecting specific market segments.

7.2   Why is forecasting important to market segmentation?

Forecasting is important because it can define a preliminary go or no-go decision based on sales potential. It can help a firm avoid a disastrous move or point out opportunities.

8.1   Explain the difference between undifferentiated and differentiated marketing strategies.

Undifferentiated marketing promotes a single product line to all customers with a single marketing mix. Differentiated marketing promotes numerous products with different marketing mixes designed to satisfy smaller segments.

8.2   What are the benefits of concentrated marketing?

Concentrated marketing can allow a firm to focus on a single market segment, which is especially appealing to smaller firms and those that offer highly specialized goods and services.

9.1   What are the four determinants of a market-specific strategy?

The four determinants are company resources, product homogeneity, stage in the product lifecycle, and competitors' strategies.

9.2   What is the role of positioning in a marketing strategy?

Positioning places a product in a certain position in the minds of prospective buyers so marketers can create messages that distinguish their offerings from those of competitors.

Marketing Terms You Need to Know

market 274
target market 275
consumer products 275
business products 275
market segmentation 276

geographic segmentation 277
demographic segmentation 280
psychographic segmentation 290
product-related segmentation 294
undifferentiated marketing 296

differentiated marketing 297
concentrated marketing 297
micromarketing 298
positioning 299

Other Important Marketing Terms

core based statistical area (CBSA) 278
metropolitan statistical area (MSA) 279
micropolitan statistical area 279
consolidated metropolitan statistical area (CMSA) 279
primary metropolitan statistical area (PMSA) 279

core region 279
geographic information system (GIS) 280
cohort effect 282
9/11 Generation 282
baby boomers 283
family lifecycle 287
Engel's laws 289

AIO statements 290
VALS 291
80/20 principle 294
niche marketing 297
positioning map 300
repositioning 300

Assurance of Learning Review

1. Classify each of the following as a business product or a consumer product:
   a. computer workstation
   b. tube of toothpaste
   c. fleet of delivery trucks
   d. bulk order of flour
   e. diamond earrings
   f. Jason Mraz music CD

2. What are core regions? Why do marketers try to identify these regions?

3. What is the cohort effect? What event—or events—do you consider significant enough to have influenced and bound together your generation?

4. What is the fastest-growing racial/ethnic minority group in the United States? What types of things do marketers need to know about this group to market successfully to these consumers?

5. How is segmentation by family lifecycle and household type useful to marketers? Briefly describe your own family in these terms, identifying characteristics that might be helpful to marketers for a firm selling HDTVs.

6. What are AIO statements? How are they used by marketers?

7. Identify a branded product to which you are loyal, and explain why you are loyal to the product. What factors might cause your loyalty to change?

8. Choose another branded product. Create a relevant profile for the marketing segment that product serves.

9. What are the six categories generally used to position a product?

10. How does a positioning map work? What are its benefits?

Projects and Teamwork Exercises

1. On your own or with a partner, choose one of the following consumer products and think about how it could be used as a business product. Then create a business advertisement for your product.
   a. pet care products
   b. gardening tools
   c. shampoo
   d. bottled water
   e. laptop computer
   f. vacuum cleaner

2. With a classmate, choose one of the following products you believe is generally targeted for either men or women and create an advertisement for the product aimed at the opposite gender.
   a. tickets to a NASCAR race
   b. hunting or fishing supplies
   c. day spa
   d. minivan
   e. large-screen TV

3. Create a chart showing how your family's income and expenditure patterns have changed over the years as the family life-cycle changed. You don't need exact figures, just the general picture. If possible, interview one or two family members for additional information.

4. With a classmate, choose a product and come up with a slogan representing each of the six positioning approaches for the product.

5. On your own or with a classmate, select one of the following products. Visit the firm's Web site to see how the product is positioned, then create an advertisement showing how you think marketers could reposition the product to gain greater market share.
   a. Odwalla nutrition bars
   b. Kleenex tissue
   c. Axe body wash
   d. Under Armour clothing
   e. Hallmark cards

Critical-Thinking Exercises

1. Create a profile of yourself as part of a market segment. Include the following:
   a. geographic location
   b. gender, age, and membership in any minority group
   c. household type
   d. income and spending habits

2. Select one of the following products and explain how you would use segmentation by income and expenditure patterns to determine your targeted market.
   a. Busch Gardens theme parks
   b. Sony Cyber-shot camera
   c. Stouffer's Lean Cuisine
   d. Porsche Boxster

3. How do you think the Internet has affected differentiated marketing techniques?

4. Choose one of the following products and describe a marketing approach that segments the target market by benefits sought:
   a. Vespa motorcycle
   b. Nikon Cool Pix camera
   c. Andersen windows and doors
   d. Water Country water park
   e. Cold Stone Creamery ice cream

5. Visit the Web site for a large company such as General Mills, Kraft Foods, Ford, Sony, or Wal-Mart. Look for ways the firm practices differentiated marketing. How do you think this approach benefits the firm?

Ethics Exercise

Marketers are making a new pitch to men—at the risk of political incorrectness. Marketers for firms such as Unilever and Wendy's were frustrated at their inability to reach young male consumers with their messages. After searching for clues about what this crowd likes, these firms created marketing campaigns designed to grab their attention—perhaps at the expense of other consumers. Some advertising is designed to appeal to "bad boy" attitudes, low-brow humor, and sex.

1. What are some of the pitfalls of this kind of segmentation?

2. Do you think these ads will be successful in the long run? Why or why not?

3. Should marketers be concerned about offending one market segment when trying to reach another? Why or why not?

Internet Exercises

1. **Segmenting markets.** Visit the Web site of Canon (usa.canon. com). How does Canon segment its markets, such as geographic, product related, demographic, or brand loyalty? Does the firm use more than one method of product segmentation? Why or why not?

2. **Strategies for reaching target markets.** Choose a consumer-products company such as Procter & Gamble, Unilever, or Colgate. Visit that company's Web site. What strategy or strategies does the firm employ for reaching its target markets? Does it rely more on undifferentiated or differentiated marketing?

3. **Demographic segmentation.** As noted in the chapter, the U.S. Census Bureau is an important source of data used by marketers when making demographic segmentation decisions. Visit the Web site of the *Statistical Abstract of the United States* (www.census.gov/compendia/statab/) and access the most recent edition you can find. Under the "population" section, find the current distribution of the U.S. population by age, race, and gender and the projected distribution in 20 years. Assume the role of a marketer at a consumer-products company. Prepare a report summarizing the demographic trends and how your firm could better segment its target markets to reflect these trends.

Note: Internet Web addresses change frequently. If you don't find the exact site listed, you may need to access the organization's home page and search from there or use a search engine such as Google.

Case 9.1 Food Allergies: Feeding a Growing Niche

The increase in food allergies, among children in particular, has created a growing niche for food producers and marketers.

About 12 million people in the United States suffer from food allergies, while another 2 million have an immune disorder that reacts to gluten, a protein widespread in products containing wheat, barley, and rye. The number of children with peanut allergies has doubled in a decade. These sensitivities and allergies can have mild to deadly effects, meaning that consumers and food producers are now working together to create a market for allergen-free foods.

According to one research firm, the market for food products for consumers with food allergies will soon reach $4 billion. The market for gluten-free foods and beverages is expected to reach $1.3 billion by 2010, an increase of $600 million over a period of only four years. Whereas in the past, these foods might have occupied a single supermarket shelf—with obscure brand names and dubious flavors—marketing foods free of eggs, gluten, dairy, peanuts, sugar, and other potentially harmful substances has grown far more mainstream. The Girl Scouts now make three kinds of milk-free cookies for those who are lactose intolerant. Anheuser Busch sells a gluten-free beer, and Kellogg's makes its Pop-Tarts in factories where no nuts are used. General Mills reformulated its Rice Chex cereal to be gluten free.

Labeling for these foods is now part of companies' marketing strategy. Although the federal government requires ingredient labels to include milk, eggs, peanuts, tree nuts (like almonds and cashews), fish, shellfish, soy, and wheat, many companies have taken the mandate a step farther. "We know there is a great demand among consumers to have free-from labeling," explains Kevin Farnum of General Mills. Stonyfield Farm, which makes organic yogurt products, uses gluten-free labeling in its marketing as well.

An increase in these offerings and the marketing to support them has had an unexpected side effect: more consumers are buying these products, whether or not they actually have food sensitivities or allergies. Some want to be on the safe side; others believe these products provide more health benefits than those containing gluten, dairy, or nuts. "This trend toward self-diagnosis has widened the 'free from' market from those who have to avoid certain foods to those who make a lifestyle choice for whatever reason," observes one marketing researcher.

Regardless of an individual's reasons for the choice, grocery stores are experiencing a huge increase in demand for these foods. "We've seen a dramatic increase in the number of customers looking for these types of products, really in the last few years," reports a spokesperson for the supermarket chain Safeway. "We've greatly increased the number and types of products we are offering."

Questions for Critical Thinking

1. We already know this market can be segmented according to people with food allergies. But if you were a marketer for one of the food companies, how would you segment your products by benefits sought? As a marketer for a large firm that wants to reach consumers with its new food formulation, such as the General Mills new formula for Rice Chex, would you choose an approach of micromarketing, niche marketing, or differentiated marketing? Why?

2. Choose a product such as Stonyfield Yogurt, General Mills Rice Chex, Kellogg's Pop-Tarts, or any other food containing free-from labeling and identify a positioning strategy for the product according to one of the six categories described in the chapter. Then, create a slogan for it that reflects the strategy.

Sources: "Food Allergies Facts," *Healthy Woman Guide*, January 1, 2009, http://healthywomanguide.com; Madeline Ellis, "Alarming Increase in Food Allergies Fuels Specialty Markets," *Health News,* June 13, 2008, www.healthnews.com; Annys Shin, "Food Allergies Trigger Multibillion-Dollar Specialty Market," *The Washington Post,* June 8, 2008, www.washingtonpost.com; "Market for Allergy Foods Quickly Growing," *UPI,* June 8, 2008, www.upi.com.

Video Case 9.2   Targeting and Positioning at Numi Tea

The written case on Numi Tea appears on page VC-9. The Numi Tea video is designed to expand and highlight the concepts in this chapter and the concepts and questions covered in the written video.

CHAP 10 TER

Relationship Marketing and Customer Relationship Management (CRM)

© Roam Images/Jupiterimages

Recycled Energy Development Turns Partnerships Green

Money is disappearing into thin air. No one is actually stealing it from company bank accounts, but firms are losing a valuable resource in the form of waste heat and steam. Despite their many

efforts to weed out inefficiencies in their business and manufacturing operations, many U.S. factories are still wasting billions of dollars—and more than half the energy they consume—every year through lost heat and steam instead of recycling it. Utility companies recycle some of their heat energy, but they could still power all of Japan's electricity needs with the amount of energy they lose. And most industrial firms are prevented from recycling energy, either by regulations that make it difficult for them to compete with utility monopolies or by lack of equipment and engineering that would make it possible. So what's to be done?

Recycled Energy Development (RED), a father-son firm in Westmont, Illinois, is trying to change U.S. energy use. For about 30 years, company chairman Thomas Casten has been championing heat-capturing technologies that already exist. Now joined by his son Sean, who serves as president and CEO, the duo is trying to recapture some of the 200,000 megawatts of heat the United States throws away each year. That's enough to replace 400 coal plants and supply almost 20 percent of the electricity the country currently produces. With mounting fuel costs, energy recycling is getting a fresh look.

RED finances most of the energy recycling projects and then sells the harvested energy back to the customer at substantially lower rates than off the power grid. RED recently obtained $1.5 billion in funding from a private investment firm in Boston. With those funds, RED partnered with Globe Specialty Metals near Charleston, West Virginia, to improve Globe's furnace operations at its West Virginia Alloys plant. The system taps the hot gas escaping from the firm's 2,000-degree furnaces to generate power. Converting that heat into electricity should yield enough power—with no additional fuel use—to yield one-third of the energy needs for the silicon plant, or enough to supply 25,000 homes.

Globe and RED have negotiated a fixed low price for the energy for the next 25 years, enabling Globe to avoid laying workers off in the summer as it's done in the past and helping it save enough money to open another furnace and add 30 jobs. The president of West Virginia Alloys says, "It will be one of the most efficient [silicon] facilities in the world."

Meanwhile, the Castens hope to use their new partnership with Globe as a model for others to spread the word about the power of recycling energy. Denmark, an early pioneer in energy recovery, has kept its energy use stable for 25 years in a growing economy because 55 percent of the country's power comes from recycled heat energy. So RED is using Google Earth images with emissions figures from the EPA to help others "see" the wasted energy from smokestacks around the country. And the Castens are exploring ways to help firms make their way through the thicket of state and federal legislation that currently shields utility companies from competition and prevents the wider use of recycled energy. Says Thomas Casten, "I always thought that if we were successful, people would emulate us and I'd be happy at the end of the day. I just didn't think it would take 30 years."[1]

evolution of a brand

Recycled Energy Development has built more than 250 energy projects around the United States. The firm sees its mission as "profitably reducing greenhouse-gas emissions by developing and owning energy recycling facilities." Its goals are to help manufacturers find cheaper and more reliable energy sources; take full advantage of allowed emissions credits; and benefit society by reducing costs, use of fossil fuels, and greenhouse-gas emissions.

- Unless we reduce greenhouse gases, the company says, "we leave the world a worse place than we found it." But the firm must be profitable to grow. What do you think RED looks for in potential business partners to help it reach its environmental and profit goals?

- According to Thomas Casten, one of the reasons why RED hasn't sold recovered energy to any utilities firms is because the energy loss from transmitting power over long distances makes the idea less feasible. What do you think utilities companies' view of a partnership with RED might be?

chapter overview

transaction-based marketing Buyer and seller exchanges characterized by limited communications and little or no ongoing relationship between the parties.

relationship marketing Development, growth, and maintenance of long-term, cost-effective relationships with individual customers, suppliers, employees, and other partners for mutual benefit.

Marketing revolves around relationships with customers and with all the business processes involved in identifying and satisfying them. The shift from **transaction-based marketing,** which focuses on short-term, onetime exchanges, to customer-focused relationship marketing is one of the most important trends in marketing today. Companies know they cannot prosper simply by identifying and attracting new customers; to succeed, they must build loyal, mutually beneficial relationships with both new and existing customers, suppliers, distributors, and employees. This strategy benefits the bottom line because retaining customers costs much less than acquiring new ones. Building and managing long-term relationships between buyers and sellers are the hallmarks of relationship marketing. **Relationship marketing** is the development, growth, and maintenance of cost-effective, high-value relationships with individual customers, suppliers, distributors, retailers, and other partners for mutual benefit over time.

Relationship marketing is based on promises: the promise of low prices, the promise of high quality, the promise of prompt delivery, the promise of superior service. A network of promises—within the organization, between the organization and its supply chain, and between buyer and seller—determines whether or not a relationship will grow. A firm is responsible for keeping or exceeding the agreements it makes, with the ultimate goal of achieving customer satisfaction.

This chapter examines the reasons why organizations are moving toward relationship marketing and customer relationship management, explores the impact this move has on producers of goods and services and their customers, and looks at ways to evaluate customer relationship programs.

❚ Contrast transaction-based marketing with relationship marketing.

The Shift from Transaction-Based Marketing to Relationship Marketing

Since the Industrial Revolution, most manufacturers have run production-oriented operations. They have focused on making products and then promoting them to customers in the hope of selling enough to cover costs and earn profits. The emphasis has been on individual sales or transactions. In transaction-based marketing, buyer and seller exchanges are characterized by limited communications and little or no ongoing relationships. The primary goal is to entice a buyer to make a purchase through such inducements as low price, convenience, or packaging. The goal is simple and short term: sell something—now.

Some marketing exchanges remain largely transaction based. In residential real estate sales, for example, the primary goal of the agent is to make a sale and collect a commission. While the agent may seek to maintain the appearance of an ongoing buyer–seller relationship, in most cases, the possibility of future transactions is fairly limited. The best an agent can hope for is to represent the seller again in a subsequent real-estate deal that may be several years down the line or, more likely, gain positive referrals to other buyers and sellers.

Today, many organizations have embraced an alternative approach. Relationship marketing views customers as equal partners in buyer–seller transactions. By motivating customers to enter a long-term relationship in which they repeat purchases or buy multiple brands from the firm, marketers obtain a clearer understanding of customer needs over time. This process leads to improved goods or customer service, which pays off through increased sales and lower marketing costs. In addition, marketers have discovered it is less expensive to retain satisfied customers than it is to attract new ones or to repair damaged relationships.

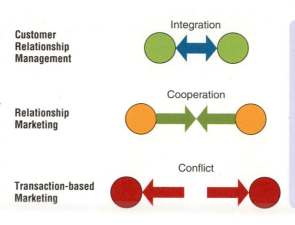

figure 10.1

Forms of Buyer–Seller Interactions from Conflict to Integration

The move from transactions to relationships is reflected in the changing nature of the interactions between customers and sellers. In transaction-based marketing, exchanges with customers generally are sporadic and in some instances disrupted by conflict. As interactions become relationship oriented, however, conflict changes to cooperation, and infrequent contacts between buyers and sellers become ongoing exchanges.

As Figure 10.1 illustrates, relationship marketing emphasizes cooperation rather than conflict between all of the parties involved. This ongoing collaborative exchange creates value for both parties and builds customer loyalty. Customer relationship management goes a step further and integrates the customer's needs into all aspects of the firm's operations and its relationships with suppliers, distributors, and strategic partners. It combines people, processes, and technology with the long-term goal of maximizing customer value through mutually satisfying interactions and transactions.

Twenty-first-century marketers now understand they must do more than simply create products and then sell them. With so many goods and services to choose from, customers look for added value from their marketing relationships. PetSmart not only charges lower prices than grocery stores for pet products, but also offers a huge selection—everything from premium and national brands of food, toys and bedding, leashes, and other supplies to comprehensive services like dog training, grooming, day and overnight boarding, and even veterinary care and hospitalization. You can even buy your pet there. These offerings help build customer loyalty in the pet ownership market, where the number of consumers and the level of spending per pet are both rising and competitors like Petco are struggling.[2]

In general, the differences between the narrow focus of transaction marketing and the much broader view of relationship marketing can be summarized as follows:
Relationship marketing:

▷ focuses on the long term rather than the short term

▷ emphasizes retaining customers over making a sale

▷ ranks customer service as a high priority

▷ encourages frequent customer contact

▷ fosters customer commitment with the firm

▷ bases customer interactions on cooperation and trust

▷ commits all employees to provide high-quality products

PetSmart offers a huge selection of pet supplies as well as services such as dog training, grooming, boarding, and veterinary care. These offerings help build customer loyalty.

© AP Images/Gerry Broome

As a result, the buyer–seller bonds developed in a relationship marketing partnership last longer and cover a much wider scope than those developed in transaction marketing.

assessment check

1. What are the major differences between transaction-based marketing and relationship marketing?

ELEMENTS OF RELATIONSHIP MARKETING

To build long-term customer relationships, marketers need to place customers at the center of their efforts. When a company integrates customer service and quality with marketing, the result is a relationship marketing orientation.

But how do firms achieve these long-term relationships? They build them with four basic elements.

1. They gather information about their customers. Database technology, discussed later in this chapter, helps a company identify current and potential customers with selected demographic, purchase, and lifestyle characteristics.

2. They analyze the data collected and use it to modify their marketing mix to deliver differentiated messages and customized marketing programs to individual consumers.

3. Through relationship marketing, they monitor their interactions with customers. They can then assess the customer's level of satisfaction or dissatisfaction with their service. Marketers can also calculate the cost of attracting one new customer and figure out how much profit that customer will generate during the relationship. Information is fed back, and they then can seek ways to add value to the buyer–seller transaction so the relationship will continue.

4. With customer relationship management (CRM) software, they use intimate knowledge of customers and customer preferences to orient every part of the organization—including both its internal and external partners—toward building a unique company differentiation based on strong, unbreakable bonds with customers. Sophisticated technology and the Internet help make that happen.

INTERNAL MARKETING

The concepts of customer satisfaction and relationship marketing usually are discussed in terms of **external customers**—people or organizations that buy or use a firm's goods or services. But marketing in organizations concerned with customer satisfaction and long-term relationships must also address **internal customers**—employees or departments within the organization whose success depends on the work of other employees or departments. A person processing an order for a new piece of equipment is the internal customer of the salesperson who completed the sale, just as the person who bought the product is the salesperson's external customer. Although the order processor might never directly encounter an external customer, his or her performance can have a direct impact on the overall value the firm is able to deliver.

Internal marketing depends on managerial actions that enable all members of an organization to understand, accept, and fulfill their respective roles in implementing a marketing strategy. Good internal customer satisfaction helps organizations attract, select, and retain outstanding employees who appreciate and value their role in the delivery of superior service to external customers. At General Mills, employees in all areas of the company on cross-functional teams enroll in week-long, hands-on training programs designed to teach the fine points of building and maintaining the company's brands. The company's director of organization effectiveness hails the program because it allows all employees to gain a different perspective on company products. "A person from human resources, for instance, would ask a provocative question [because] she wasn't a marketer," she explains. "And you'd see the look on the marketers' faces: 'Whoa, I never thought of that.'"[3]

Employee knowledge and involvement are important goals of internal marketing. Companies that excel at satisfying customers typically place a priority on keeping employees informed about corporate goals, strategies, and customer needs. Employees must also have the necessary tools to address customer requests and problems in a timely manner. Companywide computer networks

aid the flow of communications between departments and functions. Several companies also include key suppliers in their networks to speed and ease communication of all aspects of business from product design to inventory control.

Employee satisfaction is another critical objective of internal marketing. Employees can seldom, if ever, satisfy customers when they themselves are unhappy. Dissatisfied employees are likely to spread negative word-of-mouth mes-

Upscale hotel chain Four Seasons pampers its customers but also relates its high service standards directly to maintaining satisfied employees. This Florida Four Seasons employee is a restaurant hostess.

© Jeff Greenberg/Alamy

sages to relatives, friends, and acquaintances, and these reports can affect purchasing behavior. Satisfied employees buy their employer's products, tell friends and families how good the customer service is, and ultimately send a powerful message to customers. One recommended strategy for offering consistently good service is to attract good employees, hire good employees, and retain good employees. Upscale hotel chain Four Seasons pampers its customers and generates a loyal following. But the company relates its high service standards directly to its hiring policies and to maintaining satisfied employees. Founder Isadore Sharp says the chain succeeds "by hiring more for attitude than experience, by establishing career paths and promotion from within, by paying as much attention to employee complaints as guest complaints … by pushing responsibility down and encouraging self-discipline, by setting performance high and holding people accountable, and most of all, [by] adhering to our credo, generating trust." Turnover among full-time employees is half the industry average, and the company ranks among the best companies to work for in the United States.[4]

assessment check

1. What are the four basic elements of relationship marketing?

2. Why is internal marketing important to a firm?

The Relationship Marketing Continuum

3 Identify the three levels of the relationship marketing continuum.

Like all other interpersonal relationships, buyer–seller relationships function at a variety of levels. As an individual or firm progresses from the lowest level to the highest level on the continuum of relationship marketing, as shown in Table 10.1, the strength of commitment between the parties grows. The likelihood of a continuing, long-term relationship grows as well. Whenever possible,

table 10.1 Three Levels of Relationship Marketing

Characteristic	Level 1	Level 2	Level 3
Primary bond	Financial	Social	Structural
Degree of customization	Low	Medium	Medium to high
Potential for sustained competitive advantage	Low	Moderate	High
Examples	Fast-food dollar-menu items	TiVo-YouTube partnership	Southwest Airlines business traveler program

Source: Adapted from Leonard L. Berry, "Relationship Marketing of Services—Growing Internet, Emerging Perspectives," *Journal of the Academy of Marketing Science,* Fall 1995, p. 240.

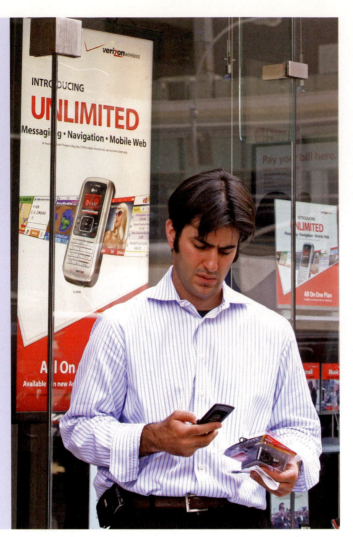

Verizon's unlimited calling plans focus on price, offering customers low flat rates for unlimited calls anytime, anywhere in the United States.

marketers want to move their customers along this continuum, converting them from Level 1 purchasers, who focus mainly on price, to Level 3 customers, who receive specialized services and value-added benefits that may not be available from another firm.

FIRST LEVEL: FOCUS ON PRICE

Interactions at the first level of relationship marketing are the most superficial and the least likely to lead to a long-term relationship. In the most prevalent examples of this first level, relationship marketing efforts rely on pricing and other financial incentives to motivate customers to enter into buying relationships with a seller. Fast-food chains, for instance, regularly use value- and dollar-menu promotions, offering more food for less, to attract fickle customers. With gasoline and other prices on the rise, "people are looking for premium items, but there's also a push for value," one industry expert says. That makes the lower prices especially attractive.[5] Service providers offer price savings, too. Verizon's unlimited calling plans offer new and existing customers low flat rates for unlimited calls anytime, anywhere in the United States.[6]

Although these programs can be attractive to users, they may not create long-term buyer relationships. Because the programs are not customized to the needs of individual buyers, they are easily duplicated by competitors. The lesson? It takes more than a low price or other financial incentives to create a long-term relationship between buyer and seller.

SECOND LEVEL: SOCIAL INTERACTIONS

As buyers and sellers reach the second level of relationship marketing, their interactions develop on a social level, one that features deeper and less superficial links than the financially motivated first level. Sellers have begun to learn that social relationships with buyers can be very effective marketing tools. Customer service and communication are key factors at this stage.

Social interaction can take many forms. The owner of a local shoe store or dry cleaner might chat with customers about local events. A local wine shop may host a wine-tasting reception. The service department of an auto dealership might call a customer after a repair to see whether or not the customer is satisfied or has any questions. An investment firm might send holiday cards to all its customers. Even television watching, once passive, is getting more social: TiVo and YouTube have partnered to bring Web videos to users' televisions, enhancing the social interaction characteristics of the Web site by featuring the most widely seen, and talked about, videos on the Internet.[7] Marketers are beginning to see the potential for more precise targeting through the use of social networking sites like Facebook and MySpace, but are still finding their way. The "Solving an Ethical Controversy" feature looks at the potential pitfalls of marketing through social networking sites.

Solving an ethical controversy

Are Social Networking Sites Abusing Their Customer Relationships?

facebook and MySpace, the two most popular social networking sites on the Internet, both introduced features that let them target users according to preferences shown on their profiles, such as shopping and other likes and dislikes. Collecting such information allows the sites to better serve their advertisers, who want to reach only those who might be interested in their goods and services. But a storm of protest greets the introduction of each new marketing tool, and both sites have ended up backtracking and apologizing for their activities. Facebook had to quickly add an opt-in feature and other restrictions to its Beacon tool, which tracked its 55 million users' activity at dozens of shopping sites and let their listed friends access the same information without their consent. MySpace allows dozens of leading advertisers to target its users in at least 10 different categories like movies, travel, and autos based on their profile pages.

Are ad targeting programs on social networking sites a betrayal of users' trust?

PRO

1. Users at the sites are there for social purposes, not for commercial ones. The executive director of the Center for Digital Democracy speaks for many when he calls Facebook's Beacon a "significant privacy problem."

2. Users say they think the ad tools are unwelcome and annoying, with the potential to create personal embarrassment.

CON

1. MySpace executives believe ad targeting grows revenue for the site by improving response rates for advertisers. Increased revenue allows the site to provide better service for users.

2. Since users have to live with ads, says MySpace owner Fox Interactive, many prefer ads that are relevant, which only targeting can provide. Targeting reduces the number of ads users see overall.

Summary

Facebook, believed to earn $150 million a year, has stumbled twice already, including an earlier "news feed" tool that tracked changes users made in their profiles. But although privacy advocates will be watching all networking sites more closely, targeting tools don't seem to keep any users away from Facebook and MySpace, and they are likely here to stay.

Sources: Chris Crum, "Facebook Launches New Ad Targeting Options," *WebProNews*, March 12, 2009, http://www.webpronews.com; Zachary Rodgers, "Inside MySpace's War on Marketing Abuse," *ClickZ Network*, May 27, 2008, www.clickz.com; Kevin Poulsen, "MySpace Bug Leaks 'Private' Teen Photos to Voyeurs," *Wired*, January 17, 2008, www.wired.com; Michael Liedtke, "Facebook Lets Users Block Marketing Tool," *Associated Press*, December 6, 2007, news.yahoo.com; Michael Liedtke, "Facebook Revamps New Advertising System," *Associated Press*, November 30, 2007, news.yahoo.com; Anick Jesdanun, "MySpace Expands Program for Targeted Ads," *Associated Press*, November 5, 2007, news.yahoo.com; Stefanie Olsen, "Can Facebook Feed Its Ad Brains?" *CNet News*, November 2, 2007, www.news.com.

THIRD LEVEL: INTERDEPENDENT PARTNERSHIP

At the third level of relationship marketing, relationships are transformed into structural changes that ensure buyer and seller are true business partners. As buyer and seller work more closely together, they develop a dependence on one another that continues to grow over time. Southwest Airlines is a leader in customer satisfaction in the airline industry, but the company is reaching out to business travelers with service changes and upgrades to its normally frills-free waiting areas. Airport lounges now feature comfortable leather seats and plug-ins for computers and cell phone rechargers, and planes offer in-flight media and new international connections. For a higher ticket price, "business select" passengers board first as the airline abandons its unassigned-seating policy. They also earn more frequent-flier miles and get a free drink.[8]

assessment check

1. Identify the three levels of the marketing relationship.

2. Which level is the most complicated? Why?

Enhancing Customer Satisfaction

Marketers monitor customer satisfaction through various methods of marketing research. As part of an ongoing relationship with customers, marketers must continually measure and improve how well they meet customer needs. As Figure 10.2 shows, three major steps are involved in this process: understanding customer needs, obtaining customer feedback, and instituting an ongoing program to ensure customer satisfaction.

UNDERSTANDING CUSTOMER NEEDS

Knowledge of what customers need, want, and expect is a central concern of companies focused on building long-term relationships. This information is also a vital first step in setting up a system to measure **customer satisfaction.** Marketers must carefully monitor the characteristics of their product that really matter to customers. They also must remain constantly alert to new elements that might affect satisfaction.

Satisfaction can be measured in terms of the gaps between what customers expect and what they perceive they have received. Such gaps can produce favorable or unfavorable impressions. Goods or services may be better or worse than expected. If they are better, marketers can use the opportunity to create loyal customers. If goods or services are worse than expected, a company may start to lose customers. The American Customer Satisfaction Index (ACSI) is a nationwide tool to provide information about customer satisfaction with product quality. Based on more than 65,000 telephone interviews a year, it tracks customer responses to over 5,000 brands produced by about 300 companies and 100 federal agencies. Some of the firms ACSI rates are 1–800-FLOWERS, Amazon.com, Kraft Foods, Levi Strauss, Marriott International, AOL, Nissan, Campbell Soup, Charles Schwab, Outback Steakhouse, The Coca-Cola Company, Overstock.com, and Quaker Foods. Each rating is based on 250 customer interviews.[9] Marketers at the companies profiled can use such rankings to measure how well they satisfy customer needs.

To avoid unfavorable service gaps, marketers need to keep in touch with the needs of current and potential customers. They must look beyond traditional performance measures and explore the factors that determine purchasing behavior to formulate customer-based missions, goals, and performance standards.

OBTAINING CUSTOMER FEEDBACK AND ENSURING SATISFACTION

The second step in measuring customer satisfaction is to compile feedback from customers regarding present performance. Increasingly, marketers try to improve customers' access to their companies by including toll-free phone numbers or Web site addresses in their advertising. Most firms rely on reactive methods of collecting feedback. Rather than solicit complaints, they might, for example, monitor Usenet, other online discussion groups, and popular blogs to track customer comments and attitudes about the value received. Marketers at cable company Comcast review postings on blogs, message boards, and social networking sites. But they not only read the comments, they sometimes respond to the messages. Responses may startle the posters, but it lets them know that someone is listening to their concerns and gripes and establishes a two-way conversation.[10] Some companies hire mystery shoppers who visit or call businesses posing as customers to evaluate the service they receive. Their unbiased appraisals usually are conducted semiannually or

figure 10.2

Three Steps to Measure Customer Satisfaction

Ongoing Measurement

Customer Feedback

Understanding Customer Needs

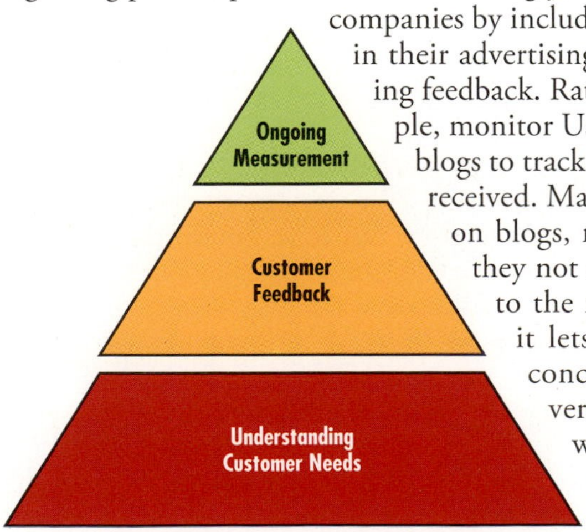

quarterly to monitor employees, diagnose problem areas in customer service, and measure the impact of employee training.

Since unhappy customers typically talk about their buying experiences more than happy customers do, the cost of dissatisfaction can be high. One instance of poor complaint handling at an upscale fitness club, for instance, could cost the gym thousands of dollars in lost membership fees; the fee is $1,000 for membership and, if the disgruntled customer tells seven people, the club could lose $7,000. So it makes sense to try to resolve problems quickly. In addition to training employees to resolve complaints, firms can benefit from providing several different ways for customers to make their dissatisfaction known, including prepaid mail questionnaires, telephone help lines, comment cards, and face-to-face exit surveys as people leave the premises.[11] Any method that makes it easier for customers to complain actually benefits a firm. Customer complaints offer firms the opportunity to overcome problems and prove their commitment to service. People often have greater loyalty to a company after a conflict has been resolved than if they had never complained at all.

Many organizations also use proactive methods to assess customer satisfaction, including visiting, calling, or mailing out surveys to clients to find out their level of satisfaction. Nokia has launched an ambitious online experiment to draw user feedback on new products that actually leads to product innovation. A cell phone application, Sports Tracker, lets runners and cyclists tap into the global positioning functions of some Nokia phones to plot their routes as well as record their speed and distance traveled. When the company posted a work-in-progress version of the application on its Web site for downloading, more than a million people used it, sometimes in ways Nokia never imagined, including hot-air ballooning and paragliding. Best of all, they provided enthusiastic feedback that helped Nokia add improvements like online groups for sharing text and photos.[12]

briefly speaking

"The way I see it, if you forget the customer, nothing much else matters. The brand deteriorates, employees lose jobs, and shareholders lose value."

—**Anne Mulcahy (b. 1952)**
CHAIRPERSON, XEROX CORPORATION

assessment check

1. How is customer satisfaction measured?

2. Identify two ways marketers may obtain customer feedback.

Building Buyer–Seller Relationships

5 Describe how companies build buyer–seller relationships.

Marketers of consumer goods and services have discovered they must do more than simply create products and then sell them. With a dizzying array of products to choose from, many customers seek ways to simplify both their business and personal lives, and relationships provide a way to do this.

One reason consumers form continuing relationships is their desire to reduce choices. Through relationships, they can simplify information gathering and the entire buying process as well as decrease the risk of dissatisfaction. They find comfort in brands that have become familiar through their ongoing relationships with companies. Such relationships may lead to more efficient decision making by customers and higher levels of customer satisfaction.

A key benefit to consumers in long-term buyer–seller relationships is the perceived positive value they receive. Relationships add value because of increased opportunities for frequent customers to save money through discounts, rebates, and similar offers; via special recognition from the relationship programs; and through convenience in shopping.

Marketers should also understand why consumers end relationships. Computerized technologies and the Internet have made consumers better informed than ever before by giving them unprecedented abilities to compare prices, merchandise, and customer service. If they perceive a competitor's product or customer service is better, customers may switch loyalties. Many consumers dislike feeling locked into a relationship with one company, and that is reason enough for them to try a competing item the next time they buy. Some customers simply become bored with their current providers and decide to sample the competition.

HOW MARKETERS KEEP CUSTOMERS

One of the major forces driving the push from transaction-based marketing to relationship marketing is the realization that retaining customers is far more profitable than losing them.

Some banking industry analysts estimate that banks acquire new customers at the rate of about 13.5 percent per year, only 1 percentage point faster than they lose them. Meanwhile, it costs five times as much to acquire a new customer as it does to keep a loyal one. This **customer churn,** or turnover, is expensive. Some estimate that banks can increase their net profits 20 percent by eliminating just 5 percent of their customer churn.[13] In the telecom industry, wireless services in the United States and Europe replace about a third of their customer base each year. That number could rise to 50 percent, according to some industry observers, based on customers' desire for the latest and most attractive handset with the most sophisticated features and impatience with any billing or service problems or gaps in network coverage. Firms that merge are paying five figures for each customer the acquired telecom provider has; at those rates, customer churn is staggeringly expensive.[14]

Also, customers usually enable a firm to generate more profits with each additional year of the relationship. For example, the Marriott Rewards program now boasts more than 17 million members who spend an average of 2.5 times as much at Marriott hotels as nonmembers and account for 40 percent of Marriott's total sales. They have more than 250 reward options, earning airline miles or points toward hotel stays and merchandise. They can receive 33 percent savings through Marriott Rewards Pointsavers, and during certain time periods, may earn double Marriott rewards or double upgrade points with rental car firm Hertz. Now they can also use points to ship their luggage door to door.[15]

frequency marketing
Frequent-buyer or -user marketing programs that reward customers with cash, rebates, merchandise, or other premiums.

Programs like Marriott's are an example of **frequency marketing.** These programs reward top customers with cash, rebates, merchandise, or other premiums. Buyers who purchase an item more often earn higher rewards. Frequency marketing focuses on a company's best customers with the goal of increasing their motivation to buy even more of the same or other products from the seller.

Many different types of companies use frequency programs: fast-food restaurants, retail stores, telecommunications companies, and travel firms. Popular programs include airline frequent-flyer programs, such as Continental's OnePass, and retail programs, such as Hallmark's Gold Crown Card.

About 84 percent of credit card purchases now include some sort of reward, such as cash back, frequent-flier miles, price rebates, and other offerings. Eighty million U.S. consumers use such cards, although credit counselors caution that their rewards aren't strictly free. Most companies charge higher interest payments and fees to finance the give-backs, making some cards more costly to consumers than the "rewards" they offer.[16]

affinity marketing
Marketing effort sponsored by an organization that solicits responses from individuals who share common interests and activities.

In addition to frequency programs, companies use **affinity marketing** to retain customers. Each of us holds certain things dear. Some may feel strongly about Eastern Michigan University, while others admire the Dallas Cowboys or the Atlanta Braves. These examples, along with an almost unending variety of others, are subjects of affinity programs. An affinity program is a marketing effort sponsored by an organization that solicits involvement by individuals who share common interests and activities. With affinity programs, organizations create extra value for members and encourage stronger relationships. And sometimes those relationships are geared toward eternity: the University of Florida is one of a handful of colleges that allow alumni to have their ashes buried on campus grounds after paying for the upkeep. "The days of someone being born in a community, staying there all their lives and dying there just doesn't happen any more," says the university's vice president. "People want to have a tie, and their tie is often their university. It's a logical resting place."[17]

Avid sports fans are another logical target for affinity programs. Bank of America offers an Extra Points card that gives pro football fans rewards linked to NFL gifts, films, and events, including the Super Bowl; the card itself is emblazoned with the logo of the fan's chosen team.[18] A few affinity debit and credit cards bear the names of celebrities, among them MasterCard's Usher card and Visa's Elvis and Hilary Duff cards. Glimpses of the celebrity's life and music accompany rewards like first-in-line ticket purchases for concerts, as well as merchandise and other perks.[19]

Not all affinity programs involve credit cards. WNET, the New York public television station, thanks members who contribute more than $40 a year with a card that entitles them to discounts at participating restaurants, museums, theaters, hotels, and car rental companies.[20]

DATABASE MARKETING

The use of information technology to analyze data about customers and their transactions is referred to as **database marketing.** The results form the basis of new advertising or promotions targeted to carefully identified groups of customers. Database marketing is a particularly effective tool for building relationships because it allows sellers to sort through huge quantities of data from multiple sources on the buying habits or preferences of thousands or even millions of customers. Companies can then track buying patterns, develop customer relationship profiles, customize their offerings and sales promotions, and even personalize customer service to suit the needs of targeted groups of customers. Properly used, databases can help companies in several ways, including:

A few affinity debit and credit cards bear the names of celebrities, such as Carmen Electra.

▷ identifying their most profitable customers;

▷ calculating the lifetime value of each customer's business;

▷ creating a meaningful dialogue that builds relationships and encourages genuine brand loyalty;

▷ improving customer retention and referral rates;

▷ reducing marketing and promotion costs;

▷ boosting sales volume per customer or targeted customer group; and

▷ expanding loyalty programs.[21]

database marketing Use of software to analyze marketing information, identifying and targeting messages toward specific groups of potential customers.

Where do organizations find all the data that fill these vast marketing databases? Everywhere! Credit card applications, software registration, and product warranties all provide vital statistics of individual customers. Point-of-sale register scanners, customer opinion surveys, and sweepstakes entry forms may offer not just details of name and address but information about preferred brands and shopping habits. Web sites offer free access in return for personal data, allowing companies to amass increasingly rich marketing information.

Google Personalized Search is a new platform that can track users' past online history and use it to improve and tailor the results of future searches. The goal is to make Google search experiences better based on the user's preferences, without the customer having to enter any additional information. The chief operating officer of one search marketing firm sees personalized search results as a breakthrough that allows the company to target its ads to those who will be most interested in them. Some users have privacy concerns, however, and some simply prefer the open-ended nature of searches without personalization. "Just because I ordered my Coke with extra ice yesterday," says one blogger about the new Google capability, "doesn't mean I want it that way for the rest of my life."[22] The "Marketing Success" feature discusses how Google continues to innovate and adopt new technology to meet marketplace demands.

NBC is another firm adding to its base of knowledge about users. Its 2,220 hours of streaming online video from the Beijing Summer Olympics were measured with about ten different tools to determine how many people visited NBCOlympics.com, what they watched, and for how long. The research was supplemented by online surveys of hundreds of consumers every day of the games as well as focus groups. For the network, the effort was a step toward comprehensive audience measurement that includes television, online viewing, video on demand, and cell phone usage.[23]

New technologies such as radio frequency identification (RFID) allow retailers to identify shipping pallets and cargo containers, but most observers anticipate that in the near future RFID will be cost effective enough to permit tagging of individual store items, allowing retailers to gather information about the purchaser as well as managing inventory and deterring theft, but also raising privacy concerns.

Interactive television delivers even more valuable data—information on real consumer behavior and attitudes toward brands. Linked to digital television, sophisticated set-top boxes already collect vast amounts of data on television viewer behavior, organized in incredible detail. As the technology makes its way into more homes, marketers receive firsthand knowledge of the kind of programming and products their targeted customers want. In addition, rather than using television to advertise to the masses, they can talk directly to the viewers most interested in their products. At a click of a button, viewers can skip ads, but they also can click to a full-length infomercial on any brand that captures their interest. About 82 percent of U.S. households subscribe to pay television, and features such as interactive program guides, on-demand content, and interactive advertising have grown to 15 percent of the content of their subscriptions.[24]

New technologies like widgets—small software applications, such as games, easily passed from friend to friend on sites like Facebook—are becoming popular marketing tools. One California job search site, Doostang, attracted 1,200 new members in three days with a game widget. Cell phone advertising is increasing, and with it the prospect that it can become highly targeted since telecom companies already have access to users' personal and credit card information and even their current location. Discount offers could be sent to users passing a particular store, for instance. Marketers can even build their own social networking sites, perhaps using a program like Ning. Kent Nichols used Ning to create a network for customers of his ninja-themed video company and figures it increased traffic and ad revenue by as much as 10 percent. The goal was to create his own social network rather than rely on MySpace or Facebook.[25]

As database marketing becomes more complex, a variety of software tools and services enable marketers to target consumers more and more narrowly while enriching their communications to selected groups. After all, a huge repository of data is not valuable unless it can be turned into information useful to a firm's marketers. **Application service providers (ASPs)** assist marketers by providing software when it is needed to capture, manipulate, and analyze masses of consumer data. One type of software collects data on product specifications and details that marketers can use to isolate products best meeting a customer's needs. This feature would be particularly important in selling expensive business products that require high involvement in making a purchase decision. Convio provides such database services to nonprofit organizations trying to cultivate a wider base of members and supporters. Convio also supplies software and online services

---

MARKETING SUCCESS   Google Stays Ahead of the Search Curve

Background. When the economy takes a downturn, everyone is affected. That was the case even for highly successful Google. Although Web users continued to search for goods and services, they weren't buying as much as they previously had. Ads on the Google site were converting to actual sales less frequently. Instead, consumers were browsing and window shopping.

The Challenge. Always known for its innovation, Google marketers had to come up with new ways to connect with

consumers wherever they are—and for consumers to connect with its advertisers. Still, the firm had to make sure to protect the privacy of consumers.

The Strategy. Recently Google introduced cutting-edge voice recognition technology to its search software for the Apple iPhone. The application is free to iPhone customers and is so sophisticated that a user can put the phone to his or her ear and ask it a wide range of questions, such as "Where's the

designed to help groups such as Easter Seals, the American Diabetes Association, the Jewish National Fund, Feeding America, museums, and other organizations identify and communicate with contributors.[26]

CUSTOMERS AS ADVOCATES

Recent relationship marketing efforts focus on turning customers from passive partners into active proponents of a product. **Grassroots marketing** involves connecting directly with existing and potential customers through nonmainstream channels. The grassroots approach relies on marketing strategies that are unconventional, nontraditional, and extremely flexible. Grassroots marketing sometimes is characterized by a relatively small budget and lots of legwork, but its hallmark is the ability to develop long-lasting, individual relationships with loyal customers.

With **viral marketing,** firms let satisfied customers get the word out about products to other consumers—like a spreading virus. Ford Models, the 60-year-old modeling agency that launched some of fashion's legendary faces, has produced more than 1,000 online videos of its models and become YouTube's third most popular destination. The videos feature informal settings and present models sharing health, beauty, and fashion tips in a candid, friendly atmosphere. With an audience that includes not only star-struck teenage girls but also ad agencies, apparel manufacturers, and retailers, Ford has increased revenue 140 percent, attracted investment capital, and become a leading digital marketer. It's currently in talks with fashion and retailing executives who want to sponsor Ford videos—costing about $200 each to produce—or place their products in them, thanks to viewership across a wide range of ages, sparked by partnerships with MySpace and iVillage.[27]

Buzz marketing gathers volunteers to try products and then relies on them to talk about their experiences with friends and colleagues. "Influencers," or early adopters of products, are ideal carriers of buzz marketing messages because their credibility makes their choices valuable among their peers. They often are recruited online through chat rooms, blogs, and instant messaging. Word-of-mouth—the idea behind buzz marketing—isn't new, but by accelerating communication, technology has made many more applications possible. "What consumers … trust are their own experiences and the words of others," says an advertising industry observer. "About 56 percent say they trust the words and recommendations of friends and family in thinking about products." Procter & Gamble's Tremor program relies on the buzz created by 225,00 recruited teens, while Vocalpoint does the same with 500,000 mothers. In one instance, Vocalpoint members were urged to talk to friends about how hard it is to get kids to help with the dishes as a way of introducing a new kind of dishwashing soap into the conversation.[28] Techniques in this area are still evolving, and the Word of Mouth Marketing Association is developing rules and standards for buzz marketing it hopes will prevent fraud and preserve the value of buzz marketing.[29]

nearest shopping mall?" or "What's the population of China?" This level of speech recognition has long been a goal of researchers trying to achieve true artificial intelligence. Another new application, called Latitude, lets smart phone users share their locations with each other and track friends who have also opted in to the service.

In response to privacy concerns associated with Latitude, Google added a shut-off feature and the capability to hide your whereabouts from others. In an effort to improve its privacy protection regarding advertisements, Google has implemented a simple technology that allows users' browsers to "remember" that the users don't want Google to remember anything about them. For those consumers who opt to allow information to be tracked or stored, Google has placed a line of text at the end of the ads it serves, showing the Internet address of the advertiser and a link to a full explanation of Google's advertising practices.

The Outcome. Because of its ability to develop and adopt new technology, and because of its willingness to change when the marketplace demands it, Google has remained a stronger business through difficult times than other marketers have. Of its speech recognition feature, Vic Gundotra, head of Google's mobile businesses, boasts, "We are dramatically increasing value to the advertiser through location and voice."

Sources: Brian Heater, "Google Labs Adds Similar Image Search," *PC Magazine*, April 21, 2009, http://www.pcmag.com; Chloe Albanesius, "Google's Schmidt Talks Privacy, Internet Domination," *PC Magazine*, April 18, 2009, http://www.pcmag.com; Saul Hansell, "A Guide to Google's New Privacy Controls," *The New York Times*, March 12, 2009, http://bits.blogs.nytimes.com; John Markoff, "Google Is Taking Questions (Spoken, via iPhone)," *The New York Times*, November 14, 2008, http://www.nytimes.com.

customer relationship management (CRM)
Combination of strategies and tools that drives relationship programs, reorienting the entire organization to a concentrated focus on satisfying customers.

Customer Relationship Management

Emerging from—and closely linked to—relationship marketing, **customer relationship management (CRM)** is the combination of strategies and technologies that empowers relationship programs, reorienting the entire organization to a concentrated focus on satisfying customers. Made possible by technological advances, it leverages technology as a means to manage customer relationships and to integrate all stakeholders into a company's product design and development, manufacturing, marketing, sales, and customer service processes.

CRM represents a shift in thinking for everyone involved with a firm—from the CEO down and encompassing all other key stakeholders, including suppliers, dealers, and other partners. All recognize that solid customer relations are fostered by similarly strong relationships with other major stakeholders. Because CRM goes well beyond traditional sales, marketing, or customer service functions, it requires a top-down commitment and must permeate every aspect of a firm's business. Technology makes that possible by allowing firms—regardless of size and no matter how far-flung their operations—to manage activities across functions, from location to location, and among their internal and external partners.

BENEFITS OF CRM

CRM software systems are capable of making sense of the vast amounts of customer data that technology allows firms to collect. With e-commerce software from SAP, Adidas created a user-friendly online store for retailers to reduce lead times and transaction costs for orders. The catalog-style store, open 24/7, improved customer service and satisfaction ratings from over 3,000 retailers worldwide that use it to place hundreds of orders every day. The software is saving about 20 percent of the normal processing costs for each order. The system checks product availability and rewards customers who order early.[30]

Another key benefit of customer relationship management systems is they simplify complex business processes while keeping the best interests of customers at heart. Discount Auto Parts, which operates in the Southeastern United States, needed to solve problems associated with its recent growth—the increasing distance between its distribution center and its new stores, and the growing number of inventory items and transactions it needed to manage. Working with Capgemini, a consulting company, Discount Auto Parts created a plan for improving forecasting and planning that in turn allowed it to reduce inventories all along its supply chain. Discount also formed new collaborative relationships with its suppliers, opened a new distribution center, instituted a transportation management system for its fleet, and reduced its total costs.[31]

Selecting the right CRM software system is critical to the success of a firm's entire CRM program. CRM can be used at two different levels: on-demand, accessed via the Internet as a Web-based service, and on-premises, installed on a company's computer system on-site.[32] A firm may choose to buy a system from a company such as SAP or Oracle or rent hosted CRM applications through Web sites such as Salesforce.com or Salesnet. Purchasing a customized system can cost millions of dollars and take months to implement, while hosted solutions—rented through a Web site—are cheaper and quicker to get up and running. But purchasing a system allows a firm to expand and customize, whereas hosted systems are more limited. Experienced marketers also warn that it is easy to get mired in a system too complicated for staff to use.

Software solutions are just one component of a successful CRM initiative. The most effective companies approach customer relationship management as a complete business strategy in which people, processes, and technology are organized around delivering superior value to customers. Successful CRM systems share the following qualities:

▷ They create partnerships with customers in ways that align with the company's mission and goals.

▷ They reduce costs by empowering customers to find the information they need to manage their own orders.

▷ They improve customer service by centralizing data and help sales representatives guide customers to information.

▷ They reduce response time and thus increase customer satisfaction.

▷ They improve customer retention and loyalty, leading to more repeat business and new business from word-of-mouth.

▷ They can provide a complete picture of customers.

▷ Their results are measurable.[33]

Once the groundwork has been laid, technology solutions drive firms toward a clearer understanding of each customer and his or her needs.

PROBLEMS WITH CRM

CRM is not a magic wand. The strategy needs to be thought out in advance, and everyone in the firm must be committed to it and understand how to use it. If no one can put the system to work, it is an expensive mistake.

Experts explain that failures with CRM often result from failure to organize—or reorganize—the company's people and business processes to take advantage of the benefits the CRM system offers. For instance, it might be important to empower salespeople to negotiate price with their customers to close more sales with CRM, but if a company does not adapt its centralized pricing system, its CRM efforts will be hampered. Second, if sales and service employees do not have input in the CRM process during its design phase, they might be less willing to use its tools—no matter how much training is offered. A third factor is some CRM "failures" are actually at least partially successful, but companies or their executives have set their expectations too high. Having a realistic idea what CRM can accomplish is as important to success as properly implementing the program. Finally, truly understanding customers, their needs, and the ways they differ from customers of the past is a critical element in any successful CRM project. "Companies lacking customer-focused strategies ... rarely succeed," says one industry expert.[34]

One of the easiest ways to lose a customer, or to damage any business relationship, is rudeness. But good manners are a two-way street. The "Etiquette Tips for Marketing Professionals" feature gives some suggestions for salvaging relationships when other people are rude to you.

RETRIEVING LOST CUSTOMERS

Customers defect from an organization's goods and services for a variety of reasons. They might be bored, they might move away from the region, they might not need the product anymore, or they might have tried—and preferred—competing products. Figure 10.3 illustrates the yearly defection rates for some industries. An increasingly important part of an effective CRM strategy is **customer winback,** the process of rejuvenating lost relationships with customers.

In many cases, a relationship gone sour can be sweetened again with the right approach. Despite well-publicized flight delays that left tens of thousands of customers stranded on the tarmac for hours, JetBlue rebounded to retain its place as first in customer satisfaction among low-cost air carriers. Part of the credit goes to the company's quick unveiling of a Customer Bill of Rights and a

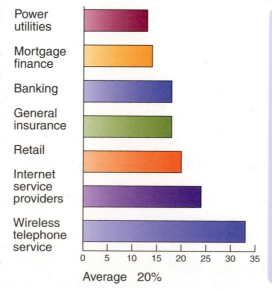

figure 10.3

Annual Customer Defection Rates

Source: Data from Andrew Greenyer, "The Danger of Defection," *CRM Today*, www.crm2day.com, accessed May 12, 2009.

Etiquette Tips for Marketing Professionals

Stopping Rudeness in Its Tracks

as more people rely on electronic devices and cell phones for communication, they may experience a disconnect with the people behind those devices. In extreme cases they can lose necessary skills in face-to-face interactions. Many believe the world is becoming a ruder place as a result. Other factors in the decline of polite interpersonal relationships might be the demand for instant gratification, the hurried pace of modern life, and a general decline of formality and rules for behavior. How can you best deal with others who are rude? Here are some tips.

In the office:

- Set the tone by always exhibiting thoughtful behavior.

- If someone is rude, control your first reaction, which might be anger or annoyance, and look for some good in the individual, or in the skills or abilities he or she brings to the workplace.

- Remember that everyone has a bad day once in a while.

- Let the person know, politely and quietly, that rudeness is counterproductive.

- Ask specific questions to try to find out the reason for a person's behavior. It might be a situation you can deal with or change.

In the retail environment:

- Ask polite questions to understand what will best satisfy the customer.

- Immediately and calmly take whatever steps you are authorized to in order to correct the situation that prompted the complaint. Refer the problem to a manager if you must.

- After ensuring you've done everything you can, thank the customer for bringing the situation to your attention.

On the road:

- If possible, on your way to the office or a meeting, avoid rush-hour traffic, where aggressive or reckless driving most often occurs.

- Allow plenty of time to get to your destination so you won't be tempted to invite rude behavior with your own anxiety.

Finally:

- Remember, other people's rudeness is not your fault. Don't let their behavior influence yours.

Sources: "How to Handle Rude People," www.sedona.com, accessed May 12, 2009; T. T. Mitchell, "Are Rude People Irritating You?" *Hodu.com*, www.hodu.com, accessed May 12, 2009; Peter Murphy, "How to Quickly and Easily Deal with Rude People," *Ezine Writer*, www.ezine-writer.com.au, accessed July 10, 2008; Jared Sandberg, "Do You Hear What I Hear? Telling Off a Colleague—Silently," *Career Journal*, October 24, 2007, www.livemint.com, accessed October 2008.

a promise of vouchers for the full airfare in case of delays that top three hours.[35] A good rule for service providers is to anticipate where problems will arise and figure out how to prevent them in the first place. The second part of this strategy is to accept that mistakes will occur in even the best system and to have a high-quality recovery effort in place that employees are empowered to enact.

assessment check

1. Define *customer relationship management.*

2. What are the two major types of CRM systems?

3. Describe two steps a firm can take to rejuvenate a lost relationship.

7 **Describe the buyer–seller relationship in business-to-business marketing and identify the four types of business partnerships.**

Buyer–Seller Relationships in Business-to-Business Markets

Customer relationship management and relationship marketing are not limited to consumer goods and services. Building strong buyer–seller relationships is a critical component of business-to-business marketing as well.

Business-to-business (B2B) marketing involves an organization's purchase of goods and services to support company operations or the production of other products. Buyer–seller relationships between companies involve working together to provide advantages that benefit both parties. These advantages might include lower prices for supplies, quicker delivery of inventory, improved quality and reliability, customized product features, and more favorable financing terms.

A **partnership** is an affiliation of two or more companies that help each other achieve common goals. Partnerships cover a wide spectrum of relationships from informal cooperative purchasing arrangements to formal production and marketing agreements. In business-to-business markets, partnerships form the basis of relationship marketing.

A variety of common goals motivate firms to form partnerships. Companies may want to protect or improve their positions in existing markets, gain access to new domestic or international markets, or quickly enter new markets. Expansion of a product line—to fill in gaps, broaden the product line, or differentiate the product—is another key reason for joining forces. Other motives include sharing resources, reducing costs, warding off threats of future competition, raising or creating barriers to entry, and learning new skills.

partnership Affiliation of two or more companies that help each other achieve common goals.

briefly speaking

"We can believe that we know where the world should go, but unless we're in touch with our customers, our model of the world can diverge from reality.... Innovation is no substitute for being in touch."

—**Steve Ballmer (b. 1956)**
CHIEF EXECUTIVE OFFICER, MICROSOFT

CHOOSING BUSINESS PARTNERS

How does an organization decide which companies to select as partners? The first priority is to locate firms that can add value to the relationship—whether through financial resources, contacts, extra manufacturing capacity, technical know-how, or distribution capabilities. The greater the value added, the greater the desirability of the partnership. In many cases, the attributes of each partner complement those of the other; each firm brings something to the relationship the other party needs but cannot provide on its own. Other partnerships join firms with similar skills and resources to reduce costs.

Organizations must share similar values and goals for a partnership to succeed in the long run. Wal-Mart has partnered with Pollo Campero, a Guatemalan fried-chicken chain that operates almost 300 restaurants in 11 countries. Both share a desire to reach more Hispanic customers in the United States. So they have formed a partnership that will allow Pollo Campero to open restaurants in 20 Wal-Mart stores around the country. "It's kind of like when we're looking at salsa versus ketchup and tortillas versus bread," said a Wal-Mart spokesperson.[36]

TYPES OF PARTNERSHIPS

Companies form four key types of partnerships in business-to-business markets: buyer, seller, internal, and lateral partnerships. This section briefly examines each category.

In a **buyer partnership,** a firm purchases goods and services from one or more providers. Apple buys Intel chips for its computers, and the two companies are working closely to share other technology innovations as well. Intel provided the unique processing chip for the top-selling MacBook Air thin laptop, and the two firms collaborated to make the Air a reality. With that success behind them, they are looking for future projects.[37]

When a company assumes the buyer position in a relationship, it has a unique set of needs and requirements vendors must meet to make the relationship successful. Although buyers want sellers to provide fair prices, quick delivery, and high quality levels, a lasting relationship often requires more effort. To induce a buyer to form a long-term

Apple buys Intel chips for its computers, forming a buyer partnership.

partnership, a supplier must also be responsive to the purchaser's unique needs. Intel, for instance, had to adjust to the faster pace at which Apple develops and introduces new products.[38]

Seller partnerships set up long-term exchanges of goods and services in return for cash or other consideration. Sellers, too, have specific needs as partners in ongoing relationships. Most prefer to develop long-term relationships with their partners. Sellers also want prompt payment.

The importance of **internal partnerships** is widely recognized in business today. The classic definition of the word *customer* as the buyer of a good or service is now more carefully defined in terms of external customers. However, customers within an organization also have their own needs. Internal partnerships are the foundation of an organization and its ability to meet its commitments to external entities. If the purchasing department selects a parts vendor that fails to ship on the dates required by manufacturing, production will halt and products will not be delivered to customers as promised. As a result, external customers will likely seek other more reliable suppliers. Without building and maintaining internal partnerships, an organization will have difficulty meeting the needs of its external partnerships.

Lateral partnerships include strategic alliances with other companies or with not-for-profit organizations and research alliances between for-profit firms and colleges and universities. The relationship focuses on external entities—such as customers of the partner firm—and involves no direct buyer–seller interactions. Strategic alliances are discussed later in this chapter.

COBRANDING AND COMARKETING

cobranding Cooperative arrangement in which two or more businesses team up to closely link their names on a single product.

Two other types of business marketing relationships include cobranding and comarketing. **Cobranding** joins two strong brand names, perhaps owned by two different companies, to sell a product. Shaner Hotels, owner of the Crowne Plaza chain, typically enters a cobranding agreement between its hotels and nearby national brand restaurants. It recently announced the opening of a Bonefish Grill in its Paramus, New Jersey, Crowne Plaza hotel, which joins a successful series of such ventures including a Starbucks at Shaner's Pittsburgh City Center Marriott hotel and an Outback Steakhouse at its Williamsburg Square complex of hotels in State College, Pennsylvania. Shaner's director of sales and marketing says most restaurants in hotels break even at best, but his firms' restaurants generate revenues because of the cobranding.[39]

comarketing Cooperative arrangement in which two businesses jointly market each other's products.

assessment check

1. What are the four key types of business marketing partnerships?
2. Distinguish cobranding and comarketing.

In a comarketing effort, two or more organizations join to sell their products in an allied marketing campaign. This store, called a Trombo, is a combination of Dunkin' Donuts, Togo's, and Baskin Robbins.

© Emile Wamsteker/Bloomberg News/Landov

In a **comarketing** effort, two organizations join to sell their products in an allied marketing campaign. A new series of ads for insurance company GEICO pairs a woman who had a car accident with Mrs. Butterworth, of pancake syrup fame. While the woman describes the broken glass during her accident, Mrs. Butterworth says it "sends shivers down my bottle." Insurance and pancake syrup might not seem an obvious pairing for a TV ad, but the spot has gained notice for both companies.[40]

Improving Buyer–Seller Relationships in Business-to-Business Markets

8 **Describe how business-to-business marketing incorporates national account selling, electronic data interchange and Web services, vendor-managed inventories (VMI), CPFaR, managing the supply chain, and creating alliances.**

Organizations that know how to find and nurture partner relationships, whether through informal deals or contracted partnerships, can enhance revenues and increase profits. Partnering often leads to lower prices, better products, and improved distribution—resulting in higher levels of customer satisfaction. Partners who know each other's needs and expectations are more likely to satisfy them and forge stronger long-term bonds. Often partnerships can be cemented through personal relationships, no matter where firms are located.

In the past, business relationships were conducted primarily in person, over the phone, or by mail. Today, businesses use the latest electronic, computer, and communications technology to link up. E-mail, the Internet, and other telecommunications services allow businesses to communicate anytime and anyplace. Chapter 4 discussed the business role of the Internet in detail. The following sections explore other ways buyers and sellers cooperate in business-to-business markets.

NATIONAL ACCOUNT SELLING

Some relationships are more important than others due to the large investments at stake. Large manufacturers such as Procter & Gamble and Clorox pay special attention to the needs of major retailers such as Wal-Mart and Target. Manufacturers use a technique called **national account selling** to serve their largest, most profitable customers. The large collection of supplier offices in northwest Arkansas—near Wal-Mart's home office—suggests how national account selling might be implemented. These offices are usually called *teams* or *support teams.*

The advantages of national account selling are many. By assembling a team of individuals to serve just one account, the seller demonstrates the depth of its commitment to the customer. The buyer–seller relationship is strengthened as both collaborate to find mutually beneficial solutions. Finally, cooperative buyer–seller efforts can bring about dramatic improvements in both efficiency and effectiveness for both partners. These improvements find their way to the bottom line in the form of decreased costs and increased profits.

BUSINESS-TO-BUSINESS DATABASES

As noted earlier, databases are indispensable tools in relationship marketing. They are also essential in building business-to-business relationships. Using information generated from sales reports, scanners, and many other sources, sellers can create databases that help guide their own efforts and those of buyers who resell products to final users.

ELECTRONIC DATA INTERCHANGE AND WEB SERVICES

Technology has transformed the ways companies control their inventories and replenish stock. Gone are the days when a retailer would notice stocks were running low, call the vendor, check prices, and reorder. Today's **electronic data interchanges (EDIs)** automate the entire process. EDI involves computer-to-computer exchanges of invoices, orders, and other business documents. It allows firms to reduce costs and improve efficiency and competitiveness. Retailers such as Wal-Mart, Dillard's, and Lowe's all require vendors to use EDI as a core **quick-response merchandising** tool. Quick-response merchandising is a just-in-time strategy that reduces the time merchandise is held in inventory, resulting in substantial cost savings. At Blue C Sushi restaurant in Seattle, an RFID tag is attached to the bottom of each sushi plate on the store's conveyor belt. It tracks the time that elapses from the moment it leaves the chef's cutting board until it is picked up by a customer, when it triggers a signal to chefs to update the inventory. The RFID tags also automate the restaurant's billing process and help it track inventory.[41] An added advantage of EDI is it opens new channels for gathering marketing information helpful in developing long-term business-to-business relationships.

electronic data interchange (EDI) Computer-to-computer exchanges of invoices, orders, and other business documents.

Web services provide a way for companies to communicate even if they are not running the same or compatible software, hardware, databases, or network platforms. Companies in a customer–supplier relationship, or a partnership such as airlines and car rental firms, may have difficulty getting their computer systems to work together or exchange data easily. Web services are platform-independent information exchange systems that use the Internet to allow interaction between the firms. They usually are simple, self-contained applications that handle functions from the simple to the complex.

Vendor-Managed Inventory

vendor-managed inventory (VMI) Inventory management system in which the seller—based on an existing agreement with a buyer—determines how much of a product is needed.

The proliferation of electronic communication technologies and the constant pressure on suppliers to improve response time have led to another way for buyers and sellers to do business. **Vendor-managed inventory (VMI)** has replaced buyer-managed inventory in many instances. It is an inventory management system in which the seller—based on an existing agreement with the buyer—determines how much of a product a buyer needs and automatically ships new supplies to that buyer. Russell Stover, the top U.S. producer of boxed chocolates, uses VMI to streamline ordering and eliminate stock-outs. "Our forecasting accuracy has greatly improved," said the company's VMI manager, "and we've seen a significant decrease in out of stocks, especially during key holiday seasons."[42]

Some firms have modified VMI to an approach called **collaborative planning, forecasting, and replenishment (CPFaR)**—a planning and forecasting technique involving collaborative efforts by both purchasers and vendors. TruServ, the wholesale hardware cooperative owned by 6,200 independent True Value retailers, relies on its more than 50 trading partners to use computer-assisted ordering. At the company's 12 distribution centers, inventory has been reduced from $600 million to $250 million, while service levels have climbed above 96 percent. Shorter lead times, more accurate forecasting, and faster reactions to marketplace trends are other benefits TruServ has realized from its CPFaR program.[43]

supply chain Sequence of suppliers that contribute to the creation and delivery of a product.

Russell Stover uses VMI to streamline ordering and eliminate stock-outs. The company's VMI manager says their forecasting accuracy has improved, especially during holiday seasons.

© Terri Miller/E-Visual Communications, Inc.

MANAGING THE SUPPLY CHAIN

Good relationships between businesses require careful management of the **supply chain,**—sometimes called the *value chain*—the entire sequence of suppliers that contribute to the creation and delivery of a product. This process affects both upstream relationships between the company and its suppliers and downstream relationships with the product's end users. The supply chain is discussed in greater detail in Chapter 13.

Effective supply chain management can provide an important competitive advantage for a business marketer that results in:

▷ increased innovation;

▷ decreased costs;

▷ improved conflict resolution within the chain; and

▷ improved communication and involvement among members of the chain.

By coordinating operations with the other companies in the chain, boosting quality, and improving its operating systems, a firm can improve speed and efficiency. Because companies spend considerable resources on goods and services from outside suppliers, cooperative relationships can pay off in many ways.

BUSINESS-TO-BUSINESS ALLIANCES

Strategic alliances—the ultimate expression of relationship marketing—are partnerships formed to create a competitive advantage. These more formal long-term arrangements improve each partner's supply chain relationships and enhance operating flexibility in today's complex and rapidly changing marketplace. The size and location of strategic partners are not important. Strategic alliances include businesses of all sizes, of all kinds, and in many locations; it is what each partner can offer the other that is important.

Companies can structure strategic alliances in two ways. Alliance partners can establish a new business unit in which each takes an ownership position. In such a joint venture, one partner might own 40 percent, while the other owns 60 percent. Alternatively, the partners may decide to form a less formal cooperative relationship that does not involve ownership—for example, a joint new-product design team. The cooperative alliance can operate more flexibly and change more easily as market forces or other conditions dictate. In either arrangement, the partners agree in advance on the skills and resources each will bring into the alliance to achieve their mutual objectives and gain a competitive advantage. Resources typically include patents; product lines; brand equity; product and market knowledge; company and brand image; and reputation for product quality, innovation, or customer service. Relationships with customers and suppliers are also desirable resources as are a convenient manufacturing facility, economies of scale and scope, information technology, and a large sales force. Alliance partners can contribute marketing skills, such as innovation and product development; manufacturing skills, including low-cost or flexible manufacturing; and planning and research and development expertise.

Companies form many types of strategic alliances. Some create horizontal alliances between firms at the same level in the supply chain; others define vertical links between firms at adjacent stages. The firms may also serve the same or different industries. NBC Sports and the Kentucky Derby share a partnership alliance that allows NBC to broadcast exclusive coverage of the annual horse race through 2010.[44] Alliances can also involve cooperation among rivals who are market leaders or between a market leader and a follower.

assessment check

1. Name four technologies businesses can use to improve buyer–seller relationships in B2B markets.

2. What are the benefits of effective supply chain management?

Evaluating Customer Relationship Programs

9 Identify and evaluate the most common measurement and evaluation techniques within a relationship marketing program.

One of the most important measures of relationship marketing programs, whether in consumer or business-to-business markets, is the **lifetime value of a customer.** This concept can be defined as the revenues and intangible benefits, such as referrals and customer feedback, a customer brings to the seller over an average lifetime, less the amount the company must spend to acquire, market to, and serve the customer. Long-term customers usually are more valuable assets than new ones because they buy more, cost less to serve, refer other customers, and provide valuable feedback. The "average lifetime" of a customer relationship depends on industry and product characteristics. Customer lifetime for a consumer product such as microwave pizza may be very short, while that for an automobile or computer will last longer.

For a simple example of a lifetime value calculation, assume a Chinese takeout restaurant's average customer buys dinner twice a month at an average cost of $25 per order over a lifetime of five years. That business translates this calculation to revenues of $600 per year and $3,000 for five years. The restaurant can calculate and subtract its average costs for food, labor, and overhead to

lifetime value of a customer Revenues and intangible benefits such as referrals and customer feedback a customer brings to the seller over an average lifetime, less the amount the company must spend to acquire, market to, and service the customer.

arrive at the per-customer profit. This figure serves as a baseline against which to measure strategies to increase the restaurant's sales volume, customer retention, or customer referral rate.

Another approach is to calculate the payback from a customer relationship, or the length of time it takes to break even on customer acquisition costs. Assume an Internet service provider spends $75 per new customer on direct mail and enrollment incentives. Based on average revenues per subscriber, the company takes about three months to recover that $75. If an average customer stays with the service 32 months and generates $800 in revenues, the rate of return is nearly 11 times the original investment. Once the customer stays past the payback period, the provider should make a profit on that business.

In addition to lifetime value analysis and payback, companies use many other techniques to evaluate relationship programs, including:

▷ tracking rebate requests, coupon redemption, credit card purchases, and product registrations;

▷ monitoring complaints and returned merchandise and analyzing why customers leave;

▷ reviewing reply cards, comment forms, and surveys; and

▷ monitoring "click-through" behavior on Web sites to identify why customers stay and why they leave.

These tools give the organization information about customer priorities so managers can make changes to their systems—if necessary—and set appropriate, measurable goals for relationship programs.

One writer suggests that, in developing the kind of loyalty that makes lifetime customers valuable, attracting the right buyers is just as important as treating them well. Lexus, for example, targets former owners of Mercedes and Cadillac cars, while Infiniti, with its focus on fashion and high performance, looks for younger drivers of sporty BMWs and Jaguars. Because these younger drivers are less loyal to car companies in general, the Infiniti repurchase rate is about 42 percent compared with 63 percent for the Lexus. Lexus is marketed to older drivers more attracted to long-term values such as service and reliability.[45]

A hotel chain may set a goal of improving the rate of repeat visits from 44 to 52 percent. A mail-order company may want to reduce time from 48 to 24 hours to process and mail orders. If a customer survey reveals late flight arrivals as the number one complaint of an airline's passengers, the airline might set an objective of increasing the number of on-time arrivals from 87 to 93 percent.

Companies large and small can implement technology to help measure the value of customers and the return on investment from expenditures developing customer relationships. They can choose from a growing number of software products, many tailored to specific industries or flexible enough to suit companies of varying sizes.

assessment check

1. Define *lifetime value of a customer.*

2. Why are customer complaints valuable in evaluating customer relationship programs?

Strategic Marketing Implications of 21st Century in the

focus on relationship marketing helps companies create better ways to communicate with customers and develop long-term relationships. This focus challenges managers to develop strategies that closely integrate customer service, quality, and marketing functions. By leveraging technology—both through database marketing and through customer relationship management applications—companies can compare costs of acquiring and maintaining customer relationships with profits received from these customers. This information allows managers to evaluate the potential returns from investing in relationship marketing programs.

Relationships include doing business with consumers as well as partners such as vendors, suppliers, and other companies. Partners can structure relationships in many different ways to improve performance, and these choices vary for consumer and business markets. In all marketing relationships, it is important to build shared trust. For long-term customer satisfaction and success, marketers must make promises they can keep.

Review of Chapter Objectives

Contrast transaction-based marketing with relationship marketing.

Transaction-based marketing refers to buyer–seller exchanges characterized by limited communications and little or no ongoing relationships between the parties. Relationship marketing is the development and maintenance of long-term, cost-effective relationships with individual customers, suppliers, employees, and other partners for mutual benefit.

Identify and explain the four basic elements of relationship marketing as well as the importance of internal marketing.

The four basic elements are database technology, database marketing, monitoring relationships, and customer relationship management (CRM). Database technology helps identify current and potential customers. Database marketing analyzes the information provided by the database. Through relationship marketing, a firm monitors each relationship. With CRM, the firm orients every part of the organization toward building a unique company with an unbreakable bond with customers. Internal marketing involves activities within the company designed to help all employees understand, accept, and fulfill their roles in the marketing strategy.

Identify the three levels of the relationship marketing continuum.

The three levels of the relationship marketing continuum are (1) focus on price, (2) social interaction, and (3) interdependent partnership. At the first level, marketers use financial incentives to attract customers. At the second level, marketers engage in social interaction with buyers. At the third level, buyers and sellers become true business partners.

Explain how firms can enhance customer satisfaction and how they build buyer–seller relationships.

Marketers monitor customer satisfaction through various methods of marketing research. They look to understand what customers want—including what they expect—from goods or services. They also obtain customer feedback through means such as toll-free phone numbers and Web sites. Then they use this information to improve. Firms build buyer–seller relationships through frequency marketing programs, affinity marketing, database marketing, and one-to-one marketing.

5 **Explain customer relationship management (CRM) and the role of technology in building customer relationships.**

Customer relationship management is the combination of strategies and technologies that empowers relationship programs, reorienting the entire organization to a concentrated focus on satisfying customers. Made possible by technological advances, it leverages technology as a means to manage customer relationships and to integrate all stakeholders into a company's product design and development, manufacturing, marketing, sales, and customer service processes.

CRM allows firms to manage vast amounts of data from multiple sources to improve overall customer satisfaction. The most effective companies approach CRM as a complete business strategy in which people, processes, and technology are organized around delivering superior value to customers. A recent outgrowth of CRM is virtual relationships, in which buyers and sellers rarely, if ever, meet face-to-face.

6 **Describe the buyer–seller relationship in business-to-business marketing and identify the four types of business partnerships.**

By developing buyer–seller relationships, companies work together for their mutual benefit. Advantages may include lower prices for supplies, faster delivery of inventory, improved quality or reliability, customized product features, or more favorable financing terms. The four types of business partnerships are buyer, seller, internal, and lateral. Regardless of the type of partnership, partners usually share similar values and goals that help the alliance endure over time. Two other types of business marketing relationships are cobranding and comarketing.

7 **Describe how business-to-business marketing incorporates national account selling, electronic data interchange and Web services, vendor-managed inventories (VMI), CPFaR, managing the supply chain, and creating alliances.**

National account selling helps firms form a strong commitment with key buyers, resulting in improvements in efficiency and effectiveness for both parties. The use of electronic data interchanges allows firms to reduce costs and improve efficiency and competitiveness. Web services are software applications that allow firms with different technology platforms to communicate and exchange information over the Internet. Vendor-managed inventory (VMI) is a system in which sellers can automatically restock to previously requested levels. The collaborative planning, forecasting, and replenishment (CPFaR) approach bases plans and forecasts on collaborative seller–vendor efforts. Managing the supply chain provides increased innovation, decreased costs, conflict resolution, and improved communications. Strategic alliances can help both partners gain a competitive advantage in the marketplace.

8 **Identify and evaluate the most common measurement and evaluation techniques within a relationship marketing program.**

The effectiveness of relationship marketing programs can be measured using several methods. In the lifetime value of a customer, the revenues and intangible benefits a customer brings to the seller over an average lifetime—less the amount the company must spend to acquire, market to, and service the customer—are calculated. With this method, a company may determine its costs to serve each customer and develop ways to increase profitability. The payback method calculates how long it takes to break even on customer acquisition costs. Other measurements include tracking rebates, coupons, and credit card purchases; monitoring complaints and returns; and reviewing reply cards, comment forms, and surveys. These tools give the organization information about customer priorities so managers can make changes to their systems and set measurable goals.

assessment check: answers

1.1 What are the major differences between transaction-based marketing and relationship marketing?

Transaction-based marketing refers to buyer–seller exchanges involving limited communications and little or no ongoing relationships between the parties. Relationship marketing is the development and maintenance of long-term, cost-effective relationships with individual customers, suppliers, employees, and other partners for mutual benefit.

2.1 What are the four basic elements of relationship marketing?

The four basic elements are database technology, database marketing, monitoring relationships, and customer relationship management (CRM).

2.2 Why is internal marketing important to a firm?

Internal marketing enables all members of the organization to understand, accept, and fulfill their respective roles in implementing a marketing strategy.

3.1 Identify the three levels of the marketing relationship.

The three levels of the relationship marketing continuum are (1) focus on price, (2) social interaction, and (3) interdependent partnership.

3.2 Which level is the most complicated? Why?

The third level is most complex because the strength of commitment between the parties grows.

4.1 How is customer satisfaction measured?

Marketers monitor customer satisfaction through various methods of marketing research.

4.2 Identify two ways marketers may obtain customer feedback.

Marketers can include a toll-free phone number or Web site address in their advertising; monitor Usenet, other online discussion groups, and blogs; and hire mystery shoppers to personally check on products.

5.1 Define *customer relationship management*.

Customer relationship management is the combination of strategies and technologies that empowers relationship programs, reorienting the entire organization to a concentrated focus on satisfying customers.

5.2 What are the two major types of CRM systems?

The two major types of CRM systems are purchased and customized.

5.3 Describe two steps a firm can take to rejuvenate a lost relationship.

Marketers can rejuvenate a lost relationship by changing the product mix, if necessary, or changing some of their processes.

6.1 What are the four key types of business marketing partnerships?

The four key types of business partnerships are buyer, seller, internal, and lateral.

6.2 Distinguish cobranding and comarketing.

Cobranding joins two strong brand names—perhaps owned by two different companies—to sell a product. In a comarketing effort, two organizations join to sell their products in an allied marketing campaign.

7.1 Name four technologies businesses can use to improve buyer–seller relationships in B2B markets.

The use of electronic data interchanges allows firms to reduce costs and improve efficiency and competitiveness. Web services provide a way for companies to communicate even if they are not running the same or compatible software, hardware, databases, or network platforms. In a vendor-managed inventory (VMI) system, sellers can automatically restock to previously requested levels. The collaborative planning, forecasting, and replenishment (CPFaR) approach bases plans and forecasts on collaborative seller–vendor efforts.

7.2 What are the benefits of effective supply chain management?

Managing the supply chain provides increased innovation, decreased costs, conflict resolution, and improved communications.

8.1 Define *lifetime value of a customer.*

In the lifetime value of a customer, the revenues and intangible benefits a customer brings to the seller over an average lifetime—less the amount the company must spend to acquire, market to, and service the customer—are calculated.

8.2 Why are customer complaints valuable in evaluating customer relationship programs?

Customer complaints give the organization information about customer priorities so managers can make changes to their systems, if necessary, and set appropriate, measurable goals for relationship programs.

Marketing Terms You Need to Know

transaction-based marketing 310
relationship marketing 310
frequency marketing 318
affinity marketing 318
database marketing 319

customer relationship management (CRM) 322
partnership 325
cobranding 326
comarketing 326
electronic data interchange (EDI) 327

vendor-managed inventory (VMI) 328
supply chain 328
lifetime value of a customer 329

Other Important Marketing Terms

external customer 312
internal customer 312
internal marketing 312
employee satisfaction 313
customer satisfaction 316
customer churn 318
interactive television 32
application service providers (ASPs) 320

grassroots marketing 321
viral marketing 321
buzz marketing 321
customer winback 323
business-to-business (B2B) marketing 324
buyer partnership 325
seller partnership 326
internal partnership 326

lateral partnership 326
national account selling 327
quick-response merchandising 327
Web services 328
collaborative planning, forecasting, and
   replenishment (CPFaR) 328
strategic alliance 329

Assurance of Learning Review

1. Describe the benefits of relationship marketing. How does database technology help firms build relationships with customers?

2. What types of factors might the firm monitor in its relationships?

3. What is an affinity marketing program?

4. What is an application service provider (ASP)? How does it work?

5. Distinguish among grassroots marketing, viral marketing, and buzz marketing.

6. Describe at least four qualities of a successful CRM system.

7. Explain how marketers can turn customers into advocates.

8. Describe each of the four types of business partnerships.

9. Give an example of cobranding and comarketing.

10. Why is it important for a firm to manage the relationships along its supply chain?

11. What is the most important factor in a strategic alliance?

12. Explain how a firm goes about evaluating the lifetime value of a customer.

Projects and Teamwork Exercises

1. With a teammate, choose one of the following companies. Create a plan to attract customers at the first level of the relationship marketing continuum—price—and move them to the next level with social interactions. Present your plan to the class.

   a. dog-grooming service
   b. health spa
   c. surfboard or snowmobile manufacturer
   d. pizza parlor

2. With a teammate, select a business you are familiar with and design a frequency marketing program for the firm. Now design a grassroots, viral marketing, or buzz marketing campaign for the company you selected. Present your campaign to the class.

3. A hotel chain's database has information on guests, including demographics, number of visits, and room preferences. Describe how the chain can use this information to develop several relationship marketing programs. How can it use a more general database to identify potential customers and personalize its communications with them?

4. Select a local business enterprise. Find out as much as you can about its customer base, marketing strategies, and internal functions. Consider whether a customer relationship management focus would sharpen the enterprise's competitive edge. Argue your position in class.

5. Suppose you and a classmate were hired by a local independent bookstore to help its owner win back customers lost to a large chain. Design a plan to win back the lost customers and rebuild those relationships. Present your plan in class.

6. Choose a company that makes great stuff—something you really like, whether it is designer handbags, electronics, the tastiest ice cream flavors, or the best jeans. Now come up with a partner for your firm that you think would make a terrific strategic alliance. Write a plan for your alliance, explaining why you made the choice, what you want the two firms to accomplish, and why you think the alliance will be successful.

7. With a teammate, interview a local business owner to find out what methods he or she uses to evaluate customer relationships. You might discover that the businessperson uses very systematic techniques or perhaps just talks to customers. Either way, you will learn something valuable. Discuss your findings in class.

Critical-Thinking Exercises

1. Suppose you were asked to be a marketing consultant for a restaurant specializing in a regional cuisine such as Tex-Mex, Cuban dishes, or New England clambake. The owner is concerned about employee satisfaction. When you visit the restaurant, what clues would you look for to determine employee satisfaction? What questions might you ask employees?

2. What types of social interaction might be appropriate—and effective—for a local bank to engage in with its customers?

3. What steps might a clothing store take to win back its lost customers?

4. Explain why a large firm such as General Mills might use national account selling to strengthen its relationship with a chain of supermarkets in the Midwest.

5. Why is it important for a company to calculate the lifetime value of a customer?

Ethics Exercise

Suppose you work for a firm that sells home appliances such as refrigerators, microwaves, and washers and dryers. Your company has been slowly losing customers, but no one seems to know why. Employee morale is sliding as well. You believe the company is run by honest, dedicated owners who want to please their customers. One day, you overhear an employee quietly advising a potential customer to shop at another store. You realize your firm's biggest problem may be lack of employee satisfaction—which is leading to external customer loss.

1. Would you approach the employee to discuss the problem?

2. Would you ask the employee why he or she is turning customers away?

3. What steps do you think your employer could take to turn the situation around?

Internet Exercises

1. **Customer loyalty programs.** Marriott has one of the oldest customer loyalty programs in the hotel industry. Visit the Web site (marriott.com/rewards/rewards-program.mi) to learn more about the Marriott Rewards program. How does the program work? What kinds of benefits are available to customers?

2. **Business marketing relationships.** Recently, Lexus introduced a "Pebble Beach" edition of the Lexus ES model. Go to the Lexus Web site (www.lexus.com) and research the marketing relationship between Lexus and the Pebble Beach Resort. What type of marketing relationship is this? How does the Pebble Beach edition of the Lexus ES differ from other models?

3. **Relationship marketing.** Review the material on relationship marketing in the chapter and then visit the three Web sites that follow. Identify at least three ways in which the brand's marketers have applied the principles of relationship marketing.
   a. Sony (www.sony.com)
   b. Swiffer (www.swiffer.com)
   c. Cannondale (www.cannondale.com)

Note: Internet Web addresses change frequently. If you don't find the exact site listed, you may need to access the organization's home page and search from there or use a search engine such as Google.

Case 10.1 Jive Software Strengthens Relationships

Jive Software CEO David Hersh has a vision of office work wedded to the social networking model, in which information

is as easy to use and share as it is on MySpace and Facebook. "We're still a long way from that," says Hirsch. "People live in e-mail and documents no one else can see." But with his company's new product, Clearspace, he wants to change the way people work.

Clearspace is a software tool that allows companies to set up and use collaboration and communication portals quickly and easily, without complicated installations or lengthy training. With these tools, employees in different departments, different divisions, and even different corporate partners in a virtual organization can use online forums, blogs, discussion rooms, and wikis to form new relationships. They can also work together by sharing documents, calendars, and ideas of all kinds.

Firms can also use Clearspace Community, a variation of the software, to communicate with their customers, trading feedback and customer support or spreading the word about new products. Nike, for instance, found Clearspace Community an effective way of turning runners looking for an Internet forum into buyers of its Nike Plus sensor, a device for tracking miles run and calories burned through sensors in Nike running shoes.

One big Clearspace client is EMC, a data-storage company with over 35,000 employees in locations as far apart as China, Russia, and India. With Clearspace technology, EMC's research and development employees can work together so effectively that new product ideas are hatched in days instead of months, with immediate input from hundreds of technical workers around the world. "This is transformational stuff," says EMC's vice president of marketing and technology. "It changes how business gets done."

Jive is no stranger to forming effective relationships. The company has made distribution deals with Oracle and other technology firms to help bundle and distribute its products in ways that have helped it grow from a Silicon Valley start-up to a profitable firm with about $20 million in sales. Jive has more than 1,600 customers, including corporate giants such as IBM, Nike, GE, Shell, Morgan Stanley, Dell, Citibank, Frito-Lay, Turner Networks, and Procter & Gamble. Another reason for its success is that it usually avoids selling to customers' corporate information technology departments, marketing directly to executives instead. One company blind-tested several brands of collaboration software, including Clearspace and Microsoft's SharePoint. Clearspace was the unanimous winner, and employees of the testing firm made bumper stickers reading, "Friends don't let friends use SharePoint."

Questions for Critical Thinking

1. Do you think the social networking model demonstrated by Facebook and MySpace can translate well into a means of building firms' relationships with their internal customers? Why or why not?

2. In what ways does Jive Software's marketing strategy rely on relationship building? Can you think of other ways it could use relationships to help grow its business?

Sources: Company Web site, http://www.jivesoftware.com, accessed May 12, 2009; Claire Cain Miller, "Higher Office," *Forbes,* June 2, 2008, pp. 62–64; Matt Asay, "Software That Sells Itself, Part II (Jive and Atlassian)," *CNet News,* May 15, 2008, news.cnet.com; Walaika Haskins, "Jive Adds Web 2.0 Rhythms to New Enterprise Collaboration Software," *TechNewsWorld,* April 7, 2008, www.technewsworld.com; "Jive Software Increases Market Share by 80%," Oracle Customer Case Study, June 2007, www.oracle.com.

Video Case 10.2   Relationship Marketing and CRM at Numi Tea

The written video case on Numi Tea appears on page VC-10. The Numi Tea video is designed to expand and highlight the concepts in this chapter and the concepts and questions covered in the written video case.

Talking about Marketing Careers with...
Libbey Paul

LIBBEY PAUL
Senior Vice President, Marketing
ACNielsen Homescan & Spectra

Getting into the heads of today's consumers—to understand their needs and offer them products when and where it best serves them—is no easy feat. But marketing research firm ACNielsen attempts to understand the behavior of consumer goods' purchasers so that its clients can meet and exceed customer expectations. ACNielsen works with some big names in consumer goods such as Wal-Mart and Kraft Foods. With literally millions of dollars at stake, those retailers and manufacturers need to target the right consumers at the right times with the right products to ensure success.

A lot of research and effort goes into what appears to be a simple product sitting on the shelf where you're shopping. We were fortunate to be able to speak with Libbey Paul, senior vice president of marketing at ACNielsen Homescan & Spectra, a global business unit of ACNielsen, to discuss her career activities and milestones and the processes involved in marketing research, market segmentation, and targeting.

Q: Tell us a bit about your background and the beginnings of your marketing career. How has your career developed through the years?

I have an undergraduate degree in business (with an art minor) and an MBA. Some of my most important business training, however, came with my first career stop in Brand Management at Procter & Gamble. P&G has a great reputation for training, and it's well deserved. Two of the lasting lessons I learned there were crisp communication skills, both written and oral, and how to create consumer-centered product concepts and marketing programs. I opted for a more entrepreneurial environment when I left P&G and joined a small, niche micromarketing firm called Spectra, where I started in a consulting and service role with direct client contact. In that role, I put my P&G training to good use and had the opportunity to support and learn from over 15 different consumer packaged goods manufacturers, ranging from Miller Brewing Company to

General Mills to Kraft to Con Agra. Six years ago, I moved back into a marketing leadership role at Spectra, helping to create new information and consulting services for this same client base. In the past year, Spectra merged with ACNielsen Homescan to form a consumer insights, segmentation, and targeting business unit.

Q: You head up the product management effort at ACNielsen Homescan & Spectra. What does your position involve? What other team members assist you and what are their roles? How does your job contribute to ACNielsen's overall goals?

Like any company, new products are the lifeblood of our company. My department creates the new solutions and software that our service team takes to our clients. Like most marketing departments, we interface with many other groups—clients, client service, research, software development, database management, legal, and finance—to create profitable, client-centered services.

Let me give you an example. Our clients came to us with a challenge: *Give us more precise consumer insights. Tell us how to grow sales in existing stores with this consumer insight. We know historical sales, but where could we sell more by better meeting local consumer needs?* We had several assets to apply to the problem—consumer trade areas tell us which consumers shop across different stores, and a demand forecasting model tells us how to project volume using consumer attributes. Marketing created business requirements with a clear statement of client needs and the kinds of reporting we'd want to provide to clients to help them solve the problem. We worked with research staff, who created and validated a new algorithm, the Navigator Model, which "consumerizes" store movement data by comparing sales rates to the people shopping in each store. The model output was then used to forecast which stores could be selling more products based on the kinds of shoppers they serve. Research and marketing worked with our

development group to build the model into end-user software, with a suite of reporting options. At the same time, marketing worked with legal and finance to develop contracts and a fee structure that created a profitable service model for Spectra. Finally, marketing worked with client service to create sales materials and a sales plan/forecast for this new service offering we called "Opportunity Finder."

Q: What types of problems do your clients typically need to solve, and how does ACNielsen help them? For instance, are they interested in setting strategic marketing plans, developing new products, or devising new advertising campaigns? Where are your clients located—in the U.S. or around the globe?

Our manufacturer and retail clients are all trying to drive efficient revenue growth in a flat to declining consumer packaged goods industry. Since many of our clients are global in reach, we are expanding our Spectra solutions beyond North America, though my focus is on the U.S. market. Across all markets, our mission is to help clients realize growth by focusing first on the needs of the consumer. We gather together many consumer insights, create a segmentation construct, called BehaviorScape, to connect those insights to each other and to our clients' marketing and trade plans, and then measure how our clients moved the needle and impacted their business.

What does this mean in plain English? We start with understanding how people buy products. Consider this example: Who buys Newman's Own Organic snack products? The consumers tend to be in the most affluent neighborhoods that we call Cosmopolitan Centers (upscale

Photo: Courtesy of ACNielsen Homescan & Spectra

cities) and Affluent Suburban Spreads (upscale communities surrounding cities). In fact, people in Cosmopolitan Centers buy at a 70 percent higher rate than the average U.S. household. This makes sense, as these are the most educated, health-oriented consumers. They're more likely to be effectively managing their weight, physically active, and consuming organic products generally. Armed with this information, we can then tell our clients how to more effectively reach these households. We know where these consumers are more likely to shop overall and, by store, where our clients should place advertising—TV, magazines, Internet. We also know what incentives these consumers respond to, what promotions they'll be interested in seeing. This information helps clients direct spending more intelligently, eliminating waste.

Q: How does ACNielsen Homescan & Spectra get the information it needs to help its clients? Do you observe shopper behavior, conduct focus groups, use telephone or fax questionnaires, collect data electronically, convene consumer panels, do mall intercept surveys—something else? Do you tap other secondary data sources such as U.S. Census Bureau data?

We get our information from many sources. With the exception of U.S. Census data and store databases, most sources are consumer panels or large-scale phone, mail, and/or Internet-based surveys.

- U.S. Census provides in-depth demographic and expenditure information down to low-level geographies.
- Trade Dimensions store database covers 350,000+ store outlets across 19 classes of trade, ranging from more conventional channels such as grocery, convenience, and mass merchandisers to emerging channels such as pet superstores.
- ACNielsen Homescan consumer panel data tells us which consumers buy what products where (how often, how much, and under what conditions), what their attitudes are, what their Internet habits are.
- Nielsen Media Research tells us what television shows people are watching.
- Mediamark Research Inc. (MRI) tells us what magazines people are reading

as well as other lifestyle and media information.

- Scarborough Research does extensive market-level surveys about local media, shopping, and lifestyle activities.
- Additionally, we integrate many client-custom data sources, from attitude and usage surveys to new product testing results. Also, we integrate store movement data either from ACNielsen or directly from retailers.

Q: You must amass a huge amount of data in your research. Does your business unit collect all of that information, or do you partner with other marketing research firms? How do clients use this data and in what form?

As indicated, Spectra collects very little information directly. We create store trading areas (called consumer trade areas) and then integrate and apply information to drive greater utility for our clients. As such, partnerships are essential to our business. We have many relationships both with our integration with Homescan and with other ACNielsen businesses that directly gather the information, as well as third-party data sources. To help our clients make sense of all this information, we provide user-friendly software applications as well as client service consultants, many of whom are on site at client offices.

Q: Do you provide information on specific market segments—based on age, gender, ethnicity, geographic location, or income levels—to your clients? Are they interested in certain target markets? Do your research methods vary from segment to segment?

We do many forms of segmentation for our clients, depending on their business needs. A key segmentation framework we have is called BehaviorScape. This segmentation was created by using millions of purchase transaction records from Homescan panel data to understand what household characteristics are associated with purchase behavior changes. From this analysis, we came up with two components for BehaviorScape, crossing BehaviorStages (which are created based on

age of head of household, age/presence of children, and size of household) by lifestyle (characterized by a neighborhood's affluence and urbanization). Take my household as an example. I live in a cosmopolitan center neighborhood and am in an older bustling family BehaviorStage. Compare that with my best friend who lives in San Francisco—she's an independent single who lives in a struggling urban core neighborhood. I guarantee that our refrigerators look totally different!

We have many other types of segmentation depending on the issues that a client is facing—boomer, Hispanic, gender, child/teen. We believe it is essential to be able to customize our segmentations based on client needs and the rapidly evolving consumer landscape. For example, a key component for Hispanic segmentation is level of acculturation. So we created a model to classify households (and geographies) based on acculturation level.

Q: What words of wisdom can you pass along to students who are preparing for their marketing careers? What work experiences or internships should they seek out to advance?

You learn by doing! Seek out classes or educational programs with the case study format; get work experience through internships. Read widely and form an opinion about what you see. *Advertising Age* and *The Wall Street Journal* are two sources, and I'm sure there are many other excellent options. Thoughtfully watch TV—what ads are working, which are not and why? What new products seem like a good idea, which are a bust? Most importantly, though, seek to make a difference in every endeavor you undertake. When talking with prospective employers, use the STAR method to describe your examples:

- Situation: Provide an overview of the situation and any relevant background information. Be specific and succinct.
- Task: Describe the tasks involved in that situation. What goal were you working toward?
- Action: Describe the action you took. How did you make a difference?
- Results: Explain the result of your actions.

GREENSBURG, INC.

This Isn't Your Father's Honda ... or Is It?

When you think about the kind of people who buy hybrid and alternative fuel cars, you're probably picturing a handful of smug, hipster vegetarians tooling around Seattle or San Francisco or Vermont. There's probably a lot of political bumper stickers on the back of the car. Maybe there's a kayak or mountain bike on the roof.

A few years ago, you'd probably be right.

When the Honda Insight, the carmaker's first consumer hybrid car hit the market in 2000, Roger Schofield, owner of Schofield Honda in Wichita, Kansas, thought he had it all figured out. For one thing, Wichita isn't exactly known as the epicenter of eco-consumerism. He'd probably sell a handful of the combination Nickel-Metal Hydride rechargeable cell/internal combustion-engine, gas-powered cars to a couple of single 20-somethings. The thing only had two seats and seemed pretty flimsy with its lightweight aluminum body. With a sticker price of $20,000, it was pretty pricey, too.

The first Insight Roger sold went to a 63-year-old.

The second person to buy one was 65.

As it turns out, Roger's experience was consistent with Honda's marketing research. They determined that the typical Insight customer was older, highly educated, probably with an engineering or science background—people who tend to be very research-driven. Nearly a decade later, almost every auto manufacturer has a hybrid car, SUV, or truck on the showroom floor.

Lee Lindquist, an employee at Schofield Honda, had always been interested in technology and the environment. As a member of the Sierra Club, an environmental group, he would often speak about the environmental impact of automobiles. He found that audiences were really interested not just in the fuel-efficient hybrids, but in alternative fuels as well. Lee did some research and learned that Honda had been selling a natural gas car to the City of Los Angeles since 1998. Because this car ran exclusively on natural gas, it was considered by the EPA to be the cleanest internal combustion motor in the market. Everything about the car was the same as a traditional Honda Civic—except the polluting emissions.

Lee asked Roger if he could try to bring a Natural Gas Civic GX to Wichita with the intention of selling the idea to large companies as a fleet car and to the City for municipal use. His pitch was simple. Once the municipality or company invested in the natural gas fueling station, fill-ups would be incredibly cheap—the equivalent of about $1.00 a gallon with the added plus of limiting their impact on the environment. It was a great value proposition.

Selling the car to the Average Joe was another matter entirely. The fueling stations cost thousands but even with the lower prices at the pump, it would be hard to justify that kind of expense.

When Roger heard the news that a tornado wiped out the small town of Greensburg, Kansas, he knew he had to help. Initially, the dealership made a generous cash donation to the relief efforts. When the news broke that the town had decided to rebuild green, Lee saw an opportunity to reintroduce the Civic GX to the people of Kansas. His thinking was simple. In rural farming communities, people are naturally greener than their city cousins; the environment is their livelihood, and the notion of conserving and recycling resources is a necessity, not a fad or a slogan on a t-shirt. It is not uncommon for farmers—large and small—to have propane or other sources of fuel to power their farming equipment. Kansas, and Greensburg in particular, provide a large percentage of the country's natural gas. About 100 of the county's residents lease parts of their land to gas companies to put in pumps and pipelines.

For Roger, it took a little more convincing. In the end, he decided to go for it. As he drove the Civic GX two hours west on Highway 54 to Greensburg, he started to have second thoughts. Wouldn't the $25,000 the car was going to set him back be better spent on a few prime-time local ads? What's a farmer going to do with a little Honda? In the end, he figured, at the very least, with all the media attention Greensburg was getting, their name would be out there.

In a well-attended ceremony, Roger handed the keys to the natural gas Civic to Daniel Wallach of Greensburg GreenTown. Residents came to check it out. No sales were made that day, but the story broadcast on KAKE, Wichita's ABC affiliate, was picked up nationwide. Before long, city and fleet managers from around the region, not just the city, were looking for the GX.

Questions

1. What are the primary market(s) for the Honda Civic GX?

2. Does it make sense for Scholfield Honda to market their alternative fuel cars to a mass audience? What are the up and downsides to this practice?

3. How important is marketing research in promoting a new product?

4. How might the Scholfield Honda brand have suffered if the Greensburg promotion was a flop?

5. Go to a few automobile dealerships and record the sticker prices of some hybrid and conventional vehicles for similar classes (sedans, SUVs). Conduct a survey of ten people from one demographic group and construct a survey to determine at what price they would purchase a hybrid over a traditional vehicle. Write a memo to Schofield about the strategies that he should use to market hybrid vehicles to the market segment you've targeted and support your conclusions with the data from your research.

© Steven J. Eliopoulos

Product Decisions

4

Chapter 11
Product and Service
Strategies

Chapter 12
Developing and
Managing Brand and
Product Categories

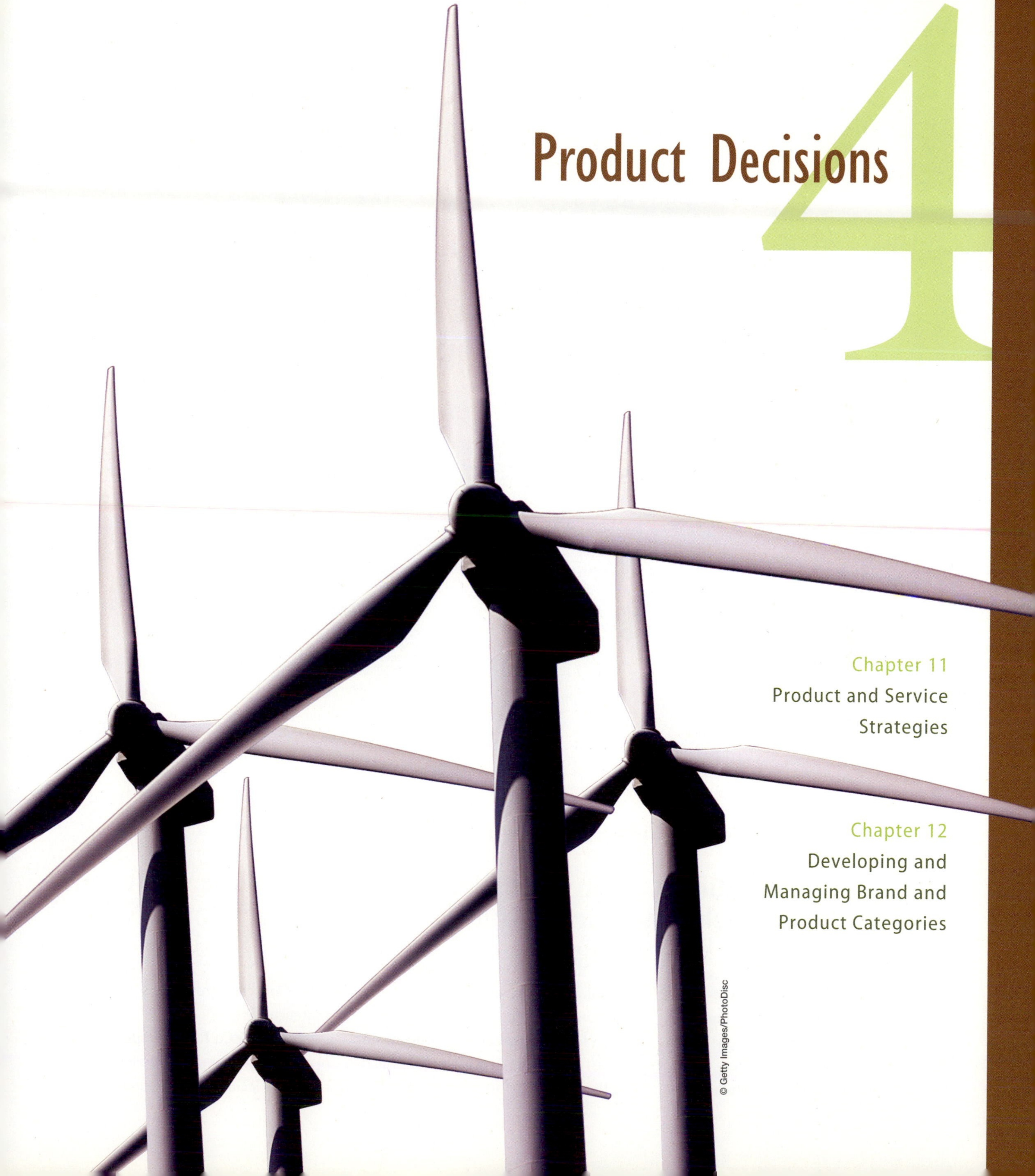

© Getty Images/PhotoDisc

CHAP**11**TER

Product and Service
Strategies

Green Works: Clorox Aims to Clean Up the Environment

When you do laundry, you want your clothes to come out clean. Add a little bleach, and those athletic socks emerge a crisp white. Clorox has been whitening socks, T-shirts, towels, and sheets—

anything needing a dose of bleach—for more than a century. While consumers are loyal to the brand, until now no one would have pointed to Clorox products as good for the environment. In fact, detergents in general, along with household cleaners, have come under fire from environmental groups for the chemicals they contain and for the residues they leave in groundwater and the soil. So why are people suddenly using *Clorox* and *green* in the same sentence?

The Clorox Co. has developed a line of natural, biodegradable household cleaners—including an all-purpose cleaner, window cleaner, bathroom cleaner, and others—called Green Works. The new products are available at traditional supermarkets like Safeway and Wal-Mart, so people don't have to travel to specialty stores to find them. They are also priced competitively. Best of all, they work. In the past, Clorox has been reluctant to join the league of green products because of the products' negative reputation among mainstream consumers. "There are four reasons this [green] category has been held back," explains Matt Kohler, brand manager for Green Works. "There's a perception that natural products don't work. They've been very expensive. People often have to go to special stores to get them. And there's not a brand that consumers know and trust." But the only growing niche of the $2.7 billion market for household cleaners that is the green one. So Clorox decided to take the plunge with a new group of products—its

first new branded line in 20 years. Company scientists came up with a line of cleaners that are at least 99 percent natural, biodegradable, nontoxic, and made from plant- or mineral-based ingredients instead of petroleum. In addition, they are not tested on animals.

Although getting these products on supermarket shelves wasn't easy, the company has another hurdle—to get skeptical consumers to buy them. Some might continue to believe the products won't work. Others might dismiss the line as an opportunistic attempt to cash in on an eco-friendly trend. Clorox, which had built a solid reputation for traditional cleaning products, didn't have expertise when it came to environmental issues. So the firm's marketers made a bold move: they approached the Sierra Club for help. If people were wary that Clorox could produce an environmentally friendly cleaner, maybe the Sierra Club

could provide some credibility. "The only way to [be successful with this] is to combine a very well-known cleaning brand with a very green brand. And we are the green brand," explains Carl Pope, executive director of the Sierra Club. After extensive testing, the Sierra Club agreed to endorse the Green Works line, which would ultimately bear the Sierra Club logo on its packaging. In return, the Sierra Club would receive a portion of the profits.

Both organizations realized the partnership would raise some eyebrows at first. But both pointed to the positive outcome for consumers, the environment, and the Clorox Co., the first major cleaning products company to launch an entire green line. "We'll definitely have some folks who are surprised by this decision," concedes Orli Cotel of the Sierra Club. "[But] we are supporting Green Works in hopes that more people will have access to these kinds of products."[1]

OBJECTIVES

 Define *product* and distinguish between goods and services and how they relate to the goods–services continuum.

 Outline the importance of the service sector in today's marketplace.

 List the classifications of consumer goods and services and briefly describe each category.

4 **Identify** each of the types of business goods and services.

5 **Discuss** how quality is used by marketers as a product strategy.

6 **Explain** why firms develop lines of related products.

7 **Describe** the way marketers typically measure product mixes and make product mix decisions.

8 **Explain** the concept of the product lifecycle.

9 **Discuss** how a firm can extend a product's lifecycle, and explain why certain products may be deleted.

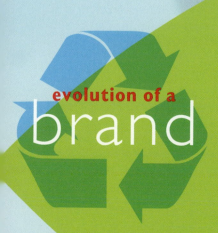

evolution of a brand

Clorox is a well-established brand, but not one traditionally associated with an environmental focus. So launching a line of green products required a boost from another well-known brand—the Sierra Club. While to some observers this may seem like an odd pairing, representatives from both organizations tout the arrangement as a win–win for both brands.

- Green Works is the first line of products ever endorsed by the Sierra Club, which is more than 115 years old. Why is this endorsement important to the development of the Green Works brand?

- In addition to the Sierra Club logo, the packaging for Green Works bears a fresh flower in bloom. These two images set Green Works items apart from other Clorox products. Is this distinction important in the minds of consumers? Why or why not?

chapter overview

We've discussed how marketers conduct research to determine unfilled needs in their markets, how customers behave during the purchasing process, and how firms expand their horizons overseas. Now our attention shifts to a company's **marketing mix,** the blend of four elements of a marketing strategy—product, distribution, promotion, and price—to satisfy the target market. This chapter focuses on how firms like Clorox Co. select and develop the goods and services they offer, starting with planning which products to offer. The other variables of the marketing mix—distribution channels, promotional plans, and pricing decisions—must accommodate the product strategy selected.

Marketers develop strategies to promote both tangible

briefly speaking

"Brand awareness is built by a thousand different interactions over time, where each one slightly builds or weakens [the customer's] impressions."

—Shelly Lazarus (b. 1947)
CEO OF OGILVY & MATHER ADVERTISING AGENCY

goods and intangible services. Any such strategy begins with investigation, analysis, and selection of a particular target market, and it continues with the creation of a marketing mix designed to satisfy that segment. Tangible goods and intangible services both intend to satisfy consumer wants and needs, but the marketing efforts supporting them may be vastly different. Many firms sell both types of products, offering innovative goods and ongoing service to attract and retain customers for the long term. Doing so can be profitable, as you'll see in this chapter.

This chapter examines the similarities and differences in marketing goods and services. It then presents basic concepts—product classifications, development of product lines, and the product lifecycle—marketers apply in developing successful products. Finally, the chapter discusses product deletion and product mix decisions.

❙ Define *product* **and distinguish between goods and services and how they relate to the goods–services continuum.**

What Is a Product?

At first, you might think of a product as an object you hold in your hand, such as a baseball or a toothbrush. You might also think of the car you drive as a product. But this doesn't take into account the idea of a service as a product. Nor does it consider the idea of what the product is used for. So a television is more than a box with a screen and a remote control. It's really a means of providing entertainment—your favorite movies, news programs, or reality shows. Marketers acknowledge this broader conception of product; they realize that people buy *want satisfaction* rather than objects.

You might feel a need for a television to satisfy a want for entertainment. You might not know a lot about how the device itself works, but you understand the results. If you are entertained by watching TV, then your wants are satisfied. If, however, the television is working just fine but you don't like the programming offered, you may need to satisfy your desire

assessment check

1. Define *product.*
2. Why is the understanding of want satisfaction so important to marketers?

for entertainment by changing your service package to include premium channels. The service—and its offerings—is a product.

Marketers think in terms of a product as a compilation of package design and labeling, brand name, price, availability, warranty, reputation, image, and customer-service activities that add value for the customer. Consequently, a **product** is a bundle of physical, service, and symbolic attributes designed to satisfy a customer's wants and needs.

product Bundle of physical, service, and symbolic attributes designed to satisfy a customer's wants and needs.

What Are Goods and Services?

Services are intangible products. A general definition identifies **services** as intangible tasks that satisfy the needs of consumer and business users. But you can't hold a service in your hand the way you can **goods**—tangible products customers can see, hear, smell, taste, or touch. Most service providers cannot transport or store their products; customers simultaneously buy and consume these products such as haircuts, car repairs, and visits to the dentist. One way to distinguish services from goods is the **goods–services continuum,** as shown in Figure 11.1.

This spectrum helps marketers visualize the differences and similarities between goods and services. A car is a pure good, but the dealer may also offer repair and maintenance services, or include the services in the price of a lease. The car falls at the pure good extreme of the continuum because the repair or maintenance services are an adjunct to the purchase. A dinner at an exclusive restaurant is a mix of goods and services. It combines the physical goods of gourmet food with the intangible services of an attentive wait staff, elegant surroundings, and perhaps a visit to your table by the chef or restaurant owner to make sure your meal is perfect. At the other extreme, a dentist provides pure service—cleaning teeth, filling cavities, taking X-rays. The dentist's office may also sell items such as night guards, but it's the service that is primary in patients' minds.

You can begin to see the diversity of services. Services can be distinguished from goods in several ways:

services Intangible tasks that satisfy the needs of consumer and business users.

goods Tangible products customers can see, hear, smell, taste, or touch.

1. *Services are intangible.* Services do not have physical features buyers can see, hear, smell, taste, or touch prior to purchase. Service firms essentially ask their customers to buy a promise—the haircut will be stylish, the insurance will cover injuries, the lawn will be mowed, and so on.

2. *Services are inseparable from the service providers.* Consumer perceptions of a service provider become their perceptions of the service itself. The name of a doctor, lawyer, or hair stylist is synonymous with the service they provide. A bad haircut can deter customers, while a good one will attract more to the salon. A house-cleaning service such as Merry Maids depends on its workers to leave each house spotless, because its reputation is built on this service.

3. *Services are perishable.* Providers cannot maintain inventories of their services. A day spa can't stockpile facials or pedicures. A travel agent can't keep quantities of vacations on a shelf. For this reason, some service providers such as airlines and hotels may raise their prices during times of peak demand—such as during spring break from school—and reduce them when demand declines.

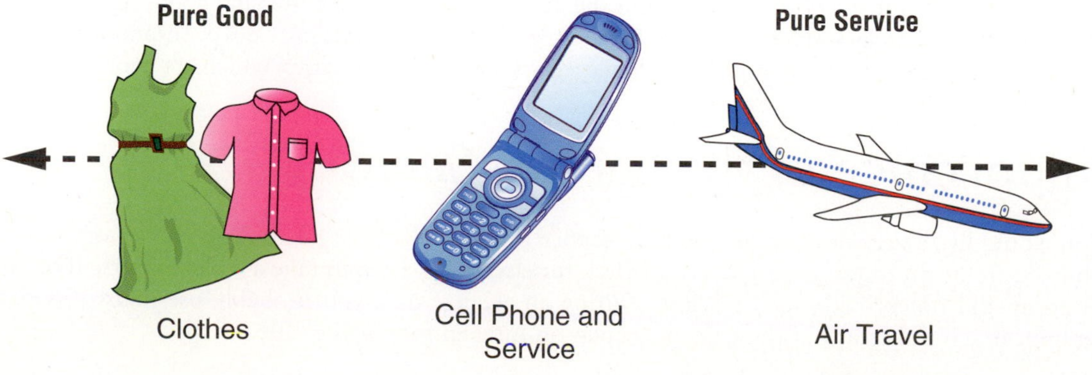

Pure Good

Clothes

Cell Phone and Service

Pure Service

Air Travel

figure 11.1

The Goods–Services Continuum

A product often blurs the distinction between services and goods. For example, U-Haul is a service that rents trucks and moving vans, which are goods.

© AP Images/Charlie Neibergall

4. *Companies cannot easily standardize services.* However, many firms are trying to change this. Most fast-food chains promise you'll get your meal within a certain number of minutes and it will taste the way you expect it to. A hotel chain may have the same amenities at each location—a pool, fitness room, free breakfast, or HBO movies.

5. *Buyers often play important roles in the creation and distribution of services.* Service transactions frequently require interaction between buyer and seller at the production and distribution stages. When a traveler arrives at the airport to pick up a rental car, he or she may have a choice of vehicle and additional amenities such as a GPS unit or car seat for a child. If the car is ready to go immediately, the customer will likely be satisfied. If the desired car is not available or is not clean or doesn't have a full tank of gas, the customer may not book with this company again.

6. *Service standards show wide variations.* New York City's posh Le Cirque and your local Pizza Hut are both restaurants. Depending on your expectations, both can be considered good restaurants. But the service standards at each vary greatly. At LeCirque, you'll experience finely prepared cuisine served by a highly trained wait staff. At Pizza Hut, you may serve yourself fresh pizza from the buffet. If you receive your dinner from attentive wait staff at LeCirque, you will be satisfied by the service standards. If the pizza at Pizza Hut is hot and fresh, and the buffet is replenished frequently, you will be satisfied by those standards as well.

Keep in mind that a product often blurs the distinction between services and goods. U-Haul is a service that rents trucks and moving vans, which are goods. LensCrafters provides eye examinations—services from optometrists—while also selling eyeglasses and contact lenses, which are goods.

Importance of the Service Sector

2 Outline the importance of the service sector in today's marketplace.

You would live a very different life without service firms to fill many needs. You could not place a phone call, log on to the Internet, flip a switch for electricity, or even take a college course if organizations did not provide such services. During an average day, you probably use many services without much thought, but these products play an integral role in your life.

The service sector makes a crucial contribution to the U.S. economy in terms of products and jobs. Three of *Fortune's* top ten most admired U.S. companies are pure service firms—Google, FedEx, and Southwest Airlines. But the other seven firms, all listed in Figure 11.2, provide highly regarded services in conjunction with the goods they sell.[2]

The U.S. service sector now makes up more than two-thirds of the economy, as the shift from a goods-producing economy to a service-producing economy continues. According to the U.S. Department of Labor, service industries are expected to account for 15.7 million new jobs by the year 2016.[3]

Services also play a crucial role in the international competitiveness of U.S. firms. While the United States runs a continuing trade deficit in goods, it has maintained a trade surplus in services every year since 1992.[4] However, although some economists believe more precise measurements of service exports would reveal an even larger surplus, others worry about the effect of offshoring service jobs such as customer-service call centers to nations such as India. While some firms have found success with offshoring their call centers, others such as Dell and U.S. Airways Group have decided to return much of their call center work to this country after receiving complaints from customers that they could not understand foreign employees' accents and did not get the quality of support or service they needed.[5] Termed *backshoring,* this trend is growing and actually becoming a marketing tool for firms. "Foreign call centers feed into the perception that companies aren't interested in their customers," notes one marketing researcher. Companies such as Royal Bank of Scotland and British energy supplier Powergen are advertising that their call centers are local, counting on the fact that the higher cost of operating local centers will be offset by the number of customers attracted and retained.[6]

In another emerging trend, firms are beginning to engage in **homeshoring,** essentially hiring contract workers to do jobs from their homes. Not only do firms save on office space, furnishings, and supplies, most also save on healthcare and other benefits. JetBlue is one well-known firm to practice homeshoring, with 900 home-based reservations agents based near Salt Lake City. Similarly, Miramar, Florida–based Arise Virtual Solutions supplies home-based employees to other companies, much the way an employment agency does. The practice is becoming so popular that some estimates expect the number of home-based call agents to reach 300,000 by the year 2010.[7] Firms that practice homeshoring are experiencing another benefit: a reduction in the use of energy and other natural resources, which decreases these firms' impact on the environment. Because employees are not commuting to work every day, and because an office does not have to be heated, cooled, and supplied with electricity and water every day, firms not only experience reduced costs but also a drop in emissions. These companies can highlight their green practices in marketing messages to customers.[8]

figure 11.2

America's Most Admired Companies

1. Apple
2. Berkshire Hathaway
3. Toyota Motor
4. Google
5. Johnson & Johnson
6. Procter & Gamble
(tie) 7. FedEx
(tie) 7. Southwest Airlines
9. General Electric
10. Microsoft

Source: "World's Most Admired Companies 2009," *Fortune,* http://money.cnn.com, accessed May 12, 2009.

homeshoring Hiring workers to do jobs from their homes.

Homeshoring entails hiring contract workers to do jobs from their homes. Firms do this to save on office space, furnishings, and supplies, as well as healthcare and other benefits.

© BananaStock/Jupiterimages

Observers cite several reasons for the growing importance of services, including consumer desire for speed and convenience and technological advances that allow firms to fulfill this demand. Services involving wireless communications, data backup and storage, and even meal preparation for busy families are on the rise. Grocery chain Trader Joe's is benefitting from this need for quick meals by offering partially cooked, fully cooked, and flash-frozen entrées that can be picked up and prepared in less time than meals made from scratch. Many traditional supermarkets offer prepared entrées and side dishes shoppers can buy at the store and heat quickly in the microwave at home. Consumers are also looking to advisors to help plan for a financially secure future and insurance to protect their homes and families.

Most service firms emphasize marketing as a significant activity for two reasons. First, the growth potential of service transactions represents a vast marketing opportunity. Second, the environment for services is changing. For instance, increased competition is forcing traditional service industries to differentiate themselves from their competitors. Providing superior service is one way to develop long-term customer relationships and compete more effectively. As we discussed earlier, relationship marketing is just one of the ways service firms can develop and solidify their customer relationships.

assessment check

1. Describe the goods–services continuum.

2. List the six characteristics that distinguish services from goods.

3. Identify two reasons why services are important to the U.S. economy and business environment.

4. Why do service firms emphasize marketing?

Classifying Goods and Services for Consumer and Business Markets

A firm's choices for marketing a good or service depend largely on the offering itself and on the nature of the target market. Product strategies differ for consumer and business markets. **Consumer (B2C) products** are those destined for use by ultimate consumers, while **business (B2B) products** (also called *industrial* or *organizational products*) contribute directly or indirectly to the output of other products for resale. Marketers further subdivide these two major categories into more specific categories, as discussed in this section.

Some products fall into both categories. A case in point is prescription drugs. Traditionally, pharmaceutical companies marketed prescription drugs to doctors, who then made the purchase decision for their patients by writing the prescription. These medications would be classified as a business product. However, many drug companies now advertise their products in consumer-oriented media, including magazines, television, and the Internet. This direct-to-consumer advertising tops $4.8 billion each year.[9]

consumer (B2C) product Product destined for use by ultimate consumers.

business-to-business (B2B) product Product that contributes directly or indirectly to the output of other products for resale; also called industrial or organizational product.

TYPES OF CONSUMER PRODUCTS

The most widely used product classification system focuses on the buyer's perception of a need for the product and his or her buying behavior. However, **unsought products** are marketed to consumers who may not yet recognize any need for them. Examples of unsought products are long-term-care insurance and funeral services.

However, relatively few products fall into the unsought category. Most consumers recognize their own needs for various types of consumer purchases and actively seek them, so the customer buying-behavior variations are key in distinguishing the various categories. The most common classification scheme for sought products divides consumer goods and services into three groups based on customers' buying behavior: convenience, shopping, and specialty. Figure 11.3 illustrates samples of these categories, together with the unsought classification.

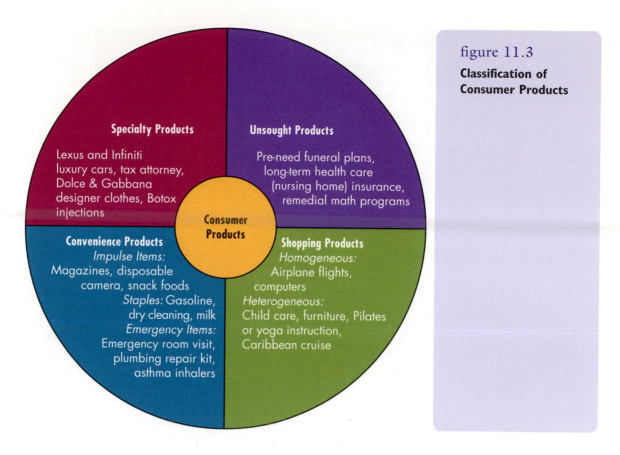

figure 11.3

Classification of Consumer Products

Convenience Products

Convenience products refer to goods and services consumers want to purchase frequently, immediately, and with minimal effort. Milk, bread, and toothpaste are convenience products. Convenience services include 24-hour quick-stop stores, walk-in hair or nail salons, copy shops, and dry cleaners.

Marketers further subdivide the convenience category into impulse items, staples, or emergency items. **Impulse goods and services** are purchased on the spur of the moment—for example, a visit to a car wash or a pack of gum picked up at the register. Some marketers have even come up with ways to make impulse shopping on the Internet attractive. Last-minute shoppers can use GiftBaskets.com's Gift Basket Emergency Service to choose and ship gifts quickly. They can select such items as the Simple & Elegant Spa Gift Basket for a new mom or someone in need of pampering or Mrs. Field's Basket of Nibblers & Brownie Bites for anyone with a sweet tooth by 1 p.m. Monday through Friday and be assured their gift will be delivered the same day. Emergency gifts don't come cheap—they range in price from about $40 to $125—but they fulfill an immediate need for goods and services. Shoppers can also sign up for the firm's reminder service, which sends them e-mail reminders of loved ones' birthdays, anniversaries, and any other occasion that might require a gift.[10]

Staples are convenience goods and services consumers constantly replenish to maintain a ready inventory: gasoline, shampoo, and dry cleaning are good examples. Marketers spend many hours and dollars creating messages for consumers about these products, partly because there are so many competitors.

Emergency goods and services are bought in response to unexpected and urgent needs. A snow blower purchased during a snowstorm and a visit to a hospital emergency room to treat a broken ankle are examples. Depending on your viewpoint, the products offered by GiftBaskets' Emergency Service could also fall into this category.

Because consumers devote little effort to convenience product purchase decisions, marketers must strive to make these exchanges as simple as possible. Store location can boost a convenience product's visibility. Marketers compete vigorously for prime locations, which can make all the difference between a consumer choosing one gas station, vending machine, or dry cleaner over another.

convenience products
Goods and services consumers want to purchase frequently, immediately, and with minimal effort.

Staples are convenience goods and services that consumers constantly replenish to maintain a ready inventory. Marketers spend a significant amount of money creating messages for consumers about these products.

© Image courtesy of The Advertising Archives

What is it about PINK that makes you feel so good?

Introducing *Passion Pink Venus.* From Gillette.

It shaves you so close, your skin stays smoother, longer.

Reveal the goddess in you.®
www.GilletteVenus.com

In addition, location *within* a store can make the difference between success and failure of a product, which is why manufacturers fight so hard for the right spot on supermarket shelves. Typically, the larger and more powerful grocery manufacturers such as Sara Lee, Kellogg, and General Mills get the most visible spots. But visibility to consumers sometimes comes at a price, often through a practice called *slotting allowances,* or *slotting fees*—money paid by producers to retailers to guarantee display of their merchandise. According to retailers, the purpose of slotting allowances is to cover their losses if products don't sell. But the Federal Trade Commission (FTC) investigated the practice of slotting allowances and found these fees vary greatly across product categories. In addition, a new trend regarding slotting allowances is emerging: growth in the private-label goods category has been so great over the last few years that retailers are will-ing to forfeit allowances they might receive so they can get into the manufacturing end themselves. This is particularly true of private-label organic and ethnic foods.

Shopping Products

shopping products
Products consumers purchase after comparing competing offerings.

In contrast to the purchase of convenience items, consumers buy **shopping products** only after comparing competing offerings on such characteristics as price, quality, style, and color. Shopping products typically cost more than convenience purchases. This category includes tangible items such as clothing, furniture, electronics, and appliances as well as services such as child care, auto repairs, insurance, and hotel stays. The purchaser of a shopping product lacks complete information prior to the buying trip and gathers information during the buying process.

Several important features distinguish shopping products: physical attributes, service attributes such as warranties and after-sale service terms, prices, styling, and places of purchase. A store's name and reputation have considerable influence on people's buying behavior. The personal selling efforts of salespeople also provide important promotional support.

Buyers and marketers treat some shopping products, such as refrigerators and washing machines, as relatively homogeneous products. To the consumer, one brand seems largely the same as another. Marketers may try to differentiate homogeneous products from competing products in several ways. They may emphasize price and value, or they may attempt to educate buyers about less obvious features that contribute to a product's quality, appeal, and uniqueness.

Other shopping products seem heterogeneous because of basic differences among them. Examples include furniture, physical-fitness training, vacations, and clothing. Differences in features often separate competing heterogeneous shopping products in the minds of consumers. Perceptions of style, color, and fit can all affect consumer choices.

Specialty Products

Specialty products offer unique characteristics that cause buyers to prize those particular brands. They typically carry high prices, and many represent well-known brands. Examples of specialty goods include Hermès scarves, Kate Spade handbags, Ritz-Carlton resorts, Tiffany jewelry, and Lexus automobiles. Specialty services include professional services such as financial advice, legal counsel, and cosmetic surgery.

Purchasers of specialty goods and services know exactly what they want—and they are willing to pay accordingly. These buyers begin shopping with complete information, and they refuse to accept substitutes. Because consumers are willing to exert considerable effort to obtain specialty products, producers can promote them through relatively few retail locations. In fact, some firms intentionally limit the range of retailers carrying their products to add to their cachet. Both highly personalized service by sales associates and image advertising help marketers promote specialty items. Because these products are available in so few retail outlets, advertisements frequently list their locations or give toll-free telephone numbers that provide customers with this information.

In recent years, makers of some specialty products, such as Coach handbags and Donna Karan clothing, have broadened their market by selling some of their goods through company-owned discount outlets. The stores attract consumers who want to own specialty items but who cannot or do not wish to pay their regular prices. The goods offered, however, usually are last season's styles. Tiffany has taken a different approach—broadening its base within its own store. Shoppers who visit the store on Fifth Avenue in New York City can take the elevator to the second floor, where they may purchase a variety of items in sterling silver at prices significantly lower than those for gold and gemstone jewelry. A number of these items are also available in Tiffany's mail-order catalog.

A WASHING MACHINE THAT'S EASIER TO UNLOAD?
(IT'S NOT MAGIC, IT'S WHIRLPOOL)

WE ASKED 40,000 PEOPLE WHAT THEY WANTED FROM A WASHING MACHINE. THE RESULT IS A BRAND-NEW MODEL WITH EVERYTHING YOU COULD ASK FOR BUILT INTO IT.

THE BIGGEST DOOR OPENING IN THE MARKET, SO IT'S EASIER TO UNLOAD.

A LARGE WASH DRUM FOR A MORE EFFICIENT WASH.

NEW SPECIAL PROGRAMME EXCLUSIVELY FOR SILK.

NEW EASY ACCESS WASH FILTER.

NEW INTEGRATED HANDLE WITH CHILD LOCK.

Whirlpool
BRINGS QUALITY TO LIFE

© Image courtesy of The Advertising Archives

Shopping products include tangible items such as appliances. Consumers buy these products after comparing competing offerings on characteristics such as price, quality, style, and color.

specialty products
Products with unique characteristics that cause buyers to prize those particular brands.

CLASSIFYING CONSUMER SERVICES

Like tangible goods, services are also classified based on the convenience, shopping, and specialty products categories. But added insights can be gained by examining several factors unique to classifying services. Service firms may serve consumer markets, business markets, or both. A firm offering architectural services may design either residential or commercial buildings or both. A cleaning service may clean houses, offices, or both. In addition, services can be classified as equipment based or people based. A car wash is an equipment-based service, whereas a law office is people based. Marketers may ask themselves any of these five questions to help classify certain services:

1. What is the nature of the service?

2. What type of relationship does the service organization have with its customers?

3 List the classifications of consumer goods and services and briefly describe each category.

3. How much flexibility is there for customization and judgment on the part of the service provider?

4. Do demand and supply for the service fluctuate?

5. How is the service delivered?[11]

A person attempting to classify the activities of a boarding kennel would answer these questions in one way; a person evaluating a lawn care service would come up with different answers. For example, customers would bring their pets to the kennel to receive service, while the lawn care staff would travel to customers' homes to provide service. Workers at the kennel are likely to have closer interpersonal relationships with pet owners—and their pets—than lawn care workers, who might not meet their customers at all. Someone assessing demand for the services of a ski resort or a food concession at the beach is likely to find fluctuations by season. And a dentist has flexibility in making decisions about a patient's care, whereas a delivery service must arrive with a package at the correct destination, on time.

APPLYING THE CONSUMER PRODUCTS CLASSIFICATION SYSTEM

The three-way classification system of convenience, shopping, and specialty goods and services helps guide marketers in developing a successful marketing strategy. Buyer behavior patterns differ for the three types of purchases. For example, classifying a new food item as a convenience product leads to insights about marketing needs in branding, promotion, pricing, and distribution decisions. Table 11.1 summarizes the impact of this classification system on the development of an effective marketing mix.

The classification system, however, also poses a few problems. The major obstacle to implementing this system results from the suggestion that all goods and services must fit within one of the three categories. Some fit neatly into one category, but others share characteristics of more than one category. How would you classify the purchase of a new automobile? Before classifying the expensive good, which is handled by a few exclusive dealers in the area as a specialty product, consider other characteristics. New-car buyers often shop extensively among competing models and dealers before deciding on the best deal. And there is a wide range of models, features, and prices

table 11.1   **Marketing Impact of the Consumer Products Classification System**

	Convenience Products	Shopping Products	Specialty Products
Consumer Factors			
Planning time involved in purchase	Very little	Considerable	Extensive
Purchase frequency	Frequent	Less frequent	Infrequent
Importance of convenient location	Critical	Important	Unimportant
Comparison of price and quality	Very little	Considerable	Very little
Marketing Mix Factors			
Price	Low	Relatively high	High
Importance of seller's image	Unimportant	Very important	Important
Distribution channel length	Long	Relatively short	Very short
Number of sales outlets	Many	Few	Very few; often one per market area
Promotion	Advertising and promotion by producer	Personal selling and advertising by producer and retailer	Personal selling and advertising by producer and retailer

to consider. At one end of the spectrum is a basic Kia or Ford that could be purchased for less than $20,000. At the other end is what people are calling European supercars such as the Porsche Carrera GT, at more than $500,000, or the Ferrari Enzo, which sells for around $1 million. These cars are fast, powerful, and hard to find—which boosts their value.[12]

So it's a good idea to think of the categorization process in terms of a continuum representing degrees of effort expended by consumers. At one end of the continuum, they casually pick up convenience items; at the other end, they search extensively for specialty products. Shopping products fall between these extremes. In addition, car dealers may offer services, both during and after the sale, which play a big role in the purchase decision. On this continuum, the new car purchase might appear between the categories of shopping and specialty products but closer to specialty products.

A second problem with the classification system emerges because consumers differ in their buying patterns. One person may walk into a hair salon and request a haircut without an appointment, while another may check references and compare prices before selecting a stylist. But the first consumer's impulse purchase of a haircut does not make hair styling services a convenience item. Marketers classify goods and services by considering the purchase patterns of the majority of buyers.

TYPES OF BUSINESS PRODUCTS

4 Identify each of the types of business goods and services.

Business buyers are professional customers. Their job duties require rational, cost-effective purchase decisions. For instance, General Mills applies much of the same purchase decision process to buying flour that Kellogg's does.

The classification system for business products emphasizes product uses rather than customer buying behavior. B2B products generally fall into one of six categories for product uses: installations, accessory equipment, component parts and materials, raw materials, supplies, and business services. Figure 11.4 illustrates the six types of business products.

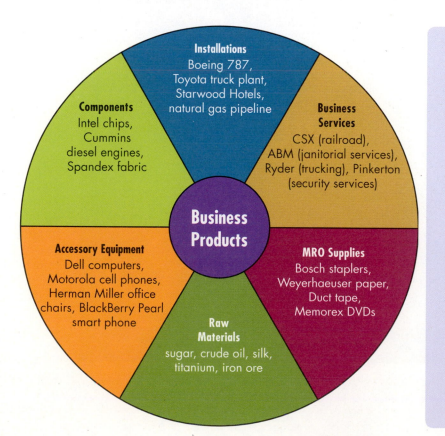

Business Products

Installations
Boeing 787, Toyota truck plant, Starwood Hotels, natural gas pipeline

Business Services
CSX (railroad), ABM (janitorial services), Ryder (trucking), Pinkerton (security services)

Components
Intel chips, Cummins diesel engines, Spandex fabric

Accessory Equipment
Dell computers, Motorola cell phones, Herman Miller office chairs, BlackBerry Pearl smart phone

Raw Materials
sugar, crude oil, silk, titanium, iron ore

MRO Supplies
Bosch staplers, Weyerhaeuser paper, Duct tape, Memorex DVDs

figure 11.4

Classification of Business Products

Installations

The specialty products of the business market are called **installations.** This classification includes major capital investments for new factories and heavy machinery and for telecommunications systems. Purchases of new Boeing 787 Dreamliner airplanes by Qantas and Kenya Airways are considered installations for those airlines.

Because installations last for long periods of time and their purchases involve large sums of money, they represent major decisions for organizations. Negotiations often extend over several months and involve numerous decision makers. Vendors often provide technical expertise along with tangible goods. Representatives who sell custom-made equipment work closely with buying firms' engineers and production personnel to design the most satisfactory products possible.

Price typically does not dominate purchase decisions for installations, although aircraft manufacturer Boeing recently landed an order from Bahrain's Gulf Air for 24 for of its 787 model passenger jets, which will be worth $6 billion. The 787 model has been extremely popular, with Boeing receiving orders for more than 800 of the aircraft.[13] A purchasing firm buys such a product for its efficiency and performance over its useful life. The firm also wants to minimize breakdowns. Downtime is expensive because the firm must pay employees while they wait for repairs on the machine. In addition, customers may be lost during downtime; in this case, travelers might choose to fly with another airline. Installations are major investments often designed specifically for the purchasers.

Training of the buyer's workforce to operate the equipment correctly, along with significant after-sale service, usually is also involved. As a result, marketers of these systems typically focus their promotional efforts on employing highly trained sales representatives, often with technical backgrounds. Advertising, if the firm uses it at all, emphasizes company reputation and directs potential buyers to contact local sales representatives.

Advertising is an important component in the marketing mix for accessory equipment, such as power tools.

© AP IMAGES/PRNewsFoto/Ridgid

Most installations are marketed directly from manufacturers to users. Even a one-time sale may require continuing contacts for regular product servicing. Some manufacturers prefer to lease extremely expensive installations to customers rather than sell the items outright, and they assign personnel directly to the lessees' sites to operate or maintain the equipment.

Accessory Equipment

Only a few decision makers may participate in a purchase of **accessory equipment**—capital items that typically cost less and last for shorter periods than installations. Although quality and service exert important influences on purchases of accessory equipment, price may significantly affect these decisions. Accessory equipment includes products such as power tools, computers, smart phones, and cell phones. Although these products are considered capital investments and buyers depreciate their costs over several years, their useful lives generally are much shorter than those of installations.

Marketing these products requires continuous representation and dealing with the widespread geographic dispersion of purchasers. To cope with these market characteristics, a wholesaler—often called an **industrial distributor**—might be used to contact potential customers in its own geographic area. Customers usually do not require technical assistance, and a manufacturer of accessory equipment often can distribute its products effectively through wholesalers. Advertising is an important component in the marketing mix for accessory equipment.

Component Parts and Materials

Whereas business buyers use installations and accessory equipment in the process of producing their own final products, **component parts and materials** represent finished business products of one producer that become part of the final products of another producer. Some materials—for example, flour—undergo further processing before becoming part of finished products. Textiles, paper pulp, and chemicals are also examples of component parts and materials. Bose supplies its luxury sound systems to auto manufacturers such as Audi, Infiniti, Cadillac, and Ferrari. Marketers for the auto manufacturers believe that Bose systems are a good match between premium sound and their top-line vehicles, comparing the high performance of the Bose sound systems to the high performance of their cars.[14]

Purchasers of component parts and materials need regular, continuous supplies of uniform-quality products. They generally contract to purchase these items for set periods of time. Marketers commonly emphasize direct sales, and satisfied customers often become regular buyers. Wholesalers sometimes supply fill-in purchases and handle sales to smaller purchasers.

Raw Materials

Farm products such as beef, cotton, eggs, milk, poultry, and soybeans, and natural resources such as coal, copper, iron ore, and lumber constitute **raw materials.** These products resemble component parts and materials in that they become part of the buyers' final products. Cargill supplies many of the raw materials for finished food products—dry corn ingredients, flour, food starch, oils and shortenings, soy protein and sweeteners, and beef and pork. Food manufacturers then take and turn these materials into finished products, including cake and barbecued ribs.[15]

Most raw materials carry grades determined according to set criteria, assuring purchasers of the receipt of standardized products of uniform quality. As with component parts and materials, vendors commonly market raw materials directly to buying organizations. Wholesalers are increasingly involved in purchasing raw materials from foreign suppliers.

Price is seldom a deciding factor in a raw materials purchase since the costs often are set at central markets, determining virtually identical transactions among competing sellers. Purchasers buy raw materials from the firms they consider best able to deliver the required quantities and qualities.

Supplies

If installations represent the specialty products of the business market, operating supplies are its convenience products. **Supplies** constitute the regular expenses a firm incurs in its daily operations. These expenses do not become part of the buyer's final products.

Supplies are also called **MRO items** because they fall into three categories: (1) maintenance items, such as brooms, filters, and lightbulbs; (2) repair items, such as nuts and bolts used in repairing equipment; and (3) operating supplies, such as printer paper and cartridges, mouse batteries, and pens. Office Max sells all kinds of supplies to small, medium, and large businesses. Companies can purchase everything from paper and labels to filing cabinets, lighting, computers, and copiers. The firm also offers print services, downloadable forms, and the production of custom artwork.[16]

A purchasing manager regularly buys operating supplies as a routine job duty. Wholesalers often facilitate sales of supplies because of the low unit prices, the small order size, and the large number of potential buyers. Because supplies are relatively standardized, heavy price competition frequently keeps costs under control. However, a business buyer spends little time making decisions about these products. Exchanges of products frequently demand simple telephone, Web, or EDI orders or regular purchases from a sales representative of a local wholesaler.

Business Services

business services
Intangible products firms buy to facilitate their production and operating processes.

The **business services** category includes the intangible products firms buy to facilitate their production and operating processes. Examples of business services are financial services, leasing and rental services that supply equipment and vehicles, insurance, security, legal advice, and consulting. As mentioned earlier, many service providers sell the same services to both consumers and organizational buyers—telephone, gas, and electricity, for example—although service firms may maintain separate marketing groups for the two customer segments.

Organizations also purchase many adjunct services that assist their operations but are not essentially a part of the final product. Cisco Systems offers its TelePresence Meeting service to businesses seeking to link people in a single interactive conference. The service combines voice, data, and video on the same network, providing an interactive and collaborative experience for participants.[17]

Price may strongly influence purchase decisions for business services. The buying firm must decide whether to purchase a service or provide that service internally. This decision may depend on how frequently the firm needs the service and the specialized knowledge required to provide it. In the case of TelePresence, firms may decide the cost of the service is offset by savings in travel expenses for meeting participants. In addition, the service offers convenience.

Purchase decision processes vary considerably for different types of business services. A firm may purchase window-cleaning services through a routine and straightforward process similar to buying operating supplies. By contrast, a purchase decision for highly specialized environmental engineering advice requires complex analysis and perhaps lengthy negotiations similar to purchases of installations. This variability of the marketing mix for business services and other business products is outlined in Table 11.2.

The purchase of the right business services can make a difference in a firm's competitiveness. The Regus Group provides businesses with facilities for meetings and conferences in 400 cities across 70 countries. The 950 facilities are fully furnished and equipped with every electronic medium and amenity a business could possibly need and are staffed by trained support personnel. Regus serves large and small companies, including those relying on mobile and home-based workers. The firm's services allow businesses to customize their office and meeting needs while saving money during periods when office space is not necessary.[18]

assessment check

1. What are the six main classifications of business products?
2. What are the three categories of supplies?

table 11.2 Marketing Impact of the Business Products Classification System

Factor	Installations	Accessory Equipment	Component Parts and Materials	Raw Materials	Supplies	Business Services
Organizational Factors						
Planning time	Extensive	Less extensive	Less extensive	Varies	Very little	Varies
Purchase frequency	Infrequent	More frequent	Frequent	Infrequent	Frequent	Varies
Comparison of price and quality	Quality very important	Quality and price important	Quality important	Quality important	Price important	Varies
Marketing Mix Factors						
Price	High	Relatively high	Low to high	Low to high	Low	Varies
Distribution channel length	Very short	Relatively short	Short	Short	Long	Varies
Promotion method	Personal selling by producer	Advertising	Personal selling	Personal selling	Advertising by producer	Varies

Quality as a Product Strategy

No matter how a product is classified, nothing is more frustrating to a customer than having a new item break after just a few uses or having it not live up to expectations. The cell phone that hisses static at you unless you stand still or the seam that rips out of your new jacket aren't life-altering experiences, but they do leave an impression of poor quality that likely will lead you to make different purchases in the future. Then there's the issue of service quality—the department store that seems to have no salespeople or the computer help line that leaves you on hold for 20 minutes.

Quality is a key component to a firm's success in a competitive marketplace. The efforts to create and market high-quality goods and services have been referred to as **total quality management (TQM).** TQM expects all of a firm's employees to continually improve products and work processes with the goal of achieving customer satisfaction and world-class performance. This means engineers design products that work, marketers develop products people want, and salespeople deliver on their promises. Managers are responsible for communicating the goals of total quality management to all staff members and for encouraging workers to improve themselves and take pride in their work. Of course, achieving maximum quality is easier said than done, and the process is never complete. Many companies solicit reviews or feedback from customers to improve their goods and services. As a customer, you can provide valuable insight to marketers by providing honest feedback, as described in the "Etiquette Tips for Marketing Professionals" feature.

WORLDWIDE QUALITY PROGRAMS

Although the movement began in the United States in the 1920s as an attempt to improve product quality by improving the manufacturing process, it was during the 1980s when the quality revolution picked up speed in U.S. corporations. The campaign to improve quality found leadership in large manufacturing firms—such as Ford, Xerox, and Motorola—had lost market share to Japanese competitors. Smaller companies that supplied parts to large firms then began to recognize quality as a requirement for success. Today, commitment to quality has spread to service industries, not-for-profit organizations, government agencies, and educational institutions.

Congress established the Malcolm Baldrige National Quality Award to recognize excellence in quality management. Named after the late secretary of commerce Malcolm Baldrige, the award is the highest national recognition for quality a U.S. company can receive. The award works toward promoting quality awareness, recognizing quality achievements of U.S. companies, and publicizing successful quality strategies.

The quality movement is also strong in European countries. The European Union's **ISO 9001:2000** standards define international, generic criteria for quality management and quality assurance. Originally developed by the International Organization for Standardization in Switzerland to ensure consistent quality among products manufactured and sold throughout the European Union (EU), the standards now include criteria for systems of management as well. Although most other ISO standards are specific to particular products or processes, ISO 9001 applies to any organization, regardless of the goods or services it produces. Many European companies require suppliers to complete ISO certification, a rigorous 14-month process, as a condition of doing business with them. The U.S. member body of ISO is the National Institute of Standards and Technology (NIST).[19]

BENCHMARKING

Firms often rely on an important tool called **benchmarking** to set performance standards. The purpose of benchmarking is to achieve superior performance that results in a competitive advantage in the marketplace. A typical benchmarking process involves three main activities: identifying manufacturing or business processes that need improvement, comparing internal processes to those of industry leaders, and implementing changes for quality improvement. The practice of benchmarking has been around for a long time. Henry Ford is known to have developed his own version of the assembly line—an improvement to gain competitive advantage—by observing the way the Armour and Swift meat-packing plants processed their meat-products.[20]

Etiquette Tips for Marketing Professionals

Giving Helpful Feedback

a s a consumer, you have positive and negative experiences with the goods and services you have purchased. When companies ask for feedback, they are looking for information that will help them improve the products they offer either by improving the items themselves or the services supporting them. You can use your training as a marketer to provide valuable feedback to companies. When doing so, keep in mind the following tips.

- *Be honest.* Describe clearly and accurately your experience with the company and its products, including salespeople, tech support, and anyone else with whom you have contact. This doesn't mean you should engage in an angry tirade if you are dissatisfied; instead, calmly outline the events.

- *Be brief and to the point.* Include the most important details relevant to the product's performance. Then the company can concentrate on exactly what needs improvement. Don't go into a long description unless you are asked for more information.

- *Be polite.* Avoid rude language or comments. The point is to find a solution to a problem, if one exists, not to offend those asking for your views.

- *Be positive.* Don't forget to tell the firm what *does* work and what you like about its products. Positive feedback lets a company know what it is doing right. Try to give specific examples—features of the products, results you've had, and so on.

- *Offer suggestions.* You might not be able to give a design engineer the specs to improve your car's interior, but you could say, "It would be great if I had a place to store my iPod," or "I wish the cup holder was easier to reach."

- *Thank the company for listening.* Even if you are taking an online survey, offer a thank-you to the firm if there is space for additional comments. The company's marketers will know you appreciate the opportunity to give feedback, and they might contact you for further insights.

Sources: "Feedback Etiquette," eBay, reviews.ebay.com, accessed May 12, 2009; "Forum Use and Etiquette," IBM, www.ibm.com, accessed July 16, 2008; "More than 650,000 Members Use Angie's List," Angie's List, www.angieslist. com, accessed May 20, 2008; Laurie Wilhelm, "Five Steps to Giving Constructive Feedback," *ArticlesBase,* March 17, 2008, www.articlesbase.com.

Benchmarking requires two types of analyses: internal and external. Before a company can compare itself with another, it must first analyze its own activities to determine strengths and weaknesses. This assessment establishes a baseline for comparison. External analysis involves gathering information about the benchmark partner to find out why the partner is perceived as the industry's best. A comparison of the results of the analysis provides an objective basis for making improvements. Large firms engaged in benchmarking include 3M, Bank of America, DuPont, General Mills, and Kraft Foods. These firms conduct formal, complex programs, but smaller firms may decide to use benchmarking as well.[21]

QUALITY OF SERVICES

Everyone has a story about bad and good service—the waiter who forgot a dinner order, a car mechanic who offered a ride to and from the repair shop. As a consumer, your perception of the quality of the service you have purchased usually is determined during the **service encounter**—the point at which the customer and service provider interact. Employees such as bank tellers, cashiers, and customer service representatives have a powerful impact on their customers' decision to return or not. You might pass the word to your friends about the friendly staff at your local breakfast eatery, the slow cashiers at a local supermarket, or the huge scoops of ice cream you got at the nearby ice cream stand. Those words form powerful marketing messages about the services you received.

Service quality refers to the expected and perceived quality of a service offering, and it has a huge effect on the competitiveness of a company. Toyota is so committed to service that it recently opened a National Customer Center (NCC) at its lift-truck manufacturing facility in Indiana. The NCC was designed specifically to serve its lift-truck customers and dealers, and it features a 360-degree showroom, a facility for live product demonstrations, a presentation theater, and a national training center.[22]

As a consumer, your perception of the quality of the service you have purchased is usually determined during the service encounter, the point at which the customer and service provider interact. Wal-Mart's "How may I help you?" vests encourage customer encounters.

© AP Images/Fick Bowmer

Unfortunately, poor service can cut into a firm's competitiveness. When Amazon.com Web Service's hosted storage service went dark one recent business day, its customers—companies who pay Amazon for the storage of data and other content—were frustrated and angry. Although service was restored within a few hours, Web entrepreneurs complained they had lost valuable business hours and might have to search for an alternative.[23] When customers receive this level of service, they often switch to a competitor.

Service quality is determined by five variables:

1. *Tangibles*, or physical evidence. A tidy office and clean uniforms are examples.

2. *Reliability*, or consistency of performance and dependability. "The right technology. Right away," asserts software solutions provider CDW.

3. *Responsiveness*, or the readiness to serve. "Citi never sleeps," say the ads for banking giant.

4. *Assurances*, or the confidence communicated by the service provider. "Let your worries go," reassures Northwestern Mutual, an investment and insurance firm.

5. *Empathy*, which shows the service provider understands customers' needs and is ready to fulfill them. "Clear your mind. Relax your soul," says Hotel Nikko San Francisco.

If a gap exists between the level of service customers expect and the level they think they received, it can be favorable or unfavorable. If you get a larger steak than you expected or your plane arrives ahead of schedule, the gap is favorable, and you are likely to try that service again. But if your steak is tiny, overcooked, and cold or your plane is two hours late, the gap is unfavorable, and you may seek out another restaurant or decide to drive the next time. The "Solving an Ethical Controversy" feature describes how the quality of service consumers expect on their cell phones can be affected by spam.

briefly
speaking

"If you can't smile, don't open a store."

—**Chinese proverb**

assessment check

1. What is TQM?

2. What are the five variables of service quality?

Development of Product Lines

Few firms today market only one product. A typical firm offers its customers a **product line**—that is, a series of related products. The motivations for marketing complete product lines rather than concentrating on a single product include the desire to grow, enhancing the company's position in the market, optimal use of company resources, and exploiting the product lifecycle. The following subsections examine each of the first three reasons. The final reason, exploiting the stages of the product lifecycle, is discussed in the section that focuses on strategic implications of the product lifecycle concept.

6 **Explain why firms develop lines of related products.**

product line Series of related products offered by one company.

Spam on Cell Phones: Who Pays?

Spam is irritating enough to receive on your computer. But what about your cell phone—especially when you pay for each text message you send or receive? U.S. consumers are receiving more than 1.5 billion unsolicited text messages—spam—each year. While that number is tiny compared with the overall number of messages sent, about 48 billion per month, consumer advocates and others expect that number to jump significantly as marketers look for new ways to reach potential customers.

Should consumers be forced to pay for unsolicited messages received on their cell phones?

PRO

1. Consumers who want to receive targeted marketing messages should be able to do so through their cell phone plans. Many companies, such as Verizon and AT&T, offer unlimited messaging plans, which would eliminate any personal cost.

2. Consumers have the option to disable incoming and outgoing text messages through most cell phone service providers, including Verizon Wireless, Sprint, T-Mobile, and AT&T. So they only pay for marketing messages if they want to receive them.

CON

1. Cell phone users are protected from spam by law—the Can-Spam Act—which prohibits firms from sending commercial messages to cell phones without "express prior authorization." Consumers who receive these illegal messages should not then be forced to pay for them by their cell phone companies.

2. Spam can attach itself to downloads—ringtones, games, and the like—opening a user's phone to unwanted messages without the user knowing it. The unwanted message arrives without authorization, and should not be charged to the consumer.

Summary

Many people agree that cell phone spam is worse than computer spam because users are stuck with the bill. "The reason this really burns people up is because they have to pay for messages they don't want, and they shouldn't have to," points out a spokesperson for Consumers Union. Fees users pay for messages represent a significant source of income for the cell phone companies, which are reluctant to absorb the cost of spam. Consumer advocates recommend that people register their cell phone numbers with the Do Not Call Registry, just as they would their home phone numbers.

Sources: J.R. Raphael, "The State of Spam: What to Expect in 2009," *PC World*, January 1, 2009, http://www.pcworld.com; Dave Cherry, "Cell Phone Spam on the Rise," *The Arizona Republic*, July 7, 2008, www.azcentral.com; Marshall Loeb, "Three Ways to Stop Cell Phone Spam," *MarketWatch*, July 7, 2008, www.foxbusiness.com; Laura M. Holson, "Spam Moves to Cellphones and Gets More Invasive," *The New York Times*, May 10, 2008, www.nytimes.com; Phuong Cat Le, "Consumer Smarts: How to Block Cell Phone Spam and Texts," *Seattle Post-Intelligencer*, June 16, 2008, seattlepi.nwsource.com.

DESIRE TO GROW

A company limits its growth potential when it concentrates on a single product, even though the company may have started that way, as retailer L.L.Bean did with its single style of boots called Maine Hunting Shoes. Now the company sells boots for men, women, and children, along with apparel, outdoor and travel gear, home furnishings, and even products for pets. The company, which has grown into a large mail-order and online retailer with a flagship store in Freeport, Maine, is nearly a century old. It is unlikely the company would have grown to its current size if the successors of Leon Leonwood Bean had stuck to manufacturing and selling a single style of his original Maine Hunting Shoes.[24]

ENHANCING THE COMPANY'S MARKET POSITION

A company with a line of products often makes itself more important to both consumers and marketing intermediaries than a firm with only one product. A shopper who purchases a tent often buys related camping items. For instance, L.L.Bean now offers a wide range of products with which consumers can completely outfit themselves for outdoor activities or travel. They can purchase hiking boots, sleeping bags and tents, fishing gear, duffel bags, kayaks and canoes, bicycles, snowshoes and skis, as well as clothing for their adventures. In addition, the firm offers Outdoor Discovery Schools programs that teach customers the basics of kayaking, fly fishing, and other sports directly related to the products they purchase from the retailer. L.L.Bean also offers many of its products sized to fit children—from fleece vests to school backpacks.[25] If children grow up wearing L.L.Bean clothes and skiing on L.L.Bean skis, they are more likely to continue as customers when they become adults.

Servicing the variety of products a company sells can also enhance its position in the market. Bean's Outdoor Discovery Schools programs are a form of service, as are its policy to accept returns—no matter what. Schoolchildren who purchase the firm's backpacks can return them anytime for a new one—even if the child has simply outgrown the pack. Policies like this make consumers feel comfortable about purchasing many different products from L.L.Bean.

L.L.Bean, a company that started with a single style of boots, now sells boots for men, women, and children, along with apparel, outdoor and travel gears, and even products for pets. They have grown into a large mail-order and online retailer.

© Susan Van Etten/Photo Edit

OPTIMAL USE OF COMPANY RESOURCES

By spreading the costs of its operations over a series of products, a firm may reduce the average production and marketing costs of each product. Hospitals have taken advantage of idle facilities by adding a variety of outreach services. Many now operate health and fitness centers that, besides generating profits themselves, also feed customers into other hospital services. For example, a blood pressure check at the fitness center might result in a referral to a staff physician.

assessment check

1. List the four reasons for developing a product line.
2. Give an example of a product line with which you are familiar.

The Product Mix

A company's **product mix** is its assortment of product lines and individual product offerings. The right blend of product lines and individual products allows a firm to maximize sales opportunities within the limitations of its resources. Marketers typically measure product mixes according to width, length, and depth.

7 Describe the way marketers typically measure product mixes and make product mix decisions.

PRODUCT MIX WIDTH

The *width* of a product mix refers to the number of product lines the firm offers. As Table 11.3 shows, Johnson & Johnson offers a broad line of retail consumer products in the U.S. market as well as business-to-business products to the medical community. Consumers can purchase over-the-counter medications, nutritional products, dental care products, and first-aid products, among others. Healthcare professionals can obtain prescription drugs, medical and diagnostic devices, and wound treatments. LifeScan, one of the firm's subsidiaries, offers an entire suite of products designed to help diabetes patients manage their condition. DePuy, another subsidiary, manufactures orthopedic implants and joint replacement products. At the drugstore, consumers can pick up some of J&J's classic products, such as Motrin and Visine.[26]

PRODUCT MIX LENGTH

The *length* of a product mix refers to the number of different products a firm sells. Table 11.3 also identifies some of the hundreds of healthcare products offered by Johnson & Johnson. Some of J&J's most recognizable brands are Band-Aid, Tylenol, and Listerine.

PRODUCT MIX DEPTH

Depth refers to variations in each product the firm markets in its mix. Johnson & Johnson's Band-Aid brand bandages come in a variety of shapes and sizes, including Finger-Care Tough Strips, Comfort-Flex and Activ-Flex for elbows and knees, and Advance Healing Blister bandages.

PRODUCT MIX DECISIONS

Establishing and managing the product mix have become increasingly important marketing tasks. Adding depth, length, and width to the product mix requires careful thinking and planning; otherwise, a firm can end up with too many products, including some that don't sell well. To evaluate a firm's product mix, marketers look at the effectiveness of its depth, length, and width. Has the firm ignored a viable consumer segment? It may improve performance by increasing product line depth to offer a product variation that will attract the new segment. Can the firm achieve economies in its sales and distribution efforts by adding complementary product lines to the mix? If so, a wider product mix may seem appropriate. Does the firm gain equal contributions from all products in its portfolio? If not, it may decide to lengthen or shorten the product mix to increase revenues. Geox is an Italian shoe manufacturer known for its patented breathable fabric that keeps feet cool and comfortable. With sales of $1.2 billion, Geox is expanding both ways—in width and

table 11.3   Johnson & Johnson's Mix of Healthcare Products

Over-the-Counter Medicines	Nutritionals	Skin and Hair Care	Oral Care	Medical Devices and Diagnostics
Motrin pain reliever	Lactaid digestive aid	Aveeno lotions	Listerine oral rinse	Ethicon surgical instruments & systems
Tylenol pain reliever	Splenda artificial sweetener	Clean & Clear facial cleansers and toners	REACH dental floss	Lifescan diabetes management products
Benadryl antihistamine	Viactiv calcium supplement	Johnson's Baby Shampoo	Rembrandt whitening toothpaste	Orthopedic joint replacement products
Mylanta antacid	Sun Crystals	Neutrogena soaps and shampoos	Efferdent	Veridex diagnostic tests

Source: Company Web site, www.jnj.com, accessed May 12, 2009.

length. The firm has added trendy new shoe styles, including strappy sandals and retro-inspired bowling shoes. In addition, Geox has launched an apparel line, including men's suits, made of similar breathable fabrics that help keep consumers cool and dry.[27]

Another way to add to the mix is to purchase product lines from other companies. Or a firm can acquire entire companies through mergers or acquisitions. Hershey acquired the organic chocolate company Dagoba to enter the premium organic chocolate market. "This business complements our premium chocolate growth platform and clearly positions Hershey as a key player within the high growth … organic market," announced Hershey president Richard H. Lenny. The purchase brings such premium products as Cacao Nibs to Hershey's cupboard.[28]

A firm should assess its current product mix for another important reason: to determine the feasibility of a line extension. A **line extension** adds individual offerings that appeal to different market segments while remaining closely related to the existing product line. In an effort to capture the interest of consumers who like to spend time outdoors, Boisset Family Estates, a French winery, began offering some of its wines in Tetra Pak bottles, which are made of recyclable cardboard. Tetra Paks are lightweight and easy to transport for picnics. In addition, marketers for the company note that the new packaging creates a carbon footprint ten times smaller than a glass wine bottle.[29]

The marketing environment also plays a role in a marketer's evaluation of a firm's product mix. In the case of Boisset, the social-cultural environment had shifted so that consumers were looking for ways to enjoy their wine outdoors, and they also wanted to purchase a product that had a reduced impact on the natural environment.

Careful evaluation of a firm's current product mix can also help marketers make decisions about brand management and new-product introductions. Chapter 12 examines the importance of branding, brand management, and the development and introduction of new products.

assessment check

1. Define *product mix*.
2. How do marketers typically measure product mixes?

The Product Lifecycle

Products, like people, pass through stages as they age. Successful products progress through four basic stages: introduction, growth, maturity, and decline. This progression, known as the **product lifecycle,** is shown in Figure 11.5.

The product lifecycle concept applies to products or product categories within an industry, not to individual brands. For instance, camera cell phones are moving rapidly from the introductory stage to the growth stage. Digital cameras are still in the growth stage, but moving toward

8 **Explain the concept of the product lifecycle.**

product lifecycle
Progression of a product through introduction, growth, maturity, and decline stages.

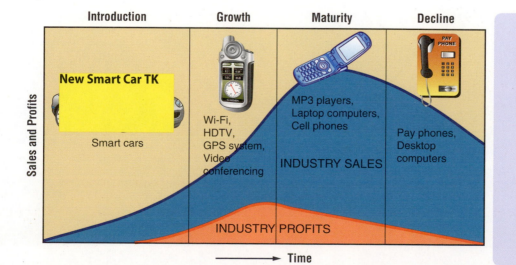

figure 11.5

Stages in the Product Lifecycle

maturity. Film cameras have declined so much that it is difficult for consumers to purchase film for their old cameras. There is no set schedule or time frame for a particular stage of the lifecycle. CDs have been around for more than a quarter of a century but are declining due to the increase in digital music downloads.[30]

INTRODUCTORY STAGE

During the **introductory stage** of the product lifecycle, a firm works to stimulate demand for the new market entry. Products in this stage might bring new technology to a product category. Because the product is unknown to the public, promotional campaigns stress information about its features. Additional promotions try to induce distribution channel members to carry the product. In this phase, the public becomes acquainted with the item's merits and begins to accept it.

A product whose introductory stage has been successful is the GPS mapping device. Although global positioning systems have been around for a number of years, their introduction to the consumer market was recent. By promoting its practical applications and making the devices easy to use, marketers have seen GPS sales increase rapidly, moving the products quickly toward the growth stage. Garmin now holds 56 percent of the U.S. consumer market for GPS devices, followed by Magellan and TomTom.[31]

Technical problems and financial losses are common during the introductory stage as companies fine-tune product design and spend money on advertising. Many users remember early problems with the Internet—jammed portals, order fulfilling glitches, dot-coms that went bust. But DVD players and camera phones experienced few of these setbacks. Users of GPS devices reported some glitches but also conceded that some problems stem from learning how to operate the devices correctly.

The GPS mapping device has had a successful introductory stage. By promoting its practical applications and making the devices easy to use, marketers have seen GPS sales increase rapidly, moving the product toward the growth stage.

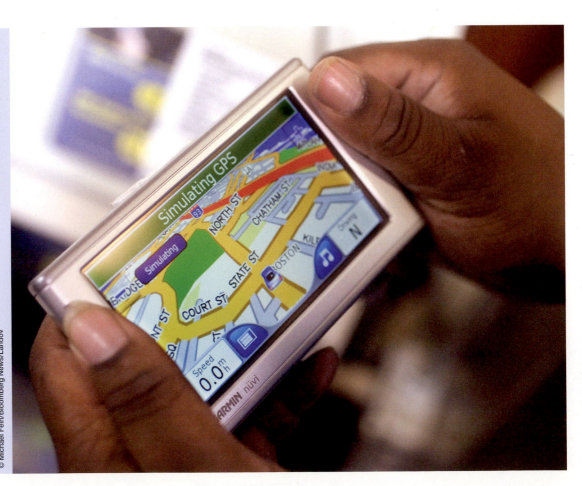

© Michael Fein/Bloomberg News/Landov

GROWTH STAGE

Sales volume rises rapidly during the **growth stage** as new customers make initial purchases and early buyers repurchase the product, such as camera phones and GPS devices. The growth stage usually begins when a firm starts to realize substantial profits from its investment. Word-of-mouth reports, mass advertising, and lowered prices all encourage hesitant buyers to make trial purchases of new products. In the case of big-screen TVs, both the plasma and LCD versions, low prices have not been a factor—many cost several thousand dollars. Big-screen now refers to a TV that is about 60 inches. As sales volume rises, competitors enter the marketplace, creating new challenges for marketers. As companies with competing technologies vied for dominance over the last few years, the TVs themselves grew larger and larger. Shoppers can purchase a 63-inch Samsung Plasma HDTV or a 65-inch Panasonic Plasma HDTV for around $5,000, or opt for the less-expensive 42-inch Toshiba at about $1,000.[32]

© Jonathan Ferrey/Getty Images for Nike

Nike running shoes could be classified in the maturity stage, but the company has unveiled the next generation of running shoes—the Flywire. Nike could be looking at a new life cycle for its shoes.

MATURITY STAGE

Sales of a product category continue to grow during the early part of the **maturity stage** but eventually reach a plateau as the backlog of potential customers dwindles. By this time, many competitors have entered the market, and the firm's profits begin to decline as competition intensifies.

At this stage in the product lifecycle, differences between competing products diminish as competitors discover the product and promotional characteristics most desired by customers. Available supplies exceed industry demand for the first time. Companies can increase their sales and market shares only at the expense of competitors, so the competitive environment becomes increasingly important. In the maturity stage, heavy promotional outlays emphasize any differences still separating competing products, and brand competition intensifies. Some firms try to differentiate their products by focusing on attributes such as quality, reliability, and service. Others focus on redesign or other ways of extending the product lifecycle. Nike running shoes could be said to be in the maturity stage. With hundreds of running shoes on the market, it is difficult to differentiate competing products. But with new technology combining materials that are both lightweight and strong, Nike has unveiled the next generation of running shoes: the Flywire. Each shoe weighs only one ounce and can take the pounding of an Olympic runner. The shoes are so simple and inexpensive to manufacture that Nike could be looking at a whole new lifecycle for its time-honored shoes.[33]

DECLINE STAGE

In the **decline stage** of a product's life, innovations or shifts in consumer preferences bring about an absolute decline in industry sales. Dial telephones became touch-tone phones, which evolved to portable phones, which are now being replaced with conventional cell phones, which in turn are being replaced with camera phones. Thirty-five-millimeter home-movie film was replaced with videotape, which is now being replaced with DVD technology.

Some manufacturers refuse to give up in the decline stage. Young consumers, accustomed to CDs and digital downloads, are beginning to turn their attention to vinyl records. They have discovered their parents' and grandparents' collections of LPs, and hauled old record turntables out of the attic. If curiosity led them to the discovery, the sound and graphics of a record seems to be holding their interest. Marketers in the music industry have taken notice, and some bands have begun to issue limited numbers of albums along with CDs and MP3 formats. They don't expect vinyl to become the primary medium for music—but are happy to resurrect a classic product for a new generation of listeners.[34] Drug manufacturer Pfizer devised a new strategy to keep itself viable when several of its name-brand drugs were facing the end of their patents, as the "Marketing Success" feature discusses. The next section of this chapter discusses more specific strategies for extending the lifecycle of a product.

It is important to remember that the traditional product lifecycle differs from fad cycles. Fashions and fads profoundly influence marketing strategies. Fashions are currently popular products that tend to follow recurring lifecycles. For example, bell-bottom pants popular in the 1960s and 1970s have returned as flares or boot-cut pants. In contrast, fads are products with abbreviated lifecycles. Most fads experience short-lived popularity and then quickly fade, although some maintain residual markets among certain segments. Webkinz are an example of a fad.

assessment check

1. Identify the four stages of the product lifecycle.

2. During which stage or stages are products likely to attract the most new customers?

⑨ **Discuss how a firm can extend a product's lifecycle, and explain why certain products may be deleted.**

Extending the Product Lifecycle

Marketers usually try to extend each stage of the lifecycles for their products as long as possible. Product lifecycles can stretch indefinitely as a result of decisions designed to increase the frequency of use by current customers, increase the number of users for the product, find new uses, or change package sizes, labels, or product quality.

INCREASING FREQUENCY OF USE

During the maturity stage, the sales curve for a product category reaches a maximum point if the competitors exhaust the supply of potential customers who previously had not made purchases. However, if current customers buy more frequently than they formerly did, total sales will rise even though no new buyers enter the market.

For instance, consumers buy some products during certain seasons of the year. Marketers can boost purchase frequency by persuading these people to try the product year round. For decades, most people used sunscreen only during warm and sunny seasons of the year. With greater warnings about the risks of sun damage and skin cancer, however, companies now advertise the benefits of using sunscreen year round. In another change, Hershey now offers its famous Hershey's Kisses with personalized messages such as "Congratulations," "It's a Boy," and "Happy Birthday" to celebrate personal events.

INCREASING THE NUMBER OF USERS

A second strategy for extending the product lifecycle seeks to increase the overall market size by attracting new customers who previously have not used the product. Marketers may find their products in different stages of the lifecycle in different countries. This difference can help firms extend product growth. Items that have reached the maturity stage in the United States may still be in the introductory stage somewhere else.

NBC Universal recently announced plans to start a 24-hour local news channel in New York. The network will rebuild the newsroom of its flagship station, WNBC Channel 4, integrating its content with the new channel, the local Web site, and on-location video displayed at gas pumps and in taxicabs. With the change, NBC hopes to gain additional viewers.[35]

FINDING NEW USES

Finding new uses for a product is an excellent strategy for extending a product's lifecycle. New applications for mature products include oatmeal as a cholesterol reducer, antacids as a calcium supplement, and aspirin for promoting heart health.

Marketers sometimes conduct contests or surveys to identify new uses for their products. They may post the results or their own new ideas on their Web sites. On its Web site, Arm & Hammer cites a variety of alternative uses throughout the house for its baking soda. Consumers can use baking soda to clean crayon off walls, as an antacid to settle an upset stomach, and as an agent to balance the pH in swimming pool water. The firm has even developed a new product—a waterproof resealable pouch—that consumers can use for poolside storage of their Arm & Hammer baking soda.[36]

CHANGING PACKAGE SIZES, LABELS, OR PRODUCT QUALITY

Many firms try to extend their product lifecycles by introducing physical changes in their offerings. Alternatively, new packaging and labels with updated images and slogans can help revitalize a product. Procter & Gamble rejuvenated its Herbal Essences shampoo line by aiming at a younger generation of consumers with new packaging and language. Instead of referring to dandruff control, marketing messages point to "no flaking away." Different hair style products were given updated names such as "totally twisted" and "drama clean." The shampoo and conditioner bottles are curved so that they fit together on the store shelf or bathroom counter.[37]

Procter & Gamble rejuvenated its Herbal Essences shampoo line by aiming at a younger generation of consumers with new packaging and language. Different hair style products were given updated names such as "totally twisted."

Changes in product size can lengthen a product's lifecycle. Food marketers have brought out small packages designed to appeal to one-person households and extra-large containers for customers who want to buy in bulk. Other firms offer their products in convenient packages for use away from home or for use at the office. Intelligentsia Coffee has stopped selling its espresso and coffee in 20-ounce sizes, opting instead for the 12-ounce cup. Company marketers reason that 20 ounces dilutes the flavor of the beverages and reduces the time the coffee and espresso remain hot. They also say that the 20-ounce size isn't as popular among its customers anyway and that eliminating it from the menu was not a difficult choice.[38]

Product Deletion Decisions

To avoid wasting resources promoting unpromising products, marketers must sometimes prune product lines and eliminate marginal products. Marketers typically face this decision during the late maturity and early decline stages of the product lifecycle. Periodic reviews of weak products should justify either eliminating or retaining them. After battling it out with Sony in the DVD player arena, Toshiba finally conceded defeat and announced it would stop making its HD DVD player. That left Sony the winner in the marketplace with its Blu-ray format.

A firm may continue to carry an unprofitable item to provide a complete line for its customers. For example, while most grocery stores lose money on bulky, low-unit-value items such as salt, they continue to carry these items to meet shopper demand.

Shortages of raw materials sometimes prompt companies to discontinue production and marketing of previously profitable items. A firm may even drop a profitable item that fails to fit into its existing product line, or fails to fit the direction in which the firm wants to grow. Some of these products return to the market courtesy of other firms that purchase these "orphan brands" from the original manufacturers. Eagle Snacks is one such brand. Reserve Brands obtained an exclusive license to market the formerly defunct Eagle Snacks brand, hoping to attract consumers nostalgic for the many flavors of potato chips once produced by Anheuser-Busch. When surveyed, many consumers never even realized that Eagle Snacks were gone, so brand awareness was still intact. In addition to the traditional Eagle favorites, Reserve Brands is launching new snacks under the Eagle name, including Poppers and Eagle Bursts.[39]

Strategic Implications of Marketing in the 21st Century

marketers who want their businesses to succeed continue to develop new goods and services to attract and satisfy customers. They engage in continuous improvement activities, focusing on quality and customer service. And they continually evaluate their company's mix of products.

Marketers everywhere are constantly developing new and better products that fit their firm's overall strategy. Technological innovations are one area in which new products quickly replace old ones. Marketers are sometimes faced with the dilemma of lagging sales for formerly popular products. They must come up with ways to extend the lives of certain products to extend their firms' profitability and sometimes must recognize and delete those that no longer meet expectations.

Marketing Success

Pfizer and Wyeth: Together They'll Live a Longer Life

Background. Several years ago, Pfizer was already the largest pharmaceutical company in the world. Its research labs enjoyed a $7 billion annual budget to develop the drugs it was well-known for: traditional oral medicines. But the pharmaceutical industry does not depend on innovation alone for its revenues; firms also rely on the life of a patent to help them recoup the money they spend developing a drug.

The Challenge. Despite a rich research budget, Pfizer recently faced the expiration of some major patents, which would allow competitors to manufacture their own versions of the drugs. In particular, the patent for anticholesterol drug Lipitor is expiring in 2011. Lipitor represented a whopping 13 percent of Pfizer's annual revenues. As Lipitor enters the next stage of the product life cycle, Pfizer did not have enough

Review of Chapter Objectives

1   Define *product* and distinguish between goods and services and how they relate to the goods–services continuum.

Marketers define a product as the bundle of physical, service, and symbolic attributes designed to satisfy customers' wants and needs. Goods are tangible products customers can see, hear, smell, taste, or touch. Services are intangible tasks that satisfy the needs of customers. Goods represent one end of a continuum, and services represent the other.

2   Outline the importance of the service sector in today's marketplace.

The service sector makes a crucial contribution to the U.S. economy in terms of products and jobs. The U.S. service sector now makes up more than two-thirds of the economy. Services have grown because of consumers' desire for speed, convenience, and technological advances.

3   List the classifications of consumer goods and services and briefly describe each category.

Consumer products—goods and services—are classified as convenience products (frequently purchased items), shopping products (products purchased after comparison), and specialty products (those offering unique characteristics that consumers prize).

4   Identify each of the types of business goods and services.

Business products are classified as installations (major capital investments), accessory equipment (capital items that cost less and last for shorter periods than installations), component parts and materials (finished business products of one producer that become part of the final products of another producer), raw materials (natural resources such as lumber, beef, or cotton), supplies (regular expenses a firm incurs in daily operations), and business services (the intangible products firms buy to facilitate their production and operating processes).

5   Discuss how quality is used by marketers as a product strategy.

Many companies use total quality management (TQM) in an effort to encourage all employees to participate in producing the best goods and services possible. Companies may also participate in ISO 9001:2000 certification or benchmarking to evaluate and improve quality. Consumers often evaluate service quality on the basis of tangibles, reliability, responsiveness, assurance, and empathy, so marketers of service firms strive to excel in all of these areas.

6   Explain why firms develop lines of related products.

Companies usually produce several related products rather than individual ones to achieve the objectives of growth, optimal use of company resources, and increased company importance in the market, and to make optimal use of the product lifecycle.

---

new medicines coming up to replace it. And other patents were also poised to expire, so Pfizer was faced with a potential loss of 70 percent of its annual revenues by the year 2015.

The Strategy. With time running out, Pfizer made a bold move—it acquired fellow drug manufacturer Wyeth. The firm didn't merge with Wyeth to knock out the competition or grow larger. The strategy was to add a whole new list of drugs—at varying stages of the product life cycle—to its roster. Most of Wyeth's products are vaccines and biotech drugs that are injectable or given intravenously. The merger of the two firms would create a pharmaceutical giant that would be balanced in its product offerings.

The Outcome. "We're well poised to deliver a whole crop of new products," said Martin Mackay, head of the restructured company's PharmaTherapeutics Group. Other firms took notice. "[This year] is set to redefine the structure and dynamics of the pharmaceutical industry in a way not seen since the year 2000," wrote one industry observer who predicted future mergers of a similar nature, which would ultimately consolidate the industry competitors.

Sources: Company Web site, http://www.pfizer.com, accessed April 24, 2009; "Pfizer/Wyeth Merger Will Force Big Pharma to Consolidate Says New Report by URCH Publishing," *Business Wire*, April 23, 2009, http://www.businesswire.com; Ransdell Pierson, "Pfizer Plans Two Research Chiefs upon Wyeth Merger," *Reuters*, April 7, 2009, http://www.reuters.com; Natasha Singer, "In Wyeth, Pfizer Sees a Drug Pipeline," *The New York Times*, January 26, 2009; Catherine Arnst, "A Pfizer-Wyeth Merger Isn't the Cure-All," *BusinessWeek*, January 24, 2009, http://www.businessweek.com.

7 **Describe how marketers typically measure product mixes and make product mix decisions.**

Marketers must decide the right width, length, and depth of product lines. Width is the number of product lines. Length is the number of products a company sells. Depth refers to the number of variations of a product available in a product line. Marketers evaluate the effectiveness of all three elements of the product mix. They may purchase product lines from other companies or extend the product line, if necessary. Firms may also acquire entire companies and their product lines through mergers and acquisitions.

8 **Explain the concept of the product lifecycle.**

The product lifecycle outlines the stages a product goes through, including introduction, growth, maturity, and decline. During the introductory stage, marketers work to stimulate demand for the new product. New customers make initial purchases and repurchases of the product in the growth stage. Sales continue to grow during the maturity stage, but eventually level off. In the decline stage, sales are reduced due to innovations or a shift in consumer preferences.

9 **Describe how a firm can extend a product's lifecycle, and explain why certain products may be deleted.**

Marketers can extend the product lifecycle by increasing frequency of use or number of users; finding new uses for the product; or changing package size, label, or quality. If none of these is successful, or if the product no longer fits a firm's line, the firm may decide to delete it from its line.

assessment check: answers

1.1 Define the term *product*.

A product is a bundle of physical, service, and symbolic attributes designed to satisfy a customer's wants and needs.

1.2 Why is the understanding of want satisfaction so important to marketers?

The understanding of want satisfaction is important to marketers because it helps them understand why people purchase certain goods and services.

1.3 Describe the goods–services continuum.

The goods–services continuum is a spectrum that helps marketers visualize the differences and similarities between goods and services.

1.4 List the six characteristics distinguishing services from goods.

The six characteristics distinguishing services from goods are the following: (1) services are intangible; (2) services are inseparable from the service providers; (3) services are perishable; (4) companies cannot easily standardize services; (5) buyers often play important roles in the creations and distribution of services; (6) and service standards show wide variations.

2.1 Identify two reasons why services are important to the U.S. economy and business environment.

The service sector makes an important contribution to the economy in terms of products and jobs. Services also play a vital role in the international competitiveness of U.S. firms.

2.2 Why do service firms emphasize marketing?

The growth of potential service transactions represents a vast marketing opportunity, and the environment for services is changing—so marketers need to find new ways to reach customers.

3.1 What are the three major classifications of consumer products?

The three major classifications are convenience products, shopping products, and specialty products.

3.2 Identify five factors marketers should consider in classifying consumer services.

Five factors are the following: (1) the nature of the service, (2) the relationship between the service organization and its customers, (3) flexibility for customization, (4) fluctuation of supply and demand, and (5) the way the service is delivered.

4.1 What are the six main classifications of business products?

The six main classifications of business products are the following: (1) installations, (2) accessory equipment, (3) component parts and materials, (4) raw materials, (5) supplies, and (6) business services.

4.2 What are the three categories of supplies?

The three categories of supplies are maintenance items, repair items, and operating supplies.

5.1 What is TQM?

TQM stands for total quality management, a process that expects all of a firm's employees to continually improve its products and work processes.

5.2 What are the five variables of service quality?

The five variables of service quality are tangibles, reliability, responsiveness, assurances, and empathy.

6.1 List the four reasons for developing a product line.

The four reasons why firms want to develop product lines are the following: (1) a desire to grow, (2) enhancing the company's position in the market, (3) optimal use of company resources, and (4) exploiting the stages of the product lifecycle.

6.2 Give an example of a product line with which you are familiar.

Product lines could include salad dressings, hybrid automobiles, sporting equipment hotel chains, and so on.

7.1 Define *product mix.*

The product mix is a company's assortment of product lines and individual product offerings.

7.2 How do marketers typically measure product mixes?

The product mix is measured by width, length, and depth.

8.1 Identify the four stages of the product lifecycle.

The four stages of the product lifecycle are introduction, growth, maturity, and decline.

8.2 During which stage or stages are products likely to attract the most new customers?

Products usually attract the most new customers during the introductory and growth stages.

9.1 Describe the four strategies for extending a product's lifecycle.

The four strategies are increasing frequency of use, increasing the number of users, finding new users, and changing packaging or quality.

9.2 Under what circumstances do firms decide to delete a product from their line?

Firms may decide to delete a product if none of their strategies work, if raw materials become unavailable, or if the product no longer fits the existing or future product line.

Marketing Terms You Need to Know

marketing mix 344
product 345
services 345
goods 345
homeshoring 347

consumer (B2C) product 348
business-to-business (B2B) product 348
convenience products 349
shopping products 350
specialty products 351

business services 356
total quality management (TQM) 357
product line 359
product lifecycle 363

Other Important Marketing Terms

goods–services continuum 345
unsought products 348
impulse goods and services 349
staples 349
emergency goods and services 349
installations 354
accessory equipment 354

component parts and materials 355
raw materials 355
supplies 355
MRO items 355
ISO 9001:2000 357
benchmarking 357
service encounter 358

service quality 358
product mix 361
line extension 363
introductory stage 364
growth stage 365
maturity stage 365
decline stage 365

Assurance of Learning Review

1. Choose one of the following products and explain how it blurs the distinction between goods and services.
   a. hip replacement surgery
   b. breakfast at a popular restaurant
   c. purchase and installation of new carpet
   d. live concert
   e. custom-made suit

2. What are the differences between consumer products and B2B products? Describe a product that could be used as both.

3. What are unsought products? Give an example of an unsought product, and explain how it might be marketed.

4. What important features distinguish shopping products from one another?

5. How does marketing for installations and accessory equipment differ?

6. How do firms use benchmarking?

7. Describe briefly how L.L.Bean achieved each of the objectives for developing a product line. Why do you think the firm has been successful?

8. What is a line extension? Describe how *one* of the following might create a line extension:
   a. Bounty paper towels
   b. Post Shredded Wheat
   c. Celestial Seasonings tea
   d. Tide laundry detergent

9. What steps do marketers take to make the introductory stage of the product lifecycle successful enough to reach the growth stage? What are some of the challenges they face?

10. Arm & Hammer extended the lifecycle of its baking soda by coming up with new uses for the product. Think of a product whose lifecycle you believe could be extended by finding new uses. Describe the product and your ideas for new uses.

Projects and Teamwork Exercises

1. On your own or with a classmate, choose one of the following goods (or choose one of your own). Visit the company's Web site to learn as much as you can about your product and the way it is marketed. Then create a marketing strategy for developing the services to support your product and make it stand out from others.
   a. Lucky Brand Jeans
   b. BlackBerry smart phone
   c. Sephora makeup
   d. HP laptop
   e. Mini Cooper car

2. On your own or with a classmate, create an advertisement for an unsought product such as flood insurance, a remedial

reading or math course, a warranty for a large-screen TV, a first-aid kit, or the like. How can your ad turn an unsought product into one actually desired by consumers?

3. Consider a customer service experience you have had in the last month or so. Was it positive or negative? Describe your experience to the class and then discuss how the firm might improve the quality of its customer service—even if it is already positive.

4. With a classmate, choose one of the following firms or another that interests you. Visit the firm's Web site and measure its product mix. Then create a chart like the one for Johnson & Johnson in Table 11.3 (on page 362), identifying the company's major product lines, along with a few specific examples.
   a. Champion athletic clothing
   b. Condé Nast magazines
   c. Hilton Hotels
   d. Sony
   e. Volkswagen

5. With the same classmate, create a plan for further extending one of the firm's product lines. Describe the strategy you would recommend for extending the line as well as new products that might be included.

Critical-Thinking Exercises

1. Draw a line representing the goods–services continuum. Then place each of the following along the continuum. Briefly explain your decision.
   a. Skype
   b. Snapfish.com
   c. Dillard's department stores
   d. Honda dealership
   e. Aura Day Spa

2. Make a list of all the convenience products you buy in a week. Does the list change from week to week based on need or your budget? What would it take to make you switch from one product to another?

3. Imagine your favorite restaurant. List as many installations, raw materials, and supplies as you can that you think the restaurant owner or manager must be responsible for purchasing.

4. Why is it important for even a small firm to develop a line of products?

5. Choose one of the following goods and services, and describe your strategy for taking it to the next stage in its product lifecycle. For products in the maturity or decline stage, describe a strategy for extending their lifecycle.
   a. Satellite radio (growth)
   b. MP3 players (maturity)
   c. Text messaging (growth)
   d. Doctors' house calls (decline)
   e. Duct tape (maturity)

6. Describe a fad that has come and gone during your lifetime, such as Beanie Babies or Pokemon. Did you take part in the fad? Why or why not? How long did it last? Why do you think it faded?

Ethics Exercise

The airline industry has suffered recent setbacks such as the high cost of fuel that have forced the major carriers to cut back on many of their services. Some firms, such as American Airlines, have started charging passengers fees for checked baggage. Others charge for in-flight snacks or don't serve any at all. Airlines have reduced the number of flights they operate to certain destinations, packing planes full to overflowing, and made restrictions on the use of frequent-flyer miles so tight that it is difficult to cash them in. Then there are the record-setting delays and lost luggage claims. All of these factors add up to less-than-enjoyable flying experiences for most travelers, many of whom are opting to find other modes of transportation or just staying home.[40]

Suppose you are a marketer for one of the major airlines. Your company is facing difficulty providing acceptable service to the passengers on its flights, but you need to find a way to emphasize the positive features of your airline's service.

1. Using the five variables of service quality as your guideline, what steps would you take—within your realm of control—to close the gap between the level of service passengers expect and the level they have been receiving?

2. How might you attract business customers? Would you give them a level of service that is different from families and other consumers who are flying for pleasure?

Internet Exercises

1. **Extending the product lifecycle.** Dozens of products have been around for years. The organizations behind these products are adept at managing and extending their product lifecycles. One example is products made from soy. Visit the United Soybean Board's Web site (www.soynewuses.org) and prepare a report on how this organization has successfully extended the life cycle of soy products.

2. **Classifying products.** Sony offers a wide variety of products. Go to Sony.com and review the firm's product offerings. Choose five different products and classify each as a convenience, shopping, or specialty product.

3. **Product deletion decisions.** As the text notes, companies occasionally decide to delete products. Use a major search engine, such as Google, to identify two recent examples of product deletions. Investigate the reasons why the firms involved made the decisions and prepare a brief report.

Note: Internet Web addresses change frequently. If you don't find the exact site listed, you may need to access the organization's home page and search from there or use a search engine such as Google.

Case 11.1 Under Armour Takes a Run at the Shoe Market

Under Armour is known for its comfortable, moisture-wicking athletic clothing. Originally made for college football players, the tops, shorts, and other items now sell across the board to professional sports teams as well as amateur tennis players and runners. Recently the company took a big step: launching a new product line of running shoes, intended to compete directly with such entrenched giants as Nike, Reebok, and Adidas. The new line features six different styles: two for trail running and four for road running. There is also a new cross-trainer, available in three models: the Proto Speed, designed for maximum performance in straight ahead running; the Proto Evade, made for side-to-side movement; and the Proto Power, a high-top sneaker. Additional styles will include models for runners with specific issues, such as pronating—those who place more weight on the inside of the foot and ankles. The shoes cost between $90 and $100, which is comparable to average running shoes made by other manufacturers.

Under Armour CEO Kevin A. Plank says adding shoes to the product mix is an important part of its strategy to grow into as fierce a contender as some of its larger rivals. He explains that his company plans to target serious recreational runners who don't have an allegiance to a specific brand, in addition to athletes who simply use running as part of their overall training. Running apparel—tanks, shorts, and other items—already is a proven winner for Under Armour, as runners appreciate the technology of the fabrics used by the firm. Plank says that Under Armour's plan is to promote the technology of the new shoes just as the company has done for its clothing. "Our goal is not for people to trade one shoe for another," he notes. "We believe we have a better shoe."

Under Armour plans to support the new shoes with customer service. Consumers who visit the company's Web site can click on a special link, type in their height and weight and a description of their typical workout routines, and be guided to the best shoe for their needs. Since many of the stores that carry Under Armour products don't provide a lot of sales support, Under Armour decided to make the shopping experience easier for consumers. The UA running shoes will be packaged in transparent boxes so shoppers can easily identify colors and styles. When a customer removes a pair of shoes from the box, more product information and assistance is visible on the inside bottom of the box.

The entire athletic footwear market represents more than $18 billion, and it is extremely competitive. Yet Under Armour believes it has the product line—and the marketing strategy—to compete effectively for customers who want a running shoe that could actually improve their performance. "We believe this signifies a tremendous opportunity for growth in the footwear category," says Raphael Peck, senior vice president of footwear and licensing for Under Armour. "Footwear will be … a major growth driver for Under Armour."

Questions for Critical Thinking

1. Do you think Under Armour's development of a new product line—running shoes—is a good move for the company? Why or why not?

2. Describe steps Under Armour can take to ensure the success of its new shoes during the introductory stage of the product lifecycle. What should marketers plan to do during the growth stage?

Sources: Company Web site, www.uabiz.com, accessed May 13, 2009; Andrea K. Walker, "Under Armour Enters Running Shoe Market," *Baltimore Sun,* May 30, 2008, www.topix.com; Ryan Sharrow, "Under Armour to Unveil a Running Shoe in 2009," *Baltimore Business Journal,* May 29, 2008, baltimore.bizjournals.com; Sean Gregory, "Under Armour's Big Step Up," *Time,* May 15, 2008, www.time.com; Darren Rovell, "Under Armour: Putting Thoughts Back 'into the Box,'" *CNBC.com,* May 2, 2008, www.cnbc.com; David Kiley, "A First Run in Under Armour Prototype," *BusinessWeek,* January 30, 2008, www.businessweek.com.

Video Case 11.2   Product and Service Strategy at Recycline

The written case on Recycline appears on page VC-11. The Recycline video is designed to expand and highlight the concepts in this chapter and the concepts and questions covered in the written video case.

Developing and Managing Brand and Product Categories

Schwinn e-Bikes Provide Pedal Power

Consumer budgets are being squeezed by the price of oil, which hikes the cost of gasoline. Fed up with their "fuel habit," Americans are doing a slow burn each time they reach for the

pump. But, with public transportation available only in certain U.S. metropolitan areas, they need other viable alternatives to driving a car. Thanks to leading bicycle makers like U.S.–based Schwinn, a green

answer may be on the way: the electric bicycle.

At first glance, an electric bicycle looks no different from a traditional bike, except for a four-pound lithium-ion battery pack

perched atop the rear wheel. The batteries power a small motor that engages when you begin to pedal the bike. As you pedal—no matter how slowly—the motor continues to run on the battery power. The motor stops when you tap the brakes.

The bicycle rider must keep pedaling to keep the motor running—an important distinction between e-bikes and scooters or mopeds, which operate without any physical input from the rider. And while scooters and mopeds are significantly more fuel-efficient than automobiles, they still require gas to power them. Another important difference: e-bikes can legally travel in the bike lane; scooters and mopeds cannot.

Are electric bicycles a new innovation? Hardly. Schwinn and other bike makers have been marketing them for nearly a decade in Europe and Asia, where the costs of fuel and car ownership have long been financially prohibitive. But it was the convergence of several events—an upward trend in world oil prices, a surge in Americans' interest in healthy living, a growing awareness of the need to protect the environment, and the aging of the baby boom generation—that helped Schwinn realize the time was right to enter the U.S. market. Since the introduction of several e-bike models in America, demand for the bikes has been so great that retailers are struggling to keep them in stock.

Fully charged, a battery-powered bike can go 40 to 60 miles, depending on riding conditions. In addition, the bike has a top cruising speed of 18 miles per hour. And it's easy to recharge the battery: simply detach it from the bike and plug it into a wall outlet. It's fully charged within three hours. Bike makers say the batteries last about three years.

Compared with a conventional bike, electric bicycles are far from inexpensive, ranging in price from $1,900 to $2,500. Scooters, on the other hand, are even more costly, priced from $2,000 to $8,000, and they still require gas. Given the cost of fill-ups, many car owners claim the e-bike's price tag is no longer out of line for what it delivers.

And although fitness enthusiasts may point out that riding a battery-assisted bicycle doesn't qualify as a true workout, the bike is attracting the attention of a broad consumer demographic, from college students to retirees. The e-bike offers freedom to users of all shapes and sizes—particularly those baby boomers whose svelte days may be behind them.[1]

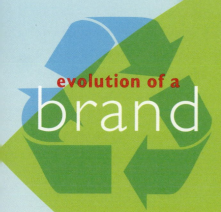

evolution of a brand

Schwinn ranks as one of the leading brands in the history of U.S. business. Founded in Chicago in 1895 by bicycle makers Ignaz Schwinn and Adolph Arnold, over time the company became the foremost name in bicycling, building some of the best-known models in cycling history for riders of all ages. In addition to its comprehensive lines of bicycles and bicycle accessories, the company's products today include jogging strollers, scooters, and skateboards.

• When the company was founded, bicycling was a new craze sweeping the nation and Schwinn was one of nearly 100 bicycle makers in Chicago alone. During the late 1980s, however, mountain biking became popular, and the company dismissed it, thinking it was merely a fad. As a result, Schwinn entered the market late but ultimately rallied by hiring some of the industry's best talent and updating its product line. What should a company like Schwinn do to stay ahead of trends?

evolution of a brand
continued

- For most of the 20th century, the Schwinn name was synonymous with the finest quality in bicycles. Yet, a series of events—including making the wrong call on mountain bikes—combined to force the company into bankruptcy in 1993 and again in 2001. What role did the Schwinn brand play in helping the company emerge from bankruptcy? What should Schwinn do to capitalize on its brand in the future?

chapter overview

Brands play a huge role in our lives. We try certain brands for all kinds of reasons: on recommendations from friends, because we want to associate ourselves with the images certain brands possess, or because we remember colorful advertisements. We develop loyalty to certain brands and product lines for varying reasons as well—quality of a product, price, and habit are a few examples. This chapter examines the way companies make decisions about developing and managing the products and product lines they hope will become consumer necessities. Developing and marketing a product and product line and building a desired brand image are costly propositions.

briefly speaking

"The man who uses Calloway golf clubs, drives a Jaguar, and wears Ralph Lauren apparel makes a statement about his identity. He is a man separate and apart from the man who uses a Penn fishing reel, drives a Dodge Durango, and wears Levi's."

—Laurence Vincent
AMERICAN AUTHOR AND BRAND
CONSULTANT

To protect its investment and maximize the return on it, a specialized marketer called a *category manager*, who is responsible for an entire product line, must carefully nurture both existing and new products.

This chapter focuses on two critical elements of product planning and strategy. First, it looks at how firms build and maintain identity and competitive advantage for their products through branding. Second, it focuses on the new-product planning and development process. Effective new-product planning and meeting the profit responsibility a category manager has for a product line require careful preparation. The needs and desires of consumers change constantly, and successful marketers manage to keep up with—or stay just ahead of—those changes.

Managing Brands for Competitive Advantage

Think of the last time you went shopping for groceries. As you moved through the store, chances are your recognition of various brand names influenced many of your purchasing decisions. Perhaps you chose Colgate toothpaste over competitive offerings or loaded Heinz ketchup into your cart instead of the store brand. Walking through the snack food aisle, you might have reached for Orville Redenbacher popcorn or Lay's potato chips without much thought.

Marketers recognize the powerful influence products and product lines have on customer behavior, and they work to create strong identities for their products and protect them. Branding is the process of creating that identity. A **brand** is a name, term, sign, symbol, design, or some combination that identifies the products of one firm while differentiating these products from competitors' offerings. The tradition of excellence created by the Gucci Group is carried through in all the brands in its lineup—Gucci, Yves Saint Laurent, Boucheron, Stella McCartney, and Balenciaga, to name a few.

As you read this chapter, consider how many brands you are aware of, both those you are loyal to and those you have never tried or have tried and abandoned. Table 12.1 shows some selected brands, brand names, and brand marks. Satisfied buyers respond to branding by making repeat purchases of the same product because they identify the item with the name of its producer. One buyer might derive satisfaction from an ice cream bar with the brand name Dove; another might derive the same satisfaction from one with the name Ben & Jerry's.

> **brand** Name, term, sign, symbol, design, or some combination that identifies the products of one firm while differentiating them from that of the competition.

BRAND LOYALTY

Brands achieve widely varying consumer familiarity and acceptance. A snowboarder might insist on a Burton snowboard, but the same consumer might show little loyalty to particular brands in another product category such as bath soap. Marketers measure brand loyalty in three stages: brand recognition, brand preference, and brand insistence.

Brand recognition is a company's first objective for newly introduced products. Marketers begin the promotion of new items by trying to make them familiar to the public. Advertising offers one effective way for increasing consumer awareness of a brand. Glad is a familiar brand in U.S. kitchens, and it drew on customers' recognition of its popular sandwich bags and plastic wraps when it introduced a new plastic food wrap that seals around items with just the press of a finger.

Other tactics for creating brand recognition include offering free samples or discount coupons for purchases. Once consumers have used a product, seen it advertised, or noticed it in stores,

> **brand recognition** Consumer awareness and identification of a brand.

table 12.1   Selected Brands, Brand Names, and Brand Marks

Brand type	Dr Pepper or A&W root beer
Private brand	Craftsman tools (Sears) or Trader Jacques French soap (Trader Joe's)
Family brand	RAID insect sprays or Progresso soups
Individual brand	Purex or Clorox
Brand name	Kleenex and Cheetos
Brand mark	Colonel Sanders for KFC or the gecko for Geico insurance

Glad, a familiar brand, drew on customers' recognition of its popular sandwich bags and plastic wraps when it introduced a new plastic food wrap that seals with the press of a finger.

© Terri Miller/E-Visual Communications, Inc.

it moves from the unknown to the known category, increasing the probability that some of those consumers will purchase it.

brand preference
Consumer reliance on previous experiences with a product to choose that item again.

brand insistence
Consumer refusal of alternatives and extensive search for desired merchandise.

At the second level of brand loyalty, **brand preference,** buyers rely on previous experiences with the product when choosing it, if available, over competitors' products. You may prefer Steve Madden shoes or Juicy Couture clothes to other brands and buy their new lines as soon as they are offered. If so, those products have established brand preference.

Brand insistence, the ultimate stage in brand loyalty, leads consumers to refuse alternatives and to search extensively for the desired merchandise. A product at this stage has achieved a monopoly position with its consumers. Although many firms try to establish brand insistence with all consumers, few achieve this ambitious goal. Companies that offer specialty or luxury goods and services, such as Rolex watches or Lexus automobiles, are more likely to achieve this status than those offering mass-marketed goods and services.

assessment check

1. What is a brand?
2. Differentiate between brand recognition, brand preference, and brand insistence.

❙ Identify the different types of brands.

TYPES OF BRANDS

generic products Products characterized by plain labels, no advertising, and the absence of brand names.

Companies that practice branding classify brands in many ways: private, manufacturer's or national, family, and individual brands. In making branding decisions, firms weigh the benefits and drawbacks of each type of brand. Some firms, however, sell their goods without any efforts at branding. These items are called **generic products.** They are characterized by plain labels, little or no advertising, and no brand names. Common categories of generic products include food and household staples. These no-name products were first sold in Europe at prices as much as 30 percent below those of branded products. This product strategy was introduced in the U.S. three decades ago. The market shares for generic products increase during economic downturns but subside when the economy improves. However, many consumers request generic substitutions for certain brand-name prescriptions at the pharmacy whenever they are available.

Manufacturers' Brands versus Private Brands

Manufacturers' brands, also called *national brands*, define the image most people form when they think of a brand. A **manufacturer's brand** refers to a brand name owned by a manufacturer or other producer. Well-known manufacturers' brands include Hewlett-Packard, Sony, Pepsi-Cola, Dell, and French's. In contrast, many large wholesalers and retailers place their own brands on the merchandise they market. The brands offered by wholesalers and retailers usually are called **private brands** (or *private labels*). Although some manufacturers refuse to produce private-label goods, most regard such production as a way to reach additional market segments. Supervalu offers many private-label products in its retail grocery stores, including Equaline over-the-counter pharmaceuticals, Homelife household goods, and President's Choice foods.

The growth of private brands has paralleled chain stores in the United States. Manufacturers not only sell their well-known brands to stores but also put the store's own label on similar products. Such leading manufacturers as Westinghouse, Armstrong Rubber, and Heinz generate ever-increasing percentages of their total incomes by producing goods for sale under retailers' private labels. In U.S. grocery stores, one of every five items sold is a private brand. Worldwide, private brands account for nearly $1 trillion in retail sales and are especially popular in western European countries such as Germany and the United Kingdom.[2]

Consistent with its corporate goal to buy and sell green products, office supply retailer Office Depot recently launched Office Depot Green, a private-label line of environmentally sound products. Over time, the line will include recycled paper and paper products, ink and toner cartridges, compact fluorescent light bulbs, and other items that create minimal impact on the environment.[3]

manufacturer's brand Brand name owned by a manufacturer or other producer.

family brand Single brand name that identifies several related products.

Captive Brands

The nation's major discounters—such as Wal-Mart, Target, and Kmart—have come up with a spinoff of the private-label idea. So-called **captive brands** are national brands sold exclusively by a retail chain. Captive brands typically provide better profit margins than private labels. Target's captive brands include housewares and apparel by Michael Graves and Mossimo Giannulli; paper collections, including party supplies such as napkins, tablecloths, and paper plates by Belgian designer Isabelle de Borchgrave; Liz Lange maternity wear; furniture collections by Sean Conway; and moderately priced clothing by Isaac Mizrahi.[4]

Family and Individual Brands

A **family brand** is a single brand name that identifies several related products. For

© Jeff Haynes/AFP/Getty Images

A family brand is a single brand name that identifies several related products. KitchenAid markets a complete line of appliances under its name.

example, KitchenAid markets a complete line of appliances under the KitchenAid name, and Johnson & Johnson offers a line of baby powder, lotions, plastic pants, and baby shampoo under its name. All Pepperidge Farm products, including bread, rolls, and cookies, carry the Pepperidge Farm brand. Frito-Lay markets both chips and salsa under its Tostitos family brand.

Alternatively, a manufacturer may choose to market a product as an **individual brand,** which uniquely identifies the item itself, rather than promoting it under the name of the company or under an umbrella name covering similar items. Unilever, for example, markets Knorr, Bertolli, Lipton, and Slim-Fast food products; Pond's and Sunsilk beauty products; and Lifebuoy, Lux, and Dove soaps. PepsiCo's Quaker Oats unit markets Aunt Jemima breakfast products, Life and Cap'n Crunch cereals, and Rice-a-Roni side dishes along with Quaker oatmeal. Its Frito-Lay division makes Lays, Ruffles, and Doritos chips and Smartfood popcorn, while the Pepsi-Cola brands include Mountain Dew, Sierra Mist, Sobe juices and teas, and Aquafina water. Individual brands cost more than family brands to market because the firm must develop a new promotional campaign to introduce each new product. Distinctive brands are extremely effective aids in implementing market segmentation strategies, however.

On the other hand, a promotional outlay for a family brand can benefit all items in the line. Family brands also help marketers introduce new products to both customers and retailers. Because supermarkets stock thousands of items, they hesitate to add new products unless they are confident they will be in demand.

Family brands should identify products of similar quality, or the firm risks harming its overall product image. If Rolls-Royce marketers were to place the Rolls name on a low-end car or a line of discounted clothing, they would severely tarnish the image of the luxury car line. Conversely, Lexus, Infiniti, and Porsche put their names on luxury sport-utility vehicles to capitalize on their reputations and to enhance the acceptance of the new models in a competitive market.

Individual brand names should, however, distinguish dissimilar products. Kimberly-Clark markets two different types of diapers for infants under its Huggies and Pull-Ups names. Procter & Gamble offers shaving products under its Gillette name; laundry detergent under Cheer, Tide, and other brands; and dishwasher detergent under Cascade.

assessment check

1. Identify the different types of brands.

2. How are generic products different from branded products?

"The right name is an advertisement in itself."

—Claude C. Hopkins (1866–1932)
AMERICAN ADVERTISING PIONEER

2 **Explain the strategic value of brand equity.**

brand equity Added value that a respected, well-known brand name gives to a product in the marketplace.

BRAND EQUITY

As individuals, we often like to say our strongest asset is our reputation. The same is true of organizations. A brand can go a long way toward making or breaking a company's reputation. A strong brand identity backed by superior quality offers important strategic advantages for a firm. First, it increases the likelihood that consumers will recognize the firm's product or product line when they make purchase decisions. Second, a strong brand identity can contribute to buyers' perceptions of product quality. Branding can also reinforce customer loyalty and repeat purchases. A consumer who tries a brand and likes it will probably look for that brand on future store visits. All of these benefits contribute to a valuable form of competitive advantage called *brand equity.*

Brand equity refers to the added value a certain brand name gives to a product in the marketplace. Brands with high equity confer financial advantages on a firm because they often command comparatively large market shares and consumers may pay little attention to differences in prices. Studies have also linked brand equity to high profits and stock returns. Service companies are also aware of the value of brand equity.

In global operations, high brand equity often facilitates expansion into new markets. Currently, Google is the most valuable—and most recognized—brand in the world.[5] Similarly, Disney's brand equity allows it to market its goods and services in Europe and Japan—and now China. What makes a global brand powerful? According to Interbrand, which measures brand equity in dollar values, a strong brand has the power to increase a company's sales and earnings. A global brand generally is defined as one that sells at least 20 percent outside its home country.

Global advertising agency Young & Rubicam developed another brand equity system called the BrandAsset Valuator. Y&R's database of consumers' brand perceptions contains more than 350,000 consumer interviews and information on 19,500 brands. According to Y&R, a firm builds brand equity sequentially on four dimensions of brand personality. These four dimensions are differentiation, relevance, esteem, and knowledge:

▷ *Differentiation* refers to a brand's ability to stand apart from competitors. Brands such as Porsche and Victoria's Secret stand out in consumers' minds as symbols of unique product characteristics.

▷ *Relevance* refers to the real and perceived appropriateness of the brand to a big consumer segment. A large number of consumers must feel a need for the benefits offered by the brand. Brands with high relevance include Microsoft and Hallmark.

▷ *Esteem* is a combination of perceived quality and consumer perceptions about a brand's growing or declining popularity. A rise in perceived quality or in public opinion about a brand enhances a brand's esteem. But negative impressions reduce esteem. Brands with high esteem include General Mills and Honda.

▷ *Knowledge* refers to the extent of customers' awareness of the brand and understanding of what a good or service stands for. Knowledge implies that customers feel an intimate relationship with a brand. Examples include Jell-O and Band-Aid.[6]

THE ROLE OF CATEGORY AND BRAND MANAGEMENT

Because of the tangible and intangible value associated with strong brand equity, marketing organizations invest considerable resources and effort in developing and maintaining these dimensions of brand personality. Traditionally, companies assigned the task of managing a brand's marketing strategies to a **brand manager.** Today, because they sell about 80 percent of their products to national retail chains, major consumer goods companies have adopted a strategy called **category management.** In this strategy, a manufacturer's *category manager* maximizes sales for the retailer by overseeing an entire product line, often tracking sales history with data from the retail checkout point and aggregating it with sales data for the entire category (obtained from third-party vendors) and qualitative data such as customer surveys.[7]

Unlike traditional product managers, category managers have profit responsibility for their product group and help the retailer's category buyer maximize sales for the whole category, not just the particular manufacturer's product. These managers are assisted by associates usually called *analysts.* Part of the shift to category management was initiated by large retailers, who realized they could benefit from the marketing muscle of large grocery and household goods producers such as Kraft and Procter & Gamble. As a result, producers began to focus their attention on in-store merchandising instead of mass-market advertising. Some manufacturers that are too small to dedicate a category manager to each retail chain assign a category manager to each major channel such as convenience stores, drugstores, grocery stores, and so on.[8]

Some of the steps companies follow in the category management process include defining the category based on the target market's needs; scoping out a consumer's decision process when shopping the category; identifying consumer groups and the store clusters with the greatest sales potential; creating a marketing strategy and performance goal for each cluster and using a scorecard to measure progress; and defining and executing the tactics, tracking progress.[9] Hershey's vending division offers category management services to its institutional customers, providing reduced inventory costs, improved warehouse efficiency, and increased sales.[10]

3 **Explain the benefits of category and brand management.**

category management
Product management system in which a category manager—with profit and loss responsibility—oversees a product line.

assessment check

1. What is brand equity?

2. What are the four dimensions of brand personality?

3. How does category management help retailers?

Organizations identify their products in the marketplace with brand names, symbols, and distinctive packaging. Iams stamps a paw print on all of its pet food packages.

4 **Discuss how companies develop strong identities for their products and brands.**

Product Identification

Organizations identify their products in the marketplace with brand names, symbols, and distinctive packaging. Almost every product distinguishable from another gives buyers some means of identifying it. Sunkist Growers, for instance, stamps its oranges with the name Sunkist. Iams stamps a paw print on all of its pet food packages. For more than 120 years, Prudential Financial has used the Rock of Gibraltar as its symbol.

Choosing how to identify a firm's output represents a major strategic decision for marketers. Produce growers have another option besides gummed paper stickers for identifying fruits and vegetables: laser coding. This new technology marks fruits and vegetables with their name, identification number, and country of origin. The food tattoo is visible but also edible—good news for consumers who tire of peeling tiny stickers from their apples and tomatoes. While the stickers provide important information in the form of four- or five-digit price look-up (PLU) codes that a supermarket cashier enters into the computer system to retrieve pricing information, the stickers must also be removed from the produce before it can be eaten. The laser codes include the PLU code and eliminate sticky labels.[11]

BRAND NAMES AND BRAND MARKS

A name plays a central role in establishing brand and product identity. The American Marketing Association defines a **brand name** as the part of a brand that can be spoken. It can consist of letters, numbers, or words and forms a name that identifies and distinguishes the firm's offerings from those of its competitors. Firms can also identify their brands by brand marks. A **brand mark** is a symbol or pictorial design that distinguishes a product such as the Jolly Green Giant for Green Giant Vegetables.

Effective brand names are easy to pronounce, recognize, and remember. Short names, such as Nike, Ford, and Bounty, meet these requirements. Marketers try to overcome problems with easily mispronounced brand names by teaching consumers the correct pronunciations. For example, early advertisements for the Korean carmaker Hyundai explained that the name rhymes with *Sunday*. Sensitivity to clear communication doesn't end with the choice of brand name; marketers should also be aware of how well they get their point across in interpersonal communications. The "Etiquette Tips for Marketing Professionals" feature provides some tips for avoiding jargon in marketing communications.

A brand name should also give buyers the correct connotation of the product's image. Nissan's X-Terra connotes youth and extreme sports to promote the off-road SUV, while Kodak's EasyShare tells consumers how simple printing digital pictures can be. ConAgra's Healthy Choice food line presents an alternative to fast foods that may be high in sodium or fat, and the iPod Nano uses a name that aptly suggests its tiny size.

A brand name must also qualify for legal protection. The Lanham Act of 1946 states that registered trademarks must not contain words or phrases in general use, such as *automobile* or *suntan lotion*. These generic words actually describe particular types of products, and no company can claim exclusive rights to them.

Marketers feel increasingly hard-pressed to coin effective brand names, as multitudes of competitors rush to stake out names for their own products. Some companies register names before they have products to fit them to prevent competitors from using them. Few, however, have found as memorable a name for their product as Louisiana pharmacist George Boudreaux, whose highly successful diaper rash cream is called Boudreaux's Butt Paste. The Butt Paste line has been extended with products for chapped lips, razor burn, bedsores, and other conditions, but nothing keeps the Butt Paste name in front of the public like its NASCAR sponsorships.[12]

When a class of products becomes generally known by the original brand name of a specific offering, the brand name may become a descriptive generic name. If this occurs, the

<div class="margin-note">

brand name Part of a brand, consisting of letters, numbers, or words, that can be spoken and that identifies and distinguishes a firm's offerings from those of its competitors.

</div>

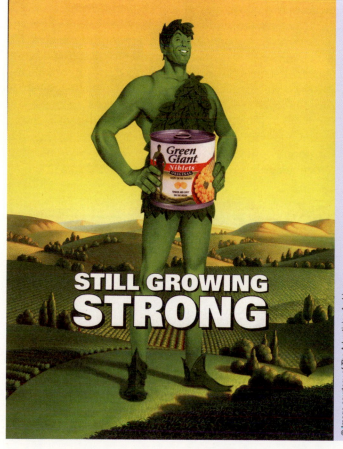

STILL GROWING STRONG

© Image courtesy of The Advertising Archives

<div class="margin-note">

A brand mark is a symbol or pictorial design that distinguishes a product, such as the Jolly Green Giant for Green Giant Vegetables.

</div>

Etiquette Tips for Marketing Professionals

IMHO … Don't Use Jargon! Seriously, I'm Not JK

Wireless technology has supercharged the pace of everyday life, and with it comes the temptation to use the shorthand common to text messaging in other everyday communications. But consider these facts:

- When you use abbreviations like "btw" and "p&c" in your communication, you're using jargon. And by its very definition, jargon can be confusing and misleading. For example, while it might be obvious to you that "btw" stands for "by the way," to another person it may mean "between." You may interpret "p&c" to mean "private and confidential," but to people in the insurance industry, it stands for "property and casualty." And think of the potential danger in using "jk" when you mean "just kidding": your reader may skip right past those two letters or mistake them for someone's initials.

- Jargon excludes. When you use jargon and people don't understand your message, they may peg you as someone who's not open or friendly. In fact, recent studies reveal that jargon users are perceived as less likable.

- Using jargon in business communication could be a deal breaker. Although the jargon of text-messaging has become increasingly common, it's too casual for business communiqués and creates a poor impression as you search for—or try to succeed at—that new job. And if your manager is older than you—say, a member of the baby boom generation—he or she is unlikely to be impressed by how cool you are.

Sources: Tim Burress, "Abbreviations Used in E-Mail," *Videojug.com*, www.videojug.com, accessed May 19, 2009; Heidi LaFleche, "Beat Business Jargon: A Veteran Bullfighter's Tips," *Monster Career Advice*, career-advice.monster.com, accessed May 19, 2009; Janienne Jennrich, "Business Text Messaging Shorthand," *Suite 101*, April 2, 2008, cell-phones.suite101.com.

briefly speaking

"The brand is the amusement park. The product is the souvenir."

—Nicholas Graham
FOUNDER AND CUO (CHIEF UNDERPANTS OFFICER), JOE BOXER, INC.

original owner loses exclusive claim to the brand name. The generic names nylon, aspirin, escalator, kerosene, and zipper started as brand names. Other generic names that were once brand names include cola, yo-yo, linoleum, and shredded wheat.

Marketers must distinguish between brand names that have become legally generic terms and those that seem generic only in many consumers' eyes. Consumers often adopt legal brand names as descriptive names. Jell-O, for instance, is a brand name owned exclusively by Kraft Foods, but many consumers casually apply it as a descriptive name for gelatin desserts. Similarly, many people use the term Kleenex to refer to facial tissues. English and Australian consumers use the brand name Hoover as a verb for vacuuming. One popular way to look something up on the Internet is now to "Google it." Xerox is such a well-known brand name that people frequently—though incorrectly—use it as a verb to mean photocopying. To protect its valuable trademark, Xerox Corporation has created advertisements explaining that Xerox is a brand name and registered trademark and should not be used as a verb.

TRADEMARKS

Businesses invest considerable resources in developing and promoting brands and brand identities. The high value of brand equity encourages firms to take steps in protecting the expenditures they invest in their brands.

trademark Brand for which the owner claims exclusive legal protection.

A **trademark** is a brand for which the owner claims exclusive legal protection. A trademark should not be confused with a trade name, which identifies a company. The Coca-Cola Company is a trade name, but Coke is a trademark of the company's product. Some trade names duplicate companies' brand names.

Protecting Trademarks

Trademark protection confers the exclusive legal right to use a brand name, brand mark, and any slogan or product name abbreviation. It designates the origin or source of a good or service.

Frequently, trademark protection is applied to words or phrases, such as *Bud* for Budweiser or *the Met* for the New York Metropolitan Opera. Robert Burck, a New York street performer who gained fame as the Naked Cowboy, sued candy maker Mars for trademark infringement. Burke, who plays guitar in Times Square wearing nothing but white cowboy boots, cowboy hat, and underpants, registered his likeness and the words "Naked Cowboy" as a trademark. Mars, the makers of M&Ms, recently erected a video billboard showing a blue M&M playing the guitar and clad only in white boots, hat, and underpants.[13]

Firms can also receive trademark protection for packaging elements and product features such as shape, design, and typeface. U.S. law has fortified trademark protection in recent years. The Federal Trademark Dilution Act of 1995 gives a trademark holder the right to sue for trademark infringement even if other products using its brand are not particularly similar or easily confused in the minds of consumers. The infringing company does not even have to know it is diluting another's trademark. The act also gives a trademark holder the right to sue if another party imitates its trademark.

The Internet is the next battlefield for trademark infringement cases. Some companies are attempting to protect their trademarks by filing infringement cases against companies using similar Internet addresses or using unauthorized versions of traditional games. Such was the case when two brothers from India posted Scrabulous, their unauthorized version of Scrabble, on Facebook. Hasbro, who owns the U.S. rights to Scrabble, moved to protect its brand by suing the brothers for copyright and trademark violations.[14] As a result, Facebook removed the game from its site.

Trade Dress

Visual cues used in branding create an overall look sometimes referred to as **trade dress.** These visual components may be related to color selections, sizes, package and label shapes, and similar factors. For example, the McDonald's "golden arches," Merrill Lynch's bull, and the yellow of Shell's seashell are all part of these products' trade dress. Owens Corning has registered the color pink to distinguish its insulation from the competition. A combination of visual cues may also constitute trade dress. Consider a Mexican food product that uses the colors of the Mexican flag: green, white, and red.

Trade dress disputes have led to numerous courtroom battles but no apparent consensus from the Supreme Court. In a recent dispute, Procter & Gamble sued Blue Cross Laboratories, a private-label manufacturer, charging trade dress infringement related to its Herbal Essences brand. According to the suit,

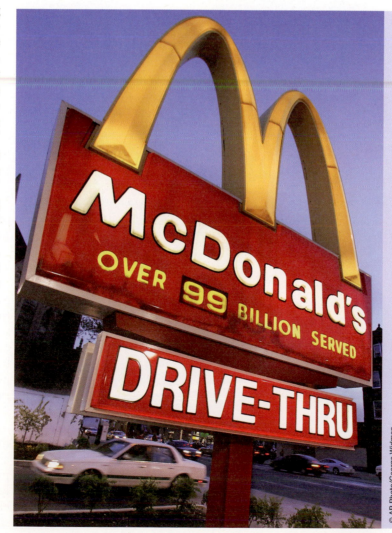

© AP Photo/George Widman

Visual cues used in branding an overall look, such as McDonald's "golden arches," are sometimes referred to as trade dress.

Blue Cross markets its "Herbal Passion" line of shampoos and conditioners, in bottles bearing the unique Herbal Essence shape, to dollar stores.[15]

DEVELOPING GLOBAL BRAND NAMES AND TRADEMARKS

Cultural and language variations make brand-name selection a difficult undertaking for international marketers; an excellent brand name or symbol in one country may prove disastrous in another. An advertising campaign for E-Z washing machines failed in the UK because the British pronounce *z* as "zed." A firm marketing a product in multiple countries must also decide whether to use a single brand name for universal promotions or tailor names to individual countries. Most languages contain *o* and *k* sounds, so *okay* has become an international word. Most languages also have a short *a*, so Coca-Cola, Kodak, and Texaco work as effective brands abroad.

A court recently awarded Adidas $65 million in a trademark and trade dress infringement suit brought against Payless ShoeSource. The suit claimed that Payless bought pairs of Adidas footwear with their distinctive three stripes, then sent the shoes to China to be copied and manufactured with two or four stripes.[16]

PACKAGING

A firm's product strategy must also address questions about packaging. Like its brand name, a product's package can powerfully influence buyers' purchase decisions.

Through marketing research, Heinz created their Picnic Pack, a packaging innovation that makes Heinz products easily portable for picnics and cookouts.

© AP Images/Paul Sakuma

Marketers apply increasingly scientific methods to their packaging decisions. Rather than experimenting with physical models or drawings, more and more package designers work on special computer graphics programs that create three-dimensional images of packages in thousands of colors, shapes, and typefaces. Another software program helps marketers design effective packaging by simulating the displays shoppers see when they walk down supermarket aisles.

Companies conduct marketing research to evaluate current packages and to test alternative package designs. Through such research, Heinz created a packaging innovation linked to usage occasions. Its Heinz Picnic Pack bundles ketchup, mustard, and pickle relish in a paperboard carrier box to make it easily portable for picnics and cookouts.[17]

A package serves three major objectives: (1) protection against damage, spoilage, and pilferage; (2) assistance in marketing the product; and (3) cost effectiveness. Let's briefly consider each of these objectives.

Protection against Damage, Spoilage, and Pilferage

The original objective of packaging was to offer physical protection for the merchandise. Products typically pass through several stages of handling between manufacturing and customer purchases, and a package must protect its contents from damage. Furthermore, packages of perishable products must protect the contents against spoilage in transit and in storage until purchased by the consumer.

Fears of product tampering have forced many firms to improve package designs. Over-the-counter medicines are sold in tamper-resistant packages covered with warnings informing consumers not to purchase merchandise without protective seals intact. Many grocery items and light-sensitive products are packaged in tamper-resistant containers as well. Products in glass jars, such as spaghetti sauce and jams, often come with vacuum-depressed buttons in the lids that pop up the first time the lids are opened.

Even prescription medicine packaging can be revolutionized for the consumer's benefit, as Target found. Its ClearRx prescription dispensing system offers bottles with easy-to-read labels, in a shape designed to fit in the palm of the hand. An information card tucked into a sleeve on the back of the bottle provides a brief summary of the medication's uses and side effects. For households where several people are taking medication, color-coded rings on the neck of the bottle help family members identify their medication at a glance.[18]

Many packages offer important safeguards against pilferage for retailers. Shoplifting and employee theft cost retailers several billion dollars each year. To limit this activity, many packages feature oversized cardboard backings too large to fit into a shoplifter's pocket or purse. Efficient packaging that protects against damage, spoilage, and theft is especially important for international marketers who must contend with varying climatic conditions and the added time and stress involved in overseas shipping.

Assistance in Marketing the Product

The proliferation of new products, changes in consumer lifestyles and buying habits, and marketers' emphasis on targeting smaller market segments have increased the importance of packaging as a promotional tool. Many firms address consumer concerns about protecting the environment by designing packages made of biodegradable and recyclable materials. To demonstrate serious concern regarding environmental protection, Procter & Gamble, Coors, McDonald's, BP Chemical, and other firms created ads that describe their efforts in developing environmentally sound packaging.

In a grocery store where thousands of different items compete for notice, a product must capture the shopper's attention. Marketers combine colors, sizes, shapes, graphics, and typefaces to establish distinctive trade dress that sets their products apart from the products of competitors. Packaging can help establish a common identity for a group of items sold under the same brand name. Like the brand name, a package should evoke the product's image and communicate its value. The design features of Folgers' AromaSeal container include a flexible cap, special handle, and concave bottom to improve freshness and make the canister easier to use. The makers of Folgers recently sued Kraft Foods, who markets Maxwell House coffee, over a Maxwell House container they claim infringes on their patented design.[19]

Other packages also enhance convenience. Pump dispensers, for example, facilitate the use of products ranging from mustard to insect repellent. Squeezable bottles of honey and ketchup make the products easier to use and store. Packaging provides key benefits for convenience foods such as meals and soups packaged in microwavable containers, juice drinks in aseptic packages, and frozen entrées and vegetables packaged in single-serving portions.

Some firms increase consumer utility with packages designed for reuse. Empty jelly jars have long doubled as drinking glasses. Parents can buy bubble bath in animal-shaped plastic bottles suitable for bathtub play. Packaging is a major component in Avon's overall marketing strategy. The firm's decorative, reusable bottles have even become collectibles.

Cost-Effective Packaging

Although packaging must perform a number of functions for the producer, marketers, and consumers, it must do so at a reasonable cost. Sometimes changes in the packaging can make packages both cheaper and better for the environment. A recent redesign of the standard gallon milk jug has cut shipping costs and lessened its environmental impact. The new squarish containers can be stacked on top of each other, eliminating the need for milk crates, and their boxy design is easier to distribute and store.[20]

Labeling

Labels were once a separate element applied to a package; today, they are an integral part of a typical package. Labels perform both promotional and informational functions. A **label** carries an item's brand name or symbol, the name and address of the manufacturer or distributor, information about the product's composition and size, and recommended uses. The right label can play an important role in attracting consumer attention and encouraging purchases.

Consumer confusion and dissatisfaction over such descriptions as giant economy size, king size, and family size led to the passage of the Fair Packaging and Labeling Act in 1966. The act requires that a label offer adequate information concerning the package contents and that a package design facilitate value comparisons among competing products.

The Nutrition Labeling and Education Act of 1990 imposes a uniform format in which food manufacturers must disclose nutritional information about their products. In addition, the Food and Drug Administration (FDA) has mandated design standards for nutritional labels that provide clear guidelines to consumers about food products. The FDA has also tightened definitions for loosely used terms such as *light, fat free, lean,* and *extra lean,* and it mandates that labels list the amounts of fat, sodium, dietary fiber, calcium, vitamins, and other components in typical servings. The latest ruling requires food manufacturers to include on nutritional labels the total amount of trans fats—hydrogenated oils that improve texture and freshness but contribute to high levels of cholesterol—in each product.

The new Food Allergen Labeling and Consumer Protection Act requires that food labeling disclose all major food allergens in terms the average consumer can understand. According to the Food and Drug Administration, eight allergens account for 90 percent of documented allergic reactions to food, and all must be identified. They are milk, eggs, peanuts, tree nuts (almonds, cashews, walnuts), fish (such as bass, cod, and flounder), shellfish (crab, lobster, shrimp), soy, and wheat.[21]

Labeling requirements differ elsewhere in the world. In Canada, for example, labels must provide information in both English and French. The type and amount of information required on labels also vary among nations. International marketers must carefully design labels to conform to the regulations of each country in which they market their merchandise.

The **Universal Product Code (UPC)** designation is another important aspect of a label or package. Introduced in 1974 as a method for cutting expenses in the supermarket industry,

MARKETING SUCCESS

Nintendo Extends Its Line and Stretches Consumers' Bodies with Wii Fit

Background. Videogame manufacturer Nintendo hit the U.S. market in 1985 with its Nintendo Entertainment System and games like "Donkey Kong," "Legends of Zelda," and the "Super Mario" series. Since then, it's been "nothing but net" for the company, whose wildly popular products—like Nintendo 64, Game Boy, and Wii—became almost instant hits worldwide.

The Challenge. Nintendo has a large user audience that consists chiefly of children, teens, and young adults. It wanted to extend its reach beyond this audience and find a way to attract a broader population that doesn't currently play videogames.

The Strategy. Noting growing worldwide concern for physical fitness and healthier living, Nintendo saw an opportunity.

UPCs are numerical bar codes printed on packages. Optical scanner systems read these codes, and computer systems recognize items and print their prices on cash register receipts. Although UPC scanners are costly, they permit both considerable labor savings over manual pricing and improved inventory control. The Universal Product Code is also a major asset for marketing research. However, many consumers feel frustrated when only a UPC is placed on a package without an additional price tag, because they do not always know how much an item costs if the price labels are missing from the shelf.

Radio-frequency identification (RFID) tags—electronic chips that carry encoded product identification—may replace some of the functions of UPC codes, such as price identification and inventory tracking. But consumer privacy concerns about the amount of information RFID tracking can accumulate may limit their use to aggregate packaging such as pallets, rather than units sized for individual sale. When the FDA decided to require drug makers and marketers to place a scannable code on all drugs sold to U.S. hospitals at the level of patient unit doses, it chose UPC codes.

BRAND EXTENSIONS

Some brands become so popular that marketers may decide to use them on unrelated products in pursuit of instant recognition for the new offerings. The strategy of attaching a popular brand name to a new product in an unrelated product category is known as **brand extension.** This practice should not be confused with **line extensions,** which refers to new sizes, styles, or related products. A brand extension, in contrast, carries over from one product nothing but the brand name. In establishing brand extensions, marketers hope to gain access to new customers and markets by building on the equity already established in their existing brands. This is the strategy behind Nautica's brand extension from fashion to furniture and bedding. Nintendo extended its participative Wii videogame line with the Wii Fit, as the "Marketing Success" feature discusses.

brand extension Strategy of attaching a popular brand name to a new product in an unrelated product category.

Targeting the 7- to 12-year-old age group, Mattel extended its Barbie fashion doll brand in an effort to sustain older children's interest. It launched the "Barbie Girls" experience, which includes a free interactive Web site and a subscription-based "VIP" version, both with opportunities for children to create a virtual world where they can design their own room, cruise a cybermall, and more. A Barbie-inspired handheld MP3 device interacts with the sites. Mattel also offers a free Web site for parents, with tools and resources for cyberspace safety. In South America, Barbie Stores offer a "fashion-tainment" experience complete with a playroom also available for parties, a kid-sized salon, and a café. Visitors to the Barbie Store can also buy Barbie-branded apparel—mostly in shades of pink.[22]

By creating a game that addressed those issues, it could attract new audience segments and help them get fit through exercise in a fun, engaging way. The company developed Wii Fit, an "exer-game" for the Wii console. Wii Fit offers four game categories: aerobics, balance games, strength training, and yoga. Users stand on Wii Fit's wireless balance board to weigh themselves, create their personal health profile, play the games, and monitor their progress. Based on the standard Body Mass Index (BMI) measure, the balance board provides verbal and visual feedback and serves as a kind of virtual personal trainer.

The Outcome. Early sales of Wii Fit show that it reaches a broad age range, from children to octogenarians. And although Nintendo hasn't marketed it in this way, Wii Fit is showing value as a physical therapy tool. A bestseller in Japan only three months after its launch, Wii Fit is also expected to get more than a few Americans off the couch.

Sources: Company Web site, www.nintendo.com, accessed May 19, 2009; Ryan Kim, "Wii Fit More Than Just a Game," *San Francisco Chronicle*, June 2, 2008, www.sfchronicle.us; David Ho, " 'Wii Fit' Exercise Game Released in U.S.," *The Atlanta Journal-Constitution*, May 19, 2008, www.ajc.com; Anita Hamilton, "Weighing Wii Fit: Serious Fun," *Time*, May 14, 2008, www.time.com; Wes Nihei and Curt Feldman, "Americans, Time to Warm Up for Nintendo's Wii Fit," *CNN*, April 16, 2008, www.cnn.com; Lindsey Tanner, "Doctors Use Wii Games for Rehab Therapy," *Associated Press*, February 8, 2008, news.yahoo.com.

Mattel has extended its Barbie fashion doll brand to include a Web site as well as a Barbie Store, where visitors can buy Barbie-branded apparel, mostly in shades of pink.

© AP Images/Natacha Pisarenko

BRAND LICENSING

A growing number of firms authorize other companies to use their brand names. Even colleges license their logos and trademarks. Known as **brand licensing,** this practice expands a firm's exposure in the marketplace, much as a brand extension does. The brand name's owner also receives an extra source of income in the form of royalties from licensees, typically 4 to 8 percent of wholesale revenues.

Brand experts note several potential problems with licensing, however. Brand names do not transfer well to all products. The PetSmart PetsHotel was a winner, as was *American Idol* camp, but recent losers were Precious Moments coffins, Donald Trump steaks, and Girls Gone Wild apparel. If a licensee produces a poor-quality product or an item ethically incompatible with the original brand, the arrangement could damage the reputation of the brand. Consider the failure of two recent Disney brand extensions: Disney cologne for children and the Disney wine collection.[23]

Overextension is another problem. In recent years, Starbucks has attempted to extend its coffee brand to a "lifestyle" brand with the sale of coffee beans in supermarkets and CDs, books, and a broad food menu in its retail outlets. By moving away from the qualities that helped make it successful, the brand suffered and market share declined. Starbucks has since closed hundreds of its stores.[24]

assessment check

1. Distinguish between a brand name and a trademark.

2. What are the three purposes of packaging?

3. Describe brand extension and brand licensing.

New-Product Planning

As its offerings enter the maturity and decline stages of the product lifecycle, a firm must add new items to continue to prosper. Regular additions of new products to the firm's line help protect it from product obsolescence.

New products are the lifeblood of any business, and survival depends on a steady flow of new entries. Some new products may implement major technological breakthroughs. Other new products simply extend existing product lines. In other words, a new product is one that either the company or the customer has not handled before. Only about 10 percent of new-product introductions bring truly new capabilities to consumers.

	Old Product	New Product
Old Market	Market Penetration	Product Development
New Market	Market Development	Product Diversification

figure 12.1

Alternative Product Development Strategies

PRODUCT DEVELOPMENT STRATEGIES

A firm's strategy for new-product development varies according to its existing product mix and the match between current offerings and the firm's overall marketing objectives. The current market positions of products also affect product development strategy. Figure 12.1 identifies four alternative development strategies as market penetration, market development, product development, and product diversification.

A **market penetration strategy** seeks to increase sales of existing products in existing markets. Firms can attempt to extend their penetration of markets in several ways. They may modify products, improve product quality, or promote new and different ways to use products. Packaged-goods marketers often pursue this strategy to boost market share for mature products in mature markets. Product positioning often plays a major role in such a strategy.

Product positioning refers to consumers' perceptions of a product's attributes, uses, quality, and advantages and disadvantages relative to competing brands. Marketers often conduct marketing research studies to analyze consumer preferences and to construct product positioning maps that plot their products' positions in relation to those of competitors' offerings.

Hyundai Motors is attempting to reposition its Hyundai and Kia brands in the United States. Although both Hyundais and Kias entered the U.S. market as economical alternatives to other cars, the company now is ratcheting up the look and feel of its sedans to take on upscale brands like Cadillac and BMW.[25]

A **market development strategy** concentrates on finding new markets for existing products. Market segmentation, discussed in Chapter 9, provides useful support for such an effort. Bank of America has succeeded in developing a new market by targeting Asian residents in San Francisco with special television commercials aimed at Chinese, Korean, and Vietnamese consumers. Tyson Foods has reached out to the Hispanic market with specially flavored versions of its chicken products that enable consumers to prepare traditional Latin dishes at home.[26]

© 2004 Coty US LLC.

STETSON

STETSON

COLOGNE FOR MEN
www.stetsoncologne.com

© Image courtesy of The Advertising Archives

5 Identify and briefly describe each of the new-product development strategies.

In addition to the classic Stetson scent, customers can choose flanker brands like Lady Stetson and Stetson Black. Flanker brands are used often in the fragrance industry.

The strategy of **product development** refers to the introduction of new products into identifiable or established markets. Hitachi entered the explosive high-definition TV market with its "1.5" brand, a line of LCD monitors only one and one-half inches thick. Thin enough to be hung on a wall, the sleek monitors are designed to appeal to consumers who can afford to pay more for style.[27]

Firms may also choose to introduce new products into markets in which they have already established positions to try to increase overall market share. These new offerings are called *flanker brands*. The fragrance industry uses this strategy extensively when it develops scents related to their most popular products. The flanker scents are related in both their smell and their names. Coty has built a family of flanker brands around its popular Stetson fragrance. The flanker brands include Lady Stetson, Stetson Sierra, Stetson Untamed, Stetson Black, and the latest in the line, Stetson Fresh.[28]

Finally, a **product diversification strategy** focuses on developing entirely new products for new markets. Some firms look for new target markets that complement their existing markets; others look in completely new directions. Cisco Systems, the networking company, expanded its presence in the consumer electronics market with Cisco-branded cable set-tops, radios, telephones, home teleconferencing systems, and home theater equipment. These products tap into its expertise in developing computer routers and mine its relationship with Internet portals such as Yahoo! and Google.[29]

In selecting a new-product strategy, marketers should keep in mind an additional potential problem: **cannibalization.** Any firm wants to avoid investing resources in a new-product introduction that will adversely affect sales of existing products. A product that takes sales from another offering in the same product line is said to cannibalize that line. A company can accept some loss of sales from existing products if the new offering will generate sufficient additional sales to warrant its investment in its development and market introduction.

assessment check

1. Distinguish between market penetration and market development strategies.
2. What is product development?
3. What is product diversification?

THE CONSUMER ADOPTION PROCESS

6 Describe the consumer adoption process.

adoption process Stages consumers go through in learning about a new product, trying it, and deciding whether to purchase it again.

In the **adoption process,** consumers go through a series of stages from first learning about the new product to trying it and deciding whether to purchase it regularly or reject it. These stages in the consumer adoption process can be classified as follows:

1. *Awareness.* Individuals first learn of the new product, but they lack full information about it.
2. *Interest.* Potential buyers begin to seek information about it.
3. *Evaluation.* They consider the likely benefits of the product.
4. *Trial.* They make trial purchases to determine its usefulness.
5. *Adoption/Rejection.* If the trial purchase produces satisfactory results, they decide to use the product regularly.

Marketers must understand the adoption process to move potential consumers to the adoption stage. Once marketers recognize a large number of consumers at the interest stage, they can take steps to stimulate sales by moving these buyers through the evaluation and trial stages. To introduce Berry Berry, a new flavor in its iced-coffee line, Dunkin' Donuts hosted a massive iced-coffee giveaway promotion. Customers who visited a Dunkin' Donuts retail outlet received a free 16-ounce iced coffee in the flavor of their choice. The company served nearly 4 million free cups of iced coffee during the promotion.[30]

consumer innovators People who purchase new products almost as soon as the products reach the market.

ADOPTER CATEGORIES

First buyers of new products, the so-called **consumer innovators,** are people who purchase new products almost as soon as these products reach the market. Later adopters wait for additional information and rely on the experiences of initial buyers before making trial purchases. Consumer innovators welcome innovations in each product area. Some computer users, for instance, rush to install new software immediately after each update becomes available.

A number of studies about the adoption of new products have identified five categories of purchasers based on relative times of adoption. These categories, shown in Figure 12.2, are consumer innovators, early adopters, early majority, late majority, and laggards.

While the adoption process focuses on individuals and the steps they go through in making the ultimate decision of whether to become repeat purchasers of the new product or reject it as a failure to satisfy their needs, the **diffusion process** focuses on all members of a community or social system. The focus here is on the speed at which an innovative product is accepted or rejected by all members of the community.

Figure 12.2 shows the diffusion process as following a normal distribution from a small group of early purchasers (*innovators*) to the final group of consumers (*laggards*) to make trial purchases of the new product. A few people adopt at first and then the number of adopters increases rapidly as the value of the product becomes apparent. The adoption rate finally diminishes as the number of potential consumers who have not adopted, or purchased, the product diminishes. Typically, innovators make up the first 2.5 percent of buyers who adopt the new product; laggards are the last 16 percent to do so. Figure 12.2 excludes those who never adopt the product.

diffusion process Process by which new goods or services are accepted in the marketplace.

IDENTIFYING EARLY ADOPTERS

It's no surprise that identifying consumers or organizations most likely to try a new product can be vital to a product's success. By reaching these buyers early in the product's development or introduction, marketers can treat these adopters as a test market, evaluating the product and discovering suggestions for modifications. Because early purchasers often act as opinion leaders from whom others seek advice, their attitudes toward new products quickly spread to others. Acceptance or rejection of the innovation by these purchasers can help forecast its expected success. New-car models are multiplying, for instance, and many are sporting a dizzying variety of options such as ports to accommodate—and integrate—the driver's iPod, wireless phone, and laptop. Improved stability controls, collision warnings, and "smart engines" that save fuel are also available.

A large number of studies have established the general characteristics of first adopters. These pioneers tend to be younger, are better educated, and enjoy higher incomes than other consumers. They are more mobile than later adopters and change both their jobs and addresses more often. They also rely more heavily than later adopters on impersonal information sources; more hesitant buyers depend primarily on company-generated promotional information and word-of-mouth communications.

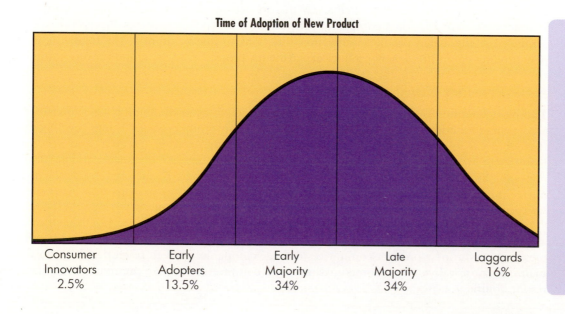

Time of Adoption of New Product

| Consumer Innovators 2.5% | Early Adopters 13.5% | Early Majority 34% | Late Majority 34% | Laggards 16% |

figure 12.2

Categories of Adopters Based on Relative Times of Adoption

Rate of Adoption Determinants

Frisbees progressed from the product introduction stage to the market maturity stage in a period of six months. By contrast, the U.S. Department of Agriculture tried for 13 years to persuade corn farmers to use hybrid seed corn, an innovation capable of doubling crop yields. Five characteristics of a product innovation influence its adoption rate:

1. *Relative advantage.* An innovation that appears far superior to previous ideas offers a greater relative advantage—reflected in terms of lower price, physical improvements, or ease of use—and increases the product's adoption rate.

2. *Compatibility.* An innovation consistent with the values and experiences of potential adopters attracts new buyers at a relatively rapid rate. Consumers already comfortable with the miniaturization of communications technology are likely to be attracted to smart phones, for instance, and the iPhone's 2- by 3-inch screen.

3. *Complexity.* The relative difficulty of understanding the innovation influences the speed of acceptance. In most cases, consumers move slowly in adopting new products they find difficult to understand or use. Farmers' cautious acceptance of hybrid seed corn illustrates how long an adoption can take.

4. *Possibility of trial use.* An initial free or discounted trial of a good or service means adopters can reduce their risk of financial loss when they try the product. A coupon for a free item or a free night's stay at a hotel can accelerate the rate of adoption.

5. *Observability.* If potential buyers can observe an innovation's superiority in a tangible form, the adoption rate increases. In-store demonstrations or even advertisements that focus on the superiority of a product can encourage buyers to adopt a product.

Marketers who want to accelerate the rate of adoption can manipulate these five characteristics at least to some extent. An informative promotional message about a new allergy drug could help consumers overcome their hesitation in adopting this complex product. Effective product design can emphasize an item's advantages over the competition. Everyone likes to receive something for free, so giving away small samples of a new product lets consumers try it at little or no risk. In-home demonstrations or trial home placements of items such as furniture or rugs can achieve similar results. Marketers must also make positive attempts to ensure the innovation's compatibility with adopters' value systems.

ORGANIZING FOR NEW-PRODUCT DEVELOPMENT

A firm needs to be organized in such a way that its personnel can stimulate and coordinate new-product development. Some companies contract with independent design firms to develop new products. Many assign product-innovation functions to one or more of the following entities: new-product committees, new-product departments, product managers, and venture teams.

New-Product Committees

The most common organizational arrangement for activities in developing a new product is to center these functions in a new-product committee. This group typically brings together experts in such areas as marketing, finance, manufacturing, engineering, research, and accounting. Committee members spend less time conceiving and developing their own new-product ideas than reviewing and approving new-product plans that arise elsewhere in the organization. The committee might review ideas from the engineering and design staff or perhaps from marketers and salespeople who are in constant contact with customers.

Because members of a new-product committee hold important jobs in the firm's functional areas, their support for any new-product plan likely foreshadows approval for further development. However, new-product committees in large companies tend to reach decisions slowly and maintain conservative views. Sometimes members compromise so they can return to their regular responsibilities.

New-Product Departments

Many companies establish separate, formally organized departments to generate and refine new-product ideas. The departmental structure overcomes the limitations of the new-product committee system and encourages innovation as a permanent full-time activity. The new-product department is responsible for all phases of a development project within the firm, including screening decisions, developing product specifications, and coordinating product testing. The head of the department wields substantial authority and typically reports to the chief executive officer, chief operating officer, or a top marketing executive.

Product Managers

A **product manager** is another term for a brand manager, a function mentioned earlier in the chapter. This marketer supports the marketing strategies of an individual product or product line. Procter & Gamble, for instance, assigned its first product manager in 1927, when it made one person responsible for Camay soap.

Product managers set prices, develop advertising and sales promotion programs, and work with sales representatives in the field. In a company that markets multiple products, product managers fulfill key functions in the marketing department. They provide individual attention for each product and support and coordinate efforts of the firm's sales force, marketing research department, and advertising department. Product managers often lead new-product development programs, including creation of new-product ideas and recommendations for improving existing products.

However, most consumer-goods companies such as Procter & Gamble and General Mills have either modified the product manager structure or done away with it altogether in favor of a category management structure. Category managers have profit and loss responsibility, which is not characteristic of the product management system. This change has largely come about because of customer preference, but it can also benefit a manufacturer by avoiding duplication of some jobs and competition among the company's own brands and its managers.

Venture Teams

A **venture team** gathers a group of specialists from different areas of an organization to work together in developing new products. The venture team must meet criteria for return on investment, uniqueness of product, serving a well-defined need, compatibility of the product with existing technology, and strength of patent protection. Although the organization sets up the venture team as a temporary entity, its flexible lifespan may extend over a number of years. When purchases confirm the commercial potential of a new product, an existing division may take responsibility for that product, or it may serve as the nucleus of a new business unit or of an entirely new company.

Some marketing organizations differentiate between venture teams and task forces. A new-product task force assembles an interdisciplinary group working on temporary assignment through their functional departments. Its basic activities center on coordinating and integrating the work of the firm's functional departments on a specific project.

Unlike a new-product committee, a venture team does not disband after every meeting. Team members accept project assignments as major responsibilities, and the team exercises the authority it needs to both plan and implement a course of action. To stimulate product innovation, the venture team typically communicates directly with top management but functions as an entity separate from the basic organization.

assessment check

1. Who are consumer innovators?

2. What characteristics of a product innovation can influence its adoption rate?

3. What is the role of a venture team in new-product development?

THE NEW-PRODUCT DEVELOPMENT PROCESS

7 List the stages in the new-product development process.

Once a firm is organized for new-product development, it can establish procedures for moving new-product ideas to the marketplace. Developing a new product often is time-consuming, risky, and expensive. Usually, firms must generate dozens of new-product ideas to produce even one successful product. In fact, the failure rate of new products averages 80 percent. Products fail for a number of reasons, including inadequate market assessments, lack of market orientation, poor screening and project evaluation, product defects, and inadequate launch efforts. And these blunders cost a bundle: firms invest nearly half of the total resources devoted to product innovation on products that become commercial failures.

A new product is more likely to become successful if the firm follows the six-step development process shown in Figure 12.3: (1) idea generation, (2) screening, (3) business analysis, (4) development, (5) test marketing, and (6) commercialization. Of course, each step requires decisions about whether to proceed further or abandon the project. And each step involves a greater financial investment.

Traditionally, most companies developed new products through phased development, which follows the six steps in an orderly sequence. Responsibility for each phase passes first from product planners to designers and engineers, then to manufacturers, and finally to marketers. The phased development method can work well for firms that dominate mature markets and can develop variations on existing products. But with rapid changes in technology and markets, many companies feel pressured to speed up the development process.

This time pressure has encouraged many firms to implement accelerated product development programs. These programs generally consist of teams with design, manufacturing, marketing, and sales personnel who carry out development projects from idea generation to commercialization. This method can reduce the time needed to develop products because team members work on the six steps concurrently rather than in sequence.

Whether a firm pursues phased development or parallel product development, all phases can benefit from planning tools and scheduling methods such as the program evaluation and review technique (PERT) and the critical path method (CPM). These techniques, originally developed by the U.S. Navy in connection with construction of the Polaris missile and submarine, map out the sequence of each step in a process and show the time allotments for each activity. Detailed PERT and CPM flowcharts help marketers coordinate all activities in the development and introduction of new products.

IDEA GENERATION

New-product development begins with ideas from many sources: suggestions from customers, the sales force, research and development specialists, competing products, suppliers, retailers, and independent inventors. BOSE Corporation has built its brand by staying at the forefront of technology. Spending an estimated $100 million a year on research, the company leads the market for products using advanced technology: sound systems for businesses, cars, and consumer home use and the award-winning Wave radio and Wave and Acoustic wave music systems.[31] The Coca-Cola Company engaged industrial designer Yves Béhar to help transform itself to a culture in which design plays a central role throughout all operations, including new-product development, merchandising strategy, the use of technology, and processes to ensure the firm is environmentally responsible.[32] Similarly, ongoing research at lawn-care industry leader ScottsMiracle-Gro helps the company fine-tune its understanding of consumer needs as it develops products and incorporates environmentally responsible behavior throughout its operations.[33]

figure 12.3

Steps in the New-Product Development Process

SCREENING

Screening separates ideas with commercial potential from those that cannot meet company objectives. Some organizations maintain checklists of development standards in determining whether

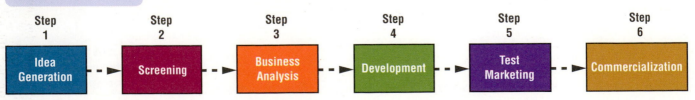

Step 1	Step 2	Step 3	Step 4	Step 5	Step 6
Idea Generation	Screening	Business Analysis	Development	Test Marketing	Commercialization

a project should be abandoned or considered further. These checklists typically include factors such as product uniqueness, availability of raw materials, and the proposed product's compatibility with current product offerings, existing facilities, and present capabilities. The screening stage may also allow for open discussions of new-product ideas among different parts of the organization.

BUSINESS ANALYSIS

A product idea that survives the initial screening must then pass a thorough business analysis. This stage consists of assessing the new product's potential market, growth rate, and likely competitive strengths. Marketers must evaluate the compatibility of the proposed product with organizational resources.

Concept testing subjects the product idea to additional study prior to its actual development. This important aspect of a new product's business analysis represents a marketing research project that attempts to measure consumer attitudes and perceptions about the new-product idea. Focus groups and in-store polling can contribute effectively to concept testing. The Eclipse 500 Very Light Jet, a six-passenger airplane about the size of an SUV, weighs under 10,000 pounds and can fly faster and higher than other aircraft in its class. Before manufacturing the plane, Eclipse Aviation spent years testing its concept. During its research phase, the company sought input from small- and large-plane pilots as well as experts from both inside and outside the aviation industry.[34]

The screening and business analysis stages generate extremely important information for new-product development because they (1) define the proposed product's target market and customers' needs and wants and (2) determine the product's financial and technical requirements. Firms willing to invest money and time during these stages tend to be more successful at generating viable ideas and creating successful products.

DEVELOPMENT

Financial outlays increase substantially as a firm converts an idea into a visible product. The conversion process is the joint responsibility of the firm's development engineers, who turn the original concept into a product, and its marketers, who provide feedback on consumer reactions to the product design, package, color, and other physical features. Many firms implement computer-aided design and manufacturing (CAD/CAM) systems to streamline the development stage, and prototypes may go through numerous changes before the original mock-up becomes a final

SOME LIKE IT HOT

THE AMAZING NEW BOSE ACOUSTIMASS LOUDSPEAKERS.
NOW PLAYING AT A DEALER NEAR YOU. FOR DETAILS RING 0795 21957/8

BOSE
Better sound through research
Bose UK Limited, Trinity Trading Estate, Sittingbourne, Kent ME10 2PD.

© Image courtesy of The Advertising Archives

BOSE Corporation has built its brand by staying at the forefront of technology. Spending an estimated $100 million a year on research, the company leads the market for products that use advanced technology, such as Wave music systems.

Sports eyeware marketer Oakley uses a design approach called sculptural physics, which it views as the discipline of wrapping science with art.

© Chip East/Bloomberg News/Landov

product. Southern California–based sports eyewear and apparel marketer Oakley uses a design approach called *sculptural physics,* which it views as the discipline of wrapping science with art. The company's ideas are born using CAD/CAM engineering and are given form as three-dimensional prototypes. New products are evaluated and field-tested by the world's top athletes. Once finalized, they are released to the general public.

TEST MARKETING

As discussed in Chapter 8, many firms test market their new-product offerings to gauge consumer reaction. After a company develops a prototype, it may decide to test market it to measure consumer reactions under normal competitive conditions. Test marketing's purpose is to verify that the product will perform well in a real-life environment. If the product does well, the company can proceed to commercialization. If it flops, the company can fine-tune certain features and reintroduce it or pull the plug on the project altogether. Industries that rely heavily on test marketing are snack foods, automobiles, and movies. Of course, even if a product tests well and reaches the commercialization stage, it may still take a while to catch on with the general public.

COMMERCIALIZATION

When a new-product idea reaches the commercialization stage, it is ready for full-scale marketing. Commercialization of a major new product can expose the firm to substantial expenses. It must establish marketing strategies, fund outlays for production facilities, and acquaint the sales force, marketing intermediaries, and potential customers with the new product.

assessment check

1. Where do ideas for new products come from?

2. What is concept testing?

3. What happens in the commercialization stage?

8 **Explain the relationship between product safety and product liability.**

Product Safety and Liability

A product can fulfill its mission of satisfying consumer needs only if it ensures safe operation. Manufacturers must design their products to protect users from harm. Products that lead to injuries, either directly or indirectly, can have disastrous consequences for their makers. **Product liability** refers to the responsibility of manufacturers and marketers for injuries and damages caused by their products. Chapter 3 discussed some of the major consumer protection laws that affect product safety. These laws include the Flammable Fabrics Act of 1953, the Fair Packaging and Labeling Act of 1966, the Poison Prevention Packaging Act of 1970, and the Consumer Product Safety Act of 1972.

Federal and state legislation play a major role in regulating product safety. The Poison Prevention Packaging Act requires drug manufacturers to place their products in packaging that is child resistant yet accessible to all adults, even ones who have trouble opening containers. The Consumer Product Safety Act created a powerful regulatory agency—the Consumer Product Safety Commission (CPSC). This agency has assumed jurisdiction over every consumer product category except food, automobiles, and a few other products already regulated by other agencies. The CPSC has the authority to ban products without court hearings, order recalls or redesigns of products, and inspect production facilities. It can charge managers of negligent companies with criminal offenses. The CPSC is especially watchful of products aimed at babies and young children.

The federal Food and Drug Administration (FDA) must approve food, medications, and health-related devices such as wheelchairs. The Food Allergen Labeling and Consumer Protection Act mentioned earlier increased the requirements for food labeling. The FDA can also take products off the market if concerns arise about the safety of these products. As the "Solving an Ethical Controversy" feature shows, food safety questions, whether true or not, can harm an entire industry.

The number of product liability lawsuits filed against manufacturers skyrocketed in recent years. Marketers' exposure to potential liability and litigation is also on the rise in many overseas markets. Many of these claims reach settlements out of court. For example, pharmaceuticals manufacturer Eli Lilly recently agreed to pay $1.2 billion to 28,500 people who claimed they were injured by Zyprexa, its drug for schizophrenia and bipolar disorder.[35] However, juries settle many other suits, often awarding multimillion-dollar settlements to individuals or their families. This threat has led most companies to step up efforts to ensure product safety. Safety warnings appear prominently on the labels of such potentially hazardous products as cleaning fluids and drain cleaners to inform users of the dangers of these products, particularly to children. Changes in product design have reduced the hazards posed by such products as lawn mowers, hedge trimmers, and toys. Product liability insurance has become an essential element for any new or existing product strategy. Premiums for this insurance have risen alarmingly, however, and insurers have almost entirely abandoned some kinds of coverage.

Volvo is well known for the safety features it designs into its automobiles, and consumers recognize that fact when they decide to purchase a Volvo.

© Bob Strong/Reuters/Landov

Solving an ethical controversy

Swine Flu: How a Name Can Hurt an Industry

When the news media broke the story about a new strain of flu recently, government agencies and consumers feared the worst—global spread of a potentially deadly disease. The virus was dubbed *swine flu*. The reason for the name is that it contains genetic material from pigs, birds, and humans. Once they heard the name, though, some consumers mistakenly believed that anyone who ate pork was at risk to contract the flu. In fact, the disease is not a food-borne illness; it is a respiratory virus. Consumers cannot catch the flu by eating pork.

People who actually contracted the flu certainly suffered. But it became rapidly apparent that hog farmers and pork products were also a casualty of the mounting fear.

Did the name given to the flu virus unfairly target pork producers?

PRO

1. Hog prices plummeted by more than 10 percent in a single week amid media reports about swine flu, as did pork sales. Hundreds of thousands of hogs were slaughtered worldwide and discarded. Because the virus originated in North America, Russia and China banned U.S. pork imports, and other countries banned imports from Canada.

2. Previously, new strains of flu have been named for their country or place of origin, such as Spanish flu and Hong Kong flu. The World Organization for Animal Health suggested the name should have been North American Influenza, while officials in Thailand, a large importer of pork, began calling it Mexican flu because the first cases were identified in Mexico.

CON

1. The pork industry was already losing money when the swine flu became news—about $3 billion over the previous 18 months. So the massive losses cited as a result of poor publicity were exaggerated.

2. Critics of the pork industry charge that many hog operations are overcrowded and imperil the health of livestock, thus creating a prime breeding ground for viral strains.

Summary

Eventually, the World Health Organization abandoned the swine flu name in favor of the neutral label H1N1, and later Influenza A. Many news organizations adopted the new labels, but the pork industry claimed that the damage was done.

Sources: Robert King, "Virus Gives Pigs a Bad Name," *Indianapolis Star*, May 4, 2009, http://www.indystar.com; Jason Markusoff, "Canada's Pork Industry Hit with Trade Bans," *Calgary Herald*, May 4, 2009, www.calgaryherald.com; Philip Rucker, "The Pork Lobbyists, Ready to Reassure," *The Washington Post*, May 4, 2009, http://www.washingtonpost.com; Bob Burgdorfer, "Flu Hits as U.S. Hog Industry Struggling to Recover," *Reuters UK*, May 2, 2009, http://uk.reuters.com; "Inaccurate `Swine Flu´ Label Hurts Industry, Pork Producers Say," *CNN*, April 30, 2009, http://www.cnn.com; Keith Bradsher, "The Naming of Swine Flu, a Curious Matter," *The New York Times*, April 28, 2009, http://www.nytimes.com.

Regulatory activities and the increased number of liability claims have prompted companies to sponsor voluntary improvements in safety standards. Many companies, including Wal-Mart and Mattel, have worked with the Consumer Product Safety Commission to improve their safety protocols. Wal-Mart uses its Retailer Reporting Model to provide CPSC with detailed weekly reports about customer product safety complaints and concerns. Safety planning is now a vital element of product strategy, and many companies now publicize the safety planning and testing that go into the development of their products. Volvo, for example, is well known for the safety features it designs into its automobiles, and consumers recognize that fact when they decide to purchase a Volvo.

Due in part to companies' voluntary policing efforts, however, the tide may be turning on liability lawsuits. In a huge decision for the medical device industry, the U.S. Supreme Court recently ruled that patients injured by medical devices could not sue the manufacturer. And with some drug makers also appealing multimillion-dollar judgments to the high court, legal observers suggest the same protection may soon be applied to the pharmaceutical industry.[36]

assessment check

1. What is the role of the Consumer Product Safety Commission (CPSC)?

2. What safety issues come under the jurisdiction of the Food and Drug Administration (FDA)?

Strategic Marketing — Implications of Marketing in the 21st Century

marketers who want to see their products reach the marketplace successfully have a number of options for developing them, branding them, and developing a strong brand identity among consumers and business customers. The key is to integrate all of the options so they are compatible with a firm's overall business and marketing strategy and ultimately the firm's mission. As marketers consider ideas for new products, they need to be careful not to send their companies in so many different directions as to dilute the identities of their brands, making it nearly impossible to keep track of what their companies do well. Category management can help companies develop a consistent product mix with strong branding, while at the same time meeting the needs of customers. Looking for ways to extend a brand without diluting it or compromising brand equity is also an important marketing strategy. Finally, marketers must continue to work to produce high-quality products that are safe for all users.

Review of Chapter Objectives

1 Explain the benefits of category and brand management.

Category management is beneficial to a business because it gives direct responsibility for creating profitable product lines to category managers and their product group. Consumers respond to branding by making repeat purchases of favored goods and services. Therefore, managing brands and categories of brands or product lines well can result in a direct response from consumers, increasing profits and revenues for companies and creating consumer satisfaction. Brand and category managers can also enhance relationships with business customers such as retailers.

2 Identify the different types of brands.

A generic product is an item characterized by a plain label, no advertising, and no brand name. A manufacturer's brand is a brand name owned by a manufacturer or other producer. Private brands are brand names placed on products marketed by a wholesaler or retailer. A family brand is a brand name that identifies several related products. An individual brand is a unique brand name that identifies a specific offering within a firm's product line to avoid grouping it under a family brand.

3 Explain the strategic value of brand equity.

Brand equity provides a competitive advantage for a firm because consumers are more likely to buy a product that carries a respected, well-known brand name. Brand equity also smoothes the path for global expansion.

4 Discuss how companies develop strong identities for their products and brands.

Effective brands communicate to a buyer an idea of the product's image. Trademarks, brand names, slogans, and brand icons create an association that satisfies the customer's expectation of the benefits that using or having the product will yield.

5 Identify and briefly describe each of the new-product development strategies.

The success of a new product can result from four product development strategies: (1) market penetration, in which a company seeks to increase sales of an existing product in an existing market; (2) market development, which concentrates on finding new markets for existing products; (3) product development, the introduction of new products into identifiable or established markets; and (4) product diversification, which focuses on developing entirely new products for new markets.

6   Describe the consumer adoption process.

In the adoption process, consumers go through a series of stages from learning about the new product to trying it and deciding whether to purchase it again. The stages are called awareness, interest, evaluation, trial, and adoption/rejection.

7   List the stages in the new-product development process.

The stages in the six-step process are (1) idea generation, (2) screening, (3) business analysis, (4) development, (5) test marketing, and (6) commercialization. These steps may be performed sequentially or, in some cases, concurrently.

8   Explain the relationship between product safety and product liability.

Product safety refers to the goal of manufacturers to create products that can be operated safely and will protect consumers from harm. Product liability is the responsibility of marketers and manufacturers for injuries and damages caused by their products. Major consumer protection laws are in place to protect consumers from faulty products.

assessment check: answers

1.1   What is a brand?

A brand is a name, term, sign, symbol, design, or some combination that identifies the products of one firm while differentiating these products from competitors' offerings.

1.2   Differentiate between brand recognition, brand preference, and brand insistence.

Brand recognition is a company's first objective for newly introduced products and aims to make these items familiar to the public. Brand preference means buyers rely on previous experiences with the product when choosing it over competitors' products. Brand insistence leads consumers to refuse alternatives and to search extensively for the desired merchandise.

2.1   Identify the different types of brands.

The different types of brands are manufacturer's (or national) brands, private brands, captive brands, family brands, and individual brands.

2.2   How are generic products different from branded products?

Generic products are characterized by plain labels, little or no advertising, and no brand names.

3.1   What is brand equity?

Brand equity refers to the added value a certain brand name gives to a product in the marketplace.

3.2   What are the four dimensions of brand personality?

The four dimensions of brand personality are differentiation, relevance, esteem, and knowledge.

3.3   How does category management help retailers?

Category management helps retailers by providing a person—a category manager—to oversee an entire product line and maximize sales for that retailer. It teams the consumer goods producer's marketing expertise with the retailer's in-store merchandising efforts to track and identify new opportunities for growth.

4.1   Distinguish between a brand name and a trademark.

A brand name is the part of the brand consisting of letters, numbers, or words that can be spoken and that forms a name distinguishing a firm's offerings from competitors. A trademark is a brand for which the owner claims exclusive legal protection.

4.2   What are the three purposes of packaging?

A package serves three major objectives: (1) protection against damage, spoilage, and pilferage; (2) assistance in marketing the product; and (3) cost effectiveness.

4.3   Describe brand extension and brand licensing.

Brand extension is the strategy of attaching a popular brand name to a new product in an unrelated product category. Brand licensing is the strategy of authorizing other companies to use a brand name.

5.1   Distinguish between market penetration and market development strategies.

In a market penetration strategy, a company seeks to increase sales of an existing product in an existing market. In a market development strategy, the company concentrates on finding new markets for existing products.

5.2   What is product development?

Product development refers to the introduction of new products into identifiable or established markets.

5.3   What is product diversification?

A product diversification strategy focuses on developing entirely new products for new markets.

6.1   Who are consumer innovators?

Consumer innovators are the first buyers of new products—people who purchase new products almost as soon as these products reach the market.

6.2   What characteristics of a product innovation can influence its adoption rate?

Five characteristics of a product innovation influence its adoption rate: relative advantage, compatibility, complexity, possibility of trial use, and observability.

6.3   What is the role of a venture team in new-product development?

A venture team gathers a group of specialists from different areas of an organization to work together in developing new products.

7.1   Where do ideas for new products come from?

New-product development begins with ideas from many sources: suggestions from customers, the sales force, research-and-development specialists, assessments of competing products, suppliers, retailers, and independent inventors.

7.2   What is concept testing?

Concept testing subjects the product idea to additional study prior to its actual development.

7.3   What happens in the commercialization stage?

When a new-product idea reaches the commercialization stage, it is ready for full-scale marketing.

8.1   **What is the role of the Consumer Product Safety Commission (CPSC)?**

The Consumer Product Safety Commission is a powerful regulatory agency with jurisdiction over every consumer product category except food, automobiles, and a few other products already regulated by other agencies.

8.2   **What safety issues come under the jurisdiction of the Food and Drug Administration (FDA)?**

The Food and Drug Administration must approve food, medications, and health-related devices such as wheelchairs.

Marketing Terms You Need to Know

brand 379
brand recognition 379
brand preference 380
brand insistence 380
generic products 380

manufacturer's brand 381
family brand 381
brand equity 382
category management 383
brand name 385

trademark 386
brand extension 391
adoption process 394
consumer innovator 394
diffusion process 395

Other Important Marketing Terms

private brand 381
captive brand 381
individual brand 382
brand manager 383
brand mark 385
trade dress 387
label 390

Universal Product Code (UPC) 390
line extension 391
brand licensing 392
market penetration strategy 393
product positioning 393
market development strategy 393
product development 394

product diversification strategy 394
cannibalization 394
product manager 397
venture team 397
concept testing 399
product liability 400

Assurance of Learning Review

1. What are the three stages marketers use to measure brand loyalty?

2. Identify and briefly describe the different types of brands.

3. Why is brand equity so important to companies?

4. What are the characteristics of an effective brand name?

5. What role does packaging play in helping create brand loyalty and brand equity?

6. What is category management and what role does it play in the success of a product line?

7. Describe the different product development strategies.

8. What are the five stages of the consumer adoption process?

9. Describe the different ways companies can organize to develop new products.

10. List the six steps in the new-product development process.

Projects and Teamwork Exercises

1. Locate an advertisement for a product that illustrates an especially effective brand name, brand mark, packaging, and overall trade dress. Explain to the class why you think this product has a strong brand identity.

2. With a classmate, go shopping in a grocery store for a product you think could benefit from updated or new package design. Then sketch out a new package design for the product, identifying and explaining your changes as well as your reasons for the changes. Bring the old package and your new package design to class to share with your classmates.

3. What category of consumer adopter best describes you? Do you follow the same adoption pattern for all products, or are you an early adopter for some and a laggard for others? Create a graph or chart showing your own consumer adoption patterns for different products.

4. With a classmate, choose a firm that interests you and together generate some ideas for new products that might be appropriate for the company. Test your ideas out on each other and then on your classmates. Which ideas make it past this review? Which don't? Why?

5. Consider the steps in the new-product development process. Do you think this process accounts for products that come into being by chance or accident? Why or why not? Defend your answer.

6. With a classmate, visit a couple of grocery stores and look for generic products. How many did you find and in what product categories? Are there any products you think could be successfully marketed as generics that are not now? Why do you think they would be successful?

7. Which product labels do you read? Over the next several days, keep a brief record of the labels you check while shopping. Do you read nutritional information when buying food products? Do you check care labels on clothes before you buy them? Do you read the directions or warnings on a product you haven't used before? Make notes about what influenced your decision to read or not read the product labels. Did you think they provided enough information, too little, or too much?

8. Some brands achieve customer loyalty by retaining an air of exclusivity and privilege, even though that often comes with high pricetags. Louis Vuitton, the maker of luxury leather goods, is one such firm. "You buy into the dream of Louis Vuitton," says one loyal customer. "We're part of a sect, and the more they put their prices up, the more we come back. They pull the wool over our eyes, but we love it." What kind of brand loyalty is this, and how does Vuitton achieve it?

9. Visit a grocery store, look at print ads, or view television advertising to develop a list of all the different brands of bottled water. How do the producers of bottled water turn this commodity item into a branded product? How does each differentiate its brand from all the others?

10. After its ReNu MoistureLoc contact lens solution was linked with cases of severe fungal eye infections, Bausch & Lomb pulled the product from shelves throughout the world. With a partner, research the steps the company went through to investigate the problem. Why was the product discontinued? What was the FDA's involvement in the case? How did the company handle the recall and how did it make the public aware of the problem?

Critical-Thinking Exercises

1. In this chapter, you learned that Mattel has launched a "Barbie Girls" experience in an attempt to sustain the interest of older girls in the Barbie brand. Do you think this strategy will work for Mattel? Why or why not? Identify another well-known product that appeals to a specific age group. Do you think a similar strategy would be successful? Why or why not?

2. General Mills and several other major food makers have begun producing organic foods. But they have deliberately kept their brand names off the packaging of these new products, thinking that the kind of customer who goes out of his or her way to buy organic products is unlikely to trust multinational brands. Other companies, however, such as Heinz, PepsiCo, and Tyson Foods, are betting that their brand names will prove to be persuasive in the $11 billion organic foods market. Which strategy do you think is more likely to be successful? Why?

3. After the terrorist attacks of 9/11, an ad hoc task force of DDB Worldwide advertising professionals in seventeen countries set out to discover what people abroad thought of the United States. In the course of their research, they developed the concept of "America as a Brand," urged U.S. corporations with overseas operations to help "restore" positive impressions of Brand America around the world, and urged the United States to launch Al Hurra as an alternative to the popular Al Jazeera network. Do you think foreigners' perception of a country and its culture can be viewed in marketing terms? Why or why not?

4. Brand names contribute enormously to consumers' perception of a brand. One writer has argued that alphanumeric brand names, such as the Toyota RAV4, Jaguar's X-Type sedan, the Xbox game console, and the GTI from Volkswagen, can translate more easily overseas than "real" names like Golf, Jetta, Escalade, and Eclipse. What other advantages and disadvantages can you think of for each type of brand name? Do you think one type is preferable to the other? Why?

Ethics Exercise

As mentioned in the chapter, some analysts predict bar codes may soon be replaced by a wireless technology called *radio-frequency identification (RFID)*. RFID is a system of installing tags containing tiny computer chips on, say, supermarket items. These chips automatically radio the location of the item to a computer network where inventory data are stored, letting store managers know not only where the item is at all times but also when and where it was made and its color and size. Proponents of the idea believe RFID will cut costs and simplify inventory tracking and reordering. It may also allow marketers to respond quickly to shifts in demand, avoid under- and overstocking, and reduce spoilage by automatically removing outdated perishables from the shelves. Privacy advocates, however, think the chips provide too much product-preference information that might be identified with individual consumers. In the meantime, Wal-Mart is requiring its top suppliers to begin using the new technology on products stocked by the giant retailer.

1. Do you think RFID poses a threat to consumer privacy? Why or why not?

2. Do you think the technology's possible benefits to marketers outweigh the potential privacy concerns? Are there also potential benefits to consumers, and if so, what are they?

3. How can marketers reassure consumers about privacy concerns if RFID comes into widespread use?

Internet Exercises

1. **Packaging.** Visit the Web site of a major food company such as ConAgra or Kraft Foods. (www.kraft.com, www.conagra-foods.com). Write a report on how the firm has used packaging as part of its brand management strategy.

2. **Product diversification strategies.** Computer company Hewlett-Packard recently embarked on a product diversification strategy. Go to the firm's Web site (www.hp.com). Click on "Company Information" and then "Newsroom" to obtain details about the firm's product diversification strategy. What are its key elements? What is the rationale for it?

3. **Trademarks.** In the United States, the Patent and Trademark Office is responsible for the registration of trademarks. Visit the USPTO Web site (www.uspto.gov). Click on "Trademarks" and answer the following questions:

   a. Do trademarks, copyrights, and patents protect the same things?

   b. What is a "standard character" drawing?

   c. What is the so-called Madrid Protocol concerning the international registration of marks? Does the Madrid Protocol make it easier for U.S. firms to resolve international trademark disputes?

Note: Internet Web addresses change frequently. If you don't find the exact site listed, you may need to access the organization's home page and search from there or use a search engine such as Google.

Case 12.1 Ferrari Runs on Brand Power

Who *wouldn't* want to own a Ferrari? Since its founding in 1947, Ferrari has worked to build a tradition of uncompromising

quality. Its ultraelegant motorcars, with their sleek lines, high-performance engines, and hand-tooled leather interiors, are almost unbelievably deluxe.

The Ferrari tradition is also built on exclusivity: the company limits its annual production. And with a robust menu of customizable features, literally every car it makes is unique. Discriminating buyers can select the Bose radio-navigator, which includes radio, audio and video DVD, Bluetooth, and satellite radio systems. Another optional feature is a satellite antitheft system integrated with the car alarm and approved by all the major international insurance companies. The backlog on some models is up to two years.

Despite this demand, with a starting price of just under $200,000, a Ferrari is out of reach for most of us. Even so, the Ferrari Company has managed to capture the attention of wistful car owners the world over by carefully nurturing its brand and offering an array of extensions like die-cast model kits, pocket-sized Hot Wheels cars, branded apparel, wristwatches, audio systems—even a $10,000 Segway transporter.

The company's ongoing sponsorship of Formula One Grand Prix racing has helped generate worldwide awareness of the brand. So, while owning one of these legendary vehicles or driving a Formula One racecar through the European countryside may not be possible for most people, they can still experience the Ferrari lifestyle by buying a piece of branded paraphernalia: a hat, jacket, T-shirt, key ring, or other collectible emblazoned with the distinctive Ferrari rearing stallion logo. The Ferrari Store, a retail chain, has outlets in select major cities across Asia, Europe, and the United States. The stores have been a smash hit. During a recent Formula One racing event in Shanghai, the local Ferrari store sold over $100,000 in merchandise in a single day.

Ferrari also licenses its name to dozens of partner companies who put the Ferrari name on a wide variety of products, from hand-held games to fitness equipment to perfumes to teddy bears. In a recent year, revenues from licensing royalties and the sale of Ferrari merchandise alone totaled $725 million.

Want more entertainment? The Ferrari theme park near Abu Dhabi in the United Arab Emirates offers an assortment of family rides, virtual simulations, and a racing school for wannabe speedsters, plus the usual array of Ferrari-branded merchandise.

Questions for Critical Thinking

1. Through the years, Ferrari has been very successful at brand extension. Do these extensions hurt the brand? Why or why not? What else can the company do to extend the brand?

2. Even though most of the world's consumers can't afford its product, Ferrari has managed to build a strong brand with loyal followers who aspire to the Ferrari lifestyle. By opening a Ferrari theme park in Abu Dhabi, the company hopes to further extend its brand. But not all concepts are seamlessly transferable, as the Walt Disney Company discovered when it opened its Euro Disney themepark outside Paris. It was three years before Euro Disney had a profitable quarter. In your opinion, what should Ferrari do to ensure success at its theme park?

Sources: Company Web site, http://www.ferrari.com, accessed May 19, 2009; David Menzies, "You Too Can Own a Ferrari," *National Post*, July 7, 2008, autos.canada.com; "Gameloft Licenses Ferrari; Fast Mobile Games Coming Soon!" *Intomobile*, March 20, 2008, www.intomobile.com; Robert Frank, "Gentlemen, Start Your Dishwashers," *The Wall Street Journal*, February 15, 2008, blogs.wsj.com; "Ferrari Revs into Retail, Announcing Plans for 40 Store Openings," *Edmunds*, October 22, 2007, www.edmunds.com; Tim Urquhart, "Leveraging the Legend," *World Motor Sport Marketplace*, October 2007, pp, 60–63; Noah B. Joseph, "At Park Opening in '09, It's All Ferrari, All the Time," *The New York Times*, June 10, 2007, www.nytimes.com; Frank Filipponio, "Ferrari Store–Los Angeles Opens in the Beverly Center," *Autoblog*, March 27, 2007, www.autoblog.com; "Ferrari at the Geneva Auto Show," *Easier Motoring*, March 7, 2007, www.easier.com.

Video Case 12.2   Developing and Managing Brand and Product Categories at Maine Media Workshops

The written video case on Maine Media appears on page VC-11. The Maine Media video is designed to expand and highlight the concepts in this chapter and the concepts and questions covered in the written video case.

part 4 voice of experience

Talking about Marketing Careers with...
Mark A. Mercurio

MARK A. MERCURIO
Assistant Brand Manager, Mr. Clean
Marketing
Procter & Gamble

Innovation and growth are two key words that best express Procter & Gamble's approach to the consumer goods market. The company is a global powerhouse, with nearly 98,000 employees working in 80 countries and product lines that include 22 billion-dollar brands. P&G focuses its product development and marketing efforts in four major segments: beauty, family health, household care, and its newest shaving products division, Gillette. If you walk down a supermarket or drugstore aisle, you'll see dozens of P&G brands—such as Cover Girl, Ivory, Pampers, ThermaCare, Tide, Folgers, and Dawn, to name just a few—all created to help simplify your daily life.

One of the tried-and-true brands in P&G's family is Mr. Clean. With a history stretching back nearly 50 years, consumers have come to depend on Mr. Clean products to help maintain their homes and autos. The feeling is mutual—the company relies on and values the trust that consumers place in the brand and want to build on that relationship. To do so, P&G has a dedicated marketing team to oversee its Mr. Clean product line. We were fortunate to be able to have a one-on-one exchange with one of those team members: Mark Mercurio, Assistant Brand Manager for Mr. Clean Marketing. He was kind enough to spend some time to help us understand what is involved in the day-to-day activities in brand management.

Q: Heading up the marketing team for such a recognized brand as Mr. Clean is a great career opportunity. Tell us a little about yourself—what academic and work experiences led you to your current position at Mr. Clean Marketing?

I took a roundabout track into brand management. I studied civil engineering at the University of Cincinnati for my undergraduate degree. I realized early in my school years that I didn't want to be an engineer but completed the degree and searched for a job in business. I found my engineering degree really helped with the quantitative nature of my future jobs. After UC, I took a job with Accenture—then Andersen Consulting—doing IT management consulting. I really enjoyed the project management nature of that job, and it gave me a chance to experience a number of different industries. After three years, I decided to go back to school to study marketing, as I wanted to get out of the back-office work of IT and more in the front end of the business, driving business strategies and planning. So I went to the Darden Graduate School of Business at the University of Virginia to get my MBA. Between my first and second years of MBA school, I took an internship in marketing research at P&G. I really loved the aspect of using research techniques to determine the best course for the business—it was a great mix of qualitative and quantitative work. After a couple years, though, I moved into marketing at P&G because it had more strategy setting and overall profit-and-loss business responsibility. And that's where I am today. Definitely the long road there, but I am absolutely certain this is the place for me.

Q: Students will be curious about what is involved in marketing consumer products such as those under the Mr. Clean family brand. How many people are on the Mr. Clean team? Would you outline the different functions of the members and their roles in marketing the brand? What is your role in the overall effort of bringing Mr. Clean products to consumers?

Brand management is all about leveraging your team's strengths to get the most out of your team. Within marketing, there are five of us—four assistant brand managers and the brand manager. Marketing's role is to set the strategy for the brand—both in how we communicate and in what we communicate to consumers. We oversee marketing planning and work with our agencies to develop world-class marketing. We also typically lead the new product initiatives for the brand—keeping the team on track, navigating the project through management reviews, etc. Marketing interacts with quite a few functions, including R&D, sales, product supply, marketing research, finance, and increasingly directly with sales teams to coordinate more closely with our retailers.

Q: We often talk about product lines in marketing. Procter & Gamble is a giant in its industry, offering several product lines for consumers. How does Mr. Clean fit into the mix of lines that P&G offers? How does it support the company's overall strategy?

Generally, different brands play different roles in the company. Mr. Clean's role in the overall company strategy is to drive discontinuous growth. With innovations like Magic Eraser, AutoDry, and Mr. Clean Magic Reach, we have been successful in that role.

Q: Mr. Clean as a brand name and brand mark has been around nearly 50 years now. How do you and your team keep the brand fresh and relevant in such a competitive marketplace as consumer household goods? How do you decide when and how to add a new product to the line? Do consumers have any input in the process? Can you give us an example?

Consumers are at the forefront of our decisions on what to bring to market and how. In fact, we have a mantra at P&G—Consumer Is Boss—representing that exact thought. Awhile back, P&G brought in business in new markets by first discovering a new technology and then figuring out how to make it work for consumers. Now, we're much better at letting the consumer drive the innovation. Our product researchers, marketing researchers, marketers, and agencies are constantly engaging in conversations with consumers through our research to understand what they need to make their lives easier. A perfect example of this is our Multi-Surface spray. We observed consumers cleaning their homes and found they have a different cleaner for every surface in their house. So we developed a spray that was suitable for every hard surface—it cleans glass, cuts grease, and kills germs all in one. Once we determine a direction for a new product, we involve the consumers in every aspect of bringing it to market, including how we name it, what benefit we talk about with consumers, what the packaging looks like, how to price it, etc.

Q: In textbooks and in the daily news, we hear about the importance of ensuring the quality of a product. That must be critical to consumer goods such as those you market. What goes into the formulation, testing, and production of a new product?

R&D staff have consumers with them the entire way as they formulate the product. Typically, they will have an "expert" panel of consumers who try iteration after iteration of formula design to help us optimize the formula. We also typically do one or two very large quantitative research tests to make sure the product meets all of our standards before releasing it to market.

Q: Mr. Clean is a true celebrity in the marketing world. Nearly everyone would instantly recognize his smiling face and bulging muscles. Could you talk a little about his value to Procter & Gamble? How do you protect his image and name?

I don't think I could put a value on Mr. Clean, the icon. In these days of fragmented marketing media, consumers are being drowned with messages—it's hard to stand out and be remembered. But with Mr. Clean, consumers are so accustomed to hearing about new ways to clean your home from Mr. Clean that our commercials are instantly recognized and easily remembered. It is a great asset we leverage in all of our marketing. At the same time, we do have distinct rules on how to use and not use the icon so that we can maintain the integrity of that asset. We have design and advertising development managers who help keep us marketing folks in line with how we want to leverage the icon, and they are constantly reviewing our work to make sure it fits with our objectives. We also track our brand's equity consistently to look for movement in how consumers view our brand.

Q: Many marketers get their start in the industry through work experience and internships. Did that help you on your career path? What advice can you give to students who are interested in getting started in a marketing career?

There are a number of ways to get into marketing—some more traditional than others. I took a pretty typical route—through an MBA program after having a few years' work experience. My advice would be to think about the kind of marketing you would like to do and focus on that industry. Then build a network. Try joining the marketing club at school or working on research projects with a professor—anything to help you understand the industry better and increase your chances of meeting a hiring manager. And when you get a chance to interview for a job, make sure you prepare yourself and be confident.

Interview from "Mr. Clean Marketing," Procter & Gamble. Used with permission.

GREENSBURG, INC.

Green: It's Not Just for Earth Day Anymore

© Steven J. Eliopoulos

Honda has always enjoyed a reputation as being a fuel-efficient economical brand. As early as 1974, Honda has been changing the way we look at cars with the low emission/fuel-efficient Civic CVCC. In the years since, Honda's commitment to the environment has spawned a line of Good, Better, Best, and Ultimate vehicles. Regular gas cars are Good, with about 30 mpg; hybrids are Better at about 45 mpg; and their Best solution is a natural gas-powered Civic GX that gets about 220 miles to a tank. Honda has Ultimate solutions in the works, including the new Honda FCX Clarity, a hydrogen fuel cell car in which hydrogen reacts with oxygen, both renewable resources, to create electricity. The only emissions you get are a little steam. You can buy the natural gas Civic GX and Clarity today, but neither vehicle is practical for the average driver as the fueling stations are hard to come by.

Roger Schofield of Schofield Honda in Wichita, Kansas, has been promoting Honda as a good and good-for-you vehicle for years. Gas mileage, safety, and brand loyalty are all important parts of Schofield's marketing. Unfortunately, despite the increasing interest in the environment, alternative fuel vehicles make up a very small part of his business. Even the Civic hybrid, a car with a lot of buzz, only makes up about 4 percent of his annual sales.

Sales figures on alternative fuel cars as they were, Roger wanted to reposition the Schofield *brand* in the green marketplace, rather than focus on particular products. When the dealership did some renovations to their buildings, they created the Honda Green Zone, a rental space for organizations to hold meetings about green projects. Internally, Roger holds weekly meetings with his Green Team to brainstorm new projects, marketing, and products. They were at work on several other project ideas when an F5 tornado hit Greensburg on May 4, 2007. At that moment, the idea of going green at Schofield Honda took on a whole new life.

The news of the green rebuilding initiative in Greensburg really drove home the need to become a leader in promoting more environmentally friendly technology. With any new technology, it takes a few early adopters to help lay the infrastructure for the rest of us. Well aware of the media attention surrounding Greensburg, Schofield decided to donate a natural gas Honda Civic GX to the town and a fueling station to go with it. The car would be made available to the residents to check out and try for themselves. The world would get to see the car in use by average people, and the town would have its own natural gas fueling station.

He admits questioning his decision even as he was driving into Greensburg on the day of the presentation, but when all was said and done, it was the right thing to do. When customers come into the dealership, they are more interested in alternative fuel and high efficiency vehicles and recognize Schofield Honda's commitment to the people of Greensburg and the green movement as a whole.

Visit Schofield Honda today, and you're going green—regardless of which type of vehicle you purchase. Employees will be drinking from ceramic coffee mugs "sponsored" by other local businesses. When you clean out your trade-in, you can use the recycling bins and take your important stuff with you in a Schofield Honda reusable shopping bag. If you're just there for an oil change, your old oil will be recycled to heat the shop.

Despite the media coverage on Greensburg and Schofield's green marketing efforts, sales are still slow on the alternative fuel vehicles, but Roger is okay with that. Making the products available to those on the cutting edge will earn him a reputation as cutting edge himself. When Wichita is ready for a change, Schofield Honda will be there and waiting.

Questions

1. Do you think repositioning the dealership as a green business will have a positive impact on their products' lifecycles?

2. What impact, if any, will going green have on brand loyalty? Discuss the Honda brand as well as the Schofield Honda brand.

3. Would you consider "green" to be a line extension at Schofield Honda? Why or why not?

4. Write a memo (3 to 5 pages) about which "businesses" on your campus (i.e., the food court, the bookstore, athletic center) could incorporate some of the initiatives that Schofield has taken with his dealership.

© Getty Images

PART

5

Distribution Decisions

CHAP 13 TER Marketing Channels and Supply Chain Management

© AP Images/Donna McWilliam

Burlington Northern Santa Fe Rides Green Rails

Railroads helped build the United States, and they are chugging into the nation's future. In an era in which fuel economy and reduced impact on the natural environment are major concerns

for businesses, consumers, and communities, rail transport is getting a new look. Why? Railroad travel is cleaner and more efficient than most other modes of transportation. A train can transport one ton of freight

more than 420 miles on a single gallon of fuel—a more economic, greener way of moving goods than trucking. "Rail has long been the most efficient means humankind has ever created for moving freight over

land," observes John Lanigan, executive vice president and chief marketing officer of Burlington Northern Santa Fe (BNSF) Railway.

Many firms depend on BNSF and other railroads to transport their goods, ranging from lumber to new automobiles, from one destination to another. BNSF, which operates over 32,000 miles of track across the western two-thirds of the United States, has taken its environmental role a step farther by implementing green processes and better equipment. Recently, the company announced plans to build a $300 million railyard closer to the California ports of Los Angeles and Long Beach, where cargo containers coming in on ships could be loaded directly onto trains instead of trucked up the highway to another yard. The plan should dramatically reduce the amount of air pollution and traffic congestion on the nearby Long Beach Freeway. The new facility not only reduces the impact of transporting goods on the environment, it also allows BNSF to grow larger to handle the surge of Asian goods arriving in these two ports. "We need to grow, but grow green," observes Matthew K. Rose, CEO of BNSF,

about his firm's commitment to the environment.

Locomotives, trucks, and other vehicles at the new facility will be powered by natural gas, which burns cleaner than other fuels. The natural gas "hostling" trucks or tractors reduce nitrous oxide and particulate matter emissions by 90 percent, compared with diesel railroad-yard transport trucks. In addition, new idle-reduction technology and hybrid switch engines reduce even more the amount of emissions produced by the railroad yard equipment. With the new technology, locomotives no longer need to idle for hours while they sit in the railroad yard. And the hybrid switcher—called the Green Goat—combines a micro-turbine and batteries for better fuel efficiency. BNSF already operates two locomotives powered by liquefied natural gas (LNG) and plans to increase the number.

BNSF combined the announcement of its plan for the

green facility with BNSF Goes Green, a promotional event that invited public officials and community leaders to view the new equipment. BNSF executives pointed out a sound wall being built around the yard so that nearby neighbors—including a school—would not be disturbed by noise. In addition, trees will be planted between the facility and the surrounding neighborhood to provide an additional sound barrier and landscaping. BNSF also distributed an English- and Spanish-language DVD to nearby residents and community officials that provides details about the project, including potential new jobs for local workers. The project received a positive response. "I commend the BNSF Railway," notes one Los Angeles city council member, "for stepping up to the challenge of developing a green intermodal facility that efficiently moves cargo while working to protect the quality of life for communities and neighborhoods."[1]

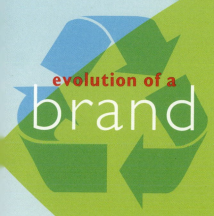

evolution of a
brand

BNSF Railway is well known as a transportation giant; the firm transports more than 10 million shipments each year. Although engaged in increasingly green practices, such as operating the two LNG locomotives in the United States, the firm has accelerated its push toward eco-friendly operations and become more public about it.

- BNSF makes an effort to have as little impact as possible on wilderness areas and national parks through which its tracks and trains pass. Because Glacier National Park in Montana receives an average of 64 trains per day, BNSF has founded the Great Northern Environmental Stewardship Area (GNESA), an organization committed to preserving the beauty and habitat of Glacier National Park. The organization provides a forum for communication and collaboration among industries, agencies, and the park. Do you think this type of action is necessary for BNSF? How does it help develop the future of the brand?

- Within its facilities, BNSF promotes as much recycling as possible—paper and

evolution of a brand

continued

cardboard, batteries, used oil, used filters, scrap metals, fluorescent bulbs, circuitboards, and the like. Over the years, the firm's employees have recycled tens of millions of pounds of these items. In what ways might BNSF use this practice as a marketing tool?

chapter overview

distribution Movement of goods and services from producers to customers.

marketing (distribution) channel System of marketing institutions that enhances the physical flow of goods and services, along with ownership title, from producer to consumer or business user.

logistics Process of coordinating the flow of information, goods, and services among members of the distribution channel.

supply chain management Control of the activities of purchasing, processing, and delivery through which raw materials are transformed into products and made available to final consumers.

physical distribution Broad range of activities aimed at efficient movement of finished goods from the end of the production line to the consumer.

Distribution—moving goods and services from producers to customers—is the second marketing mix variable and an important marketing concern. Firms depend on companies like BNSF to move their goods from one destination to another. A distribution strategy has two critical components: (1) marketing channels and (2) logistics and supply-chain management.

A **marketing channel**—also called a **distribution channel**—is an organized system of marketing institutions and their interrelationships that enhances the physical flow and ownership of goods and services from producer to consumer or business user. The choice of marketing channels should support the firm's overall marketing strategy. By contrast, **logistics** refers to the process of coordinating the flow of information, goods, and services among members of the marketing channel. **Supply chain management** is the control of activities of

briefly
speaking

"How tomorrow moves"

—CSX Corporation motto

purchasing, processing, and delivery through which raw materials are transformed into products and made available to final consumers. Efficient logistical systems support customer service, enhancing customer relationships—an important goal of any marketing strategy.

A key aspect of logistics is physical distribution, which covers a broad range of activities aimed at efficient movement of finished goods from the end of the production line to the consumer. Although some marketers use the terms *transportation* and *physical distribution* interchangeably, these terms do not carry the same meaning. **Physical distribution** extends beyond transportation to include such important decision areas as customer service, inventory control, materials handling, protective packaging, order processing, and warehousing.

Well-planned marketing channels and effective logistics and supply-chain management provide ultimate users with convenient ways for obtaining the goods and services they desire. This chapter discusses the activities, decisions, and marketing intermediaries involved in managing marketing channels and logistics. Chapter 14 looks at other players in the marketing channel: retailers, direct marketers, and wholesalers.

The Role of Marketing Channels in Marketing Strategy

A firm's distribution channels play a key role in its overall marketing strategy because these channels provide the means by which the firm makes the goods and services available to ultimate users. Channels perform four important functions. First, they facilitate the exchange process by reducing the number of marketplace contacts necessary to make a sale. Suppose you've had a Nintendo DS handheld game player in the past and been satisfied with it, so when you see an ad for the Nintendo Wii, you are interested. You visit the Nintendo Web site where you learn more about the Wii and its unique features. You are particularly drawn to the games "NCAA Football All-Play" and "Rock Band." But you want to see the game console in person, so you locate a dealer near enough for you to visit.[2] The dealer forms part of the channel that brings you—a potential buyer—and Nintendo—the seller—together to complete the exchange process. It's important to keep in mind that all channel members benefit when they work together; when they begin to disagree or—worse yet—compete directly with each other, everyone loses.

Distributors adjust for discrepancies in the market's assortment of goods and services via a process known as *sorting*, the second channel function. A single producer tends to maximize the quantity it makes of a limited line of goods, while a single buyer needs a limited quantity of a wide selection of merchandise. Sorting alleviates such discrepancies by channeling products to suit both the buyer's and the producer's needs.

The third function of marketing channels involves standardizing exchange transactions by setting expectations for products, and it involves the transfer process itself. Channel members tend to standardize payment terms, delivery schedules, prices, and purchase lots, among other conditions. Standardization helps make transactions efficient and fair.

The final marketing channel function is to facilitate searches by both buyers and sellers. Buyers search for specific goods and services to fill their needs, while sellers attempt to learn what buyers want. Channels bring buyers and sellers together to complete the exchange process.

Hundreds of distribution channels exist today, and no single channel best serves the needs of every company. Instead of searching for the best channel for all products, a marketing manager must analyze alternative channels in light of consumer needs to determine the most appropriate channel or channels for the firm's goods and services.

Describe the types of marketing channels and the roles they play in marketing strategy.

If you are interested in learning more about the Nintendo Wii, you may want to see the game console in person by visiting a local dealer.

© AP Images/Paul Sakuma

Marketers must remain flexible because channels change over time. Dell products, originally available only through direct-to-customer selling, are now sold at Best Buy.

© AP Images/Ric Francis

Marketers must remain flexible because channels may change over time. Today's ideal channel may prove inappropriate in a few years, or the way a company uses that channel may have to change. Two decades ago, Michael Dell came up with a revolutionary way to sell computers: by telephone, directly to consumers. Later, Dell added Internet sales to its operations. Now the firm has a new channel through which its computers can reach consumers: retailer Best Buy. Selected models of Dell's PCs are now available at 900 Best Buy stores around the United States. The agreement with Best Buy represents a huge shift in Dell's method for getting its goods to consumers. But many industry experts praise the move because Dell recognized that it needed greater distribution to grow, and Best Buy is one of the biggest U.S. electronics retailers.[3]

The following sections examine the diverse types of channels available to marketers and the decisions marketers must make to develop an effective distribution strategy that supports their firm's marketing objectives.

Types of Marketing Channels

The first step in selecting a marketing channel is determining which type of channel will best meet both the seller's objectives and the distribution needs of customers. Figure 13.1 depicts the major channels available to marketers of consumer and business goods and services.

Most channel options involve at least one **marketing intermediary.** A marketing intermediary (or **middleman**) is an organization that operates between producers and consumers or business users. Retailers and wholesalers are both marketing intermediaries. A retail store owned and operated by someone other than the manufacturer of the products it sells is one type of marketing intermediary. A **wholesaler** is an intermediary that takes title to the goods it handles and then distributes these goods to retailers, other distributors, or sometimes end consumers. Although some analysts believed that the Internet would ultimately render many intermediaries obsolete, that hasn't happened. Instead, it has enabled many such businesses to enhance customer service. Bikeworld, a firm that makes high-end bicycles and components, embraced e-business early on, but the company's founder initially viewed the Internet as a tool for attracting customers away from the larger, more established mail-order companies. This strategy proved successful, but Bikeworld faced a related problem: how to fulfill the increasing number of orders it was receiving. So the company enlisted the help of FedEx. Integrating the shipper's PowerShip system with its own Web server, Bikeworld was able to achieve a seamless transmission of information from online orders to fulfillment and delivery.[4]

A short marketing channel involves few intermediaries. By contrast, a long marketing channel involves several intermediaries working in succession to move goods from producers to consumers. Business products usually move through short channels due to geographic concentrations and comparatively fewer business purchasers. Service firms market primarily through short channels because they sell intangible products and need to maintain personal relationships within their channels. Haircuts, manicures, and dental cleanings all operate through short channels. Not-for-profit organizations also tend to work with short, simple, and direct channels. Any marketing intermediaries in such channels usually act as agents, such as independent ticket agencies or fund-raising specialists.

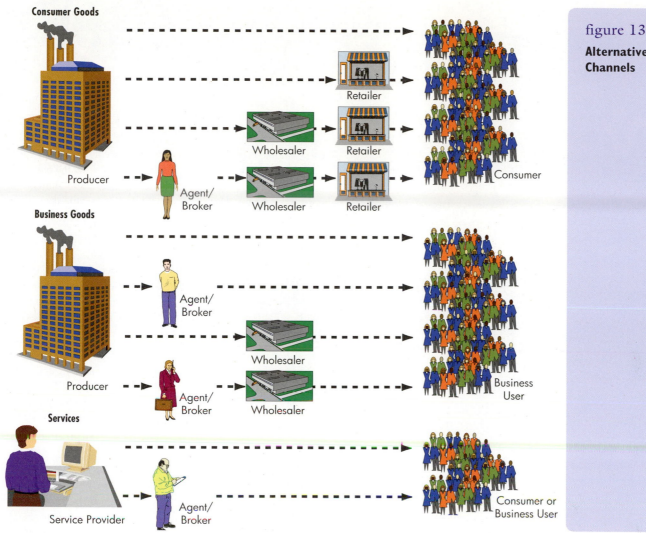

figure 13.1

Alternative Marketing Channels

DIRECT SELLING

The simplest and shortest marketing channel is a direct channel. A **direct channel** carries goods directly from a producer to the business purchaser or ultimate user. This channel forms part of **direct selling,** a marketing strategy in which a producer establishes direct sales contact with its product's final users. Direct selling is an important option for goods requiring extensive demonstrations in persuading customers to buy. The "Etiquette Tips for Marketing Professionals" feature contains suggestions for making successful sales calls.

Direct selling plays a significant role in business-to-business marketing. Most major installations, accessory equipment, and even component parts and raw materials are sold through direct contacts between producing firms and final buyers. Many people in business enjoy successful sales careers. According to the *Occupational Outlook Handbook* published by the U.S. Department of Labor, about 2 million people are employed as sales representatives in manufacturing and wholesaling industries.[5]

Direct selling is also important in consumer-goods markets. Direct sellers such as Avon, Pampered Chef, and Tastefully Simple sidestep competition in store aisles by developing networks of independent representatives who sell their products directly to consumers. Many of these companies practice a direct selling strategy called the *party plan,* originally popularized by Tupperware. Beijo Bags is one such business. Launched by entrepreneur Susan Handley, the bags are sold at home-based parties, called Beijo Collection Showcase Parties, by independent sales representatives who are mostly stay-at-home moms—and customers themselves. The bags, which appeal to women of all ages, are made from synthetic materials—no leather—and can be recycled by returning them to the manufacturer. Beijo Bags has topped $10 million in sales.[6]

Anatomy of a Successful Sales Call

When you make a sales call to a potential or existing customer, you are the face and voice of your firm. The way you are perceived is the way the customer perceives your company. So you want to make a good first impression as well as a positive lasting impression. Most likely you will be trained by your supervisor or someone else at the company in the fine art of a successful sales call. Here are a few additional tips to help you on your way.

- *Do your homework.* Be sure you know the correct spelling and pronunciation of the company you are visiting—and the person you are scheduled to meet. Familiarize yourself with the company's goods or services and past history with your company.

- *Assess the company's potential needs.* Don't launch into a presentation of your products before learning what the customer needs. If you have made yourself familiar with the customer's goods and services, you should be able to ask questions and produce answers about what types of products could provide the best solutions for the customer.

- *Dress appropriately and arrive on time.* Wear the proper business attire for your industry, whether it's a business suit or business casual clothing. Cover any tattoos or body piercings and wear conservative jewelry. In short, play it safe. Always arrive a few minutes before the scheduled time. Doing so shows respect for your customer's time and indicates you are serious about doing business.

- *Be conservative in your behavior.* Always stand to greet your customer. Smile, shake hands, and follow the customer to wherever the meeting will take place. Address him or her with the title "Mr." or "Ms.," and do not assume the person wishes to be called by first name until you are asked to do so.

- *Turn off your cell phone.* If possible, turn off your cell phone before entering the building for your meeting. At least turn it off when you enter the meeting. Never take a call during the meeting, and only make one if it will help the progress of the meeting. For example, a customer might have a question only your supervisor can answer. A successful sales call requires your total attention on the customer.

- *Follow up the meeting with a thank-you.* After the sales call, be sure to follow up with a phone call, e-mail, or note to thank the person—regardless of the outcome. Even if the call did not produce a sale or other immediate results, it could possibly have laid the groundwork for a future relationship.

Sources: "Telephone Manners," *Salary.com*, www.salary.com, accessed May 19, 2009; Dan Seidman, "Your Sales Technique," *Monster Career Advice*, career-advice. monster.com, accessed May 19, 2009; Dan Seidman, "Practice What You Preach in Sales," *Monster Career Advice*, career-advice.monster.com, accessed May 19, 2009; "Training Sales Force in Business Etiquette," *Reaction Search International*, December 1, 2007, www.executivesearchfirmnews.com.

The Internet provides another direct selling channel for both B2B and B2C purchases. Consumers who want to sport designer handbags, but don't want to pay full price for them, can rent them from Bagborroworsteal.com. For those who like to change bags often but can't or won't pay the hundreds or thousands of dollars for Chanel's, Prada's, or Gucci's latest, the site may be a real bargain. Customers become members at $9.95 for the first month, with a reduced membership fee for subsequent months. In addition to designer handbags, members can find sunglasses and jewelry to complete their look.[7]

Direct mail can also be an important part of direct selling—or it can encourage a potential customer to contact an intermediary such as a retailer. Either way, it is a vital communication piece for many marketers.

CHANNELS USING MARKETING INTERMEDIARIES

Although direct channels allow simple and straightforward marketing, they are not practical in every case. Some products serve markets in different areas of the country or world or have large numbers of potential end users. Other categories of goods rely heavily on repeat purchases. The producers of these goods may find more efficient, less expensive, and less time-consuming alternatives to direct channels by using marketing intermediaries. This section considers five channels that involve marketing intermediaries.

Producer to Wholesaler to Retailer to Consumer

The traditional channel for consumer goods proceeds from producer to wholesaler to retailer to user. This method carries goods between thousands of small producers with limited lines and local retailers. A firm with limited financial resources will rely on the services of a wholesaler that serves as an immediate source of funds and then markets to hundreds of retailers. On the other hand, a small retailer can draw on a wholesaler's specialized distribution skills. In addition, many manufacturers hire their own field representatives to service retail accounts with marketing information. Wholesalers may then handle the actual sales transactions.

Producer to Wholesaler to Business User

Similar characteristics in the organizational market often attract marketing intermediaries to operate between producers and business purchasers. The term *industrial distributor* commonly refers to intermediaries in the business market that take title to the goods.

Producer to Agent to Wholesaler to Retailer to Consumer

In markets served by many small companies, a unique intermediary—the agent—performs the basic function of bringing buyer and seller together. An agent may or may not take possession of the goods but never takes title. The agent merely represents a producer by seeking a market for its products or a wholesaler, which does take title to the goods, by locating a supply source.

Producer to Agent to Wholesaler to Business User

Like agents, brokers are independent intermediaries who may or may not take possession of goods but never take title to these goods. Agents and brokers also serve the business market when small producers attempt to market their offerings through large wholesalers. Such an intermediary, often called a **manufacturers' representative,** provides an independent sales force to contact wholesale buyers. A kitchen equipment manufacturer may have its own manufacturer's representatives to market its goods, for example.

Producer to Agent to Business User

For products sold in small units, only merchant wholesalers can economically cover the markets. A merchant wholesaler is an independently owned wholesaler that takes title to the goods. By maintaining regional inventories, this wholesaler achieves transportation economies, stockpiling goods and making small shipments over short distances. For a product with large unit sales, however, and for which transportation accounts for a small percentage of the total cost, the producer-agent-business user channel is usually employed. The agent in effect becomes the producer's sales force, but bulk shipments of the product reduce the intermediary's inventory management function.

DUAL DISTRIBUTION

Dual distribution refers to movement of products through more than one channel to reach the firm's target market. Nordstrom, for instance, has a three-pronged distribution system, selling through stores, catalogs, and the Internet. Marketers usually adopt a dual distribution strategy either to maximize their firm's coverage in the marketplace or to increase the cost-effectiveness of the firm's marketing effort. Microsoft and Netflix recently partnered to offer entertainment through more than one channel. Traditionally, customers could order their favorite movies online and have the DVDs delivered to their mailboxes. Under the new agreement, Netflix subscribers who also have Microsoft's Xbox Live Gold membership can download movies and TV programs and view them on their game system at no extra cost.[8]

REVERSE CHANNELS

While the traditional concept of marketing channels involves the movement of goods and services from producer to consumer or business user, marketers should not ignore **reverse channels**—channels designed to return goods to their producers. Reverse channels have gained increased

Staples utilizes reverse channels by collecting empty printer cartridges in its stores.

© Tim Boyle/Getty Images

importance with rising prices for raw materials, increasing availability of recycling facilities, and passage of additional antipollution and conservation laws. Purchase a new set of tires, and you'll find a recycling charge for disposing of the old tires. The intent is to halt the growing litter problem of illegal tire dumps. Automotive batteries contain potentially toxic materials, including 25 pounds of lead, plastic, and sulfuric acid. Despite this, 99 percent of the elements in a spent battery can be reclaimed, recycled, and reused in new batteries. Thirty-eight states have now passed laws requiring consumers to turn in their old batteries at the time they purchase new ones. To help in this effort, the American Automobile Association (AAA) holds an annual AAA Great Battery Roundup in the United States and Canada, during which consumers can drop off their dead batteries.[9]

Some reverse channels move through the facilities of traditional marketing intermediaries. In states that require bottle deposits, retailers and local bottlers perform these functions in the soft-drink industry. For other products, manufacturers establish redemption centers, develop systems for rechanneling products for recycling, and create specialized organizations to handle disposal and recycling. Staples collects empty printer cartridges at its stores, and some Nike retail outlets collect worn-out sneakers for recycling. Home Depot has begun collecting used compact fluorescent lightbulbs (CFLs) for recycling. This program greatly increases the convenience for consumers who want to recycle their old bulbs but until now had to take them to municipal hazardous waste collection sites because of the mercury they contain. The Home Depot recycling effort is likely to help build loyalty among customers.[10]

Reverse channels also handle product recalls and repairs. An appliance manufacturer might send recall notices to the buyers of a washing machine. An auto manufacturer might send notices to car owners advising them of a potential problem and offering to repair it at no cost through local dealerships.

assessment check

1. Distinguish between a marketing channel and logistics.

2. What are the different types of marketing channels?

3. What four functions do marketing channels perform?

2 **Outline the major channel strategy decisions.**

Channel Strategy Decisions

Marketers face several strategic decisions in choosing channels and marketing intermediaries for their products. Selecting a specific channel is the most basic of these decisions. Marketers must also resolve questions about the level of distribution intensity, assess the desirability of vertical marketing systems, and evaluate the performance of current intermediaries.

SELECTION OF A MARKETING CHANNEL

Consider the following questions: What characteristics of a franchised dealer network make it the best channel option for a company? Why do operating supplies often go through both agents and merchant wholesalers before reaching their actual users? Why would a firm market a single product through multiple channels? Marketers must answer many such questions in choosing marketing channels.

A variety of factors affect the selection of a marketing channel. Some channel decisions are dictated by the marketplace in which the company operates. In other cases, the product itself may be a key variable in picking a marketing channel. Finally, the marketing organization may base its selection of channels on its size and competitive factors. Individual firms in a single industry may choose different channels as part of their overall strategy to gain a competitive edge. Book publishers, for instance, may sell through bookstores, directly to consumers on their own Web sites, or through nontraditional outlets including specialty retailers such as craft stores or home improvement stores.

Market Factors

Channel structure reflects a product's intended markets, for either consumers or business users. Business purchasers usually prefer to deal directly with manufacturers (except for routine supplies or small accessory items), but most consumers make their purchases from retailers. Marketers often sell products that serve both business users and consumers through more than one channel.

Other market factors also affect channel choice, including the market's needs, its geographic location, and its average order size. To serve a concentrated market with a small number of buyers, a direct channel offers a feasible alternative. But in serving a geographically dispersed potential trade area in which customers purchase small amounts in individual transactions—the conditions that characterize the consumer-goods market—distribution through marketing intermediaries makes sense.

Product Factors

Product characteristics also guide the choice of an optimal marketing channel strategy. Perishable goods, such as fresh fruit and vegetables, milk, and fruit juice, move through short channels. Trendy or seasonal fashions, such as swimsuits and skiwear, are also examples.

Vending machines represent another short channel. Typically, you can buy Skittles, Sun Chips, or a bottle of Dasani water from a vending machine. But how about bike parts? Trek Bicycle recently installed its first Trek Stop, a vending machine that dispenses basic bike parts. Items include tire patch kits, spare tubes, and air pumps. Riders can also purchase water bottles and energy bars from the machines. The kiosk is located outside a bike shop not far from Trek's headquarters.[11]

Instead of selling directly to customers, entrepreneur Sara Blakely relies on big retail partners to get her product, Spanx, into consumers' hands.

© Lee Celano/WireImage for Silver Spoon/Getty Images

Complex products, such as custom-made installations and computer equipment, often are sold directly to ultimate buyers. In general, relatively standardized items that are also non-perishable pass through comparatively long channels. Products with low unit costs, such as cans of dog food, bars of soap, and packages of gum, typically travel through long channels. Perishable items—fresh flowers, meat, and produce—require much shorter channels.

Organizational and Competitive Factors

Companies with strong financial, management, and marketing resources feel less need for help from intermediaries. A large, financially strong manufacturer can hire its own sales force, warehouse its own goods, and extend credit to retailers or consumers. But a small firm with fewer resources may do better with the aid of intermediaries. Entrepreneur Sara Blakely knew she had a unique idea when she cut the feet off her pantyhose and created the first pair of Spanx underwear. Blakely says she wants her power shapers to empower women, and scores of women—including celebrities such as Gwyneth Paltrow and Tyra Banks—are loyal customers. Consumers write to Spanx thanking the company for giving them the confidence to wear the form-fitting clothes they always wanted to wear. But Blakely doesn't sell her shapers directly to customers. Instead, she relies on big retail partners such as Neiman Marcus, Nordstrom, and Target to get her product into consumers' hands.[12]

A firm with a broad product line can usually market its products directly to retailers or business users because its own sales force can offer a variety of products. High sales volume spreads selling costs over a large number of items, generating adequate returns from direct sales. Single-product firms often view direct selling as unaffordable.

The manufacturer's desire for control over marketing its products also influences channel selection. Some manufacturers sell their products only at their own stores. Manufacturers of specialty or luxury goods, such as scarves from Hermès and watches from Rolex, limit the number of retailers that can carry their products.

Businesses that explore new marketing channels must be careful to avoid upsetting their channel intermediaries. In the past decade, conflicts frequently arose as companies began to establish an Internet presence in addition to traditional outlets. Today, firms look for new ways to handle both without damaging relationships. NBC and Apple struck a deal in which NBC would sell its television programs through the iTunes store, but the agreement turned sour over issues of price and piracy. However, the two resumed their alliance after figuring out a way to add antipiracy features and reworking the price agreement for NBC's programming.[13]

Table 13.1 summarizes the factors that affect the selection of a marketing channel and examines the effect of each factor on the channel's overall length.

DETERMINING DISTRIBUTION INTENSITY

Another key channel strategy decision is the intensity of distribution. *Distribution intensity* refers to the number of intermediaries through which a manufacturer distributes its goods in a particular market. Optimal distribution intensity should ensure adequate market coverage for a product. Adequate market coverage varies depending on the goals of the individual firm, the type of product, and the consumer segments in its target market. In general, however, distribution intensity

table 13.1 Factors Influencing Marketing Channel Strategies

	Characteristics of Short Channels	Characteristics of Long Channels
Market Factors	Business users	Consumers
	Geographically concentrated	Geographically dispersed
	Extensive technical knowledge and regular servicing required	Little technical knowledge and regular servicing not required
	Large orders	Small orders
Product Factors	Perishable	Durable
	Complex	Standardized
	Expensive	Inexpensive
Organizational Factors	Manufacturer has adequate resources to perform channel functions	Manufacturer lacks adequate resources to perform channel functions
	Broad product line	Limited product line
	Channel control important	Channel control not important
Competitive Factors	Manufacturer feels satisfied with marketing intermediaries' performance in promoting products	Manufacturer feels dissatisfied with marketing intermediaries' performance in promoting products

varies along a continuum with three general categories: intensive distribution, selective distribution, and exclusive distribution.

Intensive Distribution

An **intensive distribution** strategy seeks to distribute a product through all available channels in a trade area. Because Campbell Soup practices intensive distribution for many of its products, you can pick up a can from its microwavable line just about anywhere—the supermarket, the drugstore, and even Staples. Usually, an intensive distribution strategy suits items with wide appeal across broad groups of consumers.

Selective Distribution

In another market coverage strategy, **selective distribution,** a firm chooses only a limited number of retailers in a market area to handle its line. Italian design firm Gucci sells its merchandise only through a limited number of select boutiques worldwide. By limiting the number of retailers, marketers can reduce total marketing costs while establishing

Gucci practices selective distribution, selling its merchandise only through a limited number of boutiques worldwide.

© Image courtesy of The Advertising Archives

strong working relationships within the channel. Moreover, selected retailers often agree to comply with the company's strict rules for advertising, pricing, and displaying its products. *Cooperative advertising*—in which the manufacturer pays a percentage of the retailer's advertising expenditures and the retailer prominently displays the firm's products—can be used for mutual benefit, and marginal retailers can be avoided. Where service is important, the manufacturer usually provides training and assistance to the dealers it chooses.

Exclusive Distribution

When a producer grants exclusive rights to a wholesaler or retailer to sell its products in a specific geographic region, it practices **exclusive distribution.** The automobile industry provides a good example of exclusive distribution. A city with a population of 40,000 probably has a single Ford dealer. Exclusive distribution agreements also govern marketing for some major appliance and apparel brands.

Marketers may sacrifice some market coverage by implementing a policy of exclusive distribution. However, they often develop and maintain an image of quality and prestige for the product. If it's harder to find a Free People silk dress, the item seems more valuable. In addition, exclusive distribution limits marketing costs because the firm deals with a smaller number of accounts. In exclusive distribution, producers and retailers cooperate closely in decisions concerning advertising and promotion, inventory carried by the retailers, and prices.

Legal Problems of Exclusive Distribution

Exclusive distribution presents potential legal problems in three main areas: exclusive dealing agreements, closed sales territories, and tying agreements. Although none of these practices is illegal per se, all may break the law if they reduce competition or tend to create monopolies.

intensive distribution
Distribution of a product through all available channels.

selective distribution
Distribution of a product through a limited number of channels.

exclusive distribution
Distribution of a product through a single wholesaler or retailer in a specific geographic region.

As part of an exclusive distribution strategy, marketers may try to enforce an **exclusive dealing agreement,** which prohibits a marketing intermediary (a wholesaler or, more typically, a retailer) from handling competing products. Producers of high-priced shopping goods, specialty goods, and accessory equipment often require such agreements to ensure total concentration on their own product lines. Such contracts violate the Clayton Act only if the producer's or dealer's sales volumes represent a substantial percentage of total sales in the market area. While exclusive distribution is legal for companies first entering a market, such agreements violate the Clayton Act if used by firms with a sizable market share seeking to bar competitors from the market.

Producers may also try to set up **closed sales territories** to restrict their distributors to certain geographic regions, reasoning that the distributors gain protection from rival dealers in their exclusive territories. Some beverage distributors have closed territories, as do distributors of plumbing fixtures.[14] But the downside of this practice is that the distributors sacrifice opportunities to open new facilities or market the manufacturers' products outside their assigned territories. The legality of a system of closed sales territories depends on whether the restriction decreases competition. If so, it violates the Federal Trade Commission Act and provisions of the Sherman and Clayton Acts.

The legality of closed sales territories also depends on whether the system imposes horizontal or vertical restrictions. Horizontal territorial restrictions result from agreements between retailers or wholesalers to avoid competition among sellers of products from the same producer. Such agreements consistently have been declared illegal. However, the U.S. Supreme Court has ruled that vertical territorial restrictions—those between producers and wholesalers or retailers—may meet legal criteria. The ruling gives no clear-cut answer, but such agreements likely satisfy the law in cases in which manufacturers occupy relatively small parts of their markets. In such instances, the restrictions may actually increase competition among competing brands; the wholesaler or retailer faces no competition from other dealers carrying the manufacturer's brand, so it can concentrate on effectively competing with other brands.

The third legal question of exclusive distribution involves **tying agreements,** which allow channel members to become exclusive dealers only if they also carry products other than those they want to sell. In the apparel industry, for example, an agreement might require a dealer to carry a comparatively unpopular line of clothing to get desirable, fast-moving items. Tying agreements violate the Sherman Act and the Clayton Act when they reduce competition or create monopolies that keep competitors out of major markets.

WHO SHOULD PERFORM CHANNEL FUNCTIONS?

A fundamental marketing principle governs channel decisions. A member of the channel must perform certain central marketing functions. Responsibilities of the different members may vary, however. Although independent wholesalers perform many functions for manufacturers, retailers, and other wholesaler clients, other channel members could fulfill these roles instead. A manufacturer might bypass its wholesalers by establishing regional warehouses, maintaining field sales forces, serving as sources of information for retail customers, or arranging details of financing. For years, auto manufacturers have operated credit units that offer new car financing; some have even established their own banks.

An independent intermediary earns a profit in exchange for providing services to manufacturers and retailers. This profit margin is low, however, ranging from 1 percent for food wholesalers to 5 percent for durable goods wholesalers. Manufacturers and retailers could retain these costs, or they could market directly and reduce retail prices—but only if they could perform the channel functions and match the efficiency of the independent intermediaries.

To grow profitably in a competitive environment, an intermediary must provide better service at lower costs than manufacturers or retailers can provide for themselves. In this case, consolidation of channel functions can represent a strategic opportunity for a company.

assessment check

1. Identify four major factors in selecting a marketing channel.

2. Describe the three general categories of distribution intensity.

Channel Management and Leadership

Distribution strategy does not end with the choice of a channel. Manufacturers must also focus on channel management by developing and maintaining relationships with the intermediaries in their marketing channels. Positive channel relationships encourage channel members to remember their partners' goods and market them. Manufacturers also must carefully manage the incentives offered to induce channel members to promote their products. This effort includes weighing decisions about pricing, promotion, and other support efforts the manufacturer performs.

Increasingly, marketers are managing channels in partnership with other channel members. Effective cooperation allows all channel members to achieve goals they could not achieve on their own. Keys to successful management of channel relationships include the development of high levels of coordination, commitment, and trust between channel members.

Not all channel members wield equal power in the distribution chain, however. The dominant member of a marketing channel is called the **channel captain.** This firm's power to control a channel may result from its control over some type of reward or punishment to other channel members such as granting an exclusive sales territory or taking away a dealership. Power might also result from contractual arrangements, specialized expert knowledge, or agreement among channel members about their mutual best interests.

channel captain Dominant and controlling member of a marketing channel.

In the grocery industry, food producers once were considered channel captains. Today, however, the power has shifted to the retail giants. Kroger, Supervalu, and Safeway operate about 6,500 supermarkets nationwide. To survive in the competitive grocery industry, supermarket owners are diversifying their retail formats from traditional stores to include natural and organic and upscale specialty stores to satisfy a wider variety of customers. Supervalu now operates its Sunflower Market, while Kroger has Fresh Fare and Safeway has Safeway Lifestyle.[15] But the pressure on traditional chains is coming from another strategy: supercenters like Wal-Mart and Target. Wal-Mart is continuing its expansion in the grocery market; in fact, its grocery receipts now account for a whopping 31 percent of its total sales.[16]

CHANNEL CONFLICT

Marketing channels work smoothly only when members cooperate in well-organized efforts to achieve maximum operating efficiencies. Yet channel members often perform as separate, independent, and even competing forces. Two types of conflict—horizontal and vertical—may hinder the normal functioning of a marketing channel.

Horizontal Conflict

Horizontal conflict sometimes results from disagreements among channel members at the same level, such as two or more wholesalers or two or more retailers, or among marketing intermediaries of the same type, such as two competing discount stores or several retail florists. More often, horizontal conflict causes problems between different types of marketing intermediaries that handle similar products. In an effort to resolve such a situation, Australia and the United States recently announced an "open skies" agreement, abolishing restrictions on U.S. and Australian air carriers and clearing the path for increased competition. Airlines from both countries will be allowed to choose routes based on demand within government limitations and will be able to set prices and capacity without interference. Airlines such as Qantas, United Airlines, and Virgin Blue will be affected. Negotiators on both sides predict more cooperative marketing arrangements among the carriers.[17]

Vertical Conflict

Vertical relationships may result in frequent and severe conflict. Channel members at different levels find many reasons for disputes, as when retailers develop private brands to compete with producers' brands or when producers establish their own retail stores or create mail-order operations that compete with retailers. Producers may annoy wholesalers and retailers when they attempt to bypass these intermediaries and sell directly to consumers. After years of conflict, cable companies have reached an agreement with the electronics industry so that manufacturers can produce TVs and other electronic devices that will work—regardless of the cable provider. Comcast and Time Warner are participating in

The resolution of vertical conflict between cable companies and electronics manufacturers paved the way for "tru2way," an initiative that will allow devices not only to receive but to send digital information.

© AP Images/PRNewsFoto/Panasonic

the initiative, called "tru2way," which will allow devices to receive *and send* digital information. The new standardization across the cable networks should foster the development of two-way communication from TVs to set-top boxes to PCs and other devices.[18]

The Gray Market

Another type of channel conflict results from activities in the so-called *gray market.* As U.S. manufacturers license their technology and brands abroad, they sometimes find themselves in competition in the U.S. market against versions of their own brands produced by overseas affiliates. These **gray goods,** goods produced for overseas markets often at reduced prices, enter U.S. channels through the actions of unauthorized foreign distributors. While licensing agreements usually prohibit foreign licensees from selling in the United States, no such rules inhibit their distributors. Kraft Foods lost a bid in the Canadian courts to stop a competing importer, Euro Excellence, from selling chocolates in packaging that looks exactly like Kraft's Toblerone and Cote D'Or brands—designs that Kraft's European units copyrighted. So both Kraft's chocolates and those of Euro Excellence, which are imported from an undisclosed European country, will appear in Canadian markets in identical packaging. The court ruled that Euro Excellence had obtained the rights to the packaging legally, although it did not have permission to use it in Canada, an issue of licensing versus copyright. Kraft may seek to obtain the copyright from the European units so that it can enforce it in Canada.[19]

ACHIEVING CHANNEL COOPERATION

The basic antidote to channel conflict is effective cooperation among channel members. Cooperation is best achieved when all channel members regard themselves as equal components of the same organization. The channel captain is primarily responsible for providing the leadership necessary to achieve this kind of cooperation.

The NFL Network and sports marketer ESPN are forming a joint venture that will allow the NFL Network access to more cable systems—through the clout of ESPN. Although the NFL Network has been available in more than 40 million homes via DirecTV and Verizon FiOs, it has not been accessible on Time Warner Cable, Cablevision, or many other cable providers. So the association with ESPN should give the smaller network's distribution a significant boost.[20]

4 **Identify and describe the different vertical marketing systems.**

vertical marketing system (VMS) Planned channel system designed to improve distribution efficiency and cost-effectiveness by integrating various functions throughout the distribution chain.

assessment check

1. What is a channel captain? What is its role in channel cooperation?

2. Identify and describe the three types of channel conflict.

Vertical Marketing Systems

Efforts to reduce channel conflict and improve the effectiveness of distribution have led to the development of vertical marketing systems. A **vertical marketing system (VMS)** is a planned channel system designed to improve distribution efficiency and cost effectiveness by integrating various functions throughout the distribution chain.

A vertical marketing system can achieve this goal through either forward or backward integration. In **forward integration,** a firm attempts to control downstream distribution. For example, a manufacturer might set up a retail chain to sell its products. **Backward integration** occurs when a manufacturer attempts to gain greater control over inputs in its production process. A manufacturer might acquire the supplier of a raw material the manufacturer uses in the production of its products. Backward integration can also extend the control of retailers and wholesalers over producers that supply them. The recession created problems with backward integration, as the "Marketing Failure" feature discusses.

A VMS offers several benefits. First, it improves chances for controlling and coordinating the steps in the distribution or production process. It may lead to the development of economies of scale that ultimately saves money. A VMS may also let a manufacturer expand into profitable new businesses. However, a VMS also involves some costs. A manufacturer assumes increased risk when it takes control of an entire distribution chain. Manufacturers may also discover they lose some flexibility in responding to market changes.

Marketers have developed three categories of VMSs: corporate systems, administered systems, and contractual systems. These categories are outlined in the following sections.

CORPORATE AND ADMINISTERED SYSTEMS

When a single owner runs an organization at each stage of the marketing channel, it operates a **corporate marketing system.** Phillips auctioneers runs a corporate marketing system. An **administered marketing system** achieves channel coordination when a dominant channel member exercises its power. Even though Goodyear sells its tires through independently owned and operated dealerships, it controls the stock these dealerships carry. Other examples of channel captains leading administered channels include McKesson and Costco.

CONTRACTUAL SYSTEMS

Instead of common ownership of intermediaries within a corporate VMS or the exercising of power within an administered system, a **contractual marketing system** coordinates distribution through formal agreements among channel members. In practice, three types of agreements set up these systems: wholesaler-sponsored voluntary chains, retail cooperatives, and franchises.

Wholesaler-Sponsored Voluntary Chain

Sometimes an independent wholesaler tries to preserve a market by strengthening its retail customers through a wholesaler-sponsored voluntary chain. The wholesaler adopts a formal agreement with its retailers to use a common name and standardized facilities and to purchase the wholesaler's goods. The wholesaler may even develop a line of private brands to be stocked by the retailers. This practice often helps smaller retailers compete with rival chains—and strengthens the wholesaler's position as well.

IGA (Independent Grocers Alliance) Food Stores is a good example of a voluntary chain. Other wholesaler-sponsored chains include Associated Druggists, Sentry Hardware, and Western Auto. Because a single advertisement promotes all the retailers in the trading area, a common store name and similar inventories allow the retailers to save on advertising costs.

Retail Cooperative

In a second type of contractual VMS, a group of retailers establishes a shared wholesaling operation to help them compete with chains. This is known as a **retail cooperative.** The retailers purchase ownership shares in the wholesaling operation and agree to buy a minimum percentage of their inventories from this operation. The members typically adopt a common store name and develop common private brands.

Franchise

A third type of contractual vertical marketing system is the **franchise,** in which a wholesaler or dealer (the franchisee) agrees to meet the operating requirements of a manufacturer or other franchiser. Franchising is a huge and growing industry—more than 1,500 U.S. companies distribute goods and services through systems of franchised dealers, and numerous firms also offer franchises in international markets. Nationwide, about 750,000 retail outlets represent franchises.[21] Table 13.2 shows the 20 fastest-growing

assessment check

1. What are vertical marketing systems (VMSs)? Identify the major types.

2. Identify the three types of contractual marketing systems.

table 13.2   The Top 20 Fastest-Growing Franchises

Rank	Company and Product
1	Jan-Pro Franchising International; commercial cleaning
2	Subway; sandwiches and salads
3	Instant Tax Service; retail tax preparation and electronic filing
4	Stratus Building Solutions; commercial cleaning
5	Snap Fitness; 24-hour fitness center
6	Dunkin' Donuts; coffee and doughnuts
7	Jazzercise; dance/exercise classes
8	Bonus Building Care; commercial cleaning
9	Anytime Fitness; fitness center
10	Vanguard Cleaning Systems; commercial cleaning
11	Jani-King; commercial cleaning
12	Domino's Pizza; pizza, breadsticks, buffalo wings
(tie) 13	Choice Hotels International; hotels, inns, suites, and resorts
(tie) 13	McDonald's; hamburgers, chicken, salads
15	Liberty Tax Service; income-tax preparation
16	Long John Silver's Restaurants; fish and chicken
17	ExpressTax; tax preparation and electronic filing
18	System4; commercial cleaning
19	Anago Cleaning Systems; commercial cleaning
20	Massage Envy; therapeutic massage services

Source: "2009 Fastest-Growing Franchises Rankings," *Entrepreneur,* http://www.entrepreneur.com, accessed May 19, 2009.

MARKETING FAILURE   Recycling Programs Trashed by Recession

Background. Recycling garbage is easy for consumers and good for the environment. Local governments and companies do the heavy lifting—removing glass, paper, and plastic and selling it to recyclers in a kind of reverse supply chain for reuse in manufacturing. Many were happy to do it while demand was high. They earned as much as $200 a ton for recyclables, adding hundreds of thousands of dollars to their budgets. For instance, Berkeley, California, earned $1 million from recycling last year.

The Challenge. The global drop in manufacturing caused by the recession has slashed demand for raw materials of all types. Especially painful is the slowing economy in China, the world's largest market for U.S. recyclables. The price for glass and paper plummeted to around $20 a ton, reflecting the recycling industry's drastically reduced incentive to collect what no one is buying. Some recycling plants lost tens of thousands of dollars; some stopped accepting material. Others, like Dream Sanitation in Atlanta, simply

franchises in the United States, with Jan-Pro, Subway, and Instant Tax topping the list.

Franchise owners pay anywhere from several thousand to more than a million dollars to purchase and set up a franchise. Typically, they also pay a royalty on sales to the franchising company. In exchange for these initial and ongoing fees, the franchise owner receives the right to use the company's brand name as well as services such as training, marketing, advertising, and volume discounts. Major franchise chains justify the steep price of entry because it allows new businesses to sell winning brands. But if the brand enters a slump or the corporation behind the franchise makes poor strategic decisions, franchisees often are hurt.

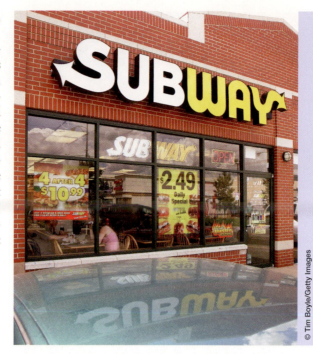

Subway is one of the 20 fastest-growing franchises in the United States.

Logistics and Supply Chain Management

Pier 1 imports its eclectic mix of items from 600 vendors in more than 50 countries, most representing small companies. If high-demand items or seasonal products are late into its warehouses or are shipped in insufficient quantities, the company may miss opportunities to deliver popular shopping choices to its 1,100 retail stores and could lose ground to competitors such as Pottery Barn and Crate & Barrel. The situation facing Pier 1 Imports illustrates the importance of logistics. Careful coordination of Pier 1's supplier network, shipping processes, and inventory control is the key to its continuing success. In addition, the store's buyers develop relationships with suppliers in all participating countries.[22]

Effective logistics requires proper supply chain management, control of the activities of purchasing, processing, and delivery through which raw materials are transformed into products and made available to final consumers. The **supply chain,** also known as the *value chain,* is the complete sequence of suppliers and activities that contribute to the creation and delivery of goods and services. The supply chain begins with the raw material inputs for the manufacturing process of a product and then proceeds to the actual production activities. The final link in the supply chain is the movement of finished products through the marketing channel to customers. Each link of the chain benefits the consumers as raw materials move through manufacturing to distribution. The chain encompasses all activities that enhance the value of the finished goods, including design, quality manufacturing, customer service, and delivery. Customer satisfaction results directly from the perceived value of a purchase to its buyer.

5 **Explain the roles of logistics and supply chain management in an overall distribution strategy.**

supply chain Complete sequence of suppliers and activities that contribute to the creation and delivery of merchandise.

shut down. "Our fear when the market crashed was that we wouldn't be able to move the material at all. If people stop buying altogether," said the director of one California pickup service, "what would we do?"

The Outcome. Burning or dumping trash in a landfill is still more expensive than recycling, so some communities are stockpiling towers of material, waiting for the price to revive. Others are scaling back on pickups or raising collection fees. Atlanta is saving $3 million a year by using its own trucks and crews instead of a service, but some residents are frustrated by allegedly unreliable results. "People are trying to recycle, and it's not easy," said one. "I wish it was easy to do what we all feel strongly about." Residents in some towns are driving recyclables to neighboring

communities, while Boston, which once earned $112 a ton, now pays recyclers $5.50 a ton to take the trash away. Tiny Frackville, Pennsylvania, suspended its program to avoid raising new taxes to pay for it. Soon local governments may cut spending to make up for lost recycling revenue.

Lessons Learned. Industry watchers say recycling is cyclical and will revive. "We feel confident that there will be a recovery," said a spokesperson for Waste Management Recycle America. "But, you know, when?"

Sources: Valerie Streit, "Recession Squeezes Recycling Programs," *CNN*, March 19, 2009, http://www.cnn.com; Amanda Ruggeri, "Could the Recession Kill the Recycling Industry?" *US News & World Report*, March 13, 2009, http://www.usnews.com; Bina Venkataraman, "Collected Recyclables Pile Up as Profits They Generate Fall," *The Boston Globe*, December 14, 2008, http://www.boston.com.

Pier 1 imports its eclectic mix of items from 600 vendors in more than 50 countries, most representing small companies. To run the operation successfully, logistics are very important.

To manage the supply chain, businesses must look for ways to maximize customer value in each activity they perform. Supply chain management takes place in two directions: upstream and downstream, as illustrated in Figure 13.2. **Upstream management** involves managing raw materials, inbound logistics, and warehouse and storage facilities. **Downstream management** involves managing finished product storage, outbound logistics, marketing and sales, and customer service.

Companies choose a variety of methods for managing the supply chain. They can include high-tech systems such as radio frequency identification (discussed in the next section) and regular person-to-person meetings. Summit Logistics International helps other businesses track and manage their global supply chains. Using software developed by LOG-NET, Summit assists its customers in supporting customer service and improving inventory management.[23]

Logistics plays a major role in giving customers what they need when they need it, and thus is central in the supply chain. Another important component of this chain, *value-added service,* adds some improved or supplemental service that customers do not normally receive or expect. The following sections examine methods for streamlining and managing logistics and the supply chain as part of an overall distribution strategy.

radio frequency identification (RFID)
Technology that uses a tiny chip with identification information that can be read by a scanner using radio waves from a distance.

RADIO FREQUENCY IDENTIFICATION (RFID)

One tool marketers use to help manage logistics is **radio frequency identification (RFID)** technology. With RFID, a tiny chip with identification information that can be read by a radio frequency scanner from a distance is placed on an item. These chips are already widely used in

figure 13.2

The Supply Chain of a Manufacturing Company

Source: Adapted from Figure 2.2, Ralph M. Stair and George W. Reynolds, *Principles of Information Systems: A Managerial Approach,* 8th Edition, Boston: Course Technology. © 2008 South-Western, a part of Cengage Learning, Inc. Reproduced by permission. www.cengage.com/permissions.

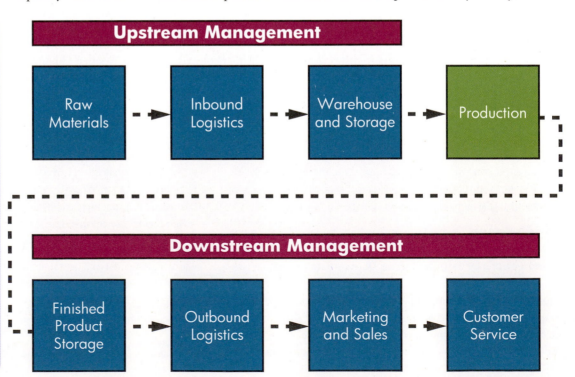

tollway pass transmitters, allowing drivers to zip through tollbooths without stopping or rolling down their windows to toss change into baskets. They are also embedded in employee ID cards workers use to open office doors without keys. But businesses such as retail giant Wal-Mart, manufacturer Procter & Gamble, credit card firms MasterCard and American Express, and German retailer Metro AG are eagerly putting the technology to wider use; they say it will speed deliveries, make consumer bar codes obsolete, and provide marketers with valuable information about consumer preferences. Wal-Mart requires its biggest suppliers to attach RFID tags to pallets and cases of products such as Coca-Cola and Dove soap, saying the technology vastly improves its ability to track inventory and keep the right amount of products in stock.

Boeing is implementing RFID tags and wireless Internet (Wi-Fi) technology to track and locate aircraft parts at its huge manufacturing plants. Each aircraft is made up of 2 to 3 million individual parts. Boeing's manufacturing site in Everett, Washington, is actually the largest building in the world—It covers 100 acres—so the RFID tags are vital to keeping track of components. The technology uses Wi-Fi access points to pick up signals from an RFID tag and pinpoint the precise location of a part.[24]

ENTERPRISE RESOURCE PLANNING

Software is an important aspect of logistics management and the supply chain. An **enterprise resource planning (ERP) system** is an integrated software system that consolidates data from among the firm's units. Roughly two-thirds of ERP system users are manufacturers concerned with production issues such as sequencing and scheduling. German software giant SAP offers systems that allow businesses to manage their customer relations. eBay uses an SAP system to interact with its top customers in Europe.[25]

As valuable as it is, ERP and its related software aren't always perfect. For example, ERP failures were blamed for Hershey's inability to fulfill all of its candy orders during one Halloween period when a fall-off in sales was blamed on a combination of shipping delays, inability to fill orders, and partial shipments while candy accumulated in warehouses. The nation's major retailers were forced to shift their purchases to other candy vendors.

LOGISTICAL COST CONTROL

In addition to enhancing their products by providing value-added services to customers, many firms focus on logistics for another important reason: to cut costs. Distribution functions currently represent almost half of a typical firm's total marketing costs. To reduce logistical costs, businesses are re-examining each link of their supply chains to identify activities that do not add value for customers. By eliminating, reducing, or redesigning these activities, they can often cut costs and boost efficiency. As just described, new technologies such as RFID can save businesses millions—or even billions—of dollars.

Because of increased security requirements in recent years, businesses involved in importing and exporting have faced a major rise in logistical costs. By law, 50 percent of all cargo on passenger planes must now be screened, increasing the cost of transporting goods even more.[26]

Third-Party Logistics

Some companies try to cut costs and offer value-added services by outsourcing some or all of their logistics functions to specialist firms. **Third-party (contract) logistics firms** (3PL firms) specialize in handling logistical activities for their clients. Third-party logistics is a huge industry, estimated at $390 billion worldwide, $113.6 billion of which takes place in the United States alone.[27] Penske Logistics, UPS, and European-based Schenker are three of the largest 3PL firms worldwide, with major operations in China and Russia.

Through such outsourcing alliances, producers and logistical service suppliers cooperate in developing innovative, customized systems that speed goods through carefully constructed manufacturing and distribution pipelines. Although many companies have long outsourced transportation and warehousing functions, today's alliance partners use similar methods to combine their operations.

assessment check

1. What is upstream management? What is downstream management?
2. Identify three methods for managing logistics.

Physical Distribution

A firm's physical distribution system is an organized group of components linked according to a plan for achieving specific distribution objectives. It contains the following elements:

1. *customer service*—level of customer service the distribution activities support;

2. *transportation*—how the firm ships its products;

3. *inventory control*—quantity of inventory the firm maintains at each location;

4. *protective packaging and materials handling*—how the firm packages and efficiently handles goods in the factory, warehouse, and transport terminals;

5. *order processing*—how the firm handles orders; and

6. *warehousing*—the distribution system's location of stock and the number of warehouses the firm maintains.

All of these components function in interrelated ways. Decisions made in one area affect efficiency in others. The physical distribution manager must balance each component so the system avoids stressing any single aspect to the detriment of overall functioning. A firm might decide to reduce transportation costs by shipping its products by less costly—but slow—water transportation. But slow deliveries would likely force the firm to maintain higher inventory levels, raising those costs. This mismatch between system elements often leads to increased production costs. So balancing the components is crucial.

The general shift from a manufacturing economy to a service economy in the United States has affected physical distribution in two key ways. First, customers require more flexible—yet reliable—transportation service. Second, the number of smaller shipments is growing much faster than the number of large shipments. Although traditional, high-volume shipments will continue to grow, they will represent a lower percentage of the transportation industry's revenues and volume.

THE PROBLEM OF SUBOPTIMIZATION

Logistics managers seek to establish a specified level of customer service while minimizing the costs of physically moving and storing goods. Marketers must first decide on their priorities for customer service and then figure out how to fulfill those goals by moving goods at the least cost. Meshing together all the physical distribution elements is a huge challenge that firms don't always meet.

Suboptimization results when the managers of individual physical distribution functions attempt to minimize costs, but the impact of one task leads to less than optimal results on the others. Imagine a hockey team composed of star players. Unfortunately, despite the individual talents of the players, the team fails to win a game. This is an example of suboptimization. The same thing can happen at a company when each logistics activity is judged by its own accomplishments instead of the way it contributes to the overall goals of the firm. Suboptimization often happens when a firm introduces a new product that may not fit easily into its current physical distribution system.

Effective management of the physical distribution function requires some cost trade-offs. By accepting relatively high costs in some functional areas to cut costs in others, managers can minimize their firm's total physical distribution costs. Of course, any reduction in logistical costs should support progress toward the goal of maintaining customer-service standards.

assessment check

1. What are the six major elements of physical distribution?

2. What is suboptimization?

CUSTOMER SERVICE STANDARDS

Customer service standards state the goals and define acceptable performance for the quality of service a firm expects to deliver to its customers. Internet retailers such as Zappos.com and Giftbaskets.com thrive because of their ability to ship within hours of receiving an order. 1-800-FLOWERS.com offers same-day delivery, every day of the week, nationwide, with a 100 percent guarantee of satisfaction. The firm's fulfillment system includes a network of about 9,000 florists—one reason why the company can guarantee its deliveries.[28] A pizza parlor might set a standard to deliver customers' pizzas hot and fresh within 30 minutes. An auto repair shop might set a standard to complete all oil changes in a half hour.

Designers of a physical distribution system begin by establishing acceptable levels of customer service. These designers then assemble physical distribution components in a way that will achieve this standard at the lowest possible total cost. This overall cost breaks down into five components: (1) transportation, (2) warehousing, (3) inventory control, (4) customer service/order processing, and (5) administrative costs.

TRANSPORTATION

The transportation industry was largely deregulated a number of years ago. Deregulation has been particularly important for motor carriers, railroads, and air carriers. Today, an estimated 15.5 million trucks are transporting goods throughout the United States; 1.9 million of these are tractor-trailers. An estimated 360,000 trucking companies and more than 3 million truck drivers operate in the country.[29] Railroads are enjoying a new boom: once hauling mostly commodities like corn and grain, they now transport cross-country the huge loads of goods coming from China through West Coast ports. Railroads can move a greater amount of freight for less fuel than trucks. In a recent year, the railroad industry spent nearly $10 billion on new track and other projects, and the U.S. Department of Transportation estimates that freight tonnage will increase about 90 percent by 2035.[30]

Typically adding about 10 percent to the cost of a product, transportation and delivery expenses represent the largest category of logistics-related costs for most firms. Also, for many items—particularly perishable ones such as fresh fish or produce—transportation makes a central contribution to satisfactory customer service.

Many logistics managers have found that the key to controlling their shipping costs is careful management of relationships with shipping firms. Freight carriers use two basic rates: class and commodity rates. A class rate is a standard rate for a specific commodity moving between any pair of destinations. A carrier may charge a lower commodity rate, sometimes called a *special rate,* to a favored shipper as a reward for either regular business or a large-quantity shipment. Railroads and inland water carriers frequently reward customers in this way.

In addition, the railroad and motor carrier industries sometimes supplement this rate structure with negotiated, or contract, rates. In other words, the two parties finalize terms of rates, services, and other variables in a contract.

Classes of Carriers

Freight carriers are classified as common, contract, and private carriers. **Common carriers,** often considered the backbone of the transportation industry, provide transportation services as for-hire

© Getty Images

1-800-FLOWERS.com strives for high customer-service standards, offering same-day delivery, every day of the week, nationwide, with a 100 percent guarantee of satisfaction.

briefly speaking

"Timely service, like timely gifts, is doubled in value."

—**George MacDonald (1824–1905)**
SCOTTISH NOVELIST, POET, AND CLERGYMAN

carriers to the general public. The government still regulates their rates and services, and they cannot conduct their operations without permission from the appropriate regulatory authority. Common carriers move freight via all modes of transport. FedEx is a major common carrier serving businesses and consumers. One way the firm remains competitive is by developing new methods for enhancing customer service. FedEx has a service called InSight, a free online service that essentially reverses the package-tracking process—instead of following a package from shipment to delivery, customers can go online to find out what will be delivered to them that day. One FedEx customer that has benefited greatly from this new service is Mexican printing company Grupo de Integración Digital, which ships more than 20 tons of instruction manuals, CD-ROMS, and software publications every month. With InSight, the firm obtained comprehensive information about the status of its supply and distribution shipments.[31]

Contract carriers are for-hire transporters that do not offer their services to the general public. Instead, they establish contracts with individual customers and operate exclusively for particular industries, such as the motor freight industry. These carriers operate under much looser regulations than common carriers.

Private carriers do not offer services for hire. These carriers provide transportation services solely for internally generated freight. As a result, they observe no rate or service regulations. The Interstate Commerce Commission (ICC), a federal regulatory agency, permits private carriers to operate as common or contract carriers as well. Many private carriers have taken advantage of this rule by operating their trucks fully loaded at all times.

7 Compare the major modes of transportation.

MAJOR TRANSPORTATION MODES

Logistics managers choose among five major transportation alternatives: railroads, motor carriers, water carriers, pipelines, and air freight. Each mode has its own unique characteristics. Logistics managers select the best options by matching the situation features to their specific transportation needs.

Railroads

Railroads continue to control the largest share of the freight business as measured by ton-miles. The term *ton-mile* indicates shipping activity required to move one ton of freight one mile. Rail shipments quickly rack up ton-miles because this mode provides the most efficient way for moving bulky commodities over long distances. Rail carriers generally transport huge quantities of coal, chemicals, grain, nonmetallic minerals, lumber and wood products, and automobiles. The railroads have improved their service standards through a number of innovative concepts such as unit trains, run-through trains, **intermodal operations,** and double-stack container trains. Unit trains carry much of the coal, grain, and other high-volume commodities shipped. They run back and forth between single loading points (such as a mine) and single destinations (such as a power plant) to deliver a commodity. Run-through trains bypass intermediate terminals to speed up schedules. They work similarly to unit trains, but a run-through train may carry a variety of commodities.

In piggyback operations, one of the intermodal operations, highway trailers and containers ride on railroad flatcars, thus combining the long-haul capacity of the train with the door-to-door flexibility of the truck. A double-stack container train pulls special rail cars equipped with bathtub-shaped wells so they can carry two containers stacked on top of one another. By nearly doubling train capacity and slashing costs, this system offers enormous advantages to rail customers.

As mentioned earlier, the railroad industry is enjoying a resurgence—this also means it must build a better infrastructure to handle the increase in demand. Cities such as Chicago are making large investments in track and switching improvements, while the Norfolk Southern Railway is undertaking projects such as raising the roof of one of its railroad tunnels in southwestern Virginia to make room for the new double-stacked container cars.[32]

Motor Carriers

The trucking industry is still an important factor in the freight industry—the American Trucking Association (ATA) reports that trucks haul about 10.7 billion tons of freight each year. Although more costly than rail delivery, trucks can make deliveries to areas railroads simply can't reach. "Trucking is the driving force behind our great economy," insists ATA president and CEO Bill Graves.[33]

intermodal operations Combination of transport modes, such as rail and highway carriers (piggyback), air and highway carriers (birdyback), and water and air carriers (fishyback), to improve customer service and achieve cost advantages.

Trucking offers some important advantages over the other transportation modes, including relatively fast shipments and consistent service for both large and small shipments. Motor carriers concentrate on shipping manufactured products while railroads typically haul bulk shipments of raw materials. Motor carriers therefore receive greater revenue per ton shipped, because the cost for shipping raw materials is higher than shipping manufactured products.

Technology has also improved the efficiency of trucking. Many trucking firms now track their fleets via satellite communications systems. In-truck computer systems allow drivers and dispatchers to make last-minute changes in scheduling and delivery. The Internet is also adding new features to motor carrier services.

Even so, the trucking industry must adjust to changes in the marketing environment. Trucking firms report a shortage of long-haul drivers, causing delays in some deliveries and higher costs, along with the rising cost of fuel, to customers. Large firms such as Swift Transportation and Knight Transportation are offering drivers regional runs and dedicated routes for more predictable work hours, as well as better pay. They also recruit husband-wife teams for the long-haul routes, which is becoming a more popular practice.[34]

Water Carriers

Two basic types of transport methods move products over water: inland or barge lines and oceangoing, deepwater ships. Barge lines efficiently transport bulky, low-unit-value commodities such as grain, gravel, lumber, sand, and steel. A typical lower Mississippi River barge line may stretch more than a quarter mile across. Large ships also operate on the Great Lakes, transporting materials such as iron ore from Minnesota and harvested grain for market. These lake carrier ships range in size from roughly 400 feet to more than 1,000 feet in length. Oceangoing supertankers from global companies such as Maersk Line are the size of three football fields, almost doubling the capacity of other vessels. At full capacity, the ships can cut the cost by a fifth of shipping a container across the Pacific Ocean. Shippers that transport goods via water carriers incur very low costs compared with the rates for other transportation modes. Standardized modular shipping containers maximize savings by limiting loading, unloading, and other handling.

Ships often carry large refrigerated containers called "reefers" for transporting everything from fresh produce to medical supplies. These containers, along with their nonrefrigerated counterparts, improve shipping efficiency because they can easily be removed from a ship and attached to trucks or trains. Although shipping by water has traditionally been less expensive than other modes of transportation, as explained earlier, costs for this mode have increased dramatically because of tightened security measures. Freight rates are based on the size of the vessel, the cost of fuel, and security measures. Industry experts predict these costs will continue to climb over the next several years.[35]

FedEx is now offering an alternative shipping method that allows customers to move their cargo from Asia to varying U.S. destinations via one integrated process. The FedEx Trade Networks Ocean-Ground Distribution system combines its ocean freight forwarding and customs brokerage services with its U.S. transportation and delivery services: FedEx Freight, FedEx Ground, and FedEx Express. Customers can initiate and track the entire process through one FedEx point of contact, reducing costs and the chance for error.[36]

Pipelines

Although the pipeline industry ranks third after railroads and motor carriers in ton-miles transported, many people scarcely recognize its existence. More than 2 million miles of pipelines crisscross the United States in an extremely efficient network for transporting energy products—enough to circle the planet 83 times. The pipelines are operated by more than 3,000 large and small firms.[37] Oil pipelines carry two types of commodities: crude (unprocessed) oil and refined products such as gasoline, jet fuel, and kerosene. In addition, one so-called *slurry pipeline* carries coal in suspension after it has been ground up into a powder and mixed with water. The Black Mesa Pipeline, owned by Union Pacific, moves the coal mined by Peabody Coal from northern Arizona 290 miles south into southern Nevada.

Although pipelines offer low maintenance and dependable methods of transportation, a number of characteristics limit their applications. They have fewer locations than water carriers, and they can accommodate shipments of only a small number of products. Finally, pipelines represent a relatively slow method of transportation; liquids travel through this method at an average speed of only three to four miles per hour. The "Solving an Ethical Controversy" feature discusses another issue related to pipelines—bringing water to thirsty communities.

Solving an ethical controversy

The Battle over "Blue Gold"

the discovery of gold in the mid-1800s in the United States prompted a rush of prospectors who furiously mined and panned for wealth. When oil was discovered, a handful of smart entrepreneurs sunk their savings into drilling for "liquid gold" or "black gold," as it was called. Now a new gold standard is emerging: blue gold. Blue gold is water, which in some areas of the country is decreasing in supply. Droughts in widespread areas from the Southwest to the Southeast have caused concern about water shortages among private users and municipal officials alike. Pipelines have been developed and others are being considered to divert water to needy areas. The cost of water is rising, and the issue of who owns water, who controls it, and who should pay for it is coming to a boil.

Should water rights be under the control of one governing body?

PRO

1. Businesses could charge communities whatever price they want for access to water if they have the single source in an area. T. Boone Pickens, an oil entrepreneur, bought the rights to a huge underground aquifer, about 200,000 acres of water, in Texas. He wants to sell the water—about 65 billion gallons a year—to the city of Dallas, where it is needed.

2. States and cities are fighting for access to the same water in their areas. Alabama, Florida, and Georgia have been locked in a conflict over millions of gallons of water used for drinking, hydropower, recreation, and agriculture. Members of all sides continue to point fingers of blame at each other, arguing that each has a greater need for the water. "While we are all suffering from this drought, relief for metro Atlanta cannot come at the expense of the people of Alabama," insists one Alabama official.

CON

1. Control wielded by a single agency can result in too much power for that agency. The U.S. Army Corps of Engineers has long been criticized for its unilateral decisions involving water use. In the case of the three southern states currently enduring a drought, all three believe the power held by the corps—to release or not release millions of gallons of water from river basins—is too great.

2. If bills are passed at the federal level to resolve local water problems, mandatory spending might be increased, driving the cost of accessing water even higher. This issue has been raised in New Mexico, where water pipeline construction has been proposed to serve rural families.

Summary

With so many local and regional water projects underway concurrently, water officials and other experts worry that coherent, cost-effective, environmentally friendly standards will not be developed. In addition, many people don't want to think water can be bought and sold just like land. "The idea that water can be sold for private gain is still considered unconscionable by many," notes James M. Olson, an attorney who specializes in water and land-use law. "But the scarcity of water and the extraordinary profits that can be made may overwhelm ordinary public sensibilities." T. Boone Pickens sees the situation as a business opportunity. "There are people who will buy the water when they need it. And the people who have the water want to sell it. That's the blood, guts, and feathers of the thing," he observes.

Sources: Bill Ibelle, "Water Water Everywhere . . . ," *Michigan Today*, February 2009, http://michigantoday.umich, edu; Jerd Smith, "Water Expansion Builds Worries for Some," *Rocky Mountain News*, July 18, 2008, www.rockymountainnews.com; Susan Berfield, "There Will Be Water," *BusinessWeek*, June 23, 2008, pp. 40–46; Mark Clayton, "Is Water Becoming 'the New Oil'?" *Christian Science Monitor*, May 29, 2008, features.csmonitor.com; Frank Byrt, "Water Emerging as a Precious Commodity," *Financial Week*, December 17, 2007, www.financialweek.com.

Air Freight

Although the air freight industry grew steadily for many years, recently that growth has dropped off—at least in certain market sectors such as overnight delivery service. But firms are adapting. UPS recently revamped its services, now offering an expanded international express service called UPS Express Freight. The service provides guaranteed time-definite, overnight to three-day door-to-door delivery, including customs clearance, to large global metropolitan areas. UPS is also offering two less-expensive, nonguaranteed services: UPS Air Freight Direct and UPS Air Freight Consolidated. Both are available worldwide and provide package pickup, delivery, and customs clearance.[38]

Firms are adapting to the recent drop in the air freight industry. UPS recently revamped its services, now offering an expanded international express service called UPS Express Freight.

© John Summers II/Reuters/Landov

Comparing the Five Modes of Transport

Table 13.3 compares the five transportation modes on several operating characteristics. Although all shippers judge reliability, speed, and cost in choosing the most appropriate transportation methods, they assign varying importance to specific criteria when shipping different goods. For example, while motor carriers rank highest in availability in different locations, shippers of petroleum products frequently choose the lowest-ranked alternative, pipelines, for their low cost.

Examples of types of goods most often handled by the different transports include:

▷ *Railroads*—lumber, iron, steel, coal, automobiles, grain, and chemicals;

▷ *Motor carriers*—clothing, furniture, fixtures, lumber, plastic, food, leather, and machinery;

▷ *Water carriers*—fuel, oil, coal, chemicals, minerals, and petroleum products; automobiles and electronics from foreign manufacturers; and low-value products from foreign manufacturers;

▷ *Pipelines*—oil, diesel fuel, jet fuel, kerosene, and natural gas; and

▷ *Air freight*—flowers, medical testing kits, and gourmet food products sent directly to consumers.

assessment check

1. Identify the five major modes of transport.

2. Which mode of transport is currently experiencing a resurgence, and why?

FREIGHT FORWARDERS AND SUPPLEMENTAL CARRIERS

8 Discuss the role of transportation intermediaries, combined transportation modes, and warehousing in improving physical distribution.

Freight forwarders act as transportation intermediaries, consolidating shipments to gain lower rates for their customers. The transport rates on less-than-truckload (LTL) and less-than-carload (LCL) shipments often double the per-unit rates on truckload (TL) and carload (CL) shipments.

table 13.3   Comparison of Transport Modes

Mode	Speed	Dependability in Meeting Schedules	Frequency of Shipments	Availability in Different Locations	Flexibility in Handling	Cost
Rail	Average	Average	Low	Low	High	Average
Water	Very slow	Average	Very low	Limited	Very high	Very low
Truck	Fast	High	High	Very extensive	Average	High
Pipeline	Slow	High	High	Very limited	Very low	Low
Air	Very fast	High	Average	Average	Low	Very high

Freight forwarders charge less than the highest rates but more than the lowest rates. They profit by consolidating shipments from multiple customers until they can ship at TL and CL rates. The customers gain two advantages from these services: lower costs on small shipments and faster delivery service than they could achieve with their own LTL and LCL shipments.

In addition to the transportation options reviewed so far, a logistics manager can ship products via a number of auxiliary, or supplemental, carriers that specialize in small shipments. These carriers include UPS, FedEx, and the U.S. Postal Service.

INTERMODAL COORDINATION

Transportation companies emphasize specific modes and serve certain kinds of customers, but they sometimes combine their services to give shippers the service and cost advantages of each. *Piggyback* service, mentioned in the section on rail transport, is the most widely used form of intermodal coordination. *Birdyback* service, another form of intermodal coordination, sends motor carriers to pick up a shipment locally and deliver that shipment to local destinations; an air carrier takes it between airports near those locations. *Fishyback* service sets up a similar intermodal coordination system between motor carriers and water carriers.

Intermodal transportation generally gives shippers faster service and lower rates than either mode could match individually because each method carries freight in its most efficient way. However, intermodal arrangements require close coordination between all transportation providers.

Recognizing this need, multimodal transportation companies have formed to offer combined activities within single operations. Piggyback service generally joins two separate companies: a railroad and a trucking company. A multimodal firm provides intermodal service through its own internal transportation resources. Shippers benefit because the single service assumes responsibility from origin to destination. This unification prevents disputes over which carrier delayed or damaged a shipment.

WAREHOUSING

Products flow through two types of warehouses: storage and distribution warehouses. A storage warehouse holds goods for moderate to long periods in an attempt to balance supply and demand for producers and purchasers. For example, controlled-atmosphere—also called *cold storage*—warehouses in Yakima and Wenatchee, Washington, serve nearby apple orchards. By contrast, a distribution warehouse assembles and redistributes goods, keeping them moving as much as possible. Many distribution warehouses or centers physically store goods for less than 24 hours before shipping them to customers.

Logistics managers have attempted to save on transportation costs by developing central distribution centers. A manufacturer might send a single, large, consolidated shipment to a break-bulk center—a central distribution center that breaks down large shipments into several smaller ones and delivers them to individual customers in the area. Many Internet retailers use break-bulk distribution centers.

Caterpillar Logistics Services recently opened a huge parts distribution center in Texas. The new facility covers 500,000 square feet, employs more than 140 people, and provides repair or replacement parts to six Caterpillar dealers in North America that sell construction and mining equipment, engines, and machinery. The new warehousing facility replaces several smaller, regional distribution centers in Texas and Missouri. The center can process dealer stock and emergency orders, in addition to incoming parts directly from suppliers.[39]

Automated Warehouse Technology

Logistics managers can cut distribution costs and improve customer service dramatically by automating their warehouse systems. Although automation technology represents an expensive investment, it can provide major labor savings for high-volume distributors such as grocery chains. A computerized system might store orders, choose the correct number of cases, and move those cases in the desired sequence to loading docks. This kind of warehouse system reduces labor costs, worker injuries, pilferage, fires, and breakage.

Warehouse Locations

Every company must make a major logistics decision when it determines the number and locations of its storage facilities. Two categories of costs influence this choice: (1) warehousing and materials handling costs and (2) delivery costs from warehouses to customers. Large facilities offer economies of scale in facilities and materials handling systems; per-unit costs for these systems decrease as volume increases. Delivery costs, on the other hand, rise as the distance from warehouse to customer increases.

Warehouse location also affects customer service. Businesses must place their storage and distribution facilities in locations from which they can meet customer demands for product availability and delivery times. They must also consider population and employment trends. For example, the rapid growth of metropolitan areas in the southern and western United States has caused some firms to open more distribution centers in these areas. Nike is building a new distribution center on 125 acres in Memphis. The 1 million-square-foot facility is adding nearly 600 jobs, bringing the firm's total number of workers in Memphis to 1,800. Nike estimates the distribution center will account for more than $200 million in savings in reduced shipping times and increased service capabilities.[40]

INVENTORY CONTROL SYSTEMS

Inventory control captures a large share of a logistics manager's attention because companies need to maintain enough inventory to meet customer demand without incurring unneeded costs for carrying excess inventory. Some firms attempt to keep inventory levels under control by implementing just-in-time (JIT) production. Others are beginning to use RFID technology, discussed earlier in this chapter.

Retailers often shift the responsibility—and costs—for inventory from themselves back to individual manufacturers. **Vendor-managed inventory (VMI)** systems like this are based on the assumption that suppliers are in the best position to spot understocks or surpluses, cutting costs along the supply chain that can be translated into lower prices at the checkout. Procter & Gamble has practiced VMI, and recently began using an *inventory optimization system,* which uses software that allows planners simultaneous views of inventory across several stages of the supply chain. Mathematical models that rely on probability give P&G logistics staff a more realistic and complex view of the inventory situation, offering an opportunity for more sophisticated planning.[41]

ORDER PROCESSING

Like inventory control, order processing directly affects the firm's ability to meet its customer service standards. A company may have to compensate for inefficiencies in its order-processing system by shipping products via costly transportation modes or by maintaining large inventories at many expensive field warehouses.

Order processing typically consists of four major activities: (1) conducting a credit check; (2) keeping a record of the sale, which involves tasks such as crediting a sales representative's commission account; (3) making appropriate accounting entries; and (4) locating orders, shipping them, and adjusting inventory records. A stockout occurs when an order for an item is not available for shipment. A firm's order-processing system must advise affected customers of a stockout and offer a choice of alternative actions.

As in other areas of physical distribution, technological innovations improve efficiency in order processing. Many firms are streamlining their order-processing procedures by using e-mail and the Internet. Outdoor-gear retailer REI, for example, pushes customers toward Web ordering—its least costly fulfillment channel—in its catalogs, store receipts, signs, mailers, and membership letters.

PROTECTIVE PACKAGING AND MATERIALS HANDLING

Logistics managers arrange and control activities for moving products within plants, warehouses, and transportation terminals, which together compose the **materials handling system.** Two important concepts influence many materials handling choices: unitizing and containerization.

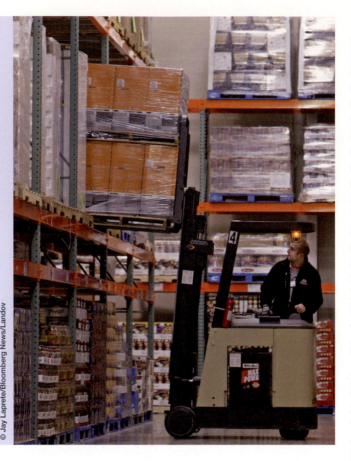

Unitizing combines as many packages as possible into each load that moves within or outside a facility. Unitizing systems often lash materials in place with steel bands or shrink packaging.

© Jay Laprete/Bloomberg News/Landov

Unitizing combines as many packages as possible into each load that moves within or outside a facility. Logistics managers prefer to handle materials on pallets (platforms, generally made of wood, on which goods are transported). Unitizing systems often lash materials in place with steel bands or shrink packaging. A shrink package surrounds a batch of materials with a sheet of plastic that shrinks after heating, securely holding individual pieces together. Unitizing promotes efficient materials handling because each package requires minimal labor to move. Securing the materials together also minimizes damage and pilferage. Pompeian, the century-old importer, bottler, and distributor of olive oil and wine vinegars, is implementing a new process for packing cases of its products. Using robots to fill and stack cases onto pallets, then wrap them, Pompeian reduces labor costs and downtime while increasing the efficiency of its production. Pallets can be stacked in different configurations, at a greater rate of speed. Prior to the change, all the work was done by hand. Switching to robotics doesn't mean losing workers, however: the company was able to switch them to another line, increasing capacity. "This system has provided flexibility in ways we didn't completely see when we began the project," says Kevin Lydon, vice president of operations. "Our operators are able to reduce the stress and strain on their bodies, and we are able to utilize their intelligence instead of their brawn."[42]

Logistics managers extend the same concept through **containerization**—combining several unitized loads. A container of oil rig parts, for example, can be loaded in Tulsa and trucked to Kansas City, where rail facilities place the shipment on a high-speed run-through train to New York City. There, the parts are loaded on a ship headed to Saudi Arabia.

In addition to the benefits outlined for unitizing, containerization also markedly reduces the time required to load and unload ships. Containers limit in-transit damage to freight because individual packages pass through few handling systems en route to purchasers.

assessment check

1. What are the benefits of intermodal transportation?

2. Identify the two types of warehouses and explain their function.

Strategic
Implications of
Marketing
21st Century
in the

everal factors, including the e-business environment, security issues, and the cost of fuel, are driving changes in channel development, logistics, and supply chain management. As the Internet continues to revolutionize the ways manufacturers deliver goods to ultimate consumers, marketers must find ways to promote cooperation between existing dealer, retailer, and distributor networks while harnessing the power of the Web as a channel. This system demands not only delivery of goods and services faster and more efficiently than ever before, it also provides superior service to Web-based customers.

In addition, increased product proliferation—grocery stores typically stock almost 50,000 different items—demands logistics systems that can manage multiple brands delivered through multiple channels worldwide. Those channels must be finely tuned to identify and rapidly rectify problems such as retail shortfalls or costly overstocks. The trend toward leaner retailing, in which the burden of merchandise tracking and inventory control is switching from retailers to manufacturers, means that to be effective, logistics and supply chain systems must result in cost savings.

Review of Chapter Objectives

1   Describe the types of marketing channels and the roles they play in marketing strategy.

Marketing (distribution) channels are the systems of marketing institutions that enhance the physical flow of goods and services, along with ownership title, from producer to consumer or business user. In other words, they help bridge the gap between producer or manufacturer and business customer or consumer.

Types of channels include direct selling, selling through intermediaries, dual distribution, and reverse channels. Channels perform four functions: facilitating the exchange process, sorting, standardizing exchange processes, and facilitating searches by buyers and sellers.

2   Outline the major channel strategy decisions.

Decisions include selecting a marketing channel and determining distribution intensity. Selection of a marketing channel may be based

on market factors, product factors, organizational factors, or competitive factors. Distribution may be intensive, selective, or exclusive.

3   Describe the concepts of channel management, conflict, and cooperation.

Manufacturers must practice channel management by developing and maintaining relationships with the intermediaries in their marketing channels. The channel captain is the dominant member of the channel. Horizontal and vertical conflict can arise when

disagreement exists among channel members. Cooperation is best achieved when all channel members regard themselves as equal components of the same organization.

4   Identify and describe the different vertical marketing systems.

A vertical marketing system (VMS) is a planned channel system designed to improve distribution efficiency and cost-effectiveness by integrating various functions throughout the distribution chain. This coordination may be achieved by forward integration or

backward integration. Options include a corporate marketing system, operated by a single owner; an administered marketing system, run by a dominant channel member; and contractual marketing systems, based on formal agreements among channel members.

5   Explain the roles of logistics and supply chain management in an overall distribution strategy.

Effective logistics requires proper supply chain management. The supply chain begins with raw materials, proceeds through actual production, and then continues with the movement of finished products through the marketing channel to customers. Supply

chain management takes place in two directions: upstream and downstream. Tools that marketers use to streamline and manage logistics include radio-frequency identification (RFID), enterprise resource planning (ERP), and logistical cost control.

6   **Identify the major components of a physical distribution system.**

Physical distribution involves a broad range of activities concerned with efficient movement of finished goods from the end of the production line to the consumer. As a system, physical distribution consists of six elements: (1) customer service, (2) transportation, (3) inventory control, (4) materials handling and protective packaging, (5) order processing, and (6) warehousing. These elements are interrelated and must be balanced to create a smoothly functioning distribution system and to avoid suboptimization.

7   **Compare the major modes of transportation.**

The five major modes of transport are railroads, motor carriers, water freight, pipelines, and air freight. Railroads, enjoying a recent surge in use, rank high on flexibility in handling products; average on speed, dependability in meeting schedules, and cost; and lower on frequency of shipments. Motor carriers are relatively high in cost but rank high on speed, dependability, shipment frequency, and availability in different locations. Water carriers balance their slow speed, low shipment frequency, and limited availability with lower costs. The special nature of pipelines makes them rank relatively low on availability, flexibility, and speed, but they are also lower in cost. Air transportation is high in cost but offers very fast and dependable delivery schedules.

8   **Discuss the role of transportation intermediaries, combined transportation modes, and warehousing in improving physical distribution.**

Transportation intermediaries facilitate movement of goods in a variety of ways, including piggyback, birdyback, and fishyback services—all forms of intermodal coordination. Methods such as unitization and containerization facilitate intermodal transfers.

assessment check: **answers**

1.1   **Distinguish between a marketing channel and logistics.**

A marketing channel is an organized system of marketing institutions and their interrelationships designed to enhance the flow and ownership of goods and services from producer to user. Logistics is the actual process of coordinating the flow of information, goods, and services among members of the marketing channel.

1.2   **What are the different types of marketing channels?**

The different types of marketing channels are direct selling, selling through intermediaries, dual distribution, and reverse channels.

1.3   **What four functions do marketing channels perform?**

The four functions of marketing channels are (1) facilitating the exchange process by reducing the number of marketplace contacts necessary for a sale; (2) sorting; (3) standardizing exchange transactions; and (4) facilitating searches by buyers and sellers.

2.1   **Identify four major factors in selecting a marketing channel.**

The four major factors in selecting a marketing channel are market, product, organizational, and competitive.

2.2   **Describe the three general categories of distribution intensity.**

Intensive distribution seeks to distribute a product through all available channels in a trade area. Selective distribution chooses a limited number of retailers in a market area. Exclusive distribution grants exclusive rights to a wholesaler or retailer to sell a manufacturer's products.

3.1   **What is a channel captain? What is its role in channel cooperation?**

A channel captain is the dominant member of the marketing channel. Its role in channel cooperation is to provide the necessary leadership.

3.2   Identify and describe the three types of channel conflict.

Horizontal conflict results from disagreements among channel members at the same level. Vertical conflict occurs when channel members at different levels disagree. The gray market causes conflict because it involves competition in the U.S. market of brands produced by overseas affiliates—often lower priced than the same U.S. manufactured goods.

4.1   What are vertical marketing systems (VMSs)? Identify the major types.

Vertical marketing systems are planned channel systems designed to improve the effectiveness of distribution, including efficiency and cost. The three major types are corporate, administered, and contractual.

4.2   Identify the three types of contractual marketing systems.

The three types of contractual systems are wholesale-sponsored voluntary chains, retail cooperatives, and franchises.

5.1   What is upstream management? What is downstream management?

Upstream management involves managing raw materials, inbound logistics, and warehouse and storage facilities. Downstream management involves managing finished product storage, outbound logistics, marketing and sales, and customer service.

5.2   Identify three methods for managing logistics.

Methods for managing logistics include RFID technology, enterprise resource planning (ERP) systems, and logistical cost control.

6.1   What are the six major elements of physical distribution?

The major elements of physical distribution are customer service, transportation, inventory control, materials handling and protective packaging, order processing, and warehousing.

6.2   What is suboptimization?

Suboptimization occurs when managers of individual functions try to reduce costs but create less than optimal results.

7.1   Identify the five major modes of transport.

The five major modes of transport are railroads, motor carriers, water carriers, pipelines, and air freight.

7.2   Which mode of transport is currently experiencing a resurgence, and why?

Railroad transport is currently experiencing a resurgence because of the cost of fuel and its efficiency in transporting large amounts of freight for less fuel.

8.1   What are the benefits of intermodal transportation?

Intermodal transportation usually provides shippers faster service and lower rates than a single mode could offer.

8.2   Identify the two types of warehouses and explain their function.

The two types of warehouses are storage and distribution. Storage warehouses hold goods for moderate to long periods of time to balance supply and demand. Distribution warehouses assemble and redistribute goods as quickly as possible.

Marketing Terms You Need to Know

distribution 416
marketing (distribution) channel 416
logistics 416
supply-chain management 416
physical distribution 416

intensive distribution 425
selective distribution 425
exclusive distribution 425
channel captain 427
vertical marketing system (VMS) 428

supply chain 431
radio frequency identification (RFID) 432
intermodal operations 436

Other Important Marketing Terms

marketing intermediary (middleman) 418
wholesaler 418
direct channel 419
direct selling 419
manufacturers' representative 421
dual distribution 421
reverse channel 421
exclusive dealing agreement 426
closed sales territory 426
tying agreement 426

gray goods 428
forward integration 429
backward integration 429
corporate marketing system 429
administered marketing system 429
contractual marketing system 429
retail cooperative 429
franchise 429
upstream management 432
downstream management 432

enterprise resource planning (ERP) system 433
third-party (contract) logistics firm 433
suboptimization 434
common carriers 435
contract carriers 436
private carriers 436
vendor-managed inventory (VMI) 441
materials handling system 441
containerization 442

Assurance of Learning Review

1. What is a marketing intermediary? What is the intermediary's role?

2. Explain why the following firms might choose a dual distribution strategy:
   a. Netflix
   b. Home Shopping Network
   c. Target

3. Describe the three levels of distribution intensity. Give an example of a product in each level.

4. Compare and contrast the two types of channel conflict. Why is channel conflict damaging to all parties?

5. What are the benefits of owning a franchise? What are the drawbacks?

6. Why do firms choose to streamline their supply chains? Describe two or three ways a firm might achieve this.

7. What are the five components associated with the cost of achieving customer service standards in a physical distribution system?

8. Which mode of transport would probably be selected for the following goods?
   a. clean diesel fuel
   b. lumber
   c. local fresh produce
   d. automobiles made in Germany
   e. T-shirts manufactured in India
   f. grain grown in the U.S. Midwest

9. Which two categories of costs influence the choice of how many storage facilities a firm might have and where they are located?

10. Describe the two concepts that influence materials handling choices. Give an example of a product that would be appropriate for each.

Projects and Teamwork Exercises

1. The traditional channel for consumer goods runs from producer to wholesaler to retailer to user. With a classmate, select a product from the following list (or choose one of your own) and create a chart that traces its distribution system. You may go online to the firm's Web site for additional information.
   a. kayak from the L.L.Bean catalog or Web site
   b. tickets to a Major League baseball game
   c. DVD recorder/player from Best Buy

2. On your own or with a classmate, identify, draw, and explain a reverse channel with which you are familiar. What purpose does this reverse channel serve to businesses? To the community? To consumers?

3. With a classmate, choose a product you think would sell best through a direct channel. Then create a brief sales presentation for your product and present it to class. Ask for feedback.

4. With a classmate, choose one of the franchises listed in Table 13.2 (on page 430) or another franchise that interests you. Visit the Web site of the company to learn more about how its goods and services are distributed. Create a chart outlining the firm's physical distribution system.

5. It takes a lot to move an elaborate stage performance like Cirque du Soleil, Big Apple Circus, or a rock band from one location to another while it is on tour. With a classmate, choose a touring performance that interests you—a music group, a circus, a theater performance, a NASCAR race, or the like—and imagine you are in charge of logistics. Create a chart showing what modes of transportation you would select to move the performance, how you would warehouse certain items during downtime, and what methods you would use to control costs.

Critical-Thinking Exercises

1. Imagine a vending machine that would charge more for hot drinks—coffee, tea, and cocoa—during cold weather. What is your opinion of a temperature-sensitive vending machine? Consumers who live in colder climates might pay more over a longer time period each year than consumers who live in warmer climates. Would your opinion change if alternatives were nearby, say, a convenience store or a vending machine that is not temperature sensitive? Do you think such a machine would be successful? Why or why not?

2. Auto dealerships often have exclusive distribution rights in their local markets. How might this affect the purchase choices consumers make? What problems might a dealership encounter with this type of distribution?

3. Choose one of the following firms and identify which marketing channel or channels you think would be best for its goods or services. Then explain the market factors, product factors, and organizational and competitive factors contributing to your selection.
   a. Barnes & Noble
   b. Outback Steakhouse
   c. *Wired* magazine
   d. Sea World
   e. Banana Republic

4. In their most basic form, RFID tags track the progress of products from warehouse to retail shelf to checkout counter. But they have great potential to provide marketers with more information about consumers' purchase patterns. In what ways might RFID technology be used to serve customers better? What problems might arise?

5. After a trip to India, where you were inspired by the craftsmanship of artisans who make jewelry and decorative artifacts, you decided to establish an import business focusing on their work. How would you determine distribution intensity for your business? What mode or modes of transportation would you use to get the goods to the United States? How and where would you warehouse the goods? Explain your answers.

Ethics Exercise

As more and more firms do business globally, transporting goods from one part of the world to another, there has been a surge in piracy—criminals making off with cargo shipments filled with everything from component parts to finished goods. A tractor-trailer loaded with electronics might be stolen from a truck stop; a warehouse stacked with pallets of new clothing, TVs, or just about anything else might be susceptible to theft. Large, sophisticated cargo theft gangs have been identified by law enforcement authorities in California, New Jersey, New York, and Texas and in cities such as Atlanta, Chicago, and Miami. However, members of the supply chain can work together to close the net around would-be thieves, developing stronger relationships with each other.[43]

1. What steps might manufacturers take to achieve the kind of channel cooperation that could reduce or prevent cargo theft?

2. How might transportation firms use security measures to build trust with customers and strengthen their position in the marketplace?

Internet Exercises

1. **Marketing channels.** Visit the Web site of footwear company Merrell (www.merrell.com). What channels does Merrell use to distribute its products? How does it avoid channel conflict?

2. **RFID.** Go the Web site of the *RFID Journal* (www.rfidjournal.com) and click on "News." Review two or three recent articles pertaining to RFID. Write a report summarizing the articles and bring it to class so you can participate in a discussion on the topic.

3. **Rail statistics.** The *Statistical Abstract of the United States* contains summary data on railroads and other transportation modes. Visit the following Web site (census.gov/compendia/statab/) and click on "Transportation." Access the tables related to railroads and answer the following questions:

a. What is a class 1 railroad? How many so-called "class 1" railroads are in operation in the United States? Has this number increased or decreased in recent years?

b. Has freight revenue increased or decreased over the past few years? How much revenue is collected per ton mile? Has this increased or decreased over the past few years?

c. Which products are transported most frequently by rail? Are there any noticeable trends in the types of products distributed by rail?

Note: Internet Web addresses change frequently. If you can't find the exact site listed, you may need to access the organization's home page and search from there, or use a search engine such as Google.

Case 13.1 XM and Sirius Merge: A New Channel for Radio Listeners

With the merger of XM and Sirius—the only two U.S. satellite radio companies—18 million subscribers are learning to live with each other's listening preferences. Despite a delay largely caused by objections from the land-based radio industry, consumer groups, lawmakers, and broadcasters, the Federal Communications Commission (FCC) approved the merger nearly one and a half years after the two companies announced they wanted to join.

The most important result of the merger is what it means to the two companies' customers. The FCC approved the deal, adding several conditions. First, the new company must cap its prices for three years, allowing customers to choose the channels they want and pay less for bundled channels. Second, existing radios must still function, and the company must begin offering radios that receive the channels broadcast by both stations. In addition, both companies will begin offering radios that allow à la carte channel choices, considered an area of growth by marketers. Finally, the newly formed company is offering more educational and minority programming and allowing any manufacturer of radio devices to build and sell transmitters, giving consumers greater choice.

Beyond the conditions laid out by the FCC, Sirius and XM have to make additional changes in order for the merger to work. The two services have different types of programming. XM offers Major League Baseball games, while Sirius has NFL games. XM touts Bob Dylan, while Sirius broadcasts shock jock Howard Stern. Some subscribers hope the merger will give them the best of both services, while others fear they will lose access to their favorite channels. Many wonder if they'll have to buy new radios to get the channels they want. Sirius and XM announced they would work together to create new programming options for their subscribers.

Both companies note it will take awhile to adjust, as they experiment with adding and dropping channels. They intend to compress the bandwidth of their channels to get more into their assigned broadcast spectrum. The new company plans to focus on service packages for new car radios, believing that consumers who obtain a satellite radio unit with the purchase of a car are likely to become subscribers. And while critics contend the merger essentially eliminates competition in the satellite radio industry, supporters say consumers benefit from more choices in programming—in the car and at home.

Questions for Critical Thinking

1. Why would XM and Sirius decide to merge considering the obstacles they face in dovetailing their devices and services? Do you think consumers will benefit from the merger? Why or why not?

2. Do you believe the land-based radio industry can continue to compete with satellite radio in its ability to deliver service? Why or why not?

Sources: "Sirius and XM Complete Merger," company Web site, http://investor
.sirius.com, accessed May 19, 2009; Kim Hart, "Satellite Radio Merger Approved," *The Washington Post,* July 26, 2008, www.washingtonpost.com; Frank Ahrens, "Subscribers' Options to Change with Merger," *The Washington Post,* July 26, 2008, www.washingtonpost.com; David Lieberman, "Sirius, XM Radios Will Still Be OK after Merger," *USA Today,* July 26, 2008, www.usatoday.com; "FCC Approves Sirius, XM Satellite Radio Merger," *USA Today,* July 26, 2008, www.usatoday.com.

Video Case 13.2 — Marketing Channels and Supply Chain Management at Recycline

The written video case on Recycline appears on page VC-12. The Recycline video is designed to expand and highlight the concepts in this chapter and the concepts and questions covered in the written video case.

CHAP14TER Retailers, Wholesalers, and Direct Marketers

© Kim Karpeles/Alamy

OfficeMax Thrives at Third

How do you define marketing success when you're the third-ranked player in a three-player market? The runner-up position is where office supply retailer OfficeMax has long found itself. But

the company thrives on come-from-behind marketing strategies and unending creativity, despite spending far less on advertising than its giant rivals, Staples and Office Depot. With more than 40,000 employees—called *associates*—in nearly 1,000 super-stores in the United States and Mexico, and with corporate customers of all sizes all over the world, OfficeMax fights a relentless battle against consumers' perception of the office-supply market as "totally beige" and its retailers as indistinguishable.

To avoid being confused with its rivals, OfficeMax recently began a turnaround marketing effort under new Senior Vice President for Advertising and Marketing Bob Thacker. Thacker's marketing strategies are concocted from equal parts perseverance and human insight. For instance, he says of advertising's tendency to intrude, "If I came and screamed at you, would you want me in your home?" On the other hand, "If I said something funny or something that touched your heart, you might let me stay."

OfficeMax certainly tickled funny bones with its innovative "Elf Yourself" holiday campaign, a bit of online silliness that allows consumers to use photos of themselves or friends to create a dancing Christmas elf and send it to others. More than 17 million people visited the Elf Yourself site in a recent Christmas season. The animated elf made its way to *The Today Show* and has returned to the Internet in upgraded versions for the past few years, outlasting more than a dozen other holiday-themed online gags the company created to grab attention during the year's biggest selling season. Most recently, the promotion featured a software widget for adding Elf videos to users' profile pages on Facebook, MySpace, LiveJournal, and iGoogle.

Combined, its many Web sites cost the company less than the price of one 30-second television ad. That suits OfficeMax's marketing budget just fine, and its online presence also sits well with members of the company's target audience, who use the Internet heavily to research many of the products OfficeMax sells. "You're talking to people [who are] already interested," says Thacker of the company's online efforts. "They've already knocked at your door finding you through search engines. . . . To open the door on the other side and make them feel welcome, that's the next step."

Its viral marketing efforts notwithstanding, OfficeMax doesn't ignore traditional advertising. In a recent year it spent nearly $15 million on newspaper ads, although that was less than half what Office Depot spent and about a quarter of Staples's ad budget. Still, says Thacker, "My mantra is, 'Don't make ads. Make news.'" In another series of ads that is part of its ongoing campaign to woo female consumers, who are known to dislike office-supply stores, OfficeMax targeted new video ads called "Life Is Beautiful" that are now playing, frugally enough, at local movie theaters.

One surefire way to make news is to give money away—as the company did recently at Minnesota's Mall of America. Going one step further than its competitors, which were slashing the prices of a few school-supply items to a penny, OfficeMax employees gave away 2 million pennies during the important back-to-school season, an event called "Power to the Penny." The giveaway lives on, along with other staged "penny pranks" promotions, in a series of YouTube videos.

True to its maverick low-budget creative image, OfficeMax recently unveiled a new product line—a coordinated series of document organizers and files—by producing a 40-minute live blogcast for an invited audience of more than 200 bloggers. Said a company spokesperson, "We want to keep pushing the envelope and continue to do things like that in future campaigns."[1]

evolution of a brand

The OfficeMax mission is to "help our customers do their best work" by offering products through retail stores, direct sales, catalogs, field salespeople, and an online store. Its customers include individuals and home office workers in Australia, Canada, Europe, Mexico, New Zealand, and the United States and corporations large and small in 36 countries through a distribution partnership.

- Founded as one store in Cleveland, Ohio, in 1988, OfficeMax expanded a year later to 11 stores in four states. By 1993, through acquisitions, it operated 300 stores in 38 states. In 2003 OfficeMax was acquired by Boise Cascade Corporation but kept its name. Do you think the OfficeMax name distinguishes the company from its competitors, or does it contribute to consumers' tendency to mistake them for each other?

- OfficeMax keeps step with Internet users by developing low-cost marketing promotions that rely not just on e-business but also on innovations like viral marketing, social networking, blogging, and animation technology. Why are technophiles an attractive market segment for the firm? What other communication technologies might OfficeMax exploit for marketing purposes?

chapter overview

In exploring how today's retailing sector operates, this chapter introduces many examples that explain the combination of activities involved in selling goods to ultimate consumers. Then the chapter discusses the role of wholesalers and other intermediaries who deliver goods from the manufacturers into the hands of retailers or other intermediaries.

Finally, the chapter looks at nonstore retailing. Direct marketing, a channel consisting of direct communication to consumers or business users, is a major form of nonstore retailing. It includes not just direct mail and telemarketing but also direct-response advertising, infomercials, and Internet marketing. The chapter concludes by looking at a less pervasive but growing aspect of nonstore retailing—automatic merchandising.

Retailing

retailing Activities involved in selling merchandise to ultimate consumers.

Retailers are the marketing intermediaries in direct contact with ultimate consumers. **Retailing** describes the activities involved in selling merchandise to these consumers. Retail outlets serve as contact points between channel members and ultimate consumers. In a very real sense, retailers represent the distribution channel to most consumers because a typical shopper has little contact with manufacturers and virtually no contact with wholesaling intermediaries. Retailers determine locations, store hours, number of sales personnel, store layouts, merchandise selections, and return policies—factors that often influence the consumers' images of the offerings more strongly than consumers' images of the products themselves. Both large and small retailers perform the major channel activities: creating time, place, and ownership utilities.

Retailers act as both customers and marketers in their channels. They sell products to ultimate consumers, and at the same time, they buy from wholesalers and manufacturers. Because of their critical location in the marketing channel, retailers often perform a vital feedback role. They obtain information from customers and transmit that information to manufacturers and other channel members.

❙ **Explain the wheel of retailing.**

Retail outlets such as Saks Fifth Avenue serve as contact points between channel members and ultimate consumers.

© AP Images/Chitose Suzuki

EVOLUTION OF RETAILING

The development of retailing illustrates the marketing concept in operation. Early retailing in North America can be traced to the establishment of trading posts, such as the Hudson Bay Company, and to pack peddlers who carried their wares to outlying settlements. The first type of retail institution, the general store, stocked a wide range of merchandise that met the needs of an isolated community or rural area.

Supermarkets appeared in the early 1930s in response to consumers' desire for lower prices. In the 1950s, discount stores delivered lower prices in exchange for reduced services. The emergence of convenience food stores in the 1960s satisfied consumer demand for fast service, convenient locations, and expanded hours of operation. The development of off-price retailers in the 1980s and 1990s reflected consumer demand for brand-name merchandise at prices considerably lower than those of traditional retailers. In recent years, Internet-enabled retailing has increased in influence and importance.

A key concept, known as the **wheel of retailing,** attempts to explain the patterns of change in retailing. According to the wheel of retailing, a new type of retailer gains a competitive foothold by offering customers lower prices than current outlets charge and maintains profits by reducing or eliminating services. Once established, however, the innovator begins to add more services, and its prices gradually rise. It then becomes vulnerable to new low-price retailers that enter with minimum services—and so the wheel turns. The retail graveyard is littered with the likes of Circuit City, Ben Franklin, Montgomery Ward, Wieboldt's, Woolworth's, W.T. Grant, and Zayre.

Many major developments in the history of retailing appear to fit the wheel's pattern. Early department stores, chain stores, supermarkets, discount stores, hypermarkets, and catalog retailers all emphasized limited service and low prices. Most of these retailers gradually increased prices as they added services.

Some exceptions disrupt this pattern, however. Suburban shopping centers, convenience food stores, and vending machines never built their appeals around low prices. Still, the wheel pattern has been a good indicator enough times in the past to make it an accurate indicator of future retailing developments.

In an interesting twist, the wheel of retailing may be turning at Wal-Mart as well. From the company's beginnings in the 1960s, founder Sam Walton held mandatory weekly Saturday morning meetings for Wal-Mart executives. It was at these legendary assemblies that managers planned strategy, debated business philosophy, and built competitive advantage—in short, where the company culture was formed. Recently, however, Wal-Mart reduced the meetings to one a month. Why the change? Some observers speculate the meetings no longer served their purpose. Whatever the reason, Wal-Mart's change from weekly to monthly Saturday morning meetings signals the end of an era.[2]

wheel of retailing
Hypothesis that each new type of retailer gains a competitive foothold by offering lower prices than current suppliers charge; the result of reducing or eliminating services.

assessment check

1. What is retailing?
2. Explain the wheel-of-retailing concept.

Retailing Strategy

Like manufacturers and wholesalers, a retailer develops a marketing strategy based on the firm's goals and strategic plans. The organization monitors environmental influences and assesses its own strengths and weaknesses in identifying marketing opportunities and constraints. A retailer bases its key decisions on two fundamental steps in the marketing strategy process: (1) selecting a target market and (2) developing a retailing mix to satisfy the chosen market. The retailing mix specifies merchandise strategy, customer service standards, pricing guidelines, target market analysis, promotion goals, location/distribution decisions, and store atmosphere choices. The combination of these elements projects a desired retail image. Retail image communicates the store's identity to consumers. Kohl's, for instance, counts on its trendy, contemporary image to attract consumers. As Figure 14.1 points out, components of retailing strategy must work together to create a consistent image that appeals to the store's target market.

figure 14.1

Components of Retail Strategy

Kohl's counts on its trendy, contemporary image to attract consumers, aligning with celebrities such as Avril Lavigne.

© Michael Tran/FilmMagic/Getty Images

Offering high-quality local produce at low prices is the strategy of Sunflower Farmers Market, a growing chain of supermarkets in five states in the West and Southwest. Launched a few years ago under the slogan "Serious food, silly prices," Sunflower targets consumers who look for quality but can't afford to pay boutique prices. In the face of rising food prices worldwide, Sunflower emphasizes affordable organic produce. In fact, it is trying to take on Wal-Mart in its own game. Currently, about 80 percent of Sunflower's merchandise undercuts Wal-Mart's prices. Same-store year-over-year revenues show double-digit increases.[3]

SELECTING A TARGET MARKET

A retailer starts to define its strategy by selecting a target market. Factors that influence the retailer's selection are the size and profit potential of the market and the level of competition for its business. Retailers pore over demographic, geographic, and psychographic profiles to segment markets. In the end, most retailers identify their target markets in terms of certain demographics.

2 Discuss how retailers select target markets.

The importance of identifying and targeting the right market is dramatically illustrated by the erosion of department store retailing. While mall anchor stores struggle to attract customers, stand-alone store Target makes a memorable splash with edgy advertising that incorporates its signature red doughnut-shaped logo in imaginative ways. And although Target can be categorized as a discount retailer, it has successfully differentiated itself from competitors like Wal-Mart and Kmart by offering trendy, quality merchandise at low prices. In addition, Target enjoys a reputation for having a clean, orderly store environment that appeals to shoppers.[4]

Deep-discount chains like Deal$, Dollar General, Dollar Tree, Family Dollar Stores, and 99¢ Only, with their less glamorous locations and low-price merchandise crammed into narrow aisles, target lower-income bargain hunters. Attracted by cents-off basics such as shampoo, cereal, and laundry detergent, customers typically pick up higher-margin goods—toys or chocolates—on their way to the checkout.

By creating stores with wide aisles and clean presentation and offering friendly service and high-end product lines like Laura Ashley paints, home improvement chain Lowe's competes with archrival Home Depot. Lowe's ambiance helps make the store more appealing to female shoppers, who account for half of all home improvement store customers.[5]

After identifying a target market, a retailer must then develop marketing strategies to attract these chosen customers to its stores or Web site. The following sections discuss tactics for implementing different strategies.

assessment check

1. How does a retailer develop a marketing strategy?

2. How do retailers select target markets?

MERCHANDISING STRATEGY

A retailer's merchandising strategy guides decisions regarding the items it will offer. A retailer must decide on general merchandise categories, product lines, specific items within lines, and the depth and width of its assortments. Shoe retailer DSW characterizes its product assortment as "very broad and shallow," with high-fashion, high-quality footwear.[6] Big box electronics retailer Best Buy recently expanded its product offerings to include a full line of musical instruments.[7]

To develop a successful merchandise mix, a retailer must weigh several priorities. First, it must consider the preferences and needs of its previously defined target market, keeping in mind that the competitive environment influences these choices. The retailer must also consider the overall profitability of each product line and product category.

Category Management

As mentioned in Chapter 12, a popular merchandising strategy is *category management,* in which a category manager oversees an entire product line for both vendors and retailers and is responsible for the profitability of the product group. Category management seeks to improve the retailer's product category performance through more coordinated buying, merchandising, and pricing. Rather than focusing on the performance of individual brands, such as Flex shampoo or Kleenex tissue, category management evaluates performance according to each product category. Laundry detergent, skin-care products, and paper goods, for example, are each viewed as individual profit centers, and different category managers supervise each group. Those that underperform are at risk of being dropped from inventory, regardless of the strength of individual brands. To improve their profitability, for example, some department stores have narrowed their traditionally broad product categories to eliminate high-overhead, low-profit lines such as toys, appliances, and furniture.

The Battle for Shelf Space

As discussed in Chapter 13, large-scale retailers are increasingly taking on the role of channel captain within many distribution networks. Some have assumed traditional wholesaling functions, while others dictate product design and specifications to manufacturers. The result is a shift in power from the manufacturers of top-selling brands to the retailer who makes them available to customers.

3 Show how the elements of the marketing mix apply to retailing strategy.

A retailer must decide on the depth and width of its merchandise assortments. Shoe retailer DSW characterizes its product assortment as "very broad and shallow," with high-fashion, high-quality footwear.

Adding to the pressure is the increase in the number of new products and variations on existing products. To identify the varying items within a product line, retailers refer to a specific product offering as a **stock-keeping unit (SKU).** Within the skin-care category, for example, each facial cream, body moisturizer, and sunscreen in a variety of sizes and formulations is a separate SKU. The proliferation of new SKUs has resulted in a fierce battle for space on store shelves.

Increasingly, major retailers such as JCPenney make demands in return for providing shelf space. They may, for example, seek pricing and promotional concessions from manufacturers as conditions for selling their products. Retailers, such as Wal-Mart, also require that manufacturers participate in their electronic data interchange (EDI) and quick-response systems. Manufacturers unable to comply may find themselves unable to penetrate this marketplace.

Slotting allowances are just one of the range of nonrefundable fees grocery retailers receive from manufacturers to secure shelf space for new products. Manufacturers may pay a national retailer thousands of dollars to get their new product displayed on store shelves.[8] Other fees include failure fees that are imposed if a new product does not meet sales projections; annual renewal fees, a "pay to stay" inducement for retailers to continue carrying brands; trade allowances; discounts on high-volume purchases; survey fees for research done by the retailers; and even fees to allow salespeople to present new items.

CUSTOMER SERVICE STRATEGY

Some stores build their retailing strategy around heightened customer services for shoppers. Gift wrapping, alterations, return privileges, bridal registries, consultants, interior design services, delivery and installation, and perhaps even electronic shopping via store Web sites are all examples of services that add value to the shopping experience. A retailer's customer service strategy must specify which services the firm will offer and whether it will charge customers for these services. Those decisions depend on several conditions: store size, type, and location; merchandise assortment; services offered by competitors; customer expectations; and financial resources. The "Solving an Ethical Controversy" feature discusses the implications of using part-time employees to provide customer services.

The basic objective of all customer services focuses on attracting and retaining target customers, thus increasing sales and profits. Some services—such as convenient restrooms, lounges, and complimentary coffee—enhance shoppers' comfort. Other services are intended to attract customers by making shopping easier and faster than it would be without the services. Some retailers, for example, offer child-care services for customers. Consumers can also get "virtual assistance" from companies like Virtuosity and CallWave, which manage phone calls by allowing users to switch between voice mail, e-mail, and real-time cell and landline calls using voice commands. Virtuosity's Virtual Assistant software can answer, screen, and route calls much like a living, breathing administrative assistant. CallWave's Vtxt automated transcription service converts voice-mail to text and e-mails or text-messages the content to the user.[9]

A customer service strategy can also support efforts in building demand for a line of merchandise. Despite the trend toward renovation, redecorating, and do-it-yourself home projects, Home

Target's gift registry system is a customer-service strategy.

© Jerry S. Mendoza/Detroit Free Press/KRT/Newscom

Solving an **ethical** controversy

Who Benefits with a Part-time Workforce?

When retailers struggle to make a profit, they scramble to trim operating costs. One strategy is to increase the number of part-time workers, either by hiring more part-timers or reducing the hours of full-time employees. Such maneuvers can cut costs because part-timers typically are ineligible for insurance and other benefits accorded to full-time workers.

Is it right to hire part-time workers?

PRO

1. When a retailer finds its margins trimmed to the bone, hiring part-time workers or reducing employees' hours may be the only way to stay in business. While few employees enjoy having their hours cut, most would prefer receiving a smaller paycheck to getting laid off.

2. Some people actually prefer working part-time: experienced workers nearing retirement, mothers with kids in school, and college students. Careful screening and hiring practices can help identify the employees who fit the organization best.

CON

1. Cutting full-time employees' hours to part time only hurts employees both financially and psychologically. They lose faith in their employer and are motivated to look for a new job.

2. Hiring part-time workers for positions that were originally full time sends the wrong message and creates poor morale because existing employees perceive—rightly—that their own jobs may be in danger.

Summary

Hiring part-time workers for formerly full-time positions or reducing full-time employees' hours to part time are risky strategies. Workplace studies suggest that part-time employees, on average, are less committed to an organization and don't stay as long as the average full timer. Lack of commitment has a direct impact on company culture, signalling that an organization is a less attractive place to work. Whether accurate or not, perceptions are hard to dispel, and the company may be saddled with this reputation long after its finances improve, making it difficult to attract and retain high performers.

Sources: Mike Hall, "Winning Full-Time Rights for Part-Time Workers," *America@ work*, www.aflcio.org, accessed May 22, 2009; Shari Roan, "Sick at Work," *Los Angeles Times*, July 29, 2008, www.latimes.com; Peter S. Goodman, "A Hidden Toll on Employees: Cut to Part Time," *The New York Times*, July 31, 2008, www.nytimes.com; Allan Beckmann, "Comparing Employer-Provided Medical Care Benefits for Lower and Higher Wage Full-Time Workers," Bureau of Labor Statistics, U.S. Department of Labor, December 19, 2007, www.bls.gov.

Depot was experiencing slowing sales until it decided to revamp its stores, improve customer service, offer a decorating service, and upgrade its marketing efforts. Home Depot experienced solid growth with the strategy, assuring its customers with its familiar slogan, "You can do it; we can help."

PRICING STRATEGY

Prices reflect a retailer's marketing objectives and policies. They also play a major role in consumer perceptions of a retailer. Consumers realize, for example, that when they enter a Gucci boutique in Milan, New York, or Tokyo, they will find such expensive merchandise as $275 belts and $2,000 handbags. Customers of the retail chain Dollar Discount Store expect a totally different type of merchandise; true to the name, every product in the store bears the same low price.

Everyone said it would be too much for a single mom to handle. But Amy bought the old house anyway. Then she went to her Home Depot® and learned how to hang cabinets. She repainted, tore out floors, added on a room, and finished the entire attic. Herself. And she proved just how much she really can handle.

See Amy's story, and others, at homedepot.com/truestories

You can do it. We can help.®

© The Home Depot

When they started experiencing slowing sales, Home Depot decided to revamp its stores, improve customer service, offer a decorating service, and upgrade its marketing efforts. It has seen solid growth using the slogan, "You can do it; we can help."

Markups and Markdowns

markup Amount a retailer adds to the cost of a product to determine its selling price.

The amount a retailer adds to a product's cost to set the final selling price is the **markup.** The amount of the markup typically results from two marketing decisions:

1. *Services performed by the retailer.* Other things being equal, stores that offer more services charge larger markups to cover their costs.

2. *Inventory turnover rate.* Other things being equal, stores with a higher turnover rate can cover their costs and earn a profit while charging a smaller markup.

A retailer's markup exerts an important influence on its image among present and potential customers. In addition, the markup affects the retailer's ability to attract shoppers. An excessive markup may drive away customers; an inadequate markup may not generate sufficient revenue to cover costs and return a profit. Retailers typically state markups as percentages of either the selling prices or the costs of the products.

markdown Amount by which a retailer reduces the original selling price of a product.

Marketers determine markups based partly on their judgments of the amounts that consumers will pay for a given product. When buyers refuse to pay a product's stated price, however, or when improvements in other items or fashion changes reduce the appeal of current merchandise, a retailer must take a **markdown.** The amount by which a retailer reduces the original selling price—the discount typically advertised for a sale item—is the markdown. Markdowns are sometimes used to evaluate merchandisers. For example, a department store might base its evaluations of buyers partly on the average markdown percentages for the product lines for which they are responsible.

The formulas for calculating markups and markdowns are provided in the "Financial Analysis in Marketing" appendix at the end of the text.

LOCATION/DISTRIBUTION STRATEGY

Retail experts often cite location as a potential determining factor in the success or failure of a retail business. A retailer may locate at an isolated site, in a central business district, or in a planned shopping center. The location decision depends on many factors, including the type of merchandise, the retailer's financial resources, characteristics of the target market, and site availability.

In recent years, many localities have become saturated with stores. As a result, some retailers have re-evaluated their location strategies. A chain may close individual stores that do not meet sales and profit goals. Other retailers have experimented with nontraditional location strategies. Starbucks cafés are now found in grocery stores, Barnes & Noble, and Target.

planned shopping center Group of retail stores planned, coordinated, and marketed as a unit.

Locations in Planned Shopping Centers

Over the past several decades, retail trade has shifted away from traditional downtown retailing districts and toward suburban shopping centers. A **planned shopping center** is a group of retail stores designed, coordinated, and marketed to shoppers in a geographic trade area. Together, the stores provide a single convenient location for shoppers as well as free parking. They facilitate shopping by maintaining uniform hours of operation, including evening and weekend hours.

There are five main types of planned shopping centers. The smallest, the *neighborhood shopping center,* is likely to consist of a group of smaller stores such as a drugstore, a dry cleaner, a card and gift shop, and perhaps a hair

Some retailers have experimented with nontraditional location strategies. Starbucks cafés are now found in grocery stores and book stores.

© Terri Miller/E-Visual Communications, Inc.

salon. This kind of center provides convenient shopping for 5,000 to 50,000 shoppers who live within a few minutes' commute. It contains five to 15 stores, and the product mix usually is confined to convenience items and some limited shopping goods.

A *community shopping center* serves 20,000 to 100,000 people in a trade area extending a few miles from its location. It contains anywhere from 10 to 30 retail stores, with a branch of a local department store or some other large store as the primary tenant. In addition to the stores found in a neighborhood center, a community center probably encompasses more stores featuring shopping goods, some professional offices, a branch bank, and perhaps a movie theater or supermarket. Community shopping centers typically offer ample parking, and tenants often share some promotion costs. With the advent of stand-alone, big-box retailers, some community shopping centers have declined in popularity. Some department stores are also moving away from the strategy of locating in shopping centers and opting for freestanding stores.

A *regional shopping center* is a large facility with at least 300,000 square feet of shopping space. Its marketing appeal usually emphasizes major department stores with the power to draw customers, supplemented by as many as 200 smaller stores. A successful regional center needs a location within 30 minutes' driving time of at least 250,000 people. A regional center—or a superregional center such as Minnesota's Mall of America—provides a wide assortment of convenience, shopping, and specialty goods, plus many professional and personal service facilities. Some shopping centers are going green, working to reduce their carbon footprint with mandatory recycling programs, maximizing the use of natural light, and installing heat-reflecting roofing that reduces the need for air conditioning.[10]

A *power center,* usually located near a regional or superregional mall, brings together several huge specialty stores, such as Sports Authority, Home Depot, and Bed Bath & Beyond, as stand-alone stores in a single trading area. Rising in popularity during the 1990s, power centers offered value because they underpriced department stores while providing a huge selection of specialty merchandise. Heated competition from cost-cutter Wal-Mart and inroads from more upscale discounters such as Target and Kohl's are currently hurting the drawing power of these centers.

Recently, a fifth type of planned center has emerged, known as a *lifestyle center.* This retailing format seeks to offer a combination of shopping, movie theaters, stages for concerts and live entertainment, decorative fountains and park benches in greenways, and restaurants and bistros in an attractive outdoor environment. At around 300,000 to 1 million square feet, the centers are large, but they seek to offer the intimacy and easy access of neighborhood village retailing with a fashionable cachet. Convenience, safety, and pleasant ambiance are also part of the appeal. Here, shoppers find a mix of just the right upscale tenants—Williams-Sonoma, Eddie Bauer, Banana Republic, Ann Taylor, Pottery Barn, and Restoration Hardware, for instance. Some lifestyle centers include office parks, townhouses, and condominiums. Well-heeled customers currently flock to such lifestyle centers as Santana Row in San Jose, California; Kierland Commons in Scottsdale, Arizona; Oak Brook Promenade in Oak Brook, Illinois; Ridge Hill Village Center, in Yonkers, New York; and St. John's Town Center in Jacksonville, Florida.[11]

Retail analysts say the decline of shopping malls and the rising market for luxury goods is fueling the rapid growth of lifestyle centers. Others, however, see the entertainment aspect of the lifestyle center as the biggest drawing card. Rayzor Ranch Town Center in Denton, Texas, includes shops, a cinema, hotels, and open-air amenities like an amphitheater, fountains, and parkland that attract prospective residents of its apartments, townhomes, senior housing, and single-family homes.[12]

PROMOTIONAL STRATEGY

To establish store images that entice more shoppers, retailers use a variety of promotional techniques. Through its promotional strategy, a retailer seeks to communicate to consumers information about its stores—locations, merchandise selections, hours of operation, and prices. If merchandise selection changes frequently to follow fashion trends, advertising typically is used to promote current styles effectively. In addition, promotions help retailers attract shoppers and build customer loyalty.

Innovative promotions can pay off, as retailer JCPenney can testify. Launching its own spin on the 1985 cult movie *The Breakfast Club,* the retailer's back-to-school ad campaign introduced five new brands over the tagline "Get that look" and one of the film's classic tunes, "Don't You Forget About Me," performed by New Found Glory.[13]

National retail chains often purchase advertising space in newspapers, on radio, and on television. Other retailers promote their goods over the Internet or use wireless technology to send marketing messages to customers' cell phones. Consumers are increasingly using their smart phones to surf the Web. To promote its bands, Warner Music Group launched a Wireless Application Protocol (WAP)–based site designed specifically for mobile browsing. Special analysis software enables Warner to analyze the browsing data by the user's device, origin of the session, and other criteria.[14]

Retailers also try to combine advertising with in-store merchandising techniques that influence buyer behavior at the point of purchase. Spain-based Zara stores offer fast fashion—inexpensive but trendy apparel that changes frequently. Merchandise arrives directly from the factory on plastic shipping hangers and already tagged. Clerks move items immediately to the selling floor, later switching out the plastic hangers for Zara's traditional wooden ones. Items typically sell out before they need to be marked down, creating a sense of exclusivity. Zara shoppers tend to visit often, sometimes even daily, to check out the new arrivals on the plastic hangers. Meanwhile, store managers wielding handheld computers identify the best-sellers and can reorder them in minutes instead of the hours it once required.[15]

A friendly, well-trained, and knowledgeable salesperson plays a vital role in conveying the store's image to consumers and in persuading shoppers to buy. To serve as a source of information, a salesperson must possess extensive knowledge regarding credit policies, discounts, special sales, delivery terms, layaways, and returns. To increase store sales, the salesperson must persuade customers that the store sells what those customers need. To this end, salespeople should receive training in selling up and suggestion selling.

By *selling up,* salespeople try to persuade customers to buy higher-priced items than originally intended. For example, an automobile salesperson might persuade a customer to buy a more expensive model than the car the buyer had initially considered. Of course, the practice of selling up must always respect the constraints of a customer's real needs. If a salesperson sells customers something they really do not need, the potential for repeat sales dramatically diminishes.

Another technique, *suggestion selling,* seeks to broaden a customer's original purchase by adding related items, special promotional products, or holiday or seasonal merchandise. Here, too, the salesperson tries to help a customer recognize true needs rather than unwanted merchandise. Beauty advisors in upscale department stores are masters of suggestion selling. Beauty retail chain Sephora creates a spa mood by treating customers like royalty. Sephora employees, called "cast members," receive special training before they hit the sales floor. Customers are encouraged to take their time, sample the wares, and indulge their senses in a stress-free environment.[16] For some retailers, the pampering strategy reaches a higher level of customer service, as seen in the "Etiquette Tips for Marketing Professionals" feature.

Just as knowledgeable and helpful sales personnel can both boost sales and set retailers apart from competitors, poor service influences customers' attitudes toward a retailer. Increasing customer complaints about unfriendly, inattentive, and uninformed salespeople have prompted many retailers to intensify their attention to training and motivating salespeople. Older training methods are giving way to online learning in many firms.

STORE ATMOSPHERICS

While store location, merchandise selection, customer service, pricing, and promotional activities all contribute to a store's consumer awareness, stores also project their personalities through **atmospherics**—physical characteristics and amenities that attract customers and satisfy their shopping needs. Atmospherics include both a store's exterior and interior décor.

A store's exterior appearance, including architectural design, window displays, signs, and entryways, helps identify the retailer and attract its target market shoppers. The Saks Fifth Avenue script logo on a storefront and McDonald's golden arches are exterior elements that readily identify

atmospherics
Combination of physical characteristics and amenities that contribute to a store's image.

Etiquette Tips for Marketing Professionals

Getting Personal with Your Customers

Seattle-based Nordstrom is famous for providing the highest level of customer service. Legend has it that in Alaska, the local Nordstrom once processed the return of a set of auto tires from a dissatisfied customer, this despite the fact that the fashion retailer did not sell—and has never sold—tires. At a time when most marketing tactics can be quickly replicated by competitors, customer service seems to be the last dimension on which businesses can differentiate themselves. And yet, while many retailers preach good service, few actually deliver it in a way that sets them apart and builds customer loyalty. What can you do to be more like the few?

- *Commit yourself to the idea of customer satisfaction.* The merchandise may be flawless and operate exactly as it's supposed to, but if your customer isn't happy, it's irrelevant. Do what it takes to satisfy the customer; your effort will reap dividends.

- *Take a genuine interest in your customers.* This goes beyond greeting visitors at the door and offering a perfunctory "thank you" as they make a purchase. Ask yourself: What can I do to help my customers find what they're looking for or at least enjoy their shopping experience while they're here? If you're stumped, a good rule of thumb is to treat each customer as you'd want your mother or grandmother to be treated.

- *Make yourself useful.* In the good old days, shoppers could rely on store clerks to know something about the merchandise they sold. Take time to learn about the products you're selling so that you can answer customers' questions and help them make an informed buying decision. If you don't know the answer to a question, find someone who does. That's the essence of providing excellent customer service.

Sources: "Do What You Love to Do: Personal Shopper," CareerBuilder, www.careerbuilder.com, accessed May 22, 2009; "Get Paid to Shop as a Personal Shopper," Fabjob.com, www.fabjob.com, accessed May 22, 2009; Randall Frost, "Welcome to the Pacific Northwest," *BrandHome*, October 22, 2007, www.brandchannel.com; Maria Palma, "Eight Reasons Why Nordstrom Is a Customer Service Legend," Customersarealways Web site, February 22, 2007, www.customersarealways.com.

these retailers. Other retailers design eye-catching exterior elements aimed at getting customers' attention. Colorful, lifelike recreations of jungle animals flank the theatrically lit entrances of the popular Rainforest Cafés, and the tropical motif carries over to the interiors, decorated with wall-sized aquariums.

The interior décor of a store should also complement the retailer's image, respond to customers' interests, and most important, induce shoppers to buy. Interior atmospheric elements include store layout, merchandise presentation, lighting, color, sounds, scents, and cleanliness. After more than three decades providing essentially the same menu offerings on dark wood tables, the Shakey's Pizza chain recently sought to capitalize on Americans' penchant for snacking by introducing its Triplets concept. The food items, all presented in groups of three, include Pizzatrios mini-pizzas; Striplets, breaded chicken strips; and Muncheese, cheese-stuffed breadsticks. But the chain also remodeled its stores to update their look and is considering other formats, such as food courts and walk-up service, to dovetail with its Triplets menu.[17]

When designing the interior and exterior of a store, marketers must remember that many people shop for reasons other than just purchasing needed products. Other common reasons for shopping include escaping the routine of daily life, avoiding weather extremes, fulfilling fantasies, and socializing with family and friends. Retailers expand beyond interior design to create welcoming and entertaining environments that draw shoppers. In a unique alliance, Apple offers "store within a store" boutiques in 500 Best Buy stores. Apple's freestanding stores have long been known for their innovative design. Shoppers who visit Best Buy to purchase a Mac or other Apple product can enjoy the intimacy and user-friendliness of the Apple display in a prime location within the big-box store.[18]

assessment check

1. What is an SKU?

2. What are the two components of a markup?

3. What are store atmospherics?

Apple's freestanding stores have long been known for their innovative design.

© George Frey/Bloomberg News/Landov

Types of Retailers

Because new types of retailers continue to evolve in response to changes in consumer demand, a universal classification system for retailers has yet to be devised. Certain differences do, however, define several categories of retailers: (1) forms of ownership, (2) shopping effort expended by customers, (3) services provided to customers, (4) product lines, and (5) location of retail transactions.

As Figure 14.2 points out, most retailing operations fit in different categories. A 7-Eleven outlet may be classified as a convenience store (category 2) with self-service (category 3) and a relatively broad product line (category 4). It is both a store-type retailer (category 5) and a member of a chain (category 1).

figure 14.2

Bases for Categorizing Retailers

Shopping Effort Expended by Customers
Convenience Retailers
Shopping Stores
Specialty Outlets

Services Provided for Customers
Self-Service
Self-Selection
Limited Service
Full-Service

Form of Ownership
Corporate Chain
Independent Retailer

Location of Retail Transactions
Retail Stores
Nonstore and Internet Retailing

Product Lines
Specialty Retailer
Limited-Line Retailer
General Merchandise Retailer

CLASSIFICATION OF RETAILERS BY FORM OF OWNERSHIP

Perhaps the easiest method for categorizing retailers is by ownership structure, distinguishing between chain stores and independent retailers. In addition, independent retailers may join wholesaler-sponsored voluntary chains, band together to form retail cooperatives, or enter into franchise agreements with manufacturers, wholesalers, or service provider organizations. Each type of ownership has its own unique advantages and strategies.

Chain Stores

Chain stores are groups of retail outlets that operate under central ownership and management and handle the same product lines. Chains have an advantage over independent retailers in economies of scale. Volume purchases allow chains to pay lower prices than their independent rivals must pay. Because a chain may have hundreds of retail stores, it can afford extensive advertising, sales training, and computerized systems for merchandise ordering, inventory management, forecasting, and accounting. Also, the large sales volume and wide geographic reach of a chain may enable it to advertise in a variety of media.

Independent Retailers

The second-largest industry in the United States by number of establishments as well as number of employees, the retailing structure supports a large number of small stores, many medium-size stores, and a small number of large stores. It generates about $3.8 trillion in retail sales every year and accounts for more than 12 percent of all business establishments in the United States.[19]

Independent retailers compete with chains in a number of ways. The traditional advantage of independent stores is friendly, personalized service. Cooperatives offer another strategy for independents. For instance, cooperatives like Best Western Hotels and Valu-Rite Pharmacies help independents compete with chains by providing volume buying power as well as advertising and marketing programs.

CLASSIFICATION BY SHOPPING EFFORT

Another classification system is based on the reasons consumers shop at particular retail outlets. This approach categorizes stores as convenience, shopping, or specialty retailers.

Convenience retailers focus their marketing appeals on accessible locations, extended store hours, rapid checkout service, and adequate parking facilities. Local food stores, gasoline stations, and dry cleaners fit this category. GreenStop, Canada's chain of alternative-fuel stations, features convenience stores that sell solar-roasted coffee and organic veggie wraps instead of candy and cigarettes.

Shopping stores typically include furniture stores, appliance retailers, clothing outlets, and sporting goods stores. Consumers usually compare prices, assortments, and quality levels at competing outlets before making purchase decisions. Consequently, managers of shopping stores attempt to differentiate their outlets through advertising, in-store displays, well-trained and knowledgeable salespeople, and appropriate merchandise assortments.

Specialty retailers combine carefully defined product lines, services, and reputations in attempts to persuade consumers to expend considerable effort to shop at their stores. Examples include Bergdorf Goodman, Neiman Marcus, Nordstrom, and Von Maur.

CLASSIFICATION BY SERVICES PROVIDED

Another category differentiates retailers by the services they provide to customers. This classification system consists of three retail types: self-service, self-selection, or full-service retailers.

The AM PM Mini-Mart is classified as a self-service store, while Safeway grocery stores and A&P Future Stores are examples of self-selection stores. Both categories sell convenience products people can purchase frequently with little assistance. In the clothing industry, catalog retailer Lands' End is a self-selection store. Full-service retailers such as Neiman Marcus focus on fashion-oriented merchandise, backed by a complete array of customer services. A new type of retailing that includes social networking is described in the "Marketing Success" feature.

CLASSIFICATION BY PRODUCT LINES

Product lines also define a set of retail categories and the marketing strategies appropriate for firms within those categories. Grouping retailers by product lines produces three major categories: specialty stores, limited-line retailers, and general-merchandise retailers.

Specialty Stores

A *specialty store* typically handles only part of a single product line. However, it stocks this portion in considerable depth or variety. Specialty stores include a wide range of retail outlets, including fish markets, grocery stores, men's and women's shoe stores, and bakeries. Although some specialty stores are chain outlets, most are independent, small-scale operations. They represent perhaps the

greatest concentration of independent retailers who develop expertise in one product area and provide narrow lines of products for their local markets.

Specialty stores should not be confused with specialty products. Specialty stores typically carry convenience and shopping goods. The label *specialty* reflects the practice of handling a specific, narrow line of merchandise. For example, Lady Foot Locker is a specialty store that offers a wide selection of name-brand athletic footwear, apparel, and accessories made specifically for women. Gloria Jean's Coffees sells whole-bean coffees, beverages, and gift baskets.[20]

Limited-Line Retailers

Customers find a large assortment of products within one product line or a few related lines in a **limited-line store.** This type of retail operation typically develops in areas with a large enough population to sufficiently support it. Examples of limited-line stores are IKEA (home furnishings and housewares) and Rubenstein's of New Orleans (clothing). These retailers cater to the needs of people who want to select from complete lines in purchasing particular products.

A unique type of limited-line retailer is known as a **category killer.** These stores offer huge selections and low prices in single product lines. Stores within this category—such as Best Buy, Barnes & Noble, Bed Bath & Beyond, and Home Depot—are among the most successful retailers in the nation. Category killers at first took business away from general merchandise discounters, which were not able to compete in selection or price. Recently, however, expanded merchandise and aggressive cost cutting by warehouse clubs and Wal-Mart have turned the tables. Competition from Internet companies that can offer unlimited selection and speedy delivery has also taken customers away. While they still remain a powerful force in retailing, especially for local businesses, category killers are not invulnerable.

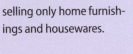

IKEA is a limited-line store, selling only home furnishings and housewares.

© Pat Goh Seng/Bloomberg News/Landov

General Merchandise Retailers

General merchandise retailers, carrying a wide variety of product lines stocked in some depth, distinguish themselves from limited-line and specialty retailers by the large number of product lines they carry. The general

MARKETING SUCCESS

Threadless Fits Web Shoppers to a "T"

Background. The year was 2000, and the Internet was exploding. When he wasn't clerking at CompUSA or taking graphic design courses, 20-year-old Jake Nickell sat hunched over his computer in his tiny Chicago apartment, playing with Web design. It had become an all-consuming hobby, and Nickell was discovering more about the design work he could do online. Chatting on Dreamless.org, a community for designers, Nickell began designing T-shirts online for fun.

But one day it struck him that he could probably sell T-shirts to other Dreamless members.

The Challenge. Nickell and his friend Jacob DeHart each kicked in $500 to fund their new venture, which they called Threadless. They began by sponsoring an online design contest, promising two free shirts as the prize. Contestants submitted designs and members of the virtual community voted

store described earlier in this chapter was a primitive form of a general merchandise retailer. This category includes variety stores, department stores, and mass merchandisers such as discount houses, off-price retailers, and hypermarkets.

Variety Stores

A retail outlet that offers an extensive range and assortment of low-price merchandise is called a *variety store*. Less popular today than they once were, many of these stores have evolved into or given way to other types of retailers such as discount stores. In recent years, many pharmacies have become drugstore–variety store combinations. Walgreens, for example, has more than 6,800 stores nationwide and fills more than 580 million prescriptions a year.[21] The nation's variety stores now account for less than 1 percent of all retail sales. However, variety stores remain popular in other parts of the world. Many retail outlets in Spain and Mexico are family-owned variety stores.

Department Stores

In essence, a **department store** is a series of limited-line and specialty stores under one roof. By definition, this large retailer handles a variety of merchandise, including men's, women's, and children's clothing and accessories; household linens and dry goods; home furnishings; and furniture. It serves as a one-stop shopping destination for almost all personal and household products.

Department stores such as Bloomingdale's built their reputations by offering wide varieties of services such as charge accounts, delivery, gift wrapping, and liberal return privileges. As a result, they incur relatively high operating costs, averaging about 45 to 60 percent of sales.

Department stores have faced intense competition over the past several years. Relatively high operating costs have left them vulnerable to retailing innovations such as discount stores, Internet retailers, and hypermarkets. In addition, department stores' traditional locations in downtown business districts have suffered from problems associated with limited parking, traffic congestion, and population migration to the suburbs.

Department stores have fought back in a variety of ways. Many have closed certain sections, such as electronics, in which high costs kept them from competing with discount houses and category killers. They have added bargain outlets, expanded parking facilities, and opened major branches in regional shopping centers. Marketers have attempted to revitalize downtown retailing in many cities by modernizing their stores, expanding store hours, making special efforts to attract the tourist and convention trade, and serving the needs of urban residents.

Over the years, U.S. department stores have undergone massive consolidation, with only a handful of companies owning many department-store chains that were once freestanding. Such acquisitions don't always sit well with shoppers. For example, Federated's acquisition of May

---

for their favorites, which Nickell and DeHart commercially printed and sold online for $12 each.

The Strategy. Fueled by this revenue stream, the design contests continued, always with customers directing which merchandise would be offered. In a couple of years, Threadless.com had attracted more than 10,000 visitors and sold over $100,000 in T-shirts. All of its merchandise is created—and vetted—by its audience.

The Outcome. In what seems like pure common sense to its founders, Threadless grew through user innovation—that is, the company develops its inventory by asking its customers what they'd

like to buy. And Threadless continues to grow: sales in a recent year topped $18 million, with $6 million in profits. The company has never advertised and employs no professional designers to create the merchandise. There's no field sales force or distribution network. The Web, it seems, has done most of the heavy lifting.

Sources: Company Web site, http://www.threadless.com, accessed May 22, 2009; Max Chafkin, "The Customer Is the Company," *Inc.*, June 2008, www.inc.com; "Threadless—The Full Story: Inc. Magazine Feature on Threadless," *Mass Customization & Open Innovation News*, May 24, 2008, mass-customization.blogs.com; Emily Maltby, "Startup Skills for a T-Shirt Company," *Fortune Small Business*, January 31, 2008, money.cnn .com; Rebecca Little, "Threadless, Now in Store," *Chicago*, September 11, 2007, www .chicagomag.com; Alan Sipress, "T-Shirt Maker's Style, Drawn from Web Users," *The Washington Post*, June 18, 2007, www.washingtonpost.com.

Department Stores several years ago included the 64-store Marshall Field chain. In an attempt to create a national brand, Federated changed its name to Macy's and announced the iconic Marshall Field stores would be renamed Macy's as well. The renaming caused a furor in Chicago, home of the first Marshall Field stores. Macy's recently announced it would attempt to localize more of its stores across the nation, so that buying activities would no longer be consolidated in New York. Instead, merchandise would reflect local needs and tastes.[22]

Mass Merchandisers

Mass merchandising has made major inroads into department store sales by emphasizing lower prices for well-known brand-name products, high product turnover, and limited services. A **mass merchandiser** often stocks a wider line of items than a department store but usually without the same depth of assortment within each line. Discount houses, off-price retailers, hypermarkets, and catalog retailers are all examples of mass merchandisers.

Discount Houses A **discount house** charges low prices and offers fewer services. Early discount stores sold mostly appliances. Today, they offer soft goods, drugs, food, gasoline, and furniture.

By eliminating many of the "free" services provided by traditional retailers, these operations can keep their markups 10 to 25 percent below those of their competitors. Some of the early discounters have since added services, stocked well-known name brands, and boosted their prices. In fact, many now resemble department stores.

A discount format gaining strength is the *warehouse club*. Costco, BJ's, and Wal-Mart's Sam's Club are the largest warehouse clubs in the United States. These no-frills, cash-and-carry outlets offer consumers access to name-brand products at deeply discounted prices. Selection at warehouse clubs includes gourmet popcorn, fax machines, peanut butter, luggage, and sunglasses sold in vast warehouselike settings. Attracting business away from almost every retailing segment, warehouse clubs now even offer fresh food and gasoline. Customers must be members to shop at warehouse clubs.

Off-Price Retailers Another version of a discount house is an *off-price retailer*. This kind of store stocks only designer labels or well-known brand-name clothing at prices equal to

Warehouse clubs are a type of discount house that sell name-brand products at deeply discounted prices. Merchandise at the clubs is sold in vast warehouse-like settings.

© Jay Laprete/Bloomberg News/Landov

or below regular wholesale prices and then passes the cost savings along to buyers. While many off-price retailers are located in outlets in downtown areas or in freestanding buildings, a growing number are concentrating in *outlet malls*—shopping centers that house only off-price retailers.

Inventory at off-price stores changes frequently as buyers take advantage of special price offers from manufacturers selling excess merchandise. Off-price retailers such as Loehmann's, Marshalls, Ross, Stein Mart, and T.J. Maxx also keep their prices below those of traditional retailers by offering fewer services. Off-price retailing has been well received by today's shoppers. France-based retailer Vente-privée.com sells high-fashion overstock merchandise through invitation-only clearance sales conducted solely on the Web.[23]

Hypermarkets and Supercenters Another innovation in discount retailing is the creation of **hypermarkets**—giant, one-stop shopping facilities that offer wide selections of grocery and general merchandise products at discount prices. Store size determines the major difference between hypermarkets and supercenters. Hypermarkets typically fill up 200,000 or more square feet of selling space, about a third larger than most **supercenters.** Ohio-based Bigg's Hypermarket Shoppes offer a vast array of items in dozens of departments, including housewares, groceries, apparel, drugs, hardware, electronics, and photo finishing in stores that average 165,000 square feet. Customer service is enhanced by wireless phones carried by key employees at each store.[24]

The newest type of hypermarket now being tested in New Mexico is AutoCart, a 24-hour drive-through superstore of about 130,000 square feet that can serve up to 12,000 cars a day. Although critics say it lacks the entertainment value of a store like Wal-Mart, AutoCart allows shoppers to phone in their orders ahead of time and offers such diverse services as dry cleaning, DVD rentals, event tickets, groceries, office supplies, and prescription drugs.[25]

Showroom and Warehouse Retailers These retailers send direct mail to their customers and sell the advertised goods from showrooms that display samples. Backroom warehouses fill orders for the displayed products. Low prices are important to catalog store customers. To keep prices low, these retailers offer few services, store most inventory in inexpensive warehouse space, limit shoplifting losses, and handle long-lived products such as luggage, small appliances, gift items, sporting equipment, toys, and jewelry.

CLASSIFICATION OF RETAIL TRANSACTIONS BY LOCATION

Although most retail transactions occur in stores, nonstore retailing serves as an important marketing channel for many products. In addition, both consumer and business-to-business marketers rely on nonstore retailing to generate orders or requests for more information that may result in future orders.

Direct marketing is a broad concept that includes direct mail, direct selling, direct-response retailing, telemarketing, Internet retailing, and automatic merchandising. The last sections of this chapter consider each type of nonstore retailing.

RETAIL CONVERGENCE AND SCRAMBLED MERCHANDISING

Many traditional differences no longer distinguish familiar types of retailers, rendering any set of classifications less useful. **Retail convergence,** whereby similar merchandise is available from multiple retail outlets distinguished by price more than any other factor, is blurring distinctions between types of retailers and the merchandise mix they offer. A few years ago, a customer looking for a fashionable coffeepot might have headed straight for Williams-Sonoma or Starbucks. Today, she's just as likely to pick one up at Target or her neighborhood Sam's Club, where she can check

4 **Explain the concepts of retail convergence and scrambled merchandising.**

retail convergence
Situation in which similar merchandise is available from multiple retail outlets, resulting in the blurring of distinctions between types of retailers and merchandise offered.

out new spring fashions and stock up on paper goods. The Gap is no longer pitted only against Eddie Bauer or American Eagle Outfitters but against designer-label brands at department stores and Kohl's, too. Grocery stores compete with Super Wal-Mart, Sam's Club, and Costco. In turn, Wal-Mart broadened its product mix to include more electronics and a line of fine jewelry, and introduced a prepaid debit card intended to serve low-income shoppers.[26]

scrambled merchandising Retailing practice of combining dissimilar product lines to boost sales volume.

Scrambled merchandising—in which a retailer combines dissimilar product lines in an attempt to boost sales volume—has also muddied the waters. Drugstores not only fill prescriptions but sell cameras, cards, housewares, magazines, and even small appliances. In addition, Walgreens, CVS, Wal-Mart, and other stores have discovered another consumer need: in-store health clinics that diagnose and treat minor illnesses and injuries quickly and affordably.[27]

assessment check

1. How do we classify retailers by form of ownership?

2. Categorize retailers by shopping effort and by services provided.

3. List several ways to classify retailers by product line.

Wholesaling Intermediaries

Recall from Chapter 13 that several distribution channels involve marketing intermediaries called **wholesalers.** These firms take title to the goods they handle and sell those products primarily to retailers or to other wholesalers or business users. They sell to ultimate consumers only in insignificant quantities, if at all. **Wholesaling intermediaries,** a broader category, include not only wholesalers but also agents and brokers who perform important wholesaling activities without taking title to the goods.

wholesaler Channel intermediary that takes title to goods it handles and then distributes these goods to retailers, other distributors, or B2B customers.

wholesaling intermediary Comprehensive term that describes wholesalers as well as agents and brokers.

5 Identify the functions performed by wholesaling intermediaries.

FUNCTIONS OF WHOLESALING INTERMEDIARIES

As specialists in certain marketing functions, as opposed to production or manufacturing functions, wholesaling intermediaries can perform these functions more efficiently than producers or consumers. The importance of these activities results from the utility they create, the services they provide, and the cost reductions they allow.

Creating Utility

Wholesaling intermediaries create three types of utility for consumers. They enhance time utility by making products available for sale when consumers want to purchase them. They create place utility by helping deliver goods and services for purchase at convenient locations. They create ownership (or possession) utility when a smooth exchange of title to the products from producers or intermediaries to final purchasers is complete. Possession utility can also result from transactions in which actual title does not pass to purchasers, as in rental car services.

Providing Services

Table 14.1 lists a number of services provided by wholesaling intermediaries. The list clearly indicates the marketing utilities—time, place, and possession utility—that wholesaling intermediaries create or enhance. These services also reflect the basic marketing functions of buying, selling, storing, transporting, providing marketing information, financing, and risk taking.

Of course, many types of wholesaling intermediaries provide varying services, and not all of them perform every service listed in the table. Producer-suppliers rely on wholesaling intermediaries for distribution and selection of firms that offer the desired combinations of services. In general, however, the critical marketing functions listed in the table form the basis for any evaluation of a marketing intermediary's efficiency. The risk-taking function affects each service of the intermediary.

Ingram Micro is a leading technology distributor with business clients in more than 150 countries and vendors all over the world. Ranking number 69 in the *Fortune* 100, it offers a wide range of information technology services for order management and fulfillment, contract

table 14.1 Wholesaling Services for Customers and Producer-Suppliers

Service	Beneficiaries of Service	
	Customers	Producer-Suppliers
Buying Anticipates customer demands and applies knowledge of alternative sources of supply; acts as purchasing agent for customers.	Yes	No
Selling Provides a sales force to call on customers, creating a low-cost method for servicing smaller retailers and business users.	No	Yes
Storing Maintains warehouse facilities at lower costs than most individual producers or retailers could achieve. Reduces risk and cost of maintaining inventory for producers.	Yes	Yes
Transporting Customers receive prompt delivery in response to their demands, reducing their inventory investments. Wholesalers also break bulk by purchasing in economical carload or truckload lots, then reselling in smaller quantities, thereby reducing overall transportation costs.	Yes	Yes
Providing Marketing Information Offers important marketing research input for producers through regular contacts with retail and business buyers. Provides customers with information about new products, technical information about product lines, reports on competitors' activities and industry trends, and advisory information concerning pricing changes, legal changes, and so forth.	Yes	Yes
Financing Grants credit that might be unavailable for purchases directly from manufacturers. Provides financing assistance to producers by purchasing products in advance of sale by promptly paying bills.	Yes	Yes
Risk Taking Evaluates credit risks of numerous, distant retail customers and small-business users. Extends credit to customers that qualify. By transporting and stocking products in inventory, the wholesaler assumes risk of spoilage, theft, or obsolescence.	Yes	Yes

manufacturing and warehousing, transportation management, and credit and collection management, as well as distributing and marketing information technology products to businesses worldwide.[28]

Lowering Costs by Limiting Contacts

When an intermediary represents numerous producers, it often cuts the costs of buying and selling. The transaction economies are illustrated in Figure 14.3, which shows five manufacturers marketing their outputs to four different retail outlets. Without an intermediary, these exchanges create a total of 20 transactions. Adding a wholesaling intermediary reduces the number of transactions to nine.

United Stationers is a wholesale distributor of business products ranging from paper clips to technology equipment and office furniture. It serves discount chains, independent stores, and Internet resellers. While big-box retailers buy in bulk directly from manufacturers, they can order low-volume specialty goods faster and more efficiently from United Stationers. By ordering online, mom-and-pop

assessment check

1. What is a wholesaler? How does it differ from a wholesaling intermediary?

2. How do wholesaling intermediaries help sellers lower costs?

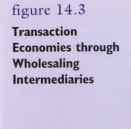

figure 14.3

Transaction Economies through Wholesaling Intermediaries

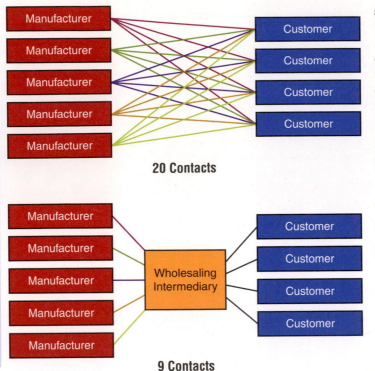

20 Contacts

9 Contacts

 Outline the major types of independent wholesaling intermediaries and the appropriate situations for using each.

stores have access to more than 100,000 items from about 1,000 manufacturers, delivered either to the store or directly to customers overnight. A one-stop warehousing, logistics, and distribution network, United Stationers' product mix even includes industrial products and janitorial and breakroom supplies.[29]

TYPES OF WHOLESALING INTERMEDIARIES

Various types of wholesaling intermediaries operate in different distribution channels. Some provide wide ranges of services or handle broad lines of goods, while others specialize in individual services, goods, or industries. Figure 14.4 classifies wholesaling intermediaries by two characteristics: ownership and title flows—whether title passes from manufacturer or wholesaling intermediary. The three basic ownership structures are as follows: (1) manufacturer-owned facilities, (2) independent wholesaling intermediaries, and (3) retailer-owned cooperatives and buying offices. The two types of independent wholesaling intermediaries are merchant wholesalers, which take title of the goods, and agents and brokers, which do not.

figure 14.4

Major Types of Wholesaling Intermediaries

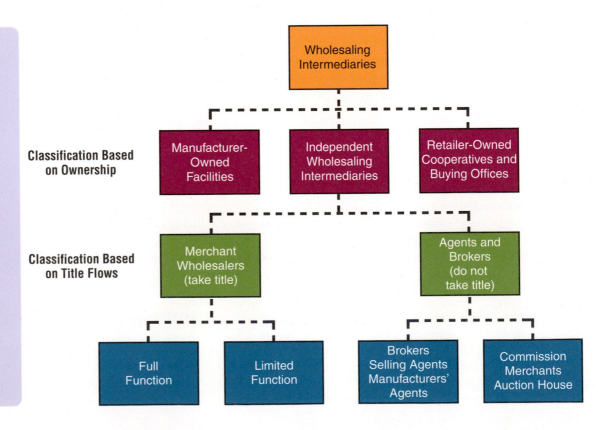

Manufacturer-Owned Facilities

Several reasons lead manufacturers to distribute their goods directly through company-owned facilities. Some perishable goods need rigid control of distribution to avoid spoilage; other goods require complex installation or servicing. Some goods need aggressive promotion. Goods with high unit values allow profitable sales by manufacturers directly to ultimate purchasers. Manufacturer-owned facilities include sales branches, sales offices, trade fairs, and merchandise marts.

A *sales branch* carries inventory and processes orders for customers from available stock. Branches provide a storage function like independent wholesalers and serve as offices for sales representatives in their territories. They are prevalent in marketing channels for chemicals, commercial machinery and equipment, and petroleum products.

A *sales office,* in contrast, does not carry inventory, but it does serve as a regional office for a manufacturer's sales personnel. Locations close to the firm's customers help limit selling costs and support effective customer service. For example, numerous sales offices in the Detroit suburbs serve the area's automobile industry.

A *trade fair* (or trade exhibition) is a periodic show at which manufacturers in a particular industry display their wares for visiting retail and wholesale buyers. The world's largest consumer technology trade show and the largest trade show of any kind in America, the annual International Consumer Electronics Show (CES), takes place in January in Las Vegas. CES typically attracts more than 140,000 attendees and features 2,700 exhibitors in 30 product categories.[30]

A *merchandise mart* provides space for permanent showrooms and exhibits, which manufacturers rent to market their goods. One of the world's largest merchandise marts is Chicago's Merchandise Mart Center, a 7-million-square-foot complex with its own zip code that hosts more than 30 seasonal buying markets each year.

Independent Wholesaling Intermediaries

Many wholesaling intermediaries are independently owned. These firms fall into two major categories: merchant wholesalers and agents and brokers.

A trade fair is a periodic show at which manufacturers in a particular industry display their wares for visiting retail and wholesale buyers, such as the annual International Consumer Electronics Show (CES).

© Robyn Beck/AFP/Getty Images

Merchant Wholesalers

A **merchant wholesaler** takes title to the goods it handles. Merchant wholesalers account for roughly 60 percent of all sales at the wholesale level. Further classifications divide these wholesalers into full-function or limited-function wholesalers, as indicated in Figure 14.4.

A full-function merchant wholesaler provides a complete array of services for retailers and business purchasers. Such a wholesaler stores merchandise in a convenient location, allowing customers to make purchases on short notice and minimizing inventory requirements. The firm typically maintains a sales force that calls on retailers, makes deliveries, and extends credit to qualified buyers. Full-function wholesalers are common in the drug, grocery, and hardware industries. In the business-goods market, full-function merchant wholesalers—often called *industrial distributors*—sell machinery, inexpensive accessory equipment, and supplies.

A **rack jobber** is a full-function merchant wholesaler that markets specialized lines of merchandise to retailers. A rack jobber supplies the racks, stocks the merchandise, prices the goods, and makes regular visits to refill shelves. Sometimes rack jobbers also work the sales floor—as in the case of Wal-Mart, which partners with Anderson Merchandisers, a rack jobber in the entertainment sector—for sales help in its electronics department. Product specialists from Anderson Merchandisers lend their expertise on high-definition TVs and other consumer electronics in about 100 Wal-Mart supercenters, answering customer questions and helping to close the sale.[31]

Limited-function merchant wholesalers fit into four categories: cash-and-carry wholesalers, truck wholesalers, drop shippers, and mail-order wholesalers. Limited-function wholesalers serve the food, coal, lumber, cosmetics, jewelry, sporting goods, and general merchandise industries.

A *cash-and-carry wholesaler* performs most wholesaling functions except for financing and delivery. Although feasible for small stores, this kind of wholesaling generally is unworkable for large-scale grocery stores. Today, cash-and-carry operations typically function as departments within regular full-service wholesale operations. Cash-and-carry wholesalers are commonplace outside the United States, such as in the United Kingdom.

A **truck wholesaler,** or **truck jobber,** markets perishable food items such as bread, tobacco, potato chips, candy, and dairy products. Truck wholesalers make regular deliveries to retailers, perform sales and collection functions, and promote product lines. Regional wholesale distributor S. Abraham & Sons delivers brand-name groceries, health and beauty aids, and other merchandise to convenience, drug, and grocery stores in the Midwest.[32]

A **drop shipper** such as ONE, Inc., of Tampa, Florida, accepts orders from customers and forwards these orders to producers, which then ship the desired products directly to customers. Although drop shippers take title to goods, they never physically handle or even see the merchandise. These intermediaries often operate in industries selling bulky goods, such as coal and lumber, that customers buy in large lots.

A **mail-order wholesaler** is a limited-function merchant wholesaler that distributes physical or online catalogs as opposed to sending sales representatives to contact retail, business, and institutional customers. Customers then make purchases by mail, by phone, or online. Such a wholesaler often serves relatively small customers in outlying areas. Mail-order operations mainly exist in the hardware, cosmetics, jewelry, sporting goods, and specialty food lines as well as in general merchandise. Some popular mail-order products are pharmaceuticals, roasted bean coffee, Christmas trees and wreaths, and popcorn.

Table 14.2 compares the various types of merchant wholesalers and the services they provide. Full-function merchant wholesalers and truck wholesalers rank as relatively high-cost intermediaries because of the number of services they perform, while cash-and-carry wholesalers, drop shippers, and mail-order wholesalers provide fewer services and set lower prices because they incur lower operating costs.

Agents and Brokers

A second group of independent wholesaling intermediaries, agents and brokers, may or may not take possession of the goods they handle, but they never take title. They normally perform fewer services than merchant wholesalers, working mainly to bring together buyers and sellers. Agents and brokers fall into five categories: commission merchants, auction houses, brokers, selling agents, and manufacturers' representatives (reps).

table 14.2 **Comparison of the Types of Merchant Wholesalers and Their Services**

Service	Full-Function	Limited-Function Wholesaler			
		Cash-and-Carry	Truck	Drop Shipper	Mail-Order
Anticipates customer needs	Yes	Yes	Yes	No	Yes
Carries inventory	Yes	Yes	Yes	No	Yes
Delivers	Yes	No	Yes	No	No
Provides marketing information	Yes	Rarely	Yes	Yes	No
Provides credit	Yes	No	No	Yes	Sometimes
Assumes ownership risk by taking title	Yes	Yes	Yes	Yes	Yes

Commission merchants, which predominate in the markets for agricultural products, take possession when producers ship goods such as grain, produce, and livestock to central markets for sale. Commission merchants act as producers' agents and receive agreed-upon fees when they make sales. Because customers inspect the products and prices fluctuate, commission merchants receive considerable latitude in marketing decisions. The owners of the goods may specify minimum prices, but the commission merchants sell these goods at the best possible prices. The commission merchants then deduct their fees from the sales' proceeds.

An *auction house* gathers buyers and sellers in one location and allows potential buyers to inspect merchandise before submitting competing purchase offers. Auction house commissions typically reflect specified percentages of the sales prices of the auctioned items. Auctions are common in the distribution of tobacco, used cars, artwork, livestock, furs, and fruit. The Internet has led to a new type of auction house that connects customers and sellers in the online world. A well-known example is eBay, which auctions a wide variety of products in all price ranges.

Brokers work mainly to bring together buyers and sellers. A broker represents either the buyer or the seller—but not both—in a given transaction, and the broker receives a fee from the client when the transaction is completed. Intermediaries that specialize in arranging buying and selling transactions between domestic

broker Agent wholesaling intermediary that does not take title to or possession of goods in the course of its primary function, which is to bring together buyers and sellers.

The Internet has led to a new type of auction house that connects customers and sellers in the online world. A well-known example is eBay.

Don't sit on it. Sell it.
You've got dozens of things in your home that millions of buyers on eBay would love to buy. You just need to decide what to sell first. List them. And then watch the bids roll in. eBay.co.uk

© Image courtesy of The Advertising Archives

producers and foreign buyers are called *export brokers.* Brokers operate in industries characterized by large numbers of small suppliers and purchasers such as real estate, frozen foods, and used machinery. Because they provide onetime services for sellers or buyers, they cannot serve as effective channels for manufacturers seeking regular, continuing service. A firm that seeks to develop a more permanent channel might choose instead to use a selling agent or manufacturer's agent.

A **selling agent** typically exerts full authority over pricing decisions and promotional outlays, and it often provides financial assistance for the manufacturer. Selling agents act as independent marketing departments because they can assume responsibility for the total marketing programs of client firms' product lines. Selling agents mainly operate in the coal, lumber, and textiles industries. For a small, weakly financed, production-oriented firm, such an intermediary might prove the ideal marketing channel.

While a manufacturer may deal with only one selling agent, a firm that hires **manufacturers' representatives** often delegates marketing tasks to many of these agents. Such an independent salesperson may work for a number of firms that produce related, noncompeting products. Manufacturers' reps are paid on a commission basis, such as 6 percent of sales. Unlike selling agents, who may contract for exclusive rights to market a product, manufacturers' agents operate in specific territories. They may develop new sales territories or represent relatively small firms and those firms with unrelated lines.

Standard Plumbing Supply of Salt Lake City is a manufacturer's representative serving the plumbing industry in eight western states. Recently named Wholesaler of the Year by *Supply House Times,* the company pioneered the concept of self-service in plumbing supply distribution. Standard Plumbing Supply carries about 20,000 SKUs, and its self-serve warehouses more closely resemble retail stores than supply houses.[33]

The importance of selling agents in many markets has declined because manufacturers want better control of their marketing programs than these intermediaries allow. In contrast, the volume of sales by manufacturers' agents has more than doubled and now accounts for 37 percent of all sales by agents and brokers. Table 14.3 compares the major types of agents and brokers on the basis of the services they perform.

manufacturers' representative
Agent wholesaling intermediary that represents manufacturers of related but noncompeting products and receives a commission on each sale.

assessment check

1. What is the difference between a merchant wholesaler and a rack jobber?
2. Differentiate between agents and brokers.

RETAILER-OWNED COOPERATIVES AND BUYING OFFICES

Retailers may assume numerous wholesaling functions in an attempt to reduce costs or provide special services. Independent retailers sometimes band together to form buying groups that can achieve cost savings through quantity purchases. Other groups of retailers establish retailer-owned

table 14.3   **Services Provided by Agents and Brokers**

Service	Commission Merchant	Auction House	Broker	Manufacturers' Agent	Selling Agent
Anticipates customer needs	Yes	Sometimes	Sometimes	Yes	Yes
Carries inventory	Yes	Yes	No	No	No
Delivers	Yes	No	No	Sometimes	No
Provides marketing information	Yes	Yes	Yes	Yes	Yes
Provides credit	Sometimes	No	No	No	Sometimes
Assumes ownership risk by taking title	No	No	No	No	No

wholesale facilities by forming cooperative chains. Large chain retailers often establish centralized buying offices to negotiate large-scale purchases directly with manufacturers.

Direct Marketing and Other Nonstore Retailing

7 Compare the basic types of direct marketing and nonstore retailing.

Although most retail transactions occur in stores, nonstore retailing is an important marketing channel for many products. Both consumer and business-to-business marketers rely on nonstore retailing to generate leads or requests for more information that may result in future orders.

Direct marketing is a broad concept that includes direct mail, direct selling, direct-response retailing, telemarketing, Internet retailing, and automatic merchandising. Direct and interactive marketing expenditures amount to hundreds of billions of dollars in yearly purchases. The last sections of this chapter consider each type of nonstore retailing.

direct marketing Direct communications, other than personal sales contacts, between buyer and seller, designed to generate sales, information requests, or store or Web site visits.

DIRECT MAIL

Direct mail is a major component of direct marketing. It comes in many forms: sales letters, postcards, brochures, booklets, catalogs, house organs (periodicals published by organizations to cover internal issues), and DVDs and CDs. Both not-for-profit and profit-seeking organizations make extensive use of this distribution channel.

Direct mail offers several advantages such as the ability to select a narrow target market, achieve intensive coverage, send messages quickly, choose from various formats, provide complete information, and personalize each mailing piece. Response rates are measurable and higher than other types of advertising. In addition, direct mailings stand alone and do not compete for attention with magazine articles and television programs. On the other hand, the per-reader cost of direct mail is high, effectiveness depends on the quality of the mailing list, and some consumers object to direct mail, considering it "junk mail."

Direct-mail marketing relies heavily on database technology in managing lists of names and in segmenting these lists according to the objectives of the campaign. Recipients get targeted materials, often personalized with their names within the ad's content.

Catalogs are a popular form of direct mail, with more than 10,000 different consumer specialty mail-order catalogs—and thousands more for business-to-business sales—finding their way to almost every mailbox in the United States. In a typical year, about 20 billion mail-order catalogs are mailed, generating more than $400 billion in sales. Catalog marketing continues to grow at a faster rate than brick-and-mortar retailers.[34] Catalogs can be a company's only or primary sales method. Spiegel, Herrington, Charles Keath, and Boston Proper are well-known examples. Brick-and-mortar retailers such as L.L.Bean, Coldwater Creek, Nordstrom, and Macy's also distribute catalogs.

Environmental concerns and new technologies are changing catalog marketing. More than 400,000 American consumers have registered with Catalog Choice, a nonprofit organization, to have their names removed from catalog mailing lists. Most cite a desire to save natural resources for their decision to stop receiving a blizzard of paper catalogs by mail.[35] By moving a catalog online, a merchant can update content easily and quickly, providing consumers with the latest information and prices. Online technology also allows marketers to use video and other techniques to display their merchandise. For example, Nordstrom's online shoe store catalog allows browsers to zoom in and out and view a shoe from different angles and in different colors.

DIRECT SELLING

Through direct selling, manufacturers completely bypass retailers and wholesalers. Instead, they set up their own channels to sell their products directly to consumers. Avon, Pampered Chef, Dell, and Tupperware are all direct sellers. This channel was discussed in detail in Chapter 13.

DIRECT-RESPONSE RETAILING

Customers of a direct-response retailer can order merchandise by mail or telephone, by visiting a mail-order desk in a retail store, or by computer or fax machine. The retailer then ships the merchandise to the customer's home or to a local retail store for pickup.

Many direct-response retailers rely on direct mail, such as catalogs, to create telephone and mail-order sales and to promote in-store purchases of products featured in the catalogs. Some firms, such as Lillian Vernon, make almost all their sales through catalog orders. Mail-order sales have grown at about twice the rate of retail store sales in recent years.

Direct-response retailers are increasingly reaching buyers through the Internet and through unique catalogs that serve special market niches. Many catalogs sell specialty products, such as kitchenware for the professional cook, art supplies, or supplies for the home renovator.

Direct-response retailing also includes home shopping, which runs promotions on cable television networks to sell merchandise through telephone orders. One form of home shopping, the *infomercial,* has existed for years. Infomercials can be short—one to two minutes—or run up to 30 minutes. Both have demonstrated success at generating revenues. Recent infomercials tout a wide variety of products from Johnny Carson DVDs to Drill Doctor tools to the Contour Core Belt, an exercise product.[36] TV networks such as Home Shopping Network and QVC have successfully focused exclusively on providing shopping opportunities. Programming ranges from extended commercials to call-in shows to game show formats. Shoppers call a toll-free number to buy featured products, and the retailer ships orders directly to their homes.

assessment check

1. What is direct marketing?
2. What is direct mail?

TELEMARKETING

Telemarketing refers to direct marketing conducted entirely by telephone. It is the most frequently used form of direct marketing. It provides marketers with a high return on their expenditures, an immediate response, and the opportunity for personalized two-way conversations. Telemarketing is discussed in further detail in Chapter 17.

8 Describe how much the Internet has altered the wholesaling, retailing, and direct marketing environments.

INTERNET RETAILING

Internet-based retailers sell directly to customers via virtual storefronts on the Web. They usually maintain little or no inventory, ordering directly from vendors to fill customer orders received via their Web sites. In recent years, conventional retailers have anxiously watched the rise—and then the demise—of many poorly planned, financed, and marketed Internet-based retailers. During the dot-com bust, 130 e-tailers failed. Even early successes such as Ezshop, an online home furnishings retailer, eventually ran aground. Traditional retailers, using the Web to support brick-and-mortar stores—the so-called *brick-and-click retailers*—have had much better staying power. The Gap, Best Buy, and Lands' End, for example, succeeded in extending their expertise to the Web. Office Max offers thousands of office supply products on its Web site, which also offers e-mail alerts, favorite-item lists, and a customer loyalty program. Chapter 4 discussed Internet retailing and other forms of e-business in more detail.

AUTOMATIC MERCHANDISING

The world's first vending machines dispensed holy water for five-drachma coins in Egyptian temples around 215 B.C. This retailing method has grown rapidly ever since; today, nearly 6,000 vending

assessment check

1. Describe Internet-based retailers.
2. Explain how the Internet has enhanced retailers' functions.

machine operators sell more than $7 billion in convenience goods annually to Americans.[37]

Although U.S. vending machines primarily sell items like snacks, soft drinks, or lottery tickets, Japanese consumers use automatic merchandising for everything including fresh sushi and new underwear. Recently, U.S. marketers have begun to realize the potential of this underused marketing tool. Organic yogurt and smoothie marketer Stonyfield Farms is helping schools convert their traditional vending machines to ones that offer healthy alternatives for children.[38] The three major soft-drink companies recently agreed to remove sweetened drinks such as soda and iced tea from vending machines in elementary and high schools nationwide. The calorie-laden drinks will be replaced by bottled water, low-fat milk, and 100 percent fruit juice or sports drinks. Technological advances and the ability to accept credit cards have made it possible for vending machines to sell even higher-cost items like iPods, headphones, and Sony PlayStation games. The high-end vending machines can be found in some shopping malls and in U.S. airports from coast to coast.[39]

© PRNewsFoto/Newscom

Recently, U.S. marketers have begun to realize the potential of vending machines. Stonyfield Farm is helping schools convert their traditional vending machines to ones that offer healthy alternatives for children.

Strategic Implications of Marketing in the 21st Century

as the Internet revolution steadily becomes a way of life—both for consumers and for the businesses marketing goods and services to them—technology will continue to transform the ways in which retailers, wholesalers, and direct marketers connect with customers.

In the retail sector, the unstoppable march toward lower prices has forced retailers from Neiman Marcus to dollar stores to re-evaluate everything, including their logistics and supply networks and their profit margins. Many have used the power of the Internet to strengthen such factors as store image, the merchandising mix, customer service, and the development of long-term relationships with customers.

Although manufacturers first anticipated that Internet technology would enable them to bypass such intermediaries as wholesalers and agents, bringing them closer to the customer, the reality is quite different. Successful wholesalers have established themselves as essential links in the supply, distribution, and customer service network. By leveraging technology, they have carved out new roles, providing such expert services as warehousing and fulfillment to multiple retail clients.

The Internet has empowered direct marketers by facilitating ever more sophisticated database segmentation. Traditional catalog and direct-mail marketers have integrated Internet sites, Web advertising, and e-mailing programs into a cohesive targeting, distribution, and repeat-buying strategy.

Review of Chapter Objectives

1   Explain the wheel of retailing.

The wheel of retailing is the hypothesis that each new type of retailer gains a competitive foothold by offering lower prices than current suppliers and maintains profits by reducing or eliminating services. Once established, the innovator begins to add more services, and its prices gradually rise, making it vulnerable to new low-price retailers. This turns the wheel again.

2   Discuss how retailers select target markets.

A retailer starts to define its strategy by selecting a target market. The target market dictates, among other things, the product mix, pricing strategy, and location strategy. Retailers deal with consumer behavior at the most complicated level, and a clear understanding of the target market is critical. Strategies for selecting target markets include merchandising, customer services, pricing, location/distribution, and promotional strategies.

3   Show how the elements of the marketing mix apply to retailing strategy.

A retailer must first identify a target market and then develop a product strategy. Next, it must establish a customer-service strategy. Retail pricing strategy involves decisions on markups and markdowns. Location is often the determining factor in a retailer's success or failure. A retailer's promotional strategy and store atmosphere play important roles in establishing a store's image.

4   Explain the concepts of retail convergence and scrambled merchandising.

Retail convergence is the coming together of shoppers, goods, and prices, resulting in the blurring of distinctions between types of retailers and the merchandise mix they offer. Similar selections are available from multiple sources and are differentiated mainly by price. Scrambled merchandising refers to retailers' practice of carrying dissimilar product lines in an attempt to generate additional sales volume. Retail convergence and scrambled merchandising have made it increasingly difficult to classify retailers.

5   Identify the functions performed by wholesaling intermediaries.

The functions of wholesaling intermediaries include creating utility, providing services, and lowering costs by limiting contacts.

6   Outline the major types of independent wholesaling intermediaries and the appropriate situations for using each.

Independent wholesaling intermediaries can be divided into two categories: merchant wholesalers and agents and brokers. The two major types of merchant wholesalers are full-function merchant wholesalers, such as rack jobbers, and limited-function merchant wholesalers, including cash-and-carry wholesalers, truck wholesalers, drop shippers, and mail-order wholesalers. Full-function wholesalers are common in the drug, grocery, and hardware industries.

Limited-function wholesalers are sometimes used in the food, coal, lumber, cosmetics, jewelry, sporting goods, and general-merchandise industries. Agents and brokers do not take title to the products they sell; this category includes commission merchants, auction houses, brokers, selling agents, and manufacturers' reps. Companies seeking to develop new sales territories, firms with unrelated lines, and smaller firms use manufacturers' reps. Commission merchants are common in the marketing of agricultural products. Auction houses are used to sell tobacco, used cars, livestock, furs, and fruit. Brokers are prevalent in the real estate, frozen foods, and used machinery industries.

7   Compare the basic types of direct marketing and nonstore retailing.

Direct marketing is a distribution channel consisting of direct communication to a consumer or business recipient. It generates orders and sales leads that may result in future orders. Because direct marketing responds to fragmented media markets and audiences, growth of customized products, and shrinking network broadcast audiences, marketers consider it an important part of their planning efforts. While most U.S. retail sales take place in stores, such nonstore retailing activities as direct mail, direct selling, direct-response retailing, telemarketing, Internet retailing, and automatic merchandising are important in marketing many types of goods and services.

8 **Describe how much the Internet has altered the wholesaling, retailing, and direct marketing environments.**

The Internet has affected everything, including how supply networks operate and how relationships are formed with customers. Successful wholesalers have carved out a niche as a source of expertise offering faster, more efficient, Web-enabled distribution and fulfillment. The Internet has allowed retailers to enhance their merchandising mix and their customer service by, among other things, giving them access to much broader selections of goods. Direct marketers have merged their traditional catalog or direct-mail programs with an Internet interface that allows for faster, more efficient, and more frequent contact with customers and prospects.

assessment check: **answers**

1.1   What is retailing?

Retailing refers to the activities involved in selling merchandise to ultimate consumers.

1.2   Explain the wheel-of-retailing concept.

The wheel of retailing is the hypothesis that each new type of retailer gains a competitive foothold by offering lower prices than current suppliers and maintains profits by reducing or eliminating services.

2.1   How does a retailer develop a marketing strategy?

A retailer develops a marketing strategy based on its goals and strategic plans.

2.2   How do retailers select target markets?

Strategies for selecting target markets include merchandising, customer services, pricing, location/distribution, and promotional strategies.

3.1   What is an SKU?

An SKU, or stock-keeping unit, is a specific product offering within a product line.

3.2   What are the two components of a markup?

A markup consists of the product's cost and an amount added by the retailer to determine its selling price.

3.3   What are store atmospherics?

Store atmospherics are physical characteristics and amenities that attract customers and satisfy their shopping needs.

4.1   How do we classify retailers by form of ownership?

There are two types of retailers by form of ownership: chain stores and independent retailers.

4.2   Categorize retailers by shopping effort and by services provided.

Convenience retailers and specialty retailers are classified by shopping effort; self-service, self-selection, and full-service describe retailers in terms of services provided.

4.3   List several ways to classify retailers by product line.

Retailers classified by product line include specialty stores, limited-line retailers, and general merchandise retailers. General merchandise retailers include variety stores, department stores, and mass merchandisers.

5.1 What is a wholesaler? How does it differ from a wholesaling intermediary?

A wholesaler is a channel intermediary that takes title to goods it handles and then distributes these goods to retailers, other distributors, or B2B customers. A wholesaling intermediary can be a wholesaler, an agent, or a broker and perform wholesaling activities without taking title to the goods.

5.2 How do wholesaling intermediaries help sellers lower costs?

Wholesaling intermediaries lower the number of transactions between manufacturers and retail outlets, thus lowering distribution costs.

6.1 What is the difference between a merchant wholesaler and a rack jobber?

A merchant wholesaler takes title to the goods it handles. A rack jobber is a full-function merchant wholesaler that markets specialized lines of merchandise to retailers.

6.2 Differentiate between agents and brokers.

Agents and brokers may or may not take possession of the goods they handle, but they never take title. Brokers work mainly to bring together buyers and sellers. A selling agent typically exerts full authority over pricing decisions and promotional outlays and often provides financial assistance for the manufacturer.

7.1 What is direct marketing?

Direct marketing is a distribution channel consisting of direct communication to a consumer or business recipient. It generates orders and sales leads that may result in future orders.

7.2 What is direct mail?

Direct mail is a form of direct marketing that includes sales letters, postcards, brochures, booklets, catalogs, house organs, and DVDs and CDs.

8.1 Describe Internet-based retailers.

Internet-based retailers sell directly to customers via virtual storefronts on the Web. They usually maintain little or no inventory, ordering directly from vendors to fill customers' orders.

8.2 Explain how the Internet has enhanced retailers' functions.

The Internet has allowed retailers to enhance their merchandising mix and their customer service by, among other things, giving them access to much broader selections of goods. Direct marketers have merged their traditional catalog or direct-mail programs with an Internet interface that allows for faster, more efficient, and more frequent contact with customers and prospects.

Marketing Terms You Need to Know

retailing 452	planned shopping center 458	wholesaling intermediary 468
wheel of retailing 453	atmospherics 460	broker 473
stock-keeping unit (SKU) 456	retail convergence 467	manufacturers' representative 474
markup 458	scrambled merchandising 468	direct marketing 475
markdown 458	wholesaler 468	

Other Important Marketing Terms

convenience retailer 463

specialty retailer 463

limited-line store 464

category killer 464

general merchandise retailer 464

department store 465

mass merchandiser 466

discount house 466

hypermarket 467

supercenter 467

merchant wholesaler 472

rack jobber 472

truck wholesaler (truck jobber) 472

drop shipper 472

mail-order wholesaler 472

commission merchant 473

selling agent 474

Assurance of Learning Review

1. Find some examples of retailers that demonstrate the concept of the wheel of retailing. Explain the stages they went through and are in currently.

2. How do retailers identify target markets? Explain the major strategies by which retailers reach their target markets.

3. Explain the importance of a retailer's location to its strategy.

4. What is retail convergence?

5. Define *scrambled merchandising*. Why has this practice become so common in retailing?

6. What is a wholesaling intermediary? Describe the activities it performs.

7. Distinguish among the different types of manufacturer-owned wholesaling intermediaries. What conditions might suit each one?

8. Differentiate between direct selling and direct-response retailing. Cite examples of both.

9. In what ways has the Internet changed direct-response retailing?

10. Define *automatic merchandising* and explain its role in U.S. retailing today and in the future.

Projects and Teamwork Exercises

1. Research and then classify each of the following retailers:
   a. Ace Hardware
   b. Petite Sophisticate
   c. Limited
   d. Ethan Allen Galleries
   e. Dillard's

2. Visit a local Wal-Mart store and observe product placement, shelf placement, inventory levels on shelves, traffic patterns, customer service, and checkout efficiency. Discuss what makes Wal-Mart the world's most successful retailer.

3. Target has become known for trendy clothes and stylish housewares, all readily available in spacious stores at reasonable prices. Visit a local Target store or the company's Web site and compare its product selection to that of your local hardware store or a department store. Make a list of each store's advantages and disadvantages, including convenience, location, selection, service, and general prices. Do any of their product lines overlap? How are they different from each other?

4. Match each industry with the most appropriate type of wholesaling intermediary.

   ___hardware   a. drop shipper

   ___perishable foods   b. truck wholesaler

   ___lumber   c. auction house

   ___wheat   d. full-function merchant wholesaler

   ___used cars   e. commission merchant

5. In teams, develop a retailing strategy for an Internet retailer. Identify a target market and then suggest a mix of merchandise, promotion, service, and pricing strategies that would help a retailer

reach that market via the Internet. What issues must Internet retailers address that do not affect traditional store retailers?

6. With a classmate, visit two or three retail stores that compete with one another in your area and compare their customer service strategies. (You might wish to visit each store more than once to avoid making a snap judgment.) Select at least five criteria and use them to assess each store. How do you think each store sees its customer service strategy as fitting into its overall retailing strategy? Present your findings in detail to the class.

7. Visit a department store and compare at least two departments' pricing strategies based on the number of markdowns you find and the size of the discount. What, if anything, can you conclude about the success of each department's retailing strategy?

8. Think of a large purchase you make on a nonroutine basis, such as a new winter coat or expensive clothing for a special occasion. Where will you shop for such items? Will you travel out of your way? Will you go to the nearest shopping center? Will you look on the Internet? Once you have made your decision, describe any strategies used by the retailer that led you to this decision. What might make you change your mind about where to shop for this item?

9. Outlet malls are a growing segment of the retail market. Visit a local outlet mall or research one on the Internet. What types of stores are located there? How do the product selection and price compare with typical stores?

10. Torrid is a national chain of about 50 stores that feature clothing for plus-size women. Recommend an appropriate retailing strategy for this type of retailer.

Critical-Thinking Exercises

1. Talbots made its name as a retailer of classic sportswear for women, but it has recently expanded its target market to include men and children. Men, however, typically don't enjoy shopping for clothes, and children shop with their parents. Visit www.talbots.com and assess how well Talbots is reaching men through its Web site. Do you think Talbots' target market is still women who shop for the men in their lives? Why or why not? How can Talbots widen its appeal on the Internet?

2. Several major retailers have begun to test the extreme markdown strategy that lies behind popular dollar stores such as Dollar General and Family Dollar Stores. Kroger, A&P, Wal-Mart, and others have opened sections in selected stores that feature items from snacks to beauty supplies priced at $1. Is this experiment simply a test of pricing strategy? What else might motivate these retailers to offer such deep discounts?

3. When Tower Records filed for bankruptcy, it was only one symptom of the general decline of the retail music store. Industry watchers blame everything including music downloading programs and changes in consumers' tastes. Most, however, feel that music stores will somehow remain viable. What are some changes these retailers could make in their merchandising, customer service, pricing, location, and other strategies to try to reinvent their business?

4. McDonald's has traditionally relied on a cookie-cutter approach to its restaurant design. One store looked essentially like every other—until recently. The chain has decided to loosen its corporate design mandate to fit within special markets and to update its image with customers. Research McDonald's makeover efforts. What types of changes has the company made and where? How have changes in atmospherics helped the chain with customers? Have the changes you researched modified your perception of McDonald's at all? If so, how?

Ethics Exercise

As the largest company in the world, with more than a million employees worldwide and more than $400 billion in sales in a recent year, Wal-Mart has become big and powerful enough to influence the U.S. economy. It is responsible for 10 percent of total U.S. imports from China and for about 12 percent of U.S. productivity gains since the late 1990s. Some observers believe Wal-Mart is also responsible for the low U.S. inflation rates of recent years. However, its unbeatable buying power and efficiency have forced many local stores to close when Wal-Mart opens a new store in their area.

1. Some economists fear what might happen to the U.S. economy if Wal-Mart has a bad year (so far it has had more than four decades of nonstop growth). Should retailers have that much influence on the economy? Why or why not?

2. Wal-Mart is selective about what it sells—refusing, for instance, to carry music or computer games with mature ratings, magazines with content it considers too adult, or, in some of its stores, handguns. Because of its sheer size, these decisions can become influential on the culture. Do you think this is a positive or negative effect of the growth of this retailer? Why?

Internet Exercises

1. **Lifestyle centers.** Using a search engine, find the Web sites of at least three lifestyle centers. Visit each Web site. In what ways do lifestyle centers differ from more traditional shopping malls? Do the differences appeal to you? Why or why not?

2. **Retailing strategy.** Go the Web site of kitchen and cooking retailer Williams-Sonoma (www.williams-sonoma.com). This site is classified as a shopping site, or online store. Review the material in the chapter on retailing strategy and store atmospherics, and answer the following questions:
   a. How does the design and layout of the Williams-Sonoma Web store appeal to the company's target market?
   b. How would you describe the atmospherics created by the online store? If you can visit a brick-and-mortar store, compare the store's atmospherics to the Web site's.

3. **Retailing statistics.** The U.S. Census Bureau reports regularly on the state of retailing. Visit the Bureau's Web site (www.census.gov), do a search for "retail sales," and answer the following questions:
   a. What is the current level of retail sales in the United States? By how much have retail sales increased during the past year?
   b. Which categories of retail sales are growing the fastest? Which categories are growing the slowest?
   c. Given projected demographic trends, which categories of retail sales would you expect to grow the fastest in the coming years?

Note: Internet Web addresses change frequently. If you don't find the exact site listed, you may need to access the organization's home page and search from there or use a search engine such as Google.

Case 14.1   Green Packaging: Is the Price Right?

Environmentalists and others have long pointed out the waste caused by the excess use of paper and plastic in packaging

U.S. goods. In recent years, some companies have worked to reduce the amount of excess packaging and, in fact, most major food and beverage companies have rallied to the cause.

McDonald's responded to the complaints about waste by discontinuing plastic foam or cardboard boxes for many of its food items and by designing packaging that can be recycled or composted. Many Micky D's sandwiches are now wrapped, simply, in paper. Although it has cut back substantially on unnecessary packaging, the company plans to do more in the future.

The Coca-Cola Company, many of whose products are sold in plastic bottles, spent $60 million to build the world's largest plastic-bottle recycling plant. The company's goal is to recycle or reuse 100 percent of the plastic bottles it uses in the United States. The firm has also redesigned its emblematic glass contour bottle to make it lighter, less expensive, and more impact-resistant. Introduced in 2000, the "Ultra Glass" bottle has already saved 52,000 metric tons of glass and reduced carbon dioxide in the atmosphere by 26,000 tons.

Wal-Mart has worked to promote sustainable packaging in both its Wal-Mart and Sam's Club outlets. Pledging to "remove, reduce, and reuse," the company has adopted a multipoint approach to sustainable packaging and aims to be "packaging neutral by 2025." In other words, it plans to boost the amount of packaging Wal-Mart and Sam's Club stores recover or recycle to equal the amount used by the products on its shelves.

But in the continuing debate over green packaging, some critics assert that sustainable packaging is more expensive—due to higher freight or transit costs, higher manufacturing costs, and the like. And because green packaging is more costly, they argue, it shouldn't be pursued as an alternative.

Others point to the tried-and-true fact of supply and demand. People's demand for green packaging, they say, will lead to greater supply and, ultimately, lower costs. Throughout modern history, businesses have sought ways to produce their goods more efficiently and more cost-effectively to enhance profits. And while the costs of green packaging may not have bottomed out just yet, they claim, the more people understand and embrace the concept, the sooner it will become the norm.

Questions for Critical Thinking

1.   With most food and beverage companies now developing sustainable packaging, is it possible for them to use this concept as a competitive advantage?

2.   Into what aspects of its retailing strategy could a marketer incorporate the notion of green packaging?

Sources: Company Web sites, www.mcdonalds.com, www.thecoca-colacompany.com, and www.walmartstores.com, accessed May 22, 2009; John Kalkowski, "Opening the Package: An Overview of Trends in Packaging Claims," *Packaging Digest*, accessed at the Federal Trade Commission Web site, www.ftc.gov, May 22, 2009; Dennis Salazar, "Sustainable Packaging: Cost vs. Price," *GreenBizSite*, June 16, 2008, www.greenbiz.com; Brian Reilly, "Transportation: Driving Sustainable Results," *Packaging World*, November 14, 2007, www.packworld.com; Kevin T. Higgins, "Packaging Trends Survey: The Year of Living Sustainably," *Food Engineering*, September 5, 2007, www.foodengineeringmag.com.

Video Case 14.2   Retailing at Flight 001

The written video case on Flight 001 appears on page VC-13. The Flight 001 video is designed to expand and highlight the concepts in this chapter and the concepts and questions covered in the written video case.

Talking about Marketing Careers with...

Richard Yoo

The Golden Arches are one of the most recognized brand marks in the world. McDonald's Corporation holds a unique—and enviable—place in the quick-service food retailing industry. The firm is a global leader, with more than 32,000 local restaurants serving nearly 50 million people daily in 118 countries around the world. But McDonald's built its reputation by serving one customer at a time, and it still focuses on the local aspect of its business through strong relationships with its owner/operators, suppliers, and employees.

Key to the chain's success is its emphasis on adapting to local tastes and customs—to serve the needs of its many markets. Here today to talk with us about McDonald's retail strategy and its global supply chain is Richard Yoo, Senior Director, Global Menu Management.

Q: Richard, McDonald's is a true global corporation with worldwide reach. Working for such a visible firm must be both challenging and satisfying. What milestones in your education and career led you to your current position with one of the world's top brands?

It truly is a privilege to work on a brand that has global reach and touches the hearts, minds, (and appetites!) of so many people everyday. My overall approach to problem solving has been shaped by both my liberal arts training at the University of Michigan (BA in English) and my formal business school training at the University of Notre Dame (MBA). I like to think of my education as a powerful combination of right-brain and left-brain development. From a career perspective, my path has taken a similar path in that I started as a brand management generalist and now specialize in product innovation. My marketing

experiences in the toy industry (at LEGO) and in retail food (Kraft Foods, Keebler Company) have built a solid foundation of general management skills and also led to my interest in and passion for new product development/product innovation. From my point of view, the on-the-job influence, a creative approach to problem solving, collaboration with other functional areas, and value-based leadership have been important career drivers for me.

Q: Overseeing global menu choices is a huge undertaking for such a large restaurant chain. What is involved in planning and adapting menus for different countries? What types of team members at the corporate and local level help suggest and select menu choices? How does the process work?

The process is a collaborative effort, and generally speaking, our development process consists of three stages: discovery, development, and deployment. During the discovery stage, we develop consumer insights; monitor culinary, technology, and cultural trends; collect competitive intelligence; and brainstorm. These ideas are made more powerful by involving cross-functional teams at our home office and collaborating with our Menu Centers of Excellence and our suppliers. These centers are THE development hubs in Latin America, Europe, Asia, and North America that do the heavy lifting of taking Menu Strategies and ideas and bringing them to life for consumers. It is at this stage that broader food platforms are made locally relevant by developing and testing products that have components that sing at the country level, and that can be executed well in our restaurants to delight our guests.

RICHARD YOO
Senior Director,
Global Menu Management
McDonald's Corporation

Q: Students read in this text about the importance of selecting the right target markets. What proportion of your corporation's sales come from global operations? How does your firm decide which markets to enter? Is it still expanding into new countries?

At this time, roughly half of our sales are generated outside the U.S. As you might expect, the decision to enter a market is driven by a number of factors. Since 2003, our focus has shifted from growth via new restaurants to growth by serving more customers in our existing restaurants.

Q: Local partners—people who can help bring a firm's marketing vision to life—are critical to a global business such as yours. Because nearly 85 percent of McDonald's restaurants are locally owned and operated, your firm relies heavily on its owner/operators to "localize" the brand. How do their efforts contribute to the success of the firm? What contribution do employees make?

Our franchisees are clearly a key pillar of our business. Their energy and passion are critical to our growth and brand sustainability. We engage them in almost every facet of our business. The local store marketing plans that they create and execute bring the corporate vision to life in their respective communities. Our managers and crew are our brand ambassadors and are the key element in delivering our brand promise of uncompromised QSC and V (quality, service, cleanliness and value) to every customer. QSC and V was the foundational operating philosophy of Ray Kroc and still is today.

Q: Suppliers of food and other restaurant products must be critical to the quality of McDonald's menu items. Are your suppliers local or global—or a mix? What efficiencies can your firm achieve by having global operations?

We've developed a coordinated supply chain "engine" that provides the ability to leverage global trade dynamics and drive efficiencies at the local level. From food and paper products to media buys, this engine, complemented by our scale and our commitment to social responsibility, is one of our competitive advantages. Wherever possible, we do purchase locally in the countries where we do business.

Q: In the past few years, McDonald's has shifted its marketing strategy to fit the needs of today's health- and quality-conscious but time-pressed consumer. Can you tell us a little bit about the changes featured in the "i'm lovin' it" campaign and the firm's Plan to Win strategy? How do you get the message out to the public? Does this effort extend to global operations, too?

"i'm lovin' it"™ is our brand attitude and spirit. It celebrates real people, real passions, and real stories around the globe. The campaign will shift focus from the "i" (consumer-centric stories) to the "it" (the reasons why consumers love their McDonald's experiences). Our customers have told us what "it" is—it is our food. It is the moments they share at our restaurants and the feelings they get before, during, and after they visit McDonald's. We are putting the "it" in "i'm lovin' it." We are also deepening our relationships by connecting customers with the facts about our brand— our food, our people, and our values.

Our Plan to Win Strategy is all about delivering a delightful experience to our customers by creating strategies for and executing the key pillars of our business: People, Product, Promotion, Place, and Price. Since the Plan to Win was implemented in 2003, our business results have been robust.

Q: Many students today are interested in running their own businesses. One of their career paths might involve running a franchise, such as a McDonald's restaurant. What types of educational experiences, training, or internships might help students get a foothold in your industry or advance their marketing career?

I often coach students to seek out their career sweet spot, where passion meets capability, and to not necessarily chase a career for the money, prestige, or perks but because you LOVE the content, the people, and the brand. Everything else has a way of falling into place along the way. I'm also a big fan of broad-based curricula, complemented by specialized "trade content" because a balanced thinker who knows how to connect and collaborate is an effective one.

GREENSBURG, INC.

A Little Hope for the Little Guy

© Steven J. Eliopoulos

John Miggins was 12 when Neil Armstrong took his first steps on the moon. It was on that day John knew he wanted to be an astronaut. He spent all his free time reading and researching his future career. He thought one of the coolest things, aside from walking on the moon, was how they got electricity all the way up in space. As early as 1905, Einstein discussed harnessing the sun's energy in a paper on the photoelectric effect; and, by 1964, NASA's Nimbus spacecraft launch was powered by a solar array.

The astronaut thing didn't quite work out for John, but all that research didn't go to waste.

Flash forward about 25 years. Miggins was at a turning point in his life. Recently laid off and with a family to support, John decided to go off the grid and start his own business. He purchased a small 800-square-foot bungalow on a busy Tulsa street—for a song—and opened Harvest Solar & Wind Power.

Unfortunately, passion wasn't enough to keep Harvest Solar energized. Even though plenty of people were aware of solar and wind power, for many it was little more than a solution to heat your pool or a back-up battery for rural homeowners. Miggins and his partner took plenty of calls, but few jobs panned out. On the jobs that did, they were always under the gun—scrambling to get what they needed when they needed it, hiring extra hands and subcontractors, keeping just enough money in the bank to make it all happen while putting in 80-hour weeks. If a customer was late on payment, or didn't pay at all, it could be catastrophic for the business.

In January 2008, Miggins received a call from Studio 804, a design group made up of students from the University of Kansas School of Architecture and Urban Planning. The students were on a semester-long project to build an art and community center in Greensburg, Kansas. The 547 Art Center, aptly named for the date of the devastating tornado that struck the town on May 4, 2007, would be the town's first completed building. As with most projects in Greensburg, they were looking for donations. Lots of them. They were hoping John, who was still operating as Harvest Solar at the time, would be able to do the solar and wind power systems for the building. John was in no position to donate the $50,000 it would cost, but submitted a bid and worked with the students on some plans, "just 'cause it was cool."

The frustrations were mounting. Miggins was doing his taxes one day and thought, "I show my income, but I don't know where it all goes." Around that same time, an old friend from his hometown of Houston called with an offer John couldn't refuse. A new company called Standard Renewable Energy was looking to expand and needed experienced regional sales managers to cover the Oklahoma and Kansas territories. Miggins knew the area and definitely knew his stuff, so it was a perfect fit. Standard Renewable could provide the corporate infrastructure, financial backing, logistics, and purchasing power Miggins lacked while allowing him some of the freedoms he enjoyed while running his own show.

Although Miggins was confident in his decision to join Standard Renewable Energy, some of his customers didn't understand the need for him to be part of a larger organization. Solar homeowner Emily Priddy purchased her system from Harvest Solar in early 2007 and was very happy with the level of service received from John on his own. Shortly after Priddy's system was installed, John joined Standard. An ardent supporter of independent local businesses, Priddy has mixed feelings about the market share large companies have nowadays. "When the big guys catch on, at least it makes the technology more widely available," says Priddy. Miggins still provides customer support for Priddy's system, but now as Standard Renewable Energy.

On April 1, 2008, Studio 804 called again. They were ready to go and hoped John was still interested in their project. The thing was, he had less than a month to engineer, take delivery of the necessary components, and install the system. May 4, 2008 was to be the grand opening and everything had to be perfect. President George W. Bush was to be the guest of honor. Oh, and they still needed at least some of the installation for free.

The next call was to Standard Renewable Energy in Houston. They agreed that the Studio 804 project was a worthy cause and gave Miggins the green light to make it happen. A normal installation takes at least 60 days to turn around. They had half of that. The building, the first of its kind in Kansas, needed to be special, so last-minute changes and upgrades had them down to the wire. The three wind turbines were so new that they had to be special ordered from Australia and shipped via air to the rural Kansas town. None of it could have been done without the backing of the larger and more well-heeled Standard Renewable Energy.

Their participation in the project has paid off. John has projects pending with several of the architecture firms he met while working in Greensburg. He's hopeful the referrals will keep coming—and isn't looking back to the old days at Harvest Solar.

Questions

1. Compare the logistics and supply chain systems of Harvest Solar with that of Standard Renewable Energy.

2. What kind of marketing channel is Standard Renewable Energy?

3. Do you prefer to shop at big box stores, like Best Buy and Wal-Mart, or local independent merchants? What are the pros and cons of each?

4. Visit a local big box store, ask for a meeting with a store manager, and write a report (3 to 5 pages) on the green initiatives they are involved in.

Promotional Decisions

© Getty Images

CHAP**15**TER
Integrated Marketing
Communications

© Joe Robbins/Getty Images

Major League Baseball Joins the Green Team

America's pastime appeals to fans who enjoy sitting in the fresh air, cheering for their team. Whether the players are sporting their home jerseys or traveling grays, they all have a new team color: green.

Major League Baseball is getting into the environmental game. Take the Cincinnati Reds. On opening day, the team purchased carbon credits to offset its energy usage. The grounds crew recycles grass clippings to fertilize landscaping outside the ballpark. When energy demand is high,

generators save electricity by powering the lights during night games; solar cells power the scoreboard. Computers monitor the stadium's energy use and automatically shut off air conditioning in nonessential office areas. "We like to say, 'It's not just the grass that's green,'" says the

team's vice president for ballpark operations. "Even down to the programs and yearbooks—we're recycling it all."

Cincinnati is not alone. Teams are adding solar panels to their stadiums, encouraging patrons to recycle food and beverage containers, adding energy-saving light bulbs and water-saving restrooms, building bicycle parking lots to encourage alternative transportation, recycling steam from incinerators for heating and cooling systems, and considering the ecological impact of their travel plans and the environmental track records of the hotels they use. The red carpet that graced New York's Avenue of the Americas for the 2008 Hall of Fame parade was a mile-long stretch of 100 percent recycled fibers, manufactured with wind and solar power that saved 6,300 pounds of petroleum-based fiber and almost 200,000 gallons of water. In fact, MLB has partnered with nonprofit group the Natural Resources Defense Council to implement an online tool—the Team Greening Program—making it easier for every team in the league to run greener operations.

MLB games draw about 80 million spectators every year. According to the president of GreenMark, an environmental marketing company that also works with MLB, sports teams can use their high visibility to bring green issues to the public consciousness "in a way that is far more efficient than most other industries." The resulting positive publicity is a bonus

that also helps teams win sponsorships and strengthen their bottom lines.

Those are just some of the ways MLB gets the word out about its green operations. It also uses a mix of written, media, and event promotions such as press releases to announce the unrolling of New York's "green" red carpet. In-person NRDC "Green Teams" promoted recycling at All-Star events, which also included the use of hybrid buses to transport fans between events and distribution of free reusable tote bags. The All-Star planning team sponsored a playground made from recycled materials. Free MLB-NRDC literature throughout ballparks promotes ecofriendly steps fans can take at home and at work. Each team's Web site also includes NRDC's Team Greening Advisor—a guide with ideas, suggestions, and proposed policies for all Major League clubs.

Television coverage and articles in the news media and wire services touted such achievements as the opening of the Washington Nationals' new stadium, a $611 million structure that is the first

major league ballpark to meet the U.S. Green Building Council's Leadership in Energy and Environmental Design (LEED) standards by being built with 95 percent recycled steel and using high-efficiency lighting and plumbing, water-absorbing planted "green" roof, preferred parking for high-mileage cars— not to mention its convenient location near public transit systems. MLB has made sure reporters also know Nationals Park may soon be eclipsed by such new green achievements as the New York Mets' new park, approved by the EPA, the Minnesota Twins' new field, which hopes to top Nationals Park in its LEED certification rating, and the Florida Marlins' future ecofriendly home in Miami.

MLB has plenty to communicate. "This is signaling a cultural shift that I think is unprecedented," said NRDC's senior scientist of MLB's green partnership. "It's apple pie, it's motherhood, it's baseball, it's environmentalism."[1]

OBJECTIVES

1 Explain how integrated marketing communications relates to the development of an optimal promotional mix.

2 Describe the communication process and how it relates to the AIDA concept.

3 Explain how the promotional mix relates to the objectives of promotion.

4 Identify the different elements of the promotional mix and explain how marketers develop an optimal promotional mix.

5 Describe the role of sponsorships and direct marketing in integrated marketing communications.

6 Discuss the factors that influence the effectiveness of a promotional mix.

7 Contrast pushing and pulling strategies.

8 Explain how marketers budget for and measure the effectiveness of promotion.

9 Discuss the value of marketing communications.

evolution of a brand

Baseball commissioner Bud Selig recently told the league, "Just as baseball took a leading role in the development of relations between the races in the United States, with the appearance of Jackie Robinson for the Brooklyn Dodgers in 1947, so must it turn its attention, efforts and influence to . . . the environment."

- Do you think an organization like MLB is a good channel for promoting a social cause like environmental awareness to the general public? Why or why not? What else could MLB say and do to get the word out to baseball fans?

- A spokeswoman for NRDC says environmentally aware sports teams "ask for changes from their vendors that trickle through the supply chain." Can this trickle effect among its suppliers also help MLB publicize its green efforts? How?

chapter overview

promotion
Communication link between buyers and sellers; the function of informing, persuading, and influencing a consumer's purchase decision.

marketing communications
Messages that deal with buyer–seller relationships.

integrated marketing communications (IMC) Coordination of all promotional activities to produce a unified, customer-focused promotional message.

Two of the four components of the marketing mix—product and distribution strategies—were discussed in previous chapters. The three chapters in Part 6 analyze the third marketing mix variable—promotion. **Promotion** is the function of informing, persuading, and influencing the consumer's purchase decision.

This chapter introduces the concept of integrated marketing communications, briefly describes the elements of a firm's promotional mix—personal and nonpersonal selling—and explains the characteristics that determine the success of the mix. Next, we identify the objectives of promotion and describe the importance of developing promotional budgets and measuring the effectiveness of promotion. Finally, we discuss the importance of the business, economic, and social aspects of promotion. Chapter 16 covers advertising, public relations, and other nonpersonal selling elements of the promotional mix, including sponsorships and guerrilla advertising. Chapter 17 completes this part of the book by focusing on personal selling and sales promotion.

Throughout *Contemporary Marketing,* special emphasis has been given to new information that shows how technology is changing the way marketers approach *communication,* the transmission of a message from a sender to a receiver. Consumers receive **marketing communications**—messages that deal with buyer–seller

relationships—from a variety of media, including television, radio, magazines, direct mail, the Internet, and cell phones. Marketers can broadcast an ad on the Web to mass markets or design a customized appeal targeted to a small market segment. Each message the customer receives from any source represents the brand, company, or organization. A company needs to coordinate all these messages for maximum total impact and to reduce the likelihood that the consumer will completely tune them out.

To prevent this loss of attention, marketers are turning to **integrated marketing communications (IMC),** which coordinates all promotional activities—media advertising, direct mail, personal selling, sales promotion, public relations, and sponsorships—to produce a unified, customer-focused promotional message. As you saw earlier, Major League Baseball uses IMC to get the message out about its increasing focus on environmentally friendly operations. IMC is a broader concept than marketing communications and promotional strategy. It uses database technology to refine the marketer's understanding of the target audience, segment this audience, and select the best type of media for each segment.

This chapter shows that IMC involves not only the marketer but all other organizational units that interact with the consumer. Marketing managers set the goals and objectives of the firm's promotional strategy in accordance

briefly speaking

"You can say the right thing about a product and nobody will listen. You've got to say it in a way that people will feel it in their gut. Because if they don't feel it, nothing will happen."

—**William Bernbach (1911–1982)**
COFOUNDER OF DDB ADVERTISING AGENCY

with overall organizational objectives and marketing goals. Based on these objectives, the various elements of the promotional strategy—personal selling, advertising, sales promotion, direct marketing, publicity, and public relations—are formulated into an integrated communications plan. This plan becomes a central part of the firm's total marketing strategy to reach its selected market segments. The feedback mechanism, including marketing research and field reports, completes the system by identifying any deviations from the plan and suggesting improvements.

Integrated Marketing Communications

Stop and think for a moment about all the marketing messages you receive in a single day. You click on the television for the morning news, and you see plenty of commercials. Listen to the car radio on the way to work or school, and you can sing along with the jingles. You get catalogs, coupons, and flyers in the mail. People even leave promotional flyers under your car's windshield wiper while it sits in the parking lot. When you go online, you're deluged with banner and pop-up ads and even marketing-related e-mail. Marketers know you receive many types of communication. They know they need to compete for your attention, so they look for ways to reach you in a coordinated manner through integrated marketing communications.

Successful marketers use the marketing concept and relationship marketing to develop customer-oriented marketing programs. The customer is at the heart of integrated marketing communications. An IMC strategy begins not with the organization's goods and services but with consumer wants or needs and then works in reverse to the product, brand, or organization. It sends receiver-focused rather than product-focused messages.

Rather than separating the parts of the promotional mix and viewing them as isolated components, IMC looks at these elements from the consumer's viewpoint: as information about the brand, company, or organization. Even though the messages come from different sources—sales presentations, word of mouth, TV, radio, newspapers, billboards, direct mail, coupons, public relations, and online services—consumers may perceive them as "advertising" or a "sales pitch." IMC broadens promotion to include all the ways a customer has contact with an organization, adding to traditional media and direct mail such sources as package design, store displays, sales literature, and online and interactive media. Unless the organization takes an integrated approach to present a unified, consistent message, it may send conflicting information that confuses consumers.

Explain how integrated marketing communications relates to the development of an optimal promotional mix.

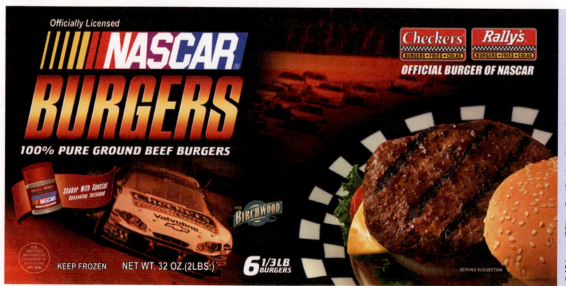

With accurate, current information about existing and potential customers, marketers can send the right messages and form the right partnerships, such as this one between Nascar and Checkers/Rally's.

© AP Images/PRNewsFoto/Checkers Drive-In Restaurants, Inc.

Today's business environment is characterized by many diverse markets and media, creating both opportunities and challenges. The success of any IMC program depends on identifying the members of an audience and understanding what they want. Without accurate, current information about existing and potential customers and their purchase histories, needs, and wants, marketers may send the wrong message. But they cannot succeed simply by improving the quality of the messages or by sending more of them. IMC must not only deliver messages to intended audiences but also gather responses from them. Databases and interactive marketing are important IMC tools that help marketers collect information from customers and then segment markets according to demographics and preferences. Marketers can then design specialized communications programs to meet the needs of each segment.

Young male consumers can be hard to pin down. That's why Totino's Pizza Rolls sponsors the ESPN Winter X Games, a favorite of extreme sports fans—usually boys 13 to 17 years of age. In its first year of sponsorship, Totino's, a General Mills brand, relied on television and print ads to direct viewers to an online Jeep sweepstakes, favorite-event poll, and blog by premier snowboarder Danny Kass. "One of the biggest things we learned after the first campaign was the importance of being relevant to our target audience," says Totino's associate marketing manager. While a Jeep makes an attractive prize, it wasn't targeted enough to young male teens too young to drive. The following year, Totino's gave away an all-expense-paid trip for four to the next year's Winter X Games.[2]

The increase in media options provides more ways to give consumers product information; however, it can also create information overload. Marketers have to spread available dollars across fragmented media markets and a wider range of promotional activities to achieve their communication goals. Mass media such as TV ads, while still useful, are no longer the mainstays of marketing campaigns. In 1960, a marketer could reach about 90 percent of U.S. consumers by advertising on the three major TV networks—CBS, NBC, and ABC. Today, even though overall TV viewing is at an all-time high, consumers spend less than 20 percent of their viewing hours watching these stations. Basic cable, with channels such as ESPN, CNN, and the Food Network, now accounts for about 50 percent of viewing time, with additional networks such as Fox, the CW, and PBS (public broadcasting) eating up hours as well.[3] So to reach targeted groups of consumers, organizations must turn to niche marketing—advertising in special-interest magazines, purchasing time on cable TV channels, reaching out through telecommunications media such as cell phones and the Internet, and sponsoring events and activities. Without an IMC program, marketers frequently encounter problems within their own organizations because separate departments have authority and responsibility for planning and implementing specific promotional mix elements.

The coordination of an IMC program often produces a competitive advantage based on synergy and interdependence among the various elements of the promotional mix. With an IMC strategy, marketers can create a unified personality for the product or brand by choosing the right elements from the promotional mix to send the message. At the same time, they can develop more narrowly focused plans to reach specific market segments and choose the best form of communication to send a particular message to a specific target audience. IMC provides a more effective way to reach and serve target markets than less coordinated strategies. Establishing an effective IMC program requires teamwork.

IMPORTANCE OF TEAMWORK

IMC requires a big-picture view of promotion planning, a total strategy that includes all marketing activities, not just promotion. Successful implementation of IMC requires that everyone involved in every aspect of promotion—public relations, advertising, personal selling, and sales promotion—function as a team. They must present a consistent, coordinated promotional effort at every point of customer contact with the organization. This way, they save time, money, and effort. They avoid duplication of efforts, increasing marketing effectiveness and reducing costs. Ultimately, it means that the result—the IMC program—is greater than the sum of its parts.

Teamwork involves both in-house resources and outside vendors. It involves marketing personnel; members of the sales force who deal with wholesalers, retailers, and organizational buyers; and customer service representatives. A firm gains nothing from a terrific advertisement featuring a great product, an informational Web site, and a toll-free number if unhelpful salespeople frustrate customers when they answer the phones. The company must train its representatives to send a single positive message to consumers and to solicit information for the firm's customer database.

IMC also challenges the traditional role of the outside advertising agency. A single agency may no longer fulfill all of a client's communications requirements, including traditional advertising and sales promotions, interactive marketing, database development, direct marketing, and public relations. To best serve client needs, an agency must often assemble a team with members from other companies.

ROLE OF DATABASES IN EFFECTIVE IMC PROGRAMS

With the explosive growth of the Internet, marketers have the power to gather more information faster and to organize it more easily than ever before. By sharing this detailed knowledge appropriately among all relevant parties, a company can lay the foundation for a successful IMC program.

The move from mass marketing to a customer-specific marketing strategy—a characteristic of online marketing—requires not only a means of identifying and communicating with the firm's target market but also information regarding important characteristics of each prospective customer. As discussed in Chapter 10, organizations can compile different kinds of data into complete databases with customer information, including names and addresses, demographic data, lifestyle considerations, brand preferences, and buying behavior. This information provides critical guidance in designing an effective IMC strategy that achieves organizational goals and finds new opportunities for increased sales and profits. This increased ability to acquire huge amounts of data poses a new challenge: how to sift through it efficiently so it becomes useful information. Newer technology allows researchers to do exactly that—work with millions of sets of data to make very specific analyses.

Direct sampling is another method frequently used to quickly obtain customer opinions regarding a particular firm's goods and services. If you've ever received a free sample of laundry detergent, air freshener, breakfast cereal, or even a new magazine in your mailbox, you've been the recipient of direct sampling.

assessment check

1. Define *promotion*.
2. What is the difference between marketing communications and integrated marketing communications (IMC)?

The Communication Process

When you have a conversation with someone, do you wonder whether the person understood your message? Do you worry that you might not have heard the person correctly? Marketers have the same concerns: when they send a message to an intended audience or market, they want to make sure it gets through clearly and persuasively. That is why the communication process is so important to marketing. The top portion of Table 15.1 shows a general model of the communication process and its application to promotional strategy.

The **sender** acts as the source in the communication system as he or she seeks to convey a **message** (a communication of information, advice, or a request) to a receiver. An effective message accomplishes three tasks:

1. It gains the receiver's attention.
2. It achieves understanding by both receiver and sender.
3. It stimulates the receiver's needs and suggests an appropriate method of satisfying them.

Table 15.1 also provides several examples of promotional messages. Although the types of promotion may vary from a highly personalized sales presentation to such nonpersonal promotions as television advertising and dollar-off coupons, each goes through every stage in the communications process.

The three tasks just listed are related to the **AIDA concept** (attention, interest, desire, action), the steps consumers take in reaching a purchase decision. First, the promotional message must gain the potential consumer's attention. It then seeks to arouse interest in the good or service.

2 Describe the communication process and how it relates to the AIDA concept.

AIDA concept Steps through which an individual reaches a purchase decision: attention, interest, desire, and action.

table 15.1 Relating Promotion to the Communication Process

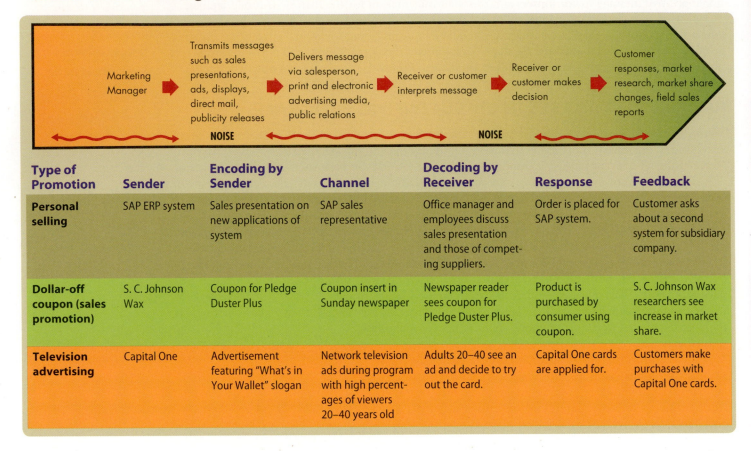

Type of Promotion	Sender	Encoding by Sender	Channel	Decoding by Receiver	Response	Feedback
Personal selling	SAP ERP system	Sales presentation on new applications of system	SAP sales representative	Office manager and employees discuss sales presentation and those of competing suppliers.	Order is placed for SAP system.	Customer asks about a second system for subsidiary company.
Dollar-off coupon (sales promotion)	S. C. Johnson Wax	Coupon for Pledge Duster Plus	Coupon insert in Sunday newspaper	Newspaper reader sees coupon for Pledge Duster Plus.	Product is purchased by consumer using coupon.	S. C. Johnson Wax researchers see increase in market share.
Television advertising	Capital One	Advertisement featuring "What's in Your Wallet" slogan	Network television ads during program with high percentages of viewers 20–40 years old	Adults 20–40 see an ad and decide to try out the card.	Capital One cards are applied for.	Customers make purchases with Capital One cards.

At the next stage, it stimulates desire by convincing the would-be buyer of the product's ability to satisfy his or her needs. Finally, the sales presentation, advertisement, or sales promotion technique attempts to produce action in the form of a purchase or a more favorable attitude that may lead to future purchases.

The message must be **encoded,** or translated into understandable terms, and transmitted through a communications channel. **Decoding** is the receiver's interpretation of the message. The receiver's response, known as **feedback,** completes the system. Throughout the process, **noise** (in such forms as ineffective promotional appeals, inappropriate advertising media, or poor radio or television reception) can interfere with the transmission of the message and reduce its effectiveness.

The marketer is the message sender in Table 15.1. He or she encodes the message in the form of sales presentations, advertising, displays, or publicity releases. The **channel** for delivering the message may be a salesperson, a public relations outlet, a Web site, or one of the numerous advertising media. Decoding is often the most troublesome step in marketing communications because consumers do not always interpret promotional messages in the same way that senders do. Because receivers usually decode messages according to their own frames of reference or experiences, a sender must carefully encode a message in a way that matches the frame of reference of the target audience. Consumers today are bombarded daily by hundreds of sales messages through many media channels. This communications traffic can create confusion as noise in the channel increases. Because the typical shopper will choose to process only a few messages, ignored messages are wasted communications expenditures.

The AIDA concept is also vital to online marketers. It is not enough to say a Web site has effective content or high response rates. Marketers must know just how many "eyeballs" are looking at the site, how often they come to view a message, and what they are examining. Most important, they must find out what consumers do besides just look. The bottom line is that if nobody is responding to a Web site, it might as well not exist. Experts advise attracting users' attention by including people in advertisements and other communications in addition to new content and

briefly speaking

"History repeats itself because no one listens the first time."

—Anonymous

formats. The 2008 Summer Olympics held in Beijing gave NBC what its research chief called "an extraordinary research opportunity" to find out how consumers watched the games. The network broadcast about 3,600 hours of coverage on its main network and 2,200 hours of streaming video on its Web site, as well as live blogging and video on demand via computers and cell phones. "The whole idea," said the research chief, "is to get the same person and to touch them across all different sorts of platforms," and then to find out what they did. NBC ran focus groups and surveyed 500 consumers online every day throughout the 17 days of events to find out what media they used and how. Network executives hoped the results would help them create a Total Audience Measurement Index, or TAMI, that gauges television, Internet, on-demand, and cell phone viewing and that can be applied to future programming of all kinds.[4]

GROCERY DELIVERY
ONE OF MANY FEATURES DESIGNED TO KEEP YOU BALANCED
MASTER THE LONG TRIP℠
RESIDENCEINN.COM

Residence Inn Marriott

© AP Images/PRNewsFoto/Marriott International, Inc.

An effective message gains the reader's attention, achieves understanding, and stimulates the receiver's needs, suggesting an appropriate method of satisfaction.

Feedback, the receiver's response to the message, provides a way for marketers to evaluate the effectiveness of the message and tailor their responses accordingly. Feedback may take the form of attitude changes, purchases, or nonpurchases. In some instances, organizations use promotion to create favorable attitudes toward their goods or services in the hope of future purchases. Other promotional communications have the objective of directly stimulating consumer purchases. Marketers using infomercials that urge the viewer to call a toll-free number to place orders for music collections, the latest fitness fad, or other products can easily measure their success by counting the number of calls they receive that result in orders.

Even nonpurchases may serve as feedback to the sender. Failure to purchase may result from ineffective communication in which the receivers do not believe the message, don't remember it, or even associate it with another firm's products. Or receivers may remember it correctly, but the message may have failed to persuade them that the firm's products are better than those of the competition. So marketers need to be keenly aware of why messages fail. Interpersonal messages can fail, too, from lack of listening skills, as the "Etiquette for Marketing Professionals" feature discusses.

Noise represents interference at some stage in the communication process. It may result from disruptions such as transmissions of competing promotional messages over the same communications channel, misinterpretation of a sales presentation or advertising message, receipt of the promotional message by the wrong person, or random events such as people conversing or leaving the room during a television commercial. Noise can also result from distractions within an advertising message itself. Buzzwords and jargon can create a linguistic jungle for consumers who are just trying to find out more about a product. AARP, for instance, surveyed about 1,200 adults and found more than half were confused by the language of the investment industry, often saving too little or making costly mistakes because they didn't understand terms like *basis point* and *expense ratio*. "What we have here," said the organization's chief investment officer, "is a failure to communicate. ... Investors need quality, not quantity, of information."[5]

Consumers today are bombarded daily by hundreds of sales messages through multiple media channels.

© Jon Arnold Images Ltd/Alamy

Noise can be especially problematic in international communications. One problem is that there may be too many competing messages. Italian television channels broadcast all advertisements during a single half-hour slot each night. Or technology may be poor, and language translations inaccurate. Nonverbal cues, such as body language and tone of voice, are important parts of the communication process, and cultural differences may lead to noise and misunderstandings. For example, in the United States, the round *O* sign made with the thumb and first finger means "okay." But in Mediterranean countries, the same gesture means "zero" or "the worst." A Tunisian interprets this sign as "I'll kill you," and to a Japanese consumer, it means "money." It's easy to see how misunderstandings could arise from this single gesture.

Perhaps the most misunderstood language for U.S. marketers is English. With 74 English-speaking nations, local terms can confuse anyone trying to communicate globally. The following examples illustrate how easy it can be for marketers to make mistakes in English-language promotional messages:

▷ *Police:* bobby (Britain), garda (Ireland), Mountie (Canada), police wallah (South Africa)

▷ *Porch:* stoep (South Africa), gallery (Caribbean)

▷ *Bar:* pub (Britain), hotel (Australia), boozer (Australia, Britain, New Zealand)

▷ *Bathroom:* loo (Britain), dunny (Australia)

▷ *Ghost or monster:* wendigo (Canada), duppy (Caribbean), taniwha (New Zealand)

▷ *Barbecue:* braai (South Africa), barbie (Australia)

▷ *Truck:* lorry (Britain and Australia)

▷ *Festival:* feis (Ireland)

▷ *Sweater:* jumper (England)

▷ *French fries:* chips (Britain)

▷ *Soccer:* football (the rest of the world)

▷ *Soccer field:* pitch (England)

Etiquette Tips for Marketing Professionals

Listen Up!

Communicating isn't just speaking; it's listening. Studies show we remember only a quarter to half of what we hear, a remarkably small percentage. We don't often practice "active listening," going beyond just hearing the message to paying conscious attention and understanding the total content. Here are some tips to help you improve your active listening skills.

- If you're attending a presentation, arrive on time, make sure you're comfortable (eat lightly, visit the restroom beforehand), and sit near the front.

- Whether it's a presentation or a conversation, pay attention. Train your eyes on the speaker and put distracting thoughts aside.

- Ignore external distractions, such as noisy neighbors or a room that's too hot or too cold. Turn off your pager and cell phone.

- Give the speaker feedback. Use body language like nods and smiles to indicate you're paying attention.

- Mentally repeat the words the speaker is saying to focus your attention and improve retention of the message.

- Suspend judgment. Whether you agree or disagree, it's harder to take in the speaker's words if you're mentally preparing your response instead of listening.

- Practice empathy. Try to understand the speaker's ideas from the speaker's point of view instead of your own.

- In conversation, remember that you can't listen if you're talking. Listen more than you speak, and restate what the other person has said to test the accuracy of your understanding.

- Resist the temptation to finish the other person's statements.

- When it's your turn to speak, be brief and open but also respectful of others' opinions and delivery.

Sources: "Active Listening," *Mind Tools,* www.mindtools.com, accessed May 27, 2009; Dalmar Fisher, "Active Listening," from *Communication in Organizations,* www.analytictech.com, accessed May 27, 2009; Vadim Kotelnkiov, "12 Active Listening Tips," *1000 Advices,* www.1000advices.com, May 27, 2009; Susie Michelle Cortright, "10 Tips to Effective & Active Listening Skills," *Jamnext,* www.jamnext .com, accessed August 8, 2008.

Faulty communications can be especially risky on a global level, where noise can lead to some interesting misinterpretations. Here are three international examples:

▷ *On a sign in a Bucharest hotel lobby*—The lift is being fixed for the next day. During that time, we regret that you will be unbearable.

▷ *From a Japanese information booklet about using a hotel air conditioner*—Cooles and Heates: If you want just condition of warm in your room, please control yourself.

▷ *In an Acapulco hotel*—The manager has personally passed all the water served here.

assessment check

1. What are the three tasks accomplished by an effective message?

2. Identify the four steps of the AIDA concept.

3. What is noise?

Objectives of Promotion

What specific tasks should promotion accomplish? The answers to this question seem to vary as much as the sources consulted. Generally, however, marketers identify the following objectives of promotion:

1. Provide information to consumers and others.

2. Increase demand.

3. Differentiate a product.

3 Explain how the promotional mix relates to the objectives of promotion.

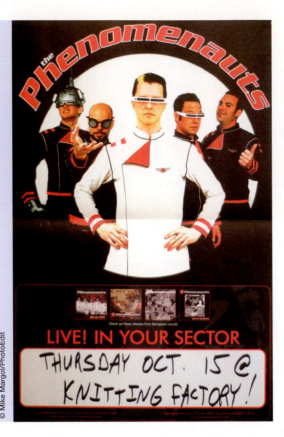

An advertisement for a concert or event typically provides information about the performer(s), time, and place.

© Mike Margol/PhotoEdit

4. Accentuate a product's value.

5. Stabilize sales.

PROVIDE INFORMATION

The traditional function of promotion was to inform the market about the availability of a particular good or service. In fact, marketers still direct much of their current promotional efforts at providing product information to potential customers. An advertisement for a concert typically provides information about the performer, time, and place. A commercial for a theme park offers information about rides, location, and admission price. Information can also help differentiate a product from its competitors by focusing on its features or benefits.

In addition to traditional print and broadcast advertising, marketers often distribute a number of high-tech, low-cost tools to give consumers product information. DVDs and online video clips are currently used for products such as cosmetics, automobiles, and exercise equipment, providing virtual demonstrations of the products. Political candidates even distribute them, packed with scenes from speeches, rallies, and the candidate on the job. Consumers still regard these media as a novelty, so they are less likely to throw them out or click elsewhere. Blogs are another channel for information. The "Solving an Ethical Controversy" feature discusses who controls bloggers' access to promotional information.

INCREASE DEMAND

Most promotions pursue the objective of increasing demand for a product. Some promotions are aimed at increasing **primary demand,** the desire for a general product category such as HDTVs or DVD players. Funding for the advertisement of agricultural commodities such as milk, sorghum, and cotton comes from mandatory fees called *checkoffs* charged to farmers on the sale of their products—in order to stimulate primary demand for the entire category of products, not just one brand.[6] The fees, totaling $750 million a year, have generated some controversy. Supporters say it's good for everyone in the industry but critics say the program is unfair, pointing out that small farmers contribute to the advertising budgets of major firms such as Hormel and Smithfield. Still, these funds have generated such memorable slogans as these:

▷ "Beef. It's what's for dinner."

▷ "Pork. The other white meat."

▷ "The incredible edible egg."

▷ "Cotton. The fabric of our lives."

Primary-demand promotions are also typical for firms holding exclusive patents on significant product improvements and for marketers who decide to expand overseas, creating new markets for their products in other parts of the world. When Procter & Gamble first introduced its Pampers disposable diapers in Hungary, most parents were using overpants with paper inserts to diaper their babies. So early Pampers television ads focused on generating interest in the novel product.

More promotions, however, are aimed at increasing **selective demand,** the desire for a specific brand. Movie studios have been looking for ways to get consumers to watch their films.

Solving an **ethical** controversy

Sports Blogs: Who Controls the Marketing Message?

When Mark Cuban, the wealthy owner of the Dallas Mavericks basketball team, recently tried to ban bloggers from the team's locker room, the National Basketball Association overruled him, saying teams could not bar bloggers from established news organizations. That was just one incident in a growing conflict between professional sports teams and the news media, centered on the question of who "owns" the news. The problem springs from the explosion of new media—in theory, anyone who sets up a blog could call him- or herself a journalist with all the rights and privileges that implies. Another provocative issue is the amount of game video media Web sites post online.

Should sports leagues be allowed to limit access to team news?

PRO

1. Leagues and teams should be able to limit news coverage like online game clips because their own Web sites bring them revenue. Major League Baseball's site is growing fast and already generates $400 million a year.

2. Some sports officials think the First Amendment right to free speech does not apply to private events like ball games, even if they are held in publicly financed stadiums.

CON

1. Media executives argue that events in publicly financed stadiums do fall under First Amendment protection, which would allow news media unlimited coverage.

2. Sports events are part of daily news and so belong to everyone. Says the editor of the Sports Illustrated Group, "S.I. does not own the sports history, but neither does Major League Baseball. That history belongs to everyone who loves the game."

Summary

The debate rolls on over the control of the sports marketing message. The head of media relations for the New York Yankees says, "The biggest danger now is that with some of these blog sites there is no structure. There is no one that [blogger] John Smith reports to." On the other hand, the executive director of the Media Law Resource Center says of sports franchises' objections to coverage, "What I see is a strident effort by a powerful monopoly to control information. They have a monopoly on the game. Now they want to have a monopoly on the information."

Sources: Brendan Funtek, "The Media's Coverage of Pro Sports," *The Olympian*, April 16, 2009, http://www.theolympian.com; Beth Krietsch, "Continued Controversy between Bloggers and the Professional Sports Community," *PR Week*, April 23, 2008, www.prweekus.com; Tim Arango, "Tension over Sports Blogging," *The New York Times*, April 21, 2008, www.nytimes.com; Barry Horn, "NBA Tells Dallas Mavericks to Allow Locker Room Access to Bloggers," *Dallas Morning News*, March 28, 2008, www.dallasnews.com.

So they've launched integrated campaigns that include Internet, video podcast, and cell phone marketing efforts. Online trailers, such as the moody teasers for Warner Brothers' second Batman film, *The Dark Knight*, and MGM's James Bond installment *Quantum of Solace*, attract wide attention. Such popular promotions have even inspired their own series of Golden Trailer Awards.[7]

DIFFERENTIATE THE PRODUCT

A frequent objective of the firm's promotional efforts is **product differentiation.** Homogeneous demand for many products results when consumers regard the firm's output as virtually identical to its competitors' products. In these cases, the individual firm has almost no control over marketing variables such as price. A differentiated demand schedule, in contrast, permits more flexibility in marketing strategy, such as price changes. As more companies try to reposition themselves as high-quality service providers, they are leaning heavily on the use of design—not only of the product but also of the consumer experience—to create emotional connections and make themselves unique and memorable. Procter & Gamble CEO Alan Lafley says, "We want to design the purchasing experience. . . . We want to design every component of the product; and we want to design the communication experience and the user experience. I mean, it's all design."[8]

ACCENTUATE THE PRODUCT'S VALUE

Promotion can explain the greater ownership utility of a product to buyers, thereby accentuating its value and justifying a higher price in the marketplace. This objective benefits both consumer and business products. A firm's promotional messages must build brand image and equity and at the same time deliver a "call to action." Advertising typically offers reasons why a product fits into the consumer's lifestyle. Today, consumers everywhere value their time; the challenge for marketers is to demonstrate how their merchandise will make their lives better.

Marketers must choose their words wisely when creating messages that accentuate their product's value. One expert advises staying away from five words: *quality, value, service, caring,* and *integrity.* These overused words are vague and tend to fall on deaf ears.[9]

STABILIZE SALES

Sales of most goods and services fluctuate throughout the year. These fluctuations may result from cyclical, seasonal, or irregular demand. Ice cream, ski trips, and swimming pools have obvious fluctuations, as do snow shovels and lawn mowers. Sales of bottled water and flashlights might spike just before a forecasted storm, while vacation rentals might be canceled in the path of the same oncoming hurricane. Stabilizing these variations often is an objective of promotional strategy. Although it may seem less obvious than ice cream, coffee sales follow a seasonal pattern, rising during colder months and dropping when the weather turns warm. Instead of turning up the temperature on its advertising for hot coffee in the summer, Dunkin' Donuts focuses on its iced coffee drinks. Recent promotions included Iced Coffee Day giveaways of 16-ounce drinks and an online instant-win game licensed by Major League Baseball played with peel-off stickers on all cold beverages.[10]

assessment check

1. What are the objectives of promotion?

2. Why is product differentiation important to marketers?

4 **Identify the different elements of the promotional mix and explain how marketers develop an optimal promotional mix.**

promotional mix Subset of the marketing mix in which marketers attempt to achieve the optimal blending of the elements of personal and nonpersonal selling to achieve promotional objectives.

Elements of the Promotional Mix

Like the marketing mix, the promotional mix requires a carefully designed blend of variables to satisfy the needs of a company's customers and achieve organizational objectives. The **promotional mix** works like a subset of the marketing mix, with its product, distribution, promotion, and pricing elements. With the promotional mix, the marketers attempt to create an optimal blend of various elements to achieve promotional objectives. The components of the promotional mix are personal selling and nonpersonal selling, including advertising, sales promotion, direct marketing, public relations, and guerrilla marketing.

Personal selling, advertising, and sales promotion usually account for the bulk of a firm's promotional expenditures. However, direct marketing, guerrilla marketing, sponsorships, and public relations also contribute to integrated marketing communications. Later sections of this chapter examine the use of guerrilla marketing, sponsorships, and direct marketing, and Chapters 16 and 17 present detailed discussions of the other elements. This section defines the elements and reviews their advantages and disadvantages.

PERSONAL SELLING

Personal selling is the oldest form of promotion, dating back as far as the beginning of trading and commerce. Traders vastly expanded both market sizes and product varieties as they led horses and camels along the Silk Road from China to Europe roughly between 300 B.C.E. and A.D. 1600, conducting personal selling at both ends. Personal selling may be defined as a seller's promotional presentation conducted on a person-to-person basis with the buyer. This direct form of promotion may be conducted face-to-face, over the telephone, through videoconferencing, or through interactive computer links between the buyer and seller.

Today, almost 16 million people in the United States have careers in sales and related occupations. They may sell real estate, insurance, and financial investments, or tractors, automobiles, and vacuum cleaners; they may work in retail or wholesaling; they may be regional managers or in the field. In other words, the range of jobs, as well as the products they represent, is huge.[11]

NONPERSONAL SELLING

Nonpersonal selling includes advertising, product placement, sales promotion, direct marketing, public relations, and guerrilla marketing. Advertising and sales promotion usually are regarded as the most important forms of nonpersonal selling. About one-third of marketing dollars spent on nonpersonal selling activities are allocated for media advertising; the other two-thirds fund trade and consumer sales promotions.

Advertising

Advertising is any paid, nonpersonal communication through various media about a business firm, not-for-profit organization, product, or idea by a sponsor identified in a message intended to inform, persuade, or remind members of a particular audience. It is a major promotional mix component for thousands of organizations—total ad spending in the United States topped $149 billion during a recent year. Online ad spending surpassed $11 billion.[12] Mass consumption and geographically dispersed markets make advertising particularly appropriate for marketing goods and services aimed at large audiences likely to respond to the same promotional messages.

Advertising primarily involves the mass media, such as newspapers, television, radio, magazines, movie screens, and billboards, but also includes electronic and computerized forms of promotion such as Web commercials, CDs and DVDs, and TV monitors at supermarkets. The rich potential of the Internet as an advertising channel to reach millions of people—one at a time—has attracted the attention of companies large and small, local and international. As consumers become increasingly savvy—and tune out messages that don't interest them—marketers are finding new ways to grab their attention. Ads on Web sites are commonplace, but now they also appear on cell phones. Consumers see them on fuel pump displays when buying gas or on their bank's ATM screens and hear audio ads embedded in vending machines and store displays.[13]

Product Placement

Product placement is a form of nonpersonal selling in which the marketer pays a motion picture or television program owner a fee to display his or her product prominently in the film or show. The practice gained attention more than two decades ago in the movie *E.T.: The Extra-Terrestrial* when Elliott, the boy who befriends E.T., lays out a trail of

Advertising is a major promotional mix component for thousands of organizations, including Burt's Bees.

Reese's Pieces for the extraterrestrial to follow, to draw the alien from his hiding place. Product sales for Reese's Pieces candies went through the roof. (Interestingly, this was not the moviemaker's first choice of candy; Mars turned down the opportunity to have its M&Ms appear in the film.) Today, hundreds of products, even B2B products such as Cisco System's TelePresence videoconferencing system, mentioned in a "CSI: NY" season finale, appear in movies and on television shows, and the fees charged for these placements have soared. A coalition of 23 advocacy and consumer groups asked the Federal Communications Commission to regulate product placement, calling the lack of adequate disclosure an "unfair and deceptive" practice, even as product placements and branded content on shows like "American Idol" grow to an average of 14 minutes per episode. "We're not saying they can't do it," says an FCC commissioner. "We're just saying they have to let the audience know what they're doing."[14]

Some firms have moved to the next generation of product placement, seeking new places for their merchandise. One popular venue for product placement is video games. Not only do these placements generate recognition and awareness, but they can also result in an immediate sale. Marketers need to be sure, however, that their product fits in the game environment, or at least doesn't interrupt the game experience. Discovery Channel successfully promoted a new show called "FutureWeapons" by giving away two levels of Microsoft's blockbuster "Gears of War" game.[15]

Sales Promotion

sales promotion
Marketing activities other than personal selling, advertising, guerrilla marketing, and public relations that stimulate consumer purchasing and dealer effectiveness.

Sales promotion consists of marketing activities other than personal selling, advertising, guerrilla marketing, and public relations that stimulate consumer purchasing and dealer effectiveness. This broad category includes displays, trade shows, coupons, contests, samples, premiums, product demonstrations, and various nonrecurring, irregular selling efforts. Sales promotion provides a short-term incentive, usually in combination with other forms of promotion, to emphasize, assist, supplement, or otherwise support the objectives of the promotional program. Restaurants, including those serving fast food, often place certain items on the menu at a lower price "for a limited time only." Advertisements may contain coupons for free or discounted items for a specified period of time. Or companies may conduct sweepstakes for prizes such as new cars or vacations, which may even be completely unrelated to the products the companies are selling.

Movie promotional tie-ins are a classic example. Although this is still a popular—and profitable—type of promotion, some companies are discovering they aren't getting the return on their investment they had hoped for. If the movie flops, it may be bad news for the product as well. And some fast-food and snack companies are growing wary of tie-ins with films bearing G and PG ratings, due to past criticism that such deals help promote junk food to children. Creative control and quick results keep television advertising attractive to marketers, while the rising cost of airing spots on such high-profile broadcasts as the Super Bowl and the Olympics grabs an ever-larger share of their advertising budgets. "It's not that it's impossible to get companies on board" with tie-ins, said one movie executive. "They all want their products on the screen. Getting them to open their wallets and promote those appearances . . . is the hard part."[16] Film studios, meanwhile, are getting more creative. One tie-in for *Spider-Man 3* paired Columbia Pictures and New York City's tourism marketing organization to create "Spider-Man Week in NYC," which held over two dozen events all over the city, including a live spider exhibit at the American Museum of Natural History.[17]

Sales promotion geared to marketing intermediaries is called **trade promotion.** Companies spend about as much on trade promotion as on advertising and consumer-oriented sales promotion combined. Trade promotion strategies include offering free merchandise, buyback allowances, and merchandise allowances along with sponsorship of sales contests to encourage wholesalers and retailers to sell more of certain items or product lines.

Direct Marketing

direct marketing Direct communications, other than personal sales contacts, between buyer and seller, designed to generate sales, information requests, or store or Web site visits.

Another element in a firm's integrated promotional mix is **direct marketing,** the use of direct communication to a consumer or business recipient designed to generate a response in the form of an order, a request for further information (lead generation), or a visit to a place of business to purchase specific goods or services (traffic generation). While many people equate direct marketing with direct mail, this promotional category also includes telemarketing, direct-response advertising and infomercials on television, direct-response print advertising, and electronic media. Direct marketing is an important element of the promotional mix, and it is discussed in depth later in this chapter.

Public Relations and Publicity

Public relations refer to a firm's communications and relationships with its various publics. These publics include customers, suppliers, stockholders, employees, the government, and the general public. Public relations programs can conduct either formal or informal contacts. The critical point is that every organization, whether or not it has a formally organized program, must be concerned about its public relations.

public relations Firm's communications and relationships with its various publics.

Publicity is the marketing-oriented aspect of public relations. It can be defined as nonpersonal stimulation of demand for a good, service, person, cause, or organization through unpaid placement of significant news about it in a published medium or through a favorable presentation of it on the radio or television. Compared with personal selling, advertising, and even sales promotion, expenditures for public relations usually are low in most firms. Because companies do not pay for publicity, they have less control over the publication by the press or electronic media of good or bad company news. But this often means consumers find this type of news source more believable than if the information were disseminated directly by the company. Of course, bad publicity can damage a company's reputation and diminish brand equity. Organizations that enjoy good publicity generally try to make the most of it. Those who have suffered from bad publicity try to turn the situation around.

Guerrilla Marketing

Guerrilla marketing uses unconventional, innovative, and low-cost techniques to attract consumers' attention. It is a relatively new approach used by marketers whose firms are underfunded for a full marketing program. Many of these firms can't afford the huge costs involved in the orthodox media of print and broadcasting, so they need to find an innovative, low-cost way to reach their market. But some large companies, such as PepsiCo and Toyota, engage in guerrilla marketing as well.

guerrilla marketing Unconventional, innovative, and low-cost marketing techniques designed to get consumers' attention in unusual ways.

As mentioned in Chapter 10, *buzz marketing* can be part of guerrilla marketing. This type of marketing works well to reach college students and other young adults. Marketing firms may hire students to mingle among their own classmates and friends, creating buzz about a product. Often called *campus ambassadors,* they may wear logo-bearing T-shirts or caps, leave Post-it Notes with marketing messages around campus, and chat about the good or service with friends during class breaks or over meals. *Time Out Chicago* relies on its Campus Ambassadors to help it promote advertisers like Macy's and the Chicago Blackhawks hockey team with parties, free event tickets, gift bags, and other giveaways.[18]

Trident sponsored a "Sweet and Sour" election in New York City to determine the flavor of the Big Apple. Hundreds of New Yorkers participated in this unconventional marketing campaign.

Viral marketing, also mentioned in Chapter 10, is another form of guerrilla marketing that has rapidly caught on with large and small firms. An online viral video called *Jumpin' In* surprised marketer Levi Strauss & Co. with its unexpected popularity, racking up 3.5 million hits in 10 days and attracting the attention of "Good Morning America" and *The Wall Street Journal.*

The success of the viral video led Levi Strauss to develop a follow-up campaign promoting the free-spirited nature of its jeans, including additional online videos, print ads, TV spots, giant three-dimensional jeans billboards, and online interactive features.[19]

The results of guerrilla marketing can be funny and outrageous—even offensive to some people. But they almost always get consumers' attention. Some guerrilla marketers stencil their company and product names anywhere graffiti might appear. Street artists are hired to plaster company and product logos on blank walls or billboards.

ADVANTAGES AND DISADVANTAGES OF TYPES OF PROMOTION

As Table 15.2 indicates, each type of promotion has both advantages and shortcomings. Although personal selling entails a relatively high per-contact cost, it involves less wasted effort than nonpersonal forms of promotion such as advertising. Personal selling often provides more flexible promotion than the other forms because the salesperson can tailor the sales message to meet the unique needs—or objections—of each potential customer.

The major advantages of advertising come from its ability to create instant awareness of a good, service, or idea; build brand equity; and deliver the marketer's message to mass audiences for a relatively low cost per contact. Major disadvantages include the difficulty in measuring advertising effectiveness and high media costs. Sales promotions, by contrast, can be more accurately monitored and measured than advertising, produce immediate consumer responses, and provide short-term sales increases. Direct marketing gives potential customers an action-oriented choice, permits narrow audience segmentation and customization of communications, and produces measurable results. Public relations efforts such as publicity frequently offer substantially higher credibility than other promotional techniques. Guerrilla marketing efforts can be innovative and highly effective at a low cost to marketers with limited funds, as long as the

table 15.2 Comparison of the Six Promotional Mix Elements

	Personal Selling	Advertising	Sales Promotion	Direct Marketing	Public Relations	Guerrilla Marketing
Advantages	Permits measurement of effectiveness; Elicits an immediate response; Tailors the message to fit the customer	Reaches a large group of potential consumers for a relatively low price per exposure; Allows strict control over the final message; Can be adapted to either mass audiences or specific audience segments	Produces an immediate consumer response; Attracts attention and creates product awareness; Allows easy measurement of results; Provides short-term sales increases	Generates an immediate response; Covers a wide audience with targeted advertising; Allows complete, customized, personal message; Produces measurable results	Creates a positive attitude toward a product or company; Enhances credibility of a product or company	Is low cost; Attracts attention because it is innovative; Is less cluttered with competitors trying the same thing
Disadvantages	Relies almost exclusively on the ability of the salesperson; Involves high cost per contact	Does not permit totally accurate measurement of results; Usually cannot close sales	Is nonpersonal in nature; Is difficult to differentiate from competitors' efforts	Suffers from image problem; Involves a high cost per reader; Depends on quality and accuracy of mailing lists; May annoy consumers	May not permit accurate measurement of effect on sales; Involves much effort directed toward non-marketing-oriented goals	May not reach as many people; If the tactics are too outrageous, they may offend some people

tactics are not too outrageous, but it is more difficult to reach people. The marketer must determine the appropriate blend of these promotional mix elements to effectively market the firm's goods and services.

Sponsorships

One of the most significant trends in promotion offers marketers the ability to integrate several elements of the promotional mix. Commercial sponsorships of an event or activity involve personal selling, advertising, sales promotion, and public relations in achieving specific promotional goals. These sponsorships, which link events with sponsors and media ranging from TV and radio to print and the Internet, have become nearly a $44 billion business. Sponsorship spending is growing more rapidly than spending for advertising.[20]

Sponsorship occurs when an organization provides money or in-kind resources to an event or activity in exchange for a direct association with that event or activity. The sponsor purchases two things: (1) access to the activity's audience and (2) the image associated with the activity. Sponsorships typically involve advertising, direct mail and sales promotion, publicity in the form of media coverage of the event, and personal selling at the event itself. They also involve relationship marketing, bringing together the event, its participants, the sponsoring firms, and their channel members and major customers. Marketers underwrite varying levels of sponsorships depending on the amount their companies wish to spend and the types of events.

Commercial sponsorship is not a new phenomenon. Aristocrats in ancient Rome sponsored gladiator competitions and chariot races featuring teams that often were supported financially by competing businesses. More than 2,000 years ago, wealthy Athenians underwrote drama, musical, and sporting festivals. Craft guilds in 14th-century England sponsored plays, occasionally insisting that the playwrights insert "plugs" for their lines of work in the scripts. During the 1880s, some local baseball teams in the United States were sponsored by streetcar companies.

Although they include both commercial and not-for-profit events, today's sponsorships are most prevalent in sports—the Olympics, the Super Bowl, the NCAA basketball championships, the Tour de France bicycle race, LPGA and PGA golf, NASCAR races, Major League Soccer, baseball farm teams, and thousands of smaller events as well. Local firms may sponsor soccer and baseball teams.

Companies may also sponsor reading and child-care programs, concerts or art exhibits, programs that support small businesses and create new jobs, and humanitarian programs such as Ducks Unlimited, the Special Olympics, and the American Cancer Society's Relay for Life.

HOW SPONSORSHIP DIFFERS FROM ADVERTISING

Even though sponsorship spending and traditional advertising spending represent forms of nonpersonal selling, they differ in a number of ways. These differences include potential cost-effectiveness, the sponsor's degree of control versus that of advertising, the nature of the message, and audience reaction.

Escalating costs of traditional advertising media have made commercial sponsorships a cost-effective alternative. Except for the really large events, which often have multiple sponsors, most are less expensive than an advertising campaign that relies on television, print, and other advertising. In addition, sponsors often gain the benefit of media coverage anyway, as associated events are covered by the news. And in the case of naming rights of such venues as sports arenas, the name serves as a perpetual advertisement. Examples include the Safeco Field (Seattle), HP Pavilion (San Jose), and the United Center (Chicago). Case 15.1 at the end of this chapter describes Dubai's leasing of the naming rights to its metro stations.

Marketers have considerable control over the quantity and quality of market coverage when they advertise. But sponsors have little control of sponsored events beyond matching the audiences

5 **Describe the role of sponsorships and direct marketing in integrated marketing communications.**

sponsorship Relationship in which an organization provides funds or in-kind resources to an event or activity in exchange for a direct association with that event or activity.

Rising costs of traditional advertising have made commercial sponsorships a cost-effective alternative. The Avon Walk for Breast Cancer has several sponsors, including Reebok.

© Kevin Mazur/WireImage/Getty Images

to profiles of their own target markets. Instead, event organizers control the coverage, which typically focuses on the event—not the sponsor. By contrast, a traditional advertisement allows the marketer to create an individual message containing an introduction, a theme, and a conclusion.

Audiences react differently to sponsorship as a communications medium than to other media. The sponsor's investment provides a recognizable benefit to the sponsored activity that the audience can appreciate. As a result, sponsorship often is viewed more positively than traditional advertising. Some marketers have tried to take advantage of this fact by practicing **ambush marketing,** in which a firm that is not an official sponsor tries to link itself to a major international event, such as the Olympics or a concert tour by a musical group. Heineken recently gave green hats to Dutch customers hoping they would wear them to the Euro 2008 soccer tournament. But Carlsberg, a rival brewer, paid $21 million to be an official sponsor of the event and stopped anyone trying to enter the stadium in the hats, asking them to remove the headgear.[21] While a vague advertisement such as hats is not illegal, some ambush practices clearly are. If a nonsponsor used the Olympic rings in an advertisement, the ad would be an illegal use of a trademark.

To assess the results of sponsorships, marketers use some of the same techniques by which they measure advertising effectiveness. However, the differences between the two promotional alternatives often necessitate some unique research techniques as well. A few corporate sponsors attempt to link expenditures to sales. Other sponsors measure improved brand awareness and image as effectiveness indicators; they conduct traditional surveys before and after the events to secure this information. Still other sponsors measure the impact of their event marketing in public relations terms.

Direct Marketing

Few promotional mix elements are growing as fast as direct marketing. Direct marketing advertising expenditures in the United States were expected to top $183 billion in a recent year. Despite the economic slowdown, direct marketers saw sales increase over 5 percent.[22] Both business-to-consumer and business-to-business marketers rely on this promotional mix element to generate orders or sales leads—requests for more information that may result in future orders. Direct marketing also helps increase store traffic, improving the chances that consumers will evaluate and perhaps purchase the advertised goods or services.

Direct marketing opens new international markets of unprecedented size. Electronic marketing channels have become the focus of direct marketers, and Web marketing is international marketing. Even direct mail and telemarketing will grow outside the United States as commerce becomes more global. Consumers in Europe and Japan are responsive to direct marketing but most global marketing systems remain undeveloped, and many are almost dormant. The growth of international direct marketing is spurred by marketing operations born in the United States.

Direct marketing communications pursue goals beyond creating product awareness. Marketers want direct marketing to persuade people to place an order, request more information, visit a store, call a toll-free number, or respond to an e-mail message. In other words, successful direct marketing should prompt consumers to take action. Because direct marketing is interactive, marketers can tailor individual responses to meet consumers' needs. They can also measure the effectiveness of their efforts more easily than with advertising and other forms of promotion. Direct marketing is a very powerful tool that helps organizations win new customers and enhance relationships with existing ones.

The growth of direct marketing parallels the move toward integrated marketing communications in many ways. Both respond to fragmented media markets and audiences, growth in customized products, shrinking network broadcast audiences, and the increasing use of databases to target specific markets. Lifestyles also play a role because today's busy consumers want convenience and shopping options that save them time.

Databases are an important part of direct marketing. Using the latest technology to create sophisticated databases, a company can select a narrow market segment and find good prospects within that segment based on desired characteristics. Marketers can cut costs and improve returns on dollars spent by identifying customers most likely to respond to messages and by eliminating others from their lists who are not likely to respond. In fact, mining information about customers is a trend boosted by the growth of e-marketing.

DIRECT MARKETING COMMUNICATIONS CHANNELS

Direct marketing uses many different media forms: direct mailings such as brochures and catalogs; telecommunications initiated by companies or customers; television and radio through special offers, infomercials, or shopping channels; the Internet via e-mail and electronic messaging; print media such as newspapers and magazines; and specialized channels such as electronic kiosks. Each works best for certain purposes, although marketers often combine two or more media in one direct marketing program. As long as it complies with current "do not call" regulations, a company might start with telemarketing to screen potential customers and then follow up by sending more material by direct mail to those who are interested.

DIRECT MAIL

As the amount of information about consumer lifestyles, buying habits, and wants continues to mount, direct mail has become a viable channel for identifying a firm's best prospects. Marketers gather information from internal and external databases, surveys, personalized coupons, and rebates that require responses. **Direct mail** is a critical tool in creating effective direct-marketing campaigns. It comes in many forms, including sales letters, postcards, brochures, booklets, catalogs, *house organs* (periodicals issued by organizations), DVDs and CDs.

Direct mail offers advantages such as the ability to select a narrow target market, achieve intensive coverage, send messages quickly, choose from various formats, provide complete information, and personalize each mailing piece. Response rates are measurable and higher than other types of advertising. In addition, direct mailings stand alone and do not compete for attention with magazine ads and radio and TV commercials. On the other hand, the per-reader cost of direct mail is high, effectiveness depends on the quality of the mailing list, and some consumers object strongly to what they consider "junk mail."

Recently, some firms have been trying a direct-mail tactic that has sparked some debate—sending marketing messages that appear to be from the government, banks, or even a personal friend. One envelope might bear a logo that looks like a government seal; inside is a solicitation for refinancing a loan. Another might have what looks like a handwritten note from a friend—but actually contains an ad for a fitness center. Some envelopes look like bank statements. All are intended to cut through the clutter that appears in consumers' mailboxes.

CATALOGS

Catalogs have been a popular form of direct mail in the United States since the late 1800s. During the early 1900s, consumers could even order a house from the famous Sears, Roebuck catalog. More than 10,000 different catalogs fill mailboxes every year. Catalogs fill so many segments that you could probably order just about anything you need for any facet of your life from a catalog. But

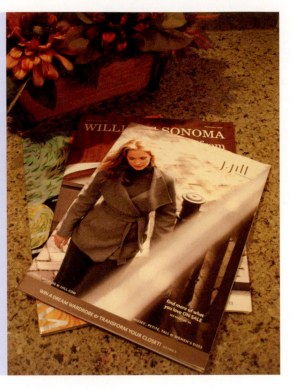

Catalogs have been a popular form of direct mail in the United States since the late 1800s. Many companies well-known for their catalogs, including J. Jill, are now creating online catalogs as well.

© Terri Miller/E-Visual Communications, Inc.

many catalog marketers are finding their business is changing. For instance, the Direct Marketing Association found in a recent survey that 44 percent of total sales are completed online or over the telephone, and about a third of the survey respondents believed their Web sites brought "incremental" sales they would not have gotten otherwise. Nearly half named their Web site as their primary marketing channel, compared with a third who listed their paper catalog in that spot. Over 80 percent planned to use e-mail promotions in the coming year, even though 60 percent reported increasing their catalog circulation.[23]

Pottery Barn, L.L.Bean, and Williams-Sonoma are well known for their catalogs. But these and other retailers have also added online catalogs to their direct marketing lineup. Upscale women's clothing retailer J. Jill created an online catalog that replicated each page of its print catalog so that consumers could flip through both and find items on the same "page." Nordstrom has begun a "buy online, pick up in-store" program for shoes, apparel, and cosmetics and is expanding to all categories.[24]

The 21st-century consumer is time-pressed and overloaded with information. To help consumers escape the barrage of mail stuffed into their boxes, the Direct Marketing Association established its Mail Preference Service. This consumer service sends name-removal forms to people who do not wish to receive direct-mail advertising.

TELEMARKETING

Although its use has been limited by a number of "do not call" restrictions enacted by the Federal Trade Commission, telemarketing remains the most frequently used form of direct marketing. It provides marketers with a high return on their expenditures, an immediate response, and the opportunity for personalized two-way conversations. In addition to business-to-consumer direct marketing, business-to-business telemarketing is another form of direct customer contact.

Telemarketing refers to direct marketing conducted entirely by telephone, and it can be classified as either outbound or inbound contacts. Outbound telemarketing involves a sales force that uses only the telephone to contact customers, reducing the cost of making personal visits. The customer initiates inbound telemarketing, typically by dialing a toll-free number firms provide for customers to use at their convenience to obtain information or make purchases.

New predictive dialer devices improve telemarketing's efficiency and reduce costs by automating the dialing process to skip busy signals and answering machines. When the dialer reaches a human voice, it instantaneously puts the call through to a salesperson. This technology often is combined with a print advertising campaign that features a toll-free number for inbound telemarketing.

Because recipients of both consumer and business-to-business telemarketing calls often find them annoying, the Federal Trade Commission passed a *Telemarketing Sales Rule* in 1996. The rule curtailed abusive telemarketing practices by establishing allowed calling hours (between 8 A.M. and 9 P.M.) and regulating call content. Companies must clearly disclose details of any exchange policies, maintain lists of people who do not want to receive calls, and keep records of telemarketing scripts, prize winners, customers, and employees for two years. This regulation was recently strengthened by the passage of amendments, creating the national Do Not Call Registry. These rules prohibit telemarketing calls to anyone who has registered his or her phone number, restrict the number and duration of telemarketing calls generating dead air space with use of automatic dialers, crack down on unauthorized billing, and require telemarketers to transmit their Caller ID information. Violators can be fined as much as $11,000 per occurrence. Exempt from these rules, however, are current customers, charities, opinion pollsters, and political candidates.

The Federal Trade Commission (FTC) recently levied penalties amounting to $7.7 million against several companies for violating the provisions of the Do Not Call Registry. One firm whose case is still pending, Global Mortgage Funding, is charged with making hundreds of thousands of calls to consumers whose names are on the registry, as well as failing to give out required caller ID information and to pay registry fees. "Consumers have made it clear that they greatly value the Do Not Call Registry," said the FTC's chair, "and they must be able to depend on its privacy protection."[25]

In further restrictions to telemarketing, after receiving many complaints about recorded sales messages left on consumers' answering machines, the FTC recently required those calls to have an "opt out" selection for recipients to stop getting those calls. After September 1, 2009, telemarketers will also be able to send recorded messages only to consumers who have provided signed written agreements to receive them. The messages exclude informational messages, such as appointment reminders or cancellations, because they are not attempting to sell products.[26]

DIRECT MARKETING VIA BROADCAST CHANNELS

Broadcast direct marketing can take three basic forms: brief direct-response ads on television or radio, home shopping channels, and infomercials. Direct-response spots typically run 30, 60, or 90 seconds and include product descriptions and toll-free telephone numbers for ordering. Often shown on cable television and independent stations and tied to special-interest programs, broadcast direct marketing usually encourages viewers to respond immediately by offering them a special price or a gift if they call within a few minutes of an ad's airing. Radio direct-response ads also provide product descriptions and addresses or phone numbers to contact the sellers. However, radio often proves expensive compared with other direct marketing media, and listeners may not pay close enough attention to catch the number or may not be able to write it down because they are driving a car, which accounts for a major portion of radio listening time.

Home shopping channels, such as Quality Value Convenience (QVC), Home Shopping Network (HSN), and ShopNBC, represent another type of television direct marketing. Broadcasting around the clock, these channels offer consumers a variety of products, including jewelry, clothing, skin-care products, home furnishings, computers, cameras, kitchen appliances, and toys. In essence, home shopping channels function as on-air catalogs. The channels also have Web sites that consumers can browse through to make purchases. In both cases, customers place orders via toll-free telephone numbers and pay for their purchases by credit card.

Infomercials are 30-minute or longer product commercials that resemble regular television programs. Because of their length, infomercials do not get lost as easily as 30-second commercials can, and they permit marketers to present their products in more detail. But they usually are shown at odd hours, and people often watch only portions of them. Nevertheless, Kodak had great success with an infomercial campaign for its EasyShare printer. "Direct response TV gave us the control we needed in telling our story, and the long-form option allowed us to roll out the right information so that consumers could absorb and process it," says the company's worldwide director for advertising and branding in the consumer digital group. "DRTV gave us the flexibility to control our message." In fact, the printers sold out during the campaign, with about half the callers closing on the purchase over the phone and another 30 percent of sales coming from the Web site promoted during the show.[27]

Infomercials provide toll-free telephone numbers so that viewers can order products or request more information. Although infomercials may incur higher production costs than prime-time 30-second ads on national network TV, they generally air on less expensive cable channels and in late-night time slots on broadcast stations.

ELECTRONIC DIRECT MARKETING CHANNELS

Anyone who has ever visited the Web is abundantly aware of the growing number of commercial advertisements that now clutter their computer screen. Web advertising is a recurring theme throughout this text, corresponding to its importance as a component of the promotional mix. In fact, Chapter 4 explained the vital role e-business now plays in contemporary marketing practices. U.S. spending on online advertising now represents almost 8 percent of total advertising spending.[28] Companies that were once skeptical—or at least slow to adopt online advertising— now embrace it.

Web advertising, however, is only one component of electronic direct marketing. E-mail direct marketers have found that traditional practices used in print and broadcast media are easily adapted to electronic messaging. You might receive e-mail notices from retailers from whom you've made past purchases, telling you about special promotions or new products. Banner ads on your cell phone might offer "click to call" options for responding. You might see a billboard or commercial promoting a code you can text to enter a sweepstakes or get a discount coupon.[29] Experts agree that the basic rules for online direct marketing mirror those of traditional practices. Any successful offline direct marketing campaign can be applied to e-mail promotions. Electronic media deliver data instantly to direct marketers and help them track customer buying cycles quickly. As a result, they can place customer acquisition programs online for less than the cost of traditional programs.

OTHER DIRECT MARKETING CHANNELS

The North Face has added in-store kiosks to boost its product selection. This kiosk screen display shows information a customer can gather.

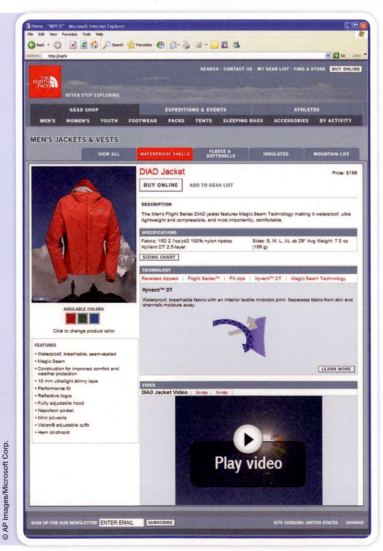

© AP Images/Microsoft Corp.

Print media such as newspapers and magazines do not support direct marketing as effectively as Web marketing and telemarketing. However, print media and other traditional direct marketing channels are still critical to the success of all electronic media channels. Magazine ads with toll-free telephone numbers enhance inbound telemarketing campaigns. Companies can place ads in magazines or newspapers, include reader-response cards, or place special inserts targeted for certain market segments within the publications. Newspapers are savvy about the Internet, producing online versions of their content that naturally include online, interactive ads.

Kiosks provide another outlet for electronic sales. In its drive to transform its business, Blockbuster adapted in-store kiosks so customers can download movies for digital delivery. Prototypes are fine-tuned to get the download time to 30 seconds, but special features like previews and recommendations are already in place.[30] Popular sports clothing company The

North Face has added in-store kiosks to boost its product selection. "You can't put a 15,000-square-foot assortment in a 3,300-square-foot box," said the company's vice president of retail. But on the kiosk, now available in all North Face U.S. stores, customers can not only see a full range of products but also watch videos of expeditions and famous athletes.[31]

Developing an Optimal Promotional Mix

6 **Discuss the factors that influence the effectiveness of a promotional mix.**

By blending advertising, personal selling, sales promotion, and public relations to achieve marketing objectives, marketers create a promotional mix. Because quantitative measures are not available to determine the effectiveness of each mix component in a given market segment, the choice of an effective mix of promotional elements presents one of the marketer's most difficult tasks. Several factors influence the effectiveness of a promotional mix: (1) the nature of the market, (2) the nature of the product, (3) the stage in the product lifecycle, (4) the price, and (5) the funds available for promotion.

NATURE OF THE MARKET

The marketer's target audience has a major impact on the choice of a promotion method. When a market includes a limited number of buyers, personal selling may prove a highly effective technique. However, markets characterized by large numbers of potential customers scattered over sizable geographic areas may make the cost of contact by personal salespeople prohibitive. In such instances, extensive use of advertising often makes sense. The type of customer also affects the promotional mix. Personal selling works better in high-priced, high-involvement purchases—for instance, a target market made up of industrial purchasers or retail and wholesale buyers—than in a target market consisting of ultimate consumers. Similarly, pharmaceuticals firms use large sales

Subway used direct marketing in the form of its popular spokesperson, Jared Fogle, who lost 245 pounds eating Subway sandwiches.

© AP Images/PRNewsFoto/SUBWAY

forces to sell prescription drugs directly to physicians and hospitals, but they also advertise to promote over-the-counter and prescription drugs for the consumer market. So the drug firm must switch its promotional strategy from personal selling to consumer advertising based on the market it is targeting.

Subway used direct marketing in the form of its popular spokesperson, Jared Fogle, who lost 245 pounds eating its sandwiches. The company had Fogle record inspirational messages on its Web site, where consumers could sign up for a time to receive them. Subway has faith that other ordinary people can also adopt healthier eating habits; it is one of the sponsors of the popular reality show "The Biggest Loser." Contestants and their trainers visit Subway during TV segments to learn healthful food selection, which consumers can view at the show's Web site, and the company also sponsors contests to win free trips to the filming of the show's season finale.[32]

NATURE OF THE PRODUCT

A second important factor in determining an effective promotional mix is the product itself. Highly standardized products with minimal servicing requirements usually depend less on personal selling than custom products with technically complex features or requirements for frequent maintenance. Marketers of consumer products are more likely to rely heavily on advertising than business products. For example, soft drinks lend themselves more readily to advertising than large pieces of business machinery.

Promotional mixes vary within each product category. In the B2B market, for example, installations typically rely more heavily on personal selling than marketing of operating supplies. In contrast, the promotional mix for a convenience product is likely to involve more emphasis on manufacturer advertising and less on personal selling. On the other hand, personal selling plays an important role in the promotion of shopping products, and both personal and nonpersonal selling are important in the promotion of specialty items. A personal-selling emphasis is also likely to prove more effective than other alternatives in promotions for products involving trade-ins.

STAGE IN THE PRODUCT LIFECYCLE

The promotional mix must also be tailored to the product's stage in the product lifecycle. In the introductory stage, both nonpersonal and personal selling are used to acquaint marketing intermediaries and final consumers with the merits of the new product. Heavy emphasis on personal selling helps inform the marketplace of the merits of the new good or service. Salespeople contact marketing intermediaries to secure interest in and commitment to handling the newly introduced item. Trade shows frequently are used to inform and educate prospective dealers and

MARKETING SUCCESS

Denny's Scores a Hit with Its Grand Slam Giveaway

Background. Both the economy and Denny's restaurants were experiencing a slump. Consumers were eating at home. Even when it came to breakfast—traditionally the least-expensive meal at a restaurant—Denny's lagged well behind competitors such as McDonald's, Burger King, and IHOP.

The Challenge. Denny's marketers wanted to bring customers back. The company's image had suffered due to unpre-

dictable service, bland food, and a lack of new products. But Denny's saw an opportunity. Because of the poor economy, other restaurants had gone out of business. "We're aggressively going after that business," said one Denny's franchisee.

The Strategy. Denny's marketers decided to attract attention with a giveaway. Between 6:00 A.M. and 2:00 P.M. one February day, customers at all but two of Denny's

ultimate consumers about its merits over current competitive offerings. Advertising and sales promotion are also used during this stage to create awareness, answer questions, and stimulate initial purchases.

As the product moves into the growth and maturity stages, advertising gains relative importance in persuading consumers to make purchases. Marketers continue to direct personal-selling efforts at marketing intermediaries in an attempt to expand distribution. As more competitors enter the marketplace, advertising begins to stress product differences to persuade consumers to purchase the firm's brand. In the maturity and early decline stages, firms frequently reduce advertising and sales promotion expenditures as market saturation is reached and newer items with their own competitive strengths begin to enter the market.

PRICE

The price of an item is the fourth factor that affects the choice of a promotional mix. Advertising dominates the promotional mixes for low-unit-value products due to the high per-contact costs in personal selling. Advertising permits a low promotional expenditure per sales unit because it reaches mass audiences. For low-value consumer goods, such as chewing gum, soft drinks, and snack foods, advertising is the most feasible means of promotion. Even shopping products can be sold at least partly on the basis of price. On the other hand, consumers of high-priced items such as luxury cars expect lots of well-presented information from qualified salespeople. High-tech direct marketing promotions such as video presentations on a laptop PC or via cell phone, fancy brochures, and personal selling by informed, professional salespeople appeal to these potential customers. Denny's held a giveaway to promote its breakfasts, as the "Marketing Success" feature discusses.

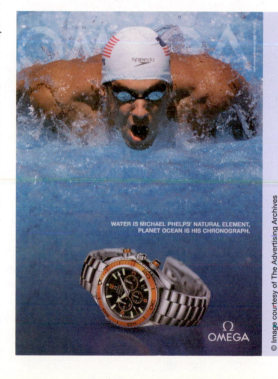

Athletes like Olympic swimming sensation Michael Phelps can earn millions of dollars in endorsements.

WATER IS MICHAEL PHELPS' NATURAL ELEMENT, PLANET OCEAN IS HIS CHRONOGRAPH.

Ω OMEGA

© Image courtesy of The Advertising Archives

FUNDS AVAILABLE FOR PROMOTION

A real barrier in implementing any promotional strategy is the size of the promotional budget. A single 30-second television commercial during the Super Bowl telecast costs an advertiser $2.7 million. While

1,500 locations received a free Grand Slam breakfast, which included two eggs, two strips of bacon, two sausage links, and two pancakes. To advertise the promotion, Denny's aired a 30-second commercial during the Super Bowl. The company predicted that about 2 million customers would show up for the free Grand Slam breakfasts, estimating that the total cost of the giveaway—including the Super Bowl ad—would be about $5 million.

The Outcome. Customers swarmed to Denny's restaurants around the country. Some waited in line for more than an hour to get in. Denny's operators heard similar stories of families devastated by economic hardship who appreciated the Grand Slam

offer. Aside from goodwill, Denny's received great press, including an estimated $50 million in free news coverage. Also, "Denny's" was one of the top search words on Google. Anticipating this online interest, the firm had purchased several search keywords on Google that included a Denny's link. The result? Denny's heard the words every marketer loves to hear: "I'll be back."

Sources: Bruce Horovitz, "2 Million Enjoy Free Breakfast at Denny's," *USA Today*, February 4, 2009, pp. B1–B2; Emily Bryson York, "Denny's Grand Slam Giveaway a Hit with 2 Million Diners," *Advertising Age*, February 3, 2009, http://adage.com; Michelle Chapman, "Denny's Gives Away Free Grand Slam Breakfasts," *San Francisco Chronicle*, February 3, 2009, http://www.sfgate.com; Jim Kavanagh, "Denny's Slammed by Breakfast Giveaway," *CNN*, February 3, 2009, http://www.cnn.com.

table 15.3 Factors Influencing Choice of Promotional Mix

	Emphasis	
	Personal Selling	**Advertising**
Nature of the market		
Number of buyers	Limited number	Large number
Geographic concentration	Concentrated	Dispersed
Type of customer	Business purchaser	Ultimate consumer
Nature of the product		
Complexity	Custom-made, complex	Standardized
Service requirements	Considerable	Minimal
Type of good or service	Business	Consumer
Use of trade-ins	Trade-ins common	Trade-ins uncommon
Stage in the product life cycle	Often emphasized at every stage; heavy emphasis in the introductory and early growth stages in acquainting marketing intermediaries and potential consumers with the new good or service	Often emphasized at every stage; heavy emphasis in the latter part of the growth stage, as well as the maturity and early decline stages, to persuade consumers to select specific brands
Price	High unit value	Low unit value

millions of viewers may see the commercial, making the cost per contact relatively low, such an expenditure exceeds the entire promotional budgets of thousands of firms, a dilemma that at least partially explains how guerrilla marketing got its start. And if a company wants to hire a celebrity to advertise its goods and services, the fee can run into millions of dollars a year. Athletes like Olympic swimming sensation Michael Phelps, LeBron James of the NBA's Cleveland Cavaliers, and tennis star Maria Sharapova earn millions of dollars in endorsements each year. Marketers estimate that Phelps's eight gold medals could earn him $30 to $40 million in product endorsements. Sharapova's game winnings amounted to only $3.8 million of her $23 million earnings in a recent year. James's endorsements brought him about half his $27 million for the same period.[33] Table 15.3 summarizes the factors that influence the determination of an appropriate promotional mix.

assessment check

1. What are the five factors that affect the choice of a promotional mix?
2. Why is the choice of a mix a difficult task for marketers?

7 Contrast pushing and pulling strategies.

pulling strategy
Promotional effort by the seller to stimulate final-user demand, which then exerts pressure on the distribution channel.

pushing strategy
Promotional effort by the seller directed to members of the marketing channel rather than final users.

Pulling and Pushing Promotional Strategies

Marketers may implement essentially two promotional alternatives: a pulling strategy or a pushing strategy. A **pulling strategy** is a promotional effort by the seller to stimulate final-user demand, which then exerts pressure on the distribution channel. When marketing intermediaries stock a large number of competing products and exhibit little interest in any one of them, a firm may have to implement a pulling strategy to motivate them to handle its product. In such instances, this strategy is implemented with the objective of building demand so consumers will request the product from retail stores. Advertising and sales promotion often contribute to a company's pulling strategy.

In contrast, a **pushing strategy** relies more heavily on personal selling. Here the objective is promoting the product to the members of the marketing channel rather than to final users. To achieve this goal, marketers employ cooperative-advertising allowances to channel members, trade discounts, personal-selling efforts by salespeople, and other dealer supports. Such a strategy is designed to gain marketing success for the firm's merchandise by motivating representatives of wholesalers and retailers to spend extra time and effort promoting the products to customers. About half of manufacturers' promotional budgets are allocated for cash incentives used to encourage retailers to stock their products.

Timing also affects the choice of promotional strategies. The relative importance of advertising and selling changes during the various phases of the purchase process. Prior to the actual sale, advertising usually is more important than personal selling. However, one of the primary advantages of a successful advertising program is the support it gives the salesperson who approaches the prospective buyer for the first time. Selling activities are more important than advertising at the time of purchase. Personal selling provides the actual mechanism for closing most sales. In the postpurchase period, advertising regains primacy in the promotional effort. It affirms the customer's decision to buy a particular good or service and, as pointed out in Chapter 5, reminds him or her of the product's favorable qualities by reducing any cognitive dissonance that might occur.

The promotional strategies used by auto marketers illustrate this timing factor. Car, truck, and SUV makers spend heavily on consumer advertising to create awareness before consumers begin the purchase process. At the time of their purchase decisions, however, the personal-selling skills of dealer salespeople provide the most important tools for closing sales. Finally, advertising is used frequently to maintain postpurchase satisfaction by citing awards such as *Motor Trend*'s Car of the Year and results of J. D. Power's customer satisfaction surveys to affirm buyer decisions.

assessment check

1. What is a pulling strategy?
2. What is a pushing strategy?

Budgeting for Promotional Strategy

8 Explain how marketers budget for and measure the effectiveness of promotion.

Promotional budgets may differ not only in amount but also in composition. Business-to-business marketers generally invest larger proportions of their budgets in personal selling than in advertising, while the reverse usually is true of most producers of consumer goods. Figure 15.1 shows estimated allocations of promotional budgets by consumer packaged-goods manufacturers.

Evidence suggests that sales initially lag behind promotional expenses for structural reasons—funds spent filling up retail shelves, boosting low initial production, and supplying buyer information. This fact produces a threshold effect in which few sales may result from substantial initial investments in promotion. A second phase might produce sales proportionate to promotional expenditures—the most predictable range. Finally, promotion reaches the area of diminishing returns, in which an increase in promotional spending fails to produce a corresponding increase in sales.

For example, an initial expenditure of $40,000 may result in sales of 100,000 units for a consumer-goods manufacturer. An additional $10,000 expenditure during the second phase may generate sales of 40,000 more units, and another $10,000 may produce sales of an additional 30,000 units. The cumulative effect of the expenditures and repeat sales will have generated increasing returns from the promotional outlays. However, as the advertising budget moves from $60,000 to $70,000, the marginal productivity of the additional expenditure may fall to 25,000 units. At some later point, the return may actually become zero or negative as competition intensifies, markets become saturated, and marketers employ less expensive advertising media.

The ideal method of allocating promotional funds would increase the budget until the cost of each additional increment equals the additional incremental revenue received. In other words, the most effective allocation procedure increases promotional expenditures until each dollar of promotional expense is matched by an additional dollar of

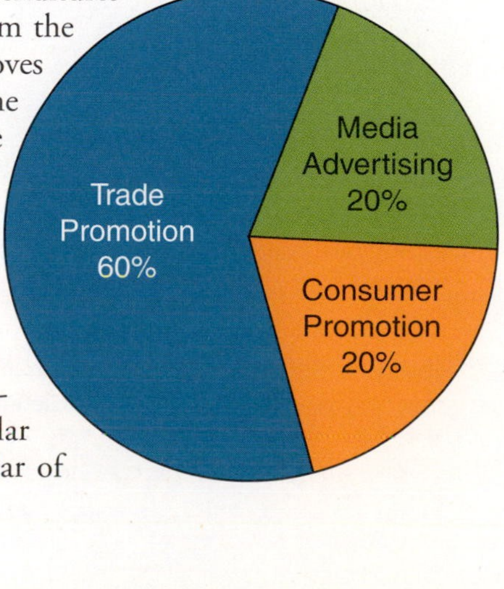

figure 15.1

Manufacturers' Promotional Budgets for Consumer Packaged Goods

Source: Data from Tom Pirovano, "Money Well Spent?: Trade Promotions in the U.S.," *Nielsen Consumer Insight Magazine*, Issue 6, January 2008, www.nielsen.com, accessed May 27, 2009

Media Advertising 20%

Trade Promotion 60%

Consumer Promotion 20%

profit. This procedure, referred to as *marginal analysis,* maximizes the input's productivity. The difficulty arises in identifying the optimal point, which requires a precise balance between marginal expenses for promotion and the resulting marginal receipts. In addition, as marketing communications become more integrated, it becomes harder to identify exact amounts that companies spend on individual elements of promotion.

Traditional methods used for creating a promotional budget include the percentage-of-sales and fixed-sum-per-unit methods, along with techniques for meeting the competition and achieving task objectives. Each method is briefly examined in Table 15.4.

The **percentage-of-sales method** is perhaps the most common way of establishing promotional budgets. The percentage can be based on sales either from some past period (such as the previous year) or forecasted for a future period (the current year). While this plan is appealingly simple, it does not effectively support the achievement of basic promotional objectives. Arbitrary percentage allocations can't provide needed flexibility. In addition, sales should depend on promotional allocation rather than vice versa.

The **fixed-sum-per-unit method** allocates a predetermined amount to each sales or production unit. This amount can also reflect either historical or forecasted figures. Producers of high-value consumer durable goods, such as automobiles, often use this budgeting method.

Another traditional budgeting approach, the **meeting competition method,** simply matches competitors' outlays, either in absolute amounts or relative to the firms' market shares. But this method doesn't help a company gain a competitive edge. A budget appropriate for one company may not be appropriate for another.

The **task-objective method** develops a promotional budget based on a sound evaluation of the firm's promotional objectives. The method has two steps:

1. The firm's marketers must define realistic communication goals that they want the promotional mix to achieve. Say that a firm wants to achieve a 25 percent increase in brand awareness. This step quantifies the objectives that promotion should attain. These objectives in turn become integral parts of the promotional plan.

2. Then the company's marketers determine the amount and type of promotional activity required for each objective they have set. Combined, these units become the firm's promotional budget.

A crucial assumption underlies the task-objective approach: marketers can measure the productivity of each promotional dollar. That assumption explains why the objectives must be carefully chosen, quantified, and accomplished through promotional efforts. Generally, budgeters should avoid general marketing objectives such as, "We want to achieve a 5 percent increase in sales." A sale is a culmination of the effects of all elements of the marketing mix. A more

table 15.4　Promotional Budget Determination

Method	Description	Example
Percentage-of-sales method	Promotional budget is set as a specified percentage of either past or forecasted sales.	"Last year we spent $1 million on promotion and had sales of $20 million. Next year we expect sales to grow to $30 million, so we are keeping our promotion allocation to 5 percent of expected sales, upping it to $1.5 million."
Fixed-sum-per-unit method	Promotional budget is set as a predetermined dollar amount for each unit sold or produced.	"Our forecast calls for sales of 14,000 units, and we allocate promotion at the rate of $65 per unit."
Meeting competition method	Promotional budget is set to match competitor's promotional outlays on either an absolute or relative basis.	"Promotional outlays average 4 percent of sales in our industry. We will match this percentage."
Task-objective method	Once marketers determine their specific promotional objectives, the amount (and type) of promotional spending needed to achieve them is determined.	"By the end of next year, we want 75 percent of the area high school students to be aware of our new, highly automated fast-food prototype outlet. How many promotional dollars will it take, and how should they be spent?"

appropriate promotional objective might be, "We want to achieve an 8 percent response rate from a targeted direct-mail advertisement."

Promotional budgeting always requires difficult decisions. Still, recent research studies and the spread of computer-based models have made it a more manageable problem than it used to be.

Measuring the Effectiveness of Promotion

Marketers know that part of a firm's promotional effort is ineffective. Evaluating the effectiveness of a promotion today is a far different exercise in marketing research than it was even a few decades ago. For years, marketers depended on store audits conducted by large organizations such as ACNielsen. Other research groups conducted warehouse withdrawal surveys of shipments to retail customers. These studies were designed to determine whether sales had risen as a direct result of a particular promotional campaign. During the 1980s, the introduction of scanners and automated checkout lanes completely changed marketing research. For the first time, retailers and manufacturers had a tool to obtain sales data quickly and efficiently. The problem was that the collected data was used for little else other than determining how much of which product was bought at what price and at what time.

By the 1990s, marketing research entered another evolutionary period with the advent of the Internet. Now marketing researchers can delve into each customer's purchase behavior, lifestyle, preferences, opinions, and buying habits. All this information can also be obtained in a matter of seconds. Consulting firm Accenture relies on computer modeling to perform "what if" analysis, helping its clients use *trade promotion management* to find out how best to spend their promotional budgets. The analysis breaks results down by customer segment, customer type, product brand, and type of promotion. In one product category, Heinz saved nearly $1 million while still growing sales by reducing inefficient spending, which the analysis revealed.[34] The next section explains the impact of electronic technologies on measuring promotional effectiveness. However, marketers today still depend on two basic measurement tools: direct sales results tests and indirect evaluations.

Most marketers would prefer to use a **direct sales results test** to measure the effectiveness of promotion. Such an approach would reveal the specific impact on sales revenues for each dollar of promotional spending. This type of technique has always eluded marketers, however, because of their inability to control other variables operating in the marketplace. A firm may receive $20 million in additional sales orders following a new $1.5 million advertising campaign, but the market success may really have resulted from the products' benefiting from more intensive distribution as more stores decide to carry them or price increases for competing products rather than from the advertising outlays.

Marketers often encounter difficulty isolating the effects of promotion from those of other market elements and outside environmental variables. **Indirect evaluation** helps researchers concentrate on quantifiable indicators of effectiveness, such as recall—how much members of the target market remember about specific products or advertisements—and readership—size and composition of a message's audience. The basic problem with indirect measurement is the difficulty in relating these variables to sales. Will the fact that many people read an ad lead directly to increased sales?

Marketers need to ask the right questions and understand what they are measuring. Promotion to build sales volume produces measurable results in the form of short-term returns, but brand-building programs and efforts to generate or enhance consumers' perceptions of value in a product, brand, or organization cannot be measured over the short term.

MEASURING ONLINE PROMOTIONS

The latest challenge facing marketers is how to measure the effectiveness of electronic media. Early attempts at measuring online promotional effectiveness involved counting hits, user requests for a file, and visits, pages downloaded or read in one session. But as Chapter 4 explained, it takes more than counting "eyeballs" to measure online promotional success. What matters is not how many times a Web site is visited but how many people actually buy something. Traditional numbers that work for other media forms are not necessarily relevant indicators of effectiveness for a Web site. For one thing, the Web combines both advertising and direct marketing. Web pages effectively

integrate advertising and other content, such as product information, that may often prove to be the page's main—and most effective—feature. For another consideration, consumers generally choose the advertisements they want to see on the Internet, whereas traditional broadcast or print media automatically expose consumers to ads.

One way marketers measure performance is by incorporating some form of direct response into their promotions. This technique also helps them compare different promotions for effectiveness and rely on facts rather than opinions. Consumers may say they will try a product when responding to a survey question yet not actually buy it. A firm may send out three different direct-mail offers in the same promotion and compare response rates from the groups of recipients receiving each alternative. An offer to send for a sample may generate a 75 percent response rate, coupons might show a 50 percent redemption rate, and rebates might appeal to only 10 percent of the targeted group.

The two major techniques for setting Internet advertising rates are cost per impression and cost per response. **Cost per impression** is a measurement technique that relates the cost of an ad to every thousand people who view it. In other words, anyone who sees the page containing the banner or other form of ad creates one impression. This measure assumes the site's principal purpose is to display the advertising message. **Cost per response,** or **click-throughs,** is a direct marketing technique that relates the cost of an ad to the number of people who click it. However, not everyone who clicks on an ad makes a purchase. So the **conversion rate** measurement was developed—the percentage of Web site visitors who actually make a purchase. All three rating techniques have merit. Site publishers point out that click-through rates are influenced by the creativity of the ad's message. Advertisers, on the other hand, point out that the Web ad has value to those who click it for additional information.

assessment check

1. What is the most common way of establishing a promotional budget?

2. What is the task-objective budgeting method? Describe its two steps.

3. What is the direct sales results test?

4. What is indirect evaluation?v

⑨ **Discuss the value of marketing communications.**

The Value of Marketing Communications

The nature of marketing communications is changing as new formats transform the traditional idea of an advertisement or sales promotion. Sales messages are now placed subtly, or not so subtly, in movies and television shows, blurring the lines between promotion and entertainment and changing the traditional definition of advertising. Messages show up at the beach in the form of skywriting, in restrooms, on stadium turnstiles, on buses, and even on police cars.

Despite new tactics by advertisers, promotion often has been the target of criticism. Some people complain that it offers nothing of value to society and simply wastes resources. Others criticize promotion's role in encouraging consumers to buy unnecessary items they cannot afford. Many ads seem to insult people's intelligence or offend their sensibilities, and they criticize the ethics—or lack thereof—displayed by advertisers and salespeople.

New forms of promotion are considered even more insidious because marketers are designing promotions that bear little resemblance to paid advertisements. Many of these complaints cite issues that constitute real problems. Some salespeople use unethical sales tactics. Some product advertising hides its promotional nature or targets consumer groups that can least afford the advertised goods or services. Many television commercials contribute to the growing problem of cultural pollution. One area that has sparked both criticism and debate is promotion aimed at children.

While promotion can certainly be criticized on many counts, it also plays a crucial role in modern society. This point is best understood by examining the social, business, and economic importance of promotion.

SOCIAL IMPORTANCE

We live in a diverse society characterized by consumer segments with differing needs, wants, and aspirations. What one group finds tasteless may be quite appealing to another. But diversity is one of the benefits of living in our society because it offers us many choices and opportunities.

briefly
speaking

"Let advertisers spend the same amount of money improving their product that they do on advertising and they wouldn't have to advertise it."

—**Will Rogers (1879–1935)**
AMERICAN HUMORIST AND SOCIAL COMMENTATOR

Promotional strategy faces an averaging problem that escapes many of its critics. The one generally accepted standard in a market society is freedom of choice for the consumer. Consumer buying decisions eventually determine acceptable practices in the marketplace.

Promotion has also become an important factor in campaigns aimed at achieving social objectives. Advertising agencies donate their expertise in creating **public service announcements (PSAs)** aimed at promoting such important causes as stopping drug abuse or supporting national parks. The Ad Council coordinates a program to raise awareness of the health of the earth's oceans that includes the National Marine Sanctuary Foundation, the National Oceanic and Atmospheric Administration, and the U.S Department of the Interior. Public service announcements feature characters from Disney's classic film *The Little Mermaid*—Disney is a volunteer participant in the campaign—and refer viewers to the related Web site, www.keepoceansclean.org.[35]

Promotion performs an informative and educational task crucial to the functioning of modern society. As with everything else in life, what is important is how promotion is used rather than whether it is used.

Advertising agencies donate their expertise in creating public service announcements aimed at promoting such important causes as stopping drug abuse.

© AP Images/PRNewsFoto/Templin Brink Design

CRYSTAL MESS

Buzz killer.

He's tweaking. His heart is racing, he's grinding his teeth, he's talking really fast and not making much sense. He thinks he's sexy and popular. And he's bumped up his risk of getting HIV by 400%.

Don't mess with crystal.
For help, visit crystalmess.net

This message brought to you by SF Dept. of Public Health HIV Prevention Program

BUSINESS IMPORTANCE

Promotional strategy has become increasingly important to both large and small business enterprises. The well-documented, long-term increase in funds spent on promotion certainly attests to management's faith in the ability of promotional efforts to encourage attitude changes, brand loyalty, and additional sales. It is difficult to conceive of an enterprise that would not attempt to promote its offerings in some manner. Most modern institutions simply cannot survive in the long run without promotion. Business must communicate with its publics.

Nonbusiness enterprises also recognize the importance of promotional efforts. The Government Accountability Office (GAO) reports that federal ad spending tops $1 billion, much of it spent for recruiting purposes by five agencies—the Departments of Defense, Health and Human Services, and the Interior; the Treasury; and the National Aeronautics and Space Administration (NASA).[36]

ECONOMIC IMPORTANCE

Promotion has assumed a degree of economic importance because it provides employment for millions of people. More important, however, effective promotion has allowed society to derive benefits not otherwise available. For example, the criticism that promotion costs too much isolates an individual expense item and fails to consider its possible beneficial effects on other categories of expenditures.

Promotional strategies increase the number of units sold and permit economies of scale in the production process, thereby lowering the production costs for each unit of output. Lower unit costs allow lower consumer prices, which in turn make products available to more people. Similarly, advertising subsidizes the information content of newspapers and the broadcast media. In short, promotion pays for many of the enjoyable entertainment and educational opportunities in contemporary life as it lowers product costs.

assessment check

1. Identify the three areas in which promotion exerts influence.

Strategic Implications of Marketing 21st Century in the

With the incredible proliferation of promotional messages in the media, today's marketers—consumers themselves—must find new ways to reach customers without overloading them with unnecessary or unwanted communications. Guerrilla marketing has emerged as an effective strategy for large and small companies, but ambush marketing has raised ethical concerns. Product placement has gained popularity in movies, television shows, and video games.

In addition, it is difficult to overstate the impact of the Internet on the promotional mix of 21st-century marketers—for small and large companies alike. Even individual entrepreneurs find the Internet to be a lucrative launchpad for their enterprises.

But even though cyberspace marketing has been effective in business-to-business transactions and, to a lesser extent, for some types of consumer purchases, a major source of Internet revenues is advertising.

Integrating marketing communications into an overall consumer-focused strategy that meets a company's promotional and business objectives has become more and more critical in the busy global marketplace. Chapter 16 will examine specific ways marketers can use advertising and public relations to convey their messages; then Chapter 17 will discuss personal selling, sales force management, and sales promotion in the same manner.

Review of Chapter Objectives

1 Explain how integrated marketing communications relates to the development of an optimal promotional mix.

Integrated marketing communications (IMC) refers to the coordination of all promotional activities to produce a unified, customer-focused promotional message. Developing an optimal promotional mix involves selecting the personal and nonpersonal selling strategies that will work best to deliver the overall marketing message as defined by IMC.

2 Describe the communication process and how it relates to the AIDA concept.

In the communication process, a message is encoded and transmitted through a communications channel; then it is decoded, or interpreted by the receiver; finally, the receiver provides feedback, which completes the system. The AIDA concept (attention, interest, desire, action) explains the steps through which a person reaches a purchase decision after being exposed to a promotional message. The marketer sends the promotional message, and the consumer receives and responds to it via the communication process.

3 Explain how the promotional mix relates to the objectives of promotion.

The objectives of promotion are to provide information, stimulate demand, differentiate a product, accentuate the value of a product, and stabilize sales. The promotional mix, which is the blend of numerous variables intended to satisfy the target market, must fulfill the overall objectives of promotion.

4 Identify the different elements of the promotional mix and explain how marketers develop an optimal promotional mix.

The different elements of the promotional mix are personal selling and nonpersonal selling (advertising, product placement, sales promotion, direct marketing, and public relations). Guerrilla marketing is frequently used by marketers with limited funds and firms attempting to attract attention for new-product offerings with innovative promotional approaches. Marketers develop the optimal mix by considering the nature of the market, the nature of the product, the stage in the product lifecycle, price, and funds available for promotion.

5 **Describe the role of sponsorships and direct marketing in integrated marketing communications.**

Sponsorship, which occurs when an organization provides money or in-kind resources to an event or activity in exchange for a direct association with the event or activity, has become a hot trend in promotion. The sponsor purchases access to an activity's audience and the image associated with the activity, both of which contribute to the overall promotional message delivered by a firm. Direct marketing involves direct communication between a seller and a B2B or final customer. It includes such promotional methods as telemarketing, direct mail, direct-response advertising and infomercials on TV and radio, direct-response print advertising, and electronic media.

6 **Discuss the factors that influence the effectiveness of a promotional mix.**

Marketers face the challenge of determining the best mix of components for an overall promotional strategy. Several factors influence the effectiveness of the promotional mix: (1) the nature of the market, (2) the nature of the product, (3) the stage in the product lifecycle, (4) price, and (5) the funds available for promotion.

7 **Contrast pushing and pulling strategies.**

In a pulling strategy, marketers attempt to stimulate final-user demand, which then exerts pressure on the distribution channel. In a pushing strategy, marketers attempt to promote the product to channel members rather than final users. To do this, they rely heavily on personal selling.

8 **Explain how marketers budget for and measure the effectiveness of promotion.**

Marketers may choose among several methods for determining promotional budgets, including percentage-of-sales, fixed-sum-per-unit, meeting competition, or task-objective, which is considered the most flexible and most effective. Today, marketers use either direct sales results tests or indirect evaluation to measure effectiveness. Both methods have their benefits and drawbacks because of the difficulty of controlling variables.

9 **Discuss the value of marketing communications.**

Despite a number of valid criticisms, marketing communications provide socially important messages, are important to businesses, and have economic importance. As with every communication in society, it is important to consider how promotion is used rather than whether it is used at all.

assessment check: answers

1.1 Define *promotion*.

Promotion is the function of informing, persuading, and influencing the consumer's purchase decision.

1.2 What is the difference between marketing communications and integrated marketing communications (IMC)?

Marketing communications are messages that deal with buyer–seller relationships, from a variety of media. IMC coordinates all promotional activities to produce a unified, customer-focused promotional message.

2.1 What are the three tasks accomplished by an effective message?

An effective message gains the receiver's attention; it achieves understanding by both receiver and sender; and it stimulates the receiver's needs and suggests an appropriate method of satisfying them.

2.2 Identify the four steps of the AIDA concept.

The four steps of the AIDA concept are attention, interest, desire, and action.

2.3 What is noise?

Noise represents interference at some stage in the communication process.

3.1 What are the objectives of promotion?

The objectives of promotion are to provide information to consumers and others, to increase demand, to differentiate a product, to accentuate a product's value, and to stabilize sales.

3.2 Why is product differentiation important to marketers?

Product differentiation, distinguishing a good or service from its competitors, is important to marketers because they need to create a distinct image in consumers' minds. If they can do so, they can then exert more control over variables such as price.

4.1 Differentiate between personal selling and nonpersonal selling.

Personal selling involves a promotional presentation conducted on a person-to-person basis with a buyer. Nonpersonal selling involves communication with a buyer in any way other than on a person-to-person basis.

4.2 What are the six major categories of nonpersonal selling?

The six major categories of nonpersonal selling are advertising, product placement, sales promotion, direct marketing, public relations, and guerrilla marketing.

5.1 Define *sponsorship*.

Sponsorship occurs when an organization pays money or in-kind resources to an event or activity in exchange for a direct association with that event or activity.

5.2 How is sponsorship different from advertising?

Although sponsorship generates brand awareness, the sponsor has little control over the message or even the coverage, unlike advertising.

5.3 Define *direct mail*.

Direct mail is communications in the form of letters, postcards, brochures, and catalogs containing marketing messages and sent directly to a customer or potential customer.

5.4 What are the benefits of electronic direct marketing?

Electronic media deliver data instantly to direct marketers and help them track customer buying cycles quickly.

6.1 What are the five factors that affect the choice of a promotional mix?

The five factors affecting the choice of a promotional mix are the nature of the market, the nature of the product, the stage in the product lifecycle, price, and the funds available for promotion.

6.2 Why is the choice of a mix a difficult task for marketers?

The choice of a mix is difficult because no quantitative measures are available to determine the effectiveness of each component in a given market segment.

7.1 What is a pulling strategy?

A pulling strategy is a promotional effort by the seller to stimulate final-user demand.

7.2   What is a pushing strategy?

A pushing strategy is an effort to promote a product to the members of the marketing channel.

8.1   What is the most common way of establishing a promotional budget?

The most common method of establishing a promotional budget is the percentage-of-sales method.

8.2   What is the task-objective budgeting method? Describe its two steps.

The task-objective method develops a promotional budget based on an evaluation of the firm's promotional objectives. Its two steps are defining realistic communication goals and determining the amount and type of promotional activity required for each objective.

8.3   What is the direct sales results test?

The direct sales results test reveals the specific impact on sales revenues for each dollar of promotional spending.

8.4   What is indirect evaluation?

Indirect evaluation helps researchers concentrate on quantifiable indicators of effectiveness.

9.1   Identify the three areas in which promotion exerts influence.

The three areas in which promotion exerts influence are society, business, and the economy.

Marketing Terms You Need to Know

promotion 490	promotional mix 500	guerrilla marketing 503
marketing communications 490	sales promotion 502	sponsorship 505
integrated marketing communications (IMC) 490	direct marketing 502	pulling strategy 514
AIDA concept 493	public relations 503	pushing strategy 514

Other Important Marketing Terms

sender 493	nonpersonal selling 501	fixed-sum-per-unit method 516
message 493	advertising 501	meeting competition method 516
encoding 494	product placement 501	task-objective method 516
decoding 494	trade promotion 502	direct sales results test 517
feedback 494	publicity 503	indirect evaluation 517
noise 494	ambush marketing 506	cost per impression 518
channel 494	direct mail 507	cost per response (click-throughs) 518
primary demand 498	telemarketing 508	conversion rate 518
selective demand 498	home shopping channel 509	public service announcements (PSAs) 519
product differentiation 499	infomercial 509	
personal selling 500	percentage-of-sales method 516	

Assurance of Learning Review

1. What is the role of integrated marketing communications (IMC) in a firm's overall marketing strategy? When executed well, what are its benefits?

2. Describe the five stages of communication.

3. What is the difference between primary demand and selective demand?

4. Differentiate between advertising and product placement. Which do you think is more effective, and why?

5. What are the benefits and drawbacks of publicity?

6. Why is sponsorship such an important part of a firm's IMC?

7. For each of the following goods and services, indicate which direct marketing channel or channels you think would be best:

   a. vacation time share
   b. denim jacket
   c. custom-made bracelet
   d. lawn care service
   e. magazine subscription

8. How does the nature of the market for a firm's goods or services affect the choice of a promotion method?

9. What is the difference between a pushing strategy and a pulling strategy?

10. What are two major ways of setting Internet advertising rates, and how do they work?

Projects and Teamwork Exercises

1. Not-for-profit organizations rely on IMC just as much as for-profit firms do. The Egyptian government, which owns the remains and artifacts of boy pharaoh King Tutankhamun, has sent the King Tut collection on a worldwide tour of selected nations and museums. Many organizers—including *National Geographic* and museums such as the Los Angeles County Museum of Art—were involved in a multimillion-dollar marketing campaign promoting the exhibit, titled Tutankhamun and the Golden Age of the Pharaohs. On your own or with a classmate, conduct online research to learn how museums and other organizers have used IMC to promote this or other tours. Present your findings to the class.

2. On your own or with a classmate, select a print advertisement that catches your attention and analyze it according to the AIDA concept (attention, interest, desire, action). Identify features of the ad that catch your attention, pique your interest, make you desire the product, and spur you toward a purchase. Present your findings to the class.

3. Watch a television show and see how many products you can find placed within the show. Present your findings to the class.

4. With a classmate, choose a good or service you think could benefit from guerrilla marketing. Imagine you have a limited promotional budget, and come up with a plan for a guerrilla approach. Outline several ideas and explain how you plan to carry them out. Present your plan to the class.

5. Evaluate two or three pieces of direct mail you received recently. Which items caught your attention and perhaps made you save the mailing? Which items did you toss in the trash without even opening or considering beyond an initial glance? Why?

Critical-Thinking Exercises

1. Choose one of the following products and discuss what you think the objective(s) of promotion should be for the product:

   a. beef
   b. Kraft Macaroni & Cheese
   c. Toyota Prius
   d. Verizon cell phone service

2. Identify a corporate sponsorship for a cause or program in your area, or find a local company that sponsors a local charity or other organization. What do you think the sponsor is gaining from its actions? Be specific. What does the sponsored organization receive? Do you think this sponsorship is good for your community? Explain.

3. What are some of the advantages and disadvantages of using a celebrity spokesperson to promote a good or service? How might this affect a firm's public relations efforts?

4. Take a careful look at a direct-mail catalog you have received recently. Who is the audience for the products? Did the firm target you correctly or not?

5. Describe a public service announcement you have seen recently. Do you believe the announcement will help the organization achieve its goals? Why or why not?

Ethics Exercise

Pop-up ads, those unsolicited messages that sometimes pop onto your computer screen and block the site or information you're looking for until you close or respond to them, are inexpensive to produce and cost nearly nothing to send. But they are so annoying to some computer users that dozens of special programs have been written to block them from appearing on the screen during Internet use.

1. Do you think that because they are unsolicited, pop-up ads are also intrusive? Are they an invasion of privacy? Explain your reasoning.

2. Do you consider the use of pop-up ads to be unethical? Why or why not?

Internet Exercises

1. **Guerrilla marketing.** Visit the Web site of Guerrilla Marketing International (www.gmarketing.com). Research at least two examples of how guerrilla marketing can fit into a firm's overall integrated marketing communication strategy. Print and bring relevant material to class so you can participate in a group discussion on the subject.

2. **Sponsorships.** Many companies use sponsorships as an important component of their integrated marketing communication strategy. One such company is Bank of America. Go to the Web site listed here (bankofamerica.com/sponsorships/) and prepare a report on how Bank of America uses sponsorships as part of its IMC strategy.

3. **AIDA.** Visit the Web sites of at least three different retailers. How does each apply the AIDA (attention, interest, desire, action) concept discussed in the chapter? Has one, in your opinion, been more successful than the others? If so, why?

Note: Internet Web addresses change frequently. If you don't find the exact sites listed, you may need to access the organization's or company's home page and search from there or use a search engine such as Google.

Case 15.1 Dubai Metro: Naming Rights Take a New Turn

The use of naming rights as a marketing communications tool goes back over half a century, when Anheuser-Busch proposed

renaming Sportsman's Park Budweiser Stadium. The resident St. Louis Cardinals rejected the idea but approved the name Busch Stadium, which Anheuser-Busch followed up with a new product called Busch Bavarian Beer.

FedEx Field in Washington, D.C., Minute Maid Park in Houston, The American Airlines Theater in New York, Coca-Cola Stadium in Xi'an, China, and the Sony Center for the Performing Arts in Toronto are just a few of the many recent multimillion-dollar naming deals, and plenty more are on the way. Perhaps none has attracted as much attention, however, as the Dubai Metro Project in the Middle East.

In full-page magazine ads in the United States and Europe, the Dubai Roads and Transport Authority (RTA) announced its lease offer of naming rights to the two lines and about half the 47 stations in its new metro system, a flagship project under construction. The rights, which the RTA calls "the ultimate branding and marketing opportunity" with "unmatched impact and visibility," will be available for at least 10 years, beginning with the 2009–2010 opening of the Metro, and the fees will help pay for the construction of the named stations. The remaining stations will be named for historic areas and landmarks in the rapidly growing city on the Persian Gulf.

"Within two weeks of launching the Dubai Metro Naming Rights project, more than 250 companies have expressed interest in getting the branding of metro stations in their name," says the RTA's chief executive. Another 120 submitted Request for Information forms. "These companies range from larger property and business firms and local and international banks, through to large multinational blue-chip corporations." The companies are headquartered in Japan, Greece, Spain, the United Kingdom, and India, among others. With bids starting at over $1.6 million a year, naming rights for at least eight stations have already been leased.

The Metro, an automatic, driverless rail system, will have stations both above ground and underground and is expected to carry about 600,000 passengers a day, with a maximum capacity of twice that number. Some Dubai residents oppose the leasing of naming rights on the grounds that the United Arab Emirates (UAE), of which Dubai is the main city, should instead name stations after prominent citizens and nearby landmarks. But a professor at UAE University says, "We are in a stage of globalization and all that it entails, including the mixing of cultures, civilizations, and nationalities. As long as the names don't contradict the values of the nation, there's nothing wrong with the idea."

Questions for Critical Thinking

1. What kind of companies do you think will be interested in leasing naming rights to the Dubai Metro stations? What benefits will they gain? Are there any drawbacks to the plan from the companies' point of view?

2. Following the RTA's announcement, the Toronto Transit Commission floated the idea of offering naming rights to some of the stations in Toronto's Metro system. Do you think the idea would work as well in an established system where familiar station names would be changed, as in a new system such as Dubai's? Why or why not?

Sources: Metro Naming Rights Web site, www.metronamingrights.com, accessed May 27, 2009; "Dubai Branding a Model for Others," *Business24/7,* August 5, 2008, www.business24-7.ae; Abbas Al Lawati, "To Name or Not to Name?" *Gulf News,* July 2, 2008, www.gulfnews.com; "Naming Rights: The Good, the Bad and the Ugly," *Kipp Report,* April 16, 2008, www.kippreport.com; "Dubai Metro Gets Huge Response to Branding Offer," *Gulf News,* April 15, 2008, archive.gulfnews.com; "Indian Firms Keen on Dubai Metro Naming Rights," *The Economic Times,* April 15, 2008, economictimes.indiatimes.com; "Dubai Metro Construction Still on Track for New Year," *Gulf News,* January 8, 2008, archive.gulfnews.com.

Video Case 15.2

Integrated Marketing Communications at Ogden Publications

The written video case on Ogden Publications appears on page VC-14. The Ogden Publications video is designed to expand and highlight the concepts in this chapter and the concepts and questions covered in the written video case.

CHAP **16** TER

Advertising and Public Relations

E*TRADE's Talking Toddler: A Media Star

Few sights are cuter than a sweet-faced cooing baby. But online brokerage company E*TRADE has showcased a different sort of child—an adorable little guy with a quick wit who seems to know

more about investing than most adults.

The irreverent E*TRADE Baby is the talkative star of a series of popular television commercials that highlight his mastery of online investing. The initial idea behind the ads was that if a baby can do it, online trading must be easy enough for a grown-up to try, too. The baby even multitasks while investing, text messaging his friends, taking calls on his Blackberry, and chatting to the camera about his active social life while confidently monitoring his online investments. He's been known to mock his baby friends for using expensive brokers instead of E*TRADE and to insult a grown-up golfing buddy for having the dismal skills of a "shankopotamus."

Making stock trading memorable, much less funny, isn't easy, especially during difficult economic times. But E*TRADE's spunky baby has helped the company succeed. He is cued during filming by his off-screen mom and assisted by an adult voice actor and a number of special-effects tricks. Despite what seems to be the complicated nature of online investing, viewers come away feeling that E*TRADE makes it so simple even a kid can do it.

Advertising during the Super Bowl, as E*TRADE has done for several years, is an expensive risk in the best of times but even more so during a recession. E*TRADE calculated that the risk was worth it to keep the visibility it needed to gain customers— and its strategy proved right. The talking baby ads consistently rank at or near the top of the industry's annual list of most memorable

Super Bowl ads. "History repeatedly has shown that those who continue to make smart marketing investments when economic times are uncertain are best positioned for success when the economy rebounds," says E*TRADE's chief marketing officer. "That's why, in this uncertain economic climate, reinforcing the strength of our brand and value proposition is critical."

The talking toddler fits well with E*TRADE's image as a maverick firm that encourages investors to take control of their own portfolios. That independence opens the door to better deals for customers because E*TRADE doesn't have the high overhead of other big, old-fashioned, brokerage firms. Fees for most trades are $9.99, with even lower rates for qualified customers. "E*TRADE has always flown in the face of traditional brokerages," says an executive of Grey New York, the agency that created the talking

baby ads. "And this little, financially savvy, street-wise baby has seemed to really tap a nerve with more independent investors." Through the baby's antics, they gain confidence that they can take charge and start managing their own financial portfolios .

Of course, a baby this smart has mastered social networking on the Web, too. He has his own branded YouTube channel showing commercial outtakes, a Twitter account, and a Facebook page. These additional media outlets build anticipation for each new ad and get people talking about it before and after it airs. All of these efforts create a buzz around the E*TRADE brand and generate interest from a wider audience than simply TV viewers. And if the baby made comments to the press about his popularity, he'd probably tell you that is exactly what a good advertising campaign is supposed to do.[1]

OBJECTIVES

 Identify the three major advertising objectives and the two basic categories of advertising.

 List the major advertising strategies.

 Describe the process of creating an advertisement.

4 Identify the major types of advertising appeals and discuss their uses.

 List and compare the major advertising media.

 Outline the organization of the advertising function and the role of an advertising agency.

7 Explain the roles of cross-promotion, public relations, publicity, and ethics in an organization's promotional strategy.

8 Explain how marketers assess promotional effectiveness.

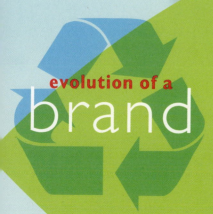
evolution of a
brand

E*TRADE, a publicly traded firm based in New York City, offers a wealth of financial products for individual investors, including trading and investing in stocks, options, mutual funds, bonds, and other financial instruments, as well as retirement planning and IRA accounts, education savings, checking and savings accounts, and credit cards. For its 2,000 corporate customers, who employ over a million people in 160 countries, it offers stock plan administration, recordkeeping, and reporting.

E*TRADE bases its business strategies on its "tireless effort to challenge the old ways of doing business" and regularly asking the question, "Can this be done better?"

• Like all firms in the financial industry, E*TRADE was hurt by the recent stock market plunge and recession. Left holding some subprime mortgage investments, the firm initially lost some customers in the crisis and missed its profit targets for several financial quarters. [Outdated statement] But with its online investing business remaining strong, emerging with record retail accounts and trading activity, the firm is making steady progress toward regaining its footing. It has even increased its market share, as investors

evolution of a brand
continued

migrate away from traditional brokerage firms. In what other ways do you think E*TRADE could use the talking baby to strengthen its brand among its 4.5 million customer accounts? Could any other industry or company benefit from the use of a similar symbol? If so, which?

- E*TRADE's corporate customers rely on its administrative services to help them set up and run their employee stock plans and comply with laws and regulations. Would you expect the talking baby to be an appropriate means of reaching more sophisticated customers like these? Why or why not? What other marketing strategies might be suited to E*TRADE's corporate business? Does E*TRADE risk anything in using the talking baby so often in its communications with the public? If so, what? Is it always a good idea for an advertiser to challenge the old ways of doing business?

chapter overview

From the last chapter, you already know the nonpersonal elements of promotion include advertising and public relations. Thousands of organizations rely on nonpersonal selling to develop their promotional mixes and integrated marketing communications strategies. Advertising is the most visible form of nonpersonal promotion, as witnessed by the success of the E*TRADE baby, and marketers often use it together with sales promotion (discussed in the next chapter) to create effective promotional campaigns. Television is probably the most obvious medium for nonpersonal selling dollars. But marketers are becoming increasingly creative in identifying new or unusual media through which to deliver their messages. General Motors has advertised its Turn-by-Turn OnStar navigation service on the seatback trays of U.S. Airways flights. The ad compares OnStar to an airplane copilot. OnStar's marketing director says his firm

chose the airline's seatback trays because consumers can't go to a store to purchase OnStar, so GM needs to go where they are to deliver its message.[2]

Other firms are banking on reaching consumers by beaming ads directly to their Bluetooth-enabled cell phones. Marketers hope the popularity of cell phones will help them reach younger consumers, who are spending less time with traditional advertising media such as television, newspapers, and magazines Even not-for-profit organizations like the Smithsonian Institution are experimenting with this medium. Two of the Smithsonian's art galleries now send messages to consumers' cell phone screens, promoting visiting exhibitions that run for specific periods of time.[3]

Marketers seeking excitement for new-product launches—and the rejuvenation of older products—pay millions for celebrities to promote their products. Glow by Jlo spawned a wave of new celebrity fragrances, while Nicole Kidman became the new face of the classic Chanel No. 5 perfume. Teenage singer Rihanna signed on to promote Totes umbrellas by singing a tune called "Umbrella" that actually became a Grammy-winning hit. Rihanna insisted that Totes create a special line of umbrellas in her honor, with sparkly fabrics and glittering charms hanging from the handles. Sales of the umbrellas, like the song, went through the roof.[4]

This chapter begins with a discussion of the types of advertising and explains how advertising is used to achieve a firm's objectives. It then considers alternative advertising strategies and the process of creating an advertisement. Next, we provide a detailed look at various advertising media channels: television, radio, print advertising, direct mail, and outdoor and interactive media. The chapter then focuses on the importance of public relations, publicity, and cross-promotions. Alternative methods of measuring the effectiveness of both online and offline nonpersonal selling are examined. We conclude the chapter by exploring current ethical issues relating to nonpersonal selling.

Advertising

Advertising in the 21st-century is closely related to integrated marketing communications (IMC) in many respects. While IMC involves a message dealing with buyer–seller relationships, **advertising** consists of paid nonpersonal communication through various media with the purpose of informing or persuading members of a particular audience. Advertising is used by marketers to reach target markets with messages designed to appeal to business firms, not-for-profit organizations, or ultimate consumers.

The United States is home to many of the world's leading advertisers. Procter & Gamble, AT&T, and Verizon Communications top the list, each spending more than $3 billion annually on advertising.[5] Advertising spending varies among industries as well as companies. Retail, automotive, and telecommunications—including Internet services and their providers—make up the top three industries, spending $10 billion to $18 billion each year.[6]

As discussed in previous chapters, the emergence of the marketing concept, with its emphasis on a companywide consumer orientation, boosted the importance of integrated marketing communications. This change in turn expanded the role of advertising. Today, a typical consumer is exposed to hundreds of advertising messages each day. Advertising provides an efficient, inexpensive, and fast method of reaching the ever-elusive, increasingly segmented consumer market.

TYPES OF ADVERTISING

Advertisements fall into two broad categories: product advertising and institutional advertising.

❚ Identify the three major advertising objectives and the two basic categories of advertising.

Procter & Gamble, which produces Oral-B toothbrushes, is one of the world's leading advertisers.

Activia yogurt ads feature Jamie Lee Curtis persuading customers to buy the product.

© AP Images/PRNewsFoto/The Dannon Company, Inc.

Product advertising is nonpersonal selling of a particular good or service. This is the type of advertising the average person usually thinks of when talking about most promotional activities.

Institutional advertising, in contrast, promotes a concept, an idea, a philosophy, or the goodwill of an industry, company, organization, person, geographic location, or government agency. This term has a broader meaning than *corporate advertising* that typically is limited to nonproduct advertising sponsored by a specific profit-seeking firm. Institutional advertising often is closely related to the public relations function of an enterprise.

advertising Paid, nonpersonal communication through various media about a business firm, not-for-profit organization, product, or idea by a sponsor identified in a message intended to inform or persuade members of a particular audience.

product advertising Nonpersonal selling of a particular good or service.

institutional advertising Promotion of a concept, an idea, a philosophy, or the goodwill of an industry, company, organization, person, geographic location, or government agency.

informative advertising Promotion that seeks to develop initial demand for a good, service, organization, person, place, idea, or cause.

OBJECTIVES OF ADVERTISING

Marketers use advertising messages to accomplish three primary objectives: to inform, to persuade, and to remind. These objectives may be used individually or, more typically, in conjunction with each other. For example, an ad for a not-for-profit agency may inform the public of the existence of the organization and at the same time persuade the audience to make a donation, join the organization, or attend a function.

Informative advertising seeks to develop initial demand for a good, service, organization, person, place, idea, or cause. The promotion of any new market entry tends to pursue this objective because marketing success at this stage often depends simply on announcing availability. Therefore, informative advertising is common in the introductory stage of the product lifecycle, for Volkswagen's Jetta TDI clean diesel auto or for the next generation of Apple's iPhone, the 3G.

Persuasive advertising attempts to increase demand for an existing good, service, organization, person, place, idea, or cause. Persuasive advertising is a competitive type of promotion suited to the growth stage and the early part of the maturity stage of the product lifecycle. Recently, Dannon launched a campaign for its Activia yogurt designed to inform consumers about digestive health and persuade them of the importance—and ease—of maintaining it by eating Activia yogurt. The ads featured actress Jamie Lee Curtis in the role of the persuader.[7]

Reminder advertising strives to reinforce previous promotional activity by keeping the name of a good, service, organization, person, place, idea, or cause before the public. It is common in the latter part of the maturity stage and throughout the decline stage of the product lifecycle. Procter & Gamble, for instance, seeks to remind consumers of the energy savings gained by washing their laundry in cold water with Tide Coldwater formula.[8]

Figure 16.1 illustrates the relationship between advertising objectives and the stages of the product lifecycle. Informative advertising tends to work best during the early stages, while reminder advertising is effective later on. Persuasive advertising, if done well, can be effective through the entire lifecycle.

Traditionally, marketers stated their advertising objectives as direct sales goals. A more current and realistic stan-

figure 16.1

Advertising Objectives in Relation to Stage in the Product Lifecycle

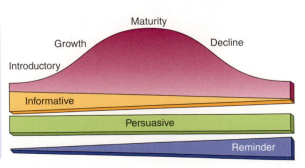

dard, however, views advertising as a way to achieve communications objectives—including informing, persuading, and reminding potential customers of the product. Advertising attempts to condition consumers to adopt favorable viewpoints toward a promotional message. The goal of an ad is to improve the likelihood that a customer will buy a particular good or service. In this sense, advertising illustrates the close relationship between marketing communications and promotional strategy.

To get the best value for a firm's advertising investment, marketers must first determine a firm's advertising objectives. Effective advertising can enhance consumer perceptions of quality in a good or service, leading to increased customer loyalty, repeat purchases, and protection against price wars. In addition, perceptions of superiority pay off in the firm's ability to raise prices without losing market share.

reminder advertising
Advertising that reinforces previous promotional activity by keeping the name of a good, service, organization, person, place, idea, or cause before the public.

assessment check

1. What are the goals of institutional advertising?

2. At what stage in the product lifecycle are informative ads used? Why?

3. What is reminder advertising?

Advertising Strategies

If the primary function of marketing is to bring buyers and sellers together, then advertising is the means to an end. Effective advertising strategies accomplish at least one of three tasks: informing, persuading, or reminding consumers. The secret to choosing the best strategy is developing a message that best positions a firm's product in the audience's mind. Among the advertising strategies available for use by 21st-century marketers are comparative advertising and celebrity advertising as well as decisions about global and interactive ads. Channel-oriented decisions, such as retail and cooperative advertising, can also be devised.

Marketers often combine several of these advertising strategies to ensure the advertisement accomplishes set objectives. As markets become more segmented, the need for personalized advertising increases. The next sections describe strategies that contemporary marketers may use to reach their target markets.

2 List the major advertising strategies.

COMPARATIVE ADVERTISING

Firms whose products are not the leaders in their markets often favor **comparative advertising**, a promotional strategy that emphasizes advertising messages with direct or indirect comparisons to dominant brands in the industry. By contrast, advertising by market leaders seldom acknowledges that competing products even exist, and when they do, they usually do not point out any benefits of the competing brands.

Wireless telecommunications carriers have been battling it out in media advertising, promoting their calling plans and inviting comparison to competitors. Some offer "in" calling, free text messaging, no roaming charges, or extended hours at reduced rates to compete against similar offers from other companies.

A generation ago, comparative advertising was not the norm; in fact, it was frowned on. But the Federal Trade Commission now encourages comparative advertising. Regulators believe such ads keep marketers competitive and consumers better informed about their choices. Generally speaking, when competition through advertising exists, prices tend to go down because people can shop around. This benefit has proved increasingly true for online consumers, who now use shopping bots to help find the best prices on goods and services.

comparative advertising
Advertising strategy that emphasizes messages with direct or indirect promotional comparisons between competing brands.

CELEBRITY TESTIMONIALS

A popular technique for increasing advertising readership in a cluttered promotional environment and improving overall effectiveness of a marketing message involves the use of celebrity spokespeople, such as New York Giants quarterback Eli Manning. About one of every five U.S. ads

briefly speaking

"As a profession advertising is young; as a force it is as old as the world. The first four words ever uttered, 'Let there be light,' constitute its charter. All nature is vibrant with its impulse."

—Bruce Barton (1886–1967)
AMERICAN AUTHOR AND ADVERTISING EXECUTIVE

WE ARE ALL WITNESSES.

CLEVELAND 23

Believe at nikebasketball.com

© AP Images/PRNewsFoto/Nike, Inc.

NBA star LeBron James is among the highest-paid product endorsers.

currently includes celebrities. This type of advertising is also popular in foreign countries. In Japan, a majority of ads use celebrities, both local and international stars. While U.S. celebrities are popular, Asian sports stars—such as basketball player Yao Ming—have risen to prominence. However, it is important for companies to be sure their brand's tie to a celebrity makes sense and is genuine.[9]

Both the number of celebrity ads and the dollars spent on those ads have increased in recent years. Professional athletes such as NBA Cleveland Cavalier's star LeBron James are among the highest-paid product endorsers, raking in millions each year. James currently claims about $170 million total in endorsement deals, including $90 million from Nike, $15 million from The Coca-Cola Company, and several-million-dollar deals with outdoor power equipment maker Cub Cadet, trading-card company Upper Deck, and Bubblicious bubble gum. Note that some of the firms, such as Nike and Upper Deck, are related to sports; others, such as Coke, Cub Cadet, and Bubblicious, have nothing to do with basketball at all.[10] The top five endorsement superstars—in recent annual earnings—are golfer Tiger Woods, $100 million; golfer Phil Mickelson, $47 million; LeBron James, $25 million; NASCAR driver Dale Earnhardt, Jr., $25 million; and golfer Michelle Wie, $19.5 million.[11]

One advantage of associations with big-name personalities is improved product recognition in a promotional environment filled with hundreds of competing 15- and 30-second commercials. Advertisers use the term *clutter* to describe this situation. As e-marketing continues to soar, one inevitable result has been the increase in advertising clutter as companies rush to market their goods and services online. But marketers need to remember that an effective online site must have meaningful content and helpful service.

Another advantage to using celebrities occurs when marketers try to reach consumers of various ethnic groups. Blockbuster Video and McDonald's have hired Hispanic stars to attract Hispanic consumers to their stores. Actress Daisy Fuentes appeared in ads for McDonald's, while John Leguizamo and Hector Elizondo advertised for Blockbuster.

A celebrity testimonial generally succeeds when the celebrity is a credible source of information for the promoted product. The most effective ads of this type establish relevant links between the celebrities and the advertised goods or services. A recent ad for Vitaminwater featured several prominent NBA players, including Kobe Bryant and LeBron James. Several studies of consumer responses show that celebrities improve the product's believability, recall of the product, and brand recognition. Celebrity endorsements also create positive attitudes, leading to greater brand equity. Although he already had about $5 million a year in endorsements—including deals with credit card firm Visa and swimming apparel maker Speedo—swimmer Michael Phelps received a rush of offers after winning eight gold medals in a single Olympics. Reasoning that people wanted to be associated with anything that Phelps represented, companies that wanted to enhance their brand recognition made all kinds of offers to him. The head of global sports management at Visa observed that Phelps "came out of [the Olympic] games a global sports icon."[12]

However, a celebrity who endorses too many products may create marketplace confusion. Customers may remember the celebrity but not the product or brand; worse, they might connect the celebrity to a competing brand. Another problem arises if a celebrity is linked with scandal or encounters legal problems. When NFL player Michael Vick was hit with charges related to dogfighting, Nike, one of Vick's most important endorsers, suspended its contract and stopped selling merchandise endorsed by the football star in its retail stores.[13]

Some advertisers try to avoid problems with celebrity endorsers by using cartoon characters as endorsers. Snoopy, a character in the popular "Peanuts" comic strip and long-running TV animated programs, has appeared in MetLife ads for years. Some advertisers may actually prefer cartoon characters because the characters can never say anything negative about the product, they do exactly what the marketers want them to do, and they cannot get involved in scandals. The only drawback is high licensing fees; popular animated characters often cost more than live celebrities. Companies may create their own cartoon characters or talking animals, which eventually become celebrities in their own right as a result of many appearances in advertisements, as is the case with the Geico gecko and Duke the dog who appears in ads for Bush's Baked Beans.

MetLife avoids possible problems with celebrity endorsers by using Snoopy cartoon characters in advertising.

© Mike Simons/Getty Images

In recent years, marketers have begun to consider celebrities as marketing partners rather than pretty or famous faces who can sell goods and services. Tiger Woods has been active in developing Nike's golf gear and apparel. Former supermodel Claudia Schiffer not only agreed to endorse a signature line of Palm Pilots but also helped position the handheld computers in the electronics market by selecting fashionable colors and her own favorite software programs.

RETAIL ADVERTISING

Most consumers are confronted daily with **retail advertising,** which includes all advertising by retail stores that sell goods or services directly to the consuming public. While this activity accounts for a sizable portion of total annual advertising expenditures, retail advertising varies widely in its effectiveness. One study showed that consumers often respond with suspicion to retail price advertisements. Source, message, and shopping experience seem to affect consumer attitudes toward these advertisements.

An advertiser once quipped that the two most powerful words to use in an ad are "New" and "Free"—and these terms often are capitalized on in retail ads. Although "Free" may be featured only in discussions of customer services, the next best term—"Sale"—often is the centerpiece of retail promotions. And "New" typically describes new product lines. However, many retail stores continue to view advertising as a secondary activity, although that is changing. Local independent retailers rarely use advertising agencies, probably because of the expense involved. Instead, store managers may accept responsibility for advertising in addition to their other duties. Management can begin to correct this problem by assigning one individual the sole responsibility and authority for developing an effective retail advertising program.

A retailer often shares advertising costs with a manufacturer or wholesaler in a technique called **cooperative advertising**. For example, an apparel marketer may pay a percentage of the cost of a retail store's newspaper advertisement featuring its product lines. Cooperative advertising campaigns originated to take advantage of the media's practice of offering lower rates to local advertisers than to national ones. Later, cooperative advertising became part of programs to improve dealer relations. The retailer likes the chance to secure advertising that it might not be able to afford otherwise. Cooperative advertising can strengthen vertical links in the marketing channel, as when a manufacturer and retailer coordinate their resources. It can also involve firms at the same level of the supply chain. In a horizontal arrangement, a group of retailers—for example, all the Ford dealers in a state—might pool their resources.

cooperative advertising
Strategy in which a retailer shares advertising costs with a manufacturer or wholesaler.

INTERACTIVE ADVERTISING

Millions of advertising messages float across idle—and active—computer screens in homes and offices around the country every day. Net surfers play games embedded with ads from the site sponsors. Companies offer free e-mail service to people willing to receive ads with their personal messages. Video screens on grocery carts display ads for shoppers to see as they wheel down the aisles of grocery stores.

Because marketers realize that two-way communications provide more effective methods for achieving promotional objectives, they are interested in interactive media. **Interactive advertising** involves two-way promotional messages transmitted through communication channels that induce message recipients to participate actively in the promotional effort. Achieving this involvement is the difficult task facing contemporary marketers. Although interactive advertising has become nearly synonymous with e-marketing and the Web, it also includes other formats such as kiosks in shopping malls and text messages on cell phones. Multimedia technology, the Internet, and commercial online services are changing the nature of advertising from a one-way, passive communication technique to more effective, two-way marketing communications. Interactive advertising creates dialogue between marketers and individual shoppers, providing more materials at the user's request. The advertiser's challenge is to gain and hold consumer interest in an environment where these individuals control what they want to see.

Interactive advertising changes the balance between marketers and consumers. Unlike the traditional role of advertising—providing brief, entertaining, attention-catching messages—interactive media provide information to help consumers throughout the purchase and consumption processes. In a sense, it becomes closer to personal selling as consumers receive immediate responses to questions or requests for more information about goods and services. Interactive advertising provides consumers with more information in less time to help them make necessary comparisons between available products.

Successful interactive advertising adds value by offering the viewer more than just product-related information. A Web site can do more than display an ad to promote a brand; it can create a company store, provide customer service, and offer additional content. And many marketers, at companies both large and small, hope such ads will soon be so finely targeted that they can cut through increasing advertising clutter and reach only consumers ready to hear their messages. In one survey, marketers learned that 80 percent of viewers who watched videos on broadcaster ABC's Web site could recall who the advertiser was, while very few could remember the names of advertisers they saw during a network TV broadcast.[14]

Most firms deliver their interactive advertising messages through proprietary online services and through the Web. And online ad spending is climbing—it increased 26 percent during a recent year, to more than $26 billion.[15]

assessment check

1. What is comparative advertising?
2. What makes a successful celebrity testimonial?
3. What is cooperative advertising?

3 **Describe the process of creating an advertisement.**

Creating an Advertisement

Marketers spend about $280 billion a year on advertising campaigns in the United States alone.[16] With so much money at stake, they must create effective, memorable ads that increase sales and enhance their organizations' images. They cannot afford to waste resources on mediocre messages that fail to capture consumers' attention, communicate their sales message effectively, or lead to a purchase, donation, or other positive action for the organization.

Research helps marketers create better ads by pinpointing goals an ad needs to accomplish, such as educating consumers about product features, enhancing brand loyalty, or improving consumer perception of the brand. These objectives should guide the design of the ad. Marketers can also discover what appeals to consumers and can test ads with potential buyers before committing funds for a campaign.

Marketers sometimes face specific challenges as they develop advertising objectives for services. They must find a creative way to fill out the intangible images of most services and successfully convey the benefits consumers receive. The "You're in Good Hands" message of Allstate Insurance is a classic example of how advertising can make the intangible nature of services tangible.

TRANSLATING ADVERTISING OBJECTIVES INTO ADVERTISING PLANS

Once a company defines its objectives for an advertising campaign, it can develop its advertising plan. Marketing research helps managers make strategic decisions that guide choices in technical areas such as budgeting, copywriting, scheduling, and media selection. Posttests, discussed in greater detail later in the chapter, measure the effectiveness of advertising and form the basis for feedback concerning possible adjustments. The elements of advertising planning are shown in Figure 16.2. Experienced marketers know the importance of following even the most basic steps in the process, such as market analysis.

As Chapter 9 explained, positioning involves developing a marketing strategy that aims to achieve a desired position in a prospective buyer's mind. Marketers use a positioning strategy that distinguishes their good or service from those of competitors. Effective advertising then communicates the desired position by emphasizing certain product characteristics, such as performance attributes, price/quality, competitors' shortcomings, applications, user needs, and product classes.

Advertising Messages

The strategy for creating a message starts with the benefits a product offers to potential customers and moves to the creative concept phase, in which marketers strive to bring an appropriate message to consumers using both visual and verbal components. Marketers work to create an ad with meaningful, believable, and distinctive appeals—one that stands out from the clutter and is more likely to escape "zapping" by the television remote control or clicking by a mouse.

Ads usually are created not individually, but as part of specific campaigns. An **advertising campaign** is a series of different but related ads that use a single theme and appear in different media within a specified time period. Retail chain Target's "Hello.... Good Buy" ads featuring the Beatles' music is one example. Different products flash across the screen in the spots, but all have the catchy song playing in the background while the familiar red bull's-eye logo appears.

In developing a creative strategy, advertisers must decide how to communicate their marketing message. They must balance message characteristics—such as the tone of the appeal, the extent of information provided, and the conclusion to which it leads the consumer—the side of the story the ad tells, and its emphasis on verbal or visual primary elements.

figure 16.2

Elements of the Advertising Planning Process

Consideration of constraints and uncontrollable factors

Research Inputs
Consumer research
Product research
Market analysis
Competitive analysis

Strategic Decisions
Setting objectives
Identifying and selecting target markets
Selecting message and media strategy
Coordinating with other marketing mix elements

Tactical Execution
Establish advertising budget
Establish controls
Write and produce ads and commercials
Select and schedule media choices
Pretest advertising alternatives

Feedback

Measuring Advertising Effectiveness
Use posttests to determine the effectiveness of advertising

Advertising Evaluation
Evaluate results of advertising
Make necessary adjustments

assessment check

1. What is an advertising campaign?
2. What are an advertisement's three main goals?

advertising campaign
Series of different but related ads that use a single theme and appear in different media within a specified time period.

ADVERTISING APPEALS

Should the tone of the advertisement focus on a practical appeal such as price or gas mileage, or should it evoke an emotional response by appealing to, say, fear, humor, sex, guilt, or fantasy? This

4 **Identify the major types of advertising appeals and discuss their uses.**

is another critical decision in the creation of memorable ads that possess the strengths needed to accomplish promotional objectives.

Fear Appeals

In recent years, marketers have relied increasingly on fear appeals. Ads for insurance, autos, health-care products, and even certain foods imply that incorrect buying decisions could lead to illness, injury, or other bad consequences. Even ads for business services imply that if a company doesn't purchase the advertised services, its competitors will move ahead or valuable information may be lost.

Pharmaceutical companies spend several billion dollars a year on advertising, much of which is directed toward consumer fears—whether it's a fear of hair loss, allergic attacks, or heart attacks and other potentially serious illnesses. These drug advertisements have flourished in both print and broadcast media after the Food and Drug Administration lifted a ban on prescription drug advertising on television. While drug firms insist these advertisements are informative to consumers, critics charge that a high percentage use fear appeals and very few provide enough details about causes and risk factors for medical conditions or lifestyle changes that might bring about the same results as the drug.[17]

Fear appeals can backfire, however. Viewers are likely to practice selective perception and tune out statements they perceive as too strong or not credible. Some consumer researchers believe viewer or reader backlash will eventually occur due to the amount of prescription drug advertising based on fear appeals.

Humor in Advertising Messages

A humorous ad seeks to create a positive mood related to a firm's goods or services. In an effort to show how innovative and cool its Macs are compared with PCs, Apple recently ran a series of ads featuring a cool dude, the Mac, upstaging a geeky PC. The ads are funny—and memorable.

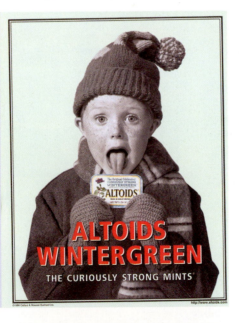

Humorous ads seek to be memorable and to create a positive mood related to a firm's goods.

ALTOIDS WINTERGREEN
THE CURIOUSLY STRONG MINTS

© Image courtesy of The Advertising Archives

But advertising professionals differ in their opinions of the effectiveness of humorous ads. Some believe humor distracts attention from brand and product features; consumers remember the humor but not the product. Humorous ads, because they are so memorable, may lose their effectiveness sooner than ads with other kinds of appeals. In addition, humor can be tricky because what one group of consumers finds funny may not be funny at all to another group. Men and women sometimes have a different sense of humor, as do people of different ages. This distinction may become even greater across cultures.

Ads Based on Sex

Ads with sex-based appeals immediately attract the consumer's attention. Advertisements for Victoria's Secret lingerie and clothing are designed this way. While many people accept these and other ads, they do not appeal to everyone. And marketers using sex-based appeals know they walk a fine line between what is acceptable to the consumers they want to reach—and what is not. Sometimes a firm's image can be hurt by its advertising approach. Clothing firm American Apparel is well known for its provocative advertising, and company head Dov Charney has received criticism for his firm's sex-based ads. But Charney insists his ads are effective with his targeted audience. "We make sexy T-shirts for young people," he argues. "Young people like honesty."[18]

DEVELOPING AND PREPARING ADS

The final step in the advertising process—the development and preparation of an advertisement—should flow logically from the promotional theme selected. This process should create an ad that becomes a complementary part of the marketing mix with a carefully determined role in the total marketing strategy. Preparation of an advertisement should emphasize features such as its creativity, its continuity with past advertisements, and possibly its association with other company products.

What immediate tasks should an advertisement accomplish? Regardless of the chosen target, an advertisement should (1) gain attention and interest, (2) inform or persuade, and (3) eventually lead to a purchase or other desired action. It should gain attention in a productive way; that is, it should instill some recall of the good or service. Otherwise, it will not lead to buying action.

Gaining attention and generating interest—cutting through the clutter—can be formidable tasks. Stimulating buying action often is difficult because an advertisement cannot actually close a sale. Nevertheless, if an ad gains attention and informs or persuades, it probably represents a worthwhile investment of marketing resources. Too many advertisers fail to suggest how audience members can purchase their products if they desire to do so. Creative design should eliminate this shortcoming.

The Head & Shoulders ad in Figure 16.3 shows the four major elements of this print advertisement: headline, illustration, body copy, and signature. *Headlines* and *illustrations* (photographs, drawings, or other artwork) should work together to generate interest and attention. *Body copy* informs, persuades, and stimulates buying action. The *signature,* which may include the company name, address, phone number, Web address, slogan, trademark, or simply a product photo, names the sponsoring organization. An ad may also have one or more headings subordinate to the main headline that either link the main headline to the body copy or subdivide sections of the body copy.

After advertisers conceive an idea for an ad that gains attention, informs and persuades, and stimulates purchases, their next step involves refining the thought sketch into a rough layout. Continued refinements of the rough layout eventually produce the final version of the advertisement design ready to be executed, printed, or recorded.

The creation of each advertisement in a campaign requires an evolutionary process that begins with an idea and ultimately results in a finished ad ready for distribution through print or electronic media. The idea itself must first be converted into a thought sketch—a tangible summary of the intended message. Advances in technology allow advertisers to create novel, eye-catching advertisements. Innovative computer software packages allow artists to merge multiple images to create a single image with a natural, seamless appearance.

CREATING INTERACTIVE ADS

Web surfers want engaging, lively content that takes advantage of the medium's capabilities and goes beyond what they find elsewhere. The Web's major advantages make it possible for advertisers to provide that, offering speed, information, two-way communications, self-directed entertainment, and personal choice. Web ads are also vibrant in their visual appeal, and some believe they will not experience the swings in spending that traditional ad media do.[19]

Web ads have grown from information-based home pages to innovative, interactive channels for transmitting messages to cyberaudiences, including banners, pop-ups, keyword ads, advertorials, and interstitials. *Advergames* are either online games created by marketers to promote their products to

figure 16.3

Elements of a Typical Ad

© Image courtesy of The Advertising Archives

targeted audiences in an interactive way or ads or product placements inserted into online video games. Automakers use these product placements to reach younger audiences—those who may not watch their TV commercials as often. JCPenney created an advergame called "Dork Dodge" to support its new Dorm Life brand of clothing and furniture. Targeted for incoming college women, the game—and the brand—hits on life situations freshmen are likely to encounter. Game players make choices in a pop-up menu, which uses humor to help freshmen women avoid guys they don't want to date. "Dork Dodge" was launched during the summer, as college students were getting ready for the upcoming school year and purchasing clothes and furnishings for their dorm rooms.[20]

Banners, advertisements on a Web page that link to an advertiser's site, are the most common type of advertising on the Web. They can be free of charge or cost thousands of dollars per month, depending on the amount of hits the site receives. Online advertisers often describe their Internet ads in terms of "richness," referring to the degree to which new technologies—such as streaming video, 3-D animation, JavaScript, and interactive capabilities—are implemented in the banners. One recent technological development is the banner with a video layer. When a user scrolls over the banner, a floating layer is displayed. When the user scrolls off the banner, the layered ad disappears.[21]

Banners have evolved into a more target-specific technique for Internet advertising with the advent of *missiles:* messages that appear on the screen at exactly the right moment. When a customer visits the site of Company A's competitor, a missile can be programmed to appear on the customer's monitor, allowing the customer to click a direct link to Company A's site. However, many people feel the use of such missiles is a questionable practice.

Keyword ads are an outcropping of banner ads. Used in search engines, keyword ads appear on the results page of a search and are specific to the searched term. Advertisers pay search engines to target their ads and display the banners only when users search for relevant keywords, allowing marketers to target specific audiences. For example, if a user searched for the term "digital camera," keyword ads might appear for electronic boutiques or camera shops that sell digital cameras and film.

Banner designs that have also evolved into larger advertising squares that closely resemble advertisements in the telephone book's Yellow Pages are called *advertorials.* Advertisers quickly expanded on these advertorials with *interstitials*—ads that appear between Web pages of related content. Interstitials appear in a separate browser window while the user waits for a Web page to download.

Then there are pop-ups—little advertising windows appearing in front of the top window of a user's computer screen—and "pop-unders" that appear under the top window. Many users complain that interstitials, like pop-ups and missiles, are intrusive and unwanted. Interstitials are more likely to contain large graphics and streaming presentations than banner ads and therefore are more difficult to ignore than typical banner ads. But despite complaints, some studies show that users are more likely to click interstitials than banners.

Perhaps the most intrusive form of online advertising is *adware,* which allows ads to be shown on users' screens via software downloaded to their computers without their consent or through trickery. Such software can be difficult to remove, and some industry experts believe that marketers should avoid dealing with Internet marketing firms that promote the use of adware.

Social network advertising on sites such as FaceBook and MySpace is a new form of online advertising receiving attention. Although firms spend an estimated $3 billion a year on this type of advertising, it is difficult to evaluate and measure its effectiveness. For example, if a virtual bottle of Coca-Cola appears on FaceBook or in an online game, how likely is it that consumers will actually purchase the bottle of Coke the next time they want something to drink?[22]

assessment check

1. What are some common emotional appeals used in advertising?

2. What are the main types of interactive ads?

5 **List and compare the major advertising media.**

Media Selection

One of the most important decisions in developing an advertising strategy is the selection of appropriate media to carry a firm's message to its audience. The media selected must be capable of accomplishing the communications objectives of informing, persuading, and reminding potential customers of the good, service, person, or idea advertised.

Research identifies the ad's target market to determine its size and characteristics. Advertisers then match the target characteristics with the media best able to reach that particular audience. The objective of media selection is to achieve adequate media coverage without advertising beyond the identifiable limits of the potential market. Finally, cost comparisons between alternatives should determine the best possible media purchase.

Table 16.1 compares the major advertising media by noting their shares of overall advertising expenditures. It also compares the advantages and disadvantages of each media alternative. *Broadcast media* include television (network and cable) and radio. Newspapers, magazines, outdoor advertising, and direct mail represent the major types of print media. Electronic media include the Internet and kiosks. A recent study projected that many firms will shift away from traditional advertising and more toward direct marketing—especially Internet and mobile media—in the next few years.[23]

TELEVISION

Television—network and cable combined—still accounts for almost one of every three advertising dollars spent in the United States.[24] The attractiveness of television advertising is that marketers can reach local and national markets. Whereas most newspaper advertising revenues come from local advertisers, the greatest share of television advertising revenues comes from organizations that advertise nationally. A newer trend in television advertising is virtual ads—banner-type logos and brief messages superimposed

table 16.1 **Comparison of Advertising Media Alternatives**

Media Outlet	Percentage of Total Spending*	Advantages	Disadvantages
Broadcast			
Broadcast television networks	17.1	Extensive coverage; repetition; flexibility; prestige	High cost; brief message; limited segmentation
Cable television networks	12.1	Same strengths as network TV; less market coverage because not every viewer is a cable subscriber	Same disadvantages as network TV, although cable TV ads are targeted to more-specific viewer segments
Radio	7.2	Immediacy; low cost; flexibility; segmented audience; mobility	Brief message; highly fragmented audience
Print			
Newspapers	18.9	Tailored to individual communities; ability to refer back to ads	Limited life
Direct mail	NA	Selectivity; intense coverage; speed; flexibility; opportunity to convey complete information; personalization	High cost; consumer resistance; dependence on effective mailing list
Magazines (consumer and business)	20.4	Selectivity; quality image reproduction; long life; prestige	Flexibility is limited
Outdoor (out of home)	2.7	Quick, visual communication of simple ideas; link to local goods and services; repetition	Brief exposure; environmental concerns
Electronic			
Internet	7.6	Two-way communications; flexibility; link to self-directed entertainment	Poor image reproduction; limited scheduling options; difficult to measure effectiveness

* Direct mail was not included in the data. In addition to broadcast network and cable TV advertising, syndicated TV totaled 2.8 percent and spot TV 11.3 percent of ad spending.

Source: Data from "Ad Spending Totals by Medium," *Advertising Age's* Data Center, June 30, 2008, www.adage.com. Reprinted with permission from the February 27, 2006, issue of *Advertising Age*. Copyright © Crain Communications, Inc., 2006.

onto television coverage of sporting events so they seem to be a part of the arena's signage but cannot be seen by anyone attending the game. Then there are streaming headlines run by some news stations and paid for by corporate sponsors whose names and logos appear within the news stream.

Other trends in television advertising include the abbreviated spot—a 15- or 30-second ad that costs less to make and buy and is too quick for most viewers to zap with their remote control—and single-advertiser shows. These advertisements work well when viewers are watching live, but as more consumers record programs with DVRs, as many as 85 percent fast-forward through even the briefest commercials.[25]

Web site Hulu has become one of the top video destinations on the Internet, where viewers can watch complete, high-resolution episodes of current TV programs on their computers. The site is free and does not require any additional wires or boxes for access. Instead, viewers see brief ads they seem to tolerate in order to watch their favorite shows. In the first three months of activity, Hulu amassed more than 700 shows that fans could watch.[26]

In the past decade, cable television's share of ad spending and revenues has grown tremendously. Satellite television has contributed to increased cable penetration; almost three-fourths of all Americans now have cable installed in their homes. In response to declining ratings and soaring costs, network television companies such as NBC, CBS, ABC, Fox, and the CW (a network formed by the merger of the WB and UPN) are refocusing their advertising strategies with a heavy emphasis on moving onto the Internet to capture younger audiences.

Because cable audiences have grown, programming has improved, and ratings risen, advertisers have earmarked more of their advertising budgets for this medium. Cable advertising offers marketers access to more narrowly defined target audiences than other broadcast media can provide—a characteristic referred to as *narrowcasting*. The great variety of special-interest channels devoted to subjects such as cooking, golf, history, home and garden, health, fitness, and various shopping channels attract specialized audiences and permit niche marketing.

Television advertising offers the advantages of mass coverage, powerful impact on viewers, repetition of messages, flexibility, and prestige. Its disadvantages include loss of control of the promotional message to the telecaster, which can influence its impact; high costs; and some public distrust. Compared with other media, television can suffer from lack of selectivity because specific TV programs may not reach consumers in a precisely defined target market without a significant degree of wasted coverage. However, the growing specialization of cable TV channels can help resolve the problem. Finally, some types of products are banned from television advertising. Tobacco goods, such as cigarettes, cigars, and smokeless tobacco, fall into this category.

Television commercials can promote more than a firm's products; they can highlight the organization's efforts to improve the environment, the communities in which the firm does business, and other causes important to the company. S.C. Johnson, manufacturer of a wide range of well-known household products, recently ran commercials showcasing the firm's commitment to the environment, as described in the "Marketing Success" feature.

MARKETING SUCCESS   S.C. Johnson's Commitment to Clean Power

Background. S.C. Johnson has been in business since 1886, when its founder first offered Johnson's Paste Wax to the marketplace. Today, the company makes hundreds of household products, including Windex and Glade. The firm has made a significant investment in developing and adopting processes that reduce waste and pollution, rely on renewable energy resources, and reuse and recycle materials.

The Challenge. Recently, company marketers decided that informing the public not just about its products but also about its green production processes would be a positive marketing message. Developing a television commercial for its products that could also showcase these efforts in just a few seconds was the objective.

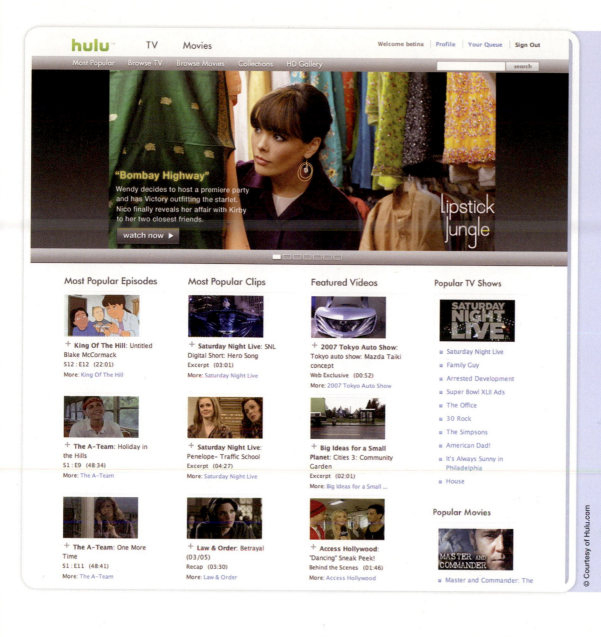

Hulu.com viewers can watch complete, high-resolution episodes of current TV programs. The only cost is time—to get to the show, they must watch brief ads.

The Strategy. The resulting commercial alluded to one of Johnson's ambitious projects—converting its Waxdale plant in Racine, Wisconsin, to power produced from garbage. The facility is now run by two turbines that get their power from methane—produced by decaying organic matter—retrieved from a local landfill. The methane gas is piped to the nearby plant, where it runs through the turbines to create power. The advertisement illustrated Johnson's commitment to both high-quality products and green processes.

The Outcome. Consumers have reacted positively to the message and are better informed about Johnson's household products and its environmental commitment. Although the ultimate goal was to create messages about products like Off! and Pledge, the advertising sent a powerful message to consumers about the company itself.

Sources: Company Web site, scjohnson.com/environment, accessed June 2, 2009; Joy LePree, "Save the Planet and Turn a Profit," *Chem.info*, www.chem.info, accessed August 12, 2008; "SC Johnson's Products and Production ... You Can Feel Good about It," *PR Newswire*, June 30, 2008, www.prnewswire.com.

RADIO

Radio advertising has always been a popular media choice for up-to-the-minute newscasts and for targeting advertising messages to local audiences. But in recent years, radio has become one of the fastest-growing media alternatives. As more and more people find they have less and less time, radio provides immediate information and entertainment at work, at play, and in the car. In addition, as e-business continues to grow globally, more people are traveling abroad to seek out new markets. For these travelers, radio stations, including those aired over the Internet, are a means of staying in touch with home—wherever that may be. Marketers frequently use radio advertising to reach local audiences. But in recent years, it plays an increasingly important role as a national— and even global—listening favorite. Thousands of online listeners use the Internet to tune in to radio stations from almost every city—an easy-listening station in London, a top 40 Hong Kong broadcaster, or a chat show from Toronto. Other listeners equip their vehicles with satellite radio to maintain contact with hometown or destination stations during long trips.

Satellite radio offers much higher-quality digital signals than regular radio stations, with many more channels mostly free of Federal Communications Commission oversight and generally commercial free. XM Radio, the first such service to be licensed, began airing commercials on a few of its nearly 200 music, sports, and talk channels. XM and its competitor, Sirius, both charged an annual subscription fee. When the two merged, they agreed initially to offer à la carte pricing, under which subscribers could select the programming they preferred. Fans of Howard Stern, Opie & Anthony, and other popular radio personalities could still get the shows they wanted.[27]

Advertisers like radio for its ability to reach people while they drive because they are a captive audience. Stations can adapt to local preferences by changing format, such as going from country and western to an all-news or sports station. The variety of stations allows advertisers to easily target audiences and tailor their messages to those listeners. Other benefits include low cost, flexibility, and mobility. Even established Internet firms see the benefit of radio advertising: Yahoo! ran radio ads in the San Francisco Bay Area touting its new features, including search assist, short cuts, and multimedia results; the company also wanted to convince consumers that it is a better alternative than Google.[28]

Disadvantages to radio advertising include highly segmented audiences (reaching most people in a market may require ads placed on multiple stations), the temporary nature of messages (unlike print ads, radio and TV ads are instantaneous and must be broadcast again to reach consumers a second time), and a minimum of research information compared with television.

While most radio listening is often done in cars or with headset-equipped portables, technology has given birth to Internet radio. Webcast radio allows customers to widen their listening times and choices through their computers. The potential for selling on this new channel is great. Recently, Clear Channel Radio, CBS Radio, Citadel Broadcasting's ABC Radio, and seven other firms formed the HD Digital Radio Alliance to launch a mobile marketing campaign. "Mobile marketing is the area that everyone wants to move to, so we came up with a mobile component to their marketing campaign to engage potential consumers," explains a spokesman for the company that created the campaign.[29]

NEWSPAPERS

Newspaper advertising continues to dominate local markets, accounting for nearly 19 percent, or slightly more than $28 billion, of annual advertising expenditures.[30] In addition to retail advertisements, classified advertising is an important part of newspaper revenues. Although some have predicted the decline of newspaper audiences, if online readers are counted in, newspapers are more popular than ever. Several thousand newspapers have their own Web sites, which attracted more than 66 million visitors, or 40 percent of all Internet users, in one quarter during a recent year. Although newspaper advertising as a whole has decreased, activity on newspaper Web sites has increased dramatically, creating new opportunities for marketers.[31]

Newspapers' primary advantages start with flexibility because advertising can vary from one locality to the next. Newspapers also allow intensive coverage for ads. Readers sometimes keep the printed advertising message, unlike television or radio advertising messages, and can refer back to newspaper ads. Newspaper advertising does have some disadvantages: hasty reading and relatively poor reproduction quality, although that is changing as technology improves. The high quality of ads in *USA Today* is an example of the recent strides in newspaper ad quality made possible by new technologies.

Newspapers have also begun to struggle to "get through the noise" of other advertisers. To retain big advertisers such as trendy designers and national retailers, some have launched their own annual or semiannual fashion magazines, taking advantage of their finely tuned distribution capabilities.

MAGAZINES

Advertisers divide magazines into two broad categories: consumer magazines and business magazines. These categories are also subdivided into monthly and weekly publications. The top five magazines in terms of circulation are *AARP The Magazine, AARP Bulletin, Reader's Digest, Better Homes and Gardens,* and *National Geographic.*[32] The primary advantages of magazine advertising include the ability to reach precise target markets, quality reproduction, long life, and the prestige associated with some magazines, such as *National Geographic.* The primary disadvantage is that magazines lack the flexibility of newspapers, radio, and television.

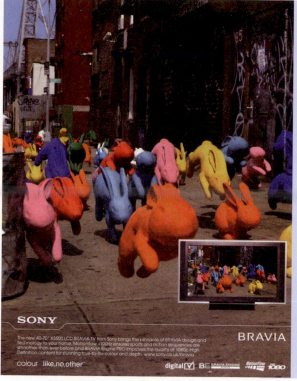

Magazines are a prime place for advertisement. This Sony Bravia ad appeared in business technology magazines.

© Image courtesy of The Advertising Archives

Media buyers study circulation numbers and demographic information for various publications before choosing optimal placement opportunities and negotiating rates. The same advertising categories have claimed the title for big spenders for several years running. Automotive, retail, and movies and media advertising have held their first, second, and third places, respectively, each year and have continued to show strong growth percentages. Advertisers seeking to promote their products to target markets can reach them by advertising in the appropriate magazines.

DIRECT MAIL

As discussed in Chapter 14, direct-mail advertising includes sales letters, postcards, leaflets, folders, booklets, catalogs, and house organs—periodicals published by organizations to cover internal issues. Its advantages come from direct mail's ability to segment large numbers of prospective customers into narrow market niches, speed, flexibility, detailed information, and personalization. Disadvantages of direct mail include high cost per reader, reliance on the quality of mailing lists, and some consumers' resistance to it.

The advantages of direct mail explain its widespread use. Data are available on previous purchase patterns and preferred payment methods as well as household characteristics such as number of children or seniors. Direct mail accounts for nearly $62 billion of advertising spending annually.[33] The downside to direct mail is clutter, otherwise known as *junk mail.* So much advertising material is stuffed into people's mailboxes every day that the task of grabbing consumers' attention and evoking some interest is daunting to direct mail advertisers. Also, many consumers find direct mail annoying.

OUTDOOR ADVERTISING

Outdoor advertising, sometimes called *out-of-home advertising,* is perhaps the oldest and simplest media business around. It represents 2.7 percent of total advertising spending.[34] Traditional outdoor advertising takes the form of billboards, painted displays such as those that appear on the walls of buildings, and electronic displays. Transit advertising includes ads placed both inside and outside buses, subway trains and stations, and commuter trains. Some firms place ads on the roofs of taxicabs, on bus stop shelters and benches, on entertainment and sporting event turnstiles, in public restrooms, and even on parking meters. A section of highway might be cleaned up by a local real estate company or restaurant, with a nearby sign indicating the firm's contribution. All these are forms of outdoor advertising.

Outdoor advertising quickly communicates simple ideas. It also offers repeated exposure to a message and strong promotion for locally available products. Outdoor advertising is particularly effective along metropolitan streets and in other high-traffic areas.

But outdoor advertising, just like every other type, is subject to clutter. It also suffers from the brevity of exposure to its messages by passing motorists. Driver concerns about rush-hour safety and limited time also combine to limit the length of exposure to outdoor messages. As a result, most of these ads use striking, simple illustrations, short selling points, and humor to attract people interested in products such as beverages, vacations, local entertainment, and lodging.

A third problem relates to public concerns over aesthetics. The Highway Beautification Act of 1965, for example, regulates the placement of outdoor advertising near interstate highways. In addition, many cities have local ordinances that set regulations on the size and placement of outdoor advertising messages, and Hawaii prohibits them altogether.

New technologies are helping revive outdoor advertising. Technology livens up the billboards themselves with animation, large sculptures, and laser images. Digital message signboards can display winning lottery numbers or other timely messages such as weather and traffic reports. Recently, Google used outdoor advertising to promote its Google Maps feature—the ads have appeared in buses and trains in San Francisco and Chicago, and an ad was placed in San Francisco's AT&T Park. Maps are now considered an important factor in grabbing a significant portion of online and mobile ad dollars, meaning that the maps themselves need to be advertised. "This is a popular consumer product, and Google is promoting it as part of its long-term strategy to win, grow, and maintain usage," observes one marketing researcher for a firm that specializes in online advertising. Traffic at Google Maps has increased more than 300 percent.[35]

INTERACTIVE MEDIA

Interactive media—especially the Internet—are growing up. Keyword ads dominate online advertising, accounting for more than 30 percent of annual online ad spending around the world.[36] Not surprisingly, interactive advertising budgets are beefing up at a growing number of companies.

Ads have already come to cell phones, as video and broadcast capabilities explode. CBS Mobile and CBS Mobile Sports have joined forces with the social networking service Loopt, through which subscribers can track participating friends and family on their cell phones. Using Loopt's GPS-based technology, CBS Mobile offers opportunities for advertisers to target promotions at consumers as they walk by certain stores and restaurants.[37]

OTHER ADVERTISING MEDIA

As consumers filter out appeals from traditional and Internet ads, marketers need new ways to catch their attention. In addition to the major media, firms use a vast number of other vehicles to communicate their messages. One such device is Total Immersion's D'Fusion system, consisting of a kiosk, Web cameras, and software that can recognize, track, and render images on the screen. At the kiosk, customers can see themselves on a screen through the Webcam while holding up a two-dimensional brochure of an advertiser's product. The system transforms the picture into a three-dimensional image of

Company logos and messages can be placed on cars for mobile advertising.

© AP Images/PRNewsFoto/Signs By Tomorrow

the consumer with the product. Marketers believe this type of system increases an advertiser's engagement with the consumer in a new way.[38]

Ads also appear on T-shirts, inlaid in store flooring, in printed programs of live theater productions, and as previews on movie DVDs. Directory advertising includes the familiar Yellow Pages in telephone books, along with thousands of business directories. Some firms pay to have their advertising messages placed on hot-air balloons, blimps, banners behind airplanes, and scoreboards at sporting events. Individuals sometimes agree to paint their own vehicles with advertising messages or tattoo them onto their bodies—for a fee. Johnson & Johnson, Yahoo!, and Dreyer's Ice Cream, among others, pay to have their logos and company messages placed on autos via Autowrapped (www.autowrapped.com). The drivers are chosen based on their driving habits, routes, occupations, and living and working locations and are paid a monthly fee for the use of the outside of their vehicles as advertising space.

Media Scheduling

Once advertisers have selected the media that best match their advertising objectives and promotional budget, attention shifts to **media scheduling**—setting the timing and sequence for a series of advertisements. A variety of factors influence this decision—sales patterns, repurchase cycles, and competitors' activities are the most important variables.

Seasonal sales patterns are common in many industries. An airline might reduce advertising during peak travel periods and boost its media schedule during low travel months. Repurchase cycles may also play a role in media scheduling—products with shorter repurchase cycles will more likely require consistent media schedules throughout the year. Competitors' activities are still other influences on media scheduling. A small firm may avoid advertising during periods of heavy advertising by its rivals.

Advertisers use the concepts of reach, frequency, and gross rating points to measure the effectiveness of media scheduling plans. *Reach* refers to the number of different people or households exposed to an advertisement at least once during a certain time period, typically four weeks. *Frequency* refers to the number of times an individual is exposed to an advertisement during a certain time period. By multiplying reach times frequency, advertisers quantitatively describe the total weight of a media effort, which is called the campaign's *gross rating point (GRP)*.

Recently, marketers have questioned the effectiveness of reach and frequency to measure ad success online. The theory behind frequency is that the average advertising viewer needs a minimum of three exposures to a message to understand it and connect it to a specific brand. For Web surfers, the "wear-out" is much quicker—hence, the greater importance of building customer relationships through advertisements.

A media schedule is typically created in the following way. Say an auto manufacturer wants to advertise a new model designed primarily to appeal to professional consumers in their 30s. The model would be introduced in November with a direct mail piece offering test drives. Outdoor, newspaper, and magazine advertising would support the direct mail campaign but also follow through the winter and into the spring and summer.

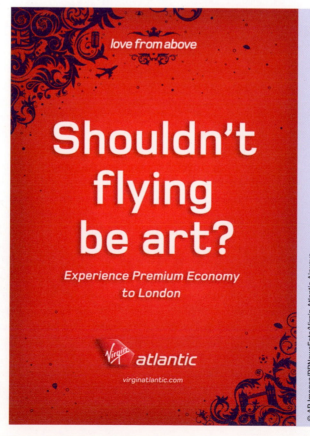

love from above

Shouldn't flying be art?

Experience Premium Economy to London

Virgin atlantic

virginatlantic.com

© AP Images/PRNewsFoto/Virgin Atlantic Airways

The airline industry often boosts its advertising during low-travel months.

Early television commercials might air during a holiday television special in mid-December, and then one or more expensively produced, highly creative spots would be first aired during the Super Bowl in late January. Another television commercial—along with new print ads—might be scheduled for fall clearance sales as the manufacturer gets ready to introduce next year's models. This example illustrates how marketers might plan their advertising year for just one product.

⑥ Outline the organization of the advertising function and the role of an advertising agency.

Organization of the Advertising Function

Although the ultimate responsibility for advertising decision making often rests with top marketing management, organizational arrangements for the advertising function vary among companies. A producer of a technical industrial product may operate with a one-person department within the company who primarily writes copy for submission to trade publications. A consumer-goods company, on the other hand, may staff a large department with advertising specialists.

The advertising function is usually organized as a staff department reporting to the vice president (or director) of marketing. The director of advertising is an executive position with the responsibility for the functional activity of advertising. This position requires not only a skilled and experienced advertiser but also an individual who communicates effectively within the organization. The success of a firm's promotional strategy depends on the advertising director's willingness and ability to communicate both vertically and horizontally. The major tasks typically organized under advertising include advertising research, design, copywriting, media analysis, and in some cases, sales and trade promotion.

ADVERTISING AGENCIES

advertising agency Firm whose marketing specialists help advertisers plan and prepare advertisements.

Most large companies in industries characterized by sizable advertising expenditures hire an independent **advertising agency**, a firm whose marketing specialists help businesses plan and prepare advertisements. Advertising is a huge, global industry. Ranked by worldwide revenue, the top five ad agencies worldwide are Tokyo-based Dentsu, followed by four New York–based agencies: BBDO, McCann Erickson Worldwide, DDB Worldwide, and TBWA Worldwide.[39]

Most large advertisers cite several reasons for relying on agencies for at least some aspects of their advertising. Agencies typically employ highly qualified specialists who provide a degree of creativity and objectivity difficult to sustain in a corporate advertising department. Smaller firms find they can benefit from the knowledge and experience of specialists as well. In the extremely competitive advertising industry, the firm Crispin Porter + Bogusky has emerged as one of the hottest agencies of this decade. Partner Alex Bogusky is known in the industry for creating ads that had car buyers flocking to the Mini Cooper. Recently, he revived Burger King's 1960s-era "King" character, making it an icon for a new generation. He even brought back the deceased Orville Redenbacher, using old footage of the popcorn tycoon in new ads. Now he faces one of his biggest assignments: to make Microsoft seem cooler than rival Apple. Crispin Porter + Bogusky is headquartered in Boulder, Colorado—far from the center of advertising action in New York. But the firm has grown to 12 times its size in the past six years and will likely continue to expand as it attracts more and more large clients.[40]

Figure 16.4 shows a hypothetical organization chart for a large advertising agency. Although job titles may vary among agencies, the major functions may be classified as creative services; account services; marketing services, including media services, marketing research, and

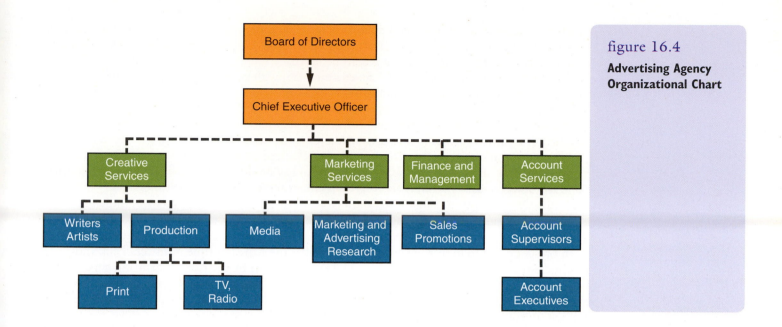

figure 16.4

Advertising Agency Organizational Chart

sales promotion; and finance and management. Whatever organization structure it selects, an agency often stands or falls on its relationships with its clients. The fast pace and pressure of ad agencies are legendary, but good communication remains paramount to maintaining that relationship.

assessment check

1. What is the role of an advertising agency?

2. What are some advantages of using an agency?

Public Relations

7 **Explain the roles of cross-promotion, public relations, publicity, and ethics in an organization's promotional strategy.**

In Chapter 15, we defined public relations as the firm's communications and relationships with its various publics, including customers, employees, stockholders, suppliers, government agencies, and the society in which it operates. Organizational public relations efforts date back to 1889, when George Westinghouse hired two people to publicize the advantages of alternating-current electricity and to refute arguments originally championed by Thomas Edison for direct-current systems.

Public relations is an efficient, indirect communications channel through which a firm can promote products, although it serves broader objectives than those of other components of promotional strategy. It is concerned with the prestige and image of all parts of the organization. Today, public relations plays a larger role than ever within the promotional mix, and it may emphasize more marketing-oriented information. In addition to its traditional activities, such as surveying public attitudes and creating a good corporate image, PR also supports advertising in promoting the organization's goods and services.

Although there are about 50,000 public relations managers in the United States, nearly 200,000 people actually work in the public relations field for both profit-centered and not-for-profit organizations.[41] Public relations is in a period of major growth as a result of increased public pressure on industries regarding corporate ethical conduct and environmental and international issues. International expenditures on public relations are growing more rapidly than those for advertising and sales promotion. Many top executives are becoming more involved in public relations as well. The public expects top managers to take greater responsibility for company actions than they have accepted in the past. Those who refuse are widely criticized.

The PR department is the link between the firm and the media. It provides press releases and holds news conferences to announce new products, the formation of strategic alliances, management changes, financial results, or similar developments. The PR department may also issue its own publications, including newsletters, brochures, and reports. When a barge accident caused an oil spill on the lower Mississippi River, the City of New Orleans issued a press release informing the public of corrective actions that would be taken.[42]

A PR plan begins much like an advertising plan, with research to define the role and scope of the firm's overall public relations and current challenges. Next come strategic decisions on short-term and long-term goals and markets, analysis of product features, and choices of messages and media channels—or other PR strategies such as speaking engagements or contests—for each market. Plan execution involves developing messages highlighting the benefits the firm brings to each market. The final step is to measure results. The Internet has changed some PR planning, as PR representatives now have more direct access to the public instead of having their messages filtered through journalists and the news media. This direct access gives them greater control over their messages.

To win its effort to merge with South Korean truck manufacturer Daewoo, Indian automaker Tata Motors launched a full-scale public relations effort. Tata executives took Korean language classes, company communications were translated into Korean, and Tata executives made in-person presentations to local Korean officials as well as the Korean prime minister. Tata, India's largest industrial group, wanted to be viewed in a positive light by the Korean firm and general public, so it used the same public relations strategy it had in its successful quest to acquire the Tetley Tea company in England. Tata's main message was respect for each firm's workers, which was a key factor in its success with both.[43]

MARKETING AND NONMARKETING PUBLIC RELATIONS

Nonmarketing public relations refers to a company's messages about general management issues. When a company makes a decision that affects any of its publics, input from public relations specialists can help smooth its dealings with those publics. A company that decides to close a plant would need advice on how to deal with the local community, while a firm dealing with a long strike might try to achieve a favorable attitude from the public. Either of these situations might be considered a crisis, as would a massive product recall. Companies that have a plan of action and can effectively handle a crisis by generating positive public relations generally can survive these types of crises, as discussed in the "Etiquette Tips for Marketing Professionals" feature. Although companies typically organize their public relations departments separately from their marketing divisions, PR activities invariably affect promotional strategies.

In contrast, **marketing public relations (MPR)** refers to narrowly focused public relations activities that directly support marketing goals. MPR involves an organization's relationships with consumers or other groups about marketing concerns and can be either proactive or reactive.

With proactive MPR, the marketer takes the initiative and seeks out opportunities for promoting the firm's products, often including distribution of press releases and feature articles. For example, companies send press releases about new products to newspapers, television stations, and relevant consumer, business, and trade publications. It is a powerful marketing tool because it adds news coverage that reinforces direct promotion activities.

Reactive MPR responds to an external situation that has potential negative consequences for an organization. As China's reputation began to slip due to recalls of toxic pet food and children's toys containing lead paint, the U.S. public relations firm Ogilvy PR got involved in helping turn the country's image around. The firm provided the Chinese government with guidance in communicating to the American public about the actions being taken to correct the situation.[44]

PUBLICITY

publicity Nonpersonal stimulation of demand for a good, service, place, idea, person, or organization by unpaid placement of significant news regarding the product in a print or broadcast medium.

The aspect of public relations most directly related to promoting a firm's products is **publicity**: nonpersonal stimulation of demand for a good, service, place, idea, person, or organization by unpaid placement of significant news regarding the product in a print or broadcast medium. It has been said that if advertising is the hammer, publicity is the nail. It creates credibility for the advertising to follow. Firms generate publicity by creating special events, holding press conferences, and preparing news releases and media kits. Many firms, such as Starbucks and Wal-Mart's Sam's Club, built their brands with virtually no advertising. Carl's Jr. and the Drycleaning & Laundry Institute

Etiquette Tips for Marketing **Professionals**

How to Handle a Business Crisis

every business faces crises during its lifetime. While most crises are relatively small—a lost order, a missed meeting with a client—some are genuinely massive in scale. Recalls such as the one for hundreds of thousands of toys manufactured overseas because they contained lead paint, warnings about the safety of such foods as tomatoes and lemons, and revelations about unethical mortgage practices create real public relations crises for individual firms as well as entire industries. But crises can be managed effectively. Here are a few tips for handling a business crisis:

- *Have a plan in place.* Establish a plan for dealing with crises before one ever arises. Appoint key people to communicate and lead.

- *Pay attention.* If a bad situation seems to be unfolding, don't ignore it. Get the facts. Put your plan into action. A lack of action and communication usually makes the situation worse.

- *Communicate.* You will probably have to communicate several times during the crisis and afterward. Be direct and concise. Provide necessary information and show concern and empathy for those affected. Do not speculate or offer untested theories. Reassure listeners that communication will continue.

- *Apologize if appropriate.* If you or your firm has made a mistake, acknowledge it. Apologize and then focus on solutions.

- *Find solutions to the problem.* Work with colleagues, customers, or others in the industry, if necessary, to correct the problem causing the crisis. This may mean finding both an immediate and a long-term solution.

- *Follow through.* If you make a promise to resolve the situation, be sure to follow through. If your firm promises to replace all defective products with new ones, do so.

Sources: "How to Maintain Control During a Crisis," *Seegert Marketing.com,* www.seegertmktg.com, accessed June 2, 2009; "How to Communicate in a Business Crisis," *eHow,* www.ehow.com, accessed June 2, 2009; Aileen Pincus, "How to Handle a Crisis," *BusinessWeek,* September 24, 2007, www.businessweek.com; Adelia Cellini Linecker, "How to Handle a Crisis," *Investor's Business Daily,* April 12, 2007, www.investorsdaily.com.

(DLI) recently generated some humorous publicity when the two launched a joint campaign telling consumers not to worry about the "messiest menu items" on Carl's menus—any stains could be removed by their local drycleaners. DLI sent "Chili Cheese Burger & Fries—A Celebration of Messy Goodness" to its drycleaning members, authorizing them to give away coupons for free Chili Cheese Burgers & Fries at Carl's restaurants. Customers ate up the challenge.[45]

While publicity generates minimal costs compared with other forms of promotion, it does not deliver its message entirely for free. Publicity-related expenses include the costs of employing marketing personnel assigned to create and submit publicity releases, printing and mailing costs, and related expenses.

Firms often pursue publicity to promote their images or viewpoints. Other publicity efforts involve organizational activities such as plant expansions, mergers and acquisitions, management changes, and research breakthroughs. A significant amount of publicity, however, provides information about goods and services, particularly new products.

Because many consumers consider news stories to be more credible than advertisements as sources of information, publicity releases often are sent to media editors for possible inclusion in news stories. The media audiences perceive the news as coming from the communications media, not the sponsors. The information in a publicity release about a new good or service can provide valuable assistance for a television, newspaper, or magazine writer, leading to eventual broadcast or publication. Publicity releases sometimes fill voids in publications, and at other times, they become part of regular features. In either case, they offer firms valuable supplements to paid advertising messages.

Unfortunately, not every item of publicity is positive for a firm. Because a company cannot control the news that surrounds its decisions and actions, sometimes negative publicity creates poor images in consumers' minds. Airline travel, once regarded as an exciting adventure, has now become more of a chore. And as the airline industry struggles to survive increased costs, many

Solving an ethical controversy

Should Airline Passengers Have to Pay for a Soft Drink?

battling a high cost structure, the airline industry has done everything from slashing the number of flights between cities to cutting routes altogether. Now many are charging fees for checking baggage including curbside check-in, a premium for window seats, even a surcharge on pillows, blankets, snacks, and nonalcoholic beverages. Adding insult to injury—in the minds of consumer advocates as well as passengers—airlines now charge a fee for booking a flight using frequent flier miles. All of this adds up to bad publicity for the airline industry, no matter how much executives say their companies are suffering.

Should passengers foot the bill for airline services that were once free of charge?

PRO

1. As costs increase or decrease, firms must pass along cost increases or decreases to customers. Fuel costs have tripled in less than a decade, and the airlines must find ways to combat these cost increases.

2. Adopting à la carte pricing—charging a small fee for specific services—allows passengers the freedom to pick and choose which services they want and pay for those, without having to pay for those they do not want.

CON

1. The $3 to $5 that US Airways now charges for in-flight snacks and the $7 that JetBlue charges for a pillow and blanket annoy customers. Similarly, the $15 that American and others charge for the first checked bag doesn't sit well with flyers. Many consumers would rather just pay a higher ticket price.

2. Implementing a cluster of new fees all at once only aggravates customers. If the industry had adopted these fees over a period of time—say, several years—they would likely be more palatable to passengers and might not generate such bad publicity.

Summary

There appears to be no end in sight for the additional service fees, and the image of the airline industry is taking a beating in the press. Rumors circulated that airlines were even considering a surcharge for passengers who weigh significantly more than the average for their height and age. Whether this actually happens, the publicity generated around the speculation is not good for the airlines. Meanwhile, some airlines are using the publicity to their advantage. Southwest Airlines, which has so far not adopted à la carte pricing for its services, is poking fun at its competitors. The airline has launched a new series of advertisements with the tag line, "Fees don't fly with us."

Sources: Company Web sites, http://www.usairways.com and http://www .jetblue.com, accessed June 2, 2009; Michael Janofsky, "Airlines May Start Treating Passengers Like Freight," *Bloomberg.com*, August 11, 2008, www.bloomberg.com; Christopher Elliott, "Four New Airline Fees and How You Can Avoid Them," *San Francisco Chronicle*, August 3, 2008, www.sfgate.com; "Overweight Passengers Cost the Airlines Fuel," *Newsweek*, August 1, 2008, current.newsweek.com.

carriers have cut flights, raised fares, and added all sorts of fees. The result has been much bad publicity, as discussed in the "Solving an Ethical Controversy" feature.

Cross-Promotion

cross-promotion
Promotional technique in which marketing partners share the cost of a promotional campaign that meets their mutual needs.

In recent years, marketers have begun to combine their promotional efforts for related products using a technique called **cross-promotion**, in which marketing partners share the cost of a promotional campaign that meets their mutual needs—an important benefit in an environment of rising media costs. Relationship marketing strategies such as comarketing and cobranding, discussed in Chapter 10, are forms of cross-promotion. Marketers realize these joint efforts between established brands provide greater benefits in return for both organizations; investments of time and money on such promotions will become increasingly important to many partners' growth prospects. Recently Coldplay's "Viva la Vida" album was cross-promoted with Apple's iTunes Web site.

Measuring Promotional Effectiveness

8 Explain how marketers assess promotional effectiveness.

Each element of the promotional mix represents a major expenditure for a firm. Although promotional prices vary widely, advertisers typically pay a fee based on the cost to deliver the message to viewers, listeners, or readers—the so-called *cost per thousand (CPM)*. Billboards are the cheapest way to spend advertising dollars, with television and some newspapers the most expensive. But while price is an important factor in media selection, it is by no means the only one—or all ads would appear on billboards!

Because promotion represents such a major expenditure for many firms, they need to determine whether their campaigns accomplish appropriate promotional objectives. Companies want their advertising agencies and in-house marketing personnel to demonstrate how promotional programs contribute to increased sales and profits. Marketers are well aware of the number of advertising messages and sales promotions consumers encounter daily, and they know these people practice selective perception and simply screen out many messages.

By measuring promotional effectiveness, organizations can evaluate different strategies, prevent mistakes before spending money on specific programs, and improve their promotional programs. As the earlier discussion of promotional planning explained, any evaluation program starts with objectives and goals; otherwise, marketers have no yardstick against which to measure effectiveness. However, determining whether an advertising message has achieved its intended objective is one of the most difficult undertakings in marketing. Sales promotions and direct marketing are somewhat easier to evaluate because they evoke measurable consumer responses. Like advertising, public relations is also difficult to assess on purely objective terms.

MEASURING ADVERTISING EFFECTIVENESS

Measures to evaluate the effectiveness of advertising, although difficult and costly, are essential parts of any marketing plan. Without an assessment strategy, marketers will not know whether their advertising achieves the objectives of the marketing plan or whether the dollars in the advertising budget are well spent. To answer these questions, marketers can conduct two types of research. **Media research** assesses how well a particular medium delivers the advertiser's message, where and when to place the advertisement, and the size of the audience. Buyers of broadcast time base their purchases on estimated Nielsen rating points, and the networks have to make good if ratings do not reach promised levels. Buyers of print advertising space pay fees based on circulation. Circulation figures are independently certified by specialized research firms.

The other major category, **message research,** tests consumer reactions to an advertisement's creative message. Pretesting and posttesting, the two methods for performing message research, are discussed in the following sections.

As the role of marketing expands in many organizations, marketers are employing increasingly sophisticated techniques to measure marketing effectiveness not only throughout the company but through the entire marketing channel. As more firms also conduct multichannel promotional efforts, keeping track of the data is a challenge. However, when they do so, they can better track which channels are most effective.[46]

Pretesting

To assess an advertisement's likely effectiveness before it actually appears in the chosen medium, marketers often conduct **pretesting.** The obvious advantage of this technique is the opportunity to

briefly speaking

"If you think advertising doesn't pay—we understand there are 25 mountains in Colorado higher than Pikes Peak. Can you name one?"

—Anonymous

evaluate ads when they are being developed. Marketers can conduct a number of different pretests, beginning during the concept phase in the campaign's earliest stages, when they have only rough copy of the ad, and continuing until the ad layout and design are almost completed.

Pretesting employs a variety of evaluation methods. For example, focus groups can discuss their reactions to mock-ups of ads using different themes, headlines, or illustrations. To screen potential radio and television advertisements, marketers often recruit consumers to sit in a studio and indicate their preferences by pressing two buttons, one for a positive reaction to the commercial and the other for a negative reaction. Sometimes proposed ad copy is printed on a postcard that also offers a free product; the number of cards returned represents an indication of the copy's effectiveness. *Blind product tests* are also frequently used. In these tests, people are asked to select unidentified products on the basis of available advertising copy.

Mechanical and electronic devices offer yet another method of assessing how people read advertising copy. One mechanical test uses a hidden camera to photograph eye movements of readers. The results help advertisers determine headline placement and copy length. Another mechanical approach measures the galvanic skin response—changes in the electrical resistance of the skin produced by emotional reactions. Audiobrain creates unique sounds that helps advertisers brand their products; when consumers hear the sound—whether it's a tune, a voice, a bird call, a drop of rain, or another sound—they automatically think of the brand. McDonald's tests some of Audiobrain's created sounds in different restaurants to evoke different moods, then evaluates how those sound-created moods affect customers. If they are successful, the sounds become a part of in-store advertising.[47]

Posttesting

Posttesting assesses advertising copy after it has appeared in the appropriate medium. Pretesting generally is a more desirable measurement method than posttesting because it can save the cost of placing ineffective ads. However, posttesting can help in planning future advertisements and in adjusting current advertising programs.

In one of the most popular posttests, the *Starch Readership Report* interviews people who have read selected magazines to determine whether they observed various ads in them. A copy of the magazine is used as an interviewing aid, and each interviewer starts at a different point in the magazine. For larger ads, respondents are also asked about specifics, such as headlines and copy. Figure 16.5 shows a magazine advertisement with its Starch scores. All such *readership tests,* also called recognition tests, assume that future sales are related to advertising readership.

Unaided recall tests are another method of posttesting the effectiveness of advertisements. Respondents do not see copies of the magazine after their initial reading but are asked to recall the ads from memory. Podcasts are fast becoming a popular medium for advertisers because posttests reveal that unaided recall among respondents can be as high as 68 percent. Podtrac conducts such posttests, and observes that this is a much higher unaided recall rate than those for other offline and online media.[48]

Inquiry tests are another popular form of posttest. Advertisements sometimes offer gifts—generally product

figure 16.5

Magazine Advertisement with Starch Scores

© General Motors Corp. Used with permission, GM Media Archives.

"Noted %" indicates the percentage of readers interviewed who saw any part of the advertisement. 64% noted this ad.

"Associated %" indicates the percentage of readers interviewed who saw any part of the ad that indicates the brand or advertiser. 62% associated this ad with Chevrolet.

"Read Most %" indicates the percentage of readers interviewed who read more than half of the body copy. 22% read most of this ad.

"Read Some %" indicates the percentage of readers interviewed who read any amount of the body copy. 61% read some of this ad.

samples—to people who respond to them. The number of inquiries relative to the advertisement's cost forms a measure of its effectiveness.

Split runs allow advertisers to test two or more ads at the same time. Although advertisers traditionally place different versions in newspapers and magazines, split runs on cable television systems frequently test the effectiveness of TV ads. With this method, advertisers divide the cable TV audience or a publication's subscribers in two; half view advertisement A and the other half view advertisement B. The relative effectiveness of the alternatives is then determined through inquiries or recall and recognition tests.

Regardless of the exact method they choose, marketers must realize that pretesting and posttesting are expensive efforts. As a result, they must plan to use these techniques as effectively as possible.

MEASURING PUBLIC RELATIONS EFFECTIVENESS

As with other forms of marketing communications, organizations must measure PR results based on their objectives both for the PR program as a whole and for specific activities. In the next step, marketers must decide what they want to measure. This choice includes determining whether the message was heard by the target audience and whether it had the desired influence on public opinion.

The simplest and least costly level of assessment measures outputs of the PR program: whether the target audience received, paid attention to, understood, and retained the messages directed to them. To make this judgment, the staff could count the number of media placements and gauge the extent of media coverage. They could count attendees at any press conference, evaluate the quality of brochures and other materials, and pursue similar activities. Formal techniques include tracking publicity placements, analyzing how favorably their contents portrayed the company, and conducting public-opinion polls.

To analyze PR effectiveness more deeply, a firm could conduct focus groups, interviews with opinion leaders, and more detailed and extensive opinion polls. The highest level of effectiveness measurement looks at outcomes: Did the PR program change people's opinions, attitudes, and behavior? PR professionals measure these outcomes through before-and-after polls (similar to pretesting and posttesting) and more advanced techniques such as psychographic analysis (discussed in Chapter 5).

EVALUATING INTERACTIVE MEDIA

Marketers employ several methods to measure how many users view Web advertisements: *hits* (user requests for a file), *impressions* (the number of times a viewer sees an ad), and *click-throughs* (when the user clicks the ad to get more information). *View-through* rates measure responses over time. However, some of these measures can be misleading. Because each page, graphic, or multimedia file equals one hit, simple interactions can easily inflate the hit count, making it less accurate. To increase effectiveness, advertisers must give viewers who click through their site something good to see. Successful Web campaigns use demonstrations, promotions, coupons, and interactive features.

Internet marketers price ad banners based on cost per thousand (CPM). Web sites that sell advertising typically guarantee a certain number of impressions—the number of times an ad banner is downloaded and presumably seen by visitors. Marketers then set a rate based on that guarantee times the CPM rate.

assessment check

1. What is CPM and how is it measured?
2. Distinguish between media research and message research.
3. Describe several research techniques used in posttesting.

Ethics in Nonpersonal Selling

Chapter 3 introduced the topic of marketing ethics and noted that promotion is the element in the marketing mix that raises the most ethical questions. People actively debate the question of whether marketing communications contribute to better lives. The final section of this chapter takes a closer look at ethical concerns in advertising and public relations.

ADVERTISING ETHICS

Even though ads geared to children, ads promoting alcohol, and ads touting prescription drugs are technically legal, these types of promotions raise ethical issues. In the case of advertising aimed at children, when it comes to influencing parents' purchase decisions, nothing beats influencing kids. By promoting goods and services directly to children, firms can sell not only to them but to the rest of the household, too. But many parents and consumer advocates question the ethics of promoting directly to children. Their argument: at a time when kids need to learn how to consume thoughtfully, they are inundated with promotional messages teaching the opposite.

Another issue is the insertion of product messages in media programs without full disclosure of the marketing relationship to audiences. To woo younger consumers, especially teens and those in their 20s, advertisers attempt to make these messages appear as different from advertisements as possible; they design ads that seem more like entertainment.

Amid accusations that its ads were misleading, drug manufacturer Pfizer—maker of the cholesterol-lowering drug Lipitor—canceled ads featuring Robert Jarvik, one of the people who pioneered the invention of artificial hearts. Critics contended the ads created the impression he was a heart specialist. However, although Jarvik does have a medical degree, he is not a cardiologist and does not have a license to practice medicine.[49]

In cyberspace ads, it is often difficult to separate advertising from editorial content because many sites resemble magazine and newspaper ads or television infomercials. Another ethical issue surrounding advertising online is the use of **cookies,** small text files automatically downloaded to a user's computer whenever a site is visited. Each time the user returns to that site, the site's server accesses the cookie and gathers information: What site was visited last? How long did the user stay? What was the next site visited? Marketers claim this device helps them determine consumer preferences and argue that cookies are stored in the user's PC, not the company's Web site. The problem is that cookies can and do collect personal information without the user's knowledge.

Puffery and Deception

Puffery refers to exaggerated claims of a product's superiority or the use of subjective or vague statements that may not be literally true. A company might advertise the "most advanced system" or claim that its product is "most effective" in accomplishing its purpose.

Exaggeration in ads is not new. Consumers seem to accept advertisers' tendencies to stretch the truth in their efforts to distinguish their products and get consumers to buy. This inclination may provide one reason that advertising does not encourage purchase behavior as successfully as sales promotions do. A tendency toward puffery does raise some ethical questions, though: Where is the line between claims that attract attention and those that provide implied guarantees? To what degree do advertisers deliberately make misleading statements?

The *Uniform Commercial Code* standardizes sales and business practices throughout the United States. It makes a distinction between puffery and any specific or quantifiable statement about product quality or performance that constitutes an "express warranty," which obligates the company to stand behind its claim. General boasts of product superiority and vague claims are puffery, not warranties. They are considered so self-praising or exaggerated that the average consumer would not rely on them to make a buying decision.

A quantifiable statement, on the other hand, implies a certain level of performance. For example, tests can establish the validity of a claim that a brand of long-life light bulbs outlasts three regular light bulbs.

ETHICS IN PUBLIC RELATIONS

Several public relations issues open organizations to criticism. Various PR firms perform services for the tobacco industry; publicity campaigns defend unsafe products. Also, marketers must weigh ethics before they respond to negative publicity. For example, do firms admit to problems or product deficiencies, or do they try to cover them up? It should be noted that PR practitioners violate the Public Relations Society of America's Code of Professional Standards if they promote products or causes widely known to be harmful to others.

Strategic Marketing Implications of 21st Century in the

g reater portions of corporate ad budgets will migrate to the Web in the near future. This trend means marketers must be increasingly aware of the benefits and pitfalls of Internet advertising. But they should not forget the benefits of other types of advertising as well.

Promotion industry experts agree that e-business broadens marketers' job tasks, though many promotional objectives still remain the same. Today, advertisers need 75 different ways to market their products in 75 countries in the world and innumerable market segments. In years to come, advertisers also agree that channels will become more homogeneous while markets become more fragmented.

Review of Chapter Objectives

1   Identify the three major advertising objectives and the two basic categories of advertising.

The three major objectives of advertising are to inform, to persuade, and to remind. The two major categories of advertising are product advertising and institutional advertising. Product advertising involves the nonpersonal selling of a good or service. Institutional advertising is the nonpersonal promotion of a concept, idea, or philosophy of a company or organization.

2   List the major advertising strategies.

The major strategies are comparative advertising, which makes extensive use of messages with direct comparisons between competing brands; celebrity, which uses famous spokespeople to boost an advertising message; retail, which includes all advertising by retail stores selling products directly to consumers; and interactive, which encourages two-way communication either via the Internet or kiosks.

3   Describe the process of creating an advertisement.

An advertisement evolves from pinpointing goals, such as educating consumers, enhancing brand loyalty, or improving a product's image. From those goals, marketers move to the next stages: creating a plan, developing a message, developing and preparing the ad, and selecting the appropriate medium (or media). Advertisements often appeal to consumers' emotions such as fear or humor.

4   Identify the major types of advertising appeals and discuss their uses.

Advertisers often focus on making emotional appeals to fear, humor, sex, guilt, or fantasy. While they can be effective, marketers need to recognize that fear appeals can backfire; people's sense of humor can differ according to sex, age, and other factors; and use of sexual imagery must not overstep the bounds of taste.

5   List and compare the major advertising media.

The major media include broadcast (television and radio), newspapers and magazines, direct mail, outdoor, and interactive. Each medium has benefits and drawbacks. Newspapers are flexible and dominate local markets. Magazines can target niche markets. Interactive media encourage two-way communication. Outdoor advertising in a high-traffic location reaches many people every day; television and radio reach even more. Direct mail allows effective segmentation.

6   **Outline the organization of the advertising function and the role of an advertising agency.**

Within a firm, the advertising department is usually a group that reports to a marketing executive. Advertising departments generally include research, art and design, copywriting, and media analysis. Outside advertising agencies assist and support the advertising efforts of firms. These specialists are usually organized by creative services, account services, marketing services, and finance.

7   **Explain the roles of cross-promotion, public relations, publicity, and ethics in an organization's promotional strategy.**

Cross-promotion, illustrated by tie-ins between popular movies and fast-food restaurants, permits the marketing partners to share the cost of a promotional campaign that meets their mutual needs. Public relations consists of the firm's communications and relationships with its various publics, including customers, employees, stockholders, suppliers, government, and the society in which it operates. Publicity is the dissemination of newsworthy information about a product or organization. This information activity is frequently used in new-product introductions. Although publicity is welcomed by firms, negative publicity is easily created when a company enters a gray ethical area with the use of its promotional efforts. Therefore, marketers should be careful to construct ethically sound promotional campaigns, avoiding such practices as puffery and deceit. In addition, negative publicity may occur as a result of some action taken—or failed to be taken—by a firm, such as a product recall.

8   **Explain how marketers assess promotional effectiveness.**

The effectiveness of advertising can be measured by both pretesting and posttesting. Pretesting is the assessment of an ad's effectiveness before it is actually used. It includes such methods as sales conviction tests and blind product tests. Posttesting is the assessment of the ad's effectiveness after it has been used. Commonly used posttests include readership tests, unaided recall tests, inquiry tests, and split runs.

assessment check: answers

1.1   **What are the goals of institutional advertising?**

Institutional advertising promotes a concept, an idea, a philosophy, or the goodwill of an industry, company, organization, person, geographic location, or government agency.

1.2   **At what stage in the product lifecycle are informative ads used? Why?**

Informative ads are common in the introductory stage of the product lifecycle.

1.3   **What is reminder advertising?**

Reminder advertising strives to reinforce previous promotional activity by keeping the name of a good, service, organization, person, place, idea, or cause before the public.

2.1   **What is comparative advertising?**

Comparative advertising makes extensive use of messages with direct comparisons between competing brands.

2.2   **What makes a successful celebrity testimonial?**

Successful celebrity ads feature figures who are credible sources of information for the promoted product.

2.3   **What is cooperative advertising?**

In cooperative advertising, a manufacturer or wholesaler shares advertising costs with a retailer.

3.1 What is an advertising campaign?

An advertising campaign is a series of different but related ads that use a single theme and appear in different media within a specified time period.

3.2 What are an advertisement's three main goals?

Advertising's three main goals are to educate consumers about product features, enhance brand loyalty, and improve consumer perception of the brand.

4.1 What are some common emotional appeals used in advertising?

Advertisers often focus on making emotional appeals to fear, humor, sex, guilt, or fantasy.

4.2 What are the main types of interactive ads?

Interactive ads include Internet banners, pop-ups, keyword ads, advertorials, advergames, and interstitials.

5.1 What types of products are banned from advertising on television?

Tobacco goods such as cigarettes, cigars, and smokeless tobacco are banned from television advertising.

5.2 What are some advantages radio offers to advertisers? What about newspapers?

Radio ads allow marketers to target a captive audience and offer low cost, flexibility, and mobility. Newspaper ads are flexible and provide nearly complete coverage of the market. Readers can also refer back to newspaper ads.

5.3 Define *media scheduling* and identify the most important factors influencing the scheduling decision.

Media scheduling sets the timing and sequence for a series of advertisements. Sales patterns, repurchase cycles, and competitors' activities are the most important variables in the scheduling decision.

6.1 What is the role of an advertising agency?

An advertising agency's role is to help businesses plan and prepare advertisements.

6.2 What are some advantages of using an agency?

Advantages of using an ad agency are the availability of highly qualified specialists who provide creativity and objectivity and sometimes cost savings.

7.1 Distinguish between marketing public relations and nonmarketing public relations.

Marketing public relations refers to narrowly focused public relations activities that directly support marketing goals. Nonmarketing public relations refers to a company's messages about general issues.

7.2 What is publicity?

Publicity is nonpersonal stimulation of demand for a good, service, place, idea, person, or organization by unpaid placement of significant news regarding the product in a print or broadcast medium.

7.3 What are the advantages of cross-promotion?

Cross-promotion divides the cost of a promotional campaign that meets the mutual needs of marketing partners and provides greater benefits for both in return.

8.1   What is CPM and how is it measured?

CPM is cost per thousand, a fee based on cost to deliver the advertisers' message to viewers, listeners, or readers.

8.2   Distinguish between media research and message research.

Media research assesses how well a particular medium delivers the advertiser's message, where and when to place the ad, and the size of the audience. Message research tests consumer reactions to an advertisement's creative message.

8.3   Describe several research techniques used in posttesting.

Commonly used posttests include readership tests, unaided recall tests, inquiry tests, and split runs.

Marketing Terms You Need to Know

advertising 531	*persuasive advertising 532*	*advertising campaign 537*
product advertising 532	*reminder advertising 532*	*advertising agency 548*
institutional advertising 532	*comparative advertising 533*	*publicity 550*
informative advertising 532	*cooperative advertising 535*	*cross-promotion 552*

Other Important Marketing Terms

retail advertising 535	*marketing public relations (MPR) 550*	*split runs 555*
interactive advertising 536	*media research 553*	*cookies 556*
banners 540	*message research 553*	*puffery 556*
media scheduling 547	*pretesting 553*	
nonmarketing public relations 550	*posttesting 554*	

Assurance of Learning Review

1. Identify and define the two broad categories of advertising. Give an example of each.

2. What are the three primary objectives of advertising? Give an example of when each one might be used.

3. Describe each of the four major advertising strategies.

4. Identify the different types of emotional appeals in advertising. What are the benefits and pitfalls of each?

5. How are interactive ads different from traditional ads? How are they similar?

6. Identify and describe the different advertising media. Which are on the rise? Which are facing possible decline?

7. What is the role of an advertising agency?

8. How can firms use marketing public relations (MPR) to their advantage?

9. Describe the ways in which marketers assess promotional effectiveness.

10. What is puffery? Where does it cross the line from ethical to unethical?

Projects and Teamwork Exercises

1. Choose a print ad to cut out and place on a poster board. With a marker, identify all the elements of the ad. Then identify what you believe is the objective of the ad—to inform, persuade, or remind. Finally, identify the strategy used—comparative, celebrity, or retail. If there is an interactive component offered, note that, too.

2. According to *Advertising Age,* some of the top advertising campaigns of all time include Nike's "Just do it" (1988), McDonald's "You deserve a break today" (1971), and Burger King's "Have it your way" (1973).[50] With a classmate, choose an ad campaign you think is effective—based on its slogan, images, storyline, or whatever strikes you. Present the ad and your evaluation of it to the class.

3. With a classmate, create your own plan for cross-promoting two products you think would be good candidates for cross-promotion.

4. Access the Internet and surf around to some sites that interest you. How many banner ads or pop-ups do you see? Do you like to view these ads, or do you find them intrusive? Which are most appealing? Which are least?

5. With a classmate, choose a product you have purchased in the past and come up with a plan for using a nontraditional advertising medium—such as balloons, T-shirts, water bottles, anything you imagine will grab people's attention and promote the product effectively. If possible, create a prototype for your ad. If not, create a sketch of your ad. Present your new ad to the class.

Critical-Thinking Exercises

1. What are some of the benefits and drawbacks of using celebrity testimonials in advertising? Identify an ad you believe makes effective use of a celebrity's endorsement, and explain why.

2. Choose one of the following products and outline a possible media schedule for advertising.
   a. toy
   b. line of bathing suits
   c. line of candles

3. Select two different advertisers' television or print ads for the same product category (cars or soft drinks, for instance) and decide what emotion each appeals to. Which ad is more effective and why?

4. Do outdoor ads and pop-up ads have any characteristics in common? What are they?

5. Think back to any good or bad publicity you have heard about a company or its products recently. If it was good publicity, how was it generated and what media were used? If it was bad publicity, where did you find out about it and how did the firm try to control or eliminate the situation?

6. One writer says that children exposed to puffery in ads grow into teens who are healthily skeptical of advertising claims. Find several print ads aimed at children, and identify what you think might be puffery in these ads. Select one ad you think children would be influenced by and rewrite the ad without the puffery.

Ethics Exercise

In an effort to target the youngest of consumers, some firms have begun to advertise tiny mobile phones sized to fit the hands of children. The MO1, developed by toy firm Imaginarium and the Spanish communications firm Telefonica, is designed specifically for the younger set—it's a real cell phone, not a toy. In Europe, where the phone is marketed, some parents and consumer groups are objecting to the marketing of the product, noting that long-term health effects of cell phone use are unknown, and young children are quickly impressed by advertising. "The mobile telephone industry is acting like the tobacco industry by designing products that addict the very young," argues one environmental advocacy group for children.[51]

1. Do you believe that Imaginarium and Telefonica are acting in an ethical manner? Why or why not? Be sure to use concepts from this chapter to build your argument.

2. What steps might Imaginarium and Telefonica take to develop good public relations and generate positive publicity surrounding their product?

Internet Exercise

1. **Preroll video ads.** Visit the Web sites listed here to learn more about preroll video ads. After reviewing the material, answer the following questions:
   a. What is a preroll video ad?
   b. How do many consumers react to preroll video ads?
   c. How effective are preroll video ads compared with more traditional forms of advertising?
   advertising.com/publishers-**video**.php
   internetadsales.com/modules/news/article.php?storyid=4360
   alleyinsider.com/2008/01/preroll-video-ads-effective-consumers-hatethem.html
   btobonline.com/apps/pbcs.dll/article?aid=/20070509/free/70509003/1078
   beet.tv/2006/10/online_video_ad.html

2. **Newspaper advertising.** Go the Web site of Newspaper Advertising.com (newspaperadvertising.com/articles.html). Read two articles on the effective use of newspaper advertising. Summarize what you learned and bring it to class in order to participate in a class discussion on the topic.

3. **Advertising history.** Visit the *Advertising Age* Web site to access information on advertising during the 20th century (adage.com/century). Answer the following questions:
   a. Who were the top ten advertisers?
   b. What were the top five advertising campaigns? What were the top three advertising jingles? What were the top two advertising slogans? What was the top five advertising icons?
   c. Are any of the top campaigns, slogans, jingles, or icons still in use today?
   d. Which current campaigns, slogans, jingles, and icons might make the list for the 21st century? Explain your answers.

Note: Internet Web addresses change frequently. If you don't find the exact site listed, you may need to access the organization's home page and search from there or use a search engine such as Google.

Case 16.1   Great Political Ads: Which Do You Remember?

Some people make a career of creating political campaign ads; others make a career of evaluating or studying them. As a

consumer, if you live in one of the states where presidential primaries are hotly contested, you get your fill of ads before the official nominations and general campaign really get rolling. The fact that there are so many political ads says something about the way presidential candidates are marketed in the United States. During the most recent presidential election, more than $800 million was estimated to be spent on TV ads alone, shattering the record of $500 million in the previous race. TV networks benefited from the dramatic increase, as auto manufacturers, real estate firms, and financial service advertisers cut back on their advertising budgets. "Every month, every quarter we're setting records," reported CBS chief financial officer Fred Reynolds in regard to political advertising.

Of course, some presidential campaign ads are memorable, and others are not. Some are memorable for their creativity, wit, or ability to persuade voters in the candidate's favor. Others are memorable for their lack of taste or their inability to convey a positive message. Some are humorous, while others are unintentionally funny. The most recent crop is no exception. Several candidates tried to portray their physical fitness by jogging for the camera, while others focused on what they supposed were their own unique qualifications. But certain words and images linked all of the ads for the recent election. Barack Obama is said to have used the word *change* in 37 percent of his ads. Flags were a popular symbol in TV ads. John McCain's ads included the American flag 77 percent of the time.

TV ads have not always been the cornerstone of U.S. presidential elections. In fact, they didn't become prominent until the early 1950s, when Dwight D. Eisenhower's campaign hired the marketer who wrote the M&M line, "Melts in your mouth, not in your hands," to create advertisements for their candidate. Since then, independent organizations have compiled lists of the best and worst ads—understanding that a good or bad TV ad could turn a campaign around. The Independent Film Channel cites an ad by President Lyndon Johnson's campaign that depicted his opponent, Barry Goldwater, as an extremist ready to use nuclear bombs at a whim as the most effective political ad in history. The ad was actually pulled from the air by Johnson, but it was aired so many times by news broadcasts because of its controversial nature that voters remembered the ad when they went to the voting booth. Another ad on the IFC's top ten list is John Kennedy's ad asking, "Is Nixon Experienced?" The tagline certainly resonates with viewers who watched commercials through the most recent election, as John McCain repeatedly questioned his opponent Barack Obama's experience and readiness to lead.

In a new trend, more and more political ads appear online. Interest groups, not-for-profit organizations, and candidates' campaigns have all jumped into the Internet advertising arena. Reviewers cite the online ads as funnier, sharper, and more intelligent than those made for television. While they may not yet reach enough voters to decide an entire election, they are entertaining—and the Internet quite likely represents the campaign advertising medium of the future.

Questions for Critical Thinking

1. Which advertisements do you remember from the most recent presidential election? Which were most effective? Which were the least effective? Why?

2. How do political advertisements compare with advertisements for goods and services? How are they similar? In what ways are they different?

Sources: Alexander Barnes Dryer, "Not for Broadcast," *Slate*, www.slate.com, accessed June 2, 2009; Sarah Scully and William Rabbe, "IFC List Month: Top 10 Presidential Campaign Ads," Independent Film Channel, July 9, 2008, ifc.com/politics; "TV Ad Spending to Set Record in Presidential Race," *Reuters*, July 2, 2008, www.reuters.com; "Presidential Campaign Ads Top $100 Million," *U.S. News & World Report*, February 4, 2008, www.usnews.com; Rick Klein, "The Year's Best Political Ads," *ABC News*, December 11, 2007, abcnews.go.com; "Top of the Ticket," *Los Angeles Times*, October 2007, www.latimesblogs.latimes.com.

Video Case 16.2   Advertising and Public Relations at Ogden Publications

The written video case on Ogden Publications appears on page VC–15. The Ogden Publications video is designed to expand and highlight the concepts in this chapter and the concepts and questions covered in the written video case.

CHAP**17**TER
Personal Selling and
Sales Promotion

© STAN HONDA/AFP/Getty Images

Vivek Gupta: IBM India's Go-to Guy

The director of IBM's communications sector in India and South Asia, Vivek Gupta doesn't fit the old mold of IBM staffers, mostly U.S. employees in blue suits and ties. A native of India who doesn't

play golf and has never been to the company's headquarters in upstate New York, Gupta is one of 65,000 new staff members IBM has added to its Indian division in recent years. He is also the company's top

salesperson for telecom accounts, IBM's fastest-growing business in one of the world's fastest-growing economies.

IBM has long been known for its dynamic sales force; now they number

40,000 highly trained people in nearly all part of the world. In fact, it has been the proving ground for six of the company's eight CEOs, including the present chief. IBM is growing despite the economic downturn, in part by putting its energies into the world's fast-growing markets. IBM stock climbed 15 percent in one recent year, while the S&P 500 lost 6 percent of its value.

One reason for its continued success is the superb salesmanship of Vivek Gupta. "I don't remember a single deal in my career which I pursued and I lost," Gupta says. "It's just a question of time. If I play very smart, I can crack the nuts very quickly. If I don't play smart, it might take some time."

Gupta defines "playing smart" strictly in terms of knowing his customers, which include Indian telecom giants Vodaphone, Bharti Airtel, and Idea Cellular. Selling to these customers isn't easy, but much is at stake—the wireless industry in India adds enough new customers each month to repopulate New York City. Gupta constantly comes up with new combinations of goods and services to pitch, including everything from chips and mainframes to call center software, intranet services, cell phone tow-

ers, and more. His ideal customer is one that allows IBM to run the entire business, except for strategy and marketing. To convince buyers he can supply all the tools and support to make that happen, Gupta becomes teacher, psychologist, diplomat, and entrepreneur when needed. "You have to understand their pain points," he says of his customers. "And they're not going to spell them out."

In closing an initial sale of 20 air-cell towers with Bharti Airtel, for instance, Gupta was laying the foundation for an account that would later lead to the sale of thousands of such towers and eventually of $1 billion worth of back-office support.

Gupta started small with Vodafone, too, selling a few laptops for employees after being told the company would never do business with IBM. A year later he had sold Vodafone some IBM servers, and four years later he had won a five-year contract for $600 million to provide a full range of business services from

customer support to finance.

The secrets of Gupta's success are simple. He gets to know his customers' business structures—and not just from their organization charts. "I start figuring out who's the fox and who's the guy who can actually swing this entire thing," he says. Then he uses patience and determination. Instead of blaming someone for not placing an order, Gupta tells himself, "'Look, he wants to give me business. Why isn't he?' Once you get tuned to that way of thinking," he says, "you'll never point fingers. Instead you'll think, 'That will probably require a little more effort. I have to jump a little more.'" Gupta also gives full credit to the rest of the sales team because "the delivery team is like the engine. They need motivation and glorification" just like the front players. Finally, he sees his customers as partners. "The moment you become a true friend to clients and start feeding them with information, you strengthen their hand, which in turn strengthens yours."[1]

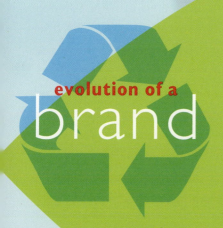

evolution of a brand

For nearly a century IBM has been at the forefront of information technology (IT) for business, putting IT to ever-growing uses as organizations and their needs have evolved and changed around the world. The company was originally incorporated in New York through a merger of three firms in 1911, when it was called the Computing-Tabulating-Recording Company, and it continued to grow by acquisitions throughout the early 1900s. The company changed its name to the International Business Machines Corporation (IBM) in 1924; by then it was already a global firm, operating three manufacturing plants in Europe.

IBM weathered the Great Depression by manufacturing a large inventory of machines that positioned it to accept a landmark government Social Security contract to record employee data in 1935; orders from other government departments soon followed. During and immediately after World War II, the company began developing a series of ever more powerful automatic calculating machines, and by the 1950s had built its first large computer. It began operations in India in 1951.

evolution of a brand
continued

- By the 1990s IBM had committed itself to being a customer-oriented IT company whose chief strength was its ability to provide customers with integrated business solutions, not just pieces or components. How does this corporate goal help IBM's sales force meet their customers' needs?

- IBM survived a slump in the 1990s by deciding not to break up into separate companies but to "commit instead to making all of IBM's parts work together," combining its expertise in both technical and business innovation. How can IBM's sales force best convey this advantage to their customers?

chapter overview

The IBM story illustrates how essential it is for salespeople and other company representatives to connect with customers, not merely sell products. In exploring personal selling strategies, this chapter gives special attention to the relationship-building opportunities that the selling situation presents.

Personal selling is the process of a seller's person-to-person promotional presentation to a buyer. The sales process essentially is interpersonal, and it is basic to any enterprise. Accounting, engineering, human resource management, production, and other organizational activities produce no benefits unless a seller matches the needs of a client or customer. The nearly 16 million people employed in sales occupations in the United States testify to the importance of selling.[2] Personal selling is much more costly and time-consuming than other types of promotion because of its direct contact with customers. This makes personal selling the single largest marketing expense in many firms.

Personal selling is a primary component of a firm's promotional mix when one or more of several well-defined factors are present: (1) customers are geographically concentrated; (2) individual orders account for large amounts of revenue; (3) the firm markets goods and services that are expensive, are technically complex, or require special handling; (4) trade-ins are involved; (5) products move through short channels; or (6) the firm markets to relatively few potential customers. For example, personal selling is an important component of the promotional mix for a car dealer, although both dealers and manufacturers also rely heavily on advertising. Because cars and trucks are expensive, customers usually like to go to a dealership to compare models, discuss a purchase, or obtain service, and trade-ins often are involved. So a dealer's salespeople provide valuable assistance to the customer. Table 17.1 summarizes the factors that influence the importance of personal selling in the overall promotional mix based on four variables: consumer, product, price, and marketing channels. This chapter also explores *sales promotion,* which includes all marketing activities—other than personal selling, advertising, and publicity—that enhance promotional effectiveness.

personal selling
Interpersonal influence process involving a seller's promotional presentation conducted on a person-to-person basis with the buyer.

table 17.1 **Factors Affecting the Importance of Personal Selling in the Promotional Mix**

Variable	Conditions That Favor Personal Selling	Conditions That Favor Advertising
Consumer	Geographically concentrated	Geographically dispersed
	Relatively low numbers	Relatively high numbers
Product	Expensive	Inexpensive
	Technically complex	Simple to understand
	Custom made	Standardized
	Special handling requirements	No special handling requirements
	Transactions frequently involve trade-ins	Transactions seldom involve trade-ins
Price	Relatively high	Relatively low
Channels	Relatively short	Relatively long

The Evolution of Personal Selling

Selling has been a standard business activity for thousands of years. As long ago as 2000 B.C., the Code of Hammurabi protected the rights of the Babylonian salesman, who was referred to as a *peddler*. Throughout U.S. history, selling has been a major factor in economic growth. Even during the 1700s, Yankee peddlers pulled their carts full of goods from village to village and farm to farm, helping expand trade among the colonies. Today, professional salespeople are problem solvers who focus on satisfying the needs of customers before, during, and after sales are made. Armed with knowledge about their firm's goods or services, those of competitors, and their customers' business needs, salespeople pursue a common goal of creating mutually beneficial long-term relationships with customers.

Personal selling is a vital, vibrant, dynamic process. As domestic and foreign competition increases the emphasis on productivity, personal selling is taking on a more prominent role in the marketing mix. Salespeople must communicate the advantages of their firms' goods and services over those of competitors. They must be able to do the following:

▷ Focus on a customer's situation and needs and create solutions that meet those needs.

▷ Follow through and stay in touch before, during, and after a sale.

▷ Know the industry and have a firm grasp, not only of their own firm's capabilities but also of their competitors' abilities.

▷ Work hard to exceed their customers' expectations, even if it means going above and beyond the call of duty.

Relationship marketing affects all aspects of an organization's marketing function, including personal selling. This means marketers in both internal and external relationships must develop different sales skills. Instead of working alone, many salespeople now unite their efforts in sales teams. The customer-focused firm wants its salespeople to form long-lasting relationships with buyers by providing high levels of customer service rather than going for quick sales. Even the way salespeople perform their jobs is constantly changing. Growing numbers of companies have integrated communications and computer technologies into the sales routine. These trends are covered in more detail later in the chapter.

❚ **Describe the role of today's salesperson.**

Personal selling is an attractive career choice for today's college students. According to the Bureau of Labor Statistics, jobs in sales and related fields are expected to grow by about 8 percent over the next decade.[3] Company executives usually recognize a good salesperson as a hard worker who can solve problems, communicate clearly, and be consistent. In fact, many corporations are headed by executives who began their careers in sales.

2 **Describe the four sales channels.**

The Four Sales Channels

Personal selling occurs through several types of communication channels: over-the-counter selling, including online selling; field selling; telemarketing; and inside selling. Each of these channels includes business-to-business and direct-to-customer selling. Although telemarketing and online selling are lower-cost alternatives, their lack of personal interaction with existing or prospective customers often makes them less effective than personalized, one-to-one field selling and over-the-counter channels. In fact, many organizations use a number of different channels.

OVER-THE-COUNTER SELLING

over-the-counter selling Personal selling conducted in retail and some wholesale locations in which customers come to the seller's place of business.

The most frequently used sales channel, **over-the-counter selling,** typically describes selling in retail and some wholesale locations. Most over-the-counter sales are direct-to-customer, although business customers are frequently served by wholesalers with over-the-counter sales reps. Customers typically visit the seller's location on their own initiative to purchase desired items. Some visit their favorite stores because they enjoy shopping. Others respond to many kinds of appeals including direct mail; personal letters of invitation from store personnel; and advertisements for sales, special events, and new-product introductions.

Marketers are getting increasingly creative in their approach to over-the-counter selling. When hardware retailing cooperative True Value discovered that, increasingly, women were making home-improvement buying decisions, it hired branding experts to help it rework store layouts and design and aspects of merchandising to become more female-friendly. For example, it expanded its mix of outdoor living merchandise beyond grills and patio furniture and emphasized new styles of lighting and plumbing fixtures that appeal to women shoppers.[4]

Retail locations typically practice over-the-counter selling.

© AP Images/Brian Branch-Price

Electronics giant Best Buy continues to outsell its competitors; with 923 stores, the firm's sales total nearly $49 billion.[5] Perhaps Best Buy's success comes from the training its salespeople receive. Training focuses on the firm's mantra: CARE Plus. *C* stands for contact with the customer. *A* means asking questions to learn what the customer needs. *R* represents making recommendations to the customer. *E* stands for encouragement, praising the customer for a wise purchase.

Clothing retailers have begun to enhance the shopping experience by expanding the capabilities of the fitting room.

Some Gap and Banana Republic stores added call buttons and delivery doors to their fitting rooms so that salespeople can offer more service. Bloomingdale's has piloted an interactive mirror and Webcam system in fitting rooms that enables shoppers to e-mail or text-message their friends with information on items they are trying on. By logging on to a special Web site, the friends can view the items and offer comments. What's more, shoppers can use the system to learn about other merchandise in the store, click on an item, and have it superimposed on their image, in short, trying on a garment virtually.[6]

Regardless of a retailer's innovation, a few things remain the same in selling. For example, customers never like hearing salespeople say the following:

▷ "That's not my department."

▷ "If it's not out (on the rack or shelf), we don't have it."

▷ "I don't know/I'm new."

▷ "I'm closing" or "I'm on a break."

▷ "The computer is down."

While these quotes may seem humorous, they also ring true. You've probably heard them, and you may have said them yourself if you've worked in a retail environment. But each statement conveys the message that the salesperson is not willing or able to serve the customer—exactly the opposite of what every retailer wants to convey.

FIELD SELLING

Field selling involves making sales calls on prospective and existing customers at their businesses or homes. Some situations involve considerable creative effort, such as the sale of major computer installations. Often the salesperson must convince customers first that they need the good or service and then that they need the particular brand the salesperson is selling. Field sales of large industrial installations such as Boeing's 787 Dreamliner jet also often require considerable technical expertise.

Largely because it involves travel, field selling is considerably more expensive than other selling options. The rising cost of fuel, air fares, car rentals, and hotel rates has forced up the average cost of a domestic business trip to more than $1,100 and an international trip to over $3,200.[7] Needing to find ways to trim costs while increasing productivity, some firms have replaced certain travel with conference calls, while others require salespeople to stay in less expensive hotels and spend less on meals. Some firms have simply shortened the time allowed for trips.

In fairly routine field selling situations, such as calling on established customers in industries such as food, textiles, or wholesaling, the salesperson basically acts as an order taker who processes regular customers' orders. But more complex situations may involve weeks of preparation, formal presentations, and many hours of postsales call work. Field selling is a lifestyle that many people enjoy; they also cite some of the negatives, such as travel delays, impact on family life, and high costs of fuel.

Some firms view field selling as a market in itself, and have developed goods and services designed to help salespeople do their jobs. Ford and Microsoft have partnered to produce the Stargate Mobile—a tablet computer loaded with Microsoft Office software, a wireless broadband card from Sprint, and a connection to Slingbox, which uses the Internet to access live television programming. In short, the two firms have created a mobile office. The computer is wrapped in a rubber case and mounted on a swiveling floor mount—but can be unlocked and carried like a laptop.[8]

Taking their cue from the successes of businesses such as Avon, Pampered Chef, and Tupperware, thousands of smaller businesses now rely on field selling in customers' homes. Often called **network marketing,** this type of personal selling relies on lists of family members and friends of the salesperson or "party host," who organizes a gathering of potential customers for an in-home demonstration of products. The Girl Scouts organization has been selling cookies for decades.

field selling Sales presentations made at prospective customers' locations on a face-to-face basis.

The Girl Scouts have been successfully field selling their cookies for decades, despite an inexperienced sales force and short selling season.

© Jeff Greenberg/PhotoEdit

telemarketing Promotional presentation involving the use of the telephone on an outbound basis by salespeople or on an inbound basis by customers who initiate calls to obtain information and place orders.

Despite being a largely inexperienced sales team that offers its product seasonally, annual revenues typically total over $700 million.[9] Mary Kay Cosmetics, with more than 33,000 sales consultants, enjoyed global sales of over $2.4 billion in a recent year.[10]

TELEMARKETING

Telemarketing, a channel in which the selling process is conducted by phone, serves two general purposes—sales and service—and two general markets—business-to-business and direct-to-customer. Both inbound and outbound telemarketing are forms of direct marketing.

Outbound telemarketing involves sales personnel who rely on the telephone to contact potential buyers, reducing the substantial costs of personal visits to customers' homes or businesses. Technologies such as predictive dialers, autodialing, and random-digit dialing increase chances that telemarketers will reach people at home. *Predictive dialers* weed out busy signals and answering machines, nearly doubling the number of calls made per hour. *Autodialing* allows telemarketers to dial numbers continually; when a customer answers the phone, the call is automatically routed to a sales representative. However, the Telephone Consumer Protection Act of 1991 prohibits the use of autodialers to contact (or leave messages) on telephone devices such as answering machines.[11] *Random-digit dialing* allows telemarketers to reach unlisted numbers and block Caller ID.

A major drawback of telemarketing is that most consumers dislike the practice, and nearly 160 million have signed up for the national Do Not Call Registry.[12] If an unauthorized telemarketer does call any of these numbers, the marketer is subject to an $11,000 fine. Organizations exempt from the fine include not-for-profits, political candidates, companies that have obtained the customer's permission, marketing researchers, and firms that have an existing business relationship with the customer.

Why do some firms still use telemarketing? The average call still costs only about $3, and companies still point to a significant rate of success. According to the Direct Marketing Association, about 6 million people are employed in telemarketing jobs.[13]

Inbound telemarketing typically involves a toll-free number that customers can call to obtain information, make reservations, and purchase goods and services. When a customer calls a toll-free number, the caller can be identified and routed to the representatives with whom he or she has done business before, creating a human touch not possible before. This form of selling provides maximum convenience for customers who initiate the sales process. Many large catalog merchants, such as Pottery Barn, L.L. Bean, Lands' End, and Performance Bike, keep their inbound telemarketing lines open 24 hours a day, seven days a week.

Some firms are taking dramatic steps to incorporate inbound telemarketing into their overall marketing strategy. JetBlue Airlines, for example, keeps operating costs low by having its reservation agents work from home.[14]

INSIDE SELLING

The role of many of today's telemarketers is a combination of field selling techniques applied through inbound and outbound telemarketing channels with a strong customer orientation, called **inside selling.** Inside sales reps perform two primary jobs: they turn opportunities into actual sales, and they support technicians and purchasers with current solutions. Inside sales reps do far more than read a canned script to unwilling prospects. Their role goes beyond taking orders to solving problems, providing customer service, and selling. A successful inside sales force relies on close working relationships with field representatives to solidify customer relationships.

The seven-member inside sales force of the NBA's Detroit Pistons supports the team's marketing efforts, such as special events for season ticket holders, including backstage tours, scavenger hunts, and privileges such as getting into games 30 minutes early. Pistons sales reps use online chat, telephone, and e-mail to stay connected.[15]

inside selling Selling by phone, mail, and electronic commerce.

INTEGRATING THE VARIOUS SELLING CHANNELS

Figure 17.1 illustrates how firms are likely to blend alternative sales channels, from over-the-counter selling and field selling to telemarketing and inside selling, to create a successful cost-effective sales organization. Existing customers whose business problems require complex solutions are likely best served by the traditional field sales force. Other current customers who need answers but not the same attention as the first group can be served by inside sales reps who contact them as needed. Over-the-counter sales reps serve existing customers by supplying information and advice and completing sales transactions. Telemarketers may be used to strengthen communication with customers or to reestablish relationships with customers that may have lapsed over a few months.

assessment check

1. What is over-the-counter selling?

2. What is field selling?

3. Distinguish between outbound and inbound telemarketing.

Trends in Personal Selling

In today's complex marketing environment, effective personal selling requires different strategies from those used by salespeople in the past. As pointed out in the discussion of *buying centers* in Chapter 6, rather than selling one-on-one, in B2B settings it is now customary to sell to teams of corporate representatives who participate in the client firm's decision-making process. In business-to-business sales situations involving technical products, customers expect salespeople to answer technical questions—or bring along someone who can. They also want representatives who understand technical jargon and can communicate using sophisticated technological tools. Patience is also a

3 Describe the major trends in personal selling.

figure 17.1

Alternative Sales Channels for Serving Customers

Over-the-Counter Selling
Customers in retail settings with typical, routine needs

Field Selling
Customers who need solutions to complex problems

Customers

Telemarketing
Outbound: Existing customers; businesses that have been contacted in the last three months; people or companies that have granted you permission to call.
Inbound: New and existing customers and customers of competitors; previous purchasers and service personnel seeking product-related information.

Inside Selling
Customers who need answers to frequently asked questions

requirement because the B2B sales cycle, from initial contact to closing, may take months or even years. To address all of these concerns, companies rely on three major personal selling approaches: relationship selling, consultative selling, and team selling. Regardless of the approach, however, experts agree on a few basic guidelines for conducting successful personal selling.

RELATIONSHIP SELLING

relationship selling
Regular contacts between sales representatives and customers over an extended period to establish a sustained buyer–seller relationship.

Most firms now emphasize **relationship selling,** a technique for building a mutually beneficial partnership with a customer through regular contacts over an extended period. Such buyer–seller bonds become increasingly important as companies cut back on the number of suppliers and look for companies that provide high levels of customer service and satisfaction. Salespeople must also find ways to distinguish themselves and their products from competitors. To create strong, long-lasting relationships with customers, salespeople must meet buyers' expectations. Table 17.2 summarizes the results of several surveys that indicate what buyers expect of professional salespeople.

The success of tomorrow's marketers depends on the relationships they build today in both the business-to-consumer and business-to-business markets. Cabela's, a leading retailer of hunting, fishing, and camping equipment, takes its customers' comments seriously. Each morning, Cabela vice chairman James W. Cabela reviews feedback from shoppers. Then, he personally delivers the messages needing follow-up to the appropriate manager. Cabela's also uses computer technology to chat online with its customers.[16]

Relationship selling is equally important in business-to-business sales, if not more so. Firms may invest millions of dollars in goods and services from a single firm, so creating relationships is vital. Barnett, a leading national distributor of plumbing, heating and air conditioning, electrical, and hardware products, uses barcode technology to keep its contractors' trucks well stocked with all sorts of supplies—just in case they are needed on a job. After a contractor finishes at a site, he or she uses a scanner to record the parts used in the job. The parts are automatically reordered at the end of the day, and Barnett replenishes the inventory.[17]

CONSULTATIVE SELLING

consultative selling
Meeting customer needs by listening to them, understanding their problems, paying attention to details, and following through after the sale.

Field representatives and inside sales reps require sales methods that satisfy today's cost-conscious, knowledgeable buyers. One such method, **consultative selling,** involves meeting customer needs by listening to customers, understanding—and caring about—their problems, paying attention to details, and following through after the sale. It works hand in hand with relationship selling in building customer loyalty. IBM Global Services trained sales staff at a European division of Sony in consultative selling techniques. Sony wanted its sales force to be more than simply product suppliers. Its sales team practiced mock phone calls, meetings, and presentations to develop their skills. As a result, the Sony salespeople were able to help customers more effectively and won new

briefly
speaking

"First, always ask for the order, and second, when the customer says yes, stop talking."

—**Michael Bloomberg**
(b. 1942)
MAYOR OF NEW YORK CITY, FOUNDER OF
BLOOMBERG LP

table 17.2   What Buyers Expect from Salespeople

Buyers prefer to do business with salespeople who:
• Orchestrate events and bring to bear whatever resources are necessary to satisfy the customer
• Provide counseling to the customer based on in-depth knowledge of the product, the market, and the customer's needs
• Solve problems proficiently to ensure satisfactory customer service over extended time periods
• Demonstrate high ethical standards and communicate honestly at all times
• Willingly advocate the customer's cause within the selling organization
• Create imaginative arrangements to meet buyers' needs
• Arrive well prepared for sales calls

Etiquette Tips for Marketing Professionals

Dressing Like a Sales Pro

although we often hear that you can't tell a book by its cover, it is human nature to form impressions about others from their appearance. If you pursue a career with sales responsibilities, pay attention to your appearance. Successful salespeople know the first hurdle is dressing in a way that makes others feel comfortable. In industries where it is important that customers feel confident about the service rendered, such as airlines and hotels, employees often wear uniforms. Other employers may specify a general dress code so their employees are easily distinguishable—think Best Buy's blue golf shirts or Target's red shirt and khaki pants.

Unfortunately, some employers don't give workers much guidance on dressing for sales calls. But the prospective customer will notice your appearance and form an impression about you. Although great latitude exists in industries like entertainment, education, and the arts, here's what's safe to wear in most other settings:

- **Men:** Two-piece suit and dress shirt, with starched collar and cuffs. Shirt and tie can be plain or patterned, as long as they complement each other. Shoes may be oxfords or loafers, and remember to shine them. Always wear socks.

- **Women:** Skirt suit or pantsuit, with a shirt or shell under the jacket, or a dress with a jacket. Low- to medium-heeled shoes with stockings. In some settings, women can wear contrasting jacket-skirt or jacket-pants combinations, and during the summer in some industries, sandals are okay.

- **For both genders:** A blazer or sport coat and dress pants, or even a golf shirt and khakis, are acceptable in some industries. Just make sure everything is clean and pressed.

- **What's *not* appropriate on a sales call:** Denim, T-shirts, bare feet, athletic shoes, or flip-flops. Anything tight fitting, low cut, or midriff baring. Avoid visible piercings, other than a couple in the earlobe, and visible tattoos.

- **One final rule of thumb:** It's better to be a bit overdressed than underdressed; it shows respect for your customer.

Sources: Lillian D. Bjorseth, "Dress for Success: Creating a Professional Image," *The Sideroad*, www.sideroad.com, accessed June 2, 2009; "All about Dressing for Sales Success," *Personal Improvement*, www.personalimprovementguide.com, accessed June 2, 2009; "Dressing Professionally for Sales Success," *Superior Sales Training*, www.superiorsalestraining.com, accessed August 18, 2008.

business.[18] One important aspect of consultative selling is being prepared for a sales call, including dressing professionally. The "Etiquette Tips for Marketing Professionals" feature provides tips on dressing for a successful call.

As rapid technological changes drive business at an unprecedented pace, selling has become more complex, often changing the role of salespeople. The commonwealth of Massachusetts issued a request for proposals for a massive new information technology system that would allow all of its health care providers to exchange clinical data. Software provider eClinicalWorks spent more than a year preparing its proposal, then traveled throughout Massachusetts demonstrating its software to the public health officials and physicians who would use it. The effort proved worthwhile: eClinicalWorks was one of four vendors selected for the multimillion-dollar contract.[19]

Online companies have instituted consultative selling models to create long-term customers. Particularly for complicated, high-priced products that

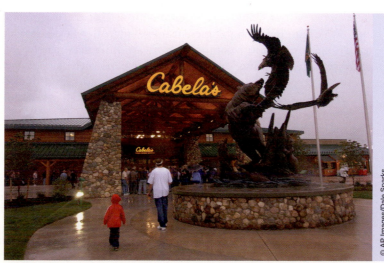

Cabela's understands the importance of customer feedback in relationship selling. Each day, James W. Cabela personally delivers shopper feedback to managers.

© AP Images/Dale Sparks

Chase cross-sells home loans to existing banking customers.

require installation or specialized service, Web sellers must quickly communicate the benefits and features of their products. They accomplish this through consultative selling.

Cross-selling—offering multiple goods or services to the same customer—is another technique that capitalizes on a firm's strengths. It costs a bank five times as much to acquire a new customer as to cross-sell to an existing one. Moreover, research shows that, the more a customer buys from an institution, the less likely that person is to leave. So a customer who opens a checking account at a local bank may follow with a safe-deposit box, retirement savings account, and a mortgage loan.

TEAM SELLING

team selling Selling situation in which several sales associates or other members of the organization are employed to help the lead sales representative reach all those who influence the purchase decision.

Another development in the evolution of personal selling is **team selling,** in which a salesperson joins with specialists from other functional areas of the firm to complete the selling process. Teams can be formal and ongoing or created for a specific, short-term selling situation. Although some salespeople have hesitated to embrace the idea of team selling, preferring to work alone, a growing number believe team selling brings better results. Customers often prefer the team approach, which makes them feel well served. Consider a restaurant meal. If the host, servers, wine steward, chef, and kitchen crew are all working well together as a team, your experience at the restaurant is likely to be positive. But if the service stops and starts, your order is recorded wrong, the food is cold, the silverware is dirty, and the staff seems grouchy, you probably won't eat at that restaurant again. In fact, you may not even finish the meal.

Another advantage of team selling is the formation of relationships between companies rather than between individuals. In sales situations that call for detailed knowledge of new, complex, and ever-changing technologies, team selling offers a distinct competitive edge in meeting customers' needs. In most computer software B2B departments, a third of the sales force is made up of technically trained, nonmarketing experts such as engineers or programmers. A salesperson continues to play the lead role in most sales situations, but technical experts bring added value to the sales process. Some companies establish permanent sales-and-tech teams that conduct all sales presentations together; others have a pool of engineers or other professionals who are on call for different client visits.

Some resourceful entrepreneurs have begun building a **virtual sales team**—a network of strategic partners, suppliers, and others qualified and willing to recommend a firm's goods or services. Merrimack, New Hampshire–based McMahon WorldWide is a small but powerful sales and management company founded a decade ago by Tim McMahon. The firm's clients include Canon USA, IBM, and The Guardian Insurance. McMahon WorldWide offers its customers strategies and software for creating their own virtual sales forces, including products such as SalesConference.Net, a fully collaborative training and consulting program. McMahon and his partners practice their own advice by conducting many virtual sessions with clients.[20]

Sales Tasks

Today's salesperson is more concerned with establishing long-term buyer–seller relationships and helping customers select the correct products for meeting their needs than with simply selling whatever is available. Where repeat purchases are common, the salesperson must be certain that the buyer's purchases are in his or her best interest; otherwise, no future relationship will be possible. The seller's interests are tied to the buyer's in a mutually beneficial relationship.

While all sales activities help the customer in some manner, they are not all alike. Three basic sales tasks can be identified: (1) order processing, (2) creative selling, and (3) missionary sales. Most of today's salespeople are not limited to performing tasks in a single category. Instead, they often perform all three tasks to some extent. A sales engineer for a computer firm may do 50 percent missionary sales, 45 percent creative selling, and 5 percent order processing. Most sales positions are classified on the basis of the primary selling task performed.

Then there's the philosophy that *everyone* in the organization, regardless of what his or her job description is, should be engaged in selling. Southwest Airlines believes delivering great customer service is paramount for every employee, from the reservations agent to the baggage handler to the flight attendant. All Southwest employees are trained to put the customer's needs first, and the airline relies heavily on technology to coordinate the effort.[21]

4 **Identify and briefly describe the three basic sales tasks.**

ORDER PROCESSING

Order processing, which can involve both field selling and telemarketing, most often is typified by selling at the wholesale and retail levels. For instance, a Pepsi-Cola route salesperson who performs this task must take the following steps:

1. *Identify customer needs.* The route salesperson determines that a store has only seven cases left in stock when it normally carries an inventory of 40 cases.

2. *Point out the need to the customer.* The route salesperson informs the store manager of the inventory situation.

3. *Complete (write up) the order.* The store manager acknowledges the need for more of the product. The driver unloads 33 cases, and the manager signs the delivery slip.

Order processing is part of most selling positions. It becomes the primary task in situations in which needs can be readily identified and are acknowledged by the customer. Even in such instances, however, salespeople whose primary responsibility involves order processing will devote some time persuading their wholesale or retail customers to carry more complete inventories of their firms' merchandise or to handle additional product lines. They also are likely to try to motivate purchasers to feature some of their firms' products, increase the amount of shelf space devoted to these items, and improve product location in the stores.

Technology now streamlines order-processing tasks. In the past, salespeople wrote up an order on the customer's premises but spent much time later, after the sales visit, completing the order and transmitting it to headquarters. Today, many companies have automated order processing. With portable computers and state-of-the-art software, the salesperson can place an order on the spot, directly to headquarters, and thus free up valuable time and energy. Computers have even eliminated the need for some of the traditional face-to-face contacts for routine reorders. JCPenney has placed kiosks in its stores that allow salespeople to select, create, and transmit accurate orders in 30 minutes or less. The kiosks are particularly useful for such transactions as orders for custom

order processing Selling, mostly at the wholesale and retail levels, that involves identifying customer needs, pointing them out to customers, and completing orders.

window blinds. The complete order is automatically transmitted electronically to a manufacturer, and a confirmation receipt is returned immediately to the salesperson. JCPenney's percentage of accurate orders has increased significantly, and the lead time required by manufacturers to fulfill custom orders has dropped by one week.[22]

CREATIVE SELLING

creative selling Personal selling in which a considerable degree of analytical decision making on the buyer's part results in the need for skillful proposals of solutions for the customer's needs.

When a considerable amount of decision making is involved in purchasing a good or service, an effective salesperson uses **creative selling** techniques to solicit an order. In contrast to the order-processing task, which deals mainly with maintaining existing business, creative selling generally is used to develop new business either by adding new customers or by introducing new goods and services. New products or upgrades to more expensive items often require creative selling. The salesperson must first identify the customer's problems and needs and then propose a solution in the form of the item offered. When attempting to expand an existing business relationship, creative selling techniques are used in over-the-counter selling, field selling, inside selling, and telemarketing.

Sometimes creative selling can rejuvenate an old product. Newell Rubbermaid's Phoenix program is designed to train young, entry-level salespeople to do whatever it takes to sell Rubbermaid products. They may be found stocking shelves, demonstrating new products, or organizing in-store scavenger hunts. Phoenix program trainees are energetic and enthusiastic, and they have helped turn the company around. As employees progress in their careers, they take part in additional training seminars that teach advanced selling skills, product and channel marketing, negotiating skills, and leadership skills.[23]

MISSIONARY SELLING

missionary selling Indirect selling method in which salespeople promote goodwill for the firm by educating customers and providing technical or operational assistance.

Missionary selling is an indirect approach to sales. Salespeople sell the firm's goodwill and educate their customers, often providing technical or operational assistance. A cosmetics company salesperson may call on retailers to demonstrate how a new product is used or to check on special promotions and overall product movement, while a wholesaler takes orders and delivers merchandise. For years, large pharmaceutical companies operated the most aggressive missionary selling, courting doctors (the indirect customer) by providing lavish restaurant meals; educational seminars; and other incentives in the hope of persuading them to prescribe a particular brand to patients. While the doctor is clearly the decision maker, the transaction is not complete until the patient hands the prescription over to a pharmacist. But recent changes in the industry code of conduct now prohibit missionary salespeople from offering any incentives of value to their customers. Instead, the Pharmaceutical Research and Manufacturers of America decreed that meetings with doctors must focus exclusively on education, not freebies.[24]

Some missionary sales may offer **sales incentives** such as trips, gas cards, free product upgrades, and other inducements. Missionary sales may involve both field selling and telemarketing. Many aspects of team selling can also be seen as missionary sales, as when technical support salespeople help design, install, and maintain equipment; when they train customers' employees; and when they provide information or operational assistance.

assessment check

1. What are the three major tasks performed by salespeople?
2. What are the three steps of order processing?

5 Outline the seven steps in the sales process.

The Sales Process

If you have worked in a retail store, or if you've sold magazine subscriptions or candy to raise money for your school or sports team, you will recognize many of the activities involved in the following list of steps in the sales process. Personal selling encompasses the following sequence of activities: (1) prospecting and qualifying, (2) approach, (3) presentation, (4) demonstration, (5) handling objections, (6) closing, and (7) follow-up.

As Figure 17.2 indicates, these steps follow the AIDA concept (attention, interest, desire, action). Once a sales prospect has been qualified, an attempt is made to secure his or her attention. The presentation

figure 17.2

The AIDA Concept and the Personal Selling Process

and demonstration steps are designed to generate interest and desire. Successful handling of buyer objections should arouse further desire. Action occurs at the close of the sale.

Salespeople modify the steps in this process to match their customers' buying processes. A neighbor who eagerly looks forward to the local symphony orchestra's new concert season each year needs no presentation except for details about scheduled performances and perhaps whether any famous musicians will be on the bill. But the same neighbor would expect a demonstration from an auto dealer when looking for a new car or might appreciate a presentation of dinner specials by the server prior to ordering a meal at a restaurant.

PROSPECTING AND QUALIFYING

Prospecting—the process of identifying potential customers—may involve hours, days, or weeks of effort, but it is a necessary step. Leads about prospects come from many sources: the Internet, computerized databases, trade show exhibits, previous customers, friends and neighbors, other vendors, nonsales employees in the firm, suppliers, and social and professional contacts. Although a firm may emphasize personal selling as the primary component of its overall promotional strategy, direct mail and advertising campaigns are also effective in identifying prospective customers.

Before salespeople begin their prospecting effort, they must be clear about what their firm is selling and create a "brand story," that is, define their product in terms of what it can do for a customer. Since customers generally are looking for solutions to problems or ways to make their lives better or businesses more successful, this focus on the customer is critical. Once they develop a brand story, the sales team must be consistent about telling it at every possible point of contact, whether in a face-to-face conversation with a prospect, in advertising, or in promoting the product to the media.[25]

In addition, salespeople must be well informed about the goods and services of the industry in general. They need to find out how other goods are marketed and packaged. They can try out a service themselves to understand how the industry operates. In these ways, they will understand what prospective customers need and want—and how they can serve them.

Qualifying—determining that the prospect really is a potential customer—is another important sales task. Not all prospects are qualified to make purchase decisions. Even though an employee in a firm might like your products, he or she might not be authorized to make the purchase. A consumer who test-drives a Porsche might fall in love with it, but not be able to afford the purchase price. Qualifying can be a two-way street. As a sales representative, you might determine that a certain prospect is qualified to make a purchase. But the prospect must agree in order for the process to go forward. If either you or the prospect determine at the outset that there's no chance for a purchase, then it's best to move on.

APPROACH

Once you have identified a qualified prospect, you need to collect all relevant information and plan an **approach**—your initial contact with the prospective customer. If your firm already has a relationship with the customer or has permission to contact the person, you may use telemarketing. But before you do so, gather as much information as you can.

Information gathering makes **precall planning** possible. As mentioned earlier, educate yourself about the industry in general, as well as goods and services offered by competitors. Read any marketing research available. Go to trade shows—you can learn a lot about many companies and their products at one location, usually in one day. Learn as much as you can about the firm you plan to approach: browse the company's Web site, find online news articles and press releases about the company, talk with other people in the industry. Know its product offerings well. If possible, buy at least one of the firm's products and use it yourself. Identify ways you can help the firm do better. Without invading an individual customer's privacy, see if you have anything in common—perhaps you grew up in the same state, or you both like to play tennis. All of this planning will help you make an effective approach.

As you plan your approach, try to answer the following questions:

▷ Who am I approaching and what are their jobs within the company?

▷ What is their level of knowledge? Are they already informed about the idea I am going to present?

▷ What do they want or need? Should I speak in technical terms or provide general information?

▷ What do they need to hear? Do they need to know more about specific products or how those products can serve them? Do they need to know how the product works? Do they need to know about cost and availability?

If you are a retail salesperson, you can ask a shopper questions to learn more about his or her needs and preferences. Say you work at a large sporting goods store. You might ask a young male shopper whether he works out at home, what equipment he already has, what his fitness goals are. The answers to these questions should lead you in the direction of a sale.

PRESENTATION

In a **presentation,** you convey your marketing message to the potential customer. You describe the product's major features, point out its strengths, and cite other customers' successes with the product. One popular form of presentation is a "features-benefits" framework wherein you talk about the good or service in terms meaningful to the buyer. If you work for a car dealership, you might point out safety features such as side airbags and built-in car seats to a young couple.

Your presentation should be well organized, clear, and concise. If appropriate, use visual sales support materials such as a chart, a brochure, a DVD, or even streaming video from your laptop. If this is your first presentation to a potential customer, it will likely be more detailed than a routine call to give an existing customer some updates. Regardless of the situation, though, be attuned to your audience's response so you can modify your presentation—even on the spur of the moment—to meet their needs.

Many presentations now use computer-based multimedia, which can offer everything from interactivity to current pricing information. CNN Headline News salespeople previously used ordinary PowerPoint presentations to sell ads to cable operators. But when the Atlanta-based company decided to change the look and feel of its 24-hour cable news network, the sales presentation material changed as well to include audio, video, and high-tech graphics.

However, technology must be used efficiently to be effective. For example, a company's Web site can be an excellent selling tool if it is easy for salespeople to present and buyers to use. A salesperson can actually use the site during a presentation by showing a potential customer how to use it to learn about and purchase products.

In a **cold calling** situation, the approach and presentation often take place at the same time. Cold calling means phoning or visiting the customer without a prior appointment and making a sales pitch on the spot. Cold calling requires nerve, skill, and creativity, but salespeople who are successful at it still point to the importance of preparation. "We link up with the best of the best," says Scott Vincent Borba, CEO and founder of Beverly Hills–based BORBA, a firm that makes

Visual sales support materials may be used in a sales presentation.

© AP Images/Steve Helber

vitamin-infused beauty products. Borba researches and selects the best companies to which he should make his pitches and admits that only about 10 percent bear fruit. But that doesn't stop him from trying. "I pick up the phone and call the president of a company. ... There's a lot of ego involved. You have to separate it and pull together to focus on the best end-product for the consumer."[26]

DEMONSTRATION

One of the most important advantages of personal selling is the opportunity to demonstrate a product. During a **demonstration,** the buyer gets a chance to try the product or at least see how it works. A demonstration might involve a test-drive of the latest hybrid car or an in-store cooking class using pots and pans that are for sale.

Many firms use new technologies to make their demonstrations more outstanding than those of their competitors. Multimedia interactive demonstrations are now common. Visitors to the Black & Decker Web site can click on video demonstrations of such products as the Alligator Lopper (an electric branch clipper) and the Scumbuster Extreme power floor scrubber.[27]

The key to an outstanding demonstration—one that gains the customer's attention, keeps his or her interest, is convincing, and stays in the customer's memory—is planning. But planning should also include time and space for free exchanges of information. During your demonstration, you should be prepared to stop and answer questions, redemonstrate a certain feature, or even let the customer try the product firsthand.

HANDLING OBJECTIONS

Potential customers often have legitimate questions and concerns about a good or service they are considering. **Objections** are expressions of resistance by the prospect, and it is reasonable to expect them. Objections might appear in the form of stalling or indecisiveness. "Let me call you back," your prospect might say, or "I just don't know about this." Or your buyer might focus on something negative such as high price.

briefly speaking

"Deliver good numbers and you earn the right for people to listen to you."

—**Mark Hurd (b. 1956)**
CHAIRMAN AND CEO,
HEWLETT-PACKARD

You can answer objections without being aggressive or rude. Use an objection as an opportunity to reassure your buyer about price, features, durability, availability, and the like. If the objection involves price, you might be able to suggest a less-expensive model or a payment plan. If the objection involves a comparison to competitive products, point out the obvious—and not so obvious—benefits of your own. If the objection involves a question about availability, a few clicks on your laptop should show how many items are in stock and when they can be shipped.

CLOSING

The moment of truth in selling is the **closing**—the point at which the salesperson asks the prospect for an order. If your presentation has been effective and you have handled all objections, a closing would be the natural conclusion to the meeting. But you may still find it difficult to close the sale. Closing does not have to be thought of in terms of a "hard sell." Instead, you can ask your customer, "Would you like to give this a try?" or, "Do I have your approval to proceed?"

Other methods of closing include the following:

1. Addressing the prospect's major concern about a purchase and then offering a convincing argument. *"If I can show you how the new heating system will reduce your energy costs by 25 percent, would you be willing to let us install it?"*

2. Posing choices for the prospect in which either alternative represents a sale. *"Would you prefer the pink sweater or the green one?"*

3. Advising the buyer that a product is about to be discontinued or will go up in price soon. (But be completely honest about this—you don't want a customer to learn later that this was not true.)

4. Remaining silent so the buyer can make a decision on his or her own.

5. Offering an extra inducement designed to motivate a favorable buyer response, such as a quantity discount, an extended service contract, or a low-interest payment plan.

Even if the meeting or phone call ends without a sale, the effort is not over. You can use a written note or an e-mail to keep communication open, letting the buyer know you are ready and waiting to be of service.

FOLLOW-UP

The word *close* can be misleading because the point at which the prospect accepts the seller's offer is where much of the real work of selling begins. In today's competitive environment, the most successful salespeople make sure that today's customers will also be tomorrow's.

It is not enough to close the sale and move on. Relationship selling involves reinforcing the purchase decision and ensuring the company delivers the highest-quality merchandise. As a salesperson, you must also ensure that customer service needs are met and that satisfaction results from all of a customer's dealings with your company. Otherwise, some other company may get the next order.

These postsale activities, which often determine whether a person will become a repeat customer, constitute the sales **follow-up.** Sales experts believe in a wide array of follow-up techniques, ranging from expensive information folders to holiday cards to online greetings. Some suggest phone calls at regular intervals. Others prefer automatic e-mail reminders when it is time to renew or reorder. At the very least, however, you should contact customers to find out if they are satisfied with their purchases. This step allows you to psychologically reinforce the customer's original decision to buy. It also gives you an opportunity to correct any problems and ensure the next sale. Follow-up helps strengthen the bond you are trying to build with customers in relationship selling. You have probably experienced follow-up as a customer—if your auto dealership called to see if you were satisfied with recent service, or if your doctor's office phoned to find out if you were feeling better.

assessment check

1. Identify the seven steps of the sales process.

2. Why is follow-up important to the sales effort?

Managing the Sales Effort

6 Identify the seven basic functions of a sales manager.

The overall direction and control of the personal selling effort are in the hands of a firm's sales managers. In a typical geographic sales structure, a district or divisional sales manager might report to a regional or zone manager. This manager in turn reports to a national sales manager or vice president of sales.

Currently, there are about 318,000 sales managers in the United States.[28] The sales manager's job requires a unique blend of administrative and sales skills, depending on the specific level in the sales hierarchy. Sales skills are particularly important for first-level sales managers because they are involved daily in the continuing process of training and directly leading the sales force. But as people rise in the sales management hierarchy, they require more managerial skills and fewer sales skills to perform well. Ann Livermore, executive vice president of Hewlett-Packard, is passionate about her job. While her company has traditionally maintained an engineering focus, she steers it toward a sales focus by hiring upper-level managers and executives with sales backgrounds. She also talks to two or three of the company's big customers every day to identify industry trends and problems. From those conversations came HP's new automated data center products.[29]

Sales force management links individual salespeople to general management. The sales manager performs seven basic managerial functions: (1) recruitment and selection, (2) training, (3) organization, (4) supervision, (5) motivation, (6) compensation, and (7) evaluation and control. Sales managers perform these tasks in a demanding and complex environment. They must manage an increasingly diverse sales force that includes more women and minorities. Women account for nearly half of U.S. professional salespeople, and their numbers are growing at a faster rate than that for men. As the workforce composition continues to change, an even more diverse blend of people will be needed to fill a growing number of sales positions. Employment opportunities for sales and related fields are expected to increase faster than the average for all occupations through the next decade.[30]

RECRUITMENT AND SELECTION

Recruiting and selecting successful salespeople are among the sales manager's greatest challenges. After all, these workers will collectively determine just how successful the sales manager is. New salespeople—like you—might come from colleges and universities, trade and business schools, other companies, and even the firm's current nonsales staff. A successful sales career offers satisfaction in all of the following five areas a person generally considers when deciding on a profession:

1. *Opportunity for advancement.* Studies have shown that successful sales representatives advance rapidly in most companies.

2. *Potential for high earnings.* Salespeople have the opportunity to earn a very comfortable living.

3. *Personal satisfaction.* A salesperson derives satisfaction from achieving success in a competitive environment and from helping customers satisfy their wants and needs.

4. *Job security.* Selling provides a high degree of job security because there is always a need for good salespeople.

5. *Independence and variety.* Salespeople often work independently, calling on customers in their territory. They have the freedom to make important decisions about meeting their customers' needs and frequently report that no two workdays are the same.

Careful selection of salespeople is important for two reasons. First, a company invests a substantial amount of time and money in the selection process. Second, hiring mistakes can damage relationships with customers and overall performance, and are costly to correct.

Most large firms use a specific seven-step process in selecting sales personnel: application screening, initial interview, in-depth interview, testing, reference checks, physical examination, and hiring decision. An application screening typically is followed by an initial interview. If the applicant looks promising, an in-depth interview takes place. During the interview, a sales manager looks for the person's enthusiasm, organizational skills, ambition, persuasiveness, ability to follow instructions, and sociability.

Next, the company may administer aptitude, interest, and knowledge tests. One popular testing approach is the assessment center. This technique uses situational exercises, group discussions, and various job simulations, allowing the sales manager to measure a candidate's skills, knowledge, and ability. Assessment centers enable managers to see what potential salespeople can do rather than what they say they can do. Before hiring a candidate, the firm checks references, reviews company policies, and may request a physical examination.

TRAINING

To shape new sales recruits into an efficient sales organization, managers must conduct an effective training program. The principal methods used in sales training are on-the-job training, individual instruction, in-house classes, and external seminars.

Popular training techniques include instructional videos or DVDs, lectures, role-playing exercises, and interactive computer programs. Simulations can help salespeople improve their selling techniques. Many firms supplement their training by enrolling salespeople in executive development programs at local colleges and by hiring specialists to teach customized training programs. In other instances, sales reps attend courses and workshops developed by outside companies.

While sales meetings often are packed with a hodgepodge of topics, they can be an excellent vehicle for sales training. Georgia-based Integra Logistics, a freight-shipping enterprise, uses its annual sales meeting as a platform for training. Recently, in one 90-minute presentation, two of Integra's top sellers outlined how they close a deal. The practical advice and give-and-take in such sessions motivates colleagues to reassess their own skills and try new techniques. One new rep applied the techniques and doubled sales for his account.[31]

Ongoing sales training is important for all salespeople, even veterans. Sales managers often conduct this type of training informally, traveling with field reps and then offering constructive criticism or suggestions. Like sales meetings, classes and workshops are other ways to reinforce training. Mentoring is also a key tool in training salespeople.

ORGANIZATION

Sales managers are responsible for the organization of the field sales force. General organizational alignments—usually made by top marketing management—may be based on geography, products, types of customers, or some combination of these factors. Figure 17.3 presents a streamlined organizational chart illustrating each of these alignments.

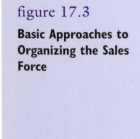

figure 17.3

Basic Approaches to Organizing the Sales Force

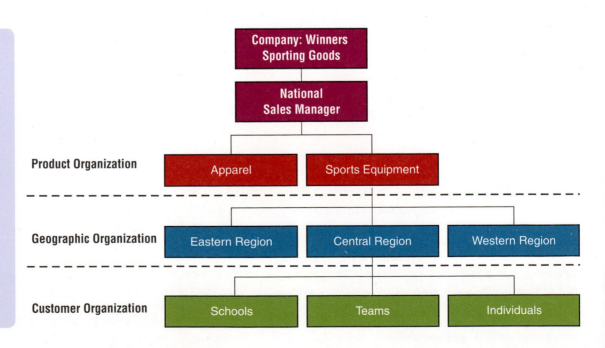

A product sales organization is likely to have a specialized sales force for each major category of the firm's products. This approach is common among B2B companies that market large numbers of highly technical, complex products sold through different marketing channels.

Firms that market similar products throughout large territories often use geographic specialization. Multinational corporations may have different sales divisions on different continents and in different countries. A geographic organization may also be combined with one of the other organizational methods.

However, many companies are moving away from using territorial sales reps as they adopt customer-focused sales forces. For example, a single territory that contains two major customers might be redefined so that the same sales rep covers both customers. Customer-oriented organizations use different sales force strategies for each major type of customer served. Some firms assign separate sales forces for their consumer and organizational customers. Others have sales forces for specific industries, such as financial services, educational, and automotive. Sales forces can also be organized by customer size, with a separate sales force assigned to large, medium, and small accounts.

Many firms using a customer-oriented structure adopt a **national accounts organization.** This format strengthens a firm's relationship with its largest customers by assigning senior sales personnel or sales teams to major accounts in each market. Organizing by national accounts helps sales representatives develop cooperation among departments to meet special needs of the firm's most important customers. An example of national account selling is the relationship between Wal-Mart and its major vendors. S. C. Johnson, Unilever, H. J. Heinz, Johnson & Johnson, Kimberly-Clark, Kraft, Nestlé, Hormel, and Colgate Palmolive are just some of the companies that have sales offices near Wal-Mart's headquarters in Bentonville, Arkansas.

As companies expand their market coverage across national borders, they may use a variant of national account sales teams. These global account teams may be staffed by local sales representatives in the countries in which a company is operating. In other instances, the firm selects highly trained sales executives from its domestic operations. In either case, specialized training is critical to the success of a company's global sales force.

The individual sales manager also must organize the sales territories within his or her area of responsibility. Factors such as sales potential, strengths and weaknesses of available personnel, and workloads are considered in territory allocation decisions.

SUPERVISION

Sales managers have differing opinions about the supervision of a sales force. Individuals and situations vary, so it is impossible to write a recipe for the exact amount of supervision needed in all cases. However, a concept known as **span of control** helps provide some general guidelines. Span of control refers to the number of sales representatives who report to first-level sales managers. The optimal span of control is affected by such factors as complexity of work activities, ability of the individual sales manager, degree of interdependence among individual salespeople, and the extent of training each salesperson receives. A 6-to-1 ratio has been suggested as the optimal span of control for first-level sales managers supervising technical or industrial salespeople. In contrast, a 10-to-1 ratio is recommended if sales representatives are calling on wholesale and retail accounts.

MOTIVATION

What motivates salespeople to perform their best? The sales manager is responsible for finding the answer to this question. The sales process involves problem solving, which sometimes includes frustration—particularly when a sale is delayed or falls through. Information sharing, recognition, bonuses, incentives, and benefits can all be used to help defray frustration and motivate a sales staff. Developing an enthusiastic sales staff who are happy at their jobs is the goal of the sales manager. Motivation is an important part of a company's success.

Creating a positive, motivating environment doesn't necessarily mean instituting complex or expensive incentive programs. Monetary rewards—cash—often is considered king. But sometimes simple recognition—a thank-you, a dinner, a year-end award—can go a long way. It is important for the sales manager to figure out what types of incentives will be most effective with his or her particular group of employees. Some firms go all out, dangling luxury items such as computers, digital cameras, or trips in front of the sales force as rewards. A Caribbean cruise, a trip to Disney World, or a long weekend in Las Vegas could be the carrot that works, particularly if family members are included. Some firms purchase gift cards from retailers such as L.L.Bean or Lowe's to distribute to sales staff who perform well.

But not all incentive programs are effective at motivating employees. A program with targets set too high, that isn't publicized, or that allows only certain sales personnel to participate can actually backfire. So it is important for sales management to plan carefully for an incentive program to succeed.

Sales managers can also gain insight into the subject of motivation by studying the various theories of motivation developed over the years. One theory that has been applied effectively to sales force motivation is **expectancy theory,** which states that motivation depends on the expectations an individual has of his or her ability to perform the job and on how performance relates to attaining rewards the individual values.

Sales managers can apply the expectancy theory of motivation by following a five-step process:

1. Let each salesperson know in detail what is expected in terms of selling goals, service standards, and other areas of performance. Rather than setting goals just once a year, many firms do so on a semiannual, quarterly, or even monthly basis.

2. Make the work valuable by assessing the needs, values, and abilities of each salesperson and then assigning appropriate tasks.

3. Make the work achievable. As leaders, sales managers must inspire self-confidence in their salespeople and offer training and coaching to reassure them.

4. Provide immediate and specific feedback, guiding those who need improvement and giving positive feedback to those who do well.

5. Offer rewards each salesperson values, whether it is an incentive as described previously, opportunity for advancement, or a bonus.

COMPENSATION

Money is an important part of any person's job, and the salesperson is no exception. So deciding how best to compensate the sales force can be a critical factor in motivation. Sales compensation can be based on a commission, a straight salary, or a combination of both. Bonuses based on end-of-year results are another popular form of compensation. The increasing popularity of team selling has also forced companies to set up reward programs to recognize performance of business units and teams. Today, about 25 percent of firms rewards business-unit performance.

A **commission** is a payment tied directly to the sales or profits a salesperson achieves. A salesperson might receive a 5 percent commission on all sales up to a specified quota, and a 7 percent commission on sales beyond that point. This approach to sales compensation is increasingly popular. But while commissions reinforce selling incentives, they may cause some sales force members to overlook nonselling activities such as completing sales reports, delivering promotion materials, and servicing existing accounts. In addition, salespeople who operate entirely on commission may become too aggressive in their approach to potential customers, which could backfire.

A **salary** is a fixed payment made periodically to an employee. A firm that bases compensation on salaries rather than commissions might pay a salesperson a set amount every week, twice a month, or once a month. A company must balance benefits and disadvantages in paying predetermined salaries to compensate managers and sales personnel. A straight salary plan gives management more control over how sales personnel allocate their efforts, but it may reduce the incentive to find new markets and land new accounts.

Many firms find it's best to develop compensation programs that combine features of both salary and commission plans. A new salesperson often receives a base salary while in training, even if he or she moves to full commission later on. If the salesperson does a lot of driving as part of the job, he or she may receive a vehicle. If the person works from home, there might be an allowance toward setting up an office there.

Total compensation packages vary according to industry, with the finance, insurance, and real estate industries coming out on top, followed closely by general services. They also vary according to years of experience in sales. Figure 17.4 reflects the findings of a recent pay survey of *account managers*—another name for a salesperson responsible for one or more customers, or *accounts*. The data show how account managers' median base pay, bonus, and commissions vary by years of experience.

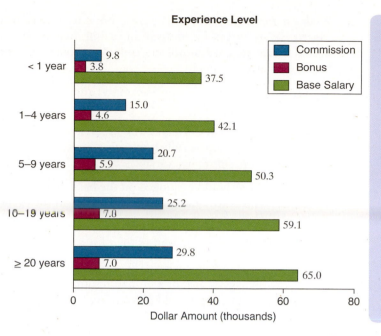

Experience Level

figure 17.4

Median Pay for Account Managers by Years of Experience

Source: Data from "Salary Survey Report," PayScale.com, http://www.payscale.com, May 24, 2009.

EVALUATION AND CONTROL

Perhaps the most difficult tasks required of sales managers are evaluation and control. Sales managers are responsible for setting standards and choosing the best methods for measuring sales performance. Sales volume, profitability, and changes in market share are the usual means of evaluating sales effectiveness. They typically involve the use of **sales quotas**—specified sales or profit targets that the firm expects salespeople to achieve. A particular sales representative might be expected to generate sales of $2.25 million in his or her territory during a given year. In many cases, the quota is tied to the compensation system. Technology has greatly improved the ability of sales managers to monitor the effectiveness of their sales staffs. Databases help sales managers to quickly divide revenues by salesperson, by account, and by geographic area.

In today's marketing environment, other measures such as customer satisfaction, profit contribution, share of product-category sales, and customer retention also come into play. This is the result of three factors:

1. A long-term orientation that results from emphasis on building customer relationships.

2. The fact that evaluations based on sales volume alone may lead to overselling and inventory problems that may damage customer relationships.

3. The need to encourage sales representatives to develop new accounts, provide customer service, and emphasize new products. Sales quotas tend to put focus on short-term selling goals rather than long-term relationships.

The sales manager must follow a formal system that includes a consistent series of decisions. This way, the manager can make fair and accurate evaluations. The system helps the sales manager answer three general questions:

1. *Where does each salesperson's performance rank relative to predetermined standards?* This comparison takes into consideration any uncontrollable variables on sales performance, such as a natural disaster or unforeseen change in the industry. Each adjusted rank is stated as a percentage of the standard.

2. *What are the salesperson's strong points?* The manager might list areas of the salesperson's performance in which he or she has performed above the standard. Or strong points could be placed in such categories as technical ability, processes, and end results.

3. *What are the salesperson's weak points?* No one likes to hear criticism, but when it is offered constructively, it can be motivation to improve performance. The manager and employee should establish specific objectives for improvement and set a timetable for judging the employee's improvement.

In completing the evaluation summary, the sales manager follows a set procedure so all employees are treated equally:

▷ Each aspect of sales performance for which a standard exists should be measured separately. This helps prevent the so-called *halo effect,* in which the rating given on one factor influences those on other performance variables.

▷ Each salesperson should be judged on the basis of actual sales performance rather than potential ability. This is why rankings are important in the evaluation.

▷ Sales managers must judge each salesperson on the basis of sales performance for the entire period under consideration, rather than for a few particular incidents.

▷ The evaluation should be reviewed by a third party, such as the manager's boss or a human resources manager, for completeness and objectivity.

Once the evaluation is complete, both manager and salesperson should focus on positive action—whether it is a drive toward new goals or correcting a negative situation. An evaluation should be motivation for improved performance.

assessment check

1. What are the seven basic functions performed by a sales manager?

2. Define *span of control.*

3. What are the three main questions a sales manager must address as part of a salesperson's evaluation?

7 **Explain the role of ethical behavior in personal selling.**

Ethical Issues in Sales

Promotional activities can raise ethical questions, and personal selling is no exception. A difficult economy or highly competitive environment may tempt some salespeople—particularly those new to the business—to behave in ways they might later regret. They might use the company car for a family trip or pad an expense report. They might give personal or expensive gifts to customers. They might try to sell a product they know is not right for a particular customer's needs. But today's experienced, highly professional salespeople know long-term success requires a strong code of ethics. They also know a single breach of ethics could have a devastating effect on their careers.

Some people believe ethical problems are inevitable because of the very nature of the sales function. And in the wake of corporate scandals in which top executives have benefited at the expense of customers, employees, and shareholders, ethical managers are working harder than ever to dispel the notion that many salespeople cannot be trusted.

Sales managers and top executives can do a lot to foster a corporate culture that encourages honesty and ethical behavior. Here are some characteristics of such a culture:

▷ *Employees understand what is expected of them.* A written code of ethics—which should be reviewed by all employees—in addition to ethics training helps educate employees in how to conduct ethical business.

▷ *Open communication.* Employees who feel comfortable talking with their supervisors are more apt to ask questions if they are uncertain about situations or decisions and to report any violations they come across.

▷ *Managers lead by example.* Workers naturally emulate the ethical behavior of managers. A sales manager who is honest with customers, doesn't accept inappropriate gifts, and leaves the company car at home during vacation is likely to be imitated by his or her sales staff.

Open communication is an important component in a corporate culture that encourages honesty and ethical behavior.

© Michael Newman/PhotoEdit

Regardless of corporate culture, every salesperson is responsible for his or her own behavior and relationship with customers. If, as a new salesperson, you find yourself uncertain about a decision, ask yourself these questions. The answers should help you make the ethical choice.

1. Does my decision affect anyone other than myself and the bottom line?

2. Is my success based on making the sale or creating a loyal customer?

3. Is my service of a customer in their best interest and not exploiting their trust?

4. What price will I pay for this decision?

assessment check

1. Why is it important for salespeople to maintain ethical behavior?

2. What are the characteristics of companies that foster corporate cultures that encourage ethical behavior?

Sales Promotion

Sales promotion includes marketing activities other than personal selling, advertising, and publicity designed to enhance consumer purchasing and dealer effectiveness. Sales promotion can be traced back as far as the ruins of Pompeii and Ephesus. In the United States, companies have been giving away trinkets and premiums for more than 100 years.

Sales promotion techniques were originally intended as short-term incentives aimed at producing an immediate response: a purchase. Today, however, marketers recognize sales promotion as an integral part of the overall marketing plan, and the focus has shifted from short-term goals to long-term objectives of building brand equity and maintaining continuing purchases. A frequent-flyer program enables a new airline to build a base of loyal customers. A frequent-stay program allows a hotel chain to attract regular guests.

Both retailers and manufacturers use sales promotions to offer consumers extra incentives to buy. These promotions are likely to stress price advantages, giveaways, or special offerings. The general objectives of sales promotion are to speed up the sales process and increase sales volume. Promotions can also help build loyalty. Through a consumer promotion, a marketer encourages consumers to try the product, use more of it, and buy it again. The firm also hopes to foster sales of related

8 **Describe the role of sales promotion in the promotional mix, and identify the different types of sales promotions.**

sales promotion
Marketing activities other than personal selling, advertising, and publicity that enhance consumer purchasing and dealer effectiveness.

Retailers use sales promotions to offer consumers extra incentives to buy.

© AP Images/Stew Milne

items and increase impulse purchases. Back-to-school sales are one type of sales promotion. Retailers run them each fall to attract shoppers who need clothing and supplies for the new academic year. In a recent campaign, Staples sold a different school item, like pencils or pocket folders, for a penny each week, as well as offering 50 percent off big-ticket items such as electronics and furniture.[32]

Today, consumers have many more choices among products than in the past, and for this reason many marketers create special programs to build loyalty among their customers. However, with loyalty programs no longer unique, other marketers work to build loyalty among their customers by ensuring every aspect of their business is customer focused.[33]

Because sales promotion is so important to a marketing effort, an entire promotion industry exists to offer expert assistance in its use and to design unique promotions, just as the entire advertising industry offers similar services for advertisers. These companies, like advertising agencies, provide other firms with assistance in promoting their goods and services. Figure 17.5 shows current spending by companies for different types of sales promotions, many of which are conducted by these firms.

Sales promotions often produce their best results when combined with other marketing activities. Ads create awareness, while sales promotions lead to trial or purchase. After a presentation, a salesperson may offer a potential customer a discount coupon for the good or service. Promotions encourage immediate action because they impose limited time frames. Discount coupons and rebates usually have expiration dates. In addition, sales promotions produce measurable results, making it relatively easy for marketers to evaluate their effectiveness. If more people buy shoes during a buy-one-get-one-free promotion at a shoe store, its owners know the promotion was successful.

figure 17.5

Current Spending by Companies for Different Sales Promotions (in billions)

Source: Data from Kathleen M. Joyce, "Higher Gear," *Promo*, www.promomagazine.com, accessed June 2, 2009.

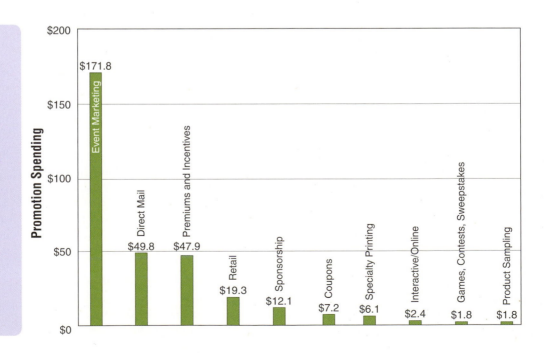

Promotion Spending

Event Marketing	$171.8
Direct Mail	$49.8
Premiums and Incentives	$47.9
Retail	$19.3
Sponsorship	$12.1
Coupons	$7.2
Specialty Printing	$6.1
Interactive/Online	$2.4
Games, Contests, Sweepstakes	$1.8
Product Sampling	$1.8

It is important to understand what sales promotions can and cannot do. They can encourage interest in both new and mature products, help introduce new products, encourage trial and repeat purchases, increase usage rates, neutralize competition, and reinforce advertising and personal selling efforts. On the other hand, sales promotions cannot overcome poor brand images, product deficiencies, or poor training for salespeople. While sales promotions increase volume in the short term, they may not lead to sales and profit growth in the long run.

Sales promotion techniques may serve all members of a marketing channel. In addition, manufacturers may use trade promotion methods to promote their products to resellers. Promotions are usually employed selectively. Sales promotion techniques include the following consumer-oriented promotions: coupons, refunds, samples, bonus packs, premiums, contests, sweepstakes, and specialty advertising. Trade-oriented promotions include trade allowances, point-of-purchase advertising, trade shows, dealer incentives, contests, and training programs.

CONSUMER-ORIENTED SALES PROMOTIONS

In the promotion industry, marketers use all types of sales promotions, including games, contests, sweepstakes, and coupons to persuade new and existing customers to try their products. Consumer-oriented sales promotions encourage repurchases by rewarding current users, boosting sales of complementary products, and increasing impulse purchases. These promotions also attract consumer attention in the midst of advertising clutter.

It's important for marketers to use sales promotions selectively; if they are overused, consumers begin to expect price discounts at all times, which ultimately diminishes brand equity. The following sections describe the various forms of consumer-oriented sales promotions.

Coupons and Refunds

Coupons, the most widely used form of sales promotion, offer discounts on the purchase price of goods and services. Consumers can redeem the coupons at retail outlets, which receive the face value of the coupon plus a handling fee from the manufacturer. The $5 billion coupon industry has been somewhat "clipped" in recent years due to more complex accounting rules that make couponing less attractive to some marketers, as well as the growing clout of retailers. In addition, consumers receive so many coupons that they cannot possibly redeem them all. In a recent year, an estimated 302 billion coupons were offered in the United States, and only 2.6 billion were redeemed.[34]

Mail, magazines, newspapers, package inserts and, increasingly, the Internet are the standard methods of distributing coupons. But another distribution channel for coupons has emerged: cell phones. Ecrio, a developer of mobile marketing technology, has pioneered a green solution to couponing with its MoBeam Barcode Service, which permits retailers to distribute coupons digitally to cell phone users, who can also redeem the coupons digitally when they shop.[35]

Refunds, or rebates, offer cash back to consumers who send in proof of purchasing one or more products. Refunds help packaged-goods companies increase purchase rates, promote multiple purchases, and reward product users. Although many consumers find the refund forms too bothersome to complete, plenty still do.

Coupons, which offer discounts on goods and services, can be redeemed at retail outlets.

© Susan Van Etten/PhotoEdit

Samples, Bonus Packs, and Premiums

Marketers are increasingly adopting the "try it, you'll like it" approach as an effective means of getting consumers to try and then purchase their goods and services. **Sampling** refers to the free distribution of a product in an attempt to obtain future sales. Samples may be distributed door-to-door, by mail, online, via demonstrations in stores or at events, or by including them in packages with other products.

Sampling produces a higher response rate than most other promotions. About three-quarters of the consumers who receive samples try them, particularly if they have requested the samples, and total annual spending on this sales promotion technique has topped $1 billion. According to a recent survey, 92 percent of consumers reported they would buy a new product after trying a free sample, assuming the price is right.[36] With sampling, marketers can target potential customers and be certain the product reaches them. Sampling provides an especially useful way to promote new or unusual products because it gives the consumer a direct product experience. It also has a "Wow!" factor. After Georgia-Pacific spent over $200 million reformulating its best-selling Brawny paper towels, the company inserted samples into Sunday newspapers so consumers nationwide could feel the new product for themselves. Georgia-Pacific followed up during the spring and summer months with live distributions of Bounty samples at festivals throughout the country.[37]

A major disadvantage of sampling is the high cost involved. Not only must the marketer give away small quantities of a product that might otherwise have generated revenues through regular sales, but the market is also in effect closed for the time it takes consumers to use up the samples. In addition, the marketer may encounter problems in distributing the samples. Hellman's marketers once annoyed consumers instead of pleasing them when the firm distributed sample packets of Italian and French salad dressing in home-delivered copies of the *New York Times*. Many of the packets burst when the papers hit the driveways.

A **bonus pack** is a specially packaged item that gives the purchaser a larger quantity at the regular price. For instance, Camay soap recently offered three bars for the price of two, and Salon Selectives is known to increase the size of its shampoos and conditioners for the same price as regular sizes. **Premiums** are items given free or at reduced cost with purchases of other products. For example, Pantene frequently attaches a purse-size bottle of hairspray to the sides of its other hair-care products. Premiums have proven effective in motivating consumers to try new products or different brands. A premium should have some relationship with the product or brand it accompanies, though. For example, a home improvement center might offer free measuring tapes to its customers.

Contests and Sweepstakes

Firms often sponsor contests and sweepstakes to introduce new goods and services and to attract additional customers. **Contests** require entrants to complete a task such as solving a puzzle or answering questions in a trivia quiz, and they may also require proofs of purchase. **Sweepstakes,** on the other hand, choose winners by chance, so no product purchase is necessary. They are more popular with consumers than contests because they do not take as much effort for consumers to enter. Marketers like them, too, because they are inexpensive to run and the number of winners is predetermined. With some contests, the sponsors cannot predict the number of people who will correctly complete the puzzles or gather the right number of symbols from scratch-off cards. But sweepstakes have generated some backlash, as the "Solving an Ethical Controversy" feature describes.

Marketers increasingly are turning to the Internet for contests and sweepstakes because of its relatively low cost and ability to provide data immediately. Interactivity is also a key part of the online experience: as consumers become more engaged in the contest or sweepstakes event, they also build a relationship with the firm's products. To promote its Delivery Intercept service, which enables anyone in the supply chain—including the customer—to redirect a package, UPS sponsored the "Delivery Intercept Challenge" video contest. The company invited contestants to submit video clips of amateur football interceptions, with viewers voting online for their favorite. UPS awarded prizes to eight finalists, with the grand-prize winner receiving $25,000 cash and a $10,000 donation to the amateur football team of his or her choice.[38] With the recent rash of

Solving an ethical controversy

Limiting Sweepstakes Fraud

The U.S. government has cracked down on telemarketers with the Do Not Call Registry and levies stiff penalties against mail fraud. Still, bogus sweepstakes flourish. Scam artists tend to prey on the elderly, and some unsuspecting seniors have been duped out of their life savings through realistic-looking but phony claims that come by regular mail, e-mail, and phone. As the Internet grows and the baby boom generation ages, criminals will have even more "fertile territory" to exploit.

Should the government ban sweepstakes to prevent fraud?

PRO

1. According to the FBI, sweepstakes fraud is increasing nation-wide and globally because it is lucrative and difficult to eliminate. Furthermore, it is underreported because victims typically are ashamed of having been tricked.

2. Because the fraud is so pervasive and some perpetrators too slick to track, law-enforcement authorities estimate that illegal sweepstakes may outnumber the lawful ones.

CON

1. Sweepstakes are legitimate vehicles for marketers to use in promoting their brand. Companies should be free to use the promotions that help them creatively engage customers and build sales.

2. Prohibiting the use of sweepstakes would only punish law-abiding businesses, not track down the criminals.

Summary

The rise of the Internet has shown us how easy it is to be tricked by false claims, and fraud can now be perpetrated on a global basis. All consumers are responsible for learning what they must do to safeguard their personal information and protect their finances, whether they are online, on the phone, or responding to their mail. And if consumers want to participate in sweep-stakes, they need to know the basics. In a legal sweepstakes, you *never* have to pay anything. Before you jump in, read the fine print. Never call a 900 number to claim a prize, and *never* give any personal information. When in doubt about a company's or organization's legitimacy, check with the Better Business Bureau. And remember, it's safer to be skeptical.

Sources: Federal Trade Commission Web site, "Sweepstakes & Lotteries Scams," www.ftc.gov, accessed June 2, 2009; "How to Avoid Sweepstakes Fraud," *eHow*, www.ehow.com, accessed June 2, 2009; United States Postal Service Web site, www.usps.com, accessed June 2, 2009; Tom Jackman, "Families Urged to Fight Elder Mail Fraud," *Chicago Tribune*, August 17, 2008, p. 6.

court rulings and legal restrictions, the use of contests requires careful administration. A firm contemplating this promotional technique might consider the services of online promotion specialists such as WebStakes or NetStakes.

Specialty Advertising

The origin of specialty advertising has been traced to the Middle Ages, when artisans gave wooden pegs bearing their names to prospects, who drove them into the walls at home to serve as convenient hangers for armor. Corporations began putting their names on a variety of products in the late 1800s, as newspapers and print shops explored new methods to earn additional revenues from their expensive printing presses. Today, just about everyone owns a cap or T-shirt with the name or logo of a company, organization, or product displayed on it.

Specialty advertising is a sales promotion technique that places the advertiser's name, address, and advertising message on useful articles that are then distributed to target consumers. Wearable products are the most popular, accounting for nearly a third of specialty advertising sales. Pens, mugs, glassware, and calendars are other popular forms.

Advertising specialties help reinforce previous or future advertising and sales messages. Consumers like these giveaways, which generate stronger responses to direct mail, resulting in three times the dollar volume of sales compared with direct mail alone. Companies use this form of promotion to highlight store openings and new products, motivate salespeople, increase visits to trade show booths, and remind customers about their products.

TRADE-ORIENTED PROMOTIONS

Sales promotion techniques can also contribute effectively to campaigns aimed at retailers and wholesalers. **Trade promotion** is sales promotion that appeals to marketing intermediaries rather than to final consumers. Marketers use trade promotions in push strategies by encouraging resellers to stock new products, continue to carry existing ones, and promote both effectively to consumers. The typical firm spends about half of its promotional budget on trade promotion—as much money as it spends on advertising and consumer-oriented sales promotions combined. Successful trade promotions offer financial incentives. They require careful timing and attention to costs and are easy to implement by retailers. These promotions should bring quick results and improve retail sales.

Trade Allowances

Among the most common trade promotion methods are **trade allowances**—special financial incentives offered to wholesalers and retailers that purchase or promote specific products. These offers take various forms. A buying allowance gives retailers a discount on goods. They include off-invoice allowances through which retailers deduct specified amounts from their invoices or receive free goods, such as one free case for every ten ordered. When a manufacturer offers a promotional allowance, it agrees to pay the reseller a certain amount to cover the costs of special promotional displays or extensive advertising that features the manufacturer's product. The goal is to increase sales to consumers by encouraging resellers to promote their products effectively.

As mentioned in previous chapters, some retailers require vendors to pay a special slotting allowance before they agree to take on new products. These fees guarantee slots, or shelf space, for newly introduced items in the stores. This practice is common in large supermarket chains. Retailers defend these fees as essential to cover the added costs of carrying the products, such as redesigning display space and shelves, setting up and administering control systems, managing inventory, and taking the risks inherent in stocking new products. The fees can be sizable, from several hundred dollars per store to many thousands of dollars for a retail chain and millions of dollars for nationally distributed products.

Point-of-Purchase Advertising

A display or other promotion located near the site of the actual buying decision is known as **point-of-purchase (POP) advertising.** This method of sales promotion capitalizes on the fact

MARKETING SUCCESS   Coast to Coast, It's the Eco Trade Show

Background. Growing concerns about climate change, rising energy costs, and new government energy mandates: these are just some of the factors contributing to the fast growth of the green products industry. Today, businesses of all kinds seek ways to reduce their use of natural resources. And consumers from all walks of life are interested in leading a greener life and reducing their personal impact on the environment.

The Challenge. For entrepreneurs, the green products industry represents a huge opportunity, estimated to be a $250 billion market. But while the number of interested buyers continues to mount, finding the right vendors in such an emerging market isn't always easy.

The Strategy. Green West, a three-day convention in Los Angeles, promotes eco-friendly business and healthy living.

that buyers make many purchase decisions within the store, so it encourages retailers to improve on-site merchandising. Product suppliers assist the retailer by creating special displays designed to stimulate sales of the promoted item. Although it is difficult to obtain concrete measures of spending on POP advertising, one estimate suggests it will hit about $27 billion a year in spending by 2010.[39]

In point-of-purchase advertising, product suppliers assist the retailer by creating special displays designed to stimulate sales, such as this special Windows Vista display.

© JAY LAPRETE/Bloomberg News/Landov

Freestanding POP promotions often appear at the ends of shopping aisles. On a typical trip to the supermarket, you might see a POP display for Disney videos, Coppertone sunscreen, or Diet Pepsi Max soda. Warehouse-style retailers such as Home Depot and Sam's Club, along with Staples and Kmart, all use POP advertising displays frequently. Electronic kiosks, which allow consumers to place orders for items not available in the store, have begun to transform the POP display industry, as creators of these displays look for ways to involve consumers more actively as well as entertain them.

Trade Shows

To influence resellers and other members of the distribution channel, many marketers participate in **trade shows.** These shows often are organized by industry trade associations; frequently, they are part of these associations' annual meetings or conventions. Vendors who serve the industries display and demonstrate their products for attendees. Industries that hold trade shows include manufacturers of sporting goods, medical equipment, electronics, automobiles, clothing, and home furnishings. Service industries include hair styling, health care, travel, and restaurant franchises. The "Marketing Success" feature discusses another popular trend in trade shows: environmentally friendly products.

Because of the expense involved in trade shows, a company must assess the value of these shows on several criteria such as direct sales, any increase in product awareness, image building, and any contribution to the firm's marketing communications efforts. Trade shows give especially effective opportunities to introduce new products and to generate sales leads. Some types of shows reach ultimate consumers as well as channel members. Home, recreation, and automobile shows, for instance, allow businesses to display and demonstrate home improvement, recreation, and other consumer products to entire communities.

The world's first trade show devoted exclusively to environmentally sustainable products, Green West is the inspiration of conference developer Green Media Enterprises, a company whose motto is "Where Green Business Is Good Business." The show features keynote speakers from business and government; educational sessions; and an expo hall with a full spectrum of exhibitors including architects, electronics firms, interior designers, technology companies, landscapers, paint manufacturers, plumbing suppliers, solar panel companies, space planners, and other green vendors. In addition, the show featured a demonstration kitchen where chefs prepared tasty dishes made without meat or dairy products.

The Outcome. In its inaugural show, Green West attracted more than 3,000 people. Attendees took advantage of the show's free "Adopt a Tree" program and networked between sessions at the Green Careers Center sponsored by staffing experts Manpower Inc. At the Sustainable Living Spaces pavilion, visitors toured a model home constructed entirely from recycled materials, less-toxic water-based paint, and fast-growing bamboo. Green West's companion expo, known as Green East, followed only months later. Plans are underway for future years' shows.

Sources: Green East Expo Web site, www.sustainablefacility.com, accessed June 2, 2009; Green West Web site, www.greenwestexpo.com, accessed June 2, 2009; Andrea Chang, "An Eco-friendly Expo in L.A.: Green West Provides a Showcase for Products That Promote Recycling and Saving Energy," *Los Angeles Times*, May 21, 2008, articles.latimes.com; "Eco-advantage Salon to Run Concurrently with Green West Expo," *Reuters*, January 8, 2008, www.reuters.com.

Dealer Incentives, Contests, and Training Programs

Manufacturers run dealer incentive programs and contests to reward retailers and their salespeople who increase sales and, more generally, to promote specific products. These channel members receive incentives for performing promotion-related tasks and can win contests by reaching sales goals. Manufacturers may offer major prizes to resellers such as trips to exotic places. **Push money**—which retailers commonly refer to as *spiffs*—is another incentive that gives retail salespeople cash rewards for every unit of a product they sell. This benefit increases the likelihood that the salesperson will try to persuade a customer to buy the product rather than a competing brand.

For more expensive and highly complex products, manufacturers often provide specialized training for retail salespeople. This background helps sales personnel explain features, competitive advantages, and other information to consumers. Training can be provided in several ways: a manufacturer's sales representative can conduct training sessions during regular sales calls, or the firm can distribute sales literature and DVDs.

assessment check

1. Define *sales promotion*.

2. Identify at least four types of consumer-oriented sales promotions.

3. Identify at least three types of trade-oriented sales promotions.

Strategic Implications of Marketing in the 21st Century

today's salespeople are a new breed. Richly nourished in a tradition of sales, their roles are strengthened even further through technology. However, as many companies are discovering, nothing can replace the power of personal selling in generating sales and in building strong, loyal customer relationships.

Salespeople today are a critical link in developing relationships between the customer and the company. They communicate customer needs and wants to coworkers in various units within an organization, enabling a cooperative, companywide effort in improving product offerings and in better satisfying individuals within the target market. For salespeople, the greatest benefit of electronic technologies is the ability to share knowledge when it is needed with those who need to know, including customers, suppliers, and employees.

Because buyers are now more sophisticated, demanding more rapid and lower-cost transactions, salespeople must be quick and creative as they find solutions to their customers' problems. Product lifecycles are accelerating, and customers who demand more are likely to switch from one product to another.

Recognizing the long-term impact of keeping satisfied buyers—those who make repeat and cross-purchases and provide referrals—versus dissatisfied buyers, organizations are increasingly training their sales forces to provide superior customer service and rewarding them for increasing satisfaction levels.

The traditional skills of a salesperson included persuasion, selling ability, and product knowledge. But today's sales professionals are also likely to possess strong communication and problem-solving skills. Earlier generations of sales personnel tended to be self-driven; today's sales professional is more likely to be a team player as well as a customer advocate who serves his or her buyers by solving problems.

The modern professional salesperson is greatly assisted by the judicious use of both consumer- and trade-oriented sales promotions. Sales promotion often is overlooked in discussions of high-profile advertising; the typical firm allocates more promotional dollars for sales promotion than for advertising. The proven effectiveness of sales promotion makes it a widely used promotional mix component for most marketers.

Review of Chapter Objectives

1 Describe the role of today's salesperson.

Today's salesperson seeks to form long-lasting relationships with customers by providing high levels of customer service rather than going for the quick sale. Firms have begun to integrate their computer and communications technologies into the sales function, so people involved in personal selling have an expanded role.

2 Describe the four sales channels.

Over-the-counter (retail) selling takes place in a retail location and usually involves providing product information and completing a sale. Field selling involves making personal sales calls on customers. Under certain circumstances, telemarketing is used to provide product information and answer questions from customers who call. Inside selling relies on phone, mail, and e-marketing to provide sales and product services for customers on a continuing basis.

3 Describe the major trends in personal selling.

Companies are turning to relationship selling, consultative selling, and team selling. Relationship selling occurs when a salesperson builds a mutually beneficial relationship with a customer on a regular basis over an extended period. Consultative selling involves meeting customer needs by listening to customers, understanding and caring about their problems, paying attention to the details, and following through after the sale. Team selling occurs when the salesperson joins with specialists from other functional areas of the firm to complete the selling process.

4 Identify and briefly describe the three basic sales tasks.

Order processing is the routine handling of an order. It characterizes a sales setting in which the need is made known and is acknowledged by the customer. Creative selling is persuasion aimed at making the prospect see the value of the good or service presented. Missionary selling is indirect selling, such as making goodwill calls and providing technical or operational assistance.

5 Outline the seven steps in the sales process.

The basic steps in the sales process are prospecting and qualifying, approach, presentation, demonstration, handling objections, closing, and follow-up.

6 Identify the seven basic functions of a sales manager.

A sales manager links the sales force to other aspects of the internal and external environments. The manager's functions are recruitment and selection, training, organization, supervision, motivation, compensation, and evaluation and control.

7 Explain the role of ethical behavior in personal selling.

Ethical behavior is vital to building positive, long-term relationships with customers. Although some people believe ethical problems are inevitable, employers can do much to foster a corporate culture that encourages honesty and ethical behavior. In addition, each salesperson is responsible for his or her own behavior and relationship with customers.

8 Describe the role of sales promotion in the promotional mix, and identify the different types of sales promotions.

Sales promotion includes activities other than personal selling, advertising, and publicity designed to enhance consumer purchasing and dealer effectiveness. Sales promotion is an integral part of the overall marketing plan, intended to increase sales and build brand equity. Promotions often produce their best results when combined with other marketing activities.

Consumer-oriented sales promotions include coupons, refunds, samples, bonus packs, premiums, contests and sweepstakes, and specialty advertising. Trade-oriented promotions include trade allowances, point-of-purchase (POP) advertising, trade shows, dealer incentives, contests, and training programs.

assessment check: answers

1.1 What is personal selling?

Personal selling is the process of a seller's person-to-person promotional presentation to a buyer.

1.2 What is the main focus of today's salespeople?

The main focus of today's salespeople is to build long-lasting relationships with customers.

2.1 What is over-the-counter selling?

Over-the-counter selling describes selling in retail and some wholesale locations. Most of these transactions take place directly with customers.

2.2 What is field selling?

Field selling involves making sales calls on prospective and existing customers at their businesses or homes.

2.3 Distinguish between outbound and inbound telemarketing.

Outbound telemarketing takes place when a salesperson phones customers; inbound telemarketing takes place when customers call the firm.

3.1 Identify the three major personal selling approaches.

The three major personal selling approaches are relationship selling, consultative selling, and team selling.

3.2 Distinguish between relationship selling and consultative selling.

Relationship selling is a technique for building a mutually beneficial partnership with a customer. Consultative selling involves meeting customer needs by listening to, understanding, and paying attention to their problems, then following up after a sale.

4.1 What are the three major tasks performed by salespeople?

The three major tasks are order processing, creative selling, and team selling.

4.2   What are the three steps of order processing?

The three steps of order processing are identifying customer needs, pointing out the need to the customer, and completing the order.

5.1   Identify the seven steps of the sales process.

The seven steps of the sales process are prospecting and qualifying, approach, presentation, demonstration, handling objections, closing, and follow-up.

5.2   Why is follow-up important to the sales effort?

Follow-up allows the salesperson to reinforce the customer's purchase decision, strengthen the bond, and correct any problems.

6.1   What are the seven basic functions performed by a sales manager?

The seven basic functions of a sales manager are recruitment and selection, training, organization, supervision, motivation, compensation, and evaluation and control.

6.2   Define *span of control*.

Span of control refers to the number of sales representatives who report to first-level sales managers.

6.3   What are the three main questions a sales manager must address as part of a salesperson's evaluation?

The three main questions a sales manager must address are the following: Where does each salesperson's performance rank relative to predetermined standards? What are the salesperson's strong points? What are the salesperson's weak points?

7.1   Why is it important for salespeople to maintain ethical behavior?

Salespeople need to maintain ethical behavior because it is vital to their firm's relationships with customers and because they are representing their company. A breach of ethics could also be detrimental to an individual's career.

7.2   What are the characteristics of companies that foster corporate cultures that encourage ethical behavior?

Characteristics of corporations fostering ethical behavior include the following: employees who understand what is expected of them, open communication, and managers who lead by example.

8.1   Define *sales promotion*.

Sales promotion includes marketing activities other than personal selling, advertising, and publicity designed to enhance consumer purchasing and dealer effectiveness.

8.2   Identify at least four types of consumer-oriented sales promotions.

Consumer-oriented sales promotions include coupons, refunds, samples, bonus packs, premiums, contests, sweepstakes, and specialty advertising.

8.3   Identify at least three types of trade-oriented sales promotions.

Trade-oriented sales promotions include trade allowances, POP advertising, trade shows, dealer incentives, contests, and training programs.

Marketing Terms You Need to Know

personal selling 566
over-the-counter selling 568
field selling 569
telemarketing 570

inside selling 571
relationship selling 572
consultative selling 572
team selling 574

order processing 575
creative selling 576
missionary selling 576
sales promotion 587

Other Important Marketing Terms

network marketing 569
outbound telemarketing 570
inbound telemarketing 570
cross-selling 574
virtual sales team 574
sales incentives 576
prospecting 577
qualifying 577
approach 577
precall planning 578
presentation 578
cold calling 578

demonstration 579
objection 579
closing 580
follow-up 580
national accounts organization 583
span of control 583
expectancy theory 584
commission 584
salary 584
sales quota 585
coupon 589
refund 589

sampling 590
bonus pack 590
premium 590
contest 590
sweepstakes 590
specialty advertising 591
trade promotion 592
trade allowance 592
point-of-purchase (POP) advertising 592
trade show 593
push money 594

Assurance of Learning Review

1. How does each of the following factors affect the decision to emphasize personal selling or nonpersonal advertising and sales promotion?
   a. geographic market concentration
   b. length of marketing channels
   c. degree of product technical complexity

2. Which of the four sales channels is each of the following salespeople most likely to use?
   a. salesperson in an American Eagle Outfitters store
   b. Coldwell Banker real estate agent
   c. route driver for Keebler snack foods (sells and delivers to local food retailers)
   d. technical support for Dell

3. What is team selling? Describe a situation in which you think it would be effective.

4. Why is it important for a salesperson to understand order processing—regardless of the type of selling he or she is engaged in?

5. What is the role of a sales incentive?

6. Suppose you are hired as a salesperson for a firm that offers prep courses for standardized tests. Where might you find some leads?

7. What is expectancy theory? How do sales managers use it?

8. What is the role of sales promotion in the marketing effort?

9. What are the benefits of sampling? What are the drawbacks?

10. What is trade promotion? What are its objectives?

Projects and Teamwork Exercises

1. Cross-selling can be an effective way for a firm to expand. On your own or with a classmate, locate an advertisement for a firm you believe could benefit from cross-selling. List ways it could offer multiple goods or services to the same customer. Then create a new ad illustrating the multiple offerings.

2. With a partner, choose one of the following sales situations. Then take turns coming up with creative ways to close the deal—one of you plays the customer and the other plays the salesperson. Present your closing scenarios to the class.
   a. You are a sales associate at a car dealership, and a potential customer has just test-driven one of your newest models. You have handled all the customer's objections and settled on a price. You don't want the customer to leave without agreeing to purchase the car.
   b. You operate a lawn-care business and have visited several homeowners in a new development. Three of them have already agreed to give your service a try. You are meeting with the fourth and want to close that sale, too.

3. As sales representatives for a cooperative of organic farmers, you and a classmate are about to make a sales presentation to a national supermarket chain. List the most important messages you wish to relate and then role-play the sales presentation.

4. On your own or with a classmate, go online and research a firm such as Kraft, General Mills, Ford, or Burger King to find out what kinds of consumer-oriented promotions the company is conducting for its various brands or individual products. Which promotions seem the most appealing to you as a consumer? Why? Present your findings to the class.

5. With a classmate, design a specialty advertising item for one of the following companies or its products, or choose one of your own. Present your design sketches to the class.
   a. Sea World or Busch Gardens
   b. Dunkin' Donuts
   c. Porsche
   d. Verizon Wireless
   e. Equal Exchange coffee
   f. Apple iPod

Critical-Thinking Exercises

1. Since the implementation of the national Do Not Call Registry, some Americans have noticed an increase in door-to-door selling as well as e-mails containing sales messages. As a marketer, do you think this type of selling is effective? Why or why not?

2. Green Mountain Coffee Roasters is well known for its specialty coffees, available in many retail outlets such as supermarkets and convenience stores. But visit a medical office or a car dealership, and you might find it there as well—in one-cup dispensers, ready for individuals to brew while waiting. This requires personal selling to office managers, doctors, and the like. What role does relationship selling play in this situation? What kind of training might Green Mountain sales reps receive?

3. Imagine you want to sell your parents on the idea of your taking a trip, buying a car, attending graduate school—something important to you. Outline your approach and presentation as a salesperson would.

4. Why is the recruitment and selection stage of the hiring process one of a sales manager's greatest challenges?

5. Food manufacturers often set up tables in supermarkets and offer free samples to shoppers, along with coupons for the promoted items. Sometimes restaurants offer free coffee or drink refills. What other products might lend themselves to sampling? Make a list. Pick one of the items and come up with a sampling plan for it. Where and when would you sample? To whom would you offer samples?

Ethics Exercise

You have been hired by a discount sporting-goods retailer in an over-the-counter sales position. You have completed a training course that includes learning about the products, assisting customers, and cross-selling. You have made several good friends in the training course and sometimes get together after work to go running, play golf, or have dinner. You've noticed that one of your friends has really taken the training course to heart and has adopted a very aggressive attitude toward customers in the store, pushing them to buy just about anything, whether they need it or not. Your friend even boasted about selling a boogie board to the father of a boy who didn't know how to swim.

1. Do you agree with your friend's actions? Why or why not?

2. Should you discuss the situation with your friend? Should you discuss it with your supervisor? Explain your response.

Internet Exercises

1. **Sales careers.** Go to the Web site of the *Occupational Outlook Handbook* (bls.gov/oco). In the left column, click on the "Sales" link and answer the following questions:
   a. How many people are currently employed in sales-related occupations?
   b. How fast is employment in sales-related occupations expected to grow over the next few years? Is this faster or slower than overall employment growth?
   c. What is the average compensation? Does it vary from industry to industry?
   d. After reviewing the material on sales occupations, are you more or less interested in a sales career? Explain your answer.

2. **Online couponing.** Visit the Web site of ValPak (www.valpak.com), a leading source of online coupons. Write a brief report summarizing what you learned, including your overall impression of online coupons.

3. **Trade shows.** Interbike is the largest bicycle industry trade show in North America. Go to its Web site (www.interbike.com). When and where is Interbike held? How many people attend? Who attends? Review the material in the chapter on trade shows. If you were a manufacturer or distributor of bicycle-related products, give three reasons why your firm should attend Interbike.

Note: Internet Web addresses change frequently. If you don't find the exact site listed, you may need to access the organization's home page and search from there or use a search engine such as Google.

Case 17.1 Chrysler Pins Its Hopes on Sales Star

After a home, a car is likely the biggest purchase most consumers ever make. And arguably, no other big-ticket item is

as dependent on the quality of personal selling to close the deal. For decades, U.S. automakers clearly dominated the auto industry, but that picture began to change in the 1970s, when the Japanese began exporting cars to the United States. Gradually, by paying close attention to consumers' changing preferences, Japanese imports gained a foothold in America, and in 2007 Toyota overtook General Motors in worldwide sales.

Surprisingly, that same year, with Toyota cruising along in the United States, the president of Toyota Motor North America left his employer of 37 years to become vice chairman and president of Chrysler. Observers described the move as a huge coup by Chrysler, to have lured Jim Press away from Toyota. Press, widely regarded as one of the industry's leading sales and marketing professionals, is credited with masterminding the sales strategy that made Toyota king of the hill in the United States.

What would have motivated Press, an executive at the top of his game, to take a leadership position with a struggling competitor? Industry insiders say Press had held many top sales jobs at Toyota. He had worked closely with dealers known to be among the industry's most profitable. In a period of only a few years, Press helped move Toyota's U.S. market share from 10 to 16 percent.

But some say once Press rose to the presidency of Toyota's North American operations and became its public face, he eventually began to miss tackling the daily challenges associated with making a company more competitive. At Chrysler, Press assumed responsibility for sales and marketing as well as its brands and dealers. And certainly, with conflict among its dealerships and flagging sales, Chrysler hopes Press can work a miracle. Before Press came aboard, Chrysler caused a deep rift among its dealer network; dealers claim the company attempted to force them to accept delivery of many more vehicles than they could sell. As a result, an estimated 100,000 cars ended up parked in lots in the Detroit area and elsewhere—Chrysler products their dealers couldn't sell. To add to the problems, industry observers claim Chrysler is unprofitable because it needs to consolidate. It appears Jim Press has his work cut out for him. Chrysler hopes the sales veteran can work magic twice in his career.

Questions for Critical Thinking

1. Jim Press spent most of his career at Toyota, where leadership follows a set of principles it calls the Toyota Way. Chrysler, on the other hand, has had a series of executives with very different styles and a history that includes time in Chapter 11 bankruptcy, an ill-fated merger with German automaker Daimler Benz and a merger with Italian firm Fiat. Do you think the cultural differences between Toyota and Chrysler will be an advantage or a disadvantage for Press in his new role? Which Toyota experiences might be helpful to Chrysler?

2. Skilled sales leadership is essential in the auto industry, particularly when an organization has profitability problems. How should Jim Press approach the issue of adding to profitability?

What attributes of a successful sales manager will be useful in solving this problem?

Sources: Ed Hellwig, "2009 New York Auto Show: Jim Press Says Chrysler/Fiat Marriage Would Be Great," *Edmunds Inside Line,* April 8, 2009, http://blogs .edmunds.com; Poornima Gupta, "Chrysler to Introduce 7 Major Models in 2010: Executive," *Reuters,* September 10, 2008, news.yahoo.com; Jim Henry, "What, Me Worry? Says Chrysler's Jim Press," *BNET Industries,* July 2, 2008, industry.bnet.com; .David Kiley, "Chrysler's Jim Press and Toyota Differ on Prius Narrative," *BusinessWeek,* April 2, 2008, www.businessweek.com; David Kiley, "The Road to a Stronger CAFÉ Standard," *BusinessWeek,* March 24, 2008, www.businessweek.com; "Chrysler's Jim Press Says Every Car Will Be Offered as a Hybrid," *eGMCarTech,* February 29, 2008, www.egmcartech.com; Jeff Yastine, "Chrysler President Jim Press Explains His Company's Shrinkage," *Nightly Business Report,* February 0, 2000, www.pbs.org; Jean Jennings, "Jim Press," *Automobile,* January 2008, www.automobilemag.com; "Jim Press Defection Shows Chrysler's Aggression (and Fear)," *Wired,* September 7, 2007, blog.wired.com; Nick Bunkley and Micheline Maynard, "Chrysler Hires a Top Toyota Executive," *The New York Times,* September 6, 2007, www.nytimes.com.

Video Case 17.2 — Personal Selling and Sales Promotion at Scholfield Honda

The written video case on Scholfield Honda appears on page VC-16. The Scholfield Honda video is designed to expand and highlight the concepts in this chapter and the concepts and questions covered in the written video case.

part 6 voice of experience

Talking about Marketing Careers with...
Andrew Swinand

ANDREW SWINAND
President, Chief Client Officer
Starcom Worldwide

Starcom Worldwide is a major player in the media marketing communications industry; in fact, it is one of the largest full-service media divisions in the world. As part of the Starcom MediaVest Group, which has global operations in 89 markets worldwide and nearly 3,500 employees, the Chicago division specializes in media selection and buying to help leading companies position and build their brands.

Starcom's media experts develop integrated marketing communications programs, providing marketing research and promotional services for their clients. Staying on top of the fragmented media market can be challenging these days because of the spread of digital and online communications. We were able to take a few minutes to discuss the changes in the advertising and media industry with Andrew Swinand of Starcom Worldwide, and he explained his role in helping clients take advantage of those new developments.

Q: Having a career in a creative field such as media communications is a job many marketing students dream of having one day. How did your educational experience prepare you to work in this field? What jobs have you held along the way, and how did they help you reach your current position?

Prior to working at Starcom, I was in the U.S. Army, worked in account management at BBDO Worldwide [advertising agency], and was in brand management at Procter & Gamble. I also majored in economics and marketing in school. All contributed to my knowledge and success. That said, I believe the two most important qualities for success in any marketing job are curiosity and discipline. You must have a curious mind to succeed. A mind that causes you to constantly ask why—Why do consumers prefer this versus us? Why is this important to them? etc. Second, you must have the discipline

to follow through on those questions with rigor. Marketing is becoming more analytical, and clients are demanding a greater degree of accountability. Successful marketers must be able to both conceptualize the ideas, and actualize the results.

Q: What are your duties and responsibilities as President and Chief Client Officer at Starcom? What strengths and skills do you draw on in your daily work? How are your work teams organized—are they specialized into different functions or units, based on the client or industry, or some other criteria?

Our agency is split into two job functions. One group works directly with the clients to manage their media strategy, media planning, consumer understanding, and accountability. The second group works directly with media vendors to activate these plans through strategic media investment by stewarding the media buys, negotiating rates, and negotiating added value such as accountability programs. My job is to ensure our client teams are delivering the best ideas, strategy, and service to our clients.

The one thing I can say about my job is that no two days are ever alike. As Chief Client Officer, I work with teams that support clients in marketing everything from technology and databases to selling cereal or dog food. Every client has different marketing challenges and a different relationship with consumers. Part of our challenge is to be flexible enough to adjust our approach to each situation yet still have enough discipline and uniformity to our process to ensure a successful result.

Q: We know that Starcom works with some very prominent clients, such as Disney, Kellogg's, Oracle, and Procter & Gamble. How do you help your clients create a cohesive marketing message? What

types of promotions do you arrange—sponsorships, event marketing, direct marketing messages?

I think the key to any effective strategy is to start with solid consumer understanding. Many people think the goal of integrated communications is to do a little of everything and ensure it looks similar. We are finding that as consumers become more and more bombarded with messages, understanding their relationship with both the brand and the media is critically important. In what context are they watching TV, searching for information on the Internet, or seeking streaming content? Then, how do we strategically place the right content into that environment to ensure consumers are captivated by our clients' messaging? The goal is not breadth of exposure but depth of experience resulting in engagement.

Q: Today's media outlets are so numerous—network and cable TV, traditional and subscriber radio, print and online newspapers, magazines and e-zines, new interactive media, to name just a few—that companies have many different avenues through which to reach their target audiences. How do you create a strategy for your clients? What relationship does your team have with the various media outlets to be able to offer expertise on media selections?

It has been said that more has changed in media in the last 36 months than the previous 36 years. I believe this to be true and find it one of the most exciting parts of the job. I think a big change is that it is not long enough for us to do research on how consumers feel about brands. We now must constantly research how consumers are interacting with media to understand both the context of the interaction and the value they are looking to get out of the experience. At Starcom, we have created a new role called Consumer Context Planning that is dedicated to researching and discovering the links between consumers' experiences with brands, media, and advertising.

Q: What objectives do your clients have in their media campaigns? Can you give us an example? How do you gauge the effectiveness of an individual media buy—or its part in a larger campaign?

Accountability in advertising has become increasingly important. Clients now expect agencies to be able to provide proof of performance for the dollars they are given. In the past, agencies provided this proof in the form of *input*-based accountabilities (i.e., a certain reach and frequency, or TRPs [television rating points]). Today, clients want *output*-based accountability in addition. They want to know if the ads achieved the desired goals of increasing awareness, driving purchase intent, capturing consumer information, or directly driving sales. To support this need, Starcom has invested in tools that allow us to better track and report what actions consumers have taken after viewing our clients' advertising. I do not believe Starcom, or the industry, has completely solved the accountability puzzle yet, and I feel that this is an exciting area of focus for the industry.

Q: Being so involved with media communications, you must have some great advice for students on developing contacts and relationships to get started in their marketing careers. What can students do now to get a good start? What types of skills would you look for in a student interested in your field?

I think there are three things that everyone starting a career in marketing should do:

1. Define your brand: I always tell people if you can't market yourself, you probably won't be able to successfully sell soap. I would encourage students to define what is their unique selling proposition and what makes them different from or better than the competition. If candidates can effectively articulate this, it goes a long way.

2. Recognize that you are a consumer: Marketers spend millions of dollars each year to talk to consumers. When you go on an interview, go with an opinion on the products the company sells or advertises. One, they will be interested in your feedback. Two, it demonstrates that you are engaged in their business (see my comments about "curiosity" at the beginning of the interview).

3. Do your homework: It is always amazing to me how many people come into an interview unprepared. If you want to be successful in the communications industry, you must be a great communicator. Great communications come from preparation (see #1 and #2 here).

Interview used by permission of Starcom Worldwide.

part 6 promotional decisions

GREENSBURG, INC.

A Town Rebounds

© Steven J. Eliopoulos

The January 2008 press release from Greensburg GreenTown read as follows:
TOWN REBOUNDING FROM TORNADO TO BECOME ECO-TOURISM DESTINATION

Greensburg, Kansas—*Greensburg is the small Kansas town that was decimated by a powerful EF-5 tornado last May, the result of which 12 residents died and the community experienced the loss of 95% of its structures. It is rebuilding as a model green community, focusing on energy self-sufficiency and other principles of sustainability, with the aim to become the greenest community in America.*

As a component of this Green Initiative, the nonprofit organization Greensburg GreenTown launched a project to oversee the building of a dozen demonstration homes in the community. Each home will show-case different designs, technologies, and products and will serve as a "living science museum" both for residents and visitors. In addition to the educational aspects of this project, these models of sustainable living will also provide bed-and-breakfast type lodging to give people the opportunity to experience green living first-hand, in true eco-tourism fashion. Homes will be constructed of a variety of wall systems including straw bale, insulated concrete forms, structural insulated panels, and traditional wood built with "advanced framing" techniques. Each home will be equipped with monitoring devices to measure the performance of green design under real-world conditions. There are plans for homes incorporating passive solar elements, photovoltaic cells, wind generated power, and myriad other technologies of sustainable design.

Cool idea, sure, but the twelve high-tech, low-impact homes were not going to build themselves. At an estimated cost of $50,000–$300,000 per structure, GreenTown's Catherine Hart and Daniel Wallach have had to hit the pavement and the phones in search of outside help. AT&T, Caroma USA, which manufactures low-flow, dual-flush toilets, Harvest Solar Energy, university architecture departments and green building experts have com-mitted time, expertise, product, and generous cash infusions to the project.

Eco-building guru and educator Dan Chiras of EverGreen Design-Build Partnership plans to build two, 1,200-square-foot wind and solar "eco lodges." He and his team of green architects, designers, and builders alone have donated approximately $50,000. "Businesses are showing an out-pouring of generosity," Chiras said in a press release dated March 17, 2008. He has received donations of wind and solar systems, to discount energy rating and LEED certification for his project.

Despite all the generous donations of product and labor the project has received, the folks at GreenTown must work hard to keep this and other Greensburg projects moving forward. Executive Director Dan Wallach is always on the lookout for like-minded organizations to help him keep Greensburg on the map.

Ogden Publications of Topeka, Kansas has been working in the greenspace for decades. Their most popular magazine, *Mother Earth News*, was started in 1970 around the time of the very first Earth Day and features projects you can do to reduce your impact on the environment. They also publish *Natural Home*, a popular decorating and lifestyle maga-zine for those interested in greening up their homes.

One day, not long after the tornado hit, publisher and editorial director Bryan Welch received a call from Daniel Wallach at GreenTown. Wallach was looking for a partner on the model homes project. *Natural Home* had recently begun work on a model green home in Brooklyn,

New York, and Ogden had experience working on similar projects in the past offering advertisers priority product placement in exchange for donations and sponsorship. "We got involved because we thought it was cool," says Welch of the Greensburg project. "If it hadn't attracted all this attention, it would still be cool, so it was a safe bet."

It may have been safe, but it hasn't been easy.

Ogden Publications and *Mother Earth News* in particular enjoy a repu-tation for being an authority on sustainable living. This gives them a lot of credibility with their readers, but to potential advertisers, it's pretty scary. Welch admits it has been a challenge explaining to advertisers and partners that we're not "a bunch of holier than thou old hippies" ready to rip their product's greenness to shreds. For the Greensburg project, he is up against another hurdle. The whole point of the demonstration homes is for them to become a destination for visitors, a resource for builders and consumers, and potentially a home for residents. If an advertiser is placing a donated prod-uct for the purposes of advertising, in six months, that product is outdated and they've moved on to another promotion. If the buildings are going to be living examples of a sustainable lifestyle, it's pretty impractical to replace the toilets or bamboo flooring every few months. Brian recognizes this is a tricky proposition and one that will take some time to work out completely.

In the meantime, *Mother Earth News* and *Natural Home* will con-tinue to reach out to their million-plus Web visitors urging them to help keep the greenest town in America moving forward.

Questions

1. What are the challenges in soliciting product placements and dona-tions for the Model Homes Project?

2. To which sales channels does Greensburg GreenTown market the Model Homes Project?

3. Why is personal selling an important aspect of Ogden Publications' approach to advertisers?

4. Why is advertising more advantageous for Ogden's ad clients?

5. Put yourself in the role of a product manager for a company (that is, low-flush toilets, solar panels) interested in donating some of their products to the Greenburg project. Your manager has asked you to comment on whether they should concentrate on the promotion opportunities this initiative provides on the consumer, business-to-business customers, or a combination of both. Write a memo (3 to 5 pages) on the approach you suggest, along with some creative ideas.

PART 7

Pricing Decisions

Pricing
Concepts

© Terri Miller/E-Visual Communications, Inc.

Private-Label Brands Pump Up Sales

Consumers used to think of private-label products as second-class citizens—their no-frills packaging and basic formulations didn't attract much attention. They were perceived as almost as good—

but not quite—as national manufacturers' brands. Those store-brand corn flakes tasted all right, but they didn't quite have the flavor or crunch of Kellogg's Corn Flakes. Nor did they have the familiar

bright-eyed rooster displayed on the box. With fewer marketing dollars spent on private-label products, retailers could price them lower than the heavily advertised national brand products. But not everyone

bought them.

Recently that has changed. With the economic downturn, consumers today are constantly looking for ways to save money. Because private-label goods are priced on average between 5 and 20 percent less than national brands, the savings can add up quickly at the supermarket checkout counter. As consumers shift their purchase decisions to consider price more frequently, the popularity and profitability of private labels are soaring.

In addition, although the price of commodities—ingredients such as corn, wheat, and sugar—has dropped from their previous heights, the major manufacturers of national brands have been slow to reduce their prices. "The prices don't seem to go down as fast as they go up," observes the CEO of grocery chain Supervalu. So consumers are turning to lower-priced private-label goods in greater numbers. According to one survey, 74 percent of consumers say that they try to get the best price on a product. More than 67 percent of these respondents agree that store brands offer "extremely good value" for the price. Only 24 percent say that national brands are worth a higher price.

Retailers are also developing much better quality private-label goods than in years past. Innovation in research and development, expansion of product offerings, and higher-quality ingredients and processes are making store

brands even stronger contenders. Wal-Mart relaunched its Great Value private brand, which is the largest food label in the United States, with more than 5,250 products. In addition to offering comparable goods at lower prices, the firm has taken steps to equal or surpass the quality of national-brand products. For instance, the firm now uses natural colorings in its ice pops and a creamier texture in its fat-free sour cream. Entirely new products include a line of all-natural ice cream, including a cake batter flavor that customers requested.

Food manufacturers like Kraft, Kellogg, General Mills, and Sara Lee are now searching for ways to lure consumers back to their brands. Although marketers for these companies once shrugged off a slight defection to private labels, they are now serious about retaining loyalty. "One thing you don't want to do is create a consumer who [has] shifted to private label and then have to spend a lot to get them back," says the CEO of Kimberly-Clark. Interestingly, some national brands are also enjoying a resurgence in loyalty

due to the familiarity of their products in uncertain times. Heinz and Smucker's recently posted an increase in earnings with sales of Heinz ketchup, Smucker's food spreads, and additional brands such as T.G.I. Friday's frozen meals and Hungry Jack potatoes and pancakes. Marketers theorize that customers are looking for the comfort foods these firms offer. Consumers are more often staying home to eat rather than dining out—so they might pay a bit more for a national brand because they are saving in the long run by cooking at home. "The number of meals prepared and consumed at home, as recent market data indicate, continues to be trending upward in this challenging economic environment," notes Tim Smucker, chairman of Smucker's. It is likely that trend will continue for some time, possibly opening the door even farther for new private-label goods.[1]

OBJECTIVES

 Outline the legal constraints on pricing.

 Identify the major categories of pricing objectives.

 Explain price elasticity and its determinants.

4 **List the practical problems involved in applying price theory concepts to actual pricing decisions.**

 Explain the major cost-plus approaches to price setting.

 List the chief advantages and shortcomings of using breakeven analysis in pricing decisions.

7 **Explain the use of yield management in pricing decisions.**

8 **Identify the major pricing challenges facing online and international marketers.**

evolution of a brand

Wal-Mart never lets a customer get away. Whether the economy is in a boom or a bust, the firm insists on offering more products for less money. So the recent decision to relaunch its private-label Great Value brand—originally introduced in 1993, during a sluggish economy—makes sense to many observers. "This is an opportunity to provide solutions to our customers at a time when they need to save money," comments Wal-Mart's senior vice president of private brands.

- Under its Great Value brand, Wal-Mart is offering 80 new products, including its line of all-natural ice cream. Do you think innovation combined with price is an important marketing strategy? Why or why not?

- Wal-Mart has also simplified the packaging on its Great Value items to feature pictures of food products against a white background. This redesign creates a streamlined, uniform look across the entire brand. How do you think this change will affect consumers' perceptions of the Great Value products in terms of price and quality?

chapter overview

One of the first questions shoppers ask is, "How much does it cost?" Marketers understand the critical role price plays in the consumer's decision-making process. For products as varied as lipstick and perfume, automobiles and gasoline, and doughnuts and coffee, marketers must develop strategies that price products to achieve their firms' objectives.

As a starting point for examining pricing strategies, consider the meaning of the term *price*. A **price** is the exchange value of a good or service; in other words, it represents whatever that product can be exchanged for in the marketplace. Price does not necessarily denote money. In earlier times, the price of an acre of land might have been 20 bushels of wheat, three head of cattle, or one boat. Even though the barter process continues to be used in some transactions, in the 21st century, price typically refers to the amount of funds required to purchase a product.

Prices are both difficult to set and dynamic; they shift in response to a number of variables. A higher-than-average price can convey an image of prestige, while a lower-than-average price may connote good value, as the trend toward consumers' purchases of private-label store brands shows. In other instances, though, a price much lower than average may be interpreted as an indicator of inferior quality, and a higher price—like the increasing price of gasoline—may reflect both high demand and scarce supply. And pricing can also be used to modify consumer behavior.

This chapter discusses the process of determining a profitable but justifiable (fair) price. The focus is on management of the pricing function, including pricing strategies, price–quality relationships, and pricing in various sectors of the economy. The chapter also looks at the effects of environmental conditions on price determination, including legal constraints, competitive pressures, and changes in global and online markets.

price Exchange value of a good or service.

❙ **Outline the legal constraints on pricing.**

Pricing and the Law

Pricing decisions are influenced by a variety of legal constraints imposed by federal, state, and local governments. Included in the price of products are not only the cost of the raw materials, processing and packaging, and profit for the business but also the various taxes governments require providers to charge. For instance, excise taxes are levied on a variety of products, including real estate transfers, alcoholic beverages, and motor fuels. Sales taxes are charged on food, clothing, furniture, and many other purchases.

In the global marketplace, prices are directly affected by special types of taxes called *tariffs*. These taxes—levied on the sale of imported goods and services—often make it possible for firms to protect their local markets while still setting prices on domestically produced goods well above world market levels. The average tariff on fruits and vegetables around the world is more than 50 percent, although it varies considerably from country to country. The United States levies tariffs of less than 5 percent on more than half its fruit and vegetable imports, and in transactions with its largest trading partners in the produce market—Mexico and Canada—tariffs for both imports and exports are minimal or zero.[2] In other instances, tariffs are levied to prevent foreign producers from engaging in a practice described in Chapter 7: *dumping* foreign-produced products in international markets at prices lower than those set in their domestic market.

The United States is not the only country to use tariffs to protect domestic suppliers. For example, China, which now surpasses Canada as the leading source of U.S. imports, recently agreed to repeal tariffs on energy services and technologies that sometimes ran as high as 16 percent. Yet the United States and other countries still contend that Chinese trade policies put them at a disadvantage. For instance, China, rapidly becoming the world's largest market for cars, taxes imported auto parts at 10 percent. But beyond a certain quantity, those same parts are taxed at the 25 percent rate that normally applies only to completed vehicles.[3] These tariffs raise the prices overseas consumers must pay to purchase U.S. goods.

Some cities and states have enacted laws prohibiting ticket scalping, a form of ticket pricing.

© Robin Nelson/PhotoEdit

Not every "regulatory" price increase is a tax, however. Rate increases to cover costly government regulations imposed on the telecommunications industry have been appearing on Internet and cell phone bills as "regulatory cost recovery fees" or similarly named costs. But these charges are not taxes, because the companies keep all the income from the fees and apply only some of it to complying with the regulations. In essence, such "recovery fees" are a source of additional revenues in an industry so price-sensitive that any announced price increase is likely to send some customers fleeing to competitors.

Almost every person looking for a ticket to a high-demand sporting or concert event has encountered an expensive, often illegal, form of pricing called *ticket scalping*. Scalpers camp out in ticket lines—or hire someone else to stand in line—to purchase tickets they expect to resell at a higher price. Although some cities and states have enacted laws prohibiting the practice, it continues to occur in many locations.

But the ticket reselling market is both highly fragmented and susceptible to fraud and distorted pricing. In response, buyers and sellers are finding that the Internet is helping create a market in which both buyers and sellers can compare prices and seat locations. Web firms such as StubHub.com and TicketsNow.com, the latter owned by Ticketmaster, act as ticket clearinghouses for this secondary market. These firms have signed deals with several professional sports teams that allow season ticket holders to sell unwanted tickets and buyers to purchase them with a guarantee. Its partnership with StubHub has been a success for the University of Southern California, among others.[4]

Pricing is also regulated by the general constraints of U.S. antitrust legislation, as outlined in Chapter 3. The following sections review some of the most important pricing laws for contemporary marketers.

ROBINSON-PATMAN ACT

The **Robinson-Patman Act** (1936) typifies Depression-era legislation. Known as the Anti-A&P Act, it was inspired by price competition triggered by the rise of grocery store chains; it is said that the original draft was prepared by the U.S. Wholesale Grocers Association. Enacted in the midst of the Great Depression, when legislators viewed chain stores as a threat to employment in the traditional retail sector, the Act was intended primarily to save jobs.

The Robinson-Patman Act was an amendment to the Clayton Act, enacted 22 years earlier, which had applied only to price discrimination between geographic areas, injuring local sellers. Broader in scope, Robinson-Patman prohibits price discrimination in sales to wholesalers, retailers, and other producers. It rules that differences in price must reflect cost differentials and prohibits

Robinson-Patman Act
Federal legislation prohibiting price discrimination not based on a cost differential; also prohibits selling at an unreasonably low price to eliminate competition.

selling at unreasonably low prices to drive competitors out of business. Supporters justified the amendment by arguing that the rapidly expanding chain stores of that era might be able to attract substantial discounts from suppliers anxious to secure their business, while small, independent stores would continue to pay regular prices.

Price discrimination, in which some customers pay more than others for the same product, dates back to the very beginnings of trade and commerce. Today, however, technology has added to the frequency and complexity of price discrimination as well as the strategies marketers adopt to get around it. For example, marketers may encourage repeat business by inviting purchasers to become "preferred customers," entitling them to average discounts of 10 percent. As long as companies can demonstrate that their price discounts and promotional allowances do not restrict competition, they avoid penalties under the Robinson-Patman Act. Direct-mail marketers frequently send out catalogs of identical goods but with differing prices for different catalogs. Zip code areas that traditionally consist of high spenders get the higher-price catalogs, while price-sensitive zip code customers receive catalogs with lower prices.

Firms accused of price discrimination often argue that they set price differentials to meet competitors' prices and that cost differences justify variations in prices. When a firm asserts it maintains price differentials as good-faith methods of competing with rivals, a logical question arises: What constitutes good-faith pricing behavior? The answer depends on the particular situation.

A defense based on cost differentials works only if the price differences do not exceed the cost differences resulting from selling to various classes of buyers. Marketers must then be prepared to justify the cost differences. Many authorities consider this provision one of the most confusing areas in the Robinson-Patman Act. Courts handle most charges brought under the act as individual cases. Therefore, domestic marketers must continually evaluate their pricing actions to avoid potential Robinson-Patman violations.

UNFAIR-TRADE LAWS

unfair-trade laws State laws requiring sellers to maintain minimum prices for comparable merchandise.

Most states supplement federal legislation with their own **unfair-trade laws,** which require sellers to maintain minimum prices for comparable merchandise. Enacted in the 1930s, these laws were intended to protect small specialty shops, such as dairy stores, from so-called *loss-leader* pricing tactics in which chain stores might sell certain products below cost to attract customers. Typical state laws set retail price floors at cost plus some modest markup.

Although most unfair-trade laws have remained on the books for decades, marketers had all but forgotten them until recently, when several lawsuits were brought against different warehouse clubs over their practice of loss-leader gasoline pricing. Most were found to violate no laws.

FAIR-TRADE LAWS

fair-trade laws Statutes enacted in most states that once permitted manufacturers to stipulate a minimum retail price for their product.

The concept of fair trade has affected pricing decisions for decades. **Fair-trade laws** allow manufacturers to stipulate minimum retail prices for their products and to require dealers to sign contracts agreeing to abide by these prices.

Fair-trade laws assert that a product's image, determined in part by its price, is a property right of the manufacturer. Therefore, the manufacturer should have the authority to protect its asset by requiring retailers to maintain a minimum price. Exclusivity is one method manufacturers use to achieve this. By severely restricting the number of retail outlets that carry their upscale clothing and accessories, designers can exert more control over their prices and avoid discounting, which might adversely affect their image.

Like the Robinson-Patman Act, fair-trade legislation has its roots in the Depression era. In 1931, California became the first state to enact fair-trade legislation. Most other states soon followed; only Missouri, the District of Columbia, Vermont, and Texas failed to adopt such laws.

A U.S. Supreme Court decision invalidated fair-trade contracts in interstate commerce, and Congress responded by passing the Miller-Tydings Resale Price Maintenance Act (1937). This law exempted interstate fair-trade contracts from compliance with antitrust requirements, thus freeing states to keep these laws on their books if they so desired.

Over the years, fair-trade laws declined in importance as discounters emerged and price competition gained strength as a marketing strategy component. These laws became invalid with the passage of the Consumer Goods Pricing Act (1975), which halted all interstate enforcement of resale price maintenance provisions, an objective long sought by consumer groups.

In a new use of the term *fair trade,* some retailers are charging higher-than-market prices for commodities such as coffee,

Some retailers are charging higher prices for "fair trade" items including coffee, bananas, and chocolate.

© Mario Tama/Getty Images

bananas, and chocolate as part of an international campaign to help farmers earn a living wage in poor countries where such products are grown. Although thousands of farmers have already benefited from the funds, which pay for education, healthcare, and training projects, it remains to be seen whether experience with the practice in U.S. stores will be similar to that in Europe, where some retailers have simply used higher markups so they can benefit as well. It's often difficult for consumers to know how much of the added price is going to help those in need. Another potential problem raised by some critics is that paying artificially higher prices for coffee could incorrectly signal more small farmers to move into the already crowded coffee market, depressing prices for all. Meanwhile, some U.S. coffee companies, such as Conscious Coffees in Colorado, see free-trade coffee not as just another "flavor" to offer but as a means to leverage social and environmental change. "Fair trade is not just about paying a fair price to the farmers, it's about taking care of our planet," says co-owner Mark Evans-Glenn. "We should have a sustainable way of roasting it, as well."[5]

assessment check

1. What was the purpose of the Robinson-Patman Act?

2. What laws require sellers to maintain minimum prices for comparable merchandise?

3. What laws allow manufacturers to set minimum retail prices for their products?

Pricing Objectives and the Marketing Mix

2 Identify the major categories of pricing objectives.

The extent to which any or all of the factors of production—natural resources, capital, human resources, and entrepreneurship—are employed depends on the prices those factors command. A firm's prices and the resulting purchases by its customers determine the company's revenue, influencing the profits it earns. Overall organizational objectives and more specific marketing objectives guide the development of pricing objectives, which in turn lead to the development and implementation of more specific pricing policies and procedures.

A firm might, for instance, set a major overall goal of becoming the dominant producer in its domestic market. It might then develop a marketing objective of achieving maximum sales penetration in each region, followed by a related pricing objective of setting prices at levels that maximize sales. These objectives might lead to the adoption of a low-price policy implemented by offering substantial price discounts to channel members.

Price affects and is affected by the other elements of the marketing mix. Product decisions, promotional plans, and distribution choices all impact the price of a good or service. For example, products distributed through complex channels involving several intermediaries must be priced high enough to cover the markups needed to compensate wholesalers and retailers for services they provide. Basic so-called *fighting brands* are intended to capture market share from higher-priced, options-laden competitors by offering relatively low prices. Those cheaper products are intended to entice customers to give up some options in return for a cost savings.

table 18.1   Pricing Objectives

Objective	Purpose	Example
Profitability objectives	Profit maximization Target return	Sony's initially high price for the Blu-ray Disc Player
Volume objectives	Sales maximization Market share	Southwest Airlines' low fares in new markets
Meeting competition objectives	Value pricing	SuperValu's lower prices on private house brands
Prestige objectives	Lifestyle Image	High-priced luxury autos such as BMW and stereo equipment by Bose
Not-for-profit objectives	Profit maximization Cost recovery Market incentives Market suppression	Reduced or zero tolls for high-occupancy vehicles to encourage carpooling

Pricing objectives vary from firm to firm, and they can be classified into four major groups: (1) profitability objectives, (2) volume objectives, (3) meeting competition objectives, and (4) prestige objectives. Not-for-profit organizations as well as for-profit companies must consider objectives of one kind or another when developing pricing strategies. Table 18.1 outlines the pricing objectives marketers rely on to meet their overall goals.

PROFITABILITY OBJECTIVES

Marketers at for-profit firms must set prices with profits in mind. Even not-for-profit organizations realize the importance of setting prices high enough to cover expenses and provide a financial cushion to cover unforeseen needs and expenses. As the Russian proverb says, "There are two fools in every market: One asks too little, one asks too much." For consumers to pay prices either above or below what they consider the going rate, they must be convinced they are receiving fair value for their money.

Economic theory is based on two major assumptions. It assumes, first, that firms will behave rationally and, second, that this rational behavior will result in an effort to maximize gains and minimize losses. Some marketers estimate profits by looking at historical sales data; others use elaborate calculations based on predicted future sales. It has been said that setting prices is an art, not a science. The talent lies in a marketer's ability to strike a balance between desired profits and the customer's perception of a product's value.

Marketers should evaluate and adjust prices continually to accommodate changes in the environment. The technological environment, for example, forces Internet marketers to respond quickly to competitors' pricing strategies. Search capabilities performed by shopping bots (described in Chapter 4) allow customers to compare prices locally, nationally, and globally in a matter of seconds.

Intense price competition, sometimes conducted even when it means forgoing profits altogether or reducing services, often results when rivals battle for leadership positions. For some years, passenger airlines cut costs to compete on pricing. Computer technology allowed them to automate many services and put passengers in charge of others, such as making reservations online and checking in at electronic kiosks. Now, thanks to increased industry concentration and the rising price of jet fuel, which climbed 71 percent in a recent year, airlines are struggling to cover their costs. As a result, passengers now pay sharply higher fares and find amenities, like in-flight meals, have all but disappeared. JetBlue and United charge between $10 and $20 extra for seats with legroom. JetBlue is charging for pillows and blankets, and US Airways passengers pay for coffee, tea, soft drinks, and even bottled water. Nearly all airlines now charge for checking bags, and fees for overweight luggage have gone up. Delta charges extra for pets and for booking seats over the phone, and many carriers now charge a fee for using frequent flier miles.[6]

Profits are a function of revenue and expenses:

$$\text{Profits} = \text{Revenue} - \text{Expenses}$$

Revenue is determined by the product's selling price and number of units sold:

$$\text{Total Revenue} = \text{Price} \times \text{Quantity Sold}$$

Therefore, a profit-maximizing price rises to the point at which further increases will cause disproportionate decreases in the number of units sold. A 10 percent price increase that results in only an 8 percent cut in volume will add to the firm's revenue. However, a 10 percent price hike that results in an 11 percent sales decline will reduce revenue.

Economists refer to this approach as **marginal analysis.** They identify **profit maximization** as the point at which the addition to total revenue is just balanced by the increase in total cost. Marketers must resolve a basic problem of how to achieve this delicate balance when they set prices. Relatively few firms actually hit this elusive target. A significantly larger number prefer to direct their effort toward more realistic goals.

Consequently, marketers commonly set **target-return objectives**—short-run or long-run goals usually stated as percentages of sales or investment. The practice has become particularly popular among large firms in which other pressures interfere with profit-maximization objectives. In addition to resolving pricing questions, target-return objectives offer several benefits for marketers. For example, these objectives serve as tools for evaluating performance; they also satisfy desires to generate "fair" profits as judged by management, stockholders, and the public.

profit maximization Point at which the additional revenue gained by increasing the price of a product equals the increase in total costs.

target-return objective Short-run or long-run pricing objectives of achieving a specified return on either sales or investment.

VOLUME OBJECTIVES

Some economists and business executives argue that pricing behavior actually seeks to maximize sales within a given profit constraint. In other words, they set a minimum acceptable profit level and then seek to maximize sales (subject to this profit constraint) in the belief that the increased sales are more important in the long-run competitive picture than immediate high profits. As a result, companies should continue to expand sales as long as their total profits do not drop below the minimum return acceptable to management.

Sales maximization can also result from nonprice factors such as service and quality. Marketers succeeded in increasing sales for Dr. Scholl's new shoe insert, Dynastep, by advertising heavily in magazines. The ads explained how the Dynastep insert would help relieve leg and back pain. Priced around $14 for two inserts—twice as much as comparable offerings—Dynastep ran over its competitors to become number one in its category.

Another volume-related pricing objective is the **market-share objective**—the goal of controlling a specified minimum share of the market for a firm's good or service. Apple applied this strategy to its recent iPhone price reduction. With 6 million phones sold in less than two years, the company set a new goal to sell 10 million in a single year and dropped the price to $199 for the cheapest, 8-gigabyte model, acknowledging that the initial price of $399 had been the biggest hurdle in the product's introduction.[7]

The PIMS Studies

Market-share objectives may prove critical to the achievement of other organizational objectives. High sales, for example, often mean more profits. The **Profit Impact of Market Strategies (PIMS) project,** an extensive study conducted by the Marketing Science Institute, analyzed more than 2,000 firms and revealed that two of the most important factors influencing profitability were product quality and market share. Companies such as outdoor gear maker REI and Best Buy, the electronics giant, introduced their loyalty programs as a means of retaining customers and protecting their market share. Faced with a slowing economy, other retailers are joining them, hoping to boost sluggish sales. Among them are Starbucks and Red Lion Hotels. Subway and Tully's Coffee plan to link loyalty programs to customers' credit cards so that membership is automatically recognized at checkout. Kroger, the supermarket giant, will let consumers add online coupons to their store loyalty cards.[8]

The relationship between market share and profitability is evident in PIMS data that reveal an average 32 percent return on investment (ROI) for firms with market shares above 40 percent. In contrast, average ROI decreases to 24 percent for firms whose market shares are between 20 and 40 percent. Firms with a minor market share (less than 10 percent) generate average pretax investment returns of approximately 13 percent.[9]

Profit Impact of Market Strategies (PIMS) project Research that discovered a strong positive relationship between a firm's market share and product quality and its return on investment.

The relationship also applies to a firm's individual brands. PIMS researchers compared the top four brands in each market segment they studied. Their data revealed the leading brand typically generates after-tax ROI of 18 percent, considerably higher than the second-ranked brand. Weaker brands, on average, fail to earn adequate returns.

Marketers have developed an underlying explanation of the positive relationship between profitability and market share. Firms with large shares accumulate greater operating experience and lower overall costs relative to competitors with smaller market shares. Accordingly, effective segmentation strategies might focus on obtaining larger shares of smaller markets and on avoiding smaller shares of larger ones. A firm might achieve higher financial returns by becoming a major competitor in several smaller market segments than by remaining a relatively minor player in a larger market.

Meeting Competition Objectives

A third set of pricing objectives seeks simply to meet competitors' prices. In many lines of business, firms set their own prices to match those of established industry price leaders.

Price is a pivotal factor in the ongoing competition between long-distance telephone services and wireless carriers. In addition to unlimited calls to the United States and Canada for $2.95 a month, Skype, the Internet calling company owned by eBay, allows unlimited calls to overseas land-line phones in 40 other countries for $12.95 a month. The countries include most of Europe as well as Australia, New Zealand, China, Japan, Korea, and Malaysia.[10]

Pricing objectives tied directly to meeting prices charged by major competitors deemphasize the price element of the marketing mix and focus more strongly on nonprice variables. Pricing is a highly visible component of a firm's marketing mix and an easy and effective tool for obtaining a differential advantage over competitors. It is, however, a tool other firms can easily duplicate through price reductions of their own. Because price changes directly affect overall profitability in an industry, many firms attempt to promote stable prices by meeting competitors' prices and competing for market share by focusing on product strategies, promotional decisions, and distribution—the nonprice elements of the marketing mix. Starbucks built its success on

Skype allows unlimited calls to overseas land-line phones in 40 other countries for $12.95 a month. Price is important in the competitive long-distance communications market.

MARKETING SUCCESS
Starbucks Takes a Shot at New Pricing and Promotions

Background. Whether it was a backlash against designer coffees or a reaction to a slowing economy, suddenly Starbucks customers were buying their cups of java elsewhere. Competition from lower-priced McDonald's and Dunkin' Donuts was cutting into sales, and Starbucks' 15,000 stores logged a surprisingly disappointing performance in 2007.

The Challenge. With ambitious plans to reinvent the Starbucks experience, chairman and former CEO Howard Schultz took back the reins to head a broad reorganization that included slowing the chain's historically rapid growth, closing underperforming stores, and refocusing product and marketing efforts on the customer's experience. That

nonprice elements but has recently experimented with beating the competition with a dollar-a-cup offer and free refills, as the "Marketing Success" feature explains.

Value Pricing

When discounts become normal elements of a competitive marketplace, other marketing mix elements gain importance in purchase decisions. In such instances, overall product value—not just price—determines product choice. In recent years, a new strategy, **value pricing,** has emerged that emphasizes the benefits a product provides in comparison to the price and quality levels of competing offerings. This strategy typically works best for relatively low-priced goods and services. The quirky Smart Fortwo microcar is a technologically advanced vehicle manufactured by Daimler AG that gets 41 miles per gallon with ultra-low emissions. Already available in 36 other countries, the Fortwo sold 10,000 units in less than six months following its U.S. debut. Priced below $17,000, the car is maneuverable in traffic at less than 9 feet long but includes the functional and safety features of many luxury cars. The president of Smart USA calls it "a powerful combination of fun-to-drive aspects, safety innovations, and functionality—all with great fuel economy." The company hopes it appeals to today's value-conscious and environmentally concerned drivers, as the VW Bug did during the 1960s and 1970s.[11]

value pricing Pricing strategy emphasizing benefits derived from a product in comparison to the price and quality levels of competing offerings.

Value-priced products generally cost less than premium brands, but marketers point out that value does not necessarily mean *inexpensive.* The challenge for those who compete on value is to convince customers that low-priced brands offer quality comparable to that of a higher-priced product. An increasing number of alternative products and private-label brands has resulted in a more competitive marketplace in recent years. Trader Joe's—a rapidly growing grocery chain that began in the Los Angeles area and has since expanded throughout the West, Midwest, and mid-Atlantic states—stands out from other specialty food stores with its cedar plank walls, nautical décor, and a captain (the store manager), first mate (the assistant manager), and the other employees (known as crew members) all attired in colorful Hawaiian shirts. The chain uses value pricing for the more than 2,000 upscale food products it develops or imports.

Trader Joe's uses value pricing to sell upscale food products.

© Michael Nagle/Getty Images

included an experiment in reducing the chain's famously high coffee prices.

The Strategy. Taking the unusual step of undercutting its competitors, the chain is testing a $1 price for an 8-ounce cup at selected stores around Seattle where it is headquartered and offering free refills to boot. In fact, some stores that were not slated to participate decided to offer the discount as well, stretching the company's "Just say yes" policy to win back local customers. After all, as Schultz says, "We have to do everything we can to demonstrate to our customers that Starbucks is an affordable luxury. We have to surprise and delight them."

The Outcome. While industry analysts warn that discounting a luxury brand can be risky and perhaps even "dilute their gross margins," customer reaction has so far been positive. Starbucks defends the experiment by saying "testing is a way of life for us." "It sounds good to me," says one customer, "because I think Starbucks is too expensive."

Sources: Company Web site, www.starbucks.com, accessed June 9, 2009; Alex McCarthy, "Starbucks Hopes to Reheat Sales," *Denver Post,* August 13, 2008, www .denverpost.com; Maria Bartiromo, "Howard Schultz on Reinventing Starbucks," *BusinessWeek,* April 9, 2008, www.businessweek.com; Craig Harris, "Starbucks— For a Buck," *Seattle Post-Intelligencer,* January 24, 2008, seattlepi.nwsource.com.

Prestige objectives help market exclusive products, like Tag Heuer watches.

© Image courtesy of The Advertising Archives

It sells wines, cheeses, meats, fish, and other unique gourmet items at everyday closeout prices, mostly under its own brand names. If the high quality doesn't persuade customers at its 280 stores to buy, they can also take comfort from the fact that Trader Joe's tuna are caught without environmentally dangerous nets, its dried apricots contain no sulfur preservatives, and its peanut butter is organic.[12]

Value pricing is perhaps best seen in the personal computer industry. In the past few years, PC prices have collapsed, reducing the effectiveness of traditional pricing strategies intended to meet competition. Falling prices have helped sales grow as much as 15 percent worldwide in a recent quarter, and about 4 percent in the United States. A recent sharp decline in the price of NAND flash memory chips, which store photos and music, is expected to further reduce prices in PCs and other devices as well as increase storage capability.[13]

PRESTIGE OBJECTIVES

The final category of pricing objectives, unrelated to either profitability or sales volume, is prestige objectives. Prestige pricing establishes a relatively high price to develop and maintain an image of quality and exclusiveness that appeals to status-conscious consumers. Such objectives reflect marketers' recognition of the role of price in creating an overall image of the firm and its product offerings.

Prestige objectives affect the price tags of such products as David Yurman jewelry, Tag Heuer watches, Baccarat crystal, and Lenox china. When a perfume marketer sets a price of $400 or more per ounce, this choice reflects an emphasis on image far more than the cost of ingredients. Analyses have shown that ingredients account for less than 5 percent of a perfume's cost. Thus, advertisements for Joy that promote the fragrance as the "costliest perfume in the world" use price to promote product prestige. Diamond jewelry also uses prestige pricing to convey an image of quality and timelessness.

In the business world, private jet ownership imparts an image of prestige, power, and high price tags—too high for most business travelers to consider. Most owners are worth $10 million or more, according to one industry researcher, and include those who see private ownership enabling them to visit three cities in a day as a business need, not a luxury. Recognizing that cost is the primary factor that makes jet ownership prohibitive, companies such as NetJets have created an alternative: fractional ownership. Corporate boards of directors pressed to cut costs in a weak economy are much more willing to pay for a share in a jet than to purchase a whole new aircraft, and NetJets has seen its customer base rise 5 percent in a recent year.[14]

assessment check

1. What are target-return objectives?

2. What is value pricing?

3. How do prestige objectives affect a seller's pricing strategy?

Pricing Objectives of Not-for-Profit Organizations

Pricing is also a key element of the marketing mix for not-for-profit organizations. Pricing strategy can help these groups achieve a variety of organizational goals:

1. *Profit maximization.* While not-for-profit organizations by definition do not cite profitability as a primary goal, numerous instances exist in which they try to maximize their returns on

Solving an **ethical** controversy

Congestion Pricing: Who Really Bears the Burden?

following the example of London, Rome, and Stockholm, many U.S. city governments, including Los Angeles, Washington, D.C., and San Francisco, are considering congestion pricing, which charges extra tolls to drive into the city center during peak hours. Technology makes the price plan easy to administer, and, as in London, drivers can pay online, by mail, in person, or via cell phone. Proponents say by encouraging commuters to use public transit, variable pricing reduces traffic snarls, improves air quality, and helps raise funds for mass-transit improvements. A recent congestion pricing proposal for New York City was defeated, although rejecting it cost the city $350 million in federal assistance funds.

Is congestion pricing really fair to those who must bear the cost?

PRO

1. Everyone benefits from reduced traffic and less pollution, as observed in London and Stockholm. Traffic jams reappeared in Stockholm the first day after a trial run of congestion pricing ended.

2. Variable pricing can generate substantial revenues for improving mass transit, which further reduces congestion and pollution and benefits everyone who lives or works in a city.

CON

1. Congestion pricing adds another layer of tax on working-class commuters. Because it is a flat rate per car, the less you make, the bigger a percentage of your income it represents.

2. Few people benefit from the policy. Also, because congestion pricing is so costly to operate, the British government abandoned plans to implement London's system nationwide.

Summary

Although defeated, New York City's variable pricing proposal may not be dead. In other cities like Los Angeles, geography and traffic conditions—and therefore congestion pricing proposals—will be very different. It seems certain that variable pricing will continue to generate much discussion in city halls around the country and possibly even become law.

Sources: "S.F.'s Half-Baked Congestion Pricing Plan," *San Francisco Chronicle*, January 15, 2009, www.sfgate.com; "Congestion Pricing," *Popular Science*, August 4, 2008, www.popsci.com; Peter Gordon and Bart Reed, "High Traffic, High Toll," *Los Angeles Times*, April 30, 2008, www.latimes.com; Joseph Berger, "Congestion Pricing: Just Another Regressive Tax?" *The New York Times*, April 20, 2008, www.nytimes.com; Steve Hymon, "Tolls on Freeway a Tough Sell," *Los Angeles Times*, April 14, 2008, www.latimes.com.

single events or a series of events. A $1,000-a-plate political fund-raiser is a classic example. The "Solving and Ethical Controversy" feature discusses congestion pricing, a profit-maximizing strategy for major cities.

2. *Cost recovery.* Some not-for-profit organizations attempt to recover only the actual cost of operating the unit. Mass transit, toll roads and bridges, and most private colleges and universities are common examples. The amount of recovered costs often is dictated by tradition, competition, or public opinion. A more original solution is Indiana's decision to lease its 157-mile toll road to a team of Australian and Spanish companies for the next 75 years, creating a source of almost $4 billion in revenue to fund needed transportation projects in the state. Similar projects are under way or under consideration in other states and are common throughout the world; however, one concern among citizens of Pennsylvania, for instance, is that leaseholders of its roads will be able to raise tolls whenever they want to.[15]

3. *Market incentives.* Other not-for-profit groups follow a lower-than-average pricing policy or offer a free service to encourage increased usage of the good or service. Seattle's bus system offers free service in the downtown area in an attempt to reduce traffic congestion and pollution, encourage retail sales, and minimize the effort required to access downtown public services.[16]

briefly speaking

"A thing is worth whatever the buyer will pay for it."

—Publilius Syrus (first century B.C.E.)

LATIN WRITER OF MIMES

4. *Market suppression.* Price can also discourage consumption. High prices help accomplish social objectives independent of the costs of providing goods or services. Illustrations include tobacco and alcohol taxes—the so-called *sin taxes*—parking fines, tolls, and gasoline excise taxes. The New York State legislature recently approved an increase in the state's cigarette tax, making it the highest in the country at $2.75 a pack. Some of the increased revenue is earmarked for financing children's health insurance.[17]

Methods for Determining Prices

Marketers determine prices in two basic ways: by applying the theoretical concepts of supply and demand and by completing cost-oriented analyses. During the first part of the 20th century, most discussions of price determination emphasized the classical concepts of supply and demand. During the last half of the century, however, the emphasis began to shift to a cost-oriented approach. Hindsight reveals certain flaws in both concepts.

customary prices
Traditional prices that customers expect to pay for certain goods and services.

Treatments of this subject often overlook another concept of price determination—one based on the impact of custom and tradition. **Customary prices** are retail prices consumers expect as a result of tradition and social habit. Candy makers have attempted to maintain traditional price levels by greatly reducing overall product size. Similar practices have prevailed in the marketing of soft drinks, chips, mayonnaise, soap, and ice cream as manufacturers attempt to balance consumer expectations of customary prices with the realities of rising costs.

Hellman's mayonnaise is now sold in 30-ounce bottles rather than the old 32-ounce size, and Edy's Slow Churned ice cream, made by Dreyer's, has shrunk, along with its major competitors, from 1.75 quarts to 1.5 quarts for the same price. Ice cream makers had already reduced the traditional half-gallon container by half a quart a few years ago and held the price constant. Although some Edy's customers were angry enough to complain about the most recent shrinkage, "We felt it was better to openly reduce the package size than to take the price of the package up and make ice cream unaffordable," says Dreyer's CEO. Not everyone agrees. "Downsizing is nothing but a sneaky price increase," according to a former Massachusetts assistant attorney general who now edits a consumer Web site. "I'm waiting to open a carton of eggs and see only eleven."[18] In some cases, customers can haggle with firms to lower prices or provide extras, as the "Etiquette Tips for Marketing Professionals" feature explains.

The changing price of U.S. gasoline presents another example of supply and demand. When average prices for a gallon of gas near the $4-a-gallon mark, frustrated drivers begin demanding to know who, if anyone, is cashing in on the price spike. Even though the United States is the world's largest refiner of gasoline, strong demand leads to an increase in oil imports.

Higher gas prices have effects on other consumer costs as well. The U.S. Department of Energy counts 57 different major uses of petroleum in addition to gasoline, in products ranging from cosmetics to chewing gum. Consumer product companies, such as Procter & Gamble and Colgate-Palmolive, anticipate raising product prices, along with Dow Chemical, which recently announced price hikes for all its products, from antifreeze to pharmaceuticals. Grocery chain Wegmans also raised prices on many items. "We're talking increased raw materials, packaging, transportation, the whole ball of wax," says a company spokesperson. Even the price of asphalt rose 65 percent in a recent year, which may mean cutbacks in roadwork and repairs in many communities.[19]

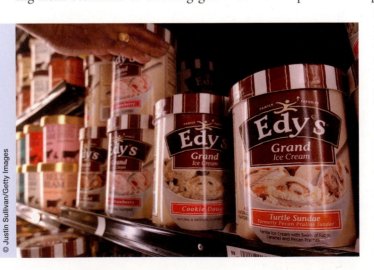

Package size for certain Edy's ice cream products has shrunk so pricing can be held constant.

© Justin Sullivan/Getty Images

Etiquette Tips for Marketing Professionals

How to Negotiate a Price

ost consumers are used to paying the posted price for everything. But you might be surprised to learn that even doctors will sometimes take 5 to 10 percent off their fees if the patient pays up front. Big-ticket items like appliances and even contractors' services often can be negotiated downward. Negotiating price takes practice. Here are some tips.

- Remember, you're entitled to a good deal.

- Establish your walk-away point—the price above which you won't go—and be prepared to leave empty-handed if you can't motivate the seller to work with you.

- Find out beforehand everything you can about the item you want, including exact specifications, manufacturer's price, warranty terms, common customer complaints, and other details. Know what the item is really worth.

- Help the salesperson sell the discount to his or her manager—bring evidence of a lower price or better terms offered elsewhere or online.

- Be flexible. If the seller can't lower the price, will he or she extend the warranty at no cost or deliver and install the item free?

- Phrase your negotiation as a friendly request. One writer suggests saying, "What can you do for me to make it easier to buy this from you?"

- Take your time; resist the temptation to take any offer because it's lower than the asking price. If you don't immediately respond, the seller may come back with a better proposal.

- Repeat the seller's offer aloud to make sure you both are clear what the terms are.

- If a seller disappoints you by providing goods or services late, don't hesitate to ask for some kind of compensation in return.

- Remember, something that sounds too good to be true usually is.

Sources: Donna L. Montaldo, "Top 10 Tips on Learning How to Haggle," *About. com*, couponing.about.com, accessed June 9, 2009; "How to Negotiate Like a Pro," *Essortment*, www.essortment.com, accessed June 9, 2009; Kelly Housen, "11 Tips toward Happy Haggling," *Delaware Online*, May 6, 2008, www.delawareonline .com; "How to Negotiate Anything," *CNN*, February 13, 2008, www.cnn.com; "The Art of Negotiating the Lowest Price," *ProBargainHunter.com*, March 24, 2007, www.probargainhunter.com.

With fuel at record highs, hybrid cars are in greater demand than ever before, and some dealers have months-long waiting lists even at premium prices. Retail businesses that use trucks and cars to deliver their products, such as pizza restaurants and florists—and even not-for-profits like Meals on Wheels—feel the pinch at the pump. Meals on Wheels also copes with increases in the price of food and paper goods such as plates and napkins. "Where we would normally have a 3 to 5 percent increase in food costs," says the nutrition director of Meals on Wheels in Sioux City, Iowa, "we've been hit with anywhere from 15 to 30 percent," the largest increase in 35 years. In the meantime, high fuel prices have sent many motorists to the bus stop, as such cities as San Diego, Boston, and Quebec City record increases in public transportation ridership.[20]

assessment check

1. What goals does pricing strategy help a not-for-profit organization achieve?

2. What are the two basic ways in which marketers determine prices?

Price Determination in Economic Theory

Microeconomics suggests a way of determining prices that assumes a profit-maximization objective. This technique attempts to derive correct equilibrium prices in the marketplace by comparing supply and demand. It also requires more complete analysis than actual business firms typically conduct.

Demand refers to a schedule of the amounts of a firm's product that consumers will purchase at different prices during a specified time period. **Supply** refers to a schedule of the amounts of

In the name of product differentiation, many U.S. ranchers have switched their beef herds to an all-grass diet.

© Image courtesy of The Advertising Archives

KEEP ON THE GRASS

ANCHOR® believe that the best tasting butter comes from cows that are fed on fresh green grass all year round.

a good or service that will be offered for sale at different prices during a specified period. These schedules may vary for different types of market structures. Businesses operate and set prices in four types of market structures: pure competition, monopolistic competition, oligopoly, and monopoly.

Pure competition is a market structure with so many buyers and sellers that no single participant can significantly influence price. Pure competition presupposes other market conditions as well: homogeneous products and ease of entry for sellers due to low start-up costs. The agricultural sector exhibits many characteristics of a purely competitive market, making it the closest actual example. But many U.S. ranchers have switched their beef herds to an all-grass diet in an attempt to differentiate their product from those raised in feedlots.

Monopolistic competition typifies most retailing and features large numbers of buyers and sellers. These diverse parties exchange heterogeneous, relatively well-differentiated products, giving marketers some control over prices.

Relatively few sellers compete in an **oligopoly.** Pricing decisions by each seller are likely to affect the market, but no single seller controls it. High start-up costs form significant barriers to entry for new competitors. Each firm's demand curve in an oligopolistic market displays a unique kink at the current market price. Because of the impact of a single competitor on total industry sales, competitors usually quickly match any attempt by one firm to generate additional sales by reducing prices. Price cutting in such industry structures is likely to reduce total industry revenues. Oligopolies operate in the petroleum refining, automobile, tobacco, and airline industries.

Despite strong demand from air travelers, rising fuel prices have led the leading U.S. airlines not only to raise prices but also to cut capacity, which means American, United, Delta, Continental, and US Airways will limit flights to major cities and eliminate service to some less-profitable or heavily discounted locations, particularly Florida. Southwest, which hedged its fuel costs and is operating profitably, will make up for some of its competitors' service cuts.[21]

A **monopoly** is a market structure in which only one seller of a product exists and for which there are no close substitutes. Antitrust legislation has nearly eliminated all but temporary monopolies such as those created through patent protection. Regulated industries constitute another form of monopoly. The government allows regulated monopolies in markets in which competition would lead to an uneconomical duplication of services. In return for such a license, government reserves the right to regulate the monopoly's rate of return.

The four types of market structures are compared in Table 18.2 on the following bases: number of competitors, ease of entry into the industry by new firms, similarity of competing products, degree of control over price by individual firms, and the elasticity or inelasticity of the demand curve facing the individual firm. Elasticity—the degree of consumer responsiveness to changes in price—is discussed in more detail in a later section.

COST AND REVENUE CURVES

Marketers must set a price for a product that generates sufficient revenue to cover the costs of producing and marketing it. A product's total cost is composed of total variable costs and total fixed costs. **Variable costs,** such as raw materials and labor costs, change with the level of production,

table 18.2 Distinguishing Features of the Four Market Structures

Characteristics	Type of Market Structure			
	Pure Competition	**Monopolistic Competition**	**Oligopoly**	**Monopoly**
Number of competitors	Many	Few to many	Few	No direct competitors
Ease of entry into industry by new firms	Easy	Somewhat difficult	Difficult	Regulated by government
Similarity of goods or services offered by competing firms	Similar	Different	Can be either similar or different	No directly competing goods or services
Control over prices by individual firms	None	Some	Some	Considerable
Demand curves facing individual firms	Totally elastic	Can be either elastic or inelastic	Kinked; inelastic below kink; more elastic above	Can be either elastic or inelastic
Examples	Indiana soybean farm	Best Buy stores	Verizon Wireless	Waste Management

and **fixed costs,** such as lease payments or insurance costs, remain stable at any production level within a certain range. **Average total costs** are calculated by dividing the sum of the variable and fixed costs by the number of units produced. Finally, **marginal cost** is the change in total cost that results from producing an additional unit of output.

The demand side of the pricing equation focuses on revenue curves. Average revenue is calculated by dividing total revenue by the quantity associated with these revenues. Average revenue is actually the demand curve facing the firm. Marginal revenue is the change in total revenue that results from selling an additional unit of output. Figure 18.1 shows the relationships of various cost and revenue measures; the firm maximizes its profits when marginal costs equal marginal revenues.

Table 18.3 illustrates why the intersection of the marginal cost and marginal revenue curves is the logical point at which to maximize revenue for the organization. Although the firm can earn a profit at several different prices, the price at which it earns maximum profits is $22. At a price of

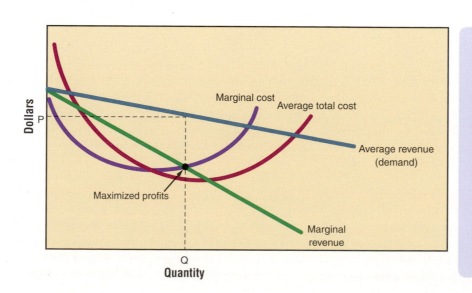

figure 18.1

Determining Price by Relating Marginal Revenue to Marginal Cost

table 18.3 Price Determination Using Marginal Analysis

Price	Number Sold	Total Revenue	Marginal Revenue	Total Costs	Marginal Costs	Profits (Total Revenue Minus Total Costs)
–	–	–	–	–	–	($50)
$34	1	$34	$34	57	$7	(23)
32	2	64	30	62	5	2
30	3	90	26	66	4	24
28	4	112	22	69	3	43
26	5	130	18	73	4	57
24	6	144	14	78	5	66
22	7	154	10	84	6	70
20	8	160	6	91	7	69
18	9	162	2	100	9	62
16	10	160	(2)	101	11	50

$24, $66 in profits is earned—$4 less than the $70 profit at the $22 price. If a price of $20 is set to attract additional sales, the marginal costs of the extra sales ($7) are greater than the marginal revenues received ($6), and total profits decline.

3 **Explain price elasticity and its determinants.**

elasticity Measure of responsiveness of purchasers and suppliers to a change in price.

THE CONCEPT OF ELASTICITY IN PRICING STRATEGY

Although the intersection of the marginal cost and marginal revenue curves determines the level of output, the impact of changes in price on sales varies greatly. To understand why it fluctuates, one must understand the concept of elasticity.

Elasticity is the measure of the responsiveness of purchasers and suppliers to price changes. The price elasticity of demand (or elasticity of demand) is the percentage change in the quantity of a good or service demanded divided by the percentage change in its price. A 10 percent increase in the price of eggs that results in a 5 percent decrease in the quantity of eggs demanded yields a price elasticity of demand for eggs of 0.5. The price elasticity of supply of a product is the percentage change in the quantity of a good or service supplied divided by the percentage change in its price. A 10 percent increase in the price of shampoo that results in a 25 percent increase in the quantity supplied yields a price elasticity of supply for shampoo of 2.5.

Consider a case in which a 1 percent change in price causes more than a 1 percent change in the quantity supplied or demanded. Numerically, that means an elasticity measurement greater than 1.0. When the elasticity of demand or supply is greater than 1.0, that demand or supply is said to be elastic. If a 1 percent change in price results in less than a 1 percent change in quantity, a product's elasticity of demand or supply will be less than 1.0. In that case, the demand or supply is called *inelastic*. For example, the demand for cigarettes is relatively inelastic; research studies have shown that a 10 percent increase in cigarette prices results in only a 4 percent sales decline.

In some countries whose economies are in shambles, price levels bear little resemblance to the laws of elasticity or supply and demand. Prices in Zimbabwe are rising at unheard-of rates, the result of hyperinflation that rose to more 7,600 percent in a recent *month*—estimated to be as high 12.5 million percent a year. What consumers would spend for a dozen new cars 10 years ago now buys a single loaf of bread. Banks and stores are unable to handle transactions in which prices come with 15 zeroes attached—a new laptop costs 1.2 quadrillion Zimbabwe dollars—and manufacturing is 30 percent below capacity because workers cannot afford bus fare to get to work. Shortages of food, fuel, and medicine are rampant, and international observers believe the economy is at the brink of collapse. Although it is against the law, those who can do so are conducting more and more transactions in U.S. dollars.[22]

Determinants of Elasticity

Why is the elasticity of supply or demand high for some products and low for others? What determines demand elasticity? One major factor influencing the elasticity of demand is the availability of substitutes or complements. If consumers can easily find close substitutes for a good or service, the product's demand tends to be elastic. A product's role as a complement to the use of another product also affects its degree of price elasticity. For example, the relatively inelastic demand for motor oil reflects its role as a complement to a more important product, gasoline. High prices for gasoline, in turn, are fueling a search for alternative fuels. Consumers are even turning away from bottled water as price hikes have them reconsidering the nearly free stuff that comes from the tap.[23]

As increasing numbers of buyers and sellers complete their business transactions online, the elasticity of a product's demand is drastically affected. Take major discounters and other price-competitive stores, for example. Small businesses and individual do-it-yourselfers shop Lowe's for tools, such as wheelbarrows; parents look for birthday gifts at Wal-Mart; and homeowners go to Home Depot for new refrigerators or stoves. Today, however, the Internet lets consumers contact many more providers directly, often giving them better selections and prices for their efforts with service sites such as Shopzilla.com for consumer goods and electronics, Net-a-Porter.com for high fashion clothing, Kayak.com for travel bargains, and Shoebuy.com for shoes from dozens of different manufacturers. The increased options available to shoppers combine to create a market characterized by demand elasticity.

Elasticity of demand also depends on whether a product is perceived as a necessity or a luxury. The Four Seasons chain of luxury hotels and resorts enjoys a strong reputation for service, comfort, and exclusiveness and is a favorite among affluent individual travelers and business professionals.

Most people regard high-fashion clothes, such as a $2,800 Escada embroidered dress at Neiman Marcus, as luxuries. If prices for designer outfits increase dramatically, people can respond by purchasing lower-priced substitutes instead. In contrast, medical and dental care are considered necessities, so price changes have little effect on the frequency of visits to the doctor or dentist.

Elasticity also depends on the portion of a person's budget spent on a good or service. For example, people no longer really need matches; they can easily find good substitutes. Nonetheless, the demand for matches remains very inelastic because people spend so little on them that they hardly notice a price change. In contrast, the demand for housing or transportation is not totally inelastic, even though they are necessities, because both consume large parts of a consumer's budget.

Elasticity of demand also responds to consumers' time perspectives. Demand often shows less elasticity in the short run than in the long run. Consider the demand for home air conditioning. In the short run, people pay rising energy prices because they find it difficult to cut back on the quantities they use. Accustomed to living with specific temperature settings and dressing in certain ways, they prefer to pay more during a few months of the year than to explore other possibilities. Over the long term, though, they may consider insulating their homes and planting shade trees to reduce cooling costs.

Elasticity and Revenue

The elasticity of demand exerts an important influence on variations in total revenue as a result of changes in the price of a good or service. Assume, for example, that San Francisco's Bay Area Rapid Transit (BART) officials are considering alternative methods of raising more money for their budget. One possible method for increasing revenues would be to change rail pass fares for commuters. But should BART raise or lower the price of a pass? The correct answer depends on the elasticity of demand for subway rides. A 10 percent decrease in fares should attract more riders, but unless it stimulates more than a 10 percent increase in riders, total revenue will fall. A 10 percent increase in fares will bring in more money per rider, but if more than 10 percent of the riders stop using the subway, total revenue will fall. A price cut will increase revenue only for a product with elastic demand, and a price increase will raise revenue only for a product with inelastic demand. BART officials seem to believe the demand for rapid rail transit is inelastic; they raise fares when they need more money.

4 List the practical problems involved in applying price theory concepts to actual pricing decisions.

PRACTICAL PROBLEMS OF PRICE THEORY

Marketers may thoroughly understand price theory concepts but still encounter difficulty applying them in practice. What practical limitations interfere with setting prices?

First, many firms do not attempt to maximize profits. Economic analysis is subject to the same limitations as the assumptions on which it is based—for example, the proposition that all firms attempt to maximize profits. Second, it is difficult to estimate demand curves. Modern accounting procedures provide managers with a clear understanding of cost structures, so managers can readily comprehend the supply side of the pricing equation. But they find it difficult to estimate demand at various price levels. Demand curves must be based on marketing research estimates that may be less exact than cost figures. Although the demand element can be identified, it is often difficult to measure in real-world settings.

5 Explain the major cost-plus approaches to price setting.

Price Determination in Practice

The practical limitations inherent in price theory have forced practitioners to turn to other techniques. **Cost-plus pricing,** the most popular method, uses a base-cost figure per unit and adds a markup to cover unassigned costs and to provide a profit. The only real difference among the multitude of cost-plus techniques is the relative sophistication of the costing procedures employed. For example, a local apparel shop may set prices by adding a 45 percent markup to the invoice price charged by the supplier. The markup is expected to cover all other expenses and permit the owner to earn a reasonable return on the sale of clothes.

In contrast to this rather simple pricing mechanism, a large manufacturer may employ a complex pricing formula requiring computer calculations. However, this method merely adds a more complicated procedure to the simpler, traditional method for calculating costs. In the end, someone still must make a decision about the markup. The apparel shop and the large manufacturer may figure costs differently, but they are remarkably similar in completing the markup side of the equation.

Cost-plus pricing often works well for a business that keeps its costs low, allowing it to set its prices lower than those of competitors and still make a profit. Wal-Mart keeps costs low by buying most of its inventory directly from manufacturers, using a supply chain that slashes inventory costs by quickly replenishing inventory as items are sold and relying on other intermediaries only in special instances such as localized items. This strategy has played a major role in the discounter's becoming the world's largest retailer.

ALTERNATIVE PRICING PROCEDURES

The two most common cost-oriented pricing procedures are the full-cost method and the incremental-cost method. **Full-cost pricing** uses all relevant variable costs in setting a product's price. In addition, it allocates fixed costs that cannot be directly attributed to the production of the specific priced item. Under the full-cost method, if job order 515 in a printing plant amounts to 0.000127 percent of the plant's total output, then 0.000127 percent of the firm's overhead expenses are charged to that job. This approach allows the marketer to recover all costs plus the amount added as a profit margin.

The full-cost approach has two basic deficiencies. First, no consideration of competition or demand exists for the item; perhaps no one wants to pay the price the firm has calculated. Second, any method for allocating overhead (fixed expenses) is arbitrary and may be unrealistic—in manufacturing, overhead allocations often are tied to direct labor hours; in retailing, the square footage of each profit center is sometimes the factor used in computations. Regardless of the technique employed, it is difficult to show a cause–effect relationship between the allocated cost and most products.

One way to overcome the arbitrary allocation of fixed expenses is with **incremental-cost pricing,** which attempts to use only costs directly attributable to a specific output in setting prices. Consider a very small-scale manufacturer with the following income statement:

Sales (10,000 units at $10)		$ 100,000
Expenses:		
Variable	$50,000	
Fixed	40,000	90,000
Net Profit		$ 10,000

Suppose the firm is offered a contract for an additional 5,000 units. Because the peak season is over, these items can be produced at the same average variable cost. Assume the labor force would otherwise be working on maintenance projects. How low should the firm price its product to get the contract?

Under the full-cost approach, the lowest price would be $9 per unit. This figure is obtained by dividing the $90,000 in expenses by an output of 10,000 units. The incremental approach, on the other hand, could permit any price above $5, which would significantly increase the possibility of securing the additional contract. This price would be composed of the $5 variable cost associated with each unit of production plus a $0.10-per-unit contribution to fixed expenses and overhead. With a $5.10 proposed price, the income statement now looks like this:

Sales (10,000 at $10; 5,000 at $5.10)		$ 125,500
Expenses:		
Variable	$75,000	
Fixed	40,000	115,000
Net Profit		$ 10,500

Profits thus increase under the incremental approach.

Admittedly, the illustration is based on two assumptions: (1) the ability to isolate markets such that selling at the lower price will not affect the price received in other markets and (2) the absence of legal restrictions on the firm. The example, however, does illustrate that profits can sometimes be enhanced by using the incremental approach.

assessment check

1. What is full-cost pricing?
2. What is incremental-cost pricing?

BREAKEVEN ANALYSIS

Breakeven analysis is a means of determining the number of goods or services that must be sold at a given price to generate sufficient revenue to cover total costs. Figure 18.2 graphically depicts this process. The total cost curve includes both fixed and variable segments, and total fixed cost is represented by a horizontal line. Average variable cost is assumed to be constant per unit as it was in the example for incremental pricing.

The breakeven point is the point at which total revenue equals total cost. In the example in Figure 18.2, a selling price of $10 and an average variable cost of $5 result in a per-unit contribution to fixed cost of $5. The breakeven point in terms of units is found by using the

6 List the chief advantages and shortcomings of using breakeven analysis in pricing decisions.

breakeven analysis Pricing technique used to determine the number of products that must be sold at a specified price to generate enough revenue to cover total cost.

following formula, in which the per-unit contribution equals the product's price less the variable cost per unit:

$$\text{Breakeven Point (in units)} = \frac{\text{Total Fixed Cost}}{\text{Per-Unit Contribution to Fixed Cost}}$$

$$\text{Breakeven Point (in units)} = \frac{\$40,000}{\$5} = 8,000 \text{ units}$$

The breakeven point in dollars is found with the following formula:

$$\text{Breakeven Point (in dollars)} = \frac{\text{Total Fixed Cost}}{1 - \text{Variable Cost per Unit Price}}$$

$$\text{Breakeven Point (in dollars)} = \frac{\$40,000}{1 - (\$5/\$10)} = \frac{\$40,000}{0.5} = \$80,000$$

Sometimes breakeven is reached by reducing costs. Faced with declining sales and revenues, Ford Motor Co. recently met a 15 percent cost-reduction goal by reducing its North American workforce using both normal attrition and some layoffs.[24]

Once the breakeven point has been reached, sufficient revenues will have been obtained from sales to cover all fixed costs. Any additional sales will generate per-unit profits equal to the difference between the product's selling price and the variable cost of each unit. As Figure 18.2 reveals, sales of 8,001 units (1 unit above the breakeven point) will produce net profits of $5 ($10 sales price less per-unit variable cost of $5). Once all fixed costs have been covered, the per-unit contribution will become the per-unit profit.

Target Returns

Although breakeven analysis indicates the sales level at which the firm will incur neither profits nor losses, most firms' managers include a targeted profit in their analyses. In some instances, management sets a desired dollar return when considering a proposed new product or other marketing strategy. A retailer may set a desired profit of $250,000 in considering whether to expand to a second location. In other instances, the target return may be expressed in percentages, such as a 15 percent return on sales. These target returns can be calculated as follows:

$$\text{Breakeven Point (including specific dollar target return)} = \frac{\text{Total Fixed Cost} + \text{Profit Objective}}{\text{Per-Unit Contribution}}$$

$$\text{Breakeven Point (in units)} = \frac{\$40,000 + \$15,000}{\$5} = 11,000 \text{ units}$$

If the target return is expressed as a percentage of sales, it can be included in the breakeven formula as a variable cost. Suppose the marketer in the preceding example seeks a 10 percent return on sales. The desired return is $1 for each product sold (the $10 per-unit selling price multiplied by the 10 percent return on sales). In this case, the basic breakeven formula will remain unchanged, although the variable cost per unit will be increased to reflect the target return, and the per-unit contribution to fixed cost will be reduced to $4. As a result, the breakeven point will increase from 8,000 to 10,000 units:

$$\text{Breakeven Point} = \frac{\$40,000}{\$4} = 10,000 \text{ units}$$

figure 18.2
Breakeven Chart

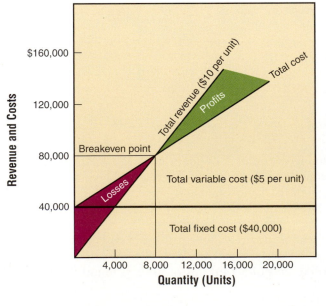

Evaluation of Breakeven Analysis

Breakeven analysis is an effective tool for marketers in assessing the sales required for covering costs and achieving specified profit levels. It is easily understood by both marketing and nonmarketing executives and may help them decide whether required sales levels for a certain price are realistic goals. However, it has its shortcomings.

First, the model assumes costs can be divided into fixed and variable categories. Some costs, such as salaries and advertising outlays, may be either fixed or variable depending on the particular situation. In addition, the model assumes per-unit variable costs do not change at different levels of operation. However, these may vary because of quantity discounts, more efficient use of the workforce, or other economies resulting from increased levels of production and sales. Finally, the basic breakeven model does not consider demand. It is a cost-based model and does not directly address the crucial question of whether consumers will purchase the product at the specified price and in the quantities required for breaking even or generating profits. The marketer's challenge is to modify the breakeven analysis and the other cost-oriented pricing approaches to incorporate demand analysis. Pricing must be examined from the buyer's perspective. Such decisions cannot be made by considering only cost factors.

The Modified Breakeven Concept

Traditional economic theory considers both costs and demand in determining an equilibrium price. The dual elements of supply and demand are balanced at the point of equilibrium. In actual practice, however, most pricing approaches are largely cost oriented. Because purely cost-oriented approaches to pricing violate the marketing concept, modifications that add demand analysis to the pricing decision are required.

Consumer research on such issues as degree of price elasticity, consumer price expectations, existence and size of specific market segments, and buyer perceptions of strengths and weaknesses of substitute products is necessary for developing sales estimates at different prices. Because much of the resulting data involves perceptions, attitudes, and future expectations of present and potential customers, such estimates are likely to be less precise than cost estimates.

The breakeven analysis method illustrated in Figure 18.2 assumes a constant $10 retail price, regardless of quantity. But what happens at different retail prices? As Figure 18.3 shows, a more sophisticated approach, **modified breakeven analysis,** combines the traditional breakeven analysis model with an evaluation of conumer demand.

Table 18.4 summarizes both the cost and revenue aspects of a number of alternative retail prices. The $5 per-unit variable cost and the $40,000 total fixed cost are based on the costs used in the basic breakeven model. The expected unit sales for each specified retail price are obtained from marketing research. The table contains the information necessary for calculating the breakeven point for each of the five retail price alternatives. These points are shown in Figure 18.3(a).

The data shown in the first two columns of Table 18.4 represent a demand schedule that indicates the number of units consumers are expected to purchase at each of a series of retail prices. As Figure 18.3(b) shows, these data can be superimposed onto a breakeven chart to identify the range of feasible prices for the marketer to charge.

Figure 18.3 reveals that the range of profitable prices exists from a low of approximately $8 (TR4) to a high of $10 (TR2), with a price of $9 (TR3) generating the greatest projected profits. Changing the retail price produces a new breakeven point. At a relatively high $15 (TR1) retail price, the breakeven point is 4,000 units; at a $10 retail price, it is 8,000 units; and at the lowest price considered, $7 (TR5), it is 20,000 units.

modified breakeven analysis Pricing technique used to evaluate consumer demand by comparing the number of products that must be sold at a variety of prices to cover total cost with estimates of expected sales at the various prices.

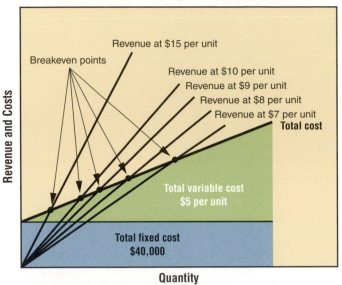

(a)
Five Breakeven Points for Five Different Prices

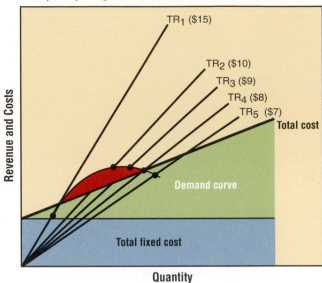

(b)
Superimposing a Demand Curve on the Breakeven Chart

> figure 18.3
>
> **Modified Breakeven Chart: Parts A and B**

The contribution of modified breakeven analysis is that it forces the marketer to consider whether the consumer is likely to purchase the number of units required for achieving breakeven at a given price. It demonstrates that a large number of units sold does not necessarily produce added profits, because—other things equal—lower prices are necessary for stimulating additional sales. Consequently, it is important to consider both costs and consumer demand in determining the most appropriate price.

7 **Explain the use of yield management in pricing decisions.**

yield management
Pricing strategy that allows marketers to vary prices based on such factors as demand, even though the cost of providing those goods or services remains the same.

Yield Management

When most of a fim's costs are fixd over a wide range of outputs, the primry determinant of profitability will be the amount of revenue generated by sales. **Yield management** strategies allow marketers to vary prices based on such factors as demand, even though the cost of providing those goods or services remains the same. Hotels use software to track customer patterns and help determine attractive

table 18.4 **Revenue and Cost Data for Modified Breakeven Analysis**

	Revenues		Costs			Breakeven Point (Number of Sales Required to Break Even)	Total Profit (or Loss)
Price	Quantity Demanded	Total Revenue	Total Fixed Cost	Total Variable Cost	Total Cost		
$15	2,500	$37,500	$40,000	$12,500	$52,000	4,000	$(15,000)
10	10,000	100,000	40,000	50,000	90,000	8,000	10,000
9	13,000	117,000	40,000	65,000	105,000	10,000	12,000
8	14,000	112,000	40,000	70,000	110,000	13,334	2,000
7	15,000	105,000	40,000	75,000	115,000	20,000	(10,000)

discounts that fill their spas during off-peak hours such as weekdays and lunchtime. The lowered prices also reduce unprofitable downtime for specialized spa employees. New to the spa business, many hotels in the past "weren't able to maximize their revenues because they weren't doing any yield management," says one industry observer. "They'd just book their staff without looking at customer flow during the week. Now more hotel operators have gotten involved and are being driven to push more revenues."[25]

Similar yield management strategies typify the marketing of such goods and services as the following:

▷ *Sports teams*—the San Francisco Giants charge more for weekend games, and the Colorado Rockies raise ticket prices based on the crowd-pleasing power of visiting teams

▷ *Lodging*—lower prices in the off-season and higher prices during peak-season periods; low-priced weekend rates (except in locations such as Las Vegas, New Orleans, and Charleston, with high weekend tourist visits)

▷ *Auto rental*—lower prices on weekends when business demand is low and higher prices during the week when business demand is higher

▷ *Airfares*—lower prices on nonrefundable tickets with travel restrictions such as advance-purchase and Saturday-night stay requirements and penalties for flight changes and higher prices on refundable tickets that can be changed without penalty

The following example from the airline industry demonstrates how yield management maximizes revenues in situations in which costs are fixed.[26]

Airlines constantly monitor reservations on every flight. Beginning approximately 330 days before the flight, space is allocated between full-fare, discount-fare, and free tickets for frequent flyers who qualify for complimentary tickets. This allocation is monitored and adjusted at regular intervals until the flight departs.

Assume, for example, that American Airlines has scheduled a 136-seat plane as Flight 2332 with a 9:15 A.M. departure from Dallas–Fort Worth to Chicago's O'Hare Airport on October 23. When Flight 2332 leaves its gate, all costs associated with the flight (fuel, crew, and other operating expenses) are fixed. The pricing that maximizes revenues on this flight will also maximize profits. An examination of past sales indicates that American could sell 30 to 40 round-trip, full-fare tickets at $500 per passenger and 100 to 110 round-trip restricted-fare tickets at $200 per passenger. Demand for frequent-flyer space should be at least 10 seats.

If American reserves 40 seats for full-fare passengers and accepts reservations for 86 restricted-fare tickets but sells only 30 full-fare tickets (leaving 20 vacant seats), total revenues will be as follows:

$$\text{Revenues} = (30 \times \$500) + (86 \times \$200) = \$32,200$$

On the other hand, if American's pricing decision makers want to reduce vacancies, they might decide to reduce the number of full-fare tickets to 15 and increase the restricted-fare tickets to 111. If the plane leaves the gate at full capacity, the flight will generate the following total revenues:

$$\text{Revenues} = (15 \times \$500) + (111 \times \$200) = \$29,700$$

Instead of rigidly maintaining the allocations established nearly a year before the flight, though, American will use yield management to maximize the revenue per flight. In this example, the airline initially holds 40 full-fare seats and accepts reservations for up to 86 restricted-fare seats. Thirty days before the October 23 departure, updated computer projections indicate that 27 full-fare seats are likely to be sold. The allocation is now revised to 27 full-fare and 99 restricted-fare tickets. A full flight leaves the gate and revenues are as follows:

$$\text{Revenues} = (27 \times \$500) + (99 \times \$200) = \$33,300$$

Applying yield management for the Dallas–Chicago flight increases revenues by at least $1,100 over the inflexible approach of making advance allocations and failing to adjust them based on passenger reservations and other data.

assessment check

1. What is modified breakeven analysis?

2. Explain the goal of yield management.

Global Issues in Price Determination

It is equally important for a firm engagng in global marketing to use a pricing strategy that reflects its overall marketing strategy. Prices must support the company's broader goals, including product development, advertising and sales, customer support, competitive plans, and financial objectives.

In general, firms can use five pricing objectives to set prices in global marketing. Four of them are the same pricing objectives we discussed earlier in the chapter: profitability, volume, meeting competition, and prestige. In addition, international marketers work to achieve a fifth objective: price stability.

In the global arena, marketers may choose profitability objectives if their company is a price leader that tends to establish international prices. Profitability objectives also make sense if a firm is a low-cost supplier that can make a good profit on sales.

Volume objectives become especially important when nations lower their trade barriers, exposing domestic markets to foreign competition. During the Beijing Olympics, Nike and Adidas faced off in a multibillion-dollar battle for the huge Chinese audience. In sportswear, as in many other industries, China is the fastest-growing market in the world. Adidas sponsored the games and the Chinese Olympic committee, while Nike sponsored 22 of 28 Chinese teams in the competition. China's own sportswear brand, Li Ning, meanwhile, used the events to woo worldwide viewers with sponsorships from countries including Sweden and the United States. "We don't have as strong a brand" as Nike or Adidas, says the head of the company's footwear division. "We need to have an international image."[27]

Increased competition in Europe has spurred firms to work toward the third pricing objective of meeting competitors' prices. The widespread adoption of the euro, the currency of the European Union, has become a driving force in price convergence. When Slovakia prepared to adopt the euro, the transition was expected to be smooth based on past experience, with only slight effects and with price increases in just a few industries, such as tourism and recreation. Consumer prices would rise by only about 3 percent in the short term, according to the Organization for Economic Cooperation and Development (OECD). "Slovakia's view corresponds with the results of the OECD study and confirms the thesis that the euro does not directly equal price increases," says the country's finance secretary.[28]

Prestige is a valid pricing objective in international marketing when products are associated with intangible benefits, such as high quality, exclusiveness, or attractive design. The greater a product's perceived benefits, the higher its price can be. Marketers must be aware, however, that cultural perceptions of quality can differ from one country to the next. Sometimes items that command prestige prices in the United States are considered run-of-the-mill in other nations;

Adidas and Nike faced off in a multi-billion-dollar battle for the huge Chinese audience during the Beijing Olympics.

© Feng Li/Getty Images

与隋菲菲一起2008
没有不可能 IMPOSSIBLE IS NOTHING

sometimes products that are anything but prestigious in America seem exotic to overseas consumers. American patrons, for instance, view McDonald's restaurants as affordable fast-food eateries, but in China, they are seen as fashionable and relatively expensive.

The fifth pricing objective, price stability, is desirable in international markets, although it is difficult to achieve. Wars, terrorism, economic downturns, changing governments and political parties, and shifting trade policies can alter prices. A retailer can even be the victim of its own success. British international supermarket giant Tesco faces fierce competition at home and abroad, as well as a backlash among UK consumers against its growing dominance in so-called *Tesco towns*. One of every seven British pounds spent in shops in Great Britain is spent in a Tesco's store. The chain argues that, thanks to the Internet and the emergence of farmers' markets, the grocery market is now a national, not a local, one and that "we and all the other major grocery multiples have national strategies on pricing, branding, advertising, quality, range and service." Tesco's defense against accusations that it is growing into a monopoly says, in part, that the market should be defined in terms of consumers' willingness to switch retailers in response to price hikes.[29]

Price stability can be especially important for producers of commodities—goods and services that have easily accessible substitutes that other nations can supply quickly. Countries that export international commodities, such as wood, chemicals, and agricultural crops, suffer economically when their prices fluctuate. A nation such as Nicaragua, which exports sugarcane, can find that its balance of payments changes drastically when the international price for sugar shifts. This makes it vulnerable to stiff price competition from other sugarcane producers.

In contrast, countries that export value-oriented products, rather than commodities, tend to enjoy more stable prices. Prices of electronic equipment and automobiles tend to fluctuate far less than prices of crops such as sugarcane and bananas.

assessment check

1. What are five pricing objectives in global and online marketing?
2. Why is price stability difficult to achieve in online and global marketing?

Strategic Marketing in the 21st Century
Implications of

this chapter has focused on traditional pricing concepts and methods—principles critical to all marketing strategies, especially in e-business. Consumers can now compare prices quickly, heightening the already intense competitive pricing environment. The Web allows for prices to be negotiated on the spot, and nearly anything can be auctioned. For products as varied as sports tickets and automobiles, the Web allows consumers to name their price.

While Internet shopping has not resulted in massive price cutting, it has increased the options available for consumers. Online price comparison engines, known as *shopping bots,* promise to help consumers find the lowest price for any good or service. Reverse auctions offered by sites such as Priceline.com, which allow customers to submit the highest price they are willing to pay for airline tickets, could conceivably be extended to other types of goods and are already gaining in popularity in business-to-business purchasing.

Electronic delivery of music, books, and other goods and services will only lead to further price reductions. E-business has smoothed out the friction of time, which kept pricing relatively static. The current obsession with time and the ability to measure it will change the perceptions and pricing of tangible goods. A growing number of products are not made until they are ordered, and increasingly, their prices are no longer fixed; instead, prices can shift up and down in response to changing market conditions.

Review of Chapter Objectives

 Outline the legal constraints on pricing.

A variety of laws affect pricing decisions. Antitrust legislation provides a general set of constraints. The Robinson-Patman Act amended the Clayton Act to prohibit price discrimination in sales to other producers, wholesalers, or retailers not based on a cost differential. This law does not cover export markets or sales to the ultimate consumer. At the state level, unfair-trade laws require sellers to maintain minimum prices for comparable merchandise.

These laws have become less frequently enforced in recent years. Fair-trade laws represented one legal barrier to competition that was removed in the face of growing price competition. These laws permitted manufacturers to set minimum retail prices for products and to require their dealers to sign contracts agreeing to abide by such prices. The Consumer Goods Pricing Act banned interstate use of fair-trade laws.

 Identify the major categories of pricing objectives.

Pricing objectives are the natural consequence of overall organizational goals and more specific marketing goals. They can be classified into four major groups: (1) profitability objectives, including profit maximization and target returns; (2) volume objectives, including sales maximization and market share; (3) meeting competition objectives; and (4) prestige objectives.

 Explain price elasticity and its determinants.

Elasticity is an important element in price determination. The degree of consumer responsiveness to price changes is affected by such factors as (1) availability of substitute or complementary goods, (2) the classification of a good or service as a luxury or a necessity, (3) the portion of a person's budget spent on an item, and (4) the time perspective.

 List the practical problems involved in applying price theory concepts to actual pricing decisions.

Three problems are present in using price theory in actual practice. First, many firms do not attempt to maximize profits, a basic assumption of price theory. Second, it is difficult to accurately estimate demand curves. Finally, inadequate training of managers and poor communication between economists and managers make it difficult to apply price theory in the real world.

5 **Explain the major cost-plus approaches to price setting.**

Cost-plus pricing uses a base-cost figure per unit and adds a markup to cover unassigned costs and to provide a profit. It is the most commonly used method of setting prices today. There are two primary cost-oriented pricing procedures. Full-cost pricing uses all relevant variable costs in setting a product's price and allocates those fixed costs that cannot be directly attributed to the production of the priced item. Incremental-cost pricing attempts to use only those costs directly attributable to a specific output in setting prices to overcome the arbitrary allocation of fixed expenses. The basic limitation of cost-oriented pricing is that it does not adequately account for product demand.

 List the chief advantages and shortcomings of using breakeven analysis in pricing decisions.

Breakeven analysis is a means of determining the number of goods or services that must be sold at a given price to generate revenue sufficient for covering total costs. It is easily understood by managers and may help them decide whether required sales levels for a certain price are realistic goals. Its shortcomings are as follows. First, the model assumes cost can be divided into fixed and variable categories and ignores the problems of arbitrarily making some allocations. Second, it assumes that per-unit variable costs do not change at different levels of operation, ignoring the possibility of quantity discounts, more efficient use of the workforce, and other possible economies. Third, the basic breakeven model does not consider demand. It is a cost-based model and fails to directly address the crucial question of whether consumers will actually purchase the product at the specified price and in the quantities required for breaking even or generating profits.

7   Explain the use of yield management in pricing decisions.

Breakeven analysis is a means of determining the number of products that must be sold at a given price to generate sufficient revenue to cover total costs. The modified breakeven concept combines traditional breakeven analysis with an evaluation of consumer demand. It directly addresses the key question of whether consumers will actually purchase the product at different prices and in what quantities. Yield management pricing strategies are designed to maximize revenues in situations in which costs are fixed such as airfares, auto rentals, and theater tickets.

8   Identify the major pricing challenges facing online and international marketers.

In general, firms can choose from among five pricing objectives to set prices in global marketing. Four of these objectives are the same pricing objectives discussed earlier: profitability, volume, meeting competition, and prestige. The fifth objective is price stability, which is difficult to achieve because wars, border conflicts, terrorism, economic trends, changing governments and political parties, and shifting trade policies can alter prices. The same types of changes can alter pricing in online marketing.

assessment check: answers

1.1   What was the purpose of the Robinson-Patman Act?

The Robinson-Patman Act amended the Clayton Act to prohibit price discrimination in sales to other producers, wholesalers, or retailers that are not based on a cost differential.

1.2   What laws require sellers to maintain minimum prices for comparable merchandise?

At the state level, unfair-trade laws require sellers to maintain minimum prices for comparable merchandise.

1.3   What laws allow manufacturers to set minimum retail prices for their products?

Fair-trade laws permitted manufacturers to set minimum retail prices for products and to require their dealers to sign contracts agreeing to abide by such prices.

2.1   What are target-return objectives?

Target-return objectives are short-run or long-run goals usually stated as percentages of sales or investment.

2.2   What is value pricing?

Value pricing emphasizes the benefits a product provides in comparison to the price and quality levels of competing offerings.

2.3   How do prestige objectives affect a seller's pricing strategy?

Prestige pricing establishes a relatively high price to develop and maintain an image of quality that appeals to status-conscious customers. The seller uses price to create an overall image of the firm.

2.4   What goals does pricing strategy help a not-for-profit organization achieve?

Pricing strategy helps not-for-profit organizations achieve a variety of goals: profit maximization, cost recovery, market incentives, and market suppression.

2.5   What are the two basic ways in which marketers determine prices?

Marketers determine prices by applying the theoretical concepts of supply and demand and by completing cost-oriented analysis.

3.1   What are the determinants of elasticity?

The degree of consumer responsiveness to price changes—elasticity—is affected by such factors as (1) availability of substitute or complementary goods, (2) the classification of a good or service as a luxury or a necessity, (3) the portion of a person's budget spent on an item, and (4) the time perspective.

3.2   What is the usual relationship between elasticity and revenue?

A price cut increases revenue only for a product with elastic demand, and a price increase raises revenue only for a product with inelastic demand.

4.1   List the three reasons why it is difficult to put price theory into practice.

A basic assumption of price theory is all firms attempt to maximize profits. This does not always happen in practice. A second reason is demand curves can be extremely difficult to estimate. Finally, managers can be inadequately trained, causing poor communication between economists and managers, making it difficult to apply price theory in the real world.

5.1   What is full-cost pricing?

Full-cost pricing uses all relevant variable costs in setting a product's price.

5.2   What is incremental-cost pricing?

Incremental-cost pricing attempts to use only costs directly attributable to a specific output in setting prices to overcome the arbitrary allocation of fixed expenses.

5.3   Give the formula for finding the breakeven point, in units and in dollars.

Breakeven point in units = Total fixed cost/Per-unit contribution to fixed cost. Breakeven point in dollars = Total fixed cost/(1 − Variable cost per unit price).

5.4   What adjustments to the basic breakeven calculation must be made to include target returns?

Breakeven point (including specific dollar target return) = (Total fixed cost + Profit objective)/Per-unit contribution.

6.1   What are the advantages of breakeven analysis?

Breakeven analysis is easily understood by managers and may help them decide whether required sales levels for a certain price are realistic goals.

6.2   What are the disadvantages of breakeven analysis?

First, the model assumes cost can be divided into fixed and variable categories and ignores the problems of arbitrarily making some allocations. Second, it assumes per-unit variable costs do not change at different levels of operation, ignoring the possibility of quantity discounts, more efficient use of the workforce, and other possible economies. Third, the basic breakeven model does not consider demand.

7.1   What is modified breakeven analysis?

The modified breakeven concept combines traditional breakeven analysis with an evaluation of consumer demand. It directly addresses the key question of whether consumers will actually purchase the product at different prices and in what quantities.

7.2 Explain the goal of yield management.

Yield management pricing strategies are designed to maximize revenues in situations in which costs are fixed such as airfares, auto rentals, and theater tickets.

8.1 What are five pricing objectives in global and online marketing?

Five pricing objectives in global and online marketing are profitability, volume, meeting competition, prestige, and price stability.

8.2 Why is price stability difficult to achieve in online and global marketing?

Price stability is difficult to achieve because wars, border conflicts, terrorism, economic trends, changing governments and political parties, and shifting trade policies can alter prices.

Marketing Terms You Need to Know

price 608
Robinson-Patman Act 609
unfair-trade laws 610
fair-trade laws 610
profit maximization 613

target-return objective 613
Profit Impact of Market Strategies (PIMS) project 613
value pricing 615
customary prices 618

elasticity 622
breakeven analysis 625
modified breakeven analysis 627
yield management 628

Other Important Marketing Terms

marginal analysis 613
market-share objective 613
demand 619
supply 619
pure competition 620

monopolistic competition 620
oligopoly 620
monopoly 620
variable costs 620
fixed costs 621

average total costs 621
marginal cost 621
cost-plus pricing 624
full-cost pricing 624
incremental-cost pricing 625

Assurance of Learning Review

1. Distinguish between fair-trade and unfair-trade laws. As a consumer, would you support either fair-trade or unfair-trade laws? Would your answer change if you were the owner of a small store?

2. Give an example of each of the major categories of pricing objectives.

3. What are the major price implications of the PIMS studies? Suggest possible explanations for the relationships the PIMS studies reveal.

4. Identify each factor influencing elasticity and give a specific example of how it affects the degree of elasticity in a good or service.

5. What are the practical problems in applying price theory concepts to actual pricing decisions?

6. Explain the advantages and drawbacks of using incremental-cost pricing rather than full-cost pricing.

7. How can locating the breakeven point assist in price determination?

8. Explain the advantage of modified breakeven analysis over the basic breakeven formula.

9. Explain how the use of yield management can result in greater revenue than other pricing strategies.

10. How do pricing objectives for a global firm differ from those used generally?

Projects and Teamwork Exercises

1. In small teams, categorize each of the following as a specific type of pricing objective. Suggest a company or product likely to use each pricing objective. Compare your findings.
   a. 5 percent increase in profits over the previous year
   b. prices no more than 6 percent higher than prices quoted by independent dealers
   c. 5 percent increase in market share
   d. 25 percent return on investment (before taxes)
   e. setting the highest prices in the product category to maintain favorable brand image

2. In pairs, discuss the market situations that exist for the following products. Defend your answers and present them to the class.
   a. MP3 players
   b. golf clubs
   c. soybeans
   d. remote control car alarms
   e. razors

3. How are the following prices determined and what do they have in common?
   a. ticket to a local museum
   b. your college tuition
   c. local sales tax rate
   d. printing of business cards
   e. lawn mowers

4. WebTech Development of Nashville, Tennessee, is considering the possible introduction of a new product proposed by its research and development staff. The firm's marketing director estimates the product can be marketed at a price of $70. Total fixed cost is $278,000, and average variable cost is calculated at $48.
   a. What is the breakeven point in units for the proposed product?
   b. The firm's CEO has suggested a target profit return of $214,000 for the proposed product. How many units must be sold to both break even and achieve this target return?

5. The marketing research staff at Cleveland-based Cyber Novelties has developed the following sales estimates for a proposed new item the firm plans to market through direct mail sales:

Proposed Selling Price	Sales Estimate (units)
$ 8	55,000
10	22,000
15	14,000
20	5,000
24	2,800

The new product has a total fixed cost of $60,000 and a $7 variable cost per unit.
   a. Which of the proposed selling prices would generate a profit for Cyber Novelties?
   b. Cyber Novelties' director of marketing also estimates an additional $0.50 per-unit allocation for extra promotion will produce the following sales increases: 60,000 units at an $8 unit selling price; 28,000 units at $10; 17,000 units at $15; 6,000 units at $20; and 3,500 units at $24. Indicate the feasible range of prices if this proposal is implemented and results in the predicted sales increases.
   c. Indicate the feasible price or prices if the $0.50 per-unit additional promotion proposal is not implemented but management insists on a $25,000 target return.

6. Research the price schedule at your local movie theater multiplex. What pricing strategy accounts for any price differentials you discover? Why don't matinee prices constitute price discrimination against those who don't qualify for the discounts?

7. Why is it more expensive to buy beer and a hot dog at a Major League Baseball game than at local retail stores?

8. Public funding of national parks has been declining for many years. What would you expect to happen to entry and use fees in this case? Research fees at parks in your state or region to verify your answer and report to the class.

9. How do cell phone companies make money by charging a flat rate per month for a set number of minutes, such as $35 for 300 minutes? Can you think of a more profitable plan? Would it appeal to consumers?

10. Some sports marketers believe simpler pricing for tickets will earn goodwill from customers and send a clear marketing message that they are ready to attract fans. But few teams are embracing a new pricing system, frequently opting to place premium tickets online and charging seat licenses for season ticket holders, who then own the rights to those seats. Why do you think the teams are reluctant to change?

Critical-Thinking Exercises

1. Prices at amusement parks are expected to rise because operators such as Disney and Universal Studios are adding new rides and coping with the rising cost of fuel. List as many things as you can think of that parks like these offer patrons in return for their money. Which of these do you think are directly reflected in the price of admission?

2. Musical artists earn only about 9 percent in royalties per CD, using a royalty base of retail price less 25 percent for packaging costs. The rest goes to the producer and to cover recording costs, promotion, copies given away to radio stations and reviewers, and other costs such as videos. What do you think happens to the artist's royalties when a CD is marked down to sell faster? Consider two cases: (1) the marked-down CD sells more copies, and (2) it sells the same number of copies as before.

3. Some finance experts advise consumers not to worry about rising gasoline prices, the cost of which can easily be covered by forgoing one takeout meal a month, but to worry about how high energy prices will affect the rest of the economy. For example, each dollar-a-barrel price increase is equivalent to a $20 million-a-day "tax" on the economy. Explain what this means.

4. Ajax Motor Company recently announced that it will rely less on high-volume strategies such as discounts and rebates to improve its profitability. Another strategy it will employ is to sell fewer cars to rental fleets, which eventually return the cars to Ajax for sale at low auction prices. How do these types of sales affect Ajax's profitability?

Ethics Exercise

You work for a major restaurant in your town. The manager is facing cost pressures from rising food prices and says she needs to raise revenues. She decides to reduce the size of the meal portions and use cheaper cuts of meat and fish in some entrées while holding the menu prices constant. She tells you and other staff members not to mention the changes to customers and to deflect any questions or complaints you hear. The descriptions in the menu will not be changed, she says, "because the printing costs would be too high."

1. You know the restaurant advertises the quality of its ingredients widely in the local media. But the menu changes are not advertised, and it bothers you. What course of action would you take?

2. A customer mentions the beef in the dish he ordered is "tough and dry" and the order seems smaller than before. What would you do?

Internet Exercises

1. **Real estate commissions and the Internet.** Critics have long contended that the flat 6 percent commission that real estate agents charge sellers is a form of price fixing. In response, entrepreneurs have started online real estate brokerage services, which charge sellers lower commissions. One of the largest online real estate brokerage firms is Zip Realty (www.ziprealty.com/). Visit the company's Web site. In comparison with a traditional real estate brokerage firm, how does Zip Realty work? What impact do you think online real estate brokers will have on real estate commissions? How have the real estate industry and government regulars responded to online brokers?

2. **Yield management.** Airlines, hotels, and rental car companies all practice yield management. Visit at least two airline Web sites. Pick a roundtrip flight between two cities served by the airline and price the fares. By how much do fares vary? Do they vary by the day of the week, time of the day, or both? Summarize your findings and relate your experience to the discussion of yield management found in the chapter.

3. **Dumping.** Many trade disputes between nations involve a practice called *dumping*—selling a product globally for less than the cost of production. Visit the Web sites of the World Trade Organization (wto.org/english) and the Office of the U.S. Trade Representative (www.ustr.gov) to learn more about dumping, including several recent cases. Summarize your findings in a one-page report.

Note: Internet Web addresses change frequently. If you don't find the exact site listed, you may need to access the organization's home page and search from there or use a search engine such as Google.

Case 18.1 Impact Fees: Who Pays, Who Profits?

Commercial and residential developments are signs of progress that bring new residents or new jobs, or both, to a city or county

and increase tax revenues for the local government. Such developments also tax the area's existing resources in several ways: they lead to increased demands on area roads, parks, schools, libraries, waste and water systems, and police and fire departments.

To help pay for expanded services to avoid these potential strains, local governments charge developers one-time impact fees that can run into hundreds of thousands of dollars per project. In some areas, for instance, the impact fee charged to a developer for building one new 2,500-square-foot home could be as much as $5,000. While developers lobby to keep such fees as low as possible, some government agencies think they are not nearly high enough when it can cost close to $16,500 to make the required improvements in a city's or county's infrastructure.

Most local governments charge impact fees that are only a fraction of the cost they estimate new developments will have on their community. One reason for keeping the fees low is fear that the cost will be passed directly to the consumer, in this case the homebuyer. "Everyone views this [impact fees] as the cost of development," said one city councilman. "It's not. It's really put onto the end consumer." Another homeowners' advocate said even a small passed-on cost could raise home prices beyond the reach of many.

A further consideration is that high impact fees could stifle development in an area by making it too expensive for developers to build there. The ripple effects are many. "The building industry drives a significant number of ancillary business in the county," says one observer. "It affects real estate, it affects construction, surveyors, bankers, insurance agencies. ... The ripple effect of a high impact fee is that it depresses the entire real estate industry."

Many developers of commercial properties like offices and shopping malls believe they cannot pass high impact fees on to their customers. "The fact is that we're having to eat those costs—you can't get the market to accept those costs," says one developer. And local government officials are constrained in setting impact fees. Commercial developments bring needed jobs and business tax revenues, relieving the real estate tax burden on residents, and some can also raise surrounding land values. No mayor or county executive wants to be the one who turns such opportunity away. "Impact fees are integral to our quality of life," explains one county council chairperson. "If my roads are bad and my schools are bad, then we're not keeping up with the expectations citizens had when they bought their homes. When impact fees aren't properly set, the taxpayers bear the brunt."

Questions for Critical Thinking

1. Who really pays the final cost of impact fees? Why? What other ways can you think of to distribute these costs?

2. If impact fees on a residential development were set too low, how might the local government make up the revenue needed to expand and maintain its infrastructure? What effect would your solution have on the average price of homes in the area? Why?

Sources: Company Web site of Duncan Associates, www.impactfees.com, accessed June 9, 2009; Christopher Curry, "Builders Want in on Impact Fee Reduction," *Star-Banner,* August 20, 2008, www.ocala.com; Jason Flanagan, "High Impact Fees Could Hurt Anne Arundel's Economy, Developers Say," *The Examiner,* August 20, 2008, www.baltimoreexaminer.com; Michael D. Bates, "Impact Fee Debate Heats Up," *Hernando Today,* August 2, 2008, www.impactfees.com; Erin Cos, "Why Should You Care about Impact Fees?" *The Capital Online,* April 27, 2008, www.hometownannapolis.com.

Video Case 18.2 | **Pricing Concepts at Evogear.com**

The written video case on Evogear appears on page VC-16. The Evogear video is designed to expand and highlight the concepts in this chapter and the concepts and questions covered in the written video case.

CHAP**19**TER

Pricing
Strategies

© AP Images/Amy Sancetta

Starbucks Ices Its Prices

With 400 billion cups consumed each year, coffee is the second-most-traded commodity in the world, second only to oil. In this gigantic market, Starbucks built its success and its reputation by

offering customers premium coffee and top-quality ingredients in all its food and beverage products. The chain grew internationally by leaps and bounds, eventually expanding from 4 to nearly 17,000 stores

worldwide and forever changing the way we think of coffee. No longer a mere commodity, coffee became what Starbucks called an "affordable luxury." The chain's runaway success allowed it to charge pre-

mium prices for its specialty drinks and essentially cede the rest of the market to lower-priced chains like Dunkin' Donuts.

The recession that hit in 2008 changed all that, as consumers began to look at a

$3.95 coffee drink as a luxury they couldn't afford after all. Starbucks saw its earnings drop early in the downturn, and it was one of the first retailers to react. The company abruptly shelved expansion plans, closed hundreds of stores—eventually shuttering over 1,000 locations worldwide—and laid off thousands of employees. Yet in a recent quarter its profit declined 77 percent as store traffic continued to fall and the value of the average transaction dropped 3 percent. Clearly, weathering the downturn without losing a large share of its customer base would require Starbucks to do more.

So, just as McDonald's rolled out a national advertising campaign offering new low-priced lattes, cappuccinos, and mocha coffee drinks at most of its 14,000 U.S. stores, Starbucks undertook a full reevaluation of its pricing strategy. The company announced it would raise the

price of a few of its more complicated drinks but lower many more. One example: the grande size iced coffee will sell for under $2, saving consumers as much as 45 cents off the original price. The company also introduced its own Via brand of instant coffee, which provides Starbucks quality at home for less than $1 a cup. And since many consumers choose their breakfast supplier based on their coffee preference, Starbucks targeted McDonald's popular breakfast menu with a coffee-plus-egg-sandwich combo of its own, for a discounted price of $3.95 that used to buy just a coffee. "It's less than four bucks," said the company's chief marketing officer, "and it's not just a drink, but food to go with it."

The company is also changing the menus posted in its stores to highlight its $2 hot and iced coffees and downplay the expensive Frappuccinos that used to be its headliners. Starbucks is also

reminding its servers that most of its drinks sell for under $3, training them to spread the word among customers and help counter the impression that the chain is interested only in those willing to pay any price for quality.

The chain is serious about recasting itself as an affordable brand. And although McDonald's claims the timing of its introduction of McCafé specialty coffees is just a coincidence, Starbucks is fighting back. "Speculation that Starbucks is losing retail market share to competitors has been grossly exaggerated," said company CEO Howard Schultz. "We know customers are looking for meaningful value, not just a lower price. . . . We're going to arm our consumers and partners with the facts about Starbucks Coffee."

Some of those facts are couched in a new multimillion-dollar ad campaign touting the benefits not just of the company's

evolution of a brand

Starbucks CEO Howard Schultz says, "If we are a premium brand, it doesn't mean we can't provide value. We believe when we come out of this, we will be stronger because we maintained our core customers and, through providing value, will bring on new customers."

- One marketing researcher comments on Starbucks's new pricing strategy: "Trading down is necessary, but they have to be very careful that they are not going to trade away the prestige the brand was built on. It's a hard needle to thread." Is there a risk Starbucks could damage its brand image if it goes too far down the "value" road? Or is a reevaluation of its pricing strategy necessary if, as some observers believe, shoppers have permanently adopted more frugal spending habits as a result of the recession?

- Some industry observers believe the coffee war between Starbucks and McDonald's isn't real. "I think it's a bit naïve to think that all of those Starbucks customers are running across the street to McDonald's," says one. "Just as

evolution of a brand
continued

quality products but of buying into its commitment to its free-trade coffee suppliers and its protection

of part-time workers, who enjoy full health-care benefits at a company still considered one of the best employers in the United States.

And then consider Starbucks's atmosphere, with its comfy chairs and wireless Internet access. When was the last time you were tempted to linger over your keyboard at McDonald's?[1]

Starbucks will always be a beverage destination, McDonald's will always be known as a food destination." Do you agree? Do you think consumers perceive more differences between the two chains than just price? If so, what are they, and how can Starbucks maintain these differences as advantages?

- Starbucks's new advertising campaign promotes the company's commitment to quality and, despite recent layoffs, to its employees. Do you think the ads about what consumers are "buying into" with their cup of coffee will help reinforce the loyalty of existing customers? Will it attract new ones? Why or why not?

chapter overview

- ### Setting prices is neither a one-time decision nor a standard routine.

As illustrated by the changes Starbucks has undertaken, pricing is just one aspect of the overall marketing effort. Pricing is a dynamic function of the marketing mix. While about half of all companies change prices once a year or less frequently, one in ten does so every month. Online companies, facing enormous price pressures, may adjust prices more often depending on what they are selling. Some firms negotiate prices on the spot, as in the case of a car dealership or an antique shop.

Companies translate pricing objectives into pricing decisions in two major steps. First, someone takes responsibility for making pricing decisions and administering the resulting pricing structure. Second, someone sets the overall pricing structure—that is, basic prices and appropriate discounts for chan-

nel members, quantity purchases, and geographic and promotional considerations.

The decision to make price adjustments is directly related to demand. Most businesses slowly change the amounts they charge customers, even when they clearly recognize strong demand. Instead of raising prices, they may scale down customer service or add fees to cover rising costs. They may also wait to raise prices until they see what their competitors do.

Significant price changes in the retail gasoline and airline industries occur in the form of a **step out,** in which one firm raises prices and then waits to see if others follow suit. If competitors fail to respond by increasing their prices, the company making the step out usually reduces prices to the original level. Fuel is one of the biggest expenses for most airlines, accounting for approximately 40 percent of their operating costs. As they try to juggle the rising costs, most have been forced to offset their expenses with increased fares and fuel surcharges, along with additional fees for checked baggage and bottled drinking water. "Fuel is eating [the airlines] alive, right now," notes one expert. "It's not surprising to see air fares double." However, as demand for flights begins to soften, carriers are rolling back some increases to remain competitive. Although airlines are prohibited by law from collectively setting prices, they can follow each other's example.[2]

Few businesses want the distinction of being the first to charge higher prices. Because many firms base their prices on manufacturing costs rather than consumer demand, they may wait for increases in their own costs before responding with price changes. These increases generally emerge more slowly than changes in consumer demand. Finally, because many business executives believe steady prices help preserve long-term rela-

tionships with customers, they are reluctant to raise prices even when strong demand probably justifies the change.

Chapter 18 introduced the concept of price and its role in the economic system and marketing strategy. This chapter examines various pricing strategies and price structures, such as reductions from list prices, and geographic considerations. It then looks at the primary pricing policies, including psychological pricing, price flexibility, product-line pricing, and promotional pricing, as well as price–quality relationships. Competitive and negotiated prices are discussed, and one section focuses entirely on transfer pricing. Finally, the chapter concludes by describing important factors in pricing goods and services for online and global markets.

Pricing Strategies

The specific strategies firms use to price goods and services grow out of the marketing strategies they formulate to accomplish overall organizational objectives. One firm's marketers may price their products to attract customers across a wide range; another group of marketers may set prices to appeal to a small segment of a larger market; still another group may simply try to match competitors' price tags. In general, firms can choose from three pricing strategies: skimming, penetration, and competitive pricing. The following sections look at these choices in more detail.

❚ Compare the alternative pricing strategies and explain when each strategy is most appropriate.

SKIMMING PRICING STRATEGY

Derived from the expression "skimming the cream," **skimming pricing strategies** are also known as **market-plus pricing.** They involve intentionally setting a relatively high price compared with the prices of competing products. Although some firms continue to use a skimming strategy throughout most stages of the product lifecycle, it is more commonly used as a market entry price for distinctive goods or services with little or no initial competition. When the supply begins to exceed demand, or when competition catches up, the initial high price is dropped.

Such was the case with high-definition televisions (HDTVs), whose average price was $19,000, including installation, when they were first introduced. The resulting sticker shock kept them out of the range of most household budgets. But nearly a decade later, price cuts have brought both LCD and plasma models into the reach of mainstream consumers. At Best Buy, shoppers can pick up a Sharp 20-inch, flat-panel LCD model for $499.99. On the higher end, they can purchase a Sharp 52-inch, flat-panel LCD model for $1,899.99.[3]

A company may practice a skimming strategy in setting a market-entry price when it introduces a distinctive good or service with little or no competition. Or it may use this strategy to market higher-end goods. British vacuum cleaner manufacturer Dyson has used this practice. Offering an entirely new design and engineering, Dyson sells several of its vacuum cleaner models

skimming pricing strategy
Pricing strategy involving the use of a high price relative to competitive offerings.

When first introduced, high-definition televisions were so expensive that most households could not afford them. Now that they've been on the market for several years, prices have dropped.

© AP Images/Paul Sakuma

for between $400 and $550, significantly more than the average vacuum. Even iRobot's Roomba vacuum sells for around $200, and the company claims it does all the work for you.[4]

In some cases, a firm may maintain a skimming strategy throughout most stages of a product's lifecycle. The jewelry category is a good example. Although discounters such as Costco and Home Shopping Network (HSN) offer heavier gold pieces for a few hundred dollars, firms such as Tiffany and Cartier command prices ten times that amount just for the brand name. Exclusivity justifies the pricing—and the price, once set, rarely falls.

Sometimes maintaining a high price through the product's lifecycle works, but sometimes it does not. High prices can drive away otherwise loyal customers. Baseball fans may shift from attending major league games to minor league games because of ticket, parking, and food prices. Amusement park visitors may shy away from high admission prices and head to the beach instead. If an industry or firm has been known to cut prices at certain points in the past, consumers—and retailers—will expect it. If the price cut doesn't come, consumers must decide whether to pay the higher tab or try a competitor's products. This has been the case with General Motors, which recently returned to its employee pricing strategy: offering consumers the same discounts employees receive on most of its cars and trucks. Although the discount is real, GM actually is offering the lower price to divert customers from expectations of rock-bottom sale prices around holidays like Labor Day.[5]

Despite the risk of backlash, a skimming strategy does offer benefits. It allows a manufacturer to quickly recover its research and development (R&D) costs. Pharmaceuticals companies, fiercely protective of their patents on new drugs, justify high prices because of astronomical R&D costs: an average of 16 cents of every sales dollar, compared with 8 cents for computer makers and 4 cents in the aerospace industry. To protect their brand names from competition from lower-cost generics, drug makers frequently make small changes to their products—such as combining the original product with a complementary prescription drug that treats different aspects of the ailment.

A skimming strategy also permits marketers to control demand in the introductory stages of a product's lifecycle and then adjust productive capacity to match changing demand. A low initial price for a new product could lead to fulfillment problems and loss of shopper goodwill if demand outstrips the firm's production capacity. The result will likely be consumer and retailer complaints and possibly permanent damage to the product's image. Excess demand occasionally leads to quality issues, as the firm strives to satisfy consumer desires for the product with inadequate production facilities.

During the late growth and early maturity stages of its lifecycle, a product's price typically falls for two reasons: (1) the pressure of competition and (2) the desire to expand its market. Figure 19.1 shows that 10 percent of the market may buy Product X at $10.00, and another 20 percent could be added to its customer base at a price of $8.75. Successive price declines may expand the firm's market size and meet challenges posed by new competitors.

A skimming strategy has one inherent chief disadvantage: It attracts competition. Potential competitors see innovative firms reaping large financial returns and decide to enter the market. This new supply may force the price of the original product even lower than its eventual level under a sequential skimming procedure. However, if patent protection or some other unique proprietary ability allows a firm to exclude competitors from its market, it may extend a skimming strategy.

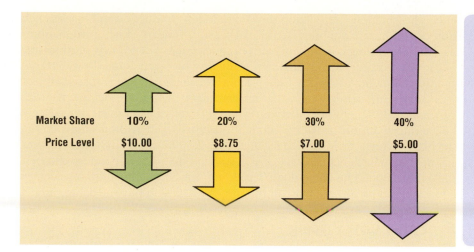

figure 19.1

Price Reductions to Increase Market Share

Market Share	10%	20%	30%	40%
Price Level	$10.00	$8.75	$7.00	$5.00

PENETRATION PRICING STRATEGY

A **penetration pricing strategy** sets a low price as a major marketing weapon. Marketers often price products noticeably lower than competing offerings when they enter new industries characterized by dozens of competing brands. Once the product achieves some market recognition through consumer trial purchases stimulated by its low price, marketers may increase the price to the level of competing products. Marketers of consumer products such as detergents often use this strategy. A penetration pricing strategy may also extend over several stages of the product lifecycle as the firm seeks to maintain a reputation as a low-price competitor.

A penetration pricing strategy is sometimes called *market-minus pricing* when it implements the premise that a lower-than-market price will attract buyers and move a brand from an unknown newcomer to at least the brand-recognition stage or even to the brand-preference stage. Because many firms begin penetration pricing with the intention of increasing prices in the future, success depends on generating many trial purchases. Penetration pricing is common among credit card firms, which typically offer low or zero interest rates for a specified introductory period, then raise the rates. If competitors view the new product as a threat, marketers attempting to use a penetration strategy often discover that rivals will simply match their prices.

When plasma TVs were retailing for around $8,000, William Wang decided he could do better. By outsourcing every process from tech support to research and development, Wang trimmed his own costs as far as possible and offered a comparable TV for about $4,000. He began with the help of Gateway but quickly went out on his own, introducing his unknown brand to the public via Costco. Now, Sony has taken notice. "I would never imagine four or five years ago that Sony would look at us as a competitor," observes Wang.[6]

Retailers may use penetration pricing to lure shoppers to new stores. Strategies might take such forms as zero interest charges for credit purchases at a new furniture store, two-for-one offers for dinner at a new restaurant, or an extremely low price on a single product purchase for first-time customers to get them to come in and shop.

Penetration pricing works best for goods or services characterized by highly elastic demand. Large numbers of highly price-sensitive consumers pay close attention to this type of appeal. The strategy also suits situations in which large-scale

penetration pricing strategy Pricing strategy involving the use of a relatively low entry price compared with competitive offerings, based on the theory that this initial low price will help secure market acceptance.

© Jeff Greenberg/Alamy

Because the market already contains so many competing brands, detergent marketers often use a penetration pricing strategy when they enter the market, pricing products noticeably lower than the competition.

operations and long production runs result in low production and marketing costs. Finally, penetration pricing may be appropriate in market situations in which introduction of a new product will likely attract strong competitors. Such a strategy may allow a new product to reach the mass market quickly and capture a large share prior to entry by competitors. Research shows that about 25 percent of companies use penetration pricing strategies on a regular basis.

Some auto manufacturers have been using penetration pricing for some new models to attract customers who might not otherwise consider purchasing a vehicle during a given year or who might be looking at a more expensive competitor. India's Tata Motors launched the world's cheapest car: the Nano, which carries a price tag of about $2,500. Although the firm has yet to announce plans to sell the Nano in the United States, it is still half the price of the next-cheapest vehicle in the world, the Maruti 800. The Nano doesn't have any frills: no radio and no passenger-side mirror or other add-ons. And if you want air conditioning, you have to buy the deluxe model at a higher price.[7]

Everyday Low Pricing

Closely related to penetration pricing is **everyday low pricing (EDLP),** a strategy devoted to continuous low prices as opposed to relying on short-term, price-cutting tactics such as cents-off coupons, rebates, and special sales. EDLP can take two forms. In the first, retailers such as Wal-Mart and Lowe's compete by consistently offering consumers low prices on a broad range of items. Through its EDLP policy, Lowe's pledges not only to match any price the consumer sees elsewhere but also to take off an additional percentage in some cases. Wal-Mart states that it achieves EDLP by negotiating better prices from suppliers and by cutting its own costs. Wal-Mart recently launched an online guide designed to help consumers save and stretch their hard-earned dollars a little farther. The company's advertising tagline—"Save More. Live Better"—embraces its EDLP policy.[8]

The second form of the EDLP pricing strategy involves its use by the manufacturer in dealing with channel members. Manufacturers may seek to set stable wholesale prices that undercut offers competitors make to retailers, offers that typically rise and fall with the latest trade promotion deals. Many marketers reduce list prices on a number of products while simultaneously reducing promotion allowances to retailers. While reductions in allowances mean retailers may not fund such in-store promotions as shelf merchandising and end-aisle displays, the manufacturers hope stable low prices will stimulate sales instead.

Some retailers oppose EDLP strategies. Many grocery stores, for instance, operate on "high–low" strategies that set profitable regular prices to offset losses of frequent specials and promotions. Other retailers believe EDLP will ultimately benefit both sellers and buyers. Supporters of EDLP in the grocery industry point out that it already succeeds at two of the biggest competitors: Wal-Mart and warehouse clubs such as Costco.

One popular pricing myth is that a low price is a sure sell. Low prices are an easy means of distinguishing the offerings of one marketer from other sellers, but such moves are easy to counter by competitors. Unless overall demand is price elastic, overall price cuts will mean less revenue for all firms in the industry. In addition, low prices may generate an image of questionable quality.

competitive pricing strategy Pricing strategy designed to deemphasize price as a competitive variable by pricing a good or service at the general level of comparable offerings.

Wal-Mart employs everyday low pricing, a strategy devoted to continuous low prices instead of special sales and other short-term pricing tactics.

© Tim Boyle/Getty Images

COMPETITIVE PRICING STRATEGY

Although many organizations rely heavily on price as a competitive weapon, even more implement **competitive pricing strategies.** These organizations try to reduce the emphasis on price competition by matching other firms' prices and concentrating their own marketing efforts on the product, distribution, and promotion elements of the marketing mix. As pointed out earlier, while price offers a dramatic means of achieving competitive advantage, it is also the easiest marketing variable for competitors to match. In fact, in industries with relatively homogeneous products, competitors must match each other's price reductions to maintain market share and remain competitive.

Retailers such as The Home Depot and Lowe's both use price-matching strategies, assuring consumers that they will meet—and beat—competitors' prices. Grocery chains such as Kroger's and Stop & Shop may compete with seasonal items: soft drinks and hot dogs in the summer, hot chocolate and turkeys in the winter. As soon as one store lowers the price of an item, the rest follow suit.

Another form of competitive pricing is setting an **opening price point** within a category. Retailers often achieve this by pricing a quality private-label product below the competition. Grocery giants Publix and Kroger have begun actively advertising their private-label goods, most of which are priced below those of manufacturers' brands. However, Kroger also has a Private Selection brand for more upscale shoppers, including gourmet brownies and caramel swirl ice cream.[9]

Prices can really drop when companies continually match each other's prices, as evident in the airline and computer industries. But competitive pricing can be tricky; a price reduction affects not only the first company but also the entire industry as other firms match the reduction. Unless lower prices can attract new customers and expand the overall market enough to offset the loss of per-unit revenue, the price cut will leave all competitors with less revenue. Research shows that nearly two-thirds of all firms set prices using competitive pricing as their primary pricing strategy. Firms forced to the edge by competitive pricing strategies may decide to declare Chapter 11 bankruptcy to become more competitive in their markets.

What happens when one discounter undercuts another? Although many retailers fear competition from Wal-Mart, one type of store seems well positioned against the powerful chain: the so-called dollar stores. Today's equivalent of the five-and-dime variety stores of the 20th century, dollar stores sell inexpensive items such as cleaning supplies, paper plates, toothpaste, greeting cards, and other household products—and compete on price and convenience, especially parking and easy access to the goods. Although these stores have yet to threaten Wal-Mart's position, the retail giant is paying attention. As these dollar store chains expand, adding more brand-name products and attracting more price-conscious customers, Wal-Mart is likely to take some competitive action.

Once competitors are routinely matching each other on price, marketers must turn away from price as a marketing strategy, emphasizing other variables to develop areas of distinctive competence and to attract customers. That might mean offering personalized service such as gift wrapping or a customer service associate who knows the type of clothing or books you like.

assessment check

1. What are the three major pricing strategies?
2. What is EDLP?

Price Quotations

2 Describe how prices are quoted.

The choice of the best method for quoting prices depends on many industry conditions, including competitive trends, cost structures, and traditional practices, along with the policies of individual firms. This section examines the reasoning and methodology behind price quotation practices.

Most price structures are built around **list prices**—the rates normally quoted to potential buyers. Marketers usually determine list prices by one or a combination of the methods discussed in Chapter 18. The sticker price on a new automobile is a good example: it shows the list price for the basic model and then adds the prices of options. The sticker price for a new Toyota Prius Touring Edition sedan is $23,770. But you can add such features as a navigation system, satellite radio, and child seat anchors—all at additional cost. Most car manufacturers bundle features into packages for one price. So if you order package number 5 on the Prius, you'll automatically get a backup camera and Bluetooth wireless capability, among other add-ons.[10]

The price of oil is equally important to consumers—particularly those who drive cars—because it directly affects the list price of gasoline. Disruptions such as hurricanes and wars affect the price of oil, and ultimately the price that drivers pay at the pump. Prices may also

list price Established price normally quoted to potential buyers.

figure 19.2

Components of Retail Gasoline Prices

Source: Data from Energy Information Administration, "Gasoline and Diesel Fuel Update," April 2009, tonto.eia. doe.gov, accessed June 9, 2009.

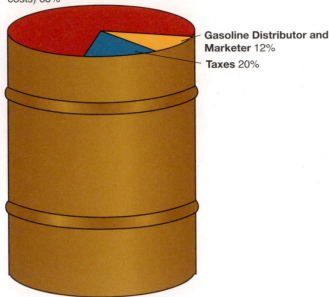

Who gets the money from retail gas sales?

Oil Wholesaler (includes crude oil price and refinery costs) 68%

Gasoline Distributor and Marketer 12%

Taxes 20%

Note: Percentages are rounded to nearest percent.

market price Price a consumer or marketing intermediary actually pays for a product after subtracting any discounts, allowances, or rebates from the list price.

fluctuate seasonally, as demand for gasoline rises and falls. Figure 19.2 illustrates where the money from a gallon of gas goes on its journey from the oil field to your gas tank.

REDUCTIONS FROM LIST PRICE

The amount a consumer pays for a product—its **market price**—may or may not equal the list price. Discounts and allowances sometimes reduce list prices. A list price often defines a starting point from which discounts set a lower market price. Marketers offer discounts in several classifications: cash, trade, and quantity discounts.

Cash Discounts

Consumers, industrial purchasers, or channel members sometimes receive reductions in price in exchange for prompt payment of bills; these price cuts are known as **cash discounts.** Discount terms usually specify exact time periods, such as 2/10, net 30. This notation means the customer must pay within 30 days, but payment within 10 days entitles the customer to subtract 2 percent from the amount due. Consumers may receive a cash discount for immediate payment, say, paying with cash instead of a credit card at the gas pump or paying the full cash amount up front for elective healthcare services such as orthodontia. Cash discounts represent a traditional pricing practice in many industries. They fulfill legal requirements provided that all customers can take the same reductions on the same terms.

In recent years, sellers have increasingly attempted to improve their own liquidity positions, reduce their bad-debt losses, and cut collection expenses by moving to a form of *negative cash discount.* Confronted with purchasers who may defer paying their bills as long as possible, another notice has begun to appear on customer statements:

Due on Receipt. A FINANCE CHARGE of 1.5% per month (18% A.P.R.) is computed on and added to the unpaid balance as of the statement date.

Past-due accounts may be turned over to collection agencies.

Trade Discounts

Payments to channel members for performing marketing functions are known as **trade discounts,** or functional discounts. Services performed by various channel members and the related costs were discussed in Chapters 13 and 14. A manufacturer's list price must incorporate the costs incurred by channel members in performing required marketing functions and expected profit margins for each member.

Trade discounts initially reflected the operating expenses of each category, but they have become more or less customary practices in some industries. The Robinson-Patman Act allows trade discounts as long as all buyers in the same category, such as all wholesalers or all retailers, receive the same discount privileges.

Figure 19.3 shows how a chain of trade discounts works. In the first instance, the trade discount is "40 percent, 10 percent off list price" for wholesalers. In other words, the 40 percent discount on the $40 product is the trade discount the retailer receives to cover operating expenses and earn a profit. The wholesaler receives 10 percent of the $24 price to retailers to cover expenses and earn a profit. The manufacturer receives $21.60 from the wholesaler for each order.

"40 PERCENT, 10 PERCENT OFF" TRADE DISCOUNT				
List Price	− Retail Trade Discount	− Wholesale Trade Discount	=	Manufacturer Proceeds
$40	− $16 ($40 x 40%)	− $2.40 ($24 x 10%)	=	$21.60 ($40 − $16 − $2.40)

"45 PERCENT" TRADE DISCOUNT			
List Price	− Retail Trade Discount	=	Manufacturer Proceeds
$40	− $18 ($40 x 45%)	=	$22 ($40 − $18)

figure 19.3

Chain of Trade Discounts

In the second example, the manufacturer and retailer decide to bypass the wholesaler. The producer offers a trade discount of 45 percent to the retailer. In this instance, the retailer receives $18 for each product sold at its list price, and the manufacturer receives the remaining $22. Either the retailer or the manufacturer must assume responsibility for the services previously performed by the wholesaler, or they can share these duties between them.

Quantity Discounts

Price reductions granted for large-volume purchases are known as **quantity discounts.** Sellers justify these discounts on the grounds that large orders reduce selling expenses and may shift some costs for storage, transportation, and financing to buyers. The law allows quantity discounts provided they are applied on the same basis to all customers.

Quantity discounts may specify either cumulative or noncumulative terms. **Cumulative quantity discounts** reduce prices in amounts determined by purchases over stated time periods. Annual purchases of at least $25,000 might entitle a buyer to a 3 percent rebate, and purchases exceeding $50,000 would increase the refund to 5 percent. These reductions are really patronage discounts because they tend to bind customers to a single supply source.

Noncumulative quantity discounts provide onetime reductions in the list price. For example, a firm might offer the following discount schedule for a product priced at $1,000 per unit:

1 unit	List: $1,000
2–5 units	List less 10 percent
6–10 units	List less 20 percent
More than 10 units	List less 25 percent

Many businesses have come to expect quantity discounts from suppliers. Online photo supply retailer Shutterfly offers volume discounts for photo books and discounts of 25 to 30 percent on prepaid orders.[11] Marketers typically favor combinations of cash, trade, and quantity discounts. See's Candies offers a quantity discount for a minimum purchase of $547.50, plus continued savings throughout the year.[12]

Allowances

Allowances resemble discounts by specifying deductions from list price. The major categories of allowances are trade-ins and promotional allowances. **Trade-ins** often are used in sales of durable goods such as automobiles. The new product's basic list price remains unchanged, but the seller accepts less money from the customer along with a used product—usually the same kind of product as the buyer purchases.

Promotional allowances reduce prices as part of attempts to integrate promotional strategies within distribution channels. Manufacturers often return part of the prices buyers pay in the form of

allowance Specified deduction from list price, including a trade-in or promotional allowance.

Shutterfly, an online photo supply retailer, offers quantity discounts on photo books and additional discounts on prepaid orders.

advertising and sales-support allowances for channel members. Automobile manufacturers frequently offer allowances to retail dealers to induce them to lower prices and stimulate sales. In an effort to alert consumers to the difference between a car's sticker price and the price the dealer actually pays to the manufacturer, *Consumer Reports* sells car and truck buyers a breakdown on dealers' wholesale costs. The information reveals undisclosed dealer profits such as manufacturers' incentives, rebates from the dealer-invoice price, and "holdbacks"—amounts refunded to the dealer after sales are completed.[13] Dealers dislike the move to reveal their markups, arguing that no other retail sector is forced to give consumers details of their promotional allowances.

Minimum advertised pricing (MAP) occurs when a manufacturer pays a retailer not to advertise a product below a certain price. Recently, the U.S. Supreme Court ruled that retailers are required to stick to their MAPs on items. However, some retailers invite shoppers to call or e-mail for lower—unpublished—prices on items ranging from espresso machines to desktop computers.[14]

Rebates

In still another way to reduce prices, marketers may offer a **rebate**—a refund of a portion of the purchase price. Rebates appear everywhere—on appliances, electronics, and auto promotions—by manufacturers eager to get consumers to try their products or to move products during periods of slow sales. Mattress manufacturer Sealy has successfully used rebates to move consumers up to more expensive models in its product line, offering the biggest rebates for its top-priced mattresses.

Rebates can have their problems. Many consumers complain about the paperwork they have to fill out to get a rebate, particularly on larger items such as computers and kitchen appliances. Some say they fill out the paperwork only to be denied the claim on a technicality. Others report never receiving the rebate—or even a response—at all. The Better Business Bureau notes that the number of complaints filed relating to rebates has grown significantly in the past few years. Some state legislators have moved to require companies to fulfill rebate requests within a certain period of time while also requiring consumers to file their request promptly. Yet companies argue that many consumers never even apply for their legitimate rebates.[15]

GEOGRAPHIC CONSIDERATIONS

In industries dominated by catalog and online marketers, geographic considerations weigh heavily on the firm's ability to deliver orders in a cost-effective manner at the right time and place. In other instances, geographic factors affect the marketer's ability to receive additional inventory quickly in response to demand fluctuations. And although geographic considerations strongly influence prices when costs include shipping heavy, bulky, low-unit-value products, they can also affect lightweight, lower-cost products.

Buyers and sellers can handle transportation expenses in several ways: (1) the buyer pays all transportation charges, (2) the seller pays all transportation charges, or (3) the buyer and the seller share the charges. This decision has major effects on a firm's efforts to expand its geographic coverage to distant markets. How can marketers compete with local suppliers in distant markets who are able to avoid the considerable shipping costs that their firms must pay? Sellers can implement several alternatives for handling transportation costs in their pricing policies.

Rebates refund a portion of the purchase price for items such as automobiles. Marketers offer rebates as a way to reduce the price paid by customers.

© Justin Sullivan/Getty Images

FOB Pricing

FOB (free on board) plant, or **FOB origin,** prices include no shipping charges. The buyer must pay all freight charges to transport the product from the manufacturer's loading dock. The seller pays only to load the merchandise aboard the carrier selected by the buyer. Legal title and responsibility pass to the buyer after the seller's employees load the purchase and get a receipt from the representative of the common carrier. Firms such as Wal-Mart often handle freight charges over the entire supply chain. Because Wal-Mart sources so many products from China, "FOB China" is now becoming common.

Many marketing intermediaries sell only on FOB plant terms to downstream channel members. These distributors believe their customers have more clout than they do in negotiating with carriers. They prefer to assign transportation costs to the channel members in the best positions to secure the most cost-effective shipping terms.

Sellers may also quote prices as **FOB origin-freight allowed,** or **freight absorbed.** These terms permit buyers to subtract transportation expenses from their bills. The amount such a seller receives for its product varies with the freight charged against the invoice. This alternative is popular among firms with high fixed costs because it helps them expand their markets considerably by quoting the same prices regardless of shipping expenses.

Uniform-Delivered Pricing

When a firm quotes the same price, including transportation expenses, to all buyers, it adopts a **uniform-delivered pricing** policy. This method of handling transportation expenses is the exact opposite of FOB origin pricing. The uniform-delivered system resembles the pricing structure for mail service, so it is sometimes called **postage-stamp pricing.** The price quote includes a transportation charge averaged over all of the firm's customers, meaning that distant customers actually pay a smaller share of shipping costs while nearby customers pay what is known as *phantom freight*— the amount by which the average transportation charge exceeds the actual cost of shipping.

Zone Pricing

Zone pricing modifies a uniform-delivered pricing system by dividing the overall market into different zones and establishing a single price within each zone. This pricing structure incorporates average transportation costs for shipments within each zone as part of the delivered price of goods sold there; by narrowing distances, it greatly reduces but does not completely eliminate phantom freight. The primary advantage of zone pricing comes from its simplified administration that helps a seller compete in distant markets. The U.S. Postal Service's parcel rates depend on zone pricing.

Zone pricing helps explain why gasoline can cost more in one suburb than in a neighborhood just two or three miles down the road. One way in which gasoline marketers boost profits is by mapping out areas based on formulas that factor in location, affluence, or simply what the local market will bear. Dealers are then charged different wholesale prices, which are reflected in the prices paid at the pump by customers. Some dealers argue that zone pricing should be prohibited. When drivers shop around for cheaper gas in other zones, stations in high-price zones are unable to compete.

Basing-Point Pricing

In **basing-point pricing,** the price of a product includes the list price at the factory plus freight charges from the basing-point city nearest the buyer. The basing point specifies a location from which freight charges are calculated—not necessarily the point from which the goods are actually shipped. In either case, the actual shipping point does not affect the price quotation. Such a system seeks to equalize competition between distant marketers because all competitors quote identical transportation rates. Few buyers would accept a basing-point system today, however.

For many years, the best-known basing-point system was the Pittsburgh-plus pricing structure common in the steel industry. Steel buyers paid freight charges from Pittsburgh regardless of where the steel was produced. As the industry matured, manufacturing centers emerged in Chicago; Gary, Indiana; Cleveland; and Birmingham. Still, Pittsburgh remained the basing point for steel pricing, forcing a buyer in Atlanta who purchased steel from a Birmingham mill to pay phantom freight from Pittsburgh.

assessment check

1. What are the three major types of discounts?
2. Identify the four alternatives for handling transportation costs in pricing policies.

3 Identify the various pricing policy decisions marketers must make.

Pricing Policies

Pricing policies contribute important information to buyers as they assess the firm's total image. A coherent policy provides an overall framework and consistency that guide day-to-day pricing decisions. Formally, a **pricing policy** is a general guideline that reflects marketing objectives and influences specific pricing decisions.

Decisions concerning price structure generally tend to focus on technical, detailed questions, but decisions concerning pricing policies cover broader issues. Price-structure decisions take the firm's pricing policy as a given, from which they specify applicable discounts. Pricing policies have important strategic effects, particularly in guiding competitive efforts. They form the basis for more practical price-structure decisions.

Firms implement variations of four basic types of pricing policies: psychological pricing, price flexibility, product-line pricing, and promotional pricing. Specific policies deal effectively with various competitive situations; the final choice depends on the environment within which marketers must make their pricing decisions. Regardless of the strategy selected, however, marketers sometimes must raise prices. Although it is never easy to deliver this news to customers, if it is accomplished with honesty and tact, customers are likely to remain loyal. The "Etiquette Tips for Marketing Professionals" feature provides some pointers on communicating price increases.

PSYCHOLOGICAL PRICING

psychological pricing
Pricing policy based on the belief that certain prices or price ranges make a good or service more appealing than others to buyers.

Psychological pricing applies the belief that certain prices or price ranges make products more appealing than others to buyers. No research offers a consistent foundation for such thinking, however, and studies often report mixed findings. Nevertheless, marketers practice several forms of psychological pricing. Prestige pricing, discussed in Chapter 18, sets a relatively high price to convey an image of quality and exclusiveness. Two more psychological pricing techniques are odd pricing and unit pricing.

In **odd pricing,** marketers set prices at odd numbers just under round numbers. Many people assume that a price of $4.95 appeals more strongly to consumers than $5.00, supposedly because

Etiquette Tips for Marketing **Professionals**

How to Handle a Price Increase

no marketer likes to hand bad news to customers, but sometimes it is necessary, as in the case of a price increase. If your firm has exhausted every alternative to a price increase, then it's time to face the challenge. If you find yourself in this situation, use these tips to soften the blow:

- *Know your customers.* Understand who your customers are, why they purchase your firm's products, and what they need. If you approach them with understanding, they will be more willing to listen and accept what you have to say.

- *Explain what the price increase is and why.* Be honest. Tell them which products—if only a few—will increase in price and why. Without revealing every detail of your business, explain which of your costs has increased; perhaps it's the price of lumber or the cost of shipping.

- *Give customers fair warning.* If possible, notify customers well before the increase takes place so they can make adjustments in their budgets. If a product is being phased out and replaced by a new product at a higher price, notify customers of this as well.

- *Work with customers to find alternatives.* Perhaps your firm has similar products comparable to the ones a particular customer has been using and will not be increasing in price.

- *Create new pricing packages, bundles, or groupings of products.* By regrouping certain products—or separating products if they were previously grouped—you might be able to give your customers a better price despite the increase.

- *Emphasize value.* The price might have increased, but your firm may provide a better value overall. A product might be more concentrated to last longer, or packages might contain more items.

- *Use promotions.* Offer a promotional price, discount coupon, or rebate for a short period of time prior to the increase.

Sources: "A Precarious Road: How Retailers Can Navigate Inflation's Hazards," *Knowledge@Wharton*, August 6, 2008, knowledge.wharton.upenn.edu, accessed June 9, 2009; Andrea Cooper, "Think Fast," *Entrepreneur*, September 2008, pp. 19–20; John Quelch, "Seven Tips for Managing Price Increases," *Working Knowledge*, June 16, 2008, Harvard Business School, hbswk.hbs.edu.

buyers interpret it as $4.00 plus change. Odd pricing originated as a way to force clerks to make change, thus serving as a cash-control device, and it remains a common feature of contemporary price quotations.

Some producers and retailers practice odd pricing but avoid prices ending in 5, 9, or 0. These marketers believe customers view price tags of $5.95, $5.99, or $6.00 as regular retail prices, but they think of an amount such as $5.97 as a discount price. Others, such as Wal-Mart, avoid using 9s as ending prices for their items.

Unit pricing states prices in terms of some recognized unit of measurement (such as grams and liters) or a standard numerical count. Unit pricing began to be widely used during the late 1960s to make price comparisons more convenient following complaints by consumer advocates about the difficulty of comparing the true prices of products packaged in different sizes. These advocates thought posting prices in terms of standard units would help shoppers make better-informed purchases. However, unit pricing has not improved consumers' shopping habits as much as supporters originally envisioned. Instead, research shows standard price quotes most often affect purchases only by relatively well-educated consumers with high earnings.

PRICE FLEXIBILITY

Marketing executives must also set company policies that determine whether their firm will permit **price flexibility**—that is, whether or not to set one price that applies to every buyer or to permit variable prices for different customers. Generally, one-price policies suit mass-marketing programs, whereas variable pricing is more likely to be applied in marketing programs based on individual bargaining. In a large department store, customers do not expect to haggle over prices with retail salespeople. Instead, they expect to pay the amounts shown on the price tags. Usually, customers pay less only when the retailer replaces regular prices with sale prices or offers discounts on damaged merchandise. Variable pricing usually applies to larger purchases such as automobiles, real estate, and hotel room rates. While variable pricing adds some flexibility to selling situations, it may conflict with provisions of the Robinson-Patman Act. It may also lead to retaliatory pricing by competitors, and it may stir complaints among customers who find they paid higher prices than necessary.

Recently, some Internet service providers began setting usage caps on their customers and requiring the subscribers who download the most content to pay the most. Frontier Communications says it plans to set a cap at 5 gigabytes per month, or the equivalent of about three DVD-quality movies. Not surprisingly, its subscribers are upset about the policy, which was not in effect when they signed up for service. "We go through that in a week," says one customer. "If they start enforcing the caps, we're going to have to change service." Meanwhile, Time Warner Cable—a competitor of Frontier's in certain markets—is trying out metered Internet access in select markets. Under that plan, customers receive metered bills much like those they receive for electricity or long-distance phone calls. Time Warner argues that this is the fairest way to distribute the company's rising costs.[16]

PRODUCT-LINE PRICING

product-line pricing
Practice of setting a limited number of prices for a selection of merchandise and marketing different product lines at each of these price levels.

Because most firms market multiple product lines, an effective pricing strategy must consider the relationships among all of these items instead of viewing each in isolation. **Product-line pricing** is the practice of setting a limited number of prices for a selection of merchandise. For example, one well-known clothier might offer three lines of men's suits: one priced at $450, a second at $695, and the most expensive at $1,295. These price points help the retailer define important product characteristics that differentiate the three product lines and help the customer decide on whether to trade up or down.

Retailers practice extensive product-line pricing. In earlier days, five-and-dime variety stores exemplified this technique. It remains popular, however, because it offers advantages to both retailers and customers. Shoppers can choose desired price ranges and then concentrate on other product variables such as colors, styles, and materials. Retailers can purchase and offer specific lines in limited price categories instead of more general assortments with dozens of different prices.

promotional pricing
Pricing policy in which a lower-than-normal price is used as a temporary ingredient in a firm's marketing strategy.

Sunglasses have become a hot fashion item in recent years, and prices for designer glasses have jumped from an average of $250 per pair to as much as $750 for Ray-Ban Wayfarers at Bergdorf Goodman in New York. While sales of other luxury goods have softened, sunglass sales are getting long looks from retailers. Younger consumers—teens and young women—seem to be snapping up designer shades most often. "The youth of America has discovered sunglasses to be the aspirational and prestige item of the moment," notes one fashion expert. Karl Lagerfeld, Giorgio Armani, Stella McCartney, Proenza Schouler, and Thakoon all offer high-end glasses carried by luxury retailers. And for those who want their shades studded with diamonds, they can grab a pair of Gold & Wood sunglasses for $1,395.[17]

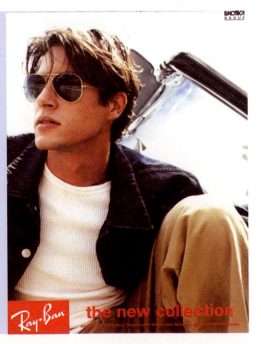

The price for designer sunglasses has jumped in recent years as consumer demand has increased.

© Image courtesy of The Advertising Archives

A potential problem with product-line pricing is that once marketers decide on a limited number of prices to use as their price lines, they may have difficulty making price changes on individual items. Rising costs, therefore, force sellers to either change the entire price-line structure, which results in confusion, or cut costs through production adjustments. The second option opens the firm to customer complaints that its merchandise is not what it used to be.

PROMOTIONAL PRICING

In **promotional pricing,** a lower-than-normal price is used as a temporary ingredient in a firm's marketing strategy. Some promotional pricing arrangements form part of recurrent marketing initiatives, such as a shoe store's annual "buy one pair, get the second pair for one cent" sale. Another example would be "7 CDs for 1 cent." This artificially low price attracts customers who must then agree to purchase a set number of CDs at regular prices within a specified time limit.

Another firm may introduce a promotional model or brand with a special price to begin competing in a new market.

Managing promotional pricing efforts requires marketing skill. Customers may get hooked on sales and other promotional pricing events. If they know their favorite department store has a one-day sale every month, they will likely wait to make their purchases on that day. Car shoppers have been offered so many price incentives that it

In promotional pricing, a lower-than-normal price is used as a temporary ingredient in a firm's marketing strategy.

© AP Images/David Zalubowski

is becoming harder and harder for manufacturers and dealers to take them away—or to come up with new ones. As gas prices soared during a recent period, Chrysler decided to launch a campaign called "Let's Refuel America," in which people who bought or leased new vehicles also got a deal that capped gas at $2.99 a gallon for three years.[18] A later drop in prices illustrates the need for flexibility in promotional pricing.

Loss Leaders and Leader Pricing

Retailers rely most heavily on promotional pricing. In one type of technique, stores offer **loss leaders:** goods priced below cost to attract customers who, the retailer hopes, will also buy regularly priced merchandise. Loss leaders can form part of an effective marketing program, but states with unfair-trade laws limit the practice. The fruit in season at your grocery store is likely a loss leader. Corn on the cob might be priced at 10 for $5. Cantaloupe might be offered at 10 for $10. Pint containers of blueberries, strawberries, and raspberries could be sold in "two for the price of one" pricing.[19]

Retailers frequently use a variant of loss-leader pricing called **leader pricing.** To avoid violating minimum-markup regulations and to earn some return on promotional sales, they offer so-called *leader merchandise* at prices slightly above cost. Among the most frequent practitioners of this combination pricing/promotion strategy are supermarkets and mass merchandisers such as Wal-Mart, Target, and Kmart. Retailers sometimes treat private-label products, such as Sam's Choice colas at Wal-Mart stores, as leader merchandise because prices of the store brands average 5 to 60 percent less than those of comparable national brands. While store brand items generate lower per-unit revenues than national brands, higher sales volume will probably offset some of the difference as will related sales of high-margin products such as toiletries and cosmetics.

Digital camcorders are a good example. Once priced at an average of more than $1,000, they are now on shelves for a few hundred dollars. Canon, Sony, and Panasonic have slashed prices on a wide range of models, sometimes by several hundred dollars. Shoppers can pick up a Samsung SC-D382 mini-DVD camcorder at Best Buy for just under $170. Although this is one of the simpler models in the firm's line, it still illustrates how prices have dropped.[20]

But marketers should anticipate two potential pitfalls when making a promotional pricing decision:

1. Some buyers are not attracted by promotional pricing.

2. By maintaining an artificially low price for a period of time, marketers may lead customers to expect it as a customary feature of the product. That is the situation currently faced by U.S. car manufacturers: sales of their models lag when they do not offer price incentives.

loss leader Product offered to consumers at less than cost to attract them to stores in the hope that they will buy other merchandise at regular prices.

leader pricing Variant of loss-leader pricing in which marketers offer prices slightly above cost to avoid violating minimum-markup regulations and earn a minimal return on promotional sales.

assessment check

1. Define *pricing policy*.

2. Describe the two types of psychological pricing other than prestige pricing.

3. What is promotional pricing?

4 Relate price to consumer perceptions of quality.

PRICE–QUALITY RELATIONSHIPS

One of the most thoroughly researched aspects of pricing is its relationship to consumer perceptions of product quality. In the absence of other cues, price serves as an important indicator of a product's quality to prospective purchasers. Many buyers interpret high prices as signals of high-quality products. Prestige is also often associated with high prices. In an effort to test the reliability of this relationship, researchers conducted a study in which participants were placed in an MRI machine and given tastes of red wine. The participants all responded that they preferred the wine labeled with a higher price, even though in some cases the same wine was presented with two different price tags. The MRI showed a change in brain activity when the participants thought they were drinking the expensive wine.[21]

A new type of prestige surrounds ecofriendly products. Many consumers are willing to pay more for green goods and services—those made with environmentally friendly materials and processes, as described in the "Marketing Success" feature. These purchases make consumers feel good about themselves and convey status among others.

Despite the appeal of prestige, nearly every consumer loves a good deal. Marketers work hard to convince consumers they are offering high-quality products at the lowest possible price. Whereas motels used to be considered both cheap and seedy, a new crop of boutique motels has sprung up around the country where guests can find comfortable accommodations, individual service, and reasonable prices. Some are steeped in retro-style decorating, others are nestled amid lush gardens, and a few offer amenities such as complimentary cocktails to their guests. They have trendy names like Orbit in Oasis, Casa Morada, and El Morocco, reflecting their décor. Although these motels aren't cheap, they do offer a customized experience at much lower prices than most hotels.[22]

Probably the best statement of the price–quality connection is the idea of price limits. Consumers define certain limits within which their product-quality perceptions vary directly

Goods made with environmentally friendly materials and processes have a new prestige. Many consumers are willing to pay more for these eco-friendly products.

© Image courtesy of The Advertising Archives

---

with price. A potential buyer regards a price below the lower limit as too cheap, and a price above the higher limit seems too expensive. This perception holds true for both national brands and private-label products.

Competitive Bidding and Negotiated Prices

5 Contrast competitive bidding and negotiated prices.

Many government and organizational procurement departments do not pay set prices for their purchases, particularly for large purchases. Instead, they determine the lowest prices available for items that meet specifications through **competitive bidding.** This process consists of inviting potential suppliers to quote prices on proposed purchases or contracts. Detailed specifications describe the good or service the government agency or business organization wishes to acquire. One of the most important procurement tasks is to develop accurate descriptions of products the organization seeks to buy. This process generally requires the assistance of the firm's technical personnel such as engineers, designers, and chemists.

Colleges and universities routinely invite competitive bids for their food-service suppliers and negotiate prices for meal packages, service, and so forth. With the cost of everything related to academic life soaring, schools are looking for ways to save money on food service, as described in the "Solving an Ethical Controversy" feature.

A select group of state troopers test potential police cars every year to determine the best model—and price—for their organization. While Ford's Crown Victoria Police Interceptor has come out on top for many years, recently the Dodge Charger and Magnum models have grown in popularity. In addition, some police forces have selected the Dodge Durango and Jeep models.[23]

In some cases, business and government purchasers negotiate contracts with favored suppliers instead of inviting competitive bids from all interested parties. The terms of such a contract emerge through offers and counteroffers between the buyer and the seller. When only one supplier offers a desired product or when projects require extensive research and development, buyers and sellers often set purchase terms through negotiated contracts. In addition, some state and local governments permit their agencies to skip the formal bid process and negotiate purchases under certain dollar limits—say, $500 or $1,000. This policy seeks to eliminate economic waste that would result from obtaining and processing bids for relatively minor purchases. New York state law requires the New York State Fair to get bids for any contract worth more than $50,000. Since the State Fair includes everything from live concerts by major acts to food vendors, contracts can run much higher than that.[24]

briefly speaking

"I have discovered in 20 years of moving around a ballpark that the knowledge of the game is usually in inverse proportion to the price of the seats."

—**Bill Veeck (1914–1986)**
AMERICAN BASEBALL TEAM OWNER

Publicity generated about environmental concerns, as well as consumers' genuine wish to do something concrete to better the environment, contributed to a change in attitude toward green products. In addition, firms have taken steps to develop the highest-quality green products to compete with more traditional items. Hybrid cars are now more reliable, and bamboo flooring is both durable and fashionable.

The Outcome. Across many industries, consumers are willingly paying more for green goods, regardless of their income level. "Many American consumers, even in the face of economic uncertainty, express a willingness to pay more for environmentally friendly products," observes one professor. "Toyota can't make the Prius fast enough to meet consumer demand, to cite just one example, and many see

green products as the wave of the future." One survey revealed that homeowners would pay more for home improvement products if the products were made from renewable resources or other ecofriendly materials. Other research showed that U.S. consumers would pay a premium for locally produced foods, giving a boost to smaller farms. As a result, the business of making and marketing green products is good for everyone—companies, consumers, and the environment.

Sources: "Several Studies Say Conscious Consumers Willing to Pay More for Green," *GreenBiz.com*, June 3, 2009, www.greenbiz.com; "Americans Willing to Pay More for Eco-Friendly Products," *CSRwire*, July 29, 2008, www.csrwire.com; "Survey Shows Homeowners Willing to Invest More in Green Home Improvement Products," *Reuters*, June 25, 2008, www.reuters.com; Martin LaMonica, "Most Consumers Willing to Pay for Hybrid Cars," *CNet News*, June 24, 2008, news.cnet.com; "Average Shoppers Are Willing to Pay a Premium for Locally Produced Food," *Science Daily*, June 8, 2008, www.sciencedaily.com.

Solving an ethical controversy

Ditching Cafeteria Trays—Does It Really Save Dough?

The cafeteria tray has been the mainstay of college dining rooms for decades. Hungry students grab those plastic trays and file through the serving line, piling their plates and trays higher and higher with everything from turkey and mashed potatoes to ice cream and brownies. Recently, a number of colleges and universities decided to do away with the trays for two reasons: to save energy and money. Regarding energy savings, food-service experts argue that the dining room is a great source of waste, including the water and detergent required to wash hundreds of trays every day. "Dining facilities on campuses take up five times more water, five times more energy, five times more waste per square foot than the dorm," notes Monica Zimmer of Sodexo, a company that serves meals at about 600 campuses nationwide. As for money savings, college administrators claim that without trays, students eat less—and less food is wasted.

Should colleges ban the use of cafeteria trays as a cost-cutting measure?

PRO

1. Without trays—using dinner plates only—students are less apt to wander around the dining hall loading up on food. They will make better choices and waste less food if they have to make several trips, thus reducing the amount of food the school pays for in the meal plan.

2. Less food means the dining hall needs less storage and cleanup, another reduction in cost. "If we create less waste, we don't even have to consider a need for back-end technologies," notes one food-service provider. Refrigeration, hot water for washing, and hauling away or treating garbage are all reduced, representing a drop in cost.

CON

1. Students claim that if they are hungry enough, they'll eat just as much. "I'll just keep coming back for seconds," says one student. So the cost for food may remain the same. Also, one college has already experienced an increase in the breakage of plates and glasses because students have loaded them up and been unable to juggle them successfully. This represents an added cost.

2. Colleges could come up with other ways to address food waste and cost, such as reducing the size of serving dishes and portions. Carrying smaller plates—with smaller amounts of food—could cut down on collisions and spillage and the amount of food lost.

Summary

Although colleges and universities should examine every means to reduce waste and cut costs, the jury is still out on whether eliminating cafeteria trays will actually create savings. Meanwhile, college students will adapt. And those who live in colder climates will have to find something else to sit on while sledding down a snowy hill.

Sources: Stephen J. Dubner, "What Happens when College Cafeterias Go Trayless?" *The New York Times*, January 13, 2009, http://freakonomics.blogs.nytimes.com; Maya Curry, "The War on College Cafeteria Trays," *Time,* August 25, 2008, www .time.com; John Raby, "U.S. Colleges Moving to Retire Cafeteria Trays," *Associated Press,* August 25, 2008, news.yahoo.com.

NEGOTIATING PRICES ONLINE

Many people see the Internet as one big auction site. Whether it's toys, furniture, or automobiles, an online auction site seems to be waiting to serve every person's needs—buyer and seller alike. Auctions are the purest form of negotiated pricing.

Ticket sales are an online auction favorite. Consumers can bid on tickets for all sorts of events: a Broadway show, a baseball playoff game, or a major rock concert. Ticketmaster and StubHub are two online ticket sellers, offering tickets to events such as NFL games, Disney On Ice shows, *Mamma Mia!* stage productions, and Dave Matthews Band concerts. Ticketmaster has a link devoted to online auctions. StubHub focuses on offering consumers the opportunity to buy and resell tickets, setting their own prices. Ticketmaster entered the resale market by purchasing TicketsNow.[25]

Online auctions also take place at sites such as eBay and uBid.com, where consumers can snap up items as varied as Italian gold cufflinks and a home in upstate New York. Recently, eBay reported that many of its transactions now take place at fixed prices through the "Buy It Now" option, signaling that perhaps consumers prefer to secure an item by paying a set price for it or that they do not want to wait up to a week for an auction to close. Regardless of how it is purchased, merchandise on eBay continues to move at astonishing speed: a pair of women's jeans sells every 40 seconds, while a cell phone sells every seven seconds.[26]

assessment check

1. What is competitive bidding?

2. Describe the benefits of an auction—to the buyer and the seller.

The Transfer Pricing Dilemma

6 **Explain the importance of transfer pricing.**

A pricing problem peculiar to large-scale enterprises is the determination of an internal **transfer price**—the price for moving goods between **profit centers,** which are any part of the organization to which revenue and controllable costs can be assigned, such as a department. As companies expand, they tend to decentralize management and set up profit centers as a control device in the newly decentralized operation.

In a large company, profit centers might secure many needed resources from sellers within their own organization. The pricing problem thus poses several questions: What rate should profit center A (maintenance department) charge profit center B (production department) for the cleaning compound used on B's floors? Should the price be the same as it would be if A did the work for an outside party? Should B receive a discount? The answers to these questions depend on the philosophy of the firm involved.

Transfer pricing can be complicated, especially for multinational organizations. The government closely monitors transfer pricing practices because these exchanges offer easy ways for companies to avoid paying taxes on profits. For example, Congress passed a bill outlawing federal contractors from hiring workers through offshore "shell"—nonexistent—companies and thus avoiding having to pay Social Security and Medicare taxes.

Figure 19.4 shows how this type of pricing manipulation might work. Suppose a South Korean manufacturer of DVD players sells its machines to its U.S. subsidiary for distribution to dealers. Although each unit costs $25 to build, the manufacturer charges the distributor $75. In turn, the distributor sells the DVD players to retailers for $125 each. This arrangement gives the South Korean manufacturer a $50 profit on each machine, on which it pays taxes only in South Korea. Meanwhile, the American distributor writes off $50 for advertising and shipping costs, leaving it with no profits—and no tax liability.

assessment check

1. Define *transfer price.*

2. What is a profit center?

Global Considerations and Online Pricing

7 **Compare the three alternative global pricing strategies.**

Throughout this course, we have seen the impact of the Internet on every component of the marketing mix. This chapter has touched on the outer edges of the Internet's influence on pricing practices. Remember: every online marketer is inherently a global marketer that must understand the wide variety of internal and external conditions affecting global pricing strategies. Internal influences include the

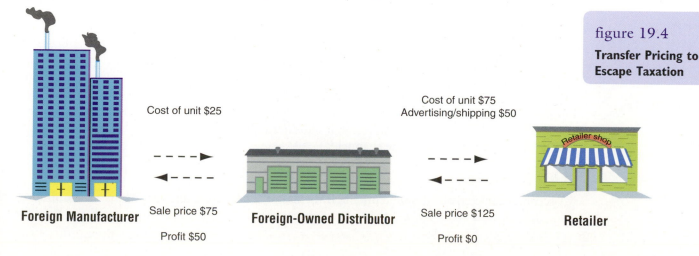

figure 19.4

Transfer Pricing to Escape Taxation

Cost of unit $25

Cost of unit $75
Advertising/shipping $50

Foreign Manufacturer   Sale price $75   **Foreign-Owned Distributor**   Sale price $125   **Retailer**

Profit $50   Profit $0

firm's goals and marketing strategies; the costs of developing, producing, and marketing its output; the nature of the products; and the firm's competitive strengths. External influences include general conditions in international markets, especially those in the firm's target markets; regulatory limitations; trade restrictions; competitors' actions; economic events; and the global status of the industry.

TRADITIONAL GLOBAL PRICING STRATEGIES

In general, a company can implement one of three export pricing strategies: a standard worldwide price, dual pricing, or market-differentiated pricing. Exporters often set standard worldwide prices, regardless of their target markets. This strategy can succeed if foreign marketing costs remain low enough that they do not affect overall costs or if their prices reflect average unit costs. A company that implements a standard pricing program must monitor the international marketplace carefully, however, to make sure domestic competitors do not undercut its prices.

The dual pricing strategy distinguishes prices for domestic and export sales. Some exporters practice cost-plus pricing to establish dual prices that fully allocate their true domestic and foreign costs to product sales in those markets. These prices ensure an exporter makes a profit on any product it sells, but final prices may exceed those of competitors. Other companies opt for flexible cost-plus pricing schemes that allow marketers to grant discounts or change prices according to shifts in the competitive environment or fluctuations in the international exchange rate.

The third strategy, market-differentiated pricing, makes even more flexible arrangements to set prices according to local marketplace conditions. The dynamic global marketplace often requires frequent price changes by exporters who choose this approach. Effective market-differentiated pricing depends on access to quick, accurate market information.

assessment check

1. What are the three traditional global pricing strategies?
2. Which is the most flexible global pricing strategy?

8 Relate the concepts of cannibalization, bundle pricing, and bots to online pricing strategies.

CHARACTERISTICS OF ONLINE PRICING

To deal with the influences of the Internet on pricing policies and practices, marketers are applying old strategies in new ways and companies are updating operations to compete with electronic technologies. Some firms offer online specials that do not appear in their stores or mail-order catalogs. These may take such forms as limited-time discounts, free shipping offers, or coupons that are good only online.

The Cannibalization Dilemma

cannibalization Loss of sales of an existing product due to competition from a new product in the same line.

By pricing the same products differently online, companies run the risk of **cannibalization.** The new twist on an old tactic is companies self-inflicting price cuts by creating competition among their own products. During the first decade of e-business, marketers debated whether it was worth taking the risk of alienating customers and channel members by offering lower prices for their products online—then an unproven retail outlet. But today, marketers are more savvy about integrating marketing channels, including online sites and affiliated stores—different stores owned by the same company. The trend is moving toward standardizing pricing across channels.

Wal-Mart recently introduced such features as "Ship to Store" and "Find It in a Store" to its Web site so shoppers can choose how and where they want to make purchases, all at the same price. Sears has increased its investment in online and multichannel operations with similar goals. Experts agree this is a good strategy because consumers like to shop the retailers they prefer both online and off, and they expect the retailer to recognize them as regular shoppers—no matter what channel they choose. In addition, research indicates that multichannel shoppers are more profitable than those who stick to one channel.[27]

Use of Shopbots

A second characteristic of online pricing is the use of search programs called **bots** or **shopbots**—derived from the word *robots*—that act as comparison shopping agents. Bots search the Web for a specific product and print a list of sites offering the best prices. In online selling, bots force marketers to keep prices low. However, marketing researchers report that the majority of online shoppers check out several sites before buying, and price is not the only variable they consider when making a purchase decision. Service quality and support information are powerful motivators in the decision process. Also, while price is an important factor with products such as books and DVDs, it is not as important with complex or highly differentiated products such as real estate or investment banking. Brand image and customer service may outweigh price in these purchase decisions.

BUNDLE PRICING

As marketers have watched e-business weaken their control over prices, they have modified their use of the price variable in the marketing mix. Whenever possible, they have moved to an approach called **bundle pricing,** in which customers acquire a host of goods and services in addition to the tangible products they purchase.

bundle pricing Offering two or more complementary products and selling them for a single price.

Nowhere is bundle pricing more prevalent than in the telecommunications industry. Consumers are bombarded daily by advertisements for all kinds of Internet, cell phone, and cable TV packages. AT&T recently offered a package called AT&T Net Reach, a bundle that provides both home and away high-speed Internet service. A package like this appeals to residential consumers, owners of small businesses, or sales representatives who are on the road.[28]

But sometimes consumers resist the practice of bundling, claiming they are forced to pay for services they don't want to receive the ones they do. This is particularly the case with cable television. Cable companies insist they have spent billions of dollars to expand their networks and technology and would be left with unused capacity if they sold only a few channels at a time to each customer. Consumer advocates argue that customers are not only forced to pay for unwanted services but also wind up paying inflated prices. The solution seems to be à la carte pricing—allowing consumers to pick and choose the shows or channels they want. But some industry experts warn that bundling actually keeps prices low, in effect leveling the playing field for all network players. "Unmoored from the cable bundle, individual networks would have to charge vastly more money per subscriber," explains one writer.[29]

assessment check

1. What is cannibalization?
2. What is bundle pricing?

Strategic Implications of Marketing in the 21st Century

Price has historically been the marketing variable least likely to be used as a source of competitive advantage. However, using price as part of a marketing program designed to meet a firm's overall organizational objectives can be a powerful strategy.

Technology has forever changed the marketplace, which affects the pricing function. Traditional geographic boundaries that allowed some businesses to operate have been broken by the Internet as well as mass merchandisers who offer a larger selection and lower prices. A customer in Wyoming might want to purchase a hand-carved walking cane from Kenya or an ornamental fan from Kyoto. Not a problem—the Web connects buyers and sellers around the globe. Similarly, the cost of shipping an overnight FedEx package from New York to California is no more than shipping it to a nearby city.

Not only is it possible to escape the boundaries of time and space on the Internet, but price is no longer a constant in the marketing process. With the increasing number of auction sites and search technologies such as bots, customers now have more power to control the prices of goods and services. Consumers can find the lowest prices on the market, and they can also negotiate prices for many of the products they buy. To succeed, marketers will continue to offer value—fair prices for quality goods and services—and superior customer service. Those traditions will always be in style.

Review of Chapter Objectives

1   Compare the alternative pricing strategies and explain when each strategy is most appropriate.

The alternative pricing strategies are skimming pricing strategy, penetration pricing strategy, and competitive pricing strategy. Skimming pricing is commonly used as a market-entry price for distinctive products with little or no initial competition. Penetration pricing is used when a wide array of competing brands exists. Everyday low price.

pricing (EDLP), a variant of penetration pricing, is used by discounters attempting to hold the line on prices without having to rely heavily on short-term coupons, rebates, and other price concessions. Competitive pricing is employed when marketers wish to concentrate their competitive efforts on marketing variables other than

2   Describe how prices are quoted.

Methods for quoting prices depend on such factors as cost structures, traditional practices in the particular industry, and policies of individual firms. Price quotes can involve list prices, market prices, cash discounts, trade discounts, quantity discounts, and allowances such as trade-ins, promotional allowances, and rebates. Shipping costs often figure heavily into the pricing of goods. A number of alternatives

for dealing with these costs exist: FOB plant pricing, in which the price includes no shipping charges; FOB origin-freight allowed, or freight absorbed, which allows the buyer to deduct transportation expenses from the bill; uniform-delivered price, in which the same price, including shipping expenses, is charged to all buyers; and zone pricing, in which a set price exists within each region.

3   Identify the various pricing policy decisions marketers must make.

A pricing policy is a general guideline based on pricing objectives and is intended for use in specific pricing decisions. Pricing policies

include psychological pricing, unit pricing, price flexibility, product-line pricing, and promotional pricing.

4   Relate price to consumer perceptions of quality.

The relationship between price and consumer perceptions of quality has been the subject of considerable research. In the absence of other cues, price is an important influence on how the consumer perceives the product's quality. A well-known and accepted concept

is that of price limits—limits within which the perception of product quality varies directly with price. The concept of price limits suggests that extremely low prices may be considered too cheap, thus indicating inferior quality.

5   Contrast competitive bidding and negotiated prices.

Competitive bidding and negotiated prices are pricing techniques used primarily in the B2B sector and in government and organizational markets. Sometimes prices are negotiated through competitive bidding, in which several buyers quote prices on the same service

or good. Buyer specifications describe the item the government or B2B firm wishes to acquire. Negotiated contracts are another possibility in many procurement situations. The terms of the contract are set through negotiations between buyer and seller.

6   Explain the importance of transfer pricing.

A phenomenon in large corporations is transfer pricing, in which a company sets prices for transferring goods or services from one company profit center to another. The term *profit center* refers to any part of the organization to which revenue and controllable

costs can be assigned. In large companies whose profit centers acquire resources from other parts of the firm, the prices charged by one profit center to another will directly affect both the cost and profitability of the output of both profit centers.

7   Compare the three alternative global pricing strategies.

Companies can choose from three export pricing strategies: a standard worldwide price, dual pricing, or market-differentiated pricing. A standard worldwide price may be possible if foreign marketing costs are so low that they do not affect overall costs or if the price is based on an average unit cost. The dual pricing approach establishes separate price strategies for domestic and exported products. Some

exporters use cost-plus pricing methods to establish dual prices that fully allocate their true domestic and foreign costs to their product; others choose flexible cost-plus pricing. Market-differentiated pricing is the most flexible export pricing strategy because it allows firms to price their products according to marketplace conditions. It requires easy access to quick, accurate market information.

8 **Relate the concepts of cannibalization, bundle pricing, and bots to online pricing strategies.**

To deal with the influences of the Internet on pricing policies and practices, marketers are applying old strategies in new ways, and companies are updating operations to compete with electronic technologies. Cannibalization secures additional sales through lower prices that take sales away from the marketer's other products. Bots, also known as shopbots, act as comparison-shopping agents. Bundle pricing is offering two or more complementary products and selling them for a single price.

assessment check: **answers**

1.1 What are the three major pricing strategies?

The three major pricing strategies are skimming, penetration, and competitive.

1.2 What is EDLP?

EDLP stands for everyday low pricing. It is a variation of penetration pricing often used by discounters.

2.1 What are the three major types of discounts?

The three major types of discounts are cash discounts, trade discounts, and quantity discounts.

2.2 Identify the four alternatives for handling transportation costs in pricing policies.

The four alternatives for handling transportation costs are FOB pricing, uniform-delivered pricing, zone pricing, and basing-point pricing.

3.1 Define *pricing policy*.

A pricing policy is a general guideline that reflects marketing objectives and influences specific pricing decisions.

3.2 Describe the two types of psychological pricing other than prestige pricing.

The two additional types of psychological pricing are odd pricing, in which marketers set prices at odd numbers just under round numbers; and unit pricing, which states prices in terms of a recognized unit of measurement.

3.3 What is promotional pricing?

Promotional pricing is a lower-than-normal price for a set period of time.

4.1 Describe the price–quality connection.

Price serves as an important indicator of a product's quality. However, many marketers now work hard to convince consumers they are offering high-quality products at the lowest possible price.

4.2 What are price limits?

Price limits indicate certain boundaries within which consumers' product-quality perceptions vary directly with price. A price set lower than expected seems too cheap, and one set above the expected limit is seen as too expensive.

5.1 What is competitive bidding?

Competitive bidding consists of inviting potential suppliers to quote prices on proposed purchases or contracts.

5.2   Describe the benefits of an auction—to the buyer and the seller.

An auction can provide buyers with opportunities to buy goods and services at very low prices. It can also offer the seller an opportunity to sell to a wider audience (online) perhaps at a higher price than otherwise would be possible, if the item is particularly popular.

6.1   Define *transfer price*.

A transfer price is the price for moving goods between profit centers.

6.2   What is a profit center?

A profit center is any part of the organization to which revenue and controllable costs can be assigned.

7.1   What are the three traditional global pricing strategies?

The three global pricing strategies are standard worldwide pricing, dual pricing, and market-differentiated pricing.

7.2   Which is the most flexible global pricing strategy?

The most flexible global pricing strategy is market-differentiated pricing, which allows firms to set prices according to actual conditions.

8.1   What is cannibalization?

Cannibalization involves cutting prices in one selling channel, which creates direct competition with a firm's own products.

8.2   What is bundle pricing?

Bundle pricing involves combining a number of goods or services together and offering them at a set price.

Marketing Terms You Need to Know

Other Important Marketing Terms

Assurance of Learning Review

1. What is the difference between a skimming price strategy and a penetration pricing strategy? Under which circumstances is each most likely to be used?

2. Why is competitive pricing risky for marketers?

3. What is the difference between a list price and a market price?

4. What are allowances? How do they work?

5. Describe the three ways buyers and sellers handle transportation expenses.

6. How is product-line pricing helpful to both retailers and their customers?

7. What is the difference between loss-leader and leader pricing? When do retailers use each?

8. What is the difference between a competitive bid and a negotiated price?

9. Describe briefly the three traditional global pricing strategies. Give an example of a firm or product that would be likely to adopt one of the three approaches, and explain why.

10. Although cannibalization generally forces price cuts, in what ways can it actually benefit a firm?

Projects and Teamwork Exercises

1. With a classmate, create two advertisements for the same product. One advertisement should feature a high price, the other advertisement should feature a low price. Present your advertisements to students in your class. Record students' perceptions of the price/quality relationship.

2. Figure out how much it will cost to buy and own one of the following new cars from a dealership, or select another model. What is the list price? What price could you negotiate?
   a. Ford Escape hybrid
   b. Mercedes E350
   c. Hyundai Santa Fe
   d. Scion tC

3. Assume a product sells for $100 per ton and Pittsburgh is the basing-point city for calculating transportation charges. Shipping from Pittsburgh to a potential customer in Cincinnati costs $10 per ton. The actual shipping costs of suppliers in three other cities are $8 per ton for Supplier A, $11 per ton for Supplier B, and $10 per ton for Supplier C. Using this information, answer the following questions:
   a. What delivered price would a salesperson for Supplier A quote to the Cincinnati customer?
   b. What delivered price would a salesperson for Supplier B quote to the Cincinnati customer?
   c. What delivered price would a salesperson for Supplier C quote to the Cincinnati customer?
   d. How much would each supplier net (after subtracting actual shipping costs) per ton on the sale?

4. On your own or with a classmate, visit a local supermarket to find examples of promotional pricing and loss leaders. Note instances of both. Does the promotional pricing make you more apt to purchase a product? Does knowing the store uses loss leader pricing of bananas or apples make you more inclined to by them? Present your findings and opinions to the class.

5. Decide on a trip you'd really like to take. Then go online to several of the travel sites—Orbitz, Travelocity, Priceline.com, or others—and compare prices for your trip, including airfares, hotels, car rental, and so forth. Does bundling the different components give a price break? Note any coupons or promotions for restaurants and attractions as well. Decide which trip is the best deal, and explain why.

Critical-Thinking Exercises

1. Dell launched four new computer models aimed at the Chinese and Indian consumer markets to create loyal customers as these markets emerge. Using a penetrating pricing strategy, Dell priced the new computers under $500, significantly less than its computers sell for in the United States.[30] Do you think this will be a successful pricing strategy? Why or why not? What steps do you predict Dell will take as it sets prices for products in these markets in the future?

2. As a consumer, would you rather shop at a store that features a sale once a month or a store that practices everyday low pricing (EDLP)? Why?

3. Staples recently established its Easy Rebates program in which customers can submit most of their rebate applications online for products purchased over the Internet, through the catalog, and in Staples stores. Customers may also submit several rebates at once and receive e-mails about the status of their

rebates at every stage. In addition, Staples claims the rebates are processed much faster than those of other companies.[31] Do you think the Easy Rebates program will increase the number of rebates customers actually submit? Why or why not? Do you think other firms will follow with similar programs?

4. Go online to a shopping site you use regularly and note the prices for different types of products. Does the firm use psy-chological pricing? Product line pricing? Note any pricing strategies you can identify. Do any of these strategies make you prefer the site over a competitor's site?

5. Why is competitive bidding an important factor in major purchase decisions like vehicles for a police force, the construction of a bridge, or the manufacture of military uniforms?

Ethics Exercise

The law allows companies in a variety of industries to add what many refer to as "hidden" charges to customers' bills. Phone bills, airline tickets, and hotel receipts often contain charges that are difficult to iden-tify. A visitor who stays in a hotel might be hit with a "hospitality fee," a "resort fee," and an "automatic gratuity" to name just a few. These charges are not taxes, and although they are itemized, it is difficult for the average traveler to make sense of them. Most people either don't check their bills thoroughly or are in a hurry to check out and don't bother to dispute the charges, which may be only a few dollars.

But these charges add up over the course of hundreds or thousands of visitors each year, and hotels are pocketing them—legitimately.[32]

1. Do you think adding hidden charges to hotel visitors' bills is a smart marketing strategy? Why or why not?

2. Visit the Web site of a hotel chain with which you are familiar to learn if it gives any information about additional surcharges. If consumers were informed about the charges ahead of time, would you feel differently about them? Why or why not?

Internet Exercises

1. **Private label pricing.** Visit the following Web site: us.acnielsen.com/pubs/2005_q4_ci_privatelabel.shtml. It contains a recent report on private label pricing. Review the report and answer the following questions:
    a. Which region of the world has the highest concentration of private labels?
    b. In which region of the world are private label sales growing the fastest?
    c. Which product category has the highest percentage of pri-vate label sales?
    d. Which type of consumer is the most likely to purchase private labels? Which type of store relies most heavily on private label sales?
    e. What is the typical price difference between a private label and a manufacturer's label? How much does this discount vary from product to product?

2. **Price markups.** Visit Edmunds.com (www.edmunds.com) to obtain invoice and retail price information on new and used vehicles. Choose three different makes and models of new vehicles and research their prices.

    a. Does the difference between the invoice and suggested retail price vary from model to model? What, in your opin-ion, explains the differences?
    b. Are certain options subject to higher markups than other options? Again, in your opinion, what explains any differ-ences you find?

3. **Transfer pricing.** Visit the following Web site: www.ey.com/ global/content.nsf/International/2007-2008_Transfer_ Pricing_Global_Survey. It contains a link to a recent report on transfer pricing prepared by the accounting firm of Ernst & Young. Download the report and prepare a brief summary on the pertinent issues relating to transfer pricing affecting global business. (Note: The report is a .pdf document and requires Adobe Acrobat or Acrobat Reader.)

Note: Internet Web addresses change frequently. If you don't find the exact site listed, you may need to access the organiza-tion's home page and search from there or use a search engine such as Google.

Case 19.1   Restaurants Try to Serve Appetizing Deals

When the economy falters, consumers naturally tighten their belts. They drive fewer miles, make smaller purchases, and eat

out less often. None of this is good news for the restaurant industry, which serves more than 70 billion meals each year and employs more than 13 million workers. But restaurant owners and marketers are familiar with the concept of making lemonade when handed lemons. So, when times are tough, many come up with ways to attract diners to their tables.

Food costs might be high, but instead of raising prices, some restaurant owners adjust their menus. Filet mignon is replaced by less expensive cuts of meat—and the savings can then be passed along to consumers. At the 200 East in Chicago, house specials on pork and chicken—instead of veal and beef—have become the new norm. Offering promotions such as a three-course meal for $29, free beverages, or early-bird specials has become more popular for many restaurants. "I see how people are these days," says Carmine Marzano, owner of Luigino in Washington, D.C. "They are saving pennies everywhere they can. I try to be good to them, and hopefully they will be good to me and come back again."

Another strategy is reducing waste as much as possible. When it comes to chicken, that means being creative enough to find ways to economize. "You just have to know how to use the whole bird," says Equinox restaurateur Ellen Kassoff-Gray. "We told our staff, 'save money.'" At Equinox, located in Washington, D.C., the chef not only uses the white breast meat of the chicken but also makes a chicken salad. The legs are roasted for staff meals. The bones go into chicken stock for soups and gravy. In addition, restaurants make a bigger effort to make sure perishable items are used quickly and not thrown in the trash. "We're very focused on rotating our product through the facility quickly—not letting things sit on the shelves," says Paul Baldasaro, owner of the Buckhead Life Restaurant Group in Atlanta. "Ultimately, it ends up being better for our guests."

Most restaurant owners are sensitive to the wallets of their customers, but it is also a good marketing strategy. At Equinox, waiters routinely suggest that customers order a few side items or appetizers as a meal instead of splurging on an expensive entrée.

Restaurants that can afford to serve moderately priced meals still have an opportunity to reel in the customers. Pepe's Mexican Grill in Arizona is one such eatery. "It [is] upscale Mexican food at lower prices," says owner Oscar Lee. "It [isn't] fast food, but it is good food fast." Pepe's serves fresh food, mostly on a takeout basis, thereby saving on the expense of a waitstaff and a large space for seating. The savings are passed along to customers.

But some restaurants are sticking to their original marketing strategy, intending to distinguish themselves from the competition in other ways. There's no reason to cut portions, argues Paul Baldasaro of Buckhead Life. "There's no reason to cut quality if you want to stay in business. The customer is very savvy. Our guests would know if they came in one of our restaurants and we changed something." Instead, Buckhead Life offers promotions like the three-course *prix fixe* dinner for those patrons who are interested, and it has stuck to its regular menu pricing in general. In fact, every restaurant owner knows that temporary cost- and price-cutting measures only work for the short term; over the long term, it is creativity—with menu choices, recipes, food quality, and service—that counts.

Questions for Critical Thinking

1. In addition to those described, discuss other pricing promotions restaurants might offer to attract customers.

2. How do you think the price–quality relationship affects the restaurant industry?

Sources: "Restaurant Industry—Facts at a Glance," National Restaurant Association, www.restaurant.org, accessed June 9, 2009; Aaron Smith, "Weak Economy Takes Bite Out of Casual Dining," *CNN Money*, July 29, 2008, money.cnn.com; Luci Scott, "2 New Restaurants Buck Economic Downturn," *The Arizona Republic*, August 21, 2008, www.azcentral.com; Cheryl V. Jackson, "Weak Economy Biting Restaurants," *Chicago Sun-Times*, August 19, 2008, www.suntimes.com; Michael S. Rosenwald, "Economy Raises the Heat in the Kitchen," *The Washington Post*, June 16, 2008, www.washingtonpost.com; Joe Guy Collier, "Restaurants Feel Squeeze from Both Ends of Economy," *The Atlanta Journal-Constitution*, June 9, 2008, www.ajc.com.

Video Case 19.2   Pricing Strategy at Standard Renewable Energy

The written video case on Standard Renewable Energy appears on page VC-17. The Standard Renewable Energy video is designed to expand and highlight the concepts in this chapter and the concepts and questions covered in the written video case.

Talking about Marketing Careers with...
Paul Williams

PAUL WILLIAMS
Founder
Idea Sandbox

Inspiration is found in some unexpected places—a garage where entrepreneurs tinker with new technology that revolutionizes business, an accidental meeting of the best and brightest minds that sparks an idea. But do we need a garage or face-to-face meetings? Finding creative solutions to marketing problems is the essence of a Web site called Idea Sandbox. The site combines the free flow of ideas of a brainstorming session with the ease of communicating in the virtual world. It also offers resources—lists of other Web sites, publications, and a blog—to which marketers can turn for inspiration and creative problem solving. The purpose, as the site says, is to help businesses create *wicked good ideas*, which are "innovative, support [a company's] key strategy, and are truly remarkable."

Idea Sandbox is the brainchild of Paul Williams, a marketing professional who has brought a fresh perspective and new strategies to such giants as Disney and Starbucks. He is here to give us some background on his activities.

Q: You've worked for some pretty high-profile companies in your career. How did your education and professional experiences lead you to form Idea Sandbox? Did you always want to be an entrepreneur?

I've always considered myself in business for myself. Even when I was working at corporations, in the back of my mind I was working for myself—just at that company. Yes, I was totally loyal, but it allowed me to manage my *own* brand. Having this mindset allowed me to manage my career growth. I've always paid attention to my professional growth. If I hadn't grown in responsibility, maturity, or skills, I would work with my boss to put a plan together. If my growth was stagnant, I would first try to fix it within the company. If that

wouldn't work, it indicated that I needed to find a challenge elsewhere.

I graduated in '91 with a bachelor of science degree with a double major in public relations (speech communication program) and business marketing/management. I also had a minor in art with emphasis in commercial and graphic design. Like many students, I didn't really know what I wanted to do when I graduated, so I built my program around subjects that I had enthusiasm for and saw a practical potential for. Public relations helped me be a better problem solver. Business courses helped me think more strategically. Art course work allowed me to communicate with creative people and understand visual composition.

One of my most valuable experiences was doing an internship my final year in college. I worked in the PR department of a medical center, which gave me real experience that could be reflected in my résumé. I recommend that you do as much work related to your potential field as possible. It doesn't matter if it's volunteer or unpaid—you'll get paid with experience.

Q: Students read about different pricing strategies for companies—reaching or maintaining profitability, meeting the competition, and establishing prestige for a product. How did you set a strategy for your company?

At Idea Sandbox, I use two different pricing strategies. Occasionally, when working with a smaller client, I may charge a per-day fee or perhaps a flat fee based on how many days' work a project will take. But the key pricing strategy I use is called value-based fees. Hourly rates and even day rates force your work based on the cost of time and materials. Value-based fees are based on the value of the outcome to the client, not the cost of your tasks.

Q: Who are Idea Sandbox clients? What range of services do they obtain? How are your fees set?

Idea Sandbox specializes in innovative/creative problem solving for medium to large English-speaking companies in the U.S. and Europe that lack internal expertise or resources or want an external perspective for innovative ideas essential to business success.

We offer problem solving/strategy sessions—a forum where you bring the challenge—and after sessions ranging from several hours to several weeks, we emerge with an effective and meaningful strategy. I also assist companies in improving their innovation process. Finally, other services range from creativity and innovation courses to designing space conducive for brainstorming.

My fees are primarily based on the anticipated value of implementing the programs or ideas I'm assisting to build—value-based fees. While I use key tools and pull from a proven process, every client situation is different. So, each proposal is unique.

Q: In this text, students have seen examples of companies that are shifting their strategies to better serve customers and remain competitive. How common is it for companies to switch marketing strategies?

The best-run companies have created a mission statement that guides their choices. I'm not talking about some words on paper or posted in the company lunchroom, rather a living mission that everyone in the company believes—its reason for being. When a company faces change, its staff may alter their short-term plans to better meet customer needs, to keep up with technology, to outdo their competitor, etc. But they should stay true to their reason for being. The mission statement serves as a compass to keep the company on the right path.

Q. Today's marketers are using some innovative methods to reach their customers—enlisting consumers in buzz marketing campaigns to serve as brand champions, sending text messages to cell phones—and get the word out cost-effectively. What is the most creative idea you've seen companies use in a marketing campaign?

The most creative ideas brands execute are ideas that entertain, make a point, are memorable, are genuine, and connect with me as a customer. It is extremely difficult to do all these things and easy to take a short-cut and go for the quick blast of attention. But ultimately the brand will suffer. Truly understanding your customers and communicating through an appropriate channel is a lot of work—but extremely rewarding both financially and for the brand's reputation. A company that does a great job of this is Apple Computer. Everything they do from the design of the computer to the design of their shipping boxes and shopping bags clearly says "Apple" and "think different."

You may be tempted to do a media stunt to gain attention. But think about the brand of the company as if it were a person with a reputation to uphold. Is the tactic you are considering going to help or hurt that reputation? There are a million cheap and easy ideas out there, but they're just that—cheap and easy.

Q. Because you help marketers generate creative ideas, you must have some unique insight to pass along. What can students do to gain skills and make themselves stand out from the crowd?

Gain experience! On your first marketing job interview, they're going to ask you if you have ever managed a budget, created a marketing plan, led an event, led people, managed multiple priorities, taken care of details, increased sales, increased attendance (the same stuff written into an entry-level job description). Now you won't be surprised, and you have plenty of time between now and graduation to work on these skills. Be the treasurer for an organization, write the plan to help the volunteer group gain awareness, be in charge of student elections, raise your hand and be team captain, learn to prioritize and effectively juggle tasks, pay attention to the details, come up with ways to drive sales, get more student participation in an event than in the past. Finally, keep notes of all these activities. It doesn't matter where or for what cause you did these things. It matters that you can say, "Yes, I have," during your first interview.

Read. I know, you're probably sick of reading. I was by the time I finished school. But the more you read, the faster you can read and the more you can process. You may not have to read something because it's on a syllabus but rather because your boss says you could use more organization skills or should be better at managing projects. You'll want to quickly and effectively learn these skills, and reading is your best ally. I recommend reading everything that interests you and is related to your job (or potential job). It's also great to read stuff you would never normally pick up.

Add value. Your boss asks you to enter some figures in a spreadsheet and you only need to return to her with a completed spreadsheet. But what if you found a way to graph the data so it reads easier than a column of numbers or reformatted the spreadsheet so it fits better in her planner? Or what if you corrected some inconsistencies in the formulas? Bottom line: Always look for a way to add value—to add the brand called YOU to the projects you work on. Leave them better than when you found them.

Arrive with the solution. One of the first mistakes I made early in my career was alerting my boss to a problem with one of our marketing programs. I thought I was being smart in discovering the issue. What I hadn't done was to think through the steps to fix it. Yes, I raised the issue, but I simply became part of the problem. From that point on, I learned to arrive with the solution to any problem I discovered. If I could, I'd fix the problem and report that. "Hey, the tracking sheets weren't calculating properly, but I reworked the formulas, reran the numbers, and it's all better now." If I couldn't fix it, I'd recommend an approach. It taught me to think through issues and align myself with my boss as a problem solver.

Be passionate. I've always followed the philosophy, "It's not enough to be good when you dream of being great." Being passionate about what you're doing helps you to get great. Sometimes in your professional career you can skate by—going through the motions gets you where you need to go. But I argue that if you don't have passion for what you are doing, it isn't worth doing. If you aren't challenged, you aren't growing and getting better—you're becoming stagnant. Perhaps it's time to try a new project, take on more work, or find a different role. I know statistics indicate only a small percentage of workers enjoy their jobs. But that's something totally within your control. If you're not passionate about your job, either find a way to make it exciting or do something different. It's up to you.

part 7 pricing decisions

GREENSBURG, INC.

Watt's the Deal?

Pricing on most items isn't all that mysterious. Fast food lunch: $5.37. Hamburger: $2.49; fries: $1.89; drink: $.99. Those prices pretty much break down into operating expenses, food cost, and profit. It is what it is. When it comes to pricing an alternative energy system for your home, it's a different story.

The first thing you have to understand is what you're buying. First, you pay for the materials and labor, and you can count on a 20 percent mark-up for the company's profit and operations. Next comes the idea of watts, the electric company's unit of measure for how much electricity you use. Then there are the intangibles. When pricing an energy-saving system like wind or solar, you have to look at your initial investment and what you can expect to save when the electric bill comes. If you are really good about limiting your energy use, you may be able to sell some of your extra power back to the "grid." But what if it takes 10 years to pay off the home improvement loan you took out to finance the system? What will the interest be? Is that adjusted for inflation? Is the cost of electricity always going to go up, or will it stabilize or even go down in two years? What are the maintenance and repair costs? Get through all these questions and you're still faced with the choice of wind or solar. Wind is cheaper to start, but less predictable on the return on investment—solar is the opposite.

That's just for residential. Add an Inc. after your name and there's a whole bunch of other considerations. What is the depreciation on the equipment? Can it be accelerated? Are there state, local, or federal tax credits?

John Miggins of Standard Renewable Energy in Tulsa, Oklahoma, can do these calculations in his sleep, but is quick to admit they are complicated. "The people call me and say, 'I have a 2,000-square-foot house. What do I need?'" There's no way to answer that, but what he does tell them is what the average customer *might* want. From there, all bets are off until he can do a custom quote designed for the customer's home—the location, type of construction, exposure, zoning, energy needs, what the customer realistically expects to get out of a wind or solar system and, most importantly, what the customer is willing to give up to get the most out of the system he or she wants.

When the students at the KU School of Architecture and Urban Planning's Studio 804 called Miggins looking for a solar and wind system for their 547 Art Center design-build in Greensburg, Kansas, the needs versus wants equation really came into play. The building, a community and art museum in the heart of Greensburg, was a unique project. 547 Art Center was the first building to be completed in the devastated town and is definitely one of, if not the greenest, buildings in Kansas. Like all projects in Greensburg, money was an issue, but building a truly sustainable, green LEED Platinum building was just as important. Add to that the fact that the building was going to be a showpiece for the town, so aesthetics couldn't suffer either. John quoted the project at about $50,000. Although he would have loved to give it all away for free, the studio needed to cover his costs. As they were completing the plans for

the project, the design team threw him a curveball. They wanted three smaller wind turbines to power the building rather than the one larger one John recommended. "It was a ten thousand dollar difference, easily," recalls Miggins. A frugal guy himself, he couldn't understand why they would spend the extra money on an already strapped project. "A friend of mine told me architects like threes," said John. "And you gotta admit, it looks really cool!" In the end, he got what they were going for and donated some of the extra labor involved in installing the three turbines so they could achieve their vision.

"We can't treat everybody like that," says Miggins. As a sales rep for the Oklahoma/Kansas region, John has some wiggle room in pricing jobs. Every project is carefully reviewed and he knows he'll get a talking to if he gives too much away. The return on investment in cool projects like Greensburg isn't lost on the finance department at Standard Renewable. John was recently called by Make it Right, Brad Pitt's foundation dedicated to the sustainable rebuilding of the 9th Ward of New Orleans, the area hardest hit by Hurricane Katrina. He is now involved in designing a solar system for a neighborhood playground. Standard knows they won't make a killing on the project, but the exposure will more than make up for it.

Questions

1. Why is it important for Standard Renewable Energy to allow John Miggins flexibility in pricing?

2. Why is return on investment such an important factor for the consumer choosing an alternative energy system?

3. While one can probably find a better price for the components online, what is the value of choosing John Miggins for your solar or wind system?

4. Which pricing objective best fits Standard Renewable Energy?

5. Perform a breakeven analysis for the owner of an average 2000-square-foot home. Prepare a presentation using a spreadsheet, powerpoint slides, and handouts that John Miggins could use when discussing solar with potential customers.

VIDEO CASE CONTENTS

Video Case 1.2

Marketing: Satisfying Customers at Flight 001

"We came up with this concept out of need," says Brad John, co-founder of Flight 001. Brad and fellow co-founder John Sencion had, until the late 90s, worked in different aspects of the fashion industry in New York. John was a menswear designer and Brad worked behind the scenes. Both did an enormous amount of travel between the United States, Europe, and Japan. No matter how many times they set out on a trip, the days and hours before hopping a cab for JFK were spent running from office supply store to bookstore to drugstore to boutique in a mad rush for the latest laptop bag. By the time they got to the airport, they were sweaty, stressed, and miserable—not exactly the glamorous existence they envisioned when they got into the fashion industry.

On May 5, 1998, somewhere high in the sky between New York and Paris, they came up with an idea for a one-stop travel shop targeted at fashion-forward globetrotters like themselves.

Not everyone got it. "Everyone would say, 'Well, there's luggage stores, Brad, what's the difference? You're gonna sell luggage.'" Brad recalls. "We were going to sell guidebooks, cosmetics, bags, passport covers. There's really no place in the world where you can buy all these items in one place."

"You can't just open another Mexican restaurant and think you're an entrepreneur," says Sencion. "Without innovation, there's no entrepreneurship." When it came to the design and concept, it was very important that Flight 001 not be just another luggage store. John lent his design experience and Brad brought his talent for selecting product and merchandising to create a truly unique shopping experience.

The stores, shaped like airplane fuselages, are chock full of fun mid-century modern design, harkening back to a time when leg room didn't cost extra and when people dressed up to travel and actually looked forward to hanging out at the airport lounge. It's not all in the look, of course. Customer service at Flight 001 is key to the experience. Friendly and helpful staff members do whatever they can to start your trip on the right foot. Unfortunately, whatever happens once your reach the airport is out of their hands.

Brad and John both know that a cool shop and nice people will only get you so far, so they put an enormous amount of thought into selecting and designing the products they sell. Looking back at the original inspiration for the store, Flight 001 created its own line of innovative space-saving packing bags called Space Pack. Each Space Pack is designed for a specific garment and, once filled, can double the amount of space in your suitcase with the added bonus of keeping everything neat, clean, and organized. Future plans include an exclusive luggage line; ultimately, Brad would like for every product in his store to be a Flight 001 branded product.

Another important part of Flight 001's plan is careful marketing. While Brad and John are not going to turn away business, it is important to the brand that they maintain the feeling of a small boutique, so they've never done any traditional paid advertising. Instead, they rely on partnerships with airlines such as Northwest and Song, editorial spreads in magazines from *Lucky* to *Business Week,* and exclusive product deals and tie-ins with high fashion designers such as Yves Behar and automaker Mini Cooper. Unlike traditional paid advertising, they are in front of only those consumers most likely to purchase their products. Plus, it's free!

As Flight 001 celebrates its 10-year anniversary, it is clear that its success is based on more than a flashy design. With retail stores in Los Angeles, San Francisco, New York and Chicago, it is clear that they aren't targeting your average big-box shopper. At the same time, they appeal to anyone who wants to make a statement at the baggage carousel. Stop by the Greenwich Village store on any given day and you may find yourself comparing guidebooks with celebs such as Rachael Ray, meeting a retired couple shopping for lightweight ergonomic carry-on approved luggage, or seeing a preteen in search of the cutest iPod protector and a vial of anti-bacterial "Cootie Spray"—just in case. As John says, "We're trying to bring a little fun and glamour back in to travel."

Questions

1. How important are Flight 001's strategic alliances to their marketing?

2. What other companies or industries would be a good fit with Flight 001?

3. What role does the design of the store play in marketing Flight 001?

Video Case 2.2

Strategic Planning and the Marketing Process at Recycline*

When Eric Hudson started the Massachusetts-based consumer products company, Recycline, in 1996, he wasn't necessarily trying to make a "green" company. Armed with an MBA, a love of the outdoors, and a desire to be his own boss, he came up with a product and set out to find a way to make it. That product was the Preserve toothbrush. Made from recycled plastic, the brush was not only environmentally friendly, but featured a unique 45 degree angled head designed by his dad, an industrial designer specializing in automobiles and boats, with help from several dentists. It is hard to believe today, with the popularity of green products and our increased environmental awareness, but in the late 1990s, green products were considered "fringe" and could be found mostly around college towns on both coasts. Most of the products were considered less effective and low quality. Many actually were. That's why, from the beginning, Eric felt strongly that Recycline's mission would be to make it easy to be green by offering environmentally friendly products for the mass market—without sacrificing quality or performance.

For the first few years, the Preserve toothbrush was mostly available locally in natural food stores. Soon they sold in to Whole Foods, a national natural foods chain, and Trader Joe's, which specializes in unique and gourmet grocery items. Recycline was doing a lot of grassroots marketing. They were sampling products at an Earth Day celebration in Boston when an employee from Stonyfield Yogurt approached them with an idea. Stonyfield had a lot of scrap waste from the manufacture of their yogurt containers that was difficult for them to recycle. Recycline needed a reliable source of recycled plastic.

It was a match made in heaven. Stonyfield had a great piece of PR to enhance their environmentally friendly reputation, and Recycline could benefit from an association with such a mainstream, well-respected product. The yogurt container toothbrushes hit the shelves in 2001 and have been doing well for both companies ever since. Stonyfield even encourages consumers to send Recycline used yogurt containers.

"We're a pretty scrappy, upstart company going up against some very big brands," says C.A. Webb, director of marketing at Recycline. Large retailers are unwilling or unable to devote large chunks of shelf space to an unknown brand, so Recycline put a lot of effort into refining its packaging and marketing to have more of a presence and appeal to a more sophisticated consumer. "Our marketing budget pales in comparison to our competitors," s-says Webb. Even though they've been around for over a decade, Recycline still relies heavily on sampling and grassroots marketing. Finally, in 2008,

Webb persuaded the marketing department to do their first real advertising campaign. She and her small staff work closely with a PR firm and smaller marketing agencies to keep the wheels turning.

With so little money and so few resources, Recycline relies heavily on publicity to market their brand. A magazine article or television appearance can reach an incredible number of unique consumers—plus, it's free. Because the green movement is hot right now, Recycline has received great press in *The New York Times Magazine, Gourmet*, and *Everyday with Rachael Ray* as well as on "Good Morning America," "The Today Show," and on Sundance Channel's "The Green."

"One thing you can be assured of is that some part of it won't work the way you'd hoped!" says Webb of her strategic marketing plans. She attributes many of the misses to the complexities of working with outside agencies on campaigns. Sometimes it's a failure to communicate or a firm's inability to deliver on the plan. No matter the reason, "sometimes you have to figure out a way to save that investment and then other times it just becomes a learning moment when you say, 'Okay, let's do the post mortem, let's understand what went wrong and let's just be sure we don't do that again.'"

Webb admits she hasn't performed a SWOT analysis, on paper at least, since business school. But when it comes to thinking about new channels, design decisions, bringing a product to market, or just looking at the marketplace in general, "I absolutely use that thinking on a daily basis ... always," she says.

When Eric started the company in 1998, he could have only dreamed that America's desire for green products would be as strong as it is today. Of course, all good trends eventually come to an end. "The interest in green products has just been incredible. The biggest thing I'm concerned about is whether it's going to kinda have a negative backlash." He is hoping that, like the dot com trend that put a laptop on every desk and a BlackBerry in every palm, "We will all realize that we've incorporated these green activities in our lives."

Questions

1. Do you consider Recycline's strategy for the Preserve brand a first mover or second mover strategy? Explain.

2. Perform a SWOT analysis on Recycline. Identify their core competency and their weaknesses in the marketplace.

*Recycline has recently been rebranded "Preserve," with the "Recycline" name stepping into the background as the parent company. For the purposes of this case, however, because the change is occurring as we go to press, the name Recycline is retained.

Video Case 3.2   The Marketing Environment, Ethics, and Social Responsibility at Scholfield Honda

When Al Gore won Best Documentary at the 2007 Academy Awards for his 2006 film, *An Inconvenient Truth*, the environment was still seen as an issue only for activists. Jokes were made. "Saturday Night Live" had a field day. Then, Gore won a Nobel Peace Prize. Things started to change. By 2008, grocery stores around the country started filling up with organic and environmentally friendly products. Reusable bags showed up at checkout counters everywhere. More and more communities were providing curbside recycling pickup. The Discovery Channel even created a new cable network, Planet Green. Today, nearly every corporation from Frito-Lay to Ford has jumped on the green bandwagon.

Of course, there have always been companies ahead of the curve. Since the early 1970s, Honda had been producing the low-emission, fuel-efficient Civic. With so many auto manufacturers producing a dizzying line of makes and models, Honda is conscious about keeping up with the competition while staying true to their roots. The entire Honda line consists of four classes of vehicles: Good, Better, Best, and Ultimate. Their regular gas cars are Good, with about 30 mpg; hybrids are Better at about 45 mpg; and their Best solution is a natural, gas-powered Civic GX, which gets about 220 miles to a tank. Honda has Ultimate solutions in the works, including the new Honda FCX Clarity, a hydrogen fuel cell car in which hydrogen reacts with oxygen—both renewable resources—to create electricity. You can buy the natural gas Civic GX and Clarity today, but neither vehicle is practical for the average driver as the fueling stations are hard to come by.

Lee Lindquist, alternative fuels specialist at Scholfield Honda in Wichita, Kansas, had been researching alternative fuel vehicles for a presentation at a local Sierra Club meeting when he learned that, since 1998, the natural gas-powered Civic GX had been in use by municipalities and fleet customers in New York and California as a way to address air-quality issues.

Lee was aware that the Wichita market wasn't exactly teeming with green consumers, but realized that everyone these days is looking for ways to combat rising fuel prices. Lee also saw the GX as a way to promote the use of local natural resources; Kansas produces much of the natural gas available in the United States today.

Lee's boss, owner Roger Scholfield, was skeptical about the Civic GX. While he was in search of a clever way to promote the dealership as more environmentally friendly, he didn't want to muddy the waters with this new, somewhat impractical, vehicle.

He agreed to offer the car to his fleet and corporate customers and went back to work on a plan for the dealership.

They made a few small changes around the dealership—recycling the oil from oil changes to heat the shop, adding biodegradable and reusable cups at the coffee machine, and placing recycling bins everywhere. When the dealership made some renovations to their buildings, they created the Honda Green Zone—a rental space for organizations to hold meetings about green projects in the community. The space features a high-tech A/V system and contains local and environmentally friendly furnishings.

Internally, Roger holds weekly meetings with his Green Team to brainstorm new environmentally friendly community projects, marketing, and products. They were at work on several other project ideas when a massive tornado hit the small town of Greensburg, Kansas on May 4, 2007.

Roger and his family have always contributed to various causes, including a generous cash donation toward the rebuilding efforts in Greensburg. Once again, Lee Lindquist approached Scholfield about the Honda Civic GX. He wanted to donate a GX to the town and a fueling station to go with it; Roger was skeptical but soon realized that the press the donation would receive could not only benefit his business, but would raise awareness in the area about alternative fuels. The car would be made available to Greensburg residents to check out and try for themselves. The world would get to see the car in use by average people, and the town would have its own natural gas fueling station.

Scholfield is upfront about the decision to donate the car. It was a costly investment, and if he had done it solely for the PR, there are many more cost-effective ways of reaching his potential customers. When customers come into the dealership, they are more interested in alternative fuel and high-efficiency vehicles and recognize Scholfield Honda's commitment to the people of Greensburg and the green movement as a whole.

Questions

1. How does Scholfield Honda rate on the social responsibility pyramid? Do they meet all the criteria for a socially responsible company?

2. What social and cultural changes have impacted the way car manufacturers design and market their products?

3. Should governmental regulations be placed on companies' claims that their products are green? Should official classifications for environmental friendliness be defined?

Video Case 4.2

E-business at Evo

When professional skier Bryce Phillips began selling closeout ski equipment out of his garage in 2001, he was hoping to make a little extra money to fund his ski vacations. Things went well with the first garage sale, and soon he had a few employees and started selling snowboard, skateboard, and wakeboarding gear. Almost by accident, at age 20, Phillips had a company on his hands. He pulled some equity out of his house—and online retailer Evo was born. The company grew to 40 employees, then 60. Revenues came to nearly $6 million. Evogear.com became known worldwide by pros and amateurs alike looking for good deals on great stuff. They now offer all the top brands, closeouts, and used gear for every level and budget. All this success is quite surprising when you consider that buying skis or snowboards isn't the kind of thing generally done online or through a catalog. To get fully outfitted can cost $500 to $1,000, and most people need some expert help with their purchase. Through the design of the site and Bryce's desire to create a community for like-minded people, rather than simply another online discounter, Evogear.com is shredding the competition.

"Well, we want it to be functional, number one," says Molly Hawkins, affiliate program manager at Evo. "If you go to some of our competitors' sites, some of them look really cool" but, she says, "you try and navigate around their sites, they're not as intuitive."

Evogear.com is easy to use and does look cool, but adding value for the shopper is key to their business. The site offers product reviews, user accounts with all your past and current orders and preferences, tons of links to affiliate sites, events, blogs—pretty much everything you would want in a Web site, or a brick-and-mortar shop. "Aside from that," Molly says, "the *About Us* page has played a huge role." Evo has, from the beginning, wanted to create a community for lovers of water and snow sports, and the *About Us* page really offers the customer an "in" to the company; their mission, values, personal pages and video clips by each employee. Customers love the idea that they can virtually "meet" their customer service person or buyer or Bryce himself. Hawkins believes this helped to legitimize the company in the beginning. "People would get excited to find that the person that they're talking to or the people that they're buying from are actual users of this gear that we're selling," she says.

Being seen as legit and trustworthy is paramount in the land of e-commerce. You spend weeks searching for the best price on that new digital camera or gaming system and when it arrives, if it arrives, it was not what you thought you were buying. Often, there is little you can do. The people at Evo know where you're coming from and want to make sure every purchase is stress-free. They have an easy return policy: just let them know what the problem is, from buyer's remorse to a box of splintered skis, and they'll make the switch.

Once an order is placed, Evo's distribution center jumps to attention. Most orders are shipped fast, within a day or two of the order. If you're not in a hurry, they'll ship it ground for free, or overnight via a partnership with FedEx.

Trust, value, and personal service are the key elements in Evo's success, but word of mouth only gets you so far. Advertising is difficult for an e-business such as Evo, where keeping it simple with low overhead and a no-frills annual budget is what makes them able to pass the discounts on to their customers. Like many Web sites, they offer an affiliate program that places ads or links on other Web sites to drive traffic back to Evo. An affiliate program or pay-per-click program pays owners of other sites every time a user clicks on an ad. In addition to paying for each click, Evo sends a "thank you" gift of 12 percent of each completed sale at evogear.com originating from the affiliate site. To protect their brand, remain authentic to their consumers, and remain in good standing with their suppliers, Molly Hawkins and her team lay out some ground rules for each potential affiliate. Their site must be well designed, easy to navigate, and, most importantly, must not contain any references to gambling, sexually explicit material, hate speech or racist content or any other inappropriate material. Sounds obvious, but being inadvertently connected with the most obscure, unseemly Web site could mean the end of their business.

Questions

1. Aside from offering good prices, how does evogear.com offer value to the consumer?

2. Evo has opened a large brick-and-mortar store/community art space in Seattle, Washington. Go to culture.evogear.com/category/seattle/ to learn more about what the store offers. Do you think this store will distract or enhance the Web site? Consider potential channel conflicts, pricing strategy, convenience, and consumer behavior in your answer.

Video Case 5.2 — Consumer Behavior at Scholfield Honda

If you want to study consumer behavior, probably the best place to start would be a car dealership. Cars are a big investment. Most people spend upwards of $20,000 on a new car and $6,000 or more on a pre-owned vehicle. In the United States, where we drive pretty much everywhere, your car is your first contact with the world. One look at someone's car and you might get an idea of their politics, bank account, occupation, education, musical tastes, and favorite weekend activities. It's the ultimate fashion accessory. Does it have a lot of cup holders and a DVD player in the headrest? Family car. Cute little convertible? Twenty-five-year old with her first real job. That Italian sports car? Retail therapy for the mid-life crisis. That person in the 2009 Honda Fit hybrid who just stole your parking space? Likely some smug, twentysomething activist.

But looks can be deceiving.

When the Honda Insight, Honda's first consumer hybrid car, hit the market in 2000, Roger Scholfield, owner of Scholfield Honda in Wichita, Kansas, thought he had it all figured out. For one thing, Wichita isn't exactly known as the epicenter of eco-consumerism. He'd probably sell a handful of the hybrid cars to a couple of single, twentysomethings. The car only had two seats and seemed pretty flimsy with its lightweight aluminum body. And with a sticker price of $20,000, it was pretty pricey.

The first Insight he sold went to a 63-year-old.

The second person to buy one was 65.

As it turns out, Roger's experience was consistent with Honda's market research. They determined that the typical Insight customer was older, highly educated, probably with an engineering or science background—a person who tended to be very research-driven.

Vinnie Koc, a sales consultant at Scholfield Honda, relies more on his experience than the data to sell cars. "The vehicle pretty much

sells itself," says Vinnie. "Most of my customers are previous owners or someone in their family owns a Honda that wants them to buy a Honda." Vinnie's customers don't just show up and hop in the first car they see. Most of them have spent time on the Scholfield and Honda Web sites, researching and comparing models before they come in. They know what they want, are unlikely to be upsold on additional bells and whistles, and are clear on how much they are willing to pay. "Our job is to present the vehicle," says Vinnie. It usually takes a few test drives to complete the sale, but he is patient. It is all part of Scholfield Honda's low-pressure environment.

"I love my Scholfield Honda" is the tagline on many of the dealership's television and radio ads. "The Scholfield reputation is 100 percent why the customers are here," says Koc. In a market where the anonymous experience of shopping online is the norm for so many consumers, providing opportunities for customers to feel special and paid attention to can really make a difference, especially in car sales, an industry where trust so often is lacking. Owner and general manager Roger Scholfield takes the time to meet with customers, and consultants like Vinnie take the time to follow up on every meeting—from test drive to final sale. "If they see that you are able to provide the information they need, they feel comfortable with you and that makes them happy." It is not unusual for Vinnie's customers to drop by on their lunch hour just to say "thanks" and gush about how much they are enjoying their new Honda.

Questions

1. Name the top influence(s) impacting a consumer's decision to buy a car from Scholfield Honda.

2. Go to www.honda.com and view the different Hondas to select the car you would be most likely to purchase. Carefully consider all the determinants discussed in the chapter and their impact on your decision.

Video Case 6.2 — Business-to-Business Marketing at Flight 001

By the time each of us retires, we will probably have acquired thousands of useless gifts from our employers, clients, and vendors. Teeny staplers, space pens, solar desk clocks, binders, cheap calculators, and, of course, the ubiquitous tote bag emblazoned with logos and slogans for products you don't want and will never own.

The folks at Flight 001 appreciate the work we do and want our employers to reward us with some better swag, so they offer a corporate gifting program to help big business say thank you with a little more style. "Everything is for travel, everything is useful," says Brad John of his travel boutique, Flight 001. "At all these big companies, everyone travels and we're useful, so we're really the perfect item for a corporate gift." To guard against re-gifting, Flight 001's consultant works one on one with corporate clients to find just the right gift.

It's nice that Flight 001 is looking out for the workers of America, but they get a return as well from the corporate gifting program. While Flight 001 has been very successful in its first ten years in business and has plans to open at least 20 new shops in the next few years, it is important to the brand that it maintain its local, independent boutique feel. Part of that is resisting the lure of splashy paid advertising. With that off the table, the company uses programs like corporate gifting to get their products in the hands of their ultimate retail customer, the business traveler. The online travel search engine, Orbitz, recently placed a huge order for Flight 001's passport and document folder. Flight 001 agreed to print the Orbitz name on it and Orbitz gave the folder away to its best customers. The program was a huge success and Flight 001 saw an increase in requests for similar sales.

In the wholesale market, Flight 001 has been successful in identifying like-minded customers such as Northwest and Song airlines. One of their more successful partnerships has been with Jet Blue, an airline known for serving a younger, hipper traveler. Flight 001 offers some of their travel gear branded with both the Jet Blue

and Flight 001 name via the airline's store.

Flight 001 hopes to start selling its products wholesale to boutique and luxury hotel chains. While they have sold to hotels in the past, they haven't had much success. An emerging trend in boutique hotels is an expanded mini-bar offering high-end cosmetics and other travel products for that late-night impulse buy. Brad is hoping to see Flight 001 products next to the macadamia nuts and Toblerone bars soon.

In comparing Flight 001's consumer retail market with its business-to-business market, Brad says, "Is it the most exciting part? No. But it's a very easy business."

Questions

1. How does marketing Flight 001's products to companies such as Orbitz to give as gifts affect sales at Flight 001's retail stores?

2. What potential conflicts might arise between Flight 001's wholesale business to Jet Blue and Northwest and Flight 001 retail business? Do you think their wholesale/retail strategy is sound? Why or why not?

Video Case 7.2   Global Marketing at Evo

The ski and snowboard community is relatively small, so Evo—the Seattle-based snowboard, ski, skateboard, and wakeboard store—is always looking to maximize their exposure, and that means crossing borders and going global. The company started as an online outlet, selling close-outs and used gear to bargain hunters. Over the years, they have expanded their offerings to include first-quality new stuff, trips to exotic locales, and a retail store in Seattle.

"There's a ton of really exciting things that happen here at a regional level that have an impact on the global community," says Molly Hawkins, marketing and PR at Evo. One of the most effective ways they reach their consumers is through advertisements and editorial pieces in the top snow sports magazines. Publications such as *Freeskier Magazine*, *Powder*, and *The Ski Journal* all have international circulations.

International exposure is nice, but selling the gear keeps the lights on. Their expertise in e-commerce makes for a fairly easy transition into the global marketplace. Canada, not surprisingly, is one of Evo's largest international markets. "Our daily unique [visitors] for example, from July 2008, we have like, 64,000 from Canada," notes Molly. The United Kingdom, Germany, Australia, and Korea are also quite big for Evo with daily visitors to their Web sites in the 20,000 range—and that's in July!

But, here's the rub: all of the products Evo sells are name brand items that are for sale in local shops overseas. These brands often restrict the sales of their products to licensed resellers within

a particular geographical zone. With the Internet, these rules become quite complicated. Evo can't stop someone in Japan from placing an order. They are working with their resellers to come up with a way to honor the contracts, but still be able to serve customers everywhere.

The world of business is becoming increasingly borderless, but there are still cultural issues to grapple with. Marketing and advertising is a particularly difficult thing to do globally. If language were the only hurdle, it would be fairly simple to translate. Unfortunately, even among English-speaking nations, cultural subtleties and colloquialisms can turn an innocent euphemism into a deeply offensive word. "I work with a lot of our vendors in marketing, looking for ways to co-promote their products through Evo," says Molly. "Like Rossignol, they're based out of Europe. Their business style and their designs and branding and marketing ideas are definitely, ah, different." Molly and her staff tend to leave the marketing of the company pretty generic. Their main propositions: best brands, best prices, and a top-notch knowledge base really know no boundaries.

Evo has extended its commitment to a boundaryless world by offering extreme skiing and boarding expeditions to some of the world's most incredible destinations. "EvoTrip is such a natural extension of the Evo brand," says Bryce Phillips, Evo's founder, "and we're doing it with great activities—skiing, snowboarding, surfing."

"EvoTrip is definitely unique," says Molly. "There are other companies that are doing something similar, but our product is a little different in that we really take people on these extreme trips that people like Bryce and people here at Evo would actually go on. They know the intricacies of getting around these areas and so

I think without them, for someone who just wanted to go down there on their own, they wouldn't have the same kind of experience. These guys have that insider info, that connection."

"The reason why I get so excited about this concept is that it is near and dear to what all of us value," says Phillips. "It's just like, getting out there, learning more about different cultures, doing the activities in different parts of the world and seeing beautiful locations you might never have seen before." Through a partnership with online travel site JustFares.com—and local guides and professional athletes in each country—they will offer trips to South America, Japan, Indonesia, Switzerland, and many more locations. It's not all about the adventure, of course; sound business is behind

it all. Every trip allows Evo's "ambassadors" to get in front of their actual potential customers in each of the countries they visit. No translations. No miscommunications. No boundaries.

Questions

1. Why doesn't Evo need to tailor its marketing to different countries? Do you agree with their decision to present one marketing message? Why or why not?

2. What challenges do U.S. e-commerce companies face when selling their products overseas? Do you believe brands have the right to limit a company's right to sell internationally?

Video Case 8.2   Marketing Research and Sales Forecasting at Ogden Publications

"One thing we do differently here than people do in most businesses is we don't budget, we forecast," claims Bryan Welch, publisher and editorial director of Ogden Publications. Ogden Publications is a small publishing house based in Tulsa, Oklahoma. They publish 13 magazines, including *Mother Earth News, Natural Home,* and *Utne Reader.* A few years ago, these titles and others from their catalog were only available in specialty bookstores, often those with a more eco-conscious clientele. The green movement has done wonders for Ogden in the past few years. Now, many of their titles are sold at the local Barnes and Noble bookstore or at hardware stores.

"I will tell you, without a shadow of a doubt, that the five-year forecast is accurate six months out. Beyond that, it is wildly inaccurate," says Bryan. So why bother? "The reason you do it is because it is a strategic tool. It makes everyone think about 'what will we *need* to do to be successful in five years?'" Welch is a big proponent of being open and flexible enough to make what he calls "wise course corrections." He always reminds his staff that just because they assigned money to a project doesn't mean they have to do the project. "Because the world is changing so rapidly, we need to be able to not make an investment we planned nine months ago," says Welch, so they can "make an investment we never thought of nine months ago."

"We work together with advertising sales and editorial," explains Cherilyn Olmsted, circulation and marketing director at Ogden Publications. One of their most valuable tools is an online survey system called Survey Monkey that collects and stores all the data from the many online surveys they present to their readers. "We like to try to find out various things from an editorial perspective and an advertising sales perspective that will help improve the content we are providing to our readers and to make sure we are reaching the audience that our advertisers would like to reach." Much of the information is what one might expect—demographics, age, income, and psychographic information. Of course, without a

good magazine, there are no readers to count, so they also perform surveys asking for more subjective feedback on covers, style, and content. This information is reported back to the editorial staff of each magazine.

Cherilyn and her team use information from past sales and the reception from various new marketing projects to forecast future sales, both at the subscription and newsstand level and with advertisers. Like most, if not all magazines, revenue is almost exclusively from ad sales, so they have to continually track reader and advertiser responses in everything they do.

While surveys have been invaluable to Ogden's marketing research, one of the best and most valuable tools has been the Web companions to their magazines. This passive form of market research asks nothing of the reader except that she visits the site. Every visit, mouse click, advertising link, and download is tracked. With a few simple clicks, Cherilyn can even see how many minutes a user spent on each page. With a traditional magazine, they would have to wait six months or more to get all the sales returns and reader and advertiser feedback and to compile new subscription rates. Now, with the companion sites, they can instantly see if they need to include more political articles or home improvement projects, or recipes or technical articles about geo-thermal heating systems. They can make adjustments to the next editions of the print and Web products.

Ask anyone working in marketing today, and they will agree that a good portion of their lives is spent spotting trends. The editors and marketers at Ogden are no exception. Welch cautions, however, that "a lot of trends are short-lived and have no real impact in the economy." His skepticism extends to a particularly hot trend in the magazine industry today: the digital magazine. "There hasn't been good evidence, in spite of the fact that it is a cool idea, that a lot of people will pay for it." But, Bryan adds, "if someone suddenly came up with a formula that allowed us to make money doing it, it would only take us a couple of months to gear up and do it."

Questions

1. Now so many companies have Web companions and/or e-commerce components to their business, do you think that more traditional methods such as telephone surveys, focus groups, response cards, and analyzing sales data will become obsolete? Why or why not?

2. What are some of the limitations to forecasting at Ogden Publications?

Video Case 9.2

Targeting and Positioning at Numi Tea

Numi Tea founders, siblings Ahmed and Reem Rahim, immigrated to the United States when they were young children and grew up in Cleveland, Ohio. Reem became a biomedical engineer. Ahmed traveled the world as a photographer and settled for a time in Prague where he opened two tea shops. Reem eventually left her career to pursue life as an artist. In 1999, the two reconnected in Oakland, California, and started Numi Tea in Reem's apartment.

"I think in the positioning of our brand, we wanted to target a certain type of customer base, from the natural health food stores, to fine dining and hotels, to universities and coffee shops, gourmet stores," says Ahmed. "What I've been most surprised about in our growth is the mass market consumer." In recent years, demand by the average American consumer for organic and ethically produced products has exploded. At the same time, economic influences have driven the more affluent and natural foods consumers to large discounters such as Target, super-size grocery chains, warehouse clubs and online shopping.

Today, explains Jennifer Mullin, vice president of marketing for Numi Tea, the average Numi consumer is female, college educated, and buys two to three boxes of tea per month, usually green tea. She also buys organic products whenever possible. All of these details, while not surprising, are fairly new. Until Mullin joined the team and formalized their marketing department, Numi assumed their customers fit the same profile as the staff—young, cool, and urban. While many of Numi tea drinkers are all these things, Mullin's findings proved that the company needed to put some additional energy toward targeting the younger, college market. They launched an initiative to raise awareness of the product on campuses where people are more inclined to be interested in issues of sustainability, fair-trade, and organics. Because Numi teas are considered a premium product, they do have an affordable, but still higher price point than conventionally produced teas. College students in general have less money to spend, so Numi

approached the food service departments of universities such as Stanford to serve the tea as part of their prepaid meal plans. Not only does the food service contract represent a giant account, it encourages trial. Sampling is Numi's most successful marketing activity for attracting new users. Students can learn to love the product, essentially for free.

The most compelling reason for drinking Numi tea is its health benefits. The company found that they don't need to spend much time talking up the organic aspect of their product. In the premium and natural foods space where Numi operates, organic is expected. There is the threat that as the terms "organic" and "natural" invade the mainstream marketplace, a lack of trust or cynicism may arise as some products will inevitably fail to live up to their labels' claims. This is why Numi relies heavily on educating its consumers about the product. When targeting women, their most valued consumer, says Jennifer, "we have an in-house PR team that works a lot with editors [of women's magazines] to educate them on tea and make sure they understand the healthy properties of tea." They follow up with sampling at Whole Foods or events targeted toward environmentally conscious moms. Numi rounds out the education efforts on its Web site with more health information as well as in-depth articles on the benefits of specific teas.

Although still young, the Numi brand is expanding rapidly and has enjoyed success overseas as well. Whatever the marketing and PR teams do—store sampling, environmental events, or partnerships with like-minded companies such as Clif Bar—they continue to survey and assess the demographic and psychographic profiles of their consumer.

Questions

1. Which of the four basic targeting strategies does Numi Tea employ when reaching their markets?

2. Would you classify Numi Tea's marketing strategy as "concentrated"? If so, what are the plusses and minuses of using such a strategy in today's market?

Video Case 10.2   Relationship Marketing and CRM at Numi Tea

Chances are, if you've heard of Numi Tea, you heard about it from someone else. Jennifer Mullin, vice president of marketing for the company, explains that this is by design. "That person really believes in the tea and is sharing the tea," she says. "It's far more credible than us saying, 'Hey, try our tea,' because, obviously, we're Numi Tea."

Numi Tea was started in 1999 by brother and sister team Ahmed and Reem Rahim. Keeping it in the family is big at Numi. Reem's artwork adorns every box of tea. Their childhood friend, Hammad Atassi, is their director of food service. Every member of the Tea'm, as they call it, is committed to the company's core values of sustainability, creativity, and quality organics. This extends to their corporate customers and their producers, as well. Like their teas, every relationship is carefully cultivated and maintained.

"We focus on sampling versus the traditional marketing methods such as print or TV advertising because, for us, the conversion happens when people taste Numi Tea," explains Mullin. Numi has found that few remember their print ads, but they remember the taste of the tea and Reem's artwork on the package. Sampling has become a very popular marketing tactic. It is big business, too. An entire industry has popped up to place products in gift bags for events ranging from local events to the Oscars. Aware that most of their best marketing is done friend to friend, Numi started a Tea Champions program. Numi sends thank-you packages to fans and provides them with free tea and educational literature on their fair-trade producers and the health benefits of natural and organic teas they can share with their friends.

Maintaining a close relationship with their end-users has been relatively easy. Free stuff goes a long way toward winning over the average consumer. "The food service customer tends to really just have one provider that they want to partner with," says Hammad. "You're either in or you're out. So marketing to the food service customer is unique. You've gotta really make it a program that's easy for them to execute and you have to have the support to drive sales—whether it's signage, customized menu cards, a big poster."

Numi has been fortunate to be the tea of choice in high-end restaurants, hotel chains, and cruise lines. The food service industry in total makes up about 40 percent of their business. Along with that comes added pressure to deliver on price, quality, and customer service. While they clearly lead in quality, it is hard for any small company to compete with the giant food service companies on price. An important part of Numi Tea is their story. To tell that story, they need to forge very hands-on, personal relationships with restaurant food and beverage managers, giving them a natural competitive advantage. A regular teabag may be cheaper, but there's not much else to say about it. When Hammad can conduct

a private cupping (tea tasting) for the kitchen staff and explain all the different exotic teas, talk about the farms and farmers, their commitment to sustainability, organic farming and events in their local community, it's pretty much a slam dunk before the tea is even steeped. Turnover is notoriously high in the food service industry, so there's always a chance that a new chef or buyer will go another direction. Luckily for Numi, this hasn't been the case. Due in part to their excellent customer relationships, it is more common for them to keep the old client and follow the chef or buyer to his new restaurant.

Their success in the food service industry has driven retail business. The testimonials section of Numi's Web site contains hundreds of entries in which people share their "Numi Transformations." They talk about where and when they discovered the tea and how they have become true believers. While there are countless stories about experiencing the tea at a friend's house, a surprising number of Numi converts come from restaurants. As the requests from consumers wanting to know where to get Numi in their area have rolled in, Numi has needed to expand to their retail customers. Once available only at natural food stores and cafés, Numi has begun to sell teas in stores, including Target, large grocery chains, and even some warehouse club stores. While good for the consumer, this poses a tricky proposition to the Hammads' carefully maintained fine dining customer relationships. It could present a problem if the same premium tea served at a restaurant is also available at a local Target. Luckily, so far the two channels have co-existed peacefully.

As the company grows, one of the biggest challenges to its marketing model will be maintaining the family feel on a global scale. Jennifer Mullin and her team have begun tailoring email communications to newsletter subscribers to inform them about local events and are hoping to add some regional sales and marketing teams in the near future. They've also added Numi fan sites on Facebook and MySpace. The sites are monitored by a staffer to address any questions or concerns about the products. Most importantly, no matter how busy they may get, founders Ahmed and Reem will always be there, lending their personal touch through their art, personal stories, and experiences.

Questions

1. How do marketing activities such as gift with purchase, samples by mail, and product community blogs impact your purchasing decisions and loyalty? What was the last product you purchased because of sampling?

2. Do you consider Numi's relationships with its producers as important to their marketing as the relationships with its customers?

Video Case 11.2

Product and Service Strategy at Recycline*

When Eric Hudson graduated from business school with his MBA, he did what most people do. He went out and got a real job. After about six years, the daily grind in corporate America had gotten old. "My family was a bit crunchy and had been known to actually hug trees," recalls Hudson, "but it wasn't until the early 90s that I decided I wanted to marry my professional career with my love of nature."

As a teenager, he remembered his dentist reminding him to hold his toothbrush at a 45-degree angle, but he was always surprised that few toothbrushes were actually shaped for that angle. When it came time to start his own business, he enlisted his father—an industrial designer specializing in automobiles and boats—to help him design a better-shaped toothbrush. Once they came up with a design they liked, they sought the approval of several dentists.

At the same time, Eric became aware of how few environmentally friendly products there were in the marketplace. The products available may have been made of recycled or recyclable materials, but they were more expensive and usually didn't work as well. He also noticed that while more communities in his native Massachusetts were starting recycling programs, much of what people were throwing in the bins was food containers made from #5 plastic. At the time, few companies reused that type of plastic, and it often ended up in the landfill. Eric knew there had to be a clever way to reuse that plastic for his toothbrush.

He brought the idea to a plastics lab at the University of Massachusetts and, after a lot of experimenting, finally figured out a way to turn all that plastic into a material suitable for the toothbrush. The Preserve toothbrush hit the market in 1998.

Sales in the beginning were slow, but the product was well received. Green products had yet to hit the shelves of stores like Target and Wal-Mart, but Hudson definitely was on top of the emerging trend. As sales improved and consumers started asking for more environmentally friendly products, he developed a recyclable razor, a children's toothbrush, and a tongue cleaner—all made from recycled plastic. Not wanting their products to end up in the trash, Recycline takes back used toothbrushes and razors to be melted down and used again.

In late 2007, Recycline announced an exclusive deal with the Austin-based Whole Foods natural and gourmet grocery chain to partner on a new product line for the kitchen. The Preserve Kitchen line includes a Preserve Colander, Preserve Cutting Board, Preserve Mixing Bowls, and Preserve Food Storage Containers—all made from #5 plastic. They also added a Preserve 100% Post-Consumer Recycled Paper Cutting Board. Priced competitively, but slightly higher than similar conventionally produced products, Recycline knew that if they were to compete against the likes of Tupperware and Rubbermaid, they would need more than a good story. Until then, they were able to get by designing their products in-house with little help from the outside. It was time to call for backup.

Industrial design firm Evo Design was the perfect solution. Their offices were nearby in Connecticut, so Eric and his team could just hop in his "grease car"—a Volkswagen Hudson modified to run on French fry grease collected from a local Wendy's. Evo's team of designers, engineers, and business experts have earned a reputation for making really cool looking (and functioning) stuff for the competition: Crate & Barrel, Cuisinart, Kimberly Clark, Schick, and Waring.

For Recycline to make its mark in the CPG (Consumer Packaged Goods) arena, they will need to continue to come up with new products in new categories. Demand by new parents for environmentally friendly toys and products present a perfect opportunity for Recycline. The company has plans to launch their first toy line in the near future.

Questions

1. Why is the development of an entire product line critical to Recycline's growth and success?

2. At which stage are most "green" products in the product lifecycle? As these products mature, what can be done to extend their product lifecycles?

*Recycline has recently been rebranded "Preserve," with the "Recycline" name stepping into the background as the parent company. For the purposes of this case, however, because the change is occurring as we go to press, the name Recycline is retained.

Video Case 12.2

Developing and Managing Brand and Product Categories at Maine Media Workshops

Since 1973, Maine Media Workshops has seen some of the most talented filmmakers, photographers, and writers pass through its doors. The program started as a summer camp of sorts for amateurs and professionals wanting to hone their creative arts skills while enjoying a week along the beautiful coast of Rockport, Maine. Over the years, students have had the opportunity to work with and learn from Hollywood's heavy hitters: Vilmos Zsigmond, cinematographer on "Close Encounters," "The Black

Dahlia," and "The Deer Hunter," Alan Myerson, Emmy-winning director of everything from "The Love Boat" to "The Larry Saunders Show" to "Boston Public," and actor Gene Wilder. The names are impressive, but what has always set the program apart is its intensity and quality. The family style lobster dinner at the end doesn't hurt, either.

Sadly, in recent years, the workshops had lost their way and the school was in danger of closing. "When it fell on hard times, and there was the possibility of it not surviving, it was hard to imagine being here anymore," says Charles Altschul, Rockport resident and current executive director of the school. Something had to be done to revitalize this gem along the rocky Maine coast.

In 2007, the family-owned school became a non-profit educational institution. The school underwent all of the infrastructure and management changes one might expect from this kind of transition, but the biggest challenges lay ahead. While the school had always enjoyed an excellent reputation within the industry, it was losing ground. More and more universities were providing excellent opportunities for students in the creative arts. These schools had deep pockets, were able to attract top-notch faculty, and more importantly, could afford superior facilities and equipment. No longer operating as a for-profit business, the Maine Workshops could now reach out to private and corporate donors to keep things afloat. This was especially critical when it came to equipment. There would be little gained by students working in outdated facilities. The reputation of the school was at stake. Companies like Canon, Sony, and Apple could now partner with the school by donating equipment and getting a break on their taxes. The workshops could attach these sponsors' cutting-edge products and technologies to their marketing materials to attract students, and the equipment manufacturers could advertise their association with the school to attract customers.

One of their most valuable relationships is with Canon. As the Maine Workshops brands itself as a leader in digital arts, Canon desires the same thing. There isn't one product, from still film camera to HD video camera to office printer to professional printing press, in Canon's product line that isn't relevant to the Workshop's offerings.

The partnership with Canon is a great first step toward repositioning the school as a leader in digital media and arts, but it has been a challenge to rally the troops and get a unified message together. Traditionally, the departments worked independently, marketing photography to photographers, writing to writers and filmmaking to the film students. "We felt it was important, after the transition, to publish a catalog that contains all of the programs we offer," says Altschul. "It's 162 pages, we printed 165,000 copies of it, it cost most of our marketing budget to do."

Moving forward, they'll do much less of the paper catalogs, which is an obvious cash-sucker. More importantly, Altschul believes that to present themselves as a leader in digital media, they need to walk the walk in everything they do. The school's Web site recently underwent a major overhaul to better communicate that, "we're back and better than before." The site contains all the standard information one might need along with a complete course catalog and school blog, as well as a place to pay tuition, take a placement test, register for classes, or donate to the school. Links to technology partners also serve as a showcase for student work.

This new interdisciplinary approach has served the school well. Enrollment is up from past years and the phone is ringing off the hook with professionals wanting to teach a workshop. The school has also added a degree program. The full-time, 1–5 year program at Maine Media College is fully accredited to offer an MFA in Maine and is expected to receive national accreditation in the next few years.

Questions

1. What are the main elements of the Maine Media Workshops brand equity? Analyze the workshop's brand equity using the Young & Rubicam "dimensions of brand personality."

2. Would you consider the Maine Media College an extension of the Maine Media Workshops brand or a new product development strategy—or both? Explain.

3. How can the Maine Media Workshops benefit from consumers' brand recognition, preference, and insistence with companies such as Canon? Can Canon benefit from the association with the Workshops?

Video Case 13.2 — Marketing Channels and Supply Chain Management at Recycline*

"Our company was born in the natural channel—natural grocery stores, Whole Foods Market, Wild Oats, and Trader Joe's," says C.A. Webb, director of marketing for Recycline. It's a channel the company knows well. For over a decade, Recycline has been selling its Preserve line of toothbrushes and razors to eco-friendly consumers across the country.

"Whole Foods is our number one customer," says Webb. "Not only do they do an amazing job of telling our story in-store, they are the ultimate retail partner for us because they are so trusted." Customers have a sense that when they enter a Whole Foods market,

every product has been carefully hand selected in accordance with Whole Food's mission to sell organic and locally produced food and to present responsibly sourced and manufactured products.

One unique opportunity that came out of the relationship between Whole Foods and Recycline was the development of the Preserve line of kitchenware. Recycline was looking for a way to expand its recycled and recyclable product line, and Whole Foods was looking for an exclusive housewares line. "Together, we did the competitive research, we speced out the products, we developed the pricing strategy, designs," says Webb. The line of colanders, cutting boards, mixing bowls, and storage containers hit the shelves in 2007. "It created less risk on both sides, " remarks

Webb. The relatively tiny Recycline was able to take an untested product and put it in the nation's largest and most respected natural foods store, which in turn used its experience and resources in the channel to do all the legwork to ensure the product sold well. "We gave Whole Foods a 12-month exclusive on the line," says Webb, "which in turn gave them a great story to tell." That story was told everywhere. The "Today Show," *The New York Times Magazine,* "Everyday with Rachael Ray," *Gourmet* magazine, and many other natural and mainstream lifestyle publications covered the product. Today, in addition to Whole Foods, you can find the entire Preserve product line at thousands of retailers around the United States and Canada, including Target, Crate and Barrel, Trader Joe's, Wild Oats, and large regional grocery chains such as Shaws, Hannaford's, and Stop and Shop.

With the recent increase in demand for green products by the average U.S. consumer, mainstream grocery and drug stores have been knocking on the doors of companies like Recycline to stock their shelves. It is a difficult space to work in, admits Webb. It's hard to make an impact on a shelf with one or two items when companies like Gillette or Rubbermaid offer 15 or 20 products in the same category.

One of the great benefits of working with Whole Foods in the beginning was that even though they are the largest chain in the natural foods channel, in the grocery and discount chain area, they are really quite small. "The quantities that we were needing to provide them were manageable for a small company like ours and it just gave us time together to assess demand, to keep inventory levels steady," says Webb. "It was much more of a 'bump-free' launch than we would have seen if we launched in other channels."

"Heading up the sales department, I think that every single day what we are working with here is supply chain management," notes Jon Turcotte, vice president of sales at Recycline.

Large supermarkets and stores like Target have entire Plan-o-gram departments that schedule and stock the shelves on a very tight schedule. If the plans include a turnover to a 4th of July holiday special, Recycline needs to be able to supply them with exact quantities and selection of Preserve Picnic Ware to fit the Plan-o-gram for the aisle. "There aren't a lot of people in the process. Everything is controlled by computers," laments Turcotte. Just-in-time inventory systems have saved retailers millions of dollars, but as a result, there is little room for exceptions and do-overs. Failure to deliver could result in losing a tremendous opportunity to present products to literally hundreds of thousands of shoppers. "The old adage that time is money holds very true in today's world," Turcotte says. For a company like Recycline, with limited resources and very tight marketing budgets, this missed chance could spell disaster for the line.

Questions

1. As Recycline makes more headway into the larger retail chains, what challenges will it face?

2. What type of marketing channel would be best to support Recycline's growth over the next five years?

*Recycline has recently been rebranded "Preserve," with the "Recycline" name stepping into the background as the parent company. For the purposes of this case, however, because the change is occurring as we go to press, the name Recycline is retained.

Video Case 14.2

Retailing at Flight 001

There's nothing like a lazy afternoon spent browsing Main Street or the mall, latte in hand, taking in the sights, sounds, and intoxicating smell of Cinnabon. You just can't get that online at iTunes, Amazon, or eBay. That's why Flight 001 founders John Sencion and Brad John take every detail in their retail stores very seriously.

Flight 001 is all about the experience. They care deeply about the experience you have in the store and carefully select every product, whether it be a $6.00 lime green luggage tag or a $600 designer carry-on, to ensure you feel just as great once you arrive at your destination.

The company gets its name from the famous Pan Am Flight 001. The flight originated in San Francisco and continued for 46 hours, stopping in Hawaii, Tokyo, Hong Kong, Bangkok, Calcutta, Delhi, Beirut, Istanbul, Frankfurt, London, and finally landing in New York. From the late 1940s through the 1980s, Flight 001 was *the* flight for the sophisticated world traveler. Founders John and Sencion set out to create a retail experience worthy of the name. Every store features a curved interior, mimicking

the walls of an airplane fuselage. The sales desk looks like the ticket counter at an airport. It was important to Sencion that every aspect of the store design suggested First Class, from the walnut panels on the walls to the time zone clocks and top-notch customer service.

When the first store opened, one of the most unique features that came out of all of that attention to detail was a sense of intimacy, something you don't get in a large department store or discount retailer. The founders began to notice that people were exploring the store, rather than just running in and picking up what they came in for. This type of grazing is great for sales. When customers come in for a travel clock, they very often leave with something they didn't realize they needed—perhaps unique space-saving packing supplies, an interesting guide book, or a stylish document organizer.

Now in its tenth year, Flight 001 is rapidly opening new locations in selected cities in the United States. You definitely won't see them in a strip mall off the highway; that's something John feels very strongly about. While there's something for everyone in the store, their customers tend to be young, trendy, and affluent. These people prefer to shop on secondary streets with clusters of boutiques and coffee shops. "Our stores that do the best seem to be in the most hip, cool places," remarks John. "It's been a bit difficult because these kind of streets don't exist in every city in America." John acknowledges that if they want to continue to grow the company, they will eventually need to be open to other types of locations, even upscale malls, but as a relatively young brand, staying consistent in design and venue is important.

While Flight 001 has made their products available on several airline Web sites, they have yet to set up shop at the airport. With airport layovers, delays, and early arrival times getting longer, airports are rethinking the way they look at retail and are asking retailers to consider opening in their "air malls." In recent years, many larger airports have added celebrity chef restaurants, Aveda spas, wine bars, and upscale

clothing retailers. "I do think people are spending a lot more money in airports and not just picking up little items," says Brad John. "We do want to open up in airports, but we want to open up in cool airports."

Questions

1. What are the key components to Flight 001's retailing strategy?

2. Flight 001 was started in the late 1990s because the founders couldn't find all their travel needs in one place. Do you think they face any impending threat from so-called "category killers' as these stores continue to raise the bar in terms of products offered and style? Explain.

Video Case 15.2 — Integrated Marketing Communications at Ogden Publications

Integrated marketing communications is all about consistency. For some companies, that's pretty simple—slap your logo on the press kit and you're good to go. For Ogden Publications of Tulsa, Oklahoma, it's a little more complicated. The small publishing house has 13 titles, ranging from *Mother Earth News* and *Natural Home* to *Cappers,* a magazine about traditional American values and rural lifestyles, and everything from *Motorcycle Classics* to *Utne Reader,* a collection of articles about art, politics, and everything in between. In addition to its magazines, the company also offers merchandise and electronic companions to its titles.

It has been difficult to present an Ogden Publications "look," although brand manager Brandy Ernzen and Cherilyn Olmsted, Ogden's circulation and marketing director, consider this one of their many priorities as they take marketing at the company to the next level. "Each of the titles is so unique that they have their own brand identity," says Ernzen, but the common thread throughout all of Ogden's offerings is that "we tell people how to do really cool things." For Ernzen and Olmsted, the focus is on raising the bar on promotions, events, and ad sales as well as driving traffic to their Web properties and increasing circulation and awareness for each magazine.

As brand manager, Ernzen leads the charge to help maintain the integrity of all the public relations and marketing efforts at Ogden. It has actually become a pretty big job in recent years. The do-it-yourself trend started about ten years ago and has been energized by the increasing interest in environmentally and socially conscious consumerism and green living. These trends have sparked tons of interest with the company's core audiences as well as a new, more mainstream, demographic, but Ernzen is cautious. "I work really closely with all the different editorial staffs as well as advertising and the media," she says. "You're making sure everyone

on the different [marketing] teams is aware of what's going on." She is constantly running between the circulation department at *Herb Companion* and to the book warehouse to ask about a new cookbook or gardening guide to identify opportunities for tie-ins. She might then look for a green event or seminar on exotic heirloom tomatoes to raise awareness for their magazines, books, and products. That triggers a press release and, before you know it, "you can really maximize what you're doing to get the most results," says Ernzen. "There are higher newsstand sales and people are buying that product because it is a full campaign."

Communicating with consumers is really only one part of Ernzen's job. "Internal communications is also a big part that a lot of people don't think about," she says. The company recently developed an electronic newsletter to let people know what's going on in the company. "That way, everybody's on the same page." Ogden is not publicly traded, yet, like publicly traded companies listed on the stock market, it must extend the same consistency in communications and messaging to investors and the regulatory agencies watching over the market.

As Ogden continues to develop each magazine's Web site, a whole new series of challenges await. The Web sites are really another product rather than a Web version of the print counterpart, and finding an appropriate mix of content, editorial voice, and design style consistent with the branding of the print magazine can be challenging. "We're trying to have fairly loose standards, right now," says Ernzen. "Start small and evolve." The first plan of attack is to nail down the design standards, including colors, fonts, and use of buttons, icons, and layout. A larger Ogden style manual and training session is in the works for the ad sales department, production, the rest of the marketing, and PR team so everyone will be working from the same standard. "Right now, I'm that person," says Ernzen, "who takes care of everything and makes sure everything is lined up like it should be in terms of what logos we're using and colors and the whole nine yards."

Questions

1. Come up with a single marketing and PR campaign to promote three or four of Ogden's magazines. Visit www.ogdenpubs.com to learn more about each title.

2. What are the challenges of maintaining a consistent look and feel across different media? What are the editorial and design differences between a Web magazine and a print one?

Video Case 16.2 — Advertising and Public Relations at Ogden Publications

Ogden Publications of Topeka, Kansas has been working in the green space for decades. Its most popular magazine, *Mother Earth News,* reaches about 1.85 million readers annually. It was started in 1970 around the time of the very first Earth Day and features projects you can do to reduce your impact on the environment. The company's second most popular magazine, *Natural Home,* debuted in 1999. *Natural Home* is for those interested in "greening up" their suburban home. The key difference between the two magazines is that *Natural Home* is more focused on things one might buy—heating systems, cleaning products, appliances, and décor. *Mother Earth's* readers tend to be a bit more hands-on with their projects. Ogden also publishes nine other magazines, including *Motorcycle Classics* for collectors and *Utne Reader,* for alternative media junkies.

On Ogden's Web site, a quotation by publisher Bryan Welch makes the following claim: *As the world's largest publisher of magazines in the conscientious consumer category, Ogden Publications is deeply committed to the environment. Everything we do, from our editorial coverage to the ads we carry, offers readers the tools to live a healthy and sustainable lifestyle.*

Ogden Publications and *Mother Earth News* enjoy a reputation as an authority on sustainable living. This gives them a lot of street cred with their readers, but to potential advertisers, it's pretty scary. Welch admits it has been a challenge explaining to advertisers and partners that we're not "a bunch of holier than thou old hippies" ready to rip their product's greenness to shreds. On the upside, according to a 2006 study by leading advertising and marketing research firm, Signet Research, Inc., *Mother Earth* readers are on average 80–90 percent more likely to pay more money or go out of their way to purchase organic and earth-friendly products. Few publications, even mainstream magazines, could offer such a great advertising proposition.

Natural Home is an easier sell to more mainstream advertisers breaking into the green marketplace. On their pages you are likely to see Toyota Prius and Home Depot ads alongside a beautiful gourmet kitchen photo spread. A solid 95 percent of readers are willing to pay more for green products. They are almost exclusively female with a median age of 45. Many of them are married with children and own their own homes. Add to that a $90,000 average household income, and an advertiser can feel pretty good about presenting their bamboo flooring and European high-efficiency washer/dryer unit.

According to Welch, Ogden's main types of advertisers are either endemic or consumer. An endemic advertiser sells a product directly related to the editorial content of the magazine or Web site. Because the demographic for each of Ogden's magazines is pretty specific, the bulk of its ads are endemic. Endemic ads are fairly easy to sell, usually featuring a specific product—a low-flow showerhead, for instance. Advertisers know that 75 percent of the magazine's readership consists of building contractors who will likely purchase this product in the next six months. There is little gamble on the part of the showerhead manufacturer. Consumer advertising is more for products that know no specific demographic. You can sell soft drinks to pretty much anyone around the world, so it doesn't matter where you place the ad. Or does it? Do health-conscious readers with organic gardens and compost heaps in their backyards drink soft drinks? Not likely. If they do, they probably don't want to talk about it too much. The very sight of a soft drink ad in their favorite publication may cause them to stop purchasing the magazine. This puts publishers like Bryan Welch in a difficult position. Magazines are funded by ad sales and companies like Pepsi, Ford, or GE can afford big ad buys. All of these companies are looking to magazines like *Natural Home* for an "in" to their very desirable readers. And some of these large companies may be able to make inroads. "A lot of big consumer advertisers have a great authentic message. [They] have new products that are genuinely more enlightened," says Welch. He names Honda, Toyota, and Owens Corning as companies that have demonstrated a true commitment to improving the sustainability of their products. "Those are the folks we are trying to connect with," he says, "and our readers want to know about those products and bring them into their lives and the lives of their friends. That's the perfect formula."

Questions

1. Given that most of a magazine's revenue comes from ads, would you be willing to turn down a large consumer advertiser because your readers may disagree with their product or business practices? Discuss the ethical, PR, and financial implications of your decision.

2. What challenges do specialized magazines such as *Mother Earth News* face when trying to entice advertisers? Create a pitch to a potential green-product advertiser stating the benefits of advertising in *Mother Earth News.*

Video Case 17.2 — Personal Selling and Sales Promotion at Scholfield Honda

"We want our customer to have a long-term relationship with us," explains Vinnie Koc, a sales consultant with Scholfield Honda, "by providing them the service that Scholfield Honda has always provided."

Scholfield Honda of Wichita, Kansas, is the largest Honda dealer in the state, and for good reason. The *Wichita Business Journal* voted them one of 2007's Best Places to Work. Roger Scholfield, owner and general manager of the dealership, attributes their company's success, both internally and with its customers, to the simple fact that "we can train anybody to do anything, but we can't train you to be a happy person." To ensure that those on the front line of every sale are the best in the business, Scholfield takes the new hire process very seriously. Every interview is vetted by at least three senior people, and Scholfield meets each potential hire before a final decision is made. The result is a staff of sales and service people who actually want to come to work every day and who believe in the product they are selling. In sales, where trust and attitude is everything, that's a pretty big deal. Scholfield's policy of "hiring good attitudes" is simple. Lose your good attitude, and the door is just a few feet away.

"I love my job," says Koc. "I love Hondas, and my whole family drives a Honda. I love the product, and I love to help people." He also loves his generous commissions and bonuses from Scholfield and extra incentives provided by Honda. As anyone who has bought a car knows, bargaining is just part of the game, and at Scholfield, they try to make it less of a contest and more of a conversation. Koc estimates that about 75 percent of his customers know what they want and know what they want to pay. They've done research, checked Blue Book values, and looked at prices in different parts of the country. They don't want to mess around. Koc understands this and treats each customer with the same respect he would want. The dealership gives its sales consultants a reasonable amount of freedom to work with customers on price. Koc keeps a spreadsheet of prices of the different models and features for customers to compare and make a reasonable offer. He takes every offer to his managers and negotiates with them to find a price each party can live with. Sometimes, that may mean less commission for him, but he's making an investment in repeat customers and referrals.

A close second to the personal sales experience customers receive at Scholfield Honda is advertising. If you've ever been in the Wichita area, you've probably seen or heard a Scholfield Honda advertisement in print, on the radio, on television, or on a billboard. The company has its own on-site advertising agency, Scholfield Creative, dedicated to keeping every man, woman, and child abreast of sales, rebates, and incentives available at the dealership.

As soon as he sits with a client, Koc reviews all the sales. A large part of his business is driven by ads, but for those who may not be up on the latest deals, taking the time can make all the difference because "it might trigger something in their mind and we can go ahead and do the deal that day," he says.

While most walk into Scholfield Honda because of its reputation, they come back because of the experience. From test drive to trade in, every customer is treated like family, and Scholfield wouldn't have it any other way.

Questions

1. How important is sales force management in Scholfield Honda's overall success? Why?

2. Which step in the sales process is most important in a consumer's decision to purchase a car?

Video Case 18.2 — Pricing Concepts at Evogear.com

In 2007, Evo, the Seattle-based snow and water sports equipment e-tailer, made *Inc.* magazine's list of the 500 fastest-growing private companies. Founder Bryce Phillips started the company in 2001 out of his garage as a way to support his expensive ski habit. He rounded up and sold closeout and used skis in hopes that other enthusiasts would be looking for a good deal on good stuff. By 2005, Bryce had added snowboards, skateboards, wakeboards, and all the apparel and accessories one could need. He amped up the Web site and opened an 8,000-square-foot retail store in the funky Freemont neighborhood for those who want to try before they buy. The giant Seattle store also offered all the fashions you would need to look awesome in the lodge or bar after a long day on the slopes. His original three employees now numbered around 40 and, in addition to the bargains, he added top-of-the-line new stuff, too. The success of Evo and Evogear.com has been incredible, but Phillips isn't going back on what got him there in the first place: good stuff at a great price, hassle-free.

The online shopper is a different kind of shopper, and the

online retailer is different as well. The low overhead enjoyed by online retailers allows them to stock more inventory in the lower-rent warehouse. Larger orders translate into better discounts from the manufacturer or wholesaler. Evo is able to pass these savings on to the consumer.

While the hard-core rider or skier is more likely to want the latest and greatest models every year, most are happy with replacing their equipment every few years with a gently used or last year's model at an average savings of 30–75 percent off the original price. Evo maintains buying relationships with all the best brands—Burton, K2, Quicksilver, Rossignol, Powell, and many more—but also looks to resorts and pro shops for used rental and demo gear. They even hit up their own brick-and-mortar store to scoop last year's unsold merchandise. The big brands see Evo as a preferred customer and often give them first crack at their closeout and "sale" merchandise as well. This buying strategy puts Evo and Evogear.com right in front of both the pro and weekend warrior, while maintaining credibility with both.

One of the reasons why Evo enjoys such great relationships with its customers is its famous price match policy. Shop around—if you find a lower price anywhere, Evo will beat it by 5 percent. Just send customer service an email and as soon as they can verify the competitor's price, they'll lock in that lower price. Five percent might not sound like a lot, but as explained on Evo's Web site, if you see a product that lists on evogear.com for $400 offered elsewhere for $350, Evo will sell it to you for $332.50. That $67.50 could pay for your lift ticket.

What sets Evo's policy apart from many competitors is that the company will match *any* lower price (except eBay auctions), including promotions, rebates, and end-of-season blowout sales. The price guarantee doesn't stop with the competition. If Evo offers a lower price within 20 days of your purchase, they'll give you a store credit for the difference. If something goes on sale at a competitor within a week of your purchase, you get the difference, too. The way they see it, if you're *that* committed to finding a bargain, you deserve the break. It takes a little more effort on Evo's side, but "it's a small price to pay for a lifetime customer," says Molly Hawkins, affiliate program manager at Evo. "Maybe we'll sacrifice a little bit of margin, but in the end, hopefully, they'll be coming back for the rest of their life to buy their gear from us."

Questions

1. Do you believe Evo's pricing strategy for evogear.com meets the five pricing objectives outlined in the text? Provide examples for each objective.

2. Do you think the opening of the 8,000-square-foot brick-and-mortar store in Seattle distracts from their pricing strategy or enhances it? Why? To learn more about the brick-and-mortar store, visit culture.evogear.com/category/seattle/.

Video Case 19.2 — Pricing Strategy at Standard Renewable Energy

Green is hot, there's no doubt about it. Visit any large retailer from Albertson's to Wal-Mart, and you can fill your reusable shopping bag with hormone-free dairy products, organic cotton t-shirts, and environmentally friendly bathroom cleaner. Demand is so high that some chains have leveraged their purchasing power to offer store-brand organics and earth-friendly products at prices just a few cents higher than conventional products.

When the average consumer makes the decision to pay more for organic or earth-friendly products, several things should be considered. Will you get more enjoyment out of the free-range chicken or the frozen chicken nuggets? Would it be better for your health to use the bleach-free detergent? Speaking of towels, could you skip the Brawny and invest in real dishtowels to save a tree or two?

"Return on investment, that's one of our main points," says John Miggins, a Tulsa-based regional sales rep for Standard Renewable Energy (SRE). "It's on the front page of our proposal." For some customers, the return comes in the form of actual cash savings on electric bills. For others, it's more about doing good.

Headquartered in Houston, Texas, SRE specializes in providing alternative energy systems for residential, corporate, and government architects and builders. In addition to solar panels and inverters, the company designs geothermal and wind systems and performs energy audits at each customer site. The energy audit not only surveys the site and takes measurements, it also shows customers other areas in which they can improve their energy usage. SRE often asks its customers to consider new foam insulation and to update lighting and inefficient heating and air conditioning units. By providing customers with the big picture, SRE can help justify the initial expense of a new system and show how it can pay off in the long run.

"The people call me and say, 'I have a 2,000-square-foot house. What do I need?'" laments Miggins. It's just not that simple, unfortunately. Many factors must be considered—location and weather as well as expectations and energy needs, to name a few. Pricing on solar or wind systems is based on a per-watt number—use 900 kilowatts per month, and a solar system will probably cost about $40,000. Miggins understands that number can hit most consumers pretty hard, so he often helps soften the blow by offering a wind generator for about $17,500. The initial investment on wind is lower, but it can only provide about half the power. The decision then becomes pay now or pay later.

Emily Priddy and her husband own a modest, 900-square-foot home in Tulsa, Oklahoma. A teacher, writer, beekeeper, and self-described hippie child, protecting the environment has always been important to Emily. When she and her husband purchased their home, they knew they wanted to look for ways to reduce their impact on the earth, but solar seemed financially out of reach. "The last figure I had heard quoted fifteen years earlier was that a solar panel would cost you about eight hundred bucks," says Priddy. "And I knew we were going to need quite a few solar panels!" Concerned about the cost and what they could expect back in the form or lower energy bills, the couple figured they'd have to go at it one panel at a time. Working with Miggins at SRE, they learned that they could take a home improvement loan to get started and still come out on budget at the end of the month. Sure, it will take them 15 years to pay off the loan, but after that, they will be free of an electric bill. The biggest selling point for Emily is that she is well insulated from rising energy costs; her loan is fixed at $150 each month, and her electric bill went down by almost 90 percent in the first month. "It's a lot less whim-based and a lot more predictable," she says.

For customers like Emily who are in it for the long haul, return on investment is a definite selling point. "If that's the only reason they [homeowners] are talking to me, I usually pack up and go, because solar is 15, 17, even 20 years away, but on commercial, solar is very lucrative," says Miggins. For corporate customers, long-term financial planning is key, so a 15-year payback is really tempting. Because they can afford more elaborate systems to begin with, they can actually start profiting off their own energy generation earlier. Other incentives, like tax credits and bragging rights, only sweeten the deal.

Questions

1. How does John Miggins quote prices for SRE's solar systems?

2. How does SRE engage in psychological pricing?

Your Career in Marketing

One Marketer's Career

Imagine being in charge of marketing for a company that is a giant in the global consumer products market and the world's largest advertiser. That's the job of Marc Pritchard, the global marketing officer for Procter& Gamble. Think of all the major brands produced by P&G—from Cheer to Clairol, from Ivory to Olay, from Duracell to Gillette. P&G products are used by hundreds of millions of consumers in the United States and around the world. Pritchard—former president of strategy, productivity, and growth for the firm—now gets to test his marketing expertise in the largest arena.

Pritchard is not new to marketing at P&G. A decade ago, he spearheaded the firm's efforts to rejuvenate the Cover Girl brand, which P&G had purchased from Noxell. Although Cover Girl had previously been a hit with teens and young women in the late 1970s in part thanks to an advertising campaign featuring supermodel Christie Brinkley, the brand had languished for a number of years. Pritchard recognized that Cover Girl had solid brand equity, but it needed a facelift. He spearheaded development of a new campaign that carried the tagline "Easy, breezy, beautiful," and consumers rediscovered the brand.

Pritchard is also credited with launching a marketing strategy that later became known as the "consumer-driven supply network." This initiative is still in place at Procter & Gamble, and it involves identifying and removing redundant or unnecessary steps and procedures along the supply chain for more efficiency. "The idea, quite frankly, was that the consumer could care less about the value of a long, expensive supply chain," explains Phil Sheehey, P&G's global supply chain director for color cosmetics. The changes have now been incorporated into the rest of the company.

Marc Pritchard developed a new ad campaign with the tagline "Easy, breezy, beautiful" to give Cover Girl a new look.

© Image courtesy of The Advertising Archives

In his new duties, Pritchard follows in the footsteps of James R. Stengel, credited with taking P&G to the next level, strengthening its brands worldwide. To ease the transition, Pritchard and Stengel worked together for several years before Stengel retired and Pritchard stepped into the position. The company's top executives are enthusiastic about Pritchard's expertise and abilities. "His deep knowledge and experience in branding, innovation, and go-to-market capability will enable [Pritchard] to drive ongoing brand-building excellence," says chairman and CEO A.G. Lafley.

Pritchard faces many challenges in piloting the marketing function at P&G, which spent more than $7.9 billion on its advertising services worldwide in a recent year. P&G products touch the lives of an estimated 3 billion people in some way each day. Whether you drink a cup of Folger's coffee or do a load of laundry washed in Tide, it is likely you also will have contact with a P&G product sometime today. Marc Pritchard knows this, and he intends to use every resource and strategy he can possibly muster to ensure that you continue to rely on P&G products in the future.[1]

overview

• Congratulations on your decision to take this course.

As a consumer, you already know marketing is a pervasive element in our lives. In one form or another, it reaches every person. This course informed you about the different types of marketing messages, showed you how they are created, and helped you

> **briefly** speaking
>
> "People are definitely a company's greatest asset. It doesn't make any difference whether the product is cars or cosmetics. A company is only as good as the people it keeps."
>
> **—Mary Kay Ash (1915–2001)**
> FOUNDER, MARY KAY COSMETICS

understand the impact they have.

As you have seen throughout this course, marketing activities are interwoven in daily business processes, helping develop useful products consumers need, pricing them for a fair profit, promoting them so consumers are aware of their availability, and bringing them to market. But marketing also has a huge impact on society and the economy in general.

Half of the total cost consumers pay for Wii gaming consoles goes to marketing costs.

© Robyn Beck/AFP/Getty Images

MARKETING COSTS ARE A BIG COMPONENT OF A PRODUCT'S TOTAL BUDGET

Approximately 50 percent of the total costs of products you buy are marketing costs. Half of the $250 you pay for a Wii gaming console goes to marketing costs—making sure you are aware of Wii's existence and its capabilities and persuading you to buy it. Yes, the cost of the high-tech features is an important component, as is the plastic console, the remote, and interactive games. But marketing expenses also figure into the total cost of the product. The same is true of that Mini Cooper you have your eye on.

But costs alone do not indicate the value of marketing to the success of a product. Marketing sends important messages to consumers and businesses, usually expanding overall sales and spreading production costs over more items sold, reducing the total cost to bring the product to market.

MARKETERS CONTRIBUTE TO SOCIETY AS WELL AS TO INDIVIDUAL EMPLOYERS

Marketing decisions affect everyone's welfare. How much quality should be built into a product? Will people buy a safer product if it costs twice as much as the current version? Should every community adopt recycling programs? Because ethics and social responsibility are critical factors in creating long-term relationships with consumers, business customers, and the community, marketers must strive to exceed customer and government expectations of ethical behavior. The "Solving an Ethical Controversy" features included in every chapter of this book got you thinking about ethical issues in marketing and increased your awareness of the importance of maintaining high ethical standards in every dimension of marketing. These features allowed you to examine such current issues as online property rights, greenwashing (false marketing claims), fair trade, marketing to seniors, spam on cell phones, unfair targeting of pork products, control of marketing messages, and airline surcharges, to name a few. The topics also made good springboards for discussion between you and your classmates.

Not only does marketing influence numerous facets of our daily lives, but decisions regarding marketing activities also affect everyone's welfare. Opportunities to advance to more responsible decision-making positions often come sooner in marketing than in most occupations. This combination of challenges and opportunities has made marketing one of the most popular fields of academic study.

Although many paths can lead to the top of the corporate ladder, marketing remains one of the strongest and most popular. The growing global economy depends on proven market leaders in winning the fight to increase a firm's worldwide market shares. Marketing provides a solid background for developing the long-term, loyal relationships with customers that are necessary for success in the global marketplace.

YOU MAY CHOOSE A CAREER IN MARKETING

Even if you aren't sure about a career now, this course could have helped you decide on a path in marketing. In fact, of the many career paths chosen by business graduates, marketing is the largest employment category in the U.S. labor force, and job growth in the field is expected to accelerate. All firms must somehow get their goods and services into the hands of customers profitably, and doing so is becoming increasingly challenging. So marketing plays a significant role in the survival and growth of all companies—which means that, as a field, it will continue to grow.

The U.S. Bureau of Labor Statistics anticipates stiff competition for desirable jobs. College graduates having "related experience, a high level of creativity, strong communication skills, and computer skills" stand the best chance of landing these jobs. These job candidates can expect high earnings along with travel and long working hours, including evenings and weekends.[2]

Your Quest for a Successful, Rewarding Career

Selecting a career is an important life decision—your career will determine such things as where you live, how much money you make, and for what kind of company you work. That's why *Contemporary Marketing* discusses the best ways to approach career decisions and to prepare for an *entry-level position*—your first permanent employment after leaving school. We also look at a range of marketing careers and describe employment opportunities in fields related to each major part of the text.

The good news is that the job market is healthy. The average starting salary for marketing graduates is about $42,000.[3] As mentioned earlier, the field of marketing is the largest area of employment in the United States—and employers are continuing to hire. This positive outlook

briefly speaking

"Knowing others is wisdom, knowing yourself is enlightenment."

—Lao Tzu
(600 B.C.–531 B.C.)
FOUNDER OF TAOISM,
AUTHOR OF *TAO TE CHING*

does *not* mean competition isn't tough or you can be casual in your approach to your first job. You are not guaranteed anything. But if you are creative, hardworking, and determined—and if you learn everything you can about business and marketing before you begin your search—you are likely to land a good entry-level position at a company that suits you. In your coursework, you have been introduced to all the key functional areas of marketing. Armed with this knowledge, you should be able to identify areas of employment you may wish to pursue.

Education improves your prospects of finding and keeping the right job. Recent college graduates can earn nearly twice what workers with high school diplomas earn. Better-educated graduates also find jobs more quickly than others, and they have much lower unemployment rates.[4] Applying yourself in class and expanding your experiences through career-directed volunteer efforts, part-time and summer jobs, and high-quality internships—and selecting the right major—are significant steps on your way toward improving these salary statistics when you launch your career.

In addition to taking classes, try to gain related experience either through a job or by participating in campus organizations. Internships, summer and part-time jobs, and volunteer activities on campus and in your community can also give you valuable hands-on experience while you pursue your education. Work-related experience, whether paid or volunteer, lets a potential employer know you are serious about pursuing your career. It also helps you decide on your own path.

This guide to planning your career provides you with a brief look at the trends and opportunities available for future marketers in an increasingly diversified, professional field. It describes essential elements of an effective résumé and discusses the latest trends in electronic job searches. Finally, it includes a listing of primary marketing information sources that contain answers to many of the questions typically asked by applicants. This information will provide valuable career-planning assistance in this and other future courses, whether your career plans involve marketing or you decide to major in another field.

Many of the marketing positions you read about throughout this text are described here. Specifically, the job summaries describe the responsibilities and duties typically required as well as the usual career path for each of these marketing-related positions. You might follow a traditional career path, or you might wind up in one of the new types of marketing jobs emerging such as blogging for a particular company or organization. Richard Brewer-Hay spent years working for a media company and in public relations before eBay recruited him to write an unedited blog to help improve the company's image among buyers and sellers. He immediately noted the most important feature of the blog would be its direct link to eBay users. When asked about the topics he would cover, he responded, "You name it, we're going to blog it. . . . I really want it to be a conversation between eBay and the outside world—an open conversation."[5]

Marketing your skills to a prospective employer is much the same as marketing a product to a consumer. Increasingly, job seekers are selling their skills online, bypassing intermediaries such as employment agencies and leveling the playing field between applicant and potential employer. The greatest challenge for online job seekers is learning how to market themselves.

Despite the vast databases and fancy tools of the giant career sites such as Monster.com, Yahoo!HotJobs, and CareerBuilder.com, which may receive hundreds of thousands of visits each day, savvy job seekers also zero in on niche boards offering more focused listings. You can find sites that focus specifically on sales, such as SalesJobs.com, and those that emphasize positions for female profession-

Huge career sites, including Yahoo!HotJobs, receive hundreds of thousands of visits each day.

© Richard B. Levine/Newscom

als, such as WomenSportsJobs.com.[6] Regardless of which type of online job board you use—general or specific—be aware that this medium is the most often used recruiting tool among employers for hiring managers at smaller and mid-sized companies.[7]

In many instances, students seeking interviews with specific employers or in certain geographic locations go directly to the employer's or region's Web site to learn of available positions. Most employers include an employment site as part of their home page. Some offer virtual tours of what it is like to work for the firm. For example, the Enterprise Rent-a-Car Web site features profiles of young assistant managers as they perform daily work activities. The employees answer several questions about their jobs and the abilities candidates need to be a successful employee at Enterprise. The site also outlines the skills employees gain while working there, the friendships formed among workers, opportunities for involvement in the community, the management training program, and available internships.[8]

The key to finding the job you want is letting the market know who you are and what you can do. While few college graduates are hired directly based on their response to an online listing, this approach often is an important first step in zeroing in on specific employers of interest and then soliciting interviews that may lead to job offers. So you should familiarize yourself with the way online job sites work, including those of specific companies.

As you begin your career, you will apply many of the principles and concepts discussed in this text, including how to target a market, capitalize on brand equity, position a product, and use marketing research techniques. Even in jobs that seem remote from the marketing discipline, this knowledge will help you stay focused on the most important aspect of business: the consumer.

Standing Out from the Crowd of Job Seekers

Because high-quality employees provide companies the edge they need in competitive markets, employers need to be choosy in deciding which applicants will make the cut, be interviewed, and possibly be offered a position. And often the applicant's accumulated job and leadership experiences will be key criteria in determining whether he or she is given serious consideration as a potential employee.

Some students continue their studies following graduation and pursue an MBA degree or enter a master's program specially suited to their career goals. But many enter the job market right away, perhaps pursuing an advanced degree later. Experience is one factor in a prospective employee's favor, and some activities that enhance a candidate's profile are internships and volunteering.

INTERNSHIPS PROVIDE VALUABLE WORK EXPERIENCE

Internships have been described as a critical link in bridging the theory–practice educational gap. They help carry students between the academic present and the professional future. They provide students with an opportunity for learning how classroom theory is applied in real-world business environments.

Internships are gaining popularity for both employers and students or recent grads. In fact, interning is now the number one recruiting technique among employers, and 60 percent of students are hired for full-time jobs from their internships. Some internships include a salary, which may be as high as $15 to $25 per hour, depending on the industry and the level of education reached by the student. Other internships are unpaid, which means students must find other ways of earning money. But the majority of students who participate in unpaid internships still believe the experience gained is much more important than a salary would have been. They cite the actual work experience, along with references and contacts in the industry, as more valuable than pay. Employers note the importance of their relationship with interns. "Employers see their internship programs as an effective way of identifying and connecting with talent," observes Marilyn Mackes, executive director of the National Association of Colleges and Employers (NACE). "These programs are a way for the employer and the intern to test each other to see if there is a good match." Mackes also notes that employers "prize relevant work experience even if the student served an internship with another organization."[9]

Start your search for an internship at your college placement office or library. Some college Web sites have catalogs of internships available through organizations such as the American Association of Advertising Agencies, the Inroads Minority Internship Program, and the Washington Center

Résumé Blunders

The following is a list of errors that have appeared in résumés, job applications, and cover letters received by Monster.com and Yahoo!Hot Jobs:

- "Suspected to graduate early next year."

- "I will accept nothing less than $18 annually."

- "Qualifications: No education or experience."

- "Fired because I fought for lower pay."

- "I am a rabid typist."

- "I am relatively intelligent, obedient, and loyal as a puppy."

- "Finished 8th in my high school graduating class of 10."

- "Please disregard the enclosed resume—it is terribly out of date."

- "If U hire me, U will not have any regrets!"

Sources: "Resume Faux Pas," *Monster Career Center*, resume.monster.com, accessed June 10, 2009; Kim Isaacs, "Common Resume Blunders," *Monster Career Advice*, career-advice.monster.com, accessed September 3, 2008; Robert Half International, "Real-Life Resume Blunders to Avoid," *Yahoo!Hot Jobs*, hotjobs.yahoo.com, accessed September 3, 2008.

for Internships and Academic Seminars.[10] Also check with the alumni office, which may have a listing of alumni willing to talk with seniors or recent grads about their fields. You can talk with your instructors, visit the Web sites of companies that interest you, and check your local bookstore for career and internship reference guides.

YOUR RÉSUMÉ

Writing a résumé is a vital task, but it doesn't need to be daunting. Your résumé is like a verbal snapshot of you. It tells a potential employer about you, your credentials, and your goals. It provides an all-important first impression of you and may be the only written record available with which an employer can make a decision about you. Your résumé is a concise summary of your academic, professional, and personal accomplishments; it makes focused statements about you as a student and potential employee.

Three basic formats are used in preparing a résumé. A *chronological résumé* arranges information in reverse chronological order, emphasizing job titles and organizations and describing responsibilities held and duties performed. This format highlights continuity and career growth. A *functional résumé* accents accomplishments and strengths, placing less emphasis on job titles and work history, and often omits job descriptions. A functional résumé prepared by a recent graduate is shown in Figure 1. Some applicants use a *combined résumé* format, which emphasizes skills first, followed by employment history. This format highlights a candidate's potential and suits students who often have little experience directly related to their desired positions.

Regardless of which format you choose, all résumés contain certain information. And they all have the same goal: to interest an employer enough to invite you to apply formally for a job and conduct an interview. A résumé should be concise—no more than a single page. Before writing your résumé, take the time to outline your goals, skills, abilities, education, and work experience and list any relevant volunteer or extracurricular activities. You can pare these down later, but having them in front of you will make it easier to build your final résumé.

Your contact information should appear at the top of the page: full name, address, phone number, and e-mail address. If your e-mail username is "MachoDude" or "SnowboardDoll," replace it with one related to your real name or location to persuade employers to take you seriously. Likewise, avoid using a nickname. Even if all of your friends call you Smitty, cite your name as John A. Smith.

A statement of goals usually follows. Try to be somewhat specific with it. You can say, "My goal is to obtain an entry-level marketing position where I can apply my analytical and organiza-

briefly speaking

"Ambition is the path to success. Persistence is the vehicle you arrive in."

—**Bill Bradley (b. 1943)**
FORMER U.S. SENATOR, NBA PLAYER, AND U.S. OLYMPIAN

Roberto Chavez
Two Seaside Drive, Apt. 3A
Los Angeles, CA 90026
215-555-7092
RCHAVEZ@hotmail.com

Objective
Joining a growth-oriented company that values highly productive employees. Seeking an opportunity that leads to senior merchandising position.

Professional Experience
Administration
Management responsibilities in a major retail buying office included coordinating vendor relation efforts. Supervised assistant buyers.

Category Management
Experience in buying home improvement and sport, recreation, and fitness categories.

Planning
Leader of a team charged with reviewing the company's annual vendor evaluation program.

Problem Solving
Successfully developed a program to improve margins in the tennis, golf, and fishing product categories.

Work Experience
Senior Buyer
Southern California Department Stores   2010–Present

Merchandiser
Pacific Discount Stores, a division of Southern California
Department Stores   2008–2010

Education
Bachelor of Science degree in business
Double major in marketing and retailing
California State University–San Bernardino   2006–2010

Computer Skills
Proficient with IBM-compatible computers and related software, including spreadsheets, graphics, desktop publishing, and word processing.
Packages: Microsoft Word, Excel, PowerPoint, Adobe PageMaker, CorelDRAW

Familiar with Adobe Photoshop and the Macintosh.

Language Skills
Fluent in speaking and writing Spanish.

figure 1
Functional Résumé

tional skills." Don't state that your goal is to become CEO of the company—that's a long way off, and it doesn't apply to the job at hand.

Your education information generally comes next. State your most recent level of education first. There is no need to list high school unless you attended a specialized school or received particular honors. Include your degree, academic honors, and grade point average if it is above 3.0.

State your work history, including employment, internships, and related volunteer work. Include the name of the organization, the dates you worked there, your job title, and your responsibilities on the job. Provide a statement of your skills such as leadership, managing others, computer software knowledge, and the like. At the end of your résumé, add a note that you will furnish references on request—do *not* include your references' names and contact information on your résumé.

briefly
speaking

"A résumé is a balance sheet without any liabilities."

—Robert Half
(1918–2001)
AMERICAN PERSONNEL
AGENCY EXECUTIVE

Whether yours is a traditional résumé on paper or posted on an Internet résumé listing, the important point to remember in creating an effective résumé is to present the most relevant information in a clear, concise manner that emphasizes your best attributes.

COVER LETTER

Your potential employer typically is first introduced to you through a cover letter. Like gift wrapping on a present, a cover letter should attract attention and interest about what is inside. Your letter should be addressed to a specific person, not "to whom it may concern." It should include information about the job for which you are applying, why you are interested in it, a brief summary of your top accomplishments or skills, and a note that you are available for an interview. Close your letter by thanking the person for his or her time and consideration.

Here are a few additional tips to guide you.

Do

▷ Keep your letter to a single page.

▷ Customize the letter to the company or person for whom it is intended, even though you may be writing 20 such letters. Send an original letter, not a photocopy.

▷ Proofread it several times, making sure there are no typos.

▷ Remember to sign your letter.

▷ Include your contact information, including cell phone number and e-mail address.

Don't

▷ Use slang or rude language.

▷ Rehash your résumé.

▷ Address the letter "Gentlemen" or "Dear Sirs." The person reading the letter might be a woman. Instead, take the time to find out exactly to whom you should send your materials.

▷ Challenge the reader to hire you; nor should you appear desperate. Instead, briefly state what you can contribute to the workplace.[11]

LETTERS OF RECOMMENDATION

Letters of recommendation serve as testimonials to your performance in academic and work settings. The best references provide information relevant to the desired industry or marketing specialty as well as opinions of your skills, abilities, and character. You can obtain references from former or current employers, supervisors from volunteer experiences, instructors, and others who can attest to your academic and professional competencies.

An effective letter of recommendation typically contains the following elements:

1. Statement of the length and nature of the relationship between the writer and the job candidate

2. Description of the candidate's academic and career growth potential

3. Review of important achievements

4. Evaluation of personal characteristics (what kind of colleague the candidate will make)

5. Summary of the candidate's outstanding strengths and abilities

Because letters of recommendation take time and effort, it helps to provide a résumé and any other information relevant to the recommendation, along with a stamped, addressed (typed) envelope. When requesting letters of recommendation, allow ample time for your references to compose them—as long as a month is not unusual.

In addition to including a cover letter, résumé, and letters of recommendation, you should include photocopies of transcripts, writing samples, or other examples of work completed. For instance, if you are applying for a position in public relations, advertising, or sports marketing, you may want to include examples of professional writing, graphics, and audiovisual media to support written evidence of your credentials. Research and service projects that resulted in published or unpublished articles may also enhance your portfolio.

- Use a standard typeface such as Times, Courier, or Arial. Stick with 12-pt to 14-pt type size. Single space the text, but double space where appropriate between sections. The text should be clean and easy to read.

- Use punctuation where necessary, but avoid graphics, shading, underlines, or other visual distractions.

- Use white paper and black type; avoid the temptation to include color.

- Use keywords that will attract the reader's attention whether the résumé is scanned into a electronic system, indexed for an online search, or printed on paper to be distributed to the appropriate people. Examples might include *marketing, entry-level, Web-based training (WBT),* or *Microsoft Office.*

- Follow the format required by the employer or job site. Most online forms are submitted in chronological format, which pinpoints recent work history.

- A plain text file that is ready to copy and paste onto an online form or to print out is the easiest for most recipients to handle. However, if you are applying for a position in the visual arts or programming field, you may create an HTML version of your résumé.

figure 2

Tips for Preparing an Electronic Résumé

Sources: "Prepare Your Résumé for E-mail and Online Posting," *The Riley Guide: Résumés & Cover Letters,* www.rileyguide.com, accessed June 10, 2009; "Scannable Résumés," *Proven Resumes.com,* www.provenresumes.com, accessed September 3, 2008; "Scannable Résumé Design," *Technical Job Search.com,* technicaljobsearch.com, accessed September 3, 2008.

USING PAPERLESS SYSTEMS

Most large firms have moved toward electronic (paperless) résumé processing and applicant-tracking systems. In fact, some human resource experts say outright that the fastest way to get your résumé to the correct person is to use the firm's own online application system. So it's best to prepare a résumé compatible with these systems. Figure 2 contains a number of tips for preparing an effective, readable, technology-compatible résumé.

In addition, keep in mind a few overall rules. First, read the directions for completing and transmitting your résumé or application carefully—and follow them to the letter. If you try to stand out by doing something different, your application will probably be lost or ignored or you may be viewed as someone who might not follow instructions on the job. Second, complete all possible fields, even those not required. Third, if the firm offers an optional online assessment test, take it. An employer will appreciate your initiative and can evaluate some of your skills immediately.

Finally, choose effective keywords for your résumé. Employers who review electronic résumés posted on their sites and on big boards save time by using computers to search for keywords in job titles, job descriptions, or résumés to narrow the search. In fact, *manager* is the number one word for which companies search. Regardless of the position you seek, one key to an effective electronic résumé is to use exact words and phrases, emphasizing nouns rather than the action verbs you are likely to use in a print-only résumé. For example, a company looking for a marketing account manager with experience in Microsoft Office applications such as Word and Excel may conduct computer searches only for résumés that include the job title and the three software programs.

Learning More about Job Opportunities

As you continue with your application and selection process, study the various employment opportunities you have identified. Obviously, you will like some more than others, but keep an open mind; remember, this is the beginning of a long career. Examine a number of factors when assessing each job possibility:

1. Actual job responsibilities

2. Industry characteristics

3. Nature of the company

4. Geographic location

briefly speaking

"Put it to them briefly so they will read it; picturesquely, so they will remember it—and, above all, accurately, so they will be guided by its light."

—**Joseph Pulitzer (1847–1911)** AMERICAN JOURNALIST

5. Salary and opportunities for advancement

6. The contribution the job is likely to make to your long-range career opportunities

Many job applicants consider only the most striking features of a job, perhaps its location, or the salary offered. However, a comprehensive review of job openings will give you a more balanced perspective of the overall employment opportunity, including both long- and short-run factors.

JOB INTERVIEWS

Your first goal in your job search is to land an interview with a prospective employer. If the experience is new to you and you feel uncertain or nervous, you can do a lot to turn those feelings into confidence.

Preparing for the Interview

Do your homework. Learn as much as you can about the company, the industry in which it operates, the goods or services it offers, the working environment, and the like. If you are well prepared for the questions you are asked—and prepared to ask educated questions—you are much more likely to have a positive interview experience. You can prepare by researching the following basic information about the firm:

▷ How long has the firm been in business?

▷ In what industry does the firm operate? What is its role within the industry?

▷ Who are the firm's customers? Who are its competitors?

▷ How is the firm organized? How many people work there? Where are its headquarters? Does it have other offices and production facilities located around the nation or around the world?

▷ What is the company's mission? Does the company have a written code of ethics?

This information is useful in several ways. Not only will it increase your confidence about the interview, but it may also help you weed out any firms that might not be a good fit for you. You've also shown the interviewer you are motivated enough to come to the discussion prepared.

You can find this information in many of the same places you looked initially for information about companies at the beginning of your job search. Your school's career center, library, and, most important, the company's own Web site will have much of the information you need. In addition, you can find brief company profiles on business sites such as Hoovers.com, and don't forget to check the various business magazines.

What to Expect in an Interview

You've made the interview appointment, done your research on the company, and chosen the right attire for the occasion according to suggestions provided in the "Etiquette Tips for Marketing Professionals" feature. What's next?

Prepare yourself for the questions you will likely be asked. As you gain experience in interviewing, you will recognize variations of similar questions and be able to answer them comfortably. An interviewer needs to get to know you in a short period of time, so he or she will ask questions that deal with your personality, your life and work experience, and decision-making or problem-solving style. Here are a few examples:

When you prepare for an interview, think about questions you will likely be asked.

© Chabruken/Taxi/Getty Images

Etiquette Tips for Marketing Professionals

How to Dress for Your Job Interview

Landing a job interview is a big step on the road to starting your chosen career. You can make the most of the opportunity to create a good impression by presenting yourself in a professional way. You need to be prepared with knowledge about the company, project confidence and a willingness to learn, and convey that you will be a reliable employee. You also need to look the part. After all, you will be representing your company even if you do not deal directly with its customers.

Unless you are applying for a job that requires certain clothing—say, a uniform or outdoor work clothes—on most days you will be wearing business attire. So you should arrive at your interview in the clothing you would likely wear to work. The following suggestions will serve you well.

- *Dress conservatively.* A conservative suit is best for both men and women, with a long-sleeved shirt or blouse. Men should choose a traditional tie with a simple pattern and muted colors. Keep conventional jewelry and makeup to an unnoticeable minimum. Cover any tattoos and limit pierced jewelry to earrings.

- *Your clothes should be clean and pressed.* Be sure you have no runs in stockings or threadbare socks. Shoes should be clean and polished. Avoid open-toed shoes, sandals, or wild colors.

- *Be sure your hair is trimmed, washed, and well groomed.* Wear your hair in a neat, professional style—a sleek, simple cut or combed into place. Men should be clean shaven or at least have trimmed mustaches or beards.

- *Make sure your overall appearance is clean and classic.* Be sure your fingernails are clean and short. If you wear polish, use a conservative color or clear. Any makeup should be understated, not attract attention.

- *Avoid cologne or perfume.* Some people are allergic to scents, particularly in closed areas such as offices and conference rooms.

- *Empty your pockets.* Don't jingle coins, keys, or a cell phone. In addition, turn off any cell phones or pagers.

- *Carry a lightweight portfolio, briefcase, or tote.* You'll want to be able to supply an extra copy of your résumé, a sample of your writing, or copies of ads you've created.

Overall, you want to present a neat, clean, professional, and appealing appearance. Looking professional is one of the first steps to conducting a successful interview and landing a job. So think about how professionals conduct themselves—and dress accordingly. No one expects you to splurge on an expensive suit or briefcase as you start your career. But you can convey yourself as the professional you know you're going to be.

Sources: Jane Harvey, "Dressing for the Job Interview," *AllBusiness.com*, www.allbusiness.com, accessed June 10, 2009; "Dressing for a Job Interview," *College Grad.com*, www.collegegrad.com, accessed September 3, 2008; Randall S. Hansen, Ph.D., "When Job-Hunting: Dress for Success," *Quintessential Careers*, www.quintcareers.com, accessed September 3, 2008; Alison Doyle, "How to Dress for a Job Interview," *About.com*, jobsearch.about.com, accessed September 3, 2008.

▷ Why did you apply for this job? Why do you want this job?

▷ What are the requirements of the job as you understand them?

▷ What are your key strengths? What are your weaknesses?

▷ Are you an organized person? How do you manage your time?

▷ What were your responsibilities on your last job or internship? How would they apply here?

▷ What were your biggest successes or failures—in school or work?

▷ How do you make important decisions? How do you function under pressure?

▷ What do you know about this company?

▷ What are your most important long-term goals?[12]

To prepare effective answers, ask a friend or family member to role-play the interview with you, asking questions so you have an opportunity to hear yourself respond out loud before the actual interview.

When you arrive for your interview, be sure to confirm the name of the person (or people) who will conduct the interview. If this person is with the human resource department and your interview goes well, he or she will probably recommend you to a manager or supervisor for further interviewing. Some hiring decisions are made by a single supervisor, while others result from joint interviews conducted by both human resource personnel and the immediate supervisor of the prospective employee.

During a typical interview, the interviewer usually talks little. This approach, referred to as an *open-ended interview,* forces you to talk about yourself and your career goals. This is a major reason why it is important to arrive prepared. If you appear uncertain or disorganized in your thinking, the interviewer may surmise that you have not prepared or aren't serious about the job. Keep the conversation on target; don't ramble on and on. You may also ask questions of the interviewer, so be sure to listen carefully to the responses. Appropriate questions include those about job responsibilities, training, and long-range opportunities for advancement. Don't ask when you will get a raise or promotion or how many vacation days you will receive. In the end, a successful interview represents a mutual exchange of information.

A successful first interview may result in an invitation to return to take a skills test, tour the building, or even meet other managers and coworkers. All of these experiences point toward getting the right fit between a company and its potential employees. On the other hand, even after a good interview, you may not be asked back. Do not consider this a personal rejection—the job market is competitive, and companies must make their selections carefully to achieve the best match. It might not have been the right firm or job for you in the long run, and the interviewer realized this. Treat each job application and interview as a chance to build confidence and experience—and eventually, the right job will be yours.

EMPLOYMENT DECISIONS

By now, a firm that is still considering you as a strong candidate knows quite a bit about you. You should also know a lot about the company and whether you want to work there. When the interview process is complete, you may be offered a position with the firm. Your decision to accept the offer should depend on a variety of factors, including the following:

▷ Do you want to work in this industry?

▷ Do you want to be part of the company's mission? Would you be proud to work for this company?

▷ Could this particular job lead to other opportunities within the company?

▷ Will you be able to work well with your coworkers and supervisors?

▷ Can you already see ways you can learn and contribute your best efforts to the company?

If you are offered the job and decide to accept it, congratulations! Approach your new job with professionalism, creativity, and a willingness to learn. You are on your way to a successful career in marketing.

Marketing Positions

To survive and grow, an organization must market its goods or services. Marketing responsibilities vary among organizations and industries. In a small firm, the owner or president may assume many of the company's marketing responsibilities. A large firm needs experienced sales, marketing, and advertising managers, as well as staff, to coordinate these activities. The "Career Path" features that follow outline major marketing positions, providing job descriptions and projected career paths for each. Each position is also cross-referenced to the chapter in this text that discusses the marketing area in detail.

Career Path 1: Marketing, Advertising, Product, and Public Relations Managers

Related Chapters: Chapters 1 and 2 (marketing); Chapters 11 and 12 (product); Chapters 15 and 16 (advertising and public relations)

Marketing management spans a range of positions, including vice president of marketing, marketing manager, sales manager, product manager, advertising manager, promotion manager, and public relations manager. The vice president directs the firm's overall marketing policy, and all other managers report through channels to this person. Sales managers direct the efforts of sales professionals by assigning territories, establishing goals, developing training programs, and supervising local sales managers and their personnel. Advertising managers oversee account services, creative services, and media services departments. Promotion managers direct promotional programs that combine advertising with purchase incentives designed to increase the sales of the firm's goods or services. Public relations managers communicate with the firm's various publics, conduct publicity programs, and supervise the specialists who implement these programs.

Job Description

As with senior management positions in production, finance, and other areas, top marketing management positions often involve long hours and regular travel. Work under pressure is also common to solve problems and meet deadlines. For sales managers, job transfers between headquarters and regional offices may disrupt one's personal life. Nearly 600,000 marketing, advertising, promotions, public relations, and sales managers are currently employed in the United States. The Bureau of Labor Statistics estimates the number of these jobs will increase faster than average through the year 2016.[13]

Career Path

A degree in business administration, preferably with a concentration in marketing, usually is preferred for these positions, but for advertising positions, some employers want a bachelor's degree in advertising or journalism. Those looking for jobs in public relations should have a bachelor's degree in public relations or journalism. In highly technical industries, such as computers, chemicals, and electronics, employers may look for bachelor's degrees in science or engineering combined with business courses or a master's degree in business administration. Liberal arts students can also find many opportunities, especially if they have business minors. Most managers are promoted from positions such as sales representatives, product or brand specialists, and advertising specialists within their organizations. Skills or traits most desirable for these jobs include high motivation levels, maturity, creativity, resistance to stress, flexibility, and the ability to communicate persuasively. In addition, these candidates must be willing to work long hours, manage their time well, and handle meetings with clients and media representatives when necessary.[14]

Career Path 2: Sales Representatives and Sales Managers

Related Chapter: Chapter 17

Millions of items are bought and sold every day. The people in the firm who carry out this activity may have a variety of titles—sales representative, account manager, manufacturer's representative, sales engineer, sales agent, retail salesperson, wholesale sales representative, and service sales representative. Sales managers typically are selected from people in the current sales force who have demonstrated they possess the managerial skills needed to lead teams of sales representatives. In addition, many organizations require all marketing professionals to spend some time in the field to experience the market firsthand and to understand the challenges faced by front-line personnel.

Job Description

Salespeople usually develop prospective client lists, meet with current and prospective customers to discuss the firm's products, and then follow up to answer questions and supply additional information. By knowing the business needs of each customer, the sales representative can identify products that best satisfy these needs. After a customer purchase, they are likely to revisit their customers to ensure the products are meeting the customers' needs and to explore further business opportunities or referrals provided by satisfied buyers. Some sales of technical products involve lengthy interactions. In these cases, a salesperson may work with several clients simultaneously over a large geographic area. Those responsible for large territories may spend most of their workdays on the phone, receiving and sending e-mail messages or traveling to customers' locations. Sales managers direct a firm's sales program. They manage the sales force by assigning territories, setting goals, and implementing training programs for sales staff. Managers also review the performance of sales representatives and guide them toward improvement. The Bureau of Labor Statistics projects average job growth in this category, with keen competition for top jobs through the year 2016. Currently, there are more than 318,000 sales managers in the United States.[15]

Work as a sales representative or sales manager can be rewarding for those who enjoy interacting with people, are invigorated by competition, and feel energized by the challenge of expanding sales in their territories. Successful sales professionals—both individual sales reps and sales managers—should be goal oriented, persuasive, self-motivated, and independent. In addition, patience and perseverance are important qualities.

Career Path

The background needed for a position in sales varies according to the product line and market. Most professional sales jobs require a college degree, preferably with a major in business administration or marketing. Creativity and strong communications skills are a plus. Many companies run their own formal training programs that can last up to two years for sales representatives in technical industries. This training may take place in a classroom, in the field with a mentor, or most often using a combination of both methods. Sales managers usually are promoted from the field; they are likely to include successful sales representatives who exhibit managerial skills and promise. Sales management positions begin at a local or district level, then advance to positions of increased authority and responsibility such as area, regional, national, and international sales manager.[16]

Career Path 3: Advertising Specialists

Related Chapters: Chapters 15 and 16

Most companies, especially firms serving consumer markets, maintain small groups of advertising specialists who serve as liaisons between the marketer and its outside advertising agencies. The leader of this liaison function is sometimes called a *marketing communications manager*. Advertising agencies also employ specialists in account services, creative services, and media services. Account services functions are performed by account executives, who work directly with clients. An agency's creative services department develops the themes and presentations of the advertisements. This department is supervised by a creative director, who oversees the copy chief, the art director, and their staff members. The media services department is managed by a media director, who oversees the planning group that selects media outlets for ads. Currently, more than 47,000 advertising and promotions managers are employed in the United States.[17]

Job Description

Advertising can be one of the most glamorous and creative fields in marketing. Because the field combines the best of both worlds—that is, the tangible and scientific aspects of marketing along with creative artistry—advertising attracts people with a broad array of abilities. As exciting as it may seem, advertising is also stressful. Those in the creative field often have to come up with innovative plans on a tight schedule. Long hours are also common. Advertising professionals must be able to manage their time wisely, be willing to travel, and deal with a wide range of clients. Typical tasks in the advertising field include writing copy, preparing artwork and graphics, and placing ads in the media.[18]

Career Path

Most new hires begin as assistants or associates for the position they hope to acquire, such as copywriter, art director, and media buyer. Often, a newly hired employee must receive two to four promotions before becoming manager of these functions. A bachelor's degree with a broad education in courses such as graphic arts, communications, psychology, and marketing usually is required for an entry-level position in advertising. Superior communications skills, creativity, and a willingness to work long hours to complete the job are important traits for advertising candidates.[19]

Career Path 4: Public Relations Specialists

Related Chapters: Chapters 15 and 16

Specialists in public relations strive to build and maintain positive relationships with various publics. They may assist management in drafting speeches, arranging interviews, overseeing company archives, responding to information requests, and handling special events, such as sponsorships and trade shows, that generate promotional benefits for the firm.

Job Description

Public relations specialists may work hectic schedules to help a firm respond to and manage a crisis or to meet the deadline for a special event. Although public relations positions tend to be concentrated in large cities near major press services and communications facilities, this is changing as communications technologies allow more freedom of movement. Most public relations consulting firms are concentrated in New York, Los Angeles, Chicago, and Washington, D.C., and they range in size from hundreds of employees to just a handful. More than 50,000 professionals serve as public relations managers in the United States.[20]

Essential characteristics for a public relations specialist include creativity, initiative, good judgment, and the ability to express thoughts clearly and simply—both verbally and in writing. An outgoing personality, self-confidence, and enthusiasm are also recommended traits.[21]

Career Path

A college degree combined with public relations experience, usually gained through one or more internships, is considered excellent preparation for public relations. Many entry-level public relations specialists hold degrees with majors in public relations, advertising, marketing, or communications. New employees in larger organizations are likely to participate in formal training programs; those who begin their careers at smaller firms typically work under the guidance of experienced staff members. Entry-level positions carry such titles as *research assistant* or *account assistant*. A potential career path includes a promotion to account executive, account supervisor, vice president, and eventually senior vice president.

Career Path 5: Purchasing Agents and Managers

Related Chapter: Chapter 6

In today's competitive business environment, the two key marketing functions of buying and selling are performed by trained specialists. Just as every organization is involved in selling its output to meet the needs of customers, so too must all companies purchase goods and services to operate their businesses and turn out items for sale. Purchasing agents and managers represent a vital component of a company's supply chain.

Job Description

About 350,000 people work as purchasing agents and buyers for firms in the United States (excluding farms), and the Bureau of Labor Statistics projects employment to remain steady in this field over the next several years.[22] Modern technology has transformed the role of the purchasing agent. The transfer of routine tasks to computers now allows contract specialists, or procurement officers, to focus on products, suppliers, and contract negotiations. The primary function of this position is to purchase the goods, materials, component parts, supplies, and services required by the organization. These buyers ensure that suppliers deliver quality and quantity levels that match the firm's needs; they also secure these inputs at reasonable prices and make them available when needed.

Purchasing agents must develop good working relationships both with colleagues in their own organizations and with suppliers. As the popularity of outsourcing has increased, the selection and management of suppliers have become critical functions of the purchasing department. In the government sector, this role is dominated by laws and regulations that change frequently.

Most purchasing agents and their managers work in comfortable environments, but they work more than the standard 40-hour week to meet production deadlines or to be ready for special sales, conferences, or other events. Depending on the industry, these specialists may have to work extra hours prior to holidays or certain seasons, such as back-to-school, in order to have enough merchandise to meet demand. Many buyers do at least some travel. Those who work for firms with manufacturing or sources overseas—such as clothing manufacturers—may travel outside the United States.[23]

Career Path

Organizations prefer college-educated candidates for entry-level jobs in purchasing. Strong analytical and communication skills are required for these positions. New hires often begin their careers in extensive company training programs in which they learn procedures and operations. Training may include assignments dealing with production planning. Professional certification is becoming an essential criterion for advancement in both the private and the public sectors. A variety of associations serving the different categories of purchasing confer certifications on agents, including Certified Professional in Supply Management, Certified Professional Public Buyer, Certified Public Purchasing Officer, Certified Purchasing Professional, and Certified Professional Purchasing Manager.

Career Path 6: Retail and Wholesale Buyers and Merchandise Managers

Related Chapter: Chapter 14

Buyers working for retailers and wholesale businesses purchase goods for resale. Their goal is to find the best possible merchandise at the lowest prices. They also influence the distribution and marketing of this merchandise. Successful buyers must understand what appeals to consumers and what their establishments can sell. Product bar codes and point-of-purchase terminals allow organizations to accurately track goods that are selling and those that are not; buyers frequently analyze this data to improve their understanding of consumer demand. Buyers also check competitors' prices and sales activities and watch general economic conditions to anticipate consumer buying patterns.

Job Description

Approximately 157,000 people are currently employed in the United States as retail and wholesale buyers, excluding those who work in the farming industry.[24] These jobs often require substantial travel, as many orders are placed during buying trips to shows and exhibitions. Effective planning and decision-making skills are strong assets in this career. In addition, the job involves anticipating consumer preferences and ensuring the firm keeps needed goods in stock. Consequently, the people filling these positions must possess such qualities as resourcefulness, good judgment, and self-confidence.[25]

Career Path

Most retail and wholesale buyers begin their careers as assistant buyers or trainees. Larger retailers seek college-educated candidates, and extensive training includes job experience in a variety of positions. Advancement often comes when buyers move to departments or new locations with larger volumes—or become merchandise managers who coordinate or oversee the work of several buyers.

Career Path 7: Marketing Research Analysts

Related Chapter: Chapter 8

These marketing specialists provide information that helps marketers identify and define opportunities. They generate, refine, and evaluate marketing actions and monitor marketing performance. Marketing research analysts devise methods and procedures for obtaining needed decision-oriented data. Once they compile data, analysts evaluate it and then make recommendations to management.

Job Description

Firms that specialize in marketing research and management consulting employ most of the nation's marketing research analysts. Those who pursue careers in marketing research must be able to work accurately with detail, display patience and persistence, work effectively both independently and with others, and operate objectively and systematically. Significant computer and analytical skills are essential for success in this field. Deadlines are typical in this field, but these specialists tend to have fairly regular work hours compared with other marketing professionals. Marketing and survey researchers hold about 261,000 jobs in the United States, and employment opportunities are expected to grow faster than average through 2016.[26]

Marketing research analysts create methods and procedures for gathering the necessary data to serve their clients. They develop ways to find out what consumers are thinking and buying, as well as who they are and how they live. Marketing researchers may design telephone, mail, or Internet surveys to evaluate consumer preferences. They may also conduct in-person interviews or lead focus group discussions. Once they have compiled data, they evaluate information to make recommendations based on their research.[27]

Career Path

A bachelor's degree with an emphasis in marketing provides sufficient qualifications for many entry-level jobs in marketing research. Because of the importance of quantitative skills and the need for competence in using analytical software packages, this professional's education should include courses in computer science and information systems. Students should try to gain experience in conducting interviews or surveys while still in college. A master's degree in business administration or a related discipline is helpful for improving advancement opportunities.[28]

Career Path 8: Logistics: Materials Receiving, Scheduling, Dispatching, and Distributing Occupations

Related Chapter: Chapter 13

Logistics offers a myriad of career positions. Job titles under this broad heading include materials receiving, scheduling, dispatching, materials management executive, distribution operations coordinator, distribution center manager, and transportation manager. The logistics function includes responsibilities for production and inventory planning and control, distribution, and transportation.

Job Description

About 86,000 people are employed as cargo and freight agents in the United States, along with more than 760,000 shipping, receiving, and traffic clerks. In addition, U.S. firms employ thousands of production and planning specialists, dispatchers, stock clerks, and order fillers. These positions demand good communication skills and the ability to work effectively under pressure. Depending on the job, these workers are involved in planning, directing, and coordinating storage or distribution activities according to laws and regulations. A logistician analyzes and coordinates the logistical functions of a firm or organization.[29]

Career Path

Computer skills are highly valued in these jobs. Employers look for candidates with degrees in logistics and transportation. However, graduates in marketing and other business disciplines may succeed in this field.

Developing an Effective Marketing Plan

overview

- "What are our mission and goals?"

- "Who are our customers?"

- "What types of products do we offer?"

- "How can we provide superior customer service?"

briefly speaking

"Knowing your destination is half the journey."

—Anonymous

marketing plan Detailed description of the resources and actions needed to achieve stated marketing objectives.

strategic planning Process of anticipating events and market conditions and deciding how a firm can best achieve its organizational objectives.

These are some of the questions addressed by a **marketing plan**—a detailed description of the resources and actions needed to achieve stated marketing objectives. Chapter 2 discussed **strategic planning**—the process of anticipating events and market conditions and deciding how a firm can best achieve its organizational objectives. Marketing planning encompasses all the activities devoted to achieving marketing objectives, establishing a basis for designing a marketing strategy. This appendix deals in depth with the formal marketing plan, which is part of an organization's overall business plan. At the end of this appendix, you'll see what an actual marketing plan looks like. Each plan component for a hypothetical firm called Blue Sky Clothing is presented.

Components of a Business Plan

A company's **business plan** is one of its most important documents. The business plan puts in writing what all of the company's objectives are, how they will be met, how the business will obtain financing, and how much money the company expects to earn over a specified time period. Although business plans vary in length and format, most contain at least some form of the following components:

business plan Formal document that outlines what a company's objectives are, how they will be met, how the business will obtain financing, and how much money the company expects to earn.

▷ An *executive summary* briefly answers the *who, what, when, where, how,* and *why* questions for the plan. Although the summary appears early in the plan, it typically is written last, after the firm's executives have worked out the details of all the other sections.

▷ A *competitive analysis* section focuses on the environment in which the marketing plan is to be implemented. Although this section is more closely associated with the comprehensive business plan, factors specifically influencing marketing are likely to be included here.

▷ The *mission statement* summarizes the organization's purpose, vision, and overall goals. This statement provides the foundation on which further planning is based.

▷ The overall business plan includes a series of *component* plans that present goals and strategies for each functional area of the enterprise. They typically include the following:

– The *marketing plan*, which describes strategies for informing potential customers about the goods and services offered by the firm as well as strategies for developing long-term relationships. At the end of this appendix, a sample marketing plan for Blue Sky Clothing is presented.

– The *financing plan*, which presents a realistic approach for securing needed funds and managing debt and cash flows.

– The *production plan*, which describes how the organization will develop its products in the most efficient, cost-effective manner possible.

– The *facilities plan*, which describes the physical environment and equipment required to implement the production plan.

– The *human resources plan*, which estimates the firm's employment needs and the skills necessary to achieve organizational goals, including a comparison of current employees with the needs of the firm, and which establishes processes for securing adequately trained personnel if a gap exists between current employee skills and future needs.

This basic format encompasses the planning process used by nearly every successful organization. Whether a company operates in the manufacturing, wholesaling, retailing, or service sector—or a combination—the components described here are likely to appear in its overall business plan. Regardless of the size or longevity of a company, a business plan is an essential tool for a firm's owners because it helps them focus on the key elements of their business. Even small firms just starting out need a business plan to obtain financing. Figure 1 shows the outline of a business plan for Blue Sky Clothing.

briefly speaking

"You don't win on emotion. You win on execution."

—Tony Dungy (b. 1954)
FORMER PROFESSIONAL FOOTBALL COACH

Creating a Marketing Plan

Keep in mind that a marketing plan should be created in conjunction with the other elements of a firm's business plan. In addition, a marketing plan often draws from the business plan, restating the executive summary, competitive analysis, and mission statement to give its readers an overall view of the firm. The marketing plan is needed for a variety of reasons:

▷ to obtain financing, because banks and most private investors require a detailed business plan— including a marketing plan component—before they will even consider a loan application or a venture capital investment

▷ to provide direction for the firm's overall business and marketing strategies

▷ to support the development of long- and short-term organizational objectives

▷ to guide employees in achieving these objectives

▷ to serve as a standard against which the firm's progress can be measured and evaluated

In addition, the marketing plan is where a firm puts into writing its commitment to its customers and to building long-lasting relationships. After creating and implementing the plan, marketers must reevaluate it periodically to gauge its success in moving the organization toward its goals. If changes are needed, they should be made as soon as possible.

The Blue Sky Clothing Business Plan

I. Executive Summary
- Who, What, When, Where, How, and Why

II. Table of Contents

III. Introduction
- Mission Statement
- Concept and Company
- Management Team
- Product

IV. Marketing Strategy
- Demographics
- Trends
- Market Penetration
- Potential Sales Revenue

V. Financing the Business
- Cash Flow Analysis
- Pro Forma Balance Sheet
- Income Statement

VI. Facilities Plan
- Physical Environment
- Equipment

VII. Human Resources Plan
- Employment Needs and Skills
- Current Employees

VIII. Résumés of Principals

figure 1

Outline of a Business Plan

FORMULATING AN OVERALL MARKETING STRATEGY

Before writing a marketing plan, a firm's marketers formulate an overall marketing strategy. A firm may use a number of tools in marketing planning, including business portfolio analysis and the BCG matrix. Its executives may conduct a SWOT analysis, take advantage of a strategic window, study Porter's Five Forces model as it relates to their business, or consider adopting a first or second mover strategy, all of which are described in Chapter 2.

In addition to the planning strategies discussed in Chapter 2, marketers are likely to use **spreadsheet analysis**, which lays out a grid of columns and rows that organize numerical information in a standardized, easily understood format. Spreadsheet analysis helps planners answer various "what if" questions related to the firm's financing and operations. The most popular spreadsheet software is Microsoft Excel. A spreadsheet analysis helps planners

spreadsheet analysis
Grid that organizes numerical information in a standardized, easily understood format.

anticipate marketing performance given specified sets of circumstances. For example, a spreadsheet might project the outcomes of different pricing decisions for a new product, as shown in Figure 2.

Once general planning strategies are determined, marketers begin to flesh out the details of the marketing strategy. The elements of a marketing strategy include identifying the target market, studying the marketing environment, and creating a marketing mix. When marketers have identified the target market, they can develop the optimal marketing mix to reach their potential customers:

▷ *Product strategy.* Which goods and services should the company offer to meet its customers' needs?

▷ *Distribution strategy.* Through which channel(s) and physical facilities will the firm distribute its products?

▷ *Promotional strategy.* What mix of advertising, sales promotion, and personal selling activities will the firm use to reach its customers initially and then develop long-term relationships?

▷ *Pricing strategy.* At what level should the company set its prices?

THE EXECUTIVE SUMMARY, COMPETITIVE ANALYSIS, AND MISSION STATEMENT

Because these three elements of the business plan often reappear in the marketing plan, it is useful to describe them here. Recall that the executive summary answers the *who, what, when, where, how,* and *why* questions for the business. The executive summary for Google includes references to its current strategic planning process for its search services, which involves "pushing the limits of technology to provide a fast, accurate and easy-to-use search service that can be accessed from anywhere."[1] It goes on to answer such questions as who is involved (key people and organizations), what length of time the plan represents, and how the goals will be met.

The competitive analysis focuses on the environment in which the marketing plan is to be implemented. Trenton, New Jersey–based TerraCycle manufactures a wide variety of products, all made from recycled materials. Believing the green movement will eventually hold sway in consumer products, TerraCycle's business goal is to become the leading ecofriendly organic brand in

figure 2

How Spreadsheet Analysis Works

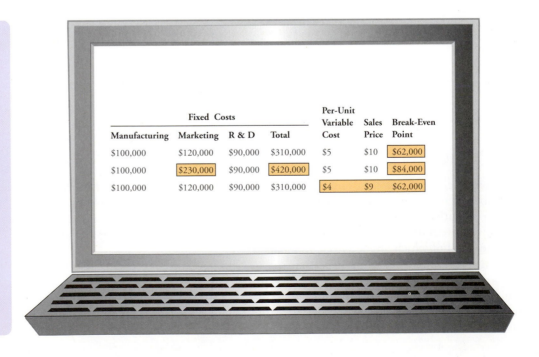

Manufacturing	Fixed Costs			Per-Unit Variable Cost	Sales Price	Break-Even Point
	Marketing	R & D	Total			
$100,000	$120,000	$90,000	$310,000	$5	$10	$62,000
$100,000	$230,000	$90,000	$420,000	$5	$10	$84,000
$100,000	$120,000	$90,000	$310,000	$4	$9	$62,000

each of the product categories in which it competes. It doesn't attempt to overpower the category leader; instead, it aims to beat other ecofriendly competitors. For example, TerraCycle wants its window cleaner to outsell green competitors Mrs. Meyers and Seventh Generation, but it is less concerned about beating Windex—the category leader.[2]

The mission statement puts into words an organization's overall purpose and reason for being. According to Nintendo's corporate mission, the company is "strongly committed to producing and marketing the best products and support services available." Not only does Nintendo strive to manufacture the highest-quality video products, but it also attempts "to treat every customer with attention, consideration and respect." Nintendo is similarly committed to its employees and believes in treating them "with the same consideration and respect that we, as a company, show our customers."[3]

DESCRIPTION OF THE COMPANY

Near the beginning of the marketing plan—typically following the executive summary and before the mission statement—a description of the company is included. The company description may include a brief history or background of the firm, the types of products it offers or plans to introduce, recent successes or achievements—in short, it consists of a few paragraphs containing the kind of information often found on the home page of a company's Web site.

STATEMENT OF GOALS AND CORE COMPETENCIES

The plan then includes a statement of the firm's goals and its core competencies—the things it does extremely well or better than anyone else. The goals should be specific and measurable and may be divided into financial and nonfinancial aims. A financial goal might be to add 75 new franchises in the next 12 months or to reach $10 million in revenues. A nonfinancial goal might be to enter the European market or to add a new product line every other year. An energy bill recently passed by the U.S. Congress mandates growth in the use of ethanol in the United States: by 2022, ethanol consumption must triple. So ethanol producers are setting specific goals to ramp up production to meet that requirement.[4]

Core competencies make a firm stand out from everyone else in the marketplace. Costco's core competency is offering a wide variety of goods at low prices, including unexpected bargains such as luxury-brand watches and Dom Perignon champagne. Costco CEO and cofounder Jim Sinegal believes his workforce is a significant differentiator in the company's success, and for that reason, Costco pays above-market wages. The average Costco hourly wage is $18.15—68 percent more than the average hourly wage at its biggest competitor, Wal-Mart.[5]

Small businesses often begin with a single core competency and build their business and reputation on it. It is important for a new firm to identify its core competency in the marketing plan so investors or banks understand why they should lend the firm money to get started or to grow to the next stage. As a college student, David Kim found he enjoyed tutoring children. When he discovered a real demand for skilled tutoring, he decided to launch a tutoring business, which he named C2 Education. Because C2's core competency is helping children to excel, employees are hired and trained according to rigorous standards. Today, C2 Education operates in 110 U.S. locations, with annual revenues estimated at $48 million.[6]

OUTLINE OF THE MARKETING ENVIRONMENT (SITUATION ANALYSIS)

Every successful marketing plan considers the marketing environment—the competitive, economic, political-legal, technological, and social-cultural factors that affect the way a firm formulates and implements its marketing strategy. Marketing plans may address these issues in different ways, but the goal is to present information that describes the company's position or situation within the marketing environment. J. Crew, for instance, has a well-known brand name and a CEO with an impressive track record, Mickey Drexler, who previously headed The Gap. The retail environment for stores like J. Crew is highly competitive. Merchandise that doesn't appeal to enough customers ends up on a clearance rack and hurts the bottom line. So Drexler advises his merchandisers, "Don't buy out of emotion. Buy less if you love something but feel it's a risky item. We don't want over-stock. … No profit, no fun!"[7] A marketing plan for J. Crew would include an evaluation of competing stores such as The Gap and Urban Outfitters; any technological advances that would affect such factors as merchandise distribution or inventory; social-cultural issues such as fashion preferences and spending habits of customers; and economic issues affecting a pricing strategy.

One such method for outlining the marketing environment in the marketing plan is to include a SWOT analysis, described in Chapter 2. SWOT analysis identifies the firm's strengths, weaknesses, opportunities, and threats within the marketing environment. A SWOT analysis for J. Crew might include strengths such as its corporate leadership, brand name, and upscale target market. Weaknesses might include the risks inherent in the business of correctly spotting fashion trends. A major opportunity lies in the fact that J. Crew can expand almost anywhere. In fact, the company recently launched a new chain, Madewell, with stores in ten U.S. cities. Madewell sells hip, casual clothes to an upscale clientele. Threats include competition from other trendy stores, sudden changes in customer preferences, and financial crises that affect spending.[8] A SWOT analysis can be presented in chart format so that it is easy to read as part of the marketing plan. The sample marketing plan in this appendix includes a SWOT analysis for Blue Sky Clothing.

THE TARGET MARKET AND MARKETING MIX

The marketing plan identifies the target market for the firm's products. In marketing its new Tide detergent and Downy fabric softener, Procter & Gamble targeted viewers of the high-fashion reality TV series "Project Runway." The reason? Innovations in their formulations brought about product improvements that help clothes keep their shape and color longer, even after repeated laundering. So those interested in purchasing upscale clothing would no doubt want to keep it looking new.[9] In another example of targeting, the Cute Overload Web site (www.cuteoverload.com) contains photos and videos of animals that visitors can share and about which they can post comments. But the site also offers a page-a-day desk calendar of the same name featuring images of puppies, kittens, birds, and chipmunks with humorous captions. Cute Overload targets women ages 18 to 34 who need a laugh and a brief escape from the real world. The calendars are also offered for sale on Amazon.com, and the retailer's inventory sold out in one day, which astonished the developer.[10]

The marketing plan also discusses the marketing mix the firm has selected for its products. Nokia is well known for product innovation and involving its customer base in its quest for technological advancement in its cell phones. But the company is looking to increase its products' ties to entertainment and social networking on the Internet. When the company recently incorporated customers and the Internet in its product-development efforts, the results were surprising. One product, Sports Tracker, is a program tied to global positioning satellites, and it allows runners and cyclists to use their Nokia phone to enter data from their workout to track speed and distance and even map out new routes. With Sports Tracker still in its early development stages, Nokia posted the application on a company Web site accessible to the public. Over 1 million people downloaded the application, using it in activities the creators never considered, such as paragliding and motorcycle riding. What's more, users provided insightful feedback that enabled Nokia to make further improvements to the program. Other upcoming products include an Internet service and online music store as well as devices that allow photo and video sharing.[11]

BUDGET, SCHEDULE, AND MONITORING

Every marketing plan requires a budget, a time schedule for implementation, and a system for monitoring the plan's success or failure. At age 21, entrepreneur Joe Cirulli of Gainesville, Florida,

made a to-do list of ten life goals, which included "Own a health club" and "Make it respected in the community." By age 33, Cirulli had achieved all ten of his life goals, including the opening of his Gainesville Health & Fitness Center. As Cirulli's business grew, however, he discovered a larger mission: to make Gainesville the healthiest community in America. Today, Gainesville is the first and only city to win the Gold Well City award from the Wellness Councils of America, and Cirulli's fitness center is widely regarded as one of the best in the industry. Whether or not he realized it at the time, Cirulli's life and business plan at age 21 had the makings of a marketing plan, with goals and budgets, setting a timeline, and measuring progress—a formula for business success.[12]

Most long-range marketing plans encompass a two- to five-year period, although companies that do business in industries such as auto manufacturing, pharmaceuticals, or lumber may extend their marketing plans further into the future because it typically takes longer to develop these products. However, marketers in most industries will have difficulty making estimates and predictions beyond five years because of the many uncertainties in the marketplace. Firms also may opt to develop short-term plans to cover marketing activities for a single year.

The marketing plan, whether it is long term or short term, predicts how long it will take to achieve the goals set out by the plan. A goal may be opening a certain number of new stores, increasing market share, or achieving an expansion of the product line. Finally, the marketing program is monitored and evaluated for its performance. Monthly, quarterly, and annual sales targets are usually tracked; the efficiency with which certain tasks are completed is determined; customer satisfaction is measured; and so forth. All of these factors contribute to the overall review of the program.

At some point, a firm may implement an *exit strategy*, a plan for the firm to leave the market. A common way for a large company to do this is to sell off a business unit. A number of these strategies have been implemented recently. Television and newspaper media company Landmark Communications of Norfolk, Virginia, sold the Weather Channel for nearly $3.5 billion to NBC Universal and two private-equity firms. The popular cable channel attracts an estimated 85 million viewers per month.[13]

Another example of an exit strategy is General Electric's sale of several of its business units to help cut costs and bolster its share price. GE sold its plastics business to Saudi firm Sabic for $11.6 billion. In another transaction, it sold its warranty management group to Assurant, an insurance company that sells warranties for consumer electronics and major appliances. Assurant paid $25 million for GE's business. Sales of other GE business units are under consideration to simplify the conglomerate's structure and concentrate on core areas.[14]

Sample Marketing Plan

The following pages contain an annotated sample marketing plan for Blue Sky Clothing. At some point in your career, you will likely be involved in writing—or at least contributing to—a marketing plan. And you'll certainly read many marketing plans throughout your business career. Keep in mind that the plan for Blue Sky is a single example; no one format is used by all companies. Also, the Blue Sky plan has been somewhat condensed to make it easier to annotate and illustrate the most vital features. The important point to remember is that the marketing plan is a document designed to present concise, cohesive information about a company's marketing objectives to managers, lending institutions, and others involved in creating and carrying out the firm's overall business strategy.

go play outside

Five-Year Marketing Plan
Blue Sky Clothing, Inc.

The executive summary outlines the *who, what, where, when, how,* and *why* of the marketing plan. Blue Sky is only three years old and is successful enough that it now needs a formal marketing plan to obtain additional financing from a bank or private investors for expansion and the launch of new products.

Table of Contents

EXECUTIVE SUMMARY

This five-year marketing plan for Blue Sky Clothing has been created by its two founders to secure additional funding for growth and to inform employees of the company's current status and direction. Although Blue Sky was launched only three years ago, the firm has experienced greater-than-anticipated demand for its products, and research has shown that the target market of sports-minded consumers and sports retailers would like to buy more casual clothing than Blue Sky currently offers. As a result, Blue Sky wants to extend its current product line as well as add new product lines. In addition, the firm plans to explore opportunities for online sales. The marketing environment has been very receptive to the firm's high-quality goods—casual clothing in trendy colors with logos and slogans that reflect the interests of outdoor enthusiasts around the country. Over the next five years, Blue Sky can increase its distribution, offer new products, and win new customers.

The company description summarizes the history of Blue Sky—how it was founded and by whom, what its products are, and why they are unique. It begins to "sell" the reader on the growth possibilities for Blue Sky.

COMPANY DESCRIPTION

Blue Sky Clothing was founded three years ago by entrepreneurs Lucy Neuman and Nick Russell. Neuman has an undergraduate degree in marketing and worked for several years in the retail clothing industry. Russell operated an adventure business called Go West!, which arranges group trips to locations in Wyoming, Montana, and Idaho, before selling the enterprise to a partner. Neuman and Russell, who have been friends since college, decided to develop and market a line of clothing with a unique—yet universal—appeal to outdoor enthusiasts.

Blue Sky Clothing reflects Neuman's and Russell's passion for the outdoors. The company's original cotton T-shirts, baseball caps, and fleece jackets and vests bear logos of different sports such as kayaking, mountain climbing, bicycling, skating, surfing, and horseback riding. But every item shows off the company's slogan: "Go Play Outside." Blue Sky sells clothing for both men and women, in the hottest colors with the coolest names—sunrise pink, sunset red, twilight purple, desert rose, cactus green, ocean blue, mountaintop white, and river rock gray.

Blue Sky attire is currently carried by small retail stores that specialize in outdoor clothing and gear. Most of these stores are concentrated in northern New England, California, the Northwest, and a few states in the South. The high quality, trendy colors, and unique message of the clothing have gained Blue Sky a following among consumers between ages 25 and 45. Sales have tripled in the last year alone, and Blue Sky is currently working to expand its manufacturing capabilities.

Blue Sky is also committed to giving back to the community by contributing to local conservation programs. Ultimately, the company would like to develop and fund its own environmental programs. This plan will outline how Blue Sky intends to introduce new products, expand its distribution, enter new markets, and give back to the community.

BLUE SKY'S MISSION AND GOALS

Blue Sky's mission is to be a leading producer and marketer of personalized, casual clothing for consumers who love the outdoors. Blue Sky wants to inspire people to get outdoors more often and enjoy family and friends while doing so. In addition, Blue Sky strives to design programs for preserving the natural environment.

During the next five years, Blue Sky seeks to achieve the following financial and non-financial goals:

Financial goals

1. Obtain financing to expand manufacturing capabilities, increase distribution, and introduce two new product lines

2. Increase revenues by at least 50 percent each year

3. Donate at least $25,000 a year to conservation organizations

Nonfinancial goals

4. Introduce two new product lines—customized logo clothing and lightweight luggage

5. Enter new geographic markets, including southwestern and mid-Atlantic states

6. Develop a successful Internet site, while maintaining strong relationships with retailers

7. Develop its own conservation program aimed at helping communities raise money to purchase open space

CORE COMPETENCIES

Blue Sky seeks to use its core competencies to achieve a sustainable competitive advantage, in which competitors cannot provide the same value to consumers that Blue Sky does. Already Blue Sky has developed core competencies in (1) offering a high-quality, branded product whose image is recognizable among consumers; (2) creating a sense of community among consumers who purchase the products; and (3) developing a reputation among retailers as a reliable manufacturer, delivering their orders on schedule. The firm intends to build on these competencies through marketing efforts that increase the number of products offered as well as distribution outlets.

By forming strong relationships with consumers, retailers, and suppliers of fabric and other goods and services, Blue Sky believes it can create a sustainable competitive advantage over its rivals. No other clothing company can say to its customers with as much conviction, "Go Play Outside"!

SITUATION ANALYSIS

The marketing environment for Blue Sky represents overwhelming opportunities. It also contains some challenges the firm believes it can meet successfully. Table A illustrates a SWOT analysis of the company conducted by its marketers to highlight Blue Sky's strengths, weaknesses, opportunities, and threats.

The SWOT analysis presents a thumbnail sketch of the company's position in the marketplace. In just three years, Blue Sky has built some impressive strengths while looking forward to new opportunities. Its dedicated founders, the growing number of brand-loyal customers, and sound financial management place the company in a good position to grow. However, as Blue Sky considers expansion of its product line and entry into new markets,

---

It is important to state a firm's mission and goals, including financial and nonfinancial goals. Blue Sky's goals include growth and profits for the company as well as the ability to contribute to society through conservation programs.

This section reminds employees and those outside the company (such as potential lenders) exactly what Blue Sky does so well and how it plans to achieve a sustainable competitive advantage over rivals. Note here and throughout the plan: Blue Sky focuses on relationships.

The situation analysis provides an outline of the marketing environment. A SWOT analysis helps marketers and others identify clearly a firm's strengths, weaknesses, opportunities, and threats. Again, relationships are a focus. Blue Sky has also conducted research on the outdoor clothing market, competitors, and consumers to determine how best to attract and keep customers.

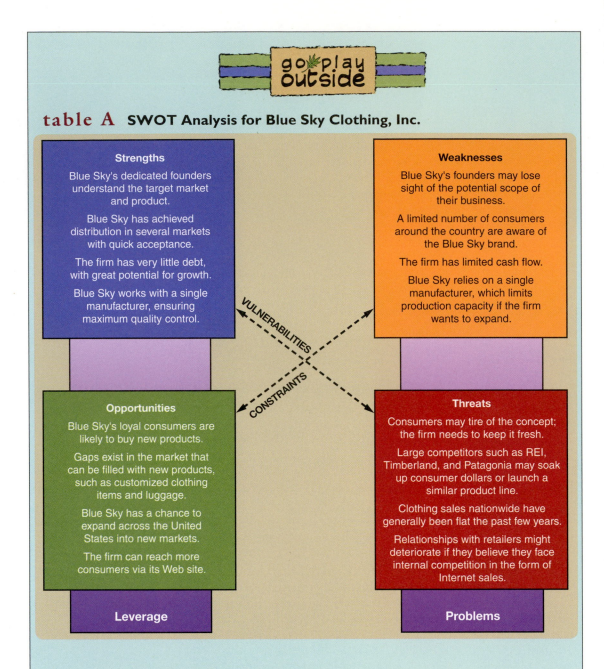

table A   **SWOT Analysis for Blue Sky Clothing, Inc.**

Strengths

Blue Sky's dedicated founders understand the target market and product.

Blue Sky has achieved distribution in several markets with quick acceptance.

The firm has very little debt, with great potential for growth.

Blue Sky works with a single manufacturer, ensuring maximum quality control.

Weaknesses

Blue Sky's founders may lose sight of the potential scope of their business.

A limited number of consumers around the country are aware of the Blue Sky brand.

The firm has limited cash flow.

Blue Sky relies on a single manufacturer, which limits production capacity if the firm wants to expand.

VULNERABILITIES

CONSTRAINTS

Opportunities

Blue Sky's loyal consumers are likely to buy new products.

Gaps exist in the market that can be filled with new products, such as customized clothing items and luggage.

Blue Sky has a chance to expand across the United States into new markets.

The firm can reach more consumers via its Web site.

Threats

Consumers may tire of the concept; the firm needs to keep it fresh.

Large competitors such as REI, Timberland, and Patagonia may soak up consumer dollars or launch a similar product line.

Clothing sales nationwide have generally been flat the past few years.

Relationships with retailers might deteriorate if they believe they face internal competition in the form of Internet sales.

Leverage

Problems

the firm will have to guard against marketing myopia (the failure to recognize the scope of its business) and quality slippages. As the company finalizes plans for new products and expanded Internet sales, its management will also have to guard against competitors who attempt to duplicate the products. However, building strong relationships with consumers, retailers, and suppliers should help thwart competitors.

COMPETITORS IN THE OUTDOOR CLOTHING MARKET

The outdoor retail sales industry sells about $5 billion worth of goods annually, ranging from clothing to equipment. The outdoor apparel market has many entries. L.L. Bean, Dick's Sporting Goods, REI, Timberland, Bass Pro Shops, Cabela's, The North Face, and Patagonia are among the most recognizable companies offering these products. Smaller competitors such as Title IX, which offers athletic clothing for women, and Ragged Mountain, which sells fleece clothing for skiers and hikers, also capture some of the market. The outlook for the industry in general—and Blue Sky in particular—is positive for several reasons. First, con-

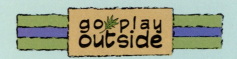

sumers are participating in and investing in recreational activities near their homes. Second, consumers are looking for ways to enjoy their leisure time with friends and family without overspending. Third, consumers tend to be advancing in their careers and able to spend more.

While all of the companies listed earlier can be considered competitors, none offers the kind of trendy, yet practical products provided by Blue Sky—and none carries the customized logos and slogans that Blue Sky plans to offer in the near future. In addition, most of these competitors sell performance apparel in high-tech manufactured fabrics. With the exception of the fleece vests and jackets, Blue Sky's clothing is made of strictly the highest-quality cotton, so it may be worn both on the hiking trail and around town. Finally, Blue Sky products are offered at moderate prices, making them affordable in multiple quantities. For instance, a Blue Sky T-shirt sells for $15.99, compared with a competing high-performance T-shirt that sells for $29.99. Consumers can easily replace a set of shirts from one season to the next, picking up the newest colors, without agonizing over the purchase.

A survey conducted by Blue Sky revealed that 67 percent of responding consumers prefer to replace their casual and active wear more often than other clothing, so they are attracted by the moderate pricing of Blue Sky products. In addition, as the trend toward health-conscious activities and concerns about the natural environment continue, consumers increasingly relate to the Blue Sky philosophy as well as the firm's future contributions to socially responsible programs.

THE TARGET MARKET

The target market for Blue Sky products is active consumers between ages 25 and 45—people who like to hike, rock climb, bicycle, surf, figure skate, in-line skate, ride horses, snowboard or ski, kayak, and other such activities. In short, they like to "Go Play Outside." They might not be experts at the sports they engage in, but they enjoy themselves outdoors.

These active consumers represent a demographic group of well-educated and successful individuals; they are single or married and raising families. Household incomes generally range between $60,000 and $120,000 annually. Despite their comfortable incomes, these consumers are price conscious and consistently seek value in their purchases. Regardless of their age (whether they fall at the upper or lower end of the target range), they lead active lifestyles. They are somewhat status oriented but not overly so. They like to be associated with high-quality products but are not willing to pay a premium price for a certain brand. Current Blue Sky customers tend to live in northern New England, the South, California, and the Northwest. However, one future goal is to target consumers in the Mid-Atlantic states and Southwest as well.

THE MARKETING MIX

The following discussion outlines some of the details of the proposed marketing mix for Blue Sky products.

Product Strategy

Blue Sky currently offers a line of high-quality outdoor apparel items including cotton T-shirts, baseball caps, and fleece vests and jackets. All bear the company logo and slogan, "Go Play Outside." The firm has researched the most popular colors for its items and given them names that consumers enjoy—sunset red, sunrise pink, cactus green, desert rose, and river rock gray, among others. Over the next five years, Blue Sky plans to expand the product line to include customized clothing items. Customers may select a logo that represents their

Blue Sky has identified its customers as active people between ages 25 and 45. However, that doesn't mean someone who is older or prefers to read about the outdoors isn't a potential customer as well. By pinpointing where existing customers live, Blue Sky can plan for growth into new outlets.

The strongest part of the marketing mix for Blue Sky involves sales promotions, public relations, and nontraditional marketing strategies such as attending outdoor events and organizing activities such as day hikes and bike rides.

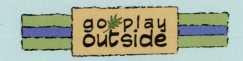

sport, say, rock climbing. Then they can add a slogan to match the logo, such as "Get Over It." A baseball cap with a bicyclist might bear the slogan, "Take a Spin." At the beginning, there would be ten new logos and five new slogans; more would be added later. Eventually, some slogans and logos would be retired, and new ones introduced. This strategy will keep the concept fresh and prevent it from becoming diluted with too many variations.

The second way in which Blue Sky plans to expand its product line is to offer items of lightweight luggage—two sizes of duffel bags, two sizes of tote bags, and a daypack. These items would also come in trendy and basic colors, with a choice of logos and slogans. In addition, every product would bear the Blue Sky logo.

Distribution Strategy

Currently, Blue Sky is marketed through regional and local specialty shops scattered along the California coast, into the Northwest, across the South, and in northern New England. So far, Blue Sky has not been distributed through national sporting goods and apparel chains. Climate and season tend to dictate the sales at specialty shops, which sell more T-shirts and baseball caps during warm weather and more fleece vests and jackets during colder months. Blue Sky obtains much of its information about overall industry trends in different geographic areas and at different types of retail outlets from its trade organization, Outdoor Industry Association.

Over the next three years, Blue Sky seeks to expand distribution to retail specialty shops throughout the nation, focusing next on the southwest and mid-Atlantic regions. The firm has not yet determined whether it would be beneficial to sell through a major national chain, as these outlets could be considered competitors.

In addition, Blue Sky plans to expand online sales by offering the customized product line via Internet only, thus distinguishing between Internet offerings and specialty shop offerings. Eventually, we may be able to place Internet kiosks at some of the more profitable store outlets so consumers could order customized products from the stores. Regardless of its expansion plans, Blue Sky fully intends to monitor and maintain strong relationships with distribution channel members.

Promotion Strategy

Blue Sky communicates with consumers and retailers about its products in a variety of ways. Information about Blue Sky—the company as well as its products—is available via the Internet, through direct mailings, and in person. The firm's promotional efforts also seek to differentiate its products from those of its competitors.

The company relies on personal contact with retailers to establish the products in their stores. This contact, whether in person or by phone, helps convey the Blue Sky message, demonstrate the products' unique qualities, and build relationships. Blue Sky sales representatives visit each store two or three times a year and offer in-store training on the features of the products for new retailers or for those who want a refresher session. As distribution expands, Blue Sky will adjust to meet greater demand by increasing sales staff to make sure its stores are visited more frequently.

Sales promotions and public relations currently make up the bulk of Blue Sky's promotional strategy. Blue Sky staff works with retailers to offer short-term sales promotions tied to events and contests. In addition, Nick Russell is currently working with several trip outfitters to offer Blue Sky items on a promotional basis. Because Blue Sky also engages in cause marketing through its contribution to environmental programs, good public relations have followed.

Nontraditional marketing methods that require little cash and a lot of creativity also lend themselves perfectly to Blue Sky. Because Blue Sky is a small, flexible organization, the firm can easily implement ideas such as distributing free water, stickers, and discount coupons at outdoor

sporting events. During the next year, the company plans to engage in the following marketing efforts:

▷ Create a Blue Sky Tour, in which several employees take turns driving around the country to campgrounds to distribute promotional items such as Blue Sky stickers and discount coupons.

▷ Attend canoe and kayak races, bicycling events, and rock climbing competitions with our Blue Sky truck to distribute free water, stickers, and discount coupons for Blue Sky shirts or hats.

▷ Organize Blue Sky hikes departing from participating retailers.

▷ Hold a Blue Sky design contest, selecting a winning slogan and logo to be added to the customized line.

Pricing Strategy

As discussed earlier in this plan, Blue Sky products are priced with the competition in mind. The firm is not concerned with setting high prices to signal luxury or prestige, nor is it attempting to achieve the goals of offsetting low prices by selling large quantities of products. Instead, value pricing is practiced so customers feel comfortable purchasing new clothing to replace the old, even if it is just because they like the new colors. The pricing strategy also makes Blue Sky products good gifts—for birthdays, graduations, or "just because." The customized clothing will sell for $2 to $4 more than the regular Blue Sky logo clothing. The luggage will be priced competitively, offering a good value against its competition.

BUDGET, SCHEDULE, AND MONITORING

An actual plan will include more specific financial details, which will be folded into the overall business plan. For more information, see the "Financial Analysis in Marketing" appendix at the end of this book. In addition, Blue Sky states that at this stage, it does not have plans to exit the market by merging with another firm or making a public stock offering.

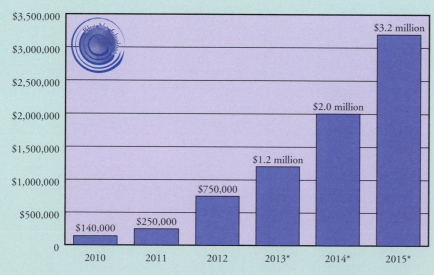

*Projected sales

figure A
Annual Sales for Blue Sky Clothing: 2010–2015

Though its history is short, Blue Sky has enjoyed a steady increase in sales since its introduction three years ago. Figure A shows these three years, plus projected sales for the next three years, including the introduction of the two new product lines. Additional financial data are included in the overall business plan for the company.

The timeline for expansion of outlets and introduction of the two new product lines is shown in Figure B. The implementation of each of these tasks will be monitored closely and evaluated for its performance.

Blue Sky anticipates continuing operations into the foreseeable future, with no plans to exit this market. Instead, as discussed throughout this plan, the firm plans to increase its presence in the market. At present, there are no plans to merge with another

figure B

Timeline for First Three Years of Marketing Plan

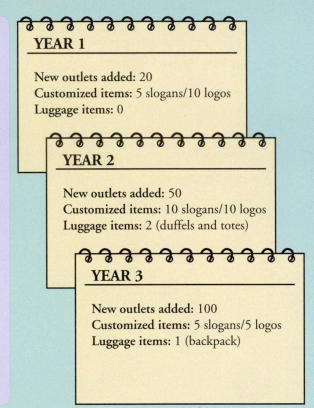

YEAR 1

New outlets added: 20
Customized items: 5 slogans/10 logos
Luggage items: 0

YEAR 2

New outlets added: 50
Customized items: 10 slogans/10 logos
Luggage items: 2 (duffels and totes)

YEAR 3

New outlets added: 100
Customized items: 5 slogans/5 logos
Luggage items: 1 (backpack)

company or to make a public stock offering.

Financial Analysis
in Marketing

A number of basic concepts from accounting and finance offer invaluable tools to marketers. Understanding the contributions made by these concepts can improve the quality of marketing decisions. In addition, marketers often must be able to explain and defend their decisions in financial terms. These accounting and financial tools can be used to supply quantitative data to justify decisions made by marketing managers. In this appendix, we describe the major accounting and finance concepts that have marketing implications and explain how they help managers make informed marketing decisions.

Financial Statements

All companies prepare a set of financial statements on a regular basis. Two of the most important financial statements are the income statement and balance sheet. The analogy of a motion picture often is used to describe an *income statement* because it presents a financial record of a company's revenues, expenses, and profits over a period of time such as a month, quarter, or year. By contrast, the *balance sheet* is a snapshot of what a company owns (called *assets*) and what it owes (called *liabilities*) at a point in time, such as at the end of the month, quarter, or year. The difference between assets and liabilities is referred to as *owner's, partners', or shareholders' equity*—the amount of funds the firm's owners have invested in its formation and continued operations. Of the two financial statements, the income statement contains more marketing-related information.

A sample income statement for Composite Technology is shown in Figure 1. Headquartered in a Boston suburb, Composite Technology is a B2B producer and marketer. The firm designs and manufactures a variety of composite components for manufacturers of consumer, industrial, and government products. Total sales revenues for 2010 amounted to $675.0 million. Total expenses, including taxes, for the year were $583.1 million. The year 2010 proved profitable for Composite Technology—the firm reported a profit, referred to as net income, of $91.9 million. While total revenue is a fairly straightforward number, several of the expenses shown on the income statement require additional explanation.

For any company that makes its own products (a manufacturer) or simply markets one or more items produced by others (an importer, retailer, or wholesaler), the largest single expense usually is a category called *cost of goods sold*. This reflects the cost, to the firm, of the goods it markets to its customers. In the case of Composite Technology, the cost of goods sold represents the cost of components and raw materials as well as the cost of designing and manufacturing the composite panels the firm produces and markets to its business customers.

The income statement illustrates how cost of goods sold is calculated. The calculation begins with the value of the firm's inventory at the beginning of 2010. Inventory is the value of raw

figure 1

**Composite Technology
2010 Income
Statement**

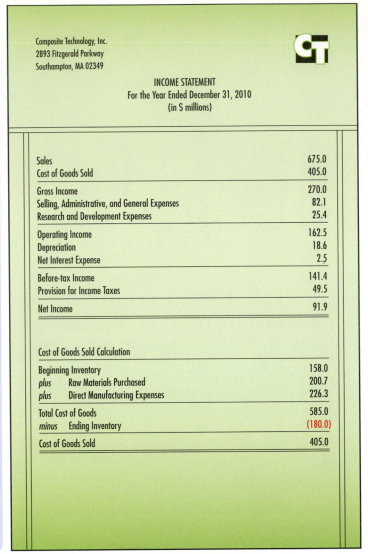

figure 1

Composite Technology 2010 Income Statement

materials, partially completed products, and finished products held by the firm at the end of some time period, say the end of the year. The cost of materials Composite Technology purchased during the year and the direct cost of manufacturing the finished products are then added to the beginning inventory figure. The result is cost of goods the firm has available for sale during the year. Once the firm's accountants subtract the value of inventory held by the firm at the end of 2010, they know the cost of goods sold. By simply subtracting cost of goods sold from total sales revenues generated during the year, they determine that Composite achieved gross profits of $270.0 million in 2010.

Operating expenses are another significant cost for most firms. This broad category includes such marketing outlays as sales compensation and expenses, advertising and other promotions, and the expenses involved in implementing marketing plans. Accountants typically combine these financial outlays into a single category with the label *Selling,*

Administrative, and General Expenses. Other expense items included in the operating expenses section of the income statement are administrative salaries, utilities, and insurance.

Another significant expense for Composite Technology is research and development (R&D). This category includes the cost of developing new products and modifying existing ones. Firms such as pharmaceuticals, biotechnology, and computer companies spend significant amounts of money each year on R&D. Subtracting selling, administrative, and general expenses and R&D expenses from the gross profit equals the firm's operating income. For 2010, Composite had operating income of $162.5 million.

Depreciation represents the systematic reduction over time in the value of certain company assets, such as production machinery, office furniture, or laptops provided for the firm's sales representatives. Depreciation is an unusual expense because it does not involve an actual cash expense. However, it does reflect the reality that equipment owned by the company is physically wearing out over time from use and/or from technological obsolescence. Also, charging a portion of the total cost of these long-lived items to each of the years in which they are used results in a more accurate determination of the total costs involved in the firm's operation each year.

Net interest expense is the difference between what a firm paid in interest on various loans and what it collected in interest on investments it might have made during the time period involved. Subtracting depreciation and net interest expense from the firm's operating profit reveals the firm's taxable income. Composite had depreciation of $18.6 million and a net interest expense of $2.5 million for the year, so its 2010 taxable income was $141.4 million.

Profit-seeking firms pay taxes calculated as a percentage of their taxable income to the federal government as well as state income taxes in most states. Composite paid $49.5 million in taxes in 2010. Subtracting taxes from taxable income gives us the firm's *net income,* $91.9 million.

PERFORMANCE RATIOS

Managers often compute a variety of financial ratios to assess the performance of their firm. These ratios are calculated using data found on both the income statement and the balance sheet. Ratios are then compared with industry standards and with data from previous years. Several ratios are of particular interest to marketers.

A number of commonly used financial ratios focus on *profitability measures.* They are used to assess the firm's ability to generate revenues in excess of expenses and earn an adequate rate of return. Profitability measures include gross profit margin, net profit margin, and return on investment (or sales).

Gross Profit Margin

The gross profit margin equals the firm's gross profit divided by its sales revenues. In 2010, Composite had a gross profit margin of

$$\frac{\text{Gross Profit}}{\text{Sales}} = \frac{\$270.0 \text{ million}}{\$675.0 \text{ million}} = 40\%$$

The gross profit margin is the percentage of each sales dollar that can be used to pay other expenses and meet the firm's profit objectives. Ideally, businesses would like to see gross profit margins equal to or higher than those of other firms in their industry. A declining gross profit margin may indicate the firm is under some competitive price pressure.

Net Profit Margin

The net profit margin equals net income divided by sales. For 2010, Composite had a net profit margin of

$$\frac{\text{Net Income}}{\text{Sales}} = \frac{\$91.9 \text{ million}}{\$675.0 \text{ million}} = 13.6\%$$

The net profit margin is the percentage of each sales dollar the firm earns in profit or keeps after all expenses have been paid. Companies generally want to see rising, or at least stable, net profit margins.

Return on Assets (ROA)

A third profitability ratio, return on assets, measures the firm's efficiency in generating sales and profits from the total amount invested in the company. For 2010, Composite's ROA is calculated as follows:

$$\frac{\text{Sales}}{\text{Average Assets}} \times \frac{\text{Net Income}}{\text{Sales}} = \frac{\text{Net Income}}{\text{Average Assets}}$$

$$\frac{\$675.0 \text{ million}}{\$595.0 \text{ million}} \times \frac{\$91.9 \text{ million}}{\$675.0 \text{ million}} = 1.13 \times 13.6\% = 15.4\%$$

The ROA ratio actually consists of two components. The first component, *asset turnover,* is the amount of sales generated for each dollar invested. The second component is *net profit margin.* Data for total assets are found on the firm's balance sheet.

Assume Composite began 2010 with $560 million in assets and ended the year with $630 million in assets. Its average assets for the year would be $595 million. As in the other profitability ratios, Composite's ROI should be compared with other firms in the industry and with its own previous performance to be meaningful.

Inventory Turnover

Inventory turnover typically is categorized as an activity ratio because it evaluates the effectiveness of the firm's resource use. Specifically, it measures the number of times a firm "turns" its inventory each year. The ratio can help answer the question of whether the firm has the appropriate level of inventory. Inventory turnover equals sales divided by average inventory. From the income statement, we see Composite Technology began 2010 with $158 million in inventory and ended the year with $180 million in inventory. Therefore, the firm's average inventory was $169 million. The firm's inventory turnover ratio equals:

$$\frac{\text{Sales}}{\text{Average Inventory}} = \frac{\$675.0 \text{ million}}{\$169.0 \text{ million}} = 3.99$$

For 2010, Composite Technology turned its inventory almost four times a year. While a faster inventory turn usually is a sign of greater efficiency, to be really meaningful the inventory turnover ratio must be compared with historical data and appropriate peer firm averages. Different organizations can have very different inventory turnover ratios, depending on the types of products they sell. For instance, a supermarket might turn its inventory every three weeks for an annual rate of roughly 16 times per year. By contrast, a large furniture retailer is likely to average only about two turns per year. Again, the determination of a "good" or "inadequate" inventory turnover rate depends on typical rates in the industry and the firm's performance in previous years.

Accounts Receivable Turnover

Another activity ratio that may be of interest to marketers is accounts receivable turnover. This ratio measures the number of times per year a company "turns" its receivables. Dividing accounts receivable turnover into 365 gives us the average age of the company's receivables.

Companies make sales on the basis of either cash or credit. Credit sales allow the buyer to obtain a product now and pay for it at a specified later date. In essence, the seller is providing credit to the buyer. Credit sales are common in B2B transactions. It should be noted that sales to buyers using credit cards such as MasterCard and Visa are counted as cash sales because the issuer of the credit card, rather than the seller, is providing credit to the buyer. Consequently, most B2C sales are counted as cash sales.

Receivables are uncollected credit sales. Measuring accounts receivable turnover and the average age of receivables are important for firms in which credit sales make up a high proportion of total sales. Accounts receivable turnover is defined as follows:

$$\text{Accounts Receivable Turnover} = \frac{\text{Credit Sales}}{\text{Average Accounts Receivable}}$$

Assume all of Composite Technology's sales are credit sales. Also assume the firm began 2010 with $50 million in receivables and ended the year with $60 million in receivables (both numbers can be found on the balance sheet). Therefore, it had an average of $55 million in receivables. The firm's receivables turnover and average age equal:

$$\frac{\$675.0 \text{ million}}{\$55.0 \text{ million}} = 12.3 \text{ times}$$

$$\frac{365}{12.3} = 29.7 \text{ days}$$

Composite turned its receivables slightly more than 12 times per year. The average age of its receivables was slightly less than 30 days. Because Composite expects its customers to pay outstanding invoices within 30 days, these numbers appear appropriate. As with other ratios, however, receivables turnover and average age of receivables should also be compared with peer firms and historical data.

MARKUPS AND MARKDOWNS

In earlier chapters, we discussed the importance of pricing decisions for firms. This section expands on our prior discussion by introducing two important pricing concepts: markups and markdowns. They can help establish selling prices and evaluate various pricing strategies, and they are closely tied to a firm's income statement.

Markups

The amount a marketer adds to a product's cost to set the final selling price is the markup. The amount of the markup typically results from two marketing decisions:

1. The services performed by the marketer. Other things being equal, retailers who offer more services charge larger markups to cover their costs.

2. The inventory turnover rate. Other things being equal, retailers with a higher turnover rate can cover their costs and earn a profit while charging a smaller markup.

A marketer's markup exerts an important influence on its image among present and potential customers. In addition, the markup affects the retailer's ability to attract shoppers. An excessive markup may drive away customers; an inadequate markup may fail to generate sufficient income to cover costs and return a profit.

Markups typically are stated as percentages of either the selling prices or the costs of the products. The formulas for calculating markups are as follows:

$$\text{Markup Percentage of Selling Price} = \frac{\text{Amount Added to Cost (Markup)}}{\text{Selling Price}}$$

$$\text{Markup Percentage on Cost} = \frac{\text{Amount Added to Cost (Markup)}}{\text{Cost}}$$

Consider a product with an invoice of 60 cents and a selling price of $1. The total markup (selling price less cost) is 40 cents. The two markup percentages are calculated as follows:

$$\text{Markup Percentage on Selling Price} = \frac{\$0.40}{\$1.00} = 40\%$$

$$\text{Markup Percentage on Cost} = \frac{\$0.40}{\$0.60} = 66.7\%$$

To determine the selling price knowing only the cost and markup percentage on selling price, a marketer applies the following formula:

$$\text{Price} = \frac{\text{Cost in Dollars}}{(100\% - \text{Markup Percentage on Selling Price})}$$

In the previous example, to determine the correct selling price of $1, the marketer would calculate as follows:

$$\text{Price} = \frac{\$0.60}{(100\% - 40\%)} = \$1.00$$

Similarly, you can convert the markup percentage from a specific item based on the selling price to one based on cost and the reverse using the following formulas:

$$\text{Markup Percentage on Selling Price} = \frac{\text{Markup Percentage on Cost}}{(100\% + \text{Markup Percentage on Cost})}$$

$$\text{Markup Percentage on Cost} = \frac{\text{Markup Percentage on Selling Price}}{(100\% - \text{Markup Percentage on Selling Price})}$$

Again, data from the previous example give the following conversions:

$$\text{Markup Percentage on Selling Price} = \frac{66.7\%}{(100\% + 66.7\%)} = 40\%$$

$$\text{Markup Percentage on Cost} = \frac{40\%}{(100\% - 40\%)} = 66.7\%$$

Marketers determine markups based partly on their judgments of the amounts consumers will pay for a given product. When buyers refuse to pay a product's stated price, however, or when improvements in other products or fashion changes reduce the appeal of the current merchandise, a producer or retailer must take a markdown.

Markdowns

A markdown is a price reduction a firm makes on an item. Reasons for markdowns include sales promotions featuring price reductions or a decision that the initial price was too high. Unlike markups, markdowns cannot be determined from the income statement because the price reduction takes place before the sale occurs. The markdown percentage equals dollar markdowns divided by sales. For example, a retailer may decide to reduce the price of an item by $10, from $50 to $40, and sells 1,000 units. The markdown percentage equals:

$$\frac{(1{,}000 \times \$10)}{(1{,}000 \times \$40)} = \frac{\$10{,}000}{\$40{,}000} = 25\%$$

NOTES

Chapter 1

1. Company Web site, http://www.colgate.com, accessed April 3, 2009; "Colgate Banks on New Product Launches," *Forbes,* http://www.forbes.com, February 22, 2008, accessed April 2, 2009; Matthew Boyle, "Colgate's World-Beating Performance," *BusinessWeek*, March 26, 2009, http://www.businessweek.com; Karl Greenberg, "Colgate Up on New Dental Hygiene Products," *Marketing Daily*, January 29, 2009, http://www.mediapost.com.

2. Ryan Kim, "iPhone's Success Spawns Generations of Imitators—and Challengers," San *Francisco Chronicle,* November 5, 2007, www.sfgate.com, accessed September 29, 2008.

3. Dylan Stableford, "Newspaper Industry Sees Biggest Ad Revenue Decline in More than 50 Years," *Folio,* March 30, 2008, www.foliomag.com; Carolyn Y. Johnson, "Newspaper Circulation Still on Decline," *The Boston Globe,* November 6, 2007, www.boston.com, accessed September 29, 2008.

4. Moneé Fields-White, "Walgreen Making More Space for Movies," *Chicago Business News,* February 27, 2008, www.chicagobusiness.com.

5. "Mattel Aims at Preteens with Barbie Web Brand," *MSNBC,* April 26, 2007, www.msnbc.com, accessed September 29, 2008.

6. Joseph P. Guiltinan and Gordon W. Paul, *Marketing Management,* 6th ed., (New York: McGraw-Hill), 1996, pp. 3–4.

7. American Marketing Association, "Resource Library," www.marketingpower.com.

8. Jonathan Ages, "Annoying Airline Charges," *MSNBC,* May 29, 2008, www.msnbc.com; "Dow Chemical to Raise Prices 20% to Combat High Energy Costs," *International Herald Tribune,* May 28, 2008, www.iht.com.

9. Bruce Einhorn, "Rolls-Royce Targets China's Really Rich," *BusinessWeek,* May 7, 2008, www.businessweek.com.

10. U.S. Census Bureau, Foreign Trade Statistics, www.census.gov, accessed May 6, 2008.

11. "Costs Driving U.S. Manufacturing Firms Out of China," *IndustryWeek,* April 29, 2008, www.industryweek.com.

12. Jack Ewing, "Telecom's Last Great Growth Markets," *BusinessWeek,* May 22, 2008, www.businessweek.com.

13. Company Web site, www.google.com, accessed May 30, 2008; Chuck Salter, "Google," *Fast Company,* February 14, 2008, www.fastcompany.com.

14. Leslie Wayne, "Airbus Superjumbo Takes a Lap Around America," *The New York Times,* March 20, 2007, www.nytimes.com, accessed September 29, 2008.

15. Michael Cai and James Kuai, "The Evolution of U.S. Mobile Broadband Wireless," *TechNewsWorld,* March 14, 2008, www.technewsworld.com; Natasha Lomas, "Ericsson CEO Hails Mobile Broadband 'Breakthrough,'" *Silicon.com,* February 11, 2008, networks.silicon.com.

16. Company Web site, www.inov8-intl.com, accessed May 30, 2008; "Bringing Green to the Restaurant Scene," company press release, May 29, 2008, www.the-mrea.org.

17. "Number of Nonprofit Organizations in the United States," National Center for Charitable Statistics, nccsdataweb.urban.org, accessed May 30, 2008; Amy Blackwood, Kennard T. Wing, and Thomas H. Pollak, "The NonProfit Sector in Brief," from *Nonprofit Almanac 2008,* National Center for Charitable Statistics.

18. Organization Web site, www.connerprairie.org, accessed May 30, 2008.

19. Organization Web site, www.stjude.org, accessed May 30, 2008.

20. Organization Web site, www.secondharvest.org, accessed May 30, 2008.

21. "Donors Make a Difference," press release, www.mdanderson.org, accessed May 30, 2008.

22. Wailin Wong, "Charities See Potential in Tapping Young Web Users to Promote Their Causes Online," *Chicago Tribune,* April 30, 2008, Section 3, pp. 1, 4.

23. Organization Web site, www.livestrong.org, accessed May 30, 2008.

24. Barry Janoff, "Eli Manning Already Scoring off MVP Showing," *BrandWeek,* February 6, 2008, www.brandweek.com; Tim Arango, "Top 10 Endorsement Superstars," *Fortune,* November 2007, money.cnn.com, accessed September 29, 2008. Tim Arango, "LeBron Inc.," *Fortune,* November 28, 2007, money.cnn.com, accessed September 29, 2008. Sarah Jane Gilbert, "Marketing Maria: Managing the Athlete Endorsement," *Working Knowledge* (Harvard Business School), October 29, 2007, hbswk.hbs.edu.

25. Gary Rivlin, "MGM Plans Huge Atlantic City Resort," *The New York Times,* October 10, 2007, www.nytimes.com, accessed September 29, 2008.

26. Miyoko Ohtake, "Virgin Galactic Preps for Liftoff at World's First Commercial Spaceport," *Wired,* September 25, 2007, www.wired.com, accessed September 29, 2008.

27. "NYC Rolls Out the Welcome Mat," *New York Daily News,* August 29, 2007, www.nydailynews.com.

28. "Skiing at Davis, West Virginia's Timberline Resort," *Ski NC,* www.skinorthcarolina.com, accessed May 30, 2008.

29. Organization Web site, www.savingpaws.com, accessed May 30, 2008.

30. Ben Rooney, "Super Bowl Ads: $2.7 Million and Worth It," *CNNMoney,* January 25, 2008, www.money.cnn.com.

31. Sarah Skidmore and Joe McDonald, "Sprint among Shoemakers Is on for Beijing Olympics," *The San Diego Union-Tribune,* October 8, 2007, beijingtoday.org.

32. Tim Tucker, "Dogs in Top 5 in Merchandising," *The Atlanta Journal-Constitution,* August 19, 2007, www.ajc.com.

33. Brad Kennedy, "Cannondale Bicycle Turns to Blogging Solution to Engage Customers and Partners," *IndustryWeek,* January 11, 2008, www.industryweek.com.

34. Karl Greenberg, "New Dunkin' Donuts Marketing Runs on Videos," Media Post Publications, www.mediapost.com/publications, January 28, 2008.

35. Liz Clarke, "NASCAR's New Marketing Strategy Is the Latest Buzz," *The Washington Post,* May 26, 2007, www.washingtonpost.com.

36. Brad Stone and Matt Richtel, "Baseball Gets into Resale of Tickets," *The New York Times,* August 2, 2007, www.nytimes.com, accessed September 29, 2008.

37. Company Web site, "CSR: Transparency & Accountability," www.timberland.com, accessed May 30, 2008.

38. Organization Web site, www.goodshepherdsistersna.com, accessed May 30, 2008.

39. Company Web site, PNC Grow Up Great Program, www.pncgrowupgreat.com, accessed May 30, 2008; "Congratulations to the Winners of CECP's Excellence Awards," press release, February 25, 2008, www.corporatephilanthropy.org.

Chapter 2

1. Company Web site, sites.target.com, accessed June 2, April 16, 2009; Jennifer Reingold, "Target's Inner Circle," *Fortune,* March 31, 2008, pp. 75–86; Eric Wilson and Michael Barbaro, "Big Names in Retail Fashion Are Trading Teams," *The New York Times,* March 8, 2008, www.nytimes.com, accessed September 29, 2008; Annual Report 2007, Target Corporation.

2. Beth Braverman, "Congress Examines Giant Airline Merger," *CNNMoney.com,* May 14, 2008, www.money.cnn.com; "Delta, Northwest Approve Merger," *CNNInternational.com,* April 14, 2008, edition.cnn.com.

3. Carol Tice, "Sell Without Selling Out," *Entrepreneur,* June 2008, pp. 19–20.

4. A. G. Lafley and Ram Charan, "Innovation: Making Inspiration Routine," *Inc. Magazine,* June 2008, www.inc.com.

5. "After Years of Squabbling, Wendy's and Arby's Unite," *The Salt Lake Tribune,* April 28, 2008, www.sltrib.com; Jeff Gelski, "Wendy's, Franchisor of Arby's Agree to Merge," *Food Business News,* April 24, 2008, www.foodbusinessnews.net.

6. Gavin O'Malley, "Study: Influencers Possess Less Clout," *MediaPost Publications,* April 3, 2008, publications.mediapost.com.

7. "Cellphone Service Providers Start to Tear Down Walls," *USA Today,* November 29, 2007, www.usatoday.com, accessed September 29, 2008.

8. "Two-thirds of Consumers Shop Online Before Buying, New Poll Reports," *Internet Retailer,* November 7, 2007, www.internetretailer.com, accessed September 29, 2008.

9. Robert Passikoff, "You Want a Latte With That? Mc D's Brews Up Coffee Strategy," *Chief Marketer,* www.chiefmarketer.com, accessed June 6, 2008; Jennifer Ordonez, "The Latte Wars," *Newsweek,* January 11, 2008, www.newsweek.com.

10. Jim Dalrymple, "iPod Success Won't Stop at 100 Million," *PC World,* April 9, 2007, www.pcworld.com.

11. "Target to Match Wal-Mart Prescription Drug Program," *Washington Business Journal,* May 6, 2008, www.washington.bizjournals.com.

12. Larry Sultan, "Streamlining HP," *Fast Company,* October 2007, www.fastcompany.com; Denise Dubie, "Hurd: Software Critical to HP Success," *Network World,* June 19, 2007, www.networkworld.com.

13. Derek F. Abell, "Strategic Windows," *Journal of Marketing,* vol. 42, no. 3 (July 1978), pp. 21–26.

14. Nandini Lakshman, "India's High-Octane Car Market," *Business Week,* April 16, 2007, www.businessweek.com.

15. Julie Jargon, "Kraft Reformulates Oreo, Scores in China," *The Wall Street Journal,* May 1, 2008, p. B1.

16. "Hispanic Population in the United States: 1970 to 2050," U.S. Census Bureau, February 8, 2008, www.census.gov.

17. Kimberly Palmer, "An Rx for Women," *U.S. News & World Report,* November 1, 2007, www.usnews.com, accessed September 29, 2008.

18. Company Web site, http://www.ford.com, accessed April 16, 2009; Bryce Hoffman, "'One Ford' Plan Will Rush Fuel-Efficient Cars to the U.S.," *The Seattle Times,* October 3, 2008, http://seattletimes.nwsource.com.

19. K. C. Jones, "Netflix Subscribers Get Unlimited Streaming Video," *Information Week,* January 14, 2008, www.informationweek.com.

20. Elizabeth M. Gillespie, "Starbucks to Give Away 50 Million Songs," *Associated Press,* September 24, 2007, www.news.yahoo.com.

21. Deidra Dukes, "Atlanta Air Travelers Hit Hard by Fare Hikes, Fees," *MyFox,* June 6, 2008, www.myfoxatlanta.com; Dave Carpenter, "US Air Travel Options Shrink Amid Carrier Strife," *Associated Press,* June 4, 2008, www.usatoday.com/money.

22. Peter Poe, "Southwest's Oil-Price Gamble Is Paying Off," *The Denver Post,* May 30, 2008, www.denverpost.com.

23. "Chinese Car Plant to be Built in Mexico," *Associated Press,* November 23, 2007, www.newsvine.com.

24. Lawrence Ulrich, "Diesel Automobiles Clean up for an Encore," *The New York Times,* May 18, 2008, www.nytimes.com.

25. Brad Stone, "Microsoft to Pay $240 Million for Stake in Facebook," *The New York Times,* October 25, 2007, www.nytimes.com, accessed September 29, 2008.

26. Catherine Holahan, "Auctions on eBay: A Dying Breed," *Business Week,* June 3, 2008, www.businessweek.com.

27. Matt Vella, "Why GE Is Getting out of the Kitchen," *Business Week,* May 16, 2008, www.businessweek.com.

28. Company Web site, www.store.apple.com, accessed June 3, 2008.

29. Andrew Ross Sorking and Steve Lohr, "Pursuing Yahoo, Microsoft Shows Need for Web Franchise," *The New York Times,* May 20, 2008, www.nytimes.com.

30. Erick Schonfeld, "Diller Wins His Court Battle—But Can IAC Succeed?," *Seeking Alpha,* April 1, 2008, www.seekingalpha.com.

Chapter 3

1. Company Web site, Peanut Corporation of America, http://www.peanutcorp.com, accessed April 3, 2009; Lyndsey Layton, "Nestlé's Inspectors Saw Rat Droppings, Rejected Peanuts," *The Washington Post*, March 20, 2009, http://www.washingtonpost.com; Kate Brumback and Greg Bluestein, "Peanut Corp. of America Files for Bankruptcy," *Yahoo! News*, February 13, 2009, http://news.yahoo.com; Jane Zhang and Julie Jargon, "Peanut Corp. E-mails Cast Harsh Light on Executive," *The Wall Street Journal*, February 12, 2009, p. A3; Michael Moss, "Peanut Case Shows Holes in Safety Net," *The New York Times*, February 8, 2009, http://www.nytimes.com; Dahleen Glanton, "Inside 'Nasty' Peanut Plant," *Chicago Tribune*, February 4, 2009, pp. 1, 4; Gardiner Harris, "Peanut Plant Knew of Contamination, Inspectors Say," *The New York Times*, January 28, 2009, http://www.nytimes.com; Roni Caryn Rabin, "Peanut Plant Had History of Health Lapses," *The New York Times*, January 26, 2009, http://www.nytimes.com.

2. "Fliers Faced with Fewer Seats," *Baltimore Sun,* June 5, 2008, www.baltimoresun.com.

3. "Report: China Halts Export of Bead Toys Tainted with Toxic Drug," *CNN,* November 9, 2007, www.cnn.com; Tim Johnson, "Chinese Toy Factories Retool after Recall," *McClatchy Newspapers,* October 23, 2007, www.mcclatchydc.com; "Mattel Issues New Massive China Toy Recall," *MSNBC,* August 14, 2007, www.msnbc.msn.com, accessed September 29, 2008.

4. "Mortgage Industry Group Spent $3.7 Million Lobbying in 2007," *Yahoo! Finance,* April 22, 2008, www.ibtimes.com.

5. Terry Frieden, "Settlement May Give Online Realtors Access to More Listings," *CNN,* May 27, 2008, www.cnn.com.

6. Chi-Chu Tschang, "Can China Take on Boeing and Airbus?" *Business Week,* May 12, 2008, www.businessweek.com.

7. Company Web site, www.costco.com, accessed April 28, 2009; "Costco January Same-Store Sales up 7 Percent," *Reuters,* February 7, 2008, www.reuters.com.

8. Candace Lombardi, "Siemens to Open Colorado Wind Turbine R&D Center," *CNET News,* June 4, 2008, news.cnet.com.

9. CNET Web site, cnet.jiwire.com, accessed June 11, 2008.

10. Queenie Wong, "Will WiMax Replace Wi-Fi and Change the Way We Live?" *McClatchy Newspapers,* April 30, 2008, www.mcclatchydc.com; Galen Gruman, "WiFi vs. WiMax," *Daily Wireless,* February 21, 2007, www.dailywireless.com.

11. "Dr Pepper Spin-Off Gets Green Light," *KWTX Daily,* April 11, 2008, www.kwtx.com.

12. Sinead Carew, "Verizon Wireless to Buy Alltel in $28.1 Billion Deal," *Yahoo! Finance,* June 5, 2008, www.yahoo.com.

13. Marc Gunther, "Stonyfield Stirs Up the Yogurt Market," *Fortune,* January 4, 2008, www.money.cnn.com.

14. "TSA Expands Paperless Boarding Pass Pilot Program to Additional Airports and Airlines," Transportation Security Administration Web site, May 28, 2008, www.tsa.gov.

15. Roy Mark, "Senate Bill Targets Cyber-Crime," *PC Magazine,* November 20, 2007, www.pcmag.com.

16. Jennifer C. Kerr, "FTC, Six Firms Settle Do Not Call Charges," *The Washington Post,* November 8, 2007, www.washingtonpost.com, accessed September 29, 2008.

17. Ransdell Pierson, "Cholesterol-Drug Rejection Rips New Gash in Merck," *Reuters,* April 29, 2008, www.reuters.com.

18. Liz Pulliam Weston, "What the New Credit Score Means to You," *MSN Money,* www.moneycentral.msn.com, accessed April 28, 2009.

19. Coalition for Fire-Safe Cigarettes Web site, www.firesafecigarettes.org, accessed June 5, 2008.

20. American Humane Association Web site, www.americanhumane.org, accessed April 28, 2009.

21. Direct Marketing Association Web site, www.dmaccc.org, accessed April 28, 2009.

22. Bureau of Economic Analysis, www.bea.gov, accessed May 21, 2008.

23. James MacPherson, "Gas Prices Knock Bicycle Sales, Repairs into Higher Gear," *Associated Press,* May 11, 2008, www.ap.google.com.

24. Ben Steverman, "Investing: Keeping Inflation at Bay," *Business Week,* June 3, 2008, www.businessweek.com.

25. Tami Luhby, "Americans $1.7 Trillion Poorer," *CNN.Money.com,* June 5, 2008, www.worldnewstrust.com.

26. "Personal Income and Outlays: April 2008," Bureau of Economic Analysis, May 30, 2008, www.bea.gov.

27. Matthew Robinson, "Oil Posts Record $6 Gain on Weak U.S. Dollar," *Yahoo! Finance,* June 5, 2008, news.yahoo.com.

28. Michelle Conlin, "Suddenly, It's Cool to Take the Bus," *Business Week,* May 5, 2008, p. 24.

29. J.P. Vettraino, "How Green Is Your Ride?" *AutoWeek,* April 21, 2008, www.autoweek.com.

30. Peter Ford and Mark Trumbull, "China's Economic Growth Can Soften U.S. Slump," *Christian Science Monitor,* February 13, 2008, www.csmonitor.com, accessed April 28, 2009; Peter Ford, "Consumer Tidal Wave on the Way: China's Middle Class," *Christian Science Monitor,* January 2, 2007, www.csmonitor.com, accessed September 29, 2008.

31. "A Catastrophe Playing Out Around the World," *U.S. News & World Report,* May 19, 2008; Daniel Workman, "Top Soybean Countries," *International Trade,* September 17, 2007, www.internationaltrade.suite101.com, accessed September 29, 2008.

32. Dennis Carter, "Study Probes RFID Use in Schools," *eSchoolNews,* May 20, 2008, www.eschoolnews.com, accessed September 29, 2008; "Dow AgroSciences Recognized for Innovative Use of RFID Technology," May 2, 2007, Corporate Web site, www.dow.com, accessed September 29, 2008.

33. Mark Clayton, "The Race for Nonfood Biofuel," *Christian Science Monitor,* June 4, 2008, www.csmonitor.com; Martin LaMonica, "Dollar-a-Gallon Ethanol Plant in U.S. Operation Next Year," *CNET News,* April 25, 2008, www.news.com.

34. Phillip Rucker, "U.S. Medical Research Gets $600 Million from Institute," *The Washington Post,* May 27, 2008, www.washingtonpost.com.

35. "Vonage Holdings 1Q Loss Narrows on Sales and Lower Costs," *Business Week,* May 8, 2008, www.businessweek.com.

36. B. Bakmaz, Z. Boykovic, and M. Bakmaz, "Internet Protocol Multimedia Subsystem for Mobile Services," *IEEE Xplore,* June 27–30, 2007, www.ieeexplore.ieee.org.

37. Laura Casey, "Baby Boomers: A New Kind of Grandparent," *Contra Costa Times,* June 3, 2008, www.contracostatimes.com; "Experts Predict Top Trends in Marketing to Baby Boomers in 2007," *Senior Journal,* March 6, 2007, www.seniorjournal.com, accessed September 29, 2008.

38. "Hispanic Media Facts," *Hispanic PR Wire,* www.hispanicprwire.com, accessed April 28, 2009; "News Corp.'s Fox Launching LatAm Online Ad Network," *Associated Press,* May 19, 2008, www.usatoday.com.

39. Telis Demos, "Bag Revolution," *Fortune,* May 12, 2008, p. 18.

40. Edith Honan, "New York Chain Eateries Must Post Calorie Counts," *Reuters,* January 22, 2008, www.reuters.com.

41. Government Web site, www.recalls.gov, accessed April 28, 2009.

42. Corporate Ethics-US Web site, www.corporate-ethics.us, accessed June 6, 2008.

43. Jane Porter, "Using Ex-Cons to Scare MBAs Straight," *Business Week,* May 5, 2008, p. 58.

44. "Justices to Review Tobacco Award," *The New York Times,* June 9, 2008, www.ihts.com.

45. "GE Money Reports Customer Data Loss," *Finextra,* January 21, 2008, www.finextra.com.

46. "HSBC Investigates after Loss of Customer Data Disc," *Brand Republic,* April 7, 2008, www.brandrepublic.com.

47. Andrew Martin, "Kellogg to Curb Marketing of Foods to Children," *The New York Times,* June 14, 2007, www.nytimes.com, accessed April 28, 2009.

48. Jake Swearingen, "Pepsi and Coke to Reform Marketing Efforts to Kids—Maybe," BNET Industries blog, May 20, 2008, industry.bnet.com.

49. Maria Glod, "Student Lender to End Deals with Colleges for Use of Logos," *The Washington Post,* December 12, 2007, www.washingtonpost.com, accessed September 30, 2008.

50. Christine Dugas, "Subprime Cards' High Fees Can Add to Debt Troubles," *USA Today,* November 27, 2007, www.usatoday.com, accessed September 30, 2008; Tony Pugh, "Crackdown Urged on 'Fee-Harvester' Credit Cards," *McClatchy Newspapers,* November 1, 2007, www.mcclatchydc.com, accessed September 30, 2008.

51. Andrea Coombes, "Some Credit Cards Get a Little Less Onerous," *MarketWatch,* March 1, 2007, www.marketwatch.com.

52. David Barboza, "China Says Abusive Child Labor Ring Is Exposed," *The New York Times,* May 1, 2008, www.nytimes.com.

53. "803 Certified Community Development Financial Institutions as of 4/1/2008," CDFI Fund, April 3, 2008, www.cdfifund.gov.

54. "Best Buy Testing Free E-Waste Recycling Program," *CNNMoney.com,* June 2, 2008, www.msnbc.msn.com.

55. James R. Healey, "Honda Upping Number of Fuel-Cell Cars on U.S. Roads," *USA Today,* October 24, 2007, www.usatoday.com.

56. "Starwood Launching Green Hotel Brand in Lexington, Mass.," *Yahoo! Finance,* April 21, 2008, www.news.yahoo.com.

57. Organic Trade Association Web site, www.ota.com, accessed April 28, 2009; Charles Abbott, "U.S. Has Huge Appetite for Organic Food: Industry," *Reuters,* April 24, 2007, www.reuters.com.

58. National Organic Program, United States Department of Agriculture Web site, www.ams.usda.gov, accessed April 28, 2009.

Chapter 4

1. Company Web site, www.amazon.com, accessed April 21, 2009; Alex Vochin, "Amazon Sold 500,00 Kindle eBook Readers, Kindle 2.0 Almost Here," *Softpedia.com,* February 4, 2009, http://gadgets.softpedia.com; "Amazon Ships Kindle 2.0 Earlier than Planned," *The Arizona Republic,* February 23, 2009, http://www.azcentral.com; Megan McArdle, "The Coming of Kindle 2.0," *The Atlantic Business Channel,* February 9, 2009, http://business.theatlantic.com; Brad Stone, "Amazon's Kindle 2 Will Debut Feb. 9," *The New York Times,* January 27, 2009, http://bits.blogs.nytimes.com; Dominic Rushe and Nic Fleming, "Amazon Kindle Buyers Rush for the iPod of Books," *TimesOnline,* June 8, 2008, http://technology.timesonline.co.uk; Andrew Nusca, "Amazon Kindle Back on the Market," *ZDNet,* May 27, 2008, http://blogs.zdnet.com; Michael Lev-Ram, "Amazon Kindle Hopes to Become the iPod of Books," *Fortune,* May 20, 2008, http://techland.blogs.fortune.cnn.com; Katherine Noyes, "Will Amazon's Kindle Spark an E-Reading Revolution?" *TechNewsWorld,* November 20, 2007, www.technewsworld.com; Steven Levy, "The Future of Reading," *Newsweek,* November 18, 2007; www.newsweek.com.

2. "E-Stats," U.S. Census Bureau, May 16, 2008, census.gov/estats.

3. "Top 20 Countries with Highest Number of Internet Users," *Internet World Stats,* March 31, 2008, www.internetworldstats.com.

4. "Top 20 Countries with Highest Number of Internet Users."

5. "India, China Propel Asia-Pacific Internet Use," *Marketing Vox,* July 3, 2008, www.marketingvox.com.

6. *Internet World Stats,* March 31, 2008, www.internetworldstats.com; Blaine Harden, "Japan's Warp-Speed Ride to Internet Future," *The Washington Post,* August 29, 2007, www.washingtonpost.com.

7. "Top Online Activities of Internet Users," *Digital Marketing & Media Fact Sheet,* www.adage.com.

8. John Horrigan, "Mobile Access to Data and Information," Pew Internet & American Life Project, March 2008.

9. Ben Worthen, "China's Very Different Internet Use," *The Wall Street Journal.com;* February 13, 2008, blogs.wsj.com.

10. "Alternative Reality: The Internet in China," *The Economist,* January 31, 2008, www.economist.com; David Barboza, "Internet Boom in China Is Built on Virtual Fun," *The New York Times,* February 5, 2007, www.nytimes.com.

11. John Tozzi, "Indie Filmmakers Hit Their Target," *BusinessWeek,* June 5, 2008, www.businessweek.com.

12. Company Web site, www.sevencycles.com, accessed April 28, 2009.

13. Company Web site, www.americanidol.com, accessed April 28, 2009.

14. "Two-thirds of Consumers Shop Online Before Buying, New Poll Reports," *Internet Retailer,* November 7, 2007, www.internetretailer.com; "Most Consumers Do Research Online Before Purchasing in Stores: Survey," *Supermarket News,* April 5, 2007, www.supermarketnews.com.

15. John B. Horrigan, "The Internet and Consumer Choice," Pew Internet & American Life Project, May 18, 2008.

16. Company Web site, www.bk.com, accessed April 28, 2009.

17. Company Web site, www.usa.canon.com, accessed April 28, 2009.

18. "E-Stats," U.S. Census Bureau, May 16, 2008, census.gov/estats.

19. Bruce Caldwell, "Harley Shifts into Higher Gear," *Information Week,* www.informationweek.com, accessed July 18, 2008.

20. Jeremy Kahn, "Pounding Keys, Not Gavels, to Sell India's Tea," *The New York Times,* April 22, 2008, www.nytimes.com.

21. William J. Angelo, "E-Procurement Process Delivers Best Value for Kodak," *Engineering News-Record,* March 17, 2008, enr.construction.com.

22. "Federal and Local Government Contracts, Bids, and RFPs in the State of Michigan," www.bidcontract.com, accessed April 28, 2009.

23. "Quarterly Retail E-Commerce Sales, 1st Quarter 2008," U.S. Census Bureau, May 18, 2008, www.census.gov.

24. John B. Horrigan, "Online Shopping: Convenient but Risky," Pew Research Center Publications, February 13, 2008, www.pewresearch.org.

25. Anne D'innocenzio, "Online Sales Expected to Rise 17% in 2008," *USA Today,* April, 8, 2008, www.usatoday.com.

26. Company Web site, www.ac.com, accessed April 28, 2009.

27. John Horrigan, "Mobile Access to Data and Information," Pew Internet & American Life Project," March 2008.

28. Laura M. Holson, "Shopping via Cellphone Slowed by Security Fears," *The New York Times,* June 23, 2008, bits.blogs.nytimes.com.

29. Dawn Kawamoto, "Amazon Rings Up Shopping via Text-Message," *CNet News,* April 2, 2008, www.news.com.

30. Company Web site, www.expedia.com, accessed April 28, 2009.

31. Company Web site, www.barnesandnoble.com, accessed April 28, 2009.

32. Jessica Mintz, "Amazon Launches Text-Message Shopping," *Associated Press,* April 2, 2008, news.yahoo.com.

33. Robert K. Elder, "Visual Search Portal Sees Bigger Picture for Web Users," *Chicago Tribune,* January 28, 2007, Section 1, pp. 1, 20.

34. "Nielsen Online Reports Topline U.S. Data," *Market Wire,* June 2008, www.findarticles.com.

35. "U.S. Online Retail Sales," Digital Marketing & Media Fact Pack, *Advertising Age,* www.adage.com, accessed April 28, 2009.

36. Joe Chung, "The Red Queen of E-Commerce," *Ecommerce Times,* July 10, 2008, www.ecommercetimes.com.

37. Company Web site, www.verisign.com, accessed April 28, 2009.

38. "Five New Online Retailers Add eBillme as a Payment Option," *Internet Retailer,* March 11, 2008, www.internetretailer.com; "Online Retailers Offering More Alternative Payment Methods," *Internet Retailer,* January 3, 2008, www.internetretailer.com.

39. Janet Kornblum, "Online Privacy? For Young People, That's Old School," *USA Today,* October 23, 2007, www.usatoday.com.

40. "Consumer Advocates Want Do Not Track Anti-Cookie Registry," *Download Squad,* April 17, 2008, www.downloadsquad.com; Catherine Rampell, "'Do Not Track' Registry Proposed for Web Use," *The Washington Post,* November 1, 2007, www.washingtonpost.com.

41. "House Panel Approves Anti-Spyware Bill," *Internetnew.com,* Septermber 22, 2004, www.news.com.internet.

42. Roy Mark, "Consumers Well Aware of Behavioral Tracking, Targeting—Don't Like It Much," *MediaBuyerPlanner,* April 1, 2008, www.mediabuyerplanner.com; Eric Auchard, "Google Wary of Behavioral Targeting in Online Ads," *Reuters,* July 31, 2007, news.reuters.com.

43. Robert Vamosi, "Reports Examine Causes, Victims of Data Breaches," *CNet News,* June 11, 2008, news.cnet.com.

44. Thomas Claburn, "Security Worries Leave Federal IT Personnel Sleep Deprived," *Information Week,* November 8, 2007, www.techweb.com.

45. Organization Web site, www.ic3.gov, accessed July 21, 2008.

46. "Phishing Related to Issuance of Economic Stimulus Checks," Internet Crime Complaint Center Intelligence Note, May 8, 2008, www.ic3.gov.

47. "Vishing," *PC Magazine,* www.pcmag.com, accessed April 28, 2009.

48. "Online Retail Sales in 2008," *The Kiplinger Letter,* March 3, 2008, www.kiplinger.com.

49. "Nielsen Reports 875 Million Consumers Have Shopped Online," Nielsen Media Research, January 28, 2008, www.nielsenmedia.com.

50. Mark Anderson, "The Gray Areas of Search-Engine Law," *IEEE Spectrum,* January 2008, spectrum.ieee.org.

51. Company Web site, www.universalmusic.com, accessed April 28, 2009; David Kraverts, "Universal Music Sues Video-Sharing Site," *ABC News,* September 5, 2007, abcnews.go.com.

52. Matt Asay, "Study: 95 Percent of All E-Mail Sent in 2007 Was Spam," *CNet Blogs,* December 12, 2007, blogs.cnet.com.

53. Company Web site, www.digg.com, accessed April 28, 2009; Catherine Holahan, "Digg Goes Deeper with Social Networking," *BusinessWeek,* September 19, 2007, www.businessweek.com.

54. "Top 10 U.S. Social-Network and Blog-Site Rankings Issued for May," *Marketing Charts,* May 2008, www.marketingcharts.com.

55. Company Web site, www.communityconnect.com, accessed April 28, 2009.

56. Mark Walsh, "EMarketer Trims Social Network Ad Forecast," *MediaPost Publications,* May 14, 2008, www.mediapost.com.

57. Wailin Wong, "Tech Firms in a Love–Hate Relationship with Bloggers," *Chicago Tribune,* June 16, 2008, Section 3, pp. 1, 6.

58. Company Web site, www.checkoutblog.com, accessed April 28, 2009; "Wal-Mart's Check Out Blog Does Not Challenge Traditional Mode," *The Employee Factor,* www.employeefactor.com, accessed July 23, 2008.

59. Greg Sandoval, "Report: YouTube Ready to Run Preroll and Postroll Ads," *CNet News,* July 8, 2008, news.cnet.com; "NBC Will Limit Pre-Roll Video Commercials to 15 Seconds for Short Clips," *BtoB,* May 9, 2007, www.usatoday.com.

60. Bill Pfleging, "Putting Widgets to Work," *Inc.,* May 2008, technology.inc.com; Jefferson Graham, "Google, MySpace Are Teaming Up," *USA Today,* November 2, 2007, news.yahoo.com.

61. *SearchEngineWatch* Web site, www.searchenginewatch.com, accessed August 15, 2008; Anick Jesdanun, "Major Internet Hubs See Lesser Influence," *Yahoo! News,* October 8, 2007, news.yahoo.com.

62. David E. Gumpert, "The Right Way to Use Web 2.0," *Yahoo! News,* August 27, 2007, www.businessweek.com.

63. "MySpace to Release Major Site Redesign," *CNet News,* June 12, 2008, news.cnet.com.

64. "Nielsen: Google Continues High But Others Rise in Share," *Search Engine Land,* April 21, 2008, www.searchengineland.com; "Web Hosting Details," *Yahoo! Small Business,* smallbusiness.yahoo.com, accessed July 23, 2008.

65. Company Web site, virginholidays.co.uk, accessed August 15, 2008; Chloe Berman, "Virgin Conversions Up After Site Rethink," *Travel Weekly,* December 7, 2007, www.travelweekly.com.

66. Kendra Marr, "Nielsen Alters Web Ratings, Favoring AOL Over Google," *The Washington Post,* July 11, 2007, www.washingtonpost.com.

67. Richard Karpinski, "Microsoft, Others Seek to Gauge Engagement," *BtoB,* April 7, 2008, www.btobonline.com.

Chapter 5

1. Company Web site, http://www.envirosell.com, accessed April 10, 2009; Josh Hunter, "Envirosell's The Science of Shopping Conference," *Transworld Business,* March 13, 2009, http://business.transworld.net; Maria Halkias, "Shoppers Departing Department Stores—and May Not Be Back," *The Dallas Morning News,* February 20, 2009, http://www.envirosell.com; Susan Berfield, "Getting the Most Out of Every Shopper," *BusinessWeek,* February 9, 2009, pp. 45–46.

2. Della de Lafuente, "Advertising: Que? An All-Spanish Ad on English Language TV?" *BrandWeek,* November 17, 2007, www.brandweek.com.

3. Cecilia Kang, "Running L8 But CU Soon. Luv, Mom," *The Washington Post,* April 11, 2008, www.washingtonpost.com.

4. Peter Gumbel, "Big Mac's Local Flavor," *CNNMoney,* May 2, 2008, money.cnn.com.

5. U.S. Census Bureau, Table 1a, "Projected Population of the United States, by Race and Hispanic Origin: 2000 to 2050," www.census.gov, accessed April 21, 2009; "U.S. Population Projection: 2005–2050," *The Pew Charitable Trusts,* February 11, 2008, www.pewtrusts.org.

6. U.S. Census Bureau, "Projected Population of the United States, by Race and Hispanic Origin."

7. "Statistical Portrait of Hispanics in the United States," *Pew Hispanic Center,* January 2008, www.pewtrusts.org.

8. Halim Trujillo, "Acculturation among Hispanics in a Changing Landscape," *Radio Business Report,* May 9, 2008, www.rbr.com.

9. Conor Dougherty and Miriam Jordan, "U.S. Hispanic Population Growth Is Driven by Domestic Birthrate," *The Wall Street Journal,* May 1, 2008, p. A3.

10. Dougherty and Jordan, "U.S. Hispanic Population Growth Is Driven by Domestic Birthrate."

11. U.S. Census Bureau, "Projected Population of the United States, by Race and Hispanic Origin."

12. "African American Market in the U.S.," *Packaged Facts,* February 1, 2008, www.packagedfacts.com.

13. "African American Buying Power Gets Star Treatment," *Marketing Vox,* October 19, 2007, www.marketingvox.com.

14. Eric Weil, "Study Looks at Habits of African American Students as Consumers," *Target Market News,* June 10, 2008, www.targetmarketnews.com.

15. U.S. Census Bureau, "Projected Population of the United States, by Race and Hispanic Origin."

16. "Marketing to Asian Americans," *Adweek,* May 29, 2008, www.adweek.com.

17. "Food For Thought," *Asian Week,* January 27, 2008, www.asianweek.com.

18. LaToyah Burke, "One Size Won't Fit All," *Happi,* October 2007, www.happi.com.

19. Todd Hale, "How the Rich Get Richer," *Nielsen,* www.nielsen.com, accessed June 10, 2008.

20. Sandra M. Jones and Deanese Williams-Harris, "Bargain Hunting Is Rule of the Day," *Chicago Tribune,* May 9, 2008, section 1, pp. 1, 24.

21. Lori Aratani, "Drool Now, Spend Later," *The Washington Post,* June 4, 2007, www.washingtonpost.com.

22. Liz Moyer, "The World's Most Exclusive Credit Cards," *Forbes,* July 20, 2007, www.forbes.com.

23. Sarah Hall, "Oprah Discovers Own Network," *EOnline,* January 15, 2008, froggy101.com.

24. Sheryll Alexander, "Women and Cars: How Women Influence Car Design and Buying Power," *AOL Autos,* March 5, 2008, autos.aol.com.

25. "Electronics Purchasers List on the Market," *DM News,* January 22, 2008, www.dmnews.com; "Women, Not Men, Are Primary Electronics Consumers," *Gizmag,* March 6, 2007, www.gizmag.com.

26. Alexander, "Women and Cars: How Women Influence Car Design and Buying Power."

27. "Technical Savvy and Increased Purchasing Power to Drive Teen Market Beyond $200 Billion by 2011," *Packaged Facts,* June 26, 2007, www.packagedfacts.com.

28. "Technical Savvy and Increased Purchasing Power to Drive Teen Marketing."

29. Stefanie Olsen, "A New Crops of Kids: Generation We," *CNET News,* January 22, 2007, news.com.com.

30. Ken Mallon, "Beating Online Ad Clutter," *MediaPostPublications,* January 29, 2008, www.mediapost.com; Louise Story, "Anywhere the Eye Can See, It's Likely to See an Ad," *The New York Times,* January 15, 2007, www.nytimes.com.

31. Story, "Anywhere the Eye Can See, It's Likely to See an Ad."

32. Lise Buyer, "Viral Marketing Key to Facebook's Success," *ABC News,* abcnews.go.com, accessed June 10, 2008.

33. Nick Carr, "Neuromarketing Could Make Mind Reading the Ad-Man's Ultimate Tool," *The Guardian,* April 3, 2008, guardian.co.uk.

34. Ernest Beck, "FedEx Ditches Kinko's," *BusinessWeek,* June 9, 2008, www.businessweek.com.

35. "The Rewards Programs with the Most Bang for Your Buck," *Smart Money,* March 9, 2007, www.smartmoney.com.

36. "Welcome to Our Free Comparison Shopping Site!" *Biz Rate,* www.bizrate.com, accessed April 21, 2009.

37. David Katzmaier, "Editors' Top HDTV Picks," *CNet,* www.cnet.com, accessed June 10, 2008.

Chapter 6

1. "Oceans Policy," *Food & Water Watch,* http://www.foodandwaterwatch.org, accessed April 21, 2009; Erica Marcus, "Burning Questions: Salmon Shortage Sparks Higher Prices," *Newsday,* May 21, 2008, www.newsday.com; Paul Tolme, "Empty-Net Syndrome," *Newsweek,* May 12, 2008, p. 49; Michael Gardner, "Harvests Banned Along Coasts of Calif., Oregon," *San Diego Union-Tribune,* April 21, 2008, www.signonsandiego.com; Alexei Barrionuevo, "Safeway Restricts Purchases of Chilean Salmon," *The New York Times,* April 17, 2008, www.nytimes.com; "Fish Industry Warns of Christmas Seafood Shortage," *ABC News,* November 21, 2007, www.abc.net.au; David Barboza, "China Vows Food-Safety Changes," *The New York Times,* June 30, 2007, www.nytimes.com; Martin Fackler, "Waiter, There's Deer in My Sushi," *The New York Times,* June 24, 2007, www.iht.com; Dennis Cauchon, "Deadly Virus Killing Great Lakes Fish," *USA Today,* April 30, 2007, p. 1A.

2. "Fiscal 2009 Department of Defense Budget Released," U.S. Department of Defense press release, February 4, 2008, www.business.att.com.

3. "E-Stats," U.S. Census Bureau, May 16, 2008, www.census.gov.

4. "AT&T OneNet Service," business.att.com, accessed April 21, 2009.

5. Jan-Pro Cleaning Systems company Web site, www.jan-pro.com, accessed April 21, 2009.

6. Office Depot company Web site, www.officedepot.com, accessed April 21, 2009.

7. "Internet Law: Pennsylvania Is Selling Airport-Confiscated Items on eBay," *IBLS Internet Law—News Portal,* www.ibls.com, March 6, 2007.

8. "E-Stats," U.S. Census Bureau, May 16, 2008, www.census.gov.

9. "How Does E-Mail Marketing Fit in with Social Media," *BtoB,* June 12, 2008, www.btobonline.com; Rich Karpinski, "Businesses Embrace Blogging," *BtoB,* June 9, 2008, www.btobonline.com.

10. Company Web site, "About the Seam," www.theseam.com, accessed April 21, 2009.

11. Company Web site, "Business 24/7," www.bankofamerica.com, accessed April 21, 2009; Kate Maddox, "Growing Influence," *BtoB,* November 12, 2007, www.btobonline.com.

12. Company Web site, TetraTech, www.tetratech.com, accessed April 21, 2009.

13. "North American Industry Classification System (NAICS)," U.S. Census Bureau, www.census.gov, accessed April 21, 2009.

14. "Government E-Rate Discounts," company Web site, www.verizonwireless.com, accessed June 12, 2008.

15. "Chapter 5, The Manufacturing Core," U.S. Department of State, www.america.gov, accessed June 12, 2008.

16. "Ford Motor Company Supplier Park," *World Business Chicago,* www.worldbusinesschicago.com, accessed June 12, 2008.

17. Company Web site, www.cdw.com, accessed April 21, 2009.

18. "Children's Miracle Network," Wal-Mart Stores, www.walmartstores.com, accessed April 21, 2009.

19. Nandini Lakshman, "Nokia's Global Design Sense," *BusinessWeek,* August 10, 2007, www.businessweek.com.

20. "Global Sourcing on the Rise," *Yahoo! Finance,* biz.yahoo.com, June 11, 2008; "Buyers with Sales of Over US$511 Billion Set to Meet Greater China Suppliers," *Yahoo! Finance,* biz.yahoo.com, June 10, 2008.

21. Rick Popely, "Parts Suppliers Crushed by Auto Plant Closings, Cuts," *Chicago Tribune,* June 5, 2008, Section 3, pp. 1, 6.

22. Company Web site, www.walmartstores.com, accessed April 21, 2009.

23. Company Web site, www.microsoft.com, accessed April 21, 2009.

24. "Fast Facts about Microsoft," company Web site, www.microsoft.com, accessed April 21, 2009.

25. Dexter Roberts, "China's Factory Blues," *BusinessWeek,* March 27, 2008, www.businessweek.com; James Fallows, "China Makes, the World Takes," *The Atlantic,* July/August 2007, www.theatlantic.com.

26. Joshua Boak, "Rain Puts a Dent in Corn Crop," *Chicago Tribune,* June 10, 2008, www.chicagotribune.com.

27. "Corporate Profile," company Web site, www.keurig.com, accessed April 21, 2009.

28. "Corporate Profile," www.keurig.com; "Green Mountain Coffee Roasters, Inc. Announces Management Transition at Keurig," *BusinessWire,* March 31, 2008, www.reuters.com.

29. Company Web site, www.ups-scs.com, accessed June 13, 2008.

30. Colin Barker, "Why HP Is Different from IBM," *CNet News,* March 31, 2008, www.news.com.

31. Joe McKendrick, "Governing IT Decisions: Who's in Charge?" *Insurance Networking.com,* June 2008, www.insurancenetworking.com.

32. "Supplier Diversity Corporate Plan, Fiscal Years 2007–2010," U.S. Postal Service Web site, www.usps.com, accessed June 13, 2008.

Chapter 7

1. Company Web site, www.mcdonalds.com, accessed May 5, 2009; Peter Gumbel, "Big Mac's Local Flavor," *Fortune,* May 5, 2008, pp. 114–121; "McDonald's Now a British Institution," *St. Petersburg Times,* January 29, 2008, www.sptimes.com.

2. Bureau of Economic Analysis, "Gross Domestic Product," National Economic Accounts, May 29, 2008, www.bea.gov.

3. U.S. Census Bureau, "U.S. Goods Trade: Imports and Exports by Related Parties," May 8, 2008, www.census.gov.

4. U.S. Census Bureau, "Annual Trade Highlights," Foreign Trade Statistics, February 14, 2008. www.census,gov.

5. Bureau of Economic Analysis, "Foreign Transactions in the National Income and Product Accounts," National Economic Accounts, May 29, 2008, findarticles.com.

6. Progressive Policy Institute, "One-Ninth of All U.S. Production Is for Export," March 19, 2008, www.ppionline.org.

7. Company Web site, www.walmartstores.com, accessed May 5, 2009.

8. Dean Foust, "Hot Growth, Against the Odds," *BusinessWeek,* May 28, 2008, www.businessweek.com.

9. Bureau of Economic Analysis, "U.S. International Trade in Goods and Services," International Economic Accounts, June 10, 2008, www.bea.gov.

10. Richard W. Fisher, "Services in the U.S. Economy: Little Bark, Big Bite," Kiplinger Business Resource Center, June 2007, www.kiplinger.com.

11. Bureau of Economic Analysis, "U.S. Services by Major Category—Exports," www.bea.gov, accessed June 19, 2008.

12. "Nearly 30 Million Chinese Travel Abroad This Year," *China Daily,* October 31, 2007, www.chinadaily.com; "China's Tourism Boom," *Property Report,* October 12, 2007, www.property-report.com.

13. Nellie Andreeva, "Foreign Production a New Reality for Fox TV Studios," *Reuters,* June 16, 2008, uk.reuters.com.

14. "Wal-Mart Says Exploring Opportunities in Russia," *Reuters,* June 6, 2008, www.reuters.com; "Wal-Mart Eyes Russia Expansion," Associated Press, February 12, 2007, www.msnbc.msn.com.

15. Bruce Shreiner, "Overseas Operations Boost Yum Brands Profit," *The Morning News,* July 17, 2008, p. 3D; Samuel Shen, "China May Be KFC's Salvation as U.S. Faces Recession," *San Diego Union-Tribune,* May 5, 2008, www.reuters.com.

16. Nancy Lacewell, "Papa's Success Comes with Global Growth," *Business First of Louisville,* June 9, 2008, louisville.bizjournals.com; company Web site, "Papa John's Signs Development Agreements to Open 57 Restaurants in Canada," April 7, 2008, ir.papajohns.com.

17. Central Intelligence Agency, *World Fact Book: 2008,* www.cia.gov, accessed June 12, 2008.

18. CIA, *World Fact Book: 2008.*

19. "Preparing for China's Urban Billion," McKinsey Global Institute, March 2008, www.mckinsey.com; Chetan Chauhan, "Urbanisation in India Faster Than Rest of the World," *Hindustan Times,* June 27, 2007, www.hindustantimes.com.

20. David Barboza, "China's Inflation Hits American Price Tags," *The New York Times,* February 1, 2008, www.nytimes.com.

21. "The Boom in India Now Heard Overseas," *Los Angeles Times,* January 14, 2008, articles.latimes.com.

22. "World Internet Users," March 2008, Internet World Stats, www.internetworldstats.com.

23. Stephen J. Hedges, "U.S. Using Food Crisis to Boost Bio-Engineered Crops," *Chicago Tribune,* May 14, 2008, www.chicagotribune.com; Andrew Pollack, "In Lean Times, Biotech Grains Are Less Taboo," *The New York Times,* April 21, 2008, www.nytimes.com.

24. Ariana Eunjung Cha, "New Law Gives Chinese Workers Power, Gives Businesses Nightmares," *The Washington Post,* April 14, 2008, www.washingtonpost.com.

25. International Organization for Standardization Web site, "ISO in Figures for the Year 2007," www.iso.org, accessed June 12, 2008.

26. Paul Wiseman, "Cracking the 'Great Firewall' of China's Web Censorship," *USA Today,* April 23, 2008, www.usatoday.com.

27. "Secretary Gutierrez to Lead CAFTA-DR Business Development Mission," U.S. Department of Commerce Web site, June 12, 2008, www.commerce.gov; "USTR Announces Agreement on Extension of Time for Costa Rica to Join the CAFTA-DR," *USTR News,* February 27, 2008, www.ustr.gov.

28. "US Holds Fire on Sanctions Against EU in Biotech Food Dispute," *Agence France Presse,* January 14, 2008, afp.google.com.

29. "European Union to Appeal Banana Ruling," *MoneyCentral,* May 20, 2008, news.moneycentral.msn.com; "EU Loses Another Battle in WTO 'Banana Wars,'" Reuters, April 7, 2008, www.flex-news-food.com.

30. Progressive Policy Institute, "Textile Quotas Aren't Working," April 23, 2008, www.ppionline.org.

31. Heejin Koo, "South Korea Lifts U.S. Beef Ban Amid Protest Rallies," *Bloomberg News,* June 26, 2008, www.bloomberg.com; NASDAQ Web site, "South Korean President Apologizes for U.S. Beef Import Deal, Bans Import of Older Beef," June 19, 2008, www.nasdaq.com.

32. Ben Rooney and David Goldman, "Oil Falls on Reports That China Will Raise Gas Prices," *Yahoo! Finance,* June 19, 2008, money.cnn.com.

33. U.S. Commercial Service Web site, "Essential Advice for Doing Business in China," www.buyusa.gov, accessed May 5, 2009.

34. "EU to Open Anti-Dumping Probe into US Biodiesel Imports," *Agence France Presse,* June 12, 2008, www.eubusiness.com.

35. Stephen Franklin, "Mexico Faces Own Job Drain," *Chicago Tribune,* December 23, 2007, Section 5, pp. 1, 4.

36. World Trade Organization Web site, "Viet Nam Joins WTO with Director-General's Tribute for True Grit," January 11, 2007, www.wto.org.

37. World Trade Organization Web site, "Liechtenstein, US, Japan, and Australia Contribute to WTO Technical Assistance," June 26, 2008, www.wto.org.

38. Frances Russell, "We Should All Support NAFTA Renegotiation," *Winnipeg Free Press,* March 5, 2008, www.winnipegfreepress.com; Julieta Mendoza, "Thousands in Mexico Urge Government to Renegotiate NAFTA," *International Business Times,* February 2, 2008, www.ibtimes.com.

39. "USTR Announces Agreement on Extension of Time for Costa Rica to Join the CAFTA-DR," *USTR News,* February 27, 2008, www.ustr.gov.

40. Central Intelligence Agency, *World Factbook: 2008,* June 10, 2008, www.cia.gov.

41. "The European Union and the Treaty of Lisbon," *EUInsight,* February 2008, www.eurunion.org.

42. "Adidas and the Beijing 2008 Olympics," China Business Network Web site, www.thechinabusinessnetwork.com, accessed June 20, 2008; Vidya Ram, "Adidas Chips at Reebok Troubles," *Forbes,* March 25, 2008, www.forbes.com.

43. Company Web site, ikea-group.ikea.com, accessed May 5, 2009; Tim Harford, "How Facebook Is Like Ikea," *Slate,* January 19, 2008, www.slate.com.

44. "WPT Enterprises, Inc. Reports First Quarter 2008 Financial Results," Company Web site, May 6, 2008, investor.shareholder.com/wpt.

45. "Indonesia to Pressure Nike to Keep Orders Local," *Industry Week,* July 16, 2007, www.industryweek.com.

46. Bureau of Economic Analysis, "U.S. Direct Investment Position Abroad on a Historical-Cost Basis," www.bea.gov, accessed June 20, 2008; Bureau of Economic Analysis, "Foreign Direct Investors' Outlay to Acquire or Establish U.S. Businesses Increased in 2007," June 4, 2008, www.bea.gov.

47. Don Lee, "Chinese Firms Bargain Hunting in U.S.," *Los Angeles Times,* May 5, 2008, articles.latimes.com; Ariana Eunjung Cha, "Weak Dollar Fuels China's Buying Spree of U.S. Firms," *The Washington Post,* January 28, 2008, www.washingtonpost.com.

48. Associated Press, "Report: Anheuser-Busch Agrees to InBev Sale," *CNN,* July 13, 2008, www.cnn.com.

49. Company Web site, "Wal-Mart in India Fact Sheet," www.walmartstores.com, accessed May 5, 2009; "Gently Does It," *The Economist,* August 9, 2007, www.economist.com.

50. "SK Telecom to Gain Management Rights in Hello," *Reuters,* November 9, 2007, www.reuters.com.

51. "Star TV," Televisionpoint.com, www.televisionpoint.com, accessed May 5, 2009.

52. Vivian Yeo, "Dell Sees 'Clearer Path' to No. 1 in Asia," *Business Week,* June 4, 2008, www.businessweek.com; Joe McDonald, "Dell to Sell PCs Through China Retailer," *The Boston Globe,* September 24, 2007, www.boston.com.

53. FedEx Web site, "FedEx Launches Global Advertising Campaign," February 15, 2008, news.van.fedex.com.

54. Company Web site, www.7-eleven.com, accessed May 5, 2009; Monica Eng, "Where Convenience Is King," *Chicago Tribune,* August 5, 2007, p. 15.

55. "Smart USA Delivers 10,000th Smart Fortwo in the United States," Company Web site, Jun 24, 2008, www.reuters.com; "Smart Microcar Dealerships Opening in U.S.," *Associated Press,* January 17, 2008, www.msnbc.msn.com; Roland Jones, "Smart's Fortwo Aiming for Big U.S. Sales," MSNBC Web site, November 21, 2007, msnbc.msn.com.

56. American Community Survey Report, www.census.gov, accessed June 20, 2008; Internal Revenue Service, Rev. Proc. 2008–19, February 29, 2008, www.irs.gov; *2008 World Factbook,* CIA, www.cia.gov, accessed January 30, 2008.

57. Company Web site, us.leg.com, accessed June 28, 2008; Company profile, *Yahoo! Finance,* biz.yahoo.com, accessed June 20, 2008.

58. Company Web site, www.toyota.com, accessed May 5, 2009; Kristi Keck, "Foreign Automakers Drive Makeover of Smalltown, USA," *CNN.com,* November 1, 2007, www.cnn.com; Micheline Maynard, "Toyota to Build $1.3 Billion Plant in the Land of Elvis," *The New York Times,* February 28, 2007, www.nytimes.com.

Chapter 8

1. "Procter & Gamble Deepens Corporate Commitment to Sustainability," company press release, March 26, 2009, http://www.pg.com; Mya Frazier, "Who's in Charge of Green?" *Advertising Age,* June 9, 2008, www.adage.com; A.G. Lafley and Ram Charan, "The Consumer Is Boss" (adapted from their book *The Game-Changer), Fortune,* March 17, 2008, pp. 121–126; "A Debate over 'Greenwashing,'" *BusinessWeek,* July 13, 2007, www.businessweek.com; Gianfranco Zaccai, "Matching Sustainability with Profits," *BusinessWeek,* February 21, 2007, www.businessweek.com.

2. Company Web site, J.D. Power and Associates, www.jdpower.com, accessed May 5, 2009.

3. Company Web site, Brain Research Group, www.brain-research.com, accessed May 5, 2009.

4. Company Web site, Nielsen Media Research, www.nielsenmedia.com, accessed May 5, 2009.

5. Company Web site, Bazaarvoice, www.bazaarvoice.com, accessed May 5, 2009.

6. Jennifer C. Kerr, "Airlines Fare Poorly in Quality Survey," Associated Press, www.usatoday.com, April 7, 2008.

7. Company Web site, California Pizza Kitchen, www.cpksurvey.com, accessed May 5, 2009.

8. Sandra J. Jones, "Kmart Tests Concepts in Out-of-Way Corners," *Chicago Tribune,* June 23, 2008, www.chicagotribune.com; Deborah Austin, "Kmart Takes Measure of Rockford," *Rockford Register Star,* October 25, 2007, www.rrstar.com.

9. Brian Hindo, "Far-flung Emerson Electric Generates Loads of Ideas. Now It Has a Way to Sort Out the Really Novel Ones," *BusinessWeek,* June 16, 2008, p. 46.

10. Jonathan Black, "Pie in the Sky," *Chicago Magazine,* January 2008, www.chicagomag.com.

11. Company Web site, Synovate, www.synovate.com, accessed May 5, 2009.

12. Stephen Ohlemacher, "Glitches Set High-Tech Census Back a Decade," *USA Today,* April 4, 2008, p. A3.

13. "Census Tracts and Block Numbering Areas," U.S. Census Bureau, www.census.gov, accessed May 5, 2009.

14. "2007 TIGER/Line Shapefiles," U.S. Census Bureau, www.census.gov, January 28, 2008.

15. Anne Broache, "Wal-Mart, Target under RFID Patent Attack," *CNet News,* February 22, 2008, news.cnet.com; Dan Nystedt, "Wal-Mart Eyes $287 Million Benefit from RFID," *PCWorld,* October 12, 2007, www.networkworld.com.

16. Company Web site, Datamonitor, www.datamonitor.com, accessed May 5, 2009; company Web site, eMarketer, www.emarketer.com, accessed May 5, 2009.

17. Michelle Quinn, "YouTube Offers More Insight on Audiences," *Chicago Tribune,* June 16, 2008, www.chicagotribune.com; Louis Story, "To Aim Ads, Web Is Keeping Closer Eye on You," *The New York Times,* March 10, 2008, www.nytimes.com.

18. David H. Freedman, "Ask, and You Shall Be Misled," *Inc.,* July 2007, pp. 63–64.

19. Burt Helm, "Online Polls: How Good Are They?" *BusinessWeek,* June 16, 2008, pp. 86–87.

20. Joan Voight, "POV: Brands in the Dark," *AdWeek,* September 4, 2007, www.adweek.com.

21. Louise Story, "Company Will Monitor Phone Calls to Tailor Ads," *The New York Times,* September 24, 2007, www.nytimes.com.

22. Company Web site, www.teenresearch.com, accessed May 5, 2009.

23. Company Web site, www.dorlandhealth.com, accessed May 5, 2009.

24. "Do Not Call Registrations Permanent and Fees Telemarketers Pay to Access Registry Set," Federal Trade Commission, April 10, 2008, www.ftc.gov.

25. Jack Aaronson, "Focus Groups 2.0," *ClickZ Network,* April 18, 2008, www.clickz.com.

26. "Fax Advertising: What You Need to Know," Federal Communications Commission, www.fcc.gov, accessed May 5, 2009.

27. Pete Blackshaw, "The Global Village, Virtually Realized," Nielsen, www.nielsen.com, accessed June 10, 2008.

28. Caroline McCarthy and Elinor Mills, "Online Ad Group: Show Us the Traffic Numbers," *CNet News,* April 23, 2007, www.cnet.com.

29. Story, "To Aim Ads, Web Is Keeping Closer Eye on You"; Miro Kazakoff, "Analyst Angle: Internet Now Key Part of Marketing," *RCR Wireless News,* April 30, 2007, www.rcrnews.com.

30. Jennifer B. Lee, "20-Something Angst, in 8-Minute Bursts, on the Web," *The New York Times,* October 19, 2007, www.nytimes.com.

31. Wailin Wong, "For Motorola Scientists, Nosiness Can Be a Virtue," *Chicago Tribune,* June 22, 2008, Section 5, pp. 1, 2.

32. Wong, "For Motorola Scientists, Nosiness Can Be a Virtue."

33. Kari Greenberg, "Consultancy Mines Data to Develop 'Vehicle DNA,'" *MediaPost Publications,* January 18, 2008, publications.mediapost.com.

34. Company Web site, SmartOrg, www.smartorg.com, accessed May 5, 2009.

Chapter 9

1. Company Web site, http://www.outback.com, accessed April 20, 2009; "OSI Restaurant Partners, LLC Company Profile," *Yahoo Finance,* http://www.biz.yahoo.com, accessed April 20, 2009; Michael Sasso, "Outback Menu Goes Leaner on Prices," *Tampa Bay Online,* February 24, 2009, http://www2.tbo.com; Andrew Martin, "Empty Tables Threaten Some Restaurant Chains," *The New York Times,* April 3, 2009, http://www.nytimes.com; "Loss at Outback Parent Swells to $739 Million," *Orlando Business Journal,* February 24, 2009, http://www.bizjournals.com/orlando; "Outback Unveils New Menu with 15 Meals under $15," *Media Post Publications,* February 19, 2009, http://www.mediapost.com; "Outback Steakhouse Goes over the Top with a New Menu and Down under with Prices," *Chain Leader,* February 19, 2009, http://www.chainleader.com; "Economic Conditions Taking a Toll on OSI Restaurant Partners," *Tampa Bay Business Journal,* November 18, 2008, http://tampabay.bizjournals.com.

2. U.S. Census Bureau, www.census.gov, accessed May 12, 2009.

3. Joanna L. Krotz, "Women Power: How to Market to 51% of Americans," *Microsoft Small Business Center,* www.microsoft.com, accessed June 26, 2008.

4. "Women Car Buyers—Declare Their Independence," *PRWeb*, www.prweb.com, June 16, 2008.

5. Nancy Mueller, "Homebuilders Urged to Keep Women in Mind," *Tennessean.com*, June 16, 2008, www.tennessean.com.

6. Bridget Thoreson, "Women's Buying Power Steals the Spotlight," *Dayton Business Journal*, October 5, 2007, dayton.bizjournals.com.

7. "State Resident Population—Projections 2010 to 2030," U.S. Census Bureau, www.census.gov, accessed June 18, 2008; "Census Bureau Announces Most Populous Cities," *U.S. Census Bureau News*, June 28, 2007, www.census.gov.

8. "State Resident Population—Projections 2010 to 2030," U.S. Census Bureau, www.census.gov, accessed June 18, 2008; "Nevada Once Again Fastest-Growing State; Louisiana Rebounds," *U.S. Census Bureau News*, December 27, 2007, www.census.gov.

9. "Countries and Areas Ranked by Population: 2008," U.S. Census Bureau, International Data Base, June 18, 2008, www.census.gov.

10. "World: Largest Cities," and "World: Metropolitan Areas," *World Gazetteer*, www.world-gazetteer.com, accessed June 26, 2008.

11. "Movers by Type of Move and Reason for Moving," U.S. Census Bureau, www.census.gov, accessed June 18, 2008; "50 Fastest Growing Metro Areas Concentrated in West and South," *U.S. Census Bureau News*, April 5, 2007, www.census.gov.

12. "Metropolitan and Micropolitan Statistical Areas: Concepts, Components, and Population," *Statistical Abstract of the United States: 2009*, U.S. Census Bureau, www.census.gov.

13. "Metropolitan and Micropolitan Statistical Areas: Concepts, Components, and Population," *Statistical Abstract of the United States: 2009*, U.S. Census Bureau, www.census.gov.

14. Kristina Cooke, "Chicago Most Caffeinated U.S. City: Survey," *Reuters*, November 6, 2007, www.reuters.com.

15. K. C. Jones, "Domino's Pizza Tracker Mixes High-Tech with Super Bowl XLII," *Information Week*, January 31, 2008, www.informationweek.com.

16. Company Web site, shine.yahoo.com, accessed May 12, 2009; Anick Jesdanun, "Yahoo Launches Site Focused on Women," *Associated Press*, March 31, 2008, www.newsvine.com.

17. Brooks Barnes, "Limiting Ads of Junk Food to Children," *The New York Times*, July 18, 2007, www.nytimes.com.

18. Bea Fields, "Marketing to Gen Y: What You Can't Afford Not to Know," *Startup Nation*, www.startupnation.com, accessed June 26, 2008.

19. Laurel Kennedy, "Why Ask Y?" *Nielsen*, www.nielsen.com, accessed May 12, 2009.

20. Company Web site, www.freepeople.com, accessed May 12, 2009.

21. Scott Schroeder, "Zeroing in on Generation X," *DM News*, January 3, 2007, www.dmnews.com.

22. Robert Levine, "Fast Talk: Green Grow the Rockers," *Fast Company*, July/August 2008, p. 27.

23. "Experts Predict Top Trends in Marketing to Baby Boomers in 2007," *Senior Journal*, March 6, 2007, www.seniorjournal.com.

24. "Experts Predict Top Trends in Marketing to Baby Boomers in 2007."

25. Mark J. Miller, "Reaching Baby Boomers on the Internet," *Small Business Trends*, April 9, 2007, www.smallbiztrends.com.

26. Company Web site, www.vespausa.com, accessed May 12, 2009.

27. "Marketing to Seniors," *Coming of Age*, www.comingofage.com, accessed May 12, 2009.

28. Company Web site, www.oattravel.com, accessed May 12, 2009.

29. "Projected Population of the United States, by Race and Hispanic Origin: 2000 to 2050," U.S. Census Bureau, www.census.gov, accessed May 12, 2009.

30. "Projected Population of the United States, by Race and Hispanic Origin: 2000 to 2050," U.S. Census Bureau, www.census.gov. accessed May 12, 2009.

31. "Population Projections for States by Age, Sex, Race, and Hispanic Origin: 1995 to 2025," U.S. Census Bureau, www.census.gov, accessed May 12, 2009.

32. "Money Income of Families—Number and Distribution by Race and Hispanic Origin," *Statistical Abstract of the United States: 2008*, U.S. Census Bureau, www.census.gov, accessed June 10, 2008.

33. Ellen McGirt, "Hola Surfers!" *Fast Company*, February 14, 2008, www.fastcompany.com.

34. "Radio One Releases Largest National Survey Conducted on African-Americans," *Target Market News*, June 30, 2008, www.targetmarketnews.com.

35. "Affluent African Americans Making Impact on Consumer Economy," *MediaBuyerPlanner*, February 12, 2008, www.mediabuyerplanner.com.

36. Armando L. Martin, "Multicultural Marketing: Turn Black Moments into Green," *Progressive Grocer*, June 3, 2008, www.progressivegrocer.com.

37. "Projected Population of the United States, by Race and Hispanic Origin: 2000 to 2050," U.S. Census Bureau, www.census.gov, accessed May 12, 2009.

38. "Marketing to Asian Americans," *Adweek*, May 26, 2008, www.adweekmedia.com.

39. Jennifer Armor, "Asian Americans Are Good for Advertisers So Why Aren't Advertisers Listening?" *USAsian Wire*, February 7, 2008, www.usasianwire.com.

40. "We the People: American Indians and Alaska Natives in the United States," *Census Special Reports*, U.S. Census Bureau, p. 1, accessed May 12, 2009.

41. "Survey of Business Owners—American Indian—and Alaska Native-Owned Firms," U.S. Census Bureau, www.census.gov, accessed May 12, 2009.

42. *Moccasin Print*, July-November, 2007, www.native-american-bus.org.

43. *Rez-Biz*, www.rez-biz.com, accessed May 12, 2009.

44. "We the People of More Than One Race in the United States," U.S. Census Bureau, www.census.gov, accessed May 12, 2009.

45. Mireya Navarro, "Who Are We? New Dialogue on Mixed Race," *The New York Times*, March 31, 2008, www.nytimes.com.

46. Liz Skinner, "Boomers Rue Lack of Retirement Planning," *Investment News*, January 7, 2008, www.investmentnews.com.

47. Melinda Liu, "China's New Empty Nest," *Newsweek*, March 10, 2008, p. 41.

48. Mike Stobbe, "Against the Trend, U.S. Births Way Up," *Associated Press*, January 15, 2008, www.brectbart.com.

49. "Marketing to Gay and Lesbian Consumers," *The Boston Globe*, March 30, 2008, www.boston.com.

50. "Food, CPI, Prices and Expenditures," *Economic Research Service*, June 17, 2008, ersu.usda.gov.

51. Alan Scher Zagier, "Food Price Inflation Changes How We Shop," *Associated Press*, March 31, 2008, www.sfgate.com.

52. Doug Anderson, "Eating Out in America," *Nielsen*, www.nielsen.com, accessed May 12, 2009.

53. Maya Roney, "The Global Millionaire Boom," *BusinessWeek*, October 18, 2007, www.businessweek.com.

54. "VALS Links Marketing Strategies to Local Efforts Through GeoVALS," SRI Consulting Business Intelligence, sric-bi.com/VALS/GeoVALS/, accessed May 12, 2009.

55. "Japan-VALS," SRI Consulting Business Intelligence, sric-bi.com/VALS/JVALS.shtml, accessed May 12, 2009.

56. "What Is LifeMatrix?" Mediamark, www.mediamark.com, accessed May 12, 2009.

57. "GfK NOP Company Profile," *Yahoo! Finance*, biz.yahoo.com, accessed May 12, 2009.

58. Jennifer Handshew, "Ahead of the Curve," *Mindset Media*, June 11, 2008, www.mindset-media.com.

59. Kelly Jane Torrance, "With Gadgets, Early Adopters Now Wary Adopters," *The Washington Times*, June 20, 2008, www.washingtontimes.com.

60. Jenn Ableson, "Sneaker Wars Are Shifting to the Smaller Sizes," *The Boston Globe*, June 18, 2008, www.boston.com.

61. Keiko Morris, "Dunkin' Donuts Tries to Snag Starbucks Customers," *Newsday*, February 25, 2008, www.newsday.com.

62. Philip Elmer-DeWitt, "Apple 2.0," *Fortune*, April 1, 2008, apple20.blogs.fortune.cnn.com.

63. Gouri Shah, "Livemint.com," *The Wall Street Journal*, March 19, 2008, www.livemint.com.

64. "George Washington's Mount Vernon Estate and Gardens," www.mountvernon.org, accessed May 12, 2009.

65. Kimi Yoshino, "Eco-Tourism Just a Short Trek Away," *Los Angeles Times*, June 29, 2008, www.latimes.com.

66. Company Web site, www.tauckbridges.com, accessed May 12, 2009.

67. Company Web site, www.ilovepeanutbutter.com, accessed May 12, 2009.

68. Jena McGregor, "At Best Buy, Marketing Goes Micro," *BusinessWeek*, May 26, 2008, pp. 52–53.

69. "Fast-Casual Chains Continue to Outperform Other Restaurants," *Restaurant News Resource*, June 19, 2008, www.restaurantnewsresource.com.

70. Saturn advertisement, *Fast Company*, July/August 2008.

Chapter 10

1. Company Web site, Recycled Energy Development, www.recycled-energy.com, accessed May 12, 2009; David Schaper, " 'Recycling' Energy Seen Saving Companies Money," *NPR Morning Edition*, May 22, 2008, www.npr.org; Danny Bradbury, "From Waste Heat to Tethered Tornados," *BusinessGreen.com*, May 21, 2008, www.businessgreen.com; Lisa Margonelli, "A Steamy Solution to Global Warming," *The Atlantic Monthly*, May 2008, www.theatlantic.com; Marianne Lavelle, "Three Ways That Firms Can Save," *U.S. News & World Report*, April 28–May 5, 2008, pp. 46–50.

2. Michael Souers, "What Makes PetSmart So Fetching," *BusinessWeek*, June 3, 2008, www.businessweek.com.

3. Company Web site, www.generalmills.com, accessed May 12, 2009; Jack Gordon, "General Mills: Building Brand Champions," *Sales & Marketing Management*, January 4, 2007, www.salesandmarketing.com.

4. Jeffrey M. O'Brien, "A Perfect Season," *Fortune*, February 1, 2008, money.cnn.com; Roger L. Martin, "Creating the Four Seasons Difference," *BusinessWeek*, January 23, 2008, www.businessweek.com.

5. "Fast Food Chains Offering More Food for Less," *MSNBC,* February 12, 2008, www.msnbc.com.

6. Company Web site, www.verizonwireless.com, accessed May 12, 2009.

7. Brian Stelter, "TiVo and YouTube to Deliver Web Video to TV," *The New York Times,* March 12, 2008, www.nytimes.com.

8. Gary Stoller, "How Satisfied Are Travelers with Their Services?" *USA Today,* May 26, 2008, www.usatoday.com; Christopher Palmeri, "Southwest: 'No More Cattle Calls,'" *BusinessWeek,* November 7, 2007, www.businessweek.com.

9. Company Web site, www.theacsi.org, accessed May 12, 2009.

10. Brian Stelter, "Griping Online? Comcast Hears and Talks Back," *The New York Times,* July 25, 2008, www.nytimes.com.

11. Jonathan Farrington, "Customer Complaints: The Income Multiplier Effect," *CRM Daily,* March 10, 2008, www.crmadvocate.com.

12. Jack Ewing, "How Nokia Users Drive Innovation," *Business Week,* April 30, 2008, www.businessweek.com.

13. "The Cost of Customer Churn," a Financial Publishing Services White Paper, www.fpsc.com, accessed May 12, 2009.

14. Accenture, "Holistic Approach Helps Cut Churn," www.accenture.com, accessed May 12, 2009.

15. Company Web site, www.marriott.com, accessed May 12, 2009; "Pack It and Ship It," *Hotels Magazine,* June 23, 2008, www.hotelsmag.com.

16. "Are Gas-Rebate Credit Cards a Good Deal?" *MSN Money,* December 21, 2007, articles.moneycentral.msn.com; Kimberly Palmer, "Putting a Price on Rewards," *U.S. News & World Report,* July 2–9, 2007, pp. 57–58.

17. Oscar Corral and Jennifer Lebovish, "Urns May Await Die-Hard Gators," *Chicago Tribune,* December 31, 2007, Section 1, p. 4.

18. Company Web site, www.bankofamerica.com, accessed May 12, 2009.

19. T. L. Stanley, "Celebs Extending Their Brand Names to Credit Cards," *BrandWeek,* November 12, 2007, www.brandweek.com.

20. Organization Web site, support.thirteen.org, accessed May 12, 2009.

21. Arthur Middleton Hughes, "The 24 Essential Database Marketing Techniques," Database Marketing Institute, July 10, 2008, www.dbmarketing.com.

22. Brian Quinton, "Google Gets Personal: Should You Care?" *Direct Magazine,* February 21, 2007, www.directmag.com.

23. David Bauder, "NBC to Use Olympics to See How People Use Media," *Associated Press,* July 7, 2008, news.yahoo.com.

24. "Gartner Says Saturation of U.S. Pay-TV Market to Create Challenges for Emerging IPTV Services," October 1, 2007, www.gartner.com.

25. Leigh Buchanan, Max Chafkin, and Ryan McCarthy, "The New Basics of Marketing," *Inc. Magazine,* February 2008, www.inc.com.

26. Company Web site, www.convio.com, accessed May 12, 2009.

27. David H. Freedman, "A Digital Makeover for the Modeling Business," *Inc. Magazine,* February 2008, www.inc.com; Jon Fine, "Ford Models' Digital Runway," *BusinessWeek,* April 30, 2007, www.businessweek.com.

28. Company Web site, www.pg.com, accessed May 12, 2009; Neda Ulaby, "State-of-the-Art Ads Are Increasingly One-to-One," *National Public Radio,* May 20, 2007, www.npr.org.

29. Organization Web site, www.womma.org, accessed May 12, 2009.

30. "SAP Customer Relationship Management: Adidas," www.sap.com, accessed May 12, 2009.

31. "Customer Relationship Management: Discount Auto Parts," us.capgemini.com, accessed May 12, 2009.

32. "Define CRM," *CRM Reports,* www.crmreports.com, accessed May 12, 2009.

33. "Benefits of a CRM System," *Customer Service Point,* www.customerservicepoint.com, accessed May 12, 2009; "Integrated CRM: 5 Benefits of Integrated CRM," Microsoft Dynamics, www.microsoft.com, accessed July 10, 2008; Paul R. Timm, "Apply the Power of CRM to Build Customer Loyalty," *Search CRM.com,* February 26, 2007, searchcrm.techtarget.com.

34. "4 Steps to Prevent CRM Failure," *Inside CRM,* July 10, 2008, www.crm-guru.com.

35. "JetBlue Airways Ranked 'Highest in Customer Satisfaction among Low-Cost Carriers in North America' by J. D. Power and Associates," company press release, June 17, 2008, biz.yahoo.com; Dan Reed, "JetBlue Tries to Make Up with Fliers," *USA Today,* February 20, 2007, www.usatoday.com.

36. Company Web site, www.campero.com, accessed May 12, 2009; Jon Gambrell, "Pollo Campero Opens Stores in U.S. Wal-Mart Locations," *The Morning News,* May 13, 2008, p. 3D.

37. John Fortt, "Apple and Intel: Best Buddies," *Fortune,* June 13, 2008, bigtech.blogs.fortune.cnn.com.

38. Fortt, "Apple and Intel: Best Buddies."

39. "Shaner Hotels Continues Restaurant Co-Branding Initiatives with Bonefish Grill Opening," *Reuters,* June 18, 2008, www.reuters.com.

40. Allison Linn, "Thick, Buttery … Insurance?" *MSNBC Ads of the Weird,* April 8, 2008, adblog.msnbc.msn.com.

41. Company Web site, www.bluecsushi.com, accessed May 12, 2009; Robert Malone, "Tracking Sushi," *Forbes,* May 23, 2007, www.forbes.com.

42. "Valentine's Day Deliveries: Vendor Managed Inventory Prevents Broken Hearts," *Manufacturing Business Technology,* February 13, 2008, www.mbtmag.com.

43. "$2 Billion Truserv Reduces Inventory 41% and Improves Service Level to Above 97% with JDA Portfolio®," JDA Software Group, Inc. www.jda.com, accessed July 11, 2008.

44. "Kentucky Derby TV Coverage," kentucky-derby.blogspot.com, April 9, 2008.

45. Arthur Middleton Hughes, "The Loyalty Effect: A New Look at Lifetime Value," *Database Marketing Institute,* July 11, 2008, www.dbmarketing.com.

Chapter 11

1. Company Web site, www.greenworkscleaners.com, accessed May 12, 2009; Elaine Korry, "Clorox Enters Booming Market for 'Green' Cleaners," *National Public Radio,* July 14, 2008, www.npr.org; Felicity Barringer, "Clorox Courts Sierra Club, and a Product Is Endorsed," *The New York Times,* March 26, 2008, www.nytimes.com; Siel, "Emerald City," *Los Angeles Times,* January 15, 2008, latimesblogs.latimes.com; Ilana DeBare, "Clorox Introduces Green Line of Cleaning Products," *San Francisco Chronicle,* January 14, 2008, www.sfgate.com; "Clorox to Launch Green Cleaning Line Across U.S.," *Reuters,* September 6, 2007, www.reuters.com.

2. "World's Most Admired Companies 2009," *Fortune,* http://money.cnn.com.

3. "Tomorrow's Jobs," *Occupational Outlook Handbook,* 2008–2009 Edition, U.S. Department of Labor, Bureau of Labor Statistics, p. 2.

4. "U.S. International Trade in Goods and Services," *International Economic Account,* Bureau of Economic Analysis, July 11, 2008, www.bea.gov.

5. Mark Scott, "Luring Customers with Local Call Centers," *Business Week,* July 24, 2007, www.businessweek.com.

6. Toni Bowers, "More Companies Realizing the Downside of Outsourcing," *TechRepublic.com,* January 23, 2008, www.techrepublic.com; Mark Scott, "Luring Customers with Local Call Centers," *Business Week,* July 24, 2007, www.businessweek.com.

7. Lynne Meredith Schreiber, "Cheaper, Better Customer Service? Try Homeshoring," *Startup Nation,* www.startupnation.com, accessed July 14, 2008.

8. Mae Kowaike, "Remote Access 'Homeshoring' Trend Shows Commitment to Green Technology," *TMCnet.com,* March 31, 2008, www.tmcnet.com.

9. Haley Westbrook, "DTC Advertising Isn't Sitting Well with Doctors in Chicago," *Medill Reports,* June 5, 2008, news.medill.northwestern.edu.

10. Gift Baskets.com, www.giftbaskets.com, accessed May 15, 2009.

11. Concept introduced by Christopher H. Lovelock, "Classifying Services to Gain Strategic Marketing Insights," *Journal of Marketing,* Summer 1983, p. 10.

12. "Car Reviews: First Look & Drive," *European Car,* www.europeancarweb.com, accessed May 15, 2009.

13. Mohammed Abbas, "Boeing Wins Gulf Air 787 Order Worth up to $6 Billion," *Reuters,* January 13, 2008, www.reuters.com.

14. Bose Web site, www.bose.com, accessed May 15, 2009.

15. Cargill Web site, www.cargillfoods.com, accessed May 15, 2009.

16. Office Max Web site, www.officemax.com, accessed May 15, 2009.

17. Cisco Systems Web site, www.cisco.com, accessed May 15, 2009.

18. Regus Web site, www.regus.com, accessed May 15, 2009.

19. "Discover ISO," International Organization for Standardization, www.iso.org, accessed May 15, 2009.

20. "Who Made America? Henry Ford," Public Broadcasting Service, www.pbs.org, accessed July 15, 2008.

21. "Improving the Quality Function: Driving Organizational Impact & Efficiency," *Benchmarking Reports,* www3.best-in-class.com, accessed July 15, 2008.

22. Toyota Web site, www.toyotaforklift.com, accessed May 15, 2009.

23. Martin LaMonica, "Amazon Storage 'Cloud' Service Goes Dark, Ruffles Web 2.0 Feathers," *CNet News,* February 15, 2008, www.news.com.

24. L. L. Bean Web site, www.llbean.com, accessed May 15, 2009.

25. L. L. Bean Web site.

26. Johnson & Johnson Web site, www.jnj.com, accessed May 15, 2009.

27. Anna Kuchment, "Holes in Your Soles," *Newsweek,* April 14, 2008, pp. E6–E7.

28. Catherine Boal, "Hershey Enters Organic Chocolate Market," *Food Production Daily,* www.foodproductiondaily.com, accessed July 15, 2008.

29. Alissa Walker, "Spin the Bottle," *Fast Company,* June 2008, pp. 54–55.

30. Toby Sterling, "Compact Disc Celebrates 25th Anniversary," *Associated Press,* August 17, 2008, news.yahoo.com.

31. Al Sacco, "Garmin GPS Dominates Consumer, Corporate Market: What's Next?" *CIO,* March 13, 2008, www.cio.com.

32. Cruchfield shopping site, www.cruchfield.com, accessed May 2009.

33. Paul Hochman, "Innovation of Olympic Proportions," *Fast Company,* July/August 2008, pp. 80–82.

34. Kristina Dell, "Vinyl Gets Its Groove Back," *Time,* January 10, 2008, www.time.com.

35. Bill Carter, "NBC to Start 24-Hour News Channel in New York," *The New York Times,* May 8, 2008, www.nytimes.com.
36. Company Web site, www.armhammer.com, accessed May 15, 2009.
37. "The Issue: How P&G Brought Back Herbal Essence," *BusinessWeek,* June 17, 2008, www.businessweek.com.
38. Monica Eng, "Small. Medium. Gone." *Chicago Tribune,* July 9, 2008, www.chicagotribune.com.
39. Ann Meyer, "Eagle Back on Shelves," *Chicago Tribune,* May 5, 2008, section 3, p. 5.
40. Del Quentin Wilber, "Less Free to Move About the Cabin," *The Washington Post,* December 3, 2007, www.washingtonpost.com.

Chapter 12

1. Company Web site, http://www.schwinnbike.com, accessed May 19, 2009; Dan Strumpf, "Electric Bikes Selling Briskly as Gas Prices Climb," *Associated Press,* August 15, 2008, news.yahoo.com; Funding Universe Web site, www.fundinguniverse.com, accessed July 10, 2008; Company Web site, www.schwinnbike.com, accessed July 8, 2008; Joel Hood, "Riders Say 'E-Bikes' Give Them Extra Spark," *Chicago Tribune,* June 7, 2008, pp. 1, 8; Joe Kafka, "Scooters Grow in Popularity," *Morning News,* May 15, 2008, pp. 1D, 2D; Jason Thomas, "Schwinn's Electric Bikes Now Available," *TreeHugger,* May 8, 2008, www.treehugger.com.
2. Consumer Goods Technology Web site, www.consumergoods.com, accessed May 19, 2009.
3. "Office Depot Unveils Eco-Friendly Private Label," *Private Label Buyer,* April 14, 2008, www.privatelabelbuyer.com.
4. Company Web site, www.target.com, accessed May 19, 2009.
5. Mark Sweney, "Google Named World's No. 1 Brand," *Guardian,* April 21, 2008, guardian.co.uk.
6. Company Web site, brandassetvaluator.com.au, accessed May 19, 2009.
7. CPG CatNet Web site, www.cpgcatnet.org, accessed May 19, 2009.
8. CPG CatNet Web site.
9. Steve Kent, "Bringing the Consumer into Category Management: Making an Old Process New Again for Today's Retail Environment," *Nielsen Trends & Insights,* www2.acnielsen.com, accessed July 7, 2008.
10. Company Web site, www.hersheys.com, accessed May 19, 2009.
11. Company Web site, "Introducing Product Laser Coding Technology," www.durand-wayland.com, accessed May 19, 2009.
12. "Boudreaux's Butt Paste Ends Diaper Rash and More," *Associated Content,* June 11, 2008, www.associatedcontent.com; "ARCA: Tom Hessert Ready for Irish Hills Debut," *Paddock Talk,* June 11, 2008, www.topix.com.
13. Ekin Middleton, " 'Naked Cowboy' Can Sue Makers of M&Ms," *CNN,* June 24, 2008, www.cnn.com.
14. Anick Jesdanun, "Creators of Popular Scrabulous Knockoff Suspended Game on Facebook after Federal Lawsuit," *Chicago Tribune,* July 29, 2008, www.newser.com; Caroline McCarthy, " 'Scrabble' on Facebook: Too Little, Too Late," *CNet News,* July 7, 2008, news.cnet.com.
15. "Procter & Gamble Files Infringement Lawsuit against Blue Cross Labs," *Reuters,* January 7, 2008, www.reuters.com.
16. Michael Hooper, "Payless Copycat Tactic at Risk," *Topeka Capital-Journal,* May 11, 2008, www.findarticles.com.
17. Scott Young, "Using Research to Guide and Support Packaging Innovation," *Brand Packaging,* January 2007, www.brandpackaging.com.
18. Company Web site, pressroom.target.com, accessed May 19, 2009.
19. Mike Hughlett, " 'Coffee Cans' No More: Patent Battle Percolates," *Chicago Tribune,* August 23, 2007, section 3, pp. 1, 5.
20. Stephanie Rosenbloom, "Users Can't Get Handle on Jug," *San Diego Union-Tribune,* June 30, 2008, www.signonsandiego.com.
21. U.S. Food and Drug Administration, "Information for Consumers: Food Allergen Labeling and Consumer Protection Act of 2004, Questions and Answers," Center for Food Safety and Applied Nutrition, cfsan.fda.gov, accessed May 19, 2009.
22. " 'Fastest Growing Virtual World,' BarbieGirls.com, Launches Subscription 'V.I.P.' Service," *Business Wire,* June 9, 2008, www.businesswire.com; Katherine Glover, "Buenos Aires: Barbie Store a Destination," *Associated Press,* November 20, 2007, money.aol.com; Anne D'Innocenzio, "Mattel's Barbie Girls Act Like Avatars, Rock Like MP3s," *USA Today,* April 27, 2007, www.usatoday.com.
23. Susan Gunelius, "Brand Extensions: A Review of 2007," *Brandcurve,* December 11, 2007, www.brandcurve.com.
24. James Bernstein, "Starbucks' Success Cools under Dollop of Overkill," *Columbus Dispatch,* July 6, 2008, www.freerepublic.com.
25. David Welch, David Kiley, and Moon Ihlwan, "My Way or the Highway at Hyundai," *BusinessWeek,* March 6, 2008, www.businessweek.com.
26. "Tyson Foods Markets Chicken to Hispanics," *Morning News,* May 21, 2008, p. 1D.
27. Antone Gonsalves, "Hitachi Launches Ultra-Thin HDTVs for U.S. Market," *InformationWeek,* January 8, 2008, www.informationweek.com.
28. Company Web site, www.stetsoncologne.com, accessed May 19, 2009.
29. "Cisco Puts Its Own Name on New Cable Set-Tops," *Multichannel News,* January 3, 2008, www.multichannel.com; Stephen Lawson, "Cisco Consumer Move Afoot?" *InfoWorld,* September 7, 2007, www.infoworld.com.
30. "Dunkin' Donuts Offers Second Iced Coffee Giveaway," *Promo Magazine,* May 15, 2008, www.promomagazine.com.
31. Barry Silverstein, "BOSE: Sound Positioning," *Brand Channel,* September 3, 2007, www.brandchannel.com.
32. Linda Tischler, "All About Yves," *Fast Company,* October 2007, p. 92.
33. Company Web site, www.thescottsmiraclegrocompany.com, accessed May 19, 2009; Ulrich Boser, "Is Grass Greener on Scotts' Side?" *U.S. News & World Report,* April 30, 2007, pp. EE6, EE8.
34. "SUVs with Wings," *Golf Digest,* April 2008, accessed at Eclipse Aviation Web site, www.eclipseaviation.com; Jessie Scanlon, "The Eclipse: Safety by Design," *BusinessWeek,* July 20, 2007, www.businessweek.com.
35. Alex Berenson, "Lilly Settles with 18,000 over Zyprexa," *The New York Times,* January 5, 2007, www.nytimes.com.
36. "High Court May Curtail Liability Lawsuits," *Boston Globe,* June 27, 2008, www.boston.com; "Los Angeles Times Examines Product Liability Lawsuits, Potential for Court to Shield Drug Makers," *Medical News Today,* March 4, 2008, www.medicalnewstoday.com.

Chapter 13

1. Company Web site, www.bnsf.com, accessed May 19, 2009; "Environmental Protection," *Communities Matter,* www.communitiesmatter.com, accessed July 28, 2008; D'Anne Hotchkiss, "BNSF Fuel-Saving Program Captures Industry Award," *Teradata,* June 4, 2008, www.teradata.com; Alex Roth, "Railroads Roll with a Greener Approach," *The Wall Street Journal,* May 29, 2008, online.wsj.com; Jeffrey L. Rabin, "Rail Chief Thinks Green at Ports," *Los Angeles Times,* February 26, 2008, www.tluc.net; "Local Leaders Praise BNSF for Its Green Technology Commitment," *Diesel Technology Forum,* September 13, 2007, www.dieselforum.org; "BNSF Debuts Natural Gas Hostler Trucks," *Market Wire,* May 2007, www.findarticles.com.
2. Company Web site, www.nintendo.com, accessed May 19, 2009.
3. Company Web site, www.dell.com, accessed May 19, 2009; "Dell: Not the PC Company You Used to Know," *CNet News,* December 6, 2007, www.news.com.
4. "Bikeworld Goes Global Using FedEx Technologies and Shipping," FedEx Web site, images.fedex.com, accessed May 19, 2009.
5. "Sales Representatives, Wholesale and Manufacturing," *Occupational Outlook Handbook 2008–2009,* Bureau of Labor Statistics, U.S. Department of Labor, www.bls.gov.
6. Company Web site, www.beijobags.com, accessed May 19, 2009; Yvette N. Coleman, "Beijo Handbags," *Fashion Edge,* June 2008, www.fashionedge.com.
7. Company Web site, www.bagborroworsteal.com, accessed May 19, 2009.
8. Mark Long, "Netflix to Stream Videos to Microsoft's Xbox 360," *Newsfactor Network,* July 16, 2008, www.newsfactor.com.
9. "Battery Recycling Benefits Environment, Education," *The Times-Standard,* April 10, 2008, www.times-standard.com; "AAA Arizona Launches Car Battery Recycling Program," *Phoenix Business Journal,* April 18, 2008, www.bizjournals.com.
10. Stephanie Rosenbloom, "Home Depot Offers Recycling for Compact Fluorescent Bulbs," *The New York Times,* June 24, 2008, www.nytimes.com.
11. Jeremy Korzeniewski, "Trek Stop: The Vending Machine for Bike Parts," *AutoblogGreen,* July 10, 2008, www.autobloggreen.com.
12. "For Spanx, the Trifecta of Culture, Creativity and Quality Is a Winning Combination," *Knowledge@Emory,* February 14, 2008, knowledge.emory.edu.
13. Katie Marsal, "NBC's iTunes Return May Hinge on Offline Piracy Filtering," *Appleinsider,* April 17, 2008, www.appleinsider.com.
14. "The Changing World of Industrial Distribution," *B2B International,* www.b2binternational.com, accessed May 19, 2009.
15. Katia Watson, "Retail Perspectives: Food Landscape in Transition," *TNS Retail Forward,* April 2007, www.retailforward.com.
16. Lauren Coleman-Lochner, "Wal-Mart Profit Climbs in Grocery, Electronics Sales," *Bloomberg News,* February 19, 2008, www.bloomberg.com.
17. "U.S., Australia Reach Open Skies Deal," *Associated Press,* February 15, 2008, news.yahoo.com.
18. Deborah Yao, "Comcast: Cable to Standardize Technology," *Associated Press,* January 7, 2008, news.yahoo.com.
19. Joe Schneider, "Kraft Loses Canada High Court Ruling on Candy Wrapper," *Bloomberg News,* July 26, 2007, www.bloomberg.com.

20. Brian Garrity and Peter Lauria, "NFL Network, ESPN Huddle on Cable TV Joint Venture," *New York Post,* June 21, 2008, www.nypost.com.

21. "Quick Franchise Facts, Franchising Industry Statistics," *A-Z Franchises.com,* www.azfranchises.com, accessed July 30, 2008.

22. Company Web site, www.pier1.com, accessed May 19, 2009.

23. "Summit Logistics International, Inc. and LOG-NET Renew Supply Chain Partnership," *Reuters Business & Finance,* June 30, 2008, www.reuters.com.

24. Company Web site, www.boeing.com, accessed May 19, 2009; Andy McCue, "Boeing Pilots RFID to Track Aircraft Parts," *ZDNet News,* March 14, 2007, www.zdnet.com.au.

25. "SAP Customers Worldwide Tout Early Success with Latest CRM Offering," *Fox Business,* July 30, 2008, www.foxbusiness.com.

26. John M. Doyle, "TSA Target 50% Cargo Screening Goal," *Aviation Week,* July 16, 2008, www.aviationweek.com.

27. David R. Butcher, "Global 3PL Industry Swells," *ThomasNet,* June 18, 2007, news.thomasnet.com.

28. Company Web site, ww21.1800flowers.com, accessed May 19, 2009.

29. "Trucking Statistics," *Truckinfo.net.* www.truckinfo.net, accessed May 19, 2009.

30. Frank Ahrens, "A Switch on the Tracks: Railroads Roar Ahead," *The Washington Post,* April 21, 2008, www.washingtonpost.com.

31. Company Web site, www.fedex.com, accessed May 19, 2009; "FedEx InSight Case Study," FedEx Web site, www.fedex.com, accessed July 30, 2008.

32. Ahrens, "A Switch on the Tracks: Railroads Roar Ahead."

33. "U.S. Trucking Industry Reaches Major Freight Transportation Milestone," *Reuters,* January 25, 2008, www.reuters.com.

34. Glen Creno and Dennis Wagner, "Trucking Industry Faces Rough Road," *USA Today,* January 24, 2008, www.usatoday.com.

35. "Higher Freight Rates May Dog Shipping Industry until 2012," *JCTrans.net,* June 23, 2008, info.jctrans.net.

36. "FedEx Trade Networks Opens New West Coast Gateways to Support Ocean-Ground Distribution Service," *MarketWatch,* June 25, 2008, www.marketwatch.com.

37. "Pipeline Basics," *PHMSA Stakeholder Communications,* primis.phmsa.dot.gov, accessed July 30, 2008.

38. Jerrel Yun, "Air Freight Volume May Have Reached Bottom," *Procurement Asia,* March 27, 2009, http://www.procurement-online.com; "UPS Launches New Global Air Freight Portfolio," *Import Industry News,* January 10, 2008, http://blogs.customhouseguide.com.

39. "Caterpillar to Create New Distribution Center in Texas," *SecurityinfoWatch.com,* July 8, 2008, www.securityinfowatch.com.

40. Company Web site, www.nike.com, accessed May 19, 2009; Trista Winnie, "Nike to Open New Distribution Center in Memphis," *NuWire Investor,* April 10, 2007, www.nuwireinvestor.com.

41. John Kerr, "Procter & Gamble Takes Inventory up a Notch," *Logistics Management,* February 1, 2008, www.logisticsmgmt.com.

42. Lauren R. Hartman, "Pompeian's Palletizing Goes Robotic," *Packaging Digest,* July 1, 2008, www.packagingdigest.com.

43. Jonathan Katz, "The Great Supply Chain Robbery," *IndustryWeek,* November 1, 2007, www.industryweek.com.

Chapter 14

1. Company Web site, http://about.officemax.com, accessed April 29, 2009; Elena Malykhina, "OfficeMax 'Blogcasts' New Product Launch," *BrandWeek,* April 13, 2009, http://www.brandweek.com; Jon Fine, "Bargain-Rate Buzz," *BusinessWeek,* February 9, 2009, pp. 65–66; Laurie Sullivan, "Many Happy Returns: OfficeMax Brings Back ElfYourself," *MediaPost Publications,* November 17, 2008, http://www.mediapost.com.

2. Kimberly Morrison, "Wal-Mart Alters Meetings," *Morning News,* January 15, 2008, pp. 1D, 6D.

3. Jessie Scanlon, "Sunflower Sprouts Fresh Stores and Consumers," *BusinessWeek,* July 25, 2008, www.businessweek.com.

4. Allison Linn, "Target Thrives in Wal-Mart's Long Shadow," *MSNBC,* June 20, 2007, www.msnbc.com.

5. Company Web site, www.lowes.com, accessed May 22, 2009.

6. "DSW Goes Smaller to Improve In-Store Experience," *BusinessWeek,* July 8, 2008, www.businessweek.com.

7. "Best Buy Stores Expanding to Musical Instruments," *Billboard,* July 28, 2008, www.billboard.com.

8. Food Marketing Institute, "Slotting Allowances in the Supermarket Industry," FMI Backgrounder, www.fmi.org, accessed July 31, 2008.

9. Company Web site, www.virtuosity.com, accessed May 26, 2009; Rafe Needleman, "Highly Useful: CallWave Transcribes Your Voicemail," *CNet News,* June 25, 2007, news.cnet.com.

10. Joan Verdon, "Malls Lauded for Going Green," *The Record,* February 23, 2008, www.northjersey.com.

11. "Lifestyle Centers Mix Best Elements of Strip Centers, Malls," *Business Ledger,* July 31, 2008, www.thebusinessledger.com.

12. Dawn Cobb, "Retail Trend Gains Ground," *Dallas Morning News,* June 17, 2007, www.dallasnews.com.

13. Kenneth Hein, "JCPenney Joins 'The Breakfast Club,'" *BrandWeek,* July 7, 2008, www.brandweek.com.

14. Barney Beal, "Smartphones Changing the Face of Web Analytics," *CRM News,* July 31, 2008, searchcrm.techtarget.com.

15. Cecilie Rohwedder and Keith Johnson, "Pace-Setting Zara Seeks More Speed to Fight Its Rising Cheap-Chic Rivals," *Fashion Spot,* February 20, 2008, online.wsj.com.

16. Jenn Gidman, "Sephora: Flawless," *BrandChannel,* May 26, 2008, www.brandchannel.com.

17. Marc S. Botts, "Shaking Things Up," *Pizza Today,* August 2008, www.pizzatoday.com.

18. Kasper Jade, "Challenges Ahead as Apple and Best Buy Expand Mac Program," *AppleInsider,* July 3, 2008, www.appleinsider.com; "Best Buy Deal May Feature Apple Boutiques," *Mac News Network,* April 5, 2008, www.macnn.com.

19. Melody Vargas, "Retail Industry Profile," *About.com,* retailindustry.about.com, accessed May 26, 2009.

20. Company Web site, www.gloriajeans.com, accessed May 26, 2009.

21. Company Web site, news.walgreens.com, accessed May 26, 2009.

22. Cathryn Creno, "Macy's Hopes to Build Customer Loyalty with a New Focus to Tailor Stores to Reflect Their Communities," *The Arizona Republic,* June 28, 2008, www.azcentral.com; Lisa Biank Fasig, "Macy's CFO: Retailer Must Ready Itself for Turnaround," *St. Louis Business Journal,* June 9, 2008, www.bizjournals.com; Martin Moylan, "Macy's Makeover of Marshall Field's Continued," Minnesota Public Radio, September 6, 2007, minnesota.publicradio.org.

23. Jennifer L. Schenker, "Vente-privee.com Refashions Closeouts," *BusinessWeek,* January 11, 2008, www.businessweek.com.

24. Company Web site, www.biggshyper.com, accessed May 26, 2009.

25. Company Web site, www.autocart.biz, accessed May 26, 2009.

26. Nicole Maestri, "New Wal-Mart Jewelry Can Be Traced from Mine to Store," *Reuters,* July 15, 2008, www.reuters.com; Michael Barbaro and Eric Dash, "Wal-Mart to Expand Banking Services," *The New York Times,* June 21, 2007, www.nytimes.com; Jayne O'Donnell, "Wal-Mart Pumps Up the Volume on Electronics," *USA Today,* May 14, 2007, www.usatoday.com.

27. "Americans Looking Near, Far to Save on Health Care," *CNN Money,* July 29, 2008, money.cnn.com; Jo Ciavaglia, "Drug Store Clinics Gaining Popularity," *Bucks County Courier Times,* July 27, 2008, www.phillyburbs.com; Marcus Kabel, "Wal-Mart Expands In-Store Health Clinics," *USA Today,* February 7, 2008, www.usatoday.com.

28. Company Web site, "Ingram Micro Fact Sheet," www.ingrammicro.com, accessed May 26, 2009.

29. Company Web site, www.unitedstationers.com, accessed May 26, 2009.

30. Organization Web site, www.cesweb.org, accessed May 26, 2009.

31. "Wal-Mart's Electronics Service Ambitions," *The Deal,* June 26, 2008, www.thedeal.com; Brent Felgner, "Wal-Mart Testing Various New CE Initiatives," *This Week in Consumer Electronics,* June 18, 2007, www.twice.com.

32. Company Web site, www.sasinc.com, accessed May 26, 2009.

33. Jim Olsztynski, "Wholesaler of the Year 2007: Standard Plumbing Supply," *Supply House Times,* December 1, 2007, www.supplyht.com.

34. Organization Web site, National Mail Order Association, www.nmca.org, accessed August 1, 2008.

35. Carol Krol, "Swelling Ranks of Consumer 'Do Not Mail' Lists Prompt DMA Response," *BtoB,* January 21, 2008, www.btobonline.com.

36. Company Web site, www.infoworx.com, accessed May 26, 2009; Bridget McCrea, "Take the Long View," *Response,* July 1, 2008, www.responsemagazine.com; Nicole Smith, "Johnny Carson Sees Success on Air Again," *DM News,* March 21, 2007, www.dmnews.com.

37. U.S. Census Bureau Web site, "Industry Statistics Sampler: Vending Machine Operators," www.census.gov, accessed May 26, 2009.

38. Company Web site, www.stonyfield.com, accessed May 26, 2009.

39. "iPod Vending Machine," *UMPC Portal,* July 26, 2008, www.umpcportal.com; Roger Yu, "iPod? Vending Machines Diversify," *USA Today,* September 4, 2007, www.usatoday.com.

Chapter 15

1. "Green Initiatives," New York Yankees Web site, http://newyork.yankees.mlb.com, accessed May 27, 2009; Keith B. Richburg, "Green Becomes Official Color of Baseball," *The Washington Post,* July 20, 2008, www.washingtonpost.com; Mike

Lee, "Sports Teams Increasingly Eco-Conscious," *The San Diego Union-Tribune*, July 15, 2008, www.signonsandiego.com; "MLB to Roll Out 'Green' Carpet for 2008 All-Star Game," *Reuters*, July 14, 2008, findarticles.com; Matthew Philips, "Not Just Greener Grass," *Newsweek*, April 14, 2008, pp. 66–67; Marc Gunther, "Major League Baseball Changes Its Colors," *Fortune*, March 28, 2008, money.cnn.com; Ben Platt, "Baseball Makes Pitch to Go Green," Major League Baseball press release, March 11, 2008, www.mlb.com; "Major League Baseball Goes Green in Collaboration with the National Resources Defense Council," Major League Baseball press release, March 11, 2008, www.mlb.com.

2. Brian Quinton, "The Joys of X, and Pizza Rolls Too," *Promo Interactive*, February 5, 2008, www.promointeractive.net.

3. Bill Gorman, "Where Did the Primetime Broadcast Audience Go?" *TV by the Numbers*, April 16, 2008, www.tvbythenumbers.com.

4. David Bauder, "NBC Uses Olympics to Measure Viewer Interest in Programming," *The San Diego Union-Tribune*, July 16, 2008, www.signonsandiego.com.

5. "When It Comes to Financial Jargon, Americans Are Befuddled," *AARP*, April 2008, www.aarp.org.

6. "Assessments Begin Under the Sorghum Checkoff Program," USDA Agricultural Marketing Service news release, July 3, 2008, ams.usda.gov.

7. Jake Coyle, "Movie Trailers Find Big Audiences Online," *Times Herald-Record*, July 3, 2008, www.msnbc.msn.com.

8. Ted Mininni, "Newest Corporate Marketing Strategy: Leveraging the Power of Design," *BrandChannel*, www.brandchannel.com, accessed May 27, 2009.

9. Steve McKee, "Five Words to Never Use in an Ad," *Ecommerce.Matrix-E.com*, ecommerce.matrix-e.com, accessed May 27, 2009.

10. "Dunkin' Donuts Swings for the Fences with New 'Bases Loaded' Summer Iced Beverage . . . ," *Reuters*, June 26, 2008, www.reuters.com; "Dunkin' Donuts Offers Second Iced Coffee Giveaway," *Promo*, May 15, 2008, www.promomagazine.com.

11. U.S. Department of Labor, "Economic News Release, Table 4, Employment by Major Occupational Group, 2006 and projected 2016," Bureau of Labor Statistics, www.bls.gov, accessed May 28, 2009.

12. "100 Leading National Advertisers," *Advertising Age*, June 23, 2008, adage.com.

13. Brent Schlender, "Advertising Everywhere," *Fortune*, January 28, 2008, money.cnn.com.

14. Stephanie Clifford, "Product Placements Acquire a Life of Their Own on Shows," *The New York Times*, July 14, 2008, www.nytimes.com; Laurie Sullivan, "23 Groups Ask FCC to Regulate Product Placement," *MediaPost Publications*, June 23, 2008, www.mediapost.com; Stuart Elliott, "Product Placement on Reality TV Seems Somehow More Realistic," *The New York Times*, January 23, 2008, www.nytimes.com.

15. Matt Story, "Video-Game Advertising: More than Just Product Placement," *ClickZ Network*, February 11, 2008, www.clickz.com.

16. Marc Graser, "Film Biz Losing Brand Wagon," *Variety*, January 25, 2008, www.variety.com.

17. "Your Friendly Neighborhood Movie Promotion," *PR Week*, April 5, 2007, thecycle.prweekblogs.com.

18. "Student Guide," *Time Out Chicago*, www.timeout.com, accessed May 28, 2009.

19. "'Live Unbuttoned' with Global Launch of New, Innovative Levi's 501 Marketing Campaign," Levi Strauss & Co. press release, July 21, 2008, www.levistrauss.com; Gregory Solman, "Viral Video Success Changes Levi's Plans," *AdWeek*, May 19, 2008, www.adweek.com.

20. "North American Sponsorship Spending Seen Up in '08," *Reuters*, January 22, 2008, www.reuters.com.

21. "Ambush Marketing: Playing the Game," *The Economist*, July 3, 2008, www.economist.com.

22. "Direct Marketing Expenditures Account for 50% of Total Ad Expenditures," Direct Marketing Association, October 16, 2007, www.the-dma.org.

23. "DMA Releases 15th Annual 'Multichannel Marketing in the Catalog Industry' Report," Direct Marketing Association, September 11, 2007, www.the-dma.org.

24. Andrea James, "Nordstrom Lets You Buy Online, Pick Up at the Store," *Seattle Post-Ingelligencer*, May 21, 2008, seattlepi.nwsource.com.

25. "National Do-Not-Call Registry," Federal Communications Commission, www.fcc.gov, accessed August 6, 2008; Jacqui Cheng, "FTC Dials Up $7.7 Million in Penalties for Do Not Call Registry Offenders," *Ars Technica*, November 8, 2007, www.arstechnica.com.

26. Christine Simmons, "FTC to Ban Prerecorded Sales Messages," *San Francisco Chronicle*, August 20, 2008, www.sfgate.com.

27. Thomas Haire, "Kodak Inks a New DRTV Blockbuster," *Response*, May 1, 2008, www.responsemagazine.com.

28. "100 Leading National Advertisers," *Advertising Age*, June 23, 2008, www.adage.com.

29. Wailin Wong, "Your Ad," *Chicago Tribune*, April 14, 2008, Section 3, pp. 1 and 4.

30. Kristen A. Lee, "Blockbuster Kicks Tires on In-Store Kiosk Strategy," *Ecommerce Times*, May 29, 2008, www.ecommercetimes.com.

31. Company Web site, www.thenorthface.com, accessed May 28, 2009; Chantal Todé, "North Face Kiosk Improves In-Store Inventory," *DM News*, March 23, 2007, www.dmnews.com.

32. NBC Web site, "The Biggest Loser," www.nbc.com, accessed May 28, 2009; Sally Squires, "Subway's Biggest Loser," *The Washington Post*, April 1, 2008, www.washingtonpost.com.

33. David Louie, "Calculating the Price of Eight Golds," *ABC News*, August 18, 2008, abclocal.go.com; "20 Under 25: The Top-Earning Young Superstars," *Forbes*, December 4, 2007, www.forbes.com.

34. "Accenture Trade Promotion Management Solution," www.accenture.com, accessed May 28, 2009.

35. "Ocean Awareness," www.adcouncil.org, accessed August 8, 2008.

36. Government Web site, www.gao.gov, accessed May 28, 2009; "Which Federal Agency Is Worst for Supplier Diversity?" *Diversity Inc.*, August 20, 2007, www.diversityinc.com.

Chapter 16

1. Company Web site, http://www.etrade.com, accessed May 12, 2009; Rick Aristotle Munarriz, "Teething Pain for the E*Trade Baby," *The Motley Fool*, April 29, 2009, http://www.fool.com; Ben Steverman, "Will E*Trade Take the TARP Tack?" *BusinessWeek*, April 29, 2009, http://www.businessweek.com; "E*Trade Financial Corporation Announces First Quarter 2009 Results," company press release, April 28, 2009; "Ad Track: E-Trade Baby, You're a Star," *USA Today*, February 19, 2008, http://www.usatoday.com; Ryan, "E*Trade Super Bowl Commercial—the Cute Baby Hook," *Ad Savvy*, http://www.adsavvy.org, accessed March 4, 2009; Charles Leroux, "E*Trade Baby Ad Puts Shankopotamus in Play," *Chicago Tribune*, February 5, 2009, http://www.chicagotribune.com; "NBC Reportedly Struggling to Sell Out Super Bowl Pregame Ads," *Sports Business Daily*, January 26, 2009, http://www.sportsbusinessdaily.com; "E*Trade Announces Super Bowl XLIII Advertisement," *Yahoo! Finance*, January 23, 2009, http://biz.yahoo.com; Rick Aristotle Munarriz, "Don't Mess with the E*Trade Baby," *The Motley Fool*, October 22, 2008, http://www.fool.com; Rafael Grillo, "The Online Brokerage Wars: E*Trade Offers Compelling Risk/Reward," *Seeking Alpha*, May 27, 2008, http://seekingalpha.com; "Talking and Trading Baby Blows Away Star-Studded Super Bowl Competition," *Reuters*, http://www.reuters.com, February 4, 2008.

2. Karl Greenberg, "GM Markets OnStar, Malibu via U.S. Airways Seatback Trays," *MediaPost Publications*, May 21, 2008, publications.mediapost.com.

3. "Smithsonian Tries Cell Phone Ads to Draw Tourists," *CNNMoney*, August 11, 2008, www.ibtimes.com.

4. Julie Creswell, "Nothing Sells Like Celebrity," *The New York Times*, June 22, 2008, www.nytimes.com.

5. "100 Leading National Advertisers," *Advertising Age*, June 23, 2008, adage.com/datacenter.

6. "U.S. Ad Spending by Category," *Advertising Age*, June 23, 2008, adage.com/datacenter.

7. "Dannon Activia Launches Thought-Provoking Advertising Campaign Featuring Jamie Lee Curtis," *Reuters*, March 3, 2008, www.reuters.com.

8. "Tide Coldwater Laundry Detergent," *Green Home*, greenhome.huddler.com, accessed June 2, 2009.

9. Martin Roll, "Sports and Celebrity Marketing in Asia," *Asian Brand Strategy*, December 18, 2007, www.asianbrandstrategy.com.

10. Tim Arango, "LeBron Inc.," *Fortune*, November 28, 2007, money.cnn.com.

11. "Top Ten Endorsement Superstars," *Fortune*, November 28, 2007, money.cnn.com.

12. John Vause, "Endorsements Pure Gold for Phelps," *CNN.com/US*, August 18, 2008, edition.cnn.com.

13. Apryl Duncan, "Companies Distance Themselves from Michael Vick," *About.com Advertising*, advertising.about.com, accessed June 3, 2009.

14. Michael Kanellos, "Are Internet Ads Better Than TV Ads?" *CNet News*, March 19, 2008, www.news.com.

15. Elinor Mills, "Online Ad Sales Rise 26 Percent in 2007," *CNet News*, May 15, 2008, www.news.com.

16. Robert Coen of Universal McCann, "Total of U.S. Ad Spending," *Advertising Age*, June 23, 2008, www.adage.com.

17. "Direct-to-Consumer Advertising Relies on Emotional Appeal," *Medical News Today*, February 1, 2007, www.medicalnewstoday.com.

18. Rob Walker, "Sex vs. Ethics," *Fast Company*, June 2008, pp. 74–78.

19. Stephen Shankland, "Will Online Ads Come Out Ahead after Recession?" *CNet News*, April 16, 2008, www.news.com.

20. David Radd, "JCPenney Targets Girls with Games," *BusinessWeek*, August 6, 2008, www.businessweek.com.

21. "Ad + Magic," *e-planning,* www.e-planning.com, accessed June 3, 2009.

22. Eric Eldon, "Social Network Ad Spending Projections Take a Dip," *Venture Beat,* May 14, 2008, www.venturebeat.com.

23. David Lieberman, "Ad Spending Forecast to Shift More to Direct Marketing," *USA Today,* August 6, 2008, www.usatoday.com.

24. "100 Leading National Advertisers," *Advertising Age,* June 23, 2008, www.adage.com.

25. Stuart Larkins, "Turn Up Your TV Ad Volume: Get More from Sponsorships Online," *Chief Marketer,* www.chiefmarketer.com, accessed June 3, 2009.

26. Scott Collins, "Where TV and the Web Converge, There Is Hulu," *Los Angeles Times,* June 16, 2008, www.latimes.com.

27. David Goldman, "XM-Sirius Merger Approved by DOJ," *CNN Money,* March 24, 2008, money.cnn.com.

28. "Yahoo Turns to Radio Ads to Lure Google Web Searchers," *CNet News,* March 19, 2008, www.news.com.

29. Dan Butcher, "Clear Channel, CBS Radio Promote HD Radio Via Mobile," *Mobile Marketer,* July 2, 2008, www.mobilemarketer.com.

30. "100 Leading National Advertisers," *Advertising Age,* June 23, 2008, www.adage.com.

31. "Newspaper Web Sites Attract Record Audiences in First Quarter," *Newspaper Association of America,* April 14, 2008, www.naa.org.

32. "Average Total Paid & Verified Circulation for Top 100 ABC Magazines," *Magazine Publishers of America,* www.magazine.org, accessed June 3, 2009.

33. John Consoli, "Magna's Coen Downgrades U.S. Ad Spending Forecast," *Media Week,* July 8, 2008, www.mediaweek.com.

34. "100 Leading National Advertisers," *Advertising Age,* June 23, 2008, www.adage.com.

35. Abbey Klaassen, "Google Maps Out Strategy for Outdoor Advertising," *BtoB,* June 9, 2008, www.btobonline.com.

36. "Worldwide Internet Advertising Spending to Surpass $106 Billion in 2011," *Marketing Charts,* June 25, 2008, www.marketingcharts.com.

37. Laura M. Holson, "CBS Mobile to Test Location-based Cellphone Ads," *International Herald Tribune,* February 6, 2008, www.iht.com.

38. Hanna "Sistek, "Want to See That Ad in 3D?" *CNet News,* April 24, 2008, www.news.com.

39. "Top 10 Worldwide Ad Agencies," *Advertising Age,* May 5, 2008, www.adage.com.

40. Danielle Sacks, "Believe It or Not, He's a PC," *Fast Company,* June 2008, pp. 64–73.

41. "Advertising, Marketing, Promotions, Public Relations, and Sales Managers," *Occupational Outlook Handbook 2008–2009 Edition,* Bureau of Labor Statistics, www.bls.gov.

42. "Mississippi Oil Spill Information Updates," City of New Orleans Web site, www.cityofno.com, accessed June 3, 2009.

43. Manjeet Kripalani, "Tata: Master of the Gentle Approach," *BusinessWeek,* February 25, 2008, p. 64.

44. Saabira Chaudhuri, "Can PR Save China?" *Fast Company,* December 19, 2007, www.fastcompany.com.

45. Ian P. Murphy, "Carl's Jr. Tie-in Garners Good Publicity," *American Drycleaner,* April 28, 2008, www.americandrycleaner.com.

46. Beth Negus Viveiros, "Paying Off," *Direct,* January 1, 2008, www.directmag.com.

47. Lucas Conley, "Strike Up the Band," *Fast Company,* June 2008, pp. 50–53.

48. Helen Leggatt, "Podcast Recall Rates Impressive," *BizReport,* April 23, 2008, www.bizreport.com.

49. Stephanie Saul, "Pfizer to End Lipitor Campaign by Jarvik," *The New York Times,* February 25, 2008, www.nytimes.com.

50. "Top 100 Advertising Campaigns," *Advertising Age,* www.adage.com, accessed June 3, 2009.

51. Doreen Carvajal, "Concern in Europe on Cellphone Ads for Children," *The New York Times,* March 8, 2008, www.nytimes.com.

Chapter 17

1. Company Web site, http://www.ibm.com, accessed May 6, 2009; "Challenges in OSS/BSS and Optimized Provisioning," *Times Global Journal,* http://www.sasken.com, accessed May 6, 2009; Jessi Hempel, "IBM's All-Star Salesman, *Fortune,* September 29, 2008, pp. 110–121; Stuti Das, "Dial IBM for IT," *DataQuest,* January 30, 2008, http://dqindia.ciol.com.

2. Bureau of Labor Statistics, *Occupational Outlook Handbook, 2008–2009 Edition,* www.bls.gov.

3. Bureau of Labor Statistics, *Occupational Outlook Handbook.*

4. "Hardware's Softer Side," *Chain Store Age,* March 1, 2008, www.chainstoreage.com.

5. Company Web site, www.bestbuyinc.com, accessed June 3, 2009.

6. Jeanine Poggi, "Dressing Rooms of the Future," *Forbes,* July 22, 2008, www.forbes.com.

7. Andrea Coombes, "Companies Crack Down on Business-Travel Policies," *The Wall Street Journal,* October 25, 2007, www.careerjournal.com.

8. Ford Motor Company Web site, media.ford.com, accessed June 3, 2009.

9. Darrell Zahorsky, "Sales Lessons from the World's Greatest Sales Force," *About.com,* sbinformation.about.com, accessed June 3, 2009.

10. Company Web site, www.marykay.com, accessed June 3, 2009; Pedro Morales, "Sales Star Driven to Succeed," *News-Press,* June 19, 2008, www.news-press.com.

11. Federal Communications Commission, "FCC Consumer Facts: Unwanted Telephone Marketing Calls," www.fcc.gov, accessed June 3, 2009.

12. Federal Trade Commission, "Do Not Call Registrations Permanent and Fees Telemarketers Pay to Access Registry Set," April 10, 2008, www.ftc.gov; Brian Burnsed, "Skirting the Do Not Call Registry," *BusinessWeek,* August 16, 2007, www.businessweek.com.

13. Direct Marketing Association, "Teleservices Fact Sheet," www.the-dma.org, accessed June 3, 2009.

14. JetBlue Airways overview, *Portfolio.com,* www.portfolio.com, accessed June 3, 2009.

15. Company Web site, www.nba.com, accessed June 3, 2009.

16. "RightNow Helps Cabela's Deliver Exceptional Customer Experiences and Support Renowned Service-Centric Brand," *Rightnow.com,* February 12, 2008, www.rightnow.com; "Customer Service Champs," *BusinessWeek,* March 5, 2007, www.businessweek.com.

17. Adam J. Fein, "Demand-Driven Customer Relationships," company Web site, www.ibm.com, accessed June 3, 2009.

18. Company Web site, "IBM Provides Consultative Sales Training for Sony Broadcast & Professional Europe," wwww-05.ibm.com, accessed June 3, 2009.

19. Amy Feldman, "My First Million: The Sale That Changed It All," *Inc.,* May 2008, pp. 33–34, 36.

20. Company Web site, www.smsap.com, accessed June 3, 2009.

21. Company Web site, www.southwest.com, accessed June 3, 2009; "Customer Service Champs," *BusinessWeek,* March 5, 2007, www.businessweek.com.

22. "Store Customers Like Having Access to JCP.com at J.C. Penney Stores," *Internet Retailer,* July 1, 2008, www.internetretailer.com.

23. Company Web site, www.newellrubbermaid.com, accessed June 3, 2009.

24. Marley Seaman, "New Pharma Ethics Rules Eliminate Gifts and Meals," *Associated Press,* July 11, 2008, news.yahoo.com; Shaili Jain, "The Relationship between Doctors, Drug Companies," *Milwaukee Journal Sentinel,* January 11, 2008, www.jsonline.com.

25. Mark Sneider, "A Better Way to Generate Leads," *Sales & Marketing Management,* July 14, 2008, www.salesandmarketing.com.

26. Leslie Benson, "Innovation through Collaboration," *Global Cosmetic Industry,* May 2008, www.gcimagazine.com.

27. Company Web site, www.blackanddecker.com, accessed June 3, 2009.

28. Bureau of Labor Statistics, *Occupational Outlook Handbook, 2008–2009 Edition,* www.bls.gov.

29. Carol Hymowitz, "HP's Ann Livermore Keeps Eye on 'Team,'" *ComputerWorld,* June 3, 2008, www.computerworld.com.

30. U.S. Department of Labor, Women's Bureau, "Quick Stats 2007," www.dol.gov, accessed June 3, 2009.

31. Susan Greco, "Let's Start with an Icebreaker: A Look at Summer Sales Meetings," *Inc.,* June 2008, pp. 47–48, 50.

32. Erin Geismar, "Retailers Back Big Back-to-School Sales," *SmartMoney.com,* July 16, 2008, www.smartmoney.com.

33. Jill Dyche, "CRM Success Drives Its Demise, and Other Aha! Moments," *CRM Today,* www.crm2day.com, accessed June 3, 2009.

34. "2008 CMS Trends Study," *CouponInfoNow.com,* www.couponinfonow.com, accessed June 3, 2009.

35. Company Web site press release, "Ecrio Announces Mobeam Digital Barcode Redemption Service Availability," May 5, 2008, www.ecrio.com.

36. "Secret Weapon?" *Promo,* December 1, 2007, www.promomagazine.com.

37. Giannina Smith, "Product Giveaways Heat Up," *Atlanta Business Chronicle,* June 6, 2008, www.atlanta.bizjournals.com.

38. "Winners Named in Search for Greatest Interception," *MSN Money,* January 14, 2008, news.moneycentral.com.

39. Thomas Franklin, "Make It POP," *Digital Output,* January 2007, www.digitaloutput.net.

Chapter 18

1. Jess Halliday, "Private Label Innovation Looms Over Big Brands," *Food Navigator,* March 19, 2009, http://www.foodnavigator.com; Ann Zimmerman, "Wal-Mart Boosts Private Label to Court Thriftier Consumers," *The Wall Street Journal,* March 17, 2009, http://www.online.wsj.com; Suzanne Kapner, "Wal-Mart's New Private-Label Look," *CNN Money,* March 16, 2009, http://money.cnn.com; Jack Neff, "Private Label Winning Battle of Brands," *Advertising Age,* February 23, 2009, http://www.adage.com; Matthew Boyle, "Slugfest in the Supermarket," *BusinessWeek,*

February 9, 2009, p. 48; Sarah Hills, "Quality Is Key to Sustaining Private Label Growth," *Food Navigator*, November 24, 2008, http://www.foodnavigator.com; Emily Fredrix, "Foodmakers Heinz, Smucker Post Higher Earnings," *Yahoo! News*, November 21, 2008, http://news.yahoo.com; "Private Label Brands Gain Favor among U.S. Consumers," *Nielsen Wire*, November 17, 2008, http://blog.nielsen.com.

2. Economic Research Service, "Outlook for U.S. Agricultural Trade," August 28, 2008, United States Department Agriculture, www. ers.usda.gov; Barry Krissoff and John Wainio, "U.S. Fruit and Vegetable Imports Outpace Exports," *Amber Waves*, May 2007 special issue, www.ers.usda.gov.

3. Mark Drajem, "WTO Challenges China on Tariffs," *The Washington Post*, July 19, 2008, www.washingtonpost.com; Ariana Eunjung Cha, "China May End Some Key Import Tariffs," *The Washington Post*, May 22, 2007, www.washingtonpost.com.

4. Company Web site, www.stubhub.com, accessed June 9, 2009; "Ticketmaster Completes Acquisition of TicketsNow," *PR Newswire*, February 26, 2008, www .ticketnews.com.

5. Gene Callahan, "Fair-Trade Coffee: Not Worth a Hill of Beans," *The Christian Science Monitor*, August 8, 2008, www.csmonitor.com; Grace Hood, "'Fair' to the Last Bean," *Entrepreneur*, March 2008, www.entrepreneur.com.

6. Micheline Maynard, "JetBlue Starts Selling Blankets and Pillows," *The New York Times*, August 5, 2008, www.nytimes.com; "Flying à la Carte," *Kiplinger's Personal Finance*, June 2008, p. 14; Julie Johnsson, "Is This the End for Cheap Airline Fares?" *The Chicago Tribune*, April 20, 2008, Section 1, pp. 1, 23; Harry R. Weber, "Delta Raising Fees for Phone Bookings," *Associated Press*, April 1, 2008, news.yahoo.com.

7. John Markoff, "Apple Aims for the Masses with a Cheaper iPhone," *The New York Times*, June 10, 2008, www.nytimes.com.

8. Kelli B. Grant, "Retailers Expand Customer-Loyalty Programs," *Smart Money*, March 31, 2008, www.smartmoney.com.

9. Robert D. Buzzell and Frederick D. Wiersema, "Successful Share Building Strategies," *Harvard Business Review*, January-February 1981, pp. 135–144.

10. Company Web site, http://skype.com, accessed June 19, 2009.

11. "Smart USA Delivers 10,000th Smart for Two in the United States," *Business Wire*, June 24, 2008, www.reuters.com; Tangi Quemener, "Tiny Smart Cars Aiming to Make It Big in USA," *Agence France Presse*, November 13, 2007, news.yahoo.com.

12. Company Web site, www.traderjoes.com, accessed June 9, 2009.

13. "PC Sales on the Rise Across the Globe," *Yahoo! Tech*, July 30, 2008, tech.yahoo.com; Agam Shah, "Intel Revenues Survive Falling Laptop Prices," *PC Advisor*, July 16, 2008, pcadvisor.co.uk; "Flash Price Drop Spurs Innovation," *The Washington Post*, February 1, 2008, www.pcworld.com.

14. Audie Lagorce, "Fractional Jet Ownership Gains Traction in Lean Times," *MarketWatch*, July 15, 2008, www.marketwatch.com; Ken Sweet, "Private Jet Ownership Remains Strong Despite Weak Economy," *FoxBusiness*, April 4, 2008, www.foxbusiness.com.

15. Jenny Anderson, "Willing to Lease Your Bridge," *The New York Times*, August 27, 2008, pp. C1, C8; Santiago Pérez, "Public Wary of Increasing Efforts to Lease Roads," *The Wall Street Journal*, May 9, 2008, corridornews.blogspot.com.

16. Victor Zak, "Going Greener and Leaner in Seattle," *Asbury Park Press*, April 23, 2008, www.app.com.

17. Kevin Sack, "States Look to Tobacco Tax for Budget Holes," *The New York Times*, April 21, 2008, www.nytimes.com.

18. Bruce Horovitz, "Products Shrink but Prices Don't," *USA Today*, June 12, 2008, Section B, pp. 1, 2.

19. Ron Scherer, "Beyond Gasoline: Prices Surge for Oil-Based Goods," *The Christian Science Monitor*, June 5, 2008, www.csmonitor.com.

20. Dolly A. Butz, "Gas Prices Hurting Meal Delivery Program, Other Charities," *Sioux City Journal*, August 20, 2008, www.siouxcityjournal.com; Eric Collins, "San Diegans Abandon Their Cars for Public Transportation," *Fox6 San Diego*, May 9, 2008, www.SanDiego6.com; "Mass Transit Gains New Appreciation," *The Republican*, May 8, 2008, www.masslive.com; Allison Lampert, "Gas Prices a Boon for Public Transit," *Canada.com*, April 22, 2008, www.canada.com.

21. Aaron Smith, "Fewer Flights, Higher Fares," *CNNMoney*, June 27, 2008, money .cnn.com; Barbara De Lollis and Barbara Hansen, "Airlines Cut Back on U.S. Flights," *ABCNews*, abcnews.go.com, December 4, 2007.

22. Macdonald Dzirutwe and Nelson Banya, "Zimbabwe Inflation Hits Record as Mugabe Tightens Grip," *Reuters*, August 22, 2008, news.yahoo.com; "Cash Crisis, Inflation Worsen in Zimbabwe," *Associated Press*, July 27, 2008, www.msnbc.com; Angus Shaw, "Zimbabwe Inflation Now Over 1 Million Percent," *Boston Globe*, May 21, 2008, www.boston.com.

23. Tali Arbel, "Taps Gushing as Bottled Water Prices Get Harder to Swallow," *Los Angeles Times*, June 18, 2008, articles.latimes.com.

24. "Ford Meets Cost-Cutting Goal," *Courier-Journal*, August 6, 2008, www .allvoices.com.

25. Suzanne Marta, "Touchy Subject: Hotel Spas Slow to Implementing Yield Management Strategies," *Hotel Online*, April 2007, www.hotel-online.com.

26. James L. McKenney, *Stouffer Yield Management System*, Harvard Business School Case 9-190-193, Boston: Harvard Business School, 1994; Anirudh Dhebar and Adam Brandenburger, *American Airlines, Inc.: Revenue Management*, Harvard Business School Case 9-190-029, Boston: Harvard Business School, 1992.

27. Tania Branigan, "The Real Olympics Competition: Nike and Adidas Claim China's Heroes," *The Guardian*, August 18, 2008, www.guardian.co.uk; Frederik Balfour, "Acting Globally but Selling Locally," *BusinessWeek*, May 12, 2008, pp. 51–52.

28. "The Cost of Euro Adoption: One Good Meal," *The Slovak Spectator*, August 4, 2008, www.spectator.sk.

29. "Tesco Nears Complete Conquest of UK," *The Guardian*, March 28, 2008, guardian .co.uk; Teena Lyons, "Ten Years of Supermarket Sweeps," *The Guardian*, October 31, 2007, guardian.co.uk; Susie Mesure, "Critics Attack Tesco's New 'Monopoly Test,'" *The Independent*, April 3, 2007, independent.co.uk; "Tesco Fights Monopoly Claim," *The Daily Mail*, April 2, 2007, dailymail.co.uk.

Chapter 19

1. Mike Hughlett, "Coffee Wars Reach Full Boil," *Chicago Tribune*, May 9, 2009, Section 1, p. 8; company Web site, http://www.starbucks.com, accessed May 8, 2009; Sean Gregory, "Latte with Fries? McDonald's Takes Aim at Starbucks," *Time*, May 7, 2009, http://www.time.com; Rick Aristotle Munarriz, "As My Barista Gently Sweeps," *The Motley Fool*, May 5, 2009, http://www.fool.com; Julie Jargon "As Profit Cools, Starbucks Plans Price Campaign," *The Wall Street Journal*, April 30, 2009, http://online.wsj.com; Laurie J. Flynn, "Starbucks, Awaiting Recovery, Says Profit Fell 77%," *The New York Times*, April 29, 2009, http://www.nytimes.com; Claire Cain Miller, "Starbucks Addresses the Price Issue, and Breakfast," *The New York Times*, March 2, 2009, http://www.nytimes.com; Janet Adamy, "Starbucks Plays Common Joe," *The Wall Street Journal*, February 9, 2009, p. B3; "Coffee Prices and Starbucks Stock," *Seeking Alpha*, January 30, 2008, http://seekingalpha.com.

2. Liz Fedor, "Airfares Unlikely to Match Oil-Price Descent," *Star Tribune*, July 31, 2008, www.startribune.com; "Major Airlines Roll Back Fare Hikes," *Associated Press*, June 10, 2008, www.cbsnews.com; "Northwest Airlines Matches Fuel Charge Increase Implemented by Other Network Carriers," *Reuters*, May 9, 2008, www .reuters.com.

3. Company Web site, www.bestbuy.com, accessed June 9, 2009.

4. Company Web site, www.bestbuy.com, accessed June 9, 2009.

5. Soyoung Kim and Kevin Krolicki, "GM Returns to Employee Pricing to Lift Sales," *Reuters*, August 18, 2008, news.yahoo.com.

6. Sara Wilson, "Picture It," *Entrepreneur*, July 2008, p. 43.

7. Gavin Rabinowitz, "Tata Unveils the World's Cheapest Car," *Associated Press*, January 10, 2008, news.yahoo.com.

8. Company Web site, "Wal-Mart Launches Online Resource Guide to Save More, Even Beyond the Store," http://walmartstores.com, accessed June 9, 2009.

9. Rachel Tobin Ramos, "Grocery Store Brands Feed on Bargain Hunter," *The Atlanta Journal-Constitution*, August 22, 2008, www.ajc.com.

10. Edmunds Web site, "Toyota Prius Styles," www.edmunds.com/toyota/prius, accessed June 9, 2009.

11. Company Web site, www.shutterfly.com, accessed August 25, 2008.

12. Company Web site, qd.sees.com, accessed June 9, 2009.

13. "The *Consumer Reports* Bottom Line Price," *Consumer Reports*, www. consumerreports.org, accessed June 9, 2009.

14. Chris Coffee Service Web site, www.chriscoffee.com, accessed June 9, 2009; "Epsom Minimum Advertised Pricing," InketArt.com, www.inkjetart.com, accessed August 25, 2008; Joseph Pereira, "Price-fixing Comes Back after Supreme Court Ruling," *TheDay.com*, August 19, 2008, www.theday.com.

15. Kimberly Palmer, "Admit It, You'll Never Send for That Rebate," *U.S. News & World Report*, March 3, 2008, p. 61.

16. Peter Svensson, "Internet Provider's Usage Cap Raises Questions," *Associated Press*, August 22, 2008, news.yahoo.com; Peter Svensson, "Time Warner Cable Tries Metering Internet Use," *Associated Press*, June 2, 2008, www.physorg.com.

17. Ruth La Ferla, "Love Your Sunglasses (Should I Know You?)," *The New York Times*, July 10, 2008, www.nytimes.com.

18. Roland Jones, "Automakers' Gas Gimmicks May Backfire," *MSNBC*, May 29, 2008, www.msnbc.com.

19. Margi Shrum, "Sauce: Taming the Wild Loss-Leader Cantaloupe," *Pittsburgh Post-Gazette*, August 14, 2008, www.post-gazette.com.

20. "Price Drops," *CNet News*, news.cnet.com, accessed June 9, 2009; Rick Broida, "Get a DVD Camcorder for $170 Shipped," *CNet News*, August 25, 2008, news .cnet.com; Best Buy Web site, http://www.bestbuy.com, accessed November 2008.

21. Deborah Stead, "Your Taste Buds Are in Your Wallet," *BusinessWeek*, April 28, 2008, p. 21.

22. Charles Gandee and Christine Ajuda, "Chic and Cheap: The New American Motel," *MSNBC*, February 8, 2008, www.msnbc.com.

23. Sam Abuelsamid, "Michigan State Police Hit the Test Track with Latest Cop Cars," *Autoblog*, www.autoblog.com, accessed August 27, 2008.

24. "NY to Bid State Fair Concert Contracts in '09," *MSN Money*, August 14, 2008, www.ibtimes.com.

25. Ticketmaster Web site, www.ticketmaster.com, accessed June 9, 2009; StubHub Web site, www.stubhub.com, accessed June 9, 2009; "Ticketmaster Branches Out," *Rock & Roll Daily*, January 15, 2009, www.rollingstone.com.

26. EBay Web site, www.ebay.com, accessed June 9, 2009; uBid Web site, www.ubid.com, accessed June 9, 2009.

27. "Krillion Adds 96 Product Categories to Its Local Shopping Search Index," *Internet Retailer*, August 19, 2008, www.internetretailer.com; Don Davis, "One Big Store," *Internet Retailer*, August 2008, www.internetretailer.com; Paul Demery, "The Big Chains Weigh In," *Internet Retailer*, August 2008, www.internetretailer.com.

28. "New 'AT&T Net Reach' Bundle Delivers High Speed Internet Solution for Customers at Home and on the Go," *AOL Money & Finance*, June 4, 2008, findarticles.com.

29. Bob Sullivan, "Cable TV: King of Misleading Come-ons," *MSNBC*, January 28, 2008, www.msnbc.com; Brian Stelter, "In Defense of Cable Bundling," *The New York Times*, November 26, 2007, tvdecoder.blogs.nytimes.com; Anne Broache, "Cable Subscribers Sue for 'à la Carte' TV Options," *CNet.news*, September 21, 2007, www.news.com.

30. Joe McDonald, "Dell Unveils New PCs Targeting Emerging Markets," *Associated Press*, August 27, 2008, news.yahoo.com.

31. Staples Web site, www.staples.com, accessed June 9, 2009.

32. Peter Greenberg, "You Charged Me for *What?*" *AARP*, May & June 2008, p. 22.

Appendix A

1. Procter & Gamble Web site, www.pg.com, accessed June 10, 2009; Elaine Wong, "All About P&G's New Global Marketing Officer," *AdWeek*, July 17, 2008, www.adweek.com; "Procter & Gamble Announces Organizational Changes," PR Newswire, July 15, 2008, money.aol.com; Andrew McMains and Todd Wasserman, "P&G's Stengel Preps Exit; Pritchard to Lead Marketing," *AdWeek*, July 15, 2008, www.adweek.com; "P&G's New Marketing Man," *Fashion Week Daily*, July 15, 2008, www.fashionweekdaily.com.

2. "Advertising, Marketing, Promotions, Public Relations, and Sales Managers," *Occupational Outlook Handbook*, 2008–2009 Edition, Bureau of Labor Statistics, www.bls.gov, accessed September 3, 2008.

3. "New Grads, Get 7.1 Percent Starting Salary Increase," *SmartPros*, July 18, 2008, accounting.smartpros.com.

4. "Employment Projections," Bureau of Labor Statistics, U.S. Department of Labor, www.bls.gov, accessed September 3, 2008.

5. Brandi Stewart, "EBay's New In-House Blogger Sounds Off," *Fortune Small Business*, March 6, 2008, money.cnn.com.

6. SalesJobs.com, www.salesjobs.com, and WomenSportsJobs.com, www.womensportsjobs.com, both accessed September 3, 2008.

7. "Online Job Boards Lead Recruiting Tools in Utilization," *Reuters Business & Finance*, August 18, 2008, findarticles.com.

8. Enterprise Rent-a-Car Web site, www.erac.com, accessed September 3, 2008.

9. Rosemary Lane, "Unpaid Interns Value Experience," *Marquette Tribune*, April 29, 2008, www.marquettetribune.org; Edwin Koc, "Paid Internships Pay Well," *National Association of Colleges and Employers*, April 7, 2008, www.naceweb.org.

10. American Association of Advertising Agencies, www.aaaa.org, accessed September 3, 2008; Inroads, www.inroads.org, accessed September 3, 2008; The Washington Center, www.twc.edu, accessed September 3, 2008.

11. Kim Isaacs, "Ten Cover Letter Don'ts," *Monster Career Advice*, career-advice.monster.com, accessed September 3, 2008; Tag and Catherine Goulet, "Seven Cover Letter Don'ts," *CareerBuilder.com*, www.careerbuilder.com, accessed September 3, 2008; Randall S. Hansen and Katharine Hansen, "Cover Letter Do's and Don'ts," *Quintessential Careers*, www.quintcareers.com, accessed September 3, 2008.

12. "Interviewing Tips," *Sam M. Walton College of Business*, waltoncollege.uark.edu, accessed September 5, 2008.

13. "Advertising, Marketing, Promotions, Public Relations, and Sales Managers," *Occupational Outlook Handbook*, 2008–2009 Edition, Bureau of Labor Statistics, www.bls.gov, accessed September 5, 2008.

14. "Advertising and Public Relations Services," *Career Guide to Industries, Occupational Outlook Handbook*, 2008–2009 Edition, Bureau of Labor Statistics, www.bls.gov, accessed September 5, 2008.

15. "Advertising, Marketing, Promotions, Public Relations, and Sales Managers," *Occupational Outlook Handbook*, 2008–2009 Edition.

16. "Advertising, Marketing, Promotions, Public Relations, and Sales Managers," *Occupational Outlook Handbook*, 2008–2009 Edition.

17. "Advertising, Marketing, Promotions, Public Relations, and Sales Managers," *Occupational Outlook Handbook*, 2008–2009 Edition; "Advertising and Public Relations Services," *Occupational Outlook Handbook*, 2008–2009 Edition.

18. "Advertising and Public Relations Services," *Occupational Outlook Handbook*, 2008–2009 Edition.

19. "Advertising, Marketing, Promotions, Public Relations, and Sales Managers," *Occupational Outlook Handbook*, 2008–2009 Edition.

20. "Advertising, Marketing, Promotions, Public Relations, and Sales Managers," *Occupational Outlook Handbook*, 2008–2009 Edition.

21. "Advertising and Public Relations Services," *Occupational Outlook Handbook*, 2008–2009 Edition.

22. "Purchasing Managers, Buyers, and Purchasing Agents," *Occupational Outlook Handbook* 2008–2009, Bureau of Labor Statistics, www.bls.gov, accessed September 5, 2008.

23. "Purchasing Managers, Buyers, and Purchasing Agents," *Occupational Outlook Handbook*, 2008–2009 Edition.

24. "Purchasing Managers, Buyers, and Purchasing Agents," *Occupational Outlook Handbook*, 2008–2009 Edition.

25. "Purchasing Managers, Buyers, and Purchasing Agents," *Occupational Outlook Handbook*, 2008–2009 Edition.

26. "Market and Survey Researchers," *Occupational Outlook Handbook*, 2008–2009 Edition, Bureau of Labor Statistics, www.bls.gov, accessed September 5, 2008.

27. "Market and Survey Researchers," *Occupational Outlook Handbook*, 2008–2009 Edition, Bureau of Labor Statistics, www.bls.gov, accessed September 5, 2008.

28. "Market and Survey Researchers," *Occupational Outlook Handbook*, 2008–2009 Edition.

29. "Cargo and Freight Agents," "Shipping, Receiving, and Traffic Clerks," "Stock Clerks and Order Fillers," "Production, Planning and Expediting Clerks," and "Dispatchers," *Occupational Outlook Handbook*, 2008–2009 Edition, Bureau of Labor Statistics, www.bls.gov, accessed September 5, 2008.

Appendix B

1. Google Corporate Web site, www.google.com, accessed August 29, 2008.

2. Kermit Pattison, "How TerraCycle Plans to Take over the Garbage Industry," *Fast Company*, August 11, 2008, www.fastcompany.com.

3. Nintendo Company Web site, www.nintendo.com, accessed August 29, 2008.

4. Justin Moresco, "Ethanol's Unsexy Dilemma," *Red Herring*, April 4, 2008, www.redherring.com.

5. Dyan Machan, "CEO Interview: Costco's James Sinegal," *SmartMoney*, March 27, 2008, www.smartmoney.com.

6. Amanda C. Kooser, Lindsay Holloway, Nichole L. Torres, and Sara Wilson, "Young Millionaires," *Entrepreneur*, September 2008, p. 66.

7. John Brodie, "Retailing Icon Mickey Drexler Doubles Down," *Fortune*, August 20, 2008, money.cnn.com.

8. Joe Nocera, "Retail Suits J. Crew's Chief Just Fines," *International Herald Tribune*, March 1, 2008, www.iht.com.

9. Dan Sewell, "Procter & Gamble Ties Laundry to Fashion," *Associated Press*, August 25, 2008, www.news.yahoo.com.

10. Dan Mitchell, "A Small Empire Built on Cuddly and Fuzzy Branches Out from the Web," *The New York Times*, August 19, 2008, www.nytimes.com.

11. Laura M. Holson, "An Unlikely Promoter Drives Nokia's Push in Hollywood," *The New York Times*, June 23, 2008, www.nytimes.com; Jack Ewing, "How Nokia Users Drive Innovation," *BusinessWeek*, April 30, 2008, www.businessweek.com.

12. Bo Burlingham, "The Believer," *Inc. Magazine*, August 2008, pp. 86–93.

13. Frank Ahrens, "Weather Channel Sold to NBCU," *The Washington Post*, July 7, 2008, www.washingtonpost.com.

14. "Analysts Say Assurant's GE Deal 'a Natural Fit,'" *CNNMoney*, September 5, 2008, money.cnn.com; Michael J. De La Merced, "GE May Spin Off Its Consumer and Industrial Unit," *International Herald Tribune*, July 11, 2008, www.iht.com.

GLOSSARY

80/20 principle Generally accepted rule that 80 percent of a product's revenues come from 20 percent of its total customers.

A

accessory equipment Capital items such as desktop computers and printers that typically cost less and last for shorter periods than installations.

acculturation Process of learning a new culture foreign to one's own.

administered marketing system VMS that achieves channel coordination when a dominant channel member exercises its power.

adoption process Stages consumers go through in learning about a new product, trying it, and deciding whether to purchase it again.

advertising Paid, nonpersonal communication through various media about a business firm, not-for-profit organization, product, or idea by a sponsor identified in a message intended to inform or persuade members of a particular audience.

advertising agency Firm whose marketing specialists help advertisers plan and prepare advertisements.

advertising campaign Series of different but related ads that use a single theme and appear in different media within a specified time period.

affinity marketing Marketing effort sponsored by an organization that solicits responses from individuals who share common interests and activities.

AIDA concept Steps through which an individual reaches a purchase decision: attention, interest, desire, and action.

AIO statements Items on lifestyle surveys that describe various activities, interests, and respondents' opinions.

allowance Specified deduction from list price, including a trade-in or promotional allowance.

ambush marketing Attempt by a firm that is not an official sponsor of an event or activity to link itself to the event or activity.

antitrust Laws designed to prevent restraints on trade such as business monopolies.

application service providers (ASPs) Outside companies that specialize in providing both the computers and the application support for managing information systems of business clients.

approach Salesperson's initial contact with a prospective customer.

Asch phenomenon Impact of groups and group norms on individual behavior, as described by S. E. Asch. People often conform to majority rule, even when it goes against their beliefs.

atmospherics Combination of physical characteristics and amenities that contribute to a store's image.

attitudes Person's enduring favorable or unfavorable evaluations, emotions, or action tendencies toward some object or idea.

average total costs Costs calculated by dividing the sum of the variable and fixed costs by the number of units produced.

B

baby boomers People born between 1946 and 1965.

backward integration Process through which a manufacturer attempts to gain greater control over inputs in its production process, such as raw materials.

banner ad Strip message placed in high-visibility areas of frequently visited Web sites.

banners Advertisements on a Web page that link to an advertiser's site.

basing-point pricing System used in some industries during the early 20th century in which the buyer paid the factory price plus freight charges from the basing-point city nearest the buyer.

benchmarking Method of measuring quality by comparing performance against industry leaders.

blog Short for *Web log*—an online journal for an individual or organization.

bonus pack Specially packaged item that gives the purchaser a larger quantity at the regular price.

bot (shopbot) Software program that allows online shoppers to compare the price of a particular product offered by several online retailers.

bottom line Business jargon referring to the overall profitability of an organization.

brand Name, term, sign, symbol, design, or some combination that identifies the products of one firm while differentiating them from that of the competition.

brand equity Added value that a respected, well-known brand name gives to a product in the marketplace.

brand extension Strategy of attaching a popular brand name to a new product in an unrelated product category.

brand insistence Consumer refusal of alternatives and extensive search for desired merchandise.

brand manager Marketer responsible for a single brand.

brand mark Symbol or pictorial design that distinguishes a product.

brand name Part of a brand, consisting of letters, numbers, or words, that can be spoken and that identifies and distinguishes a firm's offerings from those of its competitors.

brand preference Consumer reliance on previous experiences with a product to choose that item again.

brand recognition Consumer awareness and identification of a brand.

breakeven analysis Pricing technique used to determine the number of products that must be sold at a specified price to generate enough revenue to cover total cost.

broker Agent wholesaling intermediary that does not take title to or possession of goods in the course of its primary function, which is to bring together buyers and sellers.

bundle pricing Offering two or more complementary products and selling them for a single price.

business cycle Pattern of stages in the level of economic activity: prosperity, recession, depression, and recovery.

business plan Formal document that outlines what a company's objectives are, how they will be met, how the business will obtain financing, and how much money the company expects to earn.

business products Goods and services purchased for use either directly or indirectly in the production of other goods and services for resale.

business services Intangible products firms buy to facilitate their production and operating processes.

business-to-business (B2B) e-marketing Use of the Internet for business transactions between organizations.

business-to-business (B2B) marketing Organizational sales and purchases of goods and services to support production of other products, to facilitate daily company operations, or for resale.

business-to-business (B2B) marketing Organizational sales and purchases of goods and services to support production of other products, for daily company operations, or for resale.

business-to-business (B2B) product Product that contributes directly or indirectly to the output of other products for resale; also called industrial or organizational product.

business-to-consumer (B2C) e-marketing Selling directly to consumers over the Internet.

buyer Person who has the formal authority to select a supplier and to implement the procedures for securing a good or service.

buyer partnership Relationship in which a firm purchases goods or services from one or more providers.

buyer's market Market in which there are more goods and services than people willing to buy them.

buying center Participants in an organizational buying action.

buzz marketing Marketing that gathers volunteers to try products and then relies on them to talk about their experiences with their friends and colleagues.

C

cannibalization Loss of sales of an existing product due to competition from a new product in the same line.

captive brand National brands sold exclusively by a retail chain.

cash discount Price reduction offered to a consumer, business user, or marketing intermediary in return for prompt payment of a bill.

category Key business unit within diversified firms; also called a *strategic business unit (SBU)*.

category advisor (category captain) Trade industry vendor who develops a comprehensive procurement plan for a retail buyer.

category killer Store offering huge selections and low prices in single product lines.

category management Product management system in which a category manager—with profit and loss responsibility—oversees a product line.

cause marketing Identification and marketing of a social issue, cause, or idea to selected target markets.

Central American Free Trade Agreement-DR (CAFTA-DR) Trade agreement among the United States, Central American nations, and the Dominican Republic.

channel Medium through which a message is delivered.

channel captain Dominant and controlling member of a marketing channel.

channel conflicts Conflicts between manufacturers, wholesalers, and retailers.

click-through rate Percentage of people presented with a banner ad who click on it.

closed sales territory Exclusive geographic selling region of a distributor.

closing Stage of the personal selling process in which the salesperson asks the customer to make a purchase decision.

cluster sample Probability sample in which researchers select a sample of subgroups (or clusters) from which they draw respondents; each cluster reflects the diversity of the whole population sampled.

cobranding Cooperative arrangement in which two or more businesses team up to closely link their names on a single product.

cognitive dissonance Imbalance among knowledge, beliefs, and attitudes that occurs after an action or decision, such as a purchase.

cohort effect Tendency of members of a generation to be influenced and bound together by events occurring during their key formative years—roughly ages 17 to 22.

cold calling Contacting a prospect without a prior appointment.

collaborative planning, forecasting, and replenishment (CPFaR) Inventory management technique involving collaborative efforts by both purchasers and vendors.

comarketing Cooperative arrangement in which two businesses jointly market each other's products.

commercial market Individuals and firms that acquire products to support, directly or indirectly, production of other goods and services.

commission Incentive compensation directly related to the sales or profits achieved by a salesperson.

commission merchant Agent wholesaling intermediary who takes possession of goods shipped to a central market for sale, acts as the producer's agent, and collects an agreed-upon fee at the time of the sale.

common carriers Businesses that provide transportation services as for-hire carriers to the general public.

common market Extension of a customs union by seeking to reconcile all government regulations affecting trade.

comparative advertising Advertising strategy that emphasizes messages with direct or indirect promotional comparisons between competing brands.

competitive bidding Inviting potential suppliers to quote prices on proposed purchases or contracts.

competitive environment Interactive process that occurs in the marketplace among marketers of directly competitive products, marketers of products that can be substituted for one another, and marketers competing for the consumer's purchasing power.

competitive pricing strategy Pricing strategy designed to deemphasize price as a competitive variable by pricing a good or service at the general level of comparable offerings.

competitive strategy Methods through which a firm deals with its competitive environment.

component parts and materials Finished business products of one producer that become part of the final products of another producer.

concentrated marketing Focusing marketing efforts on satisfying a single market segment; also called *niche marketing*.

concept testing Method for subjecting a product idea to additional study before actual development by involving consumers through focus groups, surveys, in-store polling, and the like.

consolidated metropolitan statistical area (CMSA) Urban area that includes two or more PMSAs.

consultative selling Meeting customer needs by listening to them, understanding their problems, paying attention to details, and following through after the sale.

consumer behavior Process through which buyers make purchase decisions.

consumer (B2C) product Product destined for use by ultimate consumers.

consumer innovators People who purchase new products almost as soon as the products reach the market.

consumer orientation Business philosophy incorporating the marketing concept that emphasizes first determining unmet consumer needs and then designing a system for satisfying them.

consumer products Products bought by ultimate consumers for personal use.

consumer rights List of legitimate consumer expectations suggested by President John F. Kennedy.

consumerism Social force within the environment that aids and protects the consumer by exerting legal, moral, and economic pressures on business and government.

containerization Process of combining several unitized loads into a single, well-protected load for shipment.

contest Sales promotion technique that requires entrants to complete a task, such as solving a puzzle or answering questions on a quiz, for the chance to win a prize.

contract carriers For-hire transporters that do not offer their services to the general public.

contractual marketing system VMS that coordinates channel activities through formal agreements among participants.

controlled experiment Scientific investigation in which a researcher manipulates a test group (or groups) and compares the results with those of a control group that did not receive the experimental controls or manipulations.

convenience products Goods and services consumers want to purchase frequently, immediately, and with minimal effort.

convenience retailer Store that appeals to customers on accessible location, long hours, rapid checkout, and adequate parking.

convenience sample Nonprobability sample selected from among readily available respondents.

conversion rate Percentage of visitors to a Web site who make a purchase.

cookies Controversial techniques for collecting information about online Web site visitors in which small text files are automatically downloaded to a user's computer to gather such data as length of visit and the site visited next.

cooperative advertising Strategy in which a retailer shares advertising costs with a manufacturer or wholesaler.

core based statistical area (CBSA) Collective term for metropolitan and micropolitan statistical areas.

core competencies Activities that a company performs well and that customers value and competitors find difficult to duplicate.

core region Region from which most major brands get 40 to 80 percent of their sales.

corporate marketing system VMS in which a single owner operates the entire marketing channel.

corporate Web site Site designed to increase a firm's visibility, promote its offerings, and provide information to interested parties.

cost per impression Measurement technique that relates the cost of an ad to every thousand people who view it.

cost per response *(also called click-throughs)* Direct marketing technique that relates the cost of an ad to the number of people who click it.

cost-plus pricing Practice of adding a percentage of specified dollar amount—or markup—to the base cost of a product to cover unassigned costs and to provide a profit.

countertrade Form of exporting whereby goods and services are bartered rather than sold for cash.

coupon Sales promotion technique that offers a discount on the purchase price of goods or services.

creative selling Personal selling in which a considerable degree of analytical decision making on the buyer's part results in the need for skillful proposals of solutions for the customer's needs.

cross-promotion Promotional technique in which marketing partners share the cost of a promotional campaign that meets their mutual needs.

cross-selling Selling multiple, often unrelated, goods and services to the same customer based on knowledge of that customer's needs.

cue Any object in the environment that determines the nature of a consumer's response to a drive.

culture Values, beliefs, preferences, and tastes handed down from one generation to the next.

cumulative quantity discount Price discount determined by amounts of purchases over stated time periods.

customary prices Traditional prices that customers expect to pay for certain goods and services.

customer churn Turnover in a company's customer base.

customer relationship management (CRM) Combination of strategies and tools that drives relationship programs, reorienting the entire organization to a concentrated focus on satisfying customers.

customer satisfaction Extent to which customers are satisfied with their purchases.

customer winback Process of rejuvenating lost relationships with customers.

customer-based segmentation Dividing a business-to-business market into homogeneous groups based on buyers' product specifications.

customs union Establishment of a free-trade area plus a uniform tariff for trade with nonmember unions.

D

data mining Process of searching through customer databases to detect patterns that guide marketing decision making.

database marketing Use of software to analyze marketing information, identifying and targeting messages toward specific groups of potential customers.

decider Person who chooses a good or service, although another person may have the formal authority to complete the sale.

decline stage Final stage of the product lifecycle, in which a decline in total industry sales occurs.

decoding Receiver's interpretation of a message.

Delphi technique Qualitative sales forecasting method that gathers and redistributes several rounds of anonymous forecasts until the participants reach a consensus.

demand Schedule of the amounts of a firm's product that consumers will purchase at different prices during a specified time period.

demarketing Process of reducing consumer demand for a good or service to a level that the firm can supply.

demographic segmentation Division of an overall market into homogeneous groups based on variables such as gender, age, income, occupation, education, sexual orientation, household size, and stage in the family life cycle; also called *socioeconomic segmentation*.

demonstration Stage in the personal selling process in which the customer has the opportunity to try out or otherwise see how a good or service works before purchase.

department store Large store that handles a variety of merchandise, including clothing, household goods, appliances, and furniture.

deregulation movement Opening of markets previously subject to government control.

derived demand Demand for a resource that results from demand for the goods and services produced by that resource.

differentiated marketing Strategy that focuses on producing several products and pricing, promoting, and distributing them with different marketing mixes designed to satisfy smaller segments.

diffusion process Process by which new goods or services are accepted in the marketplace.

direct channel Marketing channel that moves goods directly from a producer to the business purchaser or ultimate user.

direct mail Communications in the form of sales letters, postcards, brochures, catalogs, and the like conveying messages directly from the marketer to the customer.

direct marketing Direct communications, other than personal sales contacts, between buyer and seller, designed to generate sales, information requests, or store or Web site visits.

direct sales results test Method for measuring promotional effectiveness based on the specific impact on sales revenues for each dollar of promotional spending.

direct selling Strategy designed to establish direct sales contact between producer and final user.

discount house Store that charges low prices but may not offer services such as credit.

discretionary income Money available to spend after buying necessities such as food, clothing, and housing.

distribution Movement of goods and services from producers to customers.

distribution strategy Planning that ensures consumers find a firm's products in the proper quantities at the right times and places.

downstream management Controlling part of the supply chain that involves finished product storage, outbound logistics, marketing and sales, and customer service.

drive Any strong stimulus that impels a person to act.

drop shipper Limited-function merchant wholesaler that accepts orders from customers and forwards these orders to producers, which then ship directly to the customers who placed the orders.

dual distribution Network that moves products to a firm's target market through more than one marketing channel.

dumping Controversial practice of selling a product in a foreign market at a price lower than what it receives in the producer's domestic market.

E

e-business Conducting online transactions with customers by collecting and analyzing business information, carrying out the exchanges, and maintaining online relationships with customers.

ecology Relationship between organisms and their natural environment.

economic environment Factors that influence consumer buying power and marketing strategies, including stage of the business cycle, inflation and deflation, unemployment, income, and resource availability.

elasticity Measure of responsiveness of purchasers and suppliers to a change in price.

electronic bulletin board Internet forum that allows users to post and read messages on a specific topic.

electronic data interchange (EDI) Computer-to-computer exchanges of invoices, orders, and other business documents.

electronic exchange Online marketplace that caters to a specific industry's needs.

electronic shopping cart File that holds items the online shopper has chosen to buy.

electronic signatures Electronic identification that allows legal contracts such as home mortgages and insurance policies to be executed online.

electronic storefront Company Web site that sells products to customers.

e-marketing Strategic process of creating, distributing, promoting, and pricing goods and services to a target market over the Internet or through digital tools.

embargo Complete ban on the import of specified products.

emergency goods and services Products bought in response to unexpected and urgent needs.

employee satisfaction Employee's level of satisfaction in his or her company and the extent to which that loyalty—or lack thereof—is communicated to external customers.

encoding Translating a message into understandable terms.

encryption The process of encoding data for security purposes.

end-use application segmentation Segmenting a business-to-business market based on how industrial purchasers will use the product.

engagement Amount of time users spend on sites.

Engel's laws Three general statements about the impact of household income on consumer spending behavior: as household income increases, a smaller percentage of expenditures goes for food; the percentage spent on housing, household operations, and clothing remains constant; and the percentage spent on other items (such as recreation and education) increases.

enterprise resource planning (ERP) system Software system that consolidates data from among a firm's various business units.

environmental management Attainment of organizational objectives by predicting and influencing the competitive, political-legal, economic, technological, and social-cultural environments.

environmental scanning Process of collecting information about the external marketing environment to identify and interpret potential trends.

e-procurement Use of the Internet by organizations to solicit bids and purchase goods and services from suppliers.

ethics Moral standards of behavior expected by a society.

European Union (EU) Customs union that is moving in the direction of an economic union by adopting a common currency, removing trade restrictions, and permitting free flow of goods and workers throughout the member nations.

evaluative criteria Features a consumer considers in choosing among alternatives.

event marketing Marketing of sporting, cultural, and charitable activities to selected target markets.

everyday low pricing (EDLP) Pricing strategy of continuously offering low prices rather than relying on such short-term price cuts as cents-off coupons, rebates, and special sales.

evoked set Number of alternatives a consumer actually considers in making a purchase decision.

exchange control Method used to regulate the privilege of international trade among importing organizations by controlling access to foreign currencies.

exchange functions Buying and selling functions of marketing.

exchange process Activity in which two or more parties give something of value to each other to satisfy perceived needs.

exchange rate Price of one nation's currency in terms of another country's currency.

exclusive dealing agreement Arrangement between a manufacturer and a marketing intermediary that prohibits the intermediary from handling competing product lines.

exclusive distribution Distribution of a product through a single wholesaler or retailer in a specific geographic region.

expectancy theory Theory that motivation depends on an individual's expectations of his or her ability to perform a job and how that performance relates to attaining a desired reward.

exploratory research Process of discussing a marketing problem with informed sources both within and outside the firm and examining information from secondary sources.

exponential smoothing Quantitative forecasting technique that assigns weights to historical sales data, giving the greatest weight to the most recent data.

exporting Marketing domestically produced goods and services in foreign countries.

extended problem solving Situation that involves lengthy external searches and long deliberation; results when brands are difficult to categorize or evaluate.

external customer People or organizations that buy or use a firm's goods or services.

F

facilitating functions Functions that assist the marketer in performing the exchange and physical distribution functions.

fair-trade laws Statutes enacted in most states that once permitted manufacturers to stipulate a minimum retail price for their product.

family brand Single brand name that identifies several related products.

family life cycle Process of family formation and dissolution.

feedback Receiver's response to a message.

field selling Sales presentations made at prospective customers' locations on a face-to-face basis.

firewall Electronic barrier between a company's internal network and the Internet that limits access into and out of the network.

first mover strategy Theory advocating that the company first to offer a product in

a marketplace will be the long-term market winner.

fixed costs Costs that remain stable at any production level within a certain range (such as lease payments or insurance costs).

fixed-sum-per-unit method Method of promotional budgeting in which a predetermined amount is allocated to each sales or production unit.

FOB (free on board) plant (FOB origin) Price quotation that does not include shipping charges.

FOB origin-freight allowed (freight absorbed) Price quotation system that allows the buyer to deduct shipping expenses from the cost of purchases.

focus group Simultaneous personal interview of a small group of individuals that relies on group discussion about a certain topic.

follow-up Post-sale activities that often determine whether an individual who has made a recent purchase will become a repeat customer.

foreign licensing Agreement that grants foreign marketers the right to distribute a firm's merchandise or to use its trademark, patent, or process in a specified geographic area.

forward integration Process through which a firm attempts to control downstream distribution.

franchise Contractual arrangement in which a wholesaler or retailer agrees to meet the operating requirements of a manufacturer or other franchiser.

free-trade area Region in which participating nations agree to the free trade of goods among themselves, abolishing tariffs and trade restrictions.

Free Trade Area of the Americas (FTAA) Proposed free-trade area stretching the length of the entire Western hemisphere and designed to extend free trade benefits to additional nations in North, Central, and South America.

frequency marketing Frequent-buyer or -user marketing programs that reward customers with cash, rebates, merchandise, or other premiums.

friendship, commerce, and navigation (FCN) treaties International agreements that deal with many aspects of commercial relations among nations.

full-cost pricing Pricing method that uses all relevant variable costs in setting a product's price and allocates those fixed costs not directly attributed to the production of the priced item.

full-service research supplier Marketing research organization that offers all aspects of the marketing research process.

G

gatekeeper Person who controls the information that all buying center members will review.

General Agreement on Tariffs and Trade (GATT) International trade accord that has helped reduce world tariffs.

general merchandise retailer Store that carries a wide variety of product lines, stocking all of them in some depth.

9/11 Generation People in their formative years at the time of the September 11, 2001, terrorist attacks.

generic products Products characterized by plain labels, no advertising, and the absence of brand names.

geographic information system (GIS) Software package that assembles, stores, manipulates, and displays data by their location.

geographic segmentation Division of an overall market into homogeneous groups based on their locations.

global marketing strategy Standardized marketing mix with minimal modifications that a firm uses in all of its domestic and foreign markets.

global sourcing Purchasing goods and services from suppliers worldwide.

goods Tangible products customers can see, hear, smell, taste, or touch.

goods–services continuum Spectrum along which goods and services fall according to their attributes, from pure good to pure service.

grassroots marketing Efforts that connect directly with existing and potential customers through nonmainstream channels.

gray goods Products manufactured abroad under license from a U.S. firm and then sold in the U.S. market in competition with that firm's own domestic output.

green marketing Production, promotion, and reclamation of environmentally sensitive products.

gross domestic product (GDP) Sum of all goods and services produced by a nation in a year.

growth stage Second stage of the product lifecycle that begins when a firm starts to realize substantial profits from its investment in a product.

guerrilla marketing Unconventional, innovative, and low-cost marketing techniques designed to get consumers' attention in unusual ways.

H

high-involvement purchase decision Buying decision that evokes high levels of potential economic or social consequence.

home shopping channel Television direct marketing in which a variety of products are offered and consumers can order them directly by phone or online.

homeshoring Hiring workers to do jobs from their homes.

hypermarket Giant one-stop shopping facility offering wide selections of grocery items and general merchandise at discount prices, typically filling up 200,000 or more square feet of selling space.

hypothesis Tentative explanation for a specific event.

I

import quotas Trade restrictions limiting the number of units of certain goods that can enter a country for resale.

importing Purchasing foreign goods and services.

impulse goods and services Products purchased on the spur of the moment.

inbound telemarketing Sales method in which prospects call a seller to obtain information, make reservations, and purchase goods and services.

incremental-cost pricing Pricing method that attempts to use only costs directly attributable to a specific output in setting prices.

indirect evaluation Method for measuring promotional effectiveness by concentrating on quantifiable indicators of effectiveness such as recall and readership.

individual brand Single brand that uniquely identifies a product.

inelastic demand Demand that, throughout an industry, will not change significantly due to a price change.

inflation Rising prices caused by some combination of excess consumer demand and increases in the costs of one or more factors of production.

influencer Typically, technical staff such as engineers who affect the buying decision by supplying information to guide evaluation of alternatives or by setting buying specifications.

infomercial Paid 30-minute or longer product commercial that resembles a regular television program.

informative advertising Promotion that seeks to develop initial demand for a good, service, organization, person, place, idea, or cause.

infrastructure A nation's basic system of transportation networks, communications systems, and energy facilities.

inside selling Selling by phone, mail, and electronic commerce.

installations Business products such as factories, assembly lines, and large machinery that are major capital investments.

institutional advertising Promotion of a concept, an idea, a philosophy, or the goodwill of an industry, company, organization, person, geographic location, or government agency.

integrated marketing communications (IMC) Coordination of all promotional activities to produce a unified, customer-focused promotional message.

intensive distribution Distribution of a product through all available channels.

interactive advertising Two-way promotional messages transmitted through communication channels that induce message recipients to participate actively in the promotional effort.

interactive marketing Buyer–seller communications in which the customer controls the amount and type of information received from a marketer through such channels as the Internet and virtual reality kiosks.

interactive television Television service package that includes a return path for viewers to interact with programs or commercials by clicking their remote controls.

intermodal operations Combination of transport modes, such as rail and highway carriers (piggyback), air and highway carriers (birdyback), and water and air carriers (fishyback), to improve customer service and achieve cost advantages.

internal customer Employees or departments within an organization that depend on the work of another employee or department to perform tasks.

internal marketing Managerial actions that help all members of the organization understand, accept, and fulfill their respective roles in implementing a marketing strategy.

internal partnership Relationship involving customers within an organization.

interpretative research Observational research method developed by social anthropologists in which customers are observed in their natural setting and their behavior is interpreted based on an understanding of social and cultural characteristics; also known as *ethnography,* or "going native."

introductory stage First stage of the product lifecycle, in which a firm works to stimulate sales of a new market entry.

ISO (International Organization for Standardization) certification Internationally recognized standards that ensure a company's goods, services, and operations meet established quality levels and its operations minimize harm to the environment.

ISO 9001:2000 Standards developed by the International Organization for Standardization in Switzerland to ensure consistent quality management and quality assurance for goods and services throughout the European Union (EU).

J

joint demand Demand for a product that depends on the demand for another product used in combination with it.

jury of executive opinion Qualitative sales forecasting method that assesses the sales expectations of various executives.

just-in-time (JIT)/just-in-time II (JIT II) Inventory practices that seek to boost efficiency by cutting inventories to absolute minimum levels. With JIT II, suppliers' representatives work at the customer's facility.

L

label Branding component that carries an item's brand name or symbol, the name and address of the manufacturer or distributor, information about the product, and recommended uses.

lateral partnership Strategic relationship that extends to external entities but involves no direct buyer–seller interactions.

leader pricing Variant of loss-leader pricing in which marketers offer prices slightly above cost to avoid violating minimum-markup regulations and earn a minimal return on promotional sales.

learning Knowledge or skill acquired as a result of experience, which changes consumer behavior.

lifetime value of a customer Revenues and intangible benefits such as referrals and customer feedback a customer brings to the seller over an average lifetime, less the amount the company must spend to acquire, market to, and service the customer.

limited problem solving Situation in which the consumer invests a small amount of time and energy in searching for and evaluating alternatives.

limited-line store Retailer that offers a large assortment within a single product line or within a few related product lines.

limited-service research supplier Marketing research firm that specializes in a limited number of research activities such as conducting field interviews or performing data processing.

line extension Development of individual offerings that appeal to different market segments while remaining closely related to the existing product line.

list price Established price normally quoted to potential buyers.

logistics Process of coordinating the flow of information, goods, and services among members of the distribution channel.

loss leader Product offered to consumers at less than cost to attract them to stores in the hope that they will buy other merchandise at regular prices.

low-involvement purchase decision Routine purchase that poses little risk to the consumer, either economically or socially.

M

mail-order wholesaler Limited-function merchant wholesaler that distributes catalogs instead of sending sales personnel to contact customers.

mall intercept Interviews conducted inside retail shopping centers.

manufacturer's brand Brand name owned by a manufacturer or other producer.

manufacturers' representative Agent wholesaling intermediary that represents manufacturers of related but noncompeting products and receives a commission on each sale.

marginal analysis Method of analyzing the relationship between costs, sales price, and increased sales volume.

marginal cost Change in total cost that results from producing an additional unit of output.

markdown Amount by which a retailer reduces the original selling price of a product.

market Group of people with sufficient purchasing power, authority, and willingness to buy.

market development strategy Strategy that concentrates on finding new markets for existing products.

market penetration strategy Strategy that seeks to increase sales of existing products in existing markets.

market price Price a consumer or marketing intermediary actually pays for a product after subtracting any discounts, allowances, or rebates from the list price.

market segmentation Division of the total market into smaller, relatively homogeneous groups.

market share The percentage of a market that a firm currently controls (or company sales divided by total market sales).

market share/market growth matrix Framework that places SBUs on a chart that plots market share against market growth potential.

marketing Organizational function and a set of processes for creating, communicating, and delivering value to customers and for managing customer relationships in ways that benefit the organization and its stakeholders.

marketing (distribution) channel System of marketing institutions that enhances the physical flow of goods and services, along with ownership title, from producer to consumer or business user.

marketing communications Messages that deal with buyer–seller relationships.

marketing concept Companywide consumer orientation with the objective of achieving long-run success.

marketing decision support system (MDSS) Marketing information system component that links a decision maker with relevant databases and analysis tools.

marketing ethics Marketers' standards of conduct and moral values.

marketing information system (MIS) Planned, computer-based system designed to provide managers with a continuous flow of information relevant to their specific decisions and areas of responsibility.

marketing intermediary (middleman) Wholesaler or retailer that operates between producers and consumers or business users.

marketing mix Blending of the four strategy elements—product, distribution, promotion, and price—to fit the needs and preferences of a specific target market.

marketing myopia Management's failure to recognize the scope of its business.

marketing plan Detailed description of the resources and actions needed to achieve stated marketing objectives.

marketing public relations (MPR) Narrowly focused public relations activities that directly support marketing goals.

marketing research Process of collecting and using information for marketing decision making.

marketing strategy Overall, company-wide program for selecting a particular target market and then satisfying consumers in that market through the marketing mix.

marketing Web site Site whose main purpose is to increase purchases by visitors.

market-plus pricing Intentionally setting a relatively high price compared with the prices of competing products; also known as *skimming pricing.*

market-share objective Volume-related pricing objective in which the goal is to achieve control of a portion of the market for a firm's good or service.

markup Amount a retailer adds to the cost of a product to determine its selling price.

mass merchandiser Store that stocks a wider line of goods than a department store, usually without the same depth of assortment within each line.

materials handling system Set of activities that move production inputs and other goods within plants, warehouses, and transportation terminals.

maturity stage Third stage of the product lifecycle, in which industry sales level out.

media research Advertising research that assesses how well a particular medium delivers an advertiser's message, where and when to place the advertisement, and the size of the audience.

media scheduling Setting the timing and sequence for a series of advertisements.

meeting competition method Method of promotional budgeting that simply matches competitors' outlays.

merchandisers Trade sector buyers who secure needed products at the best possible prices.

merchant wholesaler Independently-owned wholesaling intermediary that takes title to the goods it handles; also known as an industrial distributor in the business goods market.

message Communication of information, advice, or a request by the sender to the receiver.

message research Advertising research that tests consumer reactions to an advertisement's creative message.

metropolitan statistical area (MSA) Freestanding urban area with a population in the urban center of at least 50,000 and a total MSA population of 100,000 or more.

micromarketing Targeting potential customers at very narrow, basic levels such as by zip code, specific occupation, or lifestyle—possibly even individuals themselves.

micropolitan statistical area Area with at least one town of 10,000 to 49,999 people with proportionally few of its residents commuting to outside the area.

minimum advertised pricing (MAP) Fees paid to retailers who agree not to advertise products below set prices.

mission Essential purpose that differentiates one company from others.

missionary selling Indirect selling method in which salespeople promote goodwill for the firm by educating customers and providing technical or operational assistance.

mobile marketing Marketing messages transmitted via wireless technology.

modified breakeven analysis Pricing technique used to evaluate consumer demand by comparing the number of products that must be sold at a variety of prices to cover total cost with estimates of expected sales at the various prices.

modified rebuy Situation in which a purchaser is willing to reevaluate available options for repurchasing a good or service.

monopolistic competition Market structure involving a heterogeneous product and product differentiation among competing suppliers, allowing the marketer some degree of control over prices.

monopoly Market structure in which a single seller dominates trade in a good or service for which buyers can find no close substitutes.

motive Inner state that directs a person toward the goal of satisfying a need.

MRO items Business supplies that include maintenance items, repair items, and operating supplies.

multidomestic marketing strategy Application of market segmentation to foreign markets by tailoring the firm's marketing mix to match specific target markets in each nation.

multinational corporation Firm with significant operations and marketing activities outside its home country.

multiple sourcing Purchasing from several vendors.

N

national account selling Promotional effort in which a dedicated sales team is assigned to a firm's major customers to provide sales and service.

national accounts organization Promotional effort in which a dedicated sales team is assigned to a firm's major customers to provide sales and service needs.

nearshoring Moving jobs to vendors in countries close to the business's home country.

need Imbalance between a consumer's actual and desired states.

network marketing Personal selling that relies on lists of family members and friends of the salesperson, who organizes a gathering of potential customers for a demonstration of products.

new-task buying First-time or unique purchase situation that requires considerable effort by decision makers.

niche marketing Marketing strategy that focuses on profitably satisfying a single market segment; also called *concentrated marketing*.

noise Any stimulus that distracts a receiver from receiving a message.

noncumulative quantity discount Price reduction granted on a one-time-only basis.

nonmarketing public relations Organizational messages about general management issues.

nonpersonal selling Promotion that includes advertising, product placement, sales promotion, direct marketing, public relations, and guerilla marketing—all conducted without being face-to-face with the buyer.

nonprobability sample Sample that involves personal judgment somewhere in the selection process.

norms Values, attitudes, and behaviors a group deems appropriate for its members.

North American Free Trade Agreement (NAFTA) Accord removing trade barriers between Canada, Mexico, and the United States.

North American Industry Classification System (NAICS) Classification used by NAFTA countries to categorize the business marketplace into detailed market segments.

O

objection Expression of sales resistance by the prospect.

objectives Goals that support a firm's overall mission.

odd pricing Pricing policy based on the belief that a price ending with an odd number just under a round number is more appealing, for instance, $9.97 rather than $10.

offshoring Movement of high-wage jobs from one country to lower-cost overseas locations.

oligopoly Market structure in which relatively few sellers compete and where high start-up costs form barriers to keep out new competitors.

opening price point Setting an opening price below that of the competition, usually on a high-quality private-label item.

opinion leaders Trendsetters who purchase new products before others in a group and then influence others in their purchases.

order processing Selling, mostly at the wholesale and retail levels, that involves identifying customer needs, pointing them out to customers, and completing orders.

organization marketing Marketing by mutual-benefit organizations, service organizations, and government organizations intended to persuade others to accept their goals, receive their services, or contribute to them in some way.

outbound telemarketing Sales method in which sales personnel place phone calls to prospects and try to conclude the sale over the phone.

outsourcing Using outside vendors to provide goods and services formerly produced in-house.

over-the-counter selling Personal selling conducted in retail and some wholesale locations in which customers come to the seller's place of business.

P

partnership Affiliation of two or more companies that help each other achieve common goals.

penetration pricing strategy Pricing strategy involving the use of a relatively low entry price compared with competitive offerings, based on the theory that this initial low price will help secure market acceptance.

percentage-of-sales method Method of promotional budgeting in which a dollar amount is based on a percentage of past or projected sales.

perception Meaning that a person attributes to incoming stimuli gathered through the five senses.

perceptual screen Mental filter or block through which all inputs must pass to be noticed.

person marketing Marketing efforts designed to cultivate the attention, interest, and preferences of a target market toward a person (perhaps a political candidate or celebrity).

personal selling Interpersonal influence process involving a seller's promotional presentation conducted on a person-to-person basis with the buyer.

persuasive advertising Promotion that attempts to increase demand for an existing good, service, organization, person, place, idea, or cause.

phishing High-tech scam that uses authentic-looking e-mail or pop-up messages to get unsuspecting victims to reveal personal information.

physical distribution (functions) Broad range of activities aimed at efficient movement of finished goods from the end of the production line to the consumer.

place marketing Marketing efforts to attract people and organizations to a particular geographic area.

planned obsolescence Intentional design, manufacture, and marketing of products with limited durability.

planned shopping center Group of retail stores planned, coordinated, and marketed as a unit.

planning Process of anticipating future events and conditions and of determining the best way to achieve organizational objectives.

podcast Online audio or video file that can be downloaded to other digital devices.

point-of-purchase (POP) advertising Display or other promotion placed near the site of the actual buying decision.

political risk assessment (PRA) Units within a firm that evaluate the political risks of the marketplaces in which they operate as well as proposed new marketplaces.

political-legal environment Component of the marketing environment consisting of laws and their interpretations that require firms to operate under competitive conditions and to protect consumer rights.

population (universe) Total group that researchers want to study.

pop-up ad Separate window that pops up with an advertising message.

Porter's Five Forces Model developed by strategy expert Michael Porter that identifies five competitive forces that influence planning strategies: the threat of new entrants, the bargaining power of buyers, the bargaining power of suppliers, the threat of substitute products, and rivalry among competitors.

portfolio analysis Evaluation of a company's products and divisions to determine the strongest and weakest.

positioning Placing a product at a certain point or location within a market in the minds of prospective buyers.

positioning map Tool that helps marketers place products in a market by graphically illustrating consumers' perceptions of competing products within an industry.

postage-stamp pricing System for handling transportation costs under which all buyers are quoted the same price, including transportation expenses; also known as *uniform-delivered price*.

posttesting Research that assesses advertising effectiveness after it has appeared in a print or broadcast medium.

precall planning Use of information collected during the prospecting and qualifying stages of the sales process and during previous contacts with the prospect to tailor the approach and presentation to match the customer's needs.

premium Item given free or at a reduced cost with purchases of other products.

preroll video ad Brief marketing message that appears before expected video content.

presentation Personal selling function of describing a product's major features and relating them to a customer's problems or needs.

pretesting Research that evaluates an ad during its development stage.

price Exchange value of a good or service.

price flexibility Pricing policy permitting variable prices for goods and services.

pricing policy General guideline that reflects marketing objectives and influences specific pricing decisions.

pricing strategy Methods of setting profitable and justifiable prices.

primary data Information collected for a specific investigation.

primary demand Desire for a general product category.

primary metropolitan statistical area (PMSA) Urbanized county or set of counties with social and economic ties to nearby areas.

private brand Brand offered by a wholesaler or retailer.

private carriers Transporters that provide service solely for internally generated freight.

probability sample Sample that gives every member of the population a chance of being selected.

product advertising Nonpersonal selling of a particular good or service.

product development Introduction of new products into identifiable or established markets.

product differentiation Occurs when consumers regard a firm's products as different in some way from those of competitors.

product diversification strategy Developing entirely new products for new markets.

product liability Responsibility of manufacturers and marketers for injuries and damages caused by their products.

product lifecycle Progression of a product through introduction, growth, maturity, and decline stages.

product line Series of related products offered by one company.

product manager Marketer responsible for an individual product or product line; also called a brand manager.

product mix Assortment of product lines and individual product offerings a company sells.

product placement Form of promotion in which a marketer pays a motion picture or television program owner a fee to display a product prominently in the film or show.

product positioning Consumers' perceptions of a product's attributes, uses, quality, and advantages and disadvantages relative to competing brands.

product strategy Decisions about what goods or services a firm will offer its customers; also includes decisions about customer service, packaging, brand names, and the like.

product Bundle of physical, service, and symbolic attributes designed to satisfy a customer's wants and needs.

production orientation Business philosophy stressing efficiency in producing a quality product, with the attitude toward marketing that "a good product will sell itself."

product-line pricing Practice of setting a limited number of prices for a selection of merchandise and marketing different product lines at each of these price levels.

product-related segmentation Division of a population into homogeneous groups based on their relationships to a product.

profit center Any part of an organization to which revenue and controllable costs can be assigned.

Profit Impact of Market Strategies (PIMS) project Research that discovered a strong positive relationship between a firm's market share and product quality and its return on investment.

profit maximization Point at which the additional revenue gained by increasing the price of a product equals the increase in total costs.

promotion Communication link between buyers and sellers; the function of informing, persuading, and influencing a consumer's purchase decision.

promotional allowance Promotional incentive in which the manufacturer agrees to pay the reseller a certain amount to cover the costs of special promotional displays or extensive advertising.

promotional mix Subset of the marketing mix in which marketers attempt to achieve the optimal blending of the elements of personal and nonpersonal selling to achieve promotional objectives.

promotional pricing Pricing policy in which a lower-than-normal price is used as a temporary ingredient in a firm's marketing strategy.

prospecting Personal selling function of identifying potential customers.

protective tariff Taxes designed to raise the retail price of an imported product to match or exceed that of a similar domestic product.

psychographic segmentation Division of a population into groups having similar attitudes, values, and lifestyles.

psychological pricing Pricing policy based on the belief that certain prices or price ranges make a good or service more appealing than others to buyers.

public relations Firm's communications and relationships with its various publics.

public service announcements (PSAs) Advertisements aimed at achieving socially oriented objectives by focusing on causes and charitable organizations that are included in print and electronic media without charge.

publicity Nonpersonal stimulation of demand for a good, service, place, idea, person, or organization by unpaid placement of significant news regarding the product in a print or broadcast medium.

puffery Exaggerated claims of a product's superiority, or the use of subjective or vague statements that may not be literally true.

pulling strategy Promotional effort by the seller to stimulate final-user demand, which then exerts pressure on the distribution channel.

pure competition Market structure characterized by homogeneous products in which there are so many buyers and sellers that none has a significant influence on price.

push money Cash reward paid to retail salespeople for every unit of a product they sell.

pushing strategy Promotional effort by the seller directed to members of the marketing channel rather than final users.

Q

qualifying Determining a prospect's needs, income, and purchase authority as a potential customer.

qualitative forecasting Use of subjective techniques to forecast sales, such as the jury of executive opinion, Delphi technique, sales force composite, and surveys of buyer intentions.

quantitative forecasting Use of statistical forecasting techniques such as trend analysis and exponential smoothing.

quantity discount Price reduction granted for a large-volume purchase.

quick-response merchandising Just-in-time strategy that reduces the time a retailer must hold merchandise in inventory, resulting in substantial cost savings.

quota sample Nonprobability sample divided to maintain the proportion of certain characteristics among different segments or groups as the population as a whole.

R

rack jobber Full-function merchant wholesaler that markets specialized lines of merchandise to retail stores.

radio frequency identification (RFID) Technology that uses a tiny chip with identification information that can be read by a scanner using radio waves from a distance.

raw materials Natural resources such as farm products, coal, copper, or lumber that become part of a final product.

rebate Refund of a portion of the purchase price, usually granted by the product's manufacturer.

reciprocity Buying from suppliers who are also customers.

reference groups People or institutions whose opinions are valued and to whom a person looks for guidance in his or her own behavior, values, and conduct, such as spouse, family, friends, or celebrities.

refund Cash given back to consumers who send in proof of purchase for one or more products.

reinforcement Reduction in drive that results from a proper response.

related party trade Trade by U.S. companies with their subsidiaries overseas as well as trade by U.S. subsidiaries of foreign-owned firms with their parent companies.

relationship marketing Development and maintenance of long-term, cost-effective relationships with individual customers, suppliers, employees, and other partners for mutual benefit.

relationship selling Regular contacts between sales representatives and customers over an extended period to establish a sustained buyer–seller relationship.

remanufacturing Efforts to restore older products to like-new condition.

reminder advertising Advertising that reinforces previous promotional activity by keeping the name of a good, service, organization, person, place, idea, or cause before the public.

repositioning Changing the position of a product within the minds of prospective buyers relative to the positions of competing products.

research design Master plan for conducting marketing research.

reseller Marketing intermediaries that operate in the trade sector.

response Individual's reaction to a set of cues and drives.

retail advertising Advertising by stores that sell goods or services directly to the consuming public.

retail convergence Situation in which similar merchandise is available from multiple retail outlets, resulting in the blurring of distinctions between types of retailers and merchandise offered.

retail cooperative Group of retailers that establish a shared wholesaling operation to help them compete with chains.

retailing Activities involved in selling merchandise to ultimate consumers.

revenue tariff Taxes designed to raise funds for the importing government.

reverse channel Channel designed to return goods to their producers.

Robinson-Patman Act Federal legislation prohibiting price discrimination not based on a cost differential; also prohibits selling at an unreasonably low price to eliminate competition.

roles Behavior that members of a group expect of individuals who hold specific positions within that group.

routinized response behavior Rapid consumer problem solving in which no new information is considered; the consumer has already set evaluative criteria and identified available options.

rule of three Three dominant companies in an industry that will capture 70 to 90 percent of the market.

S

salary Fixed compensation payment made periodically to an employee.

sales analysis In-depth evaluation of a firm's sales.

sales force composite Qualitative sales forecasting method based on the combined sales estimates of the firm's salespeople.

sales forecast Estimate of a firm's revenue for a specified future period.

sales incentives Programs that reward salespeople for superior performance.

sales orientation Business assumption that consumers will resist purchasing nonessential goods and services, with the attitude toward marketing that only creative advertising and personal selling can overcome consumers' resistance and persuade them to buy.

sales promotion Marketing activities other than personal selling, advertising, guerrilla marketing, and public relations that stimulate consumer purchasing and dealer effectiveness.

sales quota Level of expected sales for a territory, product, customer, or salesperson against which actual results are compared.

sampling Free distribution of a product in an attempt to obtain future sales; process of selecting survey respondents or research participants.

scrambled merchandising Retailing practice of combining dissimilar product lines to boost sales volume.

search marketing Paying search engines, such as Google, a fee to make sure the company's listing appears toward the top of the search results.

second mover strategy Theory that advocates observing closely the innovations of first movers and then improving on them to gain advantage in the marketplace.

secondary data Previously published information.

Secure Sockets Layer (SSL) Technology that secures a Web site by encrypting information and providing authentication.

selective demand Desire for a specific brand within a product category.

selective distribution Distribution of a product through a limited number of channels.

self-concept Person's multifaceted picture of himself or herself.

seller partnership Relationship involving long-term exchanges of goods or services in return for cash or other valuable consideration.

seller's market Market in which there are more buyers for fewer goods and services.

selling agent Agent wholesaling intermediary responsible for the entire marketing program of a firm's product line.

sender Source of the message communicated to the receiver.

service encounter Point at which the customer and service provider interact.

service quality Expected and perceived quality of a service offering.

services Intangible tasks that satisfy the needs of consumer and business users.

shaping Process of applying a series of rewards and reinforcements to permit more complex behavior to evolve.

shopping products Products consumers purchase after comparing competing offerings.

simple random sample Basic type of probability sample in which every individual in the relevant universe has an equal opportunity of being selected.

skimming pricing strategy Pricing strategy involving the use of a high price relative to competitive offerings.

social responsibility Marketing philosophies, policies, procedures, and actions that have the enhancement of society's welfare as a primary objective.

social-cultural environment Component of the marketing environment consisting of the relationship between the marketer, society, and culture.

sole sourcing Purchasing a firm's entire stock of an item from just one vendor.

spam Popular name for junk e-mail.

span of control Number of representatives who report to first-level sales managers.

specialty advertising Sales promotion technique that places the advertiser's name, address, and advertising message on useful articles that are then distributed to target consumers.

specialty products Products with unique characteristics that cause buyers to prize those particular brands.

specialty retailer Store that combines carefully defined product lines, services, and reputation to persuade shoppers to spend considerable shopping effort there.

split runs Methods of testing alternate ads by dividing a cable TV audience or a publication's subscribers in two, using two different ads, and then evaluating the relative effectiveness of each.

sponsorship Relationship in which an organization provides funds or in-kind resources to an event or activity in exchange for a direct association with that event or activity.

spreadsheet analysis Grid that organizes numerical information in a standardized, easily understood format.

staples Convenience goods and services consumers constantly replenish to maintain a ready inventory.

status Relative positioin of any individual member in a group.

step out Pricing practice in which one firm raises prices and then waits to see if others follow suit.

stock-keeping unit (SKU) Offering within a product line such as a specific size of liquid detergent.

straight rebuy Recurring purchase decision in which a customer repurchases a good or service that has performed satisfactorily in the past.

strategic alliance Partnership in which two or more companies combine resources and capital to create competitive advantages in a new market.

strategic planning Process of anticipating events and market conditions and deciding how a firm can best achieve its organizational objectives.

strategic window Limited periods when key requirements of a market and a firm's particular competencies best fit together.

stratified sample Probability sample constructed to represent randomly selected subsamples of different groups within the total sample; each subgroup is relatively homogeneous for a certain characteristic.

subcontracting Contractual agreements that assign the production of goods or services to local or smaller firms.

subcultures Smaller groups within a society that have their own distinct characteristics and modes of behavior, defined by ethnicity, race, region, age, religion, gender, social class, or profession.

subliminal perception Subconscious receipt of incoming information.

suboptimization Condition that results when individual operations achieve their objectives but interfere with progress toward broader organizational goals.

subsidy Government financial support of a private industry.

supercenter Large store, usually smaller than a hypermarket, that combines groceries with discount store merchandise.

supplies Regular expenses a firm incurs in its daily operations.

supply Schedule of the amounts of a good or service that firms will offer for sale at different prices during a specified time period.

supply chain Complete sequence of suppliers and activities that contribute to the creation and delivery of merchandise.

supply chain management Control of the activities of purchasing, processing, and delivery through which raw materials are transformed into products and made available to final consumers.

survey of buyer intentions Qualitative sales forecasting method that samples opinions among groups of present and potential customers concerning their purchase intentions.

sustainable competitive advantage Superior market position that a firm possesses and can maintain for an extended period of time.

sweepstakes Sales promotion technique in which prize winners are selected by chance.

SWOT analysis Review that helps planners compare internal organizational strengths and weaknesses with external opportunities and threats.

syndicated service Organization that provides standardized data on a periodic basis to its subscribers.

systems integration Centralization of the procurement function within an internal division or as a service of an external supplier.

T

tactical planning Planning that guides the implementation of activities specified in the strategic plan.

target market Segment or group of people to whom a firm decides to direct its marketing efforts and ultimately its goods and services.

target-return objective Short-run or long-run pricing objectives of achieving a specified return on either sales or investment.

tariff Tax levied against imported goods.

task-objective method Development of a promotional budget based on evaluation of the firm's promotional objectives.

team selling Selling situation in which several sales associates or other members of the organization are employed to help the lead sales

representative reach all those who influence the purchase decision.

technological environment Application to marketing of knowledge based on discoveries in science, inventions, and innovations.

telemarketing Promotional presentation involving the use of the telephone on an outbound basis by salespeople or on an inbound basis by customers who initiate calls to obtain information and place orders.

test marketing Marketing research technique that involves introducing a new product in a specific area and then measuring its degree of success.

third-party (contract) logistics firm Company that specializes in handling logistics activities for other firms.

time-based competition Strategy of developing and distributing goods and services more quickly than competitors.

total quality management (TQM) Continuous effort to improve products and work processes with the goal of achieving customer satisfaction and world-class performance.

trade allowance Financial incentive offered to wholesalers and retailers that purchase or promote specific products.

trade discount Payment to a channel member or buyer for performing marketing functions; also known as a *functional discount*.

trade dress Visual components that contribute to the overall look of a brand.

trade industries Retailers or wholesalers that purchase products for resale to others.

trade promotion Sales promotion that appeals to marketing intermediaries rather than to consumers.

trade show Product exhibition organized by industry trade associations to showcase goods and services.

trade-in Credit allowance given for a used item when a customer purchases a new item.

trademark Brand for which the owner claims exclusive legal protection.

transaction-based marketing Buyer and seller exchanges characterized by limited communications and little or no ongoing relationships between the parties.

transfer price Cost assessed when a product is moved from one profit center in a firm to another.

trend analysis Quantitative sales forecasting method that estimates future sales through statistical analyses of historical sales patterns.

truck wholesaler Limited-function merchant wholesaler that markets perishable food items; also called a truck jobber.

tying agreement Arrangement that requires a marketing intermediary to carry items other than those they want to sell.

U

undifferentiated marketing Strategy that focuses on producing a single product and marketing it to all customers; also called *mass marketing*.

unemployment Proportion of people in the economy actively seeking work that do not have jobs.

unfair-trade laws State laws requiring sellers to maintain minimum prices for comparable merchandise.

uniform-delivered pricing Pricing system for handling transportation costs under which all buyers are quoted the same price, including transportation expenses. Sometimes known as *postage-stamp pricing*.

unit pricing Pricing policy in which prices are stated in terms of a recognized unit of measurement or a standard numerical count.

Universal Product Code (UPC) Numerical bar code system used to record product and price information.

unsought products Products marketed to consumers who may not yet recognize a need for them.

upstream management Controlling part of the supply chain that involves raw materials, inbound logistics, and warehouse and storage facilities.

user Individual or group that actually uses a business good or service.

utility Want-satisfying power of a good or service.

V

VALS Segmentation system that divides consumers into eight psychographic categories: innovators, thinkers, achievers, experiencers, believers, strivers, makers, and survivors.

value analysis Systematic study of the components of a purchase to determine the most cost-effective approach.

value pricing Pricing strategy emphasizing benefits derived from a product in comparison to the price and quality levels of competing offerings.

variable costs Costs that change with the level of production (such as labor and raw materials costs).

vendor analysis Assessment of supplier performance in areas such as price, back orders, timely delivery, and attention to special requests.

vendor-managed inventory (VMI) Inventory management system in which the seller—based on an existing agreement with a buyer—determines how much of a product is needed.

venture team Associates from different areas of an organization who work together in developing new products.

vertical marketing system (VMS) Planned channel system designed to improve distribution efficiency and cost-effectiveness by integrating various functions throughout the distribution chain.

viral marketing Efforts that allow satisfied customers to spread the word about products to other consumers.

virtual sales team Network of strategic partners, suppliers, and others who recommend a firm's goods or services.

vishing Scam that collects personal information through voice response systems, stands for *voice phishing.*

VoIP (Voice over Internet protocol) A phone connection through a personal computer with any type of broadband Internet connection.

W

Web services Platform-independent information exchange systems that use the Internet to allow interaction between the firms.

Web-to-store shoppers Consumers who use the Internet as a tool to aid them at brick-and-mortar retailers.

wheel of retailing Hypothesis that each new type of retailer gains a competitive foothold by offering lower prices than current suppliers charge; the result of reducing or eliminating services.

wholesaler Channel intermediary that takes title to goods it handles and then distributes these goods to retailers, other distributors, or business or B2B customers.

wholesaling intermediary Comprehensive term that describes wholesalers as well as agents and brokers.

widget Tiny interactive applications that Internet users can copy and add to their own pages to play music, video, or slide shows.

wiki Web page anyone can edit.

World Trade Organization (WTO) Organization that replaces GATT, overseeing GATT agreements, making binding decisions in mediating disputes, and reducing trade barriers.

Y

yield management Pricing strategy that allows marketers to vary prices based on such factors as demand, even though the cost of providing those goods or services remains the same.

Z

zone pricing Pricing system for handling transportation costs under which the market is divided into geographic regions and a different price is set in each region.

NAME & COMPANY INDEX

INTERNATIONAL INDEX